THE GOULD FAMILY

OF BOSTON

COMPILED AND EDITED BY
JAMES WARREN GOULD
&
ELEANOR GOULD BALDIC

AUGUST 2017

The authors welcome inquiries, corrections and additions:

James W. Gould, Box 161 Cotuit MA 02635 ph. (508) 428-8267,
e-mail jgCotuit@gmail.com

Eleanor G. Baldic, 35 Greengate Rd., Apt. 32E, Falmouth MA 02541,
ph. (508) 548-2681; e-mail egb61 @ aol.com

TABLE OF CONTENTS

CHARTS AND PORTRAITS

The GOULD FAMILY of BOSTON
1
for complete data see numbered charts
send corrections to J.W. Gould, Box 161, Cotuit, MA. 02635
J.W. Gould 23 IX 90

Chapter I

THOMAS[1] GOULD,

BRASS FOUNDER OF BOSTON, d. 1707.

This work traces the history of the Gould family living in Boston for three hundred years, from 1687 to 1989, for thirteen generations of the name, from Thomas[1] Gould to Lloyd[13] T. Gould, born in Boston 28 May 1988. Its purpose is to resolve a long-standing question about the ancestry of a family which was in Boston at the time of the Revolution, that of James[4] Gould, wheelwright for the Revolutionary Army and builder of the first bridge across the Charles River, in 1785-8, and father of Thomas[5] Gould, member of the first Boston City Council in 1827, abolitionist founder of Tremont Temple and his son Thomas[6] who was builder of early Boston railway equipment and stations.

The first chapter sorts out the tangle of identical names Thomas Gould, of which there were at least two living in Boston during the colonial period. The only previous work on this subject was a brief appendix to the genealogy by the astronomer Benjamin Apthorp Gould on the family of Zaccheus Gould of Topsfield, which this article corrects.

The significance of this larger family history is that it extends our knowledge of the Gould family back three generations, locates their activities and homes in colonial Boston, and identifies the many distinguished descendants, including the historian William H. Prescott, reformer John Jay Chapman, geographer Melville Grosvenor, author Cleveland Amory, art historian Martha Karolik, Civil War hospital administrator Emily Parsons, Watergate Prosecutor Archibald Cox, and many others.

In the search we have come across many new and surprising discoveries about the family: Four passengers who came over on the *Mayflower* (John Howland, Elizabeth (Tilley) Howland, Elizabeth and John Tilley, (Ch. XIV), two women condemned as witches Rachel (Haffield) Clinton, (Ch. VIII), and Mary (Perkins) Bradbury, (Ch. X), the commander of the oldest military unit in the country (Elias Waters Goddard (1803-88), commanded Columbian Artillery, Ch. XIII), victims of the massacres of Deerfield, Brookfield and Lancaster (Ch. VI, VII), two Archbishops of Canterbury (William Whitgift (ca. 1530-1605), (Ch. X), and William Juxon (1582-1663), (Ch. II), pioneer settlers of many of the towns of Massachusetts Bay including the builder of the first house in Barnstable (Thomas Dimmock in March 1639, at Mattakeese (Barnstable Village), (Ch. XIII) and the owner of the first fulling mill in Marstons Mills Shubael Dimmock, (Ch. XIII), several Puritan ministers (Rev. Thomas Welles, first pastor of Amesbury, (Ch. XIII), Rev. Joseph Hull, founder of Barnstable church, (Ch. XIV), Rev. John Smith, Barnstable, (Ch. XIV), and by marriage, Rev. Edward Bulkeley of Concord, (Ch. VIII), Rev. John Eliot, (Ch. X), the inventor of ice-shoes for oxen (William Moody of Newbury, Ch. X), many sea captains and fishermen lost at sea, the craftsman who produced the first iron in the country (Quinton Pray, at Braintree and Saugus, Ch. VIII), soldiers in every war from the Great

Swamp Fight in King Philip's War to World War II (Andrew Hidden at Swamp Fight, (Ch. X), the first civilian killed in the Revolution, (Ch. X); Nathaniel Garran killed in War of 1812 (Ch. XIV), Barnabas Turner in Indian Wars and Mexican War, (Ch. VII), Francis Gould and George E. Muzzey in Civil War, (Ch. IX), Douglas Gould in World War I, James Gould in World War II)—and a full crop of rascals, pirates, philanderers and philosophers.

The sources of this new information are original documents, principally Boston deeds and wills, church records, court files, contemporary newspaper maritime reports, as well as the extensive secondary sources in the New England Historic Genealogical Society, Massachusetts Historical Society, Boston Public Library, Massachusetts Archives, Bostonian Society, Boston Athenaeum, and local historical societies. I am particularly indebted for help from my cousin, Eleanor Gould Baldic, founder of the Falmouth Genealogical Society, who has discovered much of the evidence presented here. Our cousins Henry B. Burbank of Norton and Rehoboth, and the late Wilbur D. Raymond, Somerville historian, have been very helpful.

1. THOMAS[1] GOULD / GOLD[1], founder of brass by trade, of Boston, born perhaps London and died Boston between 1 March 1707 and 28 July 1707 (Suffolk County Massachusetts Wills, in Massachusetts Archives, [hereinafter SW]; 3049, 313). He married before 1680 to Frances (**not** Robinson), who died Boston between 8 February and 16 July 1709 (SW, 280). Note the spelling Gould/Gold: The most frequent spelling in the seventeenth century was GOLD, pronounced the same as the precious metal gold, "goold". While the noun's pronunciation has shifted to today's, the surname has stayed the same, though it was spelled erratically but phonetically, GOLD, GOOLD and finally GOULD.

ORIGINS OF THOMAS[1] GOULD.

We will show here that our first ancestor, Thomas Gould probably came to Boston from London about 1687, with the Anglican associates of Governor Andros.

The parents of Thomas Gould have not been found. Benjamin Apthorp Gould, the astronomer-genealogist (*The Family of Zaccheus Gould of Topsfield* [Thomas P. Nichols: Lynn, 1895] [hereinafter Z Gould], Appendix 17, 346) stated that as "the result of an exceptional amount of study, and yet not capable of full demonstration" that this Thomas's father was "Thomas Gould, aged 32, came on the Jonathan, with his wife Mary.... It appears to have been this Thomas, who died in Boston 1662 Oct. 26."

However, no record of birth of a Thomas to the Jonathan immigrant is found, nor of any Thomas Gould in the town or church records. There is no will for the Thomas who died 26 Oct. 1662 ([9th] *Report of the Record Commissioners...Boston Births. Baptisms. Marriages, and Deaths. 1630-1699* [Boston: Rockwell & Churchill, 1883], Document 130, [hereinafter Doc. 130], 86, Jay M. Holbrook, *Boston Beginnings. 1630-1699* [Oxford, MA: Holbrook Research Institute, 1980, 108] [hereinafter Holbrook].

The genealogist Wilton Francis Bucknam of Stoneham tried to sort out the puzzle in the *Boston Transcript* of 27 June 1917. In Note #1817 he showed that Wyman's Thomas Gould 2. and 18. were the same Baptist preacher (Thomas Bellows Wyman, *The Genealogies and Estates of Charlestown Massachusetts 1629-1818* [2 vols., Boston: David Clapp & Son, 1879] [hereinafter Wyman], 1:425, 428), but shows no Thomas Gould (1607-62) who came on the *Jonathan.* B. A. Gould distinguishes the Rev. Thomas Gould of Baptist fame (Appendix 15, 340-1) the minister had no grandchildren named Gould. We do not know if the two Thomas Goulds of early Boston, one who died 1662, the other the Baptist minister, were related, but neither seems to have been the father of our Thomas. Charles Edward Banks, *Topographical Dictionary of 2885 English Emigrants to New England. 1620-1650* [Philadelphia: Bertram Press, 1937][hereinafter Banks Topo], 67, and Charles Edward Banks, *The Planters of the Commonwealth* [Boston: Houghton Mifflin, 1930], 201) shows the *Jonathan* Thomas coming from Bovingdon, Hertfordshire, which is also the origin of the Zaccheus Gould clan of the North Shore, as well as the Quaker family of Jeremy Gould of Rhode Island, and Nathan Gould of Salisbury which spread out to Vermont and New Hampshire (Benjamin A. Gould shows these to be a cadet branch of the Bovingdon Goulds who were numerous in Hertfordshire about 1600, with eldest sons named Thomas, and younger ones William and James). It is possible that further study of Huntington wills may reveal immigrants to America or marriages of Walker and Gould (see *Register* 49:267-8).

There seem to be three possibilities for the origin of our Thomas Gould, in rising order of probability:

1. He was born in a neighboring town or colony, which seems to have been eliminated by the careful research of Benjamin A. Gould.

2. He was born in Boston before 1660, based on estimated latest date of marriage, 1680. Record of age at death would help, but neither burial nor death are recorded in Boston.

3. He immigrated from England before 1687, the first date he is definitely in Boston. Did he come with Governor Andros, who arrived 20 Dec. 1686 (Albert Bushnell Hart, ed., *Commonwealth History of Massachusetts* [5 vols., New York: States History Co., 1927] 1:583). Gould is not listed in Andros's soldiers (Massachusetts Historical Soc. Misc. Doc.) but could be among Anglican tradesmen, no list of which has been found yet.

POSSIBLE ORIGINS IN CITY OF LONDON.

Some clues exist to his origin: His will says that if his daughter Ann dies without issue his property goes to "my couzen Hannah Walker Daughter of Mr. Anthony Walker of London Hatter" or to her siblings. Perhaps Anthony Walker married a sister of Thomas Gould's mother or father, or she may have been a more distant cousin. We do not know if his mother was named Walker (a sister of Anthony, or a sister who married Walker. *The International Genealogical Index* [Compiled by the Church of Jesus Christ of the Latter Day Saints, hereinafter cited as IGI] shows a Thomas Gould or Gold married to a Frances Walker 26 Aug. 1680 at St. James's Duke's Place, London (56, 698). The marriage of Thomas Gold to Frances Bacon 30 March 1685 in the same parish may be too late for birth of William, and perhaps an older Thomas; Thomas Gould married to Frances Cole 25 Feb. 1655 at St. Peter Pauls Wharf is too early; birth of a William Gould to Thomas and Frances 23 July 1676 St. Stephens Coleman is too early for a child of Frances Walker. The parish church of St. James in Duke's Place, consecrated in 1623, but demolished in 1874, was in The City, in the north of Aldgate, which may be in the area of the brass founders (Nikolas Pevsner, *London* [London: Penguin, 1957], [hereinafter Pevsner], 1:161,

214; Peter Cunningham, *Handbook of London* [London: John Murray, 1850], 254-5).

An additional suggestion appears in the IGI: Two children are born to a Thomas and Frances Gould who are baptized in the London church of St. Stephen in Coleman Street, which was rebuilt in 1676 by Christopher Wren after the Great Fire of 1666. It lay on the west side of the street in the heart of the City of London, between the Guildhall and the Bank of London, less than a half a mile west of St. James Duke's Place (Ann Gould, baptized 18 Sept. 1674 at St. Stephen Coleman London, father Thomas, mother Francis in IGI batch CO 19662, call # 375013 film; printout 883922 film; William Gould baptized 23 July 1676 at St. Stephen Coleman, father Thomas, mother Frances; souce: LDS Ord 13 Sept. 1977 Slade [temple], same as above. (Pevsner 1: 67, 73, 76).

Most suggestive, however, is that the Armourers' and Braziers' Hall stood on Coleman Street, at the north east corner of London Wall, an 1840 building built on the site of the old Armourers' Hall which merged with the Braziers in 1708. Pevsner notes that the Hall has an important collection of silver, including six wine cups that belonged to the Braziers Company, to which Thomas Gould may have belonged (Pevsner 1:229; Cunningham 19).

BOSTON IMMIGRANTS NAMED THOMAS GOULD.

Published lists of immigrants have been searched without finding our Thomas (Meyer, eds., *Passenger & Immigrant Lists Index* [Detroit: Gale Research Co., 1981] 3 vols., plus 1984-8 supplements) refers to only three individuals, as follows:

1. <u>Charlestown 1620-50.</u> from Bovingdon, Herts, per Banks' Topo 67 (Banks' source is Banks mss. in Library of Congress, xxx, which might be checked); Massachusetts 1639 ae. 32 arrrived on the *Jonathan* 1639 with wife Hannah (Banks; NEng. 1639 ae. 45 in 1642 (Carl Boyer 180), same as next; NEng. 1652 ae. 45 per deposition Cambridge 1665, he came in *Jonathan* (Michael Tepper, *Passengers to America* [Baltimore: Genealogical Publishing Co., 1977], 140); New England 1639, ae. 45 (*Register* 10:407); Charlestown 1665, founder of Baptists (citing Shaw's *History of Boston*, 242 and Benedict's *History of Baptists*, 385-91, (John Farmer, *A Genealogical Register of the First Settlers of New England* [Lancaster, Massachusetts: Carter, Andrews & Co., 1828], 27).

2. <u>Boston 1641.</u> perhaps the freeman of 1641 was the Thomas Gold who died 26 Oct. 1662 (Farmer 127, Doc. 130:86; Holbrook 109). No will, children, deeds were found.

3. <u>New England 1680.</u> Peter W. Coldham's *The Complete Book of Emigrants 1661-1699* [Baltimore: Genealogical Publishing Co., 1990], 358 lists Thomas Gould (Gold was the spelling used by our ancestor) as passenger on the Bombay from London 7 Feb. 1680-15 March by Mr. Joseph Bartholomew and Mr. John Wood, citing PR E190/91/1.

4. <u>America 1685.</u> A rebel transported from Wiltshire to America 1685 (Peter Wilson Coldham, *Bonded Passengers to America* [9 vols., Baltimore: Genealogical Publishing Co., 1983], 5:92). There is no evidence that he arrived in Boston. Perhaps he showed up in another colony.

This appears to make the *Jonathan* immigrant and Baptist the same, despite Z Gould who calls our next entry in Boston 1641 the *Jonathan* immigrant.). Filby's list of immigrant Thomas Goulds (P. William Filby and Mary Keyser (*Passenger and Immigration Lists Index* [Detroit;

Gale Publishing, 1981]). The baptismal dates of 1674 and 1676 are close enough to the only known children of our Thomas and Frances, but the connection is not proven.

Passenger lists are obviously incomplete, and Filby's three immigrants leave unaccounted for by immigration or birth three other Thomas Goulds living in Boston before 1700:

1. One who married Frances Robinson in Boston 1656.
2. Thomas Gould, a cooper, who m. Experience Sumner about 1686 (perhaps son of the previous person) who turns up first in Boston as taxpayer in North End in 1686.
3. Our Thomas Gould, who m. Frances ____ c. 1680.

More names of immigrants may show up, but we see that there are at least four immigrants named Thomas Gould who arrived in 1639, 1641, 1680, 1685, 1686, and six seventeenth century Boston residents of the name. We will now give what biography of our ancestor that we know.

CAREER OF THOMAS[1] GOULD, BRASS FOUNDER.

1687, on 6 June, is the first notice of our Thomas Gould in America, when he appears on the Boston tax list (*First Report of the Record Commissioners of the City of Boston 1876* [Doc. 92] [Boston: Rockwell & Churchill, 1881] [hereinafter TR 1], sheet 2, 86).

A value of £ 0/1/10 is given for 1687 (99). Note that another Thomas Gould, spelled Tho Golde, also appears for the first time (On sheet 2 in Thwing, Holbrook 107, TR 1:127). This is presumably the cooper in the North End, in Ward 2. There is no previous indication that Goulds owned property in Boston (George Lamb, comp., *Plans of Boston Showing Existing ways and Owners of Property 1630-1645* [City of Boston, 1905]. Aspinwall has only one reference to a Gould 371, on 5 Dec. 1650 Thomas Gould is witness to deposition of Peter Talman (*Aspinwall Notorial Records 1644-1651* [Boston: Municipal Printing Office, 1903]. The reference to Noodles Island makes this the Baptist Rev. Thomas, not ours.

There are two possible earlier references. The first, in 1669, is when a Thomas Gould witnessed a mortgage 9 Nov. 1669 recorded (Suffolk Deeds [hereinafter SD] 6:140; Z Gould 347) from John Winthrop of Hartford to Samuel Shrimpton of Boston, executor. Since Shrimpton was a brass founder and brazier, the witness is more likely to be our Thomas Gould than the one who B. A. Gould says is "probably" the one who m. Frances Robinson. However, this may be the Rev. Thomas, since Henry Shrimpton's will of 17 May 1666 left £ 10 to Gold and Osborne's (Baptist) church on Noodles Island (Massachusetts Archives 15 B Estates 104e).

A second reference is in Suffolk County Supreme Court of Judicature files (Massachusetts Archives at Columbia Point [hereinafter Suff.Ct.] docket # 162193) recording the testimony on 12 Nov. 1680 by a Thomas Gould (a spelling not used by our Thomas at any time) age 21 and William Johannot aged 23 that they say Samuel Mattoche culled a barrel of stones for Joseph Galley. This Thomas Gould was born about 1659, a reasonable date for our Thomas, as well as the North End cooper. In its favor is the fact that Johannot's family later were neighbors of our Goulds in the South End of Boston. The spelling is against it, but we find many colonial documents where the spelling is phonetic, and varies within the same document. The birth date 1659 is too late for the other three Boston Thomas Goulds, who m. Frances Robinson in 1656, the Rev. Thomas, or the *Jonathan* immigrant (Z Gould 346, 340). Until further evidence of the age of our Thomas Gould appears we cannot accept this reference.

In 1688 Tho. Golde is shown on the Boston tax list (Sheets, TR 1:143) as a "taxable head".

In July of 1689 Thomas Gold, the founder, contributed 12 shillings to construction of King's Chapel, the first Episcopal church in Boston and in New England (Henry W. Foote, *Annals of King's Chapel* [Boston: Little, Brown, 1882], [hereinafter Foote], 1: 89 confirmed in original records of King's Chapel, Massachusetts Historical Society, [hereinafter MHS], Church Book, Minutes of Vestry (Box 1, folder 1), 2, July 1689: first contributions for erecting the church: Thomas Gould £ 0/12/-, Stephen Minot £ 1/-). King's Chapel was formally organized on 15 June 1686 and held its first service on 8 June 1689, so Thomas Gould was evidently one of the principal founders of the church. The first religious wedding in Boston was performed at Samuel Shrimpton's house by Rev. Ratcliffe, Anglican (Andre Mayer, *Kings Chapel The First Century* [Boston, 1976], 4). This is further connection of founders Shrimpton and Gould.

In 1689 the first reference is made to the trade of Thomas Gold, in the King's Chapel founding. All subsequent references are the same, "founder". At first we had assumed that he might be an iron founder, particularly since one of the first foundries was established by John[2] Gould (1635-1710) of Topsfield. However, David B. Ingram of Foxboro, who probably knows more about iron foundries than anyone, points out that there is not only no history of an iron foundry in Boston, and the physical conditions preclude it (Personal letter 14 Oct. 1989). It required a large area, trees for fuel, and a nearby source of ore (Clyde A. Sanders and Dudley C. Gould, [a descendant], *History in Cast Metal: The Founders of North America* [Cast Metals Institute: Des Plaines IL., 1976], Z Gould #7, 50).

Ingram proposed instead that Thomas Gould was a founder of non-ferrous metals like copper or brass. There is no reference to the locations of either in the standard histories of Boston and Massachusetts, nor in Massachusetts Archives, Bostonian Society or Massachusetts Historical Society. A copper works shows on the Bonner map of 1722 on the northwest point toward Cambridge, and the same on the Burgis map of 1728, but there is no connection with any Gould property until the nineteenth century, when the young Thomas[5] Gould began building houses in the West End, on Brighton Street.

Clues to the type of foundry are Thomas Gould's donation of a brass standard to King's Chapel in 1691, the presence of two brass kettles in his wife's estate of 1709, and his major repair of the town water engine in 1702. None of this is conclusive. A brass foundry had been established in Boston by 1639 by Henry Shrimpton, brazier and founder. This was such a profitable business that Shrimpton was given the grandest funeral to date in the town, and his son Samuel who inherited the business became an influential politician (councilor) and land owner on Beacon Hill and Noodles Island (*Boston Globe,* March 1900 in Bostonian Society Scrapbook G 57; Justin Winsor, *The Memorial History of Boston* [Boston: James R. Osgood, 1880, 4 vols.], [hereinafter Winsor], 1: 573, 582, 584). Gould connections with Shrimpton are Thomas Gould's witness to Shrimpton's deposition of 1669, and both were founding members of King's Chapel 1686, but no business connection has been established.

Gould Locations in Boston 1678-1804

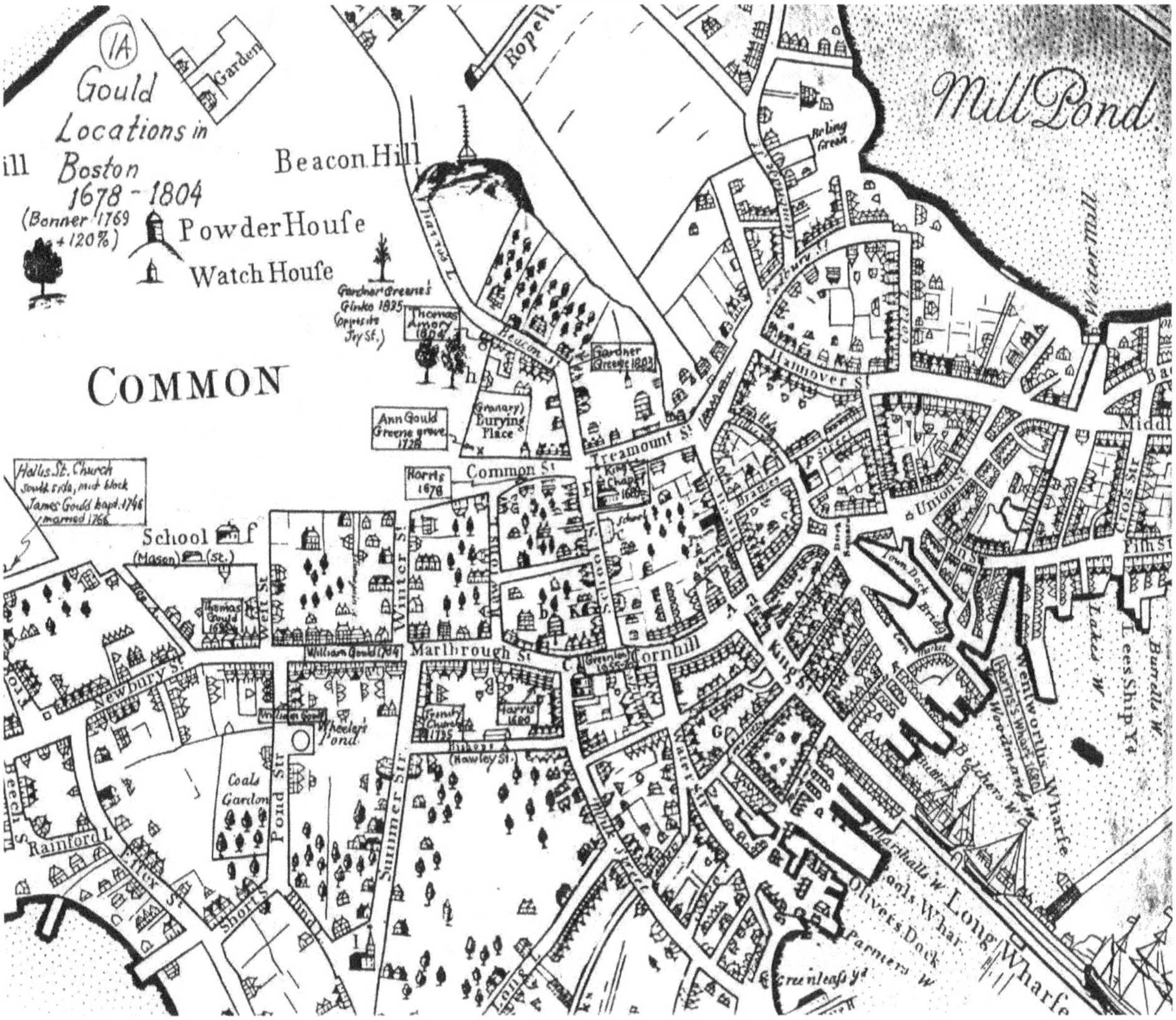

Location of Gould's foundry. In Gold's estate of 1707 in the South End there was a workshop (perhaps built in 1700) on the south half of the property close to the line of the half purchased from Shaw, near the center of the lot.

That the foundry business was profitable is indicated by the fact that Thomas Gold left an estate of three houses, and land that became part of the Greene fortune of the next century. He was also one of the largest contributors to building and extension of King's Chapel, and gave his daughter Ann an exceptionally good education.

1689 is the date of completion of first King's Chapel. There are pictures in Winsor and Greenwood (Winsor 1:214 and F. W. P. Greenwood, *A History of King's Chapel* [Boston: Carter & Henree, 1833 [hereinafter Greenwood], 215]. There is a story that the pulpit and stairs of the original Chapel were disassembled when the present building was constructed, and shipped by sea to become part of the Anglican church in Lunenburg, Nova Scotia (W. D. Raymond, 1 Sept. 1989, who cited a pamphlet "A Walk Through Old Lunenburg" which says: "There has been speculation, but no documentary proof, that the wood came from Old King's Chapel, Boston, which had been replaced about that time" of the construction of St. John's Anglican Church in 1753, 43).

In 1691 Thomas Gold is on the Boston tax list of Elizer Holyoke (#8, Holbrook 107, Bost 876:156).

On Christmas Day 1691 Thomas Golde gave a brass standard for "ye ouer-glass" of King's Chapel (Foote, 1:111; Greenwood 152). The church inventory of 19 April 1733 lists a brass hour glass given by Thomas Gold and William Weaver, and recorded with this entry: "Mr. (note honorific title reserved for prominent citizens) Thomas Gould and Mr. William Weaver gave to ye Church of England The Bras Standard for ye owerglass" (Foote 1:419, Greenwood 175, confirmed in King's Chapel records MHS, Vol. 16 Reverse "Entry Book for Church Meetings", 7). Greenwood's description of the church before 1753 says: "In the pulpit there was an hour glass, according to the old fashion, mounted on a large and elaborate stand of brass." (126). The standard is no longer in the church, and may have disappeared at the time of the Revolution when all of the records and plate were removed by the Loyalist members.

On 29 Nov. 1692 Thomas Gold, founder of Boston, sued Nathaniel Wyatt of Dorchester, carpenter. The court of common pleas awarded Gould £ 2/16 plus £2/16/7 in costs (Abstract and Index of the Records of the Inferior Court of Pleas, Boston, 1680-98, prep. by Historical Records Survey, Boston Public Library).

In May 1694 Thomas Gold paid £ 2 for his pew in King's Chapel (Foote 1:119; King's Chapel records MHS, 16:3 list of contributors to pews in May 1694: Thos. Gold 11-1-52. The first record of land owned by our family in Boston was on 10 July 1695 Thomas Gold, founder, bought a house and land of Edward Hill in the area that is today the Theater District between Washington and Tremont Streets, between West and Boylston (Annie Thwing, "Inhabitants and Estates of the Town of Boston 1630-1800" card index in MHS) [hereinafter Thwing], S.D.17.113.114=SD 17:113-114, the original deed. Suff. Ct. #1622365 is a very poor copy of this deed, starting on line 30).

The deed records that Thos. Gold, founder, paid £ 80 to Edward Hill, cordwainer and his wife Deborah, for land now occupied by Gold with houses, outhouses, shops, gardens, well-rights, etc. bounded 40 feet on the highway to Roxbury (now Washington Street), on southwest by a lot of Edward Hill, on the northwest, in the rear by the Common or Training Field 37 feet (now Mason Street, since frontage on the Common is today on Tremont), and northeast 285 feet by the land of Fearnot Shaw (which Gould bought two years later). On Clough's map of 1676 (MHS) it is the fourth lot west of Cowell's Lane (West Street). On Bonner's map of 1722 it shows as a large two story gable roof in the middle of five houses between Hog Alley and West Street (today's Avery Street; Nathaniel B. Shurtleff, *A Topographical and Historical Description of Boston* [Boston: 3d ed., Common Council, 1891], 315; Hog Alley obviously ran more in a southwesterly direction, perhaps starting a bit north of the present corner of Avery and Washington.

Well up to the American Revolution this part of Boston was out in the edges of the settled center, at the start of the Neck, the only land egress from Boston, between the mudflats of the Back Bay and Fort Point Channel. The National Register description of the area quotes an unnamed source as saying that during the colonial era this was "rural, unsettled patch of country" (Theater District (1979), significance 8, 9). The first building of any importance in the area was the Hollis Street Church, where the third generation of Goulds was baptized and married, built in 1732. Nearby, on the corner of Essex and Washington Streets was the famous Liberty Tree, planted in 1646, and the nearby tavern where the Sons of Liberty met to protest the hated Stamp Act and plan the Boston Tea Party. The area was still open and semi-rural as late as 1800. That this was on the edge of town is shown by the fact that here the stagecoaches started their run to Providence from the Lamb Tavern (1765) (John Harris, *The Boston Globe Historic Walks* [Chester CT: Pequot Press, 2d. ed. 1989], 193).

Next door to the Goulds was the well-known Lamb Tavern, which became the Adams House, where the first Scotch highball was served, now the Art Deco Paramount Theater (Massachusetts Historical Society, National Historic Register [hereinafter NHR] Washington Theater District #1). From 1835 on this area has been the core of Boston's Theater District, from the time when the former Grand Turk Tavern at 539 Washington Street (later the Lion Tavern) was converted into a theater (NHR Washington Street District #3). Renamed The Melodeon, the Handel & Haydn Society gave its early oratorios, and on Sunday opened up to the radical sermons of the dissident Unitarian preacher Theodore Parker (Samuel Adams Drake, *Old Landmarks of Boston* [Boston: James Osgood, 1874], [hereinafter Drake],394).

The Melodeon of 1844, where all the famous lecturers spoke (Harris 192), and Jenny Lind sang, became the Savoy in 1854, called "the finest theater in the world", where all of the first performances of the great operas were done, and gala receptions for royalty like the King of Siam, the Prince of Wales, as well as three U.S. Presidents. Today this is the Spanish Baroque Savoy of 1929, the flagship theater where B. F. Keith first brought both vaudeville and the moving picture, to build his chain of hundreds of theaters. His Boston agent was Henry D. Dupee (c. 1853-1915) who named Point Isabella in Cotuit for his wife Mary Isabella Dupee (NHR Cotuit OP 29). Joseph Kennedy, father of the President had his offices here In the 1970s Sarah Caldwell revived the theater for the Boston Opera. Finally, in the new century this became the focus of a major historic restoration, which I saw in progress in Oct. 2003 as the entire back-stage was demolished. I looked in vain for relics of Thomas Gould's foundry, but realized from the depth of the cellars that the demolition of the 1854 Boston Theater to make room for the Savoy in 1929 had destroyed any archaeological remains (Journal 85, 137-8, 5 Sept. 2003).

Gould's house and foundry backed up to the Boston Common, which extended to Mason St. until 1800 (Drake 316-8). Before that there was an empty field "used chiefly as a hay stand, and known as the haymarket" (Nathaniel B. Shurtleff, *A Topographical and Historical Description of Boston* [Boston: Rockwell & Churchill, 1891] [hereinafter Shurtleff], 308). At the back, on Mason and West St. was the Free School, later the Adams School, since 1722. Here the Boston Public Library opened for the first time in 1854 (Mary Caroline Crawford, *Romantic Days in Old Boston* [Boston: Little, Brown, 1910],[hereinafter Crawford], 399. Nearby on the Common were the whipping post and pillory where condemned persons were punished, as well as the Gun-House, from which the Patriots stole two brass cannons from under the noses of the

British redcoats, to be used throughout the Revolution. On the land that was once the Common, between Mason and Tremont, was built in 1811 Bulfinch's Colonnade Row, home of the most elite Bostonans like the Lowell, Lawrences and Masons, and where General Lafayette gave a gracious bow to an old friend, Mrs. Scott (Crawford 10). Behind the Colonnade was the dome of Harvard's Mass. Medical College.

Gould's house was near or at #525-527 Washington Street. Today this is the 900 seat Modern Theater in the five story Dobson Building (NHR Washington Street District #5). Here the first silent movie, "The Jazz Singer" was given its premier (Susan & Michael Southworth, *A. I. A. Guide to Boston* [Chester CT: Globe Pequot Press, 1989], 125, with photo). This was built in 1876 in Ruskinian Gothic style by Levi Dobson, as headquarters for the largest carpet maker in the world. It became the Mayflower Theater, remodeled in 1913 in the earliest extant example and the only documented building done in team by the famous Symphony Hall acoustic expert Wallace Sabine and the foremost theater architect, Clarence Howard Blacknall, who refaced the first two floors with a neoclassical front. On the south side of the theater is a little alley called Harlaem (or Harlem) Place, laid out in 1822, shortly before Newbury Street's name was changed to Washington (1824) (City of Boston *Record of Streets* (1910), 229, 333).

In that first deed, Edward Hill had to pay Gold £ 108/16 in installments of 4/16 each 16 April in the next five years, and £ 84/16 to complete the sum before 10 July 1701. The size of this debt of Hill to Gould indicates the extent of his wealth. This also shows that Gould was living in this location in the South End, then on the edge of the settled area, by 1695, and perhaps operating his foundry out of the "outhouses and shops". Gould and his wife were renting the house and living in it at the time of purchase (Suff Ct. # 3897 of 1697).

In 1695 the Thomas Gould listed as inhabitant of Ward 8 is clearly the founder (TR 1:163; "A List of Inhabitants in Boston 1695", *Bostonian Society Publications*, 10 [1913], 86). The same name in Ward 2, the North End, is the cooper.

17 July 1695 event on Boston Common: A duel fought upon the Common between Peggy and Capt. Cole (Samuel Sewall, *The Diary of Samuel Sewall* [New York: Farrar, Straus & Giroux, 1973], 1:410).

5 November "Pope Day" was celebrated on Boston Common with a bonfire, recalling the Gunpowder Plot of Guy Fawkes to blow up the Houses of Parliament in London (Mark DeW. Howe, *Boston Common* [Boston: Atlantic Monthly, 1921], 20). Douglas[8] Gould always remembered Guy Fawkes Day as his mother's birthday, and for the bonfires on the night during his youth, recalling the rhyme: November fifth, a day never to be forgot...for the Gunpowder Plot."

On 18 Nov. 1696 Thomas Gold signed a petition of Boston citizens against the requirement that buildings be made of brick (Massachusetts Archives Index 113:139; Thwing gives date 11 June 1697).

On 10 March 1697 Thomas Gold, founder of Boston, bought a second piece of property on the Common, adjoining his other one on the north (SD 14: 307-9). For 85 pounds ffearnot Shaw and his wife Bethia conveyed "all that their Messuage or Tenement with the yards[,]

Garden and Land belonging, Situate Lying and being at the southerly end of the Town of Boston aforesaid butted and bounded in the front South Easterly with the Street or Highway leading from Boston towards Roxbury, where it measureth in breadth twenty foot or therabouts... Southwesterly with the Tenement and Land of Edward Hill in the present Tenure and Occupancy of Said Gold. In the Rear Northwesterly by the Common or Trayning ffield where it measureth thirty six foot... and North Easterly with the Tenement and land of Mary Cowell widow, measuring in Depth...One hundred ninety two foot...according as it is now fenced in, which sd granted and bargained premises was formerly the Estate of the sd Jacob Leager, and was set forth unto Bethia his Daughter...Together with all and singular the Houses, Edifices, Building and ffences" etc.

On 22 March 1697 the town published a notice: No person shall ride to and fro about the Common on the Sabbath Day to water horses (Thwing citing 7.227).

On 28 April 1697 a long legal case began involving the Goulds' Washington Street property (Suff Ct. docket #3897). We quote in full the "The Deposition of Thomas Gould and ffrancess his wife both of full age, the which Deponts do testifie & say tht in the life time of Mr. William Penn they hired a dwelling house of sd Penn, in the we house the sd Deponents did dwell & but a short time before the sd Penn died the Deponts went unto the house of Edward Hill; wherein sd Penn lay sick, and coming into the Romm [sic] where Mr. Penn was, sd Thomas Gold told him they was come to pay a quarters Rent which was then due, whereupon Mr. Penn desired us to set down and called for his Cousen Edward Hill to come into that Room & he accordingly came, and then sd Penn ordered the Deponent Gould to pay the money unto sd Edward Hill and Gold accordingly did, and Edward Hill then gave receipt under his hand thereof, and at that time in the hearing of the sd Deponents the abovesaid Wm Penn did say that all he had was his Couzin Hills, saying that he gave it to him, and further said not..." In the case of *Ensor v. Gould* (below, in 1717, 6). William Gould testified that Hill occupied the house in the winter of 1688, and sold it to the Goulds in Oct. 1692. The property was claimed by Penn's niece Mary Ensor in 1717, but she lost the case on appeal to the Supreme Court in 1719.

In about 1697 The Court of Common Pleas ruled in favor of Thomas Gould, founder, in a suit of Anthony Penn of Birmingham England for illegally holding one third of the land of his uncle William Penn of Braintree located in the south end of Boston. The court awarded him cost of 16/2d. (Record Book, 1642-1701, 24, Massachusetts Archives). The will of William Penn was challenged as a forgery (Sewall, citing 5 MHS Collections 7: 88-89n). The suit came about apparently because William Penn of Braintree had bought land and house from Jacob Leager in the south end, on 5 Sept. 1679 (SD 11:229). He deeded this to Samuel Peacock, glazier, on 10 Nov. 1681 (SD 12:126). Peacock sold this to Edward Hill on 19 Sept. 1685, with mortgage of 10 Nov. 1681 (SD 13:376; also 12:336, 13:378; 21:675).

On 14 March 1698 Thos Gold was chosen Town Constable (Bos. City Doc. 50, 229; Robert F. Seabolt, *The Town Officials of Colonial Boston 1634-1775* [Cambridge: Harvard University Press, 1939], 95. The duties included enforcing town bylaws and the colony's laws, serving writs in suits, collecting colonial and town taxes, and supervising the town watchmen (G. B. Warden, *Boston 1689-1776* [Boston: Little, Brown, 1970]. Although this may have been his contemporary namesake, the cooper living in the North End, the spelling in the city document

Thomas Gold conforms to the usage of our South End resident. The term was one year through 13 March 1699.

On 20 September 1698 Gould's property adjoined to the northeast of the disputed property of Hill-Walker, in the case of Edward Hill, cordwainer versus Hannah Walker, only daughter of John Walker, Boston brick maker, who was willed half of the house and land. Hill's retention of it led to £ 150 writ of attachment dated 20 Sept. 1698, carried out that day by John Poinchombe Under Sheriff of Suffolk County. This was the estate of John Walker by will of his father John on 13 Dec. 1678 (Mass Archives 40:525; Hannah Walker, daughter of late John Walker of Boston was to inherit half his estate, 40:527.

Edward Hill sold property to Hannah Walker on 18 Aug. 1704 (SD 21:675).

On 27 Dec. 1698 Thomas Gold was witness to the mortgage of land in the south end of Boston by George Rescarricke, mariner of Boston to Gyles Dyer, merchant of Boston (SD 19:50, reported by Gail Harris, 1992). In 1700 Rescarricke was dealing with John Harrison of Pennsylvania, whose son was ordered arrested in 1699 as one of Captain Kidd's pirates (Gale Harris, "Suffolk County Deeds and Boston Tax Lists (Wheeler's Pond Neighborhood", late 1992, 4).

On 16 April 1700 Thomas Gold, founder, was given permission by the town to erect a timber building 30 x 20 x 16 next to his house in the South End, described as "rough cast" with a slate roof (Thwing). This appears to have been an extension of the brass foundry.

1701 marked the entrance of Eighteenth Century, on 1 Jan. 1700/1, with celebrations on the Common next to the Goulds': "Just about break of day Jacob Amsdan and 3 other trumpeters gave a blast with the Trumpets on the common rear of Mr. Alford's." (Sewell, I:440).

On 27 July 1702 "Thomas Gold was allowed £ 7 for worke done to ye watter Engine" of town of Boston (*Boston Report of Record Commissioners* [Boston: Rockwell & Churchill, 1884] Records of Selectmen, Doc. 75, 25).

On the same day, Thos. Gold was security for John Nichols, haberdasher, late of London, when he was given permission to reside in Boston (Bos.City Doc.50, 1, 25). Thwing indicates Nichols may be the same merchant who held town office of tithingman in 1705 and 1709, but no wife is listed. We do not know if this was a relative, and if so what his relation to Elinor Nicholls who is listed as sister of Thomas's wife Frances in her will of 1709 (see below).

On 7 March 1705 Thomas Gold, founder, paid £ 120 to Edward Hill, cordwainer, and his wife Deborah, for land and buildings located at southerly end of Boston, fronting 48 feet on the street to Roxbury (now Washington Street), 285 feet on SW by land of Joseph Blin, mariner, 37 feet northwest on the Common, and 285 feet on the northeast by land of Thomas Gold. The deed included "houses outhouses Shops Edifices buildings & fences"..."And the yards Gardens backsides well-rights", etc. There is an unusually long (over a page) guarantee that there are no encumbrances. Witness was Nathaniel Greene, his son-in-law (SD 22:177-9; There is an identical copy in Suff. Ct. # 6388.

About 1705 Thos Gold gave £ 1/- in collection of congregation of Queen's Chapel to supply debts (K. C. records, Vol. 16). During the reign of Queen Anne, 1701/2-1714, King's Chapel was dedicated to her majesty. Nathaniel Green[e], his son-in-law, gave six shillings.

On 24 May 1706 Gould's neighbor James Blin, mariner, agreed that "Thomas Gold shall have free Liberty and privilidge to Erect and build a Wall of a house of thirteen inches thick upon the land of the sd. James Blin next adjoining the Land of the sd. Thomas Gold at the south End of Boston aforesd., and to be Twentyfour foot in Length from the Street leading to Roxbury towards the Common... and to Warrant a slip of Land of thirteen Inches broad at the front and Twentyfour foot in Length running down towards the Common... for the use aforesaid unto the sd. Thomas Gold..." In consideration Gold agreed that Blin may build any house or structure adjoining the wall, that both will have equal benefit in Common, and that Gold will forever Repair it and provide the materials (SD 23:11).

Thomas Gold executed his will on 1 March 1706/7 (SW 3049, 311-312). The executrix and administrator was his widow Frances Gold. I quote the text in its original punctuation: "I do give.. .unto my beloved Wife Frances Gold the Income, use, benefit & Improvemt of all my houseing, Lands, TenemtS &...their AppurCes in Boston aforesd for & During the time & Term of her being & Continuing my Widow, But if She marry again, Then I do only give her the Use, benefit & Improvemt of my new Brick house with the Land behind the Same, during the term of her Natural Life."

After her death, he said, "I give to my Son William Gold of Boston...Founder..., my Brick house" and land. After her death or Second Marriage, which of them shall first happen, I" give my son and his heirs "my Dwelling house & Land...in the present Tenure & Occupation of James Pearson [312] Together with my Work house so called, & the Land under, before & behind the Same, reaching up unto the Common or Training Field in Boston..." and if said son dies without issue the said property to go to my daughter Ann Green. If said son leaves a widow she shall receive from said Ann £ 10 per year as long as she is a widow.

If Ann dies without issue the property goes to Hannah Walker daughter of Anthony Walker, hatter of London. He bequeaths to his daughter Ann Green all of house and land which he "bought of Fearnott Shaw reaching up to the Common... ,as formerly divided from the Northerly side of my.. .Work-house". If she dies without issue it goes to son William or his heirs; if he dies without issue the house and half of land adjoining goes to "Couzen Hannah Walker" or her heirs.

He left to his son William "all my Wearing Apparrel—both Woolen & Linnen, Together with all my Working Tools, Gearse, Implements whatsoever belonging to my Calling."

To my wife Frances I leave "All my Plate, Movables, household Goods, Shop-Goods, Debts, Trading Stock & Personal Estate."

He added a memo that if Hannah Walker died without issue, the estate would go to remaining surviving children of Anthony Walker in equal shares (Suffolk Will [hereinafter SW] 3049, 313).

Gold's will was probated in Boston on 28 July 1707, so he probably died in that month.

Comment on disposal of estate: his son William inherited the foundry business. His wife Frances kept the Brick house and half of land to south which came from Edward Hill in 1695 until her death in 1709, when it went to William, including the house occupied by James Pearson. Pearson does not show up in Thwing as possessing property, but he held town office of

Hogreeve in 1706/7 (Boston, *Report of Record Commissioners. Boston Records 1700-28* [Boston: Rockwell & Churchill, 1883], Document 137, 42), and was licensed as a retailer to sell drink on 27 July 1713 (CD 75:189). The Greene heirs of Thomas Gould yielded title to this property in 1753 to William Spearman (SD 66:120-1) as will be shown below under Thomas Greene. His daughter Ann Greene got the north half that came from Fearnot Shaw in 1696, which was inherited by the Greene children.

2. FRANCES GOULD, wife of THOMAS[1] GOULD was born perhaps in London; she died in Boston about July 1709; married about 1680 (Charles Almon Torrey, *New England Marriages Prior to 1700* [Baltimore: Genealogical Publishing Co., 1985] [hereinafter Torrey], 38). Frances's maiden name is unknown. It is mistaken by many writers to be the Frances Robinson who married another Thomas Gould of Boston 10 Sept. 1656 (Torrey 315, *Register* 11: 202). The Torrey manuscript in NEHGS shows that Frances Robinson Gould died in Guilford CT 1671? (Boston City Doc. 130:57 [9th] *Report of the Record Commissioners...Boston. Baptisms. Marriages, and Deaths. 1630-1699* [Boston: Rockwell & Churchill, 1883] [hereinafter CD 130] shows wedding by Major Atherton. Benjamin Apthorp Gould gives the correct marriage (Z Gould, 347). Though Frances Robinson Gould had three children, 1657-62, two by the names of Thomas and Ann, it is highly improbable that she was mother of two by the same names over twenty years later, in 1680-5. The historian of King's Chapel (Foote 1:92, note) makes this error, as did many in Greene Family).

Wills of women during this period are uncommon, and usually are those of some wealth. In this will dated 8 Feb. 1708/9 Frances Goold (note change of spelling from husband's consistent Gold) gave her son William "One bed, One bowlster, two pillows, one pair of Sheats, One pair of blankets, One coverlid, and my large Silver Tankard my clock and my Indian Boy called Caesar One great brass kettle, and One small kettle brass; And also ffifty pounds of Current money of New England—Item I give unto my Grand Children Thomas and Rufus Greane to each of them Ten pounds...to be Improved for them until they Come of age—Item I give unto my Sister Elinor Nicholls one piece of plate to the value of Ten pounds, if she continue in New England at my decease. And to my Son in Law Nathaniel Green, and unto my Daughter Anne Green I Do Give all the rest and residue of my whole Estate." Her son-in-law Nathaniel Green was appointed sole executor (SW 3331, 280).

It was signed with Her mark F, not necessarily a sign of illiteracy.

Frances Goold's will was probated 16 July 1709. Her death about July 1709 is not recorded in Boston or King's Chapel records. She was buried probably beside her husband in King's Chapel or Old Granary, though there is no extant record.

Three children:

3. i. WILLIAM[2] b. c. 1680 London?, d. c. 1747; m. MERCY[2] HARRIS

4. ii. ANN(E) b. c. 1685 London?, d. Boston 16 Jan. 1728, m. NATHANIEL[3] GREENE.

iii. THOMAS, b. Boston 4 July 1687 (Boston City Doc. 150 [9th] *Report of the Record Commissioners...Boston. Baptisms. Marriages, and Deaths, 1630-1699* [Boston: Rockwell & Churchill, 1881 [hereinafter CD 130], 174). d. before parents (1707), probably unmarried.

?i. THOMAS? There may have been an infant Thomas born London before 1680 who died before 1687, since the family consistently named eldest son Thomas.

Chapter II

SECOND GENERATION
CAPTAIN WILLIAM^2 GOULD

3. Capt. **WILLIAM^2 GOULD / GOLD** (Thomas^1), master mariner and founder, born perhaps in London about 1680 (Roderick Jones, Harris Papers in NEHGS MSS H3, 630); died 28 Nov. 1740 (Records of Trinity Church, 388; between 26 Oct. 1740 and 26 Jan. 1741 "Benjamin Greene Account Books 1734-1756", MHS). He married 16 April 1699 (CD 130, 251) **MERCY^2 HARRIS** (Richard^1). She was probably born Boston about 1681 (Roderick Bissell Jones, "Harrises in Boston before 1700", *Register*, 105 [1951]; hereinafter Jones, 197), and died in Boston between 11 and 29 June 1741 (SW 7623, 412-3).

William Gold married Mercy^2 Harris of Boston in King's Chapel, by Rev. Samuel Miles (1689-1728). She was eldest of three daughters of Richard Harris who died 12 April 1697 Boston, merchant of Boston and his second wife (m. before 1680, Jones, 193) Elizabeth^3 "Betty" Blackleach (b. 4 May 1659, Boston, d. after 1712), daughter of Capt. John^2 Blackleach, Jr., shipowner and his wife Elizabeth [Sheafe?]. He was a wealthy Connecticut merchant, who owned 480 acres in Middletown, and land in Stratford, Hartford, Wethersfield and Antigua. (Gale I. Harris, "John Blackleach, Merchant of London and New England" in *Register* , c. 1992,148:9 and his letter to author 19 May 1992); Robert C. Anderson, *The Great Migration Begins* [Boston: New Eng. Historic Genea. Soc., 2002] [Hereinafter Anderson], 1:313-8). He died 7 Sept. 1703 aged 77, leaving a large estate of £ 1576; his daughter Elizabeth had already received her share of £ 500 (Royal R. Hinman, *A Catalog of the Names of the Early Puritan Settlers of the Colony of Connecticut* [Hartford: Tiffany & Co., 1852], 242-3). His wife Elizabeth died 12 June 1708 aged 74.

John's father John^1 Blackleach(e) came to Chelsea (Winnisimmett) by 1634, became Massachusetts freeman that year (He and Samuel Maverick sold the ferry rights and interest in Winnisimmett; SD 1,15). By 1635 he had moved to Salem, where he was granted 350 acres of land, and became Representative for Salem in 1636. He moved to New Haven by 1658, then to Hartford where he lived at the corner of Main and Arch Sts.; he was Constable in March 1663, held land in Wethersfield 1661; died in Wethersfield 23 Aug. 1683. His wife died there 20 July 1683 (Hinman 241). John^1 Blackleach, merchant, philosopher and ship owner of London who m. before 1630 Elizabeth Bacon, daughter of Robert Bacon of Wapping and Christian Locksonne, who died in Wethersfield 20 July 1683 (There are no wills for John^1, Elizabeth or daughter Mary Olcott in Suffolk Wills).

Our Richard Harris was not the son of Mr. John Harris^2 (b. 1605/6) who came to New England 16 March 1634/5 on the *Christian*, son of Richard^1 Harris, mariner and shipowner of Leigh, Essex, d. 1607 and wife Sarah (as asserted by Roderick B. Jones papers in NEHGS, Mss.

Jones, which have been examined carefully and contain no additional Gould data; they may contain more info on Richard[1] Harris and Blackleaches and Bacons. See Gale I. Harris in TAG 64 (1989), 226). This writer believes that Richard Harris was a recent arrival in New England in 1662 (Gale I. Harris, "More Harrises of Boston", *Register* 152: 324, and letter to author 19 May 1992).

Elizabeth[2]'s sister Mary Blackleach married three times: 1) 1689 Thomas Welles Jr. who d. March 16 1695 (James Savage, *A Genealogical Dictionary of the First Settlers of New England* [4 vols. Baltimore: Genealogical Publishing Co., 1965], [hereinafter Sav.] 4: 480), 2) John Olcott who died Dec. 1711, leaving four children including Samuel b. 16 Aug. 1696; she administered his estate of £ 560, 3) Capt. Joseph Wadsworth famed for having hidden the Charter of the colony from Gov. Andros in 1687 in the Charter Oak (see W. H. Gocher, *Wadsworth or the Charter Oak* [Hartford, 1904]; cited in EB 11th ed., 6:956), he died 1729 (Frank F. Starr, *The Olcott Family of Hartford* [Hartford: James J. Goodwin, 1899], 41, 55, 61).

Richard Harris died 12 April 1697 intestate (CD 130:237; Sav. 2:363; Sewell 2:372 said "Braintry Harris".."is buried". An inventory of the estate (SW 2372) gave a total value of £ 1534/11/6, on 19 July 1697, of which the largest items were £ 650 for the brick warehouse at the Dock and a back warehouse (called Harris's Wharf later in estate; he had bought waterfront from John Woodmansey in 1679 and 1683 SD 11:339, 12:364, and dock at the mouth of the Dock from the same in 1684 SD 26:132-3).

Harris's wharf was directly south of Woodmansey's, in what is today near the east end of the North Block of Quincy Market, following the chain of title from Harris 1712 to Oliver & Welsteed, 1756 to Knight, 1760 to Williams, to Hall 1794, to Codman 1795 in part, which in 1800 is Merchants Row.), £ 450 for house and land at what is now Washington and Hawley Sts. (He bought this from Samuel Peacock in 1680 SD 12:3), and £ 160 for land at the backside of his house, probably that bought from Benjamin Blackleach in 1693 (SD 16:114). Harris also left £ 71 in silver plate and gold, including "A Salt belonging to the Eldest Daughter having her name one (Gon?) & was given by her father A long time befor his death".

At probate on 28 Oct. 1697 his widow reported debts of £ 490, including £ 3/8/4 to Thomas Gold, and £ 69 on account of Benjamin Blackleach. The house was sold for £ 430, 20 pounds under appraised value, to pay for debts leaving £ 1125 "Great part of which hath been already advanced to the deceaseds Children for their education subsistence" according to their mother.

1700 Feb. 25, William and Mercy Gold's first child, Sarah was born in Boston. ([24th] *Report of the Record Commissioners...Boston, Baptisms, Marriages, and Deaths, 1700-1800* [Boston: Rockwell & Churchill, 1894] [Document 43, 7].

1700 William Gold, cordwainer of Boston, in a petition undated but after debts for his father-in-law Richard Harris's estate were paid on 9 May 1700, and prior to division on 13 March 1701, declared "whereas the petitioner marryed with Mercy the daughter of Richard Harris late of Boston Merchant deceased who dyed intestate and left considerable Estate both in Lands houses and moveables...one fourth part of the personall and one Third part of the reall Estate, after the Widows share deducted out of the sd. reall Estate, belongs to your petitr. in right of the said wife Mercy." (SW 2372, no. 4).

On order of the probate court in 1701 a division of the real estate was proposed: The widow's third to be the Easternmost part of Harris's warehouse, the second daughter Mary's share to be the westernmost third of the warehouse, and the youngest Elizabeth's the middle third. Mercy was assigned the land between the main street and Bishops Lane in the south end of Boston and between John Walker on the south and Henery Brightman on the north. Since this was worth £ 30 more than a single share, and the land couldn't be divided without damage, Mercy should pay £ 30 to repair the warehouse "being gone to decay and much out of Repair".

1701, 30 Jan., William and Mercy Gold's second child born in Boston, named Thomas, (CD 43:7) the consistent traditional name for eldest son in subsequent generations of the family, and also in the Goulds of Bovingdon, Herts. (Z Gould, 1-23, nos. 1, 4, 17, 19. 36; *Register*, 49:265-9).

1703, 9 Feb., "Thomas Gold of Boston Founder Father of William Gold (now at Sea) who is husband of the within named Mercy Gold, and Attorney of the sd. William Gold" promised to pay the £ 30 for the estate of Richard Harris. The court then permitted the division of the estate on 9 Feb. 1702/3. In this docket 2372 we have the signatures of both Thomas and William Gold. We also have the first allusion to the maritime activity of William, who had been listed as cordwainer (leather worker) in 1700, and again 1703-4. Speaking of colonial mariners Morison says: "The shipmaster's calling has always been in high repute in Massachusetts. Only the clergy, the magistracy, and the shipowning merchants, most of whom were retired master mariners, enjoyed a higher social standing in colonial days." (Samuel Eliot Morison *The Maritime History of Massachusetts* [Boston: Houghton Mifflin, 1921], 16).

1703, 22 May, William Gold, cordwainer and his wife Mercy paid £ 130 to John Cutler for land 30 ft. on Roxbury Street (now Washington) southwest of Wheeler's Pond (Bedford Street), 87 ft. on SE bordering Benj. Thruston, on NW by James Wheeler, NE by Neh. Peirce (SD 21:260-2), today NE side of Bedford Street (Thwing). This property was mortgaged to Daniel Johannot with a brick house, 26 Feb. 1719 (SD 34:137).

1704, 2 Feb., William Gold, cordwainer, was tenant of Thomas Simpkins mariner who sold the land to John Briggs glazier on west side of Washington Street, between Winter and West Sts. The property fronted on Roxbury Street (Washington), bordered two rods by Samuel Mason's heirs on the northeast, the former pasture of late Anne Carter, now in hands of Madm Bridget Usher at the rear (NW), and two rods on southwest by land of the late Ralph Mason, late occupied by widow Sarah Mason (SD 21:498).

1704, 2 Nov., William Gould (first such spelling), cordwainer (last reference to him in this profession; some shoemaker's tools were reported in his sister's estate of 1728, see below) and wife Mercy paid £ 130 to Martha Ransford as attorney for her husband butcher of Piscataqua NJ for his title to the above property on Wheeler's Pond (SD 22:182)

1707, 1 March, Thomas Gold's will named his son William, founder (first such occupation for him) heir to his brick house on Newbury Street (now Washington) with workhouses, after his mother's death, and on his death all his clothing, tools of his founder's trade. Will was probated 28 July 1707 (SW 3049).

1707, 3 April, William Goold permitted Winsor Golding and Ephraim Fenno to erect a timber house 70 ft. from his house, and 20 ft. from Joseph Wheeler's house. (Bos. City Doc. 100, 181).

1707, 14 Aug., William Gold was neighbor to new house of Windsor Golding and Ephraim Fenno in property on Washington Street near Bedford (CR 4.452 per Thwing; CD may give his occupation, and mention of house.

1709, 8 Feb., Frances Goold's will left her son William a bed, bolster, 2 pillows, pair of sheets, blankets, coverlid, large silver tankard, clock, 2 kettles, Indian boy "Caesar" and £ 50. Her will was probated 16 July 1709 (SW 3331), so William thus inherited Thomas Gold's brick house on the Common and Newbury (Washington) on the land purchased from Edward Hill in 1695. This property, on the north side of Hog Alley seems to have gone to the Greene family after 1740, though record of transfer has not been found in the deeds.

1709, 14 March, William Gould was appointed town Hogreeve, thru 19 Dec. 1709 (CD 137 : 60; Seybolt 121) .

1709, 9 Sept., William Gold signed a petition to General Court from Boston inhabitants to restrict enlistment. (Mass Arch. Index 71:542) .

1710, 11 Oct., Queen's Chapel (today's King's, so called during reign of Queen Anne, 1702-14) was enlarged (Foote 1: 204).

1711, 31 March, William Gould and Nathaniel Green each contributed £ 4 to Queen's Chapel for enlargement of the church (Kings Chapel records, vol. 16; Foote 1:230).

1712, 11 April, William Gold founder and his wife Mercy, her two sisters Mary & Elizabeth Harris and widow Elizabeth Harris conveyed to Daniel Oliver and William Welsteed their parts of Richard Harris's estate including the brick warehouse at the mouth or entrance to the Town Dock formerly called Bonsalls Dock (or Harris's Wharf, see present location in description above) and Mercy's portion of land in south end of Boston for £ 610, £ 200 less than value appraised in 1697 (SD 26:151).

1712, 17 May, William Gold was part owner of the sloop *Four Friends* of Boston with John Henshaw, Caleb Ray co-owners and Ebenezer Elton master; she weighed 25 tons, built in Newbury 1710, square-sterned, formerly named *Kitty & Mary* (Mass Arch. 7:433). She was declared outward bound for Annapolis Royal in Nova Scotia 19-24 May under Benjamin Elton, master. (*Boston News-Letter*, 26 May). Her return is not recorded in the *News-Letter*. This is William Gold's first recorded connection with Nova Scotia, which extended until 1726.

1713, 20-27 April, William Gold arrived in a vessel from Connecticut, his first recorded voyage as master. (*News-Letter*, 27 April. In this year he was master of four voyages to Connecticut: 11 May to 22 June, a roundtrip of about six weeks; 29 June cleared again; 31 Aug. cleared again, but not recorded returning until the next year. The Peace of Utrecht on 11 April 1713 resulted in a widening of Massachusetts maritime activity (Morison, 18-19).

1714, 10 May, William Gold returned to Boston from Connecticut. We do not know if he was gone all winter, or whether the record is missing from newspapers. There is no further record of voyages this year.

1714, 6 Aug., William Gold signed as the first witness to the will of his brother-in-law Nathaniel Green who left the balance of his estate to his wife and executrix, Anne Gould Green. (Copy in Karolik Collection, MHS, Codman Family Genealogical folder Greene wills).

1716, 2 April, William Gold was outward bound for Annapolis Royal in the sloop *Caulfield*; returned 24 May with passenger "soulder" named Joseph ([29th] *A Volume of Records relating to the Early History of Boston* [Boston: Municipal Printing Office, 1900, City Document 100] [hereinafter Doc 100], 233. He made four voyages to Annapolis Royal this year: 10 June-24 July, sloop *Neptune* arr. Boston from Annapolis captained by William Goold, with passenger William Sheriff (Doc. 100, 239); 20 Aug. to 15 Oct.; left again 5 Nov., return not recorded. Sloop *Caulfield* was probably named for the first British Lieutenant Governor and acting Governor of Nova Scotia, Thomas Caulfeild.

1716, Dec. 14, The Inferior Court of Common Pleas in Boston issued a writ for the Sheriff of Suffolk County to seize £ 500 worth of goods from William Gould, ffounder, James Person, ffounder, Daniel Blin, Mariner, Nathaniel Mann, glazier, and Mary Allen, widow, all of Boston and to appear in court on the first Tuesday in January in the suit of Mary Ensor of Dritend (sp.?) near Birmingham England, she being the only daughter and heir of Guy Penn, and niece of William Penn of Braintrey, claiming the latter's land at the south end of Boston, fronting 40 ft. southeast on Roxbury Street, southwest by William Blin, northwest in the rear 37 ft. on Boston Common, and northeast by ffearnot Shaw's, 285 ft. deep. (*Ensor v. Gould*, Suff. Ct. #11206). On 15 Dec. the Sheriff Joseph Hiller stated that he "attached these of the withinnamed James Person and have taken his Bond and also attached a cask of Sugar of the withinnamed Mary Allen's Est. and an Elbow Chain of the withinnamed Na[th] Manns Estate and a Cane Chain of the withinnamed William Golds Estate and left a Summons at each of their dwelling Houses according to the Law. I also attach some Cord Wood of the withinnamed Danl Blins Estate and put a Summons in at the Keyhole of the door of his Dwelling House." (Suff. Ct. 11206 (2)).

1717, 5 Jan., Inferior Court of Common Pleas in Boston heard the case of *Ensor v. Gould* et al. (*Gould v. Ensor*, Suff. Ct. 12316 (3). Mary Ensor claimed one half of the property held by Gold, as niece of William Penn and £ 500 damages. The defendants pleaded not guilty before Gov. Dudley and his Council, "Saying that the Writ in the Body of it sounded in in the nature of a Writ of Partition." After full hearing the case was sent to the jury.

1717, 2 April, during Gould's absence on a voyage, the Inferior Court of Common Pleas in Boston found for Mary Ensor for recovery of the property, plus court costs. (Suff. Ct. 12316 (3). The defendants appealed to the next Superior Court of Judicature.

1717, 4 May, Gould and the other defendants appealed in the Superior Court in Boston thru their attorney P. Dudley on six grounds: 1) The writ should have been abated for the plea in the lower court; 2) the lower court refused official records, viz., the will of William Penn, its probate and 2 confirmations by the Governor, which refusal forced an unnecessary appeal; 3) the title is clear according to deeds (this probably ref. to Suff. Ct. # 6386, 6388); 4) the Massachusetts law assured title to anyone whose title was not challenged within 10 years of 1697, and Edward Hill took title in the winter of 1688 and held it peaceably since; 5) by common law a will once approved by a competent judge cannot be changed; 6) the jury had referred to the court its doubt whether Penn owned the property, a matter of fact which there is no question about. (Suff. Ct. 12316 (5-6).

Mary Ensor's attorney James Valentine replied that the lower court was correct, that Gould had no title, and that it was only recently that they discovered the fraud in the will of William Penn, which had always been in doubt, and correctly declared void by the Governor and Council; thus there was now no will. Evidence of this was that the appellants were cautioned about the title and bought it at half price. (Suff. Ct. 12316 (7-8).

In the Superior Court plea to abate the proceeding was rejected and Ensor ordered to trial, but there being now power of attorney, it was not decided until May 1718. (Suff. Ct. 12316 (4). A four page rebuttal of Gould's legal grounds was submitted by Ensor dated Nov. 1717. (Suff. Ct. 12316 (9); this was rejected by the court, and contains no information about Gould or the property.

1717, William Gold was master of three voyages to Annapolis Royal on unnamed vessel: 25 March-1 July; return 21 Oct.; outward bound in sloop *Marygold* for Annapolis Royal 28 Oct., cleared out 4 Nov.; its return is not recorded until 10 March 1718, so he may have wintered there.

1718, 6 May, The case of *Gould v. Ensor* came to trial in the Superior Court of Judicature in Boston (Suff. Ct. 12316 (4). Ensor's power of attorney had arrived and Gould argued insufficient proof, the court ordered the case go to trial before a jury to determine specially "If that it was within the power of the Lieut Governour & Council to null Mr. Penns will after it had been Confirmed as the Law directs and that if the Law for Quieting possession in the Province do not give Title to Gould then we find for the Applee Confirmation of the former Judgment and Cost of Court if otherwise we find for the applt Reversion of the former Judgmt & Cost of Courts." (Suff. Ct. 12316 (8).

The jury confirmed Gould's title: "We find for the Appellant reversion of the former Judgment and Costs of Courts" (Ibid.).

1718, 5 June, William Gold, merchant of Boston, received a Bill of Exchange for £ 14 at Annapolis Royal, NS, on order of John Jephson drawn on John Mulcaster, Esq., agent for HM Garrison Annapolis Royal or agent of the War Office Whitehall London, and attested to by Lieutenant Governor John Dennett; signed in blank by William Gold and George Rasin. (Suff. Ct. 12344).

1718 William Gold was master of two voyages of an unnamed vessel, probably the *Marygold* since he sails her in 1717 and 1719, for Annapolis Royal: 14 April to 23 June; cleared for Nova Scotia 7 July, no return recorded.

1718, Sept., William Gold and others were stranded in Newfoundland, whether by shipwreck or sale of ship is unknown. In Suffolk County Superior Court on 8 April 1719 William

Gold, Richard Circum made this deposition: "These deponents testifie and say that in the Month of September last past they with others being at Newfoundland and desirous to come for New England they agreed with Capt. William Arnold Commander of the Brigantine Friendship--she was then there, for their passage to Boston at the rate of three pounds per man. The said Capt. Arnold promising them good and sufficient provisions and accommodations during this Voyage Whereupon a great Number of passengers came on board viz. about one hundred. And the said arnold having not provided for such a number they had only one Bisket a man for two days & about three ounces of Meat, about seven of the said Biskets weighed a pound. And being at this short allowance near half the time of their passage. they were grown so feeble thro' fasting & other inconveniences that they could hardly stand & particularly this Deponents well know. Henry Marshall who was one of the passengers and was treated as the rest were & was brought to a very weak and low condition before their arrival at Boston." Sworn in Inferiour Court Boston 8 April 1719 by Robt. Johnston, Samuel Tucker and Willm. Gold (who signed William Gould); also signed by Richard Sladen, Richard Circum, William Perey and John Cant. (Suff. Co. Sup. Court 10274).

1719, 6 Feb., William Gold mariner and his wife Mercy mortgaged their brick house and land on Pond Street (north of Wheeler's Pond) for obligation of £ 485/4/4 to Daniel Johannot; they will pay Johannot £ 242/12/2 plus interest, and £ 49/17/3 within two months. Witness: Mary Harris. This is the last reference to Mercy's sister. (SD 34:177).

1719, 5 March, William Gold Mariner of Boston signed a note for £ 484/4/4 to Daniel Johannot, distiller of Boston; he signed Wm Gold; witnesses: Wm Walker and Zachariah Johannot. (Suff. Ct. 16190). Johannot apparently brought this to Suffolk County Court of Common Pleas in 1722, when he was awarded court costs of £ 2/12/6 (Ibid.). Note some figures at bottom of court's copy of the deed may indicate portions of the debt paid.

1719 William Gold made three voyages to Annapolis Royal: arrived Boston 22 June (clearance not recorded); 29 June outward bound for Annapolis and Canso, cleared 13 July; returned 9 Nov. on the *Marygold* from Annapolis Royal; cleared again 30 Nov., probably for the winter.

1720 William Goold's sloop *Marygold* made it back into Boston through the ice between 2-8 Feb.. The paper reported their return and "Last Week was Cold Weather, especially the last two Days extream Cold, as was also the Lords Day the first Day of this Week" [7 Feb.]. (*News-Letter*, 8 Feb.. He made another trip to Annapolis Royal 11 April to13 June, on unnamed vessel, probably the same. This was his last recorded voyage as master. In the next year the *Marygold* is captained by James Arnold for Newfoundland July 28; it is not known who owned the ship. There is no further news of any Gould as master of a vessel for a whole decade until 1729, when John Gould cleared 12 June for the West Indies. It is apparently this same captain who took voyages to the West Indies and Jamaica in 1730, Barbados in 1735, and Jamaica 1736-7. There is no known connection between these families except that they were both parishioners of King's Chapel.

1724, 3 Sept., William Gold at Canso, NS signed a promissory note to Thomas Martin, fisherman at Georgetown, York Co. NS for £ 7/10/3 payable on or before 1 July, 1725.

Witnesses: Daniel Rogers and Saml. Greene. Martin sued in Boston court in 1729, see below (Suff. Court 24029).

1724-7 William Gold was living in Canso, Nova Scotia. Canso, Guysborough County, lies at the eastern tip of the mainland of Nova Scotia at the entrance of the Strait of Canso, which separates Cape Breton from the mainland, and forms the closest passage into the Gulf of St. Lawrence. Canso was an important base for the northeastern trade, a fishing center and import center for luxury items. Faneuil established a resident agent there about 1737. (William B. Weeden, *Economic and Social History of New England* [Williamstown, Corner House, 1978] 2:614). But this was at the end of about two decades of prosperity in which Canso was the center of New England fisheries, peaking in 1729. Most of the inhabitants of Canso were New Englanders engaged in catching cod on the banks offshore and salting them on the beaches, and some illicit trade in French rum, a staple of the hard life at sea. (W. S. McNutt, *The Atlantic Provinces... 1712-1857* [London: McClelland & Stewart, 1965], 22-23; Andrew Hill Clark, *The Geography of Early Nova Scotia to 1760* [Madison, WI.: Univ. of Wisconsin, 1968], 227-8). The fishing was done by New England schooners with a crew of four, out for ten to thirty days on the banks, so Gould may have fished as well as bringing cod back to Boston. We have no record in Boston of his vessels, so he may have been assembling cargo during the winter for shipment Early in the spring.

For further information one might check Nova Scotia papers for shipping news, including his death. One might check also Nova Scotia provincial archives, unusually complete, before trying Colonial Office records in Public Record Office in London.

1725, 12 April, a William Gould was appointed town cow keeper (Boston *Report of Record Commissioners* [Boston: Rockwell & Churchill, 1885], Document 77, 136; Seabolt 167). It is not clear that this is our William. There is one other William in Boston at the time, the William of Pembroke listed in Z Gould 348, who was living in Boston briefly: On 11 Oct. 1723 William Gould of Boston bought land in Abington from Richard Williams of Bridgewater (*Register* 116:19 from Plymouth Co. Deeds 17:54); William Gould gardener and wife Rachel sold this 19 July 1725 (Ply. Deeds 19:143-4). This was probably the same William Gould who married in Boston 22 June 1719 to Rachel Atkins (*Register* 1:244).

1726, 26 Jan., Mercy Gold wife of William Gold of Boston now resident at Canso in Nova Scotia, sold their house and land at south end of Boston 30 ft. NW on Roxbury Lane from Wheeler's Pond, 87 ft. NE on late James Wheelers land, 30 ft SE on George Raizin's land, and 87 ft. SW on Samuel Adams's land to Wheeler's Pond for £ 60 to Daniel Johannot, distiller (SD 34: 124-5).

1727, 8 April, Court of Common Pleas in Boston awarded judgment against William Gold in case of Joseph Bennett et al. who sought to evict Gold from the Edward Hill property on the ground that William Penn gave the land to Hill on 18 Dec. 1688, but when Hill died in 1724 half fell to Mary Ensor, daughter of William Penn's brother Guy, and half to his niece Deborah Hill. Mary Ensor's will of 1715 left it to Joseph Bennett, Samuel ffreath, and Samuel Broughton. (Suff. Court 164302).

1727, 12 Aug., The Supreme Court of Judicature in Boston heard the appeal of William Gold against the decision of the Court of Inferior pleas in *Bennett v. Gold*. (Suff. Court 164302).

Joseph Bennet chaffindish maker of Birmingham England, Samuel ffreath whitesmith of same town, and William Walker merchant of Whittenhall, Warwick were defendants (Suff. Court 22117). The case was heard by jury, but "The Justices of the Court being dividd" after further deliberation the former judgment of the Inferior Court was reversed and "sd W G shall Recover agt ye sd JB Sf & WW Costs of Court--NB ye applicants movd for an appl to his Majestys Council which was not granted".

1728, Jan., Inferior Court in Boston admitted the case of *Gold v. Bennet* relating to the property "known by the name of William Gold's house being the North part of the sd. house, the sd house being butted and bounded upon the house & land of Widow Green; southerly upon the house of Capt. Blin; westerly upon the Comon and Easterly upon the Street." (Suff. Ct. 22117).

1728, 20 Feb., the inventory of the estate of his sister Ann Gould Green shows William Goold as her largest debtor, for £ 100/18/1 l. (SW 5574:413).

1728, 1 March, Thomas Green submitted the expenses of his mother's (Ann Green) estate including these two items: 1) £ 2/10 to John Reed for half the law charges on the House of our Unkil Mr. Willm Gold", and 2) £ 1/4 to Owen Harris "for Runing a line round our Land that I might make a fence between the Land of Willm Gold & ours." (SW 5574) 1728, Aug., Superior Court in Boston again heard the appeal of Joseph Bennet and others against William Gold. (Suff. Court 22117).

1728, 10 Oct., Superior Court in Boston denied the appeal of Bennet against Gold. (Suff. Court 22117). This apparently ended the litigation and established Gold's title to the house on Washington Street.

1728, 1 Oct., William Gold founder petitioned for payment of £ 100 rent by Benjamin Gray stationer for tenement of north end of a house bounded east by Marlborough Street (Washington), south by the tenants, and north by the house and land of Thomas Green. Thomas Gold owned this property in his will of 1 March 1706. (Misc. Bound, MHS).

1729, 11 Feb., William Gold appealed to Massachusetts Superior Court for judgment against William Gray for portion of his tenement. (Misc. Bound, MHS).

1729, 3 March, William Goold, founder of Boston sold to John Reed two houses and land on Boston Common 30 ft. to west, north on the heirs of Anne Green from Common to Newbury Street, 33 ft. on east along Newbury (Washington), and south along land of James Blin from Newbury to the Common, for 60 Pounds (SD 43:80).

1729, 8 March, Rufus Green goldsmith of Boston and wife Katherine received £ 180 from his brother Thomas merchant for his fifth of the land which he got from his parents Nathaniel and Anne, bounded 311 ft. on SW by uncle William Goold, 35 ft on NW on the Common, NE by heirs of Joseph Cowell, 21 SE on Newbury Street (SD 43:127). This is the sale Thwing erroneously gives the date of 10 Feb., citing TR 14.

1729, 16 June, Suffolk Co. Court awarded Thomas Martin, fisherman of Georgetown,

York Co. NS £ 10 damages against William Gold, founder of Boston for nonpayment of promissory note of 3 Sept. 1724, for which the court had issued a writ of attachment of Gold's estate for £ 15 (Suff. Court 24029).

1730, 18 June, Nathaniel Green shopkeeper of Boston his wife Elizabeth received £ 180 from his brother Thomas for his fifth of land he inherited from his parents Nathaniel and Anne Green, bounded 311 ft. on SW by uncle William Goold, 35 ft NW on Common, 308 ft. on NE by heirs of Jos. Cowell, and 21 ft SE on Newbury Street (SD 44:222)

1730, 18 Oct., William Gould took the King's Chapel prayer book by Clark received from King George II (for rebinding, since he was originally cordwainer by trade, and Clark's prayer book would now have had over 30 years of daily use; Foote 401: Foote is in error about its being gift of George II, the current king; rather it was William III, at time of founding. Josias Clark was the first assistant minister of King's Chapel. This book is not in the collection received in 1698 and given to the Athenaeum: see shelf list and article by Walter M. Whitehill in *Colonial Society of Massachusetts* [1945], 12:287 contains a prayer book dated 1731 and two dated 1766. King's Chapel itself retained an older prayer book which we have not seen.

1734, 10 April, Benjamin Green, goldsmith, sold his fifth of house and land at Washington and Mason Sts. which he received from parents to his brother Thomas, bounded on SW by "his uncle William Gold" (SD 46:206-7). By this deed Thomas Green had acquired all of the original property his grandfather Thomas Gold had bought from Fearnot Shaw in 1696.

1735, late May, William may have been back in Canso involved in the purchase of stone for the lighthouse. In an incomplete file of Suff. Court (41305), in the case of Gould and Spear dated 8 March 1737/8 Robert Ball deposed "that in ye year of 1735 that as I and some others coming from ye Lighthouse about ye latter end of May last mett with at Canso whereupon was Mr. Spear and some others which Mr. Indicot and Mr. Spear bargained about bringing Stones to ye lighthouse Mr. Indicott asked him how much he would have a Sum. He answered four shillings and six pence. Mr. Indicott said he would not give it for he had agreed with Mr. Wilson and some others to bring him for two Shillings and threepence Mr. Spear answered he could not afford to bring them for that for he could gett Nothing by it for he was to give fivepence a tun for ye Stone. Mr. Indicott said that was Nothing to him if..." [no more] The next document, apparently related, says "Gershom Colyer testifieth and said that he gave Joseph Spear Liberty to take Stones of ye proprity in the year 1735 but I did not give him no righten before (?) be cared the Stones of---[one sentence illegible].

1735, 5 June, William Gold, founder of Boston sued Benjamin Gray, stationer of Boston in the inferior court of appeals for Suffolk County (Court of Common Pleas, Record Books 1728-1730, microfilm 0903697 Massachusetts Archives, 56-57). The first suit was for recovery of £ 18 per month for a house, for three years ending 5 June 1734, totaling £ 54, where Gray is living (no location given). Since Gray did not appear in court, Gold was awarded recovery with £ 31 court costs. This was appealed to the next Supreme Court of Judicature (see Mass Archives). The second suit, by Gold versus Gray was for the premises bounded on the east by Marlborough Street, on the north by Thomas Green, and on south and west by William Gold, which he received from Thomas Gold in his will. Since Gray "unjustly holds the Plaint out" Gold claims £ 100 damages. When Gray did not appear in court, Gold was awarded recovery of the house and costs. This was appealed to the next Supreme Court.

1736, 16 Dec., William's son Thomas was married to Hannah Woods of Roxbury ([30th] *Report of the Record Commissioners...Boston Marriages from 1752 to 1809* [Boston: Municipal Printing Office, 1903] Doc. 101, 313).

1737, 26 July, William's nephew Benjamin Greene paid £ 8/15 quarterly rent for a house, and the same each quarter thru 1740; he charged him £ 4 for repairs to the house in 1737; in 1738 he bought from William 3 oz. 11 dm. of silver @ 26/p oz, totaling 4/12/3 and in 1739 he sold him 1½ cord of wood @ 42/ (Benjamin Greene Account Books 1734-1756, MHS).

1740, 17 Oct., Peter Blin deeded land to Martin Brimer bounded by William Gould to north; on north corner of Hog Alley (laid out 1708 from Newbury west between Sheafes Lane and West Street per SD 119; Bonner map of 1722 shows it from Newbury thru to the Common (SD 61:28).

1740, 26 Oct., Benjamin Greene recorded payment of £ 8/5 to William Gould for quarterly rent due that date, 10 shillings having been advanced on 16 Oct.. This is the last reference to William Gould until the next entry 26 Jan. [1741] when quarterly rent of £ 8/15 is recorded as "pd. Marcy Gold his Widow". William Gold thus died between 26 Oct. 1740 and 26 Jan. 1741. His wife Mercy died about June 1741. There is no record of his death in King's Chapel, or burial grounds, or town records. Perhaps he died at sea. Notice does not appear in *Boston News-Letter* 1740-1 of death or shipping disaster or capture. It is possible that he died in Canada. Nova Scotia deaths are not recorded in provincial records, parish records or newspapers at this date. No will or probate has been recorded in Boston.

1741, 10 June, Mercy Gold, widow of Boston, signed her will giving one gold ring marked W H (this could be William Harris, her half-brother, who apparently died young, or less likely, her uncle William) to Elizabeth Randell my Kinswoman in token of my Respect for her and my friend and executor Peter Thomas the whole of my personal Estate and debts. Witnesses: Thomas Newman, George Eustis and Wm Morto. (SD 7623, 206, renumbered 412-3). There is no reference to real estate, or to children, or to her sisters whose marriages do not show in Thwing. Mary had died by 1727 according to will of Ann Gould Greene, to whom she owed £ 11/5/9 (SW 5574). Mercy's will was probated 30 June, so she died between 11-29 June, about six months after her husband.

Children, b. Boston:
i. SARAH^3, b. 25 Feb. 1700 (CD 43:70).
5. ii. Thomas^3, b. 30 Jan. 1701; d. 1763?; m. HANNAH^3 WOODS.

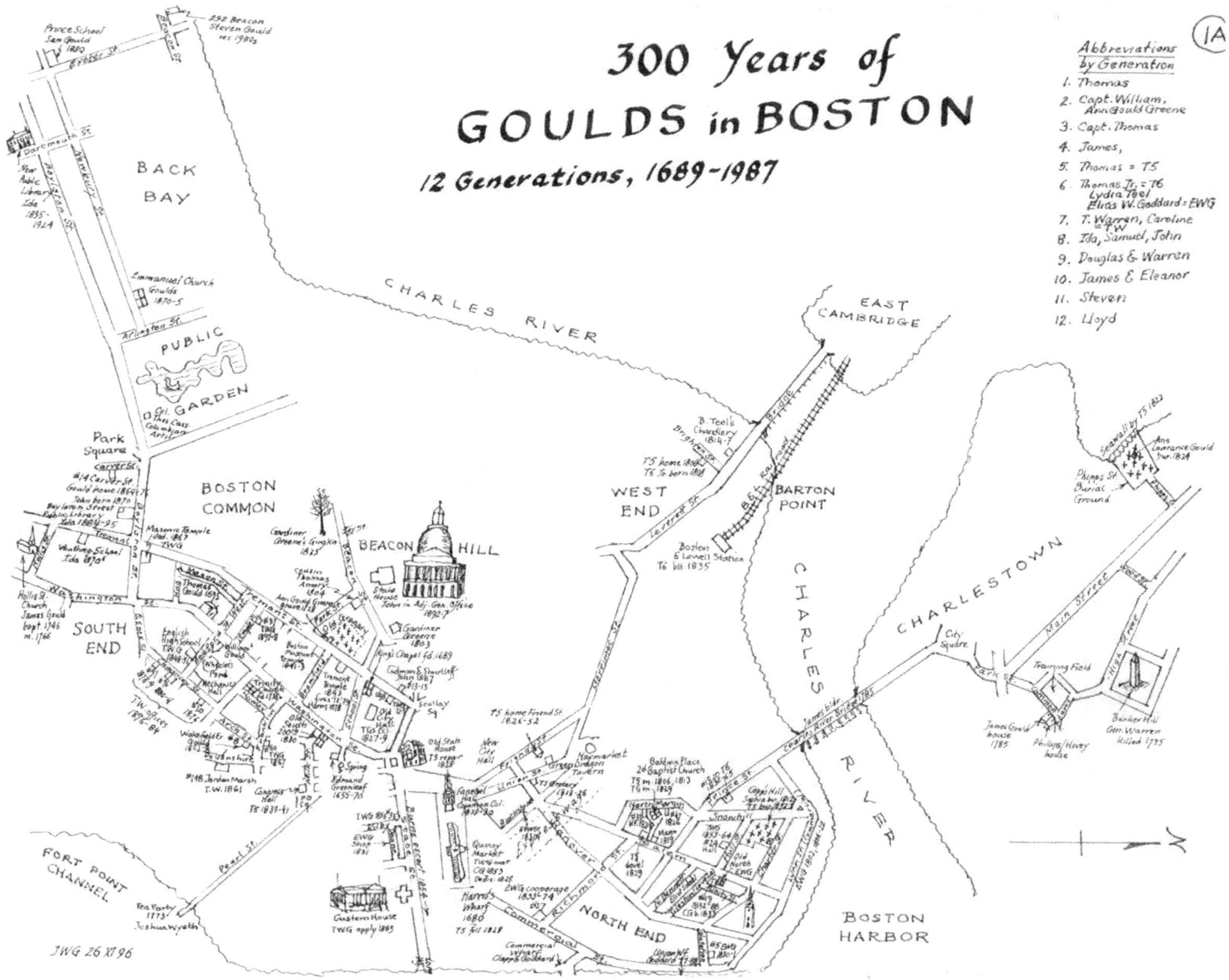
300 Years of
GOULDS in BOSTON
12 Generations, 1689-1987
1A
Abbreviations by Generation
1. Thomas
2. Capt. William, Ann Gould Greene
3. Capt. Thomas
4. James,
5. Thomas = TS
6. Thomas Jr. = T6
Lydia Teel
Elias W. Goddard = EWG
7. T. Warren, Caroline = TW
8. Ida, Samuel, John
9. Douglas & Warren
10. James & Eleanor
11. Steven
12. Lloyd
BACK BAY
CHARLES RIVER
EAST CAMBRIDGE
PUBLIC GARDEN
Park Square
BOSTON COMMON
BEACON HILL
WEST END
BARTON POINT
CHARLESTOWN
CHARLES RIVER
SOUTH END
NORTH END
BOSTON HARBOR
FORT POINT CHANNEL
JWG 26 XI 96

Chapter III

ANNE[2] GOULD GREENE, BIBLIOPHILE

4. ANN(E)[2] GOULD (*Thomas*[1]) shopkeeper and book collector of Boston, was born about 1685 (Z Gould 346), perhaps in London (see discussion of origins of her father, above 2), and died in Boston 16 January 1728, at age 43 (*Gravestone Inscriptions and Records of Tomb Burials in the Granary Burying Ground, Boston* [Salem: Essex Institute, 1918], 113; *The Family of Greene in England and America* [Boston: privately printed, 1901] [hereinafter Fam Greene], 51. She married in Boston, at King's Chapel, 27 Feb. 1704 to **NATHANIEL[3] GREENE** (*Thomas*[2], *John*[1]), merchant of Boston who was born at Warwick RI 10 April 1679 and died Boston 8 August 1714 (Fam Greene 50-10. He was first cousin once removed of the famous Revolutionary War General Nathaniel Greene (1742-1786), victor of the final battles of the War of Independence, at Cowpens, Guilford Court House and Eutaw Springs (1781) (Louise Brownell Clarke from mss. of George Sears Greene, *The Greenes of Rhode Island* [New York: privately printed, 1903] [hereinafter Greene RI] 200-21).

The size of Anne Gould's library indicates an unusual education for the date. We do not know how was she educated, but since there was no public school for girls, she could have been trained by her father or by one of his friends like a minister or schoolmaster. In any case, it shows remarkably advanced views of her father, Thomas Gould. Her mother's will is signed with the initial "F", does not indicate illiteracy. Her father, however, signed his will, though we have no writings by him. That he would have tutored her seems probable to Susan Swan. A minister or assistant at King's Chapel might have tutored her at a time when public schools did not take girls. There is a spelling book, unidentified, in her library.

The first record of Ann Gould is her wedding at King's Chapel, of which her father was a founder, by the Reverend Samuel Miles, Rector, on 27 February 1704 to Nathaniel Greene ((Boston City Doc. 150, *Report of the Record Commissioners...Boston. Baptisms. Marriages, and Deaths, 1700-1751* [Boston: Municipal Printing Office, 1898 [hereinafter CD 150], 10).

In the will of her father Thomas Gold in 1707 she was given the house and land in the South End of Boston running from what is now Washington Street to the Common (now Mason Street), lying north of her brother William's house and workshop (SW 3049:312). She was also to inherit the land to the south that went to her mother and brother in the event of both their deaths, which did not occur.

In the will of her mother Frances Goold in 1709 she and her husband received the balance of her estate after gifts to her brother William, to her mother's sister Elinor Nichols, and to two of the Greene children (SW 3331). Nathaniel Greene was sole executor.

Her husband Nathaniel Greene died in Boston on 8 August 1714 as recorded in the diary of his neighbor Justice Sewell: "Augt 9 Last night our neighbor Green died. He married Mr. Gold's daughter: was of Warwick" (Sewall 2:766). He was only 35 years old. He had made his will just two days before his death, leaving the residue of his estate to his wife and executrix,

Anne Green. Susan Swan of Winterthur Museum "found it extremely interesting that the husband should have made her 'full and sole executrix.' This was far from common so perhaps she was better educated than most. Strangely, wealthy 17th century women were academically better educated than mid-18th century women. Probably still due to the influence of Queen Elizabeth and her well educated court.". His will was probated 18 Sept. 1714 (MHS Karolik Collection: Codman Family Genealogy by Martha C. Codman, folder Greene I. Wills etc. [hereinafter Karolik].

Ann continued a member of King's Chapel, owning half of pew 56 (Greene RI 147; Foote 1:495).

Her business activity must have been successful, as shown by two recorded mortgages. On 21 April 1719 Anne Green widow and shopkeeper took a mortgage for £ 60 on the land of William Titt, tallow chandler and his wife Sarah, on the southeast side of Newbury (Washington) Street (SD 33:257). The mortgage was discharged a year later, on 28 April 1720 with her signature "Ann Green" in the margin of the record book.

Soon thereafter, on 22 September 1720 Ann Green widow and shopkeeper took a mortgage for £ 150 on the land of Nicholas Belknap 23½ ft. on the southeast side of Newbury Street, in a description which seems to resemble the previous property, but not exactly, with the addition of the orchard adjoining to the northeast (SD 34:257). The mortgage was discharged nearly four years later on 27 June 1724 with her signature "Ann Green" in the margin.

Her grandson William[4] Greene recorded his recollection of her: "My Grand Mother Greene keep [sic] an English goods shop, and my Father often tended shop for her when he could be spared from his master." (*Massachusetts Historical Society Proceedings* [1920-1] 54:93. This refers to his father Rufus[3] who was born in 1707, and would have been apprenticed after 1714.

A year before her death, on 5 January 1727, Ann Greene widow (not as shopkeeper, as earlier) bought a house and land which was southeast of hers, fronting 58 feet on Roxbury Street, 285 feet by Joseph Blin on the southwest, 37 feet on the Common at the rear (SD 40:203). She paid £ 20 to the two daughters of Edward Hill, the widow Hannah Simpson and Sarah Holiday and her husband Robert. The price is extremely low, and may represent a clearance of title of the property her father bought 7 March 1705, which differs in description only in the dimension on Roxbury Street.

We get a good idea of Ann Greene's business in English goods from the seven page inventory of her estate. The total of store goods not including her household and personal effects was £ 2421, which was a large fortune in those days. Most of it consisted of textiles, sewing materials, hardware and foodstuffs. In the following account of her inventory I have preserved the original spelling.

Of the textiles the woolen goods come first: Shalloons, a loosely women twilled worsted, worth over £ 100. There were Bristol Tameys (a woolen sieve material), Coventry stuffs (blue embroidery?), Black Russell (a ribbed or corded fabric with cotton warp and woolen weft), Drugget (a wool or wool mixture), and Callamincoes (a glossy woolen with checkered weft).

In cotton fabrics there were a variety of calicoes: checkered worth £ 118, blues, whites and narrow calicoes, and Muslins worth £ 154.

In linens she had several kinds of Holland, which is a fine variety, described as garlick, yellow, brown sheeting Hollands. There was Kenting, a fine linen, and Kenting aprons and strips. There were Checks of linen and cotton, Scotch cloth (a fine open linen like Lawn, said to be made of nettle fiber), Dowlas (a coarse French linen), narrow Diapers (white linen with diamond pattern), Shooe Tick, Fustian (a coarse cloth of cotton and flax, both flowered and fine, Crocus (a yellow linen?), Ozenbriggs (a coarse linen from Osnaburg, Germany), and Russia linen.

Silks included Cearsucker, Cheriderry, narrow and broad Persian (a thin variety) worth £ 58, flowered gause, black silk, Allamode (a thin, light, glossy black silk), Bangall (Bengali silk cloth?), Lutestring (a glossy silk), Checonees (silk?), Ardass silk (a very fine Persian variety), and Ballendine silk (with stitching silk).

In made up cloth goods there were handkerchiefs made of cotton, linen, black gause, silk and Rumalls (from Bombay). There was worsted hose and caps. Also 23 velvet masks and three Hatts. There was wadding, duffle and baye (baize). There was a gross of children's buckles, dozens of fans for women, children and girls valued at £ 64. And she also had combs made of Horne and ivory.

Sewing supplies included 2,900 needles, £ 111 worth of pins. There was thread described as colored, fine, homespun and Nun's (this kind worth over £ 100). There were buttons including Cheriday (silk?). There were also tapes, bobbin, Inkle (a linen tape) colored white, blue and red, filletings, Gartering that included clouded, folded, Jerusalem, Scotch and ordinary varieties. There was stay cord and braid, gallumes (a narrow ribbon or braid), silk ferret (a narrow tape), bindings, ribbons, and three Paddisway (silk) girdles.

But in addition to all these textiles and ladies clothing, there were groceries, house wares and paper goods. Foodstuffs included four hogsheads of molasses worth £ 45, 125 cheeses worth £ 39, starch, raisins, salt, currants, rice, butter, and sugar worth £ 119 alone. In spices we have pepper, allspice, nutmeg, cloves, cynamon and mace.

For dry goods there was shot and powder, brimstone, powder blue, indigo, beeswax, mowhair, whalebone, buttons and a reim and 8 quires of paper.

Hardware included 2½ dozen ivory knives and forks, 4 dozen knives, 4 dozen sizars, a forging anvil, a raseing anvil (for scratching), 3 boiling pans, a spoon, a skillet, 3 flasks, 6 plyers, a copper pan for boiling, a fine scratch brush, a brass stamp, 4 drawing irons, 3 spoon punches, 2 stakes for cup and tankard, a thimble stamp, 4 dozen piercing files, and 16 groce of pipes.

We do not know the location of her shop, but most shops were located in the homes of traders, so this probably faced onto Washington Street.. From the inventory of her estate it was separate from her residence on Newbury Street, but might have been in a separate building on the site. At one time it was thought she may have occupied the old Boston public schoolhouse behind King's Chapel, which was torn down for the extension of the church. The clue was "the present grammar schol then in the Occupation of the Widow Green & others". It is not known to which widow Green this refers, since there were several Green(e) families in Boston in 1748.

Only 42 years old, Ann Greene made out her will on 27 Nov. 1727 "being Sick and weak of Body but of Sound disposing Mind and Memory". According to Susan B. Swan, Curator at Winterthur museum, "the initial 'F' does not usually mean she couldn't write. Usually they have 'X her mark' (letter 2 Nov. 1990).

Her son's record of expenses for the estate gives fees due to four doctors: £ 13/14 to Docr Zebd Boylstone. Dr. Boylston was the radical pioneer of smallpox inoculation in 1721. She evidently covered her bases on cures, for there were lesser amounts of £ 10/1 to Doctr John Cutler, £ 3 to Doctr Willm Douglass, and £ 1/15/6 to Doctr Thos Bulfinch, all three of whom were with the majority in opposing Boylston's experiment. She appears to have received the best medical advice in town. Her son also recorded paying a fairly large sum of £ 15 to Mary Odlin for nursing and attendance, so she may have had a long illness.

Ann Gould Greene died in Boston 16 January 1728, aged 43 (tomb 41, Granary 113, Fam Greene 51). She was buried next to her husband in a vault constructed by William Wheelar for £ 28 in the South Burying Place, now Old Granary (estate expenses). Tomb 41 is marked "This Tomb Repaired 1807 by Gardiner Greene Grandson of Mr. Nathaniel and Mrs. Ann Green" (Granary 11). The grave is next to the sidewalk on the north side of Tremont Street, seven stones north of the Park Street Church, quite close to the grave of patriot James Otis. Although reconstructed by Gardiner Greene, the site has probably suffered from loss of ground when the sidewalk and Tremont Street were widened.

Her eldest son Thomas[3], her executor, was out of Boston when she died, and two men went to New London to notify him. He paid Richd Hunt £ 4 for horse hire "to New London to Advise me of My Hon^{d} Mother's Death", and £8 To Zach^{y} Sims for his Time & Expense in going to New London after me".

Other expenses for the funeral were £ 20/17 for rings which were given to male mourners by custom, £ 15/4 for gloves, £ 0/5/8 "To Cambrick for Wepers", that is, weepers, the hired mourners and £ 15/10 for Hatts. The use of King's Chapel cost £ 3/6, the coffin from Thos. Gibbins £ 10/10, black cloth from Benja. Atkinson £ 67/4, £ 1/16 for opening the vault, £ 7/4 for wine, and £ 0/5/6 "To makeing the Indian Womans Close (in her estate is "Indian Woman Named Flora abt 50 years of Age"). He paid Benj. Marshall 10 shillings for a newspaper ad in the *Boston Gazette*, which read: "⁎*⁎ All Persons that are Indebted to the Estate of Ann Green of Boston deceas'd are desired to come to Thomas Green of Boston aforesaid, Executor to said Estate and pay the same; and all Persons to whom the said Estate is Indebted, are desired to bring their Accompts to said Thomas Green and they shall be paid." (*Boston Gazette* #344 11-18 March 1728).

Her will of 27 November 1727, signed Ann Greene, is the only document we have left that was written by her. In it she left equal shares to her five sons, explaining "Whereas my late Husband Nathaniel Green [note different spelling]...Did ...bequeath unto my three sons namely

Rufus and Nathaniel [Thomas is omitted] all his Land lying and being in the town of Warwick...Rhode Island and unto my son Benjamin all that his half part of parcell of Land Bordering on the westerly part of Greenwich & Southward to Warwick...by [his] Will...[of] the Last day of August 1714...and foras much as the Said Lands are very much advanced and risen in value Since the // Same was given...Therefore that all my Children may have Fillial and Equal portions in my said Husbands Estate And the Personal Estate which I have by Gods blessing on my Labour acquired I Will and Order that a Just apprizement and Estimate be made of the Said Lands by Indifferent persons as shall by my Children be appointed with the other Legacys Shall be added to my personall Estate remaining after my Debts are paid...And I Give...the Same to my five Children namely Thomas Rufus Nathanael William and Benjamin Green in Equall parts to be divided to them...if any one of my Sons shall disagree and not rest Satisfied and Contented with this my Will he or they do disagreeing shall have and receive the sum of Five pounds only out of my Personal Estate as his full portion the other of my Children to have & receive his part or portion as aforesaid Equally between them."

The will was probated by Justice Samuel Sewall on 19 February 1728. There was no disagreement by the older brothers about giving up the larger inheritance, and the properties were divided equally. Thomas, the oldest son, eventually bought the fifth shares of the land and buildings on the Common. We do not know if they divided her books equally, and who got Thomas[1] Gould's portrait. If the picture and books went to Thomas[3] it seems likely to have gone to a widow or daughters, since the male line from Thomas[3] was nearly extinct in 1903 (Greene RI 576-7), and the male descent from the other brothers continued down to five male Greenes in 1903 (Greene RI 686-7).

Ann Greene left a huge estate for the time, and unusually large for a woman. Her executor, her eldest son Thomas[3], submitted an account for the total estate of £ 7522/12/01, with expenses of £ 330/15/8, which included costs of the funeral we have told above, legal expenses, medical bills, the survey of the line between her land and her brother William's to the south, taxes for 1727, £ 10 to his brother Rufus "from a Legacy left him by our hon[d] grandmother Fra[cs] Golde decs[d]". The assets were broken down into £ 5194 personal estate and £ 2328 real estate. As we have detailed above the goods in her shop came to £ 2421/10/3¼, to which £ 30/9/3 was added when found later, mostly tapes and indigo. Her household inventory came to £ 2671/6/4.

Ann Greene's personal estate is most interesting because it contains 124 books of unusual variety. The size is exceptionally large for this date, and is surely the largest known of any woman in this period. Professor Hall of Stanford commented on the collection, "They are mostly works of divinity, to be sure, but a careful look down the columns shows to one who has become familiar with seventeenth century book-lists that here is something different. Even the divinity is of lighter type. "Pilgrims Progress" and "Grace Abounding" appear, surprisingly rare in New England lists for a generation after Bunyan's death, when compared with the frequent appearance of such books as "Caryl on Job" and Mr. Preston's and Dr. Sibley's works. For a library of this size the folios are fewer [10] and less profound than in those of a generation before. The quartos and octavos have a fair proportion of history, and the list ends with a group of a // dozen titles of fiction and romance that would indicate that widow Greene and her family had found that books might serve for delight. Of all her books one quarter, including history, may fairly be called books of diversion and diverting information."

Among the romances are *The History of the Knight of the Burning Sword, Fair Rosamond, Argalus & Parthenia, Valentine & Orson, English Rogue, French Rogue*, and *Amadis de Gaul* (also perhaps *Fortunatus* and *The History of Parismus*, at total of nine. In history there are the four volumes of *Ye History of England, The Life of Leopold Emperour of Germany, The Wars of England, The Life of Lady Margaret de la Musse, Sir Francis Drake, 9 Worthies, Cromwell's Life, Queen Elizabeth & Essex, Destruction of Troy, The English Empire in America,* and *Guy Earl of Warwick*, a total of 14 volumes.

On classical subjects there are four volumes of *Athenian Oracles*, and two volumes of *Telemachus*. Practical books include a spelling book and *Maynes Practical Gaguer*, perhaps her father's, since there are a large number of scales and weights as well as anvils and tools that were probably his in her personal estate.

Then there are miscellaneous intriguing titles like *Meat out of the Eater, Laugh & be Fatt, 7 Wise masters, 7 wise Mistresses, Herberts Travels,* and *a Quarter Wagginer*.

Among the religious books are a Family bible almost new, Mather's *Life of Mr. Cotton*, two New England Psalm books, *Pilgrims Progress*, and Thomas à Kempis.

The only real property listed is "a House in Nubury Street with the Land meas^{g} 20 foot front, 36 foot Reer & 192 foot Deep", the same dimensions as the property Thomas[1] Gould bought from Fearnot Shaw in 1697 for £ 80. Thirty years later it is valued at £ 900.

In the personal effects of Ann Green were "The Picture of Mr. Tho^{S} Gold valued at £ 3. The fate of this portrait is unknown. It is an indication of the wealth and prominence of her father. Martha Karolik, one of the foremost collectors of colonial art, apparently did not find it (Inventory of her estate in Massachusetts Historical Society).

The most valuable collection is silver worth £ 278, including 5 silver tankards, 6 porringers, 5 cups & 1 Salver, 28 spoons, 1 spout cup, 1 peper box, 2 salts & sundry small things and silver buttons. There were 2 Guineas, 2 gold necklaces with rings &c, gold lace and silver fringe, a spoon & 1 Doller, and £ 52/17/6 of Silver Money bought for her son Rufus Greene.

Ann Greene's clothing included ten gowns and matching petticoats. The most expensive was her Flowered Silk Gound & Black Padusuay Petticoat worth £ 20. A Green Silk Gound with Black silk petticoat and Black Silk Gound & Petticoat are worth £ 10 each. Then there were old silk and Persian gowns, a double callico gown, a Calliminco Gown & Petticoat. She had a dozen shifts: 8 Holland (linen) and 4 second hand shifts with westcoat. She owned 23 aprons, including two silk ones with velvet tippet, 3 fine Muslin ones, 5 Kenting and 13 linen aprons. She had 27 night Capps, 7 Hed Dress, 7 old hoods, a Camblett (an oriental fabric of fine goat hair) Rideinghood, and 2 scarves. There were 16 handkerchiefs, 7 old fans, 6 pair of gloves, 4 girdles (one of silver & gold lace), 3 Sutes of old Pinners, a necklace, 3 girdles and 1 Cattgutt Shape.

The size of the Gould/Greene house may be judged from the fact that there were 12 beds. These ranged from the most expensive (£ 12/12) for a 72 pound bed & bolster to the Flock Bed & Beding for ye Indian Woman (£ 2). There were a dozen pillows, large and small. Bed linen included 28 sheets, 27½ pillowcases, 9 boulster cases, 1 pr. of white Callico Bed Curtins & Bed

Cloth, 1 Counter Pin, 1 White Cotton Quilt, 1 Coverlid, 5 Patchwork Callico Quilts, 2 Callico Quilts, 10 Homespun Blankets, 2 childrens blankets, 4 Ruggs and a Cotton Hammock.

For table linen there were 12 Damask Napkins, 1 Diaper & Damask Table Cloth valued at £ 8, 18 Napkins, 4 Towells & 2 Table Cloths, 1 Doz. of old Course Table Cloths, 3 Doz^{n} & ½ of Course Towels, 1 Doz. of Diaper Clouts. Does the fact that there were but nine window curtains mean only nine were covered, presumably on the street side. There were 7 window curtains, 1 pr. of Blew Callico Curtins & Valliants, and 1 pr. of old Serge Curtins.

She left five mirrors, both old and new fashioned, the best being a Large Old Fashioned Looking Glass worth £ 5/10. Beside the portrait of her father there were 9 small pictures, an old clock, 2 canes including a silver headed one worth £ 2. Pewter was valued at £ 15, including 14 Puter Plates, 1 Dozn of Supe Ditto, 7 Puter dishes and some old puter.

As would be expected in any household there was a lot of brass, worth about £ 27: 7 kettles, 3 skillets, a chafendish, pestle & morter, 3 pair of Brass and Irons, fireshovel, tongs, 3 candlesticks, a Standing Candlestick, warming pan, bellows with brass spouts. Also listed with the brass are 2 bell metal (copper-tin alloy) pots, a peper box, candlestick, skillet, funnel & cup. Among the iron items are cullender, tongs and fire shovels, 2 pair of and Irons, 1 pr. of Doggs, 4 Trammels (a hook for pots), 2 Ironing Boxes & Heaters, 1 Chafendish & Gridiron, 1 old Jack, 2 Spits, 1 Wale (?), 1 Dripping Pan & 1 Fender. The brass items give us a general idea of the household items that may have been made by her father Thomas Gold, founder, on this site.

Furniture in Ann Greene's estate included 25 chairs, of which a dozen were cane, 2 Armed, 6 Leather and 16 ordinary. There was one Old Fashioned Table & Chest of Drawers valued at £ 6, 1 Ovil Table £ 1/15, 1 Large Ovil Table £ 2/10, 1 old chest of drawers, 2 old tables and 1 Desk & 1 old chest, 10 trunks and 4 boxes for storage.

The glass and pottery are inventoried by the place they were apparently stored, which gives us a picture of the furnishings of colonial rooms. On one mantlepiece there was a parcell of Tea Cups & Glassware worth £ 1/5, on another mantle Glassware worth £ 1/17/8, and £ 2/16 on a third mantle. There was £ 2/4 glassware on a chest of drawers, £ 1/10 on a table, 2 glass punchbowls and one ladle worth £ 1, 5 Chancy Cups & 3 Saucers worth 6 shillings, a parcel of brown earthenware and stone pots.

Kitchen and laundry items included 1 roleing pin & 1 grater, 2 dozen old knives and forks, 2 ironing boxes and heaters, a close stool & pan, 3 close brushes, 2 old brushes, 3 washing tubs, 3 trays, 1 powdering tubb, 1 form, 1 Muff, 2 old broken cases with 8 bottles, also a lot of old bottles and barrels.

Among the tools were an old musket, a pair of garden shears, a crosscut saw, a handsaw & ax, a lot of old brass and iron, 5 pair of scales and beams, one large pair of scales and beams, 38 (pounds?) of brass weights, also iron and lead weights, 1 halfe Bushell, 1 peck, 1 pr. of Bellows, and 1 pr. of Tongs. Perhaps these were the tools of her father the founder, abandoned by her brother William. There is also "a parcell of Shoemakers Tools" valued at 5 shillings, perhaps William's cordwainer's tools. But if so, they might be in her estate if William had given them in security for a loan.

Ann Greene also left other assets. Cash in Bills of Credit & found in the house ye 20th of Feb^ry £ 852/12/3. There is a list of 197 people who owed her money totalling £ 1109/8/11. Her largest debtors were her relatives: her son Thomas owed £ 150 left him by his Father by Mother Ann Greene before she deceased; £ 100 by Nathl Greene in the same conditions; £ 102/3/11 by her brother William; her son Benjamin £ 19/8; her brother's sister-in-law Mary Harris Deceas'd £ 11/5/9. Among the male debtors were Jacob Hurd the silversmith for £ 13, and the minister Rev. Miles for £ 7. Twenty percent (41) of the debtors were women, including the famous Mother Goose (Mrs. Vergoose) who lived up the street.

Debts of her estate were relatively small, totaling £ 330/15/8, including funeral expenses. There was £ 41/2/11 in notes due, the largest, £ 14/1/9 owed to the tailor John Billings, and £ 5/4 to the shoomaker John Allen, and a small note due to a woman, Hannah Deming.

Children, born Boston, (Goulds' first cousins):

i. THOMAS[3] GREENE, merchant of Boston, born Boston 4 June 1705 (Boston: *Report of Record Commissioners* [Rockwell & Churchill, 1894, City Document 43] 34); died Boston 5 August 1763 ("The Records of Trinity Church Boston 1728-1830", *Publications of the Colonial Society of Massachusetts* [Boston: Colonial Society, 1982] [hereinafter Trinity] 61:779) ; married twice, 1) 22 Feb. 1727 (CD 150:165) ELIZABETH, daughter of John and Sarah (Chandler) GARDINER, and great-granddaughter of Lion Gardiner, first proprietor of Gardiner's Island. She died Boston 3 February 1744 (Trinity 769). He married 2) 6 Sept. 1744 MARTHA, daughter of Dr. John and Mehitable (Chandler) COIT and widow of Daniel Hubbard; she was born 1 April 1706 (Greene RI 94), and died Boston 4 Dec. 1784 (Trinity 798).

Thomas, a wealthy merchant, is best known for his foundation and endowment of Trinity Church in Boston. It was the third Episcopal church in town, built at the corner of Summer and Hawley Streets in 1735. Thomas had owned part of his mother's pew 56 in King's Chapel, but when the congregation grew there was need to establish a new church in the South End of town. The division of churches was a friendly one. Thomas continued to serve on the vestry of King's Chapel (1731-40) and as Warden (1734-6) (Foote 1:548n, 2:607). He was one of the first subscribers of Trinity, a trustee and on the building committee which built the first wooden structure 90 by 60 feet, with the finest interior in town. He was Trinity's first Warden in 1737 and vestryman for 22 years until his death (*Trinity Church in the City of Boston 1733-1933* [Boston: Wardens & Vestry of Trinity Church, 1933] 4, 20, 32, 202, 203). In his will Thomas established the Greene Foundation with £ 500 endowment which still supports the salary of the assistant minister of the church in Copley Square.

The family record erroneously claims that Thomas graduated from Yale in 1727 (Greene RI 147; he is not listed in *Catalog of Graduates of Yale* (1924), nor in Franklin B. Dexter *Yale Biographies* [NY: Henry Holt, 1885]. The error may have arisen in confusion with the famous Harvard graduate of 1726, Joseph Green (1706-1780), the noted wit, who is no relation (Clifford K. Shipton, *Sibley's Harvard Graduates* (Boston: MHS, 1951) 8:42.

There is a portrait of Thomas painted by the famous artist John Singleton Copley in 1758, now in the Cincinnati Art Museum (reproduced in Jules D. Prown, *John Singleton Copley in America* [Cambridge: Harvard Univ. Press, 1966], #56, 164), and in Fam Greene 52). Copley's portrait of Thomas's second wife Martha, also painted in 1758, is in the Lawrence Fleischman Collection in Detroit (Prown #57). Copley also painted pictures of three of their children: Mary and her husband Daniel Hubbard done in 1764, both in the Chicago Art Institute (Prown #139, 138); Joseph[4] Greene and his wife dated 1767, in the collection of Mrs. Allen Forbes of Boston (Prown #213, 214); and John[4] Greene and his wife painted in 1769, in the Currier Art Gallery in Manchester NH, and in the Cleveland Museum (wife) (Prown #261, 262).

Thomas Greene consolidated a large piece of property in the south end around the original Gould property between the Common and Washington Street (then Newbury) (SW 13304). On this land he had a mansion with stables and the first coach in Boston (Greene RI 147). His inheritance from his grandfather Thomas Gold the founder was contested as late as 1743 when the baker William Speakman (grandfather of Hannah Speakman Minot, of whom we have a silhouette) sued in the Court of Common Pleas for possession of three houses and land 53 ft. on Newbury Street. This was held by Ann's three sons Thomas, Rufus, and Benjamin, as well as two infants Nathaniel[4] and John[4] Greene of Milton under guardianship of Andrew Lane (SD 66:120-1). The property ended up in Thomas's[3] estate (see map in SW 13304).

His notable descendants include the merchants Nathaniel[4] and David[4] Greene, the botanist Benjamin[4] Greene, schoolmaster Charles[5] W. Greene, engineer Richard[7] Vose, and the wife of railway builder James[7] M. Forbes, of whom more below.

JOHN SINGLETON COPLEY (1783–1815), *Portrait of Rufus Greene* (1707–1777)
Oil on canvas; 24 x 20 3/4 inches

From Kennedy Galleries reproduction.

ii. RUFUS^3 GREENE, goldsmith of Boston, born Boston 30 May 1707 (CD 43:48); died Boston 31 Dec. 1777 (Granary 11 tomb 41); married 10 Dec. 1728 KATHARINE, daughter of Edward STANBRIDGE, born about 1709, died Boston 13 Jan. 1768 at age 59 (Trinity 781, Granary 114 tomb 41).

Like his elder brother Rufus3 was active in the Episcopal church, serving a vestryman at King's Chapel 1732-6 (Foote 2:607), then at Trinity as vestryman for 22 years (1739-50), Junior Warden 1751-64, and Senior Warden 1765-7 (Trinity 203).

In the treasures of American colonial crafts at Winterthur Museum is a silver "cann" (mug) made by Rufus about 1760. For his notable silver and pewter ware see Ralph M. and Terry H. Kovel, *A Directory of American Silver, Pewter and Silver Plate* [NY: Crown Publishers, 1968] 121.

Copley also painted portraits of him and his wife in 1758, owned in 1966 by Senator Theodore Greene of Rhode Island (Prown 164, photos # 61, 62), and of his daughter Katherine (1764) and her husband John Amory (1768) now in the Boston Museum of Fine Art (Prown 164 #140, 240). Prown comments on this collection of 14 portraits of the Greene family that 12 were Anglicans, in politics two were high Tories and 4 moderate Tories, one very high income (Thomas^{3} or Amory?), 3 high, and 3 medium. He concludes "As a family group, this is the most Anglican, the most Tory, the most married, the most paired, and the least educated." By the last phrase, he means they didn't go to Harvard.

Rufus^{3} lived in the South End, and held town offices (TR 14). An early opponent of the Revolution, he was one of 23 Addressers against the Solemn League & Covenant of 5 June 1774 and a Tory Protestor (*Massachusetts Historical Soc. Proceedings* [Oct. 1870] 11:394; Winsor 3:175). However, he remained in Boston through the Revolution.

Among his noted descendants were the merchants John^{5}, Thomas^{5} and Rufus^{5} Amory, the historians William^{7} Hickling Prescott and John^{7} C. Ropes, Georgina^{6} Lowell, Massachusetts First lady Edith^{8} Wolcott, and art collector Martha^{8} Karolik.

iii. NATHANIEL^{3} GREENE, merchant of Boston, born Boston 14 May 1709 (CD 43:61); died Boston 3 February 1791 (Trinity 805); married 27 June 1729 ELIZABETH TAYLOR (Fam Greene 51), born about 1708, died 3 October 1768 age 62. There are no portraits by Copley, and his politics appear to have been less conservative than his brothers Rufus and Nathaniel. He was ancestor of educators Charles^{7} F. Chandler and William^{7} Chandler, Civil War hospital administrator Emily^{7} Parsons, and first lady Lucretia^{7} Garfield.

iv. WILLIAM^{3} GREENE, blacksmith of Boston, born Boston 3 May 1711 (CD 43:75); died Boston 23 November 1754 (Trinity 775), unmarried; it is possible this death is another man of the same name, and our William may have died before 1743, since he is not named among the contested heirs of Thomas Gold in the Speakman suit (SD 66:170).

v. BENJAMIN^{3} GREENE, merchant and goldsmith of Boston, born Boston 11 Jan. 1712 (CD 43:83), died Boston 12 April 1776 (Trinity 788; Granary 114, tomb 41); married 7 Feb. 1737 MARY CHANDLER, daughter of Hon. John and Hannah (Gardiner) Chandler of Worcester (Fam Greene 53), born New London, 9 Sept. 1717, died Boston 28 Feb. 1756 (Granary 114 tomb 41; March 2 in Trinity 776 may be his burial).

Benjamin was also a vestryman of Trinity Church 1748 ff. (Trinity 60:112) . A high Tory in politics, he was one of the 23 Addressors against the Solemn League & Covenant of 5 June 1774, and a protestor against the move towards independence (MHS *Proceedings* 11:393, 395), but died on the eve of the war. For his silver and pewter ware see Kovel 121.

Benjamin^{3} was the progenitor of the most distinguished descendants, including the horticulturalist Gardiner^{4} Greene, botanist Benjamin^{4} Greene, philanthropist William^{5} P. Greene, clergymen John^{5} S. C. Greene and Augustine^{6} H. Amory, physician Robert^{6} Amory, manufacturer James^{6} L. Greene, artist Charles^{6} C. Perkins, feminist Anne^{6} Phillips, geographers Gardiner^{6} Hubbard and Melville^{7} Grosvenor, reformer John^{7} Jay Chapman, lawyer Gardiner^{7} Greene Jr., editors John[7] Rose Greene and Max[8] Perkins, Ace pilot Victor[8] Chapman, three successive generations of Robert Amorys, doctor[6], manufacturer[7], diplomat[8] and author Cleveland[8] Amory and Watergate prosecutor Archibald[9] Cox.

GRANDCHILDREN OF ANN GOULD GREENE (second cousins):

NATHANIEL[4] GREENE, merchant, fourth son and fifth child of Thomas[3] and Elizabeth Chandler, was Register of Deeds of Suffolk County 1786-91. He was born in Boston 12 April 1738 (CD 43:233); died Boston 3 Feb. 1791 (Trinity 805). He succeeded his father as a prominent merchant in partnership with his half-brother Joseph, and with his cousin Benjamin. Tributes applaud his enthusiastic support of the Revolution (Greene RI 248-9).

DAVID[4] GREENE, merchant, youngest son of Thomas[3], born Boston 20 June 1749 (CD 43:270), died Balston Springs NY 12 June 1812 (Greene RI 250). Harvard valedictorian for 1768 (Sibley 17:27), he earned his AM at Yale in 1772. A prominent merchant of Boston, he succeeded to the family estate on the Common, now Mason Street, west of his great grandfather Thomas Gould's house. He was elected Clerk of the Boston Market in 1772. A Tory protester in 1774, he left for England 1775, and spent the Revolution in Antigua where he married and carried on successful business. Although proscribed as a Loyalist in 1778, he returned to Boston after the peace and naturalized in 1789. He became active in promoting education, serving on Boston School Committee 1797-1812, and Justice of the Peace 1802. He served long as President of Union Insurance Co., Boston.

GARDINER[4] GREENE, merchant and horticulturalist, youngest son of Benjamin[3] and Mary Chandler, was famous for his garden on Beacon Hill, and having married the daughter of the painter John Singleton Copley, who painted his portrait (Prown 164). He was born in Boston 23 Sept. 1753 (CD 43:282); died Boston 19 Dec. 1832 (Greene RI 259). Gardiner married three times, the third in London 3 July 1800 to ELIZABETH COPLEY, daughter of the portraitist, and sister of John Copley, Baron Lyndhurst, three times Lord Chancellor of England.

Gardiner Greene returned with his third wife to Boston and in 1803 built a mansion on the east slope of Beacon Hill, then much higher, with a fine view down State Street to the harbor. He planted the terraces in front of the house rising up from Pemberton Square at Somerset Street with a variety of exotic plants, including a Chinese gingko. The garden was a showplace of Boston until his death in 1835, when the top of Beacon Hill was shaved off for fill at North Station, and the gingko moved to the Common at Joy Street (MHS *Proceedings*, 2d ser. I:312-26; Fam Greene 55-69).

Active in the Episcopal church, he was Vestryman of Trinity Church 1810 ff. (Trinity 60:292). His papers in Massachusetts Historical Society contain two genealogical references: The last folder, 1871-95, correctly refers to Nathaniel Greene "married a Gould of Boston, and settled there". A letter of Thomas C. Amory to Mrs. James S. Amory dated 15 Jan. 1881 makes two common errors: "Thomas[5] Greene of the Greene Foundation 1705-1764 Harvard College [there is no evidence of any college] was son of Nathaniel and Ann daughter of Thomas Gould by Frances Robinson [wrong maiden name].

GREAT-GRANDCHILDREN OF ANN GOULD GREENE (Goulds' third cousins):

CHARLES[5] WINSTON GREENE, (*David*[4], *Thomas*[3]) schoolmaster, born Norwich CT 3 July 1783 (Greene RI 413), died East Greenwich CT 24 Dec. 1857. A graduate of Harvard 1802, he was founder and Principal of a boys' school Jamaica Plain.

THOMAS[5] AMORY, (*Catherine*[4], *Rufus*[3]), merchant of Boston, born 9 May 1762 (CD 43:303), died Roxbury 25 Oct. 1823 (VR 2:456). He made a large fortune in partnership with his older brother John (1759-?). He had the famous architect Bulfinch build him a house that still stands at the corner of Park and Beacon Streets facing the Common and State House in 1804. The largest residence in Boston, it was called "Amory's Folly" for its size and pretentiousness. During the opening reception he was told that he had lost a fortune, but carried on anyway. The house was soon sold and divided (Mary Caroline Crawford, *Famous Families of Massachusetts* [Boston: Little, Brown 1930] 2:124n. The fourth of his eight children Julia[6] Amory married The Rt. Rev. Mark Anthony De Wolf Howe (1808-95), first Bishop of Central Pennsylvania; their daughter Mary[8] Amory Howe (1837-67) married The Rt. Rev. William Hobart Hare, first missionary Bishop to S. Dakota, "Apostle to the Sioux". The famous editor Mark Anthony Howe who summered at Cotuit was a step-brother by the third wife of the Bishop, and thus not a lineal descendant of Ann Greene.

RUFUS[5] GREENE AMORY (*Catharine*[4], *Rufus*[3]) lawyer and developer, brother of above, born Boston 20 Dec. 1760 (CD 43:298), died Boston 15 May 1833. He graduated from Harvard in 1778. He was one of the developers in the Broad Street Association (1805) which transformed the waterfront of Boston under Bulfinch's design, with the brick warehouses we see today, at India and Central Wharfs, with the wide Broad Street and Custom House (Walter M. Whitehill *Boston: A Topographical History* [Cambridge: Belknap, 1968] 84-6.

BENJAMIN[5] DANIEL GREENE (*Gardiner*[4], *Benjamin*[3]), botanist, born Demarara, British Guiana 9 Dec. 1793 (CD 43:341); died Boston 14 Oct. 1862; married MARGARET, daughter of Josiah QUINCY III (1772-1864), President of Harvard, Speaker of House of Representatives, and Mayor of Boston, with whom Thomas[5] Gould worked in improvement of Boston. She was one of the five "Articulate Sisters". Benjamin graduated from Harvard in 1812, won a L.L.B at James Gould's law school in Litchfield CT, then an MD from Edinburgh 1821. He was founder and President of Boston Society of Natural History, and botanist of note (Fam Greene 75-8; Greene RI 429).

WILLIAM[5] PARKINSON GREENE (*Gardiner*[4], *Benjamin*[3]) philanthropist, born Boston 7 Sept.1795 (CD 43:343); died Norwich CT 18 June 1864. Graduated from Harvard 1814; admitted to Suffolk Bar. He was a manufacturer in Norwich CT, of which he became Mayor. Second President of Norwich Academy (Fam Greene 78-80, Greene RI 429-30).

REV. JOHN^{5} SINGLETON COPLEY GREENE (*Gardiner*^{4}, *Benjamin*^{3}), clergyman, born Boston 27 June 1810 (Trinity 688); died Brookline MA 6 July 1872. He got his BA from Harvard 1828 and MD 1831. He was ordained a priest in the Episcopal church 1855, and became minister in Waltham and Newton MA, and Secretary of Massachusetts Church Missionary Society (Fam Greene 83-6, Greene RI 432-3).

GREAT GREAT-GRANDCHILDREN OF ANN GOULD GREENE (Goulds' fourth cousins):

WILLIAM^{6} HICKLING PRESCOTT (*Catherine*^{5} *Hickling, Sarah*^{4}, *Rufus*^{3}), historian, born Salem 14 May 1796; died Boston 28 Jan. 1859. Graduate of Harvard in 1814, author of *Conquest of Mexico* (1843), *Conquest of Peru* (1847) and histories of Spain. See extensive biographies in all encyclopedias, esp. *Dictionary of American Biography* [New York: Scribners, 1935] 8:96-200. A search of his papers and letters in MHS does not reveal any research into his family history. A recent genealogy of Prescott (Gary Boyd Roberts "The Flowering of New England...Historians...Prescott, *NEXUS* 7:29 repeats the error that Anne Gould's parents were Thomas Gould and Frances Robinson; for this he apparently cites Greene RI and Z Gould, though, as demonstrated above Z Gould 347 is correct in giving Frances Robinson to the North End family, and not to that of Ann Gould Greene.

Rev. HENRY^{6} BURROUGHS (*Catherine Amory*^{5} *Greene*, *David*^{4}, *Thomas*^{3}), Episcopal clergyman, born Boston 18 April 1815 (Greene RI 415); died 9 June 1884 ("Index to Obituary Notices in the Boston Transcript" [Worcester: typescript, 1938] 1. He graduated from Harvard 1834, and Union Theological Seminary 1838. He became rector Camden NJ, Northampton MA, then Old North (Christ Church) Boston, where Elias Goddard was parishioner after his forced deposition as Senior Warden. Burroughs was there until 1881.

GEORGINA^{6} MARGARET AMORY (*Jonathan*^{5}, *Catherine*^{4}, *Rufus*^{3}) born Boston March 1806; died Boston 27 Nov. 1830; married 6 April 1825 JOHN LOWELL, Jr. (1799-1836) founder of Lowell Institute 1836. Her death and their two children of scarlet fever within 18 months were the cause of Lowell's founding of the remarkable cultural institution (Edward Weeks *The Lowells and Their Institute* [Boston: Little, Brown, 1966].

ANNE^{6} TERRY GREENE (*Benjamin*$^{5\text{-}4\text{-}3}$), feminist and abolitionist; born Boston 19 Nov. 1814 (Greene RI 578); died Boston 24 April 1886 (*Transcript*). Introduced to her future husband Wendell Phillips (1811-84) as "a rabid Abolitionist" (1836) she was responsible for converting him to the cause of liberation of the slaves, of which he became a famous leader, in partnership with William Lloyd Garrison (Ralph Korngold *Two Friends of Man* [Boston: Little, Brown 1950] 122. They were married in Boston 12 Oct. 1837. She was a delegate to the World's Anti-Slavery Convention in London 12 June 1840, at which she took the strong stand for women's representation that "heralded the birth of the Woman's Rights Movement in America" (Ibid. 150-1).

HENRY[6] GRAFTON CHAPMAN (*Sarah*[5] *Greene, Benjamin*[4-3]), abolitionist merchant, born Boston 3 May 1804; died Boston 3 Oct. 1842; married 1830 MARIA WESTON, "Garrison's Lieutenant" or "Prime Minister", born Weymouth 25 July 1806, died 13 July 1885, co-founder of the New England Non-Resistance Society 1838, "the living spirit" of the Boston Female Anti-Slavery Society, editor of *Liberty Bell* 1839-46, and *The Liberator* in Garrison's absence (Louis Ruchames, ed. *The Letters of William Lloyd Garrison* [Cambridge: Belknap, 1971] 2: xxiv, 25). He and his wife were delegates to the World's Anti-Slavery Convention in London 1840 (*William Lloyd Garrison: The Story of His Life* [New York: Century, 1885] 2: 353, 42). He attended the Chardon Street Convention on religious reform in Boston 1840. He became a stockbroker in New York, and President of the New York Stock Exchange. He graduated from Harvard 1823. Anne Terry Greene, his niece, was raised in their home on Essex Street.

His sister ANN GREENE CHAPMAN, born 1802, died 24 March 1837, was an early abolitionist, present at the mobbing of the Anti-Slavery Convention of 1836, to whom Garrison wrote a poetic tribute on her early death at 35 (Garrison Life 2:12, 208).

Their sister MARY[6] GRAY CHAPMAN, born about 1798, died Boston 8 Nov. 1874, was also an active abolitionist leader (Garrison Letters 6:56, Life 4:360).

CHARLES[6] CALLAHAN PERKINS (*Elizabeth*[5] *Callahan, Lucretia*[4] *Greene, Benjamin*[3]) cultural leader and artist, born Boston 1 March 1823 (*Who Was Who in America* [Chicago: Marquis, 1963 f.] 405 ; died Winsor VT. 25 Aug. 1886. He was President of Boston Art Club 1869-79, one of founders of the Boston Museum of Fine Arts, and founder of Massachusetts School of Art, "by his writings and lectures materially influenced the development of art in America" (*Columbia Encyclopedia* [New York: Columbia, 1940] 1372). He was also a great patron of music, as President of Handel & Haydn Society 1850-1, 1875-86, for which he conducted and wrote music; he was the largest subscriber to Boston Music Hall, and donor of bronze statue of Beethoven in front of New England Conservatory of Music (*Dictionary of American Biography* 14:464).

MARTIN BRIMMER, husband of MARY ANN[6] "Mina" TIMMINS (*Elizabeth*[5] *Greene, Gardiner*[4], *Benjamin*[3]), married at Brimmer's home, "Wood Rock", Pride's Crossing, Beverly MA 23 May 1855, given away by her uncle John Jay Chapman. Among the ushers were her cousins Harcourt and Frederick Amory, and J. J. Storrow Jr., T. Jefferson Coolidge Jr. and Owen Wister of Philadelphia. Martin became a leading Boston art patron and politician. Born Boston 9 Dec. 1829 to Boston Mayor (1843-4) Martin Brimmer and Harriet Wadsworth of Geneseo NY, he graduated from Harvard in 1849, became Overseer about 1866 and Fellow of the Harvard Corporation 1864-8, and President of its Overseers 1887. He was first President of the Museum of Fine Arts 1870-96. He and Mary Ann lived at 47 Beacon Street, and were members of Trinity Church. He was Massachusetts state Representative 1859-61, Senator 1864, Presidential Elector 1876. He died in Boston 14 Jan. 1896.

Msgr. GEORGE[6] HOBART DOANE (*Elizabeth*[5] *Callahan, Lucretia*[4] *Greene,*

Benjamin^{3}), Catholic clergyman, born Boston 5 Sept. 1830; died about 20 Jan. 1905 (*The New York Times Obituaries Index* [New York: New York Times, 1970] [hereinafter NYT Obit] 21 Jan. 1905, 1;2; Greene RI 258). He earned his MD degree at Jefferson Medical College 1850. Converted to Catholicism 1855, he was ordained a priest in 1857 after study in Rome. He was Chaplain at First Battle of Bull Run. Secretary to Bishop Bayley of Newark, then Vicar General of Roman Catholic Diocese of Newark, NJ. Made Administrator of Newark Diocese, then made Prothonotary Apostolic by Pope Leo XIII in Rome 1890. He was responsible for several public buildings in Newark: Post Office, City Hall and Court House (Alfred Adler Doane, *The Doane Family* [Boston: A. A. Doane, 1902] 394-5.

Rev. WILLIAM^{6} CROSWELL DOANE (*Elizabeth*^{5} *Callahan, Lucretia*^{4} *Greene, Benjamin*^{3}), Episcopal clergyman and educator, born Boston 2 March 1832; d. Albany NY 17 May 1913 (*Who Was Who* 2:327; *New York Times* Obit 18 May 4:7, 20 May 11:5). He became the first Episcopal Bishop of Albany NY 2 Feb. 1869. He was Rector in Burlington 1853-60, Hartford 1860-4, and Albany 1867-9, where he founded St. Agnes School 1870 and built the Cathedral of All Saints Albany, and a children's hospital. He was Lecturer in English at Trinity College 1863-9 and Chancellor NY State University to 1909. He was warded nine honorary degrees including Oxford and Cambridge (1888) and Dublin 1901 (photo in Doane 464).

GARDINER^{6} GREENE HUBBARD (*Mary Anne*^{5} *Greene, Gardiner*^{4}, *Benjamin*^{3}), telephone pioneer, born Cambridge 25 Aug. 1822; died Washington DC 11 Dec. 1897 (Greene RI 427). Degrees from Dartmouth 1841, and Harvard Law School. He was President of first horse drawn railway in US outside NY, Cambridge to Boston. Founding president of Clarke School for the Deaf, the first permanent institution for the Deaf in US, 1867. He was also first President of Bell Telephone Co. 1878; the founder of *Science* magazine 1883; founder and first president of National Geographic Society 1888; Regent of Smithsonian Institution 1895. Hubbard Glacier in Alaska, and Hubbard Hall, home of National Geographic Society, are named for him (Who Was Who 264). His daughter MABEL^{7} HUBBARD, born 25 Nov. 1857 married 11 July 1877 ALEXANDER GRAHAM BELL, inventor of the telephone.

JAMES^{6} LLOYD GREENE (*William Parkinson*^{5}, *Gardiner*^{4}, *Benjamin*^{3}) mayor and manufacturer, born Norwich CT 17 Jan. 1827; died 18 Oct. 1883 (Greene RI 579). He was a manufacturer in Norwich, where he followed his father as mayor 1862-6, 1871-5.

ARTHUR^{6} AMORY (*Mary*^{5} *Copley Greene, Gardiner*^{4}, *Benjamin*^{3}), business executive, born Boston 6 Feb. 1841; died Boston 9 Aug. 1911 (*Harvard Class of 1862, Class Report 1912)* 3 . After graduating from Harvard in 1862 he became a partner in Amory, Brown & Co. Boston 1866 ff. (*Who Was Who* 1:21).

Dr. ROBERT^{6} AMORY (*Mary*^{5} *Copley Greene, Gardiner*^{4}, *Benjamin*^{3}), medical researcher, born Boston 3 May 1842, died Nahant MA 28 Aug. 1910 (*Who Was Who* 2:21). Earning three degrees from Harvard, AB 1863, MA, MD 1866, he became Lecturer at Harvard Medical School 1869-71. He was President of Convention to revise the US Pharmacopeia 1880 ("Amory Genealogy Descendants of Jonathan", typescript [1897?] in NEHGS G/AMO 14). He was also vestryman of Trinity Church 1899-1910 (Trinity 208).

Rev. AUGUSTINE^{6} HEARD AMORY (*Mary^{5} Copley Greene, Gardiner^{4}, Benjamin^{3}*), Episcopal clergyman, born Brookline 20 July 1852, died Lynn MA 9 April 1904 (Arthur W. Moulton *A Memoir of Augustine Heard Amory* [Salem: Newcomb & Gauss, 1909] 10. After receiving his BD 1880 from Episcopal Theological School in Cambridge he was 18 years rector of Grace Church, Lawrence 1884-1902, then rector North Andover 1880-4, and Lynn 1902-4.

HARCOURT^{6} AMORY (*Mary^{5} Copley Greene, Gardiner^{4}, Benjamin^{3}*), textile executive, born Brookline 10 Feb. 1855, died Boston 6 Nov. 1925. Graduate of Harvard 1876, he became Treasurer of Lancaster Mills & Indian Head Mills (Harvard Class of 1876, 50th class report 3. 22 years vestryman Trinity Church in Boston, 1889-1910, 1921-2, and 10 years Junior Warden (Trinity 208).

3 GREAT-GRANDCHILDREN OF ANN GOULD GREENE (Fifth cousins of Goulds):

GEORGE^{7} LEONARD VOSE (*Harriet^{6} Chandler, Lucretia^{5} Greene, Joseph^{4}, Thomas^{3}*), railway engineer, born Augusta ME 19 April 1831; died 30 March 1910 (*General Catalog of Bowdoin College* [Brunswick ME: Bowdoin, 1950] 37; *Appletons' Cyclopedia of American Biography* [New York: D. Appleton, 1888] [hereinafter Appleton] 6:307. Professor of civil engineering MIT 1881-6, and Bowdoin 1871-81, he was author of *Railway Engineering*.

JOHN^{7} ROSE GREENE HASSARD (*Augusta^{6} Greene, John Rose^{5}, David^{4}, Thomas^{3}*), editor and critic, born New York City 4 Sept. 1836; died New York City 18 April 1888 (Appleton 7:111). A graduate of St. John's in 1855 he became editor of *Catholic World* 1865, then joined the *New York Tribune* in 1866 as music and literary critic. He was author of a biography of Pope Pius IX, a popular history of US, and book on Wagner's Ring of the Niebelungen.

JOHN^{7} CODMAN ROPES (*Mary Anne^{6} Codman, Catherine^{5} Amory, Catherine^{4} Greene, Rufus^{3}*), military historian; born St. Petersburg, Russia 28 April 1836; died Boston 27 Oct. 1899 (Appleton 5:320; Cora Codman Walcott *The Codmans of Charlestown and Boston* (Brookline MA: privately printed, 1930) 68. Ropes was biographer of *The First Napoleon* (1885), one of the first historians of The Civil War: *The Army Under Pope and Campaigns of the Civil War* (1881). (His first cousin, Ogden Codman, the architect 1839-1904, son of Charles^{6} Russell, and grandson of John^{5} Codman was not a direct descendant of Ann Greene).

First Lady LUCRETIA^{7} RUDOLPH GARFIELD (*Arabella^{6} Mason, Lucretia^{5} Greene, John^{4}, Nathaniel^{3}*), wife of 20th President James A. Garfield (1831-1881), the first to be assassinated. She was born Hiram OH. 19 April 1832; married Garfield 11 Nov. 1858; died Pasadena CA 13 Jan. 1918 (Joseph N. Kane, *Facts About the Presidents* [New York: H.W.Wilson, 1974] 139; Greene RI 421).

EMILY^{7} ELIZABETH PARSONS (*Catherine^{6} Chandler, Dorothy^{5} (Dolly) Greene, John^{4}, Nathaniel^{3}*), hospital administrator, born Taunton MA 8 March 1824, died Cambridge 19 May 1880 (Greene RI 421; *Notable American Women* [Cambridge: Belknap Harvard, 1971]

3:22-3. Although partially blind and deaf and crippled, she became one of the leading hospital administrators during the Civil War. Her training as a nurse at Massachusetts General Hospital "coupled with her own executive gifts, gave her a professional competence almost unique among Civil War nurses.". First she was in charge of a ward at Ft. Schuyler near New York City Oct. 1862; then Lawson Hospital St. Louis Jan. 1863. She became Head Nurse of *City of Alton* floating hospital on the Mississippi Feb. 1863 where she caught malaria, but carried on for 16 months as Supervisor of Nurses at Benton Barracks, the largest military hospital in the West, April 1863, an appointment that was "one of the most important given to a woman in the Civil War". After the war, in 1865, she began collection of funds for a general hospital in Cambridge, opened in 1867-72, reestablished as Cambridge Hospital in 1886, now Mount Auburn Hospital.

JOHN[7] JAY CHAPMAN (*Henry*[6], *Sarah*[5] *Greene, Benjamin*[4-3]), essayist and reformer, born New York City 2 March 1862; died Poughkeepsie NY 4 Nov. 1933 (DAB Supp. I:168). Graduate of Harvard; "author two books on political reform, essays on Greek genius, on Emerson, Whitman, Balzac, Shakespeare; sketches of his contemporaries; translations and moral and religious speculations; a life of William Lloyd Garrison...original plays", and "one of the first advocates of general education" (Jacques Barzun, *The Selected Writings of John Jay Chapman* [New York: Minerva, 1968] xi, xix. He was also a poet. Biography by Mark De Wolfe Howe of Cotuit.

Dr. CHARLES[7] FREDERICK CHANDLER (*Charles Chandler*[6], *Dolly*[5] *Greene*, *John*[4], *Nathaniel*[3]), educator, born Lancaster MA 6 December 1836; died New York 25 August 1925 (Greene RI 423; *Who Was Who* 2:210; *NYTimes* Obit 26 Aug 19:4, 27 Aug 19:5; Appleton 1:572). Educated in Germany, he received his Ph.D. from Göttingen University in 1857. He became Professor at Union College 1857-64, and was one of founders of Columbia Univ. School of Mines 1864. Dean of Faculty of Science Columbia 1897; College of Pharmacy, College of Physicians & Surgeons NYC, MD NYU 1873; President of New York City Board of Health 1873, 1877, during which he initiated important reforms in public health, involving food, water and housing.

PROF. WILLIAM[7] HENRY CHANDLER (*Charles*[6] *Chandler, Dolly*[5] *Greene, John*[4], *Nathaniel*[3]), chemist, b. New Bedford MA 13 Dec. 1841 (Greene RI 423) ; d. Bethlehem PA 23 Nov. 1906 (*NYTimes* Obit 24 Nov. 11:6; Who Was Who 2:210); Professor of Chemistry Lehigh University 1871 ff.; Director of Lehigh Library 1878; Columbia Univ. School of Mines 1868-71; editor of *American Chemist* 1870-8 with his brother, above.

GARDINER[7] GREENE JR. (*Gardiner*[6], *William P.*[5], *Gardiner*[4], *Benjamin*[3]), judge and legislator, b. Norwich CT 31 Aug. 1851 (Greene RI 687), d. Norwich CT 10 Feb. 1925 (*N.Y.Times* Obit 11 Feb. 21:2; *Who Was Who* 2:482); BA Yale 1873; Columbia Law School 1877; lawyer Norwich CT; Representative of Norwich in State House of Representatives; on Commission to Revise Connecticut Laws 1899, which were adopted 1901; Judge, Superior Court of Connecticut 1910-21.

ROBERT[7] AMORY (*Robert*[6], *Mary*[5] *Greene, Gardiner*[4], *Benjamin*[3]) textile manufacturer, b. Boston 23 Oct. 1885; d. New York 20 July 1972 ; BA Harvard 1906; President, Nashua Manufacturing Co. 1930, Executive Vice President, Springs Mills (Harvard Undergraduate file

1906; *Who Was Who* 5:13; Amory 15).

HARCOURT[7] AMORY (*Harcourt*[6], *Mary*[5] *Greene, Gardiner*[4], *Benjamin*[3]), business executive, b. Beverly MA 7 July 1894; d. New York 4 Dec. 1969; BA Harvard 1916; Partner Smith, Barney 1931-42; War Production Board 1942-4; Vice President Hawaiian Pineapple, Castle & Cooke 1945-7; Smith Barney 1947-69; President Massachusetts Republican Club 1940-2 (Harvard Alum. Directory 1975, 24; *Who Was Who* 5:13).

4 GREAT-GRANDCHILDREN OF ANN GOULD GREENE (Sixth cousins of Goulds):

MARTHA[8] CATHERINE CODMAN (KAROLIK) (*John*[7] *Codman, Catherine*[6] *Amory, John*[5] *Amory, Catherine*[4] *Greene, Rufus*[3]), art historian and collector, b. Boston 24 July 1858; d. Newport RI 21 April 1948 (*NYTimes* Obit 22 April 27:1); m. 2 Feb. 1928 MAXIM KAROLIK, Russian tenor (Codmans 74). Her large collection of early American art was donated to Boston Museum of Fine Arts 1941, valued at over a million dollars before the Depression, requiring a new wing for the museum; in 1947 she gave 225 paintings by American artists 1815-65, but there is no evidence that she knew of portrait of Thomas[1] Gould (papers in MHS).

VICTOR[8] EMMANUEL CHAPMAN (*John Jay*[7], *Henry*[6], *Sarah*[5] *Greene, Benjamin*[4-3], ace aviator, b. 17 April 1890; d. France 23 June 1916; pilot with Lafayette Escadrille in World War I; exploits in combat described in *Victor Chapman's Letters from France*; killed in combat (DAB 4:21; *Columbia Ency.* 332).

MAX(WELL)[8] EVARTS PERKINS (*Edward*[7] *Perkins, Charles*[6] *C., Elizabeth*[5] *Perkins, Lucretia*[4] *Greene, Benjamin*[3]), editor and man of letters, b. New York 20 Sept. 1884; d. Stamford CT 17 June 1947 (Who Was Who 2:419; NYTimes 18 June 1947 25:3; Gary Boyd Roberts & William Reitwiesner, *American Ancestors and Cousins of the Princess of Wales* [Baltimore: Genealogical Publishing, 1984] [hereinafter Princess Di] 68, #287). Called "Dean of Book Editors" Perkins discovered Thomas Wolfe, Hemingway, Erskine Caldwell, Ring Lardner, John P. Marquand and Scott Fitzgerald. BA Harvard 1907; *New York Times* 1907-10; joined Scribner's 1910, became its editor 1914, director 1915, Secretary 1917-32; Vice President 1932 f. "probably had more books dedicated to him than any other man in his time". He published novels of Thomas Wolfe, who described him as the editor Foxhall Edwards in *You Can't Go Home Again*, and in dedication *Of Time and the River* described him as "a great editor and a brave and honest man, who stuck to the writer of this book through times of bitter hopelessness and doubt".

MELVILLE[8] BELL GROSVENOR (*Elsie*[7] *Bell, Gardiner*[6] *Hubbard, Mary Anne*[5] *Greene, Gardiner*[4], *Benjamin*[3]), geographer, born Washington DC 26 Nov. 1901 (Greene RI 428); d. Miami FL 22 April 1982 (*Current Biography* [1982, 466; *NYTimes* obit 24 April 11; Whos Who 1982 1324). He joined *National Geographic Magazine* 1924; became its editor 1957-67 and editor-in-chief 1967-77; Vice Pres. Nat. Geo. Soc. 1954-7, Pres. 1957-67; Chairman of Trustees 1967-77. He helped build membership to 10 million, and make it the world's largest private educational and scientific association., adding film and TV to its educational offerings.

EDITH^{8} PRESCOTT (*William^{7} G., William^{6} H. Prescott, Catherine^{5} Hickling, Sarah^{4} Greene, Rufus^{3}*), first lady of the Commonwealth, born 20 April 1853; d. ?, m. 2 Sept. 1874 ROGER WOLCOTT (1847-1900), Governor of Massachusetts 1896-1900, Harvard Overseer (Samuel Wolcott, *Memorial of Henry Wolcott* [New York: Anson Randolph, 1881] 418. (The Wolcott Papers in MHS contain genealogical information on her ancestry. In five places the error is perpetuated that Thomas^{1} Gould married Frances Robinson: II, N-152, Box 1 folder 1 Gov. Roger Wolcott family tree: Prescott; Box 3 folder 9 Greene family, pencil note on maternal grandfather of Catherine^{5} Greene Hickling [note that an older nineteenth century hand gives Nath. Greene m. Anne d. Thomas Gould of Boston, with no mother]; Box 3 folder 5 Hickling Genea. Sheet in ink gives error; reverse of same citing Register 4:75 repeats the error; Box 3 folder 23 Misc. on card from Union Club does the same).

ROBERT^{8} AMORY JR. (*Robert$^{7-6}$, Mary^{5} Greene, Gardiner^{4}, Benjamin^{3}*) diplomat and lawyer, b. Boston 2 March 1915 (Whos Who 1988 1:62); BA Harvard 1936; LLB 1938; Colonel World War II commanding amphibious engineering battalion and regiment, New Guinea and Philippines; Professor of Law and Accounting Harvard Law School; Deputy Director CIA 1952-62; US Delegate to international conferences Bermuda 1953, Bangkok 1955; National Security Planning Board 1953-61; Chief, International Div. Bureau of the Budget 1962-5; Harvard Board of Overseers 1963-9; member Washington law firm Corcoran, Foley, Youngman & Rowe 1965-72; advisory council of School of Advanced International Studies; Treasurer Washington Cathedral Foundation; many other civic posts.

CLEVELAND^{8} AMORY (*Robert$^{7-6}$, Mary^{5} Greene, Gardiner^{4}, Benjamin^{3}*) author and conservationist, b. Nahant 2 Sept. 1917 (*Contemporary Authors* 69:24); BA Harvard 1939; author of celebrated book on Boston Brahmins, *The Proper Bostonians* (1947) and a sequel *Proper Bostonians Revisited* (1972), also the books *Home Town* (1950), *The Last Resorts* (1952), *Who Killed Society?* (1960); editor, *Celebrity Register*; founder and President The Fund for Animals, and author of books *Man Kind? Our Incredible War on Wildlife* (1974), *Animail* (1976); radio and TV commentator; biography *The Trouble with Nowadays* (1979).

5 GREAT-GRANDCHILDREN OF ANN GOULD GREENE (Goulds' seventh cousins):

ROGER^{9} WOLCOTT, Jr. (*Edith^{8} Prescott, William$^{7-6}$, Catherine^{5} Hickling, Sarah^{4} Greene, Rufus^{3}*), state legislator, b. 25 July 1877, d. Milton MA. 21 April 1965 (Milton Town Clerk); BA Harvard 1899; Representative Massachusetts 1909-12, 1917-8; Chairman Milton Selectmen; 2 terms Harvard Overseer 1921-, Chairman Executive Committee 5 years; editor of Correspondence of his great-grandfather William Hickling Prescott (Houghton Mifflin, 1925); President Boston Athenaeum; author *Family Jottings* 1939 (*Harvard Class Report 1899*, 50th [1949] 886.

ARCHIBALD^{9} COX JR. (*Frances^{8} Braun Perkins, Edward^{7}, Charles^{6} Callahan, Elizabeth^{5} Callahan, Lucretia^{4} Greene, Benjamin^{3}*), legal authority, b. Plainfield NJ 17 May 1912; d. Brooksville ME 29 May 2004 (NYTimes obit 31 May A19); BA Harvard 1934; LLB 1937; Ropes & Gray, Boston 1946 ff., partner 1958; US Solicitor General under Presidents Kennedy and Johnson 1961-5; lecturer Harvard Law School 1945-61; Williston Professor

1965-76; Loeb Professor 1976-84; Special Prosecutor for Watergate Scandal 1974 leading to abdication of President Nixon; Harvard Overseer 1962-5 (*Whos Who* 1988 1242; Princess DI, 65, #262).

GILBERT[9] MELVILLE GROSVENOR (*Melville*[8], *Elsie*[7] *Bell, Gardiner*[6] *Hubbard, Mary Anne*[5] *Greene, Gardiner*[4], *Benjamin*[3]), geographer, b. Washington DC 5 May 1931; BA Yale 1954; joined National Geographic Society 1954, becoming Editor 1970-80 and President 1980 (*Who's Who* 1982-3, 1324).

EDWIN[9] STUART GROSVENOR (*Melville*[8], *Elsie*[7] *Bell, Gardiner*[6] *Hubbard, Mary Anne*[5] *Greene, Gardiner*[4], *Benjamin*[3]), editor and publisher, b. Washington DC 17 Sept. 1951; BA Yale 1974, MS Journalism Columbia 1976, MBA 1977, President of Grosvenor Publications, New York City 1977-83, Editor, *Portfolio* magazine 1979-83 (*Who's Who* 1988-9, 1241).

Chapter IV

THOMAS[3] GOULD, Mariner

5. **THOMAS[3] GOULD** (William[2], Thomas[1]), mariner of Boston, was born in Boston 30 January 170l (CD 43:7) and may have died at sea 1763? (SW 13214); he married 16 Dec.1736 **HANNAH[3] WOODS** (John[2], Richard[1]) of Roxbury (CD 101:313).

   This Thomas Gould is the most obscure of our Boston ancestors, and most difficult to document. For the basic descent we follow Z Gould 346 who says: "Thomas Goold perhaps son of William and Mercy [Harris]; m. 1736 Dec. 16 Hannah Woods in Roxbury. A son Thomas was born 1737 Oct. 30." We have found nothing to contradict this. The lack of a will or estate for his father makes it difficult to prove, as does lack of mention in wills of his mother and aunt. Also lack of property in Boston adds to difficulty.

The most certain fact is his wedding to Hannah Woods. Intentions are recorded 18 Nov. 1736 (CD 150:226), and wedding by Mr. Nehemiah Walter 16 Dec. 1736 with note "Int. reads [Gold]" (CD 101:313). Walter was minister of the First Church in Roxbury, so Thomas appears to have left the Episcopalian faith of his family, though his father William does not seem to have been active in any church in later years. She was admitted to the church Sept. 1737 (Thwing 135 citing Bos. City Rec. 6).

Hannah Woods was born in Roxbury 5 Dec. 1714 to John[1] and Jemima Woods (Roxbury Vital Records hereinafter Rox VR, 391). She probably died in Abington about 1775 during a smallpox epidemic, at the home of the minister of the First Church 398 Washington Street (Cyrus Nash Papers, Abington Historical Society, Dyer Mem. Library, Abington, D-36:22). She would have been 61 years old.

Her parents John[2] WOODS and Jemima[3] SEVER were married Roxbury 3 Dec. 1713 (Rox VR 445). Her father was born 6 Feb. 1690 Roxbury (Rox VR 391), died Roxbury 24 May 1747 aged 58 (Rox VR 676).

John and his wife owned the covenant Roxbury July 1714 (Roxbury City Doc. 114:144). On 17 Feb. 1723 Benjamin Woods, gunsmith of Roxbury and his wife Ann deeded to his brother John his small house and lot on Roxbury Common, measuring 33 x 21 feet, the Common on the east, the Roxbury-Dedham road on the south, their father Richard on the west, and Brookline Road on the north. (SD 37:165). In a deed of 14 Jan. 1726 his father Richard, blacksmith of Roxbury deeded to him the land where his son John a gunsmith built a house and barn, where he now lives, fronting 41 ft. on the Boston Road to Dedham, bounded on the southwest by Handshaw (from Eason), northwest by the heirs of late William Deninson, northeast by the land Richard Woods bought from Robert Dorr (SD 40:216).

On 26 July 1736 John Woods, blacksmith, eldest son of Richard, blacksmith, now deceased, and his wife Jemima, sold for £ 150 the house and shop the lot measuring 139 x 30 ft.

on Roxbury Common to James Dolbeare, brazier, witnessed by Peter Seaver. (SD 53:89). Roxbury Common is 30 ft. on west, Brookline Highway 130 ft. on north, William Mansor's house 30 ft. on east, and Dedham Highway 130 ft. on south. On 25 March 1747 John Woods, gunsmith of Roxbury and his wife Jemima deeded to their son John Jr. a lot 18 x 18 on which he had built a shop, bounded by Town Street on SE, Edmund Weld Jr. on NE and NW and John Woods's house on SW (SD 73:188).

Jno. Woods was owner of pew number 7 in the gallery of the third meeting house in Roxbury, at the cost of 12 pounds (Walter Eliot Thwing, *History of the First Church in Roxbury* [Boston: W. A. Butterfield, 1908] [hereinafter Rox Church] 140).

On 7 May 1747 John Woods Sr. gunsmith for £ 60 gave one chamber and the garret at the northeast end of his dwelling on Town Street in Roxbury to his son John Jr., gunsmith of Roxbury. (SD 89:237). This was done a day before he executed his will on 8 May 1747 giving the two lower rooms, the northeast cellar, and movables of his dwelling to his wife as long as she is unmarried. (SW 8796). Should she remarry she was to give up two thirds of the movables to be divided among their children equally. His shop tools were to be sold to pay his debts. The rest of his estate was to be divided equally among his children, except that his son John got a double share. His executors were his son John and his friend Mr. Nathaniel Felton.

The inventory of his estate on 7 Sept. 1747 showed his house and part of a shop on the Town Street worth £ 660, his most valuable possession a featherbed of 66 weight worth £ 24, then £ 17/8 of pewter, a brass kettle and 2 skillets with £ 12/12; a pair of sheets, a blanket and an old rugg £ 3, bedstead curtains and other furniture £ 8/10, 2 bolsters & pillows £ 8, a featherbed weight 78 £ 10/10, another small bed £ 2/10, a pair of sheets, a blanket, coverlid an old bedsted and underbed £ 3/2, 3 pair of sheets £ 9, 5 pillowbeers £ 2/10, a tablecloth, a dozen napkins, 2 old tablecloths and 3 towels £ 10/4, a chest and drawers £ 4, an oval table, a trunk and chest £ 4, 8 black chairs £ 4, a looking glass £ 2, and 5 ¾ oz. of silver, an iron pot and kettle £ 2, one trammel, a pair of andirons, tongs & shovel, a spit and warming pan £ 6, one chest £ 1. The tools in the shop came to £ 26: an anvil 115 weight old 3 p. pound £ 17/5; 40 weight of old iron scraps 15 sh.; a Bick iron and Lamp stamps £ 2, 4 screw plates and screws £ 4, a hand vice a brace and file £ 1/10, and a small hand hammer 10 sh.

The debts of the estate nearly ate up the assets. The funeral cost £ 47/12, including £ 21/12 to Samuel Still and £ 26 sundry. He owed Dr. Gardiner £ 4/7 for medicine. The biggest expense was £ 190 for repairs to the house, including £ 50 for clapboards, £ 36 for shingles, £ 37 for boards, £ 25 for nails, and £ 42 for glass. He owed his son and executor £ 60 for which the two rooms were security. There were debts for coal, iron and shoes. Total debts came to £ 545/1/3. The estate was probated 25 Aug. 1758 (SW 8796).

John Woods died 24 May 1747 age 58 according to his gravestone which can be seen in the Eliot burying ground Roxbury D-402, 435a. (Inventory in Bostonian Society).

The parents of John[2] WOODS were Richard[1] blacksmith of Roxbury (SD 40:211) and Hannah, who first appear in Rox VR with John's birth in 1690. They are not in Savage or Rox VR; Hannah was still living in 1726; neither name appears in stones at Eliot Cemetery.

Jemima[3] SEVER, mother of Hannah Woods, was born 1680, calculating from her age 88 at death 4 May 1768, per her gravestone in Eliot Cemetery E/D 375, 402a. She was seventh child of Joshua[2] SEAVER who m. 28 Feb.1677 Mary, widow of Joseph Pepper. (William B. Trask "The Seaver Family" *Register* [July 1872] [hereinafter Trask], 7:305). Joshua was made freeman 22 March 1690; will proved 1730. (Ibid.). He joined the First Church 31 Jan. 1674/5 (Rox Church 120). Their graves are in Eliot Cemetery: his showing death 27 March 1730, age 88; hers has only a footstone. (E/D 397). She died 22 May 1683 (Sav. 4:46).

Joshua[2] SEAVER was born Roxbury 30 Aug. 1641, twin of Caleb, third and fourth children of Robert[1] SEAVER who m. (1) 10 Dec. 1634 Elizabeth BALLARD. Robert[1] was born about 1608 probably in England, and at age 25 came from London to New England on the *Mary & John*, arriving in Roxbury before June 1634. Elizabeth Ballard, maidservant, came to Roxbury in 1633, (Rox Church 49, 51), perhaps a relative of William Ballard who came over with Seaver. Robert[1] became a freeman 18 April 1637, signed a petition of 31 May 1647 for Hugh Pritchard to be captain of militia. On 23 May 1639 the General Court exempted Robert Seaver from the requirement that homes be built within half a mile of the meeting house. Robert Seauer is listed c.1636-40 as owning 14 acres of land in Roxbury (Francis S. Drake, *The Town of Roxbury* [Roxbury: the author, 1878] 49). His homestead was on Stony River (Drake 223). He owned the land on the site of the old Crafts Homestead on Tremont Street at the foot of Parker Hill Av. (Drake 340). He was chosen selectman 15 Jan. 1665. His wife Elizabeth died 6 June 1657, and was buried the ninth per church record. He died 13 May 1683 aged about 75, and was buried 4th month, sixth day. (Trask 304; Sav 3:46). He was an original donor to the Free School, now Roxbury Latin School, founded 31 Aug. 1645 (Rox Church 51, 9). Among his descendants was the Hon. "Squire" Ebenezer Seaver (1763-1844), Harvard 1784 (Rox Church 200-l), honored as "Father of the Town" B. selectman and town moderator, member of Massachusetts legislature, and U.S. Representative 1803-1813, member of the Committee on Foreign Affairs that reported a manifesto as basis for declaration of the War of 1812, called by John Randolph "the old Warhawk of the Democracy"; he died 1844. (Drake 223-4, with portrait).

Joshua Seaver's wife was Mary MAY, widow of Joseph PEPPER, m. 4 Nov. 1675 to Joseph Pepper (Rox VR 275) Joseph[2] Pepper, born Roxbury 18 March 1649 (Rox VR 274) was killed by the Indians at Sudbury on 21 April 1676 (VR 611, Savage 392) leaving a posthumous child Bethia born 6 Nov. 1676 (Rox VR 274). Savage, 4:391 states: "PEPPER...JOSEPH, Roxbury...by w. Mary had Bethia, b. 6 Nov. 1676, posthum. he being k. by the Ind. 21 Apr. preced. at Sudbury fight. His wid. m. 28 Feb. 1678 Joshua Sever." As a widow she became member of the First Church on 10 Sept. 1676 (Rox Church 120; again after marriage 13 Oct. 1678, Rox Church 121). There is much confusion whether Mary May married Joseph Ruggles since Mary May was named in the will of her father John May of Roxbury in 1671 was married 4 Nov. 1676 to John Ruggles (Sav 2:183) but the error is corrected in Mary Walton Ferris's *Dawes-Gates Ancestral Lines* [Milwaukee: Private Printing, 1943] [hereinafter Dawes-Gates], 415.

Mary MAY was born Roxbury 7 Nov.1657, baptized 29 May 1659 (erroneously as Sarah), daughter of JOHN[2] MAY(ES) Jr., b. England c. 1630, bur. 11 Sept. 1671 Roxbury age 40 blind several months (Rox VR 588); will probated 11 Oct.. He m. 19 Nov. 1656 Sarah[2] BREWER (Sav. 1:243), born 3 March 1638 Roxbury (Sav. 1:243) to Daniel[1] BREWER b. c. 1579, who came on the *Lion* 16 Sept. 1632, became freeman 14 May 1634, died early 1646, will dated 12 Jan. 1646, and his wife Joanna who died Roxbury 7 Feb. 1689 age 87 (Sav. 1:243).

Daniel[1] BREWER, a farmer, was one of the early members of the famous Eliot church in Roxbury (Rox Church 48) and subscriber to the Roxbury Free School for 5 shillings annually (Ferris 109). He owned nearly 100 acres in Roxbury (Ferris 109) and settled at Jamaica Plain near the May family (Winsor 1:422). In his will of 12 Jan. 1646 he left £ 5 to his daughter Sarah who was also to receive on marriage "a fflock bed furnished, my new kettle & a Pewter dish. (Ferris 110, citing SD 10:186?). He died 28 March 1646 "of an Ulcer in his longes wh peed through into his bowels & emptyed thithr to his great swelling & torment." (Ferris 110). His estate came to £ 166, proved 26 May 1646. His wife was left the house, half the barn and other outhouses, a red steer, all the swine, 3 Cowes, and the plowing & soweing of the said home lott..." (Ibid.). His widow Joanna lived unmarried for another 42 years. Ferris notes that "Perhaps she was a positive lady and insisted that records be exactly right", as indicated by the fact that when Roxbury Free School hired the new teacher John Prudden Daniell Bruer's name was corrected to read "widow Bruer" (Ibid.).

John[2] May(es) was son of John[1] May(es) Sr., b.c.1590,a farmer from Mayfield Sussex, who arrived in America by 1640, became freeman 2 June 1641, died Roxbury 28 April 1670 age 80; (Dawes-Gates 1:413-5). His first wife, mother of John Jr., came with him from England, died Roxbury 18 June 1651 (Sav. 3:183). According to Drake Mayes had been master of the James sailing from London to New England by 1635. (Drake 398). May senior came to Roxbury in 1640 and settled on 14 rods of land at Gamblin's End in Jamaica Plain, to the west of Robert Gamblin, northeast of Thomas Bell's orchard, and southeast of the highway. (Drake 398). He was an original donor to the Free School, now Roxbury Latin School, founded 31 Aug. 1645. Rox Church 56 says he arrived with his wife Sarah but in this may be confused with second wife, whom he says died 3 m. 15 d. 1659 (60).

John[2] May Jr. lived on his father's farm in West Roxbury, on South Street near the Weld estate. (Drake 438), became freeman 30 May 1660, three days after joining the church (Dawes-Gates 414).

Louisa May ALCOTT was a direct descendant of John[2] May (Abigail[7], Joseph[6] (1760-1841, bio.in *Register* April 1873), Samuel[5] architect and builder of Christ Church in Cambridge, Ebenezer[4] (1692-1752), John[3] (1663-1730). Louisa May was thus fifth cousin of Thomas[7] Gould Jr. *A Genealogy of the Descendants of John May...Roxbury* [Boston: Franklin Press, 1878] [hereinafter Genea May], 13. Abigail[7] May's brother was Rev. Samuel[7] Joseph MAY (1797-1871) famous abolitionist, peace leader and reformer who worked with William Lloyd Garrison, married Garrison and Helen Benson (*William Lloyd Garrison* [New York: Century Co., 1889], 4:396), *John F. May Descendants of John May of Roxbury 1640* [2d. ed., Baltimore-Gateway Press, 1978], 19), was fourth cousin of Thomas[6] Gould. Pioneer in nonviolence, he was founder of the Windham County (CT) Peace Society in 1826, co-founder of the world's first nonviolent organization, the New England Non-Resistance Society (1838) and promoter of the League of Universal Brotherhood. (Harold Josephson, editor, *Biographical Dictionary of Modern Peace Leaders* (Westport, CT.: Greenwood Press, 1985), 613-4). He is not to be confused with his abolitionist first cousin Rev. Samuel[7] MAY (b. 1810) Jr.and his father Samuel[6] MAY (1776-1870) who married Mary Goddard MAY (1787-1882) who was active in reform causes of Garrison's supporters Maria Chapman and Lydia Maria Child. (Genea May 15).

A first cousin of Abba Alcott and Rev. Samuel May Jr. was the famous suffragist leader and educator, Abby W. MAY[7] (Samuel[6]), 1829-1888. See her biography in *Notable American Women* 2:513.

Thomas[4] GOULD, eldest of five known children of Thomas[3] and Hannah Gould, was born Roxbury 30 Oct. 1737 (Roxbury births 148).

Thomas[4] Goold took the covenant 7 Nov. 1742 at Hollis Street Church in Boston (Record of Admissions, Baptisms, Marriages and Deaths 1732-1887 (Mss. The Topsfield Historical Society, 1918), 17). The following entry records another "Thomas Goold, received into covenant and bp. Nov 7 1742", probably referring to the infant son. The other four children were baptized in the same church, John in 1742 by his mother Hannah from Roxbury (perhaps because Thomas was at sea). Hollis Street Meeting, Congregational, was founded in 1732 in the south end of Boston towards Roxbury, its minister the famous Rev. Mather Byles, who figures in several family events. The initiative to join appears to have been Hannah's (she came from a Congregational family) after the Goulds settled in Boston.

Until 1745 there is no clear indication of the occupation of Thomas Goold. Before that date there are no masters of the name in shipping news of *Boston News-Letter*. From the year of his father's last reported voyage 1720 thru 1728 there are no Goulds. Then John Gould appears in voyages to West Indies and Jamaica 1729-30; this is probably the same Capt. Gould who made trips to Barbados, West Indies and Jamaica 1735-7 and North Carolina and New Providence (Bahamas) 1744-5. We believe this is the successful merchant of Boston, member of King's Chapel who was buried there 13 Jan. 1772 age 72 (MHS King's Chapel Records, v. 40 Register of Burials, and whose daughter Sarah married the Rev. John Troutbeck (Register of Marriages, 8 May 1759). This was a prominent loyalist family of Goulds which fled at the time of the Revolution. There are ads in the Boston papers by John Gould living near the Mill Bridge offering English and European goods like tea, gloves, cloth, meat and foodstuffs (*Boston News-Letter* 20, 27 Feb. 1746, 25 March 1756). John Gould is listed as the loyalist distiller of Boston who died 1772, whose daughter Sarah married Troutbeck, with whom he left his distillery business for the benefit of his grandchildren John and William Gould; John, Samuel and Elizabeth Gould were nephews and niece of Sarah Troutbeck (Edward Alfred Jones, *The Loyalists of Massachusetts* [London: St. Catherine Press, 1930], 279, 280). There is no known connection between this wealthy loyalist Episcopalian family and ours; from membership in the church and shipping news and property records the family may have arrived about 1729. John Gould built a house in Roxbury at the corner of Pond Street in 1755 for his son-in-law Rev. John Troutbeck, assistant rector of King's Chapel for 20 years, who left Boston for London in 1776 as a loyalist (Drake 411-2).

To add to the confusion there is also a family of Thomas Gould of Roxbury listed in Clarence Winthrop Bower's *The History of Woodstock, Connecticut* [Norwood MA.: Privately Printed, 1935, *Genealogies of Woodstock* Families], 6:38-41, but it is clear that the Thomas[1]

Gould of this family is the North End family of Boston in Z Gould 347, whose son Thomas[2] married Rebecca Lyon of Roxbury in 1716 and moved to Woodstock CT about 1721-49. Thomas Gould was dismissed from West Precinct of Roxbury to the Church of Christ in Woodstock 22 Sept. 1723. (Boston Vital Records, W. Roxbury, 29).

The first possible reference to our Thomas Goold is in the *Boston Evening-Post* of 1744. On 23 April one Goold cleared for North Carolina, and a month later, 28 May, probably too early for a return, a Gould cleared for New Providence in the Bahamas. The second is probably John above. In the *Boston News-Letter* of 1744, on 23 Aug. one Gould probably John, has cleared for New Providence, and a month later, on Sept. 27, too early for a return, another Gould is outward bound for Rhode Island. In the *Evening-Post* of Dec. 31 Gould clears for North Carolina, probably the same one of the two previous trips of April 23 and Sept. 27, perhaps ours. One might check rival papers, like *Post-boy* for first names and arrivals.

The first certain reference to Capt. Thomas Goold mariner is 5 Feb. 1745 when Thomas Goold signed a receipt from Colman & Sparhawk for a stall and box, 6 sheep, 2 bags (torn) and a hogshead of water for Sir William Pepperell in Louisburg, Nova Scotia. (MHS William Pepperell Papers, microfilm 42, reel 2, 71.B.129). Two days later N. Sparhawk notified Pepperell from Boston that he was sending "by Capt. Gould 8 doz. fine weathers marked head & back, with rack ? 2 New Ozenbrigs bags with 6 Bushels corn: 7 Cabbage heads large, a hat box, & hatt & Cockade; a bundle of hay, a New hogshead with water per sheep."(129). On 10 Feb 1745 there is an invoice from Boston: "Shipped on sloop Three Sisters Thomas Goold master bound for Cape Breton by Colman & Sparhawk to Sir Wm. Pepperell 1 Beaver Hatt £ 8, 6 sheep stall @ £ 5 = £ 30, 1 bundle hay 30/6 & hogshead water 40/ = 3/14/6, 1 cockade with hat box 19/, 2 ozen baggs, 6 bushels corn @ 13/ £ 3/18/ = £ 6/10" (132). There is nothing certain to identify this person with our Boston Thomas, but the spelling Goold is consistent with Hollis Street and Boston records, and his father William was in the Nova Scotia trade 1716-1726, so it seems likely that a son would have learned the trade with him. It is perhaps coincidental that Rev. Nathaniel Walter of Roxbury, son of the minister who married Thomas and Hannah Woods, was chaplain and interpreter for Pepperell on the Louisburg Expedition (Winsor 2:346). It is clear that Thomas Goold's sloop *Three Sisters* was one of the supply ships of the famous expedition which arrived at Louisburg 30 April 1745, and may have returned before the fall of the French fortress on 16 June.

There is record of the death of a Gould whose first name is unknown at Louisburg 3 Sept., but there is no reason to suspect any relation. (MHS Parkman Collections Stephen Williams' diary 13: "one Gould—of Col. Willard's regiment that went aboard the transport, sick—dyd this day in the harbour in the evening...").

There are frequent reports of Captains Goold and Gould in shipping news 1746-52, but no first names given in *Boston News-Letter*. There were surely two Gould masters in Jan. 1746 when arrivals are reported a week apart from Philadelphia and North Carolina (16, 23 Jan.). They trade with Long Island, Connecticut, Rhode Island, New Providence, Europe, Philadelphia, etc. We assume the entry on 5 June 1751 from Annapolis Royal may have been ours.

The signature of Thomas Goold appears on two receipts for the schooner *Dutches* to Thomas Hancock, Boston 19 March 1749 for £ 150 as tenor, and March 22 for £ 100 more on account of the *Dutches*. (MHS Hancock Papers, Microfilm P 277 (1), 94 of receipt book). Papers other than *News-Letter* should be checked for clearance of Gould for what port.

Thomas Gould is on the list of soldiers enlisted for the defense of the eastern frontiers of Maine commanded by Col. John Winslow under Capt. William Flint now on Bang's Island at Falmouth, Maine 27 June 1754. (MHS Misc. Bound Documents) This is too old for our Thomases [2-3] born 1688 or 1701, but perhaps not too young (16b) for our Thomas born Oct. 1737. This person could have come from any one of the numerous Gould families of the North Shore or Maine. One might try enlistment record for Capt. Flint to see from what town they were recruited.

Thomas Goold was voted £ 8 by the Massachusetts House of Representatives on 11 April 1761 in payment "for the Hardships & suffering they underwent after they were taken in the [illegible: province Snow]" also to Joseph Leathers, Josiah Holland, and to the wives of Rouse and Atkinson.

(Massachusetts Archives, Maritime, 66:134). There is a petition of Thomas Goold of Boston dated 25 Dec. 1761 stating "he was in HM service on Province Sloop Prince of Wales, Nath. Dowse late commander...taken to Louisburgh", taken ill, then "to France where he lay sick a considerable time and underwent great Hardships and // with Difficulty got to England & from thence to Poston", so he requests an allowance. The signature might be compared to that in the Hancock Papers above for 1749; the spelling and appearance is the same. (Ibid.,162-3). Check news accounts for more detail.

Thomas Goold, master of the brigantine *Hope* of New London was murdered by his crew at Senegal 15 May 1764. (*Boston News-Letter* 7 March 1765 from Boston Newspaper Obituaries, 445). A partial account is published as "A Slave Mutiny, 1764" in *The Connecticut Historical Society Bulletin* 31:31-3 [Jan. 1966] consisting of the report in the *New London Gazette* of 17 Aug.1764 and the deposition of William Prest before the court in Boston 1 March 1765. The brig owned by the Forseys left New York, sailed from New London 24 Feb. 1764, arrived in three weeks at Goree, then to Gambia and back to Goree where they took on 30-40 slaves, then to Senegal where they got 2 or 3 more. There on 15 May Capt. Goold was murdered by the mutinous crew, thrown overboard. En route to the West Indies the slaves mutinied, but were put down with loss of life of a crew member and seven slaves. In three weeks they got to St. Vincent's, then to the Virgins, where at Spanish Town the slaves were sold to a Danish captain from Eustatia, but the Spaniards sent soldiers aboard to arrest them. They escaped in a boat to Mona, then to Santo Domingo, from which the mate got a ship to New York. The former mate William Preest was jailed in Boston early March 1765, for trial for murder of Capt. Goold, but died in Boston jail 27 March (*Boston News-Letter* 7 March, 3, 28 March, 3). There are more gory details of this episode in the sources cited. We do not know the home of Thomas Goold, though the spelling is the same as ours; it may be that other news accounts in Boston or New York will give his home, and that records of the trial will be found in Boston court records (Maritime?; Preest's deposition is before William Hutchinson).

Another Thomas Goold mariner died intestate before 9 April 1763 according to a bond of Thomas Goold mariner, Philip Master tailor and Samuel Warden peruke [wig] maker all of Boston (SW 13214). The estate was probated in Boston 9 July 1763 when Thomas was appointed administrator. The account of the estate submitted 7 Oct. claimed as assets 25 F. prize mony due to the deceased, at a rate of F. 22.10/ was £ 30. In expenses there were 10/6 for letters of administration and certificate, £ ¼ charge of receiving the money, 6/ for recording, £ 2 the administrator's trouble and expense, leaving £ 25/19/6 "allowed the widow for necessaries". The French and Indian War ended with the Treaty of Paris 10 Feb. 1763, so Thomas Goold senior appears to have been engaged in successful privateering, and brought a prize into a non-British port (also not French or Spanish, which were the enemy). It is possible that he died in Boston, though no record appears in city documents, church records or newspapers; he may have as well have died at sea or in a foreign port. We do not know for sure that this is our Thomas, except for the spelling of his name, and that he had a son of age named Thomas. Perhaps his son was the one who was victim of the slave mutiny in the following year.

Children, born Boston:

6. i. THOMAS[5], born 30 Oct. 1737 (Roxbury births 148); baptized and received into covenant Hollis Street Church 7 Nov. 1742 ("Hollis Street Church, Boston Records, 1732-1887" [Topsfield Historical Society, 1918], 1; may be the Thomas Gould who married Rachel Antine 29 Jan. 1760 (CD 101:378); death not recorded.

ii. JOHN, bp. 23 March 1739 Hollis Street; marriage and birth not recorded.

iii. JEMIMA, bp. 26 Sept. 1742 Hollis Street; perhaps married Isaac Crouch 9 Oct. 1768 (CD 101:32); the only reference to Isaac Crouch in Rider about 1750 is a Massachusetts fifer (*Massachusetts Soldiers & Sailors of the Revolution* [Boston: Wright & Potter, 1899] [hereinafter Mass Rev], 4:178); death not found; pensioners of Rev. War. may show Crouches age.

iv. HANNAH, bp. 14 Oct. 1744 Hollis Street; buried Old Granary 16 March 1745 ae. 5 months (epitaph in Thomas Bridgman, *Pilgrims of Boston*, 218; inventory of graves in Bostonian Society shows it on west side, by Park Street church, about half way to the rear.

7. v. JAMES, bp. 12 Jan. 1746 Hollis Street; m. 9 Nov. 1766 Ann(a) LAWRANCE in Hollis Street Church (*Boston Marriages 1700-1809* [reprint, Baltimore: Genealogical Pub. Co., 1977],[hereinafter BVR] 345); Charlestown 1793.

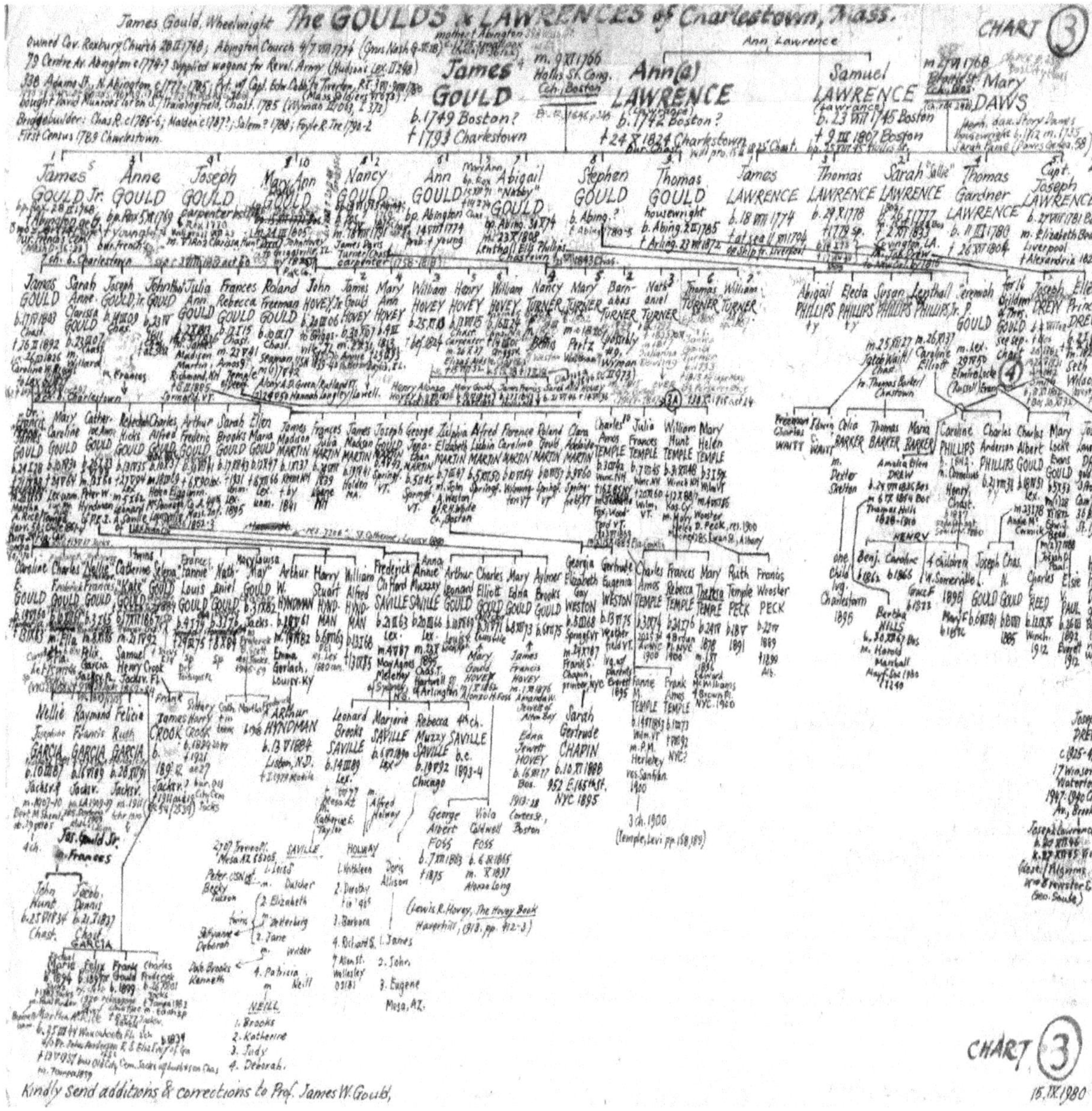

Chapter V

JAMES[4] GOULD, Bridgebuilder & Wheelwright

7. JAMES[4] GOULD (Thomas[3], William[2], Thomas[1]) was born in Boston MA, baptized at Hollis Street Church in the South End on 12 Jan. 1746 ("Hollis Street Church, Boston Records, 1732-1887", Topsfield Historical Society, vol. 1) and died in Charlestown MA late Oct. 1791 (James F. Hunnewell, *A Century of Town Life: A History of Charlestown* [Boston: Little Brown, 1884] [hereinafter Hunnewell], 256.

Hollis Street Church was from 1733-1777 the pulpit of the famous Rev. Mather Byles, who baptized and married James Gould and his wife. Though a poet and great wit, he was so conservative both politically and socially that he was finally dismissed for Tory sympathies (Arthur Eaton, *The Famous Mather Byles* [Boston: W. A. Butterfield, 1914]. The church burned down in 1787, and replaced by the second building, moved to Weymouth in 1810 (Abel Bowen, *Bowen's Picture of Boston* [Boston: Abel Bowen, 1829], 138).

Gould married in Boston, at Hollis Street Church on 9 Nov. 1766 **8.** ANN(A) LAWRANCE (BVR 1646, 345), who was probably born in Boston about 1743, sister to Samuel Lawrance (1745-1807) who was baptized at Hollis Street 25 Aug. 1745 (Hollis Street records), and direct heir of Nicholas[2] Lawrance of Dorchester. She died in Charlestown MA 24 Oct. 1824 (*Columbian Centinel* 1784-1840 [typescript: American Antiquarian Society, 1952], [hereinafter Columbian Centinel], 7 Nov. 1824) and was buried there.

While the date of James[4] Gould's birth does not appear in any town or church record, the family record is not precise, and gives the year 1749, in Boston (Charles Hudson, *History of the Town of Lexington* [Boston: Wiggin & Lunt, 1868] [hereinafter Hudson], 2:78, presumably from information given by his grandson Thomas[6] Gould, Jr. Also "Gould Family Record", c. 1895, probably compiled by Sophia Gould Bailey, in Abigail B. Bass papers held by Else Bass Jan. 30 1970, 1 [hereinafter Bass].

BOSTON TO ROXBURY, c.1763.

The first public record of James[4] Gould is his owning the covenant of the First Church in Roxbury on 28 Feb. 1768, the same date as the baptism of his first son James[5] (*Roxbury Lands & Church Records Roxbury* [Boston: Record Commissioners Report #7] [hereinafter Rox. Lands], 113, 162; *Roxbury Births, Vital Records of Roxbury* (Salem: Essex Institute, 1925), 1:152; hereinafter Rox. Births). It is logical that he would have moved from Boston after the early death of his father, assuming that it is his estate that was filed for probate 9 April 1763 (see **5.** Thomas[3] Gould, mariner, above). As a minor aged only 17 at his father's death, he might have moved to his mother's family home on Roxbury Common. Although his grandfather John[2] Woods had died in 1747, his widow Jemima[3] Seaver Woods retained right to two lower rooms and the cellar of the Woods house on Town Street as his widow as long as she lived unmarried. Grandmother Jemina Woods died 4 May 1768 age 88 (gravestone Eliot Cemetery E/D 375, 402a). The house then went to her children, with a double share to John[3] Woods who already had the upstairs. Perhaps James[4] Gould, his wife and child continued to live with his mother there, for four more children were baptized in Roxbury at the First Church: Nancy[5] 14 June 1769, Anne[5] on 5 Nov. 1769, Joseph[5] in 1770, and Mary[5] 15 Dec. 1771 (Rox. Births 163, 166). James Gould, wheelwright of Roxbury was named 20 June 1771 with John Wood Gentleman of Roxbury and William Thompson blacksmith of that town as administrators of the estate of widow Jemima Wood of Roxbury who died intestate (Massachusetts Archives Probate 70: 327 (164 in original).

THE WHEELWRIGHT'S TRADE.

James Gould probably learned the trade of wheelwright in Roxbury, perhaps apprenticed to a local craftsman. (Neither Thwing nor Winsor give Roxbury wheelwrights 1762-71). The following is a description of the wheelwright's trade by R.A. Salaman, *Dictionary of Woodworking Tools, c. 1700-1970* (Newtown CT: Taunton Press, 1990), 503-519.

"The wheelwright was not only a maker of wheels. He made wagons, carts, ploughs, agricultural implements, hay rakes, and many other things needed by the village and surrounding farms. In addition, the wheelwright often supervised the felling of local trees, and where a millwright was not available, he was called in to repair windmills and watermills. Some workshops had their own smith who made iron tyres, bonds for the hubs, and the iron cart-furniture and fittings for the vehicle [James's brother-in-law, Samuel Lawrence, the blacksmith presumably made these on the site]. But in most instances, this was done by the local blacksmith.

"A basic feature of both wheelwright's and wainwright's work was strength. Joints had to be mechanically strong in themselves, with no reliance on glue to hold them together, for glues were weakened by damp.

"In spite of the paramount need for strength, many wagons and carts are beautiful, and their graceful lines are enchanced by the practice of stop-chamfering...a finishing process [described].

It is perhaps a coincidence that the most beautiful carriages of nineteenth century America were built by James Goold of Albany NY (1790-1879), founder of the James Goold carriage works 1813-1933 (Anson J. Upson, *Memorial of James Goold*, Albany, n.p., 1879. He was born in Granby CT in 1790, no known relation to our Boston family, and learned his trade as apprentice to Obadiah Penniman of Troy NY, thus no connection professionally to our James.

"The chief woods used are...oak or ash...elm..."

Salaman continues (506) by describing "The Workshop. The buildings belonging to a wheelwright's shop usually surround a yard in which are placed those pieces of equipment which could survive the weather and are convenient to use outdoors. These include the Tyre Benders...and a Grindstone may be found mounted between two heavy posts under a lean-to or partly sheltered by a tree.

"In the main shop, the Wheel Pit may be near a window or door for good light. The Wheel Stool and Chopping Block are set in a central position; and on one side, the Lathe for turning hubs. Along one wall is a narrow bench often made from a thick plank with its waney (uneven) edge left showing at the front. Immediately behind the bench is the tool rack filled with Chisels and Gouges. Hanging above are Templets and other gear.

"The Saw Pit may be found in the workshop itself, but more often in a separate shed, adjacent to the timber store where boards and logs (for the hubs) lie for their long seasoning before use. The Smithy is separated from the woodworking shops, with the Tyring Platform placed just outside.

Salaman then describes the process of wheel making (507): "Hubs, Spokes, Felloes (which make up the rim), Tyres and finally the Axle Box. He lists special tools and equipment which are nicely illustrated.

In 1768 James Goold's signature appears on a promisory note to John Greenlaw, a Boston shopkeeper, with his brother-in-law John Woods in Greenlaw's accounts for sale of cloth in 1769 (Superior Court 101604, Mass Archives; see next Chap. VI, Lawrence for detail).

FLIGHT TO ABINGTON, 1774-1785.

By 4 Aug. 1774 James Gould had moved l8 miles south of Roxbury to Abington. This was probably caused by the closing of the port of Boston by the British on 1 June 1774, the first of the "Coercive Acts" of the British Parliament in retaliation for the Boston Tea Party of 16 Dec. 1773 and other disorders in Boston. Another coercive act that may have affected the Goulds was the Quartering Act of 2 June which permitted troops to occupy inhabited residences as well as taverns and empty buildings. The shortage of food in Boston drove many residents to the suburbs like Abington, where the plenty of produce could be bought for wagons and farm implements which Gould made.

His wife Ann joined the First Church of Abington on 4 Aug. (7 Aug. appears to be an error of transcription; "Abington, Massachusetts Church and Private Records" New England Historic Genealogical Society, MS ABI 11, Book II Register of First Church, 83, 93 [hereinafter Abington Church]. Ten days later a second Ann (the first presumably having died) "Daughr of James Gould" was baptized at the First Church (Abington Church, 84). Since another daughter of James Gould was baptized only a month and a half later (Nabby Larence, 30 Oct. 1774; Abington Church, 84), it seems probable that Ann was born in late 1773 in Roxbury, and that the move was made when the mother was pregnant with Abigail.

The Goulds' first home in Abington was at what is now 131 Centre Ave., in the village center, next to the Congregational Church (Cyrus Nash reported that "James Gould..formerly lived in this town in time of the Revolutionary War. He moved from Boston to where Capt. D. A. Ford was living in 1824; "Nash Papers", Historical Society of Old Abington, Dyer Memorial Library, 28 Centre Av., G-V:29; [hereinafter Nash]; "The house which he refers to as the D.A. Ford place was the old house at the site of present 79 Centre Av." according to Mrs. Colin A. Campbell, Curator of the Society, letter of 30 Jan. 1963. The site is now vacant.

The Gould family was struck by the tragic death of their seven year old son, James[5]. Nash G-I:1 says that the boy died in the Ford house. According to Nash (D-36:22 & 23) "James aged 6 years & three months (he was bapt. 28 Feb. 1768= about 1 June 1774) was burried at the Frenchs burrying place where there was stones erected & the other two children were burried at the same place. James Died very sudden. He with some other boyes were digging worms for bait for fishing when the end of his hoe handle struck him in the throat & he lived only about 11 hours after." "French's burying ground was to the east of Island Grove Pond on the hill in the present park. The stones that still remained were moved, some years ago, to the northern part of Mt. Vernon Cemetery in Abington." according to Mrs. Campbell, 4 Jan. 1964. In 1984 when I visited Mt. Vernon, the oldest stones were at the north end, but I found no Goulds. There are no stones left in Island Grove or Centre Burying Ground (formerly French's, on a hill in Islands Grove Park, north of the path leading from Park Street located by Ida R. Totman, "The Cemeteries of Abington" [1912] in Abington Historical Society).

SECOND HOME IN ABINGTON.

About 1775 the Goulds moved a short distance to the Niles House in Abington center, at what would be 398 Washington Street, next to the "Old Blue" Church, as the second church (1751-1819) was called. Nash says (D-36:22,23) James Gould "lived where Capt. Daniel A. Ford was residing in 1825--three or four years & worked at his trade then he took the Niles place on shears where he moved..." The Niles house was torn down for the wing of the church, but the Historical Society has three artifacts of the house: bricks from the slave pen, a spindle, and a bit of old window glass (Letter from Evelyn C. Coughlan, trustee of Dyer Memorial Library, Abington, 28 Aug. 1989). In the Niles house James's mother Hannah Wood Gould died about

1775. Nash says (D-36:22): "Widow Gould of Boston or Roxbury Died in this town with the small pox which she took in a Natural way--she Died by the meeting house where Mrs. Niles was residing in 1825. She lived there with her son James Gould, Wheelwright, who came to this town in time of the Revolutionary war..." Born in Roxbury 5 Dec. 1714 she would have been about 61 years. Her death is not recorded in town or church records, nor is there a gravestone. The probable site of burial was nearby in the Old Church Burying Ground, on the east side of Washington Street, south of Summer Street, behind house #325. There were no stones there in 1984.

Both Hudson and Bailey state that as wheelwright James Gould "supplied wagons for the army during the Revolutionary War" (Hudson 2:78; Bailey, 1). One might search in financial records of supplies for the Revolution.

MOVE TO NORTH ABINGTON c.1780.

The first record of property for a James Gould is 1778. On 2 July 1778 James Goold, Wheeler and Robert Erskin, Tanner, both of Abington paid £ 30 to Solomon Shaw, blacksmith of Abington for his Vineyard Swamp of cedar, bounded 36 rods on the south by Joshua Hows, 4 rods on the east by Micah Hunt, 36 rods on the north by Aaron Hobart, and 4 rods on the west by upland of Thomas Blancher (Plymouth Co. Deeds [hereinafter Ply Deeds] 59:163). This was sold in 1786 by James Goold, Gent. and wife Hannah et al. to Joshua Thomas of Plymouth (19 Aug.; Ply Deeds 68:76). This appears to be another James Gould, also a wheelwright living in Abington.

The Goulds' third home in the area was in North Abington, at the house that still stands at 338 Adams Street, on the west side. James bought this from Stephen Shaw and sold it to Micah Reed (Nash G-I:43; 5:29). The sale to Reed was 1785 (Ply Deeds 65:179), but the purchase cannot be found (Stephen Shaw, yeoman, bought 20¼ acres south of Elijah Bates from David French yeoman on 6 June 1771; Ply 57:232). He lived here for several years before moving to Charlestown. Two of his children died in the house and were buried with their brother at French's burying ground (Nash D-36: 22, 23). No stones remain there. Local records show no deaths; these may have been two of James and Ann's children who did not grow to maturity: Ann, baptized Abington 1774, and Stephen, whose birth is not recorded. The ninth and youngest child of the couple, Thomas[5] Gould, our ancestor, was born here on 2 Feb. 1785.

REVOLUTIONARY SOLDIER, 1780.

James Gould served as a private in the Revolution for 11 days in 1780 (Massachusetts Rev. 6:673). He served in Captain Edward Cobb's company, Major Eliphalet Cary's regiment, which marched from Abington on 30 July 1780 on an alarm at Tiverton RI. The French army of 5,000 troops under General Rochambeau had landed in Newport RI on 11 July, as part of a force that Washington hoped to recapture New York. However, the superior British naval fleet under Admirals Marriot Arbuthnot and George Rodney were able to blockade the French fleet of seven line-of-battle ships under Admiral d'Arzac de Ternay (Richard Morris, *Encyclopedia of American History* (NY: Harper, 1961) 103; *Ency. Brit.*, 11th ed., 1:846).

Tiverton lies at the north end of Newport Island at its closest point to the mainland, was clearly vulnerable to British landings which might cut off the port. The company would have marched about 45 miles south from Abington, via Taunton to reach Tiverton. Gould was discharged on 9 Aug. 1780 after 11 days service. Martha Campbell's *Abington and the Revolutions* (Abington: Abington Bicentennial Commission, 1975), 59 states that Gould was with Captain Cobb of Abington on the expedition to retake Newport in Oct. 1780, but Newport was then in French protection, and there is no record of Gould's service at this date in Massachusetts Soldiers, so this appears to be a mistaken reference to the previous expedition to Tiverton.

The Gould place in North Abington was sold 3 Oct. 1785 by James Goold and Ann Goold his wife quitting her right of dower or power of thirds, for £ 90 to Micah Reed yeoman, the dwelling house, barn and shops on 12½ acres bounded 23 rods on the west by the County Road (Washington Street), 45 rods on the south by Isaac Tirrill, and on a line 6 degrees south by Micah Hunt and on the west by a fence on the land sold recently to Hunt, on the north by Elijah Bates, then south 12½ rods along the brook, and one degree east by Amos Tirrill's land to the County Road (Ply. Deeds, 65:179).

MOVE TO BURNED OUT CHARLESTOWN.

Three days after the sale of the North Abington place James Gould wheelwright of Abington bought land on the Training Field in the center of Charlestown (Middlesex Deeds [hereinafter MD] 92:49). This pinpoints the removal of the family from Abington after eleven years residence there. That Gould paid only 18 pounds for this land in the city center that had been burned by the British probably indicates the poor condition of the property, which included "all the Buildings & Appurtenances thereto belonging".

Charlestown had been set fire during the Battle of Bunker Hill, 17 June 1775 when General William Howe ordered General John Burgoyne to fire red-hot cannonballs from Copp's Hill into Charlestown (Winsor 3:86, 546). Residents did not come back until after the British evacuation of Boston in March 1776, and Dr. Josiah Bartlett gave a description of the dismal state in Dec. 1785: "A few...were able to erect convenient buildings, whilst others, like their hardy predecessors, were only covered with temporary shelters...By a consideration of mutual sufferings, it was the endeavor of every individual to meliorate the condition of his neighbor; to cultivate harmony, and unite for the benefit of the whole" (*American Recorder*, 9 & 15 Dec. 1785, quoted by Winsor 3:547-8).

A decade later Yale's President Dwight described Charlestown: "The houses in this town are all new, many of them good, and some handsome", but "The streets are formed without the least regard to regularity", and the leaders missed making it one of the most beautiful towns in the world because "a miserable mass of prejudices prevented" the much discussed town planning to fail. (Dwight's *Travels in America* (London: 1823, 1:426-37, quoted in Winsor 3:548).

Gould bought the land for £ 18 on 7 Oct. 1785 from David Munroe, leather dresser of Northborough, executor of the estate of his brother-in-law Lovis Foye and guarantor of Louis (or Lovis) Munroe estate (SD 92/49; Wyman, 2:1063, 1:373, 429). It lay at the easterly corner of the Training Field (Winthrop Square), bounded on the south by William Leathers, around a nook of Leathers' land and by John Miller's former land to contain 50 feet from the southeast corner, 26 feet on the west, an angle of 28 feet, 22 feet on the north (on the Common?), and 26 feet on the east (Middlesex Deeds 92:49). A second deed was recorded in 1790, for the same price, but more detailed bounds, from Lovis Monroe, yeoman of Northborough (MD 101:485; 15 Oct. 1789). Since this appears to be the same property, it may be a confirmation of the previous purchase. If Gould rebuilt the house, we do not know where the family lived. Wyman lists James Gould in Charlestown from Boston in Nov. 1785, with wife and five children Nancy, Joseph,

Abigail,ThomasandPolly(Wyman1:428).

James Gould's House, 23 Common St., Charlestown,
Built 1786, Rose's Variety Store 1993.

A year after this first purchase, on 30 Aug. 1786, James Gould sold a house on the Training Field to Joseph Bird, cordwainer, bounded on the west by Leathers and Capt. Foye, for £ 6/2/6, a price that is a third of the original, showing either that nothing had been improved or that a portion of the original was sold (MD 96:314). Bird sold it back to Gould for the same price in 1790 (MD 101/487, 1 Feb.; Wyman 1:429, 84, 612?). This was the year before Gould returned from Ireland, dying in 1791, so we do not know who rebuilt the house. In 1791 the Charlestown Assessor placed a value of £ 30 on the house, almost double the original price, so substantial improvement must have been made before Gould got back from Ireland in late 1791 (Charlestown Tax Records, [1791] 1:4; City of Boston Archives, Readville).

Gould's house on the Training Field, one of the oldest in Charlestown, over 200 years old, still stands at 23 Common Street, a gambrel roofed wooden frame structure of two stories (NHR, Charlestown, C51). It has been much altered with aluminum siding, a store on the street and front door moved from center to the side. The subsequent history of the house appears under Thomas[5] Gould.

CHARLES RIVER BRIDGE, 1785.

The Goulds returned to Boston because of James's work on the Charlestown Bridge. This span across the Charles River was famous as the greatest engineering feat in America. The family record (Bailey 1) shows that Gould was foreman under Mr. Fox (Cox) building the bridge over the Foyle in Ireland in 1790. Already on 7 Feb. 1785 the town of Charlestown (and three days later the town of Boston) had petitioned the state of grant a permit to Thomas Russell and others to build a bridge across the Charles River to Charlestown to replace the ferry (Charlestown Records 1779-1804, 9:106; microfiche roll 196, Boston Public Library). Boston's petition passed overwhelmingly by 1300 votes to 2 at a meeting chaired by Samuel Adams at Faneuil Hall (Boston Town Records, 1785, 51-2; orig. 385).

Gould was evidently an associate of the famous bridge builder Lemuel Cox (1736-1806) whose biography appears in the *Dictionary of American Biography* (2:479-480). Cox was not only a wheelwright like Gould, but related to him in several ways: his mother Thankful Maudsley was a cousin of Ann Lawrance Gould, and Cox's wife was Susanna Hickling (b. 1740), whose nephew married James Gould's second cousin Sarah[4] Greene (1743-1834) ("Hickling Biographies", 11-13, 6-8, Box 3, folder 5, in Walcott Papers II N-152, Massachusetts Historical Society. Eleven years older than Gould, Cox had more experience as a wheelwright. Confined in the start of the Revolution as a Loyalist, he spent much of the war in Taunton, Massachusetts, about 17 miles farther south of Boston than Abington.

The building of the Charles River bridge in 1785-6 was one of the great engineering feats of the age. It was the first step to liberate Boston from its isolation, and its 1500 foot span the biggest in America, one of the longest in the world. Since Boston's location on a peninsula made the only land exit along the Neck to the southwest, it had been a dream since 1635 to connect to the mainland by a bridge. Plans for a bridge were supplanted by a Penny Ferry across the Charles between Prince Street in the North End, and Charlestown (Arthur B. Tourtellot, *The Charles* [N.Y.: Farrar & Rinehart, 1941] [hereinafter Tourtellot] 226-7). Tolls contributed to scholarships for indigent students at Harvard College (Boston Transit Commission, "The Ferry--1630 to 1785. The Charles River Bridge 1785" (1899) in Boston Athenaeum 964 B6.B66;

Lewis M. Hastings, "An Historical Account of Some Bridges over the Charles River", *Cambridge Historical Society Proceedings,* Cambridge 1912, 7:57). The urgency in building a bridge is seen in the years preceding when the freezing over of the Charles made ferrying impossible (Memorial from the selectmen of Charlestown to Harvard College for "abatement to Ferrymen due to severity of the winter which prevented boats passing", in 1780, 1782, 1784, and 1786 Harvard Corporation Records, 3:73, 142-3, 200, 250).

The promoters raised £ 15,000, about $75,000, by issuing 150 shares of £ 100 each ("The Ferry" 7). The incorporators were also major shareholders: Thomas Russell, Nathaniel Gorham, John Hancock, James Swan, and Eben Parsons. The main financial promoter of the bridge was John Hancock, the famous first signer of the Declaration of Independence, promoter of the Revolution, he was in 1785 first Governor of Massachusetts (1780-5), President of the Continental Congress 1775-7 and 1785), and Treasurer of Harvard College. The investment repaid the investors handsomely, and gave Harvard a big income of £ 200 a year for scholarships (James Gould's son Thomas[5] was to marry in 1806 the fourth cousin of John Hancock, Sophia Lovis, whose great-grandmother Elizabeth Hawke(s) was sister of Hancock's great-grandfather James Hawke, children of Hingham founders Matthew and Margaret Hawke; "The Ancestry of John Hancock", William M. Fowler, Jr., *The Baron of Beacon Hill: A Biography of John Hancock* [Boston: Houghton Mifflin, 1980], 4).

The Massachusetts legislature quickly passed the act authorizing the bridge, on 9 March 1785 (Massachusetts Statutes 1784, Ch. 53, 35-8). Major Samuel Sewall of Marblehead, later Chief Justice of the state (1814) was appointed architect (Walter K. Watkins, "A Medford Tax Payer, Lemuel Cox, the Bridge Builder and Inventor" [Boston: 1909] in Biographical Pamphlets #103, Boston Athenaeum 5.9B (v. 103), [hereinafter Watkins] 7). The gravestone of Capt. John Stone who died in 1791 in Concord claims he was builder of the bridge (Ibid.). Lemuel Cox was appointed master workman. Why a wheelwright? We have noted above that wheelwrights felled timber, and needed oak for their trade. Cox was also a noted inventor of a number of useful devices such as a wires for carding textiles, a mill to grind gunpowder, a machine making fishhooks, and a nail factory, and he introduced one of the first cotton spinning machines to the country. His particular interest in the bridge was the draw bridge.

This is our evidence that Gould worked for Cox on the bridge. Gould appears in Charlestown, the end from which the work began, within a few months of the start of construction. Cox would have sought workmen with skills like his own wheelwright's trade to find the heavy oak timbers, haul them to the site, use mechanical skills to drive them into the mud, tie them together, and construct a moving draw. Cox would have passed Gould's shop in North Abington on the way from Taunton to Boston, and perhaps visited him, as a relation of both his wife and mother. Gould was soon (1789) sent by Cox as his foreman to construct his first foreign project, the Foyle River bridge in Ireland. He is likely to have chosen Gould as the man who had the most experience working with him on the bridges near Boston.

Work began on 1 June 1785, the eleventh anniversary of the closing of the port of Boston (Tourtelot 239). The first pier, 14 feet 2 inches long, consisting of 7 sticks of oak timber united by a cap, was driven into the Charles bank 16½ feet off the 100 foot abutment from the old ferry landing, on 14 June 1785 (Details of construction in copy of a broadside "Charles River Bridge", printed at Charlestown Press 17 June 1786 copied by Ebenezer Barker, Middlesex County bridge commissioner and agent of the Charles River Bridge, in Barker Mss., Massachusetts Historical Society).

Successive piers of oak bundles, each about a foot longer to reach the river bed, were driven 16½ feet farther out toward Boston. Each pier was secured by a single pile on each side, driven obliquely to a solid bottom. The piers were connected by large string pieces, covered with four inch oak plank. The width was 42 feet. The bridge had a gradual rise from each end, to be two feet higher in the middle than on the ends. The floor, at highest tides, which is four feet above the water, which generally rises 12 or 14 feet. At the fourteenth span out the bridge was anchored to a strong stone wharf about 33 x 42 feet connected with three piers. The wooden spans continue on 18 piers out to a similar stone wharf in the middle of the channel.

A 30 foot drawbridge operated between two stone wharves. The design was simple, so that two men could raise it. From the west wharf the wooden spans continued over the deepest part of the river, the 44th span being 46 feet nine inches deep. After 17 spans a fourth stone wharf was reached, going on another 17 spans to the Boston abutment, for a total of 75 spans of 16½ feet each. The Boston abutment was a short 45½ feet to the old ferry landing, for a total length of 1503 feet.

The top of the bridge was finished with a foot passage of six feet width on each side, with a railing imitating a pale fence. "Forty elegant lamps are erected" on posts "to illuminate when necessary". The state legislature had required "at least 20 good lamps on each side...well supplied with oil, and lighted in due season and kept burning until 12 of the clock at night". On a contemporary drawing these are hung on the road side from tall poles at the outside edge, placed every fifth piling. Round knobs top the light poles and smaller poles at each of the three pilings in between the lamps. A shed-like structure on the Boston abutment may be the tollbooth.

Charles River Bridge, seen from Charlestown. From *Mass. Magazine* Sept. 1787, vol. I, p. 533.

We have two fine etchings of the bridge from each side, which appeared in Massachusetts Magazine. From the Boston side at Copp's Hill we see Charlestown with the new buildings clustered around the First Church, Breed's Hill which we call Bunker Hill on the right and the new mansions of Bunker Hill at the left, a two-masted vessel at the channel (*Massachusetts Magazine*, Sept. 1789, 1:533; an identical view without superscript in Athenaeum prints from *New York Magazine*, Sept. 1795, opposite 153); reproduced in Winsor 3:554, and Walter M. Whitehill, *Boston: A Topographical History* [Cambridge: Belknap Press, 1968] [hereinafter Whitehill], 49). The view from Charlestown is south from Breed's Hill shows Copp's Hill in the North End of Boston on the left, and Beacon Hill, the highest of the Tre-mont three hills on the right (*Massachusetts Magazine*, [June 1791] 3:331; identical view without superscript in Capt. Frederick L. Oliver, "The Bridges of the Charles", in *Bostonian Society Proceedings*, [1952] facing 37). The bridge appears to come into Boston west of the Mill Pond, but it is clear from the Boynton map of 1844 (Whitehill 121) that it was at the east end, like the ferry on the Bonner map of 1769 (Whitehill 45).

The seventy fifth and last pier was driven down on 31 May 1786, two weeks less than a year from the first.

"One of the greatest events in the history of Boston" is the description of the opening by one chronicler (Rev. Edward G. Porter, *Rambles in Old Boston* [Boston: Cupples & Hurd, 1887] 126). Thirteen cannon were fired in celebration on 3 June (*Massachusetts Centinel*, hereinafter *Centinel*, 31 March 1786, 3; same in *Continental Journal*, 1 June, 3). At 1,475 feet not counting approaches, this was the longest bridge in the world (Samuel Adams Drake, *Historic Mansions and Highways Around Boston* [Boston: Little, Brown] 1899, 4).

The actual cost came to only $50,000, two thirds of the capital raised (Oliver 37). Tolls set by the legislature (Ch. 53, 137) were 2/3 penny per foot passenger or extra rider, 1 2/3 penny for wheelbarrows, carts, and single horses or cattle, 4 d. for single horse cart or sled, and each dozen swine or sheep; 6 d. for sleds or carriages pulled by more than one beast; 1 shilling for coaches, chariots, phaetons and curricles; double on Sunday! A count made by a local paper 3 days after opening day showed 20 coaches at a shilling, 150 chaises at 8 d., 137 carts at 4 d., and 193 horses at 1½ d., for days toll of £ 9/7/1½, or nearly $50 (*Centinel*, 5 July, in Ferry 7).

By 1823 the shares, originally worth $500, were valued at $1,550 (Oliver 37). In 1826 Josiah Quincy estimated that the shareholder not only got back his investment, but a surplus of $ 7,000 (Ferry 7). The bridge was finally bought by the state for $25,000 in 1841 (Watkins 9; Charles River Bridge Original Dividend Books, 1786 are in Boston Public Library rare books Ms E.1.2, but cannot be read because of fragile condition after a fire).

CELEBRATION OF BRIDGE OPENING, 1786.

Actual opening day celebrations were saved until 17 June, the eleventh anniversary of the Battle of Bunker Hill. The glowing news accounts speak of it "as a day of rejoicing"..."The directors made every exertion to secure uninterrupted festivity on the day, and it fortunately happened that the weather was peculiarly agreeable, all orders were accordingly gratified and every face exhibited genuine marks of unfeigned hilarity." (*Centinel*, 21 June, 1; *Journal*, 22 June, 3).

At sunrise 13 guns were fired from Bunker Hill and Copp's Hill, as a salute to the 13 states of the Confederation. Bells in both towns pealed, and the musical chimes of Old North Church were rung.

For this first celebration of the Battle of Bunker Hill the Charlestown Artillery Company was formed under Major William Calder, composed mostly of veterans of the Battle of Bunker Hill, and to soon participate in putting down Shay's Rebellion in western Massachusetts (Harold C. Durrell, ed., *Major William Calder of Charlestown, Massachusetts, 1725-1802* [Boston: Thomas Groom, 1933], in Bostonian Society oversize F207 C26 D8, sec. H and G).

The bridge proprietors gathered at the Old State House and waited for the legislature to join them. The grand parade began at one pm, led off by the Charlestown Artillery Company under Capt. Calder, followed by the 120 artificers who had been employed on the bridge, carrying their tools, probably led by Cox and Gould. As they started directly for the bridge, down Union Street, a salute was fired from the Castle in the harbor.

Then followed the directors and proprietors, a band with fife and drum, President

Proprietor Russell, 2 County sheriffs with their officers; Governor Bowdoin, Lt. Gov. Cushing, the State Council, the President and Senate, the Speaker and members of the House, Consuls of France and Holland, Judges of the Supreme Court, Attorney General, Naval and Excise Officers, President and Corporation of Harvard, clergy, professors and tutors of the University, Chairman and Selectmen of Boston and Charlestown, Overseers of both towns, Commander of Castle William and officers of the Army, President and Directors of the Massachusetts Bank, "a great body of private gentlemen, Foreigners and citizens. A body of Civil Officers closed the procession".

When they got to the bridge the Charlestown artillery parted into two lines for the proprietors to pass through to the drawbridge. There they told Mr. Cox, the master workman, to fix the draw for all to pass over. Gould must have been close at hand, and perhaps one of the two men required to lower the span. As they did this 13 cannon were fired from Copp's Hill and as many as 6,000 people besides horses and carriages passed over to Charlestown to cheers of 20,000, a number that equaled the combined populations of Charlestown and Boston (Nathaniel Shurtleff, *A Topographical and Historical Description of Boston* [Boston: City of Boston, 1871] 418).

As the parade moved thru town, up Breed's Hill 13 more cannon were fired. At the top of the hill, where the monument now stands, the proprietors put on a dinner for 800 people seated at two tables 320 feet long, united by a semicircle at each end, the table covered by a canopy (Chronicle, 22 June, 3). 13 toasts were drunk: To the U.S., the Governor and Commonwealth, this anniversary, our foreign allies. After this fourth toast an Ode of 40 verses was sung with verses like these:

The BRIDGE is finished now I say,
Each other bridge outvies,
For London Bridge, compar'd with ours
Appears in dim disguise.

Now Boston, Charlestown nobly join,
And roast a fatted Ox
On noted Bunker Hill combine
To toast our Patriot Cox."

(Verses 3 & 23, in Watkins 9). The names of supposed architect Major Sewall and builder Captain Stone nowhere appear in the accounts of the celebration, but Cox's is everywhere the most acclaimed. After the ode was sung, there were nine more toasts to these causes: The friendship of the two towns, the Arts & Sciences, the perpetuity of the bridge, the hero General Warren who died on the battlefield here, "The Mechanick Arts", to American success in peace as in war, and finally to "All Mankind. May Peace, Harmony and happiness pervade and unite all Branches of the Mighty Family."

Festivities continued until 6 pm. The forty lamps on the bridge were lighted, "and produced not only a happy effect on the eye, but were very useful in directing the steps of some of the votaries of the rosy deity who returned to ton between ten and eleven, with a band of music before them, inspired by the collective pressure of the scene, but above all by the generous draughts they had taken to commemorate this auspicious occasion."

STRANGERS CAUTIONED OUT OF TOWN, 1787.

All 2,000 inhabitants of Charlestown had been driven out in 1774, made homeless by the fire. By 1785 many newcomers had come in their places, like the Goulds. But the town government resisted the new arrivals and ordered a census. On 19 Feb. 1787 the town records show "Cautions enter'd against Sundry Strangers who have crept into Town, that they may not become Inhabitants" (Charlestown Records, 1779-1804, 9: 2, Microfilm reel 196). Among the many were James & Ann Gould, from Abington, and four children Ann, James, Nabby and Thomas (152, col. 2). This omits the eldest surviving child, Nancy, born 1769, and now 16, and perhaps living out in domestic work. The second Ann[5] born 1773 would be 13. The first James[5] having died in 1774, this refers to a James who did not survive, or perhaps Joseph, b. 1770, now 17, who may also have been apprenticed out as a carpenter. Nabby, for Abigail, born 1774 would be 12. Thomas, the youngest, was two. The Goulds did not leave Charlestown any more than did the other cautioned strangers, and in fact became leading members of the community in the next century. James[4] Gould was probably already involved with Cox in their next bridge project.

THE MALDEN BRIDGE, 1787.

Before the Charles River bridge was opened there was already planning for a second bridge from Charlestown, north to Malden, across the broad Mystic River. On the same day the last pile was driven into the Charles, papers reported that Charlestown would petition the legislature for permit to replace the Penny Ferry (*Centinel*, 31 May 1786, 3; Journal 1 June, 3). The span would go from Charlestown Neck to Sweetser's Point in Malden.

Thomas Russell again led a financial group, with 13 of the 120 shares, incorporated by the state (Massachusetts Statutes, 1786, Ch. 69, 216-9) 1 March, this time including noted Charlestown leader Richard Devens (5 shares), Samuel Swan, Jr. (8 shares), Jonathan Simpson, Jr. (9 shares), Jonathan Harris (10 shares) and William Tudor ("Proprietors of the Malden Bridge", 24 March 1787, 13 pp. in Boston Public Library rare books *XH.89.42, and Athenaeum, on microcard Evans American Imprints 20480, has nothing re construction). Cox was engaged at once, and Gould presumably a leading craftsman.

Work began in April under master workmen Lemuel Cox and Jonathan Thompson (*Massachusetts Magazine*, Sept. 1790, 2, no. 9, 515-516, APS Microfilm, reel 15). Thompson is not identified; perhaps he is Wyman's housewright 1745-96, 941). The total length of 2,400 feet included 300 feet of abutments, with a span of 2,005 feet. It was eight feet narrower than the Charles bridge, at 32 feet. Constructed of 100 piers consisting of six oak sticks united by a cap piece, girts and braces, driven into the river bed to solid ground. It as anchored to two wharves. The 30 foot drawbridge in the middle was a wheel and axle device designed by Cox, at the deepest channel which was nine feet deep at low tide, and 20 at high. The flooring was 6 inch pine planking. There was a neat plain railing on each side. Apparently anticipating less night traffic, there were only eight lamps which burned thru the night.

We have a contemporary view of the bridge from Bunker Hill, looking west toward the hills of Somerville and Medford (*Massachusetts Magazine*, Sept. 1790, frontispiece, 513). There is a house at the Charlestown end, and a one story building on the Malden end, with a shed that may be the tollbooths at both ends, and a pair of tall poles holding lamps over each; there are four poles at the draw. A poem describes the view: "When from thy top, thou hill of deathless fame! Unnumber'd beauties rush upon the view, And the wide prospect teems as fairy ground." (no source given).

The Malden bridge now took the title of the world's longest only a year after the Charles Bridge, but the celebration was much more modest. The Malden Bridge was 60 percent longer (2400 feet against 1504), it was finished in half the time, six months, and at almost half the cost (£ 5,300 against £ 10,000). It was finished on 8 Sept. (*Salem Mercury*, 11 Sept.), and opened to traffic on 30 Sept.. On Saturday the 29th the "Malden Bridge was ceremoniously opened by firing a cannon and regaling the workmen, at the expense of the proprietors. In the afternoon the established toll was received from passengers." (*Centinel*, 3 Oct., 3; *Chronicle* 4 Oct., 3). Tolls set by the legislature were roughly a third higher than the Charles bridge, ranging from 2/3 pence for a pig or sheep to 18 pence for wheeled vehicles. As in the Charles bridge the toll gates had to be left open when the toll keeper was absent.

An indication that Gould had a part in the bridge building is payment by the town of Charlestown to Gould, Cooper and Robbins for a barn on town land leading to the Malden bridge on 1 March 1826 (Charlestown Records, 11: 272; committee appointed 2 May 1825, 252; James[4] Gould having died, this was probably paid to his son Thomas, then a town official).

THE SALEM-BEVERLY BRIDGE, 1788.

Before the Malden bridge was completed the merchants of the North Shore were agitating for a bridge from Salem to Beverly. On 17 June 1787, the second anniversary of the completion of the Charles River bridge, a subscription was begun for this one (Watkins 11). 200 shares were obtained at once. 16 towns in Essex county favored it, but Danvers and part of Salem opposed it. Among the petitioners were 85 poor women of Manchester who had been widowed by the war, with their 135 fatherless children, and wanted the road to bring their cloth to Salem (Watkins 12). The legislature authorized incorporation on 17 Nov. with George and John Cabot of Beverly, John Fisk, Israel Thorndike and Joseph White as proprietors (Massachusetts Statutes, 1787, Ch. 27, 582-6; Salem got £ 40 annually to replace the ferry, and Danvers got £ 10 annually). They signed a contract with Cox before 1 March 1788, which paid him 9 shillings a day, plus board and punch. Later they agreed to pay him $55 on completion of the bridge, and plus 10 gallons of New England rum.

The first pier was sunk on 3 May, and the last on 6 Sept., only four months later. It is clear the skills were improving, for this is a third of the time it took for the Charles River bridge, of about the same length (this was 1,484 feet against the 1,503), but 8 feet narrower, like the Malden Bridge, 32 feet wide (*Centinel*, 24 Sept. 1788, 3; *Chronicle* 25 Sept., 3). The abutments at Green's Point and Ellinwood's Wharf added 36 feet to the length. There were 93 piers, and 12 American lamps kept lighted until midnight. The draw was 30 feet wide, "which played with such ease that two boys of ten years old may raise it". The cost was $16,000. (Watkins 12). An additional feature required by the legislature was a pier at each side for vessels to tie up to securely until the draw was opened, and a hawser extending thru the draw, attached to two anchors above and below the bridge.

We have our first account of the dangers of bridge building in the news of the Salem bridge. The Boston paper reported that only three people fell during construction, two rescued by Joseph Felt; another fell in a fit, from which he recovered (*Centinel*, 24 Sept.).

The Salem bridge was opened for traffic on 24 Sept. to a celebration that included a "festive meeting at Leech's tavern in Beverly provid[ing] liberal entertainment for the workmen" (check wording; *Centinel* 24 Sept.).

Tolls reflect the change in currency from the colonial pounds/shillings/pence to the new decimal system, ranging from one cent for swine and sheep, two for pedestrians to 25 cents for large wheeled vehicles.

Only two months into the building, Cox and the bridge proprietors ended his contract (July 1788, Watkins 13). It is not known who completed the bridge (see Salem papers for July, Essex Institute for proprietors records).

TRIP TO IRELAND, 1790.

The fame of American bridge building spread across the Atlantic. After the end of his Salem contract Cox and his foreman Thompson went to Londonderry, Ireland at the invitation of the town, to see if a bridge could be built over the River Foyle. Until this time one could cross only by ferry, which travelers complained they had to wait for hours to leave (Young's "Tour of Ireland" 1776 cited in "Derry's Bridges" in Central Library Londonderry; [hereinafter Cent.Lib.]. An English engineer, Milne, had declared that the span of 900 feet, with a 40 foot depth could not be bridged (Drake 6). This was, of course, far short of the spans Cox had already done. The alternative type of bridge, the Swiss arched kind, had been designed by John Alther of Appenzell in 1773, but rejected ("Bishop Hervey and Events Leading Up to the Building of the Wooden Bridge", from Program for Opening of Craigavon Bridge, 18 July 1933, 2).

Cox declared that the bridge could be built, and estimated the cost at £ 10,000. (*Centinel*, 27 June 1789, 3). On 26 March 1789 the Londonderry corporation unanimously accepted his terms. Cox and Thompson returned by ship via Liverpool, arriving on 26 June in Boston, where they bought a ship which they loaded at Sheepscot Maine with oak piles, and 20 workmen (Watkins 13).

The Gould family record states that James Gould "Went to England in 1790 with a party of 20 skilled workmen (Mr. Fox being the architect) and built a bridge across the Foyle River at London Derry. It was finished in five months. He was never well in health after, and died soon after his return home...Died 1793" (Bass 1). The coincidence of numbers of workmen makes it probable that Gould was sent by Cox to Sheepscott to select timbers, and to make the Atlantic crossing, perhaps leaving as early as July 1789.

A delay in starting construction was caused in part by the problem of tolls, and requirement of an Act of Parliament which came in 1790. Londonderry Corporation had to petition the Irish Society which had a monopoly of tolls over the Foyle (29 April; Watkins 15). Although the Society granted the request on 15 July, it was not until 11 Dec. that they gave a perpetual lease of tolls so the town could borrow money. It is very likely Cox remained unpaid for ship's hire, lumber and salaries until credit got across the Atlantic in early 1790.

Gould and his crew of workers probably left Sheepscott after 1 Feb. when Gould bought back the house on the Training Field in Charlestown (MD 101/487).

According to Irish records the ship Nancy, Capt. Ramage, arrived in Derry at the beginning of May 1790 with the first load of timber, Cox and 20 experienced workmen. ("The Wooden Bridge, 1791", Cent.Lib.; between 4 and 11 May per *The London-Derry Journal* [hereinafter LDJ], Tues. 11 May).

The bridge was built from the foot of Ferry-quay Street, to be renamed before the bridge was done Bridge Street (LDJ 9 Nov. 1790), in front of the later Enniskillen railway depot, to the Waterside, on the west side of Lough Foyle at Walker's Place ("Derry's Bridges", booklet pub. by old Londonderry Corp. to mark opening of Craigavon Bridge 1933, in Cent.Lib.).

Work began at once, on Monday 3 May under Cox and Thompson, employing "twenty active and ingenious workmen...brought from America by Mr. Cox, and every stick of timber, and even the workmen's tools, with the purchases, machines, &c. are American. The vigour with which it is carrying on, the facility of raising the timber and piling it down, the activity of the workmen, and their extraordinary handiness in using the axe and adze, are the admiration of every beholder" raved the local paper (LDJ 1 June). The oak timbers were hewn into squares or sawed from 13 to 16 inches square, to cover a span of 1000 feet, 42 feet wide, and over a 32 foot depth at low water (Ibid.).

Oak timbers were brought from US in at least four shiploads, in the *Essex* under Capt. Young (LDJ 7 Sept.), and three in the *Nancy* 1 May, c. 15 Sept., and c. 20 Nov. under Capt. Henry Mitchell out of Kennebec, Maine, the last in 20 days, one of the fastest trans-Atlantic crossings to Londonderry (LDJ 7 Sept., 23 Nov.).

They lost a week due to a smallpox scare. *Derry Journal* of 15 June 1790 reported: "With pleasure we inform the public that the 13 Bridge huilders, who underwent inoculation with Mr. Maginnis are quite recovered, being only six days prevented from working."

The description of the construction by Watkins (15) follows: "The piles of American oak had the head of each tenoned into a cap piece forty feet long and seventeen inches square, supported by three sets of girths and braces. The piers were sixteen and one-half feet apart [same as Charles] and bound together by thirteen string-pieces, equally divided and transversely bolted, on which were laid the flooring. On each side of the platform was a railing four and a half feet high, also a broad pathway provided with gas lamps. Originally there was a drawbridge, but it was replaced by a turning bridge." 58 arches (Drake 60) made up the total length of 1,068 feet (Watkins). The width was 40 feet. On each outer edge was a footway behind a 4 foot railing.

The drawbridge and first toll booth were on the city side of the bridge. The draw was operated from below, by a large six-spoked wheel, shown in the diagram. A water main was placed below the bridge in 1809, with cutoff valves to close when the draw opened, and a gas main in 1830 (Thomas Colley, "City of Londonderry" in Memoir of the Parish of Templemore, 1837, in Cent. Lib.).

An English visitor left account of the visit of some distinguished lords during the construction: "the Marquis of Waterford, Lord Tyrone and Lord John Beresford who arrived here on Saturday last. I took the King's boat across the water for them and shewed them the different parts of the Bridge, which Cox had got dressed out with all the Ship's colours he could muster. They stayed a considerable time on the water, observing the process of sinking the piers. The Marquis was highly pleased and assured Cox that nothing on his part should be wanting to have a similar Bridge...erected at Waterford. There are now but 17 piers to sink, and Cox declared he would have it passable by the first of November at furthest. (Letter of William Lennox to his brother George 20 Sept. 1790 in Lenox-Conyngham, "An Old Ulster House", extracted by Cent. Lib.).

Local excitement rose as the bridge neared completion. On 15 Oct. they had only 12 piers to go (LDJ 15 Oct.), and eight on Oct. 26 (LDJ 26 Oct.). The local paper reported that on Saturday 6 Nov. the last pier was framed and launched into the water!" (LDJ 9 Nov.). It was temporarily opened to foot passage on Thursday 11 Nov. 1790, drawing a crowd of spectators (LDJ 23 Nov.).

However, the erection of the tollgate on 1 Dec. caused a riot. The public had been given eight or nine days of free passage, and the local newspaper reported that "an idea prevailed among the lower orders of the people, that the passage was to be entirely free...notwithstanding it must have been obvious, that a vast sum of money had been expended..." (LDJ 7 Dec.). As people came to market were charged "symptoms of discontent appeared, and towards afternoon, when the multitude became greater, and many of them heated with liquor, they refused to pay the toll. The Mayor, Sheriff...and several of the Magistrates attended, and endeavoured, by every mode of reasoning, to persuade them to refrain from their illegal opposition; all freindly remonstrances however were in vain, for increasing in numbers, they boldly proceeded to break down the toll-gate in spite of the Magistrates, who were now obliged to call for a guard of soldiers; but the violence of the rioters continuing to increase, it became necessary to bring to their support nearly the whole of the 40th Regiment now quartered here--The military charging with bayonets, drove the rioters acrss the Bridge to the Waterside, but they had no sooner got upon the street, than they turned about, and gave battle to the military with repeated vollies of stones and brick-bats. Again the Magistrates entreated the people to disperse, and warned them of the fatal consequences of their outrage; but in vain; they continued their attack. At first the military were directed to fire in the air, then at the tops of the houses; but the desperation of the mob increasing, the soldiers were ordered to level their muskets, when two men were shot dead on the spot, two desperately, and several others severely wounded. About 5 in the evening, the mob dispersed, and public tranquility was again restored."

The next day Cox made a public declaration: "I Do declare in this Public Manner, my sincerest Sorrow for the late Disturbances at the Bridge; and I do promise, that I will, with all the Expedition in my Power, go on with my Work, and assist the Corporation in their Purpose of accommodating the Public with a Passage, and collecting the Toll due to them by Law.--L:Derry, 2d Dec. 1790. LEMUEL COX" (LDJ 14 Dec.).

On 15 Dec. the town published the schedule of tolls, a seeming concession to the mob, charging nothing "For every Passenger passing over said Bridge", but a penny if he carried "a Kish (a turf-basket), Basket, Sack-load, or Pack of any Kind", the same price as an unladen horse or "For every dead Hog" (LDJ 21 Dec.). The big tolls came from flocks and big wheeled vehicles: 3 shillings for vehicles pulled by 6 or more horses, and 3/6 for every score of Drove of Oxen or Neat Cattle. The town auctioned out the tolls for 1791 for £ 1550 (LDJ 4 Jan.). The word got out that linen would be taxed when going over the bridge to the market, but the Corporation quickly squelched the rumor, saying they wanted to encourage the growing linen manufacture (LDJ 18 Jan. 1791). Strollers who walked out for pleasure were charged hapenny each way (LDJ 5 July).

Two men killed hy the soldiers were not the last deaths on the bridge. On 17 Dec. a man "very much intoxicated with whiskey, fell from the...part of the bridge (where the draw-arch is to be placed) and was drowned." LDJ 21 Dec.). A temporary railing had to be put up when two men "much intoxicated" fell off and were drowned, one a soldier of the 40th Regiment, and Hegarty, a boatman (LDJ 18 Jan. 1791).

The bridge was finally finished in slightly over a year from the start, by the end of May 1791. The basic structure was completed on 28 May 1791 (LDJ 31 May), in 13 months, delayed by shortage of timbers. It still had to be painted, lamps put up, and another toll-gate installed when Derry citizens complained that they had been paying double fare while the people on the other side went across free (LDJ 14 June). The Boston crew appears to have left at this time, for the town advertised for carpenters to build the toll-gate on 14 May (LDJ 24 May, 1, col. 2).

They may have missed the grand opening on the afternoon of Sunday 25 June. This was celehrated as was High Mall on the bridge, "the time when the throng of promenaders in the Mall was at its height--a fashionable assembly in the open air (OED #4). The paper describes the scene: "the evening was remarkably fine, and the time was full in.--We know of no place which unites so many striking beauties.--In addition to the immense and well-constructed platform which stretches across the majestic waters of the Foyle, the numerous spectators had the woods of Becken [today's Prehen, upriver], in their gayest foliage, on the left--the city of Derry, with all its picturesque objects, in front--the shipping, and the beautiful village of Troy, Pennyburn Mill [both in Pennyburn on the west bank], &tc, with the lofty mountains of Enishowen [the Donegal mountains of Inishowen], on the right--forming altogether the most charming scenery..." (Ibid., 28 June; sites identified courtesy of Christine McIvor, Librarian of Ulster-American Folk Park, Omagh, 28 June 1994).

The local paper reported on 26 July that Cox had finished his contract, and the town Corporation gave him his full sum plus 100 pounds bonus. The bridge was finished in the second week of July 1791 (*Boston Gazette*, 26 Oct. 1791, 50), nearly two years after the contract. The final cost of £ 16,594 was considerably more than Cox's £ 10,000 estimate, but the investment was a success, earning £ 3,700 tolls annually by 1839 (Watkins 15). The Londonderry Corporation was so pleased that they gave him an extra £ 100 "as a mark of their approbation of the eminent abilities of this truly ingenious Artist." ("MR.COX--The Artist", *Boston Gazette*, 26 Oct. 1791). On 22 July Derry citizens voted Cox a gold medal with this text: "TO LEMUEL COX, of Boston, in America, the builder of the Bridge of London Derry, (a work for magnitude of design, and simplicity of construction, unparalleled in the Eastern World). The cloth merchants of the town had a silver urn worth £ 60 made in Dublin to honor Cox.

We have two fine views of the bridge, including one that is strikingly like the Boston scenes, with the spire of the church on the hill and the lampposts of the bridge (engraving by J. Ford, "A View of Londonderry", 1802 in George Vaughan Simpson, *Statistical Survey of the County of Londonderry*, in Cent. Lib., and "Londonderry about 1830", lithograph orig. in Nat. Library of Ireland, Dublin). A mid-century guide to the city called the bridge "among the boasts of Derry" ("City of Londonderry, 117). There is a scale plan and elevation in *Gentleman's Magazine*, June 1791, pl. II, 505 from Index to Irish Topographical Prints and Drawings, reel 1 in Cent.Lib.).

Another account says its "story savours of romance. In the initial stages of its history it was one of the sights of Derry, and was justly regarded with pride by the citizens." "Derry's Bridges", 21).

Profitable tolls continued to be collected in 1863. One traveler complained, "One admirable custom I observed in Derry, or rather on nearing it--namely that on crossing the long wooden bridge that strides the Foyle, the gatekeeper demanded double toll for my carriage! I asked him the reason for this. 'Oh sir, if you come back we will return you half the money'. No explanation could I obtain for this most extraordinary tax on out-goers! But on reflection I would...suggest the tax be put on all absentees leaving this native soil [of Ireland]. (James Johnson, "A Tour of Ireland", 1844, quoted by Cent.Lib. account).

The bridge withstood floods, but not the pressure of ice blocks when the river Foyle froze, as in 1802 and 1814. Men were sent out in boats to break up the ice blocks with sledgehammers and mallets (Ibid.). On 6 Feb. 1814 the ice piled up so high against the bridge that 350 feet were carried away ("Bridge Fallen", *Belfast Newsletter*, 8 Feb. 1814, Cent.Lib.). It cost more than the original price to repair it, £ 18,208, with government loan ("Derry's Bridges",

21). It was the city's only bridge until replaced by the steel Carlyle Bridge, 200 yards upstream, in 1865, when the wooden bridge was dismantled piece by piece (Ibid., 19, 23; Local Studies Dept. letter 31 March 1994).

Cox was to return to Ireland to build three more bridges, at Waterford (1793), Wexford (1794) and New Ross in, and was hired as consultant on the Montrose Bridge in Scotland in 1797 (Court of Session file CS238 C9/11 in Scottish Record Office at West Registrar House copied by Cent. Library), and bid on the demolition of Christopher Wren's Monument in London. But Gould came home from Londonderry ill, probably about 26 Oct. 1791 when the news of the completion of the Londonderry bridge arrived in Boston.

RETURN TO CHARLESTOWN AND DEATH 1791.

Gould was absent from Boston during the First Census of the U.S. in 1790. Anna Gould is listed in Charlestown as head of family with two other females, probably her unmarried daughters Dolly (age 18) and Nabby (age 16); (Bureau of the Census, *Heads of Families of the First Census of the U.S. 1790, Massachusetts* [Washington: GPO, 1908] [hereinafter 1st Census],138 col. 2. Cox & wife Susannah don't appear either, unless his wife is "Mrs. Cox" with three females, 184, col. l). Wyman (1:428) lists the family in Charlestown in 1789; his source is not given.

It is not known on what ship Gould and Cox returned home, though there was little delay since many ships were sailing from Derry with immigrants to American ports of Philadelphia, Chester, New York and Charlestown. The William cleared for the latter under Capt. Stevenson before 28 June (LDJ 28 June), but the ad for carpenters on 14 May may indicate earlier departure of the workmen when the basic construction was done on 28 May. In any event, Gould should have arrived home about three weeks later, in late June or July 1791.

In 1791 James Gould's house in Charlestown lying between William Leathers and Amos Chapman (east of the Training Field) was assessed for £ 30, and a tax of £ 1/16 (Charlestown Tax Records, v. I, 4; Boston City Archives, Readville, hereinafter Chas.Tax). However, his name does not appear in 1792 assessment, indicating that he is dead. In 1793 Widow Gould was given an abatement of 15/4 for 1791 (Chas.Tax, 1793, 2), and on 4 Feb. 1793 James Gould's tax of £ 4/12/9 was abated for 1788, 1789 and 1790 (Ibid., last page). No further record of James or his widow appears in Charlestown assessor's books.

Gould died a few months after his return from Ireland. There is no town, probate or burial record of James's death. First Church in Charlestown recorded the death in Oct. 1791 of James Gould, 47, Atrophy (Hunnewell 256). Atrophy is emaciation, "a wasting away of the body, or any part of it, through imperfect nourishment: emaciation" (OED 541 b).

Gould's will and probate record is missing. It can be reconstructed partly from subsequent deeds. The Training Field property was inherited in 1819 by his son Thomas[5] Gould, from the estate of his brother-in-law James Davis Turner, who died 15 Dec. 1818, after the death of James's daughter Nancy Gould Turner on 12 Sept. 1815 (MD 68/407). From this it would appear that Nancy was the sole heir, but it is not clear if the other four children, Thomas, Joseph, Mary Ann Hovey and Abigail Phillips also had shares. This is not clarified by the wills of Turner (d. 1818), Joseph (pro. 19 Aug. 1823), and Lenthal Ells Phillips. However, Charlestown Assessor's records show that Thomas Gould, resident of Boston in 1825 owned half a house and a shop worth $800 (Chas.Tax, v. 20, 1825, 14). The following year he has a house next to Mr. Sprague worth $667, and a shop next to Varney, and an "Old House" worth $537, on which he paid a total tax of $72.06 (Chas.Tax 1826, 15).

His wife's death, burial and family origins are below under Lawrance.

Ten children:

i. JAMES[5], bapt. Roxbury 28 Feb. 1768 (Rox. Land 213; Births 152); died Abington MA age 6 years, 3 months= about 1 June 1774 of accident; buried French's burying ground, Abington (Nash D-36: 22), grave later moved to Mt. Vernon Cemetery, Abington; no stones remain.

9. ii. NANCY, bapt. Roxbury 14 June 1769; m. JAMES DAVIS TURNER of Charlestown.

iii. ANNE, bapt. Roxbury 5 Nov.1769 (Rox. Land 213; Births 152); died young, prob. Roxbury before family moved to Abington 1774, when second Ann is baptized (below).

10. iv. JOSEPH, b. Roxbury c. 1770; m. CLARISSA HUNT DREW.

v. MARY ANN, bapt. Roxbury 15 Dec. 1771; d. N. Abington, before 1781 (see namesake 12. below).

vi. ANN, prob. b. Roxbury late 1773; bapt. Abington Aug. 1774 (Nash?); died young, prob. N. Abington c. 1780-1785 (Nash D-36: 22-23): buried French's Cem.; no stones remain.

11. vii. ABIGAIL "Nabby", bapt. Abington MA 30 Oct. 1774; m. LENTHALL ELLS PHILLIPS of Charlestown.

viii. STEPHEN, b. Abington MA after 1774; died young N. Abington, c. 1780-1785 (Nash D-36:22-23).

12. ix. MARY ANN "Dolly", b. N. Abington MA c. 1780-1 (Illinois Census 1850, 1860), m. JOHN HOVEY of Charlestown.

13. x. THOMAS, bapt. Abington MA 2 Feb. 1785; m. (1) SOPHIA LOVIS of Hingham; m. (2) LYDIA PIERCE.

Chapter VI

LAWRANCE FAMILY OF DORCHESTER

8. ANN(A) LAWRANCE, was probably born in Boston about 1743, and died Charlestown MA, age 81, 24 Oct. 1824 (*Columbian Centinel*, 27 Oct. 1824 (*Deaths in Columbian Centinel 1784-1840*, F-G). She was probably buried in lot 7, First Church Charlestown (*Charlestown Record of Deeds 1800-73*, 3:460, in BPL Mss. f Bos.XC4).

She married 9 Nov. 1766 at Hollis Street Church in south end of Boston, to **7**. James[4] GOULD (Thomas[3], William[2], Thomas[1]), bridge builder and wheelwright, baptized Boston 12 Jan. 1746; died Charlestown, late Oct. 1791.

She had ten children, listed above.

Three years after the death of her husband (in 1790) she bought a small strip of land adjoining her house in Charlestown to the northwest (Middlesex Deeds, hereinafter MD, 225:520). She paid £ 7/10 to Lovise Monroe, Boston mariner, for a lot bounded on the north and west by the road thru the Training Field 24 feet, 20 feet on the west by Dr. Aaron Putnam, and 22 feet on the south and 22 feet on the east by her land. This could have been used for an extension of the house.

In 1824 the eastern boundary of the Gould land in Charlestown was altered when her neighbor Caleb Peirce, shipwright paid her £ 40 for the land on the east side of a brick wall he was building (MD 257:66-7). The line began 9 inches east of the northwest corner of the Gould house on the Training Field, ran south 26 feet, then west 26 feet 3 inches to Leathers nook (so-called), then south by her land to that of Thomas Gould. Had Thomas bought land before this or was the land subdivided?

Seven months later Ann Gould made her will, on 7 Oct. 1824 (Msx Wills 9500). She left her estate to her son ~~Joseph~~ [crossed out] and replaced by Thomas--, and Naby Phillips, wife of Lenthal Phillips, and Mary M. Hovey, wife of John Hovey, to be equally divided between them (Joseph died 1823, will probated 19 Aug. 1823). If any of them die before division, their children are to receive their share. Executor: ~~Joseph~~--crossed out and replaced by Thomas--Gould. Witnesses: Oliver Holden, M. Jarvis, Eliza A. West, Susan Phillip. Thomas received 1/6 of the house on Adams Street, where she probably lived at the time of her death (MD 387:474)

She died two weeks later, on 24 Oct. 1824, age 81 (*Columbian Centinel* 27 Oct.).

Her son Thomas had been deeded lot 7 in the First Church burial ground at Phipps Street on 2 Sept. 1822 by the Charlestown Selectmen in return for building a seawall on the river side of the cemetery (MD). Ann Lawrence was probably buried there, but no stone exists. The Gould lots still exist on the 1993 inventory, but the westernmost graves appear to have been displaced by the west wall, in which a plaque has been inserted reading "James Gould".

Ann Lawrence's parents are unknown, but we are certain that her brother was SAMUEL LAWRANCE, tailor of Boston, (1745-1807) (Norfolk Deeds 11: 7: "Samuel Lawrance" [note spelling] sold to Atherton Wales three acres in Bear Swamp in Stoughton "left me by Nicholas Lawrance & Ann Gould my sister..." on 24 May 1799, recorded 25 June.

This deed confirms a family record (Bass, c. 1895, "Lawrence Family" which states "Samuel Lawrence. Born in Boston Massachusetts Aug. 23rd 1745; Married Mary Daws June

27th 1768; By Rev. Dr. Cooper [Samuel Cooper, Minister of Brattle Street Church]; Died March 9th 1807 [*Register*, July 1924, 301 gives same date, age 62]; 5 children:

[i] James [Lanman in CD 143:325] Lawrence, Born Boston. Aug. 18th 1774; [Sea Captain on attached chart]; Died on passage from Liverpool 11 Dec. 1794.

[ii] Sallie Lawrence; Born Boston Jan. 26th 1777; Married Job Drew; She kept Coat of Arms and letters; house and all Burned at New Orleans; Died Dec. 2nd 1833 In Covington La.; [child: Joseph L[awrence] Drew married Sarah L. (witnesses to deed of his first cousin Thomas Gould Sr. 4 April 1831, SD 351/281; child 2. Ellen Prince Drew, Born 1807 Jan 2, Married Seth Wilson, 1826, per chart]; Grandchildren live at South Boston: Joseph Drew, Gold Refiner, [3] Province Court [res. Cambridgeport 1895 Boston Directory; office 36 Bromfield Street, 1925; son Henry H. Drew was Gold Refiner with father Joseph Lawrence Drew in Joseph L. Drew & Son, Boston to 1946; he resided 17 Winsor Ave, Watertown, 1915-1940; it is probably his son Joseph L. Drew, 2d. who resided 17 Winsor Av., Watertown, c. 1925-46, then 1940 Commonwealth Av., Brookline in 1947, when we lose track of descendants. A Job Drew was born 1773, one of 13 children of Job Drew who m. 21 May 1767 Thankful Prince, b. 6 March 1750, d. Thomas Prince and Lydia Delano, *Boston Transcript*, 11 June 1906, #8611; also #1336 16, 28 Nov. 1910); Thomas is fifth in line from Mayflower passenger William Brewster. Drew family genealogist Lee R. Drew, Assistant VP Utah Power, 400 E. 100 South, Salt Lake 84111; home: 254 W. 130 South, Lindon UT 84042; ph. (801) 220-6880, 1992.

[iii] Thomas Gardner Lawrence, Born Boston Oct. 29th 1778; Died 1779.

[iv] Thomas Gardner Lawrence, Born Boston March 11th 1780. Died July 26th 1804.

[v] Joseph Lawrence, Born Boston July 27th 1781; Sea captain. Married Elisabeth Beard. Liverpool; Died Alexandria, Egypt, 1826." (One might look in National Archives for U.S. Consular Records, Alexandria, for name of ship and date).

Samuel Lawrence is listed in Boston in 1790 Census with one adult male, one boy under 16, and 2 females (189c).

Mary[5] Dawes was fifth of six children of Story[4] (Thomas[3], Ambrose[2], William[1]) Dawes and Sarah Paine (Henry W. Holland, *William Dawes and His Ride With Paul Revere* [Boston: John Wilson, 1878], 58; wedding date is given 23 June 1768 rather than 27th; "no issue survive~ is correct as far as Lawrances, but is apparently unaware of Drew descendants. Story was a housewright of Sudbury Street, Boston.

Her first cousin was William Dawes[5] (William[4], Thomas[3], Ambrose[2], William[1]; 1745-99), the long-neglected companion of Paul Revere in the midnight ride to warn the colonists of the British invasion. As *The People's Almanac #1* says, "In truth, it was Dawes who rode 1st, rode longest, and who did the whole job right." (115). Gen. Joseph Warren commissioned the two to spread the alarm on 18 April 1775. He sent Dawes, a shoemaker, on the land route out Boston Neck, thru Roxbury, across the Charles on the great bridge, thru Cambridge, out Massachusetts Ave., thru Arlington to Lexington, where he met Revere about midnight (Map in Dawes-Gates 1:42). There, about 1 am on the 19th he and Revere rode toward Concord with Dr. Sam Prescott. Dawes was captured about 2.5 miles west of Lexington, but warned Revere back to Lexington, where the battle was to take place at dawn. Dawes thus rode farthest, and evaded capture. Dawes was half-brother of Ruth[5] Dawes Tidd, ancestor of Anne Garrison Gould (see Charts 20A, 18).

Further evidence of connection of James Gould and Samuel Lawrence appears in the case of *Lawrence v. Greenlaw* (1769-70; Supreme Judicial Court case 101604, Massachusetts Archives. Mrs. Marey Lawrence (receipts read Laurance) began an account with shopkeeper John Greenlaw, buying £ 26/4/10 sundries 19 Nov. 1767, £ 23/16 more on 10 March 1768, and 2¼ yards superfine cloth on 6 May, 1/8 on 12 May, and /14 cash lent in July for a total of £ 72/2/4. Greenlaw's receipt shows this was repaid £ 34/12/7 in cash, and the rest "By Sundry Works" (29 Sept. 1769). Among Greenlaw's receipts for 1769 are 4 to "Mrs. Marey Laurance" for one looking glass, 2 payments in cash and "½ dozn cheny cups & Saucers & ½ dozn tea Spoons" valued at £ 1/2. In the court file is a curious document which connects the Goulds and Lawrences:

"Boston August 17th 1768--Whereas We the Subscribers have Given our joint & Several note of hand for forty pounds to John Greenlaw payable in twelve months with interest, said note being given for Sundry Goods & Merchandize Stole (?) from said Greenlaw by Samuel Lawrance now if that s$^{d.}$ Greenlaw Shall hereafter find out that the Goods so Stolen (?) amounts to a greater Sum than Forty pounds, then we jointly & Severally promise to pay the s$^{d.}$ over---? Sum on demand as Witness our hands; Test Saml Swift; signatures of Saml Lawrence, John Fairservice, Story Dawes and James Goold."

William Dawes is also involved, with receipts from Greenlaw to him for payments on behalf of Samuel Lawrence 23-27 Feb. 1769.

Greenlaw's account with Messrs Saml Lawrance, Jno Fersarvice, Story Daw's & Jas Goold shows 2 pages of cloth sold by and to other persons (Supper fine Holland, Blue Shalloon, fine Tamie, Linnen) to a total of £ 510/12/3~ Old Tennor, or £ 68/1/9 Lawfull Money; "Mrs. Laurenc Goun not Included nor a dolar I paid Hodgon when I recd the linnen from him".

Samuel Lawrence, Taylor of Boston, sued John Greenlaw, shopkeeper of Boston in the Court of Common Pleas, for a debt of £15/2, in a plea of trespass. A summons was issued on 19 Dec. 1769 against Greenlaw, who denied the debt, so Deputy Sheriff Benj. Cudworth seized one of his chairs. On 9 Jan. 1770 the Court found for Lawrence, the plaintiff, plus costs of £3/8/4, the largest part for Jury Fees of £ 1/8/8. His attendance at court for 8 days cost 12', and witnesses travel 20 miles 3' (William Dawes trip from Watertown). Greenlaw appealed the case to the Superior Court in Feb. 1770. William Dawes, housewright of Watertown, was called as witness in the case on 12 March 1770. The court convened on 13 March and decided in favor of Lawrance, with additional costs of £1/1 for attendance, 6' for the witnesses' attendance 4 days, and 3' for 20 miles travel, and 12'/6 attorney's fee. This was executed 5 June 1770.

There is no known connection to the conviction of Anne (Amy) Lawrance for theft from Mary Fairservice in case in Superior Court of Judicature Court of Assize (102713, Massachusetts Archives) on 29 Aug. 1780 despite the coincidence of names Fairservice and Lawrance. The jury found Amy Lawrance, widow of Boston, guilty of theft from Fairservice on June 24 of a linen Patticoat worth £ 30, one Pocket worth £ 5, a check apron worth £ 50, and a pair of cotton hose worth £ 30, ordered her to pay treble the cost, or £ 366/13/4 and be whipped 15 stripes, plus costs. Note "2 years Sirvice(?)" may refer to jail.

See also case of Lawrence v. Ellis in Suffolk Court of Common Pleas (Massachusetts Archives 123B) in which Mrs. Anne Lawrence of Boston shopkeeper sued William Ellis of Boston tailor for debt of £ 40/10/9 in April 1748. No known relation.

A Mrs. Lawrence is listed as joint holder of pew #19 of the Hollis Street Church in July 1764, and again on 30 Sept. of that year as owner of one third (C. Davis collection, MHS). Since this is the place of baptism (1745) and marriage (1768) of Samuel Lawrence, this could be the widowed mother of Ann and Samuel.

On 8 Nov. 1780 a Mr. Samuel Lawrance was recommended for a liquor license at his shop on the south side of the State House (Suffolk Co. Supreme Judicial Court file 93086). Boston business directory may give location of Lawrence's tailor shop, and Census of 1790 should list other Samuel Lawrences with whom this might be confused.

In 1786 Samuel Lawrence, tailor of Boston, sued Samuel Bird, yeoman of Sharon, for a debt probably related to the Dorchester lands he sold (Suffolk Co. Supreme Judicial Court 96723). We will deal with this and other land owned by Samuel Bird below.

LAWRANCE ORIGINS.

Who then, were the parents of Samuel Lawrance and Ann Gould? Gould family tradition gives these clues:

1. Caroline[9] Gould (1890-1982) told me 22 Aug. 1966 that her aunt Ida[8] Gould (1856-1946) who worked at Boston Public Library that Capt. James Lawrence (1781-1813) of the Battle of Lake Erie was definitely a relative. Lawrence's famous last words "Don't Give Up the Ship!" were inscribed on Capt. Perry's flag at the Battle of Lake Erie on 10 Sept. 1813 after Lawrence was killed when his ship *Chesapeake* was sunk 30 miles off Boston on 1 June 1813. There is no evidence of relation in Thomas Lawrence, *Historical Genealogy of the Lawrence Family* [New York: E. O. Jenkins, 1858] [hereinafter Lawrence Gen.].

2. Caroline Gould also stated that we were related to Bishop William Lawrence, sixth Episcopal Bishop of Massachusetts (b. 1850). Again, there is no evidence in any of the Lawrence genealogies of descendants of John[1] of Watertown, nor in his biographies in *National Cyclopedia of American Biography* [1896 ed., 6:16], Mary C. Crawford, *Famous Families of Massachusetts* [Boston: Little, Brown, 1930] (2:176), *Boston Transcript* 16 Oct. 1948.

3. The diaries of Lydia Teel Gould in 1874-80 refer to the Gould family claim to a Lawrence estate in England. The first reference is 14 March 1874: "Called on James Gould [1803-92, grandson of Ann Lawrance]...[who] says there is a world of wealth waiting in England for the Goulds coming through the line of the grandmother who was a Lawrance. hurah!! for the Goulds". On 27 March she recorded: "Mr Gould called today to tell me about the fourtune!!"

If the case could be identified we might find the genealogical evidence that the family submitted. The most conspicuous case found in the *New York Times Index* is the Townley Lawrence estate, first referred to on 14 March 1874. Lydia's diary for 1880 (with John Shaw) refers to this on 19 April: "I sent brother George Gould a coppy of the history of the Townley Lawrence Estate to day with a letter". Again on 28 May 1880: "Lawyer Forbs called to see us, we had quite a chat about the Townley Estate. He staid over night...[29th] Mr. Forbs went to

Boston in the eight O'Clock train".

4. Abigail Gould Bailey (Bass 3) shows a chart giving Samuel[4] and Anna as children of John[3] Lawrence and Hannah Tarbell of Groton, son of Nathaniel[2] Lawrence and Sarah Morse, son of John[1] of Watertown, d. 1663. This is clearly mistaken since Samuel[4] was born 9 July 1700, and Anna, baptized 1702, m. Benjamin Bancroft of Charlestown (John Lawrence, *The Genealoqy of the family of John Lawrence, of Wisset...Watertown and Groton* [Boston: S.K. Whipple, 1857] [hereinafter Lawrence 1857], 20).

5. A Gould descendant, F. H. Dam, lawyer of San Francisco wrote on 24 Jan. 1913 as follows to his aunt Elizabeth[6] M. Gould of Brookline, last surviving child of Thomas[5] Gould: *"the family of Ann[5] Lawrence was not the Groton family. Her grandfather Nathaniel[2] Lawrence, was of Groton, but moved to Lexington [see Hudson 116]; John[3] Lawrence was of Lexington; Benjamin[4] Lawrence was born in Lexington, and moved to Westboro, and thence to Boston [based on Bond, 823]. Perhaps the greater part, certainly the more distinguished part, of the Lawrence family, lived in Groton; and accordingly the Lawrence name is associated with that town. Unless it can be found that Ann[5] Lawrence was married to someone else, I shall believe that she is our Ann."*

Dam was mistaken. *Boston Transcript* 11 Jan. 1904 #6818 shows that Ann Lawrence of Groton married Aaron Whitney of Harvard MA; also Benjamin[4] Lawrence (b. 1711) in Hudson 2:116, had daughter Annah, b. 19 Aug. 1742 Westboro (VR 67), bp. 26 Sept. Lexington; m. 18 Dec. 1765 Aaron Whitney (Harvard VR 189); John Lawrence, *Genealogy of the family of John Lawrence, of Wisset...Watertown* [Boston: Nichols & Noyes, 1869] [hereinafter Lawrence 1869], 402; Mercy Hale, *Genealogical Memoir of the Families of Lawrences...to Robert Lawrence of Watertown* [Stowe, Massachusetts: Mercy Hale, 1857].

6. The only published history of the Lawrence family which mentions Nicholas Lawrence is Lawrence 1857, in the Appendix, 189-190 "Brief Notices of Other Lawrences Early Settled in New England", with no indication that they are related to the Wisset-Watertown-Groton Lawrences.

7. A Mrs. Lawrence held pew #19 in Hollis Street Church in the South End of Boston in 1764, four years before the marriage of Samuel, may have been the mother of Samuel and Ann (MHS C. Davis Collection). There is no evidence that her name was Ann. It could be the Mary Lawrence found in Thwing's card index as mother of James Lanham Lawrence born 1744 in Boston to Samuel and Mary. There is no further information.

We thus conclude that there is no evidence that this family was related to the Lawrences descended from John[1] of Watertown and Wisset, but that they were heirs of Nicholas Lawrence of Dorchester. Who, then was this Nicholas?

Anderson speculates to "suggest that Nicholas Lawrence was very likely a kinsman of the former [Henry Lawrence], perhaps even a son." (Robert C. Anderson, *The Great Migration Begins* [Boston: NEHGS, 1996], 4:346. He bases this solely on the facts that Nicholas was witness to a deed of 1646 to his widow Christian and son John (citing Charlestown Land Records 138), and that Nicholas was an abutter (citing SD 1:100).

However, usually reliable traditional sources such as Savage, Bond, Lincoln and Bridges assert that he was the only son of:

THOMAS[1] LAWRENCE, born perhaps in Hingham, Kent (R. E. Thomas, *The Genealogy of Samuel W. Bridges* [Higginson Book Co. 1960] 54; error for Norfolk); died 5 Nov. 1655 Hingham, Massachusetts (LAURANCE in Hobart's journal in *Register* 1967, 105); married about 1638 ELIZABETH[1] BATE(S) (Sav. 2: 63, Torrey 455; Bridges Genealogy gives 1638, which is reasonable given Thomas's arrival in Hingham about 1637); baptized Lydd, Kent 11 March 1620/1 *(Bates Bulletin*, 2d.series, 96): died Dorchester after 1684 (Town Report 274). She was daughter of Andrew Bates (*Bates Bulletin* 2:96; Sav 2:63 and Lawrence 1857 give father as James[1], but James had no recorded child of that name, so she probably came to America with her uncle James, who left England in April 1635 on the *Elizabeth*, Capt. Staggs (Ebenezer Clapp, *History of the Town of Dorchester* [Boston: author, 1859]).

Andrew, James and Clement Bate(s) were sons of James[A] Bate, yeoman of Lydd who d. Lydd 2 March 1614, m. Lydd 6 June 1590 Mary Martine who died after him (IGI Ancestral file ver 4.02 (1992) submitted by Theresa Butterfield of 9113 Clendenen, Sacramento CA 95826 has several errors (d. 1583 Lydd Mildred Ward, Eliz. Bates' parents, etc.) states Mary Martine b. Lydd 1562, dau. of James Martin b.c.1540 Lydd, m. 27 Aug. 1562 Lydd to Joan Adam, b. 3 April 1544 Lydd, d. Lydd 1582, daughter of William Adam and Alice Baker). He was son of John[B] Bate who left will 13 May 1580, and married first at Lydd 28 Oct. 1546 Mildred Ward who was buried Lydd 1 June 1577. He was son of Andrew[C] Bate, whose will is dated 22 Feb. 1533; son of John[D] Bate, whose will probated 17 Sept. 1522; son of Thomas[E] Bate, who died Lydd, Kent, 1485 (*Bates Bulletin*, Oct. 1917, 7). Coats of arms of the Bate family appear in the Church of All Hallows, Lydd: Sable, a fess between 3 dexter hands, couped argent (Charles A. Converse, *Some of the Ancestors and Descendants of Samuel Converse Jr.* [Boston: Eben Putnam, 1905], 2:701). Ann Lawrence's son Thomas[5] Gould (1785-1872) married a descendant of immigrant Clement[1] Bates, perhaps sixth cousins, depending on number of generations of Ann Lawrence from Andrew.

Thomas[1] Lawrence had immigrated to America, residing in "Hingham, in 1637. He is given as a landholder for that year, and was admitted a freeman the year following" (Lawrence 1857, 189). The Lawrences were one of 130 families who founded the town of Hingham (Louis C. Cornish, "The Settlement of Hingham" in DAR, *Hingham* [Boston: Rockwell & Churchill for DAR, 1911], 45.

In 1638, he was given a house lot in today's Hingham Center, described in Cushing's record: ~1638//Thomas Larance have given him by the towne three acres of land for a house lot bounded with the Ceader Swampt west ward and the land of Thomas Clap eastward and with the land of Thomas Fody? northward and the land of Hendry Smith southward. (Daniel Cushing mss. 48, 1636, Hingham Histories, microfilm 76-1; abbrev. in Lawrence 1857, 189). Clapp's house was on pp. the Plain, west of today's Main Street, and Matthew Hawke's house to the south (Ibid., 48, 42; SD 4:248 Cooper to Cushing shows their five acre lot to north of Thomas Lawrence 25 Aug. 1664). Today this is on the north side of Garrison Lane in Hingham Center.

In addition he got two acres of salt marsh in Cohasset: "1647. Given him two acres of Salt Marshe at Cony Hassett being the Ninth Lott in the second Divition, and it Lies on the

Northward Sict of the great Nor? Bounded w/ the Cove? Northward, + w/ ye Towns Lan[d] West? South west" (Ibid., 48). The same lot is described as south and southeast of the sea, north of common land, and east of Josiah Coyne in 1672 (Prince to Hearsey SD 7:331). This appears to be on Cohasset's Little Harbor, though it is not shown on Bigelow's map (E. Victor Bigelow, *A Narrative History of Cohasset* [Cohasset: The Town, 1898], 156).

In 1655 Deacon Cushing was given a highway by the town between his lot and widow Lawrence's (Hingham Town Records, Cushing's record on microfiche 125, 20 March 1655). A deed of 1672 states that William Hearcie (Hersey) of Hingham bought from Thomas Lawrence two anchors of salt marsh at Cunnyhasset, north of Hingham Common, to west of Jonathan Caynes, and on the sea to the north and northwest (Hearcie to John Prince, SD 7:331).

He left a nuncupative (oral) will, to which Elder Edward Bates of Weymouth (brother to his wife) was witness (Suffolk Probate Misc. Documents, Massachusetts Arch., Docket book 5:246; Town Report 274; Sav. 2:63; Pope 280; Wyman 609).

His widow Elizabeth removed to Dorchester with her son Nicholas (Sav. 2:63). On the advice of her brother she sold about 1655 a small parcel of land to Lt. John Smith of Hingham, which she confirmed in 1675 (Suff. Prob. Misc. 5:246). This man is John Smith, a Lieutenant in King Philip's War, who lived on Main Street Hingham, opposite Leavitt Street (George Lincoln, *The History of the Town of Hingham* [Hingham: The Town, 1893] [hereinafter Lincoln], 153).

A living of £ 4/6 was paid by the town of Dorchester, to a poor person, Elizabeth Lawrence, on Dec. 12, 1679 (Town Report 237). Widow Lawrence got a town bounty in 1680 (Clapp, 239). A tax abatement is granted to the same person 1684 (Town Report 274). No record of her death has been found.

Four children, born in Hingham, MA:

i. NICHOLAS[2], Senior, born Hingham (Sav. 2:63; Lawrance 1857) about 1638-9 (Bridges Genea. 54 gives parents' marriage 1638); died early 1685 (Sav. 2:62; Wyman 609); married by 1652 MARY[2] HARRIS, daughter of Walter[1] and Mary[2] Fry.

ii. MARY, b. Hingham (Lawrence 1857); died Dorchester (2) April 1723 (21st Report of Boston Record Commissioners, *Dorchester Births* [Boston: Rockwell & Churchill, 1890] [hereinafter VR] 122; Sav. 3:179; 2:63); m. Dorchester 28 July 1658 (VR 20) THOMAS[2] MAUDESLEY (MOSELY; John[1]), b. 1636, d. Dorchester 22 Oct. 1706 (Ezra S. Stearns, *New Hampshire Genealogical Register* [Chicago: Lewis Publishing, 1908]), 3:994). She received the covenant, a ceremony similar to confirmation, at the First Church in Dorchester 3 Aug. 1652 (First Church record, 20). The covenant was usually taken at age 14, so she was probably born about 1638. She was mother of Sgt. Increase[3] Moseley who went to Canada in 1690 in King William's War against the French, and Ebenezer[3] Mosely (b. 4 July 1674; Dorchester town officer: constable 1705, Selectman 1719-21, Treasurer 1720, Clerk 1721; Ebenezer Clapp, *History of the Town of Dorchester* [Boston: the author, 1859] [hereinafter Clapp] 518), and grandmother of the Rev. Samuel Mosely, Harvard 1729 (see Sibley), and minister of the First Church in Dorchester.

iii. ELIZABETH, bp. Hingham 6 March 1641/2 (Town Record fiche I, 7; Hob. Jour.14; Lincoln); killed by Abenaki Indians, Deerfield Massacre, 28/29 Feb. 1704 during the War of the

Spanish Succession (George E. Bates, *A Bates-Breed Ancestry* [Boston: the author, 1975] A837). She m. Dorchester 31 Dec. 1658 (VR 20; Torrey 679) WILLIAM[2] SMEAD, born England, son of William[1] and Judith Stoughton (Sav. 4:109; 2:63). He was born England about 1635. (*Daughters of Founders & Patriots of America*, 21:135; 31:50). The family moved west to Northampton MA shortly after their marriage (1660), then to Deerfield 1684, where he died before the 1704 massacre (Ibid.).

In all 27 members of this family were victims of the Deerfield Massacre: 15 of the 38 killed were her family, including 8 grandchildren, a daughter, two step-grandchildren, a daughter-in-law and son-in-law (See account of massacre in George Sheldon, *History of Deerfield* [Deerfield: Historical Soc., 1896] [hereinafter Sheldon], 304). Three grandchildren burned to death in the cellar of the Nims house with their stepbrother. Three more grandchildren died with their parents Thankful and John Hawkes. Two grandchildren were smothered with her and their mother in the cellar of her son Samuel's house. Twelve of the 100 captives taken at Deerfield were family members. Four died on the march, two daughters killed because they could not keep up with the flight from the pursuing soldiers. Six of the surviving captives were eventually redeemed: granddaughters Elizabeth Hull, Sarah Warner and Waitstill Warner, grandson Ebenezer Nims, daughter-in-law Abigail Brown, and son-in-law Ebenezer Warner. But most intriguing are the two "unredeemed captives", granddaughters Waitstill Warner, age 3, and Abigail Nims age 4. The colonial view was that these were tragic figures who learned French, and were forced to become Catholics. But recent historians view them differently, perhaps assimilating happily to the Indian or French Canadian lifestyle, even marrying and producing descendants in Canada. Many years later an Indian tried to get money for Abigail, but when the money was raised she never appeared.

But the Deerfield Massacre was not the first or the last of the family's murderous encounter on the frontier. Elizabeth Lawrance Smead's eldest son William had been killed in the battle of Bloody Brook in 1675 (Sheldon 100-1), and her grandson John Nims captured the year before, but escaped in 1705 (Sheldon 287, 353). The son and namesake of her son John Smead who was wounded in 1704 in the Meadow Fight was himself captured with his wife and five children in 1746 at Ft. Massachusetts, to which they added an orphan they named Captivity. They were redeemed from Canada, but he went back to fighting and was killed by the Indians at Miller's Falls in 1747. It is not surprising that one of her grandsons became one of the leading Indian fighters, Col. John Hawkes, the hero of Ft. Massachusetts, where his cousin Elisha Nims was killed (Sheldon 542-5). The Indians had their revenge on his sister Thankful Symmes and his niece Submit (Hawks) Grout whom they captured at Ft. Bridgman in 1755 with her three children. All told we count about 45 members of the Smead family who were victims of the Indian wars. In addition to Sheldon's book Emma Coleman's *New England Captives Carried to Canada* [Portland ME: Southworth Press, 1925] gives accounts of our many Indian captives, and Rev. John Williams *The Redeemed Captive Returning to Zion* [Freeport NY: Books for Libraries reprint 1970 of the 1853 ed.] gives a firsthand account of the Deerfield Massacre and the captivity.

iv. SARAH, bp. Hingham 4 March 1643/4 (Hobart Journal 16; Lincoln; Pope 280). No record of marriage or descendants; probably died young. Check who the Sarah Lawrence was who married Joseph Winslow of Boston, of Plymouth family, with son Joseph (IGI).

NICHOLAS[2] LAWRANCE, Sr. (c.1638-1685).

Nicholas[2] Lawrance was born in Hingham (Sav. 2:63) about 1638 (given that his father arrived 1637, date in Bridges Genea. 54 is too late for his marriage 1652).

Savage is probably correct in giving two separate Nicholas Lawrences living at the same time, one in Charlestown and the other in Hingham and Dorchester, though it may turn out that they are one as Pope says (Sav.2:62; Pope 280 gives the Charlestown owner of 1648 as moving to Dorchester, dying 1685, as does Moriarty 5). The Charlestown Nicholas sold land at Sconce Point in 1648 next to the Watertown Lawrences John and Christian (Wyman 2:606, 608; SD 1:100-101), that caused Savage to speculate that the seller was brother to John (Sav. 2:63).

Nicholas, a mariner, had moved from his birthplace in Hingham to Dorchester by 1652, where he had married Mary Harris (Lawrence 1857). Bridges' date of 1638 would make him only 13 or 14 at time of marriage; if 1638 is wrong, Torrey's guess at about 1635 for his parents' marriage would make him 16 or 17 at most when wed. Perhaps he was born earlier in England.

The first child recorded there is Samuel[3], baptized Dorchester 10 Aug. 1652 (Pope 280).

Nicholas Laurence is debtor to the estate of Robert Button of Boston on 21 Nov. 1650 (debts presented to court 10 Jan. 1653; Register 8:59).

Nicholas Lawrence's signature appears on an affidavit on receipt of money from John Rigaway 9 Dec. 1655 (Photostat in MHS Mss of document in Greenough Collection in Massachusetts Archives).

Nicholas Lawrance is listed as creditor 4 May 1660 of estate of Capt. Thomas Thornhill (Register 10:175).

On 11 Jan. 1660/1 Nicholas Lawrence requested the town to grant him land near the creek (Dorchester Town Report, [hereinafter DTR], 103 [135].

He was an expert on a jury 7 March 1663 (Suffolk Supreme Judicial Court, 609).

He requested £ 3/4 for keep of Frances Tree on 19 Feb. 1666 (DTR 143).

The town paid him £ 2/5 for Frances Tree on 8 Sept. 1669 (DTR 160).

A complaint was made to the town about Nicholas Lawrence over stone horses 27 April 1670 (DTR 168).

The Town of Dorchester paid Nicholas Lawrence 14 shillings for 1000 shingles on 13 Sept. 1670 (DTR 179).

The town refused his request for a barn near the clay pits on 14 Sept. 1670 (DTR 170 [265].

On 14 April 1674, Nicholas Lawrence requested the town to permit him to build a barn near the clay pit (DTR 200).

Nicholas Lawrence contributed one shilling toward the bell for the First Church, 1675 (Register 59:106).

Nicholas Lawrence was defendant in a suit by Hudson Leverett as assignee of William Phillips Sr. who succeeded in getting payment of a note of 25 Jan. 1676 by Lawrence for £ 14. The Suffolk County court found against Lawrence on 7 Aug. 1677, adding £ 8 damages and 22 shillings court costs (Records of Suffolk Co. Court, printed, 3:834).

In 1679 the town paid him 3 shillings for keeping Frances Tree (DTR 240).

He died in early 1685, between his will of 26 Jan. (Suffolk Will 1406) and the inventory of 20 Feb. The will itself is missing from the file, but the docket states that Nicholas Laurence (no occupation or residence), executrix Mary, probated 21 May 1685; he left to his eldest son (unnamed) ¼ of his sheep, and to his four other children, Mary, Rebecca, Nicholas and Benjamin one sheep or lamb each; witnesses were Thomas Pearce and John Breck, who also did the inventory. His two youngest children (unnamed) are to be provided for until they can earn a living (Suffolk Probate Record Books, Probate Docket, Vol. 6, part 2, 796-7 of copy, 490 of original transcribed in 1900, Massachusetts Archives). He names only four other children, Mary [Patten], Rebecca [Robinson], Nicholas [Jr.], and Benjamin (Sav. 2:62; Pope 280). Since Patience and Ebenezer are unnamed, these may be the two youngest who are to be cared for. The unnamed eldest could be Samuel b. 1652, Thomas b. 1654, or Nathaniel b. 1660. Perhaps the name will show up in Dorchester deeds of abutters to the house near the wharf.

The inventory of his estate on 20 Feb. 1684 by Thomas Pears and John Brooke showed a total of £ 101/4 (Inventory 1406). The largest item was "a hous orchard and barne under mortgage" £ 40. Next in value, for £ 16/2 "In beding blanketts sheets ruggs coverlets & bedsteeds", £ 16 in "A sloop and cannoes", £9/7 in "Sheep and Swine mare colt and cow", £ 4/1 in "wearing Apparrell hatts stockins & shoes" £ 3/12 in "pewtar & brass new and old", £ 2/12/6 in "Iron potts and posnets [basins] Andirons slice & tongs", £2/10 in (silver) plate, £ 2/7/6 in wooden dishes old chests chairs tables and churn, £1/12/6 in Carpenters old tools Augers chizels plains and axes, £ 1/9 In woole a sadle pannell wheel baggs and pans & bottles, £ 0/16, in Shot, lead and lines old iron scales & steelyards, £ 0/11 In books smoothing iron & heaters.

Mary Lawrence, widow, administratrix submitted this to the probate court in Boston on 21 May 1685.

MARY HARRIS, WIFE OF NICHOLAS[2] LAWRENCE, SR.

Mary[2] Harris was baptized at Honiton, (east) Devon, 4 Feb. 1626/7, third child of Walter[1] Harris (d. 1654) and Mary[1] Fry (d. 1656) according to Douglas Richardson (Gale Harris letter 19 May 1992 citing Burton W. Spear, *Search for the Passengers of the Mary and John, 1630* [Toledo: Mary & John Clearing House, 1991] [hereinfter Spear], 16:39).

Her father Walter[1] Harris, born in England, first appears with the birth of a child in Honiton, Devon in 1621 (Spear). Prior to leaving for America, on 7 March 1631/2 he took the oath of allegiance (Charles Harris, "Walter Harris and Some of his Descendants", *Collections of Western Reserve* [Cleveland, 1922] [hereinafter C. Harris] 3. He and the family left London on the ship *William and Francis* on March 9, 1632, arriving in Boston 5 June 1632 (Ibid.). With him were his mother, widow of Walter[A] Harris, and his brother Gabriel who was lost at sea in 1684 on a return trip to England (Nathaniel Harris Morgan, *Harris Genealogy* [Hartford: Case, Lockwood & Brainard, 1878] [hereinfter Morgan], appendix. On this same ship were Rev. Thomas[1] Weld, first minister of Roxbury, progenitor of Gov. William Weld and Sarah Swan Weld, great-grandmother of Anne Garrison Gould.

Harris was one of the early settlers of Weymouth, MA, as early as 1635. On 2 June 1641 he was made a freeman of the colony (C.Harris, citing Records of Massachusetts 1:378). By 1650 he had obtained a large estate, still known in 1878 as "Harris Range". (Morgan; check loc.) This included eight acres in the Mill Furlong as well as eight acres in "Harrises Raingw" (C.Harris 4), land in the West Field first given to Robert Lovell (Weymouth Land Grants 255, cited by Georye W. Chamberlain, *History of Weymouth* [Baltimore: Genealogical Publishing Co., 1984] [hereinafter Chamberlain], 3:255-6). In 1651 he also held lot 12 of the great lots on the east side of Fresh Pond (recorded 26 Nov. per Chamberlain 3:256). In 1643 he was an appraiser of the estate of his brother-in-law William[2] Frye who died in Weymouth 26 Oct. 1642, leaving a kid goat to his sister's youngest son Thomas Harris (Lillian L. Selleck, *One Branch of the Miner Family* [New Haven: Donald Jacobus, 1928] 109).

By 1648 he had built illegally in Dorchester (C.Harris 5, citing TR 302, 4 Oct.). He made a formal request for land in 1653 (Ibid., TR 315, 14 Jan.). In 1649 we have his signature as appraiser of the estate of John Pope of Dorchester (C.Harris 5). In the same summer he is mentioned in the will of Edward Bullock of Dorchester for payment of a debt (Ibid., citing Reg. 6:356). It is thus in this period 1648-52 that his daughter would have met Nicholas[2] Lawrence, their first child being born 10 Aug. 1652, we propose a wedding in Dorchester in late 1651.

Walter and Mary Harris moved from Dorchester to New London in 1652 or 1653, where he was granted a house lot at Pequot Harbor on 20 May 1653 and granted a permit to run an inn (C.Harris, 6,7). He died there the next year, on 6 Nov. 1654 (C.Harris, 7,9, citing New London VR, 2).

His widow Mary died a year later, on 24 Jan. 1655/6 (Ibid.), having made a nuncupative will five days earlier (C.Harris 7). This is one of the oldest extant wills in America. To Mary Lawrence she left "my blue mohere peticote and my straw hatt and a fether boulster...my next brasst pan and thrum [shaggy tufts; OED 33]0] cushion...a ciffer [French coiffe, a kind of cap] and a white neck-cloth." and also "a quarter part...of the dyaper table cloth and tenn shillings" (Frances M. Caulkins, *History of New London* [New London: H.D.Utley, 1895], 270, citing New London Records, v.3; C. Harris 7-9).

Mary[1] Frye Harris's brother was William[1] Frye (m. Elizabeth[2] Humphrey (Jonas and Frances Cooley), who remarried (2) Thomas Daggett (Doggett) c. 1643). Like the Harrises they were early settlers of Weymouth by 1636, coming from Honiton, east Devon where the Frye children were born 1621-1635/6 (Spear). Frye was granted twelve acres in Weymouth in 1636. He was buried in Weymouth 26 Oct. 1642, leaving a nuncupative will dated 4 Oct. 1643 (*Register* 2:385; Chamberlain 3:244).

The parents of Mary and William Frye were William[A] Frye whose will was proved 25 Feb. 1625/6 (Spear 9, citing PCC HELE 20).

We do not know the date of death of Mary[2] Harris Lawrance. The last record of her is as a widow receiving communion of the First Church in Dorchester 23 June 1686 (First church 198, 27). In Charlestown a seat is granted by the selectmen to a widow of Nicholas Lawrence in the women's gallery behind the front pew of the meeting house (Charlestown Records 4:124, 5 May 1694, reel 192, Boston Public Library); we do not know the first name of this woman, but Mary would have been 68; her son Nicholas Jr. had moved to Charlestown by this time, after marrying Abigail Lawrence in 1689. One might find her gravestone in Phipps, or references in other town records.

12 Children of Nicholas[2] Lawrence and Mary[2] Harris, born Dorchester, MA:

i. SAMUEL[3], bp. 10 Aug. 1652 (Pope 280); paid taxes Dorchester 1676,7,8 (TR 238, 245). Old enough to marry, but wife and children not found. Not S.L. who m. widow Rebeckah Luen Charlestown 14 July 1682 (VR 118), whom Wyman says 690 moved to CT (Lawrence 1857). Not living 26 Jan. 1685 for mention in father's will (Suff. Will 1406).

ii. THOMAS, bp. 28 March 1654 (Pope 280); age 18 in 1676 (lst church, 183). Paid taxes Dorchester 1676,7,8 (4th Report of Boston Record Commissioners, *Dorchester Town Records* [Boston: Rockwell & Churchill, 1883] [hereinafter D Rec] 238, 245). He was old enough to marry, but no wife or children have been found. Not living at time of father's will 26 Jan. 1685.

?iii? son, unnamed in will of Mary Harris, 19 Jan. 1655/6. This son was not living 1676 when First Church recorded all children.

iii. MARY, b. 1656 (Pope 280); age 19 in 1676 (Records of the First Church of Dorchester [Dorchester: G. H. Ellis, 1891] [hereinafter lst church] 184); living unmarried 1685 in father's will. She married about 1692 DAVID PATTEN of Dorchester (Torrey). In both the town record and on Blake's map of the 12 Divisions he is styled "Mr.", a title that is usually reserved to persons of quality. How is he related to Nathaniel Patten of Dorchester (Savage)? He received 67½ acres of land in Stoughton (see later land grants), which Samuel Lawrence inherited (SD 154:81). This was in the 12 Divisions of Dorchester, representing 12 times his holding in the village, which must have been 5.6 acres (Dorch. records, 2:160). Patten land lay to north of Savin Hill, on Patten's Cove, south of today's *Boston Globe*. But the grant must have been to his widow since he died before 27 Aug. 1696 (lst church 230).

A David Patten of Boston and others petitioned the governor on 11 Oct. 1689 for their pay and wages for fighting Indians to the east (Maine? King William's War broke out 12 May 1689, Morris 62). The petition reads that the "Petitioners were impressed for the service of the Country to the Eastward of the Indians and have faithfully served in our several stations, and have gone through several straights & hazards by long & tedious marches & other difficulties in a cold winter..." (Massachusetts Archives Vol. 35, 53a)

Torrey's evidence for their marriage is this passage in First Church records (112 [146]: "The Same Day [5 June 1696] Sist^r Patten formerly Lawrence Made Confession of Slandring Broth^r Hix for Perjury & Lyes, casting contempt on ye ordinance of private Dealing by the s^d Hix

& ye 2 brethren, & Reflecting words & writings, to ye Elders & her often indulging ye Corruptions & passions of Her Evill heart & ye Evill Language of Her hasty tongue &c--& it was to the Satisfaction of ye Church." Although there is no mention of witchcraft this is the time of popularity of books on witchcraft by Cotton and Increase Mather (1693), Willard (1692) and Calef (1700) which gave religious justification to attacks on women (Winsor 2:158).

3 children:

i. Gershom, b. 21 Jan. 1691/2 (VR 36), bp. 24 Jan. 1691/2 (lst church 203); since 1692 is Torrey's guess, this may have been a shotgun wedding.

ii. David, b. 27 Oct. 1694 (VR 38), bp. 2 Dec. 1694 (lst church 206); this is too early for the David of Stoughton who m. Sarah Daniels 19 July 1788 (Canton VR 159). Mary Patten of Stoughton-Norton who administers the estate of her father John in 1770 (SD 118:26-8) is apparently the widow of 1786 who sold to David Patten, yeoman of Stoughton, eleven acres of her father John's estate (SD 164:263-4). The David b. Billerica 2 Aug. 1745 (David^5, Thomas^4, William^3, Thomas^2, William^1; William Baldwin Patten Genealogy, 46) is only distantly related to the Stoughton family who arrived there about 1730 when John^4 (John^3, Nathaniel^2, William^1 of Cambridge) married a Stoughton woman, Sarah Pomeroy (Ibid., 77, 55). None of the four printed Patten genealogies at NEHGS show our David of Dorchester. Not in Savage. Patten family associations in Toms River NJ and Hacienda Heights CA contacted without response.

iii. Susannah, b. 23 Sept. 1696 (DVR 40), bp. 27 July 1696, to widow Patten (lst Church 230), so she is posthumous. Marriages or children of these have not been found.

David Patten died before 27 July 1696 (lst church 230; no Suffolk will). His wife is still widow Patten 1709/10 (SD 74:89). Mary Patten, adult, was baptized in the First Church, Dorchester in the sixth year of ministry of Rev. Bownon=1735? She is still living on 17 Sept. 1747, which would make her 91 (SD 74:89).

iv.(Children of Nicholas^2 and Mary Harris, cont.):

PATIENCE, b. 13 April 1658 (VR 6, Register 11:332); bp. 20 April 1658 (lst church 169). Age 17 in 1676 (lst church 184). Died young, 2 Dec. 1677 (TR 29); unm. (Sav. 2:62).

v.NATHANIEL, b. 10 June 1660 (VR 7; Register 16:153); bp. 12 June 1660 (lst church 170; Pope 280); age 15 1676 (lst church 183); not living 1685 for father's will.

vi.NICHOLAS, Junior, b. 26 April 1662 (VR 8; Register 16:153); bp. 29 April 1662 (lst church 172); d. Charlestown MA 28 Feb. 1711/2 (VR 230), aged 49:8 (gravestone). Married twice: (1) Mary HARICE, (2) Abigail LAWRENCE. Complete details below.

vii.REBEKAH (Rebecca), b. 1 June 1664 (VR 9; Reg. 16:153); bp. 11 July 1664 (lst church 173); age 13 1676 (lst church 185); m. 23 Feb. 1686/7 THOMAS ROBINSON of Salem (Torrey 6313 Middlesex Court 1:583; Bailey 3-7). Thomas ROBBISON (Samuel^2 , William^1) b. Salem 6 July 1667 to Samuel and Martha Hawkins (*Essex Institute Historical Coll.* 3:96 from VR 3:16; printed VR 2:240).

In 1694, at the peak of the witchcraft craze she confessed to having committed fornication before her marriage (19 Aug., 1st church 206).

Nine children, born Dorchester.
In 1710 Robinson was living in Boston (SD 74:89). We do not know when he died. She was still living 1730 (SD 45:228).

viii.EBENEZER (I), b. 23 April 1667 (VR 10); died age nine, 20 Sept. 1676 Dorchester (VR 28; Register 16:153).

ix.BENJAMIN, b. 23 Aug. 1670 (VR 12; Register 16:153); bp. 3 Sept. 1671 (lst church 178). Mariner. Resident London 1730 (SD 45: 228); Gosport, Hampshire (suburb of Southampton; Lawrence v. Clifford 1734-5; Wyman 609). No marriage or children in Gosport IGI. Plaintiff in suit against Edward Clifford of Charlestown 1734-5 (Middlesex Court 147 A-1). No known wife or children.

x.ELIZABETH, d. Dorchester 18 Feb. 1679 (VR 30; Register 16:153). Probably a child, under 10.

xi.PATIENCE (II), b. 12 Aug. 1682 (VR 19; Register 16:153). At first sight she would appear to be daughter of Nicholas[3] Jr., but SD 45:228 makes clear that she is sister of Benjamin mariner, Rebeckah Robinson, and Nicholas (Jr.). Her mother would have been 55, but it is not inconceivable.

She is a child in 1686 (lst church 198). A son STEPHEN[4] LARAUNCE was born to Pachance Laraunce on 10 Dec. 1701 in Dorchester, and died there Feb. 20 1792 (TR 125), aged 2 months 10 days (City Hall Registers, [hereinafter CH], 174). On 15 April 1704 she acknowledged fornication in church (lst church 130).

She is still unmarried on 1 March 1710, but living in Boston (SD 74:89). On 3 Aug. 1710 her intentions to marry THOMAS GA(U)NT were published in Boston (CD 150:26-27?). They were married on that date by Cotton Mather, at Old North Church (CH Book 1646, 46-50). Nothing is known of him or any children.
Gaunt may have died by 1717, for she was married again in Boston on 28 Feb. 1718 to DENIS MACKAHAN of Ireland (CD 150:150:27). By 10 March 1730 she appears as PATIENCE MACMORE of Midlebury Massachusetts (CD 45:228). There is no Middlebury in the state; this is old spelling of Middleboro. Although so named three times in the deed, her signature is recorded as PATIENCE p MAKAHAN, and again as Mrs. PATIENCE MEKAHAN. There is no indication that she is a widow.

She appears to have died before Feb. 1734, as she does not appear as plaintiff with her siblings in the Clifford suit. Middleboro VR show no such name in deaths, marriages or births. We have not checked cemetery records, and records of poor. Suffolk deeds show many references to the name MACKANE or MACCANEY, but none for Patience or Denis. Norfolk Deeds have not been examined.

xii.EBENEZER (II), born 8 Jan. 1684 (VR 31), bp. 23 July 1686 (lst church 196; perhaps delay was due to father's death in early 1685). Again, this seems a very late birth for a mother, about to become 57 on 4 Feb., but is not impossible. SD 45:228 makes clear that he is brother of the other children of Nicholas[2] Sr., mariner Benjamin, Rebeckah Robinson and Patience Macmore (Makahan). He married MARY[2] BUTT. More detail below.

NICHOLAS[3] LAWRANCE, JR. (1662-1712).

Nicholas[3] Lawrance, Jr. was born Dorchester 26 April 1662 (TR 8; Register 16:153), and baptized at the First Church there three days later (lst church 172). We know nothing of his early life before his marriage at age 19, when he may have already fathered a child.

A son William[4] was born 1681, and Nicholas married MARY HARICE (or HARRIS?) in Dorchester 3 Nov. 1681 (TR 24; Register 16:153). We know nothing of this woman; she appears in none of the Harris records of Jones, and is unknown to Gail Harris who has done extensive research on Boston area Harris families. She had died before Nicholas's second marriage on Christmas Day 1689. It is possible that this is a mistaken repetition of his father's marriage.

A solution posed by George Moriarty is that Mary Harris was the second wife of Nicholas Sr., married in 1681, and mother only of the two youngest children, Patience and Benjamin II, and that Nicholas Jr. was married only once, to Abigail Lawrence (George Andrews Moriarty, "Descent of Danvers Pages from the Lawrences of Groton" [typed, 1926, in NEHGS G LAW 680], 5). But this cannot be, since Mary Fry Harris's will of 1656 mentions her daughter Mary Lawrence, as does her husband Walter's will 1654 (see above).

Child, born Dorchester:

i. WILLIAM[4], born 1681, before parents' wedding 3 Nov. 1681. Not in his father's will 1711. No further information. There is a possibility this was son of Nicholas Sr., like Patience II and Ebenezer II, born after this date.

In 1689 Nicholas[3] Lawrance, Jr. married (2) second ABIGAIL[3] (LAWRENCE) WYER, on 25 Dec. 1689 in Charlestown (CVR 151). She was born about 1661 (Sav. 2:62) in Charlestown, daughter of Susana______ and John Lawrence (John[1] of Wisset and Watertown). Her father, a mariner, was born Watertown 14 March 1636 (Sav. 2:61), to the John[1], Sr. who first came to America from Wisset, and ancestor of the famous Lawrences for whom the city is named, the naval captain James ("Don't Give Up the Ship!"), Bishop Lawrence, etc. John[2] was son by his first wife Elizabeth , who died in Groton 29 Aug. 1663 (ibid.). Her mother Susana remarried 15 Aug. 1676 to Thomas Tarbell of Groton, by whom she had children (Sav. 2:62; Bond 821; Wyman 2:606,792).

Abigail Lawrence's first husband was Edward[2] Wyer, born Charlestown to Edward[1] Wyer, a Scot who came to Charlestown by 1658, and Elizabeth Johnson, daughter of William. (William S. Appleton, *Early Wills Illustrating the Ancestry of Harriet Coffin* [Boston: David Clapp, 1893], 76). They were married 1 Sept. 1684 (Ibid., Sav. 4:662; Reg. 25:224). He died shortly after, without children.

By this second marriage for Abigail and Nicholas Jr. there was only one child, ABIGAIL[4], born Charlestown 16 Aug. 1693 (CVR 157), baptized four days later (Reg. 18:122). She died without issue in Charlestown 5 Nov. 1713 (CVR 256; copy in Middlesex Court case Lawrence v. Clifford, below), aged 20:2:9 (gravestone Phipps Street 2 N-27, which reads LARANCE; Wyman 609; Lawrence 1858).

There is a possibility that Nicholas Lawrance was a smuggler. Nicholas Lawrence, master of the ketch *Salisbury* was charged on 17 March 1691 by the Boston Collector of Customs Jahleel Brenton with importing goods from Europe via Berwick, England in violation of the Navigation Act of 1664 (John Noble, comp., *Records of the Court of Assistants of the Massachusetts Bay* [Boston: 1901], 343). He arrived on 9 Feb. 1690 with a variety of cloth (all listed), 40 barrels of powder and 5 hogsheads of nails (344). When brought to court on (date?) the jury found for the customs officer, ordering one third of the ship, guns, ammunition, furniture and apparel awarded to the crown, one third to the Governor, and one third to the customs officer (344). A committee of three was appointed to appraise the ship and goods (356). Lawrence appealed the decision on 9 Dec. 1691 (360).

On 5 July 1692 Nicholas Lawrence was witness to the mortgage of a house on the Boston neck by the distiller Michael Shaller to mariner Duncan Macfarland (SD 16:17, thanks to Gale Harris).

On 5 May 1694 Charlestown selectmen granted to the widow of Nicholas Lawrence a seat in the women's gallery next behind the front pew. (Charlestown Records, 4:124, reel 192; We do not know if this was Mary, now 78 years old, or another Nicholas related to Watertown family)

In 1695 first evidence of property in Charlestown is Nicholas Laurance's purchase from Mr. John Trumball and the heirs of Joseph Ryall of a house, backside yard and garden located as follows: "fronting upon the highway leading towards Mr. Samuel Ballalts SouthWest being from the said ffront eighty four feet unto ye ffouse North East or thereabouts, and in breadth thirty two foot and a halfe or thereabouts and bounded on the NorthWest by the house & ground of William Vine, NorthEast by the Land or garden of Daniel Smith, and on the South East by Land that was formerly John Drinkers..." which he mortgaged on 12 Dec. 1695 to Samuel Leman (Middlesex Deeds 12:466). According to marginal note the mortgage was discharged on July 11 1702 by payment of £25 to Leman. His signature is Nicolas Lawrance.

The same signature of Nicolas Lawrance appears on a court document of 1696 as witness to Capt. Jonathan Marin of Newbury's asking John Phillips Jr. of Charlestown to ask Jonathan Cutler of Charlestown to ship his negro Lawranc for £ 3 on 16 April 1696 (Suff. Co. Supreme Judicial Court, Vol. 40, #3633). Below this his name is spelled Larance in the justice of the peace's evidence taken 9 July 1696.

The following year he was in London, where he testified before an Admiralty court that he was born in Dorchester, New England, where he has lived since his birth, is now 33 years old, born 1664 (*English Origins of American Colonists* [Baltimore: Genealogical Publishing Co., 1991], 182, from New York Gen. & Bio. Registers).

In 1699 he was residing near the wharf in Dorchester (lst church 17).

In 1700 Clapp says Nicholas Lawrence Jr. was on the list of Dorchester inhabitants over 21 (146).

However, on 20 Jan. 1700 Nicholas Lawrance mariner of Charlestown paid £60 to the estate of Mark King (wife Mary) for a house and 1/8 acre of land on the north side of Wapping Row in Charlestown, bounded on the east and north by Edward Wilson and on the west by Col. John Phillips, formerly land of Edward Drinker (Middlesex Court folio 147A-1, document 5 in case *Lawrence v. Clifford*). This was recorded 14 Oct. 1702, copied from Middlesex Deeds 18: 298-300, and figured in the Clifford suit of 1734. We know that this purchaser of land in Charlestown is the Dorchester Nicholas because the property is contested by his siblings, the children of Nicholas Sr. of Dorchester.

On 17 March 1704 he was master of the bark *Endeavor* (Massachusetts Archives 7:259).

On 15 Feb. 1708 he and his wife were admitted to the First Church in Charlestown (Bond 821).

About 1708 Nicholas and Benjamin Lawrence are appointed by Charlestown Selectmen as Surveyors of damaged goods; this is cut off in microfilm; this is from index; go to original mss. (Charlestown Records 6:70, reel 193, Boston Public Library).

In 1708 Lawrance got a liquor permit in Charlestown: "At a Meeting of the Selectmen of Charlestown April 26 1708 Then Mr Nicholas Lawrance had the Aprobation of the select-men to Retail Strong drink out of Doores if the Honor^d Court sees meet to grant A Lycence therfor-" (Middlesex File Vol. 34 X-4, Mass Archives).

In 1710 he is a retailer according to Richard Frothingham Jr., *The History of Charlestown* [Boston: Little, Brown, 1852], 245.

Nicolas Lawrance (note spelling with two As), mariner of Charlestown, made a brief will, on 23 Feb. 1711, naming his wife as executrix and beneficiary: to my wife "Abigail all my Estate Real and personall during her natural life for her Comfortable Subsistence" in Case of want to Sell any part of my Estate rather then she or my daugter Should suffer and I do leave it to the discression of ^my wife to do for my daughter as she shall think proper and hath abillity and the dwelling house and Land if not disposed of for Necessity as aforesaid by my wife or for her Comfortable Subsistence I give it to my daughter Abigaill..." (Middlesex Will 13767). This clause became the subject of the suit by Nicholas's siblings against Abigail's third husband.

Of particular interest on the deed is Nicolas's seal, with the capital letters NL framing a flying swan. Witnessed by James Capen (husband of Abigail's older sister Hannah, Wyman 606), John Toocker and Nathanll Dows.

Five days after making his will, on 28 Feb. Nicolas Lawrance died (VR 230). He was buried in Phipps Street Cemetery, at 2N-26. His slate gravestone has a skull and hourglass, and the words "momento mori...Fugit hora" (remember death...time flies). The inscription reads: "Here lyes the body of Mr. Nicholas Larrance Aged 49 years and 8 months who Departed This Life the 28 day of February 1710/11" (Sec. N is in northwest corner, north of the Harvard Square monument, in second row, 26th stone).

His will was probated 19 March 1712 at Cambridge.

Only a year and a half later, on 5 Nov. 1713, their only daughter Abigail died at age 20 and was buried next to her father under a slate stone with skull and elaborate border, and this inscription: "Here lyes ye body of Abigail Larance Dautr of Mr. Nicholas & Mrs. Abigail Larance Aged 20 years 2 mo & 9 Dayes Died Novmbr ye 5th 1713" (gravestone Phipps 2N-27; VR 56; Wyman 609; Lawrence 1858).

After the death of her daughter (gravestone) Abigail married for a third time to EDWARD CLIFFORD, gunsmith of Charlestown on 1 Sept., 1684 (Wyman 2:606).

She died in Charlestown 11 Feb. 1727 (Coffin 76).

The estate of Abigail came to Middlesex County probate judge Jonathan Remington on 31 March 1729 (Middlesex Wills 4620). He ordered the heirs of Nicholas and Abigail Lawrence to appear. On 7 April Rebekah Robinson and Clifford appeared, and the judge ordered Clifford to administer the estate. On 14 April Remington confirmed this after accepting Clifford's petition: "The Petition of Edwd Clifford of Charlestown, Gunsmith Showeth That Nich^s Lawrence late of sd. Charlestown, Mariner Dec^d being seized of a house & Garden in Charlestown & posessed of a personal Estate chiefly furniture & of no Great Value by his last will dated ye 28th ffeby 1711 after Debts & funerall Charges p^d devised ye Same to his wife Abigail for life & y^t his house & Land after sd.^pl wifes decease in Case not by her Disposed of he Gave to his Daugt. Abigail his only Child as by his will more fully May appear.

That ye sd Petit[ioner]. Inter married with ye sd Abigail sd. widdow & out of his own

Estate paid several Debts of her sd. former husb^{d} as she laid out seveall Sums in repairs.

That Abigail ye Daught^{r} died with^{t} Issue & after^{wds} her sd Mother and ye sd Petit. has been at great Cost & Charge as to their respective Sicknesses & ffunerales.

That upon ye Death of ye Daug^{r} one Moyety of ye sd house and Land at Least remained in her sd. Mother by ye Province Law in fee That De Jure Lett^{r} of Admin appertain to ye sd Petit as to ye Estate of his sd Wife Deceased."

At the bottom of this is endorsed under date of 14 April 1729: "Administration of Estate of said Abigail deceacd is granted to sd Edward Clifford^ $^{\text{her Husband}}$ of Charlestown Gunsmith; Capt. Daniel Gookin & Jon^{n} Nutting Locksmith both of Cambridge Suretys 500 £". Their surety is attached. Exactly a year later Clifford submitted the inventory which is not in the file, but replaced by John Foye's inventory of Clifford's estate dated 5 Nov. 1754, which was submitted by Capt. Edw Wyer as administrator on 13 March 1755. Most of it is tools of his trade, clothing and some cash, but nothing obviously of his wife's. The administrator charged for five years, 3 months and 5 days of work, from 10 July 1749, which gives date of Clifford's death. Middlesex Wills do not contain Clifford's will and probate. However, Msx wills Lib. 35, 303 may contain Abigail's misplaced inventory in docket 4620.

Case of *Lawrence v. Clifford* (1734-5). Benjamin^{3} Lawrence of London and Gosport, was probably out of the country when this occurred, but five years later he and his sister Rebekah Robinson entered suit in Middlesex Court of Common Pleas to eject Clifford and get £ 300 damages (25 Feb. 1724, Middlesex Court Folio 147 A-1; a copy in Suffolk Court #39825, Massachusetts Archives). Benjamin, formerly of Dorchester, now of Gosport, Southampton county England, and Rebecca Robinson of Boston sued for ejection of Clifford from premises on the north side of Wapping Street in Charlestown owned by Nicholas Lawrence mariner of Charlestown on his death 23 Feb. 1711 which he left to his wife Abigail for life, to be sold if necessary, and if not sold to his daughter Abigail. The mother occupied it on his death. Daughter Abigail died in 1713 without issue. The mother having died in 1727, having made no sale, the ownership therefore "belongs to the petits. Brother & Sister of the sd. Nicholas & his Heirs...".

On 2 March 1734 the Court of Common Pleas in Charlestown ruled against them. They appealed and posted bond of ten pounds to be paid to Clifford in default, to be paid by sureties Joseph Hiller of Boston for Benjamin, and Edmund Gosse, Esq. of Cambridge and Joseph Hopkins waterman of Charlestown for Rebecca Robinson. (Suff. Court doc. #4). Clifford's plea not guilty 9 March 1734 adds no new information (Suff. doc. #2). In the court file are Nicholas's deed of 1700 and his will of 1712. Their appeal is dated 26 July 1735, heard by the Superior Court of Judicature in Cambridge 26 July 1735. The decision of the court does not appear. Court costs came to £ 1/6/6 (Suff. Ct. #4 "Recognizance").

We do not know why the will of Nicholas^{3} does not mention property in Dorchester, and refer only to his only child, Abigail. Perhaps other children had died without issue. It is possible that Clifford was not contesting the Dorchester lands, just his inheritance of the Charlestown house from his wife Abigail. If Nicholas had not sold his rights to the other heirs, the implication is that he was not the senior descendant of Nicholas^{2}. We do not know what property the father Nicholas^{2} owned, but we know who his heirs were.

PROPERTY AND HEIRS OF NICHOLAS^{2} LAWRANCE.

Samuel Lawrance became heir of Nicholas Lawrence to several parcels of land in Dorchester, now in Canton, Stoughton, Sharon, Walpole, Wrentham and Plainville. These were parts of old Dorchester, at one time the largest town in New England, extending southwest almost to Rhode Island. The exact division of these lands has never been written, but a summary is given in William Dana Orcutt, *Good Old Dorchester* [Cambridge; John Wilson, 1893] [hereinafter Orcutt], 44-47, 77-79, 114. The sequence is as follows:
1) Original grants 1636;
2) Meadows south of Neponset River, 40,000 acres "Beyond the Blew Hills" 1637, "New Grant" of 1707, including Indian grant of 1666;
3) 12 Divisions, by lot in 1668 [when Nicholas[2] lived in Dorchester], actually divided 1695. Lots were 12 times the holding of 1671;
4) In 1713 Dorchester ordered the remaining land along the Plymouth County line laid out as the 25 Divisions "so called because a Single Division or each Proprietors Proportional part which was determined before the Quantity of Land to be laid out was known, doubled Twenty five times to take up all the Land that was to be laid out" (James Blake Jr, "A Map or Plot of the Twentyfive Divisions", 8 May 1730; the original record is in Norfolk County Registry, with a copy in Foxborough Historical Commission). This was laid out by 1717.
5) Poor land of the 12 Divisions in swamp and meadow were divided 13 Feb. 1726/7.

The first two Dorchester grants do not concern us, since Nicholas[2] did not move to Dorchester until about 1652. Eight pieces of property are involved: 1. Sharon #51 of 12 Div.; 2. Sharon, Patten's #17 of 12 Div.; 3. Walpole #25 of 25 Div.; 4. Wrentham #75 of 25 Div. 5. Foxboro #52 of 25 Div.; 6. Plainville #81 of 25 Div. 7. Stoughton Bear Swamp; 8. Canton Horseshoe Swamp.

1. LAND IN SHARON WEST OF MOOSE HILL SOLD 1710.

On 29 July 1698 Nicholas Lawrance (Sr.) was granted 43 acres and two quarters in the 12 Divisions (*Dorchester Town Meeting & Selectmens Records* [Boston Public Library, rare books MS.BOS.XDI fol., 2:160]. From this we calculate his holding in the original town of Dorchester to be 3.6 acres. About 1699 Nicholas Lawrence resided near the wharf (1st church, 17). We have not found when was this sold.

A copy of the Dorchester Proprietors Book, 146 details the owners of Lot 51 (MHS Samuel Pierce papers, 1764-1820, "A List of the Lots of Land Lying in Stoughton And Dedham": Nicolas Lawrence 43 A, 2 Q; Thomas Pierce 50 A; Moses Aires 18 A; Samuel Hill 18 A, 3 Q. It concludes, "This lot lyes near Jonathan Billings House".

Lot 51 of the 12 Divisions, now in Sharon, southwest of Moose Hill, when surveyed contained 182 total acres which he shared with Samuel Hill (18 acres), Moses Eyers (18½ acres) and Thomas Pierce (98 acres).

Frederic Endicott's copy (Feb. 1891) of James Blake Jr.'s "A Map Plat or Draught of the Twelve Divisions...Dorchester--New Grant...1696 & 1697" of John Butcher (Dorchester, 1727), shows it bounded 118 rods on the north by Peter Lion's Lot 47, 166 rods on the south by Lot 63 of Wm. & Amiel Weeks, 146 rods on the east by the north-south highway (Old Post Rd.), and on the west by Lot 25 of the 25 Divisions later given to the same owners.

On 14 March 1710 48½ acres of woodland were sold by the Lawrance heirs to Thomas Pierce, yeoman of Dorchester. The acreage has expanded by five perhaps because it was larger when actually measured. It is described as bounded by Lyon on the north, Common land on the west, the Rehoboth Road (Pine Street?) on the south, omitting the eastern bounds. This is given in the deeds of Hill and Ayers, as the Country Road (Old Post Rd.), 2 miles west of Ebenezer Billings's farm at Mashapaug (west Sharon; SD 22:217, 219).

Today this lies east of the Walpole line on School Meadow Brook, west of Old Post Rd. west of Pierce Hill from the junction of Walpole Street south to Pine Street Route 1 cuts across the northwest corner diagonally as it rises across School Meadow Brook up the grade toward Boston (USGS, Walpole topographic sheet).

The five grantors were Mary Patten Widow of David Patten of Dorchester, Nicholas Lawrence of Charlestown, Ebenezer Lawrence of Dorchester, Thomas Robinson of Boston, and Patience Lawrence of Boston. These are the three children of Nicholas[2] and two children of Nicholas[3], made clear by the fact that the three wives consented and each one of them "Surrendering up their right and power of one third...Abigail the Wife of Nicholas Lawrence, Mary [Butt] the wife of Ebenezer Lawrence Rebekah the Wife of Thomas Robinson." The fact that Nicholas Junior's brothers are included implies that the land was inherited by right of Nicholas Senior, though he died in 1685, 13 years before the actual division. We have not discovered why Benjamin, brother of the three, who was alive for the Clifford suit of 1734-5, is not mentioned. Perhaps they have given him up for lost at sea, or just assuming they can act without him.

The deed was not recorded until 17 Nov. 1747, perhaps when Thomas Pierce put together the piece to the north that belonged to Lyon (SD 74:93). The document was witnessed by Ebenezer Maudsley, son of Mary[2] Lawrence, b. 1674, and Francis Price. The Register Ezekiel Goldthwaite says that Thomas Robinson Abigail Lawrance Mary Lawrence Rebecca Robinson Mary Patten Nicholas Lawrence Ebenezer Lawrence Patience Lawrence personally appeared before him in 1747, which could not be, since Nicholas died in 1711, Abigail in 1727. and Patience married a few months later in 1710.

2. SAMUEL LAWRENCE INHERITS PATTEN'S LAND IN 12 DIVISIONS.

On 7 Dec. 1785 Samuel Lawrence, tailor of Boston (wife Mary) sold to Samuel Bird, Jr., yeoman of Sharon, for £45 an unplaced piece of land described thus: "the rights of Nicholas Lawrence which fell to him the said grantor by heirship and deed being//in Dorchester new Grant as follows: the Seventeenth lot in the Twentyfive divisions the Twenty fifth lot in the twelve divisions..." (SD 154:81).

Dorchester town records show lot 17 granted to Mr. Patten, 67 acres and a quarter (2:160). In the 12 divisions this represented 5.6 acres of original land in Dorchester village. On Blake's map lot 17 becomes 72 acres, a gain of five in actual survey.

The bounds shown by Blake are a rectangle 62 by 184 rods, bounded on the northwest by lot 16 of Stephen Minot, Widdow George, Wid. Pelton, John Wales, Henry Way and Enoch Whitwell. On the northeast is lot 15 of Will. & Increase Sumner and Jeffrey Turner; on the southeast lot 18 of Price & Tilley, and on the southwest by lot 27 of Sam. Sumner.

Today this is in northwest Sharon, about 100 yards southeast of the Walpole line, between two hills southeast of the junction of US Route 1 and High Plain Street The road between Walpole Heights and Sharon Heights goes west across the parcel (Walpole topo).

Since David Patten had died before 27 Aug. 1696, this was apparently granted to his widow. It would appear that there were no Patten heirs. All of Mary and David's children may have died young. There appear to be no children of Patience Gaunt Mckanan. It is possible that all of Ebenezer[3] and Mary's children died without issue, except for our Samuel. We do not know why Ann Gould not an heir to this land. Samuel appears to have inherited it after all other heirs, including his sister Ann Gould had quitclaimed it. We have not found a previous quitclaim.

This deed may include not only the Patten lot 17, but also Patten's rights in lot 52 (in Foxboro) and lot 81 (in Plainville). The deed's description does not mention either 52 or 81, but it does say "and all his said Samuels as abovesaid falling to him lying and being in Dorchester new grant...". Since 52 and 81 are not abovesaid, I take it that they are not. A search of deeds of sale by Bird (Patten not found before 1800), and by Patten's co-owners (only 2 in lot 81: Allex. Miller and Andrew Pitcher) might reveal the connection.

What is possible, however, is that this deed includes Lawrence's direct inheritance in lot 25 of 12 Divisions.

Bird did not pay for his lot, for on 1 June 1786 Samuel Lawrance, taylor of Boston, brought suit against Samuel Bird, Jr. yeoman of Sharon in the Court of Common Pleas in Boston for recovery of a promisory note of 23 Dec. 1785 (the date of SD 154:81, above) for £15 plus interest, and £30 damages (Suffolk Co. Supreme Judicial Court file 96723, Massachusetts Archives). On 6 June Nathaniel Fisher, deputy sheriff of Suffolk served a summons on Bird, but finding him not at home, left the summons at his house and seized A Chair. William Tudor attorney for Bird claimed he was not guilty, and Lawrance replied that the debt was bad, claiming damages and court costs, thru his lawyer Thomas Dawes. The Court of Common Pleas ruled on 4 July (no holiday) for Lawrance, for £15/7/6 plus costs. Bird appealed to the Supreme Judicial Court in Aug. 1786. The file does not include the judgment, but appears to have gone to Lawrence, from the following document.

On 10 April 1787 Samuel Bird, yeoman of Sharon, quitclaimed to Samuel Lawrence, tailor of Boston, "all the rights of Nicolas Lawrence lying in Dorchester New Grant (so Excepting all that part which I have already Conveyed by deed. This would appear to have given back to Lawrence the Patten lot, but not Bird's other holdings, as damages.

We do not know what were Bird's holdings. On 15 March 1780 his father had sold him five acres of woodland 100 rods northwest of John Johnson's house (perhaps in Stoughton); SD 166:184). We do not know if he sold this before 1787. Bird holdings were extensive thru two brothers Thomas and John, the father of Samuel Sr. Assuming that Thomas's lots did not involve Samuel Jr., in 12 Divisions there were no lots except 30 acres sold to John on Mashapaog Pond, and a possible "Mr. Bird's 47 Acres" between lots 13 and 18. In the 25 Divisions there was only the 11th lot, and the waste lands, unspecified. All of these seem to be conveyed by SD 166:184, which leaves only the five acres to Samuel Jr. Suffolk deeds after 1800 may tell when Lawrance sold this.

3. TWO LOTS IN SOUTH WALPOLE 1713.

The second list in the Samuel Pierce papers is for lot 25 in the 25 Divisions, ordered by the Dorchester Proprietors on 8 Dec. 1727. This lists Nicholas Lawrence as a right to 1½ acre in single division (so-called), "being doubled twentyfive Times" making 37½ acres. The location is given as "in ye west Land among the Twelve Divisions Contiguous to ye 51 Lot...This Lot lyes upon Dedham line, to ye Westward of Jonathan Billinges."

On Endicott's map this shows as two pieces, the larger appears as "Part of Num. 25" east of the Dedham town line granted to Thos. Pierce, Nic. Lawrance, John Smith, John Hill, Moses Eyers, John Pierce and Thos Pierce Junr. SD 74:89 refers to this as "Common Land". The smaller part, of about 45 acres, to the north says "Part of No 25", lying west of the highway and Jonathan Billing's 56 acres, and separated from the larger part by lot 50.

On 10 March 1730 the four children of Nicholas Lawrence [Sr] sold for £47 37 acres of Lot 25 in the 25 Divisions to Ebenezer Robbins of Wharpol (SD 45:228). The deed description is: "all the Land that was Laid out to our Honoured father Nicholas Laurance long since of Dorchester Deceased by the Proprietors of Dorchester and Stoughton in the Twenty fifth lott in the Twenty five Divisions so called late in the Township of Stoughton containing Thirty seven acres laid out by the Proprietors afors'd in Common with the rights of Thomas Pierce and Thomas Pierce jun^{r} and others in the westland so called among the Twelve Divisions contigous to the fifty first Lott..." This agrees with the Endicott map "Part of Num. 25".

Today this lies in South Walpole south and west of School Meadow Brook, north of Pine Street, and east of the old Dedham Line, which parallels Route 1 to the west. South Street runs roughly thru the larger piece, which includes Street Francis cemetery. A smaller piece to the north, of about 40 acres was separated by lot #50 of the 12 divisions owned by Wiat, Sanders and Smith. Today it lies west of Old Post Rd. in Walpole, north of the Gund Cemetery on a hill of about 250 ft. elevation.; this is near the Walpole town forest.

The relation of the owners of this lot is of crucial interest. If we take the text literally "our Honoured father Nicholas Laurance", we have four living children: Benjamin Laurance of London, mariner; Ebenezer Laurence of Boston mariner; Rebeckah Robinson of Boston; Mrs. Patience Macmore/ Makahan of Midlebury Massachusetts The latter is the extinct name of Middleboro, south of Boston. The last name of Patience is inconsistent: Patience Macmore appears three times, but it is signed "Patience p Makahan" and "Mrs. Patience Mekahan" on 30? April 1730. She married Denis Mackahan in 1718 (Boston CD 74:89). Macmore may be a misspelling in the deed. If Patience has remarried we do not know why she still signs Mekahan or Makahan.

We must take the deed literally, and assume that Patience and Ebenezer are children of the elder Nicholas and Mary Harris. That's a childbearing span of 32 years, with the last child born when Mary was 57 years old!

4. TWO LOTS IN WRENTHAM 1713.

Endicott's map shows Nich. Lawrence sharing with Makepeace two lots of the 70th lot of the 25 Divisions, now in Wrentham. The location was then the northwest border the Old Dedham line, west of Burnt Meadow and John Gay's farm on the Wading River, and north of Fishers Mount and Samuel Scot's farm. Today this is near the junction of Route 1 and I-495 (get topo sheet and local street map).

This was granted in 1713. We have not found when the Lawrances sold it, but Makepeace's share was sold to Abigail Hawes et al 12 Jan. 1770 (SD 79:215). This was 76 3/4 acres, or 2/5 of the total of 188 acres=75.2. There is no other record of Makepeace sale, so the remaining 112 acres were presumably Lawrance land. Calculating this as 25 times the original holding we get 4.5 acres against 3.6 in the 12 divisions. The discrepancy may be due to increase in land in actual survey against the original allotment, which would be 90 acres (25 times 3.6)? Since Hales is likely to have bought from Lawrence. A search for Hales as grantor 1770 ff. might give a reference to purchase, as might deeds of abutters (nil for 25/57 Bray Wilkins, 25/71 Roger Clap & Mrs. Way).

On 15 Sept. 1786 Samuel Bird, Sr. and Jr., yeomen of Sharon sold nine acres in lot 70 of the 25 Divisions to Benjamin Hawes (SD 158:241). Since the Birds were not allocated any of this lot originally, they may have got it from Lawrence in a deed separate from the Patten lot in SD 154:81.

5. FOXBORO: PATTEN'S LOT IN 25 DIVISIONS.

If Samuel Lawrence inherited Patten's lot in the 12 Divisions (above #2), one would expect that he had inherited Patten's lots in the 25 Divisions. These are parts of lots 52 and 81, now in Foxboro and Plainville.

If Patten's original lot was 5.6 acres (see 2 above), 25 times would give him 84 acres in the 25 Divisions.

Lot 52 contains 680 acres in a large rectangle across the Walpole-Bristol highway, between the spruce swamp on the Wrentham road to the west, and Round Meadow to the west of where Billings Brook crosses the Plymouth county line on the east. The land is shared with 9 other owners: 4 Hows, Isaac, Israel and Abraham Sr. & Jr.; 3 Trotts:, James, Samuel and Thomas, as well as Benjamin Merrifield and John Minot. A check on the grantor Merrifield to whom sold this land might give a clue who consolidated this land, and refer back to that grantee for sale by Lawrence or Patton.

6. PLAINVILLE LOT 81 OF PATTEN.

Lot 81 contains 169 acres south of the Patuxsit River and James Humphrey's farm on the Wrentham-Attleboro road in today's Plainville, which borders on Rhode Island. He shared this with two others: Allex. Miller and Andrew Pitcher. Deeds of sale by Miller and Pitcher might give further clues.

There is the possibility that this is land of John Patten of Stoughton in SD 118;26-8, 1762-70, but the consistency of reference "Mr." suggests this is inheritance of David Patten of Dorchester.

7. BEAR SWAMP OF STOUGHTON 1727-99.

Finally, Nicholas Lawrence received shares of the poor lands remaining in the 12 Divisions, by the final distribution of 13 Feb. 1726/7. Both Nicholases are by then dead, so his heirs, the surviving children, Patience Macmore, Rebeckah Robinson, Benjamin Lawrance of England, and Ebenezer Lawrance of Dorchester presumably inherited the rights.

In the Samuel Pierce papers is a copy of Lot #10 in the Division of the Cedar-Swamp, now in Stoughton, Nicholas Lawrence having a right of 1i acre in the Single Division (so called), and as it was laid out, being one quarter doubled, of 1 3/4 acre, 20 rods. The location is given: "These two lots were laid out together in Bear Swamp".

This is shown on Blake's map of the 25 Divisions, combining lots 10 and 11, with the northeast border on the Braintree line, and the southwest abutting upland of Thomas Bird Sr. and Jr., James Bird Jr. and Joseph Birch.

On 24 May 1799 Samuel Lawrence, tailor of Boston (wife Mary), sold for $20 three acres of land in Stoughton "left me by Nicholas Lawrance & Ann Gould my sister" to Atherton Wales, yeoman of Randolph. The bounds are Randolph town line on the north, Ephraim Wales on the west, upland of Jonathan Wales on the south, and swamp of Jonathan and Ephraim Wales on the east. This is witnessed by Ann and Sally Rand. (ND 11:7). How did one plus acres expand to three?

That this piece was not included in the description of SD 45:28 (#3 above) indicates that separate deeds should be found for all properties.

Today this lies in the north tip of Stoughton, with Route 138 running west of Bear Swamp, and Route 24 on the east. Stoughton town records will probably give a more accurate description.

8. MEADOW IN HORSESHOE SWAMP, CANTON, 1727-1794.

In the Samuel Pierce papers is a "A List of the Lots in the Division of Meadowbottom, late in ye Township of Dorchester now now [sic] in ye Township of Stoughton containing...what Quantity belongeth to every proprietors Right, Both in a Single Division (So Called) & as it was laid Out, being one half Doubled.. No. Lots 16th...Nicholas Lawrence (single division) 1 acre 2 Q, Doubled one half 2 1q.. The places where ye Lots Lye...In ye Estermost Part of ye Horse Shoe Swamp....A Copy from ye Proprietors Records."

For a change, the same exact amount was sold, on 18 Feb. 1794 by Samuel Lawrance Taylor of Boston, for £ 9 to Joshua Fales, yeoman of Dedham (ND 3:135). No bounds or abutters are given, but described as follows: "at a place called horseshoe swamp as the same lies common & undivided with other rights in the sixteenth Lot in swamp". In Blake's map of the 12 Divisions "Eastermost [sic] part of ye Horse-Shoe swamp" lies east of the Neponset River between Mr. Stoughton's Meadow on the north and Fowl Meadows on the south, with Purgatory Swamp across the river, and Richard Baker's Lot #7 of the 12 Divisions to the east.

Today this lies on the western edge of Canton bordering the Neponset River. The Horse Shoe refers to a conspicuous bend of the river westward into Norwood, with the easternmost part of the swamp lying north of the bend and Turtle Hill. The Boston & Providence Railroad line (later N.Y.N.H.& Hartford) went directly through this swampy area in a bend just south of the Dedham Road in Canton and the railroad bridge over the Neponset River (Frederic Endicott "A Sketch of the Westerly Part of the Ponkapoag Plantation" for Canton Historical Society 1871 from Jim Rouche courtesy of Cynthia Bates of Roslindale 2005).

One could trace the deeds of other shareholders: Thomas & John Pierce, John Smith,

John Hill and Moses Aires [Eyers], but they may not refer to other shareholders.

9. PATTEN'S SHARE OF SWAMP AND MEADOW 1727.

If Lawrance inherited Patten's grants in the 12 Divisions, he probably inherited his wasteland swamp and meadow in the 1727 division. There should be evidence of Lawrance's sale.

RECAP OF LAWRANCE LANDS IN DORCHESTER.

We have record of sale of only four of nine possible Lawrance properties: 1. 51/12 in Sharon to Pierce 1710, 3. 25/25 in S. Walpole to Robbins 1730, 7. Bear Swamp to Wales 1799, 8. Horseshoe to Fales 1794. Still to be searched for are: 2. Patten 17/12 in Sharon after 1787; 4. Lawrance to Hawes after 1730? in Wrentham; 5. Patten's 52/25 in Foxboro; 6. Patten's 81/25 in Plainville; 9. Patten's swamp and meadow in 1727 wasteland. All of these are worth searching since they may give names of Lawrence heirs between Nicholas and Samuel.

EBENEZER[3] LAWRANCE, b. Dorchester 8 Jan. 1684 (TR 31); bp. 23 July 1686 (lst church 196; the delay may be due to his father's absence at sea). Married in Dorchester by Rev. John Danforth 14 June 1705 MARY[2] BUT(T) (TR 105; CH 3).

On 14 March 1710 he sold his share of land in the 12 Divisions, now Sharon (SD 74:89; details above). He is shown as resident of Dorchester, with wife Mary surrendering her claim of one third.

On 10 March 1730 Ebenezer Laurance, mariner of Boston, and his siblings sold their lot 25 in the 25 Divisions of Dorchester (SD 45:228).

In the Suffolk Court of Common Pleas in 1730 we have the case of *Lawrence v. Hayward* (32698, Mass Archives). Ebenezer Lawrence, yeoman of Boston sued Nathaniel Hayward cooper of Boston for payment of £10/8 for 8 barrels of tar sold and delivered by Lawrence on 3 June 1730. Hayward was summoned to court on 21 Sept. for trial on 2 Oct., but the verdict is not given in the file. The verdict may be found in the docket book, which is not always complete.

The deed naming the mariner of Boston is separated from the suit by the yeoman of Boston are less than three months. Perhaps we are not dealing with the same man. Note that the names are spelled differently, Lawrence and Lawrance. One possibility is that they are father and son, but one would expect the distinction of Jr. and Sr.. Perhaps this is the same Ebenezer Lawrance, who has given up the sea. A connection is suggested in the fact that it would be unusual for a farmer have gotten tar, except as a former mariner. There could not have been many places for a yeoman to farm in Boston in 1730.

We have considered the possibility that our Ebenezer is related to the farmers of Wrentham and Franklin, but extensive search by Harry Burbank in the area shows no connection. John[1] Lawrence and wife Mary appear in Wrentham in 1682 (VR 133). A son Ebenezer (James C. Johnson, Jr., *History of Franklin* [Medway: Wayside Press, 1976], 257) and wife Mary have seven children between 1709-1721, when Ebenezer Jr. is born. He married Mary Hawes in 1745, and had Ebenezer, to whom he left his estate in 1751 (Suff. Will 9792). Ebenezer, gentleman, wife Elizabeth left a will in 1766 (Suff. Will 14037). This family lived on the west side of Wrentham, in present day Franklin, and had no connection to the Dorchester lands in the east.

In the Superior Court of Judicature John Sweetser, attorney for Wigglesworth Sweetser shopkeeper of Boston, John Read Esq. and William Rollan, Gent^{n}, both of Boston as Sweetser's sureties appealed the decision of the Court of Common Pleas in Boston on 8 Jan. 1732 for £ 10/3/3 awarded to Ebenezer Lawrence, yeoman of Boston (34667, Massachusetts Archives). The verdict is not given. This may be given in the docket book. Previous *Lawrence v. Sweetser* cases may be found in the index.

The signature of Ebenezer Lawrence appears on a receipt of £ 10 paid by James Pitts in Boston 2 Feb. 1733 (38451, Massachusetts Archives). Pitts, a merchant of Boston, got an attachment of £ 15 by the sheriff of the goods of Ebenezer Lawrence of Roxbury, husbandman, to be tried in the Court of Common Pleas on 11 Jan. 1735. Court costs came to £ 2/18/9, mostly for attendance 17 days, entry fee £ 1, court fees 0/4, writ service 0/5/9. The verdict is not given and may be found in the docket book.

Ebenezer Lawrence entered into an arbitration with Samuel Waldo, assignee for Allen Wilde, in their appeal for eviction of Lawrence from a house in Roxbury (Superior Court in Boston, 43310, Massachusetts Archives). Waldo chose Capt. Robert Temple of Boston, Lawrence chose Capt. Stephen Williams of Roxbury, and the court chose Thomas Tilestone of Dorchester. As a result of the judgment Lawrence agreed on 10 Feb. 1735 (date 6 has been changed to 5, but marginal note says Feb. 1736-7) to evacuate the house and land on or before 26 March 1736. The case is continued below.

On 20 April 1736 Ebenezer Lawrence husbandman of Boston leased the Roxbury farm of William Maccarty victualer of Boston for one year beginning 25 March 1736, including 6 cows, 2 horses and yoke of oxen to be kept on the farm. The rent was one half the produce hy half yearly payments, on or before 25 Sept., and 25 March 1737, half of the money he gets for keeping horses at grass and hay, for sale of all such hay he sells, half of the increase of the cows as they calve (Indenture in Suffolk Supreme Judicial Court docket 41678, index microfilm roll 6). The property included the lean-to or back part of Maccarty's house.

Maccarty obtained a summons from the Court of Common Pleas in Boston on 14 Dec. 1737 against Lawrence, husbandman of Boston (but now of Roxbury) with attachment of £ 100 of his goods (Suffolk Supreme Judicial Court docket 45294). Lawrence gave power of attorney on 22 Dec. 1737 to John Overing (sp.?), Esq. for trial on 7 Jan. 1738. The court's decision is not recorded, but costs were allowed totaling £1/1/6, mostly 10' for attorneys fees , and 6' for three days attendance. A marginal note says: "to abate//Wr.? should have been of Roxbury writ was suit? of Dorchester writ instain? & insufficient?" The docket book should give the result. An almost illegible document appears in a later file in which Ebenezer Lawrence requests abatement, and refers to the stated place of residence in Dorchester instead of Roxbury (Suff. Court 45341; the original should be clearer). The court costs are recalculated to £ 1/12/6, adding four days attendance= 8' and abatement judgment 5'.

Samuel Waldo, merchant of Boston, reopened the case against Lawrence in the Superior Court on 31 July 1738 (Suffolk Court file 47483). He alleged that on 14 Feb. 1736 he had been awarded 20' damages against Ebenezer Lawrence, husbandman of Roxbury, and £ 13/13/9 including costs and charges, which had not been paid, Lawrence was summoned to the Superior Court in Boston on 13 Aug. 1738. Allen Wild, tobacconist of Boston also entered a suit on 29 July 1738 against Lawrence, husbandman of Roxbury, for recovery of £ 4 damages, and £ 9/19 charges and costs awarded by the court on the same day, 14 Feb. 1736 (Suff. Court 47483).

The Sheriff of Suffolk County was ordered on 13 Sept. 1738 to put Lawrence in jail in Boston until he paid the £ 4 damages, £ 9/19 costs and £ 4/19 additional costs, totaling £ 18/18 to Allen Wild, tobacconist of Boston. (Suff. Court 48670).

Ebenezer Lawrance is not in the Clifford suit of Feb. 1734, so he may have died before then. If so, the farmer of Boston and Roxbury may be his eldest son Ebenezer, Jr..

Mary[2] Butt was born Dorchester 18 March 1682 (CH); bp. Dorchester 2 July 1682 (Sav. 1:327); received covenant 22 Dec. 1701 (1st church 121). She was one of six children of Richard[1] Butt and Deliverance Hoppin, the second marriage for both, about 1676.

Richard[1] Butt was born about 1644 in England, perhaps from near Exeter, in Devon, like the Frys (Elizabeth Day McCormick, *McCormick-Hamilton Lord Day Lines* [Chicago: Private Printing, 1957] [hereinafter Day], 190). He married in Boston 1668 to a woman whose name is unknown, and had by her four children, the first Nathaniel[2], born Dorchester, 2 Dec. 1670 (TR). Another son, Samuel, who moved from Dorchester after he and his wife confessed to the sin of fornication on the same day as Patience Lawrence (9 Aug. 1702, 1st church **130?**). He was killed in the collapse of a bridge in Norwich which also killed Josiah Bates, Samuel Lawrence, and Ebenezer Harris (family of John of Brookline; 28 June 1728, Caulkins, 344).

Butt's first wife died by 1676 when he remarried (12) the widow of Robert[3] Woodward (Robert[2], Nathaniel[1]; Reg. 51:169f) who was killed at Pocasset on Cape Cod after Dec. 1675 (*Transcript* 24 Nov. 1930 #661; Harold Woodward, *Some Descendants of Nathaniel Woodward* [Boston: NEHGS, 1984], 8; Torrey). She was left with a baby, Smith[4] Woodward (b.c. 1670-2; Reg. 5:175). Smith married Thankfull[3] Pope (not "Thankful Poop" of Clemens 238) after she confessed fornication before marriage (21 Feb. 1691/2, 1st church 103).

Deliverance[2] Hoppin was born 1645 to Stephen Hoppin Sr. of Thompson's Island, off Dorchester, was in Dorchester by 1653 and Roxbury 1657 (Sav. 2:463; Transcript 4 March 1925 #1528); he testified about the Braintree line of Dorchester 30 Oct. 1666 (Mass Archives 30:1360. His will of Jan. 1676 was probated 9 May 1678 (Suff.Will 958); he died 1 Nov. 1677. She died 22 July 1699, age 54 (gravestone, *Register* 4:170).

Deliverance Hoppin Woodward Butt's mother was Hannah[2] Makepeace, sister of Waitawhile Makepeace, daughters of Elizabeth and Thomas[1] Makepeace, born in England c. 1584-5, who came to Boston in 1635 with Richard Mather on the *James*, and died Boston Jan. or Feb. 1667, aged 73 or 74 (William Makepeace, *The Genealogy of the Makepeace Family* [Boston: David Clapp, 1859]. His will of 30 June 1666 1:518) mentions Hannah and Deliverance Hoppin before her marriage to Woodward.

Thomas Makepeace (elder?) shared lot 70 in the 25 Divisions of Dorchester with Nicholas[3] Lawrance (SD 79:215, now Wrentham.

Despite 20 years' residence in Dorchester Richard Butt did not become a freeman until 18 April 1690 (Day 187). Shortly after, on 30 July he made his last will, as he departed as a sergeant in the expedition to Quebec on which Increase[3] Moseley (first cousin to Nicholas Lawrance also served as sergeant.

Richard Butt died 8 Feb. 1698 in Dorchester (TR) (Edward M. Preston, *A History of Captain Roswell Preston,* [Nevada City, CA: author, 1899], 41).

Ebenezer[3] Lawrance and Mary (Butt)'s children cont. below

i. EBENEZER[4], bp. Dorchester 15 June 1706 (lst Church 219); there is possibility that this is the farmer of Boston and Roxbury, above. One document mentions a wife without naming her (Suff. 41678).

ii. NICHOLAS, bp. Dorchester 27 Aug. 1715 (lst Church 226).

iii. MARY (I), bp. Dorchester 27 Aug. 1715 (lst Church 226). d. before next 1717.

iv. MARY (II), bp. Dorchester 11 Aug. 1717 (lst Church 228).

v. SAMUEL, bp. Dorchester 13 Aug. 1718 (1st Church 228).

?vi.? NATHANIEL, bp. Boston 15 May 1726 (New South 19; mother joined church 15 May 1726, 63).

?vii.? BENJAMIN, bp. Boston 21 May 1727 (New South 20).

Given the gap of eight years between Samuel and Nathaniel, it is possible that the last two are children of Ebenezer[4], but we have no record of his marriage. It is possible that the elder mariner lived in Boston until 1730, and became a farmer that year.

We are at the end of the historical record of the Lawrances of Hingham and Dorchester. Our Anna and Samuel could have been the children of any of the five sons of Ebenezer[3]. We know of no male descendants of other children of Nicholas[2] Sr., so it seems likely that Anna and Samuel are fifth generation, grandchildren of Ebenezer[3], great-grandchildren of Nicholas[2] Sr. from whom they inherited the Dorchester grants.

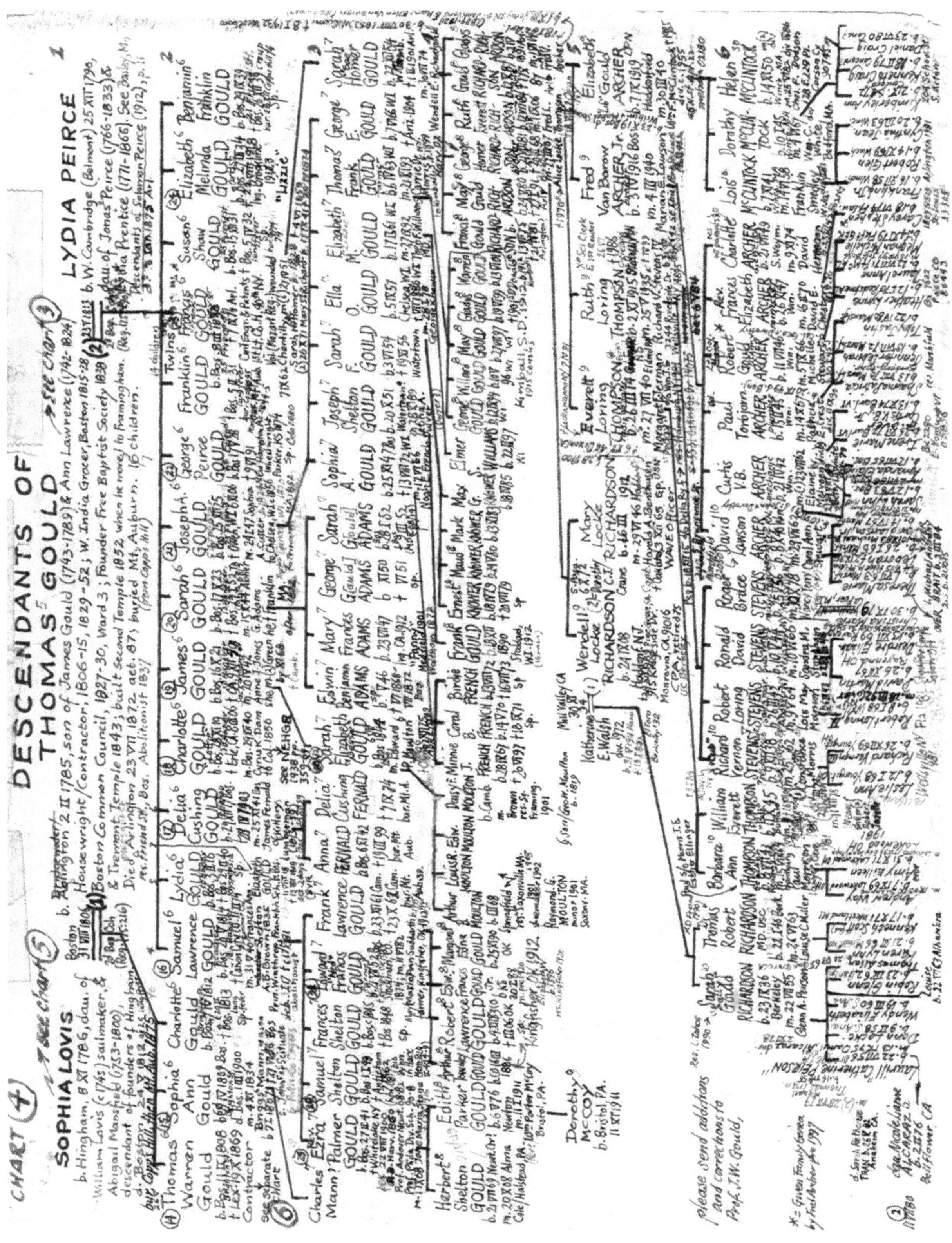
CHART 4
DESCENDANTS OF THOMAS GOULD
SOPHIA LOVIS
LYDIA PEIRCE

Chapter VII

13. Thomas[5] Gould

(1785-1872)

Boston Housewright, Politician & Abolitionist

Thomas Gould was a physically active, homely in appearance, a good Yankee by habit, poorly educated but astute, plain in speech and dress, religiously devout, loyal to family, friends and community, and stubborn in defense of human equality.

Our only portrait of Thomas Gould, when he is about 60, shows a homely man, with craggy features dominated by a bulbous nose, close-set blue eyes, wavy hair, a fringe of sideburns and whiskers below his chin. Our impression of his life is one of physical energy and activity. He surely had a better constitution than his father who died at age 47, or his sons who died younger than his 87. He was still physically active to at least 80, probably inheriting his mother's longevity (Anna Lawrance died at 81). He was manually clever, a Mr. Fixit in little repairs and on big projects like Tremont Temple, a quality he inherited from his pioneer bridge-builder father James. But he also loved working in the garden, perhaps from his years in his teens on a farm in South Reading; he retired to rural Framingham to tend his own garden, with fruit trees and hay-mowing.

At work Gould comes across as the typical good Yankee. He was frugal with resources, like writing letters on scraps of paper with pencil. He was conscientious about obligations, paying debts on time, or early, and probably demanding the same of others, so he got on fine with the murdered Dr. Parkman.

Gould was a wealthy man, ranking in the "upper class of Bostonians, according to Knights' study of the period of Gould's activity (Peter R. Knights, *The Plain People of Boston, 1830-1860* [NY: Oxford Univ., 1971], 89; from 1832 to 1866 Gould's real estate in Ward 3 alone, not counting his property in other wards, Charlestown, Framingham and Arlington came to over $10,000, Knights' cutoff, and went over $50,000 by 1851). But he was one of Knights' success examples, having started in 1807 with $1200, which made him upper middle class. Gould started with the advantage of a fifth generation Bostonian on both sides of his family, the Goulds having gone from the top of society in 1689 to genteel poverty in the third generation, but remained always in the skilled craftsman category. His mother's family went back farther to landowners and artisans. There is no evidence that Gould used family connections with the Brahmins, but he was surely part of the Boston upper class.

Thomas Gould was poorly educated, but literate. His spelling and grammar were about grade school level, which he apparently got from attending night school. But he treasured education, and paid for his children to get the best he could afford. His second son Samuel was the first in the family to go to college. He sent him to Colby and Brown, to become one of Boston's eminent schoolmasters. He sent his son George to New Hampton Academy. He sent sons James and Francis to Boston High, which the latter completed, to become an engineer. All of the other children completed grammar school.

He was plain in dress and speech. We can catch his Boston dialect in his letters where he spells Wartertown phonetically. His manner was probably direct, and perhaps tactless.

Gould had a strong set of values. He was religiously devout, a life-long Baptist of the plain New England sort. With this went Puritanical morals: T-total no alcohol, no frivolities like gambling or theater, but lover of plain prayers and uplifting sermons. Was life without enjoyment? No, fun was at home, in doing a competent job of building, working in the garden, and working for the good of the community.

He was an active politician, holding jobs of Assistant Assessor three times, Overseer of the Poor, and Member of the Boston Common Council. His politics appear to be moderately liberal. He was patriotic, naming two sons for the Boston born Benjamin Franklin, seeing a son wounded as a first lieutenant at the battle of Chantilly, and a grandson killed at Antietam. He probably annually celebrated the Battle of Bunker Hill, whose hero's name Dr. Warren he gave to his eldest son.

Gould was loyal to friends, and family, and city. Unpretentious in manner, he rarely got called "gentleman" in deeds, preferring the title "housewright", and is always called by the assessors by his first occupation, "carpenter".

He was stubborn on principle, especially of equality. He went beyond the radical abolitionists in establishing a community with Boston Blacks, by setting up the first integrated church in America, and taking the lead in giving the hand of friendship to Blacks. He made equality a physical reality by abolishing the box pews based on wealth, to establish a circle of benches of equals. His concern for the poor is evident, too.

Thomas[5] Gould was born 2 February 1785 at 338 Adams Street, North Abington MA. He was the ninth and youngest of nine children of Anna Lawrance (1742?-1824) and James Gould (1749-1791), wheelwright and bridge builder. A few months after his birth his father began work as foreman on the construction of the Boston-Charlestown bridge. The family sold the Abington house and bought property in Charlestown, where they probably moved in late 1785, when Thomas was but a few months old. He grew up in the house his father built on the east corner of the Training Field, at 25 Common Street He could not have remembered the great Bunker Hill Day celebration in 1786 when his father marched at the head of the column to open the wonderful Charlestown Bridge, but his brother, three sisters and mother must have celebrated it.

When Thomas was five his father went to Ireland to build the bridge at Londonderry (1790). James Gould died soon after his return in 1791, leaving his widow Ann with five children age six to 22. The eldest, Nancy, married that year to a carpenter James Davis Turner, but was soon to have her own family to care for. The eldest son, Joseph, age 21 was helping to support them by his earnings as carpenter, and Nabby (Abigail) at 17 was able to work. We do not know if Ann Gould worked, hut she was poor enough to get a tax abatement for several years.

Thomas's daughter wrote about her father: "There were but small means for the family support, so that at an early age the mother consented at his own earnest wish, to allow her son

Thomas to take a place as errand boy. Two such positions, he held for a time, then went to be a farmer's boy on a farm in South Reading, enjoying there the country life." ("Account of Life of Thomas Gould, prepared by his daughter, Elizabeth M. Gould, in February, 1913", l).

Of his education we know only that "Later he went to Boston to learn the carpenter's trade, serving an apprenticeship, attending also, for a while an evening school, greatly to his mother's satisfaction, she having much regretted her inability to give her boy larger advantages of education." It would seem logical to work with his elder brother Joseph as carpenter, but he lived in Charlestown, not Boston (the second Joseph Gould appears in Charlestown assessor's records in 1803, but he is difficult to distinguish from Wyman's #24 (429) who was also a carpenter and Deacon of the Universalist Church; Charlestown Tax Records, Tax Book, 6, 1803, again 1811-1825 in 11).

Elizabeth concludes, "At twenty-one [2 Feb. 1806] he was ready to establish himself as a master builder, and also set up a home of his own, in a small house, he had bought in Boston, bringing thither his wife, Sophia Lovis of Boston the marriage taking place May 1806."

Sophia, daughter of a Hingham sailmaker William Lovis and his wife Abigail Mansfield, were married at the Second Baptist Church in Boston on 31 Aug. 1806 (Reg. 75:216) This was in the North End, on the present site of the Knights of Columbus on North Margin Street This wooden building, built in 1746, had been enlarged in 1788 and 1797, had a broad aisle at the head of which was a baptismal font or cistern where church members were baptized (Abel Bowen, *Bowen's Picture of Boston* [Boston: Abel Bowen, 1829], 142. Since both Thomas and Sophia were raised in the Congregational church, their adult baptism would have taken place here. The old wooden church was torn down in 1810 and replaced by a new brick structure 80 by 75, with a tower 38 by 18. The church records are missing for this period so we have no record of construction, but it seems likely that Gould would have lent his skills as housewright to the construction, and celebrated the dedication on New Year's Day 1811.

The minister of the Second Baptist Church was the famous Rev. Thomas Baldwin, from 1790-1825. There was a friendly rivalry with the First Baptist Church under Samuel Stillman, only three short blocks away. Although the congregations celebrated holidays together, the difference was mainly political, "the Federalists naturally went to Stillman Street and the Democrats to Baldwin Place" (Rev. Henry King in Winsor, 3:423).

This gives us a clue to Gould's politics. In the early development of American parties, the Democrats were the party of Jefferson, against the more conservative Federalists of John Adams. Gould would have voted in his first presidential election in Dec. 1808 for James Madison, supporting the Jefferson Embargo which was so unpopular among the merchant class of Boston. The hot political issue of the day was Jefferson's use of nonviolent means to deal with the threat of war.

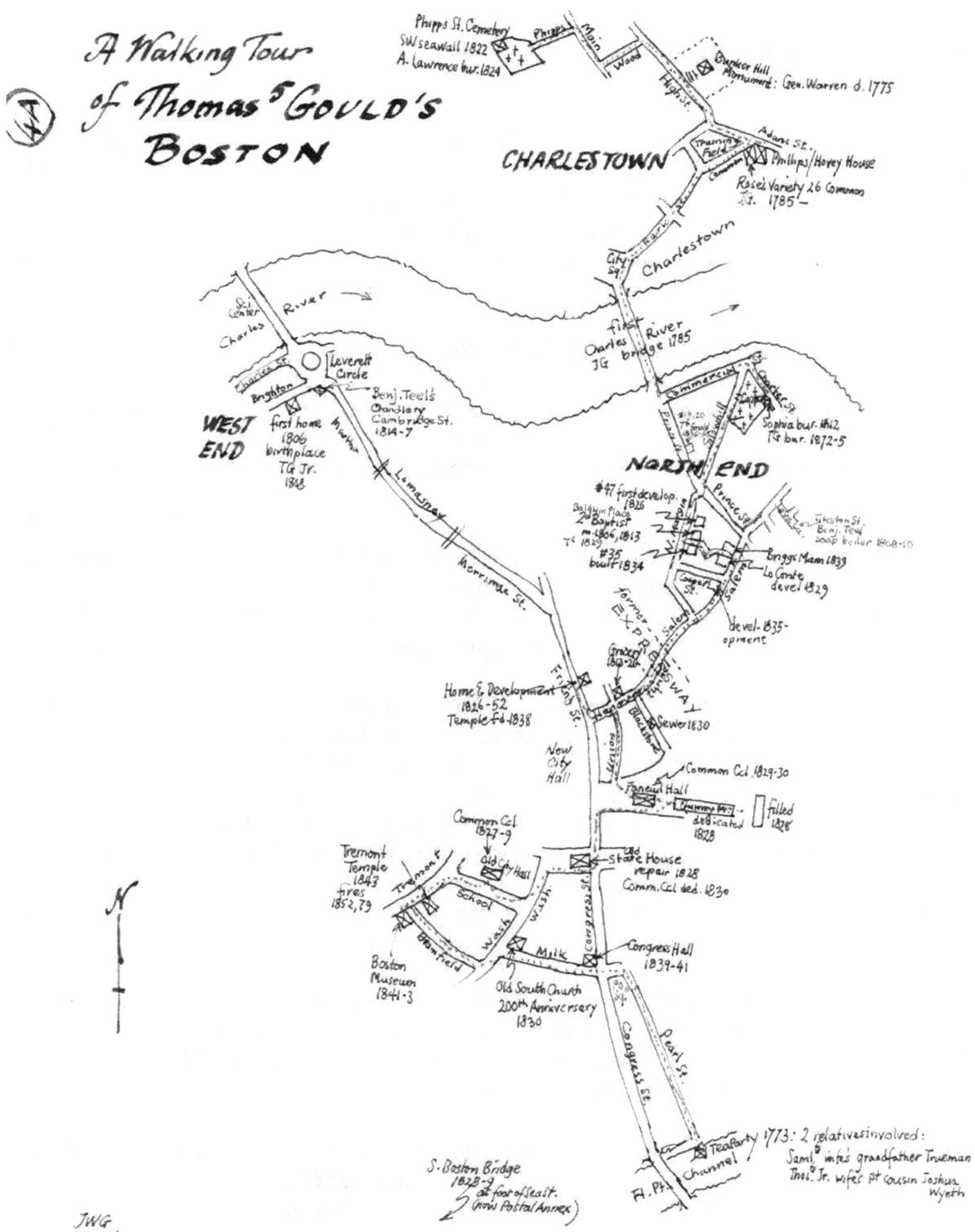
A Walking Tour of Thomas Gould's Boston
Phipps St. Cemetery
SW seawall 1822
A. Lawrence bur. 1824
Phipps
Main
Wood
High St.
Bunker Hill Monument: Gen. Warren d. 1775
Adams St.
Training Field
Common
Phillips/Hovey House
Rose's Variety 26 Common St. 1785
CHARLESTOWN
Park St.
City Sq.
Charlestown
Charles River
first Charles River JG bridge 1785
Sci. Center
Charles St.
Brighton
Leverett Circle
Benj. Teel's Chandlery Cambridge St. 1814-7
WEST END
first home 1806 birthplace TG Jr. 1818
Lomasney
Merrimac St.
Commercial St.
Copp's Hill
Charter St.
Sophia bur. 1812
TG bur. 1872-5
NORTH END
Prince St.
#47 first develop. 1826
Baldwin Place
2d Baptist m. 1806, 1813
TG 1829
#35 built 1834
Briggs Mam 1833
LeConte devel 1829
Cooper St.
Salem
devel-1835-opment
former EXPRESSWAY
Grocery 1813-26
Home & Development 1826-52
Temple Fd 1838
Friend St.
Hanover
Blackstone
Union
Sewer 1830
New City Hall
Common Ccl. 1829-30
Faneuil Hall
dedicated 1828
filled 1828
Common Ccl 1827-9
Old City Hall
Old State House repair 1828
Comm. Ccl ded. 1830
Tremont Temple 1843 fires 1852, 79
Tremont
School
Wash.
Bromfield
Boston Museum 1841-3
Milk
Congress St.
Congress Hall 1839-41
Old South Church 200th Anniversery 1830
Pearl St.
Tea Party 1773: 2 relatives involved:
Saml. wife's grandfather Trueman
Thos. Jr. wife's 1st cousin Joshua Wyeth
Channel
Ft. Pt.
S. Boston Bridge 1828-9 at foot of Sea St. (now Postal Annex)
N
JWG 18 IV 94

Part I: Thomas Gould's Homes and Landholdings
WEST END OF BOSTON

Only 17 days after his wedding to Sophia Lovis in Boston, he bought his first property. He paid the distiller Jonas Reed $1200 for a house in the West End, on Copper Street (later called Brighton Street), an area that was completely obliterated by redevelopment of the fifties, and now a park to the south of Leverett Circle near the Science Museum. The name of the street came from a colonial copper refinery at the north point of Boston. Gould later sold a well on his property, indicating the source of water. How polluted was the water by copper tailings?

We have the exact dimensions of the Gould's first house in Boston: 23 feet by 14 feet, with a door on the west courtyard, between two windows on the right (south) and one window to the left. (Plan in SD 217:41). A partition is drawn east west, giving two fifths to the north part entered by the door, a room about ten by fourteen. We can speculate that this was the living room, with the south three fifths, about 13 by 14 the bedroom. No height is shown, but a second floor is likely.

The house faced west onto a back courtyard ten feet from the house on the street, approached by a five foot wide passageway on the south side of the street house 44 feet in from the street. Gould mortgaged the house the day after the sale to the seller, Jonas Reed, for $200 less than his purchase price, $1,000 (SD 217:56) and finally discharged in 1821 (SD 217:56).

In the Boston Directories for 1807 to 1813 Thomas Gould housewright is listed as living on Copper Street, probably at this house. Therefore it is likely that it was here that his three children by Sophia Lovis were born, and that she died here. The first born was Thomas[6] Warren Gould, born 11 Feb. 1808. He was the first Gould to be given a middle name. Since there are no Warrens in the ancestry, it seems probable that he was named for the martyred hero of the battle of Bunker Hill, General Joseph Warren, who died close to the Gould homestead in Charlestown, at a battle celebrated by the opening of James Gould's bridge to Boston. However, Thomas[6] never used the middle name, always signing Thomas Gould Jr.. His son Thomas[7] Warren Gould signed Thomas Gould Jr., and his son Thomas[7] Warren Gould always called himself Warren.

Thomas[5] Gould was evidently successful in house building business, for in less than three years he bought his second property, also on the south side of Copper Street He paid Samuel Whitney, a housewright, $600 for house on a lot 20 by 62 feet to the south of Thomas Hunstable (SD 230:56; 23 Sept. 1809). We have not found when was this sold.

Three of the five Gould family died at young ages. Thomas[6] Warren Gould died in 1869 before his father, and his sister Charlotte died at less than a year of age (of lung fever), his other sister Sophia Ann Mann lived to be 91. Their mother, Sophia was only 25 when she died, on 24 May 1812, probably at the Copper Street house. She was first buried at Copp's Hill in the North End, probably at the east end near the Mathers' graves, hut moved with her husband's body to Mount Auburn in 1875.

Thomas[5] Gould remarried within a year (23 May 1813) to Lydia Peirce of West Cambridge

(Belmont), daughter of Jonas[2] Peirce (Solomon[1]) and Lydia Prentiss (Marietta P. Bailey, *Descendants of Solomon Peirce* [Arlington MA: G. H. Ellis, 1912], 11). They moved about 1835 to the center of town to open a West India Grocery (*Boston Directory* 1815; 1814 or 1815 per Elizabeth Gould). Nevertheless he continued his interest in the West End real estate until 1835 at least.

In 1816 he bought a lot fronting 31 feet on Brighton Street in front of his former residence for $300 (SD 252:195). Within a year he had sold the street half of the property to widow Lydia Dunham for $450, a gain of $150 probably representing his building own houses house here (SD 255:257).

In 1818 he had sold the inner half (SD 259:74) to the Rev. Francis A. Matignon, the second Catholic priest in Boston, who had arrived in 1792, having fled from his post as Regius professor of divinity at the College of Navarre during the French Revolution (Winsor 3:516). Matignon may have died in Gould's house, on 19 Sept. 1818, and was buried in Old Granary (Winsor 3:519). The price was $475, for a profit of $625 to Gould for both properties, probably representing his construction of two new houses.

Gould became involved in the great expansion of Boston by filling in the surrounding mudflats. His first interest in the land on the northwest side of Brighton Street, then still mudflats of the Charles, began in 1823. He bought 52 feet two inches on the street, and the same distance on the low watermark of the Charles between two lines paralleling Leverett Street (SD 283:158-161). He paid a total of $600, part to Scollay's heirs, including Dr. Jacob Bigelow, the famous scientist, then professor at Harvard Medical School, botanist, lecturer on technology, and founder of MIT and Mt Auburn Cemetery (Winsor 4:21, 567, 275), who transplanted the rare gingko tree from Gardiner Greene's garden on Beacon Hill to the Common (ibid., 611).

In 1824 Gould foreclosed on the mortgage on the property across the street, belonging to mason Thomas Hunstable with 63 feet ten inches on the street and on low watermark. The public deposition tells that Gould's North End partner Ezra Hawkes and Isaac Bowman called on his widow Susannah Hunstable, administratrix, "she was absent, but we saw her daughters, and said Gould informed them he was going to take possession of the Estate in Brighton Street which Mr. Hunstable had formerly mortgaged to Col. William Scollay deceased. We then repaired to the premises where the Mortgage Deed was exhibited to us and an Assignment of said Deed to said Gould and also an assignment of the judgement recovered by Catherine Scollay the Administratrix of said Col. William Scollay, against said Hunstable in his lifetime, upon the Bond mentioned in said Mortgage deed. Mr. Thomas Gould there being no opposition, took quiet and peaceable possession of the premises described in said Deed. We remained on and near the premises nearly one hour, and then Separated and returned to our respective places of business. And further your deponents say not, excepting that we left him in quiet and peaceable possession of said premises." (SD 265:270, 18 May 1824). Scollay had sold the lot to Hunstable (SD 207:275) who stable at the same time mortgaged it to Scollay (SD 207:278). Catherine Scollay, as administrator of her husband's estate, assigned the mortgage to Gould for $200 in 1823 (SD 283:159).

Gould then leased the waterfront for whale oil storage. He rented out a plot 50 feet deep to low watermark (60 feet on the water) for $18 a year in 1829 for ten years to oil dealer William Mills (who owned the flats to the north) (SD 345:301; 348:228). In 1832 he sold the land to Jesse P. Richardson, gentleman for a total of $3500 (a $2,900 gain on his original investment of $600 in 1823). This land was of course valuable for future expansion of Boston, in this case for new Auburn Street and North Charles Street His son Samuel Lawrence Gould, now 17 years old, was witness.

In the meanwhile, he had mortgaged the old homestead with more accurate measurements (SD 348:113) 1835, when he sold it to planemaker James Stevens for $1100, a hundred dollars less than he had paid in 1806 (SD 392:184), (though he gained rent for twenty years from 1815 to 1835).

This effectively ended Thomas Gould's interest in the West End except for a two year possession of a small (10 by 28) back lot off South Margin Street, now underneath the east wing of the State Service Center on Merrimac Street In 1839 he paid $370 for the lot with buildings and passageway to the estate of James Bullard of Sherburne (SD 439:201). In less than two years he sold it for $500 to Thaddeus Monroe, yeoman of Lexington (SD 469:212).

GOULDS' HOME IN CENTRAL BOSTON

For over a third of a century, from about 1814 to 1852, Thomas[5] Gould lived in the heart of Boston, just a block north of Faneuil Hall. Following his marriage to Lydia Peirce in 1813, he moved with his two little children and their new stepmother to # 10 Hanover Street, at the corner of Union Street where he ran a West India grocery from 1814 to 1825 (Eliz. Gould; Boston Directories for 1816 to 1821 list him as grocer at number ten Hanover Street).

His daughter told the reason for change of occupation: "A time of great business depression, extending through several years [1807-1815] had arisen from the troubles with England which culminated in the War of 1812. New York and New England being [?most affected by the depredations on the merchant fleet?] building operations were at a stand still. Thomas Gould seeing what seemed to him a favorable opening in West India goods and grocery business, opened a store for that business on the corner of Union and Hanover Streets, 1814 or 15, removed his family, not long after, to apartment in same building, continuing the business and his residence here until 1828-9..." (E.Gould, 1-2).

He rented the buildings from Abraham Babcock and may have done some improvements in 1822 Boston Assessors Records, Readville, Valuation book, Ward 3, 1822-3, 15; [hereinafter Ward 3]. This probably places the store and home on the north side, perhaps in the northeast corner, now the empty parking lot across from the Blackstone Block.

Here were born the first seven children: Samuel, Lydia, Delia, Elizabeth, Charlotte, James and perhaps Sarah. Thomas Gould's first purchase in the area was in 1821 when he bought a small lot of 37 feet on the east side of Friend Street, only 18 feet deep, with all the buildings standing on it from widow Ann Hunt for $290 (SD 273:154). By 1874 much of this block had been obliterated by the extension of Washington Street northwards into Haymarket and Friend

Street extended a block south into Dock Square. Thus, Gould's lands and homes in mid-century were located in what are today open parking lots east of the JFK Federal Building. By 1824, when he is first taxed in Ward 3 Gould's land is shown as worth $1200 on Merrimac Street (the north side of the same block), with two tenants, carpenters A. S. Johnson and Charles Roath indicating that he had built on this property, perhaps a multistoried house (Ward 3, 1824, 16).

The grocery may have failed by 1822, for in that year the directory shows him back as housewright at the same address, 10 Hanover Street In 1825 his house is at 74 Hanover Street and office at Union Street The next year the business is still on Union, but the residence is changed to Friend Street His daughter says that he changed his house and business in 1828-9, which is later than the records. Elizabeth states that as contractor he made "the family home in a house, newly built on a property he had bought on Friend Street, a considerable estate here stood several wooden dwelling houses, and where he erected four of brick, taking the first finished for his own occupancy [# 25, to north, in Business Directories 1828-36], afterwards removing from that to another of the four buildings [# 19 Friend 1837, # 21 Friend 1841-9] , the rest for rental." (2). The First Baptist Church moved to a new building on the corner of Union and Hanover Streets in June 1829 (Winsor 3:424).

Four years later, in 1825, he bought a larger lot on the same side of the street, probably closer to Faneuil Hall, from trader Washington Monroe for $1360 (SD 301:295). On this site with only 20 feet frontage on the street he was to build a house. Margaret Cooper, a widow of Andover, paid him $1000 to finish a brick house (SD 304:113), which he promised to repay in two years. The mortgage was paid off four and a half years later, in 1830. But seven months after the first mortgage he took a second one for $500 from Margaret Bradstreet for two years (SD 307:126). This deed for the first time refers to a hack building which he may have built in the meantime. The appreciation of value of the house is shown by the fact that four days before paying off the mortgage to Mrs. Cooper, Gould re-mortgaged it for $2600 to merchant Asa Richardson including a quarter interest in the well on Friend Street that he shared with his neighbor to the north, Charles Holmes (SD 344:287). He was to pay 6 % interest that was customary for the period, and to insure it against fire for $2000. His daughter Sophia Ann, now aged 21, was witness. The mortgage was discharged five years later by Richardson's estate. On the same day he re-mortgaged it with "brick dwelling and other buildings" for $ 3400 to Hannah Barker, a single woman, and widow Eliza Aplin, which he discharged two years later (SD 389:162). Six months later, in Oct. 1837 he again mortgaged it but for $ 4000 for two brick buildings and a wooden one, with privileges to a court laid out by me leading into Friend Street from the Jennings estate in back which he had bought in 1835 (SD 425:114). He agreed to pay William Faxon, gentleman, 6 percent interest and insure it for $2400. Faxon's executor Ellis Gray Loring, the well-known abolitionist lawyer, assigned the mortgage in 1854 to William Faxon of Cambridge, probably a son (SD 678:186).

Boston assessor's records show him in a $3400 house on Friend Street from May 1827 to May 1834. The new brick buildings appear between 14 May 1834 and 4 April 1835, valued at $4000, and rented to blacksmiths Artemas White, William McGinnis, Joseph Tulls and Henry Farell (Ward 3 1835, 45).

In 1845 the north boundary of this lot was straightened in an exchange of four tiny triangles with the estate of Charles Holmes (SD 587:214, 588:232). The plan in both deeds shows the exact location and approximate size of ten foot width on the plan on both deeds "T. Gould's House rear of his on Friend Street", the latter being number 25. We now know that he lived at this from 1828 to 1836 (Boston Directories), where his daughter says he built four brick houses 1828-9, changing his business from the old Union St site (Directory 1825-7). Here he moved with his seven children, Thomas, Sophia Ann, Samuel, Delia, Charlotte, James and Sarah, and here were born five more children: Joseph, George, the twins Franklin and Francis, Susan and on Friend Street for his home, but it may have been at this site at which he built the house for widow Cooper in 1825.

While Gould was on the City Council in 1829 he considered returning to the grocery business in the area, requesting leave to set up a shop over Mill Creek, which was shortly covered over by Blackstone Street as a menace to health (7 Sept. 1829; *Columbian Centinel* 9 Sept.). The permit was apparently denied, for he continued in his business as housewright on Merrimac Street from 1828 to 1836, at an undisclosed spot, perhaps in the same block as his house, but facing north on Haymarket Square (Boston Business Directories 1828-36).

In the meanwhile, in 1831, Gould had bought a larger lot at 19 and 21 Friend Street He bought two parcels with a frontage 47 feet two inches on the street, going back 86 feet to the back to the site of the famous Green Dragon Tavern. This was called by Daniel Webster "Headquarters of the Revolution", for at this place the organizers of the Boston Tea Party met, later the patriot patrollers of British troop movements, and the North End Corpus which gave the word caucus to the language; Dr. Joseph Warren was Grand Master of the first Masonic Lodge which met here. In the back yard of the Inn the boy Benjamin Franklin achieved one of his first mechanical feats, building a stone wharf, as described in his autobiography (Shurtleff 611). The inn had been torn down in Oct. 1828 for the widening of Union Street to give access to Haymarket and the Charlestown bridges (Winsor 3:64n.; Bacon, Edwin M., Boston: *A Guide Book* [Boston: Ginn, 1903] [hereinafter Bacon] 55; Harris, John, *Historic Walks in Old Boston* [2d. ed., Chester Ct.: Globe Pequot Press, 1989] [hereinafter Harris] 236-7).

Gould bought these two lots at public auction advertised in the Boston Advertiser on Jan. 31 1831, making the highest bid of $3000, paid to Susanna, widow of Joseph Couthouy, master mariner of Nantucket (SD 351:177). At the same time Gould bought separately the house on the site for $1000 (SD 351:179). In a month and a half Gould quitclaimed both house and land for the same price, $4000, back to Susanna Couthouy (SD 351:180), which she at once mortgaged to Nathaniel Williams for $2000 (SD 351:181). But three years later in 1834 Susanna Couthouy sold Gould the same land on Friend Street for $4000 subject to a mortgage to the Hospital Life Insurance Co. which Gould assumed (SD 384:85) 1835 was the peak of Gould's real estate activity, with 13 transactions in Boston and one in Charlestown. In that year he bought his fifth parcel on the northeast side of Friend Street between the second and third purchases, with nineteen feet on the street, and forty feet on the back at the Green Dragon Tavern site (SD 393:269). He paid $2000 at auction to Richard G. Wait, administrator of the estate of blacksmith Benjamin Jennings.

The big building development took place between April 1835 and June 1836, when Gould improved the Friend Street valuation from $7000 to $25,600 by laying out a new courtyard in back, called Sumner Place (Boston Street book, 350 locates it north-south between Hanover and Sudbury) with new brick buildings on Friend Street (Ward 3, 2). Gould's choice of the name Sumner may be an early appreciation of the statesmanship of Charles Sumner (1811-74), later to become the leading American political abolitionist, advocate of peace and nonviolence, and public education. At this time he was only 25, practicing law in Boston in nearby Court Street.

Sumner Place was rented to a tailor, painter, truckman, broker, watchman and assistant, in three properties valued at $6000 and two for $2000. #21 Friend, the most expensive site, worth $6500, Gould leased to Joseph Locke for a provisions shop. # 23 was rented to a painter and bookbinder. #25 was let to George H. Horn selling "galvanic instruments" (i.e., electrical gauges) and a watchman. He had eleven tenants and a home for his family.

The turnover in tenants was rapid, typical of the mobility of Boston's population, which Knights says may seem "incredible" (57). All the previous year's renters are gone, now replaced by two hardware stores, one specializing in stoves, a printer, and his son-in-law Briggs Mann, a mason who moved from the North End into what was perhaps a vacant space (Ward 32, 1837, 50). The vacancy rate is a reflection of the Panic of 1837, in which the real estate boom collapse led the depression into the mid-forties.

Despite the real estate collapse, in May 1838 Gould was building a "new brick dwelling" on twenty foot frontage on Friend Street that he had got from Couthoy and Wait, 57 feet deep on a "passage laid out by me" on the south side (SD 431:242). He was able to mortgage this to Katharine Dexter for $3,000 at 6 %, insured for $2000. She assigned the mortgage (SD 495:81, 716:95), and it was finally paid off in 1857 to W. H. Gardiner, acting for the historian and cousin of Gould's, William Hickling Prescott.

Gould's printer tenant stayed with him for three years, but the others were replaced by a dry goods shop run by William Troup who rented until 1845 or later, a gentleman Benjamin Goldsmith who stayed until 1841, and a transient laborer. Gould's son Samuel, the school teacher, moved into one of the vacant houses, and Briggs Mann stayed on (Ward 3, 1838, 43).

At the end of 1838 Gould mortgaged his house at number 19 Friend Street on an 1100 square foot lot with 20 ft. on the street, backing on the site of the Green Dragon, between a seven foot passageway to the north, and 87 feet on the south (SD 437:134). He took the mortgage of $2000 at six percent interest from an infamous lender, Dr. George Parkman, the victim of Boston's most famous murder case, in 1849. Our distant cousin, Cleveland Amory, described him in *The Proper Bostonians* [Boston: Dutton, 1947] 208 ff.): "He was a merchant at heart, one of Boston's wealthiest men, and he spent his time in the Boston manner keeping sharp accounts of his money--and a sharp eye on his debtors. He had many of the traits of character peculiar to the Proper Bostonian breed. He was shrewd and hard, but he was Boston-honest, Boston-direct and Boston-dependable. It was hard to like a man like Dr. Parkman because his manners were curt and he had a way of glaring at people that made them uncomfortable...There was no use speaking to Dr. Parkman before he went by. If you weren't his friend Dr. George Shattuck, or his brother-in-law, Robert Gould Shaw, Esq., or a Cabot or a Lowell, or perhaps a man who owed him money--and then, as someone said, God help you--the doctor would ignore you. Dr. Parkman had no need to court favor from anybody. The Parkmans cut a sizeable chunk of

Boston's social ice in 1849...a nephew of the doctor, Francis Parkman, had just published his first book and was on his way to becoming what Van Wyck Brooks has called "the climax and crown" of the Boston historical school. The Parkmans were in the Boston fashion well-connected by marriages. Dr. Parkman's sister's marriage with Robert Gould Shaw, Boston's wealthiest merchant, was a typical First Family Alliance."

Dr. Parkman was murdered at Harvard Medical School in the West End by a hounded debtor, Professor John W. Webster, who was proven guilty in a famous trial and hanged in the Leverett Street Jail in the West End in 1850.

Gould clearly had no problems with the demanding Dr. Parkman, for the mortgage was not paid off in advance according to the deed, 1837, perhaps an error for 1857 (SD 647:134). A decade later Gould went back for more from the Parkmans, and got a second $1000 mortgage on his house at 19 Friend Street from the Rev. Francis Parkman, brother of the murdered man, who had bought the doctor's first mortgage for $2000 (SD 647:237). On the minister's death in 1853 Gould's mortgage was assigned by his executors, his widow and son of the famous historian, to George R. Russell, Esq. of Roxbury and William P. Atkinson, gentleman of Brookline, who finally discharged the mortgage in 1857 (Ibid.). Gould obviously had good credit with the best lenders in Boston.

During the depression of 1837-45 Gould's tenants increased in the Friend Street houses, with his two children Samuel and Sophia continuing to live there, as did his gentleman Goldsmith and dry goods seller Troup, and his gentleman father Alexander Troup. There are often carpenters, perhaps his employees, mariners, clerks, painters, leatherworkers, coach makers, wagoners, drivers, tenders (waiters?), vegetable sellers, boot makers, sail makers, laborers, truckmen, harness makers, printers, carriage trimmers, machine makers, bakers, stone masons, wheelwrights, etc. (Ward 3, 1838-45 only). The turnover is typical of Boston in this era caused by lack of public transportation, high immigration and scarce building space in the city center (Knights 66 ff.).

Gould briefly had an interest in a lot at the north end of Friend Street, opposite what is today North Station. In 1841 he gave a mortgage of $400 to Matthew Parker, receiver for the Oriental Bank on lot number one on Mill Pond Wharf, with 17 feet frontage on Friend Street just 64 feet south of the corner of Causeway Street and 58 feet deep (SD 469:161; plan 456/end). The proprietors of Mill Pond Wharf quitclaimed the lot to Gould a few months later (SD 474:82), the mortgage was discharged by Gould's cousin Thomas Amory President of the Firemen's Insurance Co., and Gould sold it in 1844 to Grant & Co. for $1109.25 (SD 532:295) for a profit of over $600 plus mortgage payments.

In 1842 he was building on the back of the Green Dragon site, for the trustee of the estate, Henry Purkill, protested a window opened at the back, probably to prevent future claims that higher buildings erected on the Green Dragon site blocked out his light (SD 480:51). The general business recovery obviously helped Gould to increase his Friend Street tenants to 22, ranging from 3 gentlemen and 2 laborers, and a variety of shops (Ward 3, 66-67).

Eight months later a similar protest came from Washington Monroe who owned the house on the southwest corner of Friend and Deacon Street opposing the window on the north wall of merchant Charles Holmes's house. The protest is issued to Holmes as the owner of the land, and to Thomas Gould carpenter (one of the few exceptions to his being called housewright) who "is or claims to be the tenant" and laborers Phineas Bond, John G. Somes, Henry M. Ide and William N. Dow all of Boston "are the occupants" (SD 492:170). The implication is that Gould was building the house for Holmes at what was later number 107 Friend Street Munroe makes clear the reason for his protest: "the said Munroe is apprehensive that by lapse of time a right might hereafter accrue or be deemed to have accrued to you or some of you, or to some person or persons coming after or claiming by, from, through or under you or some or one of you to have such privilege of light and aid by the continuance of the use thereof for any length of time whatever..." (SD 492:171). So, under Massachusetts statute 60:28 he disputes their right and does "insist upon his right of building upon his said land in the rear of his said house immediately against the sd. North wall of the said house adjoining his said dwelling house or elsewhere upon his aid land & of obstructing + closing up the lights and windows opened as aforesaid, or any other lights or windows which may be opened in the said North wall overlooking or to overlook the land of said Munroe". This document gives us a glimpse of the names of the work crew Gould used.

In 1852 the Gould family left 21 Friend Street and moved to Framingham Center (SD 638:38 Oct. 1852 gives residence there; Eliz. Gould gives 1852; 2 empty lots in Framingham bought June 12, 1852 Msx Deeds 634:168, so they probably moved in the fall of 1852). Friend Street must have become a busier thoroughfare after its extension south to Faneuil Hall in 1854-5 (Boston Record of Streets). In 1857 he sold the north part of the Friend Street estate, including numbers 23 and 25 (89 and 91 in 1874 Atlas) to his twelfth child George Gould of Boston, then 29 years old (SD 716:1). It had nearly forty feet frontage on the street, backed up to Gould's brick house at # 2 Sumner Street, and bordered Gould's brick house to the south at 21 Friend Street The price was $14,825. George sold it at once to the neighbor to the north, the trustees of Alpheus Hardy, for $15,000 (SD: 716:2).

George[6] Peirce Gould, born at 25 Friend Street 17 May 1828, was never married. His father sent him to New Hampton Academy 1844-5. In the deeds of 1854 he has no listed occupation; later he is known as a wheelwright, like his grandfather. At the time of his father's death the executor declared his "residence unknown, last heard from at Buxton Springs, Kansas" (Msx Probate 4396). He owed his father $1400. This was presumably deducted from his inheritance which reached him in Parker KS in 1874. In 1880 he was in Colorado. He died without issue 9 June 1891.

Thomas Gould's last holding on Friend Street was sold in 1866 to George W. Berry of Charlestown (SD 883:153). This included Gould's brick house at number 21 Friend Street with 47 feet on the street and a bit wider on the Green Dragon estate at the back, and 89 feet deep. He got $20,000, for a total of $35,000 for land he paid $10,470 for plus the expense of building at least four brick houses. We do not know what happened to Sumner Ct. property. The east part of this property was taken by the city for widening of Washington Street.

Gould got out of central Boston at a good time, of general prosperity, and continuing demand for space in the inner city. Gould is a good example of a builder who took advantage of the boom in business and real estate, and the great influx of immigrants.

Chapter VII

Part II. **Thomas^5 Gould's Public Career**
and trip to visit to Hovey Family in Illinois.

Thomas Gould served four years on the City Council of Boston in its early years. His role was not controversial, though he occasionally voted with the minority. He was appointed to many of the committees dealing with building matters such as the South Boston Bridge, the Old State House and school buildings.

Boston had converted from the old town government to establish a city on 1 June 1822, only four years before he became a member of the Council. Gould served the city from the beginning of the new government as Assistant Assessor for Ward 3, doing the valuations on 20-26 June 1822 and 9-16 July 1823 (Boston Assessors Records, Readville, *Valuation* book, Ward 3, 1822, 1823).

Gould was elected to the Common Council on the second Monday in December of 1826, 11 Dec. (*Columbian Centinel* [hereinafter CC, page 2 unless cited] 13 Dec. 1826). The number of voters can be estimated from the 376 votes cast that day for mayor in Ward 3. He was elected as one of four councilors from Ward 3 which was the west side of the North End running from today's Quincy Market to North Station, including Haymarket. The Blackstone Block with the Union Oyster House is probably the only part that vaguely resembles Boston of that day, though North Margin Street and Cooper Street have some buildings of that era, including one built by Gould. The ward boundaries ran from the north side of Faneuil Hall and North Market to the harbor, north to Cross Street, and up to Hanover Street, northeast on that street to Prince Street, then northwest to the Mystic River at James Gould's bridge to Charlestown, west on Causeway Street to Friend Street, south to Hanover Street, a block east to Union Street, and south back to Faneuil Hall (*Boston City Directory, 1826*). At this time he was living on the city side of the district, on Friend Street, but had his business at the corner of Union and Hanover Streets (Ibid., 118).

Newspapers do not indicate that there was any issue on which Gould was elected, but shortly before the election a meeting of the Friends of the City Administration had voted that individuals elected to public office should have three qualifications: integrity, good habits of business and industry, and devotion to public service (CC 2 Dec. 1826). Among the famous people with whom he served on the Council were merchant prince Elias Haskett Derby, future governor Levi Lincoln, founder of the Lowell Institute John Lowell Jr. and future state senate chairman Benjamin T. Pickman.

FIRST TERM (1827).

Gould's first Common Council meeting was on New Year's Day of 1827 (no public holiday!), at which officers were sworn in by Chief Justice Parker (CC 3 Jan.). The Common Council met in temporary quarters in the County Courthouse (Mayor's address, para. 29, CC 6 Jan.) on Court Street This was the 1810 Stone Courthouse built on the site of Johnson's mansion, pictured in Snow's history (Caleb H. Snow, *History of Boston* [Boston: Abel Bowen, 1825], 37, and in Drake 59). Common Council met on the third floor of the 55 foot central octagon (Ibid., 331-2).

Mayor Josiah Quincy laid out the political issues: The million dollar city debt, two thirds of it for the new market (to be named for the mayor) under construction, location of a permanent city hall, and complaints about the voters lists used for assessments of taxes.

It took more than a year for the problem of the debt to be resolved. The solution was to sell city lands at the edge of the water for new development. The biggest piece was that east of the new (Quincy) Market. This was seaward of the mudflats that Gould's ancestor Richard Harris had developed as a wharf in the late seventeenth century. By 1827 it was worth $575,000, only $62,000 short of the debt which the city had reduced to $637,000 in 1827 (Josiah Quincy *A Municipal History of the Town and City of Boston* [Boston: Charles C. Little and James Brown, 1852] [hereinafter Quincy], 274). On 3 March 1828 the Council voted to sell this land and several lots adjoining city schools, and put Gould on the committee to lay out the lots and sell them at auction (CC 5 March 1828). The committee appointed to fill the flats east of Faneuil Hall recommended a 315 foot wharf with 57,645 square feet of space, costing the city only $19,202 (6 Oct.; CC 8 Oct.). The Council approved this 33:5, Gould voting with the majority on 13 Oct. (cc 15 Oct.). At the Council's last meeting of the year the retiring President John Adan congratulated his colleagues for achieving "the great object of the Common Council" [which] has been to reduce the debt by balancing the budget and selling public land (29 Dec.; CC 31 Dec., 3). But this hardly ended the public deficit. Councils went on spending money for schools, sewers, public buildings, street widening, fire engines and firehouses, and other improvements, and met the deficit by filling in more waterfront which they sold at a profit.

The issue of a new city hall also took over a year to solve, partly because the mayor favored converting Faneuil Hall into a meeting place, a solution that was finally rejected (Quincy 402), when the Council decided to renovate the Old State House. Early in 1828 Gould was appointed to a committee of three on public buildings (14 Jan.; CC 16 Jan., 3)· Gould was then placed on the joint committee (with the upper chamber) of three to repair the Old State House and to recommend if it be covered with cement to imitated granite or marble (13 Oct. 1828; CC 15 Oct.). We can credit our ancestor that the Old State House has retained its brick exterior, for the committee's recommendation not to stucco the brick exterior was accepted 20 Oct. (CC 22 Oct.). The Common Council first met in the new quarters on the anniversary of the founding of Boston, 17 Sept. 1830 (CC 20 Sept.).

The Old State House, 1835, in Pendleton lithograph on sheet music cover, from "Boston's Old State House" by Sinclair and Catherine Hitchings, 1975, p. 13.

The third problem, of arbitrary assessment, was quickly solved by clarifying the responsibilities of the City Assessors in preparing voters lists, an issue mainly handled by the Aldermen, in which Gould was not involved. Gould initially opposed the proposal to fix the number and choice of Assessors in a vote of 25:13 (14 April; 1828; CC 16 April), and was in the majority in a narrow vote of 17:15 which reduced the Assessor's salary from $1200 to $1000 (24 April; CC 26 April).

Before these three big issues were solved Gould was involved in the day to day problems of the Council. One of the first subjects was the contested election of George Gay for ward 12. A vote to reverse the committee's recommendation to accept Gay was narrowly defeated 18:22 with Gould voting with the majority (CC 7 Feb. 1827, 1). At the next meeting a motion to postpone the protest of David Rice against Gay's election narrowly won by 22:20 with Gould voting with the majority (CC 114 Feb., 1).

The old controversy about building a bridge to South Boston also intruded on the Mayor's agenda. Gould voted on 5 Feb. with the majority 33:9 to approve the bridge, and was appointed to a Committee of 12 (one from each ward) to settle the terms and design of the bridge (CC 7 Feb., 1). This is interesting since Gould's father James had built the first bridge out of Boston, but Gould's appointment was perhaps appropriate because of his skill as a builder. On 19 Feb.

the committee recommended following the model of Craigie Bridge to East Cambridge. The debate on this went on for nearly five and a half hours, until almost 11:30 pm on 26 Feb., ending in approval 28:10, with Gould voting with the majority (CC 28 Feb.).

Gould was then appointed to a joint committee with the Aldermen to locate the bridge (26 March; CC 28 March). The committee reported on 25 June to cross from Sea Street in Boston (CC 27 June), and a resolution of 5 July was finally passed on 16 July (CC 18 July).

On 16 Feb. of the next year the Council appointed Gould to a committee to superintend the construction of the South Boston Bridge (4 Feb. 1828; CC 6 Feb.). On 16 June the Council received notice that the bridge was finally completed (CC 18 June 1828). The bridge committee submitted its final report, giving high praise to the corporation which built it and for keeping maintenance to a third of estimated cost (CC 2 July). The opposition tried to postpone acceptance of the report, failing by a vote of 10:19, with Gould opposing, and supporting the final approval of 7 July by a vote of 21:8 (CC 9 July). Late in the year the bridge committee was asked to look into making a sidewalk on the west side of the bridge (15 Dec.; CC 17 Dec.). With this task completed, the committee could credit itself with completing the important link to South Boston which shortened the trip by a mile (Drake 25).

Early in his first term on the Council Gould was elected to the joint committee of Aldermen and Councilors headed by Mayor Quincy to apply to the state legislature for change of law to protect Boston against fires (19 Feb.; CC 21 Feb., 3). On April 2 Mayor Quincy reported for the Committee giving a clear set of building regulations against fire, setting separate requirements for factories and tall buildings (Text in CC 25 April). This passed the Council unanimously, was amended by the Legislature and submitted to a public meeting at Faneuil Hall on 26 April. Josiah Marshall moderated a public meeting which several hundred people attended (CC 28 April). Here, however, opposition developed. Mr. Clough moved to postpone action. Speeches were followed by loud calls for the question. A large majority voted for a show of hands rather than written ballot. The motion to postpone indefinitely passed nearly unanimously. However, the action permitted the city to form an independent city fire department to replace the chaotic volunteer companies. The success of the mayor's initiative in creating this department resulted in 20% reduction of fire insurance rates in Boston. (Mayor's inaugural address, Jan. 1828, para.16, Quincy 409).

The following year Mayor Quincy recommended that to build a city fire station in the North End the city buy a lot 19 feet by 74 feet on Salem and Tileston streets (two blocks north of Gould's ward 3, but covering his building projects). The Council put Gould on a committee of three, authorizing $1500 for the building and $600 for a fire engine (25 Feb. 1828; CC 27 Feb.). The vote to buy the lot failed for lack of the required two thirds, Gould probably voting with the 25:10 majority (24 March; CC 26 March).

Early in his first term on City Council Gould was appointed to another joint committee of five to repair the fence around the South Burial Ground (9 April 1827; CC 11 April).

In July 1827 the Council voted to add a second story to the Eliot School on North Bennett Street in the North End, just a block outside of Gould's district, but near his building projects, and appointed Gould to a committee of three to report a design (16 July 9; CC 11, 18 July). Gould opposed the idea of building this as a room for ward meetings, agreeing with the Aldermen who said there were only four such wardrooms in the city, including the Gun House used by wards 2 and 3, which had nothing to do with schools (CC 5 Sept.). When the Council voted on the committee's report on 3 Sept., Gould cast one of the 11 negative votes against the 14 which won (CC 5 Sept.). However, the next year Gould submitted an order to appropriate $2700 for the second story of the school, which was passed by the Council on 24 April (CC 26 April, 14 May).

SECOND TERM (1828).

Gould ran for re-election on 10 Dec. 1827 and was reelected for a second term without controversy (CC 12 Dec.). At the inauguration of the Council on 7 Jan. 1828 Mayor Quincy congratulated it on its economy and urged it on with the task of reducing the debt, warning that "cautious men began to fear lest an increase of debt would become a habit of city government." (Para.2, Quincy 406). He reported favorably on the lack of crime, and the health of the city, and the reduction of fire hazard.

Mayor Quincy added a new challenge, to expand the availability of public education to put "elementary instruction within the reach of every citizen...because they are the common right and common property of every citizen." (Ibid., para. 18, Quincy 409). He argued that primary education should be "for the benefit of the children of the whole community, and not for the benefit of the children of comparatively few".

Gould was apparently on the side of economy when it came to implementation of this liberal principle. When the Council was asked to appropriate $2400 to improve the writing departments of the Boylston Street and Bowdoin Street schools the Council split evenly 17:17, with Gould voting nay, but the President Adan [not Adams] from Gould's Ward 3 cast the deciding vote to pass it (4 June; CC 7 June, 1). In the following year, 1829, the education issue was one of establishing a separate high school for girls, for which there were funds enough for only the elite, or the alternative of adopting Mayor Quincy's insistence on high school education for both sexes in an integrated school. (Quincy 224-5). Gould voted for the latter principle with the minority of the councilors in a 24:16 vote which lost for lack of two thirds majority (13 April; CC 15 April). He was probably with the majority in establishing a new school on the Roxbury Mill Dam at the next meeting (20 April; CC 22 April).

Gould was involved in one of the minor achievements of 1828, involving Deer Island in the harbor. He was one of three councilmen on the joint committee headed by Mayor Quincy to settle the lease of Mr. Bellamy and to lease it to the U.S. to build a breakwater (17 Nov.; CC 19 Nov.) On 1 Dec. the Council ordered the lease (CC 3 Dec.), and at the next meeting the committee reported the settlement with Bellamy (8 Dec.; CC 10 Dec.).

In addition to the big issues of 1828, Gould was involved in a number of minor affairs which related to his house building business. At the second meeting of the Council he was appointed to the Committee on Public Buildings (1 Jan., CC 16 Jan., 3)· In May he was appointed to a committee of five to apply to the state legislature for a change in the law relating to measurement of boards and lumber (5 May; CC 7 May). On 4 June he was too much involved in the issue of exchange of city land for a new meetinghouse of his First Baptist Church at his office corner of Hanover and Union Streets to be put on the committee, though the unrelated councilman Frederick Gould was appointed (CC 6 June, 1). The Council later accepted the Baptist church land east of Merrimac Street and in Mill Creek to widen Green Dragon Lane behind Gould's land on Friend Street (13 Sept.; CC 10, 15 Sept.). Gould voted against giving city subsidy for a city hotel in a narrow 17:18 vote which was referred to the City Solicitor for advice (23 June 1828; 25 CC June). He again voted no, in a vote 3:35, accepting the Solicitor's advice (30 June; CC 2 July). In November he voted against the extension and widening of Common (Tremont) Street, a measure that passed 25:8 (CC 5 Nov.). His opposition may have been because this would have increased the traffic into his Friend Street property.

THIRD TERM (1829).

On 8 Dec. 1828 Thomas Gould was re-elected from Ward 3 for his third term. 295 votes cast for the mayor in Ward 3 give us the size of the electorate (CC 10 Dec.). The old council met on election day to receive the report on Deer Island and to discuss the claim of fireman Francis Oliver for injury at a fire on Canal Street in March. After a long debate in which Gould took part, Gould voted with the majority 26:5 to compensate Oliver (CC 10 Dec.).

The Common Council reconvened on 5 Jan. 1829 in its new quarters in Faneuil Hall (Quincy 280) to hear the farewell address of Josiah Quincy, and the swearing in of new mayor Harrison Gray Otis (CC 7 Jan.). Quincy lauded the achievements of his six year tenure, much of which had been done in the last year of 1828: Ending the debt by sale of public lands, finishing the new market, establishing a city fire department, and widening streets (Quincy 256). Now the senior councilman from his ward, Gould was appointed to the committee of three to wait on mayor Otis and request a copy of his speech for publication (CC 7 Jan.).

At the first working meeting of the Council the matter of paying to fill up the flats east of the market came up, and Gould was appointed to the committee (12 Jan.; CC 21 Jan.). This work was done by October for a cost of $17,300 (Quincy 289-290).

In April 1829 Gould was appointed chair of a committee for the first time, that concerning a law for weighing hay (6 April; CC 8 April). On 7 Dec. the committee reported that only two stands were needed, on Merrimac Street and Charles Street, and this was passed by the Council without dispute (CC 9 Dec.).

In mid-July Mayor Otis interrupted the usual summer vacation by calling a special meeting of the Council to consider the complaints of the stink from the old Mill Creek that ran through Gould's ward 3 from the now filled Mill Pond to the Town Dock (16 July; CC 18 July). What had once been a sixty foot wide saltwater channel had narrowed to twenty feet ditch filled with trash and out-houses hanging over the stream. It took until the stench of the next summer for the Council to appropriate $3000 to fill in the creek and put in a sewer (19 July 1830; CC 21 July).

This public health problem did not deter Gould from thinking seriously of starting a grocery nearby, or perhaps he had encouraged the improvement because of his interest. On 7 Sept. he petitioned the Council for six months leave of absence to set up a shop over Mill Creek (CC 9 Sept.). This was referred to the Aldermen and apparently refused, for he was appointed to committees on 9 and 29 Sept., and 1 Feb. 1830.

Leveling of streets caused problems for property owners, as in the case of William Redfern who claimed he lost $500 when two of his houses on the corner of May and Grove Streets were left high above the street. Gould was appointed to a committee of three to look into his claim (9 Sept; CC 11 Sept.)

On 21 Sept. Gould was appointed to a committee of three on amendments to an ordinance for sale of public lands (CC 23 Sept.) which the Council had passed on 7 Sept. to authorize appointment of commissioners to conduct such sales. These were apparently issues on which Gould's experience was essential.

The big new issue of 1829 was the prospect of railroad terminals in Boston, which the Council supported. Gould's son Thomas Jr. built some on these stations.

FOURTH TERM, 1830.

Gould was reelected for a fourth term on 14 Dec. 1829 (CC 16 Dec.). The first meeting and swearing-in on 4 Jan. 1830 had to be held at the Mayor's Mansion House because of Otis's indisposition (CC 6 Jan.).

In his inaugural address the mayor offered to have his own salary lowered if the matter came up, as he apparently anticipated (Quincy 304). Gould was chosen from Ward 3 for a committee with a representative from each ward to look into the salaries of city and county officials (1 Feb.; CC 3 Feb.). At the next meeting of the Council the committee reported and was asked to recommend which offices could be eliminated (7 Feb.; CC 12 Feb.). A month later it reported that none could be abolished (8 March; CC 10 March). In May it reported a list of proposed salaries (3 May; CC 5 May) which was later adopted.

One of Gould's last major tasks on the Council was his appointment to a committee of six headed by Mayor Otis to prepare a new ordinance for survey of lumber (15 March; CC 17 March). The committee reported on 12 April, recommending creation of the office of City Surveyor who would report annually, with power to levy fines of 10 to 50 dollars, and also setting classification of lumber, fees for surveying, and prohibition of import without survey (text CC 1 April, 3). The Aldermen first passed this on 12 April (CC 14 April), and referred it to the Council on 19 April.

The big city event of the year 1830 was the celebration of the two hundredth birthday of the founding of Boston. The day began with a 100 gun salute at sunrise of 17 Sept. (CC 20 Sept.). At 7 am the 1200 man fire department put on a historical pageant. At 8 the Common Council met for the first time in the second floor room at the west end of the Old State House, on which it had spent $5000 for refurbishment (6 Sept.; CC 8 Sept.). At 9 am a band led a parade headed by Mayor Otis followed by the 8 Aldermen and the Common Council, with Gould close behind the president Benjamin T. Pickman the Salem pepper merchant, since he was now senior to all councilors but Waters, Rice and Hatch. Behind them came the state legislators, U.S. Senators and Representatives, John Quincy Adams and other officials.

The parade marched from the Old State House, down Beacon Street, across the Common, up Tremont Street and Court Street, down and back up State Street, and down Washington Street to Old South Church. There they heard a long speech by Josiah Quincy, now President of Harvard, and songs by the Handel & Haydn Society. At one point a seat collapsed, which caused panic, some people trying to escape from the windows. But calm was soon restored. They then marched to the State House.

At 3 pm 500 citizens gathered at Faneuil Hall for a banquet prepared by Mr. Edwards of the Franklin Hotel. There were toasts to the Day, to the President, the Governor, to the foundation of Boston (followed by singing "Home Sweet Home"). More toasts, including the sixth, to "Croaking--The malady of speculators, infecting the community,--industry, economy and enterprise are an effectual cure for the disease." (followed by singing "O dear, what can the matter be). More toasts, to France, Lafayette, Carroll of Carrollton, the Laws, Poverty and Crime, the Militia and lastly the Ladies of Boston. Apples were produced from a tree planted by

Blackstone, Boston's first settler, cut into pieces and thrown to the crowd so that they might "each to taste of an original Boston Apple".

In the evening there was a reception by the Mayor, with music in the garden, and fireworks. The great day closed with a fete at the mansion of Lt. Governor Winthrop.

This was the climactic event of the year, and perhaps one of the most memorable of Thomas Gould's career. The last few months in office were uneventful. He did not run for reelection on 13 Dec. 1830, having served four yearly terms, longer than most. At the final meeting, on 20 Dec. it was reported that the city had 7,848,277 acres for sale on the Neck, an area that would create the new South End (CC 22 Dec.).

Gould's four years on Boston Council had been important ones, in the completion of Quincy Market and the South Boston Bridge, filling of new lands east of Faneuil Hall, above Charles Street, and the South End, building new sewers and waterworks, widening of streets, creation of a city fire department, moving the City Hall to the Old State House, lease of the harbor islands to the U.S. for forts, establishing the first universal public primary education. In most of these creations Thomas Gould was a positive force, and he actively supervised many.

Four years on the City Council did not end Gould's public service. Thomas Gould also served on the Boston Board of Overseers for the Poor for Ward 3 in 1834 (*Boston Directory*, 1834). He served again as Assistant Assessor for Ward 3 in 1841 (Assessors Records, Street Book, 1841). Hewick's handbook describes the office thus: "Assistant assessors...shall be sworn and shall in their respective wards or districts assist the assessors in taking a list of the ratable polls, in estimating the value of the real and personal estate in said wards or districts, and in making out lists of persons qualified to vote in elections..."(William A. Hewick, *The Powers, Duties, & Liabilities of Town & Parish Officers in Massachusetts* [Boston: Little Brown, 2d ed., 1879], 75,¶ 2).

TRAVEL TO THE WEST, about 1833.

Following his release from Council duties Gould took his only trip outside the state. His daughter Elizabeth's account is: "He was not fond of travel, but about this time--[18]33 or near that date, he started on a trip which he intended to extend to Illinois, where his youngest sister, Mrs. Mary Hovey had lived for some years, and where he had purchased two tracts of land, but altho' interested in the incidents of his journey, in those days a somewhat formidable undertaking,-- it suited neither his tastes or his health, and he went no further than Pennsylvania. One incident which he remembered with pleasure, was meeting one of the Bonapartes--Jerome probably,--with his wife, on a canal boat, and finding them cordial and friendly." (2).

Gould probably met the younger Jerome Bonaparte. Napoleon's brother Jerome (1784-1860) married Baltimore woman Elizabeth Patterson (1785-1879), but after the Emperor forced their separation he lived mainly in Italy. It seems likely to have been their son, Jerome (1805-1870), who lived in Baltimore, and looked a great like his uncle Napoleon (*Encyclopedia Britannica*, 13th ed., 4:196-7).

This era, the early thirties, before the railroads got going long distances, was the boom of canal travel, and Gould could have gone by canal from New York, across New Jersey and much of Pennsylvania with a few breaks.

The HOVEY FAMILY

The destination of Gould's visit was the Illinois home of his sister **12.** Mary Ann^6 Gould Hovey. She was born in Charlestown MA, later than 1774, and probably in 1781 (Illinois Census 1850, 1860), a namesake of the earlier Mary Ann Gould baptized in Roxbury 15 Dec. 1771, apparently died before she was ten. Mary Ann Gould married 24 March 1805 in Charlestown to John Hovey, bricklayer, born in Cambridge 1762, d. 20 Feb. 1840 Griggsville IL. (Lewis R. Hovey, *The Hovey Book* [Haverhill, the author, 1913], 412). The Hovey family was prominent in Charlestown, James Hovey being the official fireworks provider for Boston's festivities, and winner of awards for lime and chemical production at the Massachusetts Charitable Mechanics Association fairs (Front page ad in *Boston Directory* c. 1848; Massachusetts Charitable Mechanic Assn. awards in MHS).

Mary Ann and John Hovey left Charlestown sometime after the birth of their youngest child, William, on 16 Feb. 1824. But in 1830 Illinois census shows no Hovey in the whole state (Delma S. Mink letter 19 June 1985). The Seaborn family Bible says they came to Pike County IL after 1833-4. The 1872 Pike County Atlas says they came in 1837. All four of the Hovey children who married were wed in Charlestown between 1831 and 1847 (James Gould 17 Sept. 1831 to Ann R. Patterson, Mary Ann 31, May 1834 to Josiah Bryant, Henry 26 Oct. 1837 to Eliza Swett Allds, and William 2d. 19 May 1849 to Clarissa S. Sanderson), no doubt returned from Illinois in 1849, but the first two are likely not to have gone back. We thus place the Hoveys' move west about 1835. Deeds to land might confirm date of arrival, although it appears that Thomas Gould bought land there earlier.

Griggsville IL, Gould's destination, was in west-central Illinois, 50 miles west of New Salem where Abraham Lincoln was running a store and a post office before he ran first for public office, and 30 miles east of Mark Twain's boyhood home (1839-53) of Hannibal MO, on the Mississippi River. Hovey descendants still live in the area.

The eldest son *John Hovey Jr*., b. Charlestown 20 March 1806, served in the U. S. Navy 1839-40, then moved to Pike Co. IL (on the Mississippi) where he appears in the censuses of 1850, 60 and 70. With no known descendants, he probably never married.

The second son, *James Gould Hovey*, b. Charlestown 30 March 1807, m. Charlestown 17 Sept. 1831 Ann R. Patterson had a daughter *Amelia*, b. 1833, m. Charlestown 8 Dec. 1849 Daniel W. Sweetser (Info from D.R. Redman of Ithaca, NY to Delma Mink).

The third child, *William Hovey*, b. Charlestown 25 Nov. 1810, died before 1824.

The fourth child of Mary Ann Gould and John Hovey was *Mary Ann Hovey*, b. Charlestown 14 March 1813, d. Baylis IL 24 Feb. 1893; m. twice, 1) Charlestown 31 May 1834 Josiah Bryant, farmer, b. Charlestown 19 June 1809, d. Griggsville IL 19 Sept. 1840, by whom she had 3 children: one unnamed who died in infancy,

ii. *Mary Ann Bryant*, b. Griggsville 10 Jan. 1839, d. unm. Griggsville 13 April 1858;

iii. *Josiah Bryant Jr.*, b. Griggsville 1840, m. Sarah Glines, b. 1842, by whom he had 3 ch., *Mary Bryant*, b. Griggsville 1862, *Della Bryant*, b. Griggsville 1869, res. Ontario CA 1925 unm., and *Clyde Bryant*, also in CA.

On Josiah's death, Mary Ann remarried 2) Griggsville 20 July 1842 widower Robert Seaborn II, a farmer, b. Phila. 11 Oct. 1804, son of Robert Chapple Seaborn & Elizabeth Rodgers, bapt. Phila 28 Apr. 1805, d. Griggsville 19 Apr. 1880, prev. m. Caroline Bickford, b. 19 Dec. 1827, d. Griggsville 26 March 1842. By him Mary Ann had four children, b. Griggsville:

i. *David Rodgers Seaborn*, farmer, b. 1 Sept. 1843, d. New Salem IL 14 Oct. 1922, by passenger train while he walked on tracks; m. twice, 1) Pike Co. IL 22 March 1869 Emma E. Johnson, b. NJ 1852, d. after 1881, before 1897, by whom they had four children:

i. *Charles Seaborn*, b. MO Feb. 1871, d. Portland OR 2 Aug. 1950, m. twice: 1) New Salem IL 24 Feb. 1892 Maude Malvern McLaughlin b. New Salem 20 Feb. 1871; d. Los Angeles 12 March 1957, div.; he rem. 2) by 1950 when they res. Portland, name unknown, who d. Portland OR 25 March 1962, sp.; she rem. Walter Yoakum, sp. Charles and Maude had 2 ch.:

i. *Grace Muriel Seaborn*, b. New Salem 18 March 1894, d. Los Angeles CA 14 Nov. 1969, m. Los Angeles 14 March 1914 James Robinson Stull, by whom she had 3 ch. b. LA:

i. *Mary Grace Stull*, b. LA 1 Jan. 1915, d. Huntington Beach CA 1988, m. 29 Aug. 1942 Russell Myron Ioerger, b. UT 29 Aug. 1912, div. May 1955, by whom she had one ch.:*Steven Alan Ioerger*, b. Glendale CA 21 May 1943, m. 30 Sept. 1978 Linda Lou Dodge, b. Glendale 2 Dec. 1941.

Grace Seaborn & James Stull's second child was:

ii. *James Roy Stull*, b. LA 21 Nov. 1917, m. 23 Dec. 1938 Florita Bell Spaw, b. Seattle 15 Oct. 1918; div., d. 15 Oct. 1977, by whom he had 3 ch.:

i. *James Gail Stull*, b. LA 21 Feb. 1940, m. twice 1) 1960 Betty Ellen Hunter, b. Whittier CA 27 July 1940, by whom he had 2 ch. b. Whittier:

i. *James Craig Stull*, b. 6 Feb. 1961;

ii. *John Hunter Stull*, b. 10 Nov. 1962;

James Gail was div. and m. 2) 28 June 1970 Kathy Ann Giuseffi, b. Passaic NJ 22 June 1946, by whom he had one ch. *Angela Gail Stull*, b. Orange CA 1 June 1978.

ii. *William Steven Stull*, b. Glendale 27 May 1944, m. twice: 1) 15 July 1967 Barbara Jean Luhn, b. Oshkosh WI 12 July 1949, div. 20 July 1974 sp.;

he m. 2) 12 June 1985 Brigette Gawn, b. 20 Feb. 1964, div. 17 May 1986 sp..

iii. *Tommy Lee Stull*, b. Glendale 18 May 1948, m. twice, 1) 10 Aug. 1968 Deanna Vickie Vlach, div., sp., m. 2) 28 June 1975 Debi Kay Kattmeyer, by whom he had 2 ch. b. Whittier CA:

i. *Aaron Lee Stull*, b. 2 Dec. 1977,

ii. *Rachelle Kay* b. 28 Dec. 1979.

iii. *Donald Alan Stull*, b. LA 7 May 1920, m. 3 times: 1) 25 Dec. 1945 Virginia Dare Norwood., b. Hugo OK 15 May 1919, d. 4

June 1979, 3 ch.:

i. *Victor Roy Stull*, b. Inglewood CA 16 Dec. 1946, m. 13 Feb. 1979 Rebecca Sue Jacobs, b. Walla Walla WA Aug. 1947, 2 ch.:

i. *Brandy Renee*, b. Newport Beach CA 14 July 1982,

ii. *Dana Kathryn*, b. Redlands CA 12 July 198x

ii. *Christina Muriel Stull*, b. LA 8 July 1948, m. 5 Dec. 195 John Holstrum III, died by 1995.

Grace Seaborn & James R. Stull's third child was:

iii. *Donald Alan Stull Jr.*, b. LA 25 April 1951; div., m. 2) Dorothy, b. 18 June 1930, m. June 1957, div. 1969; m. 3) 29 May 1979 Theresa Elaine Stockbridge, b. San Diego 29 May 1924.

Charles & Maud Seaborn's second child was:
ii. *Wayne K. Seaborn*, b. New Salem March 1898, d. FL 1980s, buried Perry IL; m. Ellen Beatty b. New Salem 1897, dau. of Conway Beatty & Mary R. Hammitt, d. Pike Co. 1943, sp..

The second child of David & Emma Seaborn was:
ii. *Pearl Seaborn*, b. MO 9 Feb. 1874, d. Griggsville 6 Oct. 1876, age 20 mos..
Their third child was
iii. *Ruby*, b. MO March 1878, d. Chicago before 1922 in fall from balcony in her home which gave way as she leaned on it; m. Dr. Arthur H. Byers (b. IA 1871).
The fourth child of David & Emma was
iv. *Stella Seaborn*, b. New Salem IL 15 Apr. 1881, d. unm. New Salem 22 Nov. 1896, age 15.

David R. Seaborn married 2) 28 April 1898 Lucinda J. Reed, b. 27 July 1852, dau. of W. P. & Nancy Reed, d. 28 Nov. 1927 sp..

Mary Ann Hovey and Robert Seaborn's second child was:
William Hovey Seaborn, b. Griggsville IL 5 Aug. 1846, d. Baylis IL 7 Aug. 1934. He was local landowner, and served in the Civil War in 68th Ill. Infantry 1862, at Washington DC and Alexandria, guarded prisoners during Battle of Bull Run. He later served two years in the Indian Wars under Generals Sibley and Sully. He m. Pittsfield IL 16 Jan. 1872 Sarah Martah Miranda Reed, b. White Co. TN 31 March 1849, 3d. ch. of William Preston Reed & Sarah Smallman, d. 31 July 1922 Baylis IL. She wrote poetry and articles for women's magazines under the name of Sarah M. M. Seaborn.
They had 3 children:

i. *Maude Estelle Seaborn*, b. Pineville IL 31 Jan. 1876, d. from fall down cellar steps 18 Jan. 1879;

ii. *Robert Earle Seaborn*, b. Pittsfield IL 11 Jan. 1878, d. Baylis IL 13 May 1943, m. Baylis IL 18 Jan. 1903 Grace Luella Davidson, b. Pineville IL 9 Aug. 1881, third child of Hugh Davidson & Eliza Pine, d. Baylis IL 19 Jan. 1963; they lived their entire married life in the Seaborn Brick house, built by his parents 1872. 3 ch. b. Baylis IL:

i. *Donna Lavon Seaborn*, b. 12 Aug. 1912, d. 23 Feb. 1914 Baylis IL.

ii. *Delma Earline*, b. 11 Nov. 1915. She is retired teacher and family genealogist, res. 1994: Rt. 2, Box 39, Baylis IL 62314. She m. St. Charles MO 4 Sept. 1937 Leaton Eugene Mink, school principal, b. New Salem IL 4 April 1916, son of Owen Frank Mink & Lucy Mae Ervin, d. Chicago 19 Aug. 1979, div., rem. Rosalie Lazarro; One child by Delma:

i. *Darrel Lee Mink*, b. Quincy IL 13 Dec. 1940, m. twice, 1) 16 June 1961 Quincy IL Suzanne Geiker, b. 19 Feb. 1943, dau of Clyde Geiker & Sue McCreery, div.; he m. 2) Hancock MI 19 Sept. 1963 Marlene Ann Moilanen, b. Hancock MI 14 May 1939, dau. of Toivo & Ann Moilanen. He is grad. of Missouri Valley College in Business Administration; served US Air Force 6 years to rank of Capt.; empl. as special agent for Kemper Insurance.

Robert and Grace Seaborn's third child was:

iii. *Twila Doreen Seaborn*, b. 11 May 1918, d. Baylis IL 30 June 1918.

Third child of William Hovey Seaborn & Sarah Reed was: iii. *William Kyle Seaborn*, farmer, b. Pineville IL 2 Feb. 1886, d. Baylis IL 20 Aug. 1958, m. twice, 1) 1904 Myrtle Rust, b. Fairmount Twp. IL Dec. 1885, dau. of Edward R. Rust & Margaret N. Robison; div., she rem. 1908 George Hill by whom she had one ch.

William and Myrtle Seaborn's only child was:

William Edward Seaborn, b. Fishhook IL 8 April 1906, d. La Jolla CA 4 June 1980, he retired after 20 years in US Navy to establish Seaborn Del Dios Nursery, became authority on tropical plants, author of book on bromeliads, founded Quail Garden Park in Encinitas where there is a memorial honoring him. He m. Esther McBride, b. WI, 3 ch.:

i. *William George Seaborn*, b. Cook Co. IL 12 June 1931, d. Escondido CA 9 May 1983, m. Mary K. McClintock, 2 sons res. Escondido; William & Esther also had 2 dau., names unknown, with sons in S. Calif.

William Kyle Seaborn m. 2) Baylis IL 27 March 1910 Myrtle Laurel Taylor, b. 25 Dec. 1891 Fairmount Twp. IL, dau. of Wilmer Taylor & Mary Riley; d. Kinderhook IL 18 July 1977, 2 ch. b. Baylis IL, Kyle & Myrtle:

i. *Kyle Lyndell Seaborn*, b. 13 June 1914, d. Jacksonville IL 13 Feb. 1985, m. Pittsfield IL 2 Jan. 1932 Nina Bernice Orebaugh, b. Baylis 4 Jan. 1913, dau. of George Orebaugh & Nina Edith Powell; he is electrician, 4 ch.:

i. *Phyllis Nadine Seaborn*, b. Baylis 23 July 1933, m. Beardstown IL 21 April 1955 Elmer Dale Logsdon, river contractor, b. 31 May 1929 Beardstown, son of Elmer Logsdon & Blanche Smith, d. Beardstown 1 June 1986, 3 ch.:

i. *Dana Kim Logsdon*, b. Canton IL 2 Aug. 1955, m. Beardstown 13 April 1974 Tari Gail Menge, b. Beardstown IL 6 Aug. 1956, son of Charles Menge & Velma Andrews, 2 ch.:

i. *Kimberly Gail Logsdon*, b. Rushville IL 5 Oct. 1974,

ii. *Ryan Dale*, b. Rushville IL 14 March 1982.

ii. *Krysta Lynn Logsdon*, b. Beardstown IL 24 Jan. 1959, m. Milton IL 3 Dec. 1983 Robert Edward Hoover, b. Milton IL 5 Oct. 1957, son of John Otis Hoover & Clemma Zoeanne Sparks, 1 ch.: *Adam Edward Hoover*, b. Pittsfield IL 30 Oct. 1987.

iii. *Matthew Dale Logsdon*, b. Beardstown IL 30 May 1966, m. March 1987 Georgeann Buck, b. Beardstown 5 Nov. 198, dau. of George Albert Buck & Roseanne Jolly; One child: *Lacy Breeanne*, b. Rushville IL 24 March 1988.

The second child of Kyle & Nina Seaborn is:
ii. *Phillip Lynn Seaborn*, b. Baylis 3 July 1936, electrician, m. twice: 1) 27 Dec. 1959 Beardstown IL Connie DeSoller, b. Beardstown IL 27 Feb. 1939, d. John DeSoller & Alameda Crawford, 2 ch.:

i. *Krystie Ann Seaborn*, b. Huntsville AL, 7 Aug. 1961, m. 21 June 1981 Roger Schrodt, William Kirk Seaborn, b. Springfield IL 8 Aug. 1965.

Philip m. 2) Pittsfield IL 2 Feb. 1979 Gail Elaine Harbin, b. Beardstown IL 7 Nov. 1949, dau. of Keith Harbin & Rosemary Morgan; One child:

ii. *Jacob Hovey Seaborn*, b. Pittsfield, 1 Jan. 1980.

The third child of Kyle & Nina Seaborn is:
iii. *Gilbert Lloyd Seaborn*, b. Beardstown IL 15 May 1945, electrician, m. Arenzville IL 5 Sept. 1965 Patty Jean Phelps, b. Beardstown IL 29 July 1947, dau. of John K. Phelps & Gertrude Kuyper,
2 ch.:
i. *Kelly Jean Seaborn*, b. Beardstown 11 May 1973,
ii. *Shawn Kyle Seaborn*, b. Beardstown 5 July 1977.

The fourth child of Kyle & Nina Seaborn is:
iv. *Patrick Earl Seaborn*, b. Beardstown, 29 Jan. 1948, m. twice: 1) Rushville IL 20 Oct. 1968 Deborah Estes, b. 18 Feb. 1951, dau. of Maurice Estes, div.; m. 2) 5 July 1985 Lily Mae Fearneyhough b. 29 Jan. 1960, dau. of Raymond Fearneyhough & Lois Evans; 1 ch. by Deborah:

Chad Earl Seaborn, b. Rushville IL 1 June 1980.

The second child of William Kyle Seaborn & Myrtle was: ii. *Wilma Dale Seaborn*, b. Baylis 15 Dec. 1917, m. Pittsfield IL 31 Jan.1937 William Lloyd Welbourne, b. Barry IL 9 Nov. 1914, son of Melvin C. Welbourne & Larena Nichols, electrician, d. Grants Pass OR 8 Dec. 1989, one ch.:

David Lloyd Seaborn, b. Van Nuys CA 11 May 1951; div., he rem. 3 times, first to Dorothy, and thirdly to Jane.

The third child of Mary Ann Hovey and Robert Seaborn II was: iii. *Charles Carrick Seaborn*, b. Griggsville IL 5 June 1849, d. unm. 11 Sept. 1869; he was school teacher who served in Civil War as Private in Co. G, 7th Ill Inf., 17 Feb. 1865 to 9 July 1865. The fourth child of Robert Seaborn & Mary Ann Hovey was:
iv. *Howard Malcolm Seaborn*, b. Griggsville IL 25 Jan. 1852, d. Griggsville IL typhoid 4 Oct. 1869 unm.

The fifth child of Mary Ann[5] Gould and John Hovey was:
v. *Henry Hovey*, carpenter, b. Charlestown 13 July 1815, d. Charlestown 15 Aug. 1852, m. Charlestown 26 Oct. 1837 Eliza Swett Allds, b. Hollis ME 4 Sept. 1821, d. 25 Nov. 1877. They had 4 children (Hovey Book, 412-3.):

i. *Henry Alonzo Hovey*, b. 11 Dec. 1838, d. 22 Sept. 1850, age 11;
ii. *Mary Gould Hovey*, b. 19 April 1840, d. 28 July 1896, m. 1 Oct. 1862 Alonzo H. Foss; they had 2 ch.:
  i. *George Albert Foss*, b. Charlestown 7 Dec. 1863, d. Jan. 1875;
  ii. *Viola Caldwell Foss*, b. 6 Sept. 1865 Charlestown, m. Oct. 1897 Alonzo G. Long;
iii. *James Francis Hovey*, b. Hollis ME 27 Jan. 1843, m. 1 Nov. 1876 Amanda Wilson Jewett, b. Alton Bay 29 April 1841, 1 ch.:
  Edna Jewett Hovey, b. Boston 16 Dec. 1877, res. 1913 28 Cortes Street, Boston;
iv. *Sarah Alld Hovey*, b. 21 June 1846, d. 14 July 1896.

The sixth and last child of Mary Ann[5] Gould and John Hovey was: vi. *William (II) Hovey*, farmer, b. Charlestown 16 Feb. 1824, d. Griggsville IL 14 March 1901, m. Charlestown 19 May 1849 Clarissa Stetson Sanderson, sister of Johanna who m. Daniel W. Sweetser, b. Waltham 5 Sept. 1828, d. Richmond VA 17 Feb. 1918; 4 ch.:

i. *Clara S. Hovey*, b. Griggsville 1850, res. Chicago, m. Mr. DeLasso;
ii. *William H. Hovey*, b. Griggsville Nov. 1855, rancher, d. San Bernardino CA 10 Jan. 1921;
iii. *Francis S. Hovey*, b. Griggsville 1859, m. Josephine, b. 1880; they res. Springfield IL he was city railway operator in Woodside Twp., 2 ch., b. Woodside IL:
  i. *Francis Hovey*, b. 1900,
  ii. *Henry C.* b. 1902.
iv. *Lutie Ruth Hovey*, b. Griggsville 1865, to Richmond VA 1907, m. twice, 1) Dr. Sheffield (Hovey Book, 413); one ch.:
  Vernon Sheffield;
  she rem. 2) Mr. Dwyer (Obit. With Delma Mink.).

(1785-1872)

His second wife (1790-1875)

Part III. Thomas^5 Gould's Interests in North End of Boston and the Fernald and Mann Families

Thomas Gould was one of the major developers of the North End in the first half of the nineteenth century, demolishing the ancient wooden mansions and shanties, and building three story brick residences that were to house many of the incoming Irish residents after they served as homes for the old families. Though Gould himself never lived there, he built homes for his sons Thomas and Samuel, and for his daughters Delia Fernald and Sophia Mann, and perhaps his son James's wife Ann Jones. His major developments were along the west side of North Margin Street where at least one of his houses survives, in Baldwin Place, on the east side of Salem Street, and Cooper Street. He had smaller interests on Ann Street and Prince Street, and in the family burial ground on Copp's Hill. We then describe a couple of distant properties in the South End and Chelsea. This part closes with an account of the surprising scarcity of court cases.

COPPS HILL BURIAL GROUND

Gould's first purchase in the North End was lot number 74 in Copp's Hill Burial Ground, located on Charter Street, in the southeast corner near the Mathers' graves. In 1813 he paid fifty dollars for half the Jeremiah Bumstead Jr. tomb which was inscribed to Deacon John Wait. The deed is dated 5 Sept. 1813, over a year after the death of his wife Sophia, who died 24 May 1812. Presumably Sophia was buried in this plot, as he himself was in 1872 before their removal to Mt. Auburn in 1875. Today no markers can be found, but the lot 74 can be inferred to be south of #79 at the east gate onto Charter Street The location shows on the inventories of 1851 and 1878 with the inscription "Ezra Hawkes//&//Thomas Gould//Tomb.1812". Tin plate worker Ezra Hawkes who shared the tomb with Gould was a partner in the building in the West End (above, Brighton Street) and North End (below, N. Margin Street).

Although he never lived in the North End, Thomas Gould's largest investments in real estate were there, mostly in the block bounded on the west by North Margin Street, and the east by Salem Street, on the north by Noyes Place, and south by Bartlett Place. At the center of this was the Second Baptist Church of Samuel Stillman, today the Knights of Columbus Hall on North Margin Street

NORTH MARGIN STREET, 1826-1852.

At 37 North Margin Street in Boston's North End stands a three story brick house that may have been built by Thomas Gould. This has not been recorded on the National Register, but may represent one of the few remaining brick town-houses of the Federal period. In 1800 this area was east of the Mill Pond, and the north margin of the pond gave the street its name.

Gould's first land purchase in the area was in 1826 just north of the church, with 24 feet on North Margin Street, at today's #40, which replaced Gould's structures. Gould owned half of the lot with Boston trader Benjamin Kimball, who sold Gould his rights in 1829 for $1200, half of the original price. The two owners had immediately mortgaged the lot to the seller, Samuel D. Parker, Esq. for $1400. They had five tenants, mainly a blacksmith's shop, and several laborers. In 1829 Gould took a second mortgage from the same widow Katherine Bradstreet of Charlestown who had given him the mortgage on his Friend Street property. The mortgage was discharged in 1831.

On this property there was the same rapid turnover of renters that he had in the city center. The longest lease was three years to a carpenter, the others a variety of laborers and craftsmen, the most exotic, a rattan maker, working on an import of Indonesian vines that came into Boston in the East Indies trade. We get a possible clue to the rents Gould received from an assessor's note, placing $50 after widow Howard's name, and $60.80 after Asa Hamilton's.

After discharging the first mortgage in 1829 Gould again mortgaged it in 1831, this time to famous Asia trader Thomas Handasyd Perkins (whose grandson was to marry Gould's cousin Susan Timmins and build a house on Old Post Road in Cotuit), his horticulturalist brother Samuel Perkins and other heirs of James Perkins for $4,000. This was discharged in 1838, Gould having paid 5 % interest semiannually and insuring the house for a thousand dollars against fire.

The well on the lot had water to spare, for in 1833 Gould sold water rights to his neighbors to the north, Abiel Buttrick and Abijah Patch, for $150, and to the Baptist church. By 1836 this was apparently insufficient for needs of truckman Patch, who then contracted with Gould to lay a water pipe across his land from Moses Pond's well, for a hundred dollars.

By 1841 Gould had divided the property and built a house at the back, with a four foot passage that on the 1874 atlas is known as North Merion Place. He mortgaged it for $1000 at the usual rate to the estate of Boston merchant John H. Bradford, a debt not paid off until after his death, in 1873.

Later in 1841 he straightened the front of the lot, gaining 11 feet 3 inches on the street (now # 45) by paying the church $303.50 for a triangle four feet south of his brick house and 5 feet 6 inches from the church, voted by the vestry on 11 Oct.. Excluded from the sale was a "Sear pipe" which ran from the church's well, perhaps a sewer, or the water line from Gould's well.

Soon after this he mortgaged the middle part of the lot with the house (1874: 55 N. Margin Street) with rights to the water pump on the south side of his land to the blind widow Susannah Luere for $1300. She had the right to a 2½ foot passage on the east side to the back of the house; he had the right to a five foot sidewalk to the rear. Apparently she was willing to lend more, for five days later a new mortgage for the same property (except the passage now became six feet wide) at six percent was signed for $1800, the value of the house for fire insurance. This was discharged ten years later after extension and transfer.

In May 1842 Gould mortgaged the front buildings on the street (later #47) for $1000 to widow Mary Pierpont of Charlestown, with privilege to Gould's well and a 2½ foot passage to the back, and his right to the five foot passage to the street. This was discharged at 6 % in 1855.

Gould apparently built a brick house at the back of Luere's lot for John M. Cummings in 1843, for Cummings paid him $1200 for a lot 43 feet 2 inches back from the street, oddly shaped about 35 feet across and 20 feet wide, with rights to the pump and the six foot passage, and Gould reserving right to the six foot passage parallel with his adjoining estate and to the cistern on his estate . Then Cummings mortgaged it to Gould for four years at 6 % for $800, which Gould quickly discharged in less than ten months, indicating Gould's charge for building a 20 by 30 house at $400. In less than two years, in Jan. 1844, Gould bought the property back for the same $1200.

In May 1843 he built another house on the Luere lot for $2400. He sold the 35 foot 3 inches by 28 by 8 inch lot for $3000 to Boston traders John Woods and Joseph J. Bragdon, bounded on the south by the brick wall of Cummings's house, and on the north by the brick wall of his own house, in both of which they had the right to insert four inch timbers, take water from Gould's pump and drain, to use the six foot wide passage 28 feet 8 inches long on the church side, to use the arch on the west side of the house, and the "small necessary in the rear", reserving Buttrick and Patch's right to dig up and repair their water pipe across the lot. This placed the privy next to the neighborhood water supply in the southwest corner next to the church. No wonder that cholera and other water-born diseases spread so fast in Boston. The next day Gould mortgaged the lot back to Woods and Bragdon for $600 at 6 %, for a net cost of $2400 for the building. Gould discharged this in two years. Finally, two years later, in May 1845, Gould, unusually styled "Gentleman", bought from laborers John Woods and Joseph Bragdon the same lot and house. He paid $1800 and assumed Susannah Luere's mortgage of the same amount.

In 1846 Gould got a mortgage of $1000 on the whole property on North Margin Street from the estate of Elizabeth Hoppin, which he paid off in six years, in Jan. 1852.

In 1849 he lost possession of the Luere house when William Grubb and Benjamin Hudson, executors of Luere's estate, foreclosed on the mortgage "in breach of conditions".

Later that year Abijah Patch, the truckman to the north, paid him a nominal dollar to release the easement to light and air on the north side of "my wooden tenements on the rear of number 31 North Margin Street" which overlook Patch's land.

It is unclear how Gould regained the Luere lot, for in 1852 he mortgaged it with a double brick dwelling and outbuildings for $1800 to John M. Ward, gentleman, with the same passage, water from the pump, passage under the west end to the back house at # 47 owned by Gould, and the right to insert timbers of the east wall of the house as now inserted. This was discharged in 1860.

In 1852, after Gould had moved to Framingham, he sold the whole property (address # 47) for $6825 to Boston trader Gilman Caverly, subject to the mortgages which Caverly assumed, and Patch's right to move the water pipe in any other direction required. Caverly then gave Gould a 7 months mortgage for $2660 at 6 %, insuring it all for $3000; this was discharged promptly, ending a 26 year long interest in the property on North Margin Street.

Meanwhile, after 1834 Gould had probably built the houses that still stand on North Margin Street at numbers 35 and 37. In late 1834 he acquired from Samuel Beal 48 feet frontage on North Margin Street just south of the Second Baptist Church, at what is today numbers 35 and 37. The first record of his ownership is his sale in Dec. 1834 of property 23 feet fronting on North Margin near Cooper Street for $2600 to Boston trader Levi Brown, bordering his own house on the north, with which it shared a partition wall for 32 feet. This was witnessed by three of his children, Thomas 2d, Lydia age 18, and Delia age 17. The source of this property is not shown. The location is #35 which in 1993 has a three story brick house of about this age, owned by Nicolas Piso, candidate for Boston City Council in 1993. Gould may have built this, though its age is less clear than # 37 with which it shares a wall to the north.

In 1835 he sold the house to the north (# 37) which had a 25 foot front on the street, 77 feet on the Second Baptist Church on the north, 16 feet nine inches on Joseph Veazie at the back and 72 feet through the partition wall he had sold to Levi Brown. He sold it for $2900 to Joseph F. Davis, cabinetmaker. Gould at the same time gave Davis a mortgage for $1000 which he discharged two years later.

1860 (BP

IV.—Old Baldwin-Place Baptist Church. Built 1810.

The brick buildings on the right probably built by Thomas Gould. Photo by J.J.Hawes in Boston Public Library, in *Public Library Bulletin* 1860.

BALDWIN PLACE, NORTH END.

Gould then built even more substantial three-story brick houses to the east, along Baldwin Place to Salem Street. These have disappeared for late nineteenth century replacements, but the deeds give us unusually detailed descriptions of the houses he built.

In 1828, Gould had bought an empty lot on the east side of the Second Baptist Church from a Cambridge housewright, Joseph W. Welsh, in an irregularly shaped piece on the east side of Baldwin Place as it curved south to the meeting house. This included rights to pass on Baldwin Place, and to use the pump and well on the east side of the premises conveyed to the church committee, and to pay proportionate share of upkeep of the well. This cost him $2000 which he got back without profit by sale to the church five months later. This lot has remained open, now at the back of the Knights of Columbus Hall.

In 1829 he made a more permanent investment in a development by buying for only $200 buildings on a lot forty feet wide on the north side of Baldwin Place, and 28 feet deep, bounded by his old partner Benjamin Kimball, buying it from tinplate worker Ezra Hawkes, the man who had witnessed his foreclosure on widow Hunstable in 1824, and trader Ezra Eaton. A month later Gould mortgaged it back for $853.50, paying it off in less than three months. The increased value may represent replacement of old timber buildings at the west end of the old De Carteret dwelling, with new brick ones. Hawkes and Eaton then paid him $2125 for the brick building Gould was then building.

This and the following are the most detailed description we have of any houses built by Gould. He promised he will erect "within a reasonable time...a Brick dwelling three stories in heighth and build the front wall thereof with good faced bricks and underpin the same with hammered stone, and will lay the side walk in front of said building of six feet in width of brick and suitable edge stones...the steps in front of said building shall be of hammered Stone, and one of said steps only shall be on said side walk and that shall not exceed nine inches in width and shall have round corners, and that no cellar door shall be made in front of said building."

Eight months later he mortgaged it to merchant Asa Richardson for $2400 at the usual 6 % for three years, but paid it off in a year because he got the lower rate of 5 % from the Perkins estate combined with the North Margin Street property. The Perkinses carried him for over seven years, until 1838. But in 1836 he took a second mortgage for $5000 from merchant Daniel Cummings. The first mortgage was extended a year and assumed by Cummings, and all paid off at the end of 1838.

In 1829 Gould bought his fourth piece in the North End, at the southwest corner of Salem Street and Baldwin Place, where Lo Conte's restaurant is located in 1993, paying $1695.84 for 1356 2/3 square feet on which he promised he "will within a reasonable time from the date hereoff [1 April 1829] erect upon the said land a brick building three stories in height", described exactly as the previous house except that the one step is permitted in the passageway rather than in the street. He bought this from the same Hawkes and Eaton, here styled as gentlemen, while Gould is unusually called a "Carpenter".

That fall Gould lost two feet on Salem Street for the city's widening of the street, for when he mortgaged the corner building in November to housewright Joseph Ripley for $1200 it was narrowed. This was paid off in less than two months, probably marking Ripley's time building it. On the day he paid Ripley, 9 Jan. 1830, Gould, again "carpenter" mortgaged it for $3000 to merchant Benjamin P. Homer, paying $2000 off in two years, and the remainder by Dec. 1834.

Later in 1830 Gould made one of his smallest purchases, a four inch strip, 20 feet long, the east wall of his house, from his neighbor on Baldwin Place, John Symmes, paying $ 83.30. Three days before paying off the mortgage to Homer he sold the lot with brick dwelling for $6000 to gentleman Moses Pond, reserving the right to water to North Margin Street. Pond sold it at once, for half the price, to Massachusetts Hospital Life Insurance Co.. The sale was witnessed by two of his children, James, age 11 and Delia C. aged 17--an early education in real estate. From the initial investment of $2000 Gould had made $4000.

His son Thomas^6 Gould Jr. ended up with a house on Baldwin Place, valued at $3400 in 1831-3, and $4000 in 1834-5, a gain in value partly accounted for by the father's renting a shop to Thatcher R. Raymond to sell West India goods, which he switched to wooden ware in 1834.

On the day before Christmas 1836 Gould bought his ninth property in the area of the Second Baptist church, at what is now # 8 Baldwin Place, with 25 feet frontage on the south side, going forty feet deep, measuring from the center of the old Carteret entryway on the east, through the wall of the house on the east. He paid only eighty dollars to Ambrose and Sarah Nichols for the westernmost house on the Place, with rights "to a passage and staircase leading to and from the cellar and chambers" of the house, the stairs partly on Adam Thaxter's land at the back (south).

SALEM STREET PROPERTIES.

In 1830 the elder Gould was involved in a curious transaction on a house farther down Salem Street, a problem that was not settled for a whole decade. Jonathan Davis, a housewright, got $500 from Gould for a lot with 22 feet six inches on the street, going back 70 feet. Davis had got it from his wife and children, who got it from her father Thomas Page of Hawke, NH. On the same day Gould transferred it to Davis's three minor children Celestia, Mary and Juliette, reserving Davis's right to occupy the house with his wife rent free. However, although Davis had consented to this transfer he failed to record Gould's deed, took the deed from the house and hid or destroyed it. Thus it appeared in 1833 to be legally Gould's property. So the childrens' guardian asked Gould to make out a new deed, which he did, explaining the odd circumstances. But since no money is mentioned, Gould probably lost his five hundred dollars. But by 1839 the land had been sold to Gould's son-in-law Briggs Mann. Not until 1840 was the title cleared, after the Page's house had burned down, and James and Mary Graves quitclaimed to Gould for a dollar. Mary may he one of the three Davis daughters for whom Gould assumed the trust. The other Page heirs, Oren and Clarinda Page, and Daniel and Mary Jane Young all of Danville NH, also quit to Gould for a dollar. This enabled Gould to affirm his earlier sale of 17 foot 5 inch frontage on Salem St, and 52 feet back, to his son-in-law Briggs Mann, as we will see below.

With the money from these sales Gould bought in April 1835 a seventh investment in the area, this time 12 feet 3½ inches on Salem Street and north of a ten foot passageway, later widened into Cooper Street. The price he paid to merchant Page for part of China trade pioneer Elias Hasket Derby's estate was $3600 including rights to Vose's well and pump. Three years later Gould mortgaged it to Dr. Samuel Thomson, botanic physician, for $2000, including rights to Vose's well. A few months later he bought from Derby a ten foot strip to the north of this going 71 feet back to Jonathan Glazer's land, point just south of Derby's house on Salem Street, paying forty dollars. This was resold in 1856 to Sarah Pearson of Malden with the back of Page's land.

In 1839 Gould bought the next lot north with five feet front on Salem Street from his son-in-law Briggs Mann, housewright, who had married his eldest daughter Sophia in 1834, paying $800 for five feet on Salem Street, going back 71 feet to Glazer's land, and north 20 on Thomas Barnes's, and sharing the partition wall with Mann's house for 51½ feet. The deed was witnessed by 19 year old Charlotte Gould, his eighth child. Mann got this from the heirs of Jonathan Davis, for whom Gould had acted as strawman in the case of the missing deed above. It was a narrow lot bounded on the north by the brick partition wall of Mann's house on Salem Street (perhaps built by Mann to replace the old Derby house), going back to 24 feet on Jonathan Glazer's land to the west, and 20 feet on Thomas Barnes's land to the north. The price was $800. Two days later Gould mortgaged the combined frontage of 17 feet four inches on Salem Street, but only 51 feet back to trader Dexter Follett for $3000, with the buildings he was then erecting. This was discharged 6 years later.

Thomas's daughter Sophia had married Boston 4 Nov. 1834 Briggs[6] Mann (*John*[5], *Thomas*[4,3,2], *Richard*[1]), born Scituate 7 Jan. 1807, died Boston 27 June 1886; he was son of John Mann and his second wife Rebecca Briggs. He was a mason. In 1835 he shared his father-in-law's premises on Baldwin Place with Thomas Gould Jr., but moved to Friend Street by 1837, remaining in his father-in-law's house until 1839. By July 1840 Gould had given Mann the house on Salem Street and created a passage 2 feet 8 inches wide between Mann's house and the "new brick dwelling" he was building on a 19 foot frontage on Salem Street for widow Ann Jones, perhaps the same who was to marry his son James in 1842. She gave him a mortgage of $1500 for the lot 42 feet 7 inches deep north of Derby's lot. The house was insured for $1500, and the mortgage reassigned. Jones assigned the mortgage to the famous doctor moneylender Francis Parkman in 1844, perhaps on Gould's recommendation, since he already had two properties with the soon (1849) to be murdered doctor. This was not settled until 1863, when William Atkinson and George Russell foreclosed on the mortgage.

The next year, 1841, Mann got a $2400 mortgage from his father-in-law covering his lot to the north which shared a partition wall with Gould's house, facing 17½ feet on Salem Street and going back about 50 feet to Gould's land at the back, and Samuel Beal's to the north. Gould immediately assigned the mortgage for the same amount to William Minot, Esq.. Within a few months Mann sold the lot with buildings to David A. Boynton for $6000, an increase that indicates Mann (and perhaps Gould) had built a new brick house here. For the north boundary with Beal the deed speaks of bending along the north face of a brick wall conveyed with this deed. The deed was witnessed by Gould's daughter Charlotte, now married to Cyrus K. Dam. On the same day Mann (now styled a mason) paid Gould thirty dollars for a one foot wide passage under the east side of Gould's house leading north 22½ feet from Salem Street to the back of Mann's house.

In March 1842 Mann acquired a house at #29 Poplar Street where he and Sophia were to live until his death in 1886. It was appraised for $5000 in his estate. Mann's nephew Wendell E. Richardson of Arlington was administrator, reporting a total value of $14,864.22, of which his widow got $5000 personal estate plus half of the excess over $1000. Mann died intestate, with no living children, the eight listed heirs in addition to his wife being a brother and sister and children of his half-brothers and sisters. It is believed that Sophia and Briggs had a son Charles, but his birth and death have not been found. Sophia died in Boston 1 March 1900.

Gould's Salem Place house was occupied in 1844 by another daughter, **17.** Delia, married to James Fernald, mahogany dealer. They were married in Boston 25 Nov. 1841. Fernald was born in Kittery ME 1813, son of Ann Fernald, living 1851; and two brothers, Thomas C. and Elihu Fernald. Fernald was to be Assistant Assessor for the ward in 1846. He died in Boston 24 Dec. 1859, having made his will 21 Feb. 1851. At probate on 2 Jan. 1860 bond was posted by Thomas Gould, Sr. and Jr.. The inventory was done by his brother-in-law Francis Gould in March 1861, finding assets of nearly $2000 personal estate, $600 for a 12,000 foot lot on Maverick Street in East Boston, and $500 interest in the firm of Harrod & Fernald. But claims against the estate came to $3129.28, including small debts to Thomas Gould and Ezra Palmer Gould, so he was declared insolvent. His widow Delia petitioned to arbitrate the issue of his old partnership with Noah Harrod, which was given to Boston lawyers Charles F. Choate and Francis B. Hayes to arbitrate. Not until 1864 was the insolvent estate distributed, with Thomas getting $65.56 for his $75 debt and grandson Ezra getting $21.85 for his $25. Delia Cushing Gould Fernald died 28 April 1903, leaving no descendants, their two daughters having predeceased her: Anna Fernald, b. Boston 6 Nov. 1842 died 19 March 1899 unmarried; Delia Cushing Fernald d. 7 Sept. 1874; both are buried in the Gould lot in Mt. Auburn.

In early 1843 Gould sold the southern lot, now on the alley named Salem Place, and fronting 17 feet ½ inch on Salem Street to his abolitionist son teacher Samuel Lawrence Gould for $ 1200, and immediately mortgaged it back for the same price. He charged the usual rate of 6 %, for 2 years, but it was not paid off for over 12 years, in 1855. The deed was witnessed by three family members, Samuel's wife Frances A. and her sister Elizabeth, and his brother Joseph.

The back half of these lots with a 19 feet frontage on Salem Court was not sold until 1856 when Gould sold it with a depth of 42 feet subject to passage to Salem Street through an arch on the east side of Boynton's house. It was sold to Sarah A. Pearson of Malden, wife of Henry. With this he sold the ten foot wide strip 71 feet deep that he had bought from E. H. Derby in 1838. On the same New Year's Day Mrs. Pearson took a mortgage from Gould for the first parcel only, for $700, but the house (which he probably built here) insured for $1200. She discharged this 9 months later.

OTHER NORTH END PROPERTIES, 1835.

Meanwhile, in 1835, Gould made two investments in the North End outside of the Baldwin Place block. The first was in Prince Street where his son was to build, and the second in the notorious bawdy Ann Street, now called North Street

In May 1835 he bought Lot #2 Prince Street from Henry Farnham, gentleman, and Sarah

B. Farwell, administrators of the estate of Silas Atkins for $2500 with a 25 foot frontage on the street, going back 74 feet to a four foot passage. He mortgaged it back to the sellers for $2000 at 6 % payable semiannually in $ 666.66 installments; it was paid off in four years. In 1837 he sold this lot to his son Thomas Jr. for $2800 including the mortgage.

In July 1835 he made the brief investment in Ann Street. Drake describes the street named for Queen Anne as "Crowded at one time through its entire length with brothels and low dram-shops (153). Boston historian Walter Muir Whitehead tells that Ann Street had "degenerated into a rough waterfront region of disorderly houses and brawls" early in the century. He tells of the 1825 riot at the Beehive, and that "the nymphs of Ann Street" were complained about into the fifties when the name was changed to North Street.

Gould's property was a lot behind the New North Church, on Ann Court, near Bartlett (now Harris Street), called Page's Court c. 1837 according to the Boston Street Book. He had 82 feet on the court and on John Ball's land to the south, between 27 feet on Emeline Andrew's land on the west, and the respectable Robert Gould Shaw on the east, near Union Wharf. First, on 5 July 1835 Gould paid $598.38 plus $15.66 interest on Nathaniel Keith's mortgage to Robert Farley, and $3,300.87 for the property itself sold by Mary Ann Keith, administratrix of her husband Nathaniel's estate probated the previous year. Five days later he took the mortgage of one of the Irish immigrants to the North End, glass packer Michael and Margaret Haggerty, for $2,360.27. Three days later he paid her another $112.25, and five dollars to broker Thomas Robinson. The next day he got rid of the whole including the two mortgages for $3,500, having paid a total of $3,418.02 for a net gain of $81.98 in 11 days. He was assessed $3400 in May 1833, an increase of $400 over the value charged to William Jones, clothier.

A third and larger development was south of Cooper Street. In Dec. 1837 Gould paid $600 for the "mansion house and garden" of Alexander Edwards who left it by will of 1798 to his niece, wife of Hingham housewright Jedidiah Lincoln. The house was on the southwest corner of Cooper and Salem (then Back) Street. Their heirs, widow Mary Lincoln, Mary Riddle and coachmaker William O. Lincoln sold it to Gould, here called "merchant" for the only time.

Three months before this he had paid $11,228.16 at auction to Mary Smith, widow and executrix of merchant Benjamin Smith's estate on the southwest corner of Salem Street and what was to become Cooper Street, measuring fifty feet on Back (Salem) Street and 143 feet west on Cooper Street to the Mill Pond (Bartlett Street). At the end of this month Cooper Street was laid out and widened 17 feet onto Salem Street and 20 feet in 130 feet west; the city paid Gould $5,409 for the north strip of this land. Gould retained the rights to a well.

By these two transactions Gould became owner of the whole of the present day block between Cooper, Salem Streets and Bartlett Place. The widening of the street probably necessitated tearing down the Edwards mansion at the corner, perhaps then in bad repair. In early 1838 Gould took a mortgage from housewright Thomas Barnes on the remaining lot on the corner of Cooper and Salem Street for $3500 at 6 %, insured for $2000. This was witnessed by his son Samuel L. Gould. It was discharged in full just 3 years later by a guardian of an insane person.

In the middle of the block on Cooper Street, in the old Edwards garden, Gould apparently built a brick house about 23 feet wide on the street and 20 feet deep. He sold this in July 1838 to the well known East India merchant William H. Boardman, who was making good money in the trade in Sumatran pepper, Smryna opium, Northwest Coast furs, Cuban sugar and other international goods. Boardman also got rights to the six foot cistern and well on the land to the east. The sale was witnessed by three of Gould's children, his eldest son Thomas Jr., his 22 year old daughter Lydia who was to die unmarried in 1840, and his 16 year old son James.

The corner lot and the 32 foot frontage on the other side of Boardman's Gould sold for $7,800 in Oct. 1838 to the same Dr. Thomson, the botanical physician, including the six foot cistern on the west side of the corner lot. Thomson assumed the Barnes mortgage. From the three sales including the city's street Gould got $13,800, having paid $11,600, for a net gain of $2,200, which may represent his having built three houses.

Gould's final involvement in the North End was in 1843, when he became trustee for Mrs. Lois Davis of Charlestown for the property at the junctions of Endicott and Salem Streets, now lying under the former west off-ramp of the Southeast Expressway into Haymarket. The lot is a curiously shaped, with a 17 foot curve at the northwest junction of the streets, 73 feet on the east side of Endicott, 25 feet on the west side of Salem, and backing up 60 feet on a brick partition wall with Oliver's on Salem Street and 9 ft. 10 inches on a passage into Endicott separated from Bulfinch's property. Davis's trustee John Henry transferred this to Gould in 1843, but didn't record it until 1850 when merchant Andrew L. Chamberlain mortgaged it to Gould for $600, added to the first mortgage of $6000 held by James Savage. The terms were six percent, and insurance for $6000, probably the value of the building on this busy downtown corner.

Gould's daughter tells us "He took a contract for a business block on Lewis Wharf" in the North End, but there is no deed on record, so search must be made in Assessor's record for Ward 2 at the peak of his activity, 1832-48.

SOUTH END OF BOSTON

Although Gould was involved in the City Council's excitement about the development of the South End, just west of today's Theatre District, Gould took only a minor real estate interest there, a decade after his public service. His only purchase was Lot # 9 in Bay Village on the west side of Church Street, between S. Cedar Street (now Winchester) and Marion (now Melrose. He paid Roxbury bricklayer Ephraim Harrington and previous owner David A. Simmons $1000 for the 21 by 70 foot lot, with a $3000 mortgage to Dr. Parkman in 1839. Gould also paid the Bank of Norfolk in Roxbury a dollar for their interest, two days earlier. It is probable that a house was being built on the lot. Unusually identified as a carpenter, Gould quitclaimed it three and a half years later to laborer John White for a dollar, perhaps in payment for White's labor. By coincidence the site is only a couple of blocks southwest of the later Gould home of his grandson Thomas^7 Warren Gould.

CHELSEA

Gould's final piece of real estate in Boston proper was in a four story brick house on the east corner of Walnut and Fourth Streets in Chelsea. In 1866 Gould paid $3000 to Joshua Loring of Brookline for a mortgage on the property 28 feet on Fourth Street and 90 feet on Walnut. The next day Gould gave another $1000 for Loring's assignment of the mortgage he had to Alfred J. Mercer; the terms were usual six percent. This was discharged exactly three years later with the signature of Thomas Gould of Arlington.

COURT CASES

Considering the large number of real estate investments of Thomas Gould it would be surprising that there were no legal disputes. However, he does not appear to have had many, certainly compared to his litigious great grandfather William Gould. We have found no cases appealed to the Superior Judicial Court for Suffolk or Middlesex counties. The Court of Common Pleas is poorly indexed, but no cases are found 1826-8, and only two for the peak of his building activity.

In Oct. 1833 Thomas Gould, carpenter, brought a complaint against Asa Lewis, carpenter of Boston, in a writ dated 18 June 1833 for $6,974.54, requesting damages of $10,000 brought to the Court of Common Pleas on July 1833. The case was continued for years, until 18 July 1836 the agreement to refer was rescinded, and in Jan. 1837 Lewis and Gould agreed to refer it to John Pickering, Esq., Perez Loring and Edward Bell, for final decision by agreement of two of the three. Bell declined to serve, and was replaced by Calvin Bailey. The referees heard the parties and reported on 30 Sept. 1837 "do award and determine that the said Thomas Gould recover against the said Asa Lewis the sum of one hundred and ninety six dollars and thirty eight cents, in full satisfaction of the action and of all demands...and that the costs of Court shall be paid equally by the Parties...the Referees fees being two hundred and forty dollars shall be paid equally by the parties; and that each party shall pay the costs of the witnesses...". The Docket Book records that costs were paid 5 Dec.. Although he won the case, Gould lost money on court costs, plus unknown witness and lawyer's fees.

The second case was even more unfavorable. On 19 March 1838 Thomas Gould, housewright, brought a writ against Dr. Samuel Thompson, physician, to whom he had sold the two above mentioned properties on Salem Street on 21 May 1838 and the Cooper Street house on 9 Oct. 1838. His plea charged that Dr. Thompson owed him $1104.50, and also $1500 for "divers goods wares and merchandize etc", though often requested to pay has never paid it or any part, and neglects and refuses to do so. Thompson's attorney Augustus Peabody denied he had promised to pay the sum, while Gould's attorney Samuel D. Parker presented his case. The court ruled "that the Dfdt's plea aforesaid is good and sufficient. It is therefore considered by the Court that the deft Samuel Thompson, recover against the said Thomas Gould cost of suit taxed at,...". Gould then appealed to the Supreme Judicial Court. We should search for the appeal.

Part IV. THOMAS^5 GOULD'S FAMILY & HOMES IN CHARLESTOWN AND NEIGHBORING MIDDLESEX COUNTY

In addition to his holdings in Boston proper Thomas Gould owned real estate in twelve different locations in Middlesex County, northwest of Boston. These included four sites in his hometown of Charlestown, two in Cambridge, a development along the Charles River in Watertown, two lots in Framingham where he moved in 1852, his final residence in Arlington, and lots in Bedford and Newton, the latter as part of his estate. We will describe the early ones in order in which they were acquired, after 1822. The later ones after his move to Framingham will be described in Part VI. In this part we will discuss his property relations with his sisters 10. Nancy Turner, 11. Abigail Phillips and 12. Mary Ann Hovey, and his daughter Charlotte Dam. The descendants of the Turners, including the Burbank and Folsom branches, and the Phillipses will be detailed here, as the Hovey family was given in Part III.

PHIPPS STREET BURIAL GROUND, CHARLESTOWN

Gould's first acquisition of property in Charlestown came in 1822 when he built a seawall on the south side of Phipps Street Burial Ground by order of the Selectmen 4 May 1812. Peter Tufts' map of 1818 shows this faced onto the Charles River (as it did as late as 1878, King's Handbook). For this and a nominal dollar he received from the Charlestown Selectmen deeds to four cemetery lots, numbered 3,5,6 and 7 (Middlesex Deeds [hereinafter MD], 811:123, July 5, 1822). Three years later he sold # 7 to Caleb Symmes, Jr. for $100 (Charlestown *Record of Deeds 1800-73*, Boston Public Library Ms.fBos.XC4, 460, Book 3: 163). Not until 1859 did he sell lot 6, to Charles Perry, a Charlestown undertaker, a deed witnessed by his two daughters Delia Fernald and Elizabeth Gould (MD 811:124). We do not find record of sale of the other two lots 3 and 5. The 1994 location is on the north side of the cemetery, north of the short Sprague Path, facing the outer wall of Williams Street side, numbers 5 at the east end, dated July 5, 1822, and 3 at the west corner of 5, under the wall (City of Boston, map of Phipps Street Burial Ground, 1901, in inventory in Bostonian Society, c. 1985). Westward on the outer road, Austin Av., at the corner leading south to Hammond Path is Tomb No. 8, marked "Gould". We find no record of deed. Perhaps it was in exchange for lot 3 when it was cut off by the perimeter brick wall. The indication is that lots 3 and 5 are still owned in perpetuity by the heirs to Thomas Gould. We have no record of any burials here, for Thomas's first wife and he were buried in Copp's Hill, and later removed to Mt. Auburn. His mother, Anna Lawrence Gould was probably buried in lot 7, after her death 24 Oct. 1824. Of Thomas's children who died before 1822, Charlotte (1813) is more likely to have been buried with her mother Sophia on Copp's Hill. The other children who died young, Elizabeth 1818, twin Franklin 1831, Susan 1832, Benjamin 1839 may have been buried here, as might adult children and their families. Charlestown records in Boston Public Library may tell when building of wall on north side occurred, which may date exchange of lot 8 for 3. The inventory may give names on lots.

TRAINING FIELD, WINTHROP SQUARE, CHARLESTOWN

Under the will of his mother Anna Lawrence Gould, dated 7 Oct. 1824 he and his two sisters Nabby Phillips and Mary M. Hovey had received one sixth each of a lot on Adams Street, just east of the Training Field, and adjoining Thomas's lot on the east (MD 387:474). He sold half of his sixth for $150 to housewright Lenthal Phillips, husband of his sister Abigail, in 1837. The deed was witnessed by his son-in-law Briggs Mann and Thomas's wife (Ibid.). A few months before she made her will, widow Ann Gould straitened the line of this lot on the east along a wall built by her neighbor shipwright Caleb Pierce, going 26 feet south from Adams Street, then 26 feet three inches west to Leather's Nook of 5 feet 8 and 5 feet 9 (MD 257:66, 11 March 1824). This lot was divided by 1837 when the Hoveys and Phillipses exchanged halves (MD 362:241-2, 367:340). The Phillipes then sold the west side to Francis Simonds and Noah Butts for $500 (MD 367:341).

It is clear from this that Thomas had acquired the land on the Training Field before his mother's death, though the deed is not found in the Grantor index.

The house facing the Training Field at 26 Common Street, in 1993 Rose's Variety Store, was inherited by Thomas under the will of James D. Turner (MD 68:407). Turner died 15 Dec. 1818, having received it from his wife, **10.** Nancy Gould Turner who had died 12 Sept. 1818 (Letter from Barnabas Turner to his brother Nathaniel, 16 Nov. 1818, H. Burbank file RIN 52). It is doubtful that Nancy received the whole title since her sisters **12.** Mary Ann Hovey (1781-1848), and **11.** Abigail Phillips (1774-1874) were still living. We do not know if the property held in thirds, Thomas getting another third from his sister, or if it was left in 1791 to James's four living children, including Joseph, who died in 1823. The Turners' eldest son James Gould Turner, b. 1793 Charlestown (perhaps in this house), was killed in the War of 1812, on 30 Nov. 1815, off Cape May in the brig *Perseverence*, had his uncle Thomas Gould as executor (according to descendant Harry Burbank to author 17 Jan. 1994).

Thomas Gould was administrator of the elder Turner's estate in 1819 (Middlesex will 23058; Wyman 974). Gould, his Boston partner Ezra Hawkes, and his father-in-law Jonas Peirce posted bond for $10,000. Gould's son Joseph, carpenter, was one of the three who did the inventory, joining Nathaniel Crocker, shipwright, neighbor to the west.

They appraised "a part of a house with small lot of land" for $800, the same value for which Thomas Gould was assessed for half a house and shop in 1825 (Charlestown Assessors records, Readville, hereinafter referred to by Book; Vol. 20, 1825, 14). Gould sold Turner's share at auction for $380 to Sheperd Simond(s) of Charlestown (Ibid.). It had been mortgaged for $250 to Jonas Barrett 1818, discharged 1825 (Ibid.).

THE TURNER FAMILY

10. Nancy Gould m. Charlestown 28 Aug. 1791 James Davis Turner, bp. Charlestown 13 Nov. 1758 (**Wyman** 973), s. John[2] (John[1]) & Hannah Davis; d. Charlestown 15 Nov. 1818. For ancestry see Sumner A. Davis, *Descendants of Barnabas Davis,* [Talladega AL: the author, 1973], 266. Following Nancy's death, he m. (2) Charlestown 21 April 1816 widow Mary Warren of Boston (Chas. Archives 4:149; int. 3 April, VR 1:546). No children by the second marriage.

Nancy Gould and James Davis Turner had seven children, all born Charlestown except Barnabas. The eldest, James died without issue, as noted above, and the youngest two, Thomas Jefferson (bp. 26 Jan. 1805) and William (bp. 20 Sept. 1807) evidently died young.

The eldest surviving child, Barnabas, b. Cambridgeport, 21 April, 1794, bapt. 27 May, d. Charlestown 17 July 1851; m. Charlestown, 1 Jan. 1815 Sally Bodge b. Reading, 12 Jan. 1797, d. Medford 11 Dec. 1867, d. Henry Bodge of Charlestown and Jerusha Eaton. Barnabas was a professional soldier, a non-commissioned officer in U. S. Army in the Florida Indian Wars (Co. E, First Reg. Artillery 1826-36; Ft. Monroe 1832-7) and the Mexican War. He died Charlestown 17 July 1851. They had four children, i. James Gould Turner (b. Cambridgeport 11 Jan. 1816, d. New Britain CT 13 March 1884) who owned the bible of his great grandmother "Mrs. Ann Gould"; res. Dedham.

iii. Henry Bodge Turner, cordwainer, b. Cambridgeport 22 Aug. 1820; d. Malden 7 Sept. 1881, m.. Charlestown 26 Sept. 1844 Frances C. Copps of Charlestown, b. c. 1827.

iv. Harriet Turner, b. Dedham 20 Feb. 1823; m. Pierce.

THE BURBANK FAMILY

The Burbank family is descended from Barnabas & Sally Turner's second child, ii. Eliza Turner, b. Cambridgeport 9 May 1818, d. Medford 5 Dec. 1890; m. Charlestown 6 Aug. 1837 carpenter and housewright William[7] Burbank (William[6], Gershom[5], Cabel[4], Eleazer[3], Cabel[2], John[1]) b. Bethel VT 17 Sept. 1809, d. Medford 7 March 1853.

They had seven children, the first three born Charlestown, the rest in Medford:
i. William Henry b. 13 March 1838, Lt. in Union Army, died of wounds after amputation of leg, battle of White House VA 11 June 1864.

ii. James Oscar Burbank, druggist b. 6 Aug. 1840, d. Manchester NH 21 Feb. 1916, m. Manchester NH 4 March 1862 Emma Augusta Hadley, b. VT. 1846, d. 3 June 1898, d. Sidney Hadley and Mary Ann Dow; they had ten children: i. Charles Oscar, druggist, b. Manchester NH 9 Feb. 1864, d. Boston 28 Dec. 1909, m. Manchester 12 July 1884 Fanny Etta Stevens, b. E. Montpelier VT, 27 Sept. 1868, d. Daniel Stevens & Betsey Ann Chamberlin; d. Manchester 15 May 1903; bur. Manchester. They had 3 ch. b. Manchester NH:
i. Henry[10] Oscar Burbank, trucker, b. 7 Oct. 1886, d. Manchester 24 Dec. 1955, m. Cambridge 28 Nov. 1912 Mary Agnes Burke, nurse, b. Attenry, Galway, Ireland, 7 Aug. 1886, d. Patrick Burke & Dehlia Corbett; d. Weymouth MA 20 May 1968, bur. Braintree; Henry Oscar & Mary had two children: i. Henry Burke Burbank, sales exec. and genealogist, b. Brookline 9 June 1915, m. 26 Dec. 1941 Elizabeth Arend, b. Newton MA, 11 Oct. 1912, d. Frank Spener Arend & Elise Ellen Parkinson, d. Norton MA res. Box 48, Norton MA 02766. 3 ch., b. Norton: i. Betsey[12] Wilson Burbank, artist, 2 Oct. 1947, d. Norton 10 Jan. 1986 unm.; ii. David Oscar Burbank, lawyer, Dartmouth AB 1970, b. 11 Feb. 1949, m. Groton CT, 19 June 1971 Christine McCarter. Res. Pittsfield MA. 2 ch. b. Pittsfield: i. Elizabeth [13] McCarter Burbank, b. 13 Nov. 1976; ii. Margaret McCarter Burbank, b. 30 Oct. 1979.
The third child of Henry & Elizabeth Burbank is Charles Spencer Burbank,

mathematician, b. 27 Dec. 1952, m. Eugene OR 18 Dec. 1979 Karen Li of Hong Kong, b. Hongkong. Three children: i. Katherine[13] Li Burbank, b. Portland OR 24 Feb. 1984, ii. Carolyn Li, b. Norton MA 23 Nov. 1985; iii. James Spencer, b. Norton 26 March 1989. Res. Swansea MA; he works for Brown & Sharp, Providence.

The second child of Henry Oscar Burbank & Mary was Mary Elizabeth Burbank, b. Brookline 17 April 1917, d. Falmouth MA 3 May 1976, m. Brookline 3 July 1948 Howard F. Lannon, res. 260 W. Colony Rd., Falmouth MA. 3 ch. b. Brighton MA: i. Mark Burbank Lannon, medical technician, b. 27 May 1949, m. Weymouth MA, 11 July 1970 Jean Baird, Res. Florida; one ch.: Karen Lannon b. Pasco Co. FL 4 Jan. 1976. ii. Peter Burbank Lannon, engineer, b. 28 Aug. 1950, m. Weymouth MA, 19 Aug. 1972 Barbara Buckley. One ch.: James Lannon, b. Marshfield MA Nov. 1970. Res. Marshfield MA. iii. Jane Lannon, apparel designer, b. 9 April 1956, unm., res. Boston.

The second child of Charles[9] & Fanny Burbank was Betsey May Burbank, woodcarver, b. Manchester NH Nov. 1887, d. Manchester 13 June 1955, m. Manchester 28 Dec. 1910 Henry W. Sawyer, civil engineer. sp.

The third ch. of Charles & Fanny Burbank was Ira[10] Leon Burbank, railway conductor on Maine Central, b. Manchester NH 31 Aug. 1889, d. S. Portland 30 Jan, 1951, m. Mable Tibbetts, she was living Portland ME 1985. 3 ch.: i. Leon[11] Burbank, res. S. Portland, with 3 ch. incl. dau. who has 6 ch.; ii. Eleanor, iii. Marilyn.

The second ch. of James Oscar Burbank and Emma was Eva[9] Augusta Burbank, b. Boston, 16 Nov. 1865, d. Goffstown NH 21 March 1928; m. twice, (1) 18 Aug. 1888, Manley S. Adams, electrician, b. Canada 1872. m. 2) Manchester 3 April 1893 Peter F. Slavin, Eva and Manley Adams had one ch., Edward F. Adams, b.c. 1889, d. Manchester NH 20 Nov. 1945, occ? m. Ethel C. Edward & Ethel had 7 children, b. perhaps Manchester NH: i. Harold E. Adams; ii. Francis E.; iii. William O.; iv. Eva A. m. Mitchell; v. Margaret m. Wostowic; vi. Ella m. Swanson; vii. Elizabeth "Bessie" m. Robichaud, Berlin NH 1945. All ex. Bessie res. Manchester NH 1945.

Third ch. of James & Emma Burbank was William Edwin Burbank, art teacher, b. Boston 6 Oct. 1866, d. Manchester 3 March 1941 unm.

Fourth ch. of James & Emma was Walter Henry Burbank, druggist, b. Manchester 22 Sept., 1868, d. unm. Melrose 8 Jan. 1953. Res. Malden.

Fifth ch. of James & Emma was George Edgar Burbank, b. Manchester 5 Aug. 1870, d. Manchester 30 Sept. 1870, ae. one month.

Sixth ch. of James & Emma was Nellie May Burbank, b. Somerville MA 21 Sept. 1871, d. Manchester NH 9 July 1871, age 10.

Seventh ch. of James & Emma was George Alfred Burbank, b. Charlestown 4 March 1874, d. Manchester NH 12 April 1892, sp. age 18.

Eighth ch. of James & Emma was Frederick Eugene Burbank, who worked for Christian Science Publishing House and Eastern Steamship Co., b. Charlestown 15 Dec. 1877, d. Wilmington MA, 7 Feb. 1948, m. perh. Gardner ME Charlotte May Trott, sp. Res. Malden.

Ninth & Tenth ch. of James & Emma were twins: ix. Mary Elizabeth Burbank, seamstress, b. Manchester 9 May 1881, d. Portland ME, m. Portland, Harry T. Wall, sp. x. Emma Alice Burbank, d. Manchester 25 Aug. 1886, age 5.

The third child of Eliza Turner & William[7] Burbank was iii. Edwin Chapin Burbank, b. Charlestown 22 June 1843, d. Medford 23 Dec. 1928, m. 4 Sept. 1881 Hannah Alice Bowman, sp.. He was the last survivor of Co. E, 5th Mass Inf., chief librarian Medford Public Library where he worked 18 years; then pay teller at Savings Bank.

Fourth child of Eliza & William Burbank was iv. Ella Louisa Turner Burbank, teacher and genealogist, b. Medford MA, 17 Apr. 1846; d. Medford 5 May 1929, unm., Regent of DAR, teacher 40 years in Boston area, incl. 25 years at Brimmer School Boston, Somerville, Medford High School, taught Sunday School at Universalist church, Medford, 50 years.

Fifth ch. of Eliza & William Burbank was v. Ida Eaton Burbank, b. Medford, 19 May 1849; d. unm. 3 March 1911.

Sixth ch. of Eliza & William Burbank was vi . Charles Edgar Burbank, b. Medford, 22 June 1851; d. Medford 18 July 1854.

FOLSOM BRANCH

Seventh ch. of Eliza & William Burbank was vii. Eva Turner, b. Medford, 8 Aug. 1853, d. Medford 2 May 1931, m. 14 Sept. 1881 Rev. Frederick A. Folsom, b. N. Abington 6 Aug. 1852, d. Medford 13 Jan. 1905; Universalist minister. She was member of DAR. They had one child, Unitarian minister Rev. Josephine Burbank Folsom, b. Medford 4 July 1886, d. Pittsfield ME 5 Feb. 1945, m. 20 Oct. 1909 Unitarian minister Rev. Milo Garfield Folsom, b. Stockholm NY 6 Aug. 1881, d. Pittsfield 18 May 1939, Universalist minister Dolgeville NY, Heightstown NJ, Portland ME, Pittsfield ME.; grad. St. Lawrence Col., Tufts. She was ϕBK, M.Theol. Tufts, M.Theol. Tufts, ordained Gardner ME 1927. They had 3 ch.: i. Frederick Milo Folsom, b. Dolgeville NY 21 May 1912, m. 1942 Marjorie Dupres; he grad. St. Lawrence Col. 1933, grad. work Syracuse; served in US Navy WW II, went to FL, then Australia, last known res. FL 1947.

The second child of Rev. Josephine & Milo Folsom was Lois Josephine Folsom, antique dealer, b. Hightstown NJ 4 July 1913, m. Rev. William Whittemore Lewis, Unitarian minister, b. AB St. Lawrence 1934; d. Boca Raton FL 28 Oct. 1989. He was Unitarian-Universalist minister Westford MA 1936-41, Keene NH 1941-5, Portsmouth NH 1945-55, Arlington MA 1955-68. She res. May-Oct. Spofford NH 03462, Nov.-April 504 SW Second, Boca Raton FL 33432. They had 4 ch.:

i. Judith, "Judie", NMI Lewis, upholsterer, b. Westford MA 20 Feb. 1938, m. Arlington MA, 7 Sept. 1958 Prof. David Sherman Betts, prof, engineering NYSU, res. Box 175 W. Oneonta NY 13861. She is Assistamt Deputy Commissioner for Otsego County. 3 ch.: i. Kenneth Sherman Betts, P-3 pilot U. S. Navy, grad. RPI, b. Iowa City IA. 23 Sept. 1959; ii. Michael Whittemore Betts, b. Iowa City 10 Dec. 1960, AB U NC; iii. Jennifer Leah Betts, b. Oneonta NY 27 June 1963, AB Wells 1986.

The second child of Lois & William Lewis is Jonathan "Jon" Whittemore Lewis, tile businessman, b. Westford MA 22 Oct. 1940, m. Keene NH, 4 Oct. 1972 Katharine Kunz Blancato, div. Nov. 1981; one ch., Crystal Folsom Lewis, b. Keene NH 23 Feb. 1973. Res. 3590 Woodside Dr., Apt. 2, Margate FL 33063.

Third child of Lois & William Lewis is William Christopher Lewis, CPA, b. Keene NH 2 May 1943, m. Aspen CO, 2 Nov. 1970 Margaret Leclerc, therapist, res. 10706 Bordley, Houston TX 77042. One ch., Natasha (legally changed to Tasha) NMI Lewis, b. 21 May 1971.

Fourth child of Lois & William Lewis is Jefferson Walter Lewis, b. Keene NH 22 Nov. 1944, m. Aspen CO, 26 Sept. 1970 Diane McKenna, RN, res. Rt. 2, Box S V 23 E. Stroudsburg PA 18301. Two ch.: i. Patrick Anthony Lewis, b. Miami FL 6 Aug. 1975 (ad); ii. Amy Marie Lewis, b. Delray Beach FL 28 Nov. 1977.

Third child of Rev. Josephine Burbank and Milo Folsom was Ella Elizabeth Folsom, b. Portland ME 15 Sept. 1916, d. Portland 24 March 1918, age 20 months.

NATHANIEL TURNER DESCENDANTS

The third child of Nancy Gould and James Davis Turner was Nathaniel Turner, b. Charlestown Sept. 1796, bp. 2 Oct. 1797, d. Charlestown 20 Nov. 1835 (g.s.), m. Brookline, 12 Oct. 1817 Julia Ann Dowling, b. Philadelphia 23 June 1795, d. Medford 10 Dec. 1874; she was ward of Commodore William Bainbridge of USS *Constitution*. They had 7 children, born in Charlestown: i. James Davis Turner, b. March 1819; married, worked Charlestown Navy Yard.
ii. Susan Parker, b. 1821, bp. 30 Sept. 1827; d. unm. Medford? 16 July 1882.
iii.Caroline Matilda, b. 1822, bp. 30 Sept. 1827; d. Medford 5 Aug. 1899; m. Medford 9 Nov. 1841 John Russell, carpenter, b. Lexington, 31 Oct. 1814, s. of veteran of Battle of Lexington, Samuel & Betsy Small; d. Medford 1 Feb. 1894; they had 2 children, Caroline Baker Russell b. Charlestown, bp. Medford 6 Nov. 1842, d. Medford 6 Nov. 1940 unm., governess of Gen. Lawrence family Medford, DAR 1922 #175629.

Second ch. of Caroline & John Russell was John Winslow Russell, b. Medford 26 Apr. 1847, d. Medford 28 Jan. 1897, m. Chicago c. 1882 Annie Bent, b. 20 July, d. Nathaniel G.&

Elizabeth Sargent of Annisquam; their only child, Arthur E. Russell, b. Chicago 25 Feb. 1883, m. twice, (1) Bath ME Isabelle Turner, d. Edward H. & Caroline Riaby, d. 2 July 1935, sp.; perh. ad. dau. Carrie? (2) Lula Turner, res. 72 Cedar Rd., Medford; he grad. MIT 1901, and was naval architect with U. S. Navy.

iv. William Bainbridge Turner, bp. 30 Sept. 1827; m. Achasa_____; res. Polk Street, Cambridge 1866-71; 2 ch.: Carrie A. Turner, b. 14 May 1862, m. Loring E. Nichols b. 1 June; son George W. Nichols b. May, res. Okla?; second child Walter Turner b. 1852, d. 28 Oct. 1855, ae. 2, sp., buried Woodlawn Gem., Everett.

v. Sarah Elizabeth "Lizzie" Turner, b. 2 June 1828, d. Medford Feb. 1923, m. Benjamin Franklin Perkins of Medford, who had stall at Faneuil Hall market, and cousin of founders of the school for the blind (1826-93); res. cor. Central & Highland, Somerville; sp.

Twins: vi. Thomas Miller Turner, b. 8 March 1831, d. Lynn 12 Sept. 1882, bur. Woodlawn Cem.; m. Rachel___. sp.

RAYMOND BRANCH

The Raymond branch of the Turner family is descended from the youngest child, a twin, of Nathaniel & Julianna Turner: vii. Richard Devens Turner, d. Somerville 31 March 1875, m. Charlestown 1 Dec. 1849 Elizabeth Frances Pearson, b. Charlestown 2 March 1830, d. Jefferson Pearson & Harriet Mears, d. Somerville 11 Feb. 1892; 2 children b. Charlestown:

i. Hattie Devens Turner, b. 25 July 1862, d. Somerville 9 July 1933, m. Somerville 27 Oct. 1883 George Johnston Raymond, b. Woodstock NB 2 July 1852, s. Cadwallader Mallory & Judith Ann Squires, d. Hot Sprs. AK 14 Feb. 1915.

Their only child Arthur Devens Raymond, b. Cambridge 20 Aug. 1886, d. Concord 23 Oct. 1964, m. Somerville 25 June 1907 Emma Marion Graves, b. Charlestown 22 June 1887, d. David Bingham & Juliette Sabina Benson, d. Concord 18 May 1945. Arthur and Emma had 5 children, born Somerville except the last: i. Elizabeth Harriet, d. at birth 6 June 1910.

ii. Wilbur Devens Raymond, CPA and family genealogist, b. 6 June 1910, m. Melrose MA 11 June 1935 Edith Marjorie Kettell, theater archivist at Harvard's Widener Library, b. Cambridge 16 Sept. 1908, d. Oscar Alfred & Elina Persson, Radcliffe 1930, d. New London NH 11 Dec. 1993. They res. Somerville until 1991, then RR 1, Box 2640 New London NH 03257. They had one child, David Kettell Raymond, graphic designer, b. Arlington 12 Jan. 143, m. 30 Sept. 1967 Susan Carolyn Weyland, b. Malden, 30 Dec. 1945, d. Wendell Vernon & Helen Bissett. BA advertising design BU School of Fine Arts; staff artist Prudential Ins., graphic designer Digital Corp. Bio. in *Who's Who in the East*, 1983/4. Res. Littleton MA; 2 ch. Jonathan David, b. 5 Oct. 1968, Mark Christopher, b. Concord 31 Aug. 1972.

Arthur & Emma Raymond's third child was Barbara Jeanette, b. 30 Dec. 1912, m. four times: (1) Wilmot NH, 5 Oct. 1933 Robert Emerson Sheldon of Melrose, div. 1939 sp.; (2) Seabrook NH, 2 Nov. 1942 John A. Kelley of Arlington, two times winner of Boston Marathon, they res. W. Acton MA, div. 1952 sp.; (3) CA, and (4) Edwin McColl, div. twice, sp.

The fourth child of Arthur & Emma was George Johnston Raymond, toolmaker, b. 30 April 1915, m. Maynard MA, 1 June 1947 Priscilla Edwards, b. Malden MA, 9 March 1921, d. William Frederick & Ethel Florence Jamieson. They res. Acton MA where he worked for Rex Knife Co. 2 ch.: b. Concord MA: i. Louisa Raymond, b. Concord 18 April 1954, m. Wichita Falls TX 16 June 1978 David Lee Van Home, USAF, b. Malta OH, s. William L. Van Home; Res. Marquette MI; 2 ch. b. Chandler AZ: Maryann, b. 29 Jan. 1980; Matthew David, b. 29 Nov. 1981. ii. Elizabeth Anne Raymond, b. 5 March 1956, m. 31 Dec. 1983 Ronald Arthur Hersom, b. ME, res. Portsmouth NH 1984.

The fifth ch. of Arthur & Emma was Phyllis Arlene Raymond, nurse, b. Cambridge 26 Oct. 1916, m. Winchester MA, 18 Oct. 1939 Churchill Augustus Newman, b. Boston, 22 Sept. 1911, s. Edwin Augustus & Ruth Ann Churchill, d. Harvard MA 8 Nov. 1983. She grad. Northfield-Mt. Hermon. Res. 1994: 31 Still River Rd., Harvard MA 01451. 4 children: i. Charlene Newman, b. Boston 18 Oct. 1941 Boston 9 July 1967, m. Sterling MA, 20 Feb. 1965

Robert Shattuck Davis, b. Sterling MA, 10 Jan. 1938, s. Jonathan Davis & Elizabeth Maddison. She grad. Northfield-Mt. Hermon; AB Tufts 1967. He rem. (2) Jan. 1969 Sandra Digon, res. Sterling MA. 3 ch. by Charlene: unnamed twins lost 1966; iii. Sarah Elizabeth Davis, b. Worcester, 22 Feb. 1967, AB Simmons 1987.

The second child of Phyllis & Churchill Newman is Muriel Lee Newman, b. Concord 4 June 1943, AB Clark U. 1964, m. Sudbury MA, 1 March 1968 Bruce Edwin Healey, computer sales, s. Robert E. & Ruth Healey; 2 ch. Shana Ann. b. 12 Oct. 1975, Morgan Carol b. 24 July 1980. Res. Lunenburg MA.

The third and fourth children of Phyllis & Churchill were twins, b. 2 July 1947: Gregory Arthur Newman, auto mechanic, m. Harvard MA, 24 Nov. 1973 Karen Taylor, b. Harvard, 27 Aug. 1952, d. Roland Francis & Margaret Louise Poitras; res. Ayer MA. One ch.: Gary Allan Newman, b. Concord 10 Jan. 1976. The second twin was Alison Churchill Newman, m. Okinawa 22 Aug. 1969 William Gregory York, b. Bath ME, 21 July 1948, s. William Herbert & June Christine Varney. Res. Amherst NH. 2 ch.: Devon Charlene, b. Concord NH 31 Oct. 1974; Adam Tyler, b. Nashua NH 6 Aug. 1981.

The second child of Richard Turner and Elizabeth: Minnie Stimpson Turner, b. Charlestown, 27 March 1865, d. Medford MA, 17 April 1936 unm.. She was teacher at Fanny Farmer's cooking school for five years, c. 1911-5 (Obit. 24 April 1936). After Ms. Farmer's death 15 Jan. 1915 Minnie and Lucy G. Alien started their own school until the outbreak of World War I in 1917. She then contributed to the war effort by teaching food conservation under the National Civic Assn., with which she continued after the peace as director of Household occupations, and President from 1930 to her death. She was a founder of the Somerville Teachers Club, member of League of Women Voters. She was one of the first summer residents at Blodgett's Landing on Lake Sunapee NH. She taught 25 years in Somerville schools 1886-1911, at Edgerly & Burns schools. Her papers are at Schlessinger Library, Radcliffe.

The fourth child of Nancy Gould and James Davis Turner was Nancy Turner, bp. Charlestown 20 Oct. 1820 , m. Charlestown 9 March 1820 (int. 13 Feb. VR 559) Abijah Bemis of Weston. No death and children in Weston VR. A granddaughter married Mr. Pratt.

The fifth child of Nancy Gould and James Davis Turner was Mary Turner, bp. Charlestown 11 Jan. 1802 (Hunnewell 218), m. Charlestown 1820 Nichals Pertz.

The sixth child of Nancy & James Turner was Thomas Jefferson Turner, bp. Charlestown 20 Jan. 1807. He was living 1818 at his father's death, but we have no further record of him.

The seventh child of Nancy & James Turner was William Turner, bp. Charlestown 26 Sept. 1807. He was living at his father's death in 1818. It may be he, listed as William L[awrance?] Turner who m. Charlestown 30 Oct. 1845 Miss Sarah M. Beard of Charlestown (VR 700).

GOULD'S OTHER PROPERTIES IN CHARLESTOWN

Returning to Thomas Gould's property in Charlestown, a Thomas Gould residing in Boston is shown as the owner of three properties in Charlestown after 1826: a whole house by Mr. Sprague worth $667 and a shop by Varney, and an "Old House" with $534, for a total of 1201, and tax of $72.06 (1826, 15). The implication is that Gould bought out Simonds share to own the whole. In 1830 the value of the old house is reduced to 250 and the house by Sprague to $650, for a total of $900 and tax of $54, which continued thru 1833 (vol. 21, 26). In 1835 the house value went up to $800, and the store down to $200, and the next year the house up to $1000, probably reflecting the real estate boom (vol. 29, 1835, 1836).

After twenty years' possession, in 1837, Thomas sold the property to his brother-in-law and neighbor to the east, Lenthal Ells Phillips (MD 368:407) for $1200. The price was the same as the assessed value in 1836, $1000 for the house on the Training Field and $200 for the store nearby (vol. 29, 1836). Sometime before the boundary between the Adams Street and Common

Street lots had received "some little straitening of the lines by said Gould and the other legal heirs of the late James Gould's estate" (ibid.). The 1837 deed was signed by his wife and witnessed by his 20 year old daughter Delia and 17 year old son James.

PHILIPPS FAMILY

Another change occurred when Abigail Gould's husband Lenthall Ells Phillips died in 1843. **11.** Abigail Sloan married Boston 23 Oct. 1808 to Lenthall Ells Phillips, b. 17 Sept. 1787, d. Charlestown 21 July 1843 (implying second marriage for her). He was a ships carpenter and joiner who worked many years at the Charlestown Navy Yard, and in the Florida Navy Yard. (Charles H. Farnham, *History of the Descendants of John Whitman* [New Haven: Tuttle, Morehouse, 1889], 143, t 2259). Of their four children Abigail and Electa appear to have died young; Susan Harriet m. 25 Dec. 1827 Jacob Waitt of Charlestown, and had Edwin C. and Freeman Charles; Lenthall W. m. 26 Nov. 1837 Caroline Elliott (b. 19 Dec. 1816 Cambridge, VR 556) and had Charles Anderson b. 21 Aug. 1838 (prob. Charlestown) and Caroline who m. Cornelius Henry of Charlestown and had four children, living Somerville 1895. Lenthall's brother Joseph was the father of two Classical scholars, John L. T. Phillips (1827-79), Librarian of Williams College and Professor of Greek, and his sister Lucy C. Phillips, Professor of Latin and French at Williams.

Abigail declined to be administratrix of her husband's estate, resigning to her son (Middlesex Probate 39405, 15 Aug., 1843. The inventory was taken by Thomas Gould and his son Thomas Jr., appraising the house on Common and Mechanic Street at $1550. In 1843, Lenthall W. Phillips, Gentleman of Charlestown sold to Thomas Gould Jr., housewright his right in this property which he got from him in Nov. 1837, paying $700 to buy it back (MD 434:239; 348:459). In 1860 the Mayor and Aldermen of Charlestown attempted to appoint a guardian for Abigail, alleging that "by excessive drinking and idleness, so spend, waste, and lessen her estate, as to expose herself and family to want and suffering; and does thereby endanger and expose the town to a charge or expense for her and their maintenance and support" (Middlesex Probate 39393, 13 April 1860). Her brother Thomas Gould objected and the petition was dismissed on June 12.

Thomas Jr. then sold the property back to the Phillips family, for $700, to Caroline (Elliott) Phillips, wife of his nephew Lenthall W. Phillips, part of the estate of Lenthall Phillips with a straitening of the line on the east between Phillips and Pierce, being one undivided half, subject to the rights of her mother, widow Abigail Gould Phillips (MD 851:80). Caroline had already acquired one sixth held by Susan H. Waitt, wife of the painter George W. Waitt of Charlestown for $50 (MD 811:171, 1859), then paid Lewis Colby of Cambridge $500 for each sixth that had gone to Edwin C. and Freeman C. Waitt (MD 981:195). Having consolidated the family shares for $1250, she then took out a mortgage for $600 from the Warren Institution for Savings in Oct. 1866, paid off in 1878 (MD 981:197). Abigail probably remained in the house until her death on 14 Jan. 1874.

The property remained in the Gould family until as late as May 1879 (National Register Charlestown, C 71, Landmarks Commission, Boston, 2; hereinafter NHR; see MD 981:195, SD 1458:24). In 1875 Atlas #27 Common Street is shown as "Lenthall Phillips Street " (Suffolk Co. Atlas, Charlestown, 1875, v.6, plate A). NHR says that later owners were Joseph & Elizabeth A. Campbell of Boston and Edward Wentworth in early 1900s, but Wentworth and Eliz. Campbell are not in Middlesex deeds index 1881-1925. The record may show up in Suffolk deeds after annexation of Charlestown. The 1912 Atlas shows the owner as John C. Sullivan (#20 Common Street, 1157 sq.ft., 2), and the 1922 Atlas shows William H. Turner (2).

The only other property held by Thomas Gould in Charlestown was as trustee for the same widow Lois Davis whose properties he had handled in the North End. He paid the previous trustee John Henry $625 on her instruction, for lot V with 22 feet on the north side of Bartlett Street north of Bunker Hill, going back about 75 feet, assuming the mortgage for $500 and insurance from April first "on such building as was agreed to be built thereon" (MD 453:154, 9 Nov. 1844). Gould may have built the house that existed by Nov. 1844. Seven years later, in 1851 Gould acted on Mrs. Davis's written request to transfer the property to her daughter, widow Mary Ann Savage of Charlestown, and after her death to her minor children George Henry and Francis G. Savage (MD 561:540).

CAMBRIDGEPORT

Cambridgeport was a rapidly developing area between the old college town of Cambridge and Boston, separated from the city by the Charles River, now spanned by new bridges.

Three days before Christmas 1842 Gould paid $4500 to his son-in-law trader, Cyrus King Dam, who had married his daughter Charlotte "Lottie" in 1840, and had their first child Benjamin Franklin Dam (b. Boston, 15 Aug. 1840), and expecting their second child Cyrus Jr. (b. 8 Feb. 1843) (MD 422:455; Albert Lamson and Clarence Dame, "William Dam of Dover N.H., and Some of his Descendants", *Register* [Oct. 1938; hereinafter Dam], 359). He bought a 12,546 sq. ft. lot with house fronting 72 feet on the west side of the County Rd. in Cambridgeport, which was to become Prospect Street, 350 north of Broadway, going 174 feet back. Dam had bought the house eight months earlier from Madison Homer for $300 (MD 414:428).

Three years later Gould agreed to assign a mortgage of $1300 which he had received from Rev. Francis Parkman on the house, now on Prospect Street, to Steele & Dickinson (MD 474:154). The conveyance was to be made when Gould paid $3021 which he owed to Parkman.

By the birth of their fourth child Lydia in May 1848 the Dams had moved to Princeton, MA (Dam, 359), and Gould sold the house the following year, at considerable loss. He sold it for $2,925 to Cambridge druggist Joseph Studley, subject to a $1300 mortgage to Rev. Parkman at the usual six percent, which Studley took over (MD 540:469). The next year, 1850, Dam sailed to California in the Gold Rush, found land in 1852 in Wheatland, and brought his wife Lottie and their children out in 1856, where their descendants still live.

BELMONT

In 1833-6 Gould was involved in the disposal of his father-in-law Jonas Peirce's estate that had come to his wife Lydia. After the death of Peirce in 1833 he mortgaged his wife's half of the "Tavern Stand", six acres in West Cambridge (now Belmont) on the north side of the Great Road (Massachusetts Av.) back to the Old Back Road to Charlestown (Broadway) for $1900 to Seth Frost, a local farmer; it was then occupied by Charles Gordon (MD 321:563). Lydia's brother George Peirce mortgaged his half and the tavern itself to Frost on the same day (MD 321:562).

Three years later, in 1836, Gould sold the same six acres plus four on the west side of the Great Road over to the north side of Spy Pond for $1800 to Philip Whittemore, West Cambridge innholder (MD 351:95). Whittemore took over the mortgage of $3,500 from Post, discharged by his estate in 1850 (MD 351:96). Whittemore also gave them a second mortgage of $1600, a thousand for Peirce and 600 to Gould, which they discharged in 1841 (MD 3351:98). Whittemore was a distant cousin of Lydia Ann Winship Teel who was to marry Gould's son Thomas in 1839; both were descendants of Sgt. Francis Whittemore, tailor in Cambridge 1648.

Not until 1867 did Gould and his wife quitclaim her share of 24 acres on the Belmont-Arlington town line east of Prospect Street to Thomas P. Peirce who owned the Arlington land to the northeast (MD 1112:422).

WATERTOWN

Thomas Gould first acquired property on the Charles River west of the Watertown Arsenal as a result of the bankruptcy of his son-in-law Cyrus K. Dam in 1846. In the previous year Dam had joined Glover Broughton to pay $5000 for 25 ¾ acres and half measure (9 rods) in East Watertown south of Mill Dam Road to the river between John Fowle's heirs on the west and the passageway to the river of Thomas Larned from whom they bought the land (MD 461:513). On the day of purchase they had mortgaged it for $5657.10, payable $425 in six months and 12 months, and $1807 in 3 years; this was not discharged until 9 July 1849, after its assignment to Robert Steele and Prescott Dickinson (MD 461:514). Dam was unable to make the payments, for within a year Gould bought it at auction from Henry Winsor and James S. Wiggins for $370 (MD 494:3, 14 July 1846). Within six months Gould sold his half for $4000 to Isaiah Bailey, a Cambridge mason (MD 505:210). In July 1847 Dam, now a yeoman of Princeton, quitclaimed his title to his father-in-law, in this deed unusually titled "Gentleman" (MD 513:439). Shortly after this, Gould, Isaiah Bailey the mason and Isaiah Bigelow Boston merchant tenants in common sold their undivided quarter for a dollar to Robert Steele and Prescott Dickinson, Boston merchants (MD 515:168). There is no indication that any of the land was developed or built on.

On 1 June 1847 a plan was filed for a large subdivision development of 57 lots and a large wharf on the Charles in Cushingville section of Watertown running southwest along the Charles, starting on the Mill Dam Road 50 rods (82.5 feet) south of the depot of the Watertown Branch of the Fitchburg Railroad, four miles from Boston, and just west of the U.S. Arsenal (Plan of D. A. Granger, 17 Old State House, Boston, 1 June 1847, Middlesex Plan Book 2:64).

We do not know if there is a connection between this development's name and the Gould's fourth child Delia Cushing Gould, b. 10 Hanover St, Boston 29 Dec. 1817; the name does not appear on the Gould side; it may be a Peirce family name or a friend.

Gould's (quarter=about 17 lots) share included three building lots, numbers 13 to 15 on the southeast corner of Mill Dam Road and a new road to the Charles (Palmer Street?), plus lots 23, 26 and 27 on the west side of the latter road, paying $1300 to Andrew Chamberlain of Boston, and assuming the seller's mortgage of $870.10, with the restriction that no building could be erected within ten feet of the street, and correcting a surveyor's error which placed the line nine feet too far north onto Mill Dam Rd. (MD 519:4, 15 Oct. 1847). The next day Gould sold the three Mill Dam lots without buildings for $1980.80 to Wilkes Roper of Princeton (MD 54:503). When this was recorded, however, in May 1848 they appended Gould's agreement "to the evacuing [sic] of the three lot lines of this deed it not being according to agreement that was made with said Roper, Worcester Nov[r] 12, 1847". Gould's son Joseph witnessed the deed. Gould may have built on the other lots, for eight years later he mortgaged them with two intervening lots 24-25 with buildings to Catherine wife of George K. Hooper, who assumed the $1000 mortgage of Joseph Monroe of Lexington to Joseph Gould (MD 744:488), and gave Thomas a mortgage for $2000, at 6 percent, $500 to be paid in 9 and 18 months, and the rest in two years, to insure the buildings against fire for $2000 (MD 744:489). Actually Gould paid this off early, a year later. We do not know when these were finally sold.

In 1848 Gould paid the nominal dollar for a quarter of the rights to the streets of this development to Boston merchants Steele and Dickinson, the same which had earlier taken over the Dam mortgage and to which he sold his rights (MD 597:545).

Next year, 1849, he sold to his 23 year-old son Joseph, who now had a wife (Sophia A. Cutter, b 1824. m. 24 Jan. 1847) and child (Sophia A. Gould, b. Boston 25 Nov. 1847) lot number 27 (MD 597:542). Joseph probably built the house here where his second and third children were born: Joseph Shelton, b. Watertown 20 Oct. 1851, and Sarah F. who was born and died in Watertown 3 June 1854, 9 Nov. 1856. We infer this from the deed of Joseph Gould, housewright of Princeton in April 1853 selling the land AND the buildings to Thomas Gould for $2000, subject to the Joseph's mortgage to Joseph Monroe of Boston (MD 655:341). Joseph may have taken over some of the Dam's property when they left for California finally in 1856.

The sale of lots 26 and Joseph's house on 27 by Thomas Gould has not been found in the index to Middlesex Deeds. They were not found in his estate.

In 1848 Gould acquired five more lots from Dickinson & Steele: the intervening lots 24-25 on the west side of the street, and lots 47-49 on the east side. Lot 49 was first, in Sept., for $207.18 ¾ (MD 597:539), then 24, 25 and 47 in October, for $344.50 (MD 597:542-3) from John Dickinson, and 48 in 1850 from the same, for a dollar (MD 597:544). Lots 48 and 49 were sold apparently not built upon in 1867 for $400 to Michael Halleron of Middlesex, in a deed witnessed by Thomas's daughters Delia Fernald and Elizabeth (MD 1007:337). Sale of the other three lots is not found.

In 1849 Gould (titled Gentleman) bought lot 38 facing east onto the creek running into the Charles for $176.93 from Boston merchant Abel G. Peck (MD 597:540), and sold it four days later to Boston merchant William M. White for $404.40 (MD 549:385, witnessed by his daughter Sarah G. Adams who was soon to die in childbirth with her fourth child, and his 20 year old son George Peirce Gould).

In 1852 Gould bought from Steele and Dickinson empty lot 37 and the north half of 36, both facing onto the Charles River, for $316 (MD 639:401). In 1863 he paid $200 for the adjoining lots 36 and 37 to the north, with 251 feet frontage on the Charles, from Hannah, wife of David Y. Kendall (MD 905:203). He had hoped to get $500 for the six lots including the river-lots occupied by Mr. Hartford (letter to son Thomas Jr. 16 April 1866).

Four years later he sold all of these lots, 35, 36, 37, and half of 34, still unbuilt-on, at a loss, for $425, to John Dickinson (MD 1017:77). The sale of the five lots 23-27 has not been found.

In 1898 the area was still undeveloped, in large country estates. The part just south of the station and west of Prospect Av. was the Elizabeth Bleiler estate, and south of that, between North Beacon Street and the river was the large John E. Cassidy estate. Both had large mansions and barns, and no street subdivisions (Watertown Atlas 1898, 14).

Gould's other Middlesex properties, in Framingham, Arlington and Bedford will be taken up in Part VI.

Part V: **THOMAS GOULD AND FOUNDING THE FIRST INTEGRATED CHURCH** and his son SAMUEL^6 LAWRENCE GOULD, EDUCATOR

Tremont Temple is world famous as the first integrated church in America, founded in Thomas Gould's house at 31 Friend Street Boston on 26 July 1838. The founders were radical abolitionists, many coming from the same Baldwin Place Baptist Church that William Lloyd Garrison walked out of in protest, while Thomas Gould and his friends reached out the hand of friendship to Negroes, the symbol of their faith, to create a church founded on equality.

First, some background about the sources of Gould's religion. As we have seen, his family were from the majority Congregational church of Boston, where his parents married and baptized their children in the Hollis Street Church or in the First Church in Roxbury, following their parents in the Gould, Lawrance, Woods and Harris families. Unless you went back to the founder Thomas[1] Gould, staunch Episcopalian, who was followed in that faith by his daughter's descendants as founders and benefactors of Trinity Church, we find no religious radicals or Baptists.

Because of the radicalism of Thomas[5] Gould in the Baptist denomination, we had assumed some connection to the man of the same name who was a wheelwright by trade like Thomas's father, a troublemaker who founded the Baptist church in Boston in 1665, and was run out across the water to desolate exile on Noddles Island, now Logan Airport. First, all of our research above shows no relation. Second, the careful research in Zaccheus Gould shows the Rev. Thomas had no third generation of the Gould name (341), which is supported by Sav. 2:286-7, and Wyman 428. The only contradiction of this is in Charles Henry Chandler's *The History of New Ipswich, N. H.* [Fitchburg: Sentinel Printing, 1914], 445, which makes the unproven assumption that the Baptist founder Thomas was father of Thomas Gould of Salem Village (Z.Gould 342, 312). Even if Chandler were correct our Boston family cannot be linked to the Salem Village and Chelmsford Goulds. No connection has been found by Boston Baptist archivist and historian Constance C. Hanson (letter of 2 Dec. 1980), and Edward C. Starr, Curator of the American Baptist Historical Society (letter of 24 Oct. 1969). We must conclude that it is pure coincidence that there are two Boston radical Baptists named Thomas Gould who were connected with wheel making.

Garrison's wife Helen Benson had closer ties to the radical Baptists of Boston. She was a direct descendant of Rev. Obadiah Holmes (1607-82) who refused to pay his fines for Baptist preaching, was whipped so severely that he could not lie down, resting only on his elbows and knees. This happened in front of the Boston State House in 1651, and may have inspired Thomas Gould's first questions of his Cambridge neighbor, the President of Harvard.

Our Thomas's daughter Elizabeth said that he had been a member of the Boston's Second Baptist Church since his youth (3). Perhaps our Thomas Gould was attracted to Baptism by the reputation of the founder, over a century old. But the inspiration may have been a girl. We have no record of Gould in the Second, Baldwin Baptist Church until his marriage there to Sophia Lovis on 31 Aug. 1806 (Register 75:216), when she was 20, and he only 3 months older. Neither appears in the baptismal record, though a Sally Lovis is admitted 29 March 1805 and baptized Sally Lovis /Dittson 31 March (Second Baptist Church Minute Book 1 (1788-1809), 114, 176, at Andover Newton Archives). There is also a Mary Gould baptized 23 Dec. 1803 (Ibid., 94) who may be Thomas's 22 year old sister, though the name is too common to be sure.

In 1805, when these lovers were 19, Second Baptist was one of the most exciting churches in Boston. Its gifted preacher Rev. Thomas Baldwin rivaled the sermons of the famous First Baptist minister Samuel Stillman, though only a couple of blocks apart in the North End. baptizing their growing numbers in the Mill Pond at their rear. Both churches had large numbers of women and black members, though the blacks could not rent the pews on the floor, and were segregated in the galleries. Both churches encouraged the founding of the first separate black church, The African Baptist Church, in 1805 (Constance Hanson, "Baptist Beginnings in Boston" (1980, 8), and remained in supportive contact with it.

After Sophia's death Thomas married again to Lydia Peirce of Belmont, in a ceremony at the Second Baptist church on Salem Street in the North End (Reg. 175:290), on 23 May 1813.

William Lloyd Garrison, raised by an itinerant Baptist preacher mother, joined this church when he first came to Boston in Oct. 1830 (Hanson, 13, though there is no record, since the church Minute book for 1803-33 is missing, and Garrison's papers do not record it or when he left; there is no record of his dismissal in the 1833 ff. Minute Book, and none of his biographies or letters record this). Garrison helped found the New England Anti-Slavery Society in the basement of the African Baptist Church on 6 Jan. 1832 (*William Lloyd Garrison; 1805-1879: The Story of His Life: Told by His Children* [N.Y: Century Co., 1885] [hereinafter Life], 1:279).

The tradition is that Garrison walked out of the Second Baptist Church rather than be silent on "the crime of slavery" (Hanson, 13). Although this may have occurred earlier, Garrison did not notice the Baptist position in his *Liberator* (hereinafter Lib.) until 1835, when he belatedly reports that the Baptist Board of Foreign Missions in America meeting in Boston on 1 Sept. 1833 defended slavery. This stand he roundly condemned in his editorials of 14 and 21 March 1835. Garrison seems to have missed the event of 1833 when the British Baptists appealed for emancipation, to be told by the Americans that they had a different government, of federal type, and that progress was being made, if slowly (Life, 1:479). Garrison denounced as "shameful" that 19th century Christianity was "so entirely polluted" that it didn't excommunicate for MAN-STEALING! He concluded with Paul's command: "come out from among them, and be ye separate" (Life, 1:480). From this came the tag "Come-Outers", those Christians who left the corrupt church. Garrison, who acted on his convictions, probably left at this time, in 1835, though neither he nor the church recorded it.

Thomas Gould, by now a leading layman in the Second Church, was an active abolitionist, but took a different tack, and within three years founded the first integrated church in America (Gould's position is indicated by the fact that his second son has been accepted for the ministry in 1833, Second Baptist Church Record Book, 1833-47 at Andover Newton, 6, [hereinafter 2d Rec.]; and he ran the election of deacons in 1835, 39,40). The controversy in the church where there are still blacks, but in segregated galleries, is not recorded, but a harmonious cover is made when the congregation "Voted, That we observe the last Monday evening in every month as a season of prayers for the emancipation and improvement of the slavery in the United States" (11 Nov. 1834, Ibid., 23).

Headmaster Samuel Lawrence Gould (1814-1881)

By the time of Garrison's revelation of Baptist pollution, Thomas's son Samuel Lawrence Gould had become a traveling speaker for the Providence Anti-Slavery Society, speaking in Baptist churches like Olneyville, north of Providence on 12 April 1835, visiting Warwick meetings set up by his cousin Benjamin R. Greene (Lib. 2 May 1835, 2-3). When he graduated from Baptist Brown University Samuel was a delegate to the fourth convention of the New England Anti-Slavery Society in Boston 25 May 1835 (Lib. 30 May, 2). Later that year he went to the national meeting in Philadelphia where 50 persons including Lucretia and James Mott signed a resolution opposing the persecution of Garrison, epitomized in his being mobbed in front of the City Hall, a few short blocks south of Gould's home on Friend Street, 21 Oct. 1835 (Declaration of 5 Nov., Lib. 28 Nov.). The mobbing followed the meeting of the Boston Female Anti-Slavery Society, of about twenty women, including Gould's radical feminist-abolitionist third cousins, Anne Greene Chapman and Maria Weston Chapman; Life 2:12). The Goulds were no doubt outraged by the mobbing of Garrison, for as we will see, Thomas was more radical than his son Samuel.

Soon after Samuel returned from Philadelphia, Thomas was appointed by the Second Church to a committee of three to attend to the wants of the African Baptist Church (30 Nov. 1835, 2d Rec., 43). Early in 1836 he led the opening prayer (Ibid., 45). 1837 is marked in the abolitionist movement as the year of heightened controversy over the involvement of all churches in emancipation of slaves. Early in the year Garrison directly challenged: "Baptists...where are you?" (Lib. 24 March, 50).

Samuel, already an Agent of the Anti-Slavery Society, went on a month long speaking tour of southeastern Massachusetts that included his father's birthplace Abington, and on to Nantucket, Marthas Vineyard and Cape Cod, including the hospitality of a colored boatman in Falmouth (Lib. 126). His father was meanwhile helping the sister African Baptist Church, voting to pay their minister's salary (2d Rec. 65-66). Evidence that the church was moving to reconcile black members is seen in the reinstatement of Matilda Samuels and her husband in the summer of 1838 (2d Rec. 80, 83).

In 1838, when Garrison was doing the pioneer work to establish the world's first nonviolence group, the New England Non-Resistance Society, the Baptists were struggling with the issue of segregation in the churches. The open challenge seems to have come first from Rev. Timothy Tingley of the North Baptist Church on the corner of Hanover and Union, in the same block where Gould lived. The church had separated from Gould's Baldwin Place church peaceably in 1835, moving to a "missionary station" purchased by the church (2d Rec. 13,27,30). Tingley told his parishioners in 1838 that he hoped to see the day when colored people wouldn't be confined to the galleries (Guy T. Mitchell, *Historical Sketch Book...Tremont Temple* [Boston: Tremont Temple, Nov. 1953][hereinafter Mitchell], 7). When 16 of his 23 members walked out, he declared, "Are there any more that want to leave? Before I will shun to declare my true sentiments, I will beg for bread from door to door in the streets of Boston." The remaining seven started a new church. This was no doubt supported by Gould, who invited Tingley to his home to found Tremont Temple. At the same time a leader of the Charles Street Baptist Church, Timothy Gilbert, challenged the no-colored rule by inviting black members to sit in his pew. (Mitchell, 6, 36; Hanson 11). When reprimanded he moved to the tolerant Federal Street Baptist Church.

Thomas Gould invited to meet on 26 July 1838 at his home at 31 Friend Street four leaders of other Boston congregations: Tingley from North, Gilbert from Federal, future Boston Police Commissioner J. K. Hayes from Stillman (First), and future Congressman William Damrell (Mitchell 8, Hanson 11). They decided there to establish a Baptist Free Church free in the meaning of no charge for pews, but paid by subscription, thus opening seats to all races without distinction. But it was also resolved that members should be free to discuss any issue, which included Garrison's current themes of nonviolence and women's equality. Gilbert was elected to the chair, and Tingley as Secretary. A six-man organizing committee was set up with a member from each Baptist church in Boston, Gould representing Second Baldwin Place to report to the next meeting on 9 Aug. Church historians regard this as the founding meeting of Tremont Temple.

At the second meeting on 9 Aug. the committee's recommended statement of purpose was unanimously approved, "Realizing our obligations as Christians to...supply every human being with the privileges of the Gospel, and believing that the establishment of a Baptist Free Church, in this city, would draw multitudes...we...do hereby associate ourselves for the purpose of forming a Baptist Free Church to be conducted on principles similar to the Congregational Church worshiping in Marlboro Chapel. It being understood that all who make, sell, or use intoxicating drinks, and all who practice slavery or justify it, shall be excluded from the church..." (Mitchell 9).

Needing a minister, Hayes recommended a visiting Baptist lecturer in South Boston, Rev. Nathaniel Colver (1794-1870), one of Garrison's famous "Seventy" anti-slavery agents (Louis Ruchames, ed., *The Letters of William Lloyd Garrison* [Cambridge: Belknap, 1971], 2:336, 185). who was to become the first minister (Ibid.). Colver was invited to the next meeting on Aug. 21, and so pleased the committee it raised $1000 salary within a week.

Gould kept his church informed of progress, and in Nov. 1838 was given permission to attend the new church for three months (2d Rec. 95). The first meeting for worship was held on Sunday 9 Dec. 1838 in Tremont (Papanti) Hall, 31 Tremont Street, with ministers of three Boston Baptist churches preaching (Mitchell 10, Hanson 12, Charles L. Jeffrey, "Historical Sketch of Tremont Temple Baptist Church" [Boston, 6 Oct. 1906] [hereinafter Jeffrey], 2). That the first sermon, given in the morning, was by Gould's minister Rev. Barton Stowe, is credit to the diplomacy of Gould.

The close association of the Second Church and the new one is shown by the fact that Samuel L. Gould was clerk pro tempore for the Baldwin Place meeting on 15 Jan. (2d Rec. 99) and two weeks later was elected to the new church committee to solicit funds and members (Jeffrey, 2). They raised $1625 and signed up 82 who wished to transfer. Letters went out on 20 March (Mitchell 11), and on 2 April 20 members of the Second Church were peacefully discharged to the new congregation, one fifth of them Goulds: Thomas & Lydia, their daughters Delia and Charlotte, but not Samuel (2d Rec. 109)

As anticipated, "multitudes" did come to the services, and a larger place was found to seat 400 at Congress Hall, at the corner of Milk and Congress Streets, starting 17 March 1839 (Mitchell 11). Nathaniel Colver was asked to be pastor on 28 March, and installed on 11 Sept. in Congress Hall, by an official Baptist ecclesiastical council, with Rev. Stowe moderating, and Samuel Gould as official delegate from the Second Church (2d Rec. 117).

While the Goulds were preoccupied with reforming the Baptist church, Garrison had moved on to become the pioneer in nonviolence and feminism, in late 1838. Although Rev. Colver had been a friend of Garrison and radical abolitionism, he parted company on the issues of women and non-resistance (Life 2:282,297; see Gilbert's letter of 14 Oct. 1843 denying the new Baptist missionary organization's association with churches "that have gone off in favor of woman's rights, no government, etc.", in excerpt from Justin Fulton, Memoir of Timothy Gilbert (Boston: Lee & Shepard, 1866) in Andover Newton file "Anti-Slavery Agitation in the Church", typed, n.d.). At this time Gould was hiring Colver, remaining loyal to him for years, we must assume that Gould did not agree with Garrison's nonviolence and women's rights that Colver rejected.

The Baptist Free Church was formally organized at Baldwin Place on Sunday 21 April, its minister Barton Stowe giving the recognition sermon, and Thomas Gould "designated to extend the right hand of fellowship to the brethren and sisters who were now being organized as the First Baptist Free Church." (Mitchell 11). The symbol of the first integrated church in America became the clasp of two hands, black and white. That evening eight Boston area Baptist preachers gave the welcome (Jeffrey 2).

The first business meeting was held three days later, on April 24, when Gould and Gilbert made the first Deacons, though acting, since Gould refused to take the responsibility permanently (Jeffrey 2). His daughter's account is unclear about motive: "Mr. Gould for a time after joining the Tremont Temple Church, acted as Deacon, but he declined an election to the office." (4).

Meanwhile, Samuel continued to be active in the segregated Second Church, which had encouraged his youthful ministry. Although he resigned from the Executive Committee shortly after his father left (14 Jan. 1840, 2d Rec. 127), he continued to be active on committees, opening prayer, special thanksgiving services, welcome of China missionaries, and membership inquiries from 1840-1847 (2d Rec. 147, 148, 155, 161, 293, 298, 305, 308, 310, 316, 318, 321, 322, 324).

Thomas, as a builder, was constantly involved with the expansion of facilities. Having outgrown the 400 seat Congress Hall, the Free Church rented 600-700 seat space known as Tremont Chapel below Moses Kimball's Boston Museum and Gallery of Fine Arts, on the corner of Tremont and Bromfield Streets. This was rented on 4 Feb. 1841 for five years from C. H. Eldridge for $1050 a year (Mitchell 12, Jeffrey 3) in the basement of a supposed cultural exhibit that came close to being a theater (Mary Caroline Crawford, *Romantic Days in Old Boston* [Boston: Little, Brown, 1910], 251).

Among the prohibitions of good Baptists was going to the theater, shown in Samuel's recommending restoring Lebbeus S. Bates's membership after he confessed the sin of attending theatrical exhibitions (2d Rec. 322, 326). While the crowds thronged to the preaching of Great Revival ministers like Jacob Knapp, Boston theaters were closing (Jeffrey, 3). Among the dark ones was nearby Tremont Theater, on the site of the present Tremont Temple. On its stage the great Shakespearian actor Edwin Forrest had first played Hamlet in 1828, Fanny Kemble made her Boston debut of 1833, and Charlotte Cushman first sang in 1835 (Crawford, 239, 241, 243), and the first opera performed in Boston (Drake 292). It was also the scene of prize-fights, and

Baptists particularly hated the presence of three bars. But Knapp could truthfully claim that "God, through my agency, wound up the theatre" (it closed 19 Feb., 1843, after losing $10,000 in three months; Knapp's bio. cited by Mitchell 15).

Closing the theater meant the end of public events held there, like the learned blacksmith Elihu Burritt's first public antiwar speech in 1841 (Merle Curti, *Peace or War* [N.Y.: Norton, 1936], 206). Ironically, Tremont Theater was the first Boston theater to open to blacks, providing a "nigger heaven" in the central gallery "reserved for people of color" for 50 cents. Reverend Lyman Beecher, the father of the author of Uncle Tom's Cabin hated the place so much he predicted he "would yet preach" in the ungodly theater (Crawford, 249).

The building was a fine two story Greek Revival, with a plain pediment about 90 feet at its base, above two stories, the second floor of six Ionic pilasters framing three tall windows between niches with statues, and street floor with three rusticated arched doorways with two square headed windows at each side, and five lamps hanging above the street (woodcut in Mitchell 13; 1843 photo in Leonard H. Rhodes "Brief History of Tremont Temple" [Boston? 1917, in file Andover Newton], 18).

On 6 June 1843 Thomas Gould, Gilbert, Damrell and Simon Shipley purchased the theater for $55,000 from its Proprietors (SD 503:158), at once taking a mortgage from the Proprietors for $40,000 at 6 % (SD 503:160), but in less than a month switched it to the Provident Institution for Savings (SD 504:160r), from which they got a second mortgage of $15,000 in Dec. (SD 513:247), not paid off for 15 years. The four wealthy Baptists had come up with $15,000 cash. Rev. Colver raised another $8000 to convert the stage into a church with the ideal equal pews that could seat 2000 (Jeffrey 3; Mitchell 14). The purchase had included a huge chandelier whose price the Massachusetts Charitable Mechanics had balked at, but Gilbert clinched the deal by taking it too. This was the only light in the theater, so great skylights were put into the ceiling (Mitchell 16).

Outside, at the back of the 95 by 140 foot lot was the ruin of an old "barnyard wall" of an old livery stable, left partly on the neighboring estate of Nicholas Boylston, now the Parker House. Gould and the other trustees went to former President John Quincy Adams and got his signature to a deed of a ten foot strip including the fence, a privy and a drain that still goes under the Parker House out to School St (SD 506:278; Mitchell 16). They also had to get the permission of the Brooklyn owner of the Perkins estate to put eight windows on the back of the building onto her land (SD 507:124). The work was probably done by Gould. His daughter says alterations cost $24,284.54, which added to purchase price made $79,284.53 (4). Total costs were officially recorded as $73,000, including $8000 of their own money (new trust deed 1 April 1844 which gives conditions of use, sale and spending, SD 530:153-9). This may have necessitated the third mortgage of $20,000 from Charles Francis Adams, son of the President and future Minister to Britain during the Civil War (1844, SD 634:4).

Conversion was completed for the dedication of Tremont Temple, as it was called, on Thursday evening 7 Dec. 1843. The name temple seems to have been inspired by Gilbert's vision that he "might transform that theatre into a temple in which to worship Almighty God!" (Mitchell 22). The price paid to turn a wicked theater into a temple of the Lord seemed to be summed up in the opening hymn, "Lord, Let These Ransomed Walls Rejoice" (Crawford, 250).

Barton Stowe of Gould's Second Church gave the dedicatory sermon on the text "The common people heard him gladly" (Mitchell 16) .

Tremont Temple became the meeting place for some of the great reform meetings of the forties. In Dec. 1843 it was the site of a four day convention to reform society, attended by Garrison, Adin Ballou, George Ripley of Brook Farm (Walter M. Merrill, *Against Wind and Tide: A Biography of Wm. Lloyd Garrison* [Cambridge: Harvard, 1963], 216) . Garrison had the Non-Resistance Society meeting there in Dec. 1847 (Ibid., 243). The next year it was where Lincoln spoke, and became committed to the anti-slavery cause (Harris, 133).

The Trustees also rented it out to respectable performances such as Jenny Lind's debut on tour with P. T. Barnum, in 1850 (Harris's Walks, 56).

Membership of the Tremont Street Baptist Church, as it was legally called, reached a peak of 383 in 1850 and began to taper off (Mitchell 18). Deacon Gilbert felt a younger preacher was required, whereupon the founding Rev. Colver offered his resignation, and on 30 March 1852 moved to Arlington (Ibid.). The next day, 31 March, fire completely destroyed the old Greek Revival theater, defying the rescue attempts of Boston's hand pump fire engines.

The trustees immediately assembled at Gould's house at 21 Friend Street. Gould, who was not well, and about to retire to Framingham himself, was apparently opposed to rebuilding. They called together about 45 members of the church at Gilbert's home that night. The meeting was split between those who wanted to sell the property and give the amount above the mortgage to the church. Gilbert insisted on rebuilding, and Damrell agreed, but Shipley would take no more financial burden. Though Gould was opposed, the church voted full confidence in the Trustees' decision to sell or rebuild (7 April). Gould was apparently swayed by Gilbert's enthusiasm and prospect of another loan from Charles Francis Adams ($10,000 for 10 years, 31 March 1853 SD 645:41) for they agreed to rebuild 28 April (Mitchell 18) .

The reconstruction began 25 May 1852 of the Second Tremont Temple, an Italianate palace of three stories, the shortest being the street level, with six arched niches sheltered by a balustrade, then a second story of twice the height with five tall windows capped by protruding arches on rusticated bases; above that a third floor of five similar arches of three quarter the height, but with individual balustrade balconies. The building's corners on the upper stories are quoins. At the roofline was a heavy cornice with dentils below, and balustrade above, topped by an octagonal domed cupola with arched windows in each side (photo in Mitchell 20). Reconstruction cost was $126,814.26. This second Tremont Temple was dedicated on Christmas Day 1853 (Jeffrey 3).

The largest organ in the U.S. was installed in the Temple in 1853 by the Hook Company of Boston (Program of concert 27 Oct. 1868 in Andover Newton file).

In addition to Adams's mortgage, the three remaining trustees, Gould, Damrell and Gilbert (Shipley having died) raised $50,000 to repay themselves by issuing 30 thousand dollar notes and 40 five hundred dollar notes, payable in seven years with interest, secured by a mortgage of Samuel E. Sewall of Melrose who would act as trustee (10 Nov. 1853, SD 655:42). Sewall was the eminent abolitionist lawyer, and Unitarian (Letters 2:56n). Gould and the other trustees signed six other deeds dealing with Amos Baker's school on the east and other neighbors (SD 593:188, 636:214, 645:41, 641:17, 72, 662:299).

The piano business of the leading investor, Gilbert, failed in Jan. 1855, bringing him to Gould's earlier advice to sell the property (Mitchell 19, Jeffrey 3). The church put the property up for sale on June 20, but telegraphed their old minister Colver to come home from Detroit post-haste. At a farewell party for 300 Baptists Colver achieved a miracle of persuading them not to sell. Gilbert and probably Gould and Damrell went to the Boylston National Bank and made a deal (Mitchell 20).

On 28 June 1855 the three trustees took a new mortgage for $165,000 from five wealthy Baptists of the Boston area, James W. Converse of West Roxbury (founder of the Union Baptist Church 1836; Mitchell 30), Frederick Gould of Cambridge (Gould's former colleague on Common Council and deacon of the Second Church), J. Warren Merrill of Cambridge, and Thomas Richardson and George W. Chipman of Boston (later Deacon of the Temple); (SD: 684/141-3, 8 June 1855). They assumed the mortgages of Sewell and Adams, and the Providence Savings loan that had gone to Massachusetts Hospital Life, and ten leases, and got for it two organs, heaters, cushions, settees, stools, carpets, all furniture and fixtures, the privy and the sewer out to School Street.

Five years later a permanent solution was found by transferring the $165,000 debt to the Evangelical Baptist Benevolent & Missionary Society, which discharged all the mortgages to Adams, Sewall, the Hospital, on the date of the deed, 8 July 1859 (SD 760:201; the discharges have Adams's signatures). Gould was freed from his 16 year leadership and responsibility in 1855, a few months after his seventieth birthday.

This second Temple was also the scene of many famous events, such as Charles Dickens's readings in 1867-8 (Bacon guide 1910, 25; Harris 134-5), Garrison's denunciation of the execution of John Brown on the death day in 1859 at a meeting chaired by Samuel Sewall (Life, 3:490), and the first anniversary meeting which was taken over by a mob that had to be evicted by the mayor (Ibid., 505, Merrill, 274-5). It was the site for the massive celebration of the Emancipation Proclamation on New Year's Day 1863 (Hanson, 16).

The second Temple burned in 1879, to be replaced by the third building which had the same Italianate facade except for the ground floor which was opened up to large plate-glass windows (drawing in Mitchell 23). This too burned in 1893, in a third fire, to be replaced in 1896 by the nearly 100 year old structure we now see, with its Classical Greek temple on the top as a reminder of the original theater, perched high above the Venetian facade. This fourth Temple was the scene of sermons by famous evangelists like Billy Sunday, Gipsy Smith and Dwight Moody and events like the Peace Congress of 1904 (Curti).

Thomas Gould's religious leadership was carried on in the Baptist church by his son Samuel, and by his grandson Rev. Ezra Palmer Gould.

25. SAMUEL LAWRENCE GOULD.

Since we have detailed above the abolitionist stand of Thomas's son Samuel, we will complete his biography here. He was the most distinguished of the 17 children.

Born at 10 Hanover Street, Boston, on 20 May 1814, the first of the children by Thomas's second wife Lydia Pierce. He was probably named for his great-uncle, Samuel Lawrence. At age 16 he was sent to New Hampton Academy, later Colby College, 1830-1834, but did not graduate (Colby College letter 16 July 1980). He became the first member of the Gould family to attend college when he transferred to Brown University, graduating in 1835 (Brown U. Library, 21 Oct. 1969), with the intention of studying for the ministry. Before graduation he was involved in speaking in the cause of abolition, as we have seen above. He lectured in the Middle States, presumably Pennsylvania, New Jersey, Delaware, Maryland and Virginia (Obit., Providence Journal, 24 June 1874). On these tours he often had threats of violence.

In 1837 he lost his speaking voice, and gave up the career as lecturer. In the first of the year 1837 he wrote his elder half-brother Thomas[6] Gould:

Greensburg Westmoreland Co: Pa.
Jan 3d 1837.

Dear Bro Thomas,

I have just ordered our Treasurer to forward you a draft for one hundred dollars which when [you] shall recieve, I will be obliged to you to endorse on my note of last Fall. You will probably recieve it about the 12th Inst.

The other demands which you have against me, I hope to liquidate in a few months.

I think that I have heard you speak of an intention to change your present employment if one could be found-as lucrative as your present, in which you would not be compelled to perform so much bone and muscle labor as you do at present. Perhaps the permanency of your health demands such a change.

You have heard of Pittsburgh in Pennsylvania situated at the confluence of the Allegheny and Monongahela rivers, where they unite and form the Ohio. From its situation, as you will see by looking on the map of Penn: it is destned to become one of the largest cities in the country. If you were willing to settle so far away from the place which we have ever been accustomed to consider as home I have no doubt that as far as business and its profits are concerned, you would be abundantly pleased with Pittsburg. I have made inquiries of my friends who are engaged in business there concerning their pr cent profit, and as according to the best of my judgment the average does not fall below 33 pr cent, with any man possessed of the least business tact.

There is at the present time a most advantageous opening for any one who would be willing to embark in the lumber business. Timber is brought down the Allegheny river in rafts in the Spring and Fall, and is generally [~~sold~~] bought for eight dollars a thousand and is sold for twelve. As a general thing the stock may be changed twice a year. As Pittsburg has about fifty thousand inhabitants, and as the number is constantly increasing, there is of necessity a very large market there. But lumber is in immense demand//[2] from Pittsburgh, down the river to N.Orleans a distance of more than two thousand miles, and almost the whole supply has to come through Pittsburgh.

In the course of my inquiries concerning this matter I learned heard of one man, a farmer, who was no ways skilled in the lumber business, and was not at all remarkable for business tact, who engaged three or four years ago in the lumber trade and with a capital of less than a thousand dollars, and now, without any freaks of fortune, or without any remarkable speculations, is supposed to be worth ten or twelve thousand dollars.

The character of the People of Pittsburg is such as I think would please you. They are frugal, and industrious and honest, even compared with N.England people.

The only objection which I know of, to a residence here is the immense amount of coal consumed in the city. The coal is bituminous coal—and is you know smoky. It is obtained in such immense quantities and so much is consumed in the manufactories with which the city is surrounded, that really it is almost impossible to preserve one's complexion. But this disadvantage is perhaps more than made up by the abundance of fuel [, the] comfort of having fuel in abundance; cheaper than wood at a dollar and a half a cord.

Provisions are about thirty three pr ct cheaper than in Boston.

Clothing is dearer than in Boston, but laboring people here are the fashionables, and as economy is the consequent order of the day the tailors bulls and mantua makers bills are really less than in Boston.

Of course I would not have you or any other friend change his residence on the strength of any general information which I communicate, but I feel very confident that if the facilities for profitable business which Pittsburgh abounds were known in Boston there would be a flood of emigrations to this place. What say you to an exploring tour in this direction? It would not be a pleasant journey in the Winter but you could better afford such a journey at this season//[3] than in Summer. The resources of the country you might learn I suppose as well at this season as in the Summer.

I am happy to inform you of my continued good health, though from the arduousness of my labors I am constantly exhausted.

This week has been excessively cold and some snow has fallen so that sleighing is good.

How goes Lydia Ann? And your little ones are they well?

Please write to me on receiving the money above mentioned. Your letter if written previous to the 20th Institute will find me in Pittsburgh Pa.

In grateful remembrance of many kindnesses received from your hand

I am your

Mr. Thomas Gould Jr. Affectionate brother

Saml L. Gould

The letter is addressed "Mr. Thomas Gould, Boston, Massachusetts", postmarked Pittsburgh Jan. 7, Paid 25.

From this it would appear that Samuel was still on his abolitionist lecture tour, and had not yet lost his voice.

Returning to Boston in 1837 he became a teacher, first as master of a grammar school in Chelsea (Obit.). It was this year that Horace Mann became Secretary of the Board of Education of Massachusetts, creating the pioneer public education system that became a revolutionary model (Ency. Brit., 11th ed. 17: 587). Although Mann's reforms were attacked by some local masters, Gould apparently sympathized with the reforms, for after 1837-40 in Chelsea, and 1840-1 in Charlestown, he became Principal of two of the best schools in Boston, Winthrop 1841-51 and Franklin until 1865 (Obit.). In April 1841 he was chosen writing master of Winthrop School, where he taught for a decade (Dickinson, S. N., *Boston Almanac 1849*, 72; Patten, Fanny G., *History of the Winthrop School* [Boston., c.1908], 13, 50-1). When Winthrop divided in 1847 Gould continued at Winthrop South school for Girls, to which William Lloyd Garrison sent his pacifist daughter Fanny Villard in 1853, after Gould had left for Franklin in 1851 (Patten, 19, 55). In 1855 Boston became the first major city in US to have an integrated school system.

On 31 May 1840 he married Frances Ann Shelton, whose mother was a daughter of one of the Boston Tea Party protesters (Harvard Archives, 1861 Class Book, ms. 265 [hereinafter CB]). By her he had 5 children, two of whom died in infancy. The family first lived with his father on Friend Street, hut moved to one of his father's houses on Salem Place 1841-5, where the first son Ezra was born 1841 (Boston Assessor's Valuation books, Ward 3, 183R-45). They then moved to Sturgis Place, off Pearl Street c. 1845-8 (CB 25). They lived at Dover Street for 5 years, c. 1848-51, then moved to Dorchester near Mt. Pleasant in Roxbury (Ibid.). By 1861 they were living in Cambridge.

He sent his first two sons to Boston Latin in 1852 and 1853, and to Harvard College, the first in the family to go there. The two eldest sons both enlisted in the Civil War, one dying at the Battle of Antietam, the eldest rising to rank of Major.

At the age of 51 he gave up his successful career in teaching and followed the Colorado Gold Rush. In 1865 he became Superintendent of several gold mining companies near Black Hawk, Gilpin Co., 30 miles west of Denver. His trip out is described in another letter to his half-brother Thomas:

Steamer Yellowstone, Missouri River near Nebraska City N.T. Oct.31.1865
Dear Bro. Thomas,

Having left my wife and Eddie [his youngest child, age 13] at Quincy Ill. two and a half weeks ago, I have been myself engaged at St. Louis & Neb. City in getting my goods through and started by my teams over the plains. This accomplished, I am now on my way back to Q. to be joined by my family in ourselves crossing the plains. We go by rail across Mo. to the Mo. river on the North eastern border of Kanzas and thence 700 miles by stage to the Rocky Mts.

Traveling by steamer to the Mo. river is rendered unpleasant by the great rapidity of the current, the shallowness of the water the great quantity of snags, and worst of all the Perpetual shifting of the sand bars in the river. Aside from these drawbacks which are not small nor few, traveling by boat is far our most comfortable mode of trav. Travel by rail is very comfortable until you reach the Mississippi river, there being//[2] no falling off in the excellence of the roads or the cars from the time of leaving Boston. Our last stage of 700 miles by coach traveling by day and night is of course uncomfortable enough, and on acct. of my family, I must own that I fairly dread it. Just now, too the Indians are troublesome having attacked three mule trains within as many weeks. So far, however, they have not molested the mail coaches; whether because they are accompanied by an armed escort or because their plunder would be too small, I cannot tell.

My unexpected delay in getting off my goods, together with the Ind. troubles has led me to write to my wife, my consent for her and Ned to turn back and defer taking up her residence in Colorado for the present, but I cannot tell until I see her, what her choice will be.

If we reach the Mts. we propose to go to housekeeping on a small scale, furnishing, for the present, only one room besides the kitchen, and that with the plainest furniture.//

[3] This economy is especially commended by the fact that I do not propose remaining more than one or two years, for however great inducement Col. may present for a short residence, they are by no means sufficient to tempt one into a permanent residence.

Why I went there, at all, you perhaps understand. I was not dazzled by its promise of wealth. Nor did the expectation of becoming rich, either originate the plan, or lead to the determination to go. Nor was it because I had become tired of my life-long vocation, but I felt that the cares and irritations connected with that profession were wearing me out too fast and threatening to use me up long before I had md. any provision for old age. An out door life promised not only change but improvement, and while seeking such an opening, my present position offered and was accepted .

I need not tell you how much it pained me to leave N.England without visiting you, nor how great a trial it has been to make my recent visit without it, but business with its imperative demands compelled me//[4] to forego the pleasure of seeing you at your house [in Lexington]. Be assured, my dear brother, that there was no intentional neglect, and that if I am privileged again to tread New England soil, you shall have a visit.

I wish your health were adequate to embracing some of the openings for yr. business wh. our new country affords. These openings are very large. A Mr. Woodbury from Medford, a carpenter who has done much work for our Company, has in his employ near two hundred workmen, paying, I believe $6. a day as his lowest wages, and $9. to highest class workmen capable of directing others. It is my impression too, that this must be the range of wages for the present.

It is among the trials connected with leaving home, that the health of any of the family should seem precarious. In father's case, I see the signs of marked decline. Still, I cannot but hope that his life may be preserved for years to come. There are in his constitution, large elements of vitality, and if he could be persuaded to sufficient care of himself. I fully believe that ten years might yet be granted him [he had less than seven, until July 1873].

Should you find time to answer this apology for a letter, direct me at Black Hawk, Colorado. In a second letter, I may tell you of our mountain life.

With af. regards for yourself and wife and family,

Yr. af. brother To Mr. Thomas Gould Jr. Saml L. Gould

Within two years the companies found the lack of refining capacity disadvantageous, and Samuel Gould turned to a new career in stock farming (Obit.). He settled in Canon City, county seat of Fremont County, 35 miles southeast of Colorado Springs. Although never ordained, he was styled Reverend, and spoke at the Canon City Baptist church (*Canon City Times*, 4 April 1872). In early 1874 he broke a leg just below the knee, and Drs. Prentiss and Lewis amputated the leg below the joint (Ibid., 12 Feb. 1874). He seemed to be recovering when "On the morning of Feb. 11 th., he complained of great difficulty of breathing, which increased for half an hour, accompanied by great pain in his chest. He requested to be turned on his side and immediately expired." (Ibid.).

Five children:

29. i. Rev. EZRA^7 PALMER GOULD, b. Boston 27 Feb. 1841; d. White Lake NY 22 Aug. 1900; m. JANE MARIA STONE.

30. ii. SAMUEL SHELTON, b. Boston 1 Jan. 1843; d. Antietam VA 17 Sept. 1862, unm.
iii. FRANCES SHELTON, b. Boston c. 1845; d. Boston 1848, sp.

31. iv. EDWARD ERANCIS, b. Boston 21 July 1852; d. Kingfisher OK? after 1912; m. MASIE ANN SUDDARTH.

v. FRANK LAWRENCE, b. Cambridge 23 Dec. 1861; d. Cambridge 23 Oct. 1862, age 10 months; bur. Mt. Auburn.

29. Rev. EZRA^7 PALMER GOULD, b. Salem Street Boston 27 Feb. 1841. The family moved to Sturgis Place, off Pearl Street, and he attended primary school on the back of Fort Hill (CB ms. 265). When he was seven they moved to Dover Street and he attended Franklin School. At 8 he was sent to Quincy School, and 11 (1852) to Boston Latin where he studied with Messrs. Chandler and Noble (Ibid., 266; Jenks, Henry F., "Catalog of Boston Public Latin School" (1886), 202. He then studied two years at Roxbury Latin School under Mr. Buck (Class B ook 1864, 22). He entered Harvard College in the summer of 1857, at age 16, the first in his family to attend (CB ms. 267). In the summer of 1858 he went to Laconia and Centre Harbor NH. In the Winter of his Junior Year he taught school at Easton in Bristol County. He was elected OBK, and was a member of the Christian Brethren. He graduated from Harvard in 1861, shortly after the outbreak of the Civil War in April. Among his classmates were future Supreme Court Chief Justice Oliver Wendell Holmes, Jr. and Wendell P. Garrison, founder of *The Nation* and its editor 1883-1906.

At age 20, on 18 Oct. 1861 he enlisted as a private in Co. E, 24 Massachusetts Infantry. After two years he was commissioned on Christmas Day 1863 as Lieutenant in the 55th Massachusetts Volunteers, a colored regiment (CB 1864, 23). The following March he was promoted to Captain in the 59th Massachusetts in which he served to the end of the war. At the Battle of the Wilderness he was hit on the breast by a cannonball, and wounded in the left hand and forearm, May 6, 1864 (Ibid.; CB 1891, 52). He was in command of the 59th Regiment at the Battle of Petersburg in June 1864, when he was incapacitated when a horse trod on his foot (CB 1864-7, 14). He was promoted to Major 16 Dec. 1864, at which rank he was discharged 1 Aug. 1865.

On discharge he enrolled in Baptist Theological Institute in Newton MA, from which he graduated in 1868 (typed bio. in Andover Newton Records, Library; *Boston Journal* obit. 25 Aug. 1900 that he got Harvard M.A. appears incorrect, since he is not listed in Harvard printed tercentenary catalog of degrees).

On 1 Sept. 1868 he married Jane Maria Stone of Cambridge. She d. ?Bristol PA? 1 Dec. 1916. They bought a house near the campus off Glen Rd. in Newton Center where they lived until 1882. By her he had two children: i. Herbert Shelton Gould, b. Newton Center 21 July 1869, m. 20 Oct. 1908 Alma Cole of Halstead PA (Pierce Gen.); and ii. Edith Parker Gould, b. Newton 6 May 1876 Rev. William Porter McCoy of Bristol PA, who had dau. Dorothy b. Bristol PA 11 Nov. 1911 (Ibid.).

He was immediately appointed Assistant Professor of Biblical Literature and Interpretation at Newton Theological Seminary, and three years later, in 1871, at age 30 became full Professor of the same subject, a post he held for 12 years, 1870-82, with a

vacation in Europe in 1875.

Ezra was ordained in the Old Cambridge Baptist church on 6 Sept. 1869. Among his scholarly publications were articles in *Baptist Quarterly* July 1874, June 1877; *Biblia Sacra* Jan. 1875, Oct. 1878; and *Baptist Review* July 1880, but he published no book before 1885. He spent the first year in Newton, when he became editor of *Scholar's Quarterly* 1883, then the next year in Cambridge writing (1861 Class Book, 1902, 24). Finally, in Aug. 1884 he took his first parish, at the Berean Baptist Church in Burlington VT, where he stayed four years (CB 1891, 53). One of his sermons there, "God in All Things Good" was published in memory of Rev. S. H. Stackpole (Nat. Union Cat. Pre-1956 Imprints, 275). His second book was published in Philadelphia 1887 by the American Baptist Publishing Society: *Commentary on the Epistles to the Corinthians* (Ibid.). He also published articles in *Andover Review* in 1887 and 1889, and in the *Journal of the Exegetical Society*.

He seems to have ended his connection with the Baptist church with Burlington in April 1888, for he then spent several months in charge of the College Street Congregational Church (CB 1902, 25), then began study for the Protestant Episcopal ministry. He was received into the Episcopal church as Deacon by Bishop Whitaker 15 Jan. 1890, and ordained priest by the same 18 Feb. 1891 (Henry Anstice, *History of St. George's Church of...New York* [NY: Harper, 1911], 468). He then returned to teaching as Professor of New Testament Literature and Learning at Philadelphia Divinity School, 1891-9. In 1891 Columbia Univ. gave him the honorary degree of Doctor of Laws in Sacred Theology, conferred by Nicholas Murray Butler (Secretary, Columbia U. 30 Oct. 1969).

At Philadelphia the family lived at 4813 Regent Street In that city he published his most famous work, which became a standard text: *A Critical and Exegetical Commentary on the Gospel according to St. Mark* [NY: Scribner's, 1896, 3d. ed. 1901, 1903, 1907, 1913, 1922, 1948]. The next year the Church Social Union published his "Modification of Christianity by its contact with the world", Boston, 1897.

His Harvard obituary says he retired after nine years due to lack of funds (CB 1902, 25), but a funeral tribute of the minister of his next post says "He was turned out...because his views were supposed to be too broad on social matters—views which, I have the best authority for saying, he never obtruded on his class..." (Rev. W. S. Rainsford obit. St. George's Year Book 1901, 19).

Ezra was offered "asylum" as Assistant Minister to Street George's Episcopal Church at 207 E. 16th Street, New York City. Because of poor health his work was confined to training Sunday School teachers. However, his third book was published: *The Biblical Theology of the New Testament* [NY: Macmillan, 1900] and a second edition in 1901.

Prof. Gould died at the summer resort in Sullivan County, at White Lake NY of pernicious anemia, on 22 Aug. 1900. He is buried in Mt. Auburn cemetery Cambridge on Lime Av. east of the gate house, in front of his brother and mother and infant son (lot 3254).

A memorial service held at St. George's 13 Dec. included tributes by three of his Philadelphia Seminary colleagues, Rev. S. D. McConnell, D.D., Rev. Prof. Fleming Jones, and Rev. L. W. Batten, D.D.. Rector Rainsford stated "He was known all over the United States by scholars as one of the best—if not the best—New Testament exegetists we have."

(Obits. in *Boston Transcript* and *Boston Journal* 25 Aug. 1900, bios in *Who Was Who in America*, 473; Andover-Newton, S. F. Smith, *History of Newton, Massachusetts* [Boston: Amer. Logotype, 1880], 501, 548, 553 568, 569, 570. Photos in CB 1915, 92).

30. SAMUEL^{7} SHELTON GOULD, b. Boston New Year's Day 1843. He followed his brother for two years 1853-4 at Boston Latin School, and Roxbury Latin 1855-8. He entered Harvard at age 15 in 1858 (biography by his brother Ezra in *Harvard Memorial Biographies* [Cambridge: Harvard, 1866], 2:404-9)

Staying but one year, he shipped as common sailor on the *Peabody* in the Australian trade. He returned from Melbourne on another American ship, *Commonwealth* to Callao. There he learned the crew had been deceived about its destination in the Chincha Islands for guano. Failing to get a discharge from the American consul, he was beaten by the Captain and Mate. He escaped at night and shipped on the *Rival* for Cork, where he took a coastal schooner home, but nearly wrecked off Cape Hatteras, making up his sophomore year in three months he reentered Harvard as a junior in 1861.

The Civil War having broken out in April, he joined the Fourth Battalion formed at Harvard, but it was not called up. In Sept. 1862 he enlisted in the Thirteenth Massachusetts Infantry as private. The unit was sent at once to the defense of Washington. Arriving unarmed he was assigned to bear stretchers at the Battle of Antietam, 17 Sept. 1862. He picked up a musket and joined his company at the front, where he was shot through the heart, one of the 2,108 Union soldiers who were killed.

The President of Harvard declared a holiday for the Senior Class to attend his funeral, which the whole class of 1862 attended. He was buried at Mt. Auburn on Sept. 29.

27. Edward^{7} "Ned" Francis Gould, b. Boston, 21 July 1852. He probably had the benefit of the best primary education like his brothers, but at age 13 went with his father and mother to Quincy IL, and across the plains to Black Hawk Co. He was likely educated further by his schoolmaster father. They moved in 1869 to Canon City, CO, where his father died in 1874. At age 21 he probably took over the family ranch. At age 30, on 11 June 1882 he married Masie Ann Suddarth (Pierce Gen. 11). They had four children: i. Robert Lawrence Gould, b.Co. 4 Dec. 1883; d. March 1906, age 23; ii. Arthur Townley, b. Co. 16 March 1886; iii. Edward Francis, b. Kansas 20 Jan. 1888; iv. Margaret Edna, b. OK 25 Nov. 1890, all living Kingfisher, OK 1912 (Pierce Gen.). The sequence of births dates, their move from Colorado to Kansas 1886-7, and to Kingfisher, OK by late 1890, where he was a farmer. No more is known of this branch of the Gould family.

Part VI
THOMAS^{6} GOULD'S Last Years, 1852-72
RETIREMENT TO FRAMINGHAM

In 1852, at the age of 67, Thomas Gould "retired" to Framingham, a town 20 miles west of Boston on the Boston & Albany railway, but remained active in the building of Tremont

Temple in Boston, and other properties.

Elizabeth Gould's explanation is this: "Early in the fifties, came a break in his health, which altho it//[sentence missing] to be no more a man of sound health, though still possessing a good degree of strength and vigor, owing doubtless to a naturally strong constitution. He had plans for further improving his Friend Street property, but these he never carried out. The houses he held there and elsewhere, for rental, demanded considerable of his care and attention; he had gained a competence, and he had never been ambitious to acquire wealth, (2-3).

In the 1850 Census Thomas Gould is shown with no occupation, though Assessor's; records still call him "carpenter" and most deeds say "housewright". The report to the census taker, at age 63 may show retirement (Boston, Ward 3, Roll 334, house 639, family 1152). His real estate is shown at $10,000; wife Lydia 58, Francis 20 surveyor, Elizabeth 16, and Emily Walker, b. Massachusetts, probably a live-in maid.

His daughter's account of the 15 years in Framingham is: "In 1852 Mr. Gould changed his residence from Boston to Framingham, a pleasant old town about twenty miles from Boston, thus carrying out a purpose long in his mind. The new house had a good location, including three acres of land in Framingham Centre." (6).

In June of that year he bought from local "gentleman" Lothrop Wight two lots on the west side of the road to South Framingham, south of Framingham Center, an acre and 50 rods (1/32 acre), paying $3300, and assuming the mortgage of Hannah Willey of $625 plus interest (MD 634/168). At the time of purchase he took a two year mortgage for $1575 from the seller at the usual six percent, $1100 to be paid in a year, and $475 in two, the buildings to be insured for $2000 (MD 633/142). Gould discharged this mortgage in less than a year. By Oct. 15 the deeds show him resident in Framingham (SD 638/38,39), but still active in building the Tremont Temple. It is probable that he moved his family from the home in Friend St. by that date.

This land is about 100 feet south of Buckminster Square, in the angle between Maple St. and Union Av., the main road to South Framingham. The 1857 map shows "Thos Gould on South St. 20 rods (330 ft.) south of the square (Detail of Middlesex County Wall map 1857 in Framingham Hist. Society, orig. at SPNEA). Hyde's map of 1850 shows the first house south of the square approximately where #602 Union Av. is today, the house of S[tephen] L. Place, a long building with central core facing the street, an ell running westward from the northwest corner, adjoining a wider structure (barn?) at the back. (MD 633/143 names Place as having sold it to Wight in MD 603/249, Jan. 1, 1851). The most detailed plan is that of J.A.White's house in the 1908 atlas, showing a porch across the front to the street, a square core with a small projection on the north and a (kitchen?) ell to the west, connected by a narrow (one story ?) wing leading to a sguare barn to the west (Middlesex Co. Atlas 1908 in Framingham Hist. Soc.).

This was at the south edge of Framingham Centre, but less than a mile from the Baptist church on the Common, and half a mile south of the railway depot which was served by a spur that ran just west of Maple St. There was E.H Warren's store on Main St. on the other side of the square. We have no photo of the Gould house, which was near the new garrison colonial houses at 600 and 596 Union Av. (Framingham Assessor's Map 304 (1972); Josiah Temple, *History of Framinqham* (Framingham: Town, 1887), p.569; Chairman of Town Historical Commission, Steven Herring, 1, 26 Feb. 1993).

Elizabeth Gould's account continues, "He at once interested himself in the cultivation of his garden, taking both pride and pleasure in his success with fruit and vegetables for his table. He made some changes for the improvement of house and land, buying a small strip of land to straiten a boundary."

To the original acre he added a small triangle to the north, along Union Av., paying William Hastings $60 in 1854 (MD 705/66).

His daughter says only this of his civic activity: "He bought a pew in the Framingham Baptist Church taking with his wife, letters to this church; He urged alterations needed in the church building, which, carried out, gave a new and convenient vestry in place of a very unfitting one, and also an improved re-arrangement of seats in the main entrance room."

Framingham Baptist Church is a classic New England church, designed in 1825 by Boston housewright Solomon Willard, a contemporary of Gould whose carving of the capitals of Park St. Church and Federal St. Church, St. Paul's, and designs for the Boston Court House and Bunker Hill Monument Gould must have known well (National Historic Register form First Baptist Church in Framingham; hereinafter NHR). According to the record, changes in 1856-7 included closing the basement horse stalls, raising the floor of the sanctuary, and replacing box stalls with circular benches.

When Gould came to Framingham the back of the church basement was open for horses. In 1856 this was closed to provide social rooms in the basement, and horse sheds built outside (NHR p.6). The level of the "audience room" or sanctuary was raised, with access by 3 circular steps with simple round balusters, in the vestibule opposite each side front door. Around the pulpit the box pews were changed to plain benches in a semi-circle, in which Thomas Gould has one of the best seats, at bench #7 on the right aisle, four from the front, and two behind the Pastor (1857 Pew Plan, First Baptist Church, Framingham, in Framingham Hist. Soc.; NHR, 2). A recess was made behind the pulpit area, with a desk instead of a pulpit is shown. A diagram of the circular benches in 1856 shows two windows on either side of the pulpit area, now gone ("History of First Baptist Church in Framingham", vertical file, Framingham Public Library, 2 pp.)- The changes, probably supervised if not designed by Gould reflect not only practical matters, but suggest a more democratic concept of religious congregation. An indication of the abolitionist sentiment of the church is the closing of the two slave galleries on the balcony, called Negro Galleries when the openings onto the Sanctuary were plastered up in 1849 ("History"). The first organ was installed the year Gould arrived (ibid.).

The big Gould house was home to three generations of the family. Elizabeth's account says, "His new roof tree sheltered beside himself and wife, two daughters and three grandchildren,—his daughter **18.**]Charlotte [b. 1819], with her two youngest children [Lydia, b. 1848, and **21.** Joseph, b. 1845, James Gould Dam having died 1851, aged 13 months; Dam 359-360], came to her parents' home after, tho' not immediately after her husband Cyrus K. Dam, went to California, remaining in the home two or three years [before she joined her husband in Wheatland CA in 1856, arriving in San Francisco on "The Golden Age" 1 Dec. 1856 via Panama (Ibid.)]".

She adds that she, **24.** Elizabeth (age 18) came too, with "a third grandchild **32.** Sarah Elizabeth Gould, b. 1842], whom his son **19.** James had left with his parents when he went to California in April 1849,--to grow up (in their care as it proved), her father dying in California in **9** December of -49." It is unclear what became of her mother, Anne J. Jones, whom he married 20 April 1842, for she is said to have remarried a man named Green before Thomas made his will in Nov. 1868, but we have no record of her remarriage or death which may have been in Cambridge.

Sarah m. Framingham? Feb. 1866 Edward P. Moulton, s. George W. b. Framingham 1819. She may have remained in the area, for her children lived nearby: i. Arthur B. Moulton, b. Springfield March 1868, res. Saxonville 1901 (Peirce Gen.). In 1902 he is a shoemaker in Saxonville, until 1908 (Framingham Hist. Soc. 26 March 1994). ii. Louis R. Moulton, res. Saxonville 1901; iii. Edward Moulton; iv. Daisy F., b. Cambridge, m. Mr. Brown, res. S. Framingham 1901. A minor child Raymond G. Moulton is listed in Saxonville 1901. Sarah d.

Cambridge Dec. 1875.

The daughter's account goes on: "To the home came later, another little grand-daughter, [Sarah "Sae" Homer Gould, b. 27 Dec. 1854], the only child of **23.** Francis Gould [b. 1830], after her father had entered the army on the outbreak of the Civil War, her mother [Sarah Howe Homer, b. 1828] having died two years before [4 June 1859, when the daughter was only four and a half]. Her father was in active service until Sept. 7, 1862, then while acting Captain of his company he was wounded in the knee in the Battle of Chantilly, the wound disabling him for further service, so that he received honorable discharge January 1863. His daughter, however, remained at the Framingham home after his return,.until June, 68, that home was exchanged for one on Pleasant Street, Arlington, Francis Gould having built a house there."

In the Federal Census of 1860 six persons are shown in the household: Thomas Gould, 73, housewright, Lydia 68, Delia 43, Elizabeth 30, Anna Fernald 17, and Sarah E. Gould 17 (US Census 1860, Vol. XX, Framingham, house 384, family 39, 48-9).

In 1861 Gould had a small interest in land in Bedford, giving $100 mortgage to George W. Monroe, which he soon assigned to Boardman (MD 877/424).

On 23 May 1863 Lydia and Thomas celebrated their fiftieth wedding anniversary. His sisters and her brothers and sisters presented them a silver goblet with this inscription: "Presented to Thomas and Lydia Gould by their brothers and sisters on the fiftieth anniversary of their marriage, May 23d 1863" (In possession of descendant Fred V. Archer, Port St. Lucie FL 1994).

In 1867 Thomas Gould rounded off his Framingham property by paying William Hastings $500 for an acre and 3/4 fronting east on Adams St. going back to the road to Ichabod Gaines' house, adjoining his 50 rod sliver on the south (MD 1022/286). Although the bounds are not explicit, the next deed makes it appear that Gould had squared off his holding between Maple and Union by acquiring 344 feet frontage on Maple, and an ell going back to Union Av.

On 27 April 1868 Gould sold to Joseph Avery White the house in Framingham and land totaling two and 7/8 acres, apparently the combination of the four parcels, bounded on the east by Union Av. 331½ ft., on the west by Maple St. 341 ft. 9 in., on the north by William Hastings 97 ft. 3 in., on the south 233 ft. by Ichabod Gains, and southeast 270 ft. by Sydney Phillips (MD 1037/220; this coincides with the three parcels on the 1972 Assessor's map 204, 1.72 acres of Moran & Arglin, #592 Union Av. of Carolina & Pasquale Tordiglione, and #14 Maple St. of Bernard & Alice Slatkavitz). He made about $2,235 profit on the sale of $6000. Witnesses were his daughters **17.** Delia Fernald and **24.** Elizabeth M. Gould.

In June 1868, now age 83, he moved to Pleasant St. in Arlington, with his wife, age 78, so that his son Francis could care for them. This move also reunited 13 year old Sarah with her father after his return from the war.

LAST HOME IN ARLINGTON CENTRE

Both Thomas Gould and his wife Lydia died at the family home on Pleasant St. in Arlington Center, in 1872 and 1875. The first occupant was their son **23**. Francis[6] Gould, who after his marriage to Sarah Howe Homer on 27 April 1851 moved to Arlington (Frederick C. Clark, *History of the 40th (Mozart) Regiment* [Boston: F.H.Gilson, 1909], 128). Thomas gave his son a second mortgage of $1200 on his house on the west side of Pleasant St. on 16,500 sq. ft. with 102 foot frontage on the street, going back 160 and 170 feet (MD 758/281). Francis had got $1000 mortgage from Mary Pierpoint a year earlier (Ibid). However, six months later Francis gave full title to his father for a nominal five dollars, the only difference in the property being the shortening by four feet on the north boundary (MD 774/267). Eight years later, in 1865, after

Francis returned from the Civil War, wounded at the battle of Chantilly, Thomas sold it back to his son for the same five dollars (MD 968/301), shortly after Francis repaid his father the original mortgage (MD 758/281 margin autograph of Thos Gould). The 1865 deed was witnessed by Thomas's youngest child **24**. Elizabeth M. and his great-niece Anna Fernald (1842-99, daughter of **17.** Delia). This deed was recorded again in 1874 for the benefit of the Probate Court of Suffolk, attested to by his widow Lydia and daughter Elizabeth (MD 1300/575, presumably for estate of Thomas). This property remained in the Richardson family until the mid-twentieth century.

His daughter Elizabeth explained the move to Arlington in June 1868 thus: "This step, for several reasons seemed desirable. Thomas Gould was eighty-three//his [Francis's] daughter to be with himself in one home". "The four years that remained to Thomas Gould were years of failing powers, and the enforced inactivity was somewhat welcome to him, after his many busy and active days. Pleased with the new home and its surroundings, his keen interest in life was waning." Among the celebrations must have been Francis's remarriage, on 26 Sept. 1871 to Mary S. Richardson, who was to die in less than four years. Elizabeth continues, "The physical ailments from which he had long suffered had acted upon the nervous system, so that he was sometimes impatient and unreasonable; the wonder was, his physician said, that he was not so to a much greater degree."

In 1867-9 Francis Gould bought three parcels totaling three acres on the east side of Pleasant St. backing up to Spy Pond (MD 1012/18, 1036/579, 1018/381, 1042/474). His father took a second mortgage of $4000 at 7 percent for five years, payable semi-annually at Feb. 1 and Aug. 1, buildings to be insured for $4000 (MD 1126/637, 22 Aug. 1870). After Thomas's death in 1872 and Francis's in Sept. 1874 this mortgage was transferred to his daughter and co-administratix Elizabeth and to Francis's daughter Sarah H. Richardson (1854-1901) by his administrators **29.** Prof. Ezra P. Gould and Elizabeth (MD 1337/548).

Among the trials of his last years must have been the death of his eldest son **14.** Thomas Jr. in Lexington on 19 Oct. 1869. Two children were out West, **16.** Samuel in Colorado and 18. Lottie Dam in northern California. Francis was to die of his Civil War wounds shortly, and of his 17 children, only **15.** Sophia Mann, **17.** Delia Cushing and spinster **24.** Elizabeth were to survive him long.

Thomas Gould made his last will five months after moving to Arlington, on 14 Nov. 1868, prefaced by the realization, "Considering the uncertainty of human life and being of sound mind, and trusting God to direct me" (Middlesex Probate 4396, in pencil; copy in hands .of descendant Hazel LaPorte, Bedford MA 1968). He left his four sons Thomas, Samuel, George and Francis $1500 each, first deducting his debts. He left the same amount to each of his three daughters Sophia Mann, Delia Gushing and Elizabeth M. To his daughter **16.** Charlotte Dam he left only a thousand dollars, "in full for her part of the Estate, having for her sake already paid large sums of her husband's debts". He favored three of his 23 grandchildren with $600, **32.** Sarah E. wife of Edward P. Moulton, daughter of his son James; Edward B. and Mary F. Adams, children of his daughter Sarah. If Sarah Moulton were to die without children, the bequest was void, but she soon had Arthur B. and three others. If Edward or Mary Adams were to die, the other would get both; if both died, no one would get it. All legacies were to be paid within a year at 5% interest. He left $300 to Anne J. Green, widow of his son **19.** James, to be paid at times and amounts judged by his widow and executors. The interest on all the rest after paying debts, funeral expenses and legacies went to his wife for her lifetime. On Lydia's death it was to be divided equally among his eight children Thomas, Sophia Mann, Delia Fernald, Samuel, Joseph, George, Francis and Elizabeth, but the portion falling to Sophia is for her life only, then half going to his granddaughter **26.** Sophia Bailey, a quarter to her sisters **27.** Anna Muzzey and **28.** Lucy Whiting.

The favoring of five of the 23 grandchildren probably reflects their relative prosperity, for the oldest, 25. T. Warren Gould was now a successful Boston commission merchant, **29.** Rev. Ezra a prominent theologian at Andover Newton, his brother **31.** Ned a cattle rancher in Colorado, 16. Charlotte Dam's children now farmers in the Sacramento Valley, 21. Joseph's six children settled in the midwest and benefitting from their father's share, Sarah Richardson covered by her father's share and a husband, leaving only the two Fernald girls, Anna and Delia, who are covered by their mother's share.

The will was witnessed by non-family members, unlike many of Gould's deeds: Joshua and L. D. Loring (his bankers?) and Frederick Gould, his longtime colleague m the Boston Common Council and elder of the Second Stillman Baptist Church, who took over his debt at Tremont Temple, but is no known relation (but not listed in Z.Gould).

Thomas appointed his two eldest sons 14. Thomas and 16. Samuel as executors, and not anticipating the death of both, named his son **23.** Francis in one's place. Thomas was to die before his father in 1869, and both Sam lei and Francis within months of the other in 1874.

Son Samuel asked to be excused from executing the will, in a letter from Greenwood, Fremont Co. Colorado Territory, 26 Aug. 1872 (attached to bottom of will). He was to die 18 months later in Canon City Co., on 11 Feb. 1874 as a result of an accident on 21 Jan. Son Francis filed for probate, on 8 Oct. 1872 listing 14 heirs. But Francis himself was to die of his Civil War wounds only seven months after Samuel, on 7 Sept. 1874. So daughter 24. Elizabeth and grandson **29.** Prof. Ezra Palmer Gould ended up as executors. The file does not contain an inventory, so the only account we have is the executors' first account, giving total assets of $17,604.55, which included $1225 premium on US bonds, $1400 unsettled note of G.P.Gould probably on the Friend St. sale, $600 note from estate of Francis Gould, and small amounts .of interest on mortgages to Ezra and Francis, and notes to George and Samuel. Expenses included fifteen dollars for undertaker Benson, $62.17 for Mt.Auburn lot, and burial cost $8, leaving eight equal shares of $2081.82 paid to the five living children Delia, Joseph, Elizabeth, George and Sophia, and to the heirs of Samuel, Thomas Jr. and Francis (Schedule B).

Grandson Edwin B. Adams could not be found in 1874, so his sister Mary F. Adams, last surviving child of Sarah Gould Adams, petitioned for his share of $600, plus interest, stating that "Edwin B. Adams left no widow or children, and that his next of kin was his father Abner G. Adams, of said Boston... said Edwin B. Adams died without children prior to the time of the death of said Thomas Gould" (Petition of administratrix after 1885 in Pro. 4396).

Elizabeth concludes, "The 'silver thread' was wearing thin;--it parted July 23, 1872, after two weeks in which he had not the strength to rise from his bed. His wife survived him, living until January 3, 1875. She had griefs, spared to her husband, of the deaths of her eldest, and her youngest son, Samuel L. Gould, February 11, 1874, Francis Gould, September 7, 1874, dying from the effects of the wound received in the Battle of Chantilly, twelve years before, the ball having remained in the knee, causing lead poison." This was the third family death in the tragic year, for Francis's young wife Mary died April 26, at age 32, again leaving 19 year old Sarah motherless.

Thomas Gould's last real estate transaction was done for him by his executor, his son 23. Francis in 1873. He gave a $3000 mortgage to Gould's grandson **29.** Prof. Ezra Palmer Gould on his house on a new road extending southeast of Glen Av. in Newton Centre near Andover Newtown Theological Seminary where he taught (MD 1289/309). The professor had bought it for $6500 five days before from Joseph M. White of Newton (MD 1289/283). He took a second mortgage of $1400 from his aunt **24.** Elizabeth M. Gould of Arlington at the same rate of 7 %, payable also in five years (MD 128/311). Because of the executor's death Sept. 7, 1874, the first mortgage was assigned to his sister, **17.** Delia G. Fernald in 1875 (MD 1338/282), then to their half-sister **15.** Sophia Ann Mann (MD 1940/80), to whom it was finally discharged in ? (MD 2057/441).

The funeral took place at 3:30 pm 25 July 1872, at his son Francis's house on Pleasant St., Arlington (obit. *Boston Transcript*, 24 July, p.3:2). Thomas Gould was first buried in the family tomb on ;.the west side of Copp' s Hill, but moved three years later to be next to his wife Lydia in Mt. Auburn Cemetery, Cambridge. Mt. Auburn had been opened a few years before, as a pioneer "garden cemetery", that became the resting place of Boston's most famous literary, artistic and political persons. The decision to join the elite was apparently made by Thomas's son Francis (Middlesex Will 4379).

The graves are on the north side of Perella Path, close to the main entrance (turn immediately left on Garden Av. along the Mt. Auburn fence, first right on Yew Av., and left on fourth lane, Perella. About 100 feet east, on the right is Lot 4335-1, to southwest of the granite boulder "GOULD//RICHARDSON"; letter of Duncan W. Munro, Superintendent 16 Sept.,1968, and plot plan 4334-1 with record of 22 burials). Francis apparently bought the plot in 11 July 1874 to bury his second wife Mary, then was buried here with his first wife Sarah, followed by his mother Lydia. Then, on May 26 1875 the family (Sarah Gould Richardson) moved eight bodies from Copp's Hill, including Thomas and his first wife Sophia Lovis, two infant children of **18.** Charlotte Gould Dam (James and Joseph), and four children of Thomas and Lydia, Susan (1831-2), Franklin (1830-31), Benjamin (1839), and Lydia (1816-40).

Thomas's epitaph gives his dates and tribute "Blessed are the dead who die in the Lord", and Lydia's gives dates and "He giveth his beloved sleep" (Epitaphs copied by great-great grandson Fred V. Archer, letter 11 June, 1978).

17 children, all born Boston:

By his first wife, Sophia Lovis:

14. i. THOMAS[5] WARREN GOULD, b. 11 Feb. 1808; d. Lexington, 11 Feb. 1808; m. LYDIA ANN WINSHIP TEEL.

15. ii. SOPHIA ANN, b. 6 April 1809; d. Boston 1 March 1900, m. BRIGGS MANN. For descendants see above, Part III .

iii.CHARLOTTE, b. 7 April 1812; d. Boston c. 20 Feb. 1813 of lung fever.

By second wife, Lydia Peirce:

16. iv. SAMUEL LAWRENCE, b. 20 May 1814; d. Canon City CO, 11 Feb. 1874; m. FRANCES ANN SHELTON. For life and descendants see above Part V.

v. LYDIA, b. 3 Feb. 1816; d. Boston 29 Feb. 1840 sp.

17. vi. DELIA CUSHING, b. 29 Dec. 1817; d. 28 April 1903; m. JAMES FERNALD. For descendants see above Part III .

vii.ELIZABETH, b. 11 Aug. 1818; d. Boston 13 Aug. 1818.

18. viii .CHARLOTTE, b. 28 Novt 1819; d. Erie CA 8 March 1906 m. CYRUS KING DAM. For property and children, see Part IV above, and Register Oct. 1938, p. 359 ff..

19. ix. JAMES, b. 16 Oct. 1821; d. CA 9 Dec. 1850; m. ANNE J. JONES. For descendants see Part VI above.

20. x. SARAH, b. 17 Oct. 1823; d. Boston 29 Jan. 1852; m. 15 Oct. 1844 ABNER G.

ADAMS; he died after 1872 Franklin MA (Peirce Gen.; TG probate). They had 4 children surnamed ADAMS: i. Edwin Benjamin, b. May 1846, d. Boston between June 1868-July 1872 (TG estate); ii. Mary Frances, b. Boston? 23 July 1847; called "Fanny" Adams, shfe never married. Res. Waltham 1872, Medfield 1901, Calif. 1912; iii. George Gould, b. Nov. 1850; d. June 1851 (Peirce Gen.); iv. Sarah Gould, b. 28 Jan. 1852; d. Feb. 1852 (Peirce Gen.). All dying unm., there are no descendants.

21. xi. JOSEPH A., b. 25 Dec. 1825; d. Owen WI 6 Nov. 1906 m. Boston 24 Jan. 1847 SOPHIA A. CUTTER, b. 1824; they had 7 ch.:(Peirce Gen.; 1870 Census Genoa WI)

i. Sophia A. Gould, b. Boston 25 Nov. 1847; d. WI 13 Aug. 1872; m. 17 June 1866 Noah E. French, by whom she had 3 ch. b. WI: Minnie J., b. 28 Sept. 1867, d. 20 June 1897; Coral B., b. 14 May 1870, d. 18 Sept. 1871 sp; Birdie b. 13 Aug 1872, d. 16 July 1873.

ii. Joseph Shelton, b. Watertown 20 Oct. 1851 m. WI 28 Nov. 1889 Letitia A. Pulver, by whom he had one ch.: Frank Gould, b. 18 Dec. 1890, res. Stoddard WI 1912.

iii. Sarah F. b. 3 June 1854, d. Watertown 19 Nov. 1856. .

iv. Ella 0. b. Chelsea WI 5 Sept. 1657; d. WI July 1886, m. WI 28 Jan 1878 George Knower by whom she had 4 ch.: Ernest b. 18 April 1879, d. 20 April 1879.; Maud b. 24 May 1880; Mark b. 13 Nov. 1883; Max G. b. 18 April 1885.

v. Elizabeth "Lizzie" M. b. WI 17 Feb. 1861; m. 27 Sept. 1892 Theodore F. Williams MD, by whom she had Elmer S. Williams b. WI 22 Feb. 1897.

vi. (Thomas) Frank, farmer Kimball SD 1899-1915, b. WI 6 April 1863, m. 21 Nov. 1893 Carrie De Morris, b. NY 1899, by whom he had 6 ch.: George b. WI 12 Sept. 1894; Willard b. WI 10 May 1896; May b. WI 27 July 1897; Gladys b. 19 June 1899 d. 1901 SD; Warren b. Kimball 13 June 1901; Donald b. Kimball 1912 (1915 Census), vii. George E., b. WI 7 June 1866; d. Ariz.1904.

22. xii. GEORGE PEIRCE, b. 17 May 1828; d. CO? 9 June 1891. unm. He attended New Hampton Academy 1844-5; became a wheelwright; res. Parker KS on father's death 1874, Colorado 1880.

twins, b. 8 March 1830:

xiii. FRANKLIN; d. Boston 5 Feb. 1831

23. xiv. FRANCIS; d. Arlington MA 7 Sept. 1874; m. twice: (1) SARAH HOWE HOMER, (2) MARY RICHARDSON.

xv. SUSAN SHAW, b. 15 Dec. 1831; d. Boston 5 April, 1832, sp.

24. xvi. ELIZABETH MELINDA, b. 27 March 1834; d.

Brookline MA 22 Aug. 1918; Called "Lizzie". She lived with her parents in Framingham and Arlington, and continued living in the Gould house there. She was an artist, decorating teacups. Res. Brookline 1912-8 at 365 Walnut St., where she died, the last of her generation. Buried Mt. Auburn.

xvii. BENJAMIN FRANKLIN, b. 29 Sept. 1839; d. Boston 26 Dec. 1839, sp.

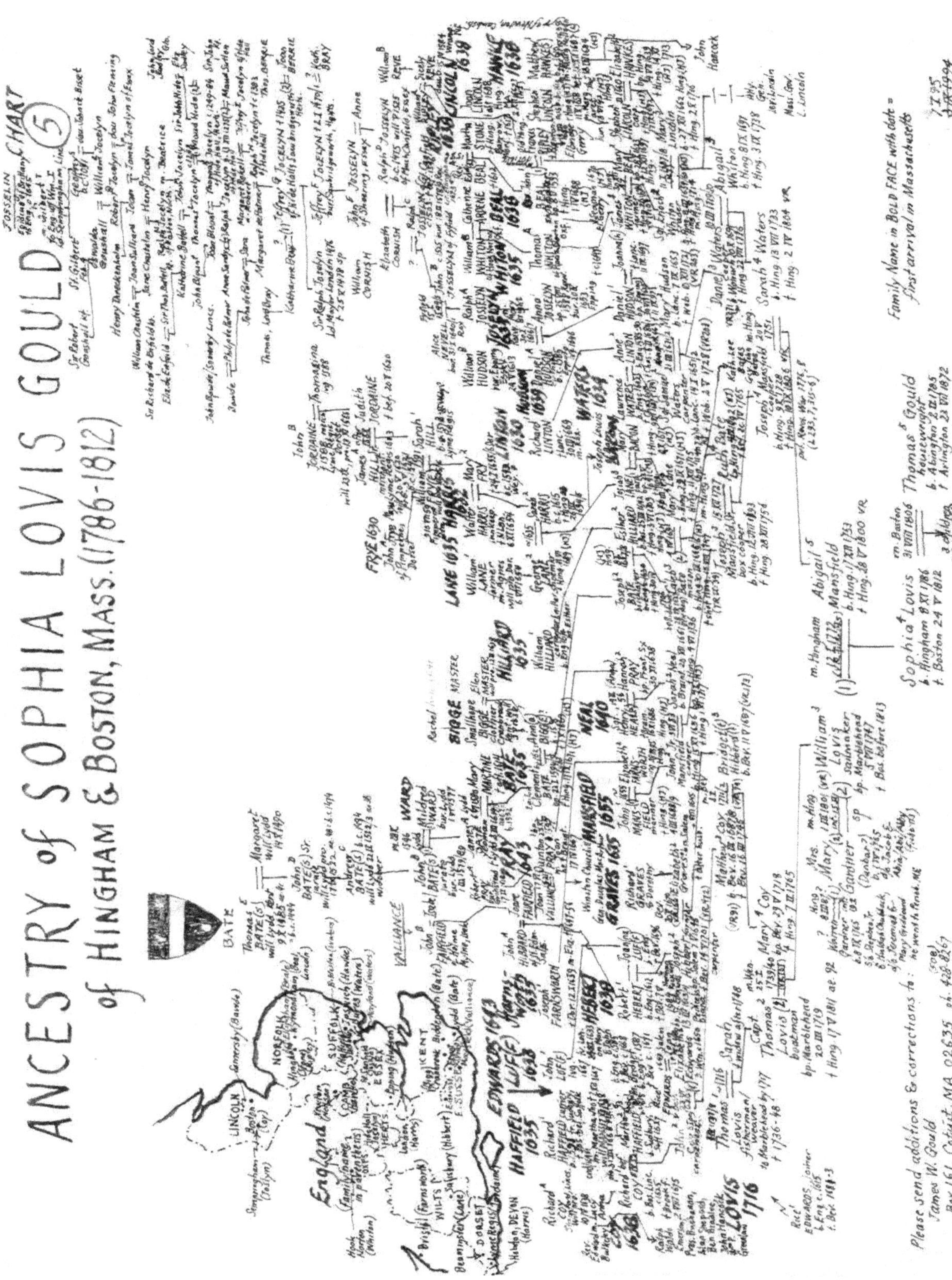
ANCESTRY of SOPHIA LOVIS GOULD CHART 5
of HINGHAM & BOSTON, MASS. (1786-1812)
Family Name in BOLD FACE with date = first arrival in Massachusetts
Please send additions & corrections to: James W. Gould Box 161, Cotuit, MA 02635 ph. 428-8367
Sophia Lovis
b. Hingham 8 XI 1786
† Boston 24 V 1812
Thomas Gould
housewright
b. Abington 2 III 1785
† Abington 23 VII 1872

Chapter VIII.

ANCESTRY OF SOPHIA LOVIS GOULD
of Hingham and Boston
(1786-1812)

This chapter tells the fascinating story of our great, great, great grandmother, Sophia Lovis, who died a young woman of only 25, almost unknown to her descendants until this research was done by Eleanor Gould Baldic and James Warren Gould in 1994. Here is the true tale of witches, Indian massacres, pioneers on the frontier, industrial innovators, and first settlers of New England towns.

SOPHIA^{4} LOVIS (William^{3}, Thomas$^{2-1}$) was born in Hingham, Massachusetts 8 Nov. 1786 (Solomon Lincoln, *History of Hingham* [Hingham: The Town, 1893] [hereinafter Lin], 44), and died in Boston 24 May 1812 (*Columbian Centinel*, 27 May; Howe records it as 26 May, *Record of Deaths in Boston, Mass. 1799-1825*, 1: 232, Online database: NewEnglandAncestors.org, NEHGS, 2006, from mss. Ledgers of William and Joseph Howe, MSS/A/5862; hereinafter Howe) at age 25. She was buried Copp's Hill tomb # 74 on Charter Street near the Mathers (SD 252:194) , and removed to Mt. Auburn Cemetery, Cambridge in 1875, north side of Perella Path (plot plan 4334-1).

She came from a modest family of sail makers, fishermen and boatmen in Hingham and Marblehead, but was allied to all the important landed families of Hingham through her mother. Her father's family, the Lovises, came over about 1715, but all of her other ancestors had been here since at least 1655, the earliest 1630 (Linton). Many were founders of towns, of Hingham, Dorchester, Braintree, Quincy, Weymouth, Beverly, Ipswich, Wenham, Salisbury, Brookfield and Lancaster. For fifteen years an ancestor sat in the State House as Representative, from 1632-59. Many held important offices in their towns, especially as Hingham Selectman for ten years between 1637 and 1712, Constable for six years, and first Schoolmaster and Town Clerk. The peak of influence is 1654 when all three Selectmen were ancestors: Beal, Lincoln and Hawke. There were also Selectmen in Dorchester and Braintree.

One relative, Rachel (Haffield) Clinton, was convicted as witch in 1692, and jailed for nine months. In this story we will find people tried for all kinds of crime: drunkenness, fornication before marriage, excessive mirth and merriment, taking God's name in vain, wearing fancy clothes, bashing a man's skull with an iron rod, tax delinquency, resisting arrest, railing in public, idleness, swearing, fighting, etc. Several relatives were victims of the Indian wars. Richard Coy was killed at Brookfield in 1676, and his family driven from town. Two ancestors, Daniel and Joanna Hudson were killed in Lancaster in 1697, when two of their daughters also died in captivity. Three of her forebears (the Lawrence Waters family) were driven out of Lancaster in 1676 by the Indians, who killed other relatives in the Josselyn family and took others captive. In the same year James Whiton's house in Hingham was burned.

All of the males of these frontier families served in the militia guarding against Indian attacks, and three ancestors were Sergeants, in effect, leaders of the local militia during the Indian wars: Henry Neal in Braintree, Samuel Waters of Woburn and Enoch Whiton in Hingham. The Whitons were soldiers in every war from King Philip's to the Civil War; several ancestors fought in the Revolution.

For work, the Lovis family had mostly maritime occupations, as captain, boatman, fisherman, blubber-boy on a whaling ship, and sailmaker. Except for the Lovises, the Mansfields and Beals most of her ancestors had land-based occupations, the most common being farmers and carpenters. Housebuilding skills like mason, bricklayer, pavior and housewright often involved them in building the first homes and public buildings in the colony, including the Old Ship Church in Hingham, which is the oldest church building in America. Some were brought to America for their special skills, in ironmaking or saltmaking. Three generations of Mansfields were coopers, a Hingham specialty. Two founders of Hingham were shoemakers. Other occupations were innkeeper, trader, school teacher, weaver, currier, and pewterer.

Most of the men were literate, and one was a student at Cambridge University in England and one a theologically trained minister. In several towns they were associated with the first educational enterprises, building the first school in Cambridge, donating the first school in Ipswich, giving Thompson's Island in Dorchester for the first school in the colonies, and teaching in the first Hingham school for half a century.

All of the ancestors whose origins can be traced came from England. But the distribution of the 20 is widespread through 12 counties: six from the West Country, out of Bristol, Devon, Wiltshire and Dorset; ten from the East counties of Essex, Suffolk, Norfork, Cambridge and Lincolnshire; and three from Kent, and three from central counties of London, Hertfordshire and Oxfordshire. The Prays may have come from Belgium. Most of these English families were probably of middle class background, although three families claimed coats of arms (Bates, Whiton and Josselyn) and the Mansfields descent from gentry. The oldest family is Josselyn which can be traced clearly back to the Norman Conquest of 1066, with links to country gentlemen of Essex, Lincolnshire, Hartfordshire, Northamptonshire and Gloucestershire. Among the Josselyn ancestors was St. Gilbert of Sepringham, founder of the only English order, of Gilbertine monks. Cloth weaving is an occupation of some. The largest number of closely associated families was the low church community from Hingham in Norfolk who came on the *Diligent* in 1638.

Sophia had a number of famous cousins: Presidents Cleveland and Bush, Ralph Waldo Emerson, Norman Rockwell, Winston Churchill, General MacArthur, John Hancock, Katherine Lee Bates, Elbridge Gerry, astronaut Neil Armstrong, editor Ben Bradlee, cabinet member Levi Lincoln, as well as two Governors of Massachusetts (Bates and Lincoln), a state supreme court justice and numerous scholars like the President of Middlebury and the first schoolmaster of Barnstable.

Long life is a notable characteristic of the family, her grandfather Lovis supposedly living to 100, actually 95, and St. Gilbert lived to over 100. But the average age is low because of early deaths of women in childbirth, like Sophia herself at 25, her grandmother Lovis died at 46.

She was probably born on North Street near Bare Cove of Hingham harbor where her father worked as a sailmaker (Lin 44). We do not know if she was educated at school, since we have no letters or other record.

Sophia probably met Thomas Gould in Boston, where several members of her family had moved. Her widowed aunt Ruth (Mansfield) Lovis ran a boarding house on Kilby Street as early as 1796 (*Boston Directory* 70; 1798, 77, 1800, 73; widowed by 29 Oct. 1778, PD 132:246; Wendell B. Cook papers, NEHGS, Mss, 64, sub-group I, series C, sub-series (3) ; hereinafter Cook, folder 3) , and her eldest brother ran a cooperage in the North End, at Creek Square in 1800 (Directory, 73), then at 15 Middle Street (1803 Directory, 85; 1805, 84; 1806, 83; 1807, 105; 1809, 93; 1810, 130).

Sophia married Thomas[5] Gould 31 Aug. 1806 (Reg. 75:216), by Rev. Thomas Baldwin at the Second Baptist Church, in the North End, on North Margin Street where the Knights of Columbus Hall now stands. Church records for that date are missing, but we know that Baldwin attracted many young people by his inspired preaching (church records at Andover Newton library).

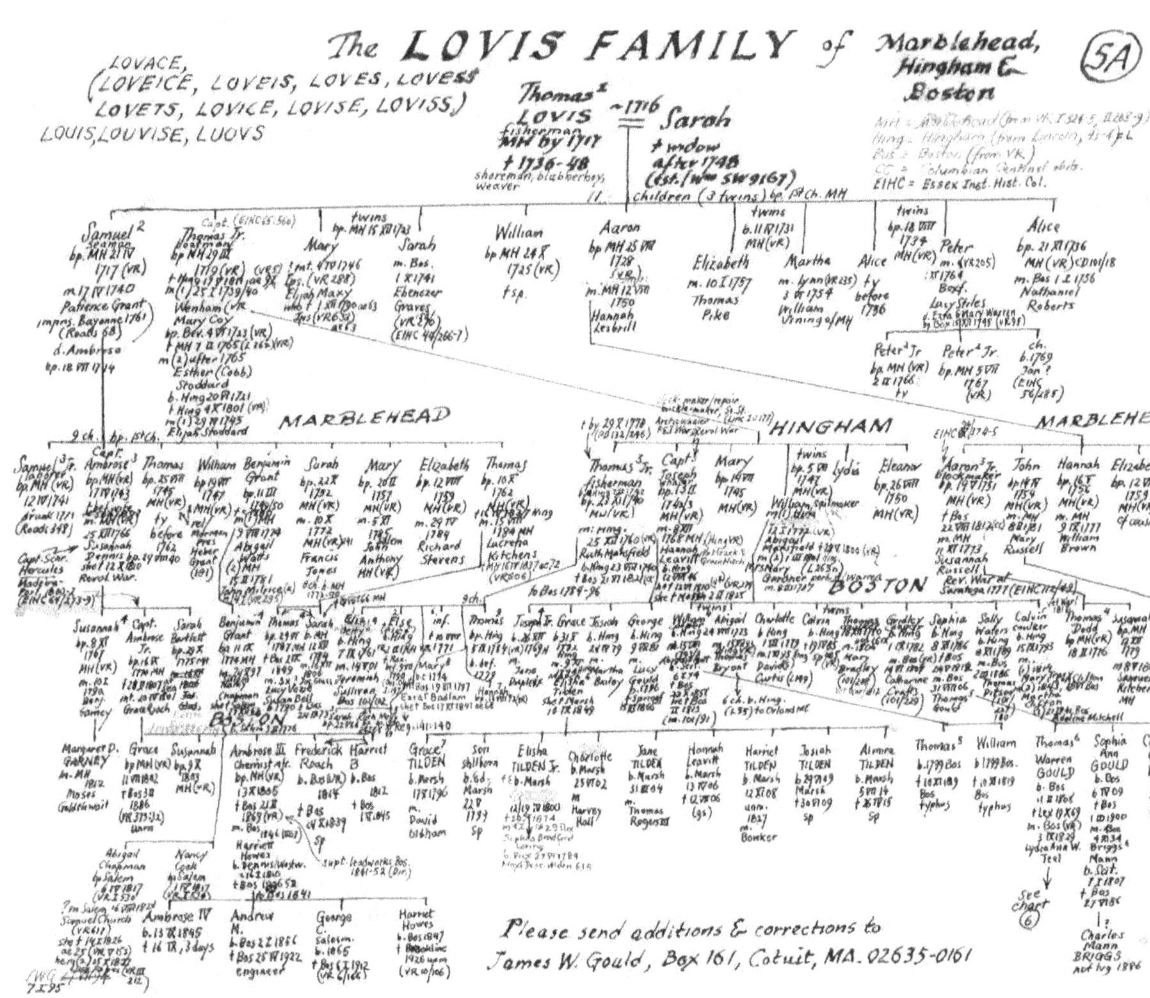

She was the seventh of nine children of WILLIAM[3] LOVIS and ABIGAIL MANSFIELD, a family of many twins. She had a brother Thomas whose twin Calvin had died at age 4; her father had a twin Lydia, and her Lovis grandfather had three sets of twins for brothers and sisters.

Her mother was the fifth generation of one of the old Hingham families, and descended from a dozen of the original settlers: Bates, Beal, Hawkes, Hilliard, Lane, Lincoln, Mansfield, Waters and Whiton, to which we will turn in order from left to right on the attached chart.

WILLIAM[3] LOVIS (Thomas[1-2]) was baptized Marblehead MA 5 July 1747 (VR 325), and came to Hingham with his parents soon after the birth of his sister Eleanor (26 Aug. 1750, Marblehead, VR 325; Lin 43). He grew up in Hingham, where his father, a boatman, lived in the Middle Ward, that is, Hingham Center. He married first, ABIGAIL[5] MANSFIELD 12 Jan. 1772 (VR fiche 145), who died 28 May 1800 age 46, 6 months (VR fiche 165).

Within nine months, on 1 March 1801 (VR fiche 145; Lin 263n) he remarried Mrs. Mary Gardner, widow perhaps of Warren Gardner, m. Hingham 8 March 1787 Mary Dunbar (VR fiche 138) , b. Hingham 1 April 1765, daughter of Jacob Gardner and Abia, Abi or Abby (fiche 113); he was son of Stephen Gardner Jr. and Huldah Chubbock, daughter of Jeremiah and Mary Goddard (fiche 138). Lincoln says he went to Penobscot ME; one might try deaths there about 1800, when widow may have returned to Hingham. There were no children by Lovis's second marriage. Their deaths are not recorded in Hingham or Boston.

Her father William Lovis was prominent as a sailmaker, the first listed by Lincoln (Lin 1/ii:174) . He built a house on the Mill Dam soon after his marriage to Hingham born Abigail Mansfield. This was on a ten rod lot, extending back to the bank, two rods back from the road to the dam, on which road he had 5 rods frontage (SD 122:188, 5 Dec. 1772) . This he bought for £ 3 from yeoman Richard Cobb, whose house was southwards, with privilege to Cobb's well. In the deed he is a fisherman, but the next year is listed as a mariner.

Sophia's birthplace can be inferred as near the Water Mill on North Street, facing the Hingham harbor, from her father's purchase of a house on a small lot which he bought in 1773 from Ann Moore within two years of his marriage, on Boston Street to North Street at the Water Mill, with right of passage to Prince Street (11 Nov. 1773, SD 124:258; 171 ft. on street leading to North Water Mills on sw, 14 ft. nw by Joseph Roberts, 175 ft. on ne by John Riordan, 14 ft. se on house and land of William Beers, with privilege to the well and pump at the end of a six foot passage, from the estate of Benjamin Browne, for which Lovis paid £ 52; Cook, f.1).

In this deed of 1773 William is known as a mariner, the same occupation that is given in a deed 16 years later, but from Boston, to a larger lot nearby with dwelling house west of the Town Cove and north of the Hingham highway to the Cove. It was sold by William to his brother Joseph Lovis 5 Feb. 1789, for £ 20/10/3, and may mark the family's move to Boston (SD 174:139; the deed states that it was bought from Samuel Johnson, but he is not found in the grantor or grantee indexes for Hingham; Cook f.1) .

Sophia had eight brothers and sisters, four of them twins. The youngest sibling was Calvin, a caulker of ships, who served twice in the War of 1812, the first time for the month of July in Capt. E. G. House's company of Osgood's regiment, and the second time for a month in the fall of 1814 with his brother Thomas, in the same company *(Records of Massachusetts Volunteer Militia...1812-1814* [Boston: Wright & Pelter, 1913], 79, 82).

Her grandfather Capt. THOMAS[2] LOVIS, Jr. was baptized at Marblehead 29 March 1719 (VR 1:325), died Hingham 17 May 1811 (VR fiche 165; Lin 43), age 95. He married twice, first in Wenham 25 Jan. 1739/40 (VR) MARY COY, who died Hingham 7 Feb. 1765 age 47 (VR fiche 165, 175; Lin 362) . He then married (not in Hing. VR) widow ESTHER (Cobb) STODDARD, b. Hingham 20 June 1721, d. Hingham 4 Oct. 1801 (VR fiche 164, nearly 80 years), who had first married 29 April 1745 Elijah Stoddard.

In 1750 he claimed the 50 pound reward for the capture of Obediah Allbey Jr. who was charged with murder of an Eastern Indian at Wiscassett, Maine (EIHC 65: 560-1). As master of a schooner of Capt. John Howard he was asked by the man's father to take him to Marblehead to visit friends to the westward, fearing his son was involved in the murder. On the way Allbey admitted he "Snapt his Gun" when he was with the Indians. As soon as Lovis arrived in Marblehead he went to Howard who showed him the proclamation of the governor for Allbey's arrest, and they went to justice Blaney to report (21 Dec. 1749). The judge told him to go home and secure Allbey until a warrant was ready. But before he got to his house Constable Mullett came and took the man to jail. Lovis was denied the reward, apparently because of his part in Allbey's flight.

We know little of Lovis in Hingham except his occupation as boatman, and residence in Hingham Center. He died 19 May 1811, age 95 (VR fiche 165), evidently reported two days before incorrectly as Mr. Joseph Lovis, about 100, in the Hingham Almshouse, on the west side of School Street, (Lin 1/ii:280).

Sophia's uncle, Thomas Jr.'s eldest son Thomas[3], a Hingham fisherman, had apparently moved to Boston by 1796 when his wife Ruth ran the boarding house on Kilby Street His death is not recorded, but Ruth is a widow in the 1813 Boston directory.

The second son, Captain Joseph of Hingham (1743-1810), also married into an old

Hingham family, the Leavitts. He fought in both French and Indian Wars and in the Revolution. He was only 16 when he went as a private to garrison Halifax NS for Pownall in March thru Nov. 1759 (Lin 1/i:267) . He is presumably the experienced soldier Joseph Levis who served in Peter Gushing's company in the defense of Dorchester, 15 March 1776 (Ibid., 293) . He was owner of a sailing vessel 1788 to 1812 (Lin 1/ii:171) . As a whaling captain Arctic waters (VR fiche 165 says Capt. Joseph Lovis, "made northern voyages for oil. Upon retirement from the sea he took up making and repairing clocks and watches, and making buckles in South Street, near the later waterworks building (Lin 1/ii:177). For the last years of his life resided in Jones' Lane at Hingham Centre, and there died" age 68, 12 June 1810) . His house, at 10 Jones Street, off Leavitt Street in Hingham Center, east of the Weir River, still stands, but much altered from its 1768 condition (Julian Loring inventory, Hingham Historical Commission, [hereinafter Loring]. Sophia must have visited this house of her uncle Joseph and aunt Hannah. Of Thomas and Mary's three daughters Mary, Lydia and Eleanor we know nothing, and may have died young or married out of Hingham.

The name LOVIS is variously spelled phonetically Lovace, Loveice, Loveis, Loves, Lovess, Lovets, Lovice, Lovise, Loviss, Louvise and Luovs. The family has not been traced to England, but James Lovis and his son Abraham appear on the list of Huguenot refugees in 1688 (SD 14:212 in Reg. 35:250). The first of our ancestors of the LOVIS name in America was THOMAS[1], who appears in Marblehead with his wife SARAH (no maiden name known) with the baptism of their first son Samuel on 21 April 1717, at the First Church (VR 325; genealogical file Lovis in Marblehead Historical Soc.). All eleven of their children, including three sets of twins were baptized there 1717-1736. There is no record of Thomas and Sarah's marriage, so it is possible that they were wed before coming to America. He died between the birth of their last child Alice in 1736 and 1748 when his wife is described as a widow in the estate of William (SW 9167, Cook f.2). The persistence of the name Alice in first and third generations makes it possible that it was a family name, perhaps the first Thomas's mother.

A warrant for Thomas Lovis, fisherman or shoreman of Marblehead, was issued by the Suffolk Court of Common Pleas in 1719 in favor of William Young of Boston, cordwainer, who claimed s 2/10 for 10 bushels of onions delivered to Lovis, and was awarded £ 2/7/6 court costs in early 1720 (Suffolk Court file 13988 in Cook f .2) . A decade later, in 1730, Thomas Lovis, fisherman or blubber boy (a whaler) of Marblehead had a writ of attachment issued by the Superior Court at Salem in favor of Andrew Tinker, shoreman of Marblehead for £ 7/1/6 damages, £ 4/19/3 costs, issued 9 Nov. 1730. Sheriff Blaney could find neither Lovis nor his goods on 19 May 1731 (Suff. file 31493 in Cook f.2).

The first record of property for Lovis in Essex deeds is 30 March 1747 when yeoman William Wheeler Jr. sold to Thomas Lovis, weaver of Marblehead a dwelling and land in the east part of town at Neek's Cove {ED 89:226). This is phonetic spelling of Nick's Cove in the Old Harbor, shown by William Perley's map #3 east of the Common, the present location of Boston Yacht Club (Sidney Perley, "Marblehead in the Year 1700", 220) . The sale for £ 120 Old Tenor Bills included three small pieces of land, a strip to the west 15 by 6 feet, another to the northeast 15 by 4 (perhaps along the road) , and a strip of marsh to the east 25 by 5. The spelling of Lovis, though indexed Lewis, is corrected and repeated in the deed, so probably refers to the elder Thomas[1], since his son would be Junior. We do not know if he changed his occupation to weaver from fisherman, or came to this country was a weaver. The deed of sale may give an answer.

Thomas[1] Lovis's eldest son Samuel (born 1717), Sophia's great-uncle, was captured by the French and imprisoned during the French and Indian War. He had sailed on the schooner *Prince of Orange* under Capt. Nathan Bowen for Spain or Portugal in early 1761. Over a month out they were captured by the French brig *Gentile* of Bayonne, and taken into St. Andreas (Tenerife in Canary Islands?), and imprisoned in Bayonne castle (Samuel Roads, Jr., *History and Traditions of Marblehead* [Boston: Houghton, Osgood, 1880], 68) .

It was his eldest son Samuel Jr., laborer, who was put into the stocks for two hours on the afternoon of 26 Aug. 1771 for "being intoxicated and misbehaving" in court (Ibid., 348). His younger brother Capt. Ambrose turned out better, serving in the Revolution and his son Ambrose

Jr. was successful captain in the Madeira-Portugal trade (EIHC 64:273-9; *Revolutionary Soldiers & Sailors* 9:1014-9) . He was the grandfather of Ambrose[5] Lovis (1805-69), chemical manufacturer of Boston (Directory 1853-69).

Sophia's great-uncle Aaron also had a son who served in the Revolution, in Capt. Glover's company at the battle of Saratoga in 1777, later became a blockmaker in Marblehead (EIHC 112:49, 91:374-5).

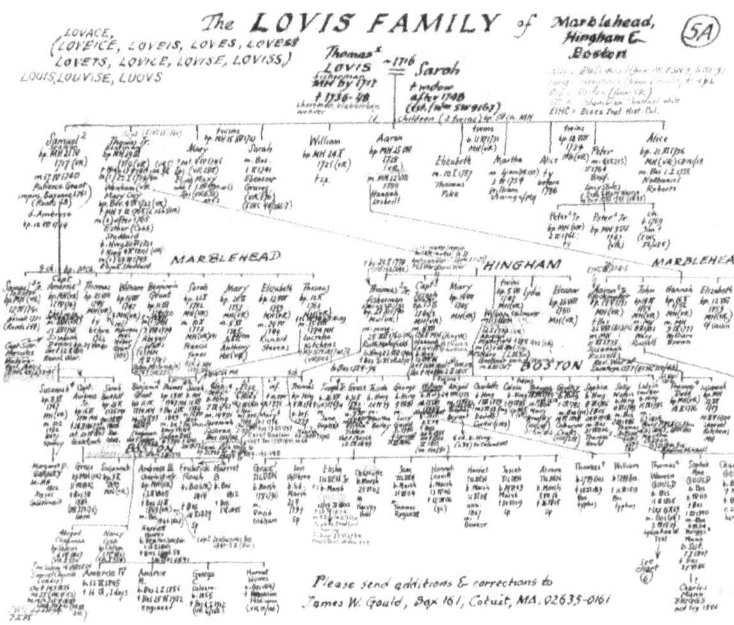

The COY FAMILY of Beverly and Wenham, 1638.

Sophia's paternal grandmother was Mary Coy of Wenham.

Our Coy ancestors were founders of the towns of Wenham and Brookfield, where place names still recall their settlement. Richard Coy was killed by the Indians at Brookfield.

Sophia's paternal grandmother was MARY[4] COY, baptized Beverly 29 May 1718 (VR); died Hingham 7 Feb. 1765, age 47 (Lin 362). She was the daughter of MATTHEW[3] COY and his wife BRIDGET[3] HIBBERD of Beverly (not of Caleb[2] Coy and Mary Wellman as erroneously stated in L. E. Roy, *Quaboag Plantation* (Worcester), 221) since their dau. Mary, bp. 1723 was too young to marry Lovis in 1740, and did marry William Richardson of Attleborough 1742).

Matthew Coy was the grandson of RICHARD[1] COY who was born in England about 1625, probably near Boston, Lincolnshire (Hoyt, David, *The Old Families of Salisbury and Amesbury* [Providence: The author, 1897], [hereinafter Hoyt], 118), came to America about 1638 and was killed by Indians at Brookfield on 2 Aug. 1675. Richard arrived in Boston aged 13 from Boston, Linconshire with his brother Matthew and sister Lucy, children of RICHARD COY, who left his children £ 5 each if their mother Lucy Anna remarried, as she did, to Rev. Edward[2] Bulkeley (1614-96) in Boston, 1638 (Reg. 113:236; her identity "Lucian" in Ply. Deed 4:293, 9 Sept. 1668 in Reg. 58:201-2).

Bulkeley (pron. Buckley) was the eldest son of the well known colonial preacher Rev. Peter[1] Bulkeley (1583-1659) , for whom Cotton Mather wrote a tribute. The son studied at Cambridge University, but did not graduate (John and J. A. Venn, *Alumni Cantabrigensis* [Cambridge: University Press, 1922], 250; matriculated St. Catherine's College, Easter 1629, when he was 14, his father and grandfather having graduated). He came to America before his father, by 1635, and studied theology under him in Concord (Donald L. Jacobus, *Rev. Peter Bulkeley* [New Haven: Tuttle, Morehouse, 1933] [hereinafter Jacobus], 111) . It is not clear whether he and Lucian were married in England or in Boston. They moved to Concord when he was dismissed from the church in Boston to Concord 15 Aug. 1641. One of the first ministers trained in America, he was licensed and ordained pastor at Marshfield 1642/3, where he served 16 years. Our ancestor Lucian lived with her minister husband at the Marshfield parsonage, built for them at 40 Parsonage Street, at the north corner of Webster Street, where the House for Independent Living now stands (Cynthia Krusell & Betty Bates, *Marshfield* [Marshfield Historical Soc., 1990], 109-110). Her husband calls her Lucey Anna in a receipt for her daughter's estate of 1679 (10 April, Ibid., 112).

Bulkeley then succeeded his father as minister at Concord, serving 35 years until his death in Chelmsford 4 Jan. 1695/6 (Sewall's diary in MHS Coll. 5th ser. 5:418, cited by Jacobus 111n.; Lemuel Shattuck, *History of the Town of Concord* [Boston: Russell, Odiorne, 1835], 161).

Lucy Ann or Lucian outlived her second husband, but record of her death has not been found in Concord or Chelmsford, so she may have died at the home of one of her children, as her husband died at a son's home in Chelmsford. By her previous husband, presumably RICHARD* Coy, she had a daughter Lucy, second wife of John[1] Lake who died 6 Aug. 1677, and whose estate she settled (text of Suff. Prob. 12:28 in Reg. 63:199, Jacobus 112. There is some confusion in Torrey about the wives' maiden names, for the John Lake who died in Boston in 1677 appears to be the same person, and if as we show Lucy's father was Coy, Mary's name is different).

By Bulkeley Lucian had five children, half-brothers and sisters of our Richard Coy, three of whom had descendants, cousins of the Coys (Jacobus 113; her son Rev. Peter was Harvard graduate 1660, Sibley 11:68, Reg. 42:276-7). Among these were the poet Ralph Waldo Emerson (William Jr., Sr., Joseph Emerson, Elizabeth Bulkeley, Lucian), fourth cousin of Sophia's father William[2] Lovis, and his father the patriot preacher who died in the Revolution, third cousin of Mary[4] Coy Lovis (*NEXUS* 6:110); Ency. Brit, 11th ed., 9: 332-3; Shattuck 162). Lucian was ancestor of the first President Bush (Prescott, Samuel P., Harriet Fay, Samuel Fay, Samuel P. F. Fay, Lucy Prescott, Rebecca Bulkeley, Peter, Lucian), also descendant of Daniel Brewer *NEXUS* 6:25). The astronaut and moon explorer Alan Shepard was also a descendant (mother Pauline Emerson, Charles, Abraham, Elias, Joseph, Ebenezer, Elizabeth Bulkeley, Lucian, *NEXUS* 11:107). *Washington Post* editor Ben Bradlee was also descended from her (father Frederick, Elizabeth Thomas, Elizabeth Rand, Isaac, John, Margaret Damon, Margaret Clarke, Mary Bulkeley, Lucian, *NEXUS* 10:165). John Hancock was also a descendant (John Jr., Elizabeth Clarke, Mary Bulkeley, Lucian, *NEXUS* 3:237) .

Richard[1] Coy Sr.'s will of 22 Dec. 1637 was proved at Stamford, Lincs. 10 April 1638 (Reg. 113:236).

There is a long biography of Richard to which new details will be added here (Richard Rutyna, "Richard Coy of Essex County, 1625-1675: A Biographical Sketch", EIHC 104:75-9; Reg. 35:337-8). Coy came from Boston in Lincolnshire to London at age 13 as unindentured servant to John Whittingham, (Benj . Muzy's testimony, Ipswich March 1655 in "Coy of Ipswich", *Putnam's Monthly* (1893-4), 11:177; Pope Essex County 121; *Records & Files of the Quarterly Courts of Essex County* [Salem: Essex Institute, 1911] [hereinafter EQ] 1:87, 381-2). Whittington was a nephew of Richard Whittington who married a brother of Rev. Edward Bulkeley (Reg. 39:172). Whittingham arrived in Ipswich in 1638 (Pope 496), where he sold Coy's service for 10 years to William Hubbard Sr. of Ipswich. Although a judge confirmed his obligation even after Coy reached the age of 21, he served only 8 years, when Hubbard agreed to pay him to stay on.

Coy was acquitted of a charge of excessive drinking, vain mirth, and singing with frequent oaths in 1649, and sued his slanderer (charged Salem 23 Dec. 1648; disch. Ips. 17 Jan. 1649; EQ 1:160-1, 163) . In May 1650 he was one of the first settlers of Salisbury, but not a townsman until 3 Dec. 1650.

Before the end of 1651 he had married MARTHA[2] HAFFIELD of Ipswich, where he lived until about 1657 (Roy, 214). In 1653 she was charged with an unstated offense and discharged (EQ 1:279, 303; 26 June, in Marion Carter, "The Coye/Coy Family of Essex County" (typesc. 1931 in NHGS, 2). In 1658 he leased the Ipswich farm and house of Peter Pelfrey, formerly John Fairfield's, occupied by William Gear (24 March; in 1660 the Fairfields got a court order for him to stop cutting timber on the land except for repair of house and fences, EQ 2:258-9).

But a week later he was licenced to run an ordinary in Wenham, and to draw wine and "strong waters" on the road to Manchester at the east end of town, near the 30 acre pond named for him (EQ 2:67; Adeline Cole, *Notes on Wenham History 1643-1943* [Salem: Wenham Historical Society, 1943], 38; license renewed 1658, 1660, EQ 2:177, 235) . In this he was successful, for he was a major contributor to the Wenham minister's salary in 1659, and served in several church and town offices (Myron O. Alien, *The History of Wenham* [Boston: Bazin & Chandler, 1860), 33, 163, 20; *Wenham Town Records* [Wenham: Historical Society, 1930], 15, 16, 18, 20).

Coy claimed ownership to the house which the town of Ipswich bought for a free school from him for £ 25, but he had to sue Ezekiel Cheever for trespass to get him out (EQ 2:232). He was involved in numerous lawsuits, including the defense of a 13 year old runaway servant, Hope Tiler, to whom he gave refuge EQ 2:403, 1662). A major controversy involved a neighbor's beating Coy's wife and stranding his children on their roof by pulling away the ladder (*Coy v. Fairefield* Oct. 1665 EQ 3:273-4; Marion W. Carter, "The Coye Coy Family" Ms. NEHGS, 3) . Soon he was in court again for not paying Frances Wainwright for a pair of pistols worth £ 8 to be paid in wheat, and scissors, pipes and salt (EQ 3:281, 296) . He apparently produced a crop in 1665, shown by his delivery of "corn", from a barn he sold on Thanksgiving day (EQ 3:307) .

By 1666 he was on the frontier farming livestock on lot number one in Brookfield, then called Quabog, 15 miles west of Worcester. He brought his family there in 1667, to become about the fifth family to settle there after the Warners, Ayres, Parsons and Wilsons (J.H. Temple, *History of North Brookfield* [Boston: Town of N. Brookfield, 1887; hereinafter Temple], 55) . Their houselot was the first allocated in the Town Plot, 20 acres bordering west on what is still known as Coy's Brook, called Massequockummis by the Indians (Temple 58-9). Coy also got 20 acres of meadow along the brooks, eight to ten acres of "Plain Land" in the Great Field west of Coy's Brook, 20 acres of upland, and rights in the unallocated Commons (Ibid.) . In addition to the brook named for him, there is also Coy's Hill north of Warren Village between West Brookfield and Warren (Temple 17).

Coy became an early leader of the settlement, empowered by the legislature "to admitt inhabitants, grant lands, & to order all the prudentiall affayres of the place in all respects" (15 May 1667, Massachusetts Col. Rec. 4/ii, 342, cited by Temple 56). He was on the committee that allocated lands to the first minister in 1668 (Temple 59), and acted as surveyor of lands (Temple 61). He was one of three "poor" petitioners for expansion of the Quabog lands to include the 600 acre Peter Tufts farm about five miles west toward Springfield, a grant that was not made (9 Oct. 1670, Massachusetts Arch. 112:212 in Temple 61-2). In 1670 he helped build a grist mill in town, and served as Constable and Surveyor. In 1673 his is the second signature on the petition to incorporate the town and change its name from Quabog to Brookfield (Temple 62-3). He was appointed a mediator with the Indians at Wickaboag Pond, and while serving as corporal in the militia he was killed in the battle with the Indians on 2 Aug. 1675.

Coy's part in the Brookfield battle is told by Peirce: The Governor sent Capt. Edward

Hutchinson to Brookfield to try to get peace with the Nipmuck Indians (Ebenezer Peirce. Indian History *Biography and Genealogy* [N. Abington: Zerviah Mitchell, 1878], 96-7). A meeting was agreed upon at 8 am 2 Aug. on the plain at the head of Wickaboag Pond, two or three miles west of Brookfield. Coy was one of three Brookfield residents who went along with Hutchinson and a guard of about 20 mounted soldiers. When they got to the rendezvous no Indians appeared, so they rode two and a half miles north towards the Nipmucks' main settlement at Wenimeset or Meninimesset, in what was to become New Braintree. They were attacked in a defile between a swamp to the north and a steep hill, above Wickabog Pond (map of Gen. Putnam, 1785 in George Bodge, *Soldiers in King Philip's War* [Leominster: the author, 1896], 111) . Eight of the party, including Coy killed; Hutchinson died of his wounds. They were buried in West Brookfield, at the south shore of the pond, where seven graves could still be seen in 1883 (Reg. 38:37) . The survivors escaped to Brookfield, pursued by the Indians.

The inhabitants including Coy's family took refuge in a fortified house while the attackers burned all the buildings. After two days of siege, the Indians set fire to a cart full of hay, which they pushed against the fort. But a providential sudden rain shower put out the fire, just as a relief party of solders arrived. Coy's wife and children fled to Boston, where she received £ 3 from an English fund for the victims set up by John Hall of Islington. It may have been she who died Boston 14 Aug. 1694 (CD 130:219).

The HAFFIELD FAMILY of Ipswich, 1635.

The Haffield family were founders of Ipswich, and included the well-known witch Rachel Clinton.

Richard Coy married before 8 April 1654 (Hoyt 699) MARTHA^2 HAFFIELD (HAFEELD, HAFFEILD, HAFFELDE, HAFFELL, HAFTEL, HAFTELL, HAIFIELD, HALFIELD, HARFEILD, HARFIELD, HAYFIELD, or HEFFIELD,) was born in Sudbury, Suffolk in 1627, and probably died in Boston 14 Aug. 1694 (CD 130:219). She was daughter of currier RICHARD^1 and his second wife Martha, all of whom came to Boston on The Planter on 7 June 1635, to settle in Ipswich (Charles E. Banks, *The Planters of the Commonwealth **162**-1640* (Baltimore: Genea. Pub. Co. reprint, 1972, hereinafter Planters], 144, citing Public Record Office (PRO) and Drake's Founders 15-21; Gary B. Roberts, *English Origins of New England Families* (Baltimore: Genea. Pub. Co., 1985], 941; Reg. 30:110-1). The ship *Planter* had sailed from London under Capt. Nicholas Trerice 10 April 1635; Haffield's age is 54, and Martha's eight.

Richard^1 was born in Sudbury, Suffolk 1581, and died in Boston, Mass, before end of 1641 (Hoyt, 102n). He brought some inherited wealth with him, in "goods and ready money, and afterwards he sold a good estate in land left him by their grandfather." (John Demos, *Entertaining Satan: Witchcraft and the Culture of Early New England* (New York: Oxford U. Press, 1982, 22). With him came his second wife, MARTHA MANSFIELD, age 42, born about 1593, perhaps Sudbury; d. Ipswich 2 Dec. 1667 (Demos 21; Hoyt 102n).

Haffield settled in Ipswich in 1635, with holdings above average of the first settlers. His house was on half an acre on the road to the mill, just north of the meeting house, in 1905 the corner of High Street and North Main, which he bought from John Whityear empty (Thomas F. Waters, *Ipswich* (Ipswich: Historical Soc., 1905, 351; diagram 2). This was sold in 1639 to Thomas Firman. He also owned an acre and a half houselot on the west side of Bridge Street (Washington Street 1905; ibid., 320; diag. 1).

Richard Haffield's will of 17 Feb. 1638/9 at Ipswich is given in Reg. 3:156, and died before the end of 1641, in Ipswich. But his estate wasn't settled for 30 years (29 Sept. 1668), Demos believes because of the dispute of Martha's stepdaughters by his first wife who claimed that much of his estate came from their mother (Demos 29; Suffolk Court case 931, *Cobham v. White,* hereinafter SC 931). Haffield had unsuccessfully tried to avoid dispute by evenhandedly giving all five daughters the same £ 30, rejecting an appeal to give the elder two more (SC 931, testimony of George Geedings, 19 May 1668; Demos 22).

In his will he mentions his daughter Martha as under 16 years. It is a small personal estate of about £ 150, but perhaps totaled £ 500 if we include the farm valued at £ 300 in his widow's estate (Demos 22). He died before the end of 1641 (on 28 Dec. his widow charged Jo. Lee with stealing a Bible, for which he was fined 10 shillings EQ 1:38; Carter 8) . In the will his name is written Riard Haffeeld, and other spellings are Haffell, Halfield and Hayfield. Demos points out that his death brought more turmoil to an already divided family, leaving five girls fatherless and quarreling (24-5).

MARTHA MANSFIELD had been a maidservant when married, her parents being very poor (her maiden name is given MANFIELD by witness Frances Nucom, age 70, living in the town where they were married, SC 931, 27 April 1668; witness Alice Tilly, age 66, also said they were very poor, SC 931, 27 Jan. 1668; George Giddings said that Richard Haffield told him that most of his estate had come from his first wife, SC 931, 19 May 1668; Demos 21). She was accused of being "very abusive and unreasonable" to her two stepdaughters, neglecting to clothe them, and giving them "many hard words and blowes" (Tilly's testimony in SC 931). Despite the neighbors' wondering about her "strang and froward behaviour" (Tilly again), she managed the estate well, as shown in her own estate inventory of £ 349 (SC 931), by leasing out farmland, and selling cloth.

She was fined 20 shillings for "a lye" that her daughter struck her, then denied it (30 March 1647; EQ 1:113; Carter 8). In 1652 the younger Martha's sisters Ruth and Rachel chose Richard Coy as guardian (5 April 1652, text in SC 931; Pope 266) . Coy defended her sister Ruth against a charge of excess apparell, winning the case by proving his mother-in-law was worth over £ 200 (EQ 1:278; *Essex Antiq.* 10:80, Jan. 1906).

Mother Martha was made commoner of Ipswich in 1641, and lived on the farm near the bridge which was still called Haffield's in 1905 (Waters 41) . In 1655 the town sold her a tiny lot of four rods near the mill dam to build a house upon, but without rights to common land (Waters 461) . This was sold before 1723 by her son-in-law Thomas White to Samuel Dutch (she is probably the Martha "Hassell", 460, 461). It may be she who was fined 20 shillings for taking the name of God in vain to witness to a lie (Waters 283). In 1657 the town laid out a new road from Chebacco Ferry to "Goodwife Haffield's bridge, called Haffield's Bridge in 1678 when a road was made from the bridge to the windmill (Joseph B. Felt, *History of Ipswich* [Bowie MD: Heritage Books, 1991, facs. of 1834 Cambridge ed.], 50-51). She had to sue Richard Brabrooke for rent in 1660 (EQ 2:266).

In Sept. 1666 she was declared non compos mentis and her daughter Ruth's husband Thomas White made her guardian (EQ 3:352, 321; Carter 8). That involved him in a messy suit against Robert Cross for £ 21 he had been paid for the release of Rachel's husband Lawrence Clinton. This brought out many family details *(White v. Crosse,* 1666, EQ 3:371-5, 456-9; Carter 8-9). She was buried Wenham 22 Dec. 1667 (EQ 3:468) . Her will dated 11 June 1662 left Martha Coye "a pot, brass skillet and two large pewter dishes, four pair of sheets, four napkins, four pillow beers (cases), one kettle and a stone jug tipped with silver" and one third of the rent paid by Richard Brabrooke for her house and land which she left to Rachell Haifield (not Clinton; EQ 4:16; copy in SC 931) . The estate inventoried 31 March 1668 at £ 350, 300 of it for the farm (Ibid.) and administered by Coy and White. Clinton surrendered his right to Thomas Fiske of Wenham "as feoffe in trust for Rachell Clenton, his wife." (EQ 4:14).

THE IPSWICH WITCH IN THE FAMILY?

Martha Haffield had been cared for by her daughter Rachel, later accused of being a witch at the height of the witchcraft furor in 1692. She was jailed at Ipswich, put into irons and tried in Salem, but only released on general amnesty after much suffering of more than nine months in prison. The case is the subject of Demos's first chapter, "A Desolate Condition", which makes the point that Rachel was a victim of poverty, reduced to begging, after her share of a good family inheritance was taken from her (19-35) . Denied a divorce from a proven adulterer, she took up with another man. At times she responded to neighbors' selfishness and gossip with abusive language.

Two years younger than her sister Martha Coy, Rachel Haffield Clenton (wife of Lawrence Clinton) had been sold a tiny lot next to the bridge near the mill dam for 12 pence in 1655. Rachel called her brother-in-law Thomas White "a cheaten Rogue" who "goese about to undoe mee. He keeps my portion from me, and strives to git all that I have" (Essex Court file 12:24, cited by Karlsen 109). He sold her cottage, making her "destitute of money and friends", so she asked the court to restore it to her so "that shee may not be forced to wander from house to house like and Indian or bruit beast" (EQ 3:458). A neighbor "found her very sad, weeping and crying" because her brother-in-law White said she'd stolen money from her mother (EQ 3:372) .

As Martha's guardian in 1666 White sued Robert Cross, Sr. for £ 21 that Cross had received to release Lawrence Clinton from bondage as his servant. In court Rachel claimed Cross had tried to marry Clinton off to "a maid worth a bushel of gold", urging that Clinton would be heir to a rich uncle worth thousands, he had £ 50 coming and a mother in Boston "and other lies to delude her" (EQ 3:457). Her sister Ruth White said she'd heard Cross telling what rich friends Clinton had in England, but couldn't dissuade Rachel from seeing him (Ibid.). Rachel skeptically remarked, "this is the man that you said was worth gold but it is not his fair Lookes that will maintain me." (Huton's testimony, EQ 3:372).

But Martha gave her daughter 31 gold pieces from her inheritance, which Clinton used to pay off his 3 year term. Close wouldn't take the money until he was sure he got it honestly. Both Rachel and Martha said was freely given.

At last Rachel and Lawrence were married in Dec. 1665, she being relatively old 36, and Clinton 14 years younger. On her wedding night Rachel was found crying, complaining of White's treatment of her (H. Symonds, EQ 3:373) . It is clear that Rachel did not get the £ 300 farm and house which her mother left her. The court ordered White to lend Clinton some of the widow's household goods: a bed, bolster, bedclothes, posnet (a small metal pot with handle and 3 legs), bason, four spoons and a skillet (EQ 3:375).

But both husband and wife were whipped publicly for telling lies, Laurance for "lying, cursing and cheating" (March 1666, EQ 3:314), and Rachel after admitting in court that she had falsely accused John Clark of "lying with her" (March 1667, EQ 3:402, 400, perhaps paid as a fine. EQ 8:303). In 1670 Laurence Clenton was "severely whipped with twenty stripes well laid on" for trying to abase [Demos finds "abuse or ravish", 30] Mary Knoulton, and ordered to bring his wife 2s. a week and "live with her, as duty binds him, and at least lodge wth her one night in a week" or be sent to jail (June 1670, EQ 4:269).

When Rachel complained that her husband hadn't paid up, the court sent him to jail until he paid 40s. for past due; she was ordered "to entertain him as husband whenever he comes" or go to jail (EQ 4:425). She failed to prove nonsupport in 1672, but got another order in 1674 after Mary Grely, Goody Wells' maid said "she was afraid that she was with child by Lorance Clinton" after he had "lain with her upon a sabbath day when her master and dame was gone to meeting"

(Demos 31) . Arter Abbit presented the town with a bill of Mary Grely's lying in: houseing and lodging and diat, £ 1, midwife 5s, nursing 15s, for sack and lickers 3s 6d, for fier wood etc 6s, totalling £ 2/10/6 (Sept. 1673, EQ 5:37, 267, 312). Three years later Mary was whipped for fornication with Clinton (Sept. 1676, EQ 5:205), and Clinton ordered to pay her 20s. a week to support his reputed son, the second child, called Jacob Clinton, born 1 April 1677 (EQ 6:278).

Rachel got another order in 1676 for Lawrence to pay her 18d. a week in corn when he was away, which he paid in wheat, pork and barley; at the same time she was ordered "to follow her work" (unspecified) or go to jail (EQ 6:137,196). But then Clinton was found guilty of fornication with a third woman, Mary Woodden, and ordered severely whipped (Sept. 1677; EQ 6:338; both he and Mary paid the town fines that month EQ 8:307) . When the whipper Jonas Gregory refused to perform his duty, he was whipped in turn. Rachel then asked for a divorce, which the court refused and ordered him to pay her 50s. (6 Sept. 1677, EQ 6:344).

Given his record, one doubts if Clinton paid, but then Rachel was jailed with John Ford for "unlawful familiarity and much cause of suspicion of uncleanness and other evil practices". She admitted giving Ford a napkin and a piece of stuff and kersey, which she said he paid for as his wife because she was divorced, as she understood it, but they had never lived together (Nov. 1677, EQ 6:374-5) . The Constable had found Ford in bed at Clinton's house, with a glass bottle of liquor at the bedside, took them both to jail in Ipswich, and sent them to prison in Salem. When witnesses said they found her standing beside the bed in which he lay with his upper clothes off, the guilty couple claimed "sometimes they sat up; sometimes she went to bed, so he sat up in the chair; and sometimes he went to bed, and she sat up" (Demos 31). The court said they deserved severe whipping, but since they'd spent a week in jail, were released on good behavior, on the condition they not meet except in company of some discreet person, and pay jail keep.

The next year Rachel had to petition again for support, saying her husband had paid no more than ten pounds in ten years, and he hadn't paid the 50s ordered by the court, so "she had suffered the loss of her estate by her husband and is now altogether neglected by him." (25 Sept. 1678, EQ 7:100). The court ordered Clinton to pay her a peck of corn a week, but in the same court Artur Abbott said he hadn't paid the bill for the birth of his child by Mary Greely (Ibid.). He was forced to work off the bill (EQ 7:181). In 1680 she had to go to court again to get an order for him to pay 20s (EQ 8:17) .

Clinton finally left town about 1680, taking Mary Greely and their two illegitimate children to Providence, where they were married in Feb. 1681 (Demos 32) . Married a third time, Clinton was ancestor of a Connecticut family of Clintons. Rachel was finally given a divorce in Oct. 1681. She remained unmarried, living in a hut on Hog Island near the harbor of Ipswich (Ibid.) . She remained on town dole (Carol F. Karlsen, *The Devil in the Shape of a Woman: Witchcraft in Colonial New England* [New York: W. W. Norton, 1987], 110). In 1686 the town paid for repairs to her house, and other services such as a load of clay (Demos 33).

One of the first incidents in which Rachel was suspected of witchcraft occurred about 1682 when the contents of a barrelful of new beer disappeared after an argument with Rachel (William Baker's testimony in Suffolk Court file 2660, 217; transcribed somewhat inaccurately by Paul Boyer and Stephen Nissenbaum, *The Salem Witchcraft Papers: Verbatim Transcripts* [New York: DaCapo Press, 1977], hereinafter Boyer, I: 217; Demos is better). She had come to Nathaniel Rust's house on the day the beer was brewed, and "met with some small affront". She then walked "bakwords and forrowords, 6 or 7 times: up & Dow[n] the Lane that Le[a]ds to our house", her accuser said. The next day Mrs. Rust found the barrel empty, and the floor dry; when filled with water the barrel did not leak, so Rachel was blamed.

The first record of public accusation as a witch came by 1687 (Knowlton's testimony in "Witchcraft 1687", mss. at Cornell, cited by Demos 20). Thomas Knowlton stated that his daughter Mary had awakened with a dreadful cry that "she was pricked in her side with pins". Was this the same Mary Knowlton that Rachel's husband had tried to ravish? Asked who pricked her she couldn't tell. When "she was out of her fits" her father asked if she'd given Rachel any pins, to which she admitted having given her about seven. After that followed another fit of being pricked.

About two months later Rachel went to John Rogers' house while the owner was away and told the maid "she must have some meat and milk". When Knowlton and two others arrived Rachel left, scolding and railing against Knowlton, calling him "hellhound", "whoremasterly rogue" and "a limb of the devil", and saying that she'd rather see the Devil than him (Knowlton did have a prison record, EQ 9:189, 1684). She then took up a stone and threw it towards him until "it fell short three or four yards off from me...and so came rolling to me, and just touched the toe of my shoe. And presently my great toe was in a great rage, as if the nail were held up by a pair of pincers".

In the Salem witchcraft trials of 1692 Rachel was the second person accused that year, on 29 March, and the only one from Ipswich (Richard Weisman, *Witchcraft. Magic & Religion* [Amherst: U. of Massachusetts, 1984], 210). She was tried at Ipswich the next day, 30 March 1692 at 8 am, "on grounded Suspision of witchcraft" (Warrant in Suff. Court 2660, 140, in Boyer 1:215). The court also ordered the Ipswich constable to call eight witnesses: Mary Fuller, Sr. and Jr., Alexander Thomson Jr. (age 61, EQ 7:292), Richard Fitts, Dr. John Bridgham (probably to examine her for witches marks), Thomas Manning, smith, age 44-45 (EQ 7:336, 8:193), Nathaniel Burnam, Thomas Knowlton Jr., age 48 (EQ 4:584), and Mary Thorne (SC 2660, 14).

Joseph Fuller, Ipswich Constable, reported on the 29th: "I have served this warrant and Read it to Rechell Clinton: this morning and sezed hur Body: and Left hur in ye hands of Samuell Ordoway her[e] in ye Court house Against your honoures shall call for hur//and I have Read the Severieall warants one the other sid[e] written this morning Save only Richard fitts and mary Thorne, and Richard fitts I could not find and mary Thorne is not well:"

Joseph Fuller's bill gives the rough schedule of the trial: 10 days (29 March-7 April) in Salem (Waters 294), but a witness on April 4 in Ipswich indicates the trial may have been transferred tp the alternate court seat for convenience of witnesses (Mary Edwards in Boyer 218).

Then, on 21 April six more witnesses were summoned, all citizens of Ipswich: James Burnam, Jonas Gregory, Mary Andrews, Sarah Rogers, Margueriet Lord and Sary Halwell (Warrant to Sergeant Johan Choate Sr. in Waters 461). They were ordered to be present at John Spark's house in Ipswich at 2 pm 22 April (same). Of the 12 witnesses summoned we have testimony of only six.

Mary Fuller, sister-in-law of the constable, testified that a year before the trial Rachel had come to her house and accused her of "Raisin Lies of hur About my Daughter and Mary Thorne" (27 Dec. 1691, Suff. Ct. 2660, 141, Boyer 216 omits two lines and mistakes several words; Demos 19) . In the midst of a quarrel Mary's nephew burst in with news that their Betty Hucking next door had dropped dead when she saw Rachel pass by the Constable's house. They rushed next door and found she wasn't dead, but in a catatonic state which lasted for three hours. Mary asked her to hold up her hand if Rachel was the cause, which she did. When she recovered her speech she said "a woman in a white cap passed by and struck me on the forehead."

Mary Fuller's nephew confirmed the story, saying that when he asked the girl the next day who made her so the night before she told him she saw something stare up at the corner of the stoop, and went a little way towards it and it looked so basely that she turned about to run away and it followed her and knocked her down (testimony of 18 year old James Fuller Jr. in Boyer 219, from Boston Public Library). The young man also elaborated on the quarrel that was going on when this happened. Rachel had arrived at the Fullers' about 9 or 10 o'clock. He asked her why she was bothered them at this time of night, and Rachel said she came to see what lies they were raising about her.

Nathaniel Fuller also testified, but his testimony is lost (Joseph Fuller's bill for 12 shillings for 3 days apiece at Salem for James and Nathaniel in Waters 294).

Thomas Boreman testified that he was asked by "Some women of worth and quality" to complain to the town Selectmen of Rachel's "hunching them with her elbow" in church on Sunday (Suff. Ct. 2660, 140; Boyer 217; Demos 19-20) . Demos points out that in this stratified society the well-to-do Haffields once held preferred pews near the front of the church, which now disdainful neighbors made Rachel unwelcome.

After Boreman reported to the Selectmen, as he was riding home at night he saw a strange animal that at first looked like a cat, then like a little dog, then, alarmingly, "a great turtle, that moved as fast as I rode." He then thought of Rachel Clinton and "the little creature and the turtle vanished away."

Evidence that the trial took place in Ipswich on 4 April 1692 comes from the testimony of Mary Edwards on that day (Boyer 218 from mss. in Boston Public Library). Rachel came to the Edwards home on 27 Dec. 1691 and asked for board, and was told that she could have no wages. Rachel was "very importinat". Rachel was sitting by the fire while Mary made blood puddings. Rachel said she loved such good food, and asked for some. When Mary gave her a pudding received it very scornfully, quickly got up from her seat and went away muttering unintelligibly.

Then, a month later five of the Edwardses litter of piglets were taken suddenly ill and died a fortnight later. The remaining three piglets which seemed very hearty were suddenly taken with unusual fits, "Jumping & Roreing till thay tumbled downe" one after the other. John Edwards swore this was true. Mary added that some of her children asked Rachel why her hands came to be so scratched and swolen. Mary heard her reply that she had two or three rogue cats that would scratch her hand when she put it down.

In the 1692 trial we have testimony of five witnesses against Rachel, with evidence of four cases of witchcraft. Two say she caused a girl to fall down after seeing Rachel--just seeing a witch is enough to scare a girl. This followed a quarrel, as did the episode of the disappearing beer. The pigs died after Mary Edwards turned down Rachel's request for board--perhaps a guilty conscience, like Boreman's" nightmare of a cat/dog/turtle after he reported Rachel's elbowing in church. Add to that her hands admittedly scratched by cats, and you have a witch. Other supernatural events attributed to Rachel were the earlier accusations of causing a man's toe to rage, and his daughter to be pricked with pins.

The personality of Rachel emerges. She is a crusty, "importunate" woman in her mid-sixties, tired of being gossiped about, and pushed around, who tells people off. She is no recluse, but shows up in the front pew of church where her family had sat, and sits at the fires of her neighbors. No thanks to a greedy brother-in-law and a spendthrift adulterous husband, she has lost a good house and fortune. Yet her economic destitution is clear: In two of the episodes, she is reduced to begging for food, and gets turned down. Rachel was one of the six witchcraft defendants whom Weisman found "either economically vulnerable or completely destitute" (Weisman 140) . When she asked for board, but was turned down without explanation, this was a violation of village morality, according to Weisman (89).

The decision of the court is not recorded, but it is clear that she was convicted of witchcraft (Demos 19, Karlsen 260). We know that Rachel was placed in irons from the bill for mending and putting on her fetters (Charles W. Upham, *Salem Witchcraft* [Williamstown: Corner House, 1971 reprint of 1867 orig.], 2:198). She was kept chained in the filthy dark jail. She was only released in the general reprieve of Jan. 1693, after nine months of imprisonment (Demos 19, Karlsen 260).

Rachel survived less than two years, living alone in a hut on Hog Island, on a piece of land inherited from her mother (Reg. 69:51). She died at about age 66 years, at the end of 1694, her sister Ruth White being given administration of her estate the next January (Reg. 69:51).

Richard and Martha Coy's second child was JOHN[2] COY, born Wenham 1657/8, where he was the eight year old chased onto the roof by John Fairfield, went with his parents to Brookfield in 1666 where his father was killed (Roy, 219). He fled to Boston with his mother, and became a carpenter in Wenham. In 1699 he sold the family lands in Brookfield. In the division of Wenham lands in 1705 Coy was awarded an eighth of the Third Lot of swamp, which he shared with John Edwards, perhaps his wife's brother (Alien 51-2).

He died in Wenham age 80, on 1 March 1737/8. His will is dated 15 March 1733/4 (Essex Wills 6463, Probate Vol. 325 (Book 25), 530-2). In this he left his entire estate to his son Richard, consisting of over 26 acres, all in Newport, part of Manchester: two acres he bought from John Winthrop, three acres he bought from a William-----, the land from the four divisions of 1718, namely ten acres in the North division of common land, five acres in the South Division lot, and an acre in the Shingle Hill Place division (531).

To his son Matthew he left only ten shillings, explaining in detail his displeasure: "The reason why *I* give to sd. Mathew Coye no more in this my last Testament is because he has proved very rebelious & Disobedient to me, and also To his mother before her Decease, and ever since to me he has continued in the practice of Rebellion, abuse, & Disobedience, & Remains so Obstinate their is no Reclaiming him, As I am his Natural Parent, the Grief & trouble, such behaviour from him Occasions, Restrains one from Setting forth his abuses in ye Largest Degree, and I am very sorry I have Reason to expose his Faults// [532] Nevertheless since he has been of age *I* have paid him considerable and have done a great deal for him & have been at a great Deal of toil and charge for him."

The EDWARDS FAMILY of Salem, 1643.

Our Edwards family, which lived on the Severly-Wenham town line, was unrelated to the many Edwardses of the colony, but distinguished by the unusual first name of the founder, Rice.

John[2] Coy married in Beverly 23 June 1679 ELIZABETH EDWARDS, by whom he had 7 children, including our ancestor, Matthew[3]. Elizabeth was born about 1650, to RICE[1] EDWARDS and his second wife JOAN(NE), whose maiden name is unknown. Rice, or Reece, Rise, Ryse or Ryce, a joiner by profession, that is, a finish carpenter who joins parts like stairs and doors.

He was born in England c. 1615 (deposed age 65 July 28, 1680, EQ 8:22), and first appeared in Salem in 1642 when he was granted ten acres next to Mr. Blackleach in what was to become Wenham (EIHC 10:116, 13 Dec. 1642; Richard Pierce, ed., *Records of the First Church in Salem* [Salem: Essex Inst., 1974], 16) appears mistaken in saying he was in Salem in 1638 when an Abraham was baptized, he being recorded of Watertown (19 Dec., Bond 756 identified the father as John). The next year he and his wife were admonished by the court for "incontinency before marriage", witnessed by Henry Walton and Mary Bourne (27 April 1643, EsCt 1:56 Court, Essex Antiq.. 4:185; *Putnam's Historical Mag.* 1:134-5).

They were in Boston briefly in 1646, when his name appears about 15 April ("Rich Coy sh Itm ten shillings on the whole", *Aspinwall Records* [Boston: Municipal Printing Off., 1903], and his wife Joan was admitted to the First Church 9 March 1647 (Sav. 3:103; Pope 152). But they returned to Wenham by 1647 (Elizabeth G. Fuess, "Gushing and Allied Families" [Andover MA: typesc., 1931] [hereinafter Fuess], 157). At the New Year's Day court in Salem Rice (or Reesse) was charged with fighting with Henry Hagott, but since now blows were struck, just struggling together, and never before been brought to court for this, were fined only costs (EQ 1:135). That was not the end of it, for nine months later Henry's wife Ann was fined "for wishing the curse of God on Rice Edwards and that fire might come down from heaven and consume his house, as it did Goodwife Ingersoll's barn." (EQ 1:152).

In 1651 he exchanged 20 acres on Mackerel Cove "towards the Cricke" which he had bought from Mr. Thorndike (earlier Richard Lambert's grant) for 20 acres next to Richard Dodge (16 April 1651, EIHC 10:168). He received land in Wenham in 1653 (Fuess) and contributed 1 shilling sixpence taxes toward "ye College" (Harvard, EIHC 19:106). In 1670 the town of Ipswich prosecuted him for cutting down 6 or 7 white oaks on town common land on the Salem line (EQ 4:224). Four years later he was named again for cutting down an Ipswich poplar (EQ 5:373).

Edwards' land was on the Wenham-Beverly line, and in 1677 he took the oath of fidelity to Beverly, listed as a pavior, or pavement layer (3 Dec., EQ 6:401). In 1679 seven families, led by Edwards, petitioned to remain in Beverly where they had been for above 26 years, objecting to the new East line running "betwixt some of Or dwelling houses & our out houses & orchards & cutts us off from *y^{e}* Common" (EQ 8:18) . But in 1679-80 Wenham claimed his farm and his two sons'. Wenham Constable Richard Hutton and two Selectmen, Fairfield and Capt. Fiske seized 3 pewter platters in neighbor John Dodge's house, and took them to Rise Edwards'. Dodge's wife came to the Edwards' and asked why they had rifled her house when no one was home, and stepped up to take back her platters. "They all three pulled her down and dragged her upon the ground, Thomas Fiske, sr. striking her a blow on the neck with his fist. Then Rise Edwards cried out, 'Rescue the woman, what [!] will you let hear be Cilld [?]'", and his son John held Fiske and Fairfield back by the shoulders (*Dodge v. Capt. Fiske et al.*, EQ 8:18, 22). In a jury trial the court found the assailants guilty, fined them, and returned the platters.

In an agreement with his children on 18 April 1681 his son Benjamin agreed to take care of his father in return for the major share of the estate (Essex Prob. 307:133-5, cited by Edward Mills, "The Edwards Family of Wenham", EIHC 56:60). The agreement is an interesting record of colonial care for the aged. It reads: [I] "doe surrender and yield up all my upland Meadows Stock of Cattle Sheep horses and swine Except my Rideing mare & all my housing only Excepting a free and Quiet subsistence in my now Dwelling house untill he build another for me, and..."[he gives] % meadow & stock to son Benjamin on condition that he clear & pay my debts & "and also that Son does Provide for me Conveniently as a Son for a father both in sickness & health both Respect to food Phisick & Cloths washing Lodgin & Attendance as my age or Weakness doth Require & also twenty shillings a year in money to be paid me If I Require it also to keep Winter & Summer in able Condition a Mare or horse for my Rideing...and not Expect any thing or labour further from me but to be at my own Pleasure, and furter itt is hereby Declared" that if he does not fulfil these terms, the donor is at Liberty to dispose of half his lands (Essex Prob., 307:134).

He must have died between that date and 15 April 1683 when his children refer to him as deceased and agreed to give Benjamin the housing, land and stock, and to share the movable furniture (eight signatures, including John Coy's, Essex Pro. 307:135). His personal estate was appraised by neighbor John Dodge and Thomas Patch for £ 21/10/--(15 June 1683; Essex Pro. 307:132). There must have been a 17 year dispute over the estate, for Benjamin's execution was not approved by the court until 1700 (6 Jan., Essex Pro. 307:132). Then, two weeks later the three sons Benjamin, Thomas and Edward settled the disposition of the land, 16 acres near the homestead, and two acres of meadow in Wenham south of Congham Brook, north of John Dodge's woods and east of Robert Bradford's meadow, and west of an acre Benjamin had sold to Thomas (18 Jan. 1700, Essex Pro. 307:136). Finally the inventory was presented in court on 7 Feb. 1700, and bills for £ 6/2/6, including four shillings for funeral costs (Essex Pro. 307:133).

The location of his house is shown on the road to Chebacco from Beverly Common near the new house of Mordecai Larkin in an agreement of his sons on 18 Jan. 1700 (Essex Pro. 307:136) .

His wife Joan is not mentioned in 1680, so probably died before that. She was a witness in court that Richard Haines of Cape Ann side violated the sabbath by carting hay (Oct. 1665, EQ 3:296).

John Coy's wife Elizabeth's (Edwards) death or remarriage after his death in 1738 has not been found. She is not the person who married Richard Hood on Salem on 1 April 1747 when she would have been about 80 (Salem VR 3:251) .

The HIBBERT FAMILY of Salem and Beverly, 1639.

The Hibberts have the distinction of spelling their name as many as 23 phonetic ways: HEBARD, HEBART, HEBBARD, HEBBART, HEBBERD, HEBBERT, HEBERT, HEBORD, HEBURD, HEIBARD, HERBERT, HIBARD, HIBBARD, HIBBART, HIBBERD, HIBBERT, HIBBIRD, HIBBITT, HIBBOARD, HIBBORD, HIBBURD, HIBERD, or HIBERT. One man can spell it three different ways in the same document. We will use the most common spelling, HIBBERT.

The fifth child of John and Elizabeth Coy was MATTHEW^{3}COY, born Beverly 16 March 1687/8 (VR 91), and died there 16 March 1745. He married three times: (1) BRIDGET(T)^3 HIBBERT at Beverly 3 Jan. 1711/2 (VR 74), born 11 May 1687 Beverly to JOSEPH^{2}and ELIZABETH HIBBERT (VR 173).

Joseph was baptized at the first church in Salem with his brother on 7 March 1648 (VR 1:427; EIHC 6: 241), son of ROBERT^1 and JOAN HIBBERT. He was a farmer in Beverly, having been given land by his father before his death (Augustine Hibbard, *Genealogy of the Hibbard Family* [Hartford: Case, Lockwood & Brainard, 1901], 17, 14). It was located on a road to Thomas Chubb's (EQ 6: 259, 252).

On 26 Feb. 1677 Joseph took the oath of fidelity in Lynn, serving under the squadron of Tithingman William Bassett Sr. and Constable Eleazer Lynzee (EQ 400, 289) . In 1677 the Hibberts were living in the house of widower John Blaine, whose children Elizabeth and her sister Hannah cared for after Blaine's wife died (EQ 6:361, 299ff.). In Oct. 1677 a summons stated "they dwell som wher about mr Kings farme." (EQ 6:389), presumably the Ralph King farm to which Blaine had moved (EQ 6:300).

That he was illiterate is shown by his mark on the bond for his father's estate and his own will (Ibid., 16) . Joseph Hibbert made his will on 19 April 1701, leaving his as yet unmarried daughter Bridgett Hibbert "three pounds in Currant or a good Cow", and naming his wife executrix (Essex Wills 7:OS, 152, in Hibbard 18). He died 14 May 1701 aged 53 in Beverly (VR 472).

The GRAVES FAMILY of Salem.

The Graves family were early settlers of the north part of Salem village, on land that was to become Topsfield.

ELIZABETH is the recorded name of Hibbert's childrens' mother, yet Beverly records show he married ABIGAIL GRAVES in Beverly 20 Oct. 1670 (*Genealogical Magaz*. (1905,

1:109; cf. VR 160). The confusion is carried on by most secondary sources. We have not found whether Abigail died young, and Joseph remarried an Elizabeth of another family. Some researchers solve this by marrying his brother John to Abigail on the same day; but this may be a mistake of transcription. Original may give a clue.

Elizabeth Graves had a sister Hannah (EQ 6:361), which makes Elizabeth the twin to Benjamin, bapt. 6 Aug. 1645 in Salem to RICHARD[1] GRAVES who came from London on the *Abigail,* captained by Richard Hackwell out of Plymouth about 1 Aug. 1636 (Planters 166, citing Founders 28, 31-8) as a husbandman or pewterer, age 23 or 33, his wife Joan age 30 following on the *Hopewell* in Sept. 1635 (Sav. 2:296; Pope 197 differ on several points: his age 23 or 33; his occupation pewterer or husbandman; his wife's arrival 1637 or 1635; Torrey differs on wife's name Dorothy v. ?Joan; these differences may be resolved by search in Salem deeds and court cases).

Richard Graves settled in Salem as a fisherman and ferryman, becoming proprietor 1637, where he was allowed two or three acres "next beyond Raph ffoggs 5 Acre Lott" (Perley 427). In 1655 he sold for 55s. to John Putnam 14 acres he had been given by Salem on the Topsfield line adjoining the farms of Capt. Hawthorne (to south), John Ruck (to west) and William Nichols? (to north), and the town confirmed his ownership of the remainder of its original 40 acre grant (26 Dec. 1654/5, deed 12 March, EQ 8:319, 322). This is a diamond-shaped property astride the Topsfield-Salem Village line, a mile west of the Indian Bridge over the Ipswich River, just north of Hawthorne Hill, and half a mile southwest of Nichols Brook (map in Upham, xxvi).

Torrey found little about Graves beyond Salem except possible residence in Boston. In 1669 widow Dorithy Graves sued John Neale as executor of Francis Lawes[1] will for her third of the house and land Richard once owned (15 April, EQ 4:169) . Elizabeth survived her husband, but her death or remarriage have not been found.

ROBERT HIBBERT was born England 1612, and died Beverly 7 May 1684 (EIHC 33:317-9). A number of sources have accepted that he was baptized St. Edmunds, Salisbury 13 March 1613/4, son of JOHN[A] HIBBARD of St. Edmunds, and his wife JOANE, daughter of JOHN[8] and ISABEL FAIRFIELD of Holme Mylne, Leek (Tingley, Raymon, Some *Ancestral Lines...Tingley...Meyers* [Rutland VT.: Tuttle, 1935], 134; Louis E. de Forest, *Our Colonial Ancestors...Dommerich* [New York: de Forest Pub. Co., 1930], 107); Paul, Edward, *The Ancestry of Katharine Choate Paul* [Milwaukee: Burdick & Allen, 1914], 76); Edith B. Sumner, *Descendants of Thomas Fair of Harpswell* [Los Angeles: American Offset, 1959], 165); Rev. R. T. Cross, *My Children's Ancestors* [Twinsburg OH: Roselle T. Cross, 1913], 43). Holme Mylne is not in Ekwall's English place names; perhaps mill island; there is Leek in Lincolnsh. and Notts.; Fairfield's will of 3 March 1612, proved 23 March, which mentions daughter Joan Hibbarde and grandchild Elizabeth Hibbarde, Paul 76).

Hibbert was an early settler of Salem, as a salt maker in 1639 (Joseph B. Felt, *Annals of Salem* [Salem: W. & S. B. Ives, 1849] 2:175). He deposed that when he was about 24 or 25 in 1643 or 4 he was living at the Salem salt house with John Winthrop (24 Feb. 1673, EQ 6:247; age about 55 in March 1671, EQ 4:332). He may have been brought over by John Winthrop Jr. who had been given a grant in 1638 to set up saltworks at Ryall side, at Salt House Point, later called Salter's Point (Ibid., 176; EIHC 33:317; Perley 11:17; map EQ 6:245). He lived in today's Beverly; on the south side of Colon Street, midway between Cabot and Heather Streets. (Perley 2:l5n).

Hibbert and his wife Joanna were admitted to the church 3 May 1646 when their three children were baptized. His autograph is in the court certificate of 13 Nov. 1644 for the birth dates of his first four children (EO 1:74n). He became a freeman 6 May 1647 (EQ 1:114). On 9 Nov. 1650 the town gave him 20 acres of common ground and woodland at the upper end of

William Dodge and Roger Haskells next to the swamp (in Beverly). By 1659 he was a bricklayer in his deed of 13 acres bought from William Haskell (ED 1:63). He bought land on Cape Ann in 1664 (18 Nov.). In 1666 he was appointed fence-viewer on the Cape Ann side. By 1670 he was a town Selectman, living in Beverly on the south side of Colon Street as bricklayer (ED 4:87; Cross 43). In 1669-71 he was Beverly's Constable, involved in replevining (suing to recover property) John Dodge whose cattle he found lying in his cornfield (EQ 4: 209, 332). He apparently encouraged his daughter to work with him, for they are paid by the town in 1672 for repairing a bridge (EQ 8:305). In 1673 he sued Nicholas Rice for not returning a service with promised £ 2 and use of two acres for tillage for a year (EQ 5:220). He was on the grand jury 1673-4 (EQ 5:245, 316). In 1674 he was paid six shillings for work on the fort at Winter Island. In 1677 he was appointed tithingman "to prevent private tippling and drunkenness" (25 June, EQ 5:289-90). He was Wenham Constable in 1683 (EQ 9 :84, 110).

Robert's will of 29 April 1684 in Beverly, of which his wife Joan was executrix is abstracted in EIHC 4:63 (Essex Will 4:87, text in EQ :296-7). In it he confirms previous grants to his three sons, including Joseph. He died 7 May 1684, age 72, leaving a goodly estate of £ 281, most of it in land: £ 60 for his homestead and orchard, £ 119 for 34 acres near the house, £ 27 for meadow and upland by the orchard-by Beaver Pond, and £ 17 for salt marsh by the Mill. Among his effects were peliberes (pillow cases), books 6s/6, "A gun, sword & other Iron geare".

Among his descendants is the illustrator Norman Rockwell (1894-1978; Jarvis, John, Orilla Sherman, Jacob, Rose Blashfield, John, Luke, Abigail[2] Hibberd; *NEXUS* 8:30).

The LUFF FAMILY of Salem, 1633.

The Luffs are examples of the poorest of early settlers, often in trouble with the law, and unable to live together.

Hibbert's wedding to JOAN(NA)[2] LUFF (LUF, LUFFE, LOOP LOOFE or LOVE) is not recorded, but must have been about 1641 in Salem, for their first child Marie was born 27 Nov. 1641 (EQ 1:74; Sumner 166). She was born in England, and died in Beverly before 1696 (when son John is named administrator of his father's estate, 6 April, on account of her death). Joan Hibbert was accused in Essex County court in 1659 of "railing and speaking several lies upon Zackary Herek, affirming that he was drunk, and went away from John Ston's house drunk about one or two o'clock at night." (EQ 2:190; de Forest 107). In court "She took God to witness that she did not" so speak, and "as she had a soul to save, it was not true", but was fined (EQ 2:221) . She paid, so the next time she was tried for saying that Liddea and Mary Grover were the "veriest lyers att bass riuer & they were able to ly the deuill out of Hell", she wouldn't deny it this time, and got a fine of ten shillings (EQ 2:222). She was daughter of JOHN[1] and BRIDGETT LUFF.

JOHN[1] LUFF was a weaver, an even earlier settler of Salem, and proprietor in 1636 (Sidney Perley, *The History of Salem* [Salem: the author, 1924], 1:391, 456; deForest 129). Luff was born in England about 1585 and died about 1668 in Beverly. John is listed alone as passenger on the *Mary & John* out of Southampton on 24 March 1633/4 with Robert Sayres as master (Planters 110, citing Founders 70-1). Many of the ship's passengers came from the south of England, but Luff signed the oath of allegiance in London on 24 March 1633 (Reg. 9:267; there is no evidence that the John Luffe of Combe Street Nicholas, Somerset, servant of John Fry, related to George Fry of Weymouth, New England in Reg. 47:420 is the same person, despite the unusual name).

Our Luff had many problems with the law. He is perhaps the John Love fined for drunkenness by the General Court 7 July 1635 (Sumner 192). Luff was sentenced to the stocks for four hours in mid-winter 1636 for resisting Constable Weston (EQ 1:5; Sumner 192). He received two acres in the division of 1637, for a single person (Ibid., 461). In 1640, 1641 and 1642 he was involved in court cases for debt, poor repair of a fence, and slander (EQ 1:19, 28, 43; de Forest 129).

In 1648-9 he and his wife were living apart, which his son-in-law Hibbert confirmed, when the Salem selectmen threatened him with jail if he did not accept the work they found for him (EQ 1:158). The problems continued into 1649, when the selectmen ordered his son-in-law Robert Hibbert to carry out their orders, presumably to find him work (EQ 1:182; Sumner 192). In 1650 he was excused from military duty because of age and disability, from which it is inferred that he had been in the Train Band or militia (EQ 1:193). In 1662 the town gave him 2 loads of wood, on request for aid.

By 1664 he was reconciled with his wife Bridgett, and moved in with the Hibberts according to an agreement: "that John Luffe delivering to Rob: Hibburd the £ 10 he sold hs house and land for at the ferry, to have for ever after his own pp. estate, that John Luffe and his wife shall live in a part of the house in which the French man now lives after his year is out to live in, for the terms of their lives, and that he will allow them a parcel of grounds for a garden of 10 cr 20 rods; if they are put at a charge to the town, that in case John Luff should be disabled by sickness or other hand of God from his work that shall come to be kept on other charge, that the town will free Rob: Hibburd from any such extraordinary charge." (Salem town records 11:84, in Sumner 192-3) .

Nearly 80 in 1665 he was still able to work for the town mending roads, for which it paid him £ 20. The next year he was old and feeble, and the town relieved him of work, and paid Edmund Batters 28 sh/ 6d. for "supplying" him. In 1668 the town gave Hibbert a 30 shilling tax abatement "for his exterordinary troble and expence about his father John Luff". Hibbert asked for more and got £ 2 "for exterordynary Charg." Luff probably died soon after this, in Beverly. Although there is no evidence of property, a 20 acre plot called "Loofes (or Luff's) Lott" in Salem may mark his occupancy (John Neal's will 3 May 1672, EQ 5:71; in 1677 this was in Salem north field, bounded by John Massey (ex Goodail), Marshal Skerrie (ex Richard Waterman) at upper end, Joshua Ray and Thomas Robins; EQ 7:167).

John Luff's wife BRIDGET does not appear on the passenger manifest of 1633, but it is apparent that the daughter Joan was born before that, in England. Since the name Bridget was given to the granddaughter Bridget[3] Hibbert it seems probable that she was the mother of Joan and another daughter who married John Tompkins (Sumner 193). She was born about 1587 in England, and died at Beverly after 1671 when she was 84. She was admitted to the church in Salem 16 May 1647 (deForest 129). "Goodwife Loofe's" name comes up in a curious case of 1650 when 16 year old Dorothy Pray testified that Jonathan Bond was so drunk one night at John Herdman's house that he dragged Loofe cut of the kitchen into another room, she called her for help, and escaped to the attic (EQ 1:198). From this it would appear that she was living with John Hardman, a coaler at the Saugus Ironworks (Hartley, E. N., *Ironworks on the Saugus* [Norman OK: Univ. of Okla., 1957], 189), perhaps to support herself as a servant. At age 84 in 1671 she was asleep in her daughter Joan Hibbert's home when two drunks broke into the house, assaulted and cruelly abused two granddaughters, for which one man was severely whipped and jailed until he paid 40s. damages (24 June 1671, EQ 5:24-5).

The MANSFIELD FAMILY of Hingham, 1655.

The Mansfield name is common in early Massachusetts, but there is no known relationship to those in Lynn and Charlestown. Ours came as late as 1655, becoming box-coopers in Hingham, and landholders.

Sophia (Lovis) Gould's mother was ABIGAIL[5] MANSFIELD (Joseph[4-3], John[2-1]). Abigail was born in Hingham Center, on Leavitt Street, on 17 Dec. 1753 (Lincoln, George, *History of the Town of Hingham* [Hingham: The Town, 1893;hereinafter Lin], 51), and died in Hingham 28 May 1800. She was the eldest surviving child in a large family of 12 children, the last born when she was 21, so she must have had a large share of her mother's childcare and housekeeping. Her parents were JOSEPH[4] MANSFIELD, third generation cooper in Hingham, and SARAH[4] WATERS, to whom we will return below.

Our Mansfields were relatively late comers to Hingham, about 1655. The name John Mansfield was quite common, for Banks shows two different ones arriving in 1634 and 1635, 124, 132. Our first in America was JOHN[1] MANSFIELD, mariner. One genealogist mistakenly makes him the son of Sir John Mansfield, Mayor of Exeter, England, whose son John came to Charlestown as a goldsmith, with claim to nobility and coat of arms (Clarissa T. Bass, *Genealogy Taylor-Snow* [Freeport IL: author, 1935], 2:317). However, it is clear that he was an older contemporary of our John Mansfield, who married Mary Gove and had a son John[2] 11 July 1678, who inherited a large estate in England and on the Merrimac, none of which came to our Hingham branch (Wyman 454). The John Mansfields of Lynn are no known connection either.

Our John first appears in Dorchester about 1655 when he married Elizabeth[2] Farnsworth. They moved to Hingham about 1656 when their first son John is born. Soon thereafter he held his first town responsibility, to join Matthew Hawke in the repair of the fence at Playne Neck, Old Planter's Hill and World's End (Hingham Town Records, Hoseah Sprague's copy, Microfiche 6, hereinafter TR, 114). He became Selectman in 1659, Constable in 1662, and Surveyor of Highways 1671, 1672, 1675).

In the first division of the common lands of 1669 he got five shares, entitling him to lot #15 (TR 158). The same shares gave him 9+ acres on the sea facing Supper Island in lot 18 in the first Cohasset division (TR 172), 14+ acres in a triangle on the Hingham line of North Cohasset, near the Maypole, in lot 51 of the second Cohasset division (TR 176), 20+ acres of lot 71 in the third division (TR 183). In the first division of the Neck fences (that is, the northeast of Bare Cove) he got ten acres in lot 27, and 8 rods 12 feet in lot 12 of the second division (TR 186). In the first part of the third division he got five acres plus 10 rods in lot #71 south of the Mast Bridge over Accord Brook, down to the Old Colony Line. His five shares plus four shares bought from Simon Peck in the Fourth Division of town lands in 1677, gave him 13 acres in lot 59 on the Weymouth town line southwest of where route 3 expressway goes in 1994 (TR 207; Hart 34).

Mansfields Cove, on the east side of Hingham Harbor, west of today's Bare Cove Lane, is probably named for him. His home was on the east side of the Common, near School Street (LH 230). He did not become a freeman until 1684. His will, made 19 Feb. 1688/9 was proved 20 Aug. 1689 (Lin 50).

He died in Hingham 4 March 1688/9 ("The Hobart Journal", Reg. 121:274, hereinafter HJ). He and his children are probably buried in Hingham Cemetery near the Old Ship Church, though no stones remain today (Lin 1:ii, 367 says his heirs bought half a rod lot #24).

The FARNSWORTH FAMILY of Dorchester, 1635.

The Farnsworths were early settlers in Dorchester, and owned land in Milton and Weymouth.

John Mansfield married about 1655 in Dorchester ELIZABETH[1] FARNSWORTH (usually spelled ffARNSWORTH), born in England, coming to Dorchester with her parents. We do not know the date she died, but she was still living on her husband's death in 1689 (Lin 51) and after 28 Sept. 1695 when she posted bond to remove a wall on the public road at Plain Neck to old Planter's Hill which her husband had fenced in (TR 272-3; the complaint came to town meeting 17 Dec. 1694, she was ordered 5 March 1695; Thaxter Coll., microfilm 76-19, 18).

Her father, JOSEPH[1] FARNSWORTH and mother ELIZABETH may have come to Dorchester as early as 1628, though not on the first ship. Perhaps they came with Richard Mather on the ship *James* out of Bristol, landing at Dorchester 17 Aug. 1635 (Ebenezer Clapp, *History of Dorchester* [Boston: author, 1859][hereinafter Clapp], 119; Moses F. Farnsworth, *Farnsworth Memorial* [Manti UT: L. A. Lauber, 1897, 2d ed. rev. by R. Glen Nye, Calif. 1974], 11:749).

Joseph was granted lands on Dorchester Neck in 1637, joined the church next year, and became freeman 14 March 1638/9 (Clapp 119). He was town Selectman in 1647.

Elizabeth's mother Elizabeth, whose maiden name is unknown, died between the birth of their llth child, Samuel on 30 March 1647, and her father's remarriage to Mary (Lane), widow of John Long and birth of their son Samuel Farnsworth on 14 July 1656 (Farns. Mem. 751). Mary Long was the daughter of another of Sophia's ancestors, William Lane of Dorchester. She was probably born in Beaminster, Dorset, like William Lane's other English-born children. Mary remarried (3) John Wilcox of Dorchester (Ibid. 749).

The Farnsworth house in Dorchester was probably northwest of the house of John Smith, sold to Elder James Penn in 1661 (SD 3:466 shows the late Joseph Farnsworth northwest of his house which was north of the highway). At Middle Hill on Dorchester Neck he was given 18 acres bounded by the sea to the south, the road to the Castle on the north, widow Batten on the east, and Thomas, John and James Bird to the west (SD 11:140). On either side of the highway on the Little Neck leading down to the Great Neck he had two lots of 50 rods each, bounded on the southwest by Isaac Jones, on the northwest by Richard Withrington, on the southeast by widow Jones, and on the northeast by Benjamin Beales (north side of road) and widow Batten (south side; SD 11:141).

In Milton the town of Dorchester gave Farnsworth 16 acres in lot #8 at Brush Hill in the first three divisions south of the Neponset River, with the Braintree line to the south (in his estate, SD 7:296; also SD 7:279; 8:32). In the Great Lots he was given 12 acres bounded by William Stoughton on the south, Ensign Richard Hall on the west, Richard Baker on the north, and widow Minot and Samuel Rigby on the east, with an access road eight feet wide between Hall and Baker to the highway (SD 10:353-4). It is perhaps this lot that is referred to as northeast of the highway through the Great Lots and northwest of the creek near Captain's Neck (Rigby to Thacher in SD 8:125). In the Third Division he got two wooded lots, #2 of 175 acres north of the Neponset River, the Roxbury line on the north, and Elder John Wiswall on the east, and Samuel Topliff on the west, and lot #72 of 5¼ acres south of Robert Stiles, and the common lands to the west and south (SD 10:355). In Milton he also got 16 acres in the three first divisions in the west side of the eighth lot south of the Neponset, south of Robert Vose's farm to the Braintree line on the south, west of George Badcock, and east of Thomas Vose and John Glover (Pond to Vose, SD 11:379).

In Braintree his daughter Elizabeth brought "considerable Estate" unspecified to her husband John Ruggles, for which the groom's father gave them a house and 30 acres with orchards (SD 13:184).

Farnsworth died in Dorchester 12 Jan. 1659, leaving a will dated ten days earlier. Elizabeth, wife of Joseph Mansfield is mentioned first, with a bequest of "£ 18.5s. wch maks vp y^{t} wch she haue allready received ye sume of £ 40" (Suff. Wills 1:327; Reg. 9:140). Part of his lands were sold by his widow to William Pond in 1660 (SD 7:296), but most of it was sold by his son Samuel after he moved to Windsor CT.

Also mentioned in his will are her sisters Mary Ripley, ancestor of Winston Churchill (Jennie Jerome, Clarissa Hall, Clarissa Wilcox, David, Sarah Smith, Eleazer, Rebecca Ripley; Farns. Mem. 752) and Rebecca Ruggles, ancestor of Gen. MacArthur (son of Gen. Arthur MacArthur, Aurelia Belcher, Benjamin B., Benjamin, Gregory, Joseph Belcher, Elizabeth Ruggles). Samuel^{8} Gould and John G. Gould were thus eighth cousins of Gen. MacArthur and Churchill.

The son of John Mansfield and Elizabeth (Farnsworth), JOHN^{2} MANSFIELD, Jr., a cooper, was born Hingham 15 Nov. 1656 (Lin 51), baptized 4 Jan. 1656/7 (HJ 106), and died there 1 Nov. 1717. He inherited much of his father's estate on his death in 1689, including 30 acres and a house at Mill Neck, between the sea at the west and highway on the east, between lands of Peter Barnes (SD 42:117 in TAG 25:158). He also inherited an acre at Beach Island and Little Harbor (SD 53:95 in same). He lived in Hingham Center on the east side of the Common in his father's house (LH 230). There is no probate record for him or his wife (TAG 25:158).

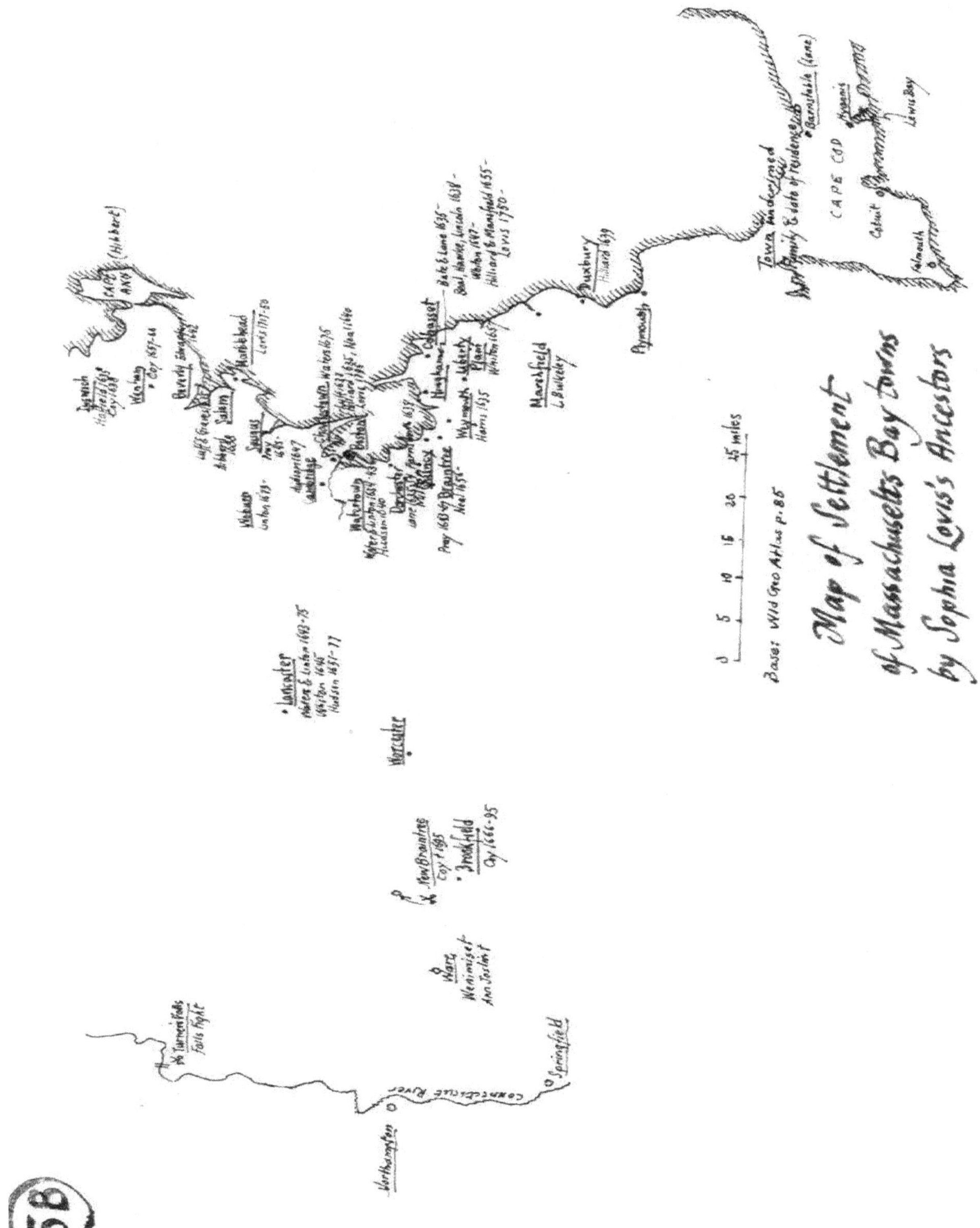
Map of Settlement
of Massachusetts Bay towns
by Sophia Lovis's Ancestors
Base: Wld Geo Atlas p. 86
0 5 10 15 20 25 miles
5B
Northampton
Springfield
Connecticut River
Turners Falls
Falls Fight
Ware
Worcester
Lancaster
Brookfield
New Braintree
Woburn
Watertown
Braintree
Weymouth
Hingham
Cohasset
Marshfield
Duxbury
Plymouth
Salem
Marblehead
Beverly
Wenham
Ipswich
Saugus
CAPE ANN
(Hibbert)
CAPE COD
Barnstable (Lane)
Hyannis
Falmouth
Lewis Bay

The NEALE FAMILY of Braintree, 1640.

The Neale family is descended from Henry Neale, father of 21 children according to his gravestone in Quincy center, one of the first settlers of Braintree.

John[2] Mansfield Jr. married in Hingham 5 June 1683 (HJ 212) SARAH[2] NEAL(E), born Braintree 20 Dec. 1661 (VR 819), died Hingham 4 June 1736, age 75 (Lin 51). She was one of 21 children of HENRY NEALE by his second wife HANNAH[2] PRAY. Henry had come to Boston by 1640 from England where he was born about 1619 (Edith Sumner, *Ancestors & Descendants of Samuel Bartlett* [Los Angeles: author, 1951], 75). On 24 Feb. 1640 he was granted 12 acres in Braintree, now Quincy (William S. Pattee, *History Of Old Braintree* [Quincy: Green & Prescott, 1878][hereinafter Pattee], 29). He was a carpenter and builder. He moved in 1647 to Braintree (Pettee 559) where he and Peter George bought 80 acres in 1648 from the trustees of William Hudson Sr. (14 May, SD 1:93; bounded nw by Furnace Brook, ne by Barnaby Derisock, se by Edward Rainsford and sw by Common land and William Letherland; Winifred Holman Lovering Mss. NEHGS Mss. AH 63, fol. Neale, fam. 2).

His house is described as east of the first meetinghouse (which was on the rise at the intersection of Cottage Street and Hancock; Daniel Wilson, *Three Hundred Years of Ouincy* [Quincy: City of Quincy, 1926], 36; the 1994 minister of the First Church) near the junction of Revere and Hancock Streets in Quincy Center (agreement of the towns of Braintree and Weymouth 25 Dec. 1648 on the layout of the highway from Dorchester to Weymouth, which skirted the church and Neal's house, in Pettee 67n). However, the town surveyor located his 100+ acre farm south of Furnace Brook, and Neale's house close to the Country Road to Boston, at about 309 Adams Street, north of the curve east of Glenwold Rd., just opposite Colonial Drive (Ezekiel Sargent Coll., book G, Quincy Historical Soc.}. This is just west of the John Quincy Adams historical site, and 3/4 mile northeast of the iron furnace. It may be that this was his second residence, when they returned to Braintree from Providence in 1660. The place where the Country Highway (Adams Street) crossed Furnace Brook became known as Neal's Bridge (SD 7:172, 1670; 10:290, 1678).

Neale's first wife Martha Noll died in childbirth 3 May 1655 (Torrey mss.), and Henry then remarried our ancestress, Hannah Pray, the daughter of the Iron Works fineryman, in Braintree 14 Feb. 1656. They moved to Providence where he was given a 6 acre lot 27 Jan. 1658 (Sumner). This was sold 23 Nov. 1660, when they returned to Braintree. In 1663 he and Samuel Deering of Block Island sold for £ 52/10 half interest in 140 acres in Braintree to Thomas Holbrook (21 March, SD 5:498, with the Monatiquot River on the east, Laurance Copeland on the north, William Tyng on the south, and common land on the west). The deal also included half interest in 454 acres of meadow or marsh to the north of a river flowing to the Monatiquot, Copeland on the east, and Holbrook to the northwest.

In 1665 he was one of eight townsmen who signed a deal for all of Braintree between Dorchester and Weymouth down to the sea, paying £ 21/10 to Josiah Wampatuck, Sagamore, son of Chickatawbut, and eight other Indian wise men (5 Aug., text in Pettee, 45-7). Excepted were the farms of Wilson, Quincy, Coddington and Hough's Neck which they had previously bought from the Indians.

Neale also owned land on Hough's Neck northeast of the house of Richard Harris, father-in-law of William[2] Gould (SD 6:202a, 1670). In 1683, five years before his death, he deeded 32 acres in Braintree to his son Joseph out of "parental love and Affection" (SD 13:61, 9 Jan. 1683). This included four acres on Hough's Neck (west of the road to the Neck, se of Tyng's swamp, northeast of a ditch separating his meadow, and northwest of John Baxter. It also included two acres of salt meadow on Salter's Farm, as yet undivided with John Penyman. The biggest part, 26 acres lay south and west of Neales Brook which separated it from the lands of Henry Crane and Alexander Marsh, with the common land and Ebenezer Owen to the south, and his own land to the east, divided from it by a line parallel to an extension of the line between Salters Farm and Henry Crane to the Braintree Common. The largest part of about 100 acres around the homestead on Adams Street remained in the Neal family for many years (Hobart Holly).

Neale was active in town government, as Selectman and Sergeant, the ranking officer of the trainband of militia. Living next to Furnace Brook, he was chosen by local buyers in 1655 to value three pieces of property at the Iron furnace and two more lots that had been given to the iron works by the town of Boston. He joined Francis Nucum for the owners to give an assessment of six pence an acre (Ironworks Papers, "A Collection of Papers Relating to the Iron Works at Lynn and more particularly to the suit between Mr. Gifford [and the owners]...1650 ff.", typescript c. 1926 in Baker Historical Collection, Harvard Business School, Mss:301 1650-1685 Lynn Iron Works Lin 909, 336, 272; the "original" in Baker appears to be a penwritten transcript from Suffolk Court files now in Massachusetts Archives).

Neale made two wills, on 11 July and 12 Aug. 1688, naming his daughter Sarah Mansfield among others. The estate was proved 27 Feb. 1691, providing for 15 surviving children (Suff. Will 1818). His gravestone is one of the oldest, but well preserved, in Hancock Cemetery in Quincy Center, across from the Church of the Presidents, among the Adamses, the Quincys, the president of Harvard and Rev. John Hancock, is in the south, but fallen in 1994. It says he died at 71 on 16 Oct. 1688, "The father of 21 children" (Pettee 117; VR 659, 665).

The PRAY FAMILY of Lynn & Braintree, 1643.

The founder of the Pray family, Quinton, was a highly skilled iron manufacturer who was responsible for the production of the first wrought iron at Braintree and Saugus.

Henry Neale was married secondly, in Braintree, to HANNAH[2] PRAY, on 14 Dec. 1655 by Capt. Torrey of Weymouth (VR in Reg. 37:286) . She was born in Britain and came to America about 1643 with her parents QUINTON[1] and JOAN PRAY. Her father was born in Britain, probably near an iron foundry, in 1597 (in June 1658 he testified his age about 61, EQ

2:94). He was brought over by John Winthrop Jr. as a finery man for the Iron Work Company in Lynn. It seem probable that he came to America as the most skilled ironworker who accompanied Winthrop on the ship *An Cleve* of London in May 1643 arriving 14 weeks later (Winthrop's draft of petition, *Massachusetts Historical Society Proceedings,* 2d. Ser. 8 (Oct. 1892): hereinafter MHS Proc.], 14n, cited by Reg. 55:280). A highly skilled workman, he may have come over as an indentured servant, that is, under contract, with high wages (Hartley 196).

His home in England has not been traced. Henry Woods noted that the name Quentin is common in Scotland where two other Lynn foundrymen came from, the name Pray derived from the French *pre,* or meadow. However, this theory seems dubious since the Scots were not brought over until seven year later, after their capture at the Battle of Dunbar in 1650, and had to be trained in ironwork (Hartley 199), and Scotland was not a center of blast furnaces. For Pray's origins one would better seek around Hammersmith, in the west end of London, after which the Lynn forge was named, the Wealde south of London, the Welsh Marches and perhaps Ireland, where furnace workers who had been recruited in Belgium were thrown out of work by the Civil War (Hartley 81).

The Hammersmith Ironworks at Saugus have the distinction of being the first large-scale industry in America, the first successful integrated ironworks, employing the first imported alien workers at contrast with the Puritan society, in the first company town, using the first Walloon process in America, the first use of gabbro (a rock from Nahant) for flux (Hartley 8-10) . However, this was preceded by a furnace and forge in Braintree in which Pray had a leading part.

The first blast furnace in America was set up by Winthrop at Furnace Brook in Braintree, at the southwest corner of the Catholic St. Joseph's Cemetery on Crescent Street, West Quincy (Hartley 101-2). Winthrop reported the first iron production in early 1644 (Marion S. Arnold paper to Braintree Historical Society, quoted in *Ouincy Patriot Ledger*, date, col. 3) . In a letter to the English investors Winthrop wrote in early 1644 that they had tried the Bogge ore at Braintree "& the finer [Pray] hath made good iron out of it divers tymes; that wch. we sent into England was made of that from Braintre" (MHS Proc., 14) .

Pray seems to have been the key craftsman, as finery man, who supervised the forge work of refining the sows and pigs of cast iron into "loops" or balls of iron which were then pounded by water-driven hammers into bars of merchant iron (Hartley 176-9, 189) . Before forge work began Pray may have been useful in assaying the iron content of bog ore and cast iron. Hartley suggests that Winthrop's finer used a small stone furnace to do this testing (Hartley 166). The Braintree furnace started work in the late Spring of 1645 (Hartley 101-2), but was abandoned within two years for lack of ore in the Quincy bogs (in Montclair per Hobart Holly), and the small flow of water from the Blue Hills (Hartley 109).

Apparently for lack of waterpower on Furnace Brook, the forge was set up by 1645 on the Monatiquot (pron. Mon-at'-ih-quot) River in present-day Braintree, about two miles south of the furnace. Hartley believes Pray built and operated the forge (Hartley 189). The river was dammed at Middle Street, forming a pond that is just a couple of blocks east of the shopping mall west of the Southeast Expressway, south of Adams Street.

The location of the forge is east of the junction of Middle, Adams and Elm Sts. (Dam site #4 in H. Hobart Holly, ed., *Braintree Massachusetts Its History* (Braintree: Historical Society, 1985, 42, 155; "Buildings and Sites in Braintree of Historical Interest", 2 (22-8) in binder, Thayer Library); Arnold, Waldo Sprague, "Iron Works in Braintree Before 1800", Braintree Historical Soc.; Lorenzo Shields, "Industries of Old Braintree--Iron Works", *Braintree Observer* 18 May 1940, col. 4 (4-12); Hartley 115; but not at the 1657 Hubbard forge site, Hartley 266, which misled earlier historians to deny the earlier forge, Pettee 458, 471-2n). The site was later

(1688-1749) used for a grist mill, then Thayer's mill (1752-1835), and Morrison's textile mill at 131 Adams Street (photo in Holly 156). Today there is an oil depot on the site behind Danny's Cleaners.

The date the forge became operational is unclear, but it was surely going by the visit of Winthrop on 4 Dec. 1645, as recorded in his diary: "Dec. 4, Thursday. Waded over Naponset the tree being carried away by the thaw flood, also a little river before. A third made a bridge over, felling a small tree. Passed over Monotiqid at twilight. Came by direction of the noise of the falls to the forge. Lodged at Th. Facksons [Faxon]. Mr. Hoffes [Atherton Hough] farmer." (MHS Proc. 12). Local historians estimate a start by the spring of 1645.

Although the company closed down in 1653 (Hartley 266), Holly believes that fineryman Pray may have continued work there, perhaps until his death in 1653 (Holly 155). Pray had a house nearby where pigs for Saugus were stored in 1653 (Ironworks records, below). Pray was using coal at the forge about 1646 to make iron (Henry Leonard 27 Oct. 1655, in Pettee 470, citing Reg. 15:146).

However, Saugus had the advantage of power and iron so that forge and furnace could be run side by side. By the Spring of 1646 a second furnace had started at Saugus in Lynn (Hartley 122), where Pray appears as finery man. This second forge was built under Winthrop's successor Richard Leader who took over in mid-1645 (Hartley 115), and operating by the spring of 1646 (Hartley 122).

Pray's role as finery man was clearly one of the most skilled and critical to the success of the first American heavy industry because the colony needed wrought iron of low carbon content compared to the impure cast or pig iron. Even 130 years later, in 1775 refining iron was regarded as "the most difficult operation in all metallurgy" (Dr. H. R. Schubert, "Wrought Iron Production at Hammersmith" *First Ironworks Gazette*, 3:1, Feb. 1953, 8). This forge used the most modern technology, the two-hearth "Walloon" process, brought over from Namur and Liege to England in the 1490s. We can see this demonstrated in the National Park middle building at Saugus, where Pray worked in the finery. The complex process of removing the impurities involved at least eight steps: 1) melting the cast iron pig in the finery hearth, and stirring with the "ringer" rod, 2) a second fusion under high heat, 3) a third cooking into a ball or "loop, 4) beating the ball with a sledge to remove scale, 5) hammering by the water-driven helve until it was a square bloom, 6) cutting into half-blooms, 7) reheating in the finery hearth to sweat out, 8) pounding again by the huge hammer into a dumbbell-shaped "anchony" (Hartley 177-8, Schubert 3:2, 6). From there it went to the chaffery hearth and pounded into the final bar shape.

All of this created great fireworks, which sightseers came from miles around to gape at until the management had to forbid it. But for the foundry worker it was dirty, grimy, without goggles or protection, blazing hot, smoky, a literal hell. No wonder that the management provided liberal supplies of beer and spirits to quench the thirst--and that tempers got hot, and the workmen swore. The manipulation of the heavy loops and blooms also required great physical strength.

Sumner says that the ironworkers were no Puritans, and often involved in fighting. In 1648 Quinton and five others were brought to Essex County Court for swearing (EQ 1:134). Two days later Pray was witness in court to say that one of his fellow swearers, iron founder Nicholas Pynyon's wife said her husband had killed five children, one of them a year old (EQ 1:135). A few months later Pynyon's evidence got Quinton or Quintweth and his wife fined 50 shillings for making five oaths (EQ 1:156).

Next year he was brought in for breaking the head of Nicholas Penion with a two foot long iron staff, and hitting Thomas Billington and swearing, for which he was fined (11 July 1649 in Essex Antiq. 6:160; he was also charged with hitting John Dimond, EQ 1:174n). In defense, Pray swore he heard Nicholas Penion coming out of his corn, and swearing on a Sabbath day: "By God, all his pumions [pumpkins] were turned to squashes, and by God's blood he had buyt one pumion of all." (deposition 1 July). The judge admonished: "Let no man make a jest at pumpkins" (EQ 1:173n; Alonzo Lewis & James Newhall, *History of Lynn* [Lynn: George Hubert, 1890], 225; Edward Joy Paul, *Ancestors of Katharine Choate Paul* [Milwaukee: Burdick & Alien, 1914], 142). Here the judge was was echoing a phrase of Edward Johnson: "Let no man make a jest at pumpkins, for with this fruit the Lord was pleased to feed his people." (*Wonder-working Providence*, 85, quoted by David H. Fisher, *Albion's Seed* [N.Y.: Oxford U. Press, 1989], 135).

Pray's importance in the Saugus works is shown in the account books which have survived from 1650-1 (Ironworks Papers; see note above on this source, under Neale Family).

In this we get the charges to Pray for the coal and fuel he used, and the baskets for carrying them, as well as his weekly rations (dyett), and for his clothing which no doubt wore out fast in the grime of the forge, as well as payments to him for moving his belongings, for drawing out bar iron and hammering blooms, and bringing in his son to help him repair the milldam. In the accounts for 1651 we find the following payments to him:

".19: To: y[e] accompte of Quintoun praye p
mendeing his bellow" (52) . . . . £ 0/04

"ye Carridge of Quintonn prayes goods" .....£ 2 (59, folio 75)

"19th ye accompte of Quintonn praye 11 Coard
1 foote-m[ta] ....£ 1/2/3
(firewood , 78)

For Dyett [food]:
"1651 19: ye accompte of Cuintonn praye p 12 weekes
dyett by ch: Hooke...(97) ....£ 3
To: Quintonn Praye p 21: Weeckes dyett
p Thomas Tower beeing from ye
9th of maye to ye 4: of October (127) ... £ 5/5 To: ye ace' of ditto, 21 Weeckes dyett
p george Adams from ye time
afore mentioned to ye 4: of 8[ber] " ......£ 5/5

For Clothing:

"To: ditto: p mackinge 2 pr of drawers
p Jn° Adams"...(Ibid.) ....£ 0/2
To: ye acc[te] of quinton Praye Soe much
pd p Thomas Tower ye Summ of" ....£ 1/4/5
To: ditto: p macking a shearte p
James gourdenn"...(128) ....£ 0/7/7

For Iron:
"To: the Accompte of Bar Ironn mackinge Viz[0]
To: Quinton Praye p macking and
draueinge out: Bar Ironn beeinge:-
$_6c,_{2q} = i_4ii$...(130) ....£ 0/10/1

To: ditto: p mackinge 5 blumes 2 = 1 = 12 .... £ 0/8

1653 for construction of the finery:
"1653 To Quinton Praye p mending y[e] finerreye bellowes and bellowewoodes (132)................£ 0/5
To: ditto p dresseinge y[e] finereye Bellowes (133) . £ 0/12 To: ditto p meale to dresse y[e] Bellowes. ....£ 0/2
To: ditto p 4 daies goinge to Bostonn for Bellowe Leathers, and nayles for his Expence. ....£ 0/9
To: ditto: p 6 1/2: dayes Worke in Laltheing & dabeinge y[e] finerreye Chimneyes. ....£ 0/16/03
To: ditto: p 100: of Larthes fo[r] ye Chimneye. .... £ 0/01/06
To: ditto: p Six dayes Worke p him Sealfe & man mending ye flood gates and damm. ....£ 0/15
To: ditto p 3 dayes Worke more p him Sealfe & Sonn about y[e] damm ....£ 0/12
To: ditto p macking one hammer gudginn of: 2[T]:2°:26[ta] ....£ 0/02/02
To: ditto p two dayes Worke Setting up Pellesados about y[e] Coale heape ....,,.........£ 0/05

To: the acc[te], of quinton Praye p 5 dayes heapings of Coales...(134) ....£ 0/12/6
To: guinton Praye p macking 3 Basketts...(Ibid) £ 0/7/6 To: Quinton Praye p him Selfe and Son three dayes Worcke about ye flood gates and damm...(135) ....£ 0/10/6

"Inventory of Stock and bootes taken away at Brantrye...octob 6: 1653 barr Iron in Quinton Prays howse-6 hundreds (194, f.288) ....£ 6/0/0

The house at Braintry measuring 30 by 18 feet is valued at £ 25; whether this refers to Pray's house or more likely *to* the company's storehouse is unclear (208).

By 1653 Pray had moved back to Braintree to work at the ironworks there, as shown in his deposition in the court files (Suff. Court 225, doc. 25, referred to in Ironworks inventory 10, #67). "Quinton Pray ffinery man aged about 58 years testifieth than mr. Gifford did give away to one ffoster a smith as he told him a pcell of Coule wch was left by Mr. Gilbourne at Brantrey fforge by estimation neer about 30 Loade & the said ffoster took away some quantity & said he had order to take them by Mr. Gifford, and took away a [ ] of them whether he would or no, *& I* refused & suffered him not to take more away, & testifieth that he did make about 8 or 10 Tun of Iron of that Coules left.

And further testifyeth y[c] there is by estimation about 500 Loade of Coales at Brantry, & ye workes there as he believeth, not much above fforty Tunns of Base Iron in a yeere wch about 150 Loud will.---make, & doe believe a great pte [part?] of these Coales will be spoyled before used up[.] further sayd depon[en]t saith that Mr. Gifford gave away the said Coles upon the information of Henery Leanard[.] taken upon oath in---27 [8] in 1653" (month is illegible; Index to Court file has tenth month; Ironworks inventory has eighth).

It is unclear what happened in Braintree after the company closed in 1655. When the Braintree works closed the workers were thrown onto the dole of the town, which petitioned the legislature for relief (Reply 26 May 1659 in Massachusetts Bay Col. Rec. 309, cited by Shields col. 2). Braintree historian Holly doubts Pray would be among these since he was a highly paid workman, and quite wealthy.

Pray apparently kept on making wrought iron, at the old site as Holly believes, and not at the new Hubbard forge on the Monatiquot (Hartley 267, 303-4) which was not built until 1682-4. There a court case in Lynn described his efforts to get iron (Sumner 96). Braintree historians have located this new site at tidewater, a mile downstream from the first 1645 forge, where Shaw Street joins Mill Lane, at the bridge, where iron could be shipped out at tidewater (Dam site #9, Holly 157). John Hubbard's deed of 13 Dec. 1684 refers to his sixth "of the Iron Workes Damm and Pond, fflume & Sawmill by me Erected and made, now standing upon or neere unto the sd River" evidently on land deeded him by Joseph Alleine 26 Dec. 1682, SD 13:361).

The clear references to Pray's house in Braintree in the Ironworks Papers do not locate his home: The first houses in Braintree were on Elm Street north and south of the 1645 site; Holly locates it west of the first forge on the north corner of Elm Street and Hawthorne Rd., near the Catholic church of St. Thomas More (Hobart Holly to author 13 Dec. 1994). We get clues from court cases. On 28 May 1657 Richard Thayer, the principal landowner in the area near the forge got a warrant of attachment against Pray on charges of "holding a legaty duren promises of 50 £" (Suff. Court 276). It is not clear whether this is a loan, but the case was referred to a jury which found for Thayer, awarding him £ 40 plus court costs of £ 7/7. In 1667 John Paine sold the Ironworks site to Richard Thayer, describing it thus: "one dwelling house and Coale house Orchards dam with the Lands adjoining thereto on the North side of the River called by the name of Manaticote, part of it formerly in the hands [309] Quinton Pray, otherwise known by the name of the Iron workes at Brantery (excepting onely...four Acres sold to John Pray" (SD 11:308-9, 12 Sept. 1667).

It appears that this is the same lot mortgaged by Thayer to Simon Lynde in 1668 as the fifth parcel described as "about one acre and a halfe of Land more wch. mr John Paine deemed or accompted as belonging to the Iron workes and comprised in the forementioned lands sold by him to me, although is and was duely and property belonging to the lands of my ffather Richard Thayer, and by him Sold unto me & never alienated to the Owners of the Iron workes, but onely licensed and permitted them of the Iron workes during his pleasure to occupy some part thereof the more to advance his Lands adjoining to the same; which sd. one acre and halfe of Land or thereabout is bounded Southerly upon or with the sd. Monataquot River, Easterly with the five acres formerly John Downhams, Northerly with the highway to the Monataquot River, and westerly with a highway from Monataquot highway downe to the Mill dam together with all and every the houseing Barnes, buildings, Corn Mill, Saw Mill, fulling Mill and Erectments, utensills, Mill stones, Iron worke thing or things..." (SD 11:80, mort. 10 April 1668, deed 29 Oct. 1678; the highway to the Mill dam, now Middle Street, appears to be the one rod wide from the end of the dam north to a three acre plot sold by John Paine to Thomas Thayer in 1665, SD 8:122,123).

From these two deeds it appears that Pray was occupying only part of the Iron Works, which themselves were claimed by the Thayers, but which they still paid Paine for.

Separate from the Iron Works proper is reference to a piece of land formerly owned by Pray himself, to the west of a 25 acre parcel which Thayer put together, lying north of the river, and perhaps west of the Iron Works (parcel #2 in SD 11:80, 1678). By 1667 Paine had also sold four acres next to the Iron Works to John Pray (excepted from 1667 sale of Iron Works, SD 11:309). This may be the same property that is south of the 80 acres which William Pen sold to Peneman & Veazy in 1675, lying east of the brook to the mill pond (west of Church Street; SD 9:201), and west of the 30 acres John Crosbey sold to Joseph Adams in 1671, northwest of the Monatiquot field (SD 9:304).

A month after Thayer bought the Iron Works in 1667 he had a warrant served on Quinton Pray (who had died six months earlier, on 17 April 1667) for "a pasture and a Barne and part of an orchard of Quinton Pray" (28 8/mo [Oct. in margin] [16]67 (SC 827) . Whether this is in collection of the debt or for trespass is unclear, as is the location.

A year after Pray died, Savage sued to eject Thayer from four rows of apple trees which once belonged to Pray, and given to him for a debt (Sup. Jud. Ct. 2053, 1885, cited by Waldo C. Sprague, "The Braintree Iron Works", Quincy, 1955, 14). Pray died in Braintree 17 April 1667 (VR 639). The only burial ground in Braintree was the present Hancock Cemetery in Quincy Center, where he and his wife were probably buried, though no stones remain, perhaps in the Pray family plot in the south part. His estate was inventoried 21 May and widow Joan made administratrix. We know no more of her.

John[2] Mansfield and Sarah Neal's sixth child and third son was JOSEPH[3] MANSFIELD Sr., a box-cooper living on Leavitt Street in Hingham Center. He was born in Hingham 12 Aug. 1693 (Lin 51), and died there 28 Dec. 1756 aged 63 (Lin 51). In 1718 he was still a laborer, selling his share of land at Underwoods Cove, apparently the same 30 acres held by his grandfather at Mill Neck (SD 71:238 in TAG 25:158). In the second part of the Fifth Division of 1745 he received lot 90 of about 18 acres, west of the Mill Pond, and Ward Street In the second part of the Sixth Division of 1744 he got a tiny 20 rod strip in lot #63 just north of Accord Pond, but separated from the water by John Fearing's strip. In 1741 his cousin Sarah Harvey gave him her 1/7 of 11 acres of land and saltmarsh inherited from their grandfather (SD 62:62 in same). By 1749 he had a good estate evaluated at £ 27/6: a house which was on the site of the Charles Lincoln house in 1929, value £ 1/5, and 68 acres of land: 10 acres homelot @ 3=1/10, 6 of orchard=/6, 28 saltmarsh= /18, 8 in Joy's Lot @2=/16, 9 at Cambridge Bar @1=/9, 7 at Mackoelows @1=7 ("Valuation of the Town of Hingham 1749", fiche 22).

The BATE FAMILY of Hingham, 1635.

The Clement Bate family of Hingham was one of the earliest to arrive there, building one of the first homes, on South Street, and becoming large landowners and civic leaders.
Joseph[3] Mansfield married in Hingham 15 Dec. 1727 (Lin 51) RUTH[4] BATE, descendant of several of the town's landed families. She was born about 1702 (*Bates Bulletin* 3d ser., 1917, 42; is she "Ruth Bate baptized 4 Sept. 1692 HJ 279), and died after her husband (28 Dec. 1756) and before 20 April 1765 (SD 110/82). She was daughter of CALEB[3] BATE, mason on South Street, and MARY[4] LANE. Caleb was born Hingham 30 March 1666 (HJ 118), and died there 15 Aug. 1747, age 81 (Lin 40). He was Constable in 1729, and lived in the ancestral homestead on South Street.

Caleb's death is one of the most curious events: both murder and suicide. The town record says: "Caleb Bate being shot, the Jury brought in willful murder. Died Aug. 15, 1747 (TR Births, Deaths & Marriages 1741-1835, 2:39). The transcript *Deaths.* (A-G 46) adds his age 82, and the note: "Jones's record says shot himself with a gun (Jones) (Town) (Gay)". Jones ref. is unknown; town refers to above, and Gay probably refers to Ebenezer Gay's interview with Caleb[6] Bate 28 Feb. 1844 who said: "My great grandfather Caleb Bates shot himself with a gun charged with a part of a nail rod in a fit of insanity--He was sick at the time--" (Microfilm 76-15) . The jury of 14 townsmen, including Sophia's relatives Elijah Beal and Stephen Mansfield reported to Coroner Francis Barker on the day of his death: "Caleb Bate was found Dead on the fifteenth day of August, AD 1747 in his owne Dwelling house Lying upon the flower,----- with his breast Shott open, and with his Gun by him, and so the Jurours aforsd. Say upon their oaths, that the said Caleb Bate in manner and form afors[d] then & their [Volent?] rily, & fallonesly as *a* fellon of his Self did kill & Murther himself[.]" (Suffolk Ct. case 63404, Sup. Jud. Ct. Vol. 395, reel 217, Massachusetts Archives).

Caleb was thrice married, (1) 26 Aug. 1689 (HJ 274) to Ruth___ , who died 20 Sept. 1690 (HJ 276), (2) 14 April 1691 to MARY[4] LANE (HJ 277), born 22 Sept. 1671 (HJ 126), died 11 Dec. 1711 (Lin 40), to whom we will return in 3 pages, and (3) 10 June 1716 to Sarah Sprague, daughter of Anthony Sprague and Sarah Bartlett. Caleb's namesakes were noted military men in Hingham: a Lieutenant fought in the French & Indian War 1762, and a Sergeant was killed at the battle of Brandywine 1777 in Capt. Burbeck, Crane's Artillery (LH 269, 314, 320).

Caleb[3]was grandson of Hingham pioneer CLEMENT[1] BATE(S) , who came to America with Caleb's father JOSEPH[2]on the *Elizabeth* from London in 1635 (Planters 145, Clement Bates, 40, tailor of Lydd, Kent, with wife Anne, 40, 5 children including Joseph, 5, and two servants, sailed from London under Capt. William Stagg in April, arrived Boston midsummer, citing PRO and Founders 18, 119, 21, 24-6, 27).

Clement was born in Lydd, Kent, and baptized there 22 Jan. 1594/5. He died in Hingham 17 Sept. 1671 (Lin 38). Clement was the son of JAMES[A] BATES, yeoman who died Lydd 2 March 1614, and married 6 June 1580 MARY MARTINE, who outlived him (Reg. 51:269-72). James was the son of Lydd Jurat, or alderman, JOHN[B] BATES, whose will was proved 13 May 1580, buried Lydd 1 March 1579, and his first wife whom he married Lydd 28 Oct. 1546, buried there 1 June 1577. John was the son of ANDREW[C] BATES, whose will is 22 Feb. 1532/3, and his wife who predeceased. Andrew was the son of JOHN[D] BATES, also Jurat of Lydd, whose will of 31 July 1522 was proved 17 Sept. John was the son of THOMAS[E] BATES, who died All Hallows Parish, Lydd, Kent in 1485, with will of 19 Oct. leaving a widow MARGARET, who left a will of 14 Oct. 1490. Robert Crother assumed that he was Junior, son of THOMAS[F], Sr. fl. 1431-58, son of JOHN[3] BATE the Elder, f1. 1411-47 (chart -25 April 1993).

The Bate family has claimed coat of arms (Colkett 22), and several relatives in Lydd were styled Gentleman (Clement will of 1623; John g.s. 1642; Richard of Dorchester), and many were Jurates, or sworn officials like Aldermen. The name Bate may come from the Anglo-Saxon word for contention, or perhaps short form of Bartholomew (Newton Bate, *Ancestors & Descendants of Asa Bates* [W. Bloomfield NY: author, 1804], 1). Lydd is a small village on the south coast of Kent, within sight of the ancient port of Rye. The stone church and graveyard have many memorials to members of the Bate family.

This Bate family from Kent is clearly NOT the same as the Edward Bate family from Buckinghamshire who went to Weymouth in 1638, ancestors of Thomas Gould through the Nicholas Lawrance family (TAG Jan. 1990, 35-6; Bates Bull.. 1st ser., 5).

Clement, his wife and five children are on the passenger list of the *Planter* which left London 6 April 1635, but actually sailed on the *Elizabeth* which left on the 13th (Banks, 144-5; Daniel Lowell, *A Munsey-Hopkins Genealogy* [Boston: author, 1920], 67-8). He went to Hingham, where he was granted houselot #5 containing five acres on the south side of South St, five lots west of Main Street (TR 7, 3 July 1636; Gushing Mss. 32; Lin 38). There he built a house, at 98 South Street, which was inherited by his son Joseph and grandson Caleb (Bates Bull. 1st ser., 5). The house became the Anchor Tavern, where Lafayette was to stay (Gilbert 0. Bert, *Bert Genealogy* [Boston: Clapp & Sons, 1903], 49; Hart 53).

In 1635 he was also granted a ten acre planting lot at Pleasant Hill (TR 4), a planting lot in Broad Cove field and three acres of meadow at the upper end of Broad Cove meadow (north of town, TR 12, Gushing).

1636. He was granted 20 acres of lot #16 in the Great Lots on the Weymouth River (TR 15), an acre of meadow and 13 of upland in lot #32 of Nataseus Division (Nantasket; TR 30).

1637. He exchanged five acres he bought from Daniel Trop for Thomas Nicholas's houselot of two acres at Bachelor River and three acres planting lot on the Neck and ten acres of Great Lot (TR 40). That year also given 1¼ acre in Crooked Meadow east of the highway to the river, between Nicholas Jacobs and Thomas Jones (5 March, Gushing), and two acres for a small planting lot on the Plain by Thomas Loring (20 Nov., Gushing).

1638. In town meeting he gave up an acre of fresh meadow to James Bate for an acre of salt marsh on the north side of Lyford's Liking (northeast corner, 3 Sept., Gushing).

1647. An acre of salt marsh, lot #21 in the first Cohasset division, was given to him, lying north of William Chapman, east of the Creek, west of Michael Perse (Gushing). In the second Cohasset division of 1647 he got lot #19 of 1½ acres of salt marsh south of the Creeke between Foy and Weir (Ibid.).

1647. The town gave him right to erect a barn on the Common "against his house" (Gushing).

1669. Division of Common lands in 1669 gave him 6 shares, which gave him lot #28 in the first division. In the division of the lands to the northeast he got lot #23, west of Foundry Pond and Weir Street But he died in 1671 in the midst of the Cohasset Division, and one of his shares was combined with his son Joseph's five, and four with his son Samuel's five to make a total of 12 for the family in lot 68 on the south side of Little Harbor (TR 171, 174). His acre in lot 11 of the first division of Neck Fences, and 14 feet in the second division (TR 186-7) probably went to his sons in the same proportion.

Clement was a tailor by trade. He was chosen one of the first of three Selectmen of Hingham in 1637, a position held many years by Sophia's ancestors in the next hundred years. He held a number of town offices, including fenceviewer in 1638, one of nine to make the original divisions of Conyhasset (Cohasset) 1640 and 1647 (TR 70, 104; E. Victor Bigelow, *History of the Town of Cohasset* [Cohasset: Town Committee, 1898], [hereinafter Big] 111, 134), Waywarden 1641, one of three to build the first bridges over the creek and to tax owners for the cost, 1640 (TR 78), Selectman again in 1647 and 1649, and fix taxes for 1649, Selectman again 1651, 1652, Surveyor 1655.

In 1637 he and three partners were given monopoly to a weir in the river at Lawford's Liking in Cohasset to catch alewives for seven years, at a maximum price of 10/6 per 1000 (TR 75; Big. 109).

Bate made his will on 12 Oct. 1669, still "being in health and perfect memory", leaving eldest son James most of the land and as executor, our ancestor Joseph getting only £ 10 from his brother Samuel and the piece of salt meadow of the first division, and a quarter of his household effects (transcript in 7:159 on microfilm 76-14) . However, the inventory was done by Joseph, the executor, 15 July 1689, showing a good estate of £ 239/11, the dwelling house and adjoining land at Ward Hill worth £ 45, 12 acres of pasture at Turkey Hill £ 75, 1½ acre of salt meadow at Broad Cove £ 30, two acres of fresh meadow by the river at Turkey Meadow £ 25, Planting lot at Turkey Hill £ 20, the rest in the usual tools, household goods, clothing, furniture, a gun, two cows, one sow & 6 pigs, "a Bible & other small books" (9:207, in same).

Clement Bate died in Hingham 17 Sept. 1671, "Aged 81 years dyed sabb: day night" (Lin 38, HJ 126). He is presumably buried under the granite marker "BATE" on the north hill of the town cemetery, where the family's graves are, but no ancient stones remain.

Clement came to America from Biddenden, Kent, about 20 miles northwest of his birthplace in Lydd. Four of his children were born there (Reg. 66:54), and it is probable that he married his wife ANNA there about 1623. Her maiden name may have been BIGG(E), a family of well-to-do clothiers of whom many came to Dorchester and Roxbury, especially Rachel (Martin) Bigge, and her daughter Prudence Foster, both of whom came over with Clement Bates on the *Elizabeth,* and perhaps the cause of their delay (Reg. 66:54-5; Roberts 178-81). Anna Bate died in Hingham 1 Oct. 1669 (HJ 124), age 74 (Lin 38), so she was born about 1595, perhaps daughter of SMALLHOPE BIGGE, clothier of Cranbrook, Kent, who left a will of 3 May 1638.

JOSEPH[2] BATE, third child of Clement and Ann, was baptized at All Saints, Biddenden, Kent, 28 Sept. 1628 (Reg. 66:54; Bates Bull. 1st ser. 107). He came with his parents to America age six. He became a bricklayer, living in the family homestead on South Street which he inherited. He became freeman in 1672, and held many town offices, including Constable in 1675-8, Selectman 1668, 1671, 1677, 1684, 1692, and served as parish sexton 1673-81.

In the big division of town lands in 1669 he got five shares, and was given one of his father's shares (TR 159, 171). In the first division he got lot #31. In the first Cohasset division he shared 12 shares with his brother Samuel, for 23 acres in lot #68 that nearly parallels Sohier Street today (TR 174). In the second Cohasset division the same arrangement gave them 34+ acres in lot #20 across North Cohasset (TR 175). In the third division they got lot #52 with 26+ acres in the southwest part of Cohasset, and 24+ acres in the southeast (TR 183). In the Neck Fence divisions he got lot 42 of three acres, and lot five of a rod and 12½ feet (TR 186). In the Fourth Division next to Weymouth he and his brother shared equally in the 18 acres of lot 71 (TR 207; west of the intersection of Whiting and Gushing Sts.). In 1678 the town commissioned him to lay out land to the grist mill at Straits Pond (TR 215, 222). In 1684 he was ordered to take a lot at Nutty Hill for a road (TR 230).

He died in Hingham 30 April 1706, at age 76. His will, made six days before, mentions his son Caleb[3].

Joseph[2] and Esther Bate were the ancestors of Katharine[9] Lee Bates (1859-1929), author of "America the Beautiful" (William[8], Joshua[7], Zealous[6], Joshua[5-4-3]) . Her grandfather Joshua[7] (1776-1854) was President of Middlebury College, and Chaplain of the U.S. House of Representatives, 26th Congress. Joseph and Esther were also ancestors of Massachusetts Governor John[9] Lewis Bates (b. 1859; Lewis[8-7], Levi[6], Joshua[5-4-3]) , who had previously served on Boston Common Council 1891-2, Representative 1894-9, Speaker 1897-9, Lt. Governor 1900-2; Governor 1903-4; *Bates Bull*., 1st ser., 110). They were also ancestors of Civil War Brig. Gen. Joshua[7] Hall Bates (1817-1908; George[6], Revol. War Major Jonathan[5], Samuel[4], Joseph[3]; William R. Cutter, *New England Families* [New York: Lewis Pub., 1915], 1080).

The HILLIARD FAMILY of Boston, Duxbury and Hingham, 1635.

The Hilliards were late-comers to Hingham, about 1655, from Duxbury, and may have moved on to Rhode Island.

Joseph[2] Bate married in Hingham 9 Jan. 1657/8 ESTHER[2] HILLIARD (HJ 107), born Boston 25 March 1642, daughter of WILLIAM[1] and ESTHER or HESTER (maiden name unknown), carpenter born in England 1614, who came to Boston on *Elizabeth & Ann* in mid-summer 1635, having sailed from London in mid-May, on the ship captained by Roger Cooper (Planters 157, citing Founders 20, 22, 24, 27-30) .

He went first to Duxbury, where, as a carpenter, he built the first mill in town, in 1639 (Dorothy Wentworth, *Settlement & Growth of Duxbury* [Duxbury: Rural & Historical Soc., 1973], 71-6). This was located on Stoney Brook, later called Mill Brook, and today Duck River, almost on the Marshfield line, where Route 3A crosses the river. Miles Standish and three others signed an agreement for the town with Hillier and George Pollard on 7 Nov. 1639 that they "att their owne PPI (personal) cost and charges, to build, frame, and set up 1 sufficient water milne to grynde corne both english and indian, within ye terme of one whole yeare next after the date hereof. As also Stampers to beate Corne att as speedily as they cann, and...shal build ye sd Milne and Stampers on a certain Brooke, called Stoney Brooke lying by ye house of Phillip Delaynoye..." (71-2). Their commission was fixed at one pottle (2 old quarts, or 1/16) per bushel ground. It was also agreed that there would be no other mill in town, and the millers be given land nearby for their farming needs.

Hillier mortgaged his half to pay Robert Carver, a sawyer, for planks, the repayment of which shows the success of the mill (73). After Pollard's death Hillier sold his share to Constant Southworth, whose mother had married Governor Bradford (74). The deed transferred "one dwelling and outhousings barn, and three acres of land...and two acres of meadow lying on the east side of the common highway, which sd Willm bought sometime of Robert Mendame. All of which dwelling, outhousings, fences and appurtenances thereto belonging being his own property, and in no way belonging to ye aforesaid partnership..." From this it appears that Hillier lived near the millsite, into which Soutworth moved, on Crab Island (74). Mendame owned the land where the mill was placed, near Mendame's Spring.

Among the lands granted to Hillier and Pollard jointly was an area around present day Church Street, north of Stoney Brook and south of Green Harbor Brook (*Copy of the Old Duxbury Records* [Plymouth: Avery & Doten, 1893], 55; 18 Oct. 1684, a:247-8).

The Hilliers moved to Hingham about 1655, when their daughter Esther was baptized by Rev. Hobart 25 June (HJ 105). They may have removed to Little Compton RI (Benjamin P. Wilbour, *Little Compton Families* [Providence: College Hill Press, 1967], 343). The "widow Milliard" who received land in the Hingham divisions (TR 181, 186, 205, etc.) is another person, whose daughter married Cornelius Cantlebury. The daughter, Esther (Milliard) Bate died Hingham 3 June 1709 (Lin 40).

The LANE FAMILY of Hingham, 1635.

The Lanes were among the earliest settlers of Dorchester and Hingham, and became leading landholders and civic leaders in the latter. They were ancestors of the Lewis family of Barnstable, which gave its name to Lewis Bay in Hyannis.

Caleb^3 Bate was married by Rev. Samuel Sewall in Hingham 14 April 1691 to his second wife, MARY^4 LANE (HJ 277) , another descendant of an old Hingham family. She was born there 29 Sept. 1671 (HJ 126), and died there 11 Dec. 1715. She was daughter JOSIAH^3 LANE and his first wife MARY BACON. He was a carpenter who lived in West Hingham, on North Street near Goold's (no known relation) Bridge over Town Brook (Lin 412). He was baptized by Rev. Hobart 23 May 1641 (HJ 14). He died in Hingham 26 March 1714, age 72 (VR 174, fiche 164). He was probably buried in Hingham Cemetery behind the Old Ship Church, in lot #15 (one rod sold to him, Lin I:ii, 367).

Mary, his first wife, died ten days after the birth of their first child Mary who was to marry Caleb Bate 6 Oct. 1671, HJ 127). Her wedding to Josiah about 1671 is not recorded by Hobart nothing in the three Bacon files. Lincoln does not relate her to the Hingham Bacons, and his Mary born 17 Sept. 1654 is too young (17) to be wed in early 1671. Given the close connections of the Lanes with Barnstable, one possibility is Mary born in Barnstable 12 Aug. 1648 (Pope; Amos Otis, *Genealogical Notes of Barnstable* [Barnstable: Goss, 1888] [hereinafter Otis], 25), bapt. 20 Aug., daughter of Nathaniel^1 Bacon and Hannah Mayo, dau. of Rev. John Mayo. No husband or death is shown, so further proof must be sought: Nathaniel left no will (Otis 24), but probate 23 Oct. 1673 mentions children; Mary Lane died before that, 1671; Barnstable probate may have reference to Lane.

He fought in the King Philip's War 1676. When Lancaster was sacked and our relatives Ann Joslin and her daughter Beatrice were captured and killed in captivity, as we will tell below, Joshua joined the company of Capt. Samuel Wadsworth of Milton and arrived at Marlborough on 1 March (Bodge, 218-25) . Wadsworth s company defended Milton, Braintree, Weymouth and

Hingham, for which Lane was paid £ 5/14 on 24 July (222).

Lane was among those detached for service in the Connecticut Valley, under Capt. William Turner, the former companion of Baptist pioneer, Rev. Thomas Gould (no relation), who was killed by the Indians after the retreat from the Falls Fight (232-45). Lane was one of the 35 soldiers who joined Turner's company when they left Marlborough 29 Feb. (240) to Quabog (Brookfield), which they left 4 March (235). They crossed the Connecticut River for the successful defense of Northampton against the Indian attack of 14 March, and another shortly afterwards. One of the soldiers killed in the defense of Westfield was Clement Bates (236). Joshua escaped the disastrous Falls Fight of 19 May at which 40 soldiers were killed, because he was with the largest force that was returned to Boston 7 April (237; James H. Fitts, *Lane Genealogies*, [Exeter NH: News-Letter Press, 1897] [hereinafter Fitts], 2:11). In addition to the pay, Joshua was given land in Narraganset Township #5, Souhegan East, which became Bedford, part of Merrimac and Manchester NH; the lot was claimed by his son John (Bodge 430-1).

On his return from the war Joshua remarried 9 May 1676 Deborah Gill (HJ 192), daughter of Thomas Gill Sr. and Hannah Otis. She died 16 April 1727.

In the great division of Hingham lands in 1669 he got 3 shares, for lot 66 of the first division (TR 159). In the Cohasset divisions this was combined with his father's large 10 shares to produce the largest grants after the minister's. He received lot # 24 on the Weymouth line (near Industrial Park Rd. 1994) in the Fourth Division of 1677, in 13 shares with his father (TR 205; Hart 34). On the opposite side of town, at the northeast corner, he got lot #24, on the south side of the pond west of Weir Rd.

As a carpenter he may have had a hand in the building of the Old Ship Meetinghouse of 1680 which still stands today, over 300 years old, the oldest church in New England. At town meeting of 3 May 1680 he voted to replace the old meetinghouse, and was assessed £ 3/16/8 on 9 Oct. This gives an idea of his wealth, for assessments ran from one to fifteen pounds (Hart 42). His status in the hierarchical society is shown by his getting seat 4 on 5 Jan. 1681. His wife got sixth seat in the women's gallery at the side (Fitts 12). In 1690 he was an owner who approved the records of the clerk of Agawam plantation or Wareham Farms.

Josiah[3] Lane was the grandson of WILLIAM[1] LANE, from Beaminster, Dorset (pron. Bemminster), 12 miles north of the coast at Bridport, and 3 miles from the home of Thomas Hollis, the benefactor of Harvard (TAG 64:214, 65:106). He sailed from Weymouth, about 25 miles southwest, on 8 May 1635 on the *Hopewell* with his wife (Pope 277), and six children. They settled in Dorchester, where he received two land grants in 1637, an acre on the Little Neck towards the harbor (2 Jan.) and 6-7 acres March 18 (Fitts 11:1). Three acres were on Dorchester Great Neck, south of the road to the Castle (SD 10:334 deed of one of his executors John Wiswall Sr., Boston shopkeeper, to Mary (Bates) Foster, whose brother James Bates had sold it to Wiswall). Before 1637 he remarried Agnes Farnsworth, perhaps sister of Sophia's ancestor Joseph (Belle Preston, *Bassett-Preston Ancestry* [New Haven: Tuttle, Morehouse & Taylor, 1930], [hereinafter Preston] 169) .

The inventory of his estate says he was a farmer. Clapp says "He was a man of humble life" (Clapp 126). Fitts says he "was a person of competent property, a freeman, a virtuous and good citizen who evidently had the esteem and confidence of the people" (Fitts 11:2). In 1641 he was one of the proprietors who gave Thompson's Island to maintain the first public school in the colonies.

He died in Dorchester at "advanced age" in 1654, before the inventory of 5 July 1654 (Preston 169). His will of 28 Feb. 1650/1 left his "new dwelling house" to his daughter Elizabeth Rider (Reg. 5:304). One of his two executors was Sophia's ancestor "Loving Brother

Joseph ffarnsworth", who had married Lane's widowed daughter Mary Lane. Mary inherited her father's great lot of 24 acres, and took in orphaned Elizabeth Farnsworth until her marriage to John[1] Mansfield about 1655. We do not know the maiden name of the mother of his children, or whether she is the same as the Agnes who became a member of the church in Dorchester about 1637 (Pope 277), and died some time before William (Bert 48).

William's son GEORGE[2] LANE was born in west of England, perhaps at Beaminster, Dorset. He was already adult when he came with his parents and married sisters to New England. A shoemaker by trade, he was one of the first 30 settlers of Hingham, by 1635. In 1641 the town charged him 8 pence a tree for 15 trees he cut on common land (TR 56).

In the first division of 1635 (18 Sept.) he was given a five acre house lot #23 on the northwest corner of Burton's Lane and Town Street (now North Street), "up in town", at the west end of the village (Hart 23; LH 225). The site of his house is now 287 North Street, built in 1781 by Joseph Beal (Loring). The land backs up to Baker's Hill, a rough piece of glacially scoured rock, with a cart track today that looks as bumpy as it must have been in his time.

As a shoemaker, he probably did not need the land to farm, but he got ten acres of Great Lot in 1637 (TR 53), two acres at Pleasant Hill, and an acre of marsh on the Weymouth River (VR Bargains & Sales, fiche 4). In 1643 the shortage of cattle feed prompted him to ask for a Great Lot farther out, so the town gave him ten acres on the Weymouth road west of the free meadow as it bends around the Great Swamp (TR 102). Given a large ten shares in each of the following divisions, more than any other settler except the minister, he got ten acres on Nutty Hill, on the west side of Hingham north of High Street (Fitts, 2:6). In the Cohasset divisions three shares were added to his ten for his son Josiah, making 13 for a wide lot of 25+ acres west of Supper Island (lot 27, TR 173), 37 acres west of Little Harbor (lot 28, TR 175), 28 acres southwest lot 8, TR 181), and 26 acres south of Scituate Pond. He shared 13 shares in the fourth division of 1677 with his son Josiah to get lot #24 of 19½ acres (TR 205; Hart 34); on the Weymouth line near Industrial Park Rd.. In 1650 he sold all of his planting lot on Old Planters Hill to Nicholas Jacob, except for an acre and a half he had earlier sold to Henry Gibbs (VR, fiche 4). In his estate he also left a great lot and parcels of saltmarsh at the Weymouth river, and "horbly fiele".

He was Hingham Selectman for 1669 and 1678, and Surveyor of Highways 1670 and 1677, Viewer of leather 1678 and 1681. He became a freeman 8 Oct. 1672. He was about the middle of incomes ranging from l to 15 when taxed for the Old Ship Meetinghouse in 1681, at £ 6/6, and rated a front pew. His will of 16 Oct. 1688 was proved 20 Aug. 1689. He died in Hingham 11 June 1689 (HJ 274), probably over 75, given that he came as an adult in 1635.

Among his descendants was Ebenezer Lane, Chief Justice of Ohio (Frank M. Hawes, *Foster Record: An Account of Thomas Foster* [Somerville: Fred Bradford, 1889], 84). George's daughter Sarah, sister of our Josiah, married Lt. James[2] Lewis of Barnstable village, and they lived on the site of the Trayser Museum where he had a blacksmith shop (Otis, 120, 125, 126). Four of their grandsons graduated from Harvard, including Joseph[4] Lewis (1702-88) who taught 60 years in Barnstable in rotation among the four districts, after preaching in Hyannis briefly, probably the first minister there, where his cousin Jonathan[3] (George[2]) gave the name to Lewis Bay (Otis 2:138, 135, 131-2).

The FAMILY OF WALTER HARRIS of Weymouth & New London, 1632.

The Walter Harris family was a founder of Weymouth and Dorchester, and became prominent innkeepers in early New London.

George Lane married about 1634-6, either in England or Massachusetts, SARAH[2]

HARRIS, eldest daughter of WALTER[1] HARRIS. She was perhaps born in Honiton, East Devon, where her siblings were born 1621 ff. (Burton W. Spear, *Search for the Passengers of the Mary & John, 1630* [Toledo: Mary & John Clearing House, 1991], [hereinafter Spear], 16:39), perhaps by an earlier wife than Mary Fry. Honiton is 20 miles west of the Lane home is Beaminster, Dorset, so it is possible they were married in Honiton before coming to America. Walter Harris took the oath of allegiance 7 March 1631/2 in London, his residence, and sailed two days later on the *William & Francis*, arriving in Boston 5 June 1632 (Planters 97, citing Winthrop's Journal 1, 80-1, Reg. 12:274; she sailed under Capt. Thomas 9 March; Charles Harris, "Walter Harris and Some of His Descendants", *Collections of Western Reserve,* [hereinafter C.Harris], Dec. 1932, 3). On the same ship was Rev. Thomas[1] Weld, first minister of Roxbury and ancestor of Massachusetts Governor William Weld and Sarah Swan Weld[9], great-grandmother of Anne Garrison Gould. With him were his mother, widow of WALTER[1] HARRIS and his brother Gabriel who was lost on a return trip to England (Nathaniel Harris Morgan, *Harris Genealogy* [Hartford: Case, Lockwood & Brainard, 1878], 199).

Harris went first to Plymouth (Planters 97), then was one of the first settlers of Weymouth, by 1635, where he owned "Eyght acres lying in Harrises Raing first given to Walter Harris", and "Eyght acres in the mill furlonge" (Harris 4). He was made freeman 2 June 1641. He also had land in the West field first given to Robert Lovell (Weymouth Land Grants 255 cited by George W. Chamberlain, *History of Weymouth* [Baltimore: Genealogical Pub., 1984], [hereinafter Cham], 3:255-6). In 1651 he also had lot 12 of the great lots on the east side of Fresh Pond (Cham 3:256) . In 1643 he was an appraiser of the estate of his brother-in-law William[2] Frye who died 26 Oct. 1642 in Weymouth, leaving a kid goat to his nephew Thomas Harris (Reg. 11:385; Lillian Selleck, *One Branch of the Miner Family* [New Haven: Donald Jacobus, 1928], 109).

By 1648 Walter Harris had built illegally in Dorchester (C. Harris 5, citing TR 302, 14 Jan. In 1649 we have his signature as appraiser of the estate of John Pope of Dorchester (C. Harris 5). That year he is paid by the will of Edward Bullock of Dorchester for a debt "a pecke of rye, for tyrmng for a hatt" (Ibid., citing Reg. 5:356). In early 1653 Dorchester granted him "a little p'cell of land...which he form'ly have enjoyed" (C. Harris citing 4th Report of Bost. Rec. Commis., 302). It was in Dorchester that his daughter Mary married in late 1651 to Nicholas[2] Lawrance, ancestor of Thomas Gould. The exact generations of Lawrances is not fixed, but this makes Sophia Lovis and Thomas Gould fifth or sixth cousins.

Walter and Mary Harris moved from Dorchester to New London in 1652 or 1653, where he was granted a house lot on Pequot Harbor (20 May 1653) and licensed to run an ordinary (C. Harris 6, 7). There is a family tradition that the house stood near the river on Pequot harbor, where an immigrant vessel took shelter, en route to New Haven. Their son Gabriel went out to the ship and invited them ashore. They landed and spent the night partying. Gabriel fell in love with one of the party, Elizabeth Abbott, followed her in his father's newly painted pinnace, in which he brought her home with her household gear (C. Harris 6-7). Walter died in New London 6 Nov. 1654 (C. Harris 7, 9 citing VR 2).

The Harrises were allied to the well-to-do English merchant families of Fry, Hill and Jordaine.

Walter Harris was married in England, perhaps near Honiton, Devon, before 1615 to MARY[1] FRYE. She was born about 1593-7 to WILLIAM[A] FRYE and SARAH HILL (Sheldon Harris Family GHAR 4304) . William's will was proved in England 25 Feb. 1625/6 (Spear, citing PCC HELE 20). Sarah was born about 1570-5 probably in Weymouth to JAMES[B] HILL and JUDITH JORDAINE, daughter of JOHN (d. Lyme Regis, Dorset 1588) and THOMAZIN JORDAINE (James K. Delapine, *Descendant Mothers of Fry Daughters* [typescript, n.p., 1969], family 5). Mary received £ 20 in the will of her grandfather James Hill, and her mother Sarah Fry the same; James Hill's son-in-law William Fry was executor and residual legatee (Henry F. Waters, *Genealogical Gleanings in England* [Baltimore: Genea. Pub. Co., 1969] 2:1075, citing

Dale 35). John[B] Jurdaine, merchant of Lyme Regis, left a will of 23 Sept. 1588, proved 13 Nov. mentions his wife Thomazin and daughter Judith as yet unmarried (Ibid. 1071, citing Leicester 7). He is related to London merchant John Jourdaine who was principal agent of the East India Company in the East Indies 1617-20 (Ibid., citing Soame 87). Mary (Fry) Harris's brother William also came to America, and settled in Weymouth.

Mary Harris was granted the license to continue to run the ordinary at Pequot on her husband's death (Preston 128). She died in New London a month after her husband, on 24 Jan. 1655/6, having made a nuncupative will five days before (C. Harris 7). Hers is one of the oldest extant wills in America. We know that our Sarah Lane was her daughter since she is named in the will, and gives her "the bigest brass Pan" and "the bigest pewter dish and one silken riben" (C. Harris 8). To Sarah's daughter Mary she gave a silver spoon and a pewter candlestick.

The WATERS FAMILY of Watertown & Lancaster, 1634.

The Waters family was early settled in Watertown, then the frontier town of Lancaster, where they survived the massacre of 1675, fleeing to Hingham where they were prominent innkeepers on North Street.

JOSEPH[4] MANSFIELD, Jr., grandfather of Sophia Lovis, was born Hingham 9 Oct. 1728 (Lin 51), and died in the Almshouse there 10 Sept. 1806, age 78 (VR 295, fiche 166; Lin 51). He was a cooper like his father and grandfather, residing on Leavitt Street in Hingham Center. He was a soldier in the Revolution, serving 3 times in Capt. Peter Gushing's company on coastal defense 15 March 1776, again on 14 May 1776 at Hull, and 27 Feb. 1778 for the garrison at Nantasket (Lin 1: 293, 297, 315-6). Later his name shows up in Capt. Theophilus Wilder's company (DAR application of Ethel Lane Hersey, #160,024, approved 20 Sept. 1927).

He married in Hingham 20 May 1751 SARAH[4] WATERS, born Hingham 13 July 1733, died there 2 April 1804, nearly 71 (VR 295, fiche 166; Lin 51, 280). She was the seventh of nine children born to DANIEL[3] WATERS and his first wife, ABIGAIL[3] WHITON, of whom more later. He was born a twin 10 Oct. 1691 Woburn (Elizabeth J. Harrell, *The New England Ancestry of Oren Waters* [Los Altos CA: author, 1988], 13, citing his letter of 23 May 1728 confirming inventory of his father Samuel's estate in Woburn), and died Hingham 22 July 1776, age 85 (Lin 280). He was a cooper, who lived on Leavitt Street, Hingham Centre. On Abigail's death 3 Sept. 1738, he married (2) 9 Oct. 1740 Mary Wilder, daughter of John and Rebecca (Doggett) Wilder, b. Hingham 30 July 1692, d. 10 Nov. 1756, age 64 (Lin 280). 22 days after her death he m. (3) 2 Dec. 1756 Elizabeth Day, who died 12 Oct. 1757, age 43. Three months later, on 12 Jan 1758 he m.(4) Mrs. Lydia Lawson, widow of James Lawson.

Sarah Mansfield's brother was Elijah[4] Waters (1729-96), owner of two Waters Taverns on North Street The older one, of 1753, is still standing at #69-71, on the northeast corner of Ship Street. In 1793 he built a larger one on the northwest corner, at # 73, now gone (Lorena and Francis Hart, *Not All is Changed* [Hingham: Hingham Historical Commission, 1993] [hereinafter Hart], 53; Julian Loring records in Hingham Historical Commission, [hereafter Loring]).

Daniel[3] Waters was the grandson of immigrant LAWRENCE[1] (or Laurence) WATERS, house carpenter. He was born in England about 1602, and died Charlestown 9 Dec. 1697, "neer 85" (Harrell 6, citing VR 139). That he had some education is shown by his signature on documents.

The unusual name Lawrance Wattar(s) has been found in Cundall, West Riding of Yorkshire, including a Lawrence Watters' will of 1594, the Mayor of York, Sir Richard Watter, and Lawrance Wattar, brother of James of Latton Essex, but the connection is unproven (EIHC 17:124-6). More recently, Roger Thompson placed Lawrence Waters in the William Pelham company which settled Watertown, coming a compact social group from the Stour Valley textile town of Bures, Suffolk ("Social Cohesion in Early New England", Reg. July 1992, 238, citing N.C.P. Tyack, "Emigration from East Anglia to New England", London Univ. Ph.D. disser. 1951).

Waters came to Watertown by 1634, where he was granted an eight acre houselot on the southwest slope of Strawberry Hill, between present-day Mason and Gushing Streets, extending up the hill to about Fairfield Street (Bond, map 1095). In the first town inventory of 1639 he owned lot #11 of four acres of plowland at Beaver Brook on the north bank of the river on the further plain (1636), lot # 94 of four acres in the remote Westpine "Meddowes" (1637), lot # 10 of 25 acres in the third division (1636), lot # 14 of twe;ve acres of upland beyond the further plaine, and a farm of 105 acres of upland in the sixth division (Frederick C. Warner, "The Ancestry of Samuel, Freda and John Warner" [typesc., Boston, 1949 in NEHGS], 4:728; Bond 1022-8; Holman 213 citing Watertown Records, 1894, 1-4, 8, 10, 13). In the second inventory of 1644 the list is the same except that the 105 acres is replaced by an acre in Patch Meadow. By 1646 he had sold all except his homestall of eight acres, which he sold in 1688 to Richard Harrington (MD 3:338). He and his wife were warned for dancing (1638, Mass Bay Col. Records 1:233 cited by Mary L. Holman, *Stearns-Miller Ancestry* [Concord NH: Rumford Press, 1948], 94).

In 1643 Waters and his father-in-law were sent to scout for a settlement at Nashaway Plantation, an Indian trading post on the Nashua River, which became the town of Lancaster in 1653 (*Worc. Magazine* 11:272 in A. Holman; Joseph Willard, *Sketches of the Town of Lancaster* [Worcester: Charles Griffin, from *Worc. Mag.*, 1826], 20, 22; he signed the compact 15 Jan. 1653, Henry Nourse, ed., *Early Records of Lancaster* [Lancaster: W.J. Coulter, 1884], 30). By 1647, after a decade in Watertown, he and his family became pioneer settlers on the frontier, 25 miles west. The first child born in the town was Ann and Lawrence's son Joseph, born 29 Feb. 1647 (*Annals of Lancaster*, "Births, Marriages, and Deaths in Lancaster Families" [hereinafter Annals], 313; the speculation that their older son Adam may have been born there in 1645, but unrecorded).

By 5 Aug. 1647 he and Linton had planted "corn" (wheat) on 50 acres which John Cowdall of Boston deeded to John Prescott in Lancaster. He was given 17 acres on The Neck, east of ford or "Wading Place" over the North Nashua River, near where route 70 crosses the river today. There he built the first dwelling (the second building after the George Hill trucking (trading) house) in that town, later the Caleb T. Symmes estate (Nourse 261). Before 1650 he sold this house to John Hall and built another a short way north on 6½ acre lot at what was in 1884 the S. J. S. Vose house.

These first houses were one-story hewn timber structures with a central chimney; later they were two-story clapboard saltbox, with catslide roof to one story at the rear (Herrell).

In 1650 he owned in addition nine acres of intervale land to the south of his father-in-law Richard Linton's, thirteen acres of upland on the east side of Swan's Swamp (east bank of Penacook), and eleven acres of intervale on the east bank of the Penacook. In 1651 he and Linton were paid expenses as witness to a court case in Cambridge involving slander against Elizabeth Hall, wife of John Hall who was in England. He signed the first laws and orders of Lancaster on 15 Jan. 1653. He was an early subscriber to the Covenant for the town, between March and May 1653 (Willard 26, 28). Later that year he and Linton were signers of an agreement with blacksmith John Prescott to build a corn mill in Lancaster, which started grinding wheat in 1654. In 1654 he and Linton petitioned to set up the town of Lancaster (Massachusetts Rec. 4:i:139 in A. Holman), and subscribed to its first laws. He became freeman in 1663 (Annals 261).

He built up an estate of over 300 acres, valued at £ 277 in 1654, having received lot #14 of eleven acres in he second division, and subsequent grants of 1657 and 1659. In 1658 the town ordered the first bridges to be built, one at Waters' ford, to be paid by the Neck residents (Willard 32).

At age 60 he began giving his land to his house carpenter sons as inducement to settle. In 1662 he gave his son Adam 85 acres and his fourth lot of the first division (MD 3:342 in Holman). To son Stephen he gave half his second division land in 1666 (MD 10:78 in same). His son Laurence sold the remaining land in Lancaster amounting to 240 acres in 1688: the seven acre upland houselot, nine acres of intervale (i.e., valley land), thirteen acres of upland, 70 acres of upland in the second division, and 50 acres of swamp in the second division, including ten acres of upland that was once Linton's houselot (MD 10:105 in same).

In King Philip's War Lancaster was sacked by the Indians and abandoned. Although relations between the Indians and the first settlers had been harmonious, by 1675 they had turned hostile. Recent historians blame the white settlers for their insults to people they called savages, and for their greedy sale of guns and rum (Safford 27-8) . More immediate causes were replacement of the Christian sachem with a resentful chief Sagamore Sam, who aligned with King Philip. After eight settlers were killed just north of the Waters, in Aug. 1675, including Anne Waters' niece's husband, George Bennett (Lydia Kibby, dau. of Rachel Linton). The Waters family had moved for security to the Cyprian Stevens garrison house, perhaps the original Waters house. On 10 Feb. 1675/6 fifty five Lancaster people were killed or captured at minister Rowlandson's house just across the Nashua River. This included their Joslin relatives. The Waters family was rescued by troops that arrived belatedly, after their home had been burned and cattle killed. The Waters family fled to their son Stephen's home in Charlestown (Wyman 997 in A. Holman 214). The town was deserted for five years.

Although Waters was 74 at the time of the Lancaster raid, he received a large sum of £ 5/16/6 for military service in defense of Lancaster in King Philip's War (paid 24 Nov. 1676, Bodge 448; Myrtle T. Emberson, *101 Ancestors of John Fay Hinckley* [Los Angeles: the author, 1928], 72). Given their siege, it would be surprising if he did not fire his gun. Lawrence's petition to the General Court in 1676 stated that he was not only elderly but blind (Massachusetts Col. Rec., 5:120 in Holman 94). He died in Charlestown 6 Feb. 1687, age nearly 85 (Lane. VR 20 in A. Holman; Annals state 9 Dec. 1687, 325) .

Lawrence and Ann Waters were ancestors of the eminent genealogist Henry Fitzgilbert Waters (Joseph Gilbert[6], Joseph[5], Benjamin[4-3], Stephen[2]) 1833-1913 (Reg. 68:3).

The LINTON FAMILY of Watertown & Lancaster, 1630.

The Lintons were the first of Sophia Lovis's ancestors to arrive in America, in 1630. Like the Waters family, the Lintons were early settlers of Watertown and Lancaster, fleeing to Woburn after the 1674 massacre.

Lawrence Waters married about 1634 in Watertown ANN(E)[2] LINTON, born in England about 1585-90, and died Charlestown 6 Feb. 1680/1. She was daughter of RICHARD[1] and ELIZABETH LINTON (LENTON, LYNTON). Richard was born in England, and died Lancaster MA 30 March 1665. They came to America by 1630 when he was called for the jury for the inquest into Austin Bratcher's death at Cradock's Plantation (Medford), but did not show up (28 Sept., Holman, 98; Massachusetts Records, Shurtleff ed. 1853, 1-78, cited by Alfred L. Nolman, *Blackman & Allied Families* [Chicago: Nathan Blackman, 1928], 127).

By 1639 he was in Watertown, when the first inventory shows a homelot of eight acres, and a 97 acre farm in the fifth division of upland (Warner, 2: 410). His son-in-law Lawrence Waters testified 8 Dec. 1646 that he had sold in July 1645 his dwelling and lot in Watertown to Robert Sanderson (SD 1:79 in Holman 99).

It was then that he probably moved to Nashaway Plantation with Waters. His house, probably built by him, was east of Lawrence Waters' on the Neck, in the center of today's Lancaster. He was an early subscriber to the Covenants of the town, 4 Sept., 1653 (Henry S. Nourse, *Early Records of Lancaster* [Bowie MD.: Heritage Press, 1993],[hereinafter Nourse] 30). He and his son-in-law had planted wheat in Lancaster by the summer of 1657. In the first division he received lot #2, 20 acres on the neck along the Penacook River (1653). He also had an intervale lot of ten acres at the south end of Quasapankim next to John Whitcomb.

We have noted above that he was involved with his son-in-law with the Hall slander case of 1653, and the building of the first mill that year, and the 1654 petition to set up the town of Lancaster.

His property was valued at £ 90 that year, when he got lot # 12 in the second division. In 1658 he swapped his homelot on which Ralph Houghton had built a house for Houghton's two homelots and 20 acres to the west of his homelot. His final residence was on the nineteenth century main street, west side between Levantia Bradley's and Henry Latham's, opposite the town buildings (Nourse 252).

Linton left no will, but gave his property to his two daughters. To the younger, Ann Waters, in 1659 he gave ten acres of the north part of his houselot including an acre of orchard next to the Waters house, and four acres of intervale the town had given him for taking the land for a highway thru Quasaponakim (now Neck Rd., northeast of center; MD 2:200 in Holman). In 1662 he gave in trust the rest of his land he had not given to Anna and Lawrence Waters to his granddaughter Lidia Bennet until her son John became 19: 45 acres at south end of Bare Hill, eight acres of intervale, six acres at the east end of his houselot, ten acres of Quasaponakim intervale next to the gate, his little meadow, the remaining ten intervale acres and the rest of his houselot with house and buildings (Msx Pro. 14103).

Richard died in Lancaster 30 March 1665 (Annals 322), in the time of peace with the Indians. Richard's wife Elizabeth (whom Holman shows not to be the mother of Ann Waters) was also spared the massacre of relatives and destruction of the town, died in Lancaster between his death and 6 Oct. 1674, probably in the latter year (Holman 100).

Richard's grandson, by his daughter Lidia, George Bennett was killed by the Indians in the first Lancaster massacre 22 Aug. 1675, as was probably their son John, for the land went to Samuel Bennett (Warner 410-411).

Sgt. SAMUEL^2 WATERS, the father of Daniel of Hingham, was the youngest surviving of the 14 children of Lawrence and Ann (Linton) Waters. He was born in Lancaster 14 Nov. 1651 (Annals 314; Harrell makes this 14 Jan. 1651/2; VR state 14 Nov. 1651 in Reg. 16:353), and died Woburn 2 May 1728 (VR 203) . He grew up at the house on the Neck, and followed his father and brothers in the trade of house carpenter (Harrell 9).

After the Lancaster massacre of 1676 he and his wife with two babies fled to his brother Stephen's in Charlestown. By 1679 they had settled in Woburn where his brother Joseph had settled about 1671. His brother seems to have returned to Lancaster in 1681, and in the following year he swapped three lots in Lancaster with his Woburn neighbor James Snow for Snow's house and two acres (Lane, town rec. 1:46 in Harrell). His home was apparently near the Snows, Pierces and Clevelands in Woburn. He also owned land in Heart's Hole in north Woburn, at Milestone Meadow in northwest near the Burlington line, in Reading, and at Maple Meadow plain (Johnson's abstracts of Woburn deeds, 72, 9; MD 12:203, 220, 21:238 in Harrell).

As Sergeant in the Woburn militia he may have taken part in the retaliation for the second massacre at Lancaster in 1697 when his wife's parents were killed and her two sisters taken captive, though his name does not show up in Bodge's exhaustive list (Harrell 11).

Samuel did work for the town on the school and church. He was not well-to-do, ranking in the middle of taxpayers (Harrell).

He died at age 76 in Woburn, on 2 May 1728 (VR 203). It is assumed he is buried next to his wife in Woburn Cemetery, though no stone remains. His will of 15 March 1725 was proved 7 May 1728, leaving £ 12 to his son Daniel in addition to what he had already given (Msx Pro. 23920 in Harrell).

Samuel was the ancestor of President Cleveland (Stephen[8], Richard[7], William[6], Aaron[5-4-3-2], Moses[1]) by his daughter Abigail[3] who m. Aaron[3] Cleveland (G.B. Roberts, Conn. Fam. 3:652 in Harrell; chart by Walter K. Watkins, 1892).

The HUDSON FAMILY of Watertown & Lancaster, 1639.

The Hudsons were also a pioneer family in the frontier at Lancaster, with the ancient English family of Josselyn which traces its roots back to the Norman Conquest, and the founding of the Order of St. Gilbert. As a bricklayer he was responsible for many of the early buildings in Watertown, Lancaster and Cambridge, including the first schoolhouse built in the last place. On the Indian frontier they suffered from repeated raids, which resulted in the deaths of Daniel and Joanna Hudson, and the captivity of several relatives.

Samuel Waters married in Lancaster 21 March 1671/2 MARY[2] HUDSON (Annals 321; Harrell), born Watertown? 7 Sept. 1653 (Lane VR, but prior to res. there), died Woburn 19 Dec. 1721, age 68 (gs; VR states 11th per Harrell). Her gravestone in the Woburn cemetery read in 1890: "Here Lyes ye Body of Mary Waters wife to Samuel Waters Dec'd Dec'mbr 10th 1721 in ye 68 Year of Her Age" (Cutter's Transcripts of Woburn Epitaphs 21, in Harrell).

Mary Hudson was the second daughter and third of eleven children of DANIEL HUDSON, Sr. and his wife JOHANNA(H) . He was baptized at Epping, Essex (about 20 miles NNE of London) 30 July 1620 (Douglas Richardson, "English Origins of Daniel Hudson of Watertown and Lancaster, Massachusetts", TAG 56: 25), the son of DANIEL[A] (Samuel) HUDSON or HUTSON, who married at Roxwell, Essex (HA)AN(N)A JOSSELYN 30 Jan. 1616/7. He was the son of WALTER[8] HUDSON, buried at Epping 24 May 1613, whose estate was administered that year by his son Daniel (Douglas Richardson, "The Grandfather of Daniell Hudson", TAG 64: 148). Daniel and Anna Hudson received gifts under the will of Joseph Joslyn, yeoman of Cranham, Essex, and Daniel was one of two executors (proved 6 Dec. 1645, Reg. 71:30). In 1646 the executors had to sue her brother-in-law Ralph and Simon Joslyn over Bollinghatch farm (30 April 1646, Reg. 71:230 ff.). The case was settled by a family agreement at Westminster 11 March 1646/7 (Diary of Rev. Ralph Josselin, vicar of Earl's Colne, Essex, in Reg. 71:235).

Anna Josselyn was baptized at Roxwell 25 Aug. 1588 (TAG 56:26), daughter of RALPH* JOSSELYN, whose descendants claim right to arms and ancestry to Charlemagne and a companion of William the Conqueror, Sir Gilbert Jocelyne (Reg. 71:235). The family began as lords of Sempringham, Lincolnshire, where the eldest son of Gilbert founded the only English monastic order, the Gilbertines in 1147, recognized by the Pope in 1148 (Ency. Brit, llth ed.12:l 1). Modeled on the Cistercians, Gilbert emphasized hard labor in the fields, which contributed to the agricultural prosperity of the time. It was a double order, of men and women living separately, but worshiping together. The founder died at Sempringham on what is now his Saint's day, 4 Feb. 1189, at age 100 or more. Miracles at his tomb in Sempringham Abbey led to his canonization in 1202 (Reg. 71:236) .

Possible royal ancestry or Magna Charta connections have been searched by Gary Boyd Roberts of NEHGS, who tells me that no evidence has been found, but that the family has been accepted by the Order of Charlemagne. He suggests caution in accepting the line published in the Register in 1912, since it appears to be cobbled together (pers. interview 5 Oct. 1994). Another American branch of the Josselin family had royal ancestry thru Philippa Bradbury-Cromwell-deSomery-d'Aubigny, but our branch is not descended from her (Frederick Weis, *Ancestral Roots of 60 American Colonists* [Baltimore: Genealogical Pub. Co., 1969], 133).

Daniel's marriage is inexplicably recorded under the name Samuel Hutt, which led earlier students to conclude that he was a second husband (TAG 44:125).

Anne's brother Thomas Josselyn came to Hingham and Lancaster, where his son Abraham[2] was killed in the first massacre of 1676, and his wife Ann (assumed without proof to be the eldest daughter of Daniell Hudson, TAG 56:27) and their only child Beatrice, age two, were both taken into captivity, and killed (massacre of 10 Feb. 1676, Annals 324). Abraham's brother Joseph Josselyn was also captured, but fortunately released (Reg. 71:255) .

Daniel[1] Hudson was a clothier in Epping, where his wife Anna was buried 30 Sept.1653 (TAG 56:26).

Daniel[1] came to New England about 1640, when he first appears in Watertown. He was named in the will of an uncle Joseph Hudson of Cranham, Essex in 1642 (TAG 56:26) . As a bricklayer and mason, he helped build the first school in Cambridge in 1647 (Ibid.). This was on the west side of Holyoke Street, halfway between Mt. Auburn and Harvard (Lucian Paige, *History of Cambridge* [Boston: N.D. Houghton, 1877], 370. The president of Harvard, Henry Dunster, hired him and two others to bring 150 cartloads of rock from Charlestown Rock within seven months, build stone foundation and walls, with two chimneys, gable ends in battlement fashion, lath and tile the roof, to be finished by 1 June 1648, with materials supplied by Dunster and Edward Goffe, accepting pay in kind, "whether corne or cattle" at rates of "Wheat at 4'. Ry at 3s6d. Indian [corn] at 3d. Pease at 3s.6d. Early mault at 4s6d. the bushell." As substantial as this sounds, the town tore it down in 1669 and used the stone in the cellar for the minister's house (Ibid., 373).

Hudson's marriage to Johanna has not been found, prior to their first child, Anna's birth 1 Jan. 1648 in Watertown (TAG 56:27). Bond found him on the tax rolls of Watertown in 1652.

But in 1651 he was on the dangerous frontier, as one of the first settlers of Nashaway Plantation (later Lancaster), where he was to die 46 years later (Marion Safford, *The Story of Colonial Lancaster*, [Rutland VT: Tuttle, 1937], 8, 21). His skills were obviously useful in building the huge brick central chimneys and brick lining of the garrison houses.

In 1653 he was back in Watertown, given two acres of common land on the condition that he make brick for the town (Bond 799). His second move from Watertown to Lancaster by 1664 is shown by his release from the brick making condition, and transfer of ten acres to John Chinery (Ibid.).

He and his family moved in 1664 back to Lancaster, on the frontier. There they lived on the opposite (west) bank of the Nashua River from the Waters (Harrell 9). Daniel paid £ 40 for proprietary right on Gibson's Hill, west of the church, bought from Major Simon Willard.

About 1672 he moved back to Cambridge, to the south side of the Charles, in present day Newton (Paige 592) . In 1673 he agreed to take care of William Clemance and his wife Ann in return for all of Clemance's land in Billerica and Newton (Ibid., 511). They may have been related to Daniel's wife Johanna, who is not otherwise identified, perhaps to Clemance's first wife Ann Taylor. In 1672 he bought 20 acres from John Moore in Lancaster, which he gave the next year for his son Daniel on his marriage (TAG 56:27).

In the Indian attack on Lancaster in 1675 his supposed daughter, Anne and her husband Abraham Joslin took refuge in the minister's garrison house, which was burned, Abraham killed, and the pregnant wife and two year old granddaughter Beatrice taken captive and killed (Annals 324; Charles Hudson, *History of the Town of Lexington* [Boston: Wiggin & Lunt, 1868],[hereinafter Hudson], 2:105-6). This foreshadowed his own fate 22 years later.

The sad story of Ann Joslin's death was told in the most famous Indian captivity narrative, that of Mary Rowlandson (*The Narrative of the Captivity and Restoration of Mrs. Mary Rowland son* [Lancaster MA: Town, 1975 annotated text of 1682 orig.]). Twenty four persons, two women and 22 children, were taken captive on 20 Feb. 1675 (6), and moved just one mile the first night to George Hill (7, 66). On 21 Feb. they travelled westward through the wilderness 12 miles to the foot of Mt. Wachusset in the western part of present day Princeton. On the third day, 22 Feb. they travelled southwest about 15 miles to the Indian village of Wenimeset, now Ware MA (9, 67), where Richard Coy was killed. There they stayed ten days when the approach of the white rescuing soldiers cause the Indians to break up the party and to move on (14).

It was here that Ann, who was only a week from giving birth talked of escaping: "The woman, viz.. Goodwife Joslin, told me she should never see me again, and that she could find in her heart to run away. I wished her not to run away by any means, for we were near thirty miles from any English town and she very big with child and had but one week to reckon, and another child in her arms, two years old, and bad rivers there were to go over, and we were feeble with our poor and coarse entertainment. I had my Bible with me; I pulled it out and asked her whether she would read. We opened the Bible and lighted on Psal. 27, in which Psalm we especially took notice of that ver.ult.: Wait on the Lord: be of good courage, and he shall strengthen thy heart; wait I say on the Lord."

Mary Rowlandson was taken northwest on 27 or 28 Feb., and soon redeemed. However, Mrs. Joslin kept pestering the Indians to let her go home for her confinement. With the rescue parties closing in, about to arrive on 2 or 3 March (69), she was unable to travel. Mary Rowlandson tells of her death, near Wenimisset about 28 Feb.:

"I must part from that little company that I had... neighbors, some of which I never saw afterward...Amongst them also was that poor woman before mentioned, who came to a sad end, as some of the company told me in my travel. She having much grief upon her spirit about her miserable condition, being so near her time, she would be often asking the Indians to let her go home. They, not being willing to do that and yet vexed by her importunity, gathered a great company together about her and stripped her naked, and set her in the midst of them. And when they had sung and danced about her (in their hellish manner) as long as they pleased, they knocked her on the head, and the child in her arms with her. When they had done that, they made a fire and put them both into it, and told the other children that were with them that if they attempted to go home, they would serve them in like manner. The children said she did not shed one tear, but prayed all the while." (15; Mrs. Bigelow's "Reminiscences of Marlborough" in Emma Coleman, *New England Captives* [Portland ME: Southworth Press, 1925], 1:306).

On 6 Oct. 1690 Daniel Hudson was admitted as townsman of Charlestown, as bricklayer. But in March 1692 he was back in Lancaster where he and his two sons were ordered to take refuge with the military garrison when danger threatened, but "at present they may Continue in their own house, it having a good Fort." (Reg. 43:371).

In July 1692 an Indian raid killed Peter Joslin's wife and three children while he was out working in the fields (Peter Joslin's account to Harrington in the "Century Sermon" of 1753, in Coleman 1:306; Annals 325). They took another child, Peter, age 6, and Mrs. Joslin's 17 year old sister Elizabeth Howe captive. Elizabeth Howe escaped her sister's fate because the "sweet sounds" of her voice captivated the captors. She was ransomed four years later, in 1696, for £ 3/18, and married to Thomas Keyes, who had promised to wait for her (Coleman 1:307) . She kept some Indian ways, such as sitting on the floor.

Daniel made his will 2 June 1695 in which he owned two houselots of 20 acres each, on Gibson's Hill and the John Moore lot, the whole extending from Mrs. Ware's Corner to the site of 1676 massacre at the Rowlandson Garrison (Annals 134).

Daniel and his wife with two grandsons were surprised while working in the fields, and killed by the Indians in the attack of 11 Sept. 1697, and their two spinster daughters Joanna age 37 and Elizabeth age 40 either killed or taken into captivity, where they died (Annals 326, Coleman 1:299). The basis for the confusion of their fate appears to be that 5 months after the massacre their bodies had not been found, for the surviving Hudson children signed an agreement in Dec. 1697 "for our sisters wearing cloaths we mutualy agree to Leave them undevided at present...hoping that one of them namely: either Johanah or Elizabeth may be yet alive...& also in case that either of our said sisters shall by Gods goodness be againe Reduced from captivity that hen we do farther oblidge our selves as aforesaid to allow & pay unto either of them that so Returne her portion double or two shares through all that would of Right have appertained to either of them..." (Middlesex Pro. cited by Coleman, 1:309; 14 Oct. 1697?). The massacre occurred because garrisons had been left open while the people were in the fields, and the Indian party of about 40 took them by surprise at noon, killing 26 including the minister (Gov. Stoughton to Gov. of Conn. 14 Sept. 1697 in Massachusetts Arch, by Hudson; see Worc. Mag. 11:296).

The WHITON FAMILY of Hingham, 1647.

Although they came to Hingham a decade after the founding of Hingham, the Whiton family became the most prominent one, and largest landholder in the south part of town called Liberty Plain, where the ancient home of our ancestor Enoch Whiton still stands as built in 1680. This was near a house burned by the Indians, the Whitons being military leaders in every war.

Daniel[3] Waters married in Hingham 10 March 1719/20 ABIGAIL[3] WHITON of Liberty Plain, South Hingham, descendant of several Hingham pioneers. She was born in Liberty Plain 8 Sept. 1697, and died in Hingham 3 Sept. 1738 (Lin 290, 280). She was granddaughter of JAMES[1] WHITON (WITON, WHITING or WYTON), who came to town relatively late, by 1647, but soon became one of the largest landholders.

James was once assumed to be the eight year old Jeremy=Jamie on the manifest of the *Elizabeth & Ann.* 1635, with his parents, Thomas and Awdry Whitton from Benendon, Kent, the home of the Bate family (Planters 156, citing PRO and Founders 20, 22, 24, 27-30; Augustus S. Whiton, *The Whiton Family in America* (New London: E. E. Darrow, 1932, 19). But Leonard Tibbetts corrected this in Reg. 123:228-30, showing that our James came from Hook Norton, Oxfordshire. A James was baptized in that Cotswold village in 1624, (Banks 134 citing Aspinwall in Bos. Rec. Comm. 30) . His father THOMAS[A] was the son of WILLIAM[B] WHITON and CATHERINE ARDE(R)NE of Hook Norton, according to a power of attorney signed by James (Ibid. 19). Descendants claim descent from William Whitton of Nethercott, Oxfordshire, who bore arms (Ibid., 18), but the claim was questioned by the NEHGS heraldry committee. The coat of arms is shown in Barry, John S., *Town of Hanover* [Boston: Bazin & Chandler, 1853], 419).

James gave a letter of attorney to Richard Betscomb of Hingham on 6 Oct. 1647 to collect a legacy of Thomas Whiton's estate in Hook Norton (Whiton citing Genea. of New England 4:172).

At age 21 James[1] signed the compact for the Nashaway Plantation, to become Lancaster, to settle there (7 April 1654, Nourse 30). However, he returned to Hingham where he had married MARY BEAL(E) on 30 Dec. 1647 (HJ 20). The town gave him land that year: half of a 3 acre lot at Nutty Hill shared with Onesephorus Marsh in compensation for land taken from their houselots for the town way; also an acre of Salt Marsh, the first lot in the Conyhasset third division, bounded by the Salt River on the south, and on other three sides by the town land (Gushing 70, confirmed 3 Dec. 1659).

He became a farmer in Liberty Plain, where he built a large estate, with holdings in neighboring Abington, Hanover and Scituate. This gave him top rank in the hierarchy that was to become the dominant elite of town (Hart 38). He became freeman in 1660.

Since many of the original lots were so narrow as to be unusable, Whiton picked up many pieces. He swapped several pieces with the town (TR 133, 136). In 1664 the town gave him title to the four acres where he had built a house on Liberty Plain (15 Aug., TR 139). In the big division of common lands in 1669 he was entitled to five shares, which gave him 5/11 share with Mathew Hawke in lot 19 (21 acres; TR 171, 173) and 80 (31 acres; TR 176). He got five separate shares in the third division, in lot #69 of ten+ acres in the first part (south of Accord Brook to the Norwell line, near Wanders Dr. 1994), and ten+ more in the southeast corner of Cohasset (TR 183, Big 139). In the fourth division of 1677 he got lot #75, west of Old Ward Street above its junction with Whiting Street (Rt. 58). In the division of the northeast corner he got lot 20, today west of Rt. 228 or Hull Street near Pine and Spruce Sts.

At this time he got into a quarrel with the town, claiming an acre of fresh meadow on Scituate Pond, which he offered to give to the town if they'd recompense him (TR 168) . The matter went to mediation in 1672, Whiton choosing Capt. John Hubbard, and the town John Jacob.

His five shares got him seven acres on the Weymouth line in lot #76 in the Fourth Division of 1677 (TR 207).

As a resident of the south side of town, he was one of the minority who had their names recorded as opposing the building of a new meetinghouse in 1680 (TR 220). He served on the jury in Boston in 1674, 1683, 1686, and Surveyor of highways in 1690, and Tithingman for 1694.

As an Indian fighter during King Philip's War the Indians somehow got his gun and coat, for which he was repaid in 1675 (LH 237), and his house in Liberty Plain was one of five burned by Indians in Hingham, on 20 April 1676 (HJ 198: LH 232, 247), less than 3 months before the war ended with Philip's death at Mt. Hope. Nevertheless, he was one of the largest contributors to the Old Ship Church building of 1681, giving £ 50.

His will of 29 Sept. 1708 mentions his son Enoch, of whom more after we deal with Whiton's wife. Among his descendants was New York yachtsman Henry[10] Devereaux Whiton (Nathan[9], William[8], Luther[7], John[6], Jonathan[5],Thomas[4-3-2], 1871-1930), for whom William Beebe named Mt. Whiton in the Galapagos in thanks for his sponsorship of the 1925 expedition; Reg.

85:430).

Enoch Whiton House, Hingham, built 1680

The BEAL FAMILY of Hingham, 1636.

The Beals were among the first settlers of Hingham, allied by marriage to the founding minister, Rev. Hobart, and large landholders and holders of town offices.

James Whiton's marriage of 1647 connected him with two of the founding families of Hingham, the Beals and the Hobarts. His wife, MARY[2] BEAL(E) was baptized Wymondham (pron. Windham) , Norfolk (about three miles east of Hingham, near Norwich) 28 Oct. 1626 (*NEXUS* 4:88), and died Liberty Plain 12 Dec. 1696, age 70 (John D. Beals, *The Beals Genealogy* [N.Y.: author, 1927]). She received 30 shillings from the will of her cousin John Beales (1658, Reg. 9:38).

She was the daughter of immigrant JOHN BEALE) and his first wife FRANCES RIPLEY, whom he married at Wymondham 11 June 1616 (*NEXUS*). Frances was sister of weaver William[1] Ripley, the immigrant from Old Hingham to Hingham on the *Diligent* in 1638 (Cushing's record in Reg. 15:27; Planters 194). The names of their parents have not been published despite promise by Torrey in TAG 13:263n. She was buried in Wymondham 16 March 1629/30 (Ibid.).

John Beal(e) was baptized 8 May 1593 in the church at Wramplingham, Norfolk, where his father Rev. JOHN[A] BEAL(ES) was Rector, and his third wife MARTHA STONE. EDWARD BEALES, Rector of Wramplingham and MARTHA STONE of Hingham Barrow were issued a marriage licence on 8 Sept. 1586--the confusion of Edward and John is not resolved. Edward Beal died 1612, and Martha 1617. After Frances's death in 1630, on 13 July John[1] remarried (2) Nazareth Hobart, sister of Rev. Peter Hobart (1604-78) who was to become first minister of Hingham, Massachusetts

John[1] Beal, shoemaker, came over on the *Diligent*, with three other ancestral families, the

Ripleys, Stephen Lincoln and Matthew Hawke. The ship sailed under Captain John Martin from Ipswich, Suffolk on the North Sea in June 1638, arriving in Boston, 10 Aug. (Planters 192-4, citing Gushing Mss.). With him was his second wife, 8 children and two servants, settling in Hingham (Hingham town clerk Daniel Cushing's record Reg. 15:26) . In a month, on 18 Sept., he was given six acres for a houselot on the southwest corner of today's South and Hersey Streets, at Goold's Bridge. This is the site today of his son John[2] Junior's 1699 house, at 184 South Street

He became freeman on 13 March 1639, and held many town offices over 44 years. As a shoemaker, it is appropriate that his first office was leatherviewer in 1644 (TR 98). He was selectman for seven years, 1649, 1651, 1654, 1658, 1667, 1668, 1679. He served as Representative for 11 years, 1649-59, which, as Hart notes was to become in the next century "government by hereditary oligarchy" dominated by wealthy landowners (Hart 52). Other offices were surveyor (1655) , waywarden (1657), setter of tax rates (1647), and odd jobs of hiring a herdsman who became the first settler of Cohasset (1647; Big 134), and juryman in Boston (1649) .

On 15 July 1639 he was granted 21 acres of land: a planting lot of ten acres on the Weymouth River, two acres of saltmarsh at the same, next to Chamberlin's planting lot, 1½ acres of fresh meadow in Turkey Meadow on the Cohasset line, and 6 acres of planting ground on Pheasant Hill abutting the sea, which he bought from his brother-in-law Joshua Hubbard, but returned all the last to Thomas Hubbard in 1654 (TR 66; confirmed 2 Feb. 1645, VR fiche 4). He consolidated a big farm on the river by swapping two pieces, eight acres on the Plain which he bought from Jarvice Gould between Bacon and Eyebrook, for six acres of upland next to his Weymouth River lot. He also gave up his 20 acre Great Lot on the Plain between Gibbs and Gushing for ten acres of planting lot on the Weymouth River (7 Feb., VR fiche 4). His father-in-law Edmund Hobart also gave him half an acre of meadow in Turkey Meadow (Ibid.). He bought four acres on Weymouth Neck from shoemaker Henry Chamberin in 1647, east of his own lot (Reg. 139:132, citing SD 8:455-8). In 1652 the town gave him "all those Swampy pieces that he hath now fenced in" on the river (TR 119). In the division of lands in 1669 his ten shares out of 700 entitled him to lot #12 (TR 158). In the second division of 1670 he got a large piece of land north of the intersection of Whiting and Gushing Streets.

In the first division of Cohasset marshes around Little Harbor the next year his 12 shares got him lot #62 of 23 acres, 2 rods, 8 rods, 2 shares of which he split with his son Jacob, the rest with his son John Jr. (TR 170, 174). In the third Cohasset Division of 1670 Beal and son got lot #20 of 26 upland acres on the south side of Great Neck, and 24 acres of marsh on the other side of the river south of Scituate Pond (TR 182, Big. 138-9), and the 39th lot of several acres of saltmarsh west of Robert Jones and the river, which went to Mathew Gannet by 1702 (Misc. Wills, reel 76-19, 44).

That same year the Neck Fences were divided in the north end of town, Beal getting ten acres in the first division and one rod 12 feet in the second (lots 34 and 4, TR 186). Most interesting is that Beal is no longer shoemaker, but a seaman, clearly referring to the original proprietor, not his son. In the fourth division of 1677 he and his son John jointly drew lot 20 with 34 acres, 2 roods and 24 rods for 12 shares on the Weymouth line close to today's interchange of Derby Street and Rt. 3 (TR 205, Big 137, Hart 34). He held lot 34 south of the junction of Turkey Hill Rd. with Leavitt Street, and lot 60, now at the west edge of Wompatuck State Park, south of Triphammer Pond and Union Street.

The Beal family became the third largest landowner in Hingham, with 437 acres, after the Hobarts and Cushings (Hart 35).

When his second wife Nazareth died 23 Sept. 1658 (HJ 108), he took a third wife, on 10 March 1659 (HJ 109), Mary, widow of his old friend and fellow immigrant from Hingham, Nicholas Jacob. He died in his garden 1 April 1688 (HJ 272; Hobart calls him uncle). Judge Sewall says he was 100, but his baptismal record makes him short of 95 (Beal 5). He made a will 27 Sept. 1687 (we have not found whether Enoch Whiton was named).

Among John Beal's descendants, and cousins of Sophia Lovis, was Elbridge Gerry, father of the Gerrymander, named for his oddly shaped Congressional district in Essex County (mother Elizabeth Greenleaf, Enoch, Sarah Beal, Nathaniel[2], John[1]; *NEXUS*, 3:237) .

The seventh child of Mary[2] Beal and James[1] Whiton was Sgt. ENOCH[2] WHITON. He was born in Liberty Plain of Hingham, 8 March 1659/60, baptized 13 March (HJ 109), and died there 5 May 1714. He inherited these parts of his father's land: half a lot of fresh meadow east of the river at Mast Bridge bought from Richard Dudley and Humphrey Johnson; part of a lot of Hingham Fourth Div. bought from Jeremiah Beal ¼ of "small share" lot; 2½ acres of Hingham common land; front part of his Third Div. land in Cohasset; and land given him for his house (Barry 420).

He built there in 1680 the two story house which still stands at 1083 Main Street, on the northwest corner of Pine Grove Rd., south of the Catholic church. The oldest house in Liberty Plain, it is compared to the John Alden house in Duxbury as "superb survivals of English folk architecture" (National Historic Register, Hingham, #695). The irregular placement of the windows, and off-center doorway suggest "medieval tolerance of asymmetry [which] persisted long after the abandonment of medieval details" according to Fiske Kimball's Domestic Architecture, 17. It is a plain farm structure, without later changes to its plain corners, simple door with seven lights above, unpainted shingle sheathing, 9 over 6 windows with thick muntins between, a stone foundation, and solid shape.

The house was then in the wilderness, beset with wolves and Indians. In 1687 Enoch Whiton killed eight wolves, earning the town bounty of £ 20 (Big 180). His father's house nearby was burned by Indians in 1676.

Enoch was a trader by profession. He served the town in a number of offices, starting in 1691 to prosecute owners of unfettered horses (TR 242), surveyor of highways (1692, 7), fenceviewer (1695), tithingman (1699), Constable in 1703 and Selectman 1712, and Sergeant in the militia. In 1709 he was one of the signers of a public defense of Mahitable Warren of Plymouth against the "sispition" that she was a witch (Whiton 24).

He died in Liberty Plain 5 May 1714, leaving a large estate of £ 1,021 (Whiton 25), most to his widow, except for £ 50 for each of four daughters, including Abigail. He was probably buried in the Liberty Plain Cemetery where most of his progeny and namesakes are buried, though no stone remains (the town sold the lot to his son Enoch and others 28 Feb. 1755, Lincoln I:ii, 375)

.

His father's military leadership was carried on by the numerous descendants buried there. There are fine gravestones of three sons of Enoch who fought in the Revolution (the first two commanders of companies: Enoch[4] 1733-78; Elias[4] 1747-1817; and Elijah[4] 1737-97. At least seven other relatives served in the Revolution, including company captain Zachariah[5], and two who were killed: Joseph[5] at Ticonderoga, and Hosea[5] on the Canada expedition. Jonathan[4], was a soldier on the Crown Point Expedition of 1755 under Capt. Thaxter (Jonathan[3], Thomas[2]) . There were three War of 1812 fighters, Capt. Elias[4], Major Walter[5] who was killed at the battle of Bridgewater (Elijah[4], Enoch[3]), and Archelaus[6] who enlisted on the frigate *Constitution* for duty on the Great Lakes, and was never heard from again (Benjamin[5-4-3], James[2]; Lin 295 7 30).

Enoch's great-grandson Levi Lincoln was Jefferson's Attorney General, 1801-5 and Acting Secretary of State (also Delegate to the Confederation Congress 1781, U.S. Representative 1800, Lt. Governor of Massachusetts 1807, declined appointment as Supreme Court Justice in 1811; Lin 1:ii, 339), and Levi's son Levi Lincoln became Governor of Massachusetts (Whiton 25).

The STEPHEN LINCOLN FAMILY of Hingham, 1638.

Our ancestry includes one of the several Lincoln families of Hingham, that of Stephen, the farmer. Although they came from the same part of England as the other Lincolns, ancestors of the President and the Revolutionary General, the connection has not been established. Nevertheless, as early proprietors of the town, our Lincolns had large landholdings and civic responsibilities. Their house, in the original settlement, was the town garrison, where Stephen Lincoln sounded the drum to change the guard at sunset and sunrise.

Enoch[2] Whiton married in Hingham 11 Jan. 1687/8 MARY[3] LINCOLN (HJ 270), granddaughter of two other Hingham pioneers who came over on the *Diligent.* She was born in Hingham 27 Dec. 1662 (HJ 114), and died there 2 Oct. 1716, two years after her husband. Her gravestone is in High Street Cemetery.

She was granddaughter of Hingham founders STEPHEN and MARGARET LINCOLN. They arrived in Boston 10 Aug. 1638 as passengers on the *Diligent*, Capt. John Martin, with their son Stephen[2] Jr., and his brother Thomas, a husbandman like himself, and settled in Hingham (Planters 194). This was a year after the ancestors of President Lincoln, Samuel, came from an area near their origin in Norfolkshire. There is no known relation of these two Hingham families except frequent intermarriages, so that we cannot claim any blood ties to the president.

Stephen and Margaret came from the Hobart's parish of Wymondham (pron. Windham), Norfolk (Gushing's Rec., Reg. 15:27; William E. Lincoln, *Some Descendants of Stephen Lincoln* [N.Y.: Knickerbocker Press, 1930], 15). They were, however, members of the low church congregation of Rev. Robert Peck of Hingham, who persuaded them to sell their possessions and go to America. The births and wedding of Stephen and Margaret have not been found in the area, though a Stephen, under 21 at his father Stephen's death in 1589 is mentioned as grandson of Robert Lynkon, a clothier of East Bergholt, Suffolk, 10 miles from Ipswich, from which the Diligent sailed (Ibid., 14-16). The marriage of his mother Joan, who is mentioned in his will, has not been found.

On arrival in Hingham, Mass, in Sept. 1638 Stephen was granted a three acre houselot at Goold's Bridge just east of John Beal, on the east side of Hersey Street (then Austin's Lane) at 182 South Street It was in his fortified garrison house where Clement Bate's granddaughter Anna[3] (Samuel[2]) was born 12 April 1676 when villagers fled here during the Indian attack (LH 224, Lin 39). The house at that site today at #182 was built by his great-grandson Matthew (David[3], Stephen[2]) .

Margaret, his wife, was buried 13 June 1642 (HJ 15), 3 weeks after the birth of their only child born in America, Susan, who was baptized Hingham 22 May 1642 (HJ 15) and died at Matthew Cushing's, age seven on 4 Nov. 1649 (HJ 22; Lin 476).

In less than six years of arrival he needed money, and sold off the land he had been given by the town: three acre houselot and house to Thomas Joslin, three acres west of John Beal, five acres of Nicholas Lobden's land he bought from Richard Ozborne, his 14 acre Great Lot #23 on the Plain, and an acre of upland north of the road to John Otis's house next to the Swamp (14 Feb. 1644, VR fiche 4).

Stephen probably had a hand in building the first meetinghouse in 1644 when the town gave him discretion on the height of the gallery (TR 100). He served as Selectman in 1654. Stephen's will was made three days before his death on 11 Oct. 1658 (HJ 108). He stated that his mother, widow Joane Lincolne, should have "the new End of my house that is to say, the Parlor, the low room only" for her lifetime, the use of his household goods, and a cow and 2 goats to be kept by his son. Except for some small gifts to his brother Thomas and his daughter, the residue went to his son, who was executor (text in reel 76-14) . The inventory of 18 Aug. 1658 by Matthew Hawke gave a modest value of £ 179/10 (Reg. 9:38). His mother Joane Lincolne, whose maiden name is unknown, may be the "widdow Lincoln dyed" in Hingham 2 Dec. 1662 (HIT 113).

Stephen's only surviving child was STEPHEN[2] Jr., born Wymondham, Norfolk before 1638, and died Hingham, Massachusetts 17 Sept. 1692 (HJ 279). He was a carpenter who lived at his father's homestead at #182 South Street, opposite Goold's Bridge.

Stephen was hired as town drummer, and given 20 shillings "to maintayne His Drum" (1659, TR 130) and 10 sh. in 1662 (LH 216). It was the duty of the town drummer to beat the change of watches at sunrise and sunset (HL 216), logically since his garrison house was the village refuge. He seems to have got careless, for 14 years later the town clerk recorded, "Stephen Lincoln the Drummer shall have but 10 sh allowed him for repairing the Drum the last year, because he did not keep the Drum in repair all the year as he ought to do." (1673, TR 196) . In 1667 he had been Constable and did some surveying, which led to his appointment as town Surveyor for the big division of town land in 1669.

In the first division of 1669 his five shares got him lot #72 (TR 152). They gave him 9+ acres in lot #14 of the first Cohasset Division, a triangle of 14+ acres in lot #50 in the second, and 10+ acres in each of the two parts of the third, in lot #77. In the northeast corner's division he got lot #21, west of Rt. 228 (Hull Street, the Cohasset line) near Walnut Street In the fourth division of 1677 his five shares gave him lot #30 of 7½ acres on the Weymouth line near Abington Street in the southwest corner of Hingham today (TR 206; Hart 34). In 1678 the town allowed him to build a dam over the run at Bear Swamp by the cartway to Nutty Hill, thus drowning some common land (TR 210).

He became a freeman in 1680, and served as Selectman in 1685, as well as Surveyor of Highways in 1689, on the committee to regulate sheep keeping in 1692, and Constable in 1698.

The rowdy behavior of boys in church caused the town to commission him "to look to the boys in the Meeting House in the time of public worship and to do thir best endeavour to keepe them from playing in meeting, or from running out of the meeting house to play abroad." (1689; TR 236).

He was evidently literate, his signature appearing on a deed of 1692 in which Elizabeth Thaxter paid him £ 10 for unsettled rights on Squirrel Hill which he had bought from John Lobdell, south of the road to Captains Tent (SD 15:185-6 in Thaxter Coll. reel 76-19). He died Hingham 17 Sept. 1692 (Lin 476).

The HAWKE FAMILY of Hingham, 1638.

Our ancestors include the second most distinguished founder of the town of Hingham, Mathew Hawke. After the minister, he was the most highly educated, so held the posts of first town clerk and schoolmaster. For his community services he received almost as much land as the other first proprietors. The site of his house in Hingham Center is today named Matthew Hawke Square.

Stephen[2] Lincoln married in Hingham Feb. 1659/60 ELIZABETH[2] HAWKE (HJ 110; Reg. 11:253). She was baptized Hingham 14 July 1639 (HJ 11), and died there 4 Nov. 1713, age 74 (L 476). She was daughter of two other passengers on the *Diligent* in 1638, MATHEW[1] and MARGARET HAWKE, who came from Cambridge, but earlier from Ipswich, Norfolk (Banks

Ms.; Cushing's Rec. Reg. 15:27). With them came a servant, John Fearing. Hawke was born about 1610, and died Hingham 11 Dec. 1684 (HJ 215), age 74 according to his gravestone (Sav. 2:381).

MATHEW (always spelled with one "T" in his records) HAWKE was one of the most distinguished early settlers of Hingham. The square in west of the Hingham Common opposite his homesite, the Hawkes-Fearing House of 1783 is named in his honor. Hawke lived at 303 Main Street in Hingham Center where he was given a four acre houselot in 1638 between the Plain and the Cedar Swamp, two lots south of Thomas Lawrance (Cushing's Mss. 42 on microfilm, Hingham Library; house where John Hancock's mother was born was torn down and replaced by the present one at 303 Main Street in Loring 89).

He was born in England about 1610, perhaps a younger brother of Winthrop Fleet immigrant Adam Hawkes of Hingham, England (Ethel F. Smith, *Hawkes Talks*, 14:63-4). He died in Hingham 11 Dec. 1684, age 74 (gravestone, Lin 294).

Hawke had married in Ipswich, England, just before the *Diligent* left, to MARGARET NELLSON of Newton, Cambridgeshire (7 miles south of Cambridge), on 21 April 1638 (Suffolk Eng. licenses cited Ibid.; her maiden name was assumed to be TOWLE (Elizabeth G. Fuess, "Gushing and Allied Families" typescript, Andover, 1931, 225, citing *Transcript* query 6797, 21 March 1928) . They arrived on the *Diligent* on 10 Aug. 1638, then went to Hingham and where he became freeman 18 May 1642 (Sav. 2:381).

In Hingham he served as first Town Clerk 18 April 1646 (VR fiche 4) and again 1666-69 (Sprague's copy, Hingham Records, 2: 141, 156; James Hawke is first clerk, 1 June 1655, 136, then Daniel Gushing, before and after Mathew). He was Selectman in 1645, 1654, 1659, 1663, 1664, and 1663, and schoolmaster 1679-83 {officially, Lin 1:ii, 110; but he was given land as early as 1639 for teaching, see below).

In divisions of town commons, Hawke became one of the major grantees of land, placing him equal to the leading proprietors. Gushing list his lands (42, reel 76-1 copied from f.78 of Great Book):

1639 [1650]. 14 acre Great Lot in the Great Plain, in the first furlong from the center, between 2 highways, south of John Foulsham, west of Jonas Ruston.

1639 [1649]. Three acre planting lot in the Playn Neck, south of John Foulsham, north of Thomas Johnson, east of John Tower and west of John Winchester. To this he added by purchase from Samuel Packer John Foulsham' s five acre lot to the north, south of Thomas Barne (reel 76-19, 46).

1639. An acre each of salt and fresh meadow at Nantasket. This was taken from him in exchange for four acres at Turkey Hill, also for "his pains" as Town Clerk (no date; Misc. Wills & Deeds, 45, reel 76-19). To this was added two more acres "in satisfaction for teaching school".

1639. ½ acre meadow in Turkey Meadow, given by Nicholas Hodgsdon, east of Thomas Hubbard and west of marsh (also TR 93).

1647. An acre of saltmarsh in the 14th lot of the first Cohasset Division, south of John Leavitt's meadow and north of Simon Burr.

1647. An acre and half a saltmarsh at Cohasset, the 29th lot of the first division, which the town first gave to John Tower, cooper, west of the Cove, south of the Creek, north of Daniel Gushing and se of John Leavitt (reel 76-19, 42-3).

1647. An acre of saltmarsh in lot 31 of the third Cohasset Division, west of the river, south of John Tower and north of Edward Runton.

1649. Two boatloads of cordwood cut on common land at the Ware River (TR 110).

1669 as pay for the job of Town Clerk he was given four acres of upland at Turkey Hill next to Francis James, in exchange for an acre of meadow at Nantasket (TR 155).

1670. Six shares in the divisions of town commons entitled him to lot #77 in the First

Division (TR 159).

1670. This was shared with James Whiton in the first division of Cohasset (TR 171: lot 19 of 21+ acres, 31 acres in lot 80 in the second).

1670. In the Second Division his lot was in Liberty Plain north of Blaisdell Rd..

1671. In the first part of the Third Division he got lot #54 of eight acres, 12 rods extending from where South Pleasant Street crosses Accord Brook southwards. In the second part of the Third Division he got a narrow strip on the Cohasset line, six acres and rods in lot #55.

1672. The share with James Whiton is separated in the third Cohasset division in which he got six shares, which gave him 13 acres on the first part, and 12+ acres of the second part (TR 173, 176, 183).

In the division of Neck fences he got lot 38 of three acres, and lot 7 of 12 rods 8 feet (TR 186).

1677. In the Fourth Division he got lot 67 of nine acres near the Weymouth line close to today's Derby Street.

At an early date he bought part of George Russell's six acre planting lot at Old Planters Hill northwest of the Salt meadow, and Thomas Andrews on the other three sides (reel 76-19, 42; not 1635 as shown, since he came in 1638).

Hawke made out a long will on 24 Sept. 1684, leaving 30 books, all religious (6:485 in reel 76-14). His son James got a dozen books with the bulk of the estate. Each daughter got a book of Norton's sermons, and Elizabeth Lincoln also got Norton's *Expositions*, a little book "the poor doubting Christian", "A Treatise of Faith", and share with her brother in "my great writing book of Mr. Goodwin's Sermons and Mr. Tory's Sermons". He preserved the notes of the minister, Rev. Norton, which he left to his son. All his children got an equal interest in his book of Martyrs " because I would have all my children acquainted with the sufferings of the Martyrs of Jesus."

His wife Margaret died nine months before her husband, in Hingham, on 18 March 1683/4 (HJ 213). He was buried in the Hingham Cemetery behind the Old Ship Church, but was removed to Central Burying Ground west of his house, with the gravestone, which Lincoln copied as follows:

HERE LYES Y^{E}
BODY OF MATHEW
HAWKE
AGED 74 YEARS
DEC^{D} DECEMBER Y^{e}
11th 1684

(Lin 1:ii, 371). She was probably buried beside him in the Hingham Cemetery.

Mathew and Margaret Hawke were ancestors of John Hancock, through his mother Mary^{4} (James$^{3-2}$, Matthew^{1}) Hawke, who married Rev. John Hancock; *NEXUS* 3:237). The patriot was third cousin of Sophia's grandmother Sarah Waters, and also a fourth cousin of her father thru the Clarke and Coy lines.

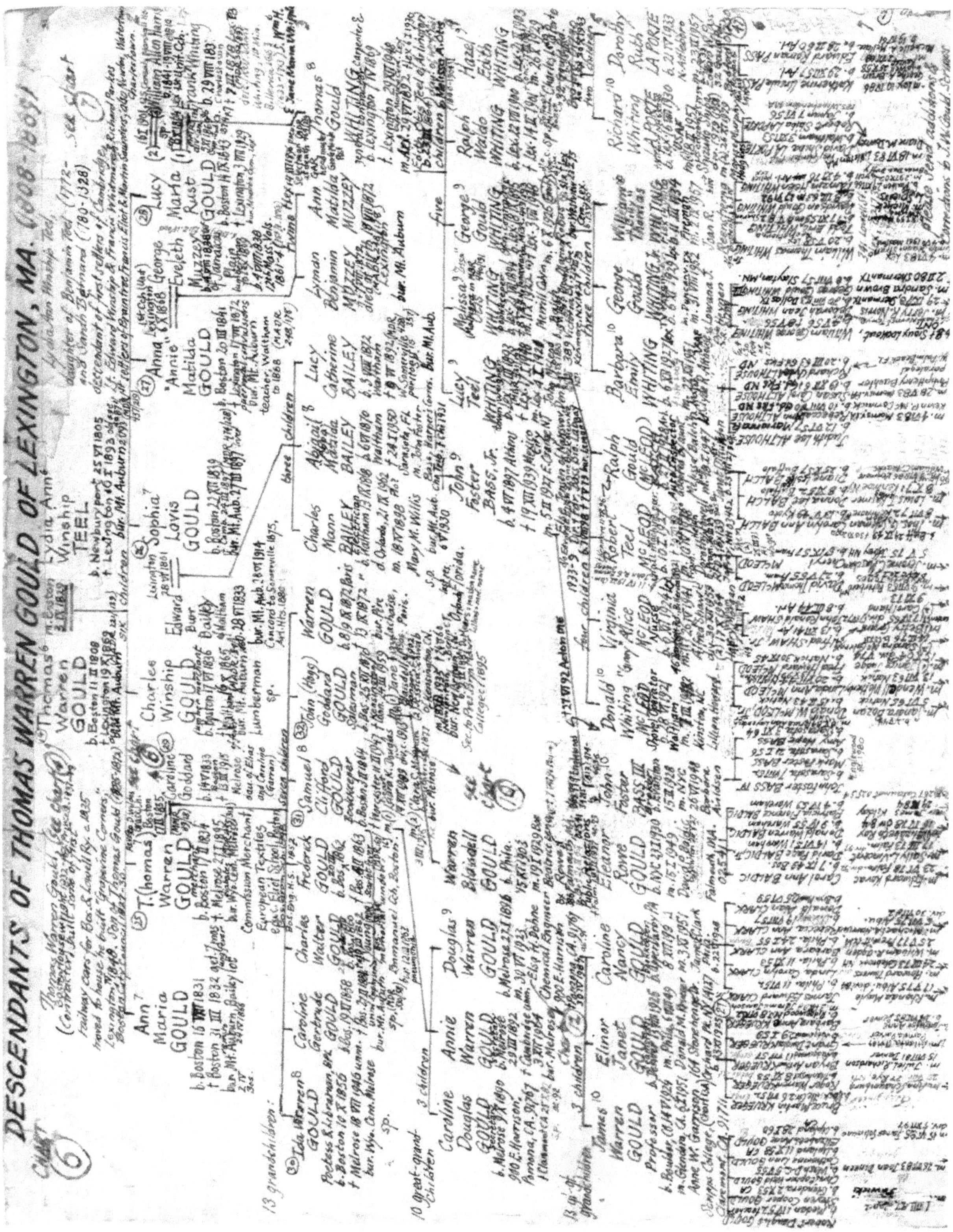
CHART 6
DESCENDANTS OF THOMAS WARREN GOULD OF LEXINGTON, MA. (1808-1889)

Chapter IX

THOMAS^6 GOULD Jr. 1808-69
Builder

THOMAS^6 WARREN GOULD (Thomas^5, James^4, Thomas^3, William^2, Thomas^1), was born in Boston, MA, 11 Feb. 1808 and died in Lexington, MA 1869 in his sixty first year, of diabetes. He was the eldest of seventeen children of Thomas^5 Gould, housewright of Boston, and his first wife Sophia Lovis. He never used the middle name Warren, always signing documents and letters as Thomas Gould Jr. The name Warren does not appear in any of the ancestors, so we infer that he was named for the famous patriot General Joseph Warren who was killed near his father's home in Charlestown, at the Battle of Bunker Hill, in 1775, an event that also marked the opening of the Charles River bridge, in 1786, the construction of which his grandfather James oversaw.

In character he seems to have been a great deal like his father: serious and sober, faithful to his wife, home loving to the extent that he never traveled, a plain and frugal Yankee who wasted no time or words. Though educated only to grade school level, he was a skillful Jack-of-all-constructions who could build a tall structure from scratch, do the carpentry, masonry and shingle the roof and sides.

He seems to have lacked some of his father's strong qualities of good health, love of family, business acumen, public spirit and religious piety that led Thomas Gould Senior to be a leader in the abolition of slavery. Poor health began early, and led to his dying before his father, of a neglected infection from a raccoon bite. Through much of his life he seems to have been in financial trouble, or at least seldom making the great investments in real estate that his father did. Yet at the end he left a modest estate of five acres and a house at Grapevine Corner, and $500 cash. He never seems to have traveled out of the state, going only as far as his wife's birthplace in Newburyport, and a trip to Cape Cod for lumber. His public service was confined to two services on jury duty. His writing was about at the grade school level of his father, and used none of the pious expressions. Early separated from his father's Baptist church, he held pews in the Universalist Church in Boston and in the First Church Unitarian of Lexington, but does not appear to have been an active member, though his children went to church most Sundays.

We get a glimpse of humor in a letter his daughter wrote during the Civil War when Lucy was living in Kentucky with her husband who would not let her go outside alone: "Father says 'whiskey makes guns go off in the wrong direction sometimes, dont sit in the doorway and get shot at'. I laugh at him and tell him you will." (Annie Gould to Lucy Whiting 2 July 1865).

Most striking were his differences with his eldest son Warren, who parted with the family to get a high school education in Boston and become a successful merchant. Who was responsible for the quarrel we cannot tell, but he clearly carried the grudge into the words of his will. His own relations with his father seem to have been close. Perhaps he was disappointed that his son did not want to follow the family trade of housewright, and seemed to be marrying for position, and seeking wealth and international travel. We can only speculate about the effect his loss of a mother at age four have, and what it meant to grow up with a demanding father who had 15 other children to care for.

Thomas was born in his parents' home in the West End of Boston, on Copper Street, later to become Brighton Street. All of this area was leveled in the twentieth century urban renewal, and is today a park south of Leverett Circle, near the Museum of Science.

His mother Sophia died when he was only four, leaving him and his three year old sister Sophia without a mother. We do not know how their father managed, perhaps with the help of their grandmother Anna Lawrance Gould, who lived in Charlestown across the bridge, and their aunts Mary Ann Hovey, Nancy Turner and Abigail Phillips, who lived in nearby Charlestown.

However, in exactly a year their father had remarried to Lydia Peirce of Belmont, who raised the two orphans with her own 14 children. Her first child arrived within a year, Samuel Lawrence Gould (1814-74). Samuel was the first of the family to be sent to college, and he became a leading abolitionist speaker as well as headmaster in the pioneering educational system of Horace Mann. There is no evidence of rivalry between brothers, and Thomas often worked on his brother's houses, but the contrast of their educations and occupations is great. While Samuel followed his father's dedication to religion and social reform, Thomas took his father's trade of housewright, or building contractor.

The family moved with their new mother to the corner of Hanover and Union Streets in Boston center, just north of the Blackstone Block, where his father ran an East India grocery for five years. However, by 1822, when young Thomas was 14, his father returned to his trade of housewright. The boy would not have had to be apprenticed out, but could learn the trade under his father. It was about this time that the father began development of a block on the west side of Friend Street backing up to the historic Green Dragon Tavern. This is now the Curley Park between City Hall and the Blackstone Block. Here the young man probably began to learn carpentry and other building skills. He also went to school, perhaps at a nearby Centre Grammar School, which required attendance to age 14.

In the next few years, he probably helped his father building the new brick houses in the North End, on North Margin Street and Salem Street, as well as Friend Street in Boston center.

MARRIAGE AND MOVE TO BALDWIN PLACE 1829

On 3 Sept. 1829, just after he came of age, he married Lydia Ann Winship Teel, a woman almost three years older. She had come from her birthplace in Newburyport to Boston with her parents, baker Benjamin Teel and Sally Barnard. Lydia's father was descended from the first settlers of Cambridge, Braintree, Newton, Charlestown and Watertown, as we will relate in the next chapter. They were married by Rev. James D. Knowles, at his father's church, Second Baptist, in Salem Street (BVR 1:343).

The newlyweds moved into his father's building in the North End on Baldwin Place, behind the Second Baptist Church (Boston Assessors Records, *Valuation,* 1830, Ward 3, 6 ("Thomas Gould Jr. 1 poll, Carpenter") . Their first child, Ann Maria was born in less than two years, on 16 Aug. 1831, but died when she was only seven months old, on 31 March 1832. Their second child, and first son, was born 17 Feb. 1834. Named for his father, Thomas Warren Gould, was never called Junior, but always Warren, and formally T. Warren Gould.

The young carpenter probably expanded the living space at Baldwin Place, for the single occupancy building valued at $3400 in 1832 was revalued for $3600 in 1833 and $4000 the next year. He first appears in the *Boston Directory* in 1832 as housewright at Baldwin Place (165).

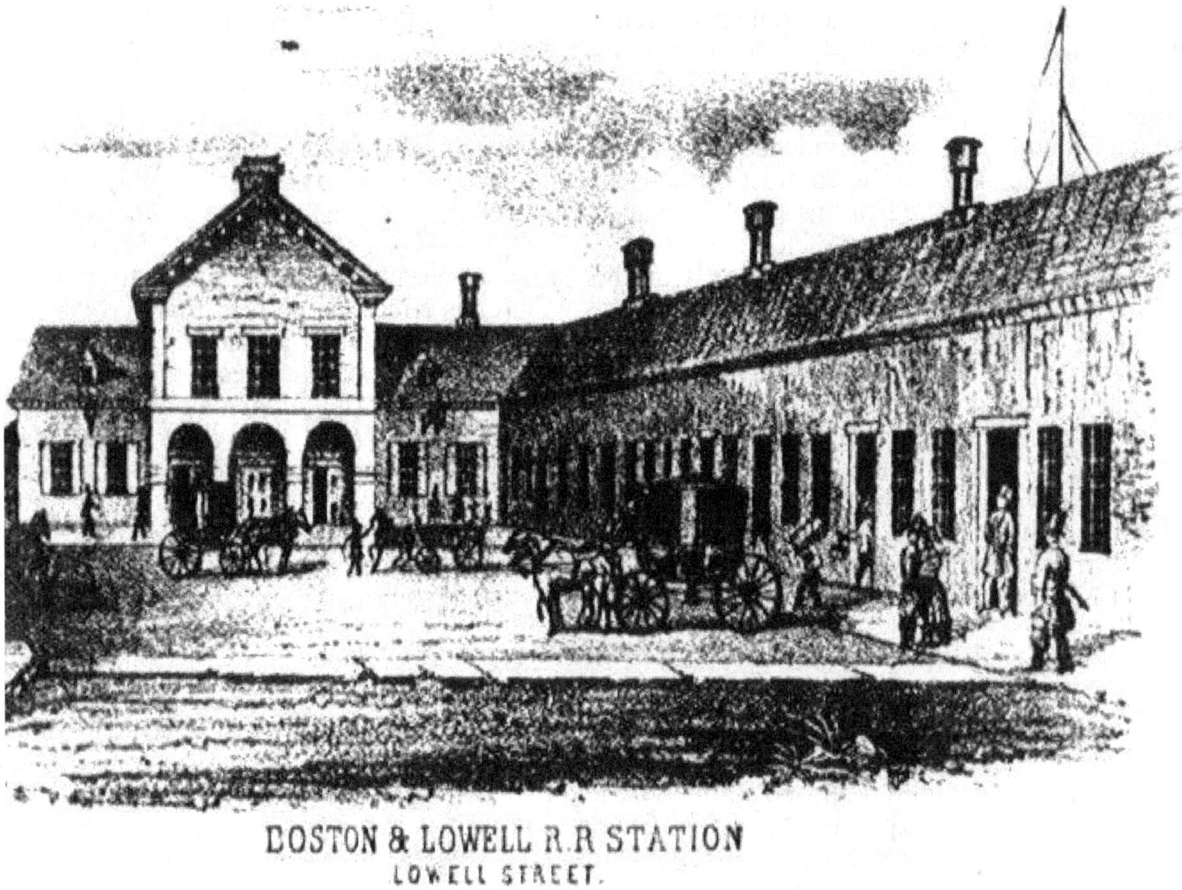

Boston & Lowell Railroad Station built by Thomas Gould Jr. c. 1836, from McIntyre's Map of Boston 1852.

BUILDING FIRST AMERICAN RAILROADS

Thomas Gould Jr.'s most notable accomplishment was the construction of some of the first railroad buildings and rolling stock in America, in 1835. Gould built the Boston Depot of the Boston & Lowell Railroad, one of the first in the city. He also built railway cars for the first two railroads in Boston.

The first railway in America had been built in Quincy in 1829, quite close to his ancestor Quinton Pray's pioneer American iron furnace of 1655. The first railroad in Boston was the Boston & Lowell, for which Gould built a depot, was chartered in 1830, and the first to be built (Charles Francis Adams, in Winsor 4:126). .He also built cars for the Boston & Worcester Railroad which was the first to run an engine, in 1834, and introduced the first passenger service in May (Winsor 4:127-8). Gould may have been working on cars before the first record we have of his work in Oct. 1834.

In 1834, at the age of 25, Gould was working for himself, building railway cars and structures for two new railroads coming into Boston. (Day Book of Thomas Gould Jr. 1834-68, last belonged to descendant Hazel LaPorte, Gould Rd., Bedford MA, who died 17 March 1987;

these notes are from extract made by J. W. Gould before her death). His first record of work is 15 Oct. 1834 when he was paid for making baggage cars for the Boston & Worcester Railroad, and painting 25 cars (l) . By Dec. 20 of the same year he was paid by the Boston & Lowell Co. for work he had begun Oct. 10, presumably for similar jobs.

The Boston Depot of the Boston & Lowell Railroad was his major stucture. The public front, facing south down Lowell Street was an early example of Greek Revival style (We have two contemporary drawings: *Boston Directory 1848-9*, 40; a vignette from McIntyre's map of Boston 1852, in Athenaeum; and Ballou's "Railway Depots in Boston", 8 March 1856). It had a two story high open pediment above plain pilasters, and blocks below the eaves. On the second floor there were three six over six windows with plain lintels. These are directly above a band between the floors. On the ground floor are three open arches between plain pilasters, leading into an open porch, behind which are three sets of double doors. Behind the peak of the gable is a low chimney. Two of the pictures show a large clock in the center of the pediment.

Ballou's Magazine described it as "a brick building, and makes no pretensions to architectural elegance". Yet the effect is dignified. A one story high wings emerge from the sides of the main building, each with two six over six windows, and shutters. Between the windows is a lighting sconce. Above each wing is a doghouse dormer. On the east, or water side, the one story wing extends southward, with at least five doorways, probably into offices of the company. In two of the pictures we can see the masts of small ships which could come up the Charles to unload at the station.

This station was the first one built in the area of North Station, and was abandoned in 1857 when a new Boston & Lowell depot was built a couple of blocks southeast, on Causeway Street to line up with the other northern line stations, the Eastern, the Boston & Maine, and the Fitchburg (text for Hill's drawing of new station in *Ballou's Pictorial*, 1856, Athenaeum). Gould's depot was thus the ancestor of all the structures that were to become North Station. It may not have been torn down at once, for there were still company buildings on the site as late as 1878 (King's Handbook).

Our statesman Charles Francis Adams points to the importance of 1835 in the turning point in Boston's history, from a provincial capital dependent on the sea and horseback, into a railway hub linked with the nation (Winsor 4:148). The lines opened up the commuter suburbs like Framingham, Lexington and Melrose, to which three generations of Goulds soon moved. It was these first railroads that made the change, and our ancestor was building at the start.

Thomas's workplace was in his father's building on Baldwin Place next to the Second Baptist Church, where his father apparently set him up on 16 Oct. 1834 (Boston Assessors Records, *Valuation* Ward 3, 1834, 5, with note "only as Jy [Journeyman?]) . For the next years he shared the shop with his brother-in-law Briggs Mann, mason, listed on tax rolls "only as Jy" in 1837 (50) . Much of the work must have been done at the railroad yards at Barton Point, and a notation in Sept. 1835 "Insurance on shop at Leevet Street" perhaps refers to Leverett Street" (37) which was then a short street running east-west near the Boston & Lowell depot. In 1836 the directory shows his workplace at Leverett Street, but for that year only. This was only two blocks northeast of Gould's birthplace on Brighton Street.

For 1835 his Day Book records almost 50 pages of detailed accounts for work for the two railroad companies, much of it located at Barton Point, the northernmost tip of Boston, where the railways came across the Charles River, east of Leverett Circle, near today's Spaulding Rehabilitation Hospital. In January he was paid $2.38 each for 24 stores (storehouses) for the Boston & Lowell (2). The rest of the year he was making various railroad structures, except in February, when he built cars, mostly cattle cars, for the Boston & Worcester Railroad, charging $12 per day, billing $544.79 on the 19th (2-5). Work for the Boston & Worcester continued thru April, probably for more cars.

In the Boston Directory of 1848 the Boston & Lowell depot is shown with simple boxcars of the type Gould probably made. *Ballou's Magazine* shows similar baggage cars on two trucks of paired wheels, and sliding door in the middle of the side, like today's freight cars.

Most of the 1835 he worked for the Boston & Lowell Co. at Barton Point, in March at the office, in April working 34 3/4 days on a carhouse in East Cambridge, in May on carhouses in Boston and Cambridge Point, in late May on the passenger house and offices, in June on stores at Barton Point, and office, Engine House, Passenger House and carhouse, and turntable; on July 11 he had done 59 days work on the engine house, work which continued through Nov. 7. In late July he was working at Barton Point on a carhouse and a baggage car box. By the end of September he was working on shops, including the Blacksmith shop which kept him occupied to the end of November, when he was also making snow shovels for trains.

Early in 1836 he had a credit of $255.92 with Boston & Lowell, and built 308 windows and 120 doors for the Barton Point Proprietors. In March he built a pleasure car for Boston & Lowell at $12 (per day?). Work for the railroad seems to have ended by mid-July when he did his last work on the Boston & Lowell depot (23 July, 77). His tools and workshop were apparently at Leverett Street, at a store on which he paid insurance, 21 Sept. 1836, 37).

EAST BOSTON INVESTMENT 1835

The railroad work having ended in 1836 he built chests for George R. Baldwin, a board maker at 2 Howard Street (Boston Directory, 1834, 5), and went back to working for his father. On 28 Oct. he was working on two houses of his father's, probably in the North End, between Salem and North Margin Streets, where his father was active at the time (94).

A measure of this 27 year old builder's success was his first purchase of land, in 1835. He and fellow housewright John Bowen paid $1,000 for a lot on City (now Maverick) Square in East Boston, where the new Cunard Line terminal was creating a boom (SD 400:26, 11 Dec. Lot #15, 45'x 80', subject to a mortgage they assumed). This was in a prime location, just opposite the new City Hotel where transatlantic travelers were to stay (plan in SD 377:end; Winsor 4:38-9) . However, Gould had to go to court to get possession from the previous owner, Boston trader Joshua H. Pollard and William Fettyplace, gentleman (Docket #680, Jan. 1837 term, Suffolk Court of Common Pleas). Gould charged $2000 damage, which may represent his costs of building. When the defendants failed to appear, the court ruled for Gould's possession unless they paid him $1,173.75 representing principal and interest, plus $4.94 costs (10 Aug. 1837; at the same time Gould also won a suit to recover $40 from Boston truckman Horace C. Close, got 60 cents damage and $4.56 court costs, docket 681, writ of 20 Dec. 1836, decided 20 March 1837) .

He must have done well working for his father, for in 1839 he bought out Bowen's interest (SD 449:206, 21 Oct.) . Today we would not recognize the booming prospect, for at #25-31 Maverick Square is a rundown four-story building of 1900 vintage housing Maverick Movies and Via Brazil travel agency. In 1841 he transferred the mortgage to the developer, the East Boston Company, of which Robert Gould Shaw (no relation) was President (SD 465:91). Next year he got a year's mortgage of $877.36 from Boston housewright Constant T. Benson (who lived nearby, at 33 Lynn Street, *Bos. Directory 1833*, 81), and renewed it for another year (SD 485:271). In 1844 he mortgaged it to Boston Counselor-at-law Edward Blake for $2000, at six percent, and engaging to insure it for the same (SD 523:157) . The increase in value indicates that he may have built on the lot shortly before June 1844. In 1846 he sold it for $5500 to Doctors Jesse Merrill and Daniel V. Folts, surgeons and physicians who had offices in East Boston at 3 Lewis Street (SD 562:206, 26 May, subject to $2000 mortgage to Blake (*Bos. Directory* 1846-7, 115, 1847, 158, 1848, 194). The doctors in turn mortgaged it to him for $2505 at 6%, which was not paid off until the end of the Civil War (1 Aug. 1865, SD 562:207) . Of particular interest are the witnesses, George Garan, brother of his son's mother-in-law Caroline Garran Goddard, and Sarah Merrill, the family name of his wife's Newburyport cousins, and L. G. Nash, the family name of a woman who sold him land in Boston.

Continued success is shown in a thousand dollar loan he made to Benjamin Kimball, Boston provision dealer, forming part of a mortgage on properties on the southwest corner of Salem Street and Baldwin Place, in the North End backing up to his father's land next to the Baldwin Place Baptist Church, sold by his father's business associates Ezra Hawkes and Ezra Eaton (9 Jan. 1836 in SD 411:216). In 1995 this was the empty Paesani Meat Market, at #120 Salem Street. In 1838 Gould may be preparing to build on the site, as a deed to Gould and stove dealer Lewis Jones sets conditions that the light of the back windows was not to be shut out as long as Kimball controlled the wooden house to the north, and they got the right to the gutters from the eves at the back over land below the gutter which they did not own (SD 432:101 7 June 1838 Gould and Jones paid $7000 to provision dealer Benjamin Kimball for property he received the same day from seven mortgage holders including Jones and Gould for $6000, SD 432:99-100). The house fronted 20 feet on Salem Street, going back 60 feet along Kimball's line on the north, and 79 feet along Baldwin Place to Thomas Gould Sr.'s lot, and included right to the water of the Second Baptist church in the rear. In 1840 Gould and Jones sold the property for $6750 to Boston victualler Samuel C. Bradshaw, but the Salem Street frontage has increased to 25 feet (SD 459:91).

PRINCE STREET ESTATE 1837-1865

Meanwhile, in 1836, the family was growing, when a second son, Charles Winship Gould was born (17 June). By 1837 Thomas Jr. moved home and business to 14 Prince Street in the North End, a short block north of his father's buildings on North Margin Street, and a block south of his grandfather's Charlestown Bridge (Directory). Today the site is the childrens' play area at the east side of the John S. Defilippo Playground, just north of the junction of Snowhill with Prince Street.

In 1835 his father had bought lot #2, with 25 feet on the street, going back about 73 feet, paying $2500 to Henry Farnham and Mary Farwell for the estate of Silas Atkins (SD 405:123, 18 May 1836; plan in SD 405:139; then mortgaged to Farnham for $2000 in SD 405:136, discharged 1839; we have the title search which shows John Osborn to Silas Atkins Jr. 7 Dec. 1776 in SD 150:238, etc.).

We still have the original deed of Thomas Gould the father to his son selling lot #2 with buildings for $2,800, including Farnham's mortgage of $2000 on 18 Feb. 1837 (SD 416:238). Three months earlier the son bought his first land in Boston proper, the lot #3, just south of his father's, from Boston ship chandler Zenas Snow for $2300, including a passage on the south side running to the back 75 feet, and along the back of both lots (orig. deed, 24 Nov. 1836 in SD 414:97; his title SD 405:141 from Farnham and Farwell as executors of Silas Atkins' estate, and with their mortgage of $1760).

Lot #3 had no building on it, so Thomas Jr. must have built the three buildings on the two lots in 1837, for he mortgaged the houses and lots for $4500 in March 1839 to Brookline farmer Elijah Corey (orig.; SD 442:57). The Day Book records that he was working on two houses for his father 28 Oct. 1836, perhaps on lot #2 (94). One of these, at 19 Prince Street he rented out for $150 a year (Day Book 99, 21 Jan. 1837).

In late 1839 Thomas Jr. built a brick dwelling on the southeast corner of lot #3, fronting 17 feet on the street, and going back only 45 of the 75 foot lot (SD 452:36, 11 Jan. 1840 mortgaged the brick dwelling "lately erected by me" to Ellis Gray Loring, Esq., trustee for heirs and widow of William Faxon, insured for $2000) . When this was discharged in 1859 he got a $1500 mortgage from Thomas Mair, executor for Hannah Barker, SD 753:120, and a second mortgage from Boston widow Eliza Aplin for $680, SD 753:116; there is no record of discharge of the second, but the first was discharged 4 Jan. 1867 to the Boston Gas Co., which was to acquire all of this area).

A few months later in 1840 he was building on the north side of the lot, having acquired 16 feet frontage on Prince Street, 22 feet deep, with a passage between this and the north side of lot #2 (orig.; SD 455:26, 30 April, for $265 from Mary G. Nash of Medford), and the gutter to the street, which he had the right to remove, to put in suction well though it was next to his privy on lot #2, and to get light into the windows of the back of the house (SD 455;27, same date and seller, for $219). Four months later Gould needed to clear out a vault at the northeast corner of Nash's lot #1, and made her an even swap of $50 pieces, acquiring a 7 1/2 by 9 foot corner for 3'8" on the street (orig.; SD 460:141, 174, 21 Sept. 1840; he sold this for $100 in 1851 to Joshua B. Stearns, who owned lot #10 to the rear, SD 623:10).

In 1840 the family had moved to one of the two buildings on the passage at the back of 19 Prince Street (*Directory 1840*), their address until 1843, when they moved to #20, perhaps the new brick house (*Directory 1841*, 250). They kept this address until they moved to Lexington in April 1849. The house at the rear of #19 was rented to a Mr. Eveleth for $175 a year or $14.58 per month (cancelled receipt 1 June 1849).

By 1849 Gould had run into hard times, and farmer Corey foreclosed on the mortgage on the three Prince Street houses (SD 599:238, 23 April). However, three years later Gould was able to get Dr. Louis J. Glover of Quincy to give him a $4500 mortgage with which he was able to pay off Corey; this included the passage and right to the well on the north (orig.; SD 632:298, 299, 1 June 1852). The doctor died within a year and the mortgage was assigned to his widow Eunice, who gave an additional mortgage of $1000 in 1856 at the usual 6% (SD 645:295, 714:279).

On a smaller scale, Gould followed the business of his father in building tenements in the North End, and renting them out to the new Irish immigrants. One gets an idea of the marginal nature of the livelihood when we look at the details that are preserved in his Day Book. He rented one house on Prince Street to James Halloran for $300 per year in 1859, and the Old Wooden House for $21 (per month?) to Halloran in 1860 and 1861. One of the two houses at the rear he rented for $200 per year to Dennis Twigg until Twigg left without notice even though Gould had deducted a dollar from his monthly rent of $15.67 "to better times" (12 June 1861 Cash Book; rent from 9 April 1860, William A. Brien as security; left 23 Jan. 1862). He paid Boston city taxes twice that year, $95.90 in Feb. (for 1859?) and $86.49 in Dec. The next year he had to pay $40 city water tax for four houses (1 March) . His insurance on the most expensive house, the brick one, cost him $24.62 for 7 years (12 Feb. 1861). Another back house tenant was a Mrs. Smith who paid $5 (per month? 26 April 1861). In 1861 he rented the old house for $300 to a McLaughlin (10 April) . Income from five rentals in Sept., Oct. and Nov. 1861 came to $80.25 a month: $25 from McLaughlin, $16 from Gilman, $15.67 from Twiggs, $13.58 from Dixon, and $10 from Muzzey (Cash Book). His city taxes went up to $105.35 in 1863 (11 June) . He rented the brick house to Mr. Ruddin for $20 (per month; 2 March 1863. In 1864 taxes went up to $124.64 (1 Dec.) . He insured the two back houses for $800, payable to Glover, the mortgager (29 Oct. 1864) . His interest payments to Glover came to $30 per month (1 Oct. 1861, 4 Nov. 1861, 1 April 1865).

Gould's Day Book records that he sold his "Prince Street Estate for $10500 to William A. Prescott, $1000 down and the rest in six months" (1 July 1865) . But the deeds show that on top of his existing $7680 mortgages Gould took two more third mortgages for $12,000 from Levi J. Prescott covering the whole area, with 47.2 feet frontage on the street, going back 75 feet on the passage, and 56.15 feet on the back passage (plan in SD 661:89,90, 1 July 1865) . This seems to have tided him over for 18 months until most of the mortgages were discharged in early 1867 to the Boston Gas Light Company which built a gas works on this site, tearing down Gould's houses. For several months after the sale Gould collected Prescott's rents on the four houses on Prince Street, one brick, one old wood, and two at the rear, at the same time notifying the tenants of a 3 dollar monthly increase and that they had to pay the water bills (1 Aug. 1865, 1 Sept., 1 March 1866). He also put in some work on the property for Prescott (3, 4, 8 Aug., 2 Sept. 1865).

Gould's Day Book skips a whole decade from 1837 to 1846, but the work on either side and the deeds cited above suggest a continuity of housewright's building for himself and his father.

Gould was surely not as religious as his father, leaving the Baptist church where he was married in 1829. By 1840 he was a member of the Rev. Sebastian Streeter's First Universalist Church on North Bennett Street near his home in the North End (Directory 1840, 29). We have a receipt dated 13 April 1840 from the First Universalist Society of Boston for pew #82, costing $145.63, for which he paid $25.63 in cash, and promise to pay $60 in six months, and $60 in 15 months. By 1844 Gould was behind in payment of his annual church assessment of $25.31, and the church auction 5 Aug. 1844, applying $36.73 to the arrears and charges, and $51.96 to a note for 6 months plus interest ("Copy of a/c sale of pew No 82 for doun-payt of taxes."). In late 1845 the Universalist Society gave him a note and mortgage for $2000 for six months, the interest on which he repaid $40.66 by a rent collected from C.H.Crafts on Nov. 22 and $60 in cash on Dec. 12 (receipt of Edward Blake 9 Dec. 1845) .

TRIP TO CAPE COD FOR LUMBER 1842

He obtained his lumber from Cape Cod, as we learn from a letter to his wife dated 14 Sept. 1842 from Boston. She was visiting her first cousin Ann Merrill, wife of David Merrill, on Water Street in Newburyport. Thomas urges her not to hurry home since the two boys (Warren 8 and Charles 6) were well cared for by Mrs. Bryant. 18 month old Annie must have gone to be shown off to relatives in Newburyport, for she is not mentioned. Thomas says "I have engaged a vessel, which is now at the wharf to take on the Lumber and will go if weather permits tommorow...! will bid you good by for three weeks, if you should write, direct it to Barnstable Cape Cod."

Lydia did not stay, and wrote to him simply addressed: "Mr. Thomas Gould Jr.//Barnstable//Cape Cod//in haste". Dated 23 Sept. and postmarked 2 days later it gives the flavor of their domestic life as well as her education: "My Dear Thomas

I recived your last letter and was happy to hear you was well, I spent one week in Newburyport I had hard work to get away, they wanted me to stay longer, but I felt huried to get home and see the boys, for I expected you was gone, I had a very pleasant visit, but it seemed very lonesome to come home and not see you here, I want you to send me word how long you think you shall stay, you said you had bought your coal but I cannot find it, it is very cold here and I must have some fuel, for I expect Ann [Merrill, her cousin with whom she stayed in Newburyport] here tomorrow to stay a few days, it was so cold to day I thought I would make a coal fire and I went down and got my kindling and put the shovel in to get my coal and behold there was none, our neighbors moved yesterday noon, Mrs. Davis [Mrs. Lois Davis, for whom his father was trustee?] come to me with the key I told her you had left orders to have it left at your fathers, she wanted to know where it was and I told her [Friend Street] and she went away, after dark I was up in the parlor and the bell rung, mary [the maid?] called me to come and when I got down the gentleman was gone, the door was open, Mary said it was a stranger he said here is the key of Mr. Goulds house and she refused to take it and called me, he was goin to through it on the floor an she took it, when I got their an I found what it I put on my things and whent to your fathers and told him how it was, he said if I would find where he kept he would go and see him, I sent a note to father [Gould] this morning and he whent to see him, and Mr. Davis said he did not hire the house of him and did not want to have any thing to do with him, and if father wanted the house he would find the key here,//he seems disposed to be ugly I advise you to have the house fixed to lett and not have any more to do with them for their tongues are as long as from here to south Boston, the two upper chambers want witewashing and papering, and the whole stairway wants papering and the kitchen wants painting, *I* would have it done before I offerd it to lett, I wish you would write me what do to directly, send by peny post for I cannot go to the post office conviently, it is very late and I am much fatigued or I would write more

Mrs Benyan and her family are well [John Benyon, shipwright, lived at 9 Prince Street, Directory 1842, 87]

Mrs Colbeth and little girl are well [A.P.Colbath, cartman, lived at 76 Prince Street, Directory 1842, 141] I have not have had time to go to Charlestown [to visit his family?] and dont know how they do

we are all well the baby goes alome [walks alone, age 18 months?]

write as soon as you get thiss yours ever
and affectionately
Lydia Ann Gould
good night"

In 1846 Gould served on a jury in Boston (Municipal Court, 17 April, Day Book), and worked for his family on building projects. In June he worked on his father's house on Friend Street, and in August on his half-brother Samuel Lawrence Gould's house on Sturgis Place (Day Book 27 June and 5 Aug.).

DIABETES AND MOVE TO LEXINGTON 1849

Business conditions in the nation were terrible in the panic of 1849, and living conditions in downtown Boston were becoming more crowded. With many of the new immigrants passing through to Boston suburbs, the old families were also moving out to more pleasant settings. These may have been factors in the Gould family's move to Lexington in 1849, when he was 41, his wife 44, and their five children 6 to 14. The eldest son, Warren, had finished Boston Grammar School in 1848, and continued on at Boston English High School when the family moved.

However, the main cause of the early retirement, at age 41 may have been diabetes. We do not know when his symptoms first appeared, for there is no reference to it until it is given as cause of his death at age 61 (Massachusetts Archives, Death Reports [hereinafter MADR] 221:139, #30), However, letters refer to his not taking sweet rolls.

At the end of the twentieth century there is still no cure for diabetes, and an effective treatment came half a century after Thomas Gould's death, with the discovery of insulin in 1922. Diabetes melitus, now believed to be an auto-immune defect, that causes the body's protective mechanisms to destroy the hormones that convert blood sugar to energy. The immediate symptoms are excessive urination, and great fatigue. In the long run it often causes blindness, kidney failure and nerve destruction. High blood sugars also cause susceptibility to infection, such as the raccoon bite which killed Thomas Gould.

Before the use of insulin there was little that could be done for diabetics, and standard remedy was logically enough, a reduction of carbohydrate intake, especially from sugar and bread. The problem with the remedy was that the body got little nourishment and energy, and the result was starvation.

In May 1847 Gould bought five acres of farmland in southwest Lexington, at Grapevine Corner, the northwest corner of the Lexington-Waltham Rd. (now Waltham Street) and Lincoln

Rd. (MD 539:366, 24 May 1847). This was near the Wellington dairy farm which provided the first milk for the Boston market (Hudson 2:256) . He paid $550 to Samuel Bridge, Lexington farmer, married to Hannah Wellington, daughter of a neighboring farmer, and first cousin of Boston Customs Appraiser (1841) Samuel Bridge and onetime partner of Robert Gould Shaw (Lincoln 11:25, 24). Three days after the deed was signed he got a receipt for $550 from Jonas C. Wellington, brother of Hannah Bridge (Hudson 2:357).

On 7 July 1847 he had a well dug on the property (Day Book). He then made a contract with his 21 year old half-brother Joseph A. Gould to build a house for $485 (contract 6 Nov. Day Book; prev. ref. 6 Sept.; relationship is not stated, but his brother was a carpenter who had married in Jan. 1847, moved to Princeton MA 1853, and to Chelsea WI c.1853, where his descendants lived 1912. It is possible that this refers to his first cousin Joseph, b. 1809, son of his uncle Joseph, carpenter who died 1823. This may become clear from Lydia Ann's diaries).

While work on the Lexington house was going on Thomas had a job working for the Boston Water Commissioners on the waterworks (began 15 May 1847, again 1 Dec., Day Book). The first city water supply had been authorized in 1846, and by 1847 iron pipes had been laid from Long Pond in Natick 22 miles up to the State House on Beacon Hill, and water turned on in a great fountain on the Common in 1848 (Rossiter, 17). The Day Book does not reveal what kind of work he did, but he was not one of the prime contractors (list in Thorndike, John H., *History of the Introduction of Pure Water into the City of Boston* [Boston: Alfred Mudge, 1968], 121).

Thomas Gould's House, Grapevine Corners, Lexington 1848
Photo taken 1963 by Eleanor Baldic

Lydia Ann recalled that they moved from Boston to Lexington in April 1848 (Diary 26 Aug. 1869). Joseph Gould must have finished the house by April 1849, when Thomas began planting potatoes and vegetables (23 April, Day Book). He sold the potatoes in the fall (10 Nov.), but was meantime building a private school in Lexington for Mr. Wait, the teacher (Day Book 1 Sept.).

In 1848 Gould mortgaged the house and land for $1200 to his neighbor Nehemiah Wellington (17 Aug. MD 545:52). Though originally for only three years, it was not paid off for nearly half a century, in 1905 (21 Oct. MD 3195:2; assigned on Nehemiah's death 1857 to his son Augustus MD 787:415, then to Benjamin Reed MD 813:501, F. W. Reed MD 854:236, Bethiah L. Reed MD 938:333, Lexington M. Fund MD 1215:528, 2645:410, Albert A. Gleason MD 3196:181).

In 1851 Wellington gave Gould a second mortgage on the house, for $400, for two years at 6% (16 Jan. 1851, MD 603:263, assigned to his son Jonas Clarke Wellington MD 787:414. He had paid off all but $100 when Wellington wrote him (E. Cambridge Feb. 14 [no year]). This was not discharged for 15 years, after the Civil War (1 Feb. 1866). In 1860 Gould got another mortgage, for $500 for three years at 6% from Lexington storekeeper James Harvey Bennett (10 Dec. I860, MD 865:307; Hudson 2:22). This was not paid off until after Gould's death (12 April 1869, MD 865:307).

WORK IN LATER YEARS OF LIFE

His half-brother James, 27 years old, worked for him most of the first year on the farm. In November 1847 he paid him for working on an unnamed client's "Estate fronting on Lexington Common" (13-23 Nov.). The next spring he was plowing (3 May).

In April 1852 Thomas took a job as salesman in James Fernald's store, at $2 per day. He gave this up four years later when his son "Charles W. Gould agreed that if *I* would leave Mr. Fernald's store that he would collect My Rents for me and do My Business in the City Gratis" (Day Book 14 Feb. 1856) . Charles was now 20, and had been given a loan by his father "against his earnings 'till he is 21" (Day Book 1853).

From 1856 until his death 13 years later he seems to have gone back to doing building and odd repair jobs for his father, brothers Samuel and Francis, and for local projects. They made a bit of money when his cousin Lenthall Phillips' family boarded in June and July 1856. He employed his brother James on a job at the corner of Bedford Rd. in 1858 (May) . His 15 year old daughter Lucy received a legacy of $300 from the estate of Enoch Burt (2 Sept. 1858; perhaps this was a godfather) . He worked for his father in Boston in 1858 and 1859 (16 Oct., 13 April). He worked for his step-brother the schoolmaster Samuel Lawrence Gould on his Sturgis Street house in 1846, 1859 (9-18 April; paid 7 July). In the last three months of 1859 he was "building a dam across Richardson land for the Lexington Skating Club" (29 Oct. thru end of year). The Lexington Literary Association paid him for a job at Town Hall (22 Feb. 1860).

We have detailed record of his work in 1861 from his Diary Cash Book (in possession of John Shaw). On 19 Feb. he began work on Walter Wellington's house on Bedford Rd (thru 9 March). From 24 to 27 May he built a barn for C. B. Johnson. On 10 June Walter Wellington agreed to have him make an addition to his barn, and to shingle one side for $125; he finished the framing and raising 27 June, and finished the barn 13 July. From 31 July to 3 Sept. he worked on George W. Robinson's store. From 26 Oct. to 2 Nov. he worked on John Haskins's cornhouse. Mr. Fairweather had him do roof repair 23 Nov.

Meanwhile there was the regular work on the farm: May 20 plowing, May 21-3 planting, 14 July haying (Lucy's diary 1857), 19 Oct. dig red potatoes.

In 1863 he had an opportunity to return to his old skill of building railway cars and buildings, and began work for the West Cambridge & Lexington Railroad Co. (31 Aug. 1863) , This line connected Arlington and Lexington in 1846, organized by George's father Benjamin. In Sept. he was working on cars and the Engine House and turntable (10, 17 Sept.). At the end of Sept. he worked on the Oil House and switch. In Jan. 1864 he again worked on the Engine

House and turntable (18 Jan.).

Between 1864 and 1868 he built two houses for his half-brother Francis Gould, the Civil War veteran who returned to become a civil engineer and surveyor. In March 1864 he worked on his house on Pleasant Street in West Cambridge (Arlington, 16-29 March). In Nov. 1867 he was superintending framing of a house in Cambridgeport, and also did work on Francis's house in Arlington (18 Nov., 29 Nov.-5 Dec.). He worked for Francis several months in 1868, earning $100 on 22 Feb., 29 May, and 26 July.

He insured his Lexington house for $2500, and the barn and tools for $300 (20 Jan. 1866), paying local taxes of $24.86 (1861, 1862) .

With the proceeds of the sale of his Prince Street property to Prescott he bought a $1,500 U.S. bond (20 Jan. 1866). But money was obviously tight. He had been given $100 gifts from his father in 1864 and 1865.

Then came the shock of the death of his 29 year old son Charles, in Walt ham on 16 Oct. 1865, of fever (MADR, 184:166, #114, age 29 years, 3 months and 30 days). His brother Warren was the administrator who had to pay off the debts. This led to disagreement between Thomas and his son Warren, which Thomas Sr. mediated.

Thomas apparently insisted on disposing of the estate. An undated letter from Warren to his mother has survived that shows the depth of the quarrel:

"All of my experience will be lost to Father if he administrates.

A trip west will be necessary to obtain satisfactory settlement of the estate, and for this Father is incompetent both by age [58] and experience [lumber buying was his business; Warren's was textiles].

Most of the parties with whom Charles had dealings are personal friends and acquaintances of mine and men who while they would esteem it a pleasure and a privilege to assist me to the utmost, would not be actuated by similar feelings in dealing with father.

I can conduct the entire business to a favorable settlement without the intervention of law or lawyers, with their bills of cost etc. which is more than Father or any other person will be able to do.

Remember Mother, *I* am not <u>dictating.</u> The dictation is Charlie's, and as such, should be responded to us all, not only as a duty, but as a pleasure.

Read this well Mother and consider it better, and with the girls.

If you can view the matter in the light of reason, let me know of it by return of bearer to-night or by your personal presense at my house at seven o'clock tomorrow morning, <u>after which time It will be too late for.</u>

Your Affectionate Son

Warren

Lydia Ann received a letter from George White of 5 Tremont Street Boston saying that the administrator "complains that you have in your possession personal property belonging to that estate--and that you refuse to give it them up. . .The Administrator has directed me to institute legal proceedings to secure such property as you may have--but I deem it best to write you before bringing any action against you--Please attend to this at your earliest convenience and save further costs and trouble." (25 Aug. 1866; orig. with J. Shaw).

Thomas Senior's letter of 20 May 1867 reflects his concern: "I was in hopes to hear from you before this how you get along with Warren [. H]ave you seen the Judge though I beleave it lays all with Warren it is his duty to pay all Charles just debts as fur as the property will pay". The family reached a three generation financial treaty in 1867 that Thomas Jr. described thus:

"T. Warren Gould agreed in the presence of Father if I would allow him for the watches and sleeve buttons to offset against one half of cost of burial lot and tombstone [Mt. Auburn] amounting to 127$ Watches valued $80 sleeve buttons>_would settle; Also paid the Bill of Mothers for [George] Muzzey [his son-in-law, married to Annie 1868], amount of 4750, also paid the note of 200$ in part, amounting to $150.-" (4 Dec. 1867).

With this is a loose note in the handwriting of Warren of the same date addressed to Thomas Gould Jr. : "By the settlement of today of the last of the accounts against my brothers estate *I* am happy to inform you that I shall close my account as admr at once, and you will receive due notice from the court, as your interests in the same. Yours truly...".

On 10 Dec. he received $54 from Warren, "said to be allowed him to pay it by the Judge on Acct of the Note". Two days before Christmas in 1867 T. Warren Gould settled in part, receiving $157.75".

In May 1866 he had settled all his debts with his father by giving him a note for $700 (11 May) . He reduced this by exchanging it for a $600 note in 1868 (11 Feb.).

POOR HEALTH AND WILL 1869

His health was poor in the final years. As early as 1862, when he was 54 his father wrote that he "would advis [sic] you to settle your [worldly business] when you can do it without too much sacrfise as you are geting in years [so] free your mind as much as you can from worldly cars for I think your Constitution will not prolong your life as you Fathers has..." (11 May 1862) . Two years later he wrote "let me know of your health and family and how is your complaint (9 Dec. 1864). In 1867 he started a letter "I have been some time ancious to hear from you and hear at last by the letter from [cousin] Anna Fernald that you are a little better bles the Lord for his goodness..." (20 May 1867).

His symptoms are not stated until 1865 when his daughter Annie wrote to her sister Lucy: "Father...is not so well, I dont think, as he was a month ago, is restless, thirsty, pale and tired all the time. He is taking <u>Iron</u> and I hope will be better soon" (4 June 1865, 10) . Four days later she wrote: "Father is better, I think, now that he is taking Iron, and I have put him on stricter diet, he doesnt complain, and I guess is convinced that it wont do for him to eat honey, bunns, and bread now and then" (7 June 1865, 4).

However ill, he put off making a will until six months before his death in 1869. The text is short. After usual introduction and general clause on executors:

"Secondly, I request to be given to my son Thomas Warren Gould the sum of five dollars from the estate it being in full for all that I shall allow him from the estate, hoping it may do him good.

<u>Thirdly.</u> All the remaining property, with that which may com to the estate after my death I request to be managed for the benefit of my Wife and children, my Wife to receive from the estate a sufficient sum for the maintenance while she lives.

<u>Fourthly.</u> All the property left at the decease of my wife and that which may come to the estate after her death, I request it to be divided equally to my three daughters, Sophia L. Bailey, wife of Edward B. Bailey, Anna M. Muzey, wife of George E. Muzzey and Lucy M. Whiting wife of Frank Whiting, first deducting what each or their husbands may be owing to the estate, that part belonging//to Lucy to be held in trust for her sole benefit, to be paid to her in such sums and at such times as the Executors think best for her good.

<u>Finally.</u> I appoint my two sons in law Edward B. Bailey of Waltham and George E. Muzzey of Jamaica Plain as executors to this my last Will and Testament..." signed 23 April 1869; witnesses: Leonard G. Babcock [Lexington's Postmaster 1867, Hudson 2:9], Charles A. Butter [s, b. Boston 1808, res. Lexington, Hudson 11:34], and H[orace] B. Davis [b. 1824, res. Lexington, Hudson 2:56].

Thomas Jr. died of infection from a raccoon bite, at his home at Grapevine Corners, Lexington, 19 Oct. 1869. This is the account in his wife's diary for 1869 (transcribed by Hazel

LaPorte 4 Oct. 1968) :

"Saturday Sept. 4, 1869

Thomas has killed a Coon that has been killing our chickens. The creature bit his hands. Hope not dangerously.

Sept. 5. Thomas dont mind his hands he is so glad he has destroyed the coon he thinks he would not missed of it for ten dollars.

Sept. 25. Thomas had a horrid night. I was up all night.

Lu sent the Dr. when she went to choir he cauterized his sore thumb.

Oct. 6. Thomas very sick, this anniversary of Annas weding day. Lucy went to spend the night but Father was so sick that I sent for the girls to come home to me.

Tuesday Oct. 12. Thomas very sick. Oct. 17. Warren came out here too. Tuesday

Oct. 19. Thomas has got through all his sorrow.

Oct. 21. I left my best friend never to look on him again in this world.
What shall I do?
Oh Father in heaven will thou pitty me protect and guide me. Oh my God."

He was buried 21 Oct. 1869 in Mt. Auburn Cemetery, Cambridge, in the Bailey lot #3634, Narcissus Path, south of Henry Wordsworth Longfellow's grave. With him are his wife and her mother, his three daughters (Lucy Whiting is in Lexington Cem.), and son Charles.

ESTATE AND TRUST FOR LUCY 1870

Bailey and Muzzey sent the will to the county Probate Court 25 Oct. (Middlesex Wills 32948, doc. 0947; will is 0944-5) . They were appointed executors 23 Nov.

The three men appointed to appraise the estate, B. M. Clark, Franklin Patch and his half-brother George P. Gould reported personal assets of $1236.50, most of which was the 1847 U.S. 5.2% bond of $1000. Real estate (the five acres and house at Grapevine Corner) was worth $3730, with a mortgage of $1200 to Wellington (4 Feb. 1870; 0958, 0960).

The first account of the executors 14 Feb. 1870 reported expenses, including funeral costs, interest on the mortgage, 1869 taxes, payment to Lydia Ann and to creditors, amounting to $878.26 (0962). It adds: "All parties interested having assented to, except one". Was son Warren holding out?

The sale of personal property realized $141.76, making total assets $1378.26. Subtracting the debts there remained only $500 to divide among the three daughters (0962).

The trust for Lucy Whiting is not explained, since she was 26 years old and married for five years with a child. The exclusion of her husband Frank as an executor and the trust suggest some doubt about the marriage, which eventually ended in divorce. In 1896 the court terminated the trust on the request of the two administrators, who were now widowers (Msx Prob. 32948, 15 Sept. 1896) . Annie Muzzey had died in childbirth with twins only three years after her father's death, leaving only her husband Lexington Selectman George E. Muzzey, who died shortly after (14 Dec. 1896) . The event that appears to have precipitated the termination was the approaching death of Sophia Bailey c.25 March 1897, and her apparent lack of desire for the family property to go to her two children Charles and Abigail Bailey. In any event, the termination of Lucy's trust resulted in conveying title of the Grapevine Corners house to Lucy (Msx Pro. 32948).

The day that Lucy's trust was terminated the court appointed Leonard A. Saville, Lexington Town Clerk, and husband of Lucy's second cousin Rebeckah[7] (James[6], James[5]) Hicks Gould (1835-94; Hudson 11:212) guardian to Lucy's three grandchildren, Lucy 3, Melissa 2, and George 1 (15 Sept. 1896, Msx Pro 32948).

Six children, born Boston, MA.:

i. ANN[7] MARIA, b. 16 Aug. 1831, d. Boston 31 March 1832, age 7 months; buried Mt. Auburn in Bailey lot.

25. ii. THOMAS WARREN, b. 17 Feb. 1834, d. Melrose 27 Jan. 1895; Boston 17 Feb. 1855 CAROLINE GODDARD.

iii.CHARLES WINSHIP, b. 17 June 1836, d. Waltham 16 Oct. 1865, age 29, 3 months and 30 days, of fever, at home of his sister Sophia Bailey, unmarried; buried Mt. Auburn under marble stone "Charlie". He was a lumberman, listed as "merchant" in official report of death {MADR, 184:166, #114).

A letter to his mother survives which tells of a business trip west: "Buffalo, n.y. July 7th 1858...I at last got started from Boston...last Thursday afternoon at half-past 5 O'clock By the Fall River Rail Rd. to New-York at which place I arrived at about half-past six o'clock the next morning[.] When I arrived at Fall River I was unable to obtain a State-room, they all having been previously engaged, therefore I was obliged to take my quarters in one of those berth in the lower cabin, or rest as I best could, but as I would not submit myself to be stowed away in such a warm place[.] I remained in the upper cabin the most of the night, getting what little rest I could by lying down on the Settee, which were so short that I was obliged to keep changing my position every five minutes, but as the weather was fair we had a very pleasant trip.

"After having got my breakfast at the Hotel I started to attend to business--but before//! had accomplished much I met a Gentleman of my acquaintance who insisted upon devoting his whole time too me by showing me around the City, and it made it very pleasant for me because he was acquainted with all the Mahogany Dealers in New York to many of which he introduced me. He invited me to dine with him, and after Dinner he got his horse and buggy out, and drove all over the principal parts of New York, not returning until towards evening, and of course I had a beautiful time.

"I left there the following forenoon for Albany viz. Hudson River Rail Rd. arriving there about six o'clock on Saturday evening after one of the most beautiful trips I have ever had. The whole scenery on the Hudson River is one of the most splendid sights I ever saw...

"After remaining in the beautiful city of Albany until Sunday afternoon, I fell in with a Gentleman who I had met in Boston, and who is one of the richest Lumber Dealers in the place. [H]e invited me to call on him Monday morning and afterwards extended an invitation to spend the day with him, it being the Fourth of July--He assured me, finding that I was not a married man, that *I* might enjoy the company of his daughter and//[3] pleanty of cousins. that he would introduce me to, therefore you see that after holding out such inducemants as those, I could not resist the temptation any longer, and finally yealded to his request, which I was not sorry for I assure you, for they live in great style, and the Daughter was charming indeed and of course I carried on quite a flirtation with, and after spending the whole day and evening with them, inevitably [asked] the Young Ladies to go and see the Fire-works, which invitation of course they accepted. I finally took leave of them at a late hour in the evening with my mind made up that the Albany Ladies could not be beat. So you see that I have not yet felt as though I was in a strange land. I spent the day Yesterday with a friend of Carrie's who is in the Lumber Business in Troy about six miles from Albany.

"I left Albany for this place last evening and after traveling all night I arrived here about seven o'clock this morning. I shall leave here by this evening's train for Cleveland Ohio. Arriving there about day light tomorrow. I am enjoying excellent health notwithstanding the warm weather...In haste as usual. Yours Truly.

Charles."

He must have been successful, for the next year he gave the family a present of a cart (27 March 1858; Sophia thanks Charles).

His brother Warren was named executor, causing a rift in the family. As we have seen above, Warren reported many of his business associates were in "the west", that is, west of the Hudson. His estate was settled by his brother in Dec. 1867.

Given the patriotism of the Goulds, and Charles's age 25 at the outbreak of the Civil War it is surprising that he was not in the army. We do not know whether he purchased exemption, or was disqualified.

iv. SOPHIA LOVIS, b. 22 Dec. 1839, d. Boston c. 25 March 1897 (VR 476:128); buried Mt. Auburn 27 March 1897. Married Lexington 28 June 1861 (LVR 330) Edward Burr Bailey of Waltham, b. 28 June 1833, buried Mt. Auburn 28 June 1914. They resided in Waltham through 1872, moved from Concord to Somerville 1875, and Arlington Heights 1880. Three children, born Waltham:

i. Charles[8] Mann Bailey, electrician, b. 13 Sept. 1868; d. Orlando FL 21 Sept. 1962; married 18 1898 Mary A. M. Willis b. c. 19 Jan. 1865, bur. Mt. Auburn 6 May 1930; he was carpenter and master electrician, last res. 2603 S.W. Moreland Dr. Orlando FL 32805; buried Mt. Auburn 6 May 1930. No issue.

ii. Abigail "Abbie" Matilda, b. 6 June 1870, d. Sarasota FL 24 Jan. 1950; m. John Foster Bass, correspondent for *Harper's.* One child: John[9] Foster Bass Jr. b. Athens, Greece, 4 June 1897, d. Mexico 19 Dec. 1939; m. East Orange NJ 5 Feb. 1927 Else Jensen of Naksvev Denmark. He was founder of Bass Biological Laboratories, Sarasota. Last res. 1980 5050 Bayshore Dr. Sarasota FL 33580. One child: John[10] Foster Bass III, real estate broker b. Evanston IL 15 Feb. 1928, m. New York City *26* June 1948 Barbara Avildson. Res. 1981 3464 Gulf of Mexico Dr. Longboat Key FL 33548; 1500 New Point Comfort Rd. Engle-wood FL 33533. 3 children born Sarasota: i. John[11] Foster Bass IV, b. 7 Aug. 1952 ii. Mark Foster, b. 21 Jan. 1956. iii. Amy Hope, b. 3 Nov. 1964. iii. Lucy Catherine Bailey, b. 3 Aug. 1872, d. West Somerville 8 June 1892, age 19; buried Mt. Auburn.

v. ANNA "ANNIE" MATILDA Gould, b. 20 March 1841, named for her mother's first cousin, Ann M. Merrill of Newburyport, d. Lexington 17 July 1872 {LVR 456; MADR 248:178 #33) , m. Lexington (First Church Unitarian) 6 Oct. 1868 (LVR 330) George Eveleth Muzzey, b. Lexington 4 Aug. 1838, son of Benjamin and Elizabeth Wood, d. Lexington 14 Dec. 1896 (LVR 456) of pneumonia. First resided 1868-9 Burroughs Street Jamaica Plain. Moved to Lexington 17 Sept. 1869. After his wife's death he lived at Grapevine Corner with his mother-in-law. He ran a lumber business as the poem "Poetical Novelty" states:

"For a large supply of lumber, I'm not afraid to state I'ts sold by GEORGE E. MUZZEY at the lowest rate. For lumber of all kinds, for lime, cement and hair, He carries a stock with which few can compare. He sells all his goods at prices of which you can't complain, You'll recommend him to your friends and surely call again." (undated printed in red).

He was town Selectman at time of death, and head master of the George G. Meade post of the GAR, having fought in the Civil War with the 12th Massachusetts Volunteers, 1861-4, as quartermaster-sergeant 1862, First Lt. 1863, and quartermaster 1864 (Hudson 2:167) . His uniform was passed down in the Whiting family to Richard LaPorte, who gave it in 1993 to Lt. Col. Robert Gould Archer who lives in Frisco CO. 1994. Anna Muzzey died of puerperal convulsions, giving birth to twins. She is buried in Bailey lot Mt. Auburn with her two children, twins, who died at birth:

i. Lyman[8] Benjamin Muzzey, d. 17 July 1872 (LVR 456; MADR 248:178 #34), and

ii. Ann Matilda, d. 18 July, the next day. Both are buried beside their mother at Mt. Auburn.

vi. LUCY MARIA RUST Gould, b. 14 Sept. 1843, d. Lexington 3 Aug. 1929, buried Municipal Cemetery Lexington; m. (1) 6 Oct. 1864 (LVR 330, 402) Lexington (First Church, Unitarian) Frank[7] Whiting, b. Charlestown 29 Aug. 1837, son of William H. and Jane Maria Whipple; he was descended from Rev. Samuel Whiting (1633-1713), first minister of the church in Billerica.

Frank was a civilian attached to the Union Army during the Civil War, c/o Capt. E. B. W. Resticaux, Chief Quartermaster. He wrote his wife from Camp in the field in Virginia during the Battle of Spotsylvania saying: "I am surrounded by suffering humanity. I have visited most of the battle field & have seen the awful results of war. day before yesterday I was within 200 yards of our line of battle and could hear the bullets whistle. Curiosity is now//satisfied (11 May 1864, orig. with John Shaw. Loose is a sketch of a battle, with Gen. Burnside's IX Corps tunnel into a rebel fort they held for 6 hours. Frank notes: "In the space between the Rebel fort and the front of the 9th Corps over 300 dead wounded & dying Rebels & our men have been lying for 24 hours. flag of truce went out today & I think get permission to bury the dead & care for the living."

Lucy spent several months with her husband at Camp Nelson 18 miles from Lexington KY in 1865. Her sister Annie accompanied her as far as Albany, left for Buffalo and Cleveland about 9 May (Annie to Lucy 10 May), arriving at camp on 14 May 1865. She wrote to her mother about taking a turn running the household for the week and other activities (28 May, 4 June 1865; orig. with Shaw) . We have several of her letters from camp, describing social life and trips in the area, including the limestone cliffs of the Ohio River. Local conditions were so unsafe her husband wouldn't let her walk outside, but finally bought her a horse to ride. She had returned to Lexington by 20 Aug. when he wrote from Camp Nelson (also note 11 Sept., both with Shaw).

He d. Lexington 7 March 1878 after divorcing Lucy. She remarried (2) 16 Jan. 1901 William Alien Harris, b. ?Providence RI 1841, d. Lexington c. 1910; this was his third marriage; he had been U.S. Consul's Marshall in Hong Kong.

When Lucy was 15 she received a legacy of $300 paid by Dr. Ingalls as trustee for the estate of Enoch Burt (Day Book 2 Sept. 1858; she anticipated it in her 1857 diary: "I hear that I have got a legacy left me." (7 July 1857). He is no known relative, and no others received money. He might be a godfather.

She had one child by her first husband:

Thomas[8] Gould Whiting, general contractor, b. Lexington 7 April 1869, d. Lexington 29 Dec. 1948, m. Arlington 29 June 1892 Edith Otis Teel of Arlington, b. 23 March 1864, dau. of William Frederic and Melissa Arabella Otis; d. Lexington c. 1928. Thomas "Tom" Whiting was born and died in the old Gould homestead at Grapevine Corners.

They had five children born there:

i. Lucy[9] Teel Whiting, b. 2 March 1893 (LVR 238), d. Lexington 17 Jan. 1948, m. Lexington 4 Jan. 1921 John McLeod, b. Ridgewood NJ 14 Sept. 1883. She was town Weigher. Four children:

i. Donald[10] Whiting McLeod, b.Waltham 28 June 1921, d. Acton (ME 7 June 1991 of cancer; m. Kinstrorf NC 1 March 1948 Lillian Howard; served in USMC; he was shovel operator, moved from Natick to E. Main Street Hopkinton MA Sept. 1962; last res. Box 613 Milton Mills Rd. Acton ME 04001; ph. (207) 636-1816. 2 children b. Natick:

i. Donald "Skip" Whiting Mc Leod Jr., b. 15 Feb. 1943, m. Natick 5 June 1965 Sandra Bozan, b. 2 May 1944; 5 children b. Natick i. Cindy Ann b. 3 Aug. 1966, m. Winnipesaukee NH 10/20 June 1986 Stephen Marshall, tractor operator Acton ME, 2 ch. b. Sanford ME: Brian Steven b. 5 Jan. 1987, Shawnadee, b. 26 April 1989. ii. Scott David, b. 20 June 1968, trucker, unm.

iii. Shawn David, b. 30 Oct. 1969; m. 31 Aug. 1991 Catherine Ann Vallee, b. 20 Sept. 1968; blackjack dealer; one ch: Evan James b. Framingham 29 Aug. 1987; he is crap dealer, res. 1994 3333 Ira Marcus Dr. Las Vegas.

iv. Corrie Ann, b. 5 Oct. 1973, m. c.1992 Timothy; one ch.: Amber Marie b. Sanford ME 24 Aug. 1993 . v. Craig David, b. 10 Jan. 1976.

ii. Linda Ann b. 20 July 1944, m. Natick 13 July 1963 Wendell Roy Wetherby of Rickford VT.; res. 9 Teresa Rd., Hopkinton MA 02147; one ch. : Wendell Roy Jr. b. Framingham 16 Sept. 1964, m. Hopkinton 23 Sept. 1989 Lani Rebecca Herrin.

iii. Fred Howard, b. 30 Sept. 1945, m. twice: 1) 15 Oct. 1964, div. May 1974 Janice Judge, of Weston; Res. 1980 19 Larabee Av. Framingham 01701 3 ch. b. Peterboro NH:

i. Christopher Michael b.3 Nov. 1965;
ii. Jeffrey Paul b.27 Dec. 1969;
iii. Lisa Ann b. 10 March 1971.

Fred m. 2) 14 Feb. 1976 Sandra Kay McGilvray b. 13 Dec.194-, 1 ch: Joshua Shain b. Peterboro, 5 Dec. 1978.

ii. Virginia "Ginny" Alice McLeod, nurse, b. Lexington 6 Dec. 1924, m. twice: 1) 26 April 1941 Alfred R. Shaw, b. Cambridge 11 April 1922, son of John R. & Emma Owens; div. 30 Dec. 1959; two ch. b. Arlington:

i. Alfred Jr. b. 13 Dec. 1941 m. 3 times: 1) CT 17 April 1965 Betty Grant, div. 17 April 1972, no ch.; m. 2) 9 Sept. 1973 Carol Hand, div. by 1991, res. Bourne MA 1992; 2 ch. : i. Scott Walter Shaw b. Norwood MA 11 July 1978; USN 1993; ii. Kevin Jason b. Denver CO 11 July 1978, res. with mother who remarried Acton 18 Dec. 1993 Michael Rinaccio, 281 Brown Bear Crossing, Acton MA 01718. He m. 3) New Hope PA 20 June 1992 Laura Elaine Robinson b. Los Angeles 17 Sept. 1962, dau. of Herbert & Elaine Lindo; no ch. He is Massachusetts State Policeman, res. 1994; 6 Carriage Circle, Bourne MA 02532, ph. (508)759-1750.

ii. John Ronald "Ron" Shaw, b. 8 March 1944. accountant, San Francisco area; he has several original family documents, including Thomas Jr.'s 1861 Cash Book. Res. 1980: 205 Monte Diablo #8C San Mateo CA 94401; ph. {415) 347-2993; (o)345-5742.

Virginia worked 28 years as nurse at Tewksbury State Hospital c. 1959-87; remarried 2) 17 Oct. 1964 Henry William Morgan b. Billerica 14 Nov. 1932 son of John Young & Nellie Trayton; he d. Billerica 19 Aug. 1982; no children. She res. 46 Morgan Rd. Billerica 01821-3438; ph. (508) 663-3954.

iii. Robert Teel McLeod, b. 10 Jan. 1927; d. Peterboro NH 30 Dec. 1989; m. 10 April 1948 Dorothy Powell; Res. 1980 Forest Park, RFD #1 box 139 Jaffrey NH 03452; 2 ch:

i. David Thomas b. 27 May 1955, m. Peterboro NH Mary Beth Jones; 2 ch. b. Peterboro: Katrina Dorothy b. 19 Feb. 1984 and Heather Elizabeth b. 17 Aug. 1988; also stepdaughter not adopted: Melissa Whipple b. 27 Aug. 1978. ii.Cheryl b. 5 Sept. 1957; m. 5 May 1975 Jerome C. Maschan; 3 ch.: i. Joshua Robert b. 5 Sept. 1977 or 13 Oct. 1978; ii. Melissa Marie b. 5 July 1979; iii. Melody Lynn b. 8 July 1982; res. 1980 Chesham Pond Rd., Harrisville NH 03450.

Robert was a nail machine operator. On his death his widow remarried 25 March 1993 Al Wager.

iv. Ralph Gould (McLeod) Balch, b. Arlington 27 Feb. 1928; he was adopted, and raised by his aunt Melissa, whose name he took at baptism Buffalo 1942. He m. 18 Jan. 1947 Janet Ruth Dyer-Hurdon, b. Buffalo, 23 July 1927; he was auto inspector at Chevrolet plant in Buffalo area, res. 1963-1991: 389 Victoria Rd., Kenmore NY 14217; ph. (316)877-3432.

3 children:

i. Carolyn Ann Balch, b. Kyoto Japan 13 May 1949 m. Kenmore NY 8 July 1972 Thomas G. Coleman; b. Buffalo 24 Sept. 1949; res. 1983 1419 Parker Blvd. Tonawanda NY 14223.

2 ch. b. Amherst NY: Scott Thomas b. 30 May 1976, and Jessica Rae b. 9 June 1978.

ii. Donna Lee, b. Buffalo 8 Nov. 1952; m. Kenmore 8 Oct. 1971 Louis J. Kasmer b. Buffalo 22 March 1949; 2 ch. : Scott Christopher b. Buffalo 6 Feb. 1973, and Sarah Melissa b. Amherst NY 18 July 1978. Res. 1983: 230 Wilmington Av. Tonawanda NY 14150. iii.Diane Leslee, b. Buffalo 25 Oct. 1957; m. Kenmore 3 Aug. 1986 William NMI Marks of Hughes Industries; 1 ch.: Adam Justin b. Kenmore 11 Jan. 1989.

ii. Melissa Otis Whiting, bookkeeper, b. Lexington 21 July 1894 (LVR 284), d. Kenmore NY 8 May 1987, m. 11 Oct. 1922 Merrill Calvin Balch he d. 12 March 1979. No children; they adopted her nephew Ralph Gould (McLeod) Balch, see above. Prior to marriage she was cashier at George W. Spaulding Grocery in Lexington center, then bookkeeper at Jefferson Union Co. (Obit., *Lexington Minute-Man*, 14 June 1984. She retired as a bookkeeping machine operator, for 20 years at Columbus-McKinnon Corp. 1937-57. res. Upper Mountain Rd., RFD #1, box 165, Sanborn NY. until 1979 when she moved to son Ralph's. Buried Mount View Cem., Kenmore.

iii. George Gould, general contractor like his father and Gould ancestors, b. Lexington 18 Sept. 1895 (LVR 284), d. Lexington 3 July 1948 in an accident; m. 6 Oct. 1926 Marion Emily Robus; she worked at Lexington Trust Co. She d. Lexington 23 Jan. 1975. He is buried Westview Cem. Lexington. Three children born Lexington:

i. Barbara Emily, b. 6 Dec. 1927, m. 22 Dec. 1951 Clyde Richard "Dick" Althouse, jet pilot, ret. Major USAF. Res. 1994: 212 Tyburn Rd. Fairless Hills PA 19030; ph. (215) 736-1791. 4 ch.:

i. Judith Lee Althouse, b. Marianna PL 12 June 1957; m. May 1995? Kevin Preuss; she is a nurse in Archer FL.

ii. Rebecca Lynn, b. Grand Forks ND 10 Aug. 1960 m. twice: 1) Morrisville PA 4 June 1983 Kevin Patrick McCormick, div. Jan. 1994; 2 ch. b. Bristol PA: Kevin Patrick Jr. b. 6 Aug. 1983, and Christopher James b. 5 May 1985. She m. 2) Morrisville PA 17 April 1994 Stephen Curtis Kent, res. 19 Independence Dr. Morrisville PA 19067.

iii.Susan Carol, b. Grand Forks ND 19 Dec. 1961; m. Morrisville PA 28 May 1983 Philip Henry Buehler, Jr., res. 1994; 620 Hood Blvd., Fairless Hills PA 19030. 3 ch.:

i. Lindsay Marie b. Bristol PA 16 Nov. 1984.

ii.Philip Henry III "Trey" b. Bristol PA 27 Dec. 1986.

iii.Morgan Elizabeth, b. Langhorne PA 26 May 1994.

iv. Richard Clyde, b. Grand Forks ND 20 March 1963; paralegal W. Palm Beach FL 1994.

ii. George Gould Whiting Jr., b. 6 Nov. 1929; m. Duncanville TX 31 Aug. 1952 Lowana J. Heynen; he was CW0 4 warrant officer USAF 1950-70, then TV repairman; res. 1980 Rt. 2 Box 2728, Pottsboro TX 75076. 3 ch.:

i. Deborah J., b. Dallas TX 30 Aug. 1953; m. Sherman TX 29 Sept. 1973 Jerry R. Norris; 2 ch.: Alan Joe Norris b. Sherman TX 5 April 1977, and J.C. b. TX c. 1984.

ii. William George, b. Sioux Lookout ONT 4 May 1956; d. there 8 May 1956, age 4 days.

iii. George Gould III, b. Slayton MN 8 Aug. 1957; m. Sherman TX 2 Feb. 1980 Sandra Brown; 1 ch.: Amanda Gail, b. Pottsville TX 27 Oct. 1980.

iii. William "Billy" Thomas, b. 11 March 1934; m. 2 Sept. 1957 Joan R. Reenstierna; he is a firefighter, res: 341 Lowell Street, Lexington 02173. 4 ch. b. Lexington?:

i. William Thomas Jr., b. 20 May 1958; m. Lexington 4 June 1983 Linda Jean Strango

ii. Todd Eric, b. 17 Nov. 1959; m. Sharon MA 8 May 1982 Cheryl Ann Roach.

iii. Davidson Gould, b. 8 March 1963; d. Lexington 18 Aug. 1994 in crash of his State police car on Rt. 128 when a NYNEX van lept center divider and hit his patrol car head on (*Boston Globe.* 19 Aug. 1994 1,29); m. 29 June 1992 Michele Louise Spiers, dau.of Richard E. & Louise M. of Lexington. Buried Westview Cem. Lexington. No children.

iv. Tamzin Helen, b. 4 Nov. 1970.

iv. Ralph Waldo Whiting, b. 22 July 1900, d. Lexington 14 Feb. 1901, age 6 months.

v. Hazel Edith Whiting, b. 21 Feb. 1903, d. Concord 17 March 1987, m. 26 Oct. 1929 Charles Louis LaPorte; res. 32 Gould Rd. Bedford 01230. She was Lexington's oldest girl scout, having joined in 1918, 5 years after its founding {Obit. *Lexington Minute-Man*, 26 March 1987) . She learned to play drum from William J. Healy at Hancock School (wedding *Gift Record,* #31), and began playing at the Patriots Day parade in 1921, winning two state drummer contests in 1922 and 1923. She inherited the Gould homestead at

Grapevine Corner on her father's death in 1948, returned from South Wales NY. Her husband fixed up the old house, tore down the old barn and wagon shed, and converted the wagon shed on the lower part to a four car garage (letter to author 12 Oct 1962). He ran the Jenny gas station at 384 Waltham Street. He d. Lexington 30 Oct. 1963.

In 1967 she reactivated the Lexington Drum and Bugle Corps for the Patriots Day celebration, leading it to parades in Bristol RI, Lexington KY, Portland ME and the nation's capitol. Her charity was marked by welcoming servicemen at nearby Hanscomb AFB at Christmas and Thanksgiving. Active in the town historical society, she preserved the Gould family documents, including Thomas Gould's Day Book and his wife's diaries.

She died at Walden nursing center in Concord, and was buried at Munroe Cemetery to the tribute of the Drum & Bugle Corps she led many years.

Two children:

i. Richard Whiting LaPorte, b. Lexington 16 Aug. 1930; m. twice: 1) Japan 18 Feb. 1951 Shizuka Shiba; div. 1958/79; joined USAF 1947; after retiring from USAF he became senior technician at Mitre Corp. res. 118 Harwood Av. Littleton MA 1962. 2 ch.:

i. David Shiba, b. Waltham 3 Dec. 1953; m. Middleton MA? c. 1987-8 Brenda; res. 1994 FL.

ii.Robert Shiba, b. 374 Station Hospital, Tachikawa, Japan 7 June 1956; m. twice: 1) Littleton MA 18 June 1983 Diane M. Downey; US Army Okinawa 1987; res. Winchendon MA; m. 2} c. 1992; res. 1994 Las Vegas, where he is stage manager for MGM Grand. Richard m. 2) Lexington 26 Nov. 1979 K. Marise (Hodgkins) Murphy of Hyannis; sp. they res. 1995 Ponemah Hill Rd. Milford NH 03055, ph. (603) 673-6857.

ii. Dorothy Ruth, b. N. Attleboro 21 April 1933; m. 23 Feb. 1957 Eduard W. Pass b. Moscow USSR 26 Oct. 1933; ed. Graz, Austria; 6 mos. USArmy; naturalized US citizen; he is owner of Pass Porsche-Audi car agency; res. 32 Gould Rd., Bedford MA 01730, ph. (617) 275-7519. 2 ch. b. Arlington MA.:

i. Katherine Ursula Pass, b. 29 Dec. 1957; m. twice 1) Lexington 10 May 1986 George A. Brun, b. Lowell 25 Oct. 1958; she grad. cum laude Johnson Wales College, Providence AA in culinary arts 11 June 1978; was a chef and caterer. She m. 2) 2003 res. VA.

ii. Eduard "Edie" Roman, b. 28 Feb. 1960; m. Revere 2 July 1988 Michelle A. Mellace; Res. 124 Tennis Plaza Rd. #14, Dracut MA 01826.

Chapter X

LYDIA ANN TEEL GOULD, 1805-1893

LYDIA ANN^6 WINSHIP TEEL (Benjamin^5, William$^{4-3-2-1}$) was born in Newburyport MA, 25 June 1805 (Lydia's diary, 1874, 1875; VR 380 states 24 June, based on 2d Presby. Church record). She died in Lexington MA 6 Jan. 1893, age 87 (Massachusetts Death Records 437:219; obit. *Transcript* 13 Jan.).

She was married in Boston 3 Sept. 1829 to THOMAS^6 WARREN GOULD Jr., housewright (Diary 1877: "Sept. 3 the Anniversary of My Weding day. I have been married fourty two years to day"; *Statesman.* 5 Sept. 1829; VR 1:343) . By him she had six children, listed above.

Lydia was descended from the first settlers of Cambridge and Arlington, Lt. Edward Winship, Francis Whitmore and Richard Parke, early immigrant of Salem and Danvers Richard Ingersoll, the founders of Braintree Francis Eliot and Martin Saunders, five pioneer families of Newbury and Newburyport, Noyes, Greenleaf, Somerby, Hale and Moody, early Rowley settler Andrew Hidden, first colonists of Ipswich William Moody and John Perkins, Dedham founder Michael Bacon, Bedford and Billerica pioneer Michael Bacon Jr., Haverhill planter Thomas Hale, New Haven settler Jasper Crane and founder of York ME and Salisbury MA Thomas Bradbury.

Several of these pioneers had distinguished connections. Michael Bacon was a cousin of the famous scientist and author Sir Francis Bacon. Jasper Crane was a leader of the Puritan government of New Haven and the first united colony of Connecticut. Colonial leader Capt. Thomas Bradbury's ancestry traced back to royalty, his mother was niece of Queen Elizabeth's Archbishop of Canterbury, and his wife Mary (Perkins) Bradbury who was tried for witchcraft in Salem.

Lydia's grandfather was a leader of the Revolutionary patriots in Newburyport, and her father's first cousin, Joshua Wyeth, was one of the "Indians" who dumped the British tea into the harbor at the Boston Tea Party. Her great uncle Josiah Teel fought in the battle of Lexington, and first cousin Jason Winship was the first civilian killed in the Revolution, in an Arlington tavern. Most of her ancestral families had Indian fighters, including two soldiers in the Great Swamp fight in King Philip's War.

Several of her ancestors were active politicians. She had a forebear in the Massachusetts legislature continuously for 16 years 1651-66, and in the stormy decade 1677-86 of "The First American Revolution", in which Caleb Moody was imprisoned f of his resistance to tyranny. She had ancestors who were selectmen and officers of all of the towns named above.

Among her cousins were four U.S. Presidents, Ford (thru John Noyes), Pierce (thru Kenrick), Fillmore (thru Story & Foster) and Hayes (thru Farnum). Also cousins were Supreme Court Justice Moody, poet John Greenleaf Whittier, noted lawyers like Harvard Law School professor Simon Greenleaf, Robert Hale of the Alabama Claims and Massachusetts Supreme Judicial Court Justices Theophilus Bradbury and Dwight Foster. Among the several U.S. Congressmen were Chairman of the House Foreign Affairs Committee Charles Ingersoll. There was a Loyalist colonial official who opposed the Revolution, Jared Ingersoll. Military leaders included Revolutionary War captain, two Civil War colonels, a Mexican War colonel, an Admiral and a Secretary of the Navy.

In the private sector Lydia had cousins who were important inventors, of cotton machinery and the world's first stamp. Industrial pioneers included the Ingersolls of the typewriter, and lockmaker Halbert Greenleaf. A partner of J. P. Morgan, and a London banker and transportation magnate were among the financier cousins. The king of the Sumatra pepper trade, Joseph Peabody, was a cousin. There were ten nationally known clergymen and theologians, mostly Unitarian. There were two editors of major newspapers in New York and Boston. Educators of national note are numerous, including Alcott's associate Elizabeth Peabody, one of the famous Peabody sisters. Three of the most important orators of the nineteenth century were cousins, Rufus Choate, Edward Bacon and Robert Ingersoll. The architect of the Lincoln Memorial was also a cousin, as was the Boston Custom House tower designer. Two important doctors, Edwin Hale and Elisha Perkins were cousins. Well-known women cousins were writer Delia Bacon, and poet Josephine Peabody. Genealogists Henry Waters, John Dean and William Whitmore were also cousins. Among her relatives was the noted musician William Bradbury.

It is doubtful if Lydia ever knew any of these people personally, but it shows what talented stock she came from. Many did grow up in Newburyport, so her parents may have sold them bread, candles and soap, and she may have gone to school with some.

Lydia's ancestors came to America from England, with the possible exception of the Farnhams and Moodys who may have come from Wales. The English counties of origin are less eastern than Sophia Lovis's. Although there are a lot of East Anglian families from Essex (Eliot, Foster, Moore, Winship and Bradbury), Suffolk (Bacon, Greenleaf, Harrington, Moody and Saunders), Norfolk (Bacon and Story) and Lincolnshire (Somerby and Whitgift), there are many more from the West Country counties of Wiltshire (Cutting and Noyes), Berkshire (Aggar and Cutting) and Hampshire (Hepburn, Knight and Poore), Devonshire (Foster) and several from the central counties of Derbyshire (Bradbury), Warwickshire (Perkins), Leicestershire (Farnum and Ingersoll), Cambridgeshire (Hale) and Hertfordshire (Aggar and Hale). And, unlike the Lovis origins there are some from the north: Winship, Foster and Wilkinson from Northumbria, Kenrick from Yorkshire or Lancashire.

Most of Lydia's ancestors arrived in the Great Migration, between 1629 and 1642. The first arrival was on the *Mayflower* voyage of 1629, by Richard Ingersoll. Last arrivals were the Hiddens about 1649, Houston by 1654 and Teels by 1680. Places of settlement were all on Massachusetts Bay, mostly on the North Shore in today's Essex County, with heaviest concentration of five families in Newbury, four in Ipswich and two in Rowley. Boston was the first place of settlement of five families, and Charlestown for three. The Charles river valley was the next center, with four families in Cambridge, spreading out to its satellite towns of Newton, Arlington, Lexington and Medford. The only South Shore towns of settlement were Braintree (Eliot and Saunders), Dedham (Bacon) and Duxbury (Hall). The most northern place of colonization was York, Maine, by Bradbury, who later went to Salisbury, Massachusetts

Most of the pioneers seem to have gone into farming and stock-raising on arrival, using skills from rural farm areas of England where most of them were born. However, three opened up ordinaries to serve liquor (Saunders, Somerby and Knight).

Where previous occupations are known most were skilled craftsmen. Four ancestors were leather workers, including two glove-makers, a currier, or leather-dresser, and a saddler. Two were in the cloth business, one a silk-dyer, and another a mercer, or merchant tailor. There were two skilled carpenters who became housewrights. Two founding pioneers were master seamen, Captains Blaney and Cutting. There was also the merchant Richard Park. We also had a barber and a tailor.

Most were middle class. Although some may have had ties with gentry, they were younger sons without titles, like Bradbury. Two family founders were sons (Noyes) or brothers (Eliot) of Puritan ministers.

In religion all were members of the Puritan church, and none seem to have been members of dissenting groups of Baptists, Quakers or Hutchinsonians until the Presbyterian conversion of the 1750s.

A striking characteristic of Lydia's ancestry was the great age of many at death. Her great-grandmother Anna Whitmore Winship died just short of 100. The longest lived was Sarah Houston Hidden, who died in Rowley at age 103. Elizabeth Knight Noyes, at 92, was the oldest person in Newbury. Many others lived into their eighties and nineties, though there are a number of short-lived ancestors.

In a society where punishment for adultery and pre-marital sex was not uncommon, it is notable that there is none of this recorded for Lydia's ancestors. Marriages appear to have been stable. The major exception may be the mystery of Lydia's grandfather John Barnard. His marriage to Jemima Hidden is recorded only 20 years later, and the family never mentioned him or anything about him. There is the possibility that he was the playboy minister's son who went to Harvard, who jilted women, and fled the country as a Tory. But nothing can be proved about him.

In this chapter we will tell first of Lydia's father, and his ancestors, then of his wife and her family, and ancestors, and conclude with what we know of Lydia's own life.

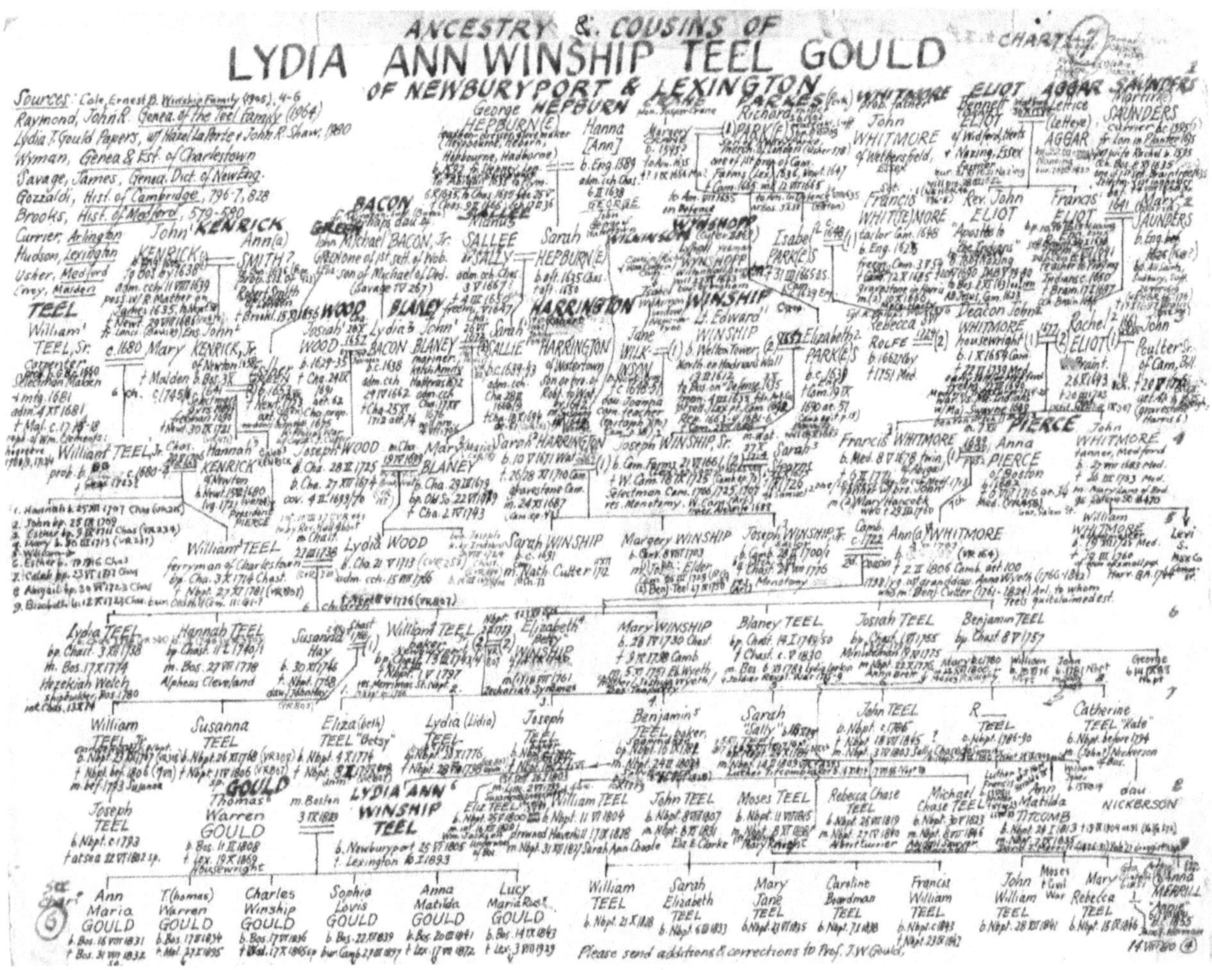

LYDIA'S ANCESTRY

Lydia's father BENJAMIN^{5} TEEL (William$^{4\text{-}3\text{-}2\text{-}1}$), a baker and soapmaker, was a pioneer in the soapmaking business in Louisville KY about 1818. He was born in Newburyport, and baptized at North Church 16 Sept. 1781 (VR 380; Lydia Gould's handwritten record in John Shaw's possession, San Mateo CA, hereinafter LG) , fourth child of WILLIAM^{4} TEEL and his second wife ELIZABETH^{4} "Betty" WINSHIP (Joseph$^{3\text{-}2}$, Edward^{1}; John M. Raymond, *Genealogy of the Teel Family* [Palo Alto: Runnymede Press, 1964] [hereinafter Raymond], 9). We will tell more of his life after telling about his parents and ancestry.

Benjamin's father, WILLIAM^{4} TEEL Jr. (William$^{3\text{-}2\text{-}1}$) , baker of Newburyport, was the third of six children of WILLIAM^{3} TEEL of Charlestown and LYDIA^{3} WOOD, of whom more below under Wood Family. He was born Charlestown 12 March 1743/4 (LG) and baptized there the next day (Wyman 935).

William Teel was a member of the Newburyport Committee of Safety and Correspondence that led the patriots at the start of the American Revolution (23 Sept. 1774, Mrs. E. Vale Smith, *History of Newburyport* [Newburyport: the author, 1854], 81); Hurd 2:1744). The committee organized the Minute Men that marched to Lexington and Bunker Hill, bought cannon and gunpowder, and organized the town watch. His brother Josiah Teel was one of the Minutemen of Newburyport under Captain Nowell who responded to the alarm at Lexington (Hurd 2:1745; is it he who served with Capt. Barnard in 1776 as "Tool" in Hurd 2:1746b; see Revol. War records).

William Teel Jr. had two wives, the second one our ancestor. He had married in Charlestown firstly on 30 Oct. 1766 Susanna Hay (VR 497, int. 24 Oct. VR 485; Nbpt. VR 468), daughter of John Hay & Mercy Sutton, born 30 Nov. 1746 (VR 389; Wyman 486). The Teels had moved to Newburyport by the end of 1767, when their first son William^{5} Teel, Jr. was born (23 Dec. 1767, VR 380). This son died before July 1806, having married a Susanna, and fathered Joseph^{6} Teel, born Newburyport about 1793 (VR 380) and died at sea 22 June. 1802 without issue (VR 807) . William's wife Susanna (Hay) died at the end of 1768 after giving birth to their second child, Susanna, 26 Nov. 1768 (VR 380) . This child died at age 38 in Newburyport 1 April 1806 (VR 807) without issue.

William Jr. then remarried in Newburyport 2 Feb. 1773 (VR 468) to ELIZABETH "Betty"^{4} WINSHIP SYMMES, widow of Zechariah Symmes (d. 1766). Of her, more shortly under Winship Family. They had eight children in Newburyport.

William Teel was not only a baker, but candlemaker and merchant in meat and other foods. In the Teel Account Book 1791-1825 (kept by John Shaw of San Mateo, CA) we have receipts of William Teel for tallow, flour, candle moulds, yeast, wood, beef, and candle boxes, for a five year period, dated 20 Dec. 1791 to 24 Dec. 1796 which shows that in addition to his bakery, Teel was involved in candle making in the building next to his home on Merrimac Street Items that clearly relate to the bakery are twelve receipts for flour, and one for carting 16 barrels of flour from Salem, for which he paid $8 to Ipswich farmer Jacob Manning (3 Oct. 1796). One receipt specifies Philadelphia flour 17 Jan, 1793). There are nine receipts for wood, for the oven. There are two for salt, and one each for sugar, molasses, butter, yeast and hegg [sic].

Some of the wood he bought probably went into fires for candle making. The biggest cost was tallow, for which there are 43 receipts, some specifying rendered or tryd tallow, or good rough tallow. His major suppliers of tallow were Capt. Nathaniel Thurston of Bradford for whom there are eleven unspecified deliveries, and the brothers Richard and Levi Bean of Brintwood for whom there are nine deliveries, also probably tallow. On 2 April 1792 he paid John Nicoll £ 22/10/1 for four dozen #4 candle moulds, 4 dozen #5s, and an iron pan. Moses Somerby was his main supplier of candle boxes @ a shilling each. There are four receipts for "work" from John Adams, Richard Wright and Samuel Beede, and Richard Hunniwell seems to have been on the payroll for $20 a month for most of 1796.

Teel was also in the business of selling locally raised beef to Philadelphia, for there are 13 receipts for beef, one which the supplier guaranteed "to be Sweat & good Marchintate Beef" (18 Feb. 1794) . The Philadelphia destination appears in two receipts, 5 Feb. 1794 and "sold for me in Philadelphia" 28 Oct. 1794 for Nathaniel Garland. There is one purchase of pork, some lamb, and frequent meat scraps that went along with the tallow.

Then there are building items in his accounts, like a house frame for which he paid Jon[a] Abbot Jr. £ 11, and the same amount again a month later (18 May, 20 June 1792). In 1793 he paid Jon[a] Dale £ 1/1 to build a stone wall 3 rods and half a link (50 feet) beginning at his northeast corner and running half way across his land (4 Nov.). Six chairs bought from Daniel Somerby for £ 2/8 may have been for resale (18 Nov. 1794).

Some items are personal, like two watches, a silver one with the day of the month, bought three days before Christmas for £ 7, and another for £ 5/8 from David Wood (21 Dec. 1793, 7 Oct. 1794). There are other items like $20 for eight barrels of syder bought from Henry Little (11 Nov. 1794), and £ 3 for five hogsheads of rum from Zebulon Rowe (16 April 1792) that were probably for resale like the beef.

William Teel also owned an interest in an oil mill at the foot of the falls of the Merrimac River in Amesbury, which he held in partnership with Amesbury gentleman Timothy[5] Barnard (1741-98; Jonathan[4], Samuel[3], Thomas[2-1], no known relation) : and Newburyport painter Joseph Pearson (Essex deed 154:97, 21 Nov. 1791). Pearson and Teel sold out their interest to Barnard 21 Nov. 1791.

William Teel's home, where Benjamin probably grew up, was on the northeast corner of Merrimac Street (the waterfront street of town) and Summer Street, facing Patch's Wharf (Harden map 1851) , which has been torn down and replaced by Country Driving School in 1995.

William Teel Jr. died in Newburyport 1 May 1797 (not in VR; LG) age 54. The last entry in his account book is made the day before Christmas 1796. His last illness was reported by his daughter Betsey in a letter to her cousin Anne Cutter also gives the order of his children as he insisted on their lining up for church: "Newbury-port 3 July 1794...my father is indispos'd. . .The week afterwards came home he was very delirious and has remain'd in the same situation ever since...! knew not felt nothing of his illness before now, when he was sick before, *I* was young, and threw off ene trouble, which I find is now impossible, Mam [her mother] has a great degree of fortitude, I hope I am thankful for it I am sure I know not what we cou'd do without her if I cou'd be but half so insensible as mam appears I shou'd be in some measure happy to what I am at present, sometimes I wish I had no feeling at all, my Father has two Doc[rs] but they can do nothing for him but to converse with and try to sooth him, but after all advice he will follow his own inclination//...

The first Sunday after my father was taken our minister happen'd to be out of town and, Sunday morn, he insisted upon it that every one of the family shou'd go to Mr. Andrews with him and walk in order (he is very fond of order and regularity whenever [illegible word]...ell) he'd head my-self next Lydia Joseph Benj[n] Sally John R-R--and Kate to bring up the rear. *I* pleaded indisposition and in fact was truly sick [she died of TB four years later] . Sick or well we must all attend I found how it was and determin'd not to be one but went into one of the neighbours and spent the day, the procession began their walk about eleven oclock all except Jo--- and proceeded to the meeting house, was there stopt which made my father quite outragious, he made them all run home as fast as they coud come--poor souls a tedious day it was [.] Some nights we have little or no sleep and for four or five nights when he was first taken he never went into his bed and eat barely sufficient to keep him alive.--

Mams arm has not recover'd she cannot yet lift it to he head...Eliza Teel"

We have not found where he was buried, perhaps with his parents at Old Hill.

His wife was executor of his estate. His real estate included his "mansion house" on Merrimac Street, the adjoining candle works, which was heavily mortgaged to local baker John Berry Titcomb (as seen in documents below). The family home on Merrimac Street and the barn behind it on Summer Street were left to his wife, as appears from Benjamin's quitclaim of Sept. 1816 quoted below. There were numerous claims against his estate by Benjamin Moody Sr. and Jr. who agreed to forego their claims in a document in John Shaw's collection:

"Newbury-Port, Decr 21st '98.

This day looked over all accounts between Mr. William Teel, late of Newbury-Port aforesaid & Benjamin Moody Senior; and owing to Dates omitted & other difficulties occurring which makes it impossible to come to the right of the matter, we have agreed, each on our own part & on the part of those for whom we act, entirely to give up all demands, dues, charges, Bill or any other matter thereto appertaing, & do acknowledge as aforesaid each for ourselves & for those we act, never to demand any thing each of the other, but to consider all accounts settled, & all matters adjusted to our mutual satisfaction as witness our hands--Signed in behalf of Benjamin Moody Senior,

Benjamin Moody Junr

In behalf of Elizabeth Teel Administratrix

Joseph Teel [her son]"

In 1803 Benjamin was still dealing with the estate, his brother Joseph having died 22 June 1802 (VR 807). In the account book he recorded under 27 Jan. 1803: "this day looked it over and setled all accounts with John Berry Titcomb Relative to My Father's Estate and gave Susan ten Dollars for her Dower in the Herbert Land adjoining to the tallow house" (Account Book).

The settlement of the estate of his brother Joseph, who died intestate, gives an account of William Teel's property which Benjamin acquired. Levi Mills, trader, as administrator of Joseph's estate declared 17 Jan. 1803 that Benjamin bought at auction, as highest bidder, for one dollar, on 5 Jan. 1803, "a certain Tenement in...Newburyport which is under mortgage to John Berry Titcomb of Said Newburyport Baker-for the sum of" $914.20 with interest up to 5 Jan. $1026.50 "and in consideration of his discharging the above Mortgage, and of the above sum of one dollar"...sold to Benjamin "a certain lot of Land with the building thereon Situated in Newbury port (called the Candle Manufactory) adjoining the mantion house of William Teel dece^{d} on Merrimac Street--It being fifty two feet six inches in length and twenty feet five inches in width with the land under said Buildings--and a privilege of the passage way from thence to Merrimac Street".

"Likewise by virtue of the above Order [for disposal of the estate], have Sold to...Benjamin Teel, for forty Dollars--About four rods of Land more or less with the incumbrance of the widow Susanna Teel Dower--Adjoining on the Southwest End of the Above mentioned piece of Land it being a piece of Land Deeded by John Herbert to Joseph Teel...In Consideration of ten Dollars I Susanna Teel Relinquish my right of Dower in the above Mentioned piece of Land." [signed] Levi Mills

Susan Teel (Recorded in Essex Deeds 2 Feb. 1803 171:164)."

William Teel Jr.'s father was WILLIAM^{3} TEEL Sr. (William$^{2-1}$), ferryman of Charlestown and Newburyport. He was baptized Charlestown 3 Oct. 1714 (not in VR; Wyman 935), son of WILLIAM^{2} TEEL Jr. of Malden and HANNAH KENRICK, of whom more under Kenrick Family, below. He was married in Charlestown 27 March 1738 (VR 330) by Rev. Hull Abbot to LYDIA^{3} WOOD of Charlestown, their intentions recorded 10 March 1738 (VR 463) . They had six children, all born in Charlestown. Two sons served in the American Revolution, Blaney (1750-c. 1830) served five years 1775-9, and Josiah was a Minuteman 19 April 1775 (Revol. War Records 15: 469-470). William^{3} died in Newburyport 27 Nov. 1781 (VR 807), age 67. He was buried in Old Hill Cemetery, Newburyport Sec., off Pond Street, third row from street, F-7, lot 17, grave 1.

He was the fifth of eight children of WILLIAM² TEEL Jr., whose birth and death is not recorded, but probably born in Great Britain, or perhaps Malden c.1680-4 (Raymond 3).

William² Jr. married in Charlestown 20 May 1706 (VR 210) HANNAH³ KENRICK of Newton, of whom more under Kenrick Family, shortly. They had eight children between 1707 and 1723. He died in Charlestown after 1723, when his last child Elizabeth was born 12 Oct. 1723 (VR 279; Raymond 6).

He was eldest of six children of the family founder, WILLIAM¹ TEEL Sr., carpenter of Malden. The father was a relatively poor man, a late immigrant about 1680. He was born in Great Britain about 1660 (Deloraine Corey *The History of Malden* [Malden: the author, 1899] [hereinafter Corey] 396-402. The name is inconsistently spelled TEAL, TEALE, TEEL, TEELE, TELLE and THEALE. One family tradition is that they were Orangemen, that is Protestants, from Northern Ireland (Frank H. Teal, cited by Raymond 1). The time of their appearance in America, the 1680s, was when many immigrants were coming from the border area of England and Scotland, or from Northern Ireland (David H. Fischer, *Albion's Seed* [Oxford: Oxford Univ. Press, 1989], 606.

Other Teels of the time have not been connected with William: John Teel, a schoolmaster of Charlestown (Raymond 3, citing Wyman 937), and Alice Teel who married William Man 11 June 1657 (Raymond Supp. 2 citing Cambridge VR, Sav. 3:146; Reg. 13:325n; Paige 601) . Raymond demonstrates that William has no known connection with the Connecticut Teel family.

Our only clue to the first William's origin is that he was a nephew of a William Clements (4 Col. RL 360; Wyman 2:934-5; Boutelle 3:245-53; Teall (3) 50, cited by Raymond 2; Raymond has done extensive research on this connection, and cannot distinguish which of three William Clements this is, or the exact relation--see his letter 20 Aug. 1980).

Teel first appeared in America in Malden records on 4 Nov. 1681, when "Will Teale" was one of ten men named "to cut and cart wood for Mr. Chevis", the minister Rev. Thomas Cheever (Corey 259) . He held a minor town office of Hawerd, or hogreeve, in 1709 and 1714 (4 March 1708/9, March 1713/4, Corey 352). His duties were described "to se to the swine that thay [be] yoked and Ringed that thay may not do damige in the medowes." (Corey 352).

His wife's name was Mary, but we do not know her maiden name. She probably married him in the old country. Mary outlived him, and died in Malden about 1745 (not in VR; Raymond 6).

Teel was among the poor of Malden, who received public assistance from the town. William received a grant of six acres in today's Melrose, at the end of the 300 acres in the third division, between Swain's Pond and Scadan in 1695, but not as freeholder or proprietor (Corey 378, 397) . This land he sold to Philip Atwood in 1706 (MD 14:147 in Corey 397), evidently in need of cash. He owed the local doctor, Samuel Wigglesworth in 1711 (Corey 610n). He was twice excused from taxes, in 1702 and 1714 (Corey 397).

In 1709 the town gave Teel the right to put a fence across the road leading down to the Sandy Bank landing on the Malden River, with right to the "fede" in the fenced area (March 1708/9, Corey 459) . This was renewed every year, and continued to his widow, who in 1719 was permitted "To hang a gate a thort sandy-bank high-way neer her hous, and to haue ye benefit of ye feed or paster in ye buring place." (Corey 460).

In Aug. 1713 the town gave him and his wife a life tenure of a small lot at the south corner of the Great Road (Main) and Burying Ground Lane (later called Poor House Lane, today's Madison Street) (Corey 397, 399n, 99n). This was near the first burying ground at Sandy Bank, now Bell Rock Cemetery (Corey 158n). There he built a house (Corey 378, 397) . The next year the town gave him a piece of land near Sandy Bank below the clay pits, between Parsons and Samuel Green, a privilege that continued under his widow (Corey 397) .

Teel died in Malden about 1714-8 (last entry in town record=l March 1713/4, Raymond 1,6; his wife is widow 1719, Corey 459). There are no wills or estates for him or his wife. She survived him, and was helped by the town to repair her house in 1736 (16 Jan. 1735/6) . She had died by 3 March 1745/6 when another poor person, Edward Hallowell, was given "liberty to live in the house that was the teels" (Corey 398) . They are probably buried near their house in Bell Rock Cemetery, but too poor to afford gravestones.

THE KENRICK FAMILY

The son of the immigrant married well. William^{2} Teel Jr.'s wife HANNAH^{3} KENRICK was born in Newton MA 5 Dec. 1680 (VR 124; dup. 15 Dec.) to JOHN^{2} KENRICK Jr. of Newton and his wife ESTHER^{2} (GREEN) HALL. Hannah was born in Boston 3 Oct. 1641 (CD 130:11) to JOHN^{1} KENRICK Sr. and his first wife ANN(E) SMITH. The parents had married in Boston about 1638, and she had been sent to America in 1636 by her brother, wine cooper Robert Smith of London (Deposition of Elizabeth Scott 4 Dec. 1663 in Massachusetts Arch. 15 A:11 in Origins 3:632; John W. Linzee, *Peter Parker and Sarah Ruggles* [Boston: the author, 1913], 275; Pope 423 citing Scarbarrow and Reg. 40:63; Isaac B. Dodge, *Descendants of John Kendrick* [Milford NH: Cabinet Print, 1894], 2; Banks, Topo, 105 citing Reg. 40:63; Banks cited another Robert Smith who came from Manton, county Rutland, 136) . She was admitted to the First Church in Boston 18 July 1640 (Linzee 275), and died at Muddy River (Brookline) 15 Nov. 1656 (Bos.CD 130:56). He married secondly Judith who died Roxbury 23 Aug. 1687 (VR 2:567); Francis Jackson, *History of Newton* [Boston: Stacy & Richardson, 1854]; Lucius R. Paige, *History of Cambridge* [Boston: Houghton, 1877], 595).

The family name is variously spelled KENDERICK, KENDRICK, KENDRICKS, KENERICKS, KENNARICKS, KENRICK, KENRICKS, KINDRICK, KINNERICK, KINRICK. The senior John Kenrick may have come over on the *James* out of Bristol, with Richard Mather in 1635, from Lancashire (Topo. 89, citing Sav. [3:11]). He was born in York (Jackson, corrections, 7) about 1605 (Jackson 354; will of 1683 says his age was about 78) . He died Newton 29 Aug. 1686 age 82 (VR 471; Paige 596; town monument says age 82 at death; Jackson says 81, 355).

Kenrick was in Boston by 1638, where he was admitted to the church on 11 Aug. 1639, as "John Kenricke, a Laborer" (Winsor 1:573), and made freeman 1640 (Jackson 354; S. F. Smith, *History of Newton* [Boston: Amer. Logotype, 1880], 99-100, 144; Mary Elizabeth (Crosby) Kendrick in Elizabeth B. Hall, "The Genealogy of John^{8} William Kendrick" (typesc. Great Barrington MA, 1979, 37). He is listed in the Boston Book of Possessions about 1645 (Winsor 1:559).

His house and garden in Boston were on the south side of Milk Street, about halfway down from Washington to the creek (Winsor 2: xxix, map #51 xxv; #71 on George Lamb's "Plan of Boston...1635") . Lamb shows Kenrick also in 1635 owning two sites on Trimount, between Beacon Hill and Pemberton Hill in the area of Ashburton Place. Lamb also credits him with land in 1635 in the West End near today's Shriners Hospital. He owned Tyng's Wharf on the east side of the Town Dock in Boston, which he sold to Richard Brecke of Dorchester for £ 28 in 1652 (8

Jan. SD 1:323). He may also have owned the house of Valentine Hill on the north side of Hanover Street, just west of Union Street, close to the later house and store of Thomas[5] Gould in today's Haymarket (Winsor 2: v, map #6, iv) . This may be the property next to which Simon Bradstreet built a house in 1649 next to Kenrick, and "adjoining the lane that goes down to the mill pond." (SD 1:130).

Kenrick was living as a farmer in Muddy River (Brookline) by 1651 when he and his wife are named as "brother and sister" in the will of Thomas Sawtell, whether brother-in-law or brother is unclear (will of 14 May 1651, pro. 18 Sept., Suff. Will 111 in Reg. 126:3, 4:286; Suff. 1: 64-5 in Linzee 275; he calls himself yeoman in SD 1:323). He sold his estate in Muddy River (Brookline) and moved a few miles west to Newton by 1658 (**SD;** Dodge 2).

In 1658 Kenrick was one of the first settlers (sixteenth per Jackson 10) of Newton, then part of Cambridge. He paid £ 200 for a house and barn on 250 acres east of the Charles River from Richard Parker (hence called "Parker's Farm") of Boston, who had acquired it from Thomas Mayhew (MD cited by Jackson 27, 354; Hall 37). Today the farm is still mostly open land between the Charles River and Winchester Street, and Wallace and Nahanton Streets, with the north end nicely preserved as Nahanton Park.

The Kenrick house was on the south side of today's Nahanton Street near where Wells Av. enters Newton Industrial Park (map in Jackson 112). The continuation of Nahanton Street westward across the Charles at "Kenrick's Bridge" is still called Kendrick Street in Needham.

In 1659 he was granted a historic piece of land in the village, on the southeast slope of Nonantum Hill. It was here on 28 Oct. 1646 that the Apostle John Eliot began preaching to the Indians at the wigwam of the first convert, Waban or Waanton (Smith 170-1; map Jackson). A fountain marked the spot in 1880 where the first Protestant mission in America had begun, today a plaque on a concrete railing at the end of Eliot Memorial Av., which runs east off of Waverly Av. Also present was Anne Garrison Gould's ancestor Daniel Gookin, who built a wigwam on the site in 1666 (Smith 170). The property continued down in the Kenrick family, thru J. A.[6] Kenrick, John[5] Esq. (1755-1833), and Edward Junior (1742). John Kenrick Esq. was a noted abolitionist (founder and second president of N.E.Anti-Slavery Society), and donor of the town's Kenrick Fund for the poor (Smith 358, 277; W. P. & F. J. Garrison, *William Lloyd Garrison...Life* [4 vols., NY: Century, 1885], 1:419, 425) . There is no evidence that the Indians gave title to Kenrick, who apparently got it directly from the town of Cambridge which claimed "what land the Indians possessed and improved, by subduing the same, they have just right unto." according to the colony law of 1633 (Jackson 84) . Waban and friends moved off the land in 1651 to the 6,000 acre reservation in Natick (Jackson 85). It is unclear to me if this is the property west and south of the 60 acre lot sold by Samuel & Mary Truesdale of New Cambridge (Newton) to William Gilbert of Boston 23 June 1679 (SD 9:218; Jackson's maps may clarify this).

In 1671 he was chosen as one of three Cambridge Constables, presumably for the Newton side of the river (CR 196; Paige 464). In 1673 Cambridge appointed "olde goodman kendrick" hogreeve "on the other side of the water for the swine." (CR 209). Both he and his son signed the petition of 1678 to separate Cambridge Village (Newton) from the town of Cambridge (text in Jackson 50; Paige 80).

Kenrick died Newton 29 Aug. 1686 (VR 471), age 82. His name appears on the Newton town monument to the first settlers in the Center Street Cemetery, on the northwest corner of Cotton and Center Streets, between Newton Corner and Newton Center. On the west face of the obelisk is inscribed: "John Kenrick 1658 [time of settlement]-1686 [date of death]-82 [age at death] (Edith Alien, "Tombstone Records of Newton Mass" (1937), 24).

His will of 21 Jan. 1683 gives his age "about 78" (Jackson 355). He left the west end of the house to his widow Judith, and to his son John Jr., his executor the house and barn and residue of the estate. He left his son-in-law Jonathan Metcalf who had married his daughter Hannah 50 acres in the southeast of his farm which he had bought from first settler Deacon John Jackson before he died in 1675 (Jackson 327). He also gave Metcalf ten acres of meadow at Cow

Island. He also left four acres of meadow by the Charles to the second minister, Rev. Nehemiah Hobart, or £ 10, at the discretion of his son John Jr. The will was proved 23 Sept. 1686.

His founder's son, the junior John Kenrick, was settled on his father's estate in south Newton, at Mr. Parker's farm 1 March 1659 (Dodge 2). At age 23 went to England for a year (1667-8; Dodge 3 citing "[Benjamin[4]] Kenrick's Memorandum, 1772"). Because of his father's age (73), it is probably the son whom Cambridge made a surveyor in 1677 (CR 236).

He was Selectman of Newton for nine years, 1689 ff. (Jackson 216; Sav.), and freeman by 1678 when he signed the petition for separation from Cambridge (Jackson 52; Smith 63; Paige 80) . In 1702 he was given in trust for the town a half acre lot at Oak Hill for a school, by Sgt. Jonathan Hyde, Sr. (Jackson 30-1; 317; at south corner of Carlson Av. and Dedham Street today) . In 1713 the town laid out a road on the east side of his land, today called Winchester Street, giving Kenrick and a neighbor the right to hang two gates on the way (Jackson 38) . In 1720 the town renewed the bounds on today's Nonantum Street from Kenrick's farm to the Dedham Road (Jackson 39-40). In 1714 he was on the committee to confirm the highways, including the one by his land (Smith 162, 163). It was not until 1761 that the Charles River was spanned at "Kenrick's Bridge" (Jackson 44).

His grandson Benjamin Kenrick's memorandum of 1772 recorded some of his aphorisms:

"A wise man which values himself upon the score of virtue, and not of opinion, thinks himself neither better or worse for the opinion of others."

"Never imploy yourself to discern the faults of others, but be careful to mend and prevent your own."

"Say what is well, and do what is better; be what you appear, and appear what you are."

"He makes himself a servile wrech,
To others evermore, Who tells his secrets
unto such As knew them not before."

"Thy credit wary keep, tis quickly gone, Being got by many
actions lost by one." (Dodge 3).

Kenrick died at Parker Farm in south Newton 30 Sept. 1721, age 27 days, 11 months and 79 years (VR 471; Dodge 2; Paige 596), and was buried on his 81st birthday, 3 Oct. (Hall 37). His tombstone is in Center Street Cemetery (Alien 24). His will of 1721 mentions his daughter Hannah Teale (Jackson 355; Dodge 3).

John Kenrick married 23 Oct. 1673 (Kenrick's Memo; not in Cam., Newt, or Wat. VR; ESTHER (GREEN), widow or daughter of John Hall whose death cannot be found in VR. She was born 1653 (g.s.; not in Cam., Newt., Wat. Brain. VR) to JOHN and ELIZABETH GREEN (Roberts' Presidents 30 gives them without dates or places. They may be the couple in Dorchester cited by Torrey).

Almira Blake believed that she was the Esther Hall born Braintree 23 Oct. 1654 to Edward[1] and Esther Hall (Almira Blake, *Nathan Blake 3rd and Susan (Torrey) Blake* [Boston: Stanhope Press, 1916], 49; Rev. David B. Hall, *The Halls of New England* [Albany: Joel Munsel's Sons, 1883], 527, 695). Hall had probably come to Salisbury by 1636 when he became freeman, but moved to Duxbury 1636-8, then Braintree 1640, Taunton 1641, back to Duxbury 1642-3, and Bridgewater 1644-52. As proprietor in settlement of Bridgewater he got land on 28 March 1645 in l/54th proportion, but withdrew from the town in 1652. He was in Rehoboth 1655, and got £ 50 right of commonage in 1658, and was #41 of 49 receiving meadow on the north side of Rehoboth. He drew lots in the North Purchase (now Attleboro, Cumberland RI and part of Mansfield and Norton) on 26 May 1668. His will of 23 Nov. 1670 was made four days before his death in Rehoboth on 27 Nov. (VR 832). His estate was a mere £ 84. He was survived by his wife Esther or Hester, who received the £ 50 commonage in 1671. It is possibly she who married Thomas Jorden in Rehoboth 24 Dec. 1674 (VR 168), or his daughter Esther (no death in VR).

The Kenrick Memo may have confused generations and families. There was a contemporary John Hall in Cambridge 1656 ff. (born England 1627, son of widow Mary Hall; he lived in Concord 1658, 1666, but had come to Cambridge before 1675, when he moved to Medford until his death there 18 Oct. 1701, Paige 570, Rev. Hall 296) who married 4 April 1656 Elizabeth Green, born Cambridge April 1639, daughter of Percival[2] and Ellen Green, who lived in Cambridge (John[1]) , Paige 567).

There was also a Hall family in Newton immediately to the east of the Kenrick farm, on the same side of the Nonantum Street, but the family head Andrew did not arrive there until 1695; he had a son John born that year; this could have been a relative of his wife (Jackson 295).

Esther and John Kenrick had 12 children (Dodge 3) . Esther died in Newton 10 Sept. 1723 age 70, and is buried at Center Street Cemetery (VR 471; Paige 596).

Hannah Kenrick's brother Caleb[3] was great-grandfather of President Franklin Pierce (1804-69; Anna[5] Kendrick m. Gen. Benjamin Pierce, Caleb[4-3], John[2-1]; Jackson 357; Roberts Presidents 29) . Lydia's father was third cousin of the President (as was Sally Fletcher Garran, grandmother of Caroline Goddard Gould).

THE JOSIAH WOOD FAMILY

William[3] Teel's wife LYDIA[3] WOOD, probable namesake of our Lydia Ann Gould, who probably got her name from her own grandmother Lydia (Bacon) Wood. Lydia was born in Charlestown 21 May 1713 (VR 253) to JOSEPH[2] WOOD and his wife MARY or MARIE[2] BLANEY. Lydia died in Newburyport 8 May 1776 age 63 (VR 807), and was buried in Old Hill Cemetery next to her husband in Sec. G-7, Lot 11, grave 2.

Her father JOSEPH[2] Wood was born Charlestown 27 Dec. 1674 (VR 185) to immigrant JOSIAH[1] WOOD and his wife LYDIA[3] BACON. He was baptized there 27 10th month (Dec.) 1674 (Wyman 1045). He owned the covenant of the church in Charlestown on 4 Feb. 1699/1700.

In 1701 he bought five acres of woods in Charlestown from John Call. In 1703-4 he bought some woodlots from the town. In 1712 a final division of his father's estate gave him his parents' house, which had been bought from the widow of Solomon Phipps in 1678 (where?). He also inherited about 20 acres of land. Much of this was soon sold: the house to R. Miller in 1712-3, a lot near the burying hill to Joseph Frost the same year, the Richbell &c. woods in 1716, ten acres to William Rand in 1723-4. However, he did get a quitclaim on the Blaney lot from John Frothingham in 1719.

Joseph[3] Wood was married Charlestown 19 April 1699 to MARY BLANEY (VR 185), of whom more below. Lydia's brother Joseph Wood was killed by the Indians Charlestown 3 Aug. 1724 (VR 290).

Joseph died in Charlestown 28 Feb. 1725, age 51 (age about 50 in VR 289; g.s. in Wyman 1045). He may be buried Phipps Street Cemetery.

His will of 1 Jan. 1722/3 was proved on 23 April 1725. His daughter Lydia, unmarried, is mentioned. The estate was a scattered one, for his widow sold off 13 different properties in the following 20 years, seven of them to her sons Thomas and David (Wyman).

Joseph's father Josiah[1] Wood was born in England about 1629 (age 32 in 1667; Wyman 1045; age 60 in 1691 per Msx Ct. depos. in Reg. 85:455), and died in Charlestown 24 Sept. 1691, age 62 (VR 152, citing Co. Rec. 4/187; Wyman 1045) . He served in King Philip's War under Capt. J. Cutter (See *Transcript* 22 July 1914, #4205; *Society of Colonial Wars Index*, [hereinafter SCW], 548).

Josiah was a proprietor of Charlestown in 1681 when the town gave him four shares of commons, for which he drew lot #24 of six acres (Wyman). He evidently came into a good bit of capital about 1675, for he bought property in Charlestown from five persons: two lots from Elizabeth Chalkley 1675, 1676; 3/4 cow common from William Foster 1676-7; one common from A. Ludkin 1676-7; M common from S. Carter 1677; a house from Solomon Phipps's widow 1681; four acres from Thomas Brattle 1682 (Wyman).

The Wood's house as described in Solomon[1] Phipps's deed of 1678 was between the highway on the southwest, the field highway on northeast, Phipps's land northwest, and Jacob Green southeast (Wyman 748). It is unclear if this is Phipps's house at Moulton Point or the one bought from Rev. Zechariah Symmes.

He made his will 19 May 1691, which was proved 29 Dec. In it he left most of his estate to his sons Joseph and Samuel. This was evidently contested, with inventories separated by 20 years. The first one in 1691 showed a goodly total of £ 378. The inventory of 17 March 1711/2 reflected final division, in which our Joseph got the old house on an acre (£ 91), the southwest half of four acres in Brattle's close on the Cambridge road (£ 22), the west half of six acres of orchard (£ 49), northeast part of 21 acres of pasture (£ 52), and the west part of eight acres of woodland (£ 5). His brother Samuel's children got the other half of these lots plus the two acres bought from Chalkley (£ 32). Samuel, who died in 1711, must have been close to the Winship family, though not related, for Edward and Joseph Winship were sureties for his estate (19 Nov. 1711, Wyman 1045).

THE BACON FAMILY

Josiah[1] Wood married in Charlestown 28 Oct. 1657 LYDIA[3] BACON (not in VR; Wyman 1045), born about 1638 (died age 74, g.s.), perhaps daughter of MICHAEL[2] BACON Jr. (Sav, 4:627), and son of MICHAEL[1] BACON of Dedham one of the founders and first settlers of Woburn in 1641 (Henry A. Hazen, *History of Billerica,* [Boston: A. Williams, 1883], 5. Savage's doubt about her parents seems resolved in Reg. 90:302).

Lydia (Bacon) Wood was admitted to Charlestown church 29 June 1662 (Sav. 4:627), and died Charlestown 25 Nov. 1712 age 74 (not in VR; Wyman 1045) . Her finely carved gravestone is photographed in the Museum of Fine Arts in Boston, taken from the Charlestown burial ground (Cutter 2:1130).

Michael Bacon Jr. was probably born in Winston, Suffolk about 1608-9 (age about 60 in 1668; 67 in 1676 in case vs. Benj. Simonds in Msx. Ct., Reg. 90:302). He married first in Winston 31 Aug. 1624 MARIE (Mary) JOBO (Reg. 57:330) who died Woburn 26 Aug. 1655 (VR 8) . He came to America in 1640 with his father, who settled in Dedham. The son went to Charlestown where he signed the "Town Orders" for the formation of the settlement of Woburn, of which he was a founder (Reg. 51:365; Samuel Sewall, *History of Woburn* [Boston: Wiggin & Lunt, 1868], 25.

Michael Jr. was surveyor of Woburn highways in 1644. A grant to Cambridge in 1644 involved him in a suit by the Artillery Company of Boston against him and William Simonds (D. Hamilton Hurd *History of Middlesex County* [Philadelphia: J. W. Lewis, 1890, 3 vols.], [hereinafter Hurd] 1:350 and Msx Ct. Rec. 1:224 cited by Woburn VR 14n). In 1648 he bought from Roger Shaw a farm in today's Bedford near the Shawsheen River, in the east corner of Concord, including the meadow by the Great Swamp (Cutter 990; Hurd 2:813 believes this to be his second purchase in Bedford) . In 1653 he and William Simms bought 200 acres in Bedford part of Cambridge northwest of Capt. Cook's farm, including the meadow next to the Great Swamp at the east corner of Concord (Thomas W. Baldwin, *Michael Bacon of Dedham* [Cambridge: Murray & Emery, 1915], 29). He was evidently living on the land granted to Rev. Joseph Mitchell before he bought it (Hurd 2:815). His home, evidently unfortified, was in Bedford, for during the Indian raids Timothy Brooke's house was designated as a garrison house for Brooks "& to entertain Michael Bacon's family" (town meeting 14 Oct. 1675 in Hurd 2:815) . Sometime before 1663 he built a saw and gristmill on the Shawsheen which was burned by the Indians in King Philip's War, and replaced by a structure that was still standing in 1902 (Hurd 2:815. In King Philip's War Michael he served in Timothy Brooks's garrison ten in Billerica, of which he was a citizen in 1675 (Baldwin 29; SCW 20).

He served as Woburn Selectman for ten years, 1659-70 except for 1667 and 1669 (Baldwin 29). After Mary's death he married secondly 26 Oct. 1655 Mary Richardson (VR 14) , widow of Thomas[1] Richardson of Sudbury who had died Woburn 28 Aug. 1651 (Belle Preston, *Bassett-Preston Ancestors* [New Haven: Tuttle, More house & Taylor, 1930], 233; Reg. 90:302; John A. Vinton, *The Vinton Memorial* [Boston: Portland ME, 1856] 506). She died Woburn 19 May 1670 (VR 2:8). He then married 28 Nov. 1670 Mary Noyes (VR 14), widow of Thomas Noyes of Sudbury, and daughter of Walter and Eliza Haines.

Bacon died in Woburn 4 July 1688 (VR 2:8).

Michael Bacon Sr. was baptized at Winston, Suffolk 6 Dec. 1579 (Reg. 57:330; Topo 164, citing Reg. 58:302). Son and father both went to northern Ireland 1633-40, from which they came to New England with Samuel Cooke and John Smyth (Dedham approved settlement 26 May and 23 June 1640, town records 3:69; Reg. 57:330) . The father was proprietor of Dedham 23 May 1640 where he signed the famous Dedham Covenant (list of proprietors 16 Feb. 1643 in town rec. 1:81 per Herman Mann, *Historical Annals of Dedham* [Dedham: the author, 1847], 84). At the same time, however, he paid eight shillings of ship money in Suffolk, England (27 March 1640 in Baldwin 25) . His house site can be inferred as south of the first cart bridge over the Charles from his deed of 1644 when he gave Dedham a strip three rods wide across his planting lot for a highway from the Training Ground to the Cart Bridge, and received in exchange ten acres on the Island in north part of town] , and meadow east of it, and the upland between the ten acre plot and the Charles (Baldwin 26; Reg. 56:364; Mann 119).

His wife Alice, whose maiden name has not been found, was born in England about 1608 (Reg. 90:301). She went to Dedham ahead of him, and was admitted to the church there 17 Sept. 1641. Alice died in Dedham 2 April 1648 (Woburn VR 2:8; Reg. 57:330).

He died in Dedham 18 April 1648 (VR 128). His will, signed four days before his death, is in Suff. Pro. 70, Reg. 7:230-1. The inventory of his estate 20 April 1649 shows value of only £ 55, but includes "one tipped pott [worn] silver spoones" which had been bequeathed by his father in England.

Michael Bacon's genealogy traces back 14 generations (Thomas Baldwin, *Bacon Genealogy* (Cambridge: Murray & Emery, 1915, 1-31; Reg. 90:300-2). His father Michael[A] Bacon married first at Helmingham, Suffolk (8 mi. north of Ipswich) to Elizabeth Wylie. He remarried widow Grace Blomosale 30 Sept. 1607, who is named in his will. His will of 24 Oct.

1624, proved 20 April 1615 left "A pott Tipped with silver Six silver spoones marked wth M and B", similar to those left in the will of Michael[1] in 1649, and may have been the silver tipped pot in the will of Thomas Bacon of Helmingham (Howard's *Miscellanea Genealogica et Heraldica*. 2d Ser. 6:298-302, 11:349 cited in Reg. 57:330). He was buried 25 March 1615. He was third cousin to the famous Sir Francis Bacon.

Michael's parents were John[B] & Margaret Bacon; his will probated 19 March 1557. He was son of Thomas[c] of Helmingham, will probated 18 Feb. 1555; wife Joan(e) died 1540, will 30 July 1540, probated 12 Dec. He was son of John[D] & Agnes, daughter of Sir Thomas Cockfield; both great-grandparents of Sir Francis Bacon. He was son of Edmund[E] of Drinkston, Suffolk and Elizabeth Crofts. He was son of John[F] Bacon & Margery Thorpe, daughter and heir of John Thorpe, Commander in the wars of Edward II and III, son of William[8] Thorpe & Margaret Quaplade; he was son of Sir William" Thorpe & Beatrix Bacon, daughter of Sir Roger Bacon. John[F] Bacon was son of John[G] Bacon & his first wife Helena Tillot, daughter of Sir George Tillot of Rougham, Norfolk. John was son of John[H] Bacon & Helena Goading. Son of John[I] Bacon & Cicily Hoo or How. Son of John[J] & Alice Bacon of Hertset, Suffolk. Son of Robert[K], first of the surname Bacon, of Hessett, Suffolk and his wife Alice Burgate. He was son of Roger[1], son of Ranulf" (Reynolds) of Thorpe, Norfolk (just east of Norwich) . He was son of Grimbaldus[N] the Norman who came to England in 1066, and held lands near Letherigsete, Holt, Norfolk (8 miles west of Cromer). The Bacons of Hessett, Suffolk bore arms described as "Argent on a fesse engrailed between three escutcheons gules, 3 mullets or." (Cutter 990).

There are seven descendants of Michael by the name of Bacon in the *Dictionary of American Biography* [NY: Scribners, 1964, 20 vols.] [hereinafter DAB]. Five of these are the remarkable family of Congregational ministers: David (1771-1817), missionary to the Michigan Indians (DAB 1:474) , his author daughter Delia (1811-59; DAB 1:475), his son Leonard (1802-81), Professor of Divinity at Yale 1866-81 and 41 years minister of the First Church in New Haven (DAB 1:479-80), his son Rev. Leonard W. (1830-1907 (DAB 1:481), and daughter Alice (1858-1918), author of books on Japan and teacher at Hampton Institute. In addition, there is Rev. John Bacon (1738-1820), pastor of Old South Church in Boston, US Congressman 1801-3, and noted as the opponent of racist clauses in the draft Massachusetts constitution of 1778 which led to its defeat (DAB 1:478-9) . Finally, architect Henry Bacon (1866-1924), designer of the Lincoln Memorial and many other public monuments and buildings (DAB 1:477-8).

THE BLANEY FAMILY OF CHARLESTOWN

Joseph Wood's wife MARY or MARIE (VR 107) BLANEY was born Charles town 29 March 1679 (VR 107) to JOHN[1] BLANEY and SARAH[2] SALLIE. Mary was baptized at Old South Church 22 June 1679 {Wyman 1:92). She was admitted to the church 30 Sept. 1733. Mary died Charlestown 2 April 1743, age 64 (not in VR; Wyman 1045).

Mary's father Captain JOHN[1] BLANEY, was a mariner master of the ketch *Amity* at Cape Hatteras in 1672 (SD per Wyman 92) . He was admitted to the Charlestown church 17 Dec. 1676. In 1675 he bought the house built in Charlestown by Thomas Hett north of the creek, between B. Lothrop's house on the east, and Ann Hett's land leased to W. Hurry (MD 7:134; Wyman 93) . In 1681 he was granted two acres, land drew lot #59 of three acres. In 1685 the town gave him seven acres southwest of the road to Dickson's. In 1698 he sold the same seven acres to Peter Tufts.

Blaney's will of 28 Jan.1705/6 was probated 15 March 1705/6 (Wyman makes one of his rare mistakes, confusing the estates of father who died 1706, 93, and the son who died 1715/6, 92) gave his son the new east end of his house, wharf and three acres, plus two near the mill, to his daughter Susan Cook the old, west end of the house with right of way past the brew-house, and to his daughter Katharine (later Cutler) his brick house and shop, and to our Mary Wood two acres of marsh by the Mystic River (Wyman 93, from Msx. Pro. #1933).

THE SALLEE FAMILY OF CHARLESTOWN

Captain Blaney was married in Charlestown 26 June 1672 (VR 82) to SARAH (SALLIE) POWELL. She was the widow of John Powell, Charlestown mariner whom she had married in Charlestown 20 May 1667 (VR 24), who died June 1658 (VR 82; Wyman 2:768). She was born about 1639-43 (g. s. age 51; age 54 in 1693 per archives vol. xl), daughter of MANUS[1] SALLEE, SALLY, SALLIE or SOLLY. Sarah was admitted to the Charlestown church 28 Feb. 1688/9, after her marriage to Powell on 20 May 1667 (VR 24). She had one child by Powell, John Jr., born Charlestown 2 April 1668 (VR 67). She died in Charlestown 18 Oct. 1694, age 51 (VR 163).

Her father Manus Sallee had come to Charlestown by May 1647 when he was admitted to the church 3 May and became freeman 29 May (Pope 397; Wyman 2:842). The following year, on 9 July 1648, a Mary Sallee was admitted to the church, probably a relative. We have not found whether she was a sister or mother.

In 1649/50 Manus sold Jacob Green ten acres on Mystic side which he had bought from W. Mirable. The same year he exchanged lots with L. Dowse, and bought a house near the water mill from W. Phillips.

Manus Sallee died Charlestown 4 March 1650 (VR 14). His will dated 10 Oct. 1649 (Wyman 842) left his daughter Sarah his house assessed at £ 35 on ten acres near the water mill, along with three cow commons (£ 6) and two hay lots on Mystic side (£ 5), which she sold to R. Lowden in 1666. Our Sarah also shared with her mother and sister Rebecca (later Jones) £ 15/50 in cash. The town gave Sarah and Rebecca three acres of commons in 1656/7.

THE HEPBURN FAMILY OF CHARLESTOWN

Manus Sallee married in Charlestown SARAH[2] HEPBURN, born Charlestown after 1635 to GEORGE[1] and (H)ANN(A) HEPBURN(E), leather-dresser and glovemaker of Charlestown. HEPBURN, variously spelled HADBORN, HEBORN, HEIPBOURN, HEPBOURNE or HEYPBOURNE was born about 1592 (age 43 in 1635). He came from St. Saviour's church, Southwark (London), and Stepney on the *Abigail* to Plymouth on 6 Oct. 1635 (Winthrop's Journal), moved to Charlestown where he became a freeman 25 May 1636, and member of the church there 17 Feb. 1636 (Wyman 1:495; Sav. 2:227, 404; Topo 168 citing Banks mss.). His wife Hannah or Ann who was born in England about 1589 (age 46 in 1635) was admitted to the Charlestown church 6th 2d. mo. 1638 (April, Sav. 2:227). She probably died before he made his will in Aug. 1665.

He was town bell-ringer in 1658, paid £ 4 for the year "to ring the bell on the Lord's days and lecture days, and to make and keep cleane the meeting-house" (8th 12 mo., Wyman 495).

In 1637 he had a lot of ten acres on Mystic side. The next year he owned seven properties: 1) a house on Middle Row on the west corner of Mill Lane and Back Street, 2) an acre of arable land in Southfield near Beecher's Cove, 3) one cow commons, 4) two acres in Linefield, next to the Mystic River, 5) five acres of woods, 6) 36 acres in Waterfield, 7) ten acres of swampland in Eastfield which he exchanged in 1655 with John March for an acre in Eastfield, north of the Training place. In 1649-50 he sold a lot to L. Dowse. In 1650 he sold Alice Rand 3/4 acre in

Great Field south of the river, within the Neck. In 1660 he bought part of a barn from John Cutter. In 1661 he gave Aaron Ludkin (his business partner, and perhaps his daughter Hannah's husband) the house where widow Ludkin lived, on the Training place by the highway to the Neck, on one acre plus part of a barn. In 1665/6 he sold Thomas Rand one acre in Eastfield, southwest of the river (last deed in MD I) . The same year he sold A. Ludkin eight rods of land, one of which he had lately bought from the town at the lower end or corner of his own garden, with a building recently erected (perhaps for his daughter).

Hepburn died Charlestown 9 Feb. 1665/6 (VR 14) . His will of 27 Aug. 1665 was probated 3 April 1666, in which his wife is not mentioned. He mentions his daughter Sarah Sally and her sister Rebecca (Msx Will 1186 per Pope; Sav. 2:227).

THE WINSHIP FAMILY

William[4] Teel was married in Newburyport 2 Feb. 1773 {VR 468; LG) to ELIZABETH[4] "BETTY" WINSHIP SYMMES, born Charlestown 17 Sept. 1740 (VR 468; LG), one of eleven children of JOSEPH[3] WINSHIP, Jr. and ANN(A)[4] WHITMORE. She married first in Medford 28 July 1761 mariner Zechariah Semmes (Symmes in VR 300; int. Charlestown 18 July, VR 479) who died at the end of 1765, having made his will 20 Aug. 1762 leaving everything to Elizabeth, probated 6 Jan. 1766 (not in VR; Wyman 930) . Symmes was a close cousin of two presidents, William Henry and Benjamin Harrison (the first married Anna[6] Symmes, dau. of U.S. Rep. John[5], Rev. Timothy[4], Timothy[3] of Charlestown 1683-1710, William[2] of Charlestown d. 1691, Rev. Zechariah[1], Roberts 12-15). We do not know where she died (not in Arl. Cam. Med. VR) "half past four, Sabath afternoon", 23 Dec. 1815 (LG), age 75. We get an intimate idea of the way she raised her children from a letter of 16 March 1798 her son Joseph wrote to his cousin Anna Wyeth on that date from Newburyport about the death of his oldest sister Eliza(beth) or "Betsey" Teel aged 23 (b. 4 Oct. 1774, d. 13 Jan. 1796, 10 minutes before seven, evening, LG):

"You ask me, cousin, How was Betsey's mind & the events previous to her death. You know she enjoy'd but little health since the death of our tender Father, her greatest attention to him & his constant wish to have her with him, we sometimes think originated her disorder, & planted those seeds within her breast, that could not be rooted out but by earth & worms.

In the first part of her disorder she was anxious to know if she was in a consumption & as ''soon as she knew, she could talk with the calmness of Death, though several months before her dissolution, & willingly resign herself to the Ruler of the Universe who can do no wrong. Though her disorder often subjected her to intense pain, yet the excellent Sister bore it with more patience than I have ever seen her "the fever of the mind." What could be pleasanter than reflections upon her past life! often have I look'd to her as a pattern from which to choose a partner for life. Her noble principles, the dignity of her manners, her truly tender & affectionate heart, her temper that dissis'd, while she strove" »y example to correct the littleness of others, served for to make me, in my heart, love her as well as Adam his extracted ribb.

About 11 O'clock of the 13th Jany, her friends apprehending her near her worldly end, were call'd around her bed: her stuff'd throat & her feeble smile told us , that she was, by extreme weakness, unable to raise the flem that rattled in her throat. Without the use of voice the expressive eyes & estended hand convey'd the most excurtiating feelings to her faithful friends! What could they do? And is all hope cut off? With a squeeze of the hand thou bid me farewell be virtuous & happyl The Dear Girl had her senses perfectly clear & never was she depriv'd of the sense of that pain, with which her body was afflicted, till her soul wing'd its way to that seat of bliss where we shall forget to mourn the loss of friends.

My Father died the 1st Day of May. Eliza"Burroushs the 13th of Nov. '97. Eliza Teel the 13th Jany ~98 [VR 807 says 15th] & as we have but a mournful prspect of the Life of my other Sister [Lydia who died Newburyport 28 June 1798, age 22, VR 807 says 29th; at 3 minutes before 1 morn, LG], I will leave a [blank space] sacred to her memory...

Betsy, we may ask, what had she to repent of? of real sins I believe but few; The sins of the heart we must leave to God! but we may presume she had not many. She believed in the Christian religion, and those religious truths impressed'd on her mind when young, where only, in the prospect of Death, more profoundly interesting & more deeply engavin. Once disappointed in her posses'n of happiness, she was careless on whom she confer'd her person & all but her heart, she was resolv'd, should be interested in his happiness. Indeed, my cousin, she always posses'd that refinement, that delivery, so pleasing in the sex, & all the qualities necessary for the happiness of the other. I think it a wrong notion that Brothers should not be permitted without censure to praise their sister...". In this letter the writer also makes clear that his mother Elizabeth (Winship) Teel was called "Betty", and her daughter Eliza(beth) Teel, "Betsy".

The writer of this letter, Joseph, was himself to die only three years later. That his was a life surrounded by death is seen in a beautiful piece of calligraphy which he did at the age of 13 which survives: "A Poem composed by a Christian a few Days before his Death. I Christs dazzling glory shines so bright
No mortal here can tell But those that in him take
delig[ht] And in his presence dwell.

II Oh! what transforming joys are seen In that bright
world above In Shining robes they all appear With
hearts inflam'd with love.

III Dear lord send down that Heavenly Dove That we a sinful
race Might fly above on Wings of love And see thy
glorious Face.

IV Dear~[lord] when will thou call me home This world is
not my treasure I long to be with all above

To praise thy name forever.

V I am a child I cannot speak The Glories of the Place
Send some kind Angel for my guide To see thy
glorious Face.

JOSEPH TEEL *Newbry*
Port March XXIII 1791

Joseph[3] Teel was born Newburyport 11 Dec. 1777 (not in VR; LG) . He married in Lincoln 2 June 1799 Susan(na) Underwood of Lincoln (VR 138) . As his letter of advice to his brother Benjamin indicates, he was trading in 1801, but his estate shows he was a baker, like his father. He died Newburyport 21 June 1802, age 25 (not in VR; LG) . His widow remarried there 13 May 1807 William Wood (VR 468).

Elizabeth (Winship) Teel's sister Mary Winship (1730-99), who married Ebenezer Wyeth of Charlestown, was mother of Boston Teaparty "Indian" Joshua Wyeth born 6 Oct. 1752 (E. Wyeth's record of births and deaths, mss. in Teel Papers with John Shaw, which also contains four autographed letters from Wyeth from Vermont 1806 and Cincinnati, 1813, 1827, two of which were reproduced in Cutter's *History of Arlington,* (Benjamin & William Cutter, *History of the Town of Arlington* [Boston: David Clapp, 1880], 332-3; originals in possession of John Shaw).

Betsy's father JOSEPH[3] WINSHIP, Jr., sailor, was born Cambridge 28 Feb. 1700/1 (VR 775) to JOSEPH[2] WINSHIP Sr. and his first wife SARAH[2] HARRINGTON. He was baptized at the First Church 2 March 1701 (1st ch. 50) . He married Cambridge about 1722 his second cousin, ANN(A)[4] WHITMORE, of whom more below. He owned the covenant of the First Church 11 Aug. 1723 (1st ch. 66), as did his wife Anne 19 Jan. 1723/4 (1st ch. 92) . They lived at Menotomy, today's Arlington (Cutter 326), probably at his parents' homestead near Spy Pond. He must have inherited the large tracts of land owned by his father in Arlington. In his only mention in Cambridge Proprietors Records he is respectfully styled "m[r]. Joseph Winshipp" when he was placed on a land committee (1730, CP 320) . The distance of Arlington from the church in Cambridge led to building a church there in 1734. Joseph was one of the 16 men who held the first pews (Cutter 23) . He and his wife were among the 83 signatories of the church covenant in 1739, in which there were nearly twice as many women as men (Ibid., 27, 28).

On 12 March 1742 he bought the Charlestown estate of David Dunster, grandson of Harvard President, who had moved to Narragansett Twp., Worcester. The location of the house was confusingly listed as Charlestown, Medford, Metonomy and West Cambridge. It was northwest of the road from Medford to Arlington (Medford Street), west and southwest of the pond (Lower Mystic Lake) and Medford River weirs, close to the 1798 house of Benjamin Cutter where Anna Winship died (Cutter 326, 218; Near the end of life he lived in Cambridge close to Charlestown per Paige 697).

He died intestate in Charlestown (Arlington) 24 July 1761, age 60 (Arl VR 158; Wyman 1041; Cutter 326) . His wife was made administratrix, and his son Captain Joseph[4], mariner in Norwich Ct. surety. His estate included 30 lots sold to George Cutter, 15 acres sold to John Cutter (1749; Wyman 1041). The inventory included a house and 26 acres south of the Medford River and pond, of which his widow got 10½ acres. His gravestone has not been recorded in Arlington.

His first cousin's grandson was one of the first civilians killed in the Revolution. Jason[3] Winship (Jason[4], Edward[3-2-1]) was brutally killed by the British soldiers on 19 April 1775 as they retreated from Lexington and entered Cooper's Tavern in Arlington, where Jason and his brother-in-law Jabez Wyman were sitting (Cutter 74, 327) .

Joseph Winship Junior's father JOSEPH[2] Sr. was born at Cambridge Farms (Arlington) 21 June 1661 (VR 774), fifth child of immigrant Lt. EDWARD[1] WINSHIP and his second wife ELIZABETH[2] PARK(E)S. He was baptized at the First Church 25 Aug. 1661 (Cambridge First Church, *Records* [ed. by Stephen Sharples, Boston: Eben Putnam, 1906], 22). He lived at Menotomy, West Cambridge, now Arlington. In the census of 1688, taken before his father died, he was taxed in the Menotomy (Arlington district) £ 3 shillings one pence, on personal and estate value of £ 36 (Paige 443) . On his father's death in 1688 he and his brothers inherited a large estate, but was entitled to large grants as a Proprietor in his own right. In 1689 he got lot #87 of eight acres in Cambridge Rocks First Division and #63 of the same in the Second (CP 182, 194). From his mother he inherited six acres in Charlestown fields (Wyman 1041) . In 1694 he got permission to fence a lot he bought from widow [Edward] Mitchelson (CP 204, 170, 192) . In 1703 the Proprietors gave eight of their members including Joseph and his brother "liberty for y[e] Erecting a Conveniency (against y[e] Colledge fence Northard of e[r] meeting house) for y[e] : Standing of their Horses on Saboth Dayes." (CP 218). In 1705 he paid the town 30 shillings for four acres of upland north of his land at Alewife Brook (CP 224-5). In 1707 a survey was made of the land he bought at Cambridge Rocks from Nicholas Fessenden, and let Winship fence it but reserved a right of way for the road to Watertown near Black Brook (CP 232-3) . In the division of 1707 he got 3¾ acres in lot #26 of the third squadron (CP 240). In the Ninth Squadron of Hunting Swamp he got lot #4 of three acres (CP 258). In 1720 he was on a committee of five to lay out an acre of Spy Pond reserved for Proprietors' fishing, to place weirs and enforce the privilege (CP 285). In the division of common lands in 1724 he drew lot #53 of 2¼ acres at Mills' Ware (CP 308).

Joseph was apparently acquainted with the Samuel Wood family of Charlestown, for he and his brother Edward were sureties to his estate in 1711 (Wyman 1045) .

Joseph was Selectman in Cambridge 1706, 1707 and 1725. He died in West Cambridge (Arlington) 18 Sept. 1725, age 65 (Cam. VR 798; g.s.) and his epitaph is recorded in William T. Harris, *Epitaphs from the Old Burying-Ground in Cambridge* [Cambridge: John Owen, 1845], [hereinafter Harris], 73). The stone stands near the north fence, west of the Vassal table. In the same row is the stone of his half-sister which has one of the better epitaphs recorded by Harris 38:

> "This good School Dame
> No longer School must keep
> Which gives us cause
> For Childrens sake to weep".

Joseph[2] Winship Sr. married firstly 24 Nov. 1687 (Mary Gozzaldi, *History of Cambridge...Supplement* [Cambridge: Camb. Historical Soc., 1930],[hereinafter Gozzaldi] 351; VR) SARAH[2] HARRINGTON, born Watertown 10 May 1671 ("Sary" in VR 34; Gozzaldi 351) 12th child of ROBERT[1] ARRINGTON, ERRINGTON or HARRINGTON and SUSANNA[2] GEORGE. Robert had settled in Watertown by 1642, where he had a homestall given by Thomas Hastings (1605-82), a possible relative (Bond 285; Cutter 1425). Hastings had come to Watertown in 1635, having come over from Ipswich, Suffolk in 1634, age 29.

Robert Harrington (1616-1707) came from Ipswich, Suffolk to Watertown 1643, where he married 1 Oct. 1649 Susan(nan) George (VR 14).

Robert Harrington took the oath of fidelity in 1652 and became freeman in Watertown 27 May 1663, and was Deacon and Selectman of the town. He also owned a mill on the Charles River (Pope 214; Cutter 1425).

Sarah's father is mistakenly given as "George" Harrington because of an error in Bond 272 which mixes his wife's last name with Robert's children. Sarah's brother was killed by the Indians at Lancaster 1675/6, when Sophia Lovis's ancestors died.

It is unclear if his ancestry is as given in George H. Harrington, "*Harrington Family Genealogical Gazeteer*" [Typescript: author, 1942], 377. Robert might be son of Robert Herrington, Bailiff of Southwold, Suffolk, who married 7 March 1613 Joan, daughter of William and Agnes Jentilman (Valentine Harrington, "*Harrington Family*" [W. Newton: author, n.d.][3]). Cutter states without evidence that Robert Harrington of Watertown was probably descended from Robert de Harington, younger son of Robert de Haverington who moved to an estate of Aldingham, Lancashire which his wife Agnes de Cancefield had inherited from her mother Agnes de Fleming (Cutter 1423) . This family began in Haverington, Cumberland under its lord Oswulf or Osulphus, whose son Robert was great-grandfather of the Robert de Haverington who took over Aldingham.

Robert Harrington's will of 1 Jan. 1704/5 mentions Sarah Winship (Bond 272). He left an estate of 16 lots totalling 642 acres, valued at £ 717. His homestead, on the western half of the Oldham farm, was sold for £ 90 to Boston goldsmith Jeremiah Dummer (24 Dec. 1684, Cutter 1425). The farm continued in the hands of descendants until the twentieth century (Cutter 1425).

Harrington's wife Susan George was probably born in England about 1632, the daughter of JOHN[1] GEORGE, an early settler of Watertown, by a wife unknown to Savage (Sav. 2:242; Reg. 3:239; *Amer. Ancestry* 40:99). After her mother's death about 1638 John remarried Ann, or Hannah, b. c. 1589, age 45 on departure Ipswich April 1634, Bond 774; or 1591 age 79 at death 1670), widow of Henry Goldstone (1591-1638) whom she married in England (Suffolk?) before 1615 (dau. Anna bapt. Wickam Skeith, Suffok 16 May 1615, Bond 774).

John George died Watertown about 1 June 1647 (Bond) , his estate inventoried 12 June and probated by his widow 29 June, in which there were debts to Susan (Suff. Pro. 11:33 per Bond; Reg. 7:172, 8:57; Pope 184) . Ann was appointed guardian to her two step-children Susan and Robert George. Bond considers it "not improbable" but not ascertained that the Baptist pioneer of Charlestown, John George, was an older brother of Susan and Robert (Bond 774n, Wyman 404, Sav. 2:242 is unsure if this is the John George apprenticed March 1641 for eight years to Governor Winthrop). Ann died 26 April 1670, age 79 (Bond; deposed age about 64 in 1654, Arch. 38 B per Pope 184).

Hannah George died Watertown 26 April 1670, age 79 (Bond 235, 774) . Susanna (George) Harrington died Watertown 6 July 1692 (Bond 272) .

Sarah (Harrington) Winship died Cambridge 26/28 Nov. 1710, age 39 (VR 430), and is buried there, in the graveyard north of Harvard Square. Her epitaph is reproduced in Harris 43.

Joseph Winship remarried four years later, in Cambridge, on 27 Oct. 1714 to Sarah[3] Stearns (VR 798), born Watertown 23 April 1675 (VR 14), daughter of Samuel[2] Stearns (Isaac[1]) and Hannah[3] Manning. She died Sept. 1726, her estate administered by Samuel Jennison of Watertown (Paine 696).

CAMBRIDGE PIONEER EDWARD WINSHIP.

The founder of the Winship line was Lt. EDWARD[1] WINSHIP who came over in 1635. The family name is inconsistently spelled WENSHEP, WENSHEPPE, WINCHEP, WINCHEPP, WINCHIP, WINCHOPE, WINDSHIP, WINSHAPE, WINSHAPP, WINSHEP, WINSHEPE, WINSHIP, WINSHIPE, WINSHIPP, WINSHOP and WINSHOPE in early Cambridge records.

He was born 13 March 1612 at Welton Tower, Northumberland, on Hadrian's Wall bordering Scotland, 8 miles west of Newcastle-on-Tyne, an area of constant warfare (Gozzaldi 828; Topo 130 citing Reg. 61:69). His father was LYONEL[A] WINSHIP or WYNSHOPP, yeoman of Wilton Hall, Ovington, North., whose will of 22 Nov. 1633 makes Edward co-executor and residuary legatee, and is buried at Ovington (Cutler 11:869). The Winship descendants have claimed arms of 4 birds, 2 argent in dexter field azure, and 2 azure in sinister field argent, surcharged with a scallop or, but give no evidence that Lyonel was entitled to them, or any other ancestry.

Among his friends in Newcastle-on-Tyne was Giles Bittleston who was arrested in 1638 for having adopted the Scotch covenant and in whose house the authorities found a loving letter from him addressed to his friends in New Town (Cambridge) , New England, including Edward Winshop, Thomas Cheasman, William Cutter and Guy Bainbridge (1 Sept. 1638 in Origins 6).

Edward is said to have come from Harwich, Essex to Boston on the *Defence* 3 Oct. 1635, but Gozzaldi corrects the ship's name to *Defiance.* He came with his first wife Jane Wilkinson, born Newcastle-on-Tyne, and died Cambridge c.1648-51, daughter of ISABEL (or Izbell) WILKINSON, widow of Newcastle who was a cousin of Richard and William Cutler of Cambridge. Isabel Wilkerson in 1637 shared a house with the Winships on two acres in the west end of Cambridge just inside the west pallisado, and gate to the town, on a triangle between the Watertown-Charlestown road (Mason Street) and Watertown Rd. (Brattle) , just northwest of Henry Dunster's barn and "out out house", today west of James Street and the Radcliffe campus *(Cambridge Proprietors' Records* [Cambridge: The town, 1896], [hereinafter CP], 94, 74). With this went six acres on Jones Hill. Isabel also owned two acres in the New West Field (south of Garden Street), six acres south of the river, and six acres in the 24th lot of the Upper Division (Ibid.) and two acres of planting ground in the New West Field (CP 56). In the Shawshine Division of 1652 she got 60 acres in lot #23, in today's Billerica (Paige 58). She died in Cambridge 23 Feb. 1655 (Paige 691) . Her property was apparently inherited by her two daughters, Margaret Goffe (wife of Edward Goffe and John Witchfield; Paige 313, 561) and Isabel, wife of our ancestor Edward Winship.

Winship was in the company of Rev. Thomas Shepherd of Northumberland, who arrived in the *Defence* in Oct. 1635 (Paige 35). But Winship arrived ahead of the minister, and settled at once in Cambridge where he became freeman 4 March 1635/6. This was granted after a year's residence, so he must have arrived before the trip of the *Defence* came in Oct. 1635.

The first town record him was 20 Aug. 1635, when he was giver} a share in the division of meadows *(Records of the Town of Cambridge* [Cambridge: City Council, 1901], hereinafter CR 13). Five months later he got two acres in the Pyne Swamp (north of the Common, between Massachusetts Av. and Kirkland; Ibid. 15). As one of the first Proprietors of Cambridge he already had 64 acres in 1637: seven in the Pyne Swamp Field, 14 in the Ox Pasture toward Metonomy (Arlington), 11 in the Great Marsh (now MIT), two beyond Alewife meadow, ten south of the Charles in the Lower Division, ten in the Upper Division, and ten Fresh Pond meadow (CP 94-5) . In 1638 he acquired the three acres between the Commons and Brattle and Mason Streets, now the triangle west on James Street and Radcliffe Campus, evidently from his wife's inheritance. In 1639 the town gave him two more acres north of the Alewife (CP 47) . That year he bought John Clark's house on two acres in Cow Common (betwen Garden Street and Massachusetts Av.), six acres from William Jones on Jones Hill, half an acre from George Stocking, M acre from Nicholas Clark, two acres from James Hosmer and three acres from James Ensigne in the Ox Pasture behind the Pine Swamp, to which the town added another two acres (CP 56). He was given 40 acres of upland at Alewife Brook next to his meadow in 1641 (CR 45). That year he bought 11 more acres of Great Marsh (MIT) bordering on Oyster Bank Bay from Robert Sanders (CP 70) . The town in 1645 gave him 12 acres in Menotomy (Arlington) next to the lands of Thomas Marrett and John Russell that he had bought (CR 68) . and another three acres west of the Menotomy River (CP 128) . In 1646 he bought 20 acres from John Betts in Alewife Meadows (CP 132).

The huge Shawshine tract (today's Billerica) was divided first in 1652, with Winship getting lot #49 of 200 acres (CR 98). This he sold with one share that "was his father Parks" (Pope 507).

Winship probably lived near Spy Pond, in today's Arlington. In 1653 he got two acres of wood lots in the 4th Sguadrant by the pond (CR 65). He apparently lived in today's Arlington, as the town order of 1657 states, "that Ensigne Edward Winship shall have the swampy piece of land annent his house, towards Spy Pond, prvided he shall not take in the Well...(CR 120). Spy Pond was popular for its good fishing, attracting revered fishers of men like Cotton Mather, who fell in one day (Hurd 3:174). But it was also dangerous, for Sewell tells of two people being killed by Mohawks there at one o'clock one night (Diary, 8 July 1680).

In 1662 Winship got two acres on the south side of the Charles in the Second Squadrant (CP 141) . But in 1665 he forfeited his lot on the south side of the Charles after he confessed to selling wood out of town (CR 161). That year, however, he got 50 acres in lot #49 of the Cow Common (between Garden & Massachusetts Av.) and right to five cow commons (CP 146) . In 1683 he got another 50 acres in lot #51 between the Eight Mile Line and the Concord boundary (Lincoln, CP 161). In 1689, just after his death, he was granted lot 98 of 12 acres in Cambridge Rocks First Division (CP 184) and lot 60 of the same in the Second Division (CP 193).

Soon after arrival Winship became a political leader, first elected Surveyor of Highways 7 Nov. 1636, Townsman (Selectman) 4 Sept. 1637, and Constable 1638 (CR 23, 29, 34). For years after that he was appointed to town committees that laid out boundaries of the town and land grants, and other matters. He was 14 years Selectman of Cambridge between 1637 and 1684, and eight years Representative to the General Court 1663, 1664, 1681 to 1686 (Paige 463, 460). He was also a military leader, one of the founders of the Ancient & Honorable Artillery Co. in Boston in 1638, and first called Sergeant who led the Cambridge militia in 1642 (CR 46), of which he was commissioned Ensign in 1657, and Lieutenant in 1660 (SCW 343; Gozzaldi 828).

A leader in the church as well, he was on the committee to raise taxes to pay the £ 240 debt of "matchless Mitchell", who succeeded Shepherd as minister of the Cambridge church (Mather's name for him, Paige 260-2). After Mitchell's death he and another ancestor, Francis Whitmore were appointed to catechize youth on the west side of the Winottime (the Menotomy, or Alewife Brook; Paige 269). He and his wife were both members 1658 (Pope 507).

In the census of 1688 he is listed as in the Arlington district, taxed at three shillings, on an estate and person valued at £ 36 (Paige 443).

Edward was one of the first landowners of Lexington, then called Cambridge Farms, about 1642 (Hudson, 1:40, 2:267). Although he did not live there, he did build the first mill, which made lumber, about 1650, in the east side of Lexington, on Mill Brook, site of the fur factory in 1868 (Hudson 40). In 1648 the town of Cambridge gave him 96 acres "on the Rocks, on the North side of the River" for "his owne house", to the west of Edward Parks who had bought Capt. Cook's house (CP 138). This is apparently in Lexington, for it refers to houses of other Lexington pioneers, the Marretts and Russells. Hudson places his lands north of the Arlington line and Massachusetts Ave., including Gilboa and Mt. Ephraim which remained in the Winship family until the nineteenth century.

Lt. Edward Winship died Lexington (Cambridge) 2 Dec. 1688, age 76 (Lex. VR 210; Cam VR 798, g.s.) . He is buried in Cambridge with his wife under a single stone that is unusually thick. It is located on the west side of the Old Burial Ground, southeast of the tall red slate stone of the Puritan John Bridge.

His will of 16 Sept. 1685, proved 1 Oct. 1689, left a large estate covering parts of Lexington, Arlington and Cambridge (Pope 507) . It mentions his son Joseph[2] to whom he left land on Alewife Brook. His widow's will of 18 Oct.. 1689 also names Joseph.

Among his descendants is Albert E. Winship (1845-1933), editor of the *Journal of Education* and author of books on education (DAB 10:391), and his son Laurence L. (1890-1975), editor of the *Boston Globe* 1937-65 (*Who Was Who* 6: 443).

THE PARKE FAMILY

After the death of his first wife Winship remarried 1657 to his neighbor ELIZABETH[2] PARK(ES) , who had come over from her English birthplace with her parents on the *Defence* at age 4 (George Willison, John Camden Hotton, ed., “The Original Listes” in Frank S. Parks, *Genealogy of the Parke Families of Mass.* [Washington: n.p., 1909, 25], Bond 384, Banks 169 lists Richard age 33 and Marjorie, age 30, but not Elizabeth). Her father was RICHARD[1] PARK(E)S, or PERK, a miller, born about 1602 (33 in July 1635) , and baptized Watfield (not in Ekwall), Suffolk 8 Aug. 1609, the son of HENRY[A] PARKE, merchant of London. Gozzaldi says he was from Hadleigh, Suffolk 561), which is ten miles east of Sudbury, in southern West Suffolk. Jackson 383 speculates that London merchant Henry Park who conveyed land in Cambridge in 1650 was brother of Richard; Sylvester Parks, *Parke Family in Connecticut* (Washington DC: Columbia Poly., 1906) says that Richard was son of Winthrop's friend Sir Robert Parke, who came with Winthrop on the *Arabella* in 1630, but this is unproven.

Her mother was MARGERY[2] CRANE, daughter of Hon. JASPER CRANE, who came to America about 1635 from Spaxton, Somerset to New Haven and Newark NJ (Topo 145 citing Banks Mss.). Crane went from Massachusetts to New Haven in 1639, where he became Representative for New Haven in 1650, then Assistant of New Haven Colony for ten years, during a time of theocratic Puritan government (Sav. 1:472) . He then became Assistant of the United Colony of Connecticut for three years (united 1665 under Charter of 1662, with capital at Hartford). Crane moved to Branford in 1668.

Margery was 40 on arrival in 1635, and may have died Cambridge (Newton) 1 Sept. 1656. Parke arrived with Winship in 1635 according to Parks, but was in Rev. Thomas Shepherd's company of 1636, according to Paige (36). He settled in Cambridge before Shepherd arrived. His first house in Feb. 1635 was by Fresh Pond (CR 19), but he soon moved closer to the village, on half an acre on the Cow Common (between today's Garden Street and Massachusetts Av.) southwest of the Pine Swamp, between Percival (Hellen) Green and John Wilcox (1639, CP 53; 1642, CP 103). He settled on the east side of North Street (now Massachusetts Av.), near the Common (Paige 623).

Richard Park built a house on the north side of "the Little Common" (Sumner Square and the tunnel into the Red Line stop) in the middle of what became Holmes Place, east of the Harvard Law Review's Gannett House, about 1638 (DAR, *An Historic Guide to Cambridge* [Cambridge: DAR, 1907], 154, map C #57, 124). The house was later (c. 1760) owned by another ancestor, Francis[3] Whitmore, who inherited it from his second wife Mary (Hancock) Parker, daughter of its previous owner, shoemaker Nathaniel Hancock (Ibid.). The house, which had a long lean-to roof sloping almost to the ground at the back (north) , was torn down by the college about 1849 for the short lived Fitchburg Railroad station, later Harvard's Thayer Commons, and today the open space west of Littauer Center.

Park was elected Cambridge Constable in 1656 (CR 3), and served on several town committees.

In 1639 he owned two acres and ten poles of planting ground on the north side of Jones Hill, west of Winship (CP 53), what is called New West Field in 1642 (CP 103). In 1645 he got lot #23 next to the Charlestown fence (CP 153) . In 1646 the town gave him three acres on the other side of the Menotomy (Alewife) bridge (CR 66) , and use of five acres for woodlot (CR 65). In 1647/8 he got 7 rods 8 feet in the West Field (CP 336) . In the big Shawshine division (later Billerica) of 1652 he got 100 acres of lot #78, next to Francis Whitmore (CP 98).

Park became with Winship one of the first proprietors of Cambridge Farms, today's Lexington, where he had eleven acres near the Common in 1636 (Hudson 40).

Park moved to Newton in 1647, as one of the founders of the church and settlement, on the 1852 monument on the site of the first meetinghouse (listed as seventh settler in Jackson 9). In 1645-1647/8 he got eleven acres south of the Charles near Watertown mill, at the southeast of Newton Corner (CR 69; Jackson 382) . Much of the land he owned in Nonantum or Newton Village became part of today's Waltham (Hurd 3:19) . He built a house about at the site of today's Eliot Church in Newton (Jackson 382) on the east side of the Dedham road (CP 136) which was laid out across his land in 1647 (Jackson 24). The house he built survived until 1800. In 1652 he was granted 600 acres south of the Charles River in Newton, probably bought from Rev. Thomas Shepard. This huge tract extended from the river south to West Newton, east of Cheesecake Brook (Jackson 383; map 112).

He served as Newton Constable in 1656, and surveyor of highways the next year, to lay out the roads of Cambridge Village (Newton) . He was a member of the committee of inquest into the accidental death of Stephen Holden in 1679, which found that he died of a skull crushed by a tree he was felling (Paige 587) . He was a signer of the Cambridge petition of loyalty to the king in 1664 (Paige 75), and of the petition for the separation of Newton from Cambridge in 1678 (Paige 81).

After his wife died in 1656, Park remarried secondly Sarah[2] (Collier) Brewster (1612-91), widow of Mayflower passenger Love[2] Brewster [*The Mayflower Descendant* (Boston: Mass. Society of Mayflower Descendants, 1901), 3:192] and daughter of merchant William and Jane Collier (Gozzaldi 561). She married Brewster at Plymouth 15 May (new style; 25 May O.S.) 1634, and Brewster died Jan. or Feb. 1651 [Anderson, Robert, *The Pilgrim Migration* (Boston: NEHGS, 2004), 279]. After Park's death Sarah returned to the South Shore, for in 1676 when she sold her share of the estate she was "relict of Richard Parke, late of Cambridge

Village" in Duxbury (Jackson 383). She died Plymouth 26 April 1691, age 76 [*First Book of Plymouth First Church Records,* (Boston: Colonial Society of Mass., 1920), 3: 22; 22:271].

Park was one of the founders of the church in Newton, about 1658 (Jackson 118), its first minister Rev. John Eliot, nephew of our ancestor Francis of Braintree. The first church was built in 1661, and Park was one of its organizers in 1664 (Smith 85), but Park petitioned the General Court in 1661 to retain his membership in the Cambridge church (Jackson 119).

In 1663 he was released from military training on account of age, indicating he was over 60 (Smith 92). He died in Newton part of Cambridge 1665 (Newton VR 486 gives year only) . His will dated 12 July 1665 names both of our ancestors Elizabeth Winship and Isabel Whitmore, who inherited all of his estate except the 600 acres and homestead that went to their brother Thomas (Msx Pro. 16442) . The inventory of the estate 18 Aug. 1665 came to £ 972, mostly in Newton real estate (£ 660), with only 29 acres outside of Newton (£ 100; Jackson 382) . In 1666 Nicholas Wythe complained that he had been cheated of land next to the Boston line by the town's grant to Park (CR 166), but it is not clear how this was settled.

Among Richard Park's descendants are two men famous enough to be listed in the *Dictionary of American Biography*. Edward Amasa Park (1808-1900), son a Prof. Calvin Park of Brown was Professor of Theology at Amherst, then at Andover Theological Seminary for 45 years, 1836-81, where he "ranked with the greatest preachers and orators of his time" (DAB 7:204-5). Treanor W. Park (1823-82) was legal expert on California land titles and financier of railroads, the Pacific Mail Line, and sold his controlling interest in the Panama railway to deLesseps in 1881 (DAB 7:208-90).

Elizabeth (Park) Winship died Cambridge 19 Sept. 1690, age 58 (VR 798; g.s.), and buried with her husband in the Old Burial Ground in Cambridge. Her epitaph is transcribed in Harris 15. Her will of 18 Oct. 1689 mentions our ancestor, Joseph (Pope 507).

THE WHITMORE FAMILY

ANN (A)[4] WHITMORE was born in Medford 4 May 1707 (VR 164; Wyman 1020; Brooks, *History of Medford* [Boston: Rand & Avery, 1886], 80; 1706 in Paige 685) to FRANCIS[3] WHITMORE and ANNA PIERCE. She died Cambridge (Arlington) 2 Feb. 1806 (not in VR; Wyman 1041; Wyeth family dates; Cutter 326 makes her 101), three months short of 100 years. She is listed in the Charlestown census of 1789, having moved from Cambridge in 1786 (Wyman under Joseph 2). After 1784 the heirs of Joseph Winship quitclaimed their rights to the area of Arlington west of the Medford bridge, in exchange for Benjamin Cutter assuming Anna's care (Cutter 218) . In her nineties she was cared for by her granddaughter Anna (Wyeth) Cutter of Arlington, as a letter from Joseph Teel explains:

Newburyport, March 15,1798

"What is old age but pain & regret! but how has that of my Grandma'am's been softened by the attentive kindness of my cousins! . . .With what pleasure can Grandma'am look back, survey each past year of her life, dispell the prejudices that such sick bed & long confinement are apt to engender, & of consequence be what you say she is "happy & serene". May Heaven grant her happiness to all eternity!"

She died in the three-story brickend mansion built in 1798 by Benjamin and Anna (Wyeth) Cutter a few feet west of the bridge over weir on the Mystic River (Medford Street, Arlington; Cutter 217-8).

Her father FRANCIS[3] WHITMORE, tanner of Medford, was born in Medford 8 May 1678 with his twin Abigail (VR 165), to Deacon JOHN[2] WHITMORE and his first wife RACHEL[2] ELIOT. He was one of 15 elders who founded the First Church in Medford 1713. He was joined in the tannery business by his brother John, who had been a housewright (W. H.

Whitmore, *Record of the Descendants of Francis Whitmore of Cambridge* [Boston: J. Wilson, 1855],[hereinafter Whitmore], 4) . He bought land from Stephen Willis for a tanyard, and also owned land near Marbey Brook. [More on Whitmores after Pierce].

THE PIERCE PUZZLE

Francis Whitmore was twice married, firstly, in Boston 7 Dec. 1699 (CD 150:252) to ANNA PIERCE of Boston, born about 1681/2. She was mother of our ANN(A) WHITMORE WINSHIP. She died in Medford 6 Aug. 1716, age 35 (VR 458; 34 in Paige 685), and was buried in Salem Street Cemetery.

Anna Pierce's birth is not recorded in Boston, and an exceptional amount of research in possible sources has not disclosed her ancestry. Two possibilities are that she was daughter of Richard or John Pierce. John is based on an undocumented assertion in *Boston Transcript* 31 Aug. 1927 #5980 which states: "5. PIERCE. Anna Pierce of Boston who married about 1699 Francis Whitmore of Medford. Her father was John. Was he of family of Michael Pierce of Hingham, 1646, who names daughter Ann in his will. . . J.B.M.E." We find no reply to this, or confirmation. Lincoln's Hingham 108 merely lists a John Peirce as inheriting land from his father who was killed in the Indian fight at Rehoboth 27 March 1676, but gives no more. The author of the query is unknown.

The other claim is that Anna was the daughter of Richard Pierce, Boston printer (*Transcript* 27 Oct. 1930, # 844) : "PEIRCE. For some time I have endeavored to learn more about my ancestor Richard Peirce a printer of Boston, Massachusetts I would like to have the names of his parents and when and where he died. He married Aug. 27, 1680, Sarah Cotton, daughter of Rev. Seaborn and Dorothy (Bradstreet) Cotton. Anna Peirce, daughter of Richard, married Dec. 7, 1699, Francis Whitmore of Medford, Massachusetts M.B.B.W."

Richard Pierce, whose dates are unknown, was noted as the publisher of the first newspaper in America, "Public Occurrences Both Foreign and Domestick" in 1690 (Benjamin Franklin V, ed., *Boston Printers* (Boston: G. K. Hall, 1980, 412-4). It had only one number, however, because of its suppression by the government, and does not quite qualify as does multi-issued *The Boston News-Letter* which started in 1704. Pierce was the fifth printer in Boston, who flourished 1684-91, notably for the first edition of *The New-England Primer* (1680), and for printing the works of Cotton and Increase Mather. His last publication was 1691, when Littlefield believed he died, perhaps of small pox (best biography is George E. Littlefield, *The Early Massachusetts Press* (Boston: Club of Odd Volumes, 1907, esp. 11:43-7) . He married 27 Aug. 1680 Sarah Cotton, daughter of Rev. Seaborn Cotton and Dorothy Bradstreet, daughter of Gov. Bradstreet, thus allying himself with the elite families of the colony. She died 2 Aug. 1690.

There is no evidence of any children in any town, church or family record. That a couple would have had no children is unusual for the day, and children of anyone so well connected would have been noted (e.g., John W. Thornton, "Genealogies: The Cotton Family" *Register* 1:164-5; "A Partial List of the Descendants of the Rev. John Cotton in America", NEHGS G COT 222; John Dean & Dean Dudley, "Descendants of Gov. Bradstreet", Reg. April 1855, 113; Seaborn Cotton, Class of 1651, Sibley 1:286-93) . Sarah does appear in the will of her father dated 1684, but it gives no married name or children, as it might be expected to (Albert S. Batchellor, ed., *Probate Records of the Province of New Hampshire* [Concord NH: Rumford Printing Co., 1907], 1: 278) . None of Torrey's mss. sources gives any child. We conclude that there is no evidence that Anna was child of printer Richard Pierce and Sarah (Bradstreet).

One additional possibility is considered, that she was indeed daughter of a Richard Pierce, but one of the many others of the day:

1. Richard Peirce, servant of Anne Batchelder of Portsmouth, named in her will 5 Nov.

1660, N.H. Probate Records 1:51; we have no idea what happened to him.

2. Richard Pierce, eldest son of Maine carpenter of Muscongus, born about 1647 (Libby, 554).

3. One of the Essex County families.

It does not seem worthwhile searching all of these possibilities unless we could be sure that her father was indeed Richard, and that is asserted only by M.B.B.W. who says he was the printer. Here are some possible sources: Mss. genealogies of MBBW(hitmore?) and MBME; Suffolk Deeds for Pierce, Peirce, Pearse for poss. ref. to Anna Whitmore (starting with printed vols., then mss.); Massachusetts Court records 1680-91 for ref. to Anna; MHS for Richard Pierce; Sibley's refs 1:293 for possible clue; Harvard alum mss. for S. Cotton addenda re Pierce.

Francis[3] Whitmore remarried Medford 6 Aug. 1716 widow Mary (Hancock) Parker (not in VR; IGI fiche), daughter of Nathaniel[3] Hancock of Cambridge, and widow of John Parker, whom she had married 20 Dec. 1711, and who had died 2 Nov. 1712 at the young age of 22 years, 10 months and 11 days (g.s., Paige 623, 572). She died Medford 29 March 1760 age 71 (VR 458 from g.s.; Whitmore, 4) . Francis then became owner of the old Richard Park house east of the Cambridge Common (DAR 155). This became the Gannett House, torn down for the brief existence of the railroad station, and later Harvard's Thayer Commons eating hall, and today the open space between the Harvard Law Review's New Gannett House and the Littauer Center for Public Administration (Harris, 256-7). On Francis's front lawn the troops assembled before the Battle of Bunker Hill, only five years after Francis's death. He died Medford 6 Feb. 1771 (VR 458). His burial in the family plot in Salem Street Cemetery in Medford is not inventoried, so he may be buried across the common in the Old Burial Ground. Paige quotes his obituary in *Boston New Letter* of 14 Feb. 1771: "he was the father of 10 children, 41 grandchildren, 96 great-grandchildren, and 8 of the fifth generation, in all 155" (Paige 685).

Francis[3] was the son of Deacon John[2] WHITMORE, housewright and carpenter of Medford, born Cambridge 1 Oct. 1654 (Sav. 4:527; VR ; Whitmore 2; Jessie Purdy, *The Whitmore Genealogy* [Cambridge: author, 1907],[hereinafter Purdy], 13) to Sgt. FRANCIS[1] WHIT(TE)MORE and his first wife ISABEL[2] PARK(ES), sister of Elizabeth Park, the wife of Lt. Edward[1] Winship, whose parents we have above. While living in Arlington he was given permission with 11 others, including Edward Winship, to build another gallery on the north side of the Cambridge meeting house (CR 212) . He had moved out of Cambridge by August 1688, for he does not appear on the town census of that date (Paige 440ff.) . Deacon Whitmore became freeman in Medford 22 March 1690. He was impressed into fighting in the war against the Maine Indians 1689 with Major Swayne beyond Piscataqua (SCW 331; Magn. 11:67) . On 6 June 1711 he quitclaimed 3+ acres on the Concord Road (Massachusetts Av.) in Cambridge to his brother Samuel. An early settler of Medford, he was Deacon of its First Church 11 March 1713, and Treasurer of the town for a decade, 1714-25. He died 22 Feb. 1739 age 87 (g.s.), and is buried in the family plot on the east side of Salem Street Cemetery, Medford center, west of the municipal parking facility on River Street, the building of which seems to have moved the family footstones closer to the headstones (Oak Grove inven. #478) .

The founder of the Whitmore Family in America was FRANCIS[1] WHIT(TE)MORE, a tailor, born in England about 1623 (g.s. died Oct.. 1685 age 62) or (1625 (dep. about 35 on 18 Oct. 1660, Msx files per Pope 494; Whitmore 24 citing two Cambridge affidavits; Purdy 13), probably son of John Whitmore of Wethersfield, Essex (Sav. 4:526). He is supposed to have come to America as early as the 1630s (Purdy 13).

He was a proprietor of Cambridge in 1648, became freeman 7 May 1654 (Gozzaldi 796), and signed the loyalty petition of 1664 (Paige 75) . He held minor town offices like hogreeve (1662/3, CR 143; 1663, CR 151), surveyor (1663, CR 147), fenceviewer (1667/8, CR 169), and most importantly, "Katechiseing the youth of this Towne" west of Alewife Brook with our other ancestor Edward Winship (1668, CR 175; 1669, CR 188; Paige 269; Purdy 14 says he was Selectman 1668). When William Wilcox died in 1653 he left 20 shillings to Whitmore as one of his "loving brethren that were of my family meeting" (Paige 691). When three single men were loose on the town, one of them, Jacob Coale "submitted himselfe to the family goventf of francis whitmore, who engaged to respond to his rates [taxes], & orderly cariage dureing his abode their." (1665, CR 161; Paige 511).

As early as 1648 he lived in Lexington (Cambridge Farms) just above the Arlington (Menotomy) line according to the account of the division (Hudson 40; Whitmore 23; Purdy 13; Paige 685). Settlers of this part of Cambridge were called "Farmers" (Hurd 1:607) . In 1682 he was one of eight residents of the Farms who petitioned for a separate church there because of the distance from Cambridge center (Paige 121) . In 1682 he was chosen "farme Counstable", that is, a deputy for the outlying Arlington area and beyond (CR 260).

He owned land near the Plains in Cambridge, and in Arlington at Menotomy near Dendrick Meadows (Purdy citing Brooks; Dunbarke in Whitmore 23). The first land record of him is in 1652 when he got a relatively small 50 acre lot #59 in the huge Shawshine division (today's Billerica; CR 98; divided 1698, CP 321; Paige 59). The next year he was given a woodlot of 3/4 acre near Spy Pond in Arlington (CR 65) . In 1662 he got two acres south of the Charles (CP 141) . In 1664 the town gave him two acres of swamp north of the Menotomy River on the condition that he clear it for meadow within five years (CR 154). In the division of the Cow Common in 1664/5 he drew lot #125 measuring 12 acres, with rights to one cow common (CP 148) . In the 1682 division of the land between the eight mile line and Concord he drew lot #82, of 12 acres (CP 162) . He had land on the Mystic River, for in 1685 John Rolfe gave 1/12 right in a sawmill on Sergt. Francis Whitmore's land to William Cutter (MD 9:366 in Cutter 14).

In 1682 his taxes came to £ 9/11/5, of which he had to pay a quarter in money, £ 1/1/6, the rest in produce (CR 261-2).

Francis served in the Indian wars under Major Simon Willard, then against the Saco Indians under Major Swayne (Whitmore 23 citing Treasurer's Book; SCW 531; Levi Gould, *Ancient Middlesex* [Somerville MA: Journal Print, 1905], 125).

The family's liberal views are shown by testimonials which he and his wife signed to secure Mary Holman's acquittal of a charge of witchcraft (1660, Paige 363-4; Whitmore 23; Purdy 13).

He married first, about 1648, Isabel Park, daughter of Richard, and sister of Elizabeth Winship (Paige 684, 623; Pope 494 says she was dau. of Thomas Parks citing Msx files 1672). After her death on 31 March 1665 (Cam. VR 789) he remarried Lexington 10 Nov. 1666 to Margaret Harty (Cam. VR 418; Paige 684; Purdy 13; Torrey mss.; Howard W. Carter, *A Genealogy of the Descendants of Thomas Carter* [Norfolk: author, 1909], 18 suggests alternative spelling Hartz), whose parents and family are unknown. She died Cambridge {Lexington) 1 March 1685/6 (Lex. VR 209; Paige 685; Whitmore 1).

He died in Cambridge (Arlington/Medford) 12 Oct. 1685 age 62 (g.s.; Med. VR 458; Cam VR 789 from g.s. Harvard Square). His gravestone is on the east side of Salem Street Cemetery, between Salem and River Streets, Medford center, (Oak Grove inven. #467). His epitaph on the gravestone, supposedly in Cambridge, is recorded by Harris 11. His will, dated 8th of 8th month (Oct.) 1685 left an estate valued at £ 305/9/0 (Msx Pro. 6:270; text in Reg. 9:134, Whitmore 23, Purdy 137).

Among his descendants was the noted genealogist and antiquarian William H. Whitmore (1836-1900) who edited the diary of Samuel Sewall and other historical works (DAB 9:153) . He was also ancestor of Levi S. Gould, b. 1835 (mother Elizabeth Whitmore. . .John$^{3-2}$) ,

Chairman of Middlesex County Commissioners 1897-1905 ff., first mayor of Melrose 1900, town Moderator for 35 years (1865-99), Massachusetts Representative 1868-9, and President of Melrose Co-Operative Bank (L. Gould 123-5).

THE ELIOT FAMILY

John Whitmore married twice, firstly in 1677 to the mother of our Francis[3], RACHEL[2] (ELIOT) POULTER. She was born in Braintree 26 Oct. 1643 (VR 633) to Deacon FRANCIS[1] ELIOT and MARY[2] (MARIA) SAUNDERS. She had married firstly in Billerica 29 Dec. 1662 (Billerica VR 250, 301; Cam VR 384) to John[2] Poulter (1635-76; John[1] and Mary) of Cambridge and Billerica (Reg. 141:219; estate Msx Pro 17818 in Reg. 141:220). Poulter died in Cambridge 20 May 1676, age 41 (VR 700). His epitaph is in Harris 6. Her petition to the government reads:

"The humble petition of Rachael Whitmore wife of John Whitmore,
Whereas, your Petitioner's husband was impressed into the countrye's service against the Indian enemy, and is now with Major Swayne at Newechawanick, and your petitioner and her children are very weak and ill, and unable to help ourselves and do anything for our relief and the rest of the family, as several of the neighbors can and have informed your honors,
Doth therefore humbly request for favor from hour Honors that her husband, John Whitmore may be dismissed the present service and that yours Honors would please to pass your order for the same, that he may return to his sick family. . .Rachael Whitmore" (Reg. 9:307 from Massachusetts Records 35:34; also Whitmore 24).

Rachel died in Medford 20 March 1723/4 at age 80 (VR 459; g.s. reads 1723), and is buried in Salem Street Cemetery next to her husband (Reg. 141:219; Oak Grove inven. #469). A year after her death Deacon John Whitmore married secondly Cambridge June 1724 (VR 421; Cutter 316) Rebecca (Rolfe) Cutter, widow of William[2] Cutter (Richard[1]) of Cambridge, who had died there 1 April 1723 (VR 521; Cutter 316; Paige 521). Rebecca was born Newbury 9 Feb. 1661 (Roafe in VR 439; Cutter 316; Paige 645) to John Rolfe of Nantucket, Newbury and Cambridge, and his wife Mary Scullard. She and Cutter were admitted to the church in Cambridge 28 July 1700, and had ten children. As Rebecca Whitmore she donated £ 6 toward silver for the communion at the first church Arlington, which are inscribed, "The gift of Rebeckah Whitmore to the 2d Church of Christ in Cambridge, 1739" (Cutter 316). She died Medford (Menotomy/Arlington per Paige 686) 13 Nov. 1751 age 90 (Arl VR 155; Cutter 316).

Rachel was niece of the famous Rev. John Eliot, "Apostle to the Indians" whose first conversion was made in Newton on Nonantum Hill, soon purchased by John Kenrick, and marked by a plaque at the end of Eliot Memorial Av. in east Newton Corner (1603-90; see DAB 5:79-80). Her father Francis was also a teacher of the "Praying Indians" under his brother about 1650 (Reg. 36:292 in Pope 153; L. Gould 125) . He was baptized at Nazeing, Essex, 10 April 1615 (Topo 50 citing Pope).

Francis settled in Braintree 29 Jan. 1638 as one of its first "Planters". There is no earlier town grant than his 16 acres on that date (Pettee 28). His house appears to be between Elm and Sea Streets, along Miller's Stile, laid out by 1655 across his land and by the foreside of his barn (Pettee 68). They sold the house, on land which probably belonged to his wife's father, Martin Saunders, west of the brook, in 1662 (SD 4:57, see below). He became freeman 2 July 1641, joined the church in Braintree 1645, of which he became Deacon 12 Oct. 1653. When the minister's house burned down in 1644 he and three others bought land near Knight's Neck for the benefit of Rev. Henry Flint, paying five shillings an acre, to be paid in kind, "in corne or cattle" within one month (Pettee 13, 30) . Francis was one of the eight men of Braintree, with Henry Neal, who signed the deed of Indian land by chief Wampatuck in 1665 (text in Pattee 45-6) . But in 1679 he owned land east of the 11 acre plot that Stephen Willis sold to John Ruggles that year, in a deed that he witnessed (SD 11:312, 313). He died Braintree 17 Jan. 1697. His widow Mary presented his estate 13 Nov. 1677, with inventory of 29 Oct. (Pope 153). His estate came to £

321/17 (see ref. to will above).

Francis[1] Eliot and his brother Rev. John were children of Bennett[A] (Benit) Eliot and Lettice (Letteye) Aggar. Bennett was a farmer of Widford, Hertfordshire and Nazeing, Essex (Reg. 48:396-8; more promised in Reg. 2007). It is believed that he was related in some unproved way to the Eliot family of Bishop's Stortford, Herts. (Origins 3:178). He was buried at Nazeing 21 Nov. 1621. His will of 5 Nov. was probated 28 March 1622 left a large estate of extensive lands in several villages. It mentions his son Francis, to whom he left four silver christening spoons in trust, and five pieces of land: two acres Crottwell Croft, one acre Coles Croft, Dameter in Great Hyfield, one acre in Little Westney, and an acre in Sowters Common Meade (text in Reg. 48:396-8 from Com. Ct. of London 24:85). He was married St. John's Church, Widford, Herts. 30 Oct. 1598 to Lettice Aggar. She was buried Nazeing 16 March 1620. Lettice Algor was baptized at Nazeing 22 March 1578/9, daughter of yeoman Francis Alger who died between the writing of his will on 24 May 1582 and its probate on 5 July (Reg. 160: 181-4). Francis was the son of Robert Algore of Nazeing and his wife Joane. Lettice's mother was Lettice Peacock, daughter of yeoman Thomas Peacock of Waltham Holy Cross, Essex, who died between his will of 1 Nov. 1583 and its proof on 4 Dec. She subsequently married John Miller in Nazeing on 3 Sept. 1582, and William Fentecoote on 13 April 1613 in Colchester, Essex.

THE SAUNDERS FAMILY

Francis[1] Eliot married Braintree before 1641 (VR) MARY[2] (MARIA) SAUNDERS. She was born Sudbury, Suffolk 1618 (age 15 on departure from London in Spring 1635), where she was baptized at All Saints Church 26 Aug. 1619 (Reg. 66:176), first daughter and eldest child of MARTIN(E)[1] SAUNDERS and RACHEL WHEATLEY.

Mary was probably illiterate, for her mark "M" appears with her husband's signature on a deed of sale of their house and orchard in Braintree for £ 50 to mariner John Ke(a)ne of Braintree. It included three acres west of the brook, east of a private road to Henry Pennyman's land on the south, and Rev. Henry Flint's on the north (4 May 1662, SD 4:57). This same house was sold six months later for the same price to another ancestor, Richard[1] Harris, father of Mercy Harris Gould, with ffrancis Elliot witnessing the takeover "giuen by turfe & twig" (17 Nov. 1662, SD 5:376-7).

She died Braintree 17 Jan. 1697 (VR 301), age 77. She is probably buried in Braintree's first graveyard, the Hancock Cemetery in Quincy Center, probably in the Eliot plot.

Martin was born in England, perhaps Suffolk about 1593-5 (40 on departure from London in Spring, 1635, Hotten's lists 47,48 cited by Reg. 10:87), worked as a currier, or leather-dresser (Origins 1:194). He married twice, firstly in England, probably Sudbury, Suffolk, about 1618 to RACHEL (WHEATLEY) BRACKETT, born about 1590, who had married first about 1607 to Peter Brackett (1590-1616) of Sudbury, by whom she had four children before his death in Sudbury, Suffolk 16 Aug. 1616 (TAG 55:215-7) . Martin and Rachel lived in Sudbury 1619 to 1634 where their seven children were baptized and one buried 1 Aug. 1634 (Origins 194-5).

Saunders came via London on the *Planter,* Capt. Nicolas Tradice, in the Spring of 1635 with his wife and three daughters and son Martin Jr. and three teenage servants, which indicate some wealth (Pope 399; Origins 194; Banks 141) . He joined the church in Boston 8 Nov. 1635 at the same time as his wife (Winsor 1:570). I have not found evidence of where they lived in Boston. The Martin Saunders who had ¼ acre and house at the south end of the Common before 1677 was probably his son (SD 10:119a).

He was one of the first settlers of Braintree, when he moved there in 1639 to become freeman 13 March 1640. He was the first innholder of town, licensed 6 June 1639, and the following year to "draw wine" (Pettee 164) . His inn was a convenient place for town meetings, held after incorporation in 1640 (Pettee 568, 534) . Saunders served as Selectman and in many important town committees. He was among those who took the first town action to prevent fires, in 1641, requiring every householder to keep a ladder against his chimney (Pettee 74). In 1642 he was put in charge of making sure there was enough saltpeter to make gunpowder (Pettee 358).

Saunders was one of the eight men who signed the Covenant that created the First Church in Braintree 16 Sept. 1639 which began: "We poor unworthy creatures, who have sometime lived without Christ and without God in the world, and have deserved rather fellowship with the devil and his angels, than with God and his saints...renounce the devil, and the wicked world, a sinful flesh with all the remnants of Anti-Christian pollution, wherein sometimes we have walked, and all our former evil ways...and we give up ourselves also one to another...promising...to walk in brotherly love...(text in Pattee 194).

In 1648 the gunner of the *Peregrine,* Edward ffilpot, gave a power of attorney to William Cotton of Boston to recover a debt of £ 6/12/8 in cattle in the hands of Martin Saunders of Braintree (25 Dec. in *Aspinwall Notarial Records* [Boston: Municipal Printing Office, 1903], 288) . The ship was in Boston lading for England under Capt. Nicholas Trerice (Ibid., 181, 189, 199).

Just a year before he died, on 11 Aug. 1657, he made a contract with his son John prior to his marriage to Mary Mujoy, giving him ten pieces of property:

1) Half of the Mill Playne, 16 acres east of the highway, west of Stephen Payne, south of John Hakbone and north of Willjam Ellis;
2) The other half within 40 days of his death, or £15;
3) Half of his barn, which he calls "Barron";
4) Half of the orchard at the east end, next to Peter Brackett's house;
5) "a litle Garden plott" adjoining the orchard and the highway;
6) Four acres in the Great field of Braintree, called Stony Bottom;
7) Half the oxehowse next to the west end of the Barron;
8) The land on which John Saunders house stands with the inclosed garden on the backside of it and a sufficient way on the back side of the house to the water brook;
9) Five acres of saltmarsh in Dorchester, lately possessed by Christopher Gibson;
10) 12 acres a little distant from the Garden, called the Outland (SD 3:40-1).

His wife Rachel died Braintree 15 July 1651 (not in VR), and Martin remarried in Braintree 23 May 1654 Elizabeth Bancroft of Cambridge (Brain. VR 716; whose husband Roger had made his will two days before his death in Cambridge 28 Nov. 1653 (Cam VR 459) . She lived in one of the oldest houses in Cambridge, the 1642 Vassall House at 94 Brattle Street on the east side of Longfellow Park (DAR 95; although extensively remodelled about 1742 the core dates back to Elizabeth's time).

Martin died in Braintree 4 Aug. 1658 (not in VR ; Pope 399), having made his will 5 July 1658 (Reg. 10:87). The value of his estate was £ 321/17, mostly for the house (£ 60), 16 acres at Pumpkin Hill (£ 40), a meadow (£ 40), and a dozen cows (£ 51). Pettee reprints the inventory, noting that the inn had no knives and forks, or plates, and only three beds, four chairs and a table (164-5). An agreement of his heirs on 10 Aug. 1658 divided his property. Francis Eliot thru his wife got six acres on the Neck and £ 7. This did not settle the estate, for Francis found an earlier will, so the probate court did "advise ye children to come to a Loving agreement".

His widow Elizabeth remarried twice more, first on 2 Sept. 1659 (VR 49 incomplete 1648=1648/9), to Deacon John Bridge of Cambridge who died 15 April 1665 (VR 484) , and whose statue by Daniel French was placed on Cambridge Common in 1882 to represent "the ideal puritan" (DAR 126, 59) . Elizabeth, who had lived in the Vassal House as Mrs. Bancroft, moved back to the area of Tory Row, to John Bridge's house on the north corner of Brattle and Mason Streets, now the site of Episcopal Divinity School's Shepard Memorial Church (DAR 93) . Her wedding date of 2 Sept. 1659 is inferred from her mark, first a big "F" between the name

Elizab: Sanders, and on the same date a big "C" appears between the name Elizabeth Bridge on the marriage contract with her son John Saunders and her son-in-law Francis Eliot (SD 3:280-1). In this the men promise to pay her £ 8 annually, half in cattle either in milch cows or steers under 6 years, the other half in merchantable corn, all sorts of ordinary grain at merchantable prices, the corn by next 25 March, the other half in fatt cattle at the following Michaelmas. They also deeded to her 36 acres in Braintree: 16 acres of the Mill Playne, 14 acres in the Great Field called Pumping Hill, and six acres of meadow. She is also to get £ 44, of which £ 40 in household goods according to the previous covenant, the mare, coult and cow at Deacon Ellis's, a cow at Joseph Adams's, and £ 11 in Martin Saunders[1] hand, and a two year old and vantage heifer, ast the price set by the appraisers. In return they cancel all previous contracts of Martin Saunders and his wife.

Finally she married in Reading 22 Jan. 1673 (VR 292) to Edward Taylor who died Reading 4 Sept. 1694 (VR 572) . She died in Reading 22 Jan. 1696 (VR 572).

CAREER AND MARRIAGE OF LYDIA'S FATHER

Having concluded the ancestry of Benjamin Teel, we return to his career and marriage.

Lydia's father Benjamin Teel was trained as a baker under his father, but at age 19 was unsure of his career, while working unhappily in the shipping business out of Portsmouth NH. A letter from his brother Joseph, four years older than he, in 1801 has been preserved in the family (1995 with John R. Shaw of San Mateo).

"Newburyport, Feby 11, 1801 Dear

Brother,

I reed yours of the 6th Instant & am sorry you are discontented in your situation, especially as it was your own choice. It grieves our Parent that you cannot fix on a situation in which you would be happy & hansomely support yourself.--With a little thought, you might attain content by only acquiring an established principle within. We all come into the world with fashions too discordant for others, & consequently for our own happiness, these fashions it is our duty to subdue, & the greater the conquest, the greater is our merit.--If we examine ourselves, & think how others conduct effects us, we can easily conjecture how ours will effect others--& then you will say thus to yourself--"! have relations whose happiness is affected by mine, consequently *I* will be happy & that will make them so". This would a patriotic & noble principle & worthy a prince.--

It has always been my opinion that you would do better at the southward than in this town, but Ma'am being of a contrary opinion, I have seldom mentioned it.

I still think that if you were to go in the Sloop, which I expect home the middle of March & go in such a manner as to have your own Liberty, when there, that it would be for your benifit & should cost you nothing but the loss of time--You could there not only carry on Baking but by having a communication with me transact business the commissions of which would be almost sufficient for your expenses.

If you are really much discontented I would when Henry comes to Portsmouth come round with him & then we will have another trip to Kennebunk.

If Noyes is ready to sail before Henry arrives I wish you to put the Rum aboard him, but, by all means have Henry come directly here. Write me of Henry's business--! have heard from Bassett & he is doing well. Your shirts were left at Charles Pierce's a week ago--John [their brother b. c. 1786] has no money at present--has his runners still on hand. Enquire what Board ClapBoard & Shingle nails will sell for by the Cask--Tarr also. With my best wishes & the love of us all be assured I am (as usual) your Brother."

Portsmouth & Newburyport maritime reports may give news of Capt. Noyes, and sloop.

He apparently continued buying tallow and trading in soap. In the Teel Account Book we get his entries 1801-5 that give some idea of Benjamin's activity:

3 Jan. 1801 $200 for labor Newburyport for Philip Butler.

30 Jan. 1802 for 100 wt. Rozin soap sold in West Indies by Nehemiah Pitman.

26 March 1802 paid Enoch Tappan $ 7 for keeping his horse Feb. 1 to March 1.

6 July 1802 8 Barrells of herrin to be carried to West Indies M cost & commission to Christopher Bassett.

13 Jan. 1803 $200 for 764 Ibs. Tallow from Christian? Brock. 13 Jan. 1803 $50 for Tallow

from J[signature torn].

18 Jan. 1803 "Mr. Rutly this day moved from my small House in Sumer Street I Haveing Sold It to Mr Ebenezer Noyes."

27 Jan, 1803 "this day looked of over and [settled?] all accounts with John Berry Titcomb Relative to My Father's Estate and gave Susan ten Dollars for her part in the Herbert Land adjoining the end of the tallow house."

We will return to Benjamin's career after telling about his wife.

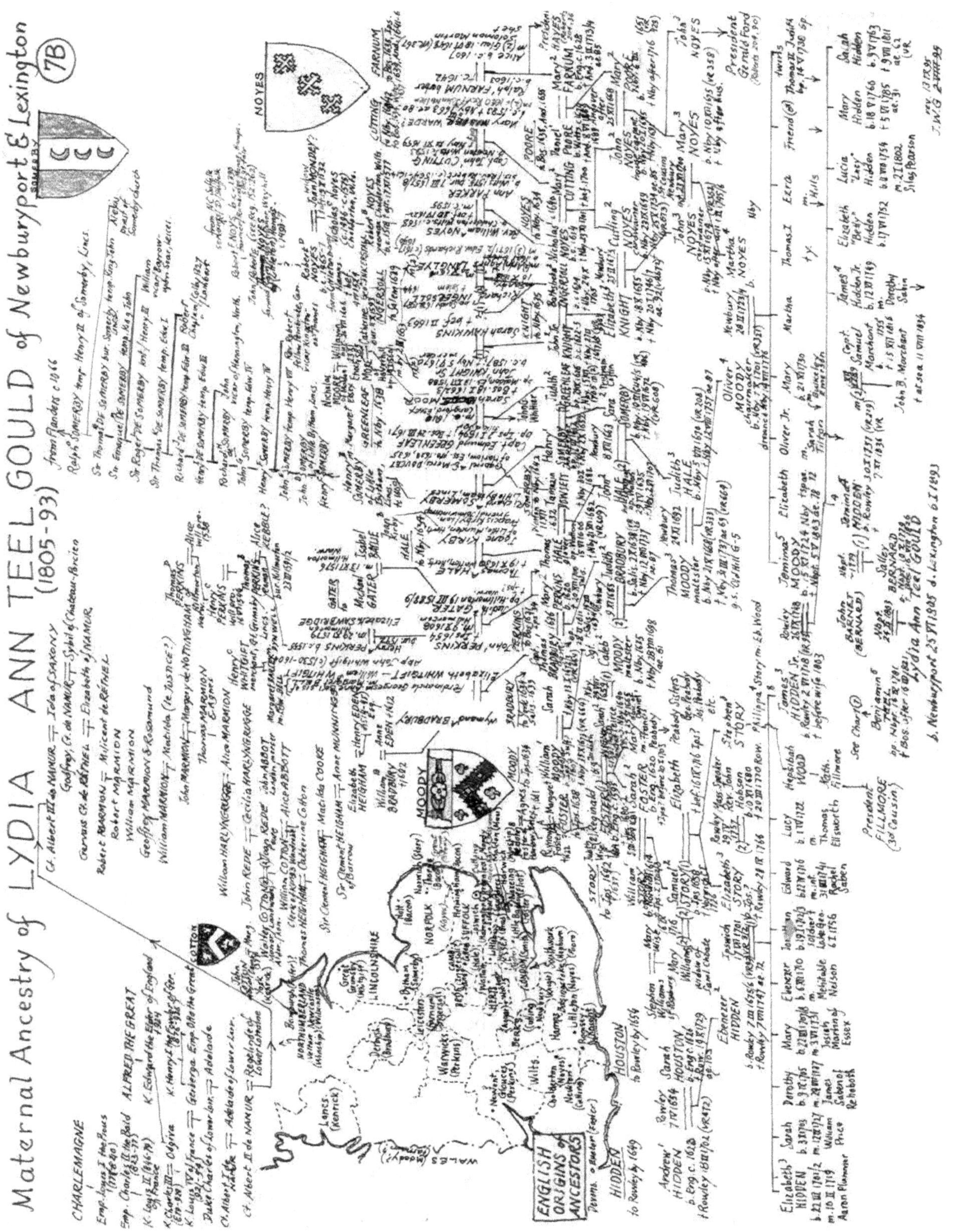

Maternal Ancestry of LYDIA ANN TEEL GOULD (1805-93) of Newburyport & Lexington
7B
CHARLEMAGNE
ALFRED THE GREAT
ENGLISH ORIGINS of ANCESTORS
COTTON
MOODY
NOYES

THE BARNARD FAMILY

On 24 Feb. 1803 in Newburyport Benjamin Teel was married to SALLEY BERNARD (VR 468). She was born in Newburyport as recorded in the "Record of Baptisms" of the Second Presbyterian Church there, in the Newburyport Library, 17 (also VR 27: "Sally Barnet, an adult person). - -Daughter of the late John Barnet and Miner His Wife, was born October 10, 1779 & Baptized October 4, 1801 by Rev[3] John Boddily." She died in Boston 16 Aug. 1826, age 47 (Lydia's diary 1875: "fourty seven years ago to day My Mother Died it was eight O'clock in the Morn and Saturday, she was buried on Sunday after meeting about five O'clock").

Sally's father is a complete mystery. We can find no record of his birth, parents, occupation, property, or death. Although Sally's baptismal record shows the name Barnet, she consistently signed her name Bernard. There are numerous Barnard families in the area which often used the spelling Barnet:

1. Descendants of Thomas Barnard of Salisbury & Amesbury, towns immediately north of Newburyport ("Barnard Genealogy", *Essex Antiquarian,* 6 (1902) 120-5; we have checked these thoroughly in wills, deeds and local histories, and find only the possibility that Thomas[4] (Thomas[3-2-1]) would be expected to have more than one child, but he disappears after Essex Deed 95:101 7 April 1739 and birth of son Thomas[5] on 9 June 1739. Perhaps he had other children who were unrecorded.

2. Descendants of Robert Barnard, most of whom lived in Andover (Ibid., 125-8). We have checked these also, particularly the line of Johns, but our John does not fit.

3. Descendants of Rev. Thomas Barnard of Andover (Ibid., 129-31). A possibility, for which we have NO evidence is that he was the John[4] Barnard #16, the Loyalist who was in Newburyport in 1779, dealing with a distillery he owned. He may not have been married to Sarah Ramsdell of Salem though they recorded intentions 10 July 1773 (*Sibley's Harvard Graduates* [Boston: MHS, 1970], 15:174-5). No marriage record is found, and she completely disappeared. John is supposed to have married in Canada, at a date unrecorded, to a Chloe Butler, daughter of Loyalists Eleazer and Lydia (Durkee) . This minister's son had a "mixed" career at Harvard, became a successful West India merchant in Boston, but aroused resentment by "a scurrilous piece" in the Boston press condemning the nonviolent acts preceding the Revolution, served in the English corps against the Patriots, and fled on Evacuation Day to Canada, single.

He was in Newburyport in 1772 when he was one of the first members admitted to the Marine Society of Newburyport (20 Nov. 1772 (William Bayley & Oliver Jones, *History of the Marine Society* [Newburyport: private printing, 1906], 10). He had returned to Newbury by March 1778, recovering his extensive property. He sold his distillery in Newburyport. The Marine Society expelled him with this note: 6 Dec. 1781...Voted, that whereas Capt. John Barnard, a member of the Marine Society has been present in the society but one evening since his admission in the year 1772, has not paid his dues regularly, is now greatly in arrears and in our opinion has been guilty of a breach of the thirteenth article of the standing laws, and sustains a character unworthy of a member of this society and also absconded from, and left his native country and taken part with enemies thereof.

Therefore, that he the said John Barnard be deemed unworthy of any dependence from the society and excluded from the benefit of the box. (30) . He had returned to Canada for good, to St. John NB, where he died in 1785, age 43 (David Maas, comp. *Divided Hearts: Massachusetts Loyalists* [Boston: NEHGS, 1980], 9) ; Lorenzo Sabine, *Loyalists of the American Revolution* [Boston: Little, Brown, 1864], 1:209. His merchant brother Benjamin administered his estate 5 Dec. 1807, and took guardianship of his minor son John[5] (Barnard Mss., Essex Institute, #5).

We find no record of the actual marriage of John and "Miner", but the possibility that Sally's birth was illegitimate is dismissed by local historians, who believe Rev. Boddily would not have recorded an illegitimate birth, even 21 years after the event. Rev. Richard J. Link of the First Presbyterian Church accounted for the lack of many other records of the church due to the senility of the current minister.

The identity of Sally's mother "Miner" is also a mystery, but somewhat easier to solve. In Lydia's diary for 7 Feb. 1874 she wrote: "Newburyport...Anna & I called on Miss Emerson [perhaps her second cousin, whose grandmother Mary Moody, sister of Jemima Hidden, married Bulkeley Emerson, whose son of the same name was town librarian; Rolfe 3]. She told me my Great Grandmother's name was Hidden[,] and Moody before she was married."

JEMIMA[5] MOODY of Newbury, born 15 Nov. 1724 (Moodey in VR 327) married in Rowley 26 Sept. 1748 (Rowley VR 312; Newbury VR 2:229) to JAMES[4] HIDDEN Sr. born Rowley 2 June 1718 (VR 93), and had a daughter JEMIMA[5] HIDDEN, born Rowley 30 Jan. 1757 (VR 1:219, citing CR9=First Presbyterian Church, Old South, Newburyport). We believe that the Minister recorded her familiar name "Miner", short for "Jemimer".

That John Barnard actually did marry Jemima is shown by the fact that Jemima (Hidden) used the name when she remarried Newburyport Samuel Marchant 1 Dec. 1789 (VR 29), after Barnard's death (not in VR) . Capt. Samuel Marchant died 15 Dec. 1816, age 61 (VR 715; Rolfe 823). It is unclear how they are related to two John Marchants, who were born too late to be Jemima's children, one who died 17 April 1824, age 21 (g.s. Old Burying Hill), or John B. Marchant who died at sea 11 Aug. 1834, age 21 (Nbypt VR 2: 712; Rolfe 823) . Jemima (Hidden) Marchant died in Newburyport on 7 Nov. 1836 (VR 2: 715) at the age of 79. Further record of her has not been found, but correspondence of her brothers and sisters in the Greenleaf, Pearson and Pettigall families may reveal more.

James Hidden was the grandson of ANDREW[1] HIDDEN, born in England about 1623 (he deposed he was about 40 years 23 June 1662 per court record EQ 2:397; the round number is suspect, and in March 1663 he gave the same age, EQ 3:22; about 55 in both Sept. 1678 and June 1679, EQ 7:83-84n, 208). Most of the settlers of Rowley came from Yorkshire, but his origin has not been found. One descendant supposed that he was descended from a Hidden family that came from Clydesdale, Scotland to Hungerford, Berkshire by 1465 (Robert & Margaret Hidden, "A Hidden Memorial" (typesc. Vancouver WA, 1953 in NEHGS, 1-5). However, the connection is unsubstantiated. New England onomastics (naming procedures) suggests that his parents may have been Andrew and Margaret, for whom his first children of each sex are likely to have been named.

In the records the name is spelled HADON, HAEDEN, HEADEN, HADDEN, HEDDAN, HEDDEN, HEIDEN, HEYDEN, HIDEN, etc. See more in Richard Hunt's "The Hiddens Have Gone to Newburyport" in *The Essex Genealogist*, Aug. 2004, 165-8.

Andrew's first appearance in America is 31 May 1649 when he was brought to Essex county court for striking "another man's servant", who is not named, though he had to pay Richard Swan's witness fees (31 May 1639 EQ 1:168; George B. Blodgette, *Early Settlers of Rowley* [Rowley: Amos Jewett, 1933, hereinafter Blodgette], 150). It is no surprise that Hidden's next appearance in court was when he testified that Robert Swann told him in 1653 that unless Nehemiah Abbott brought out the lost heifer he would accuse Hidden of being negligent in his calling of cattle tender, and that he would speak more of it to the town than Robart Hesseltine had done (Ipswich April 1654, EQ 1:345) . The main point of his testimony was about lost cattle, about which Hidden expertly testified that many had crossed the river between Haverhill and Rowley in 1652.

Hidden was not only literate, but well educated, for before early 1649 he was among several citizens of Rowley who were paid (19 sh./ 10 d.) for teaching the village children (Richard Dummer's account of Thomas Nelson's estate of 25 March 1649 in EQ 2:16; Jewett 130) . Although the account lists him with the title of "Mr. Hidden", we cannot assume this was more than an honorific, not necessarily a sign of college degree, as Hidden Memorial does. Nor is there any evidence of connection with Rev. Ebenezer Hidden of Salem and Portsmouth, though that may be.

In 1653 he was hired by the town of Rowley to keep "Young cattell" (25 April 1653, Amos & Emily Jewett, *Rowley, Massachusetts* [Rowley: Jewett Family, 1946],[hereinafter Jewett], 120, 122), a job he seems to have held for most of the next 25 years. He was hired to care for calves on 26 Jan. 1653 (*The Early Records of the Town of Rowley* [Rowley: the town, 1894], [hereinafter RR], 84). His fellow townsmen paid him in "corn and butter", as shown in his suit in 1674 against James Bailey and Ezekiell Northend (EQ 5:275).

On 7 April 1654 he married SARAH HOUSTON or HOUSTIN (EIHC 6:37) . Her parents have not been traced. One might check this name in Mass. towns. She was born about 1626 if her age at death was indeed 103, as given in Rowley church records 19 Oct. 1729 (Blodgette 150). The couple had 12 children, whose dates are listed by Blodgette.

Hidden continued to be paid by the town for keeping cattle, being the largest payee, £ 7, "at marchants" on 24 May 1654, and £ 11/2/11 at 1^s-10^d apeace" for "young catell" (RR 89; index says "Andrew" is Hidden). Later in the year he was officially appointed town Finder, the Yorkshire word for "pounder" of cattle (12 Dec., RR 91).

The next month he was given a cow gate (a grant of common land--OED) "vpon the plain lieing beyond the pine plain joyning vpon elder rainers midow" for the land given him on that plain (RR 93). The next year he was given a cow gate "in Lue of 4 acers of land that he laid Downe, beyond long medow bridge" (3 Dec. 1656, RR 96). In 1661 the town survey showed him possessing two gates (grants), one which he got in exchange for his previous town grant, and another he bought from Danniell Rouse (4 Feb. 1661, RR 122; text in Hurd 2:1134 from 86 of town record). As a charge for one gate he was assessed 30 shillings to lease land to Rev. Ezekiel Rogers of Ipswich (16 Feb. 1661, RR 128). The town then gave him two acres on the east side of William Law's marsh (4 Aug. 1661, RR 3). Next year they gave him another acre and a half, west of Simonds Brook, south and east of the highway that comes down on the south side of the brook, east of John Pearson's meadow, and abutting the common land on the hillside (30 Jan. 1662, RR 144) . Later the year he got another acre south of John Todd and north of Henory Royoly (26 Nov. 1662, RR 136). He sold his share in Plum Island to the Jewetts for £ 1 before 1665 (EQ 8:167). His taxes for 1662 were fifth lowest in the village, only 4 shillings 3 pence (19 June, RR 132).

In 1656 he was in debt to the estate of Francis Parrat of Rowley for £ 6/10 (EQ 2:5).

Hidden was hired as messenger. He was sent by Samuel Bellingham "to the Bay" (Boston) to ask Richard Bellingham to come to a family funeral, and was paid a red waistcoat of the dead man for his trip (1662, EQ 2:397).

In 1663, after repeated town complaints about loose cattle, he was appointed one of four town Finders for the East Field and farm (12 Aug. 1663, RR 146). This was renewed for "our end" in 1665 and 1666 (9 Jan. 1665, RR 159) . In 1672 he was reappointed Finder for the northeast field and farm (15 Jan., RR 226).

Hidden's homestead is first identified in 1666 at the east end of Rowley, at the southwest corner of Pleasant and Main Sts. (Essex Deeds 4 Ips. 44 cited by Blodgette) . This was land originally given to William, John and Thomas Harris in 1639 (Jewett, 21 and frontis. map). Hidden bought 3/4 acre from James Barker Jr. (Ips. Deed 4:44 cited by Joseph N. Dummer, "Rowley: 1640-1936" [Rowley: The Town, 1936], 35). By 1648 there was a tavern here owned by John Todd (Ibid., 257) . In the twentieth century it may have been the site of Henry Boynton's house (Ibid., 114) . In 1995 there is a sign on the second house from the corner of Pleasant and

Main Streets identifying it as site of home of "Andrew Hidden, Pinder".

In 1666 the town paid him 1 sh./4 d. to bury a horse (RR 162), and 5 sh. for an unspecified task (RR 168).

In 1667 he was given half an acre of meadow near the old calf pen in compensation for shortage of the land given him near the mill (10 April, RR 169-170) . In the division of Hog Island upland and marsh that year he got a plot between Charles Broome and Samuel Plats (20 May 1667, RR 170). In the division of Hog Island marsh he got 2 gates east of Mark Prime on the end abutting the river, and the other end against a creek that is short of the creek where Prime's land ends, and west of Samuel Platts' (15 Nov. 1666, RR 171, 178-9). In the 1673 division of common lands of Rowley Hidden got the next to smallest allotment, only one rod and 9 feet wide in Lot #XII, between Simon Chapman and "Rebecca Law & hir sisters" land near Mrs. Crosby's cross fence (14 March 1672/3, RR 230-1).

In 1675 he was brought to court at Ipswich of breach of the peace with Thomas Ally, but discharged (Andrew Heiden, EQ 6:26). But he was at once charged with "telling a lie in public town meeting" as witnessed by 3 townsmen, but merely admonished "for suspicion of a lie" (EQ 6:27).

In King Philip's War Hidden was a foot soldier along with his 20 year old son John in the local militia Train Band under Capt. Philip Nelson (Jewett 54). His name is listed as "Andrew Heding" for £ 2/10/6 base pay in Major Samuel Appleton's division in an "army, the largest and best organized that had ever been in the field in the American colonies" at the Great Swamp Fight of 19 Dec. 1675 (10 Dec., in Massachusetts Arch. 68:104, George Bodge, *Soldiers in King Philip's War* [Boston: the author, 1891]; [hereinafter Bodge], 107). Hidden's name does not appear in the company rosters, which makes it likely he was in the First Company which Appleton commanded personally, seconded by Lt. Jeremiah Swain, with men who had been impressed from Rowley, Ipswich and Newbury (135).

The division mustered at Dedham 9 Dec. 1675, marched to Attleboro (Woodcock's Garrison) that day, arriving at Sekonk 11 Dec., crossed the Patuxet River the 12th, thru Providence to Smith's Garrision at Wickford that night. On the 18th they were joined by Connecticut forces, and spent a miserable night in the open in a snowstorm. The Massachusetts forces led the way the next day thru deepening snow, thru rough terrain to the Great Swamp where the Narragansetts had built their fort (Ibid., 105-6). Today this is west of Kingston, RI (map in Bodge 131).

The Christian blessing of the fight was no doubt made by one of the three chaplains, Rev. Nicholas[2] Noyes, son of our immigrant ancestor {Bodge 136).

The Massachusetts division led the attack on 19 Dec. across the frozen cedar swamp, attacking from the north east side, where least expected (137-8). The Mass, troops found a gap in the log palisade, fought thru, and after several hours of desperate fighting, set fire to the wigwams which caught fire to the whole fort, burning women, children and aged within. The Indians counted 700 dead. At night the whites retreated to Wickford, thru a snowstorm, carrying wounded and dead. 68 died, 150 were wounded. Having led the way, Appleton's company had the most casualties, 22, with four dead, one Hidden[1]'s fellow villager Samuel Tiller (108, 142). The campaign ended 5 Feb. 1676 (Ibid., 160), When Andrew got home to Rowley, his wife was eight months pregnant, giving birth to our ancestor Ebenezer a month later.

At Dedham muster the soldiers had been promised land in the area, which 840 veterans received (Bodge 149 says list is in Narragansett Historical Reg. 1:145).

Andrew's son John died in Philip Nelson's company when it was sent to Canada in 1690 in King William's War (Blodgette #87-2).

Acting under the colony law of 1677 the town placed him as one of ten families under the supervision of a Tithingman, in his case, Sgt. John Palmer (1623-95), ancestor of William Lloyd Garrison and Anne Garrison Gould (chart 14; Jewett 124).

Hidden was in court in 1678 complaining that a boy, John Bailey, had come into Rowley mill and set his bag on top of Hidden's corn, with the end of the bag into the hopper, without waiting his turn. When Hidden laid his hand on the boy's mouth he bit him (EQ 7:101n).

At the Rowley town meeting of April 1679 Hidden had his name recorded as dissenting from the decision of the town to sue William Longfellow in dispute over Merrimac land, in which he testified (EQ 7:208, 213).

In the April 1679 term of the Ipswich Quarterly Court he was paid 12 shillings for whipping two Indians (EQ 8:306). These may be the same ones who were brought from Gloucester by Constable William Sargent.

Andrew Hidden died 18 Feb. 1702, age about 80 (VR 472; Church record says 20 Feb. 1701/2, "an old man", Blodgette 150, Hurd, 2:1132) . He made his will on 18 Feb. 1702 (Essex Pro. 307:418, Blodgette, proved 1 April, Hurd 2:1132), mentioning only his widow and his youngest son Ebenezer.

EBENEZER[2] HIDDEN, our ancestor, was the twelfth and last child of Andrew and Sarah. He was born in Rowley 7 March 1675/6 (VR 93).

Ebenezer lived in the family homestead at the southwest corner of Pleasant & Main Sts., next to the Northeast Field in 1728 (Jewett 148).

He died in Rowley 7 July 1748, age 72 (VR 474), having made his will the day before (Essex Pro. 328:99). He mentions his son James, who was not to marry for another two months.

Ebenezer and Elizabeth (Story) Hidden had nine children, of whom our James was the next to youngest (list in Blodgette 151). One son, Jonathan, died as a soldier at Lake George 6 Jan. 1756 (Blodgette #87-24).

Elizabeth outlived Ebenezer, and remarried 29 April 1757 in Rowley to Rev. John Hobson, Esq. (VR 312) . Hobson (John[2], William[1], born 10 Nov. 1680; died 20 March 1770 was Justice of the Peace and Speaker of the Massachusetts House in 1741 (Blodgette 154; Essex Pro. 346:453). She died in Rowley 28 Sept. 1766, age 85 (church record). She probably died in the Hobson house on the north side of Wethersfield Street, which was replaced by today's 1787 Hobson house, two houses west of the Rowley Library (Dummer, 92). We have not found her gravestone.

THE STORY FAMILY OF IPSWICH

Ebenezer Hidden married in Ipswich 17 July 1701 ELIZABETH[3] STORY (Int. Rowley VR 312) , daughter of SAMUEL[2] and ELIZABETH STORY of Ipswich. She was born prob. Ipswich (VR). Her father Samuel Story had settled in Ipswich by 1678 (Thomas F. Waters, *Ipswich* [Ipswich: Historical Soc. 1905], 105), probably at Chebacco (Hidden Mem. 7).

There was a Samuel Story from Chebacco who fought in King Philip's War. He would have been 17 when the company of Captain Joseph Gardiner of Salem was mustered at Dedham 10 Dec. 1675 (Hurd 2:1179; Bodge 116). The company marched to Wickford RI, and had three stragglers killed by Stone-wall-John's men before they reached the Narragansett Indian fort in the Great Swamp of South Kingston in Dec. 1675. Gardiner's company was one of the leading companies that made its way thru the gap in the east end of the fort where their commander was killed, with three of his men, and ten wounded (19 Dec., Bodge 119). In the final battle of the Narragansett Swamp command was taken over by Lt. William Hathorn, under whom Story was paid £ 4/5/8 (Bodge 118) . The company was discharged 7-10 Feb. 1676.

We know nothing more of Samuel's life, but given his youth at this battle, it would be surprising not to find him in later Indian wars.

Samuel Story's estate was administered at Norwich CT In 1726 where he and his wife had moved by 1722 (Francis Caulkins, *History of Norwich* [Norwich: author, 1874], 241; Hidden Mem. 7) . The will mentions our Elizabeth Hidden by name.

It is not known what her mother's name was (Torrey mss.). She died probably in Ipswich before 16 Sept. 1716 when Samuel remarried Mary (Williams) Choate (VR). Mary, born Roxbury 20 Dec. 1669 (VR 381), was the daughter of Stephen Williams and Sarah Wise, and widow of Samuel[2] Choate (John[1]) , whom she had married Roxbury 23 Nov. 1688 (VR 381; he died about 1713), (Nora Snow, *The Snow-Estes Ancestry* [Hillburn NY: author, 1939], 1:107; Abraham Hammatt, *The Hammatt Papers: Early Inhabitants of Ipswich* [Baltimore: Genea. Pub. Co., 1980], [hereinafter Hammatt], 52-3).

Samuel and Elizabeth's most famous descendant was our thirteenth President Millard Fillmore (1800-74; Roberts 20, #44,45). The Storys' son Stephen[3] (22) had Philippa[4] Wood (11), mother of Hepzibah (Wood) Fillmore (5), the president's grandmother. This made him third cousin of Lydia's mother.

Samuel Story was the youngest son of Ipswich pioneer WILLIAM[1] STORY and SARAH[2] FOSTER, born Ipswich 1658 (Samuel testified his father was William 1699, EQ 7:204n; VR; Snow 107).

William Story was born England about 1613-4 (twice deposed age about 55 Nov. 1668, EQ 4:67n, 69n; about 66 June 1676, EQ 6:155; Massachusetts Historical Col. 5:97 cited by Snow 106). Choate says he was son of Andrew Story who came to Ipswich by 1636, but corrected this to say he was a probably a brother (David Choate, *History of the Town of Essex* [Essex: The town, 1868], 236, 478) . He came from Norwich, county Norfolk (Sav. 4:212; Pope 437) . He was 23 at the time of departure, 8 April 1637, as apprentice to joiner Samuel Dix of Norwich (Pope 437) . They arrived in Boston 8 June 1637 on either the *John and Dorothy* of Ipswich, Capt. William Andrews, or the *Rose* of Yarmouth, Capt. William Andrews, Jr. (Charles E. Banks, *The Planters of the Commonwealth* [Boston: Riverside, 1930], 185 citing PRO and Winthrop's Jour. 1:222).

He first appears in Ipswich records in 1642, as a proprietor (Pope 437), and sold a lot to William Knowlton before 12 Feb. 1643 (Hammatt 351). In 1647 he lost a suit by Mr. Samuel Symonds for breaking down a fence and had to pay £ 3 damages as well as repairing the fence (EQ 1:124). In 1648 he is one of eight known inhabitants of Essex, then known as Chebacco, who paid 2 shillings to the town of Ipswich for military instruction by Major Daniel Dennison (Hurd 2:1156). On 8 May 1649 he bought 90 acres of farmland beyond Chebacco Falls that included the nineteenth century farm of David Low from Henry and Elizabeth Archer (10 May, Hurd 2:1208) . The William Story estate in Chebacco (today's Essex) was described as extending from the southern part of Belcher's Lane to the river, west of White's Hill and Deacon Thomas Low's land, east and northeast of Reynold Foster's land (Choate, 236-7) . In 1650 he held *a* mortgage as security for a debt (Pope 437) . In 1652 he had land in Chebacco next to John Webster. In 1655 he bought two more lots next to land he bought from Robert Kinsman (from William Symonds, Gent, and John West, yeoman) . He also had a share in Plum Island (1664) and a lot on the river bank.

William Story is listed as carpenter and contractor in 1648 when he subscribed to the military defense fund for Major Dennison (Hammatt 352). One of the apprentices he took on was the son of John Leeds, whom he promised to "teach him his trade, also to read and write and give him a set of tools when his time is out" at age 21 (1674 EQ 5:37).

He is believed to have built the first sawmill in the town of Ipswich, in 1656 (Hurd

2:1208).

In Jan. 1656 the town appointed him to prevent persons from cutting trees on the south side of the river (EQ 2:141n). 14 years later he was still reporting such violations as William Fairfield's running away when Story caught him chopping down a poplar on the Ipswich common land; Fairfield objected that Story was to get half the fines of those convicted (1670, EQ 5:373-4).

He was made freeman at Ipswich in March 1658 (EQ 2:67). In 1659 he got a writ against John Smith and Shoreborne Willson for debt, but the outcome is not printed (EQ 2:189n). The next year he sued Edward Bragg "For withholding one parcel of his land without any right, it being part of the farm which plaintiff bought of Henry Archer." (EQ 2:254), and got a writ of attachment of property (EQ 2:260). In 1664 he won a judgment against William Whittred for not paying for a fence, plus court costs (EQ 3:183). Then the two sued each other for slander, and Story again won (1667, EQ 3:441).

He was trial juror in 1653, 1664 and 1676 (EQ 1:276, 3:119, 6:196), and grand juror 1669 and 1682 (EQ 4:175; 8:373). He was Tithingman in 1678 (EQ 6:441).

Story signed the petition of loyalty in 1666. In the petition of 1668 in favor of ships carpenter Thomas Wells he placed his mark next to the name Weluame Stori (EQ 4:76n).

In 1671 he got permission for a mill on the Chebacco River, which he set up to saw timber (Choate 60). The next year Abraham Perkins complained that he had taken green timber over his land from his property or the town commons.

He had to sue another of our relatives, Ruth (Haffield) White for the £ 5 her husband Thomas owed him on his death in 1672. Story lost the case, since White left only £ 131 of the Haffield inheritance which had been withheld from Rachel Clinton unjustly, and which the court ordered distributed at 13 sh. 4 d. to the pound (EQ 5:230, 213; he got £ 3/6/8, EQ 6:57).

Story was a soldier in King Philip's War, paid at Ipswich. He was the first citizen after the Minister to sign the unsuccessful petition in favor of John Proctor, who was executed for witchcraft in 1692 (text Pierce 125-6 from Upham 2:304-7).

In his last years Story was cared for at his home by his son Seth under agreement of 1693 when he gave most of his property to his sons Seth and William (31 March 1693 ED 5:596) . On 3 April 1693 he gave his son Samuel all of his upland and swamp on the south side of the Chebacco Falls River, and half of the salt marsh he bought from Henry Archer, on the condition that Samuel pay 40 shillings each on his death to his sister Susanna Browne and his niece Ruth Walker. Our ancestor Elizabeth Story is named in the same deed with a gift of "a little iron Kettle & a pewter bowle and a broad box that useth to stand in ye bed Leantow." (Pierce 123).

William Story died Ipswich Jan. 1702/3 (VR). Administration was granted to his son Seth 20 Jan. 1702/3. Seth's grandson Jesse Jr. was killed at the Battle of Bunker Hill.

John Prince, historian of Essex, claimed that William Story was the ancestor of US Supreme Court Justice Joseph Story (1779-1845), and father of William Wetmore Story (1819-95), well-known sculptor and poet, but DAB reliably states that he was descended from an immigrant of c.1700, Elisha Story.

THE FOSTER FAMILY OF IPSWICH

William Story married about 1640 SARAH^{2} FOSTER, born England 1620 (age about 48 in deposition 23 Nov. 1668 re Thomas Wells, EQ 4:80), daughter of REGINALD^{1} FOSTER and his first wife, name unknown (Pierce 120). Sarah was evidently literate, for she spelled her name Sara Store in the petition defending the character of ships carpenter Thomas Wells and his wife Naomi in 1668 (EQ 4:76). Sarah died, probably in Ipswich, before her husband's will was proven

20 Jan. 1702/3, but is not in VR (Wildes 181).

The family name is often spelled FORSTER, which was the original form, from the occupation of forester. Although the family founder signed himself Reginald, he wrote Renol in his will, which gives the pronunciation. The name has innumerable variants like Rainold, Reanalld, Reienald, Reienalld, Reienold, Reinald, Reinold, Reginall, Reginold, Regnald, Regnell, Regnold, Rejnald, Renald, Renall, Renold, Reonall, Reynold, Ringdell, etc. which suggest that the name was pronounced "Renol". Walter Davis, whose article in TAG (38:15) is given "caveat" in Colket, calls Reginald "pure Strawberry Hill Gothick", citing only nine instances where "g" is used in the records, but allowing that Reginald may be the Latinized form of the name Renold.

Reginald, as we will call him, was born in England about 1595, perhaps at Little Baddow, just south of Chelmsford, county Essex. His father was probably the yeoman Reynowld Foster of Harlow, Essex, 45 miles from Ipswich, whose will of 18 Sept. 1622 was proved the next 7 Jan. (Walter G. Davis, *The Ancestry of Dudley Wildes* [Portland Me: Anthoensen Press, 1959], [hereinafter Wildes], 178, citing Archdeaconry of Middlesex (Essex & Herts), register Bushew f. 8; Pierce 110). In this he mentions his wife Margaret, and children named Reynold, William and Sara, names which were used by the American pioneer. Reynold[A] was the son of John[B] Foster of Harlow, whose will of 10 Dec. 1601, proved 7 Jan. 1601/2 left Great Mead meadow to his son Reynold, who mentions it in his will (Foster 177 citing Archdeaconry of Middlesex (Essex & Herts) register Grove f. 187). John's wife Agnes survived him.

Others claim this family was from Bamburgh and Ethestone Castle, Northumberland, and Reginald himself was perhaps born in Brunton, Northumberland (Pierce gives birthplace without date or evidence 110, 120; TAG calls this "complete nonsense"). Currier, contradicting an earlier entry says he was son of Thomas Foster, Esq. of Brunton and his second wife Elizabeth Carr, Thomas being son of Sir Thomas Foster, Bart, of Etherston, with a lineage all the way back to the Counts of Flanders and royalty (Currier 927). Since there is no evidence of our Reginald's birth in Brunton this appears a ficticious ancestry.

Currier earlier gives an entirely different origin, Barmton, which is in Durham, but is probably a misreading of Brunton (above) or even Barnston, Essex (782).

However, Reginald's eldest son was born in Exeter, Devon, where we might look for his wife (Hammatt 105; see Reg. 1:352; Topo says Reginald was from Exeter, citing Reg. 30:83) . Wildes says the Margaret in his will was his second wife, probably Margaret Humphrey who married Renold Foster at Thaxsted, Essex in 1608 (Wildes 178).

During the American Revolution his descendants claimed Reginald[1] was a "Gentleman" related to Sir Reginald Foster, Baronet created 21 July 1661, but the claim is not substantiated (probably written by Rhode Island Senator Theodore Foster as obituary sermon for Hon. Jedidiah Foster in *Boston Gazette* 9 Nov. 1779, Pierce 118). Senator Foster's papers in the Rhode Island Historical Society claimed that Reginald was born at or near Exeter, where his children were also born (Vol. 8 "Genealogies", Foster Papers, in Pierce 118).

On 28 Sept. 1619 Reginald married JUDITH WIGNOL at Theydon Garnon, Essex, eight miles south of Harlow (Pane-Joyce Genealogy on line at http://aleph0.clarku.edu/~djoyce/gen/report/rr01/rr01_128.html; Torrey 278; Wildes 176; TAG 18:13).

He left England on a ship embargoed under proclamation of King Charles I on 30 April 1637 to prevent Puritan emigration to America, and enforced by the Privy Council on 1 May 1638 against eight ships in the Thames (Pierce 110). On petition of the ship owners the embargo was lifted within a few days, and Foster came to Ipswich with seven children by his first wife Judith (Cutter 927).

Wildes claims to have found evidence of him in Ipswich records in 1635, but does not say where (Wildes 179).

Coming to Ipswich he bought the house and lands of John Tuttell on 26 Sept. 1638 (Pope 173 cited by Reg. 90:309; Currier 782). These were on the north side of the Ipswich River, "lying near the great Cove beneath the Falls of the Town River (Wildes 179). The house had been built by Richard Brown, who sold it to Richard Saltonstall, and he to Richard Lumpkin, who sold it to Tuttell (Wildes 179).

Reginald was given a grant of land in Ipswich 6 April 1641 of eight acres in the west meadow "in consideration of a little hovel that stood at the new bridge, which was taken away for the accommodation of the passage there." (Pierce 113, 120). This was the East Bridge, replaced by the stone Choate Bridge. His home was near this East Bridge, and stood there until torn down about 1879 (picture in "Ipswich Antiquarian Papers", Dec. 1880 per Pierce 113) . In 1646 he was one of the townspeople that "promise carting voluntary toward cart Bridge, besides the rate, a day work a piece." (Hammatt 105).

In 1643 he was given charge of the town cattle herd south of the river, to be done by his son Abraham (Pope 173; Currier 782). In 1645 he subscribed to the pay of Major Dennison for the defense against Indians.

In 1648 he bought six acres on the north side of the river from Ralph Dix, who had bought from William White (8 March 1647/8, Pierce 113).

In 1655 he bought a house on the north side of the river from Roger Preston, who had got the land from John Gage (11 March, Ips. Deeds 1:211 per Wildes 179). The house, built before 1649, is one of the oldest houses in the country. Located on Water St. in Ipswich, it is known as the Renault-Foster House (HABS MA-633; a plan is on the Library of Congress list of timber frame houses: http:www.loc.gov/rr/print/list/100_tim/html).

In 1652 the town paid Reginald and Thomas Clark £ 10 to cut a canal from the Chebacco 10 feet wide and deep enough for a lighter to pass thru, and to build a ford and footbridge over it (Pierce 113).

Reginald was made freeman at Ipswich 19 Nov. 1657 (EQ 2:55). He was on the trial jury of 1651, 1655, and 1658 (EQ 1:210, 219, 397, 2:61), and grand jury of 1659 1665, 1668 and 1678 (EQ 2:168, 270, 4:46, 7:82). He was Ipswich Constable in 1661 (EQ 2:266).

In 1658 he paid Roger Preston £ 50 for his dwelling, barn and outbuildings, and also the Robert Wallis houselot and gardens, and a three acre planting lot on the north side of Town Hill (11 March 1657/8 in Reg. 90:308) . These were at the east end of High Street near the old house of Rev. Norton in 1899 (Pierce 113-4). Foster also had a houselot near the meetinghouse green.

In 1663 Forster paid Richard Nicholls 16 shillings for six acres of marsh in the Hog Island marshes, which the town had granted to Nicholls (20 May, recorded 28 Jan. 1680 in ED 4:378, EQ 3:119n) . In 1664 he had a share in Plum Island (14 Feb., Pierce 114; Hammatt 105), which he and his wife sold 2 Aug. 1676 (Reg. 90:308).

In the winter of 1665 he had cattle on Red Roote Hill (EQ 3:228).

He was released from military service on condition of paying a bushel of wheat each year (1667, EQ 3:399, 1674, EQ 5:312).

In 1667 the town appointed him to see "that all swine be yoked and ringed" south of the river (EQ 4:48).

The next year he was surety for the bond of the ships carpenter Thomas Wells when Wells was accused of slander against the authorities (EQ 4:76, 77).

18 year old John Chubb was ordered by the court to pay Foster £ 5 for killing his horse,

and the same amount to Essex County, or be whipped, but having no money agreed to work four months for Thomas Low Jr. until the fines and court costs were paid off (1669, EQ 4:124-6, 157).

After Judith died Oct. 1664 in Ipswich (VR 2:558; Pierce 115, Hammatt 105), Reginald remarried in Ipswich 19 Sept. 1665 (VR 1:172, 306) Sarah Martin, widow of John Martin, ship's carpenter of Charlestown, who outlived Reginald. Sarah then married thirdly in Haverhill 21 Sept. 1682 as second wife to William White (Haverhill VR 2:330; Reg. 90:308). She died 22 Feb. 1683 (Currier 782) before White's death on 28 Sept. 1690 (Haverhill VR 492).

His last appearance on town records is as voter on 2 Dec. 1679 (Hammatt 105). Reginald died at "extreme old age", probably in Ipswich, between March and May 1681, which would make him 86 (not in VR; Pierce 115 places the date between 5 March and 30 May 1681; Hammatt 105). His will of 30 April 1680 has a codicil of 5 March 1680/1, was proved on 9 June 1681, and inventoried 30 May (copy of orig. in Ips. Records 4:402, text in Pierce 115-6; Wildes 181n cites Essex Pro. 3:419-22). The inventory gave a high value of £ 744/16, of which £ 671 was in real estate, the house and barn £150, 50 acres of upland £ 150, Jacob Foster's house and homestead £75, 20 acres of saltmarsh £ 85, 20 acres in the common field £ 76, 12 acres of pasture £ 40, ten acres at Muddy River £ 35, four acres in the common field £ 20, and eight acres of fresh meadow £ 16 (Ips. Records 4:403 in Pierce 117). In it he leaves his "daughter William Storys wife" £ 10 to be paid by his son Renol less the value of a pair of sheets and pillowcases, which came to 16 shillings.

Foster had many distinguished descendants (Pierce 122) who are Gould cousins:

The most famous was thirteenth President Millard Fillmore (1800-74; Roberts 23, #178) . The descent is through the Story family. The president's grandmother Hepzibah Wood (5) was daughter of Philippa[4] Story (11) was daughter of Stephen[3] (22), the brother of our ancestor Elizabeth (Story) Hidden. Lydia Gould was thus third cousin once removed of the president. Those named Foster include the author David (1852-1920, DAB 6:545) and Associate Justice of the Massachusetts Supreme Judicial Court Dwight, and his more famous son, the constitutional lawyer Roger (1857-1924; DAB 5:556) whose article "Treason Trials" prevented the prosecution of the Homestead strikers in 1892.

Other descendants were financier George Peabody (1785-1869; Thomas, David, David), merchant and London banker, and philanthropic endower of the Peabody Museums at Harvard and Yale, the Peabody Academy of Salem, the Peabody Institutes of Baltimore and Peabody Massachusetts, after whom town of Peabody Mass, is named (DAB 14:336).

Unitarian minister & Harvard Divinity Professor Andrew P. Peabody, who was twice acting president of Harvard, 1862, 1868-9 (1811-93, Andrew, Andrew, Zerubabel, Joseph; DAB 14:334). Two more Unitarian ministers and literary men, the twins Oliver (1799-1848) and William (1799-1847) Peabody, the first a lawyer and first American editor of Shakespeare 1836 (DAB 14: 340, 343).

International pioneer Charles A. Peabody (1814 ; Samuel, Richard, Stephen) N.Y. Supreme Court Justice who was U.S. delegate to the 1881 International Code Conference in Cologne; Ephraim Peabody, Chief Justice of the Maine Supreme Court in 1869.

Salem Revolutionary War privateer and merchant prince in the pepper trade with Sumatra and China Joseph Peabody (1757-1844; Francis, Francis; DAB 14:338) .

Col. Nathaniel Peabody (1741-1823; Jacob, Jacob), Member of the Continental Congress from NH and patriot who took one of the first military steps of the Revolution in Dec. 1774 in the capture of Fort William & Mary (DAB 14:340).

Architect Robert Peabody (1845-1917) who designed many important buildings in American cities, including the Boston Custom House tower (DAB 14:341).

Educator Selim Peabody (1829-1903) who put the University of Illinois on its feet financially (DAB 14:342).

Massachusetts Governor Endicott Peabody, liberal Republican who confronted presidential candidate Robert Dole in the NH primary campaign of 1995 with a challenge to support the United Nations.

Poet Josephine Peabody (1874-1922) who was suffragist and dramatist as well as lyric poet (DAB 14:339).

Finally, the famous Peabody Sisters of Salem (Isaac, Matthew, Nathaniel), Mary (b. 1806), who married Horace Mann, Sophia (b. 1809) who married Nathaniel Hawthorne, and Alcott's educator, Elizabeth Palmer Peabody (1804-94), one of the first Transcendentalists, who started the first American kindergarten in Boston in 1860 (DAB 14:335).

Foster was also ancestor of the famous American orator and politician Rufus Choate (1799-1859; son of Miriam Foster), noted for his speeches in the U.S. Senate (1841-5) opposing annexation of Texas, favoring tariffs (Hurd 2:1201-3, states John Perkins was also an ancestor; Ency. Brit. 6:259).

THE HIDDENS (CONTINUED)

JAMES[3] HIDDEN was born in Rowley 2 June 1718 (VR 93) . He appears to have been an independent thinker on religious matters. Shortly after his marriage he was accused of saying that part of the sermon by visiting minister Rev. Moses Hale was false, and convicted of disorderly conduct (20 Aug. 1749, Blodgette 152; Hurd 2:1138) . Forgiven two months later, he was soon accused of saying the church had not treated him fairly, and admonished (13 Feb. 1750/1). After confession, he was again restored to membership (29 April 1756).

However, he moved to Ipswich in 1753, and to Newbury in 1760. Only the birth of his first child is recorded in Rowley, 2 Aug. 1749, but his baptism recorded 12 Aug. 1749 at the First Presbyterian Church in Newburyport (Old South, on Federal Street), with that of his other children, including our Jemima (Newbury VR 1:219).

It is apparent that the Hiddens were converted from the Congregational orthodoxy of their ancestors by George Whitefield, the famous preacher (1714-70) , who was buried beneath the pulpit of the Hiddens' First Presbyterian Church in Newburyport. Our Jemima Hidden's sister recalled having walked from their home in Rowley when she was about 16 (1770) to Exeter NH with her mother to hear Rev. Whitefield preach (Russell Jackson, "The Pearsons & Their Mills", EIHC 74 (Jan. 1938), 68).

In 1765 the Presbyterian Church in Newburyport complained to his Rowley church of his "dangerous opinions" (15 Jan. 1765, Rowley church records in Blodgette).

In 1749 he paid £ 70 to Jeremiah Bennit of Hampton NH for his Rowley lands Bennit had inherited from his mother Jemima Parsons, namely, nine acres in Polepod Lots, 4½ acres in the Great Swamp, two cow rights in the East End Oxpasture, and three acres of salt marsh in Casway Marsh (Rowley Deeds 99:84, 27 April 1749, recorded 30 March 1753).

James Hidden is listed as a soldier (New England Regiments, 50:338, 345 cited by Hidden Mem. 10; not in SCW).

Mary Rolfe recorded that James Hidden signed a petition for "Dec [laration of] War at Newburyport" 16 June 1763 (Mary Rolfe Papers, Historical Society of Old Newbury, Moody 4: 818) . This presumably refers to Pontiac's War, since peace had been concluded with the French 10 June 1763.

There is no record of his death, but his wife died a widow in 1803. There is no record of probate in Essex County.

He married in Rowley on 26 Sept. 1748 to JEMIMA^{5} MOODY of Newbury (VR 312). By her he had six children, including our JEMIMA^{4} HIDDEN, their fourth child.

THE MOODY FAMILY

JEMIMA[5] MOODY was born in Newbury 15 Nov. 1724 {Moodey in VR 327; Rolfe 818) to OLIVER[4] MOODY and his wife MARTHA[4] NOYES. She died 5 May 1803 as recorded by Mary Rolfe: "In this town on Sunday last Mrs. Jemima Hidden aged 78, she was in perfect health and attended to her concern all the day previous to her death, went to bed well and slept the sleep of Death//A Solemn admonition to mortals to be at all times prepared. May 17, 1803" (Rolfe 819; VR).

Her father OLIVER[4] MOODY was a chairmaker in Newbury. He was born in Newbury 7 Oct. 1701 (VR 328) to THOMAS[3] MOODY and his wife JUDITH[3] HALE. Only five days before the publication of the Declaration of Independence he was drowned after falling from the Newbury wharf 14 July 1776 (Joshua Coffin, *History of Newbury* [Boston: Samuel Drake, 1845],[hereinafter Coffin], 253) . He was 75 years old, and "week in Body but of a Sound disposing Minde and Memory" according to his will of 1 May 1776, signed in a shaky hand (Essex Pro. 18617) . In para. 2 he names our Jemima: "I give and bequeath to my Daughter Jemima Hedin Twenty Pound in money besides what I have already given her." His wife valued his estate at £ 168/4/6, most of which, £ 126/13/4 was the value of his house and 5 1/3 rods of land (Inventory 14 Oct. 1776 in Essex Pro. 18617), but the assessors found five times that, £ 729/13/6, more than doubling the value of his house, at £ 390, and counting £ 150 for adjoining land on King Street, £ 40 for two saltmarsh lots in Newbury, £ 70 for seven cowrites in the fourth General pasture in Newbury, £ 20 for five acres in Penneyornery River, Newbury, and £ 10 for a three acre woodlot in Newbury.

On 28 Feb. 1723/4 he was married to MARTHA[4] NOYES (VR 333), born between 1706 and 1710 to JOHN[3] NOYES and MARY[3] NOYES (not in VR), of whom more below.

THOMAS[3] MOODY was a maltster, or maker of malt that all colonial families required for beer making. His factory was located on Chandler's Lane and Water Street in Newbury (Rolfe 2. Earlier, perhaps, his malt house was located on Moody's Lane, now Woodland Street (John Currier, *History of Newbury* [Boston: Damrell & Upham, 1902], [hereinafter Currier], 264, 238n). Nearby was the ferry to Salisbury, which he purchased half interest in from the town in 1706 with the ferryman Capt. Edward Serjeant (text of grant in Currier 452-3).

He was born in Newbury 21 Oct. 1668 (VR 333; EQ 4:95), the second child of CALEB[2] MOODY and his second wife, JUDITH[2] BRADBURY.

Thomas died in Newbury at age 69 on 31 March 1737 (VR 2:664) and was buried in Sec. G-5 of Old Burial Hill Newbury (Rolfe 2; Noreen Pramberg, *Etched in Stone* [Decorah IA: Anundsen Pub. Co. 1991], 277). His will was probated 18 April 1737 (Essex Pro.). On 24 Nov. 1692 he married JUDITH[3] HALE (VR 334), of whom more below. She died Newbury 12 Aug. 1757, age 87 (VR 2:663).

Thomas's father, Sergeant CALEB[2] MOODY was also a maltster. Currier claimed he was the first person born in Newbury, about 1637, though the date is not recorded (Rolfe 1; date inferred from age 41 when he took oath of allegiance 1678, EQ 7:156; Hist 180) . It is said that he walked all the way to Cambridge to take the oath of freeman 23 May 1666 (Ips.Ct.Rec. 4, pt. 2, 582; 1668 per EQ 4:24). He served as Newbury Constable 1665-6, deputy Constable 1669,

Selectman for at least five years 1669-72, 1684 (Henry Crapo, *Certain Comeovers* [New Bedford: E. Anthony, 1912],[hereinafter Crapo], 484), Recorder in 1670 and 1684-5, and Tithingman over ten families in 1681. He was on the committee of three to divide the 3000 acres of Newbury common lands, of which he got a share (5 May 1686 in Pauline Moody Schlitzer, 8410F Charles Valley Court, Ruxton MD 21204-2031, letter of 25 July 1995).

CALEB MOODY

Caleb was twice Representative to the General Court in Boston for two years, 1677-8 (24 May 1677, 9 May 1678, Schlitzer 2 citing Currier).

Caleb was a leader of what has been called "The First American Revolution", the American phase of the Glorious Revolution in England which opposed the Stuart monarchy's representative in Boston, Governor Andros. He was an associate of the liberal minister of Ipswich, Rev. John Wise (Schlitzer).

Caleb was imprisoned five weeks in 1688 by Governor Andros for being found with a paper which warned his fellow citizens of the arbitrary government; and speaking out (text of Moody's account, Coffin 150). The paper starts:

> New England alarmed, To rise and be
> armed, Let not papist you charme, I mean
> no harme..."

(Mabel H. Huse, *The Old Home* [Boston: Meador, 1957], 15; Coffin 150 in Bio. Sketches 11). Caleb claimed that in Jan. 1688 Joseph Bailey gave him the paper which he had found on the King's Highway. Caleb later wrote that the purpose of the paper "was to give notice to the people of the danger they were in, being under the sad circumstances of an arbitrary government, sir Edmund Andros having about one thousand of our soldiers, as I was informed, prest out of the Massachusetts colony and carried with him to the eastward under pretence of destroying our enemy Indians (although not one Indian killed by them had I heard of that time.)" (Coffin 150; Crapo 495) . Moody and Bailey were summoned to court, and Moody released by Judges Woodbridge and Epps, while Bailey was detained. However, a week later Moody was arrested on a justice's warrant by the same judges. In his words, "they committed me to Salem prison (though I proffered ym bayle) they would not take it but I was to be safely kept to answer what should be charged against me upon the king's account for publishing a scandalous and seditious lybell." (Coffin 150, slightly altered by Crapo 496) . After a week he was examined by Judge Palmer and King's Attorney Grayham who put him into close confinement with no outside contact, which they confirmed a week later, refusing bail again. Finally the High Sheriff, Charles Redford, came to the Salem prison and told Moody and Bailie that he had orders to examine them, and to put a new mittimus on them and charge them with treason. But when the time came for trial, there was no court. While in prison he was a Confessor (Sav. 3:225, citing Coffin 150). The Salem prison was newly built, in 1684, at the corner of Federal and St. Peter's Streets (Standard 364).

The landing in England of William of Orange 5 Nov. 1688 and flight of King James II the next month brought about the Glorious Revolution. Caleb recounted his release: "Afterwards there came news of ye happy arrival and good success of ye prince of Orange, now King of England [William II], and then, by petitioning, I got bayle." On 9 Jan. 1689/90 Caleb made a claim for £ 40 "dammage" for false imprisonment (Coffin 150 from Colonial files; Crapo 496) .

Caleb's house, built in 1659 in West Newbury, still stands, the oldest house in town, and one of the oldest in the country. It is opposite The Way to the River, at 803 Main Street, about a mile and a half west of 1-95, on the south side of Route 113. In 1658 it was far from Newbury center, in the "West Woods" of town, where William bought the land. This is now West Newbury, near Pipestave Hill, where early settlers cut oak trees for barrel staves *(Standard History of Essex County* [Boston: C. F. Jewett, 1878], [hereinafter Standard], 420).

Caleb Moody House, West Newbury, built 1658

William[1] Moody helped Caleb build the house for his bride, Sarah Pierce. Caleb I's part built in 1658 is the east and southern part, the latter containing the big seven foot wide colonial fireplace and beehive oven (Thomas Downey, "Moody-Ridgeway House"). The west side was built later by Caleb III Moody. The interior of the house, including "the prayer closet" off the south bedroom, is described in Huse 13-14. Woodwork in the house, including the original kitchen, closely resembles that of the Emery House of West Newbury, built in 1675, and burned in 1937. Both houses are illustrated in John Mead Howell' s *Architectural Heritage of the Merrimac* (cited by Downey, fig. 181, 234).

The house remained in the Moody family until 1937 when Clara Ridgeway, descendant of Joseph Ridgeway and Elizabeth Moody sold it and 100 acres to the famous writer J. P. Marquand. He intended to move it to his estate on Kent's Island in Newbury, but finally sold it in the early forties to Harvard Professor of Music Randall Thompson. From him it was purchased in 1950 and restored by Thomas Downey, whose widow, Beatrice, president of the West Newbury Historical Society, lives in the house in 1995.

Caleb had 60 head of cattle and large flocks of sheep and goats (Standard 419). It is unclear whether he personally supervised this farm, and when turned this house over to his son Caleb Jr., for by 1673 Caleb Sr. had built a malthouse at the corner of today's Federal and Water Streets in Newburyport, and may have lived near his work, in one of the Moody houses on Water Street.

Caleb was a member of the church in Newbury by 1670, and his second wife Judith in 1674 (Hoyt 249). Caleb was a participant of the Woodman faction (with his father) that criticized Rev. Parker (16 March 1670, Coffin 83), and became a major spokesman for it (19, 21 April 1670, 16 Feb., 17 March, 18 April 1671, Coffin 88, 92, 97, 103, 104). He was fined one noble (6 sh. 8 d.) for his offense (29 May 1671, Coffin 100).

In 1671 he and ten other members were ordered to build a pew in the southeast corner of the meetinghouse (30 Jan. 1670/1, in Schlitzer 2). He was on the losing side, with his father, in the attempt to censure the minister Rev. Parker, and had to pay a fine of 13 sh. 4d. for dishonoring the name of God, disturbing the peace and scandalizing the name of the loving pastor (1671 EQ 4:359, 366-7).

Caleb was Sergeant in the Newbury company of militia, in King Philip's War, listed by the Colonial Society as "Doctor" for unknown reasons, for there is no local record of medical practice (SCW 332) . Maine local historian George F. Dow suggests that the term was used for a person who had special knowledge of care for livestock (personal letter 5 Sept. 1995, Box 57, Nobleboro ME 04555-0057). Caleb submitted a modest bill for his wartime expenses: Quartering 5 sh., 13 bou. Oates 26 sh.. Conducting souldiers & expenses on ym [him] 17 sh., totalling £ 2/8 (EQ 6:448). Another accounting comes to £ 2/13, repeating the 26 sh. for oats, but the rest shown: Quartering] 4 m. 2 sh., post 4 sh., Quartering] 13 sh. 6, 3 horces 18 d., post 2 sh., bagg 2 sh. (EQ 6:453). The militia committee met at his house, where the officers Capt. Gerrish, Ensign Greenleaf and he drew up the expenses (EQ 6:443-9). The only clue to military movements in the accounts is that they went eastward with Capt. Gerrish on 15 April 1677, and the Newbury soldiers were released of 24 April (EQ 6:444).

Caleb also served usefully in the judicial system. He was on the grand jury for 1674 (EQ 5:385) and trial jury of 1676 and 1681 (EQ 6:196; EQ 8:150). He and another ancestor, John Knight (Jr.) were arbitrators in a suit of Robert Crosse v. Hugh March over pine boards (1677, EQ 6:285-6). Caleb was mediator in the quarrel between Hugh March Sr. and his son John over accounts in 1682 (EQ 8:260). He was on the board of inquest into the death of Andrew Newcomb of Boston, whose body was found washed up on Plum Island in Sept. 1682 (EQ 8:442).

Caleb and four other ancestors, John and Thomas Hale, John Knight and Nicholas Noyse signed the petition of 23 April 1677 defending the reputations of Edward Qrdway and Joshua and Caleb Richardson who were convicted of breaking into the church and smashing a pew (EQ 6:259). The petition is careful to say "that though they are far from justifying the outrageous practices of the young men. . .and they do not question the justice of the court's decision" the accused were not criminals, but dutiful sons who adventured their lives in public service, and had openly admitted their offense. It appears that the offending pew had been illegally put into the gallery, and most of the town agreed with their action.

He signed the oath of allegiance in 1678 age 41 (EQ 7:156).

Caleb and his daughter complained in court of "Wm. Fanning and his wife for misdemeanors, excessive drinking, offering violence to his wife, swearing and cursing." (EQ 7:381). Sarah Moody said that one morning when they were passing the Fanning's house to get the cows Goodwife Fanning complained that her husband had sworn at her and said he would knock out their brains.

Caleb was also a shipowner, as shown in his name at the head of a petition of 15 May 1683 to make Newbury a port of entry, which begins:

"Wee humbly crave the favour that your honors would be pleased to consider our little Zebulon and to ease us of that charge, which at present we are forced unto by our goeing to Salem to enter our vessells and thereby are forced to stay at least two days, before we can unload..." (Coffin 138; Crapo 494). The petition was successful, and Newbury was recognized as a port of entry in 1684, for customs entry (Standard 312).

In 1684 he was licensed to boil sturgeon for the market (EQ 9:219; Coffin 113). Crapo says that sturgeon 12 to 18 feet long were plentiful in the Merrimac, and were pickled for shipment to England (Crapo 494) . They sold for a good sum of about 10 shillings a keg (Coffin 113).

Moody's Indian slave Joseph was involved in the slave revolt of 1690 led by Isaac Morrill and George Major, both of New Jersey, who proposed that *"the English should be cut off, and the negroes should be free"* (Quarterly Court files cited by Coffin 153-4; Standard 419, 320) . They planned to seize a ship at a Newbury dock, sail to Canada and bring back 400-500 Indians and 300 Canadian French, to "come down upon the backside of the country and save none but the negroes and Indians", ascend the Merrimac, and land between Haverhill and Amesbury, near Indian River by Archelaus Hill behind John Emery's meadow, and easily destroy the lightly guarded towns of Amesbury and Haverhill. Morrill was arrested 29 May 1690 and sent to Ipswich for trial with Joseph and James, a negro slave of R. Dole, though Coffin could not find the result.

Caleb married first, in Newbury, on 24 Aug. 1659 to Sarah Pierce (VR 579; Peirce in EQ 2:181), born Newbury or Watertown about 1640 to blacksmith Daniel[1] and Sarah Pierce (Noreen Pramberg, "Four Generations of Daniel Pierce"), by whom he had two children. On her death in Newbury 25 May 1665 (VR 664; EQ 3:294) he married secondly, in Newbury on 9 Nov. 1665 our ancestor JUDITH[2] BRADBURY (VR 55; Salisbury VR say 9 Oct. per Hoyt 70; EQ 3:293n report of town clerk says Nov.), of whom more shortly.

Caleb Moody died in Newbury 25 Aug. 1698, age 61 (VR 661). He died intestate (pro. 18554 per index 2:621).

Caleb was son of Newbury pioneer WILLIAM[1] MOODY and his wife SARAH, who arrived from Ipswich, East Suffolk on the ship *Mary and John* which left London 10 April 1634, after an initial delay, arriving Boston 22 May (Banks Planters says it left Southampton 24 March 1633/4, citing Drake 70-1; Pope 316; Hoyt 1:248; Rolfe 1; Charles A. Wright, "The Mudie, Moodey, Moody Family" [typesc. Beloit WI, c. 1978, in NEHGS], 7; on Suffolk origins also Sav. 3:225, Sibley, Coffin 310). On the other hand, Banks's Topographical Dictionary says Moody came from King's Samborne, Hampshire, a name which does not exist in Ekwall (Topo 60, citing Banks mss.).

The parents and wife of William Moody have not been found by Sept. 1995, despite speculation by competent genealogists.

Various sources give three different names for the supposed ancestor who was knighted by Henry VIII, William, Edward or Edmund. Waters speaks of George Washington's ancestor buying "the estate of Garsdon in Wiltshire from the Moodys to whom it had been granted by King Henry VIII as a reward to one William Moody, his footman, for saving his life on the occasion of an accident that befel him in the hunting field (Henry F. Waters, *Genealogical Gleanings in England* [2 vols., Boston: NEHGS, 1901-6], 1:456, citing Aubrey's Collections for Wilts., 25.--Garesden).

One descendant claimed without evidence that our immigrant was the William Moody baptized 16 Jan. 1611 as son of Edward[A] Moodye of Ipswich, Suff., Edward being one of two sons of Rev. William[B] Moodye, rector of Cockfield, Suffolk, who was son of Sir Edward[C] Moody (Wright, 1), but there is no such knight.

Other descendants call our William son of William[A] and Agnes Collyn (m. All Saints' Sudbury 2 July 1603), he being son of Robert[B] and Mary Bacon, the ancestors of Dwight[8] Moody through the line of John[1] Moody of Connecticut (Schlitzer cites two documents on file at Nobleboro ME Historical society: 1) *a* chart from Moody Bible Institute of 820 N. LaSalle Street, Chicago IL 60610, dated 2 March 1979, which does not mention our William; and 2) Dr.. David L. Moody, 17 Skillman Lane, Street Paul MN dated 9 April 1987, who explicitly cautions that "You will need to prove that Robert was Richards son"; the most resourceful family historian Harold M. Moody, 3 Brookside Dr., Apt. 1, Exeter NH 03833-1641 to author 8 Sept. 1995, citing Pramberg; George F. Dow, Nobleboro ME town historian; one researcher claims without citation that William was born Giswock, Suffolk, not listed in Ekwall, George S. Davis & Royce W. Miller, "A Davis Family--Ancestors & Descendants of Charles Elbridge Davis" [typesc. 1994], 56). One possibility is that our William was the nephew of John[1] Moody whose descent from Sir Edmund is proven, but the source of this relation is not given (Schlitzer, verbally to author 17 Oct. 1995).

Robert Moody was claimed without proof to be in turn son of Richard[C] and Anne Pannal. Richard, buried Moulton, Suffolk 28 April 1574, was son of an actual personage, Sir Edmund[D] and Ursula Sadleir, descendant from Sir Rolff Sadlier of Apley Guise (Harold Moody citing Gary Boyd Roberts, *English Origins of New England Families* [Baltimore: Genealogical Pub. Co., 1984], 2:145-7 from Reg. 39:68-9, 4:178-80).

Since no parish registers or wills are cited for the birth of our William or his supposed father Robert, and no children of Richard named Robert, and none of Robert's named William, the connection to Sir Edmund is unproven.

There was a real Sir Edmund Moodye who was knighted by King Henry VIII on 6 Oct. 1541 "for miraculously saving" the ruler's life at Hitchin, Hertfordshire, "when leaping over a ditch with a pole which brake; that if the said Edmund, a footman in the King's retinue, had not leapt into ye water and lifted up the King's head, he had drowned; for which he was rewarded. "The Reward of Valor"" (A. W. Windsor, Herald of Arms, copy in hands of Harold Moody).

This is the source of the claim to Moody coat of arms which show two arms reaching out to hold a Tudor rose. These are displayed in Memorial Hall of Newbury: "Argent on a chevron engrailed sable between three trefoils slipped vert as many lozenges or, on a chief azure two arms issuing from clouds proper vested bendy or and gules holding in the hands a rose of the last." (taken from Burke 1878 by Wright 4; the most recent illustration from the British College of Arms came from Dr. David Moody 1987, but applies only to the John Dwight Moody line) . The crest is 2 arms embowed in saltire, the dexter vested gules, the sinister vert, each holding a cutlass argent hilted or." The mottoes are "Vincit qui patitur", "The patient man wins". The coat of arms on the Dwight Moody chart is similar, but differs in replacing trefoils with crosses, giving a different motto and other details.

An earlier source says that our Moody came from Wales (Charles C.P. Moody,

Biographical Sketches of the Moody Family [Boston: S.G. Drake, 1847], 8 cited by Rolfe and Cutter 328).

Our Moody family first arrived in the fall of 1643 at Ipswich, then called Agawam, in Essex County. He was one of the 40 in the company of Rev. Thomas Parker of Ipswich, Suffolk. In the Spring of 1635 the company moved north, and William was one of the first settlers of Newbury, landing on the north bank of the Parker River, about 550 yards below the bridge (Bio. Sketches 8 citing Coffin). The landing place on the Lower Green near Route 1A was marked in 1902 by a granite stone with the inscription "LANDING PLACE OF THE FIRST SETTLERS 1635", and the names of nine of our ancestors on the reverse, as "First Settlers", including John Cutting, John Emery (Weld), Edmund Greenleaf, Thomas Hale, Henry Jacques (Weld), John Knight, George Little (Weld), William Moody and Nicholas Noyes (Sons & Daughters of the First Settlers of Newbury flier).

He became freeman 6 May 1635 (Massachusetts Col. Rec. 1:370; Hoyt 1:248) and as one of the 91 original proprietors of the town received 92 acres of land (Coffin 287, 292) . In 1635 Moody was given a four acre houselot in the east end of the village, five lots north of the Parker River, between Thomas Hale and Edmund Greenleaf (John Currier, *Old Newbury* [Boston: Damrell & Upham, 189], [hereinafter Old], 14).

Moody was one of the first settlers of the "New Town" on the riverside of the Merrimac that was to become Newburyport (Standard 312) . The loss of most of the town book of records before 1652 resulted in a major suit against him over ten acres of the west side of the Merrimac Ridge (EQ 1:262-3) . Heard before our ancestor Nicholas Noyes and two other commissioners, Richard Kent sued Moody at Ipswich court. Richard Kent, Jr. said he' d broken the wedge of one of the bars and broke off the lock and staple of the other bar that stood in the way. A third ancestor, John Knight said he'd heard Moody say he'd enjoyed the land for years, and one day Kent came and asked him why he was cutting his timber. Moody told Kent that he "should have the timber and his labor upon it too." One of the commissioners hearing the case and another witness said they had laid out 14 acres over Little River to compensate Kent for the ten in question. The town recorder Anthony Somerby produced the original grant to Kent, and an 1646 record of Kent's exchange. Moody was exonerated and awarded costs, but Kent appealed and got a review in 1653, but did not withdraw his suit until March 1654 (EQ 1:302, 334) . He and Kent were apparently reconciled, for their names head a petition of 1654 appealing to the General Court on behalf of Lt. Robert Pike of Salisbury who had defended the right of Quakers to religious liberty (EQ 1:366; D. Hamilton Hurd, *History of Essex County* [Philadelphia: J.W.Lewis, 1888][hereinafter Hurd], 2:1447). When ancestor Nicholas Noyes examined the petitioners for their reasons, both said they were sorry Pike had been punished by the court (EQ 1:367).

By profession Moody was a saddler, or maker of saddles, saddlebags and harnesses, but he also did some smithy work. Moody is supposed to have invented ice-shoes for oxen, which he made to cross frozen water, experimenting first with a hoof of a dead ox (Coffin says it was Samuel Moody who did this, 395).

Although he did not sign his name on the inventory of Thomas Seers (perhaps due to his absence, 16 May 1661, EQ 2:301n) he was literate and a learned man who sent his oldest son Joshua to Harvard ('53) to become a minister. His signature is reproduced in Currier 62 on a town document of 15 June 1638. He was on the grand jury in 1650 (EQ 1:197), 1656 (EQ 2:1), 1663 (EQ 3:84) and 1668 (EQ 4:46).

He appears to have been an active member of the church. He is probably the "Goodman Mowdey" who was the first to testify in Ipswich court that John Tillison had made "scandalous and reproachful speeches cast upon the elders and others in a public church meeting on the Lord's day" (10 Oct. 1650, EQ 1:225). At the end of his life he abstained on the vote to hear Woodman's complaint about Rev. Parker (29 Jan. 1670, EQ 4:355), but joined with his son Caleb in censuring the minister (16 March 1670, Coffin 83), and got fined by the court in 1671 13sh. 4 d. for disturbing the peace, dishonoring the name of the god of religion and scandalizing the good pastor (EQ 4:366-7; Coffin states that he was not fined, 100, one speculates perhaps because of his final abstention).

The month before his death he gave his estate to his son Samuel (8 Sept. 1673, Pope 316). He died Newbury 25 Oct. 1673 (VR 664; EQ 5:261).

His wife SARA(H), whose maiden name is unknown, died Newbury 13 Jan. 1672/3 (VR 664) . Pramberg says some people have speculated that her name was Coffin (cited by Schlitzer) . Another source says that her maiden name might be McMudah, which is Moody in old Scottish tongue, but why he would have taken her name to him is unexplained and the source is not given (Davis 56; erroneously copied McDudah by others).

Their eldest son, Joshua (1632-97) , who came with them from England, was sent to Harvard, graduating in 1653, and becoming a minister in Portsmouth NH. When Rev. Moody refused to give Lt. Gov. Cranfield the sacraments, the official had him imprisoned for 13 weeks. He was elected President of Harvard in 1684, but turned it down to take the pulpit of Old South Church in Boston 1684-92. Caleb[2]'s son Samuel Moody graduated from Harvard in 1697 and became a minister. Great-grandson of Caleb was Samuel[5] Moody (1720-90, Joseph[4], Samuel[3]), founding Master of Dummer Academy, the first school of its kind in Massachusetts (Hurd 2: 1720). Among the claimed descendants of William[1] was the famous preacher Dwight[8] L. Moody (1837-99), but DAB 7:103 says he was descended from John[1] Moody of Connecticut, whose relation to William is unknown.

However, Lydia may have been third cousin of Ralph Waldo Emerson (William Emerson, Mary[4] Moody, Samuel[3], Caleb[2]) if Davis and Miller are correct (56, though there appear to be too few generations).

William Moody's inventiveness was passed on to his descendants. Paul Moody (1779-1831) was the inventor of cotton machinery that had important roles in the industrial revolution of the Merrimac Valley and Waltham (DAB 7:106). Eben Moody Boynton (1840-) was inventor of the crosscut saw and the monorail who built a mansion on the land of his ancestor Caleb Moody on Pipestave Hill, West Newbury (Downey, 3; Hurd 2:1887).

More famous is Supreme Court Justice (1906-10) and Teddy Roosevelt's cabinet officer William H. Moody (1853-1917; DAB 106-7) . Born in the Moody homestead in Newbury, he graduated from Harvard in 1876, and Harvard Law School. He gained fame as the lawyer on the Lizzie Borden murder trial, served in Congress 1898-1902, became Roosevelt's Secretary of the Navy 1902-4, then as Attorney General actively pursued anti-trust cases.

William was the ancestor of one of the "giant" genealogists of the NEHGS, John Ward Dean (1815-1902), its librarian 1872-89, 1893-1902, and editor of the Register for a quarter of a century, 1876-1901 (*Nexus* 11:6, 200, 203; he was also descended from three other ancestors, Thomas Bradbury, John Perkins and Ralph Farnum (Ibid., 204, 206).

THE BRADBURY FAMILY

Sgt. Caleb[2] Moody's second wife, and mother of our Thomas[3] Moody, was JUDITH[2] BRADBURY, born Salisbury 2 Oct. 1638 (VR 26) to Captain THOMAS[1] BRADBURY and his wife MARY[2] PERKINS. She died Newbury 12 Aug. 1737, age 87 (g.s. Old Hill Cem., G-5, Pramberg 377).

Her father Captain Bradbury was one of the most important leaders of the early colony, and her mother the most socially prominent witch.

He was baptized at Wicken-Bonhunt, Essex, 28 Feb. 1611, son of WYMAND[A] BRADBURY of the "Brick House" (William[B] and Matthew[C] of Wicken-Bonhunt, William[D] and Robert[E] of Littlebury, Essex, Robert[F] of Olcersett, Derbyshire; TAG 19:36; Hidden Mem. 140 citing John M. Bradbury, *Bradbury Memorial* [Portland: Brown & Thurston, 1890]; Origins 633n). He was residing in London, St. Mary Whitechapel before he came to York, Maine (Topo 101).

His wife was ELIZABETH GILL, nee WHITGIFT (sometimes given as WICKEN), She was the niece of John Whitgift (c. 1530-1604), Archbishop of Canterbury who crowned James I king, after serving Queen Elizabeth 1583-1604 as her Privy Councillor 1586 *(Ency Brit.* llth ed. 28:608). Whitgift and Elizabeth's father were children of HENRY WHITGIFT, merchant of Great Grimsby, Lines. He was married to a DYNWELL (Marshall Kirk of NEHGS staff, a descendant, cites Threlfall's 1995 rev.). The future archbishop had been Regius Professor of Divinity at Cambridge, and Master of Trinity and Pembroke, and Vice Chancellor after complying the university statutes of 1570. As archbishop he gave the English church much of its Reformation form, including persecution of the Puritans.

The Bradbury family is descended from royalty thru Belgian nobility of the Middle Ages (Gary Boyd Roberts, *Royal Descents* (Santa Clarita CA: NEHGS, 1989, 461) as follows: 1. Thomas[1] Bradbury, 2. Wymond[A], 3. William[B] Bradbury married Anne Eden, daughter of Henry Eden and 4. Elizabeth Heigham, dau. of 5. Clement Heigham, 6. Clement Heigham, 7. Thomas Heigham m. Catherine Cotton, dau. of 8. William Cotton, 9. Walter Cotton m. Joan Rede, dau. of 10. John Rede m. Cecilia Harlyngrugge, dau. of 11. William Harlyngrugge m. Alice Marmion, dau. of 12. Thomas Marmion, 13. John, 14. William, 15. Geoffrey, 16. William, 17. Robert, 18. Robert Marmion m. Milicent de Rethel, dau. of 19. Gervais, Count of Rethel m. Elizabeth of Namur, dau. of 20. Godfrey, Ct. of Namur, 21. Count Albert III, 22. Count Albert II, 23. Count Albert I of Namur m. Adelaide of Lower Lorraine, dau. of 24. Charles, Duke of Lower Lorraine, and last of the Carolingians, heir to the throne of France who was supplanted by Hugh Capet. Charles was son of 25. Louis IV, King of France, 921-954, probable maternal grandson of Edward the Elder, King of England who d. 924, whose daughter Odgiva married Louis's father Charles III the Simple while he was in exile in England. Louis IV married Gerberga, daughter of Henry I the Fowler, German Emperor who d. 936, and sister of Emperor Otto the Great. Louis IV was a descendant of Charlemagne and Pepin the Great (26. King Charles III the Simple (879-929), 27. King Louis II the Stammerer (846-79), 28. Emperor Charles II the Bald (823-77), 29. Emperor Louis I the Pious (778-840), 30. Charlemagne). There are glorious illustrations of the personages, coats of arms and maps in John Brooks Threlfall's *The Ancestry of Thomas Bradbury and Judith Perkins* [Madison WI: author, 1988].

Another possible royal ancestry to the De La Zouche and De Cantelou families depends on establishing two unverified links in Thomas's mother's ancestry (TAG 52:176-7).

William Cotton (8. above, c. 1411-55) was Clerk of Wardrobe of King Henry VI 1432, holder of several manors (TAG 57:41-2). He was son of Walter (no. 9, d. 1445), Esq., Alderman of London, mercer and owner of Landwade Manor, Camb. who had a coat of arms: Sable a chevron between 3 griffin heads erased argent which was halved with his wife's arms quartering 3 martlets azure (pheasants) with field varry (Marmion; illus. TAG 57:40). Walter's father was John Cotton (c. 1330-93), mayor of Cambridge 1378, from the village of Coton, three miles west of Cambridge (TAG 57:35-6) .

Henry Eden (3. above, c. 1514-45) was gentleman farmer of Barningham, Suffolk, son of Thomas (1478-1533) & Joan Eden who bought the manors of Sinclair and Netherhall in Barningham from Henry VIII, and grandson of gentleman Thomas (d.c.1495) & Agnes Edon of Bury St. Edmunds, Suffolk (TAG 55:5-16). Elizabeth French related the Bradburys to the Josselyns thru Philippa Bradbury, b. Wicken-Bonhunt before 1500, but how is unclear (Gary Boyd Roberts, *English Origins of New England Families* [Baltimore: Genea. Pub. Co., 1984], [hereinafter Origins], 482n).

Bradbury was sent to America in 1634 as Agent, or steward, to his great-aunt's husband, the Proprietor of the Province of Maine, Sir Ferdinando Gorges, at Agamenticus, now York ME. He was in London 1 May 1634, but had come to America by 5 May 1636 (TAG 19:36; Gorges married Anne Bell, Thomas's mother's sister, TAG 52:177; Reg. 37:376). On that date he signed, "Gent.", one of Maine's first deeds, ceding 500 acres on the north side of the Pascataquacke (Piscataqua) River to Edward Johnson for use of John Treworgy of Dartmouth (York Deeds 1:11 in TAG 19:37; York Reg. 1:19 in Origins 3:633).

In 1639 he was one of the first settlers of Salisbury MA, settling next to Thomas Macy on the north side of the Beach road (Hurd 2:1442) . He was made freeman 13 May 1640 (Pope 63) , and was granted land in the First Division of 1640 and 1641 (Hoyt 69), and served on the committee that divided the town lands (7 Nov. 1640, 25 March 1641, Hurd 2:1443, 1463). The first road laid out in town, north from the river, passed by his land (12 Jan. 1642, Standard 402). He was one of the first Constables (1641). The bell for the first meeting house built in 1641 was hung by him in 1642 (located on the Common below the East Salisbury depot, opposite Moses French's house; 14 Jan., Hurd 2:1443), and he was on the building committee for the second meeting house in 1665 (Hurd 2:1447).

He served in the town government almost continuously from 1642 to his death half a century later. He was on the first town committees, as Assessor and highway surveyor in 1642 (4 July, Hurd 2:1443), and the first committees of seven to govern town affairs (26 Feb., 4 May 1643, 18 April 1644, 27 Jan. 1647, 2 Feb. 1648, Hurd 2:1444, 1463). This was succeeded by the Prudential Committee on which he served 1648, 1650, 1652, and as town Moderator 1654 (Hurd 2:1463) . He was on the committee that levied the first taxes in town, 1642, and was given authority to seize the property and double taxes of anyone who refused to work on town roads or bridges (Standard 402).

Bradbury was one of the foremost citizens of the town, serving as Town Clerk, Constable, Justice of the Peace, Schoolmaster, Moderator, Selectman, and 7 years Representative to the General Court in Boston, 1651-66 (16 April 1651, Hurd 2:1463).

He was also a leading county magistrate, as Essex County Recorder 1649 (EQ 1:167), and judge, Clerk of Writs 1641, Commissioner 1657, Norfolk County associate judge and commissioner. His tact is recorded in an apology to the county court "that he intended no offence to the court, and was sorry that he offended them." in representing Goodman George Goldwyer's petition (Sept. 1654 In EQ 1:367) . One of his cases was sentencing Jane Flanders to be whipped ten stripes upon lecture day for "telling lies, for making debate among neighbors and casting great reproaches upon//several, also having acknowledged that she was often 'distempered in hir head'" (May 1666, EQ 3:319-20) . The whipping post and stocks were on the town Common near the church.

He was elected the first schoolmaster of the town 10 Jan. 1652, to be paid £ 20 per year, half in good corn, and the right to teach out-of-town children, unless the overseers thought it prejudicial to the local pupils (Hurd 2:1446). Shortly later he was given £ 10 in lumber from the sawmill in part payment (1 Feb., Hurd 2:1446) . The job was taken over by another man in 1664, but late in life Bradbury again served as Schoolmaster (1680, Hurd 2:1448).

A leader of the militia, he was Clerk in 1645, Ensign in 1647 and Captain in 1661 of the Salisbury Train Band (SCW 57; EQ 1:87) . There were two captains in 1689, Bradbury being Capt of ye fort (EQ 7:283). One of his jobs was to supply each soldier with a pound of powder (1679, ibid.). Salisbury was spared Indian raids, in part because its reputation for fair dealing. Bradbury was Moderator of a town meeting which granted the Indian Ned the right to set up a weir to catch fish (6 March 1666, Hurd 2:1453).

He supported Richard Pike's effort to distribute land to newcomers, and became a member of the Prudential Committee in 1652, 1662, 1664, and 1667 to 1677, then Selectman 1678-86, 1689-92 (Hurd 2:1447-9). He was Town Clerk 1693-4 (Hurd 2:1449).

Capt. Bradbury was one of the commissioners who laid out the boundary between Hampton and Salisbury in 1653 (EQ 5:241n).

In 1663 he lost a suit over his "higlede piglede" lot on the way to Hampton, against George Goldwyer, whom he charged with mowing "and for carrying away the hay from it, and going about to alter the title of his land." (EQ 3:57).

In 1664 the town made him responsible for the tax of one out of each thousand "staves or bolts, or heading, or planks" produced in town (Standard 404).

His prominence in the church is show by his appointment in 1666 to the committee to deal with Rev. John Wheelwright over the minister's differences with the town (6 March, Standard 404). The minister got a raise the next year. The family's rank in the community is indicated by the fact that he and his wife are listed second as church members in 1687 (Hoyt 69).

In 1669 he owed the estate of his son Wymond Bradbury of Salisbury £ 60 for "ye howsing & house lott & oarchyard" (Essex Pro. 3,015 in EP 2:171). In 1677 he settled this claim for £ 16, and took guardianship of his grandson Wymond (Norf. Deed 3:ii/22, Salis. Quar. Ct. 11:71 in EP 2:132. In 1679 he and Caleb Moody were the administrators and appraisers of his son William's estate (EP 3:299-302).

In 1671 he got a writ of trespass against John Davis Sr. for cutting his grass and fodder on the east end of Ring's Island (EQ 4:452).

His taxes for 1679 were among the highest in town, £ 1/2/6, behind Rowell, Martin and Osgood (EQ 7:287). The county record of 1682 shows him having the third most valuable estate in town, £ 86/3/4 for two houses, 28 acres of meadow, 20 of pasture and six commonage (EQ 8:390).

The Bradburys' final home was on Mudnock Rd., Salisbury (Carolyn Sargent, *Salisbury History* [Newburyport: Salisbury Historical Commission, 1991], 5).

He died in Salisbury, 16 March 1694/5, age 84 (VR 530) . His will was made 14 Feb. 1693/4 and probated 26 March 1695. It included a legacy of £ 5 for the poor of the town (Standard 405). His daughter Judith Moody and his wife Mary were executrices.

Two well-known Bradburys are descended from Thomas, a jurist and a musician. Theophilus Bradbury (1739-1803) was U.S. Representative 1795-6, and Justice of the Supreme Judicial Court of Massachusetts 1797-1803 (DAB 1:548). William B. Bradbury (1816-68) was an important composer and organist, and founder with his brother Edward of the Bradbury Piano Co. in 1854 (DAB 1:550).

THE PERKINS FAMILY OF IPSWICH

In 1636 Bradbury married 16 year old MARY^2 PERKINS of Ipswich, who had come over from England where she was born in 1620 with her parents JOHN^1 PERKINS and JUDITH^2 GATER on the *Lyon* under Capt. William Pierce from Bristol 1 Dec. 1630, landing in Boston 8 Feb. 1631 (Reg.10:211-6) after a stormy crossing of 67 days (account in Prince's *Annals of New England* 1:341 quoted by Threlfall app. [31) ; Banks Planters 93 citing Winthrop's Jour. 1:57) . Threlfall claims that Mary Perkins was baptized at Hillmorton, Warwickshire 3 Sept. 1615 (appendix [l] , but this does not accord with her age on arrival. Among their fellow passengers was Rhode Island's founder Roger Williams.

The family name we always spell PERKINS was also spelled PARKINS, PEARKENS, PEARKINS, PERKEINGS, PERKENS, PERKINES, PERKINGS, PERKUS, PIRKENS, PIRRKINS and even PURCKINSE and PURKINGS.

JOHN[1] PERKINS was probably born in the village where he was baptized at St. John the Baptist church, Hillmorton, Warwickshire 23 Dec. 1583 (Threlfall app. [3] ; not in Newent, Gloucestershire in 1590 per Currier 1040 and Hurd 2:1201; deposed age above 60 in March 1650, EQ 1:187). He was the son of HENRY[A] PERKINS and ELIZABETH SAWBRIDGE (married Hillmorton 29 Nov. 1579, Threlfall [6]). Hillmorton is two miles northeast of Rugby, Warwick, near the junction of the three counties of Warwick, Northampton and Leicester, and the Leicestershire homes of Salem's first pastor, the Rev. John Higginson (Claybrooke), nonconformist minister Rev. Dillingham (Cotesbach), whose two sons came to America (Wildes 87).

The Sawbridges came from a village of that name in the parish of Wolfhamcote, Warwickshire, 6 miles from Hillmorton. Elizabeth's brother George made a will 1636 that named his nephew Thomas Perkins as overseer, and his mother Elizabeth (Threlfall [6] ; Wildes 86).

Henry[A] Perkins was born about 1555, the son of Thomas" Perkins and Alice (KEBBLE?). He was buried at Hillmorton 11 March 1608/9. Administration of his estate was given to his son Thomas 5 April 1609. The inventory came to £ 366, including a well-furnished servants quarters, grain in the field which suggests farming, and a lot furnishings that would be found in an inn (Threlfall [7-8]) . Henry's eldest son Thomas left a will styling him "gentleman" (Prerog. Court of Canterbury, 53 Pell cited by Wildes 86).

Henry[A] Perkins administered his father's will in 1592 (made Hillmorton 15 Sept. 1588, proved 11 May 1592, Lichfield Registry in Wildes 82) . Thomas[B] PERKINS was probably born Hillmorton about 1525-30. He appears to have been a well-to-do yeoman farmer. He made his will 16 Sept. 1588, and was buried 23 March 1591/2. There was once a stone in the middle aisle of the Hillmorton church reading:

Here lyeth Thomas Perkins and Alice and Elizabeth

Our Lord Save their souls from everlasting death" (Smith, *History of Warwick* quoted by Threlfall [9]). Thomas asked to be buried in an aisle of that church, but the stone could be his grandfather's inscription of 1528. He names his wife Alice, Sislye and Thomas Kebble, and "my brother Kebble's wife", which may be his wife's maiden name. The inventory of value came to less than £ 100.

Thomas[B] Perkyns's father is unsure. Thomas is supposed to be mentioned in the missing will of HENRY[C] PERKINS of Hillmorton, proved 16 June 1546, when abstracted before 1894 (Lichfield Registry, Act Book 4, 44 in Wildes 82) . Henry proved his mother Alice's will in 1538 (will 31 July, proved 15 Oct. in Lichfield Registry, Wildes 81; Threlfall [13] citing *Putnam's Historical Magazine)* . Henry was the son of THOMAS" and ALICE PERKYNS of Hillmorton (Hylmoreton). Thomas was born about 1475, died at Hillmorton April 1528, and left a will of 3 April, proved 21 April (Lichfield Registry in Wildes 81). He mentions lands and tenements in Hillmorton, Fylds and Lilbourne, Northamptonshire, about 3 miles northeast (Lichfield Registry Series II cited by Threlfall [14] from Putnam's). His widow Alice died in 1538, leaving a will also quoted by Threlfall [14], naming her son Henry executor and residuary legatee. Thomas Clerke and Richard Smyth (Smith) are both named in Thomas and Alice's wills, and may be relatives, perhaps her brother. It may be these older Perkinses who were commemorated in the stone in the church of Hillmorton, whose inscription was quoted above.

JUDITH[2] (spelled Judeth in her husband's will) GATER married John Perkins in the church of St. John the Baptist, Hilltnorton, Warwickshire 9 Oct. 1608 (Wildes 87; Threlfall, [3] citing Wildes and *Putnam's Magazine*). She was baptized there 19 March 1588/9, daughter of

MICHAEL GATER and ISABEL BAYLIE, who were married Hillmorton 13 Nov. 1576, and came to New England (Threlfall [8]). Judith died Ipswich between 28 March and 26 Sept. 1654 (not in VR; Wildes 87).

The Perkins family lived in Boston for two years, 1631-3. He became a freeman in Boston 18 May 1631 (Hammatt 244). He and his wife are listed as 107th and 108th members of the First Church in Boston (1631; Winsor 1:567). In the War with the Tarrantine Indians his son was Sergeant of the English forces and their Indian allies under Masconomaat at Agawam (Ipswich) in 1631 (Wildes 89; SCW 368) . In 1632 he was given the sole right to shoot fowl at Noodles Island (East Boston) and Pullen Point (3 April 1632 in Massachusetts Col. Rec. 1:94 [103 in Wildes] per Winsor 1:449; Threlfall [3]; Wildes says this was probably his son). That year he was one of those chosen to make the boundary between Dorchester and Roxbury (7 Nov. 1632 in Threlfall [3]).

He went to Ireland with John Winthrop Jr. (Sav. 3:396; this may refer to Winthrop's accidental shipwreck there in Oct. 1634. DAB 20:42).

The family then moved to Agawam, to be known as Ipswich, by 1634 (Waters 493). Panicked by rumors that the Jesuits were coming, Governor Winthrop sent in March 1633 a company of Puritans, including an unrelated William Perkins, under his son John Winthrop to settle Agawam (Hurd 1:569). William Perkins is named by the colonial court as one of the ten families including John Winship Junior exclusively to live at Agawam (11 April 1633 in Pierce 3).

On 29 Dec. 1634 John Jr. was given right to set up a fish weir on the Parker River, but with the clear proviso that if he settled permanently he would submit to local regulation (Coffin 13). From this Coffin assumed that actual settlement followed, in early 1635, but still 1634 in the current calendar. John Sr. was granted in 1634 forty acres on Manning's Neck, to the west of Robert Coles, and north of "a small creek" (Hammatt 244; Threlfall [3]). He sold this to Thomas Hewlett in 1637 for £ 7/10 (Hammatt 244) . John Perkinses house was on the north side of the Jeffries Neck Road, at the north end of the village (Waters 401, map 3, 386) . This was the farthest extent of the village in Nov. 1634, when the town set the limits "Eastward unto a Cove of the River [including the wharves], unto the planting ground of John Pirkings the Elder." (Waters 60). In 1635 he was given 85 more acres, including the ten acres on which he had built his house, with adjoining six acres of meadow and six of upland.

In 1635 he also got fifty acres of the island called More's Point on the south side of the town river (among his lands was Perkins Island in the Ipswich River, Hoyt 281), and ten acres of meadow and three of upland at the head of Chebacco creek (Threlfall [3]) . The next year, 1636, he got forty acres of meadow and upland at Chebacco (today's Essex) which he sold to Thomas Hewlett the following year (Ibid.). In 1639 he bought the next lot south from John Sanders, and was given six acres of planting land on the south side of the river (Ibid.).

He held numerous town offices, and was Representative 1636 (Hoyt 282; Pope 354). In the first town record of Ipswich of Nov. 1634 he is one of the lot-layers who assigned land grants (Waters 56) . He is also on the first board of proto-Selectmen, called "The Seven Men" in 1637 (Waters 56) , and continued in that role thru 1641 (Waters 57). As early as 1635 he was on a town committee to settle differences over a well (Essex Co. His & Gen Reg. 185). He was on the grand jury for 1641, 1648 and 1652 (EQ 1:37, 145, 260).

Perkins probably served in the town militia until he was excused from military service in March 1650, being over 60 (EQ 1:187).

He died in Ipswich 1654, age 64 (VR 645) . His will of 28 March 1654, proved 26 Sept., leaves each of his daughters, including Mary Bradbury "one cow and one heyfer or a young steere to remaine to her & her children in theyr increase or proffits as it shall please the Lord to bless them and to be equaly Devided to the children" (text Essex Pro. 21,337 in *The Probate Records of Essex County* [Salem: Essex Institute, 1916], hereinafter EP 1:190-1; Reg. 14:120; 10:211-6) . The inventory came to only £ 250/5, of which £ 40 was the house, and £ 79 for 50 acres of land.

John's Bible and original will were preserved by his descendant Horatio N. Perkins of Melrose in 1888 (Hurd 2:1201).

His second son Deacon Thomas Perkins married Phebe[2] Gould, daughter of Zaccheus of Topsfield (no relation; Hoyt 283). His eldest son John Perkins was father of Mary[3] Perkins who married Rev. Thomas Wells (Hoyt 283). They were ancestors of our great-grandparent, Caroline Goddard Gould (Caroline Garran, Sally[5] Fletcher, Lydia[4] Wells, Obadiah[3], Luke[2], Mary[3] Perkins, John[2] Jr., John[1] Perkins) who married T. Warren Gould (Lydia[6] Teel, Sally Barnard, Jemima[4] Hidden, Jemima[5] Moody, Oliver[4], Thomas[3], Judith Bradbury, Mary[2] Perkins, John[1] Perkins), and were thus seventh cousins once removed.

There are four noted descendants of John Perkins whose biographies appear in the *Dictionary of American Biography*. Dr. Elisha (1741-99) was responsible for "Perkinism", a use of electric rods of brass and iron, called tractors, which had international attention for some time (DAB 7:466). Dr. Perkins was grandfather of the diplomat George P. Marsh, American minister to Italy and Turkey (Hurd 2:1201). Naturalist and geologist George H. Perkins (1844-1933) was professor at University of Vermont for 64 years, Vice President and Academic Dean, and Curator of its museum, as well as state geologist 1898-1933 (DAB 7:470-1) . Banker George W. Perkins (1862-1920) was member of J.P.Morgan firm 1901-10, when he led in formation of International Harvester and other important businesses. Believing in the regulation of capitalism, he was a leader in the Progressive Party (DAB 7:471-2). Inventor Jacob Perkins (1766-1849) produced the die for the first U.S. coins, invented the counterfeit-proof banknote plate, the high-pressure boiler, and the plate for the world's first postage stamp, the British penny black in 1840 (DAB 7:472-3).

Two prominent genealogists counted him as ancestor, NEHGS Librarian and *Register* editor John Dean (noted above under descendants of William Moody) and Henry F. Waters (1833-1913; *Nexus* 12:l, 25), who also shared descent from Edmund Greenleaf.

MARY PERKINS BRADBURY, CONDEMNED WITCH

Mary (Perkins) Bradbury became famous as the most socially well-placed woman accused and condemned for witchcraft in the Salem trials of 1692. She was the exception to the general rule that the accused were often poor and socially marginal characters, like our Rachel Clinton. In fact, Mary's high social status may have had influence on the repudiation of witchcraft by the authorities.

Mary was first accused of witchcraft in 1672, when she was 52 (Demos 66). Twenty years later, during the great Salem epidemic, she as tried. One of the accusations was by a young man, Richard Carr, who testified that he was riding home on a Sunday noon about 1678, passing the Bradburys' house "I saw Mrs. Bradbury go into her gate, turn the corner of, and immediately there darted out of her gate a blue boar, and darted at my father's horse's legs, which made him stumble; but I saw no more. And my father said, 'Boys, what do you see?' We both answered. 'A blue boar.'" (9 Sept. 1692, Upham 11:230; Boyer 1:123-4; Frost 123-4).

This was confirmed by the other witness, 15 year old Zerubabel Endicott. He said "I also saw the blue boar dart from Mr. Carr's horse's legs in at Mrs. Bradbury's window. And Mr. Carr immediately said, 'Boys, what did you see?[1] And we both said, 'A blue boar.' Then said he, 'From whence came it?' And we said, 'Out of Mrs. Bradbury's gate.'" (Ibid.).

The clerk of the court added that the witnesses said they discussed it on the way home, "and they all concluded that it was Mrs. Bradbury that so appeared as a blue boar." (Upham 11:231).

Another witness, Samuel Endicott, swore that about 1681 Mary Bradbury had come to Boston and sold some butter to the captain of their ship, "And after we had been at sea three weeks...it stank so and ran with maggots, which made the men very disturbed about it, and [they] would often say that they heard Mrs. Bradbury was a witch..." (Demos 59 citing Boyer 1:122).

This witness also attributed terrible storms on that voyage and bad leaks in the ship to her witchcraft, and swore she appeared one moonlit night while he was on watch. He heard a rumble, and "thought he saw the legs of some person. 'Presently he was shook, and looked over his shoulder, and saw the appearance of a woman, from her middle upwards, having a white cap and white neckcloth on her, which then affrighted him very much; and, as he was turning of the windlass, he saw the aforesaid two legs. '" (Upham 11:232; Boyer 1:122).

Richard Carr's brother James said that 20 years ago he had been afflicted by creatures running over his body, which Dr. Crosby diagnosed as "behagged". When Carr suggested it was caused by Goody Martin, the doctor countered that "he did believe Mary Bradbury was a great deal worse than Goody Martin." (McMillen 440; Frost 124-5).

Upham gave Mary Bradbury's case extra attention to show generally that some well-placed people were accused, and particularly to show that this resulted from long-standing village quarrels. The Carr family, who employed the Endicott boys, was a rival of the Bradburys. He concluded that accusations "were instigated by personal grudges and private piques, many of them of long standing, fomented and kept alive by an unhappy indulgence of unworthy feelings, always read to mix themselves with popular excitements, and leading all concerned headlong to the utmost extent of mischief and wrong." (Upham 11:238) . In particular, Ann Putnam seems to have projected onto Mary her own guilt for having prevented the marriage of John Carr, who died of a broken heart (Upham 11:235-7).

But the event that precipitated Mary's arrest and jailing in Salem 26 May 1692 was the accusation of two major witnesses in the Salem epidemic, Ann Putnam and Mary Walcott (Persis McMillen, *Currents of Malice* [Portsmouth NH: Peter Randall, 1990], 39, citing *Salem Witchcraft Papers. Verbatim Transcripts* [3 vol. comp. by Archie Frost Salem: Essex Institute, 1938], 1:117).

On 26 July she was formally indicted for bewitching Timothy Swan of Andover and Sarah Bibber of Salem (text in Boyer 1:115, 116; McMillen 439, citing Frost 115-6). This followed the confessions of three generations of "witches" from Andover, Ann Foster, her daughter Mary Lacey Sr, and her fifteen year old daughter Mary on July 21-2, in which they named Mrs. Bradbury as collaborator (McMillen 413-9, Frost 2:514-26).

Women accused of witchcraft met Cotton Mather's criterion for examination: "If a Fellow-Witch, or Magician, give Testimony of any Person to be a Witch; this indeed is not sufficient for Condemnation; but it is a fit Presumption to cause a strait Examination." (Cotton Mather, *On Witchcraft; Being the Wonders of the Invisible World* [Boston: 1692, reprint N.Y.: Dorset Press, 1991], 28).

One of the women who confessed to witchcraft, Mary Lacey, named Mary Bradbury: "About three or four years ago, she saw Mistress Bradbury, Goody Howe, and Goody Nurse baptized by the old Serpent at Newbury Falls; that he dipped their heads in water, and then said they were his, and he had power over them..." (Upham 2:400).

Mary's spunky defense is recorded in Boyer 1:116-7 and Upham 2:225 (Frost 116-7): 'The Answer of Mary Bradbury in the charge of Witchcraft or familliarity with the Divell

"I doe plead not guilty. I am wholly inocent of any such wickedness through the goodness of god that have kept mee hitherto I am the servant of Jesus Christ and have given my self up to him as my only lord & saviour: and to the dilligent attendance upon him in all his holy ordinances, in utter contempt & defiance of the divell, and all his works as horid & detestible; and accordingly, have endevo'red to frame my life; & conversation according to the rules of his holy word, & in that faith & practise resolve by the help and assistance of god to contineu to my lifes end.

for the truth of what I say as to matter of practiss I humbly refer myself to my brethren & neighbors that know mee and unto the Searcher of all hearts for the truth & uprightness of my heart therein (human frailties and unavoydable infirmities excepted) of which i bitterly complayne every day:"

Her husband's defense gives a nice picture of her character: "July 28, 1692 .--Concerning my beloved wife, Mary Bradbury, this is what I have to say: We have been married fifty-five years, and she hath been a loving and faithful wife to me. Unto this day, she hath been wonderful laborious, diligent, and industrious, in her place and employment, about the bringing-up of our family (which have been eleven children of our own, and four grandchildren) . She was both prudent and provident, of a cheerful spirit, liberal and charitable. She being now very aged and weak, and grieved under her affliction, may not be able to speak much for herself, not being so free of speech as some others may be. I hope her life and conversation have been such amongst her neighbors as gives a better and more real testimony of her than can be expressed by words." (Frost 117-8; Boyer 117-8).

117 neighbors signed a testimonial of her good character (22 July; text in Boyer 1:119, Upham 2:226, Frost 119-20) . Her minister, Rev. James Allin, swore "I, having lived nine years at Salisbury in the work of the ministry, and now four years in the office of pastor, to my best notice and observation of Mrs. Bradbury, she hath lived according to the rules of the gospel amongst us; was a constant attender upon the ministry of the word, and all the ordinances of the gospel; full of works of charity and mercy to the sick and poor: neither have I seen or heard any thing of her unbecoming the profession of the gospel." (Upham 11:226; Boyer 1:121). This testimonial was supported by one of the top colonial officials, Robert Pike, who was judge, representative and member of the provincial council (Upham 11:228, Boyer 1:121).

Mary was tried in Salem 9 Sept. 1692. Among the witnesses was a maid, Mary Warren, who had been one of the leading accusers of others, and swore that day that "Mis Bradbury is [a witch] and that she has very often afflicted [me] and several others by her acts of witchcraft." (Boyer 1:123; McMillen 439; Frost 123).

Also testifying were Mary Walcott, Elizabeth Hubbard and Sarah Bibber (Boyer 1:125-8; McMillen 440; Frost 125-9) . Ann Putnam Jr. said the ghost of her dead uncle John Carr appeared to her in his winding sheet and told her "that Mrs. Bradbury had murdered him and that his blood did call for vengeance against her." (Boyer 1:127; McMillen 440; Frost 127). She also accused her of killing her father's horse and sheep.

Upham states that testimony in defense was excluded, the court having made up its mind in advance (11:235).

On the day of her trial, 9 Sept., she was condemned to death, with six other women (Upham 11:324). Four of these were executed 22 Sept. by hanging on Witches Hill. But somehow, Mary escaped, after six months in prison (petition of Henry & Jane True 11 Sept. 1710 in Massachusetts Arch. 135:120, Boyer 3:981). McMillen concluded, "the records show that the Court showed leniency to persons of wealth. Then, as now, there was one law for the rich and one for the poor." (McMillen 441).

Mary (Perkins) Bradbury died Salisbury on 20 Dec. 1700 (VR), at age 80. Her heirs petitioned for reversal of her sentence, and finally, 11 years after her death, Governor Dudley ordered compensation of £ 20 on 7 Dec. 1711, but not paid until 24 March 1712 (Upham 2:480; Boyer 3:103).

THE HALE-DOWSETT-KIRBY FAMILIES

Thomas[3] Moody's wife, and mother of Oliver[4] Moody, was JUDITH[3] HALE, born Newbury 5 July 1670 to JOHN[2] HALE and his second wife SARA[2] SOMERBY (VR 208; EQ 4:320; Reg. 31:97).

The name HALE is spelled phonetically in the records HALLE, HEALL, HEILL and even HELL (EQ 4:402).

John was baptized at Watton-at-Stone, Hertfordshire on 29 April 1635 (Reg. 35:375; Rolfe; Topo 71) , and came to America with his parents in 1637-8 on the . He is easily confused with the contemporary Rev. John Hale of Beverly, who was the same age, but ours was usually called Sergeant.

He was a housewright or carpenter by trade (Reg. 31:85).

One of our ancestor's first appearances in court was as a witness to a fight at John Knight's farm, in 1659 when he said "I saw matthew moores ty his Horse to the fence & took up an axe & with the helve struck Robert Downer three tymes upon the thygh." (EQ 2:154). Later that year he was witness in his father's suit against Muzzey for grain (EQ 2:175, 176).

He was a member of the Newbury church in 1662 when he was seated in the foreseat of the North Gallery next to Caleb Moody and in 1668 when he was seated on the long seat next to the north gallery (EQ 4:140, 138) . In the long church controversy he was in the conservative faction supporting the minister (13 March 1669, Coffin 74) when his son was in the dissident Woodman party that voted to censure Rev. Parker and was fined 13sh. 4 d. for "dishonor to the name of god of religion. . .as also the disturbance of the peace the scandalizing of a venerable pious and loving pastor" (EQ 4:366-7; Coffin states fine at one noble, or 6 sh. 8 d., 100). Later that year he was authorized to build a pew in the southeast corner of the Newbury church (Currier 318).

He owned a negro slave, who was fined by the court in Nov. 1674 (EQ 8:306). In 1677 he was licensed to make sturgeon at Nubury (EQ 6:249). The next year the town paid him £ 1/4 to repair the bridge over Newbury River (EQ 8:47n).

He took the oath of allegiance in Newbury, age 42, in 1678 (EQ 7:156; Currier 180). He signed his name "Jno." on the petition of 1681/2 to protect his land title (Currier 194) . John was Constable in 1682 (EQ 8:419n, 442), Tithing man for 1683 (Currier 118), and fenceviewer Sgt. Jno. in 1685 (Currier 116). In 1688 Serj. Hale was assessed for two houses, seven acres of plowland, 2 horses, 4 oxen, 4 cows, 4 calves, 16 sheep and 5 hoggs (Currier 203).

He died Newbury 2 June 1707 (VR 607), age 62. There is no record of will or probate, like his father (Reg. 31:86).

John Hale was married to Sara Somerby in Newbury 8 Dec. 1663 (VR 215) after the death of his first wife Rebecca Lowle on 1 June 1662 (Newbury VR 608; they were married Newbury 5 Dec. 1660, VR 215; she was daughter of Richard, b. Newbury 27 Jan. 1641, VR 29).

On Sara's death in Newbury 19 June 1672 (VR 609) he married a third time, probably in 1673 (m. not in VR) to Sarah (Simonds) Cottle, a widow born about 1647, who died 19 Jan. 1699/1700 (Reg. 31:86). It is this third wife who probably testified in the witchcraft hearings of 1680 about alleged wizard Caleb Powell (Reg. 31:86).

John was son of THOMAS[1] HALE (HALLE) , a glover, who was baptized at Watton-at-Stone, Hertfordshire, 15 June 1606, son of THOMAS[A] HALE and his wife JOANE KIRBY, a sister of Winthrop's friend Francis Kirby (Rolfe; Pope 207; In April 1662 he deposed that he was about 50, a round number that is suspect EQ 2:206n; 74 in Nov. 1678, EQ 7:156). Kirby's recommendation of the son to Gov. Winthrop is reproduced in Ould 86 (10 May 1637 from MHS Coll. 4, ser., vii:19; also in Reg. 35:369) . It states that he has nearly £ 200, half of which he spent on the passage across the Atlantic. He came on the ship *Hector* (Topo 71 citing Reg. 35:370, 67:186, Banks mss.). The elder Thomas[A] Hale, yeoman, was buried at Watton 19 Oct. 1630, having made his will on the l lth (summarized in Reg. 35:37l; 367 ff. refutes previous Reg. 31:83 speculation that he was son of William Hale, Esq. of King's Walden, Herts, as stated by Coffin 393; for relation to Thomas[1] Hale also b. Watton 27 June 1610 who went to Connecticut, see TAG 398:237).

His mother, Joane Kirby, daughter of Joan Kirby, came from Little Munden, Herts., where she was probably married (Reg. 35:370). She returned to Little Munden and remarried June 1637 to John (?) Bydes or Bides, and made her will Oct. 1640, but had died by the time of her brother Francis's will of July 1660 (Reg. 35:372). Her brother Francis Kirby was a skinner of leather who became a London merchant engaged in shipping supplies to the colonies, and at his death bridgemaster of London Bridge, living in the Bridgemaster's House at St. Olave, Southwark (his letters to the Winthrops in MHS Coll. 7:13-22, series 3, 9: 237-67 per Reg. 35:373).

Thomas[1] Hale was among the first settlers of Newbury, but no earlier than 1637, despite claims of Newbury historians who confuse him with three contemporaries of the same name. He was not the one of that name admitted as freeman 14 May 1634 (Currier 98, citing Massachusetts Col. Rec. 1:368, 369; 7 Sept. 1638 per Ould 86). His first appearance in Newbury is 10 Aug. 1638 when he was appointed hayward, with "speciall care of the impounding of swine" (Coffin 28; Currier 132; Reg. 35:368).

His houselot of about 1635 was just north of William Moody's in the east end, six lots north of the Parker River (Ould 14). But he subsequently lived south of the river (Coffin 393) . On 6 Oct. 1638 Hale sold his house to Richard Dummer, with lands on both sides of Merrimac Ridge (Historical 649 citing Old 315, 86) . In 1640 he sold 52 more acres on Merrimac Ridge to Joseph Carter (Old 86, citing Ips. Deeds 1:2) . He is listed as a proprietor of Newbury 7 Dec. 1642 as one entitled to commons (Old 86; Reg. 31:84). In 1642 he was appointed by the town to decide about disposal of common land (23 Feb., Coffin 35), then made one of the committee of three that divided the ox and cow commons (Currier 53, 55, Ould 86) . In 1645 he was assigned a lot in the New Town (later Newburyport) , but may not have taken it (Currier 89: Thos. Haile).

He was on the county trial jury for 1647, 1650-1 and 1654 (EQ 1:111, 201, 232, 262). Hale was rarely in trouble with the law. The one case in the printed record is for "reproachful speeches concerning the birth of the plaintiff", Thomas Davis who sued him for slander, and won the court's admonishment of Hale (1651, EQ 1:222) .

About 1645-6 he resettled in Haverhill, then called Pentucket, which had been settled by Newbury families in 1641. He was one of 32 men who had land there in 1645 (Hurd 2:1916) . Hale is one of the first 31 landholders in 1645 (Standard 166) . He was the first Selectman elected by the town, 29 Oct. 1646, for which he was paid 50 shillings (Standard 167, 169, 182; Hurd 2:1918) . The next year he was named to the town's first court, as judge for small claims under 40 shillings, and layer of the road to Andover (May 1647, Hurd 2:1918; Standard 182).

Hale was appointed ferryman across the Merrimac in 1648 (Hurd 2:1918) after he had complained to court against Haverhill "for want of a convenient ferry for their river." (28 Dec. 1647, EQ 1:129). The ferry started from a point a little east of Kent Street. He was allowed "one penny for a passenger, two pence for cattel under two years old, and four pence for each as were over that age." (Hurd 2:1918).

He was the first Constable elected by Haverhill, in 1649 (Hurd 2:1921; Reg.31:83-4; Ould 86). In 1650 he was appointed by Haverhill to set the boundary with Newbury. In the next year "Little River" of Haverhill is called "Thomas Hale's River" where a sawmill was to be built about 1650 that gave it the name of Saw-Mill River (16 Dec., Reg. 31:83 citing Mirick's Haverhill and Chase's Haverhill; Little River flows south from NH into the Merrimac ¼ mile west of the nineteenth century Haverhill bridge, at Winter Street, Hurd 2:1904, 1923; Standard 168, 169). Some of his meadow land bordered Merries Creek, north of the highway (Hurd 2:1913). His lot is named in 1651 as bound of the fencible area on the west side of Little River (Hurd 2:1921). He had left Haverhill by mid-1652, for his name is not among the 41 grantees of the second division of plowlands (7 June, Hurd 2:1924). Yet in 1667 he was fourth largest grantee, receiving 20 acres (July, Hurd 2:1921).

But Hale returned to Newbury about 1652. He was named judge for small claims in Newbury in 1647, and received several grants of land there, including ten acres of marsh on the Neck over the great river (Ips. Deeds 1:227 (607), and ten acres next to this (Ibid). In 1652 he bought a house, barn and 70 acres south of the Newbury River which he then occupied, from Stephen and Anne Kent in exchange for his farm in Haverhill (Ips. Deeds. 1:236 (629) in Old 87). In 1655 he had power of attorney from Joseph Carter to sell a psll of land (EQ 1:386). About 1656 he mowed the hay in the marsh of a cove on Plum Island on land he had been granted by the town, and by 1681 owned by Richard Kent (EQ 8:171).

Hale was Sergeant of the Newbury militia 1652-7 (SCW 214) . He was one of those dissenting at Newbury town meeting of 14 May 1653 to raise a tax to maintain a school and pay the schoolmaster (EQ 2:70n).

He then moved to Salem in 1656 or 1657, where he was Clerk of the Market (Reg.31:84 citing town records). There he was employed as a glover, and bought John Smith's house (ED 1:48 per Old 87). He was on the trial jury there in April 1657 (EQ 2:42) and Nov. 1658 (EQ 2:124), but paid a fine for not attending (EQ 2:133), again in 1660 (EQ 2:202). He acted as an attorney in court for Mr. Thomas Burnap of Reading in a suit for debt owed by Zaccheus Gould of Topsfield, who appointed "my Cozan John Putnam the yonger" his attorney (1658, EQ 2:126). In 1659 he won a judgment against Corporal John Andrews for debt of wheat (EQ 2:147). Later that year he had two more suits, against Joseph Muzzey for ten bushels of wheat he promised to deliver to John Webb of Boston (EQ 2:175). Muzzey counter-sued for "unjust molestation", but lost, and had to pay £ 28/10 "to be paid in a mare of his, now in the woods, and the remainder in young cattle, as soon as she can be found" (EQ 2:176). On 6 May two men went with Muzzey and "drove a yearling horse colt and twenty sheep to Goodman Kale's in payment of bill" (EQ 2:177n).

Hale returned again to Newbury in 1661, living with his son in his second homestead, which he had sold him the previous year (Ips. Deeds 11:215 (396). A photo of his big house on Newbury Neck is shown in Old 83 as it appeared about 1896. In 1663 the town agreed to pay him and Daniel Pierce £ 30 in goods semiannually to build and maintain a causeway for the road to Rowley, but were released from this in 1673 (Currier 421) . He was on the trial jury of 1664,

1667, 1669 and 1678 at Ipswich (EQ 3:119, 387, 4:100; 7:83).

He was one of the petitioners of Newbury in 1666 on government of the colony (Currier 176). For many years he was fenceviewer for the old village of Newbury: 1666, 1670, 1670, 1671, 1672, 1675, 1679 (Currier 115-6). In 1670 he was surveyor of highways (Currier 110), in 1674 way warden (Currier 111), surveyor again 1676 and 1677 (Currier 111).

Thomas was a member of the church faction of Rev. Parker who supported Rev. John Woodbridge in the long controversy in the Newbury church, as shown by his signature with elders Nicholas Noyes and Ensign (John Jr.) Knight expressing "great grief" at Edward Woodman's charges that Woodbridge was "an intruder, brought in by craft and subilty", and that Parker "was an apostate and backslider from the truth, that the would set up a prelacy, and have more power than the pope.. ." (30 March 1669 in Coffin 74) . On the other side, supporting Woodman's criticism were his son Thomas Jr. and ancestors William and Caleb Moody (Coffin 83).

Hale was a major witness in the trespass case of Benjamin Rolfe against John Emery Sr. for cutting grass on a five acre lot that once belonged to John Muslwhite, who had paid Hale to watch the field. Hale had witnessed Muslwhite's refusal to sell to Emery, and the transfer to Rolfe "by turf and twig" (1670, EQ 4:225-8).

Hale, whose name is spelled Heall and Heill, was in the majority opposing censure of Rev. Parker, though his son was in the Woodman party, but not fined as were the leaders (23 March 1669, Coffin 86, 100). Most interesting is that he is listed as not "a regular member" of the church (EQ 4:360-1).

He was 74 when he signed the oath of allegiance in 1678 (EQ 7: 156; Currier 180). He died Newbury 21 Dec. 1682 (VR 609). No will or probate could be found in 1877 (Reg. 31:84).

Thomas married at Watton apud Stone, Herts., 11 Dec. 1632 (Reg. 6:162, 64:186 in Origins 698) THOMASINE, TAMOSIN, TAMAZIN, or THOMAZIN DOWSETT, the mother of John; her parents were GABRIEL[A] & MARIE DOUCET of Harlow, Essex, he a miller whose will was probated Jan. 1627/8, leaving £ 10 to his daughter Tomazen (Archdeaconry of Middlesex, Somerset House, Reg. Browne, f. 176, in Origins 698) . Her mother's,_ Mercie Dowsett's estate at Watton-at-Stone, Herts, administered' by her daughter Thomasine, wife of Thomas Hale 25 June 1635 (Archdeaconry of Hunts., Somerset House, Act Book 5, f. 8). She died Newbury 30 Jan. 1682/3 (VR 609), the forty days later called "the widow's quarantine" (Reg. 31:84; this excluded his having remarried Margaret, daughter of Sir Henry Tamorin, per Virkus cited by Rolfe).

Three well-known Hales are descended from Thomas, an educator, a homeopathic doctor, and a international lawyer. Benjamin Hale (1797-1863) founded a progressive school in Maine on the principles of Pestalozzi, became professor of chemistry at Bowdoin (1827) and 23 years president of Hobart (then Geneva) College 1836-58 (DAB 4: 96-7) . Dr. Edwin M. Hale (1829-99) was a leader in homeopathic medicine, as professor at Hahnemann in Chicago (DAB 7:101-2). Robert S. Hale (1822-81) was U.S. Congressman from New York 1865-6 and 1873-4, and in between was American Counsel for the Alabama Claims at the Hague 1871-3 (DAB 7:110-1).

THE SOMERBY & MOORE FAMILIES

Sara (Somerby) Hale, born Newbury 10 Feb. 1644/5 (VR 486) , was the daughter of immigrant HENRY[1] SOMERBY and his wife JUDITH[2] GREENLEAF (Rolfe) . She died Newbury 19 June 1672 (VR 609) , age 27.

The family name is spelled variously SOMERSBY, SOMMERSBEY, SUMERBY, SUMERSBY, SUMERSBYE, SUMMERBY, etc. inconsistently even by his brother, the college-educated town clerk Anthony Somerby (Ould 27).

Her father Henry Somerby was baptized 17 March 1612 at Little Bytham, Lincolnshire, brother of Anthony Somerby, graduate of Clare Hall, Cambridge 1635, who became Newbury town clerk (William Cutter, *Genealogy of Boston and Massachusetts* [4 vols., NY: Lewis Historical, 1908] 2:1014; evidence that he came from Little Bytham in his brother Anthony's statement in Newbury records, per Pope 425) . They were sons of Richard[A] Somerby who died Little Bytham 1 March 1639, and grandson of Henry[B] (d.c. 1609) and Margaret Somerby. Little Bytham is in South Heath, 8 miles from Stamford, Lines. (Coffin 668). The Newbury historian said the family name came from the village of Somerby, Lincolnshire, where the first record is in the Doomsday Book of Adam de Somerby, but the connection is unproven (668).

Henry[B] Somerby was son of Henry[C], son of John[D] both of Little Bytham. The lineage traces back to John[E], brother of Robert Somerby, fellow of Pembroke Hall, Cambridge in 1463, and vicar of Kingston-on-Thames who d. 1502. They were sons of Henry[F], son of John[G] , son of Richard[H] de Somerby, brother of John, vicar of Hannington, Northamptonshire. They were sons of Henry[I], son of Richard[J] who was brother of Robert, chaplain of Colby in 1327, and Lambert. They were sons of Sir Thomas[K] de Somerby, brother of William, vicar of Barrow-on-Soar, Leicester. They were sons of Sir Roger[L], son of Sir Emanuel[M], son of Sir Thomas[N], buried in the reign of King John in Somerby church, of which his brother Alexis was priest. His marble effigy rests under a canopy in a niche in the church has his legs crossed on an unusual cushion of a saddled horse reined by a squire (Cutter 1013). They were sons of the first known member, Roger[0] Somerby of Somerby, near Grantham, Lincolnshire, in the reign of Henry II (1154-89).

The family is supposed to have come from Flanders at the time of the Norman Conquest. The arms are "Per pale argent and vert three crescents countercharged. Crest: a talbot sejeant proper collared or resting his dexter forepaw on an escallop argent." (Cutter 1013).

It is claimed that Henry came to Boston on the *Jonathan* with his brother Anthony in 1639 (Greenleaf 74).

Henry[1] Somerby was in Newbury as early as 29 March 1642 when he appears as defendant in a suit of John Ilsley and plaintiff against others (EQ 1:40, 41). They apparently settled in the "New Town" on Merrimac riverside, in what became Newburyport (Standard 312).

Henry[1] became freeman 18 May 1642 (Hist, from Massachusetts Col. Rec. 11:291) . Later that year he was named one of the citizens entitled to common land in the proposed new settlement that was to become Newburyport (Currier 84). He was on the trial jury of 1647 (EQ 1:111) .

Henry was licensed as an innkeeper in Newbury 24 Sept. 1650, in the place of Edmund Greenleaf, probably operating in the old part of the old Coffin house on High Street Newburyport (EQ 1:199; Old 109, photo 168). In 1647 he bought a lot of four acres in new Newbury (Newburyport) on the west side of Federal Street (earlier Chandler's Lane) from the estate of Gyles Badger (Old 150, 119). Just before his death in 1652 Somerby agreed to sell it to the eventual owner, William Chandler, a sale that was completed by his widow Judith Coffin in 1654 Ips. Deeds 3:24 (17) in Old 150). Backing up to this he had another four acre lot in 1648, on the east side of State Street (then Greenleaf's Lane) which went to Edward Richardson by 1660 (Old 146, 119). Currier tells of the local tradition that before his death Henry built the rear part of the Tristram Coffin house, where she was living as a widow on remarriage to Coffin (Old 170; photo 168). When built, it probably faced south, with the present side door in front.

He died Newbury 2 Oct. 1652 (YR 726), age only 40. He died intestate, for his widow Judith petitioned the court to give their son Daniel six acres in the little field and half the marsh and meadow and £ 5 when he was 18, and their two daughters Sarah and Elizabeth £ 13 and *a* noble (6 shillings 8 pence) when they were 16 (Essex Ct. Rec. 3:46 in EP 1:150; EQ 1:271) . The inventory was taken 6 Nov. by his wife's father, Edmund Grenlefe, his brother Anthony and Richard Browne, coming to a total of £ 164/4, mostly of the house £ 45, and 25 acres of land, £ 29. The only distinctive sign of the inn's furnishings is "a copper and brewing vessels" £ 6/10. Debts came to £ 62 (EQ 1:271-2). When the estate of Elizabeth Lowell came to probate Judith testified that her husband Sumerby bought five pewter platters marked IL, I^{M}L, I^{E}G, I^{E}G, IG, a mortar and two blankets..."worth about £ 5 which she thought he had bought from Thomas Miller, and they had belonged to Mrs. Lowell" (EQ 4:380).

THE GREENLEAF FAMILY

Henry Somerby was the first husband of Judith Greenleaf, born Ipswich, Suffolk, 2 Sept. 1625, and baptized St. Margaret's Ipswich 29 Sept. 1626 (Reg. 122:31). She was daughter of Capt. EDMUND[I] GREENLEAF, a silk dyer, perhaps the one baptized at St. Mary's la Tour, Ipswich 2 Jan. 1594 (Origins gives 1574, which is too early for the immigrant) , the son of JOHN[A] and MARGARET GREENLEAF (of Brixham, Devon, Rolfe 9-10; Origins 396 and Topo 155 give Ipswich). Another possible parent is EDMUND[A] GREENLEAF of Street Mary-at-the-Tower, Ipswich, whose wife Elizabeth is named in a suit of her half-brother Richard Fryeth alias Norman against her mother Agnes widow of John Fryeth alias Norman (who died Sept. 1590) over land in St. Marys Parish, Ipswich in 1603 (PRO Court of Requests, unindexed records, Bundle 466 in Origins 396; Reg. 38:299).

The name Greenleaf is unusual in England, appearing only in Ipswich, so Cutter states that it is a French Huguenot name Feuillevert who were refugees from the revocation of the Edict of Nantes in 1685, which is an obvious error (Cutter 638) . John Greenleaf Whittier repeated the origin of the name in his poem, "A Name", which starts:

The name the Gallic exile bore,
Street Malo! from thy ancient mart,d Became
upon our Western shore
Greenleaf for Feuillevert."

Whittier later admitted that he was not sure they came from St. Malo, but since many Huguenots left from there he took the liberty (letter quoted in Greenleaf 189).

If there is any basis for the claim that they were Huguenots, it would be during the persecutions prior to the Edict of Nantes in 1598, which culminated in the St. Bartholomew's Day Massacre of 1573. That would be a more likely approximate date for emigration to England. Origins in France might be sought in Huguenot centers like La Rochelle and Paris. Edmund's unusual skill of silk-dyer suggests that he may have been a recent immigrant among the skilled textile workers driven from France.

The family name is variously spelled GREENLEAFE, GREENLEF, GREENLEIFE, GREENLIF, GREENLIFE, GREENLYF, GRENLEFE, GRENLIFF, GRINLEAF, etc. in early colonial records. Among the family heirlooms said to have come from England with Edmund Greenleaf is a cane with a silver band near the head, with initials "J. G.", perhaps his father's, John, a name given to Edmund's first son (Cutter 638; Reg. 122:30; James E. Greenleaf, *Genealogy of the Greenleaf Family* [Boston: Frank Wood, 1896], [hereinafter Greenleaf], 71).

It was long supposed that Edmund's wife was Sarah Dole, but it has been proven that he married at Langford, Essex 1611 SARA MOOR (Boyd Marriage Index, Women's Vol. 33 in Reg. 122:28, correcting Reg. 38:100) . She was baptized 13 Dec. 1588 at All Saints, Maldon, Essex. She is named as wife of Edmund Grinleaf of Ipswich, Suffolk in the will of her brother, which also names their father ENOCH[A] MORE of Haverhill, West Suffolk in 1615. Enoch, baptized St. Peter's, Maldon, Essex 19 Jan. 1560/1, married a CATHERINE 23 Nov. 1585 at All Saints,

Maldon, who was buried there 11 Oct. 1593. He was son of NICHOLAS[B] (buried Maldon 8 Oct. 1594) and WILLAMIN MOORE (buried 20 July 1606) of Fulbridge Street, Maldon, a seaport in central Essex.

Greenleaf was the main military leader of Newbury, as Captain of the militia, for which he was also to superintend production of saltpeter "in some out house for poultry, or the like" (Historical 76). An early leader of the Newbury train band, Edmund was appointed head of one of the four militia companies 15 June 1638 (document signed by our ancestors Thomas Moody and John Knight reproduced in Currier 63, Coffin 1, 26) . They were required to have the militiamen show up on Sundays and Lecture days to guard the meeting house "to stand sentinell at the doores all the time of the publick meeting" (Old 16-17; text in Currier 63). The next year he was commissioned Ensign (9 Nov. 1639 in Massachusetts Col. Rec. 1:249 cited by Historical 493), Lieutenant in 1642 and Captain in 1645 (SCW 208) . He was discharged from military service in 1647, at his request (Greenleaf 172).

Immigrant Edmund was made freeman of Newbury 13 March 1639 (Massachusetts Col. Rec. 1:375 in Historical 99). He was licensed as innkeeper "to keepe a house of intertainment." (22 May 1639 in Historical 71; renewed 28 March 1648, EQ 1:142). His home and tavern were near the town bridge of Newbury (Greenleaf 71).

Greenleaf is listed fifth of the 91 original Proprietors of Newbury in 1642 (7 Dec. 1642 in Proprietors' Book f. 44 in Coffin 291). In addition to the four acre houselot he got one of the largest grants, of 122 acres (Coffin 287) . He was given a houselot next to William Moody on the east side of the new settlement, four lots north of the Parker River (Old 14) . In 1641 he was given four stint in the Ox and Cow Common (Currier 55) . The next year the town ordered him "to send home an Indian woman" (8 Sept., Greenleaf 72) . In 1645 he was granted lot #7 next to Nicholas Noyes in the New Town of future Newburyport (Currier 88) . Yet he was one of those who protested moving the meetinghouse there, arguing mainly "it cannot be imagined that we, ould, feeble men, women and children of all sorts, can possibly many of ym goe above three miles to meeting..." (Remonstrance of 2 Jan. 1645/6 text in Coffin 44-6; Currier 87, 93; Ould 24 citing Massachusetts Arch. 10:27-30).

He was a judge, as commissioner of the general court to judge small claims in 1642, and frequently in court during the early years, usually suing or being sued for unpaid debts (*Greenleaf v. Waldron* in EQ 1:53, 109; *Paine v. Greenleaf* 1650 in EQ 1:199; *Short v. Greenleaf* 1652 in EQ 1:248) . Isaack Couzens sued him "for not delivering a colt, for which he had bargained", having asked £ 12, even shaking hands on the deal, but refused to deliver until the buyer saw the colt (EQ 1:277) . Greenleaf would not let the buyer take goods unseen!

In 1651 he sold his house on the farm of 150 acres of upland and 50 acres of meadow in Newbury on the other side of Little River, bounded on the south by John Hull and a creek of 8 score rods, on the east by Richard Kent, divided in the marsh by a creek and a trench running from the creek to the upland of Richard Dole, and north from the trench to the new highway (deed 22 May 1651 in EQ 5:225n) . In 1653 he sold his Newbury house with the still and fixtures, located on an acre at the corner of two streets, east of Tristram Coffin Jr., north of Stephen Swett to Capt. Paul White (Currier 262, Ould 177 citing Ips. Deeds 1:143 (402).

Greenleaf and his wife Sarah moved about 1650 to Boston, where he established his silk-dying shop "by the spring" on 30 July 1655 (Cutter 638; Pope 199; Reg. 6:102). The Spring was located south of High Street (today's Washington Street), at Spring Lane (maps 1640-50 in Whitehill 9, 10). His house was just south of that of merchant Peter Oliver which faced west onto Washington Street, and was on land that Greenleaf had bought from Henry Webb (SD 11:308) . Spring Street was "a narrow lane leading from the market to the spring", at the southwest end of which was Greenleaf's, below the property which Robert and Penelope Turner left to their son

Joseph who sold it in a deed witnessed by Greenleaf in 1670 (SD 6:200, 200a, 223).

He also owned 46 acres of land in Malden which he had bought with a new house from William Luddington, and then gave to his eldest son Enoch in 1663 (10 July, Msx Deeds 8:2 quoted by Greenleaf 75-6; also mortgage of 1683 in Msx Deeds 8:425; Hoyt 183).

He continued to have business in Newbury, as shown in the suit by his attorney Robert Lord Sr. against Nathaniel Boulter "For withholding two calves, two muskets and a bushel of Indian corn, taken by execution and appraised." (March 1662, EQ 2:358). He lost a suit by John Godfrey for an old debt that the plaintiff had tried to collect in 1659, claiming he had sold him some English goods, "kersey and stuff", worth £ 11 that our ancestor Thomas Hale Sr. had given to Godfrey about 1642 for a heifer (EQ 3:370).

Sarah (Moore) Greenleaf died in Boston 18 Jan. 1662/3 (CD 130:86).

Greenleaf then married secondly and unhappily to Sarah (Jurdaine) Hill, baptized St. Mary Arches, Exeter, 4 March 1598, daughter of Ignatius Jurdaine of Exeter, England and his wife Elizabeth Baskerville, and widow (perhaps of a Wilson) , and William Hill of Fairfield CT. whom she had married in Exeter 28 Oct. 1619 (Origins 3:654, and Reg. 38:300, 49:493, 50:398). His quarrels with his step-children are recorded in "a queer memoranda" appended to his will on Christmas Day 1668 (quoted in Coffin 393; Cutter 639; Greenleaf 190, 73).

Greenleaf died in Boston 24 March 1670/1 (**VR** ; Hoyt 183), leaving a will of 22 Dec. 1668, proved 12 April 1671 which mentions our ancestor Judith Coffin (Suff. Pro. 1667-74, 112 per Greenleaf 72; Cutter 638; Pope 199) . The inventory came to £ 131/5/9 (Greenleaf 73).

Edmund Greenleaf was ancestor of many notable Americans. The most famous was the Quaker poet John Greenleaf Whittier (1807-92; John^{4} Whittier, son of Sarah^{5} Greenleaf, Nathaniel^{4}, Tristram^{3}, Stephen^{2}, Greenleaf 156, 451; thus fifth cousin of our Jemima Hidden).

He was great-grandfather of the father of the Gerrymander, U. S. Vice President (1812-14), Massachusetts Governor Elbridge Gerry (1744-1814), Signer of the Declaration of Independence, and Member of the Constitutional Convention, and American diplomat to France in the XYZ Affair (1797)(his mother was Elizabeth^{4}, Enoch$^{3-2}$; Greenleaf 77; Ency Brit, 11th ed. 11:903-4).

Joseph^{5} Greenleaf (1720-1809; William^{4}, Enoch$^{3-2}$) Revolutionary Patriot, author of the Abington Resolves and Chairman of the Boston Committee of Correspondence (Greenleaf 77; Reg. 30:382) . His son Thomas^{6} Greenleaf (1755-98; Joseph^{5},etc.) was a noted Boston printer 1773-85, then owner of the *New York Journal* (1787 ff.) (DAB 7:584-5). Moses^{7} Greenleaf (1777-1834; Moses^{6}, Jonathan^{5}, Daniel^{4}, John^{3}, Stephen^{2}) was noted Maine mapmaker and author of book on Indian languages (DAB 7:582-3). His brother Simon^{7} (1783-1853) as associate of Justice Story helped make Harvard Law School famous (DAB 7:583-4). Benjamin^{7} Greenleaf (1786-1864; Caleb^{6}, Timothy^{5}, John^{4}, Samuel^{3}, Stephen^{2}) was the first person to give popular lectures on science, as teacher at Bradford Academy and founder of Bradford Teachers Seminary. He was author of widely used texts like *National Arithmetic* (1836) (DAB 7:581). Halbert^{9} Greenleaf (1827-1906), son of another textbook author, Jeremiah^{8} (1791-1864; Daniel^{7}, Stephen^{6}, Dr. Daniel^{5}, Rev. Daniel^{4}, Stephen$^{3-2}$) founded Yale & Greenleaf Lock Co. in 1861 and headed its successor companies. In the Civil War he was Colonel of the 52d Massachusetts Infantry which fought in the Gulf Campaign. He served as U.S. congressman (Democrat) 1882-4, 1890-2 (DAB 7:581-2). Also descended from Edmund was the painter and poet Christopher P. Cranch (1813- ; Anna^{6}, Hon. William^{5}, Rev. Daniel^{4}, Stephen$^{3-2}$) Greenleaf 104).

Five months after Somerby's death, Judith (Greenleaf) remarried Newbury 2 March

1652/3 (VR 112) to Deacon Tristram[2] Coffin, Jr. (1632-1704) , by whom she had two ancestors of Anne Garrison Gould. Sharing the common ancestor Judith Greenleaf makes Anne ninth cousin of James Gould. Judith Coffin died Newbury 15 Dec. 1705 (VR 570), age 79. She is buried in old Town Cemetery under a stone with this epitaph: "To the memory of Mrs. Judith, late virtuous wife of Deac. Tristram Coffin, Esqr., who having lived to see 177 of her children and children's children to the 3d generation died Dec. 13, 1705, ae. 80//

Graue, sober, faithful, fruitfull vine was she,
A rare example of true piety.
Widow'd awhile she wayted, wished-for rest
With her dear husband in her Savior's breast." (Spelling and punctuation of Coffin 402, not Greenleaf 75).

THE NOYES FAMILY

The mother of our Jemima[5] Moody, and wife of Oliver[4] Moody was MARTHA[4] NOYES. She was born Newbury between 1706 and 1710 (Henry & Harriette Noyes, *The Noyes Descendants...Descendants of Nicholas*, [Boston: author, 1904], [hereinafter Desc.], 1:53, 204); not in VR , which gives Martha born 14 March 1696/7, dau. of Timothy and Mary VR 364; she married Thomas Smith) to JOHN[3] NOYES and his wife who was his first cousin MARY[3] NOYES, to whom we will return.

We have not found when Martha (Noyes) Moody died.

Her father John[3] Noyes was born Newbury 15 Nov. 1674 to CUTTING[2] NOYES and his wife ELIZABETH[3] KNIGHT (VR 362; EQ 5:440), who were married in Newbury 25 Feb. 1673 (VR 355). John was a cordwainer like his father, that is, worker in leather. He married his first cousin, Mary[3] Noyes, daughter of his uncle John[2], deceased, declaring their intentions at Newbury 6 April 1700 (VR 358; Reg. 55:197). He inherited the south part of the family homestead. John's house in 1729 was on the east side of High Street, at the north end of the village (map #92, Old 393). His will of 1 Feb. 1745/6 must have been made shortly before his death at age 71 (not in VR; Desc. 204; Reg. 55:197), for the estate was inventoried 22 March 1746, and on 24 March his widow Mary was made administratrix of his estate. His daughter Martha Moody is named. The estate was a mere £ 76, mostly in six acres of pasture and 1¼ salt meadow. His widow's death was not recorded in Newbury, but she was 70 at his death, and probably did not remarry.

CUTTING[2] NOYES was born in Newbury 23 Sept. 1649 (VR 358), the fifth of 14 children of founder NICHOLAS[1] NOYES and his wife MARY[2] CUTTING who were married about 1640 (Coffin 204). Cutting Noyes was a cordwainer, or leather worker. In 1673 he made a property agreement with his parents (ED 27:8, 1 April 1673 per Desc. 46). When he was ten his grandfather Capt. Cutting had left him the Thomas Bloomfield farm of 50-75 acres and house valued at £ 300 in care of his mother (EP 1:309, below).

He was made freeman 9 Jan. 1673/4 (Massachusetts Col. Rec. 4, ii/587; sworn 31 March, Ips. Ct. Rec. 2:240 cited by Currier 102; EQ 5:288) . He was 29 when he took the oath of allegiance in 1678 (Currier 179). He was on the grand jury for 1683 and 1684 (EQ 9:86, 103, 168). In 1686 he was on the committee that recommended how to divide the common land (Currier 210) . He was Selectman 1686 (Currier 112), and in that office signed the town petition to Gov. Andros to appoint an official to confirm titles (5 Jan. 1686/7 in Currier 200). He also served as Deacon of the first parish church.

He also served as Captain-Lieutenant of the militia (Reg. 55:196; SCW 348). However, his small bill of 3 sh. 8 d. in 1678 indicates short service in King Philip's War (EQ 6:454). In 1690 he was elected by the militia company as its Lieutenant (2 Dec. 1690 in Historical 499) . I am unsure if it is Cutting who was the captain Noyes of Newbury who was thanked by Major

Robert Pike for "preservation of our towns of Salisbury and Amesbury in the day of our distress by assaults of the enemy" when "dunt" (saying no) "which is common pay in the country, may//hinder any advised man from doing thayr duty..." (1691 in Coffin 155-6; perhaps Capt. Thomas Noyes, 166) . By 1712 he had a company of "snowshoo men" in the North Essex Regiment who had to "keep snow-shoes and mogginsons" (22 Sept. 1712 from Massachusetts Arch. 71:495-8 in Currier 542).

Cutting was 29 when he took the oath of allegiance at Newbury in 1678 (EQ 7:156). In 1688 he was assessed for four houses, 16 acres of plowland, 30 acres of meadow, four acres of pasture, two horses, four oxen, nine cows, ten calves, 33 sheep and six hoggs (Dec. Noyes in Currier 203) . In 1709 he had land at Indian Hill in West Newbury next to the Poores (Old 350 citing book 32/185). In 1724 a lane that is now Middle Street was laid out thru his land in downtown Newburyport (ED 42:247 in Old 629).

He was one of five town representatives who signed the deed confirming the purchase of 10,000 acres from the Indians for a mere £ 10 (10 Jan. 1700/1 in Currier 185; Coffin 364). He served five terms as Deputy to the General Court in Boston, 1704, 1709, 1710, 1711 and 1712, for which the town paid him four shillings per diem (Currier 680).

Cutting was a pallbearer for Rev. Samuel Sewall's mother in 1701 (Diary 14 Jan. in Old 251). He was wealthy enough to own a slave, for in 1713 he sold Richard Kelly "a Spanish ingon boy named Sesor...under 10 yers old" for £ 38 (Currier 254).

Cutting Noyes died Newbury 25 Oct. 1734, age 85 (VR 673) . His will of 16 July 1730 was proved 18 Nov. 1734, leaving the south half of his house to eldest son John[3], to be used by his wife as long as she is a widow (Reg. 55:196). John also got half of other properties, including Indian Hill.

NICHOLAS[1] NOYES was born in Cholderton, Wiltshire (8 miles north of Salisbury) about 1614 (age 60 in 1674, Ips. Deeds 4:187; age about 55 in Nov. 1671, EQ 4:433; 63 in April 1679 EQ 7:165n) the son of Rev. WILLIAM[A] NOYES (c. 1568-d. 1616) and his wife ANN(IE) PARKER. The name is variously spelled NOIC, NOICE, NOIES, NOIS, NOISE, NOISS, NOYCE, NOYS or NOYSE. The name seems to have rhymed with Choice, as epitaphs on two family gravestones in the first parish burying ground show (Daniel d. 1716, Timothy d. 1718, in Historical 114, 115).

On the basis of a coat of arms on the gravestone of Nicholas's nephew, Rev. James Noyes, in Palmer burying ground, Connecticut, dated 1720 (facsim. in Desc. 17), the Noyes family in America has claimed arms similar to the Noy family of Cornwall and Noyes of East Mascalls, Sussex: Azure 3 crosses crosslett in bend argent (James A. Noyes in Desc. 16-19). The pretention to gentry seems to be upheld by his fellow colonists, who referred to him as "Mr. Nicholas Noyes of Newbury, gent." (Essex Q. file 3:35 in EP 1:215) . The same title is used in a power of attorney given him by Thomas Noyes of Sudbury in Essex court files (20 Sept. 1656, EQ 1:407).

Rev. William[A] Noyes was eldest son of Robert[B] Noyes, yeoman of Cholderton, born there about 1518, and died after 17 Nov. 1577. He married before 1568 when he was about 50 to a woman whose name is unknown.

Robert was the second son of Nicholas[C] Noyes, probably born Littleton, Hampshire about 1496, and died Cholderton about 1575. He inherited land in Cholderton, Wilts, from his father, and lived there while the family contested their right to the manor of Littleton. He married about 1515 a woman whose name is unknown.

Nicholas was younger son of Robert[D] Noyes, born Littleton parish, Kimpton, Hampshire about 1465, and died there about 1524. In 1516 he leased the manor of Littleton from the Abbey of St. Peter's, Gloucester. He married about 1488 JOAN MONDEY?, perhaps sister of William Mondey; she died after making her will 15 Oct. 1532. Robert may have been son of Thomas

Noyes of Littleton about 1490, the first of the name in the Kimpton area. He was cousin of the wealthy Noyeses of Urchfont, Wilts., who married into the minor gentry. The name is commonly spelled NOYSE.

Rev. William became rector of Cholderton in 1602, a post in which he was succeeded by his son Nathan, and later by the famous William Stubbs. William entered University College, Oxford 15 Nov. 1588 at age 20, and received his BA 31 May 1592 (Reg. Univ. Oxon. 2:166, 3:171 cited by Reg. 53:35) . He died intestate before 30 April 1622, the date of his inventory. His widow was appointed administratrix 28 May 1622.

About 1595 he married ANN PARKER, sister of Rev. Robert Parker (c.1564-1614), a family that one source claims to have born arms, though his parents and birth are unknown in *Dictionary of National Biography* (DAB 15:269-70; David Smith & Paul Reed, "Four Generations of English Ancestry for the Noyes Families of New England", Reg. 149 (April 1995), 105 ff.; Ann's brother Cuthbert, Gent, of Whitchbury, Wilts, and Nether Clatford, S.Hants, note 45; Withington suggested without proof that Rev. Robert might be related to the Essex yeoman Robert Parker of Rumford, who names a son Robert in his will of 1591, Origins 3:432). Mather's Magnalia called Robert one of the greatest scholars of the English nation (Rolfe). He was surely an influential Puritan minister and theologian. His son Rev. Thomas Parker, was the Puritan minister who led a company of parishioners to found Newbury. Ann (Parker) Noyes's will of 18 March 1655 was proved London 21 April 1658 mentions her son Nicholas, "now of New England" (Wooton 130 at Somerset House per Noyes Desc. 18) . She was born 1575 and was buried at Cholderton 7 March 1657/8, age 82.

Our Nicholas came over on the *Mary & John,* under Capt. Robert Sayres, out of Southampton 24 March 1633/4, arriving in Boston May 1634 (Banks Planters 110, citing Drake 70-1; from London per Reg. 1855:265). He was one of the first settlers of Newbury, and the first person to leap ashore, on the north bank of the Quascacunquen (Parker) River, about 100 rods below where the bridge was in 1845 (Ould 10; Coffin 15; Emery 112).

He came over with his brother Rev. James Noyes, Oxford graduate, and later pastor of Old North Church, Boston. It is James's house on Parker Street Newbury, built about 1646, that is the oldest in town (Ould 166). Among James's children was Sarah (Noyes) Hale, accused of witchcraft in 1692, and ancestor of Revolutionary hero Nathan Hale (Coffin 533).

Nicholas had one of the first houselots in Old Town, the first on High Street, running south to the Parker River (Ould 14).

Nicholas was involved in liberal politics all his life. One of his first acts was in 1637, when he walked the 40 miles to Cambridge to qualify as freeman and vote for Governor Winthrop rather than the unpopular Sir Henry Vane (Coffin 23 citing Sewall's Diary). He was made freeman in Cambridge 17 May 1637 (Massachusetts Col. Rec. 1:373 in Currier 99, 41).

Nicholas was fined 2/6 "for being absent from the towne meeting, having lawful warning, and so forth." (21 April 1638). But he evidently went back to England in 1638 and returned the next year on the *Jonathan* with Anthony Somerby, first schoolmaster and town clerk (Currier 311n, 395; trip per deposition of Peter Noyes in Blanchard case, Salem 1652, Reg. 32:407 in Pope 333). The scandalous conduct of Henry and Hannah "Strumpet" Phelps on that voyage came out in a court case in which Noyes testified about a collection taken up for Thomas Blanchard of Charlestown while they were waiting for a month to sail from London (EQ 1:268) .

He is listed with the original 91 Proprietors of the town (Coffin 292) . In 1642 he was given

4 shares of the ox and cow common (Currier 54). In 1645 he was given lot #6 in the New Town of what became Newburyport, which was exchanged for "an house lot at the new town joyning South Street" (Currier 88-9) . The old homestead was still standing in 1903 when it was owned by Nathaniel Little. In 1663 he owned land southwest of the mill at Little River, in 1896 known as Four Rock Bridge (Deeds 11:196 (361) in Old 104) .

John Lowell named him one of five "Christian deare Loving freinds & brethren" to be his executor and administrator and "be the overseers of my wife & children in a freindly Christian way...", a task that was not completed until 1684 (1647, EQ 5:327; 9:410; 1:118).

In 1654 he received a curious legacy. Richard Kent Sr. gave "the first Samon that is caught in my wire, yearly to m^{r} Noice. . .til my sonne be of the age nineteene" (Essex Pro. 15,378 in EP 1:187).

In 1646 the town appointed him to replace Capt. Cutting on the committee of two dealing with the new settlement (Currier 91, 92). In 1648 and 1675 he was on the prudential committee of the town (Currier 109, 111). He was appointed Clerk of the Market in 1651 (EQ 1:233).

Nicholas's interest in education is shown in the fact that he was on the committee to build and manage the first school in town in 1652 (EQ 2:70n; Currier 395; Coffin 56). In 1677 he and Daniel Pierce were elected to find a new schoolmaster (Currier 397).

He was a signer of the petition of 1666 on the Charter (Currier 176). He also signed the petition for confirmation of land titles in 1682 (Currier 194).

It is clear that Nicholas was respected for his judicial temperament. As early as 1652 he was serving as Commissioner in the land case involving William Moody described above (Sept. 1652, EQ 1:262-3). In 1654 he was appointed one of the special commissioners to hear the petition in favor of Lt. Robert Pike, who had defended religious freedom of the Quakers (EQ 1:367; Historical 163-4 citing Massachusetts Col. Rec. 4:i/194). He had served on grand jury in 1646, 1648 and 1649 (EQ 1:103, 146, 164), in the special jury for Mr. Samuel Symonds in 1647 (EQ 1:124), and trial jury for 1651 (EQ 1:210). For most of 15 years 1654-68, and again 1673-7 and 1681 he was Commissioner to end small causes, that is, a small claims judge (Currier 104-6; EQ 1:336, 420; 8:232). In 1657 he was appointed arbitrator in a dispute about roads (Currier 420) . He was often appointed arbitrator in disputes of neighbors (EQ 4:12). In 1678 the town made him one of the commissioners to go to the Ipswich court to settle a dispute with Richard Dummer (Currier 650).

Nicholas Noyes was chosen Selectman in 1678, 1681, 1684 (Currier 111-2). He was one of the first Tithingmen in 1679, and served again in 1680, 1683 and 1686 (Currier 117-8). When a stranger, "a Jarsie man", Peeter Youter died casually in Newbury, the court made him administrator of his estate (1683, EQ 9: 23). And when a black woman named Juneper asked to live in Newbury, the Selectmen appointed Noyes its attorney to see that she obeyed their order to leave town (1683 EQ 9:105).

Clearly one of the leaders of the church, Noyes joined the selectmen in building new seats in the church (1660, EQ 4:139). Nicholas was a member of the conservative faction supporting the founding minister Rev. Parker and his assistant Rev. Woodbridge, along with Thomas Hale and John Knight Jr. (13 March 1669 in Coffin 74; 23 March 1670, Coffin 86) . He was major witness against Edward Woodman's attempt to censure Rev. Parker in 1670 (EQ 4:359-67). He became Deacon of the church 20 March 1683/4, and as such was chosen by the town as one of three Overseers of the Poor (21 Nov. 1686, Coffin 147). He was Moderator of a town meeting to choose a new minister in 1685 (Currier 332).

He was four times Representative to the General Court in Boston, 1660, 1679, 1680 and 1681 (Currier 677, 679; Reg. 53:36). He was Newbury Selectman in 1681 (EQ 8:148).

Although in his sixties he put in long service in King Philip's War, shown in his bill for quartering 3 sh., post to Rowley 9 sh. (EQ 6:446), horc & man 3 d., Andiver 5 sh., horc hier 4 sh. 8 d., p[ro]vi[sions] 6:1, Quartering 16 m[onths] 8 sh., gun 26 sh. 8 d., home 1 sh., totalling £ 2/10/9 (EQ 6:453), and 3 days & his mare to Andiver 1 sh. 3 d. (EQ 6:456). At age 63 Nicholas was excused from service in the militia in King Philip's War, on condition of paying a bushel of Indian corn each year (EQ 7:263-4) .

1698 he deeded property to his grandson Nicholas (ED 15:41).

Just before his death, at 85, he was pallbearer for his old friend Henry Sewall (Diary of Samuel Sewall 17 May 1700 in Old 250). Sewall referred to him in his book *New Heaven upon the New Earth* (1697) as witness to the sermon of founding pastor Parker saying that the first settlers "came over upon good Grounds, and that God would multiply them as he did the children of Israel. His text was Exodus 1:7. And the children of Israel were fruitful and increased abundantly, and multiplied, and waxed exceeding might; and the land was filled with them." (Coffin 368).

Nicholas died in Newbury 23 Nov. 1701, age 86 (Sewall Diary 1:458; not in VR; Desc. 46; Coffin 312 gives age 83), having made his will 4 July 1700, proved 29 Dec. 1701 (Essex Pro. 307:233, 336). He left a large estate worth £ 2,691, of which £ 1531 was personal estate, and £ 1160 real estate.

One of the leading ministers who examined the accused witches was Rev. Nicholas[2] Noyes (1647-1717) of Salem, elder son of Nicholas[1] and brother of our Cutting Noyes (Desc. 49; Sav. 3:297-8; Reg. 53:37). When seven women and an alleged wizard were hung on Gallows Hill 22 Sept. 1692 Rev. Noyes declared, "What a sad thing to see eight firebrands of hell hanging there." (Robert Calef, *More Wonders of the Invisible World* in Burr's *Narratives of the Witchcraft Cases,* 369 cited by Marion Starkey, *The Devil in Massachusetts* [N.Y.: Knopf, 1949], 213) . At the hanging of five others on 19 July Noyes pressed Sarah Good to confess, since she knew she was a witch. Sarah replied: "You're a liar! I am no more a witch than you are a wizard! If you take my life away, God will give you blood to drink." (Calef 358 in Starkey 176) . Nicholas had the previous distinction of being the Chaplain at the Great Swamp Fight of 19 Dec. 1675, the slaughter that ended the first war against the Native Americans.

There are three descendants of Nicholas of the Noyes name who are notable in American history. Crosby S. Noyes (1875-1905) was publisher and editor of the *Washington Star* (DAB 7:586). Prof. George R. Noyes (1798-1868), Unitarian clergyman, was Professor of Oriental Languages at Harvard, and 30 years leader of Harvard Divinity School (DAB 7:587-8) . The most famous is John H. Noyes (1811-86) founder of the Utopian Oneida community in 1848 (DAB 7:589).

There are three well-known Noyeses descended from Nicholas's brother James, and also Lydia's cousins. Edwin F. Noyes (1832-90) was Governor of Ohio and Minister to France (DAB 7:587). LaVerne Noyes (1849-1919) was an inventor of farm machinery (DAB 7:590). Lawyer William C. Noyes (1805-64) was an endower of Hamilton College in New York state, and a delegate to the Washington Peace Conference that tried to settle the quarrel between the states in 1861 (DAB 7:592).

THE CUTTING FAMILY

In common New England onomastic (naming) practice, Cutting Noyes was named for his mother, MARY[2] CUTTING, who married Nicholas[1] Noyes about 1640, and died Newbury before 1700. Mary was accused of violating the Puritan sumptuary laws by wearing a silk hood and scarf, but she was able to prove that her husband was worth over £ 200, and won acquittal (Sept. 1653, EQ 1:303; Reg. 149:120; Historical 122; Coffin 58). Mary was evidently educated, for we have her signature on a court document defending Henry Greenland against charges of adultery with Mary Rolfe in 1663 (EQ 3:53).

Mary Noyes was the daughter of Capt. JOHN[1] CUTTING, shipmaster of London, and Newton, Wiltshire (the most common English place name, of which there are three in Wilts, per Ekwall). Pope lists him as "gent." for reasons unknown (128) . He had come to Newbury about 1642 from Charlestown, originally London (Coffin 300) . He died Newbury 20 Nov. 1659 (VR 577).

The town historian states: "He was a man of a great deal of humor, and many stories are told to this day (1845) concerning his peculiarities, which afforded much diversion to himself and others, but which want of room compels me to omit." (391).

Capt. Cutting crossed the Atlantic 13 times, including a voyage of 1637 in which he carried the Indian captive Pequot to England (Winthrop cited by Hidden Mem. 142; Coffin 391) . He was master of the *Francis of* Ipswich which left there the last of April 1634 (Banks Planters 121 citing PRO). Cutting was master of the ship *Advent* of Boston 19 Oct. 1647 (Pope 128 citing "A."). In 1653 he carried letters from Robert Keene to the proprietors of the Saugus Ironworks in London on his ship *John Adventure* (EQ 2:75).

He was listed seventh of the original proprietors of Newbury in 1642, and received the seventh largest grant of land, 220 acres plus house lot of four acres (Coffin 291, 287; Currier 84). One of his first appearances in Essex County was in Salem court where he sued Henry Sewell (27 Dec. 1642, EQ 1:45).

His maritime occupation naturally drew him to the Merrimac side of town, and he was on the town committee of eight to consider removing to what became Newburyport in 1642 (Coffin 36) . This committee decided to give four acre lots available for four years (Coffin 37). Capt. Cutting received a large grant of land in Newbury, a farm of 200 acres north of the Falls River and east of Greenleaf (Currier 64). He was among the settlers who got lots in what was to become Newburyport in 1645, "an house lot at the new town joyning Hill Street" (Currier 89), and actually moved there (Ibid. 90). Cutting's land was south of Woodland Street (Poor's Lane 1707, Currier 438). He was on the Newbury committee of 2 Jan. 1646 that settled the location of the meetinghouse on the knoll by Abraham Toppan's barn, that is, at the northwest corner of the first burial ground (Coffin 44, Old 93, Currier 86). He sold his Newbury lands to John Hull 20 June 1651 (Pope 128).

He bought a house in Charlestown in 1648 from John Alien, formerly Thomas Cortmore's land, lying north of the town common, between the common on the east and highway on the west, and south of Robert Cooke (SD 1:92 in Wyman 17, 271). He had power of attorney to sell land in Dedham in 1651 for shoemaker Ferdinando Adams of St. Katherine's, London (SD in Wyman 271).

Captain Cutting obviously had some un-Puritan habits. In 1659 he was brought before Ipswich court and fined "for taking tobacco in bell yard", and "respitted till court takes further notice." (EQ 2:149).

John Cutting died Newbury 20 Nov. 1659 (Essex Pro. 6,984 in EP 1:309; EQ 2:182n). His will made 22 Oct. 1659 mentions "my Daughter Mary the wife of Nicholas Noyes" (Reg. 53:36) to whom he left £ 5 a year, and her son Cutting Noyes who got the house and 55 acres east of the highway then in possession of Thomas Bloomfield. The inventory taken 16 Dec. found a goodly estate worth £ 737, mostly in real estate: £ 100 for his house and 12 acres of land and 20 acres of saltmarsh (which he left to his daughter Sara Browne); £ for the house of John Davis with 25 acres of pasture and plowland and six acres of meadow (which went to his granddaughter Mary Moody); £ 300 for the farm rented by Thomas Bloomfield containing 70 to 75 acres of upland, meadow and pasture; £ 132 for livestock.

His widow Mary remarried shortly to John Miller (Pope 128; Walter Goodwin Davis 1:360 assumed that this was Rev. John Miller), who joined with her in selling land that Cutter had bought from Stephen Dummer, the buyer being her son-in-law Nicholas Noyes (Pope citing Topsfield records). Miller died soon afterwards (12 June 1663, Groton VR 2:245), as shown in her will of 26 Nov. 1663, in which she mentions her daughter Mary the wife of Nicholas Noyes (Essex Pro. 18,445 In EP 1:437). Her estate came to £ 79, mostly in livestock, but also a silver spoon, a silver wine cup and a silver dram cup worth £ 1 (Ibid., 438). MARY MILLER died Newbury 6 March 1663 (VR 2:660; Coffin 300) at age 80.

THE KNIGHT FAMILY OF NEWBURY

Cutting[2] Noyes married Newbury 25 Feb. 1673 (VR 355; EQ 5:260) ELIZABETH[3] KNIGHT, born Newbury 18 Oct. 1655 (VR 267) to JOHN[2] KNIGHT Jr. and BATHSHEBA[2] INGERSOLL of whom more below. Elizabeth died Newbury 20 Jan. 1746/7 (VR 674), at age 92, one of the oldest persons in town (Coffin 404).

John[2] Knight was born about 1622-5 in England (Newbury, Berks.?; 1622, deposed age about 47 in Nov. 1669 EQ 4:207; about 48 in Jan. 1671, EQ 4:332; about 50 in Sept. 1673, EQ5:224n; about 50 March 1675, EQ 6:11n; about 51 in March 1676, EQ 6:125n, 128n; about 51 June 1676, EQ 6:165n; 48 in Nov. 1683, EQ 9:108n), son of pioneer JOHN[1] KNIGHT Sr. and his first wife SARAH HAWKINS.

The Knights had come to Newbury from Romsey, Hampshire on *the James* on 3 June 1635, having left Southampton 5 April (Currier 32 citing Winthrop's History (1853), 1:192-3; Topo 62 cites Pope; Coffin 307).

The junior John Knight became freeman at Newbury 7 Sept. 1650 (Ips. Ct. Rec. 1:21 in Historical 100). In 1652 the town extended freehold rights to him, and he bought Richard Littlehale's rights (sale 23 Nov. in Currier 94). John Jr. was Constable in March 1654 (EQ 1:336) . The records do not clearly distinguish the father, son and grandson named John, but the senior John was active in town affairs in the thirties and forties, while we have assumed that most of the offices in the sixties and seventies were the son, even if not designated junior. We will assume that "Ensign" John Knight refers to t;he son, since the father would be in his seventies and too old for military service. He was discharged from service as a common soldier in June 1670, "having been in office in the foot company" (EQ 4:267). He is already called John Knight Sr. soon after his father's death, when he voted to support the minister Rev. Parker in the vote of censure supported by William and Caleb Moody and John Hale Jr. of the Woodman party (16 March 1671, EQ 4:359; also 30 March 1669 in Coffin 74).

In mid-century both gave the town the right of way to the mill in exchange for eight acres of saltmarsh and two other acres (Prop. Rec. 22 in Currier 415). Before his father's death in 1670 he bought two acres on the west side of the road to the New Town from Nicholas Noyes (EP 11:191).

Both father and son signed the petition about town rights in 1666 (Currier 170). They were both owed money by the manager of the Saugus ironworks for services in the fifties, one for £ 3/10 and the other, undistinguished, 10 sh. (EQ 4:392, 437).

Ensign John Knight was appointed to lay out the road to Rowley in 1668 (Currier 421, 422) . He and Tristram Coffin were appointed by the town in 1673 to measure the bounds of the large grant to Richard Dummer (EQ 6:40-1). He was lotlayer of the Higglety-Piggelty lots near

Fox Island in Salisbury before 1662 (EQ 9:108-9).

John Jr. was town Selectman in 1668 and 1669 (Currier 110), fenceviewer in 1675 (Currier 115) . In the former year he joined with the other selectmen to sign a petition to allow Capt. Paul White to draw and sell wine out of doors "for the necessary releif of Some Sick & other indigent psons by whom the Churches Exigencies haue Sundry times been Supplied", a permit that was granted for one year because no one else was licensed to keep an ordinary (EQ 4:37).

Ensign Knight was one of the elders with Nicholas Noyes, Thomas Hale Sr. and Tristram Coffin who had to handle the complaints of Edward Woodman against the minister, Rev. Parker, and testified in court that the congregation had unanimously agreed to let the minister continue (March 1669, EQ 4:124). In the vote to censure Parker, Knight was in the opposition with Thomas Hale Sr. and Nicholas Noyes (EQ 4:359), and was a major witness in the court case (EQ 4:352, 355, 363).

He was involved in trying to settle the disputes over seats in the meeting in 1667-9, Elizabeth Randall's being eldered for "disorderly carriage in the meeting house" because Daniel Lunt's wife was given a seat less good than the one next to Goody Godfrey (EQ 4:136) and John Woolcott and Peeter Tappan making disturbance over seats (EQ 4:137) .

When widow Burt was examined in court for witchcraft he confirmed other witnesses' evidence of her mysterious comings and goings by testifying that "he saw old goody burt coming out of a swamp and shee was in her smok sleeues and a blake hancacher and black cap on her head and hee looked up and suddenly shee was gone out of sight and I looked aboute and could not see her when I came into the house I found her in the same habit as I saw her and said vnto her did I not see you in the swamp even now and she sd noe I was in the house and he tould her that she was a light headed woman." (Nov. 1699, EQ 4:208).

Knight came to the defense of a friendless "simpill boy" William Harrison who was thrown into Boston prison for failure to perform service for John Wolcott and comply with arbitration. Knight stated: "whear a seruant is in any houes where no Cristian duty is performed nor Regard to Instruckt such young ons wil be bad enouf and for a seruant to be Cept almost nakd lick a hethen and left alone in his work and none luck aftr him weeck after weeck ad so munths a man Cannot xpeckt much seruis..." (Sept. 1670, EQ 4:290).

Knight's house was on the road to the Beverly ferry, near Roger Conant's (1670, EQ 4:325). This is evidently the house he inherited from his father in 1670 (EQ 4:249).

His land and frame of a house was attached in a suit of Edmond Batter against him (writ 12 March 1671, EQ 4:413).

Knight was evidently a peacemaker in the community, as shown in his petition of 1673 in the dispute over the inheritance of Abraham Tappin (EQ 5:176) . He says, "I am much trubled to hear that ouar frends old goodman [Jacob] Toppen and his son Peetor haue soch differanc between them of late which I maruell at: Considering how louingly thay haue caried it this 20 years for I haue had much Aquintance with them and Acording too my observation the old man have bin vary pessable towards all men and vary louing to peetar: peetar haue bin vary dutiful too his father and vary carfull of his bisnis when the old man was in Ingland and at the barbaos and all along vary carfull and painfull in his labor for his father at haruest tims: his tneedow liing neer min: I haue often wrought with him: and I haue obserued his dilligenc Raeth [Counsel]: and late willing too Improu all sesons for his fathers good: as it is well knouen the care of Improument of the estat lay much vpon peetar: if not all for the generall: many years and in mattrs of delling apon acounts as ther was a prety deall beetween us: I still found peetr vary sauing and carffull in acants not willing to lay much apon his on back in Respecke of cloas which I blamd him for: and tould him: seing hee had the//care apon him: his father would bee willing to let him goe hansomly in cloes and lickwies both the old pepell and the young haue seuerall titmes bin speaking of ther content in peeters mach espesially the old man seemed to bee much pleased with the conuersation of peeters wife and I am trubled too hear what I now doe and ernestly desiar the welfair of them all."

On the other hand, he would sue for trespass, as he did when he accused John Smith and Ralph Ellinwood for carrying away dung (1673, EQ 5:218). And he won a suit against Samuel Watts of Haverhill for not delivering a black horse in payment for two oxen Knight sold him in 1672 (EQ 6:334).

He was on the trial jury in 1674, 1677 and 1684 (EQ 5:269, 6:318; 9:168). In 1674 he was appointed to a committee to enforce proper use of the town common lands (Currier 137).

About Sept. 1674 Knight made a trip to England and tried to rent his new house (per James Browne and John Rogers in EQ 6:44, 45). This was shortly after he had built a house in Beverly (part of Salem) on 24 rods or pole of land he bought from the smith Jacob Pudeator (deed 24 June 1674 in ED 4;87, EQ 6:44). Among the workers he hired was Samuel Pickworth and glazier James Browne. Knight then sold the house measuring 18 by 26 to Boston merchant Richard Bronsdon (ED 4:115 in EQ 6:44). He later got a £ 20 mortgage on it from Lt. Thomas Putnam of Salem, which resulted in a suit by Putnam against Bronsdon's agent Edward Richards (who was to marry his widow) for getting the smith to help him break down the door of the empty house with a great hammer and putting on a new lock (EQ 6:43).

Knight was a soldier in active service in King Philip's War. His residence in Beverly led to a call for his service in the militia, and a warrant for his impressment by the Constable of Manchester ordering him "to appear armed and equipped at Beverlee at John Stone's on Jan. 14 [1675] by eight of the clock in the morning (EQ 6:134-5). However, his accounts for expenses were submitted in Newbury. horse hire 4 [sh.?], post Iptswich] 6 sh. 6d. (EQ 6:447) ; horse lost £ 3, saddle and belt 30 sh., 2 bridles 1 £, 1-2 powder & bullets 3 sh., sword & belt £ 10/18 sh., chease & bread 6 sh., conducting soldiers 2:6, 1 belt 4:6, hire 6 weeks 9 sh., powder & bullets (amun) 2 sh., chease 4 sh., horse hire 4 sh., totaling £ 7/3 (EQ 6:448) . When asked to give account of half of his demands (for pay?) in Feb. 1675 he asked for £ 2/11/6 (EQ 6: 449) and repeated the above list with addition of post to Ha.[verhill] & Andtdover] 3 sh., Gun 5 sh., sword & belt burnt 22 sh., Amu 2:8, 6d., p [ro] vi [sions] 4:6, snap [sack] 2:6, post marl[borough] 3 sh. 6, Quar[taring] 48 meales 24 sh., 3 horces 18 [sh.], 20 bullets 8 d., totalling 10 £ (EQ 6:452-3). To this was added a trip to Andover (1 sh. 3d., EQ 6:456).

Back home, he lost a suit as lot layer for the town against Richard Dummer for a lot east of Dummer's residence on Easson's river near Rowley Mill on the Newbury-Rowley line, Dummer having given up his claim to the land (Sept. 1675, EQ 6:64-6; map 320). Knight was sent by the town to defend it against Richard Dummer's suit in Ipswich court in 1677 (Historical 650).

Knight evidently produced barley malt, as shown in his delivery of 23 bushels to Peter Tappan's orchard for Tappan to pay an arbitral award in 1676 (*Tappan v. Haines*, EQ 6:127-8).

He was also involved in shipbuilding at William Starling's Haverhill, as shown in the suit of Baniel Ely for his service in 1674-5 to Capt. Ben. Boongrain who was to take command (EQ 6:212). This may be the ship that appears in his inventory as bound for Barbados (below).

Knight testified in court that he had paid Benjamin Thompson of Charlestown for a debt to the accused witch John Godfrey, who maintained that Thompson had gotten his estate "by fradelant meanes, my selfe and most of the company being drunke at the same time, he engageing to pay unto me for my yearly maintenance, the full & iust sum of ten pound in silver, the which was never payd to me to the value of one farthing. . .all that ever he did for me, once when I was in Boston prisson he was occastion of my being let out... (26 July 1675, EQ 6:248n; Godfrey's trial for witchcraft 1665, EQ 4:153).

George Major was branded on the forehead with a "B" for burglary and stealing meat from his neighbor Knight's (EQ 6:253-5) . At daybreak, half an hour after Knight left for Boston his negro boy James Black heard a noise and went downstairs to find Major taking pork from the kitchen and beef from the parlor. Major told him to say nothing and he would give him something he liked. When Black went to Major's house and saw the meat on the floor, Mrs. Major said "thee art a good boy Jams; said I why: I good boay. my husband tell thee anon: when he Com horn." On returning Major said "good James Cepe Counsel and when thy mastar corns home hell mis his meat and Charge thee for stelling it but tell him thee dide never giue any body a bit and thee speckist trou: then heel Com to mee and ask mee: why i did case .his neggar to steall meat for him: and I will strongly afirm I had: nara bit of meat of thee". Black said Major had asked him to steal powder and wool from Knight, and his wife asked him to take her little white bag to steal meal and sugar, etc. John Mitchell also said Major had tried to get him to steal a cheese from his master Richard Kent.

Mary and Sara Knight asked Major's girl where her mother put the meat, so the girl asked her mother about it. Her mother hit her on the mouth and said, "Husy, you shall not tell, thay shall never know whear it is and I will make it my bisnes night and day to cep [keep] her in." Later a dog was seen near Major's house eating a fresh pork leg.

Joseph Knight went to the Major's house and asked about the meat. Mrs. Major "turned pale and then blushed as red as a red cloth." He asked what meat there was in the house and she said maybe 40 pieces of pork and 4 or 5 pieces of beef. "He asked what they had lived on all winter if she had so much left now."

John Whichar (Whittier) said George Major came to their house and talking about Knight's pork said, "If I haue his pork I wish the devill might teare mee in pecces body and soalle as small as my tobacco pipe and I wish the devill would fech away John Knight boody and soalle and all that dou belong to him. Sarah Kelly, whom Mrs. Major said had given her the meat, said to George, "how dow you dare to wish such wishes dounot you knowe that god hears you: yeas said hee: but I must wish such wishes and will wish soch wishes; saide John whichar get the[e] out of dores for if thou dust follow this coarse thou wilt Com to the gallos: saide Mogior I care not If I dow I wish I wear out of the world."

Major had previous problems with the law, having been sentenced to be fined or whipped and put in prison until he paid two shillings a week for the support of a child he had by Mary Duell--Mary was whipped for fornication (1671, EQ 4:342). The summer before the pork burglary Major chased Anthony Morse's boy into the pigsty at gunpoint, and when Anthony asked him why Major "gaue mee vary bad languidg and saied 111 shute the[e] doune presently: & presente his gun at me Redy Kokd and chargd and I did loock emediatly to bee ciled: but thoro gods prouedenc wee got away his gun and then he drad his sord and swagared with it till wee got that away also." (Morse's testimony EQ 6:255n).

John Jr. died Newbury 27 Feb. 1677/8 (VR 636) without making a will and on 26 March his widow Bathshebah was made administratrix (Essex Pro. 15,983 and Ips. Ct. Rec. 5:303, 337 in EP 3:199-200; EQ 6:424). Her inventory of 15 March presented to the court 24 Sept. showed an estate of £ 1011 of which his house and barn were worth £ 100, 75 acres @ £ 5 per acre= £ 475; "a negar man" £ 25; an eighth part of a vessel and "parte of a Cargoo gon to barbados" £ 40. The unusual number of beds (5) , napkins (36) , 9 pair of sheets suggests that he may have continued his father's innkeeping. His widow petitioned the court to divide the house (worth £ 100) and land (75 acres @ £ 5 per acre) between her three sons equally, and give each of three daughters (including our Elizabeth Moody) £ 80 apiece, and the residue for her to keep and pay off the debts, which the court permitted 24 Sept. 1678 (EQ 7:93-4).

The way Bathsheba's name is spelled in records gives some clue to possible pronunciation: Borshua and Barshua (EQ 3:131, 134). She was born about 1624, in England (deposed age about 40 March 1664, EQ 3:134). This came out in her testimony in the suit of Richard Cordin versus Joseph Muzzey for a debt. She was also a witness against Richard Knight for playing cards at Hugh Marsh's house (EQ 3:70). Bathsheba(h) Knight died Newbury 24 Oct. 1705 (VR 635; Rolfe 37, 115), about 71.

The senior John[1] Knight was born in England about 1587. He was brother of another Newbury founder, Richard Knight, mercer, who came from Romsey, Hampshire, seven miles northwest of Southampton, in June 1635 in the *James* (Coffin 307) . John Knight was also a mercer, or merchant tailor. His arrival in America is marked in 1635 by his appearance as witness in Joseph Avery's case before the General Court (Pope 273). He is easily confused with three other early settlers of the same name, John of Dorchester 1634, John the tailor who came on the *James* in 1635, and John who came in the *Bevis* in 1638 (Pope 273).

Knight was one of the 91 original proprietors of Newbury (Coffin 292). In 1635 he was assigned a houselot northeast of the Meeting House in Old Newbury (Old 14). He became a Newbury freeman 25 May 1636, and the next year became an innkeeper there licensed "to keepe an ordinary and give intertainment to such as neede" (6 June 1637; Massachusetts Col. Rec. 1:140 per Historical 71, Old 21).

His tavern would have been the meeting place for the first town government. In 1638 he was chosen with four others to manage town affairs for two quarters (Currier 48). In this capacity he made an agreement with Richard Dummer to send all of his corn to be ground at Dummer's mill (Historical 38; text in Old 20-1, Coffin 27). He was also deputed to enforce the laws against demolition (Massachusetts Col. Rec. 1:168 in Historical 56-7). Coffin and Currier reproduce his signature on the town document of 15 June 1638 ordering Edmund Greenleaf and others to form a guard for the meeting house (Coffin 1, Currier 63). He was then chosen Constable for the year, and had half his taxes abated in payment (Ibid.).

In 1642 Knight was given seven shares in the ox and cow common (Currier 55). He is listed as entitled to freeholder rights in the new town in 1642 (Currier 84). When New Town (Newburyport) was laid out in 1645 he got lot #9, separated from Nicholas Noyes and Edmund Greenleaf by one lot (Currier 88). Like Noyes's his lot was designated on South Street (Currier 89). Before 1646 he gave up 20 acres of upland beyond Little River (flowing into the Great River) which had been Nathaniel Wyer's, next to William Stevens, and got five acres of upland "in the field of exchange beyond the new town", apparently west of Merrimac Ridge (EQ 1:263). A third of "Knight's farm", worth £ 20, was in the estate of James Patch Sr. in 1658 (EQ 2:108-9n).

Knight was not litigious in early years. His first appearance in court is his suit against Mr. Cobbit "For detaining a mare and her increase", but he withdrew the suit (Sept. 1648, EQ 1:147) , He was on the trial jury for 1650 and 1658, and substitute juror in Jonathan Wade's case of 1652 (EQ 1:197, 247, 2:111). He was Clerk of Newbury market in 1655 (EQ 1:387). He was a witness in the land suit of 1652 *Kent v. Moody* tried by Commissioner Nicholas Noyes which we noted above (EQ 1:262, 263).

Knight was rich enough to afford a young boy servant, William Nef, who came into court twice in 1658 and 1659 for physical abuse by fellow workers on Knight's land. Joseph Muzzey admitted striking the boy so hard on the arm it made it black (EQ 2:116-7), and the next year Muzzey testified that Mathew Moore the Scott attacked Nef for not giving up a shovel "which he refused to deliver whereupon the Scotte flew upon him & pressed him to the ground taking him by the necke put his head & heeles together and pinched him by the throate I was afraid he wold have strangled him or at least done him some great mischeife, I seeing this rescued him whereupon he gave me many reproachfull speeches chalenging me to fight and threatening me if ever he mett me alone." (EQ 2:154n).

In 1660 Knight was on the Saugus Ironworks property where our ancestor Quinton Pray had begun the first iron refining, and helped build a dam for his forge. Knight was appointed by the court to assess the damage to Adam Hawkes's land by "damming their waters so high, which was the cause of floating his lands, well and bridge, to his great damage for several years." (EQ 2:210). Knight and Thomas Wellman reported the damage at £ 10 a year "for the meadow, plow land and in floating a bridge; in the corn field, the corn had suffered much from the water; the wells were sometimes floated with the waters of the Iron works, so that when the pond was up with the waters standing in the wells, the well water was not fit for use on account of the dirt that fouled it; the damage in the orchard, in the English grass and in the tobacco lands was also great, etc." The court nevertheless denied Hawkes damages, evidently on the basis of a previous arbitration of the matter (EQ 2:211n).

Knight's signature is on the report of the inquest into the drowning of John Balch which concluded that "sd Balch beinge constrayned to leaue the Canow in which he was bound over the riuer at Salem ferrie, by reason of the violence of the winde and waue and indeauouring to returne againe to the shore died by the extremitie of the cold with the violence of the winde and rage of the sea and so perished in the water." (16 Nov. 1661, EQ 2:42ln).

His evidence was used to convict Richard Cordin of attempting to assault Mary, the wife of John Rolfe in 1663 . Knight said that when he was at his son's house the previous summer "Goodwife Rofe and Mr. Cording came in about an hour and a half after sunset." (EQ 3:55). He was on the trial jury that year (EQ 3:84), and Grand Jury 1666 and 1667 (EQ 3:344, 387).

Knight must have been known for his knowledge of horses, for the court appointed him to appraise "a gray mare three years old and an iron gray horse" in 1665 (EQ 3:354). On his way to Haveral John Burbank "asked him to stop and see how wet his hay and corn were, for the rain came in at many places in the roof" of Philip Nelson's building (1667, EQ 3:393).

His generosity is shown in two cases separated by 14 years. In the first he saved Henry Jaques's servant Frances Usell from being whipped for using the name of God profanely by paying his fine (June 1651, EQ 1:224). In 1666 by paying £ 5 fine Knight prevented Elnor Bryer from being publicly whipped after Henry Jaques was proved to have had fornication with her. She had just given birth to twins 10 Feb. after marrying Richard Bryer 21 Dec. 1665 (26 March EQ 3:309, 293, 294).

Knight signed the petition of 1663 to allow Dr. Henry Greenland to practice in town (Historical 141). Both he and his son signed the petition of 1666 on town rights (Historical 176).

He won a suit for debt of £ 6 of wheat @ 5 sh. a bushel and barley at 4 sh. 6d. @ bushel from John Woolcott, plus £ 1/11/2 costs (1666 EQ 3:346-7).

Knight was in real trouble in 1666 when Thomas Cromwell' s house burned down, and two men swore they "heard John Knight, sr., say that he was at work in the house that day and left some fire there.", but the printed record does not record the outcome of the case (EQ 3:420-1).

Either he or John Poore were to serve on the committee of 1669 to run the boundary with Rowley; the designation of Poore may indicate doubt about Knight's health (Historical 168). He died Newbury soon after 5 May 1670 (not in VR).

His will of that date starts: "being often pained in my body and know not how sudenly I may be desolued and leaue this world. . ." (Essex Pro.15,981 in EP 2:190-2; summary in EQ 4:250-1). Beside the gifts he had already "manie years sine" given his son John Jr., he gave him his house and barn with the land it was on, and orchard, also his land next to the ox common, both plowland, pasture and meadow, and 4 or 5 "akers of marrish joyning to the Creeke by the Comon on the south East", and another piece of marsh to the north of John Pike toward little Pine Island. All of this was to be given to John Jr.'s son Joseph when he comes of age. He made his son John his executor and residuary legatee, including all of his cattle. The closeness of our ancestors' families is shown by his appointing "my thre frends", his brother Richard, Thomas Hale Sr. and Nicholas Noyes as overseers of his will; they also witnessed the signature and did the inventory which came to £ 324/11/6, of which £ 220 was house, barn and orchard, 12 acres of upland and 22 of meadow. The will was proved 23 June 1670.

Coffin states that his wife Elizabeth died 20 March 1640 (307). His wife, Sarah (Hawkins) , had died before 10 Feb. 1663 when Knight was already remarried to another ancestor, An(n) (Langlye) Ingersoll (power of attorney in EQ 4:109). Ann was provided for in the will, with £ 11 a year for maintenance, and to be allowed to live in one end of his house and use his goods. The "Wid[ow] Knight" who appears in the Newbury assessment record of 1688 owning a house, eight acres of plowland, 18 of meadow and eight of pasture, etc. is Ingersoll's widow of 1644, and John Knight's widow of 1670.

The best known descendant of the name was Rev. Henry[7] C. Knight (1789-1835) , Episcopal clergyman who was Deacon of the Massachusetts church 1827 and rector in Maryland (DAB 10:466).

THE INGERSOLL FAMILY OF SALEM AND DANVERS

Bathsheba(h) or Bathsua Knight was daughter of RICHARD[1] INGERSOLL of Salem and a woman whose name is unknown and died in England before he married at St. Swithin's church in Sandy, Bedfordshire 10 [20] Oct. 1616 to AGNES LANGLYE (Reg. 90:92; Perley 310; 20th in Origins 3:453) . Agnes was a cousin of John Spencer (Spenser) of Newbury, buried at his place of origin, Kingston on Thames, Surrey, 23 June 1648 (Origins 3:458; will in Reg. 44:390). But she appears to be the first wife, the mother of our Bathsheba, for the widow in America named Ann was born about 1621.

The family name is spelled variously ENGERSON, INGARSALL, INGARSON, INGERSELL, INGERSOL, INGERSON, INGERSULL, INGOSON, INKARSALL and INKERSELL. Great Migraton 2:1061 says the family came over from Sandy, Bedfordshire (seven miles east of Bedford; citing Walter G. Davis, *Ancestry of Abel Lunt* [Portland ME: Anthoensen Press, 1963] 63). Withington said Ingersoll wills were "as scarce as hen's teeth", and could find no Ingersoll wills in Bedfordshire 1493-1660, but did find them in the next county to the north, Huntington (Origins 3:441).

Ingersoll was one of the first of our ancestors to come to America. He arrived in 1629 with Rev. Francis Higginson, and settled in Salem (Sav. 2:521, 412). Banks says they came on the *Mayflower* of Yarmouth under Capt. William Peirce from Gravesend in March 1629, arriving 15 May, citing Bradford 2:65; Perley 1:130ff.; Pope 252 cites SD 1:xvi). Ingersoll came with the recommendation of the New England Company who had hired him (letter of 3 June 1629 in Perley 1:135).

Ingersoll was one of the first settlers of Danvers, then the northwest part of Salem. Some of the most historic spots in Danvers were once owned by him, the Nourse "witch house", Danvers Common, and the future inn next to the church. Ingersoll leased the Bishop-Nourse farm west of Governor Endicott's land, where founder Townsend Byshop built a mansion of 1635, bought by Endicott in 1648, then by Francis Nurse in 1678, whose mother Rebecca Nurse was taken from the house to be hanged as a witch (Hurd 1:428, 426). There is an engraving of the house in *Essex County Historical and Genealogical Register* 49, with account of Ingersoll's lease by William Upham, 63. At the northwest corner of Ingersoll's lease is Muddy Boo, the site of ancient wolf pits (angle of Prince Street in 1888, Hurd 1:426).

Ingersoll's Corner at the First Parish Church of Danvers, on Centre Street apparently marks where Ingersoll also owned the land next to the nineteenth century site of the First Church parsonage, and the Common (Standard 97; Hurd 1:428) . This was left to his son Nathaniel, who built an inn that became the center of village life, and gave two acres next to Ingersoll Street for a training ground where Danvers soldiers assembled in King Philips War, the French & Indian war, the Revolution and Civil War (Hurd 1:428). He also donated the land that was the last home of Deacon Edward Putnam, and 434 acres to Rev. Samuel Parris (Ibid.).

He bought the Richard Weston estate when the original grantor moved on with other Baptists to Providence RI (Harriet Tapley, *Chronicles of Danvers* [Danvers: Danvers Historical Soc. 1923], 5, 9) . This was in Danvers Highlands. It is probably the same that Hurd calls the original Francis Weston grant which extended from the Danvers church west to the turnpike, which Ingersoll and William Haynes bought in 1634 from John Pease (Hurd 1:427-8).

Richard was granted a lot in Salem next to Lawrence Leach, with whom he shared a road to the woodlots laid out in 1635 (Perley 1:293) .

He also had lands east of the Porter River, then called Frost Fish River. In 1636 he was granted 80 acres in Salem (EQ 4:110; Perley 1:456} . The 80 acre lot was laid out on Rial Side (north of the river) in 1643 with the top of the Great Hill dividing his land from Jacob Barney's, and on the west by the creek or cove below Bass Point on the Frost Fish river, now Porter's River, in Danvers (EQ 4:111). His 80 acres in Salem was on the Royall Side (north of the Danvers River) , lying east of the Frost Fish riverhead, west of the country road, south of Pasco Foote's land occupied by Jacob Barney in 1668, and north of Jacob Barney (deed of 10 April 1668 in EQ 4:109). The land was broken up and fenced with the help of a servant, Joseph Houlton (EQ 4:109).

He was granted one acre of marsh and meadow in the division of late 1637 (Roger Conant's list, Perley 1:464). It is unclear if this is the same grant of 1637 of marsh land on Frost Fish Brook next to Jacob Barney (10 April in town rec. 1:45, Perley 1:428). The boundary of the neighbors led to one of the earliest suits in Essex Court, of Inkersell v. Barney in 1639 which was settled by Col. Endicott's motion to have Jeffrey Massy and others lay out Barney's land (EQ 1:13). As frequently happened in court, Barney got back the next year with a suit against Ingersoll for "Feeding cattle in his marsh." (EQ 1:21) . Ingersoll apparently lost for he had to deliver "Two loads of hay at water side as convenient as his own was." But the dispute over the land went on for at least 30 years.

Ingersoll sold the timber on the Frost Fish river to several men who made them into staves (EQ 4:109).

In 1639 the town gave him 20 acres in the Great Meadow (23 Dec., Perley 2:77).

Richard's house in 1641 or 1642 was on Engerson's Point, next to Willistone's river, near the fishing place (John Putnam's testimony in EQ 4:110; perhaps in the southeast corner of today's Danvers).

Meanwhile the town ordered that he be paid a penny a passenger for a temporary ferry service over the North River, probably from North Street, in 1636 (12 Jan. 1636/7, Hurd 1:428; Salem town rec. 1:53 in Perley 1:406) . His wife Anne became a member of the Salem church before 1636 (Pope 252).

A Danvers historian says Richard "was another of the right sort of men", apparently basing it on the generous character of his son, Deacon Nathaniel, the peacemaker (Alden White in Hurd 1:428).

In his short residence of 15 years in Essex County Ingersoll seems to have been constantly in court. One of the first recorded cases was *Inkersell v. Jno. Norman* (3 Oct. 1637, EQ 1:6).

In 1640 Ingersoll had the town miller Capt. Traske in court and "admonished to be more careful about grinding and toll-taking." (29 July 1640, EQ 1:20) . Ingersoll "testified that he had the grists weighed before Lawrence Leech, a grand juryman, before they went to mill, and when they came back they were much short of weight wanting in two grists 71i. [pounds] each and 51i in another, besides being badly ground." The court ordered unspecified "satisfaction."

Soon Ingersoll was involved in another land controversy with a neighbor, Joshua Verrin. Verrin sued him in Sept. 1640 "to maintain his share of the fence for one acre of ground" (EQ 1:22). Ingersoll apparently appealed, for the court reviewed the decision in March 1641, and finally demanded a decision from 3 arbitrators "by 6' o'clock tomorrow", 30 June 1641 (EQ 1:29, 41; the printed abstract does not record the outcome).

In 1642 he got into a quarrel over loose cattle eating crops. He apparently started this by getting the court to appoint 3 commissioners to decide the damage done by cattle in his lot on the North River side (12 July 1642, EQ 1:42) . But five months later he and 10 others were fined for breach of a court order to keep their cattle out of the common corn (wheat) fields, in a complaint led by Lawrence Leach (Dec. 1642, EQ 1:49). Ingersoll got back at Leach with a suit for trespass by his cattle, referred to the same commissioners (EQ 1:50). But he and the offending ten were fined the next year for "putting their cattle into the North corn fields." (Dec. 1643, EQ 1:56).

Ingersoll was held responsible for the loose behavior of his son-in-law William Walcott, who had been whipped for idleness in Jan. 1641 (EQ 1:34) . Three years later the court ordered that "William Walcott"s wife, children and estate committed to Richard Inkersell, his father-in-law, to be disposed of 'according to God; & the said Wm. Walcott to bee & Remaine as his servant."

About 1645 Richard and his family were living farther west, on the 300 acre Chickering farm which John Ingersoll, gent., had leased in 1648 from Henry Chickering, the former Townsend Bishop estate and mansion, north of Governor Endicott's "Governor's Plain" (evidence of his 3 sons in EQ 7: 13-14; ED 17 Jan. 1664 in EQ 7: 16; map EQ 7:19). This was bounded on the northwest by Job Swinerton's house of 1678, the crotch of a brook on the north, the country road lying over the Crane River, the Myrie Swamp and the swamp by the wolf pits. This came to court in the dispute over the Nurse Farm in 1678. Today this is in the south side of Danvers, west of the Duck River and east of 1-95, centered on Pine Street, Danvers (map Perley 1:289).

He was named at Salem town meeting of 7 July 1644 to be one of a pair of citizens to check on those who did not come to Sunday services: "euery Lords day to walke forth in the time of Gods worshippe, to take notice of such as either lye about the meeting howse without attending to the word or ordinances, or that lye at home or in the fields, without giuing good account thereof, and to take the names of such psons to present them to the Magistrate. . ." (Perley 11:165). Since his turn, seven Sundays off, was in mid-August, he may not have made it.

Richard died in Salem about Aug. or Sept. 1644, between making his will on 21 July and its inventory of 4 Oct. (Essex Pro. 1:29 in EP 43, 458; EQ 1:76, 4:111) . He gave his youngest daughter Bathsheba two cowes. Most of the estate went to his wife Ann, except for six acres of the great meadow to his son George, a parcel with a frame on it to his son Nathaniel, his town house with ten acres of upland and meadow to his daughter Alice Walcott after his wife's death.

He had left the 80 acre lot to his widow An(n) who deeded it in 1663 to their two sons John and Nathaniel.

The whole estate came to £ 213/19. The real estate was valued at £ 40, including £ 26/7/6 for two houses, 26 acres and two acres of saltmarsh, £ 7 for a farm of 75 acres, and £ 14/13/4 for a farm of 80 acres and 20 acres of meadow. In the court case of 1669 *Ingersoll v. Barney* the court found that Barney had bought the farm in 1651 [from Ingersoll' s heirs] for a mere £ 8, and proved possession by felling timber on it (EQ 4:110).

Most interesting item on the inventory is "moose skin sute" worth £ 2. His farming activity is indicated by the variety of crops: Indian corne, ry, wheate, pease, hay and livestock. Seven cowes are the most valuable item in the estate, £ 34, with related dairy items like milke pan, milk pail, cheese, cheese fatts, churne, etc.

Soon after his death, the widow's barn was hit by lightning and burned to the ground, as we learn from a court case involving another of our ancestors, Rice Edwards, whom Henry Hagett wished the curse of God upon, "that fire might come down from heaven and consume his house, as it did Goodwife Ingersall's barn." (Nov. 1648, EQ 1:152).

His widow An(n) (Langlye) Ingersoll remarried before 10 Feb. 1663 to another ancestor, John Knight Sr., as shown in their power of attorney of that date (EQ 4: 109; Pope cites Essex files 14:29) . Her gift of her land to her sons in that year precipitated a lengthy suit, not settled for eight years, when the Knights agreed to the settlement (27 Sept. 1671 EQ 4:432-3, 219, 144, 108-12) . In addition to the Ingersoll farm, she succeeded to the lease on the Chickering farm that was the last residence of her husband Richard Ingersoll, as shown in the deed of 1664 to the farm of 300 acres "in the tenure & occupation of Richard Ingersoll deceased & in the right of his widow in the late tenner and occupation of John Knight of Newbery, together with the mansion house thereupon built by the said Townsend Bishop, together with all outhouses yards orchards or orchards meadow pasture fences bridges woods or underwoods" (17 Jan. 1664, EQ 7:16).

By Nov. 1672 she had remarried a third time to Edward Richards of Lynn (b.c.1614-7, EQ 5:107, 317), as shown in the legacy of £ 5 from the estate of Daniel Knight (EQ 5:117). Edwards had been tried for piracy and fined and forced "to acknowledge his sin and evil at Lynn" in 1645, although he denied the story that he had been the captain who seized a ship in Plymouth, England in 1631 with ten others, killed the crew and ordered the head cut off the surviving crew member, but escaped hanging because he was underage (EQ 1:83) . Richards had also been in court "for being distempered with drink at artillery" (1646, EQ 1:99, 108) . Ann and her husband were granted a license "to draw strong beer, cider and sell cakes" in Lynn (petition of 23 June 1674, granted 30 June (EQ 5:356-7; renewed to him 1675, 1677, EQ 6:51, 290) . Richards, who had built boats (EQ 6: 362) , bought the great boat of the Saugus ironworks in 1654 (EQ 5:424n) , and won a suit for debt owed by the factory manager (EQ 1:292, 300). She died 30 July 1677 (Perley 1:131n). Richards remarried to another Anne (age 62 in 1681, EQ 8:138; 9:240). She testified in court in June 1681 that she was about 63). Richards died Lynn 26 Jan. 1689/90 age 74 (VR 579).

Richard Ingersoll was ancestor of seven well-known Americans of that name. There were four generations of prominent lawyers, beginning with Jared (1722-81) , who was Connecticut Agent to London 1758-61 and Vice President of the Admiralty Court in Philadelphia 1768 ff., and Loyalist (DAB 11:467-8). His son Jared Jr. (1749-1822) argued foreign affairs cases before the U.S. Supreme Court after 1791, served in the Continental Congress 1780 and Federal Convention 1787, was Attorney General of Pennsylvania 1790-9, 1811-7, ran for Vice President in 1811 (DAB 9:468-9) . His son Charles Ingersoll (1782-1862) was a playwright and historian of the War of 1812 as well as lawyer/politician. He was U.S. Congressman for Pennsylvania 1812-4, 1840-9, serving as Chairman of the House Foreign Affairs Committee which approved a resolution for the annexation of Texas (DAB 9:465-6). His son Edward (1817-93) was also a lawyer and author, noted for his support of the Confederate position before the Civil War, which led to his brief arrest and attack by a mob (DAB 9:467).

Three other Ingersolls achieved fame. Robert G. (1833-99) earned the reputation of "one of the greatest of American orators" for his nomination of James G. Blaine for President in 1876, when his phrase "plumed knight" stuck. His brother Ebon Ingersoll was U.S. Representative from Illinois 1864-71, and Robert was Attorney General of Illinois 1867-9. His colonelcy of the 11th Illinois Cavalry in the Civil War ended with his capture by the Confederates in 1862 (DAB 9:469).

Robert H. Ingersoll (1859-1928) was founder with his brother Charles of the typewriter firm of the name, and successfully marketed millions of dollar watches and sewing machines (DAB 9: 470-1). Admiral Royal Ingersoll, a naval ordinance expert taught at Annapolis for 13 years between 1876 and 1901. On duty in the Orient he made a cruise up the Yangtze in 1902 (DAB 9:471-2).

NOYESES MARRY FIRST COUSINS

John^3 Noyes had declared intention in Newbury to marry 23 Nov. 1700 (VR 358; Desc. 204) his first cousin MARY^3 NOYES, daughter of his uncle JOHN^2 NOYES and MARY POORE, born Newbury 10 Dec. 1675 (VR 364; Desc. 53; No death in VR).

John^2 was born Newbury 20 Jan. 1645 (VR 362) . He married Newbury after 23 Nov. 1668 (VR 358) MARY POORE of Andover, of whom more below. He became freeman at the same time as his brother Cutting, on 9 Jan. 1674 in Cambridge, (Massachusetts Col. Rec. 4, ii/587 in Currier 102; Desc. 52; EQ 5:288) . He was a house carpenter by trade. In 1670 he bought the John Hull property in the "farms district" of Newbury, and there he probably built, in 1677, the house still standing in 1904 (photo Desc. op. 52). John built the house in unusually grand style, with wainscoted entry hall and elaborate balusters on the stairway. The kitchen fireplace was so huge that an ox could be roasted in it.

He was 33 when he took the oath of allegiance in 1678 (EQ 7:157; Currier 182). He was appointed Tithingman in 1681 (Currier 117), and served on the trial jury that year (EQ 8:150) . In 1688 he was assessed for one house, five acres of plowland and 12 of meadow, one horse, two oxen, four cows, three calves, 15 sheep and six hoggs (Currier 204).

He died intestate in 1691 (not in VR; Desc. 52), leaving an estate of £ 555, of which £ 309 was personal estate, and £ 246 real estate (Essex Pro. 303:158 per Reg. 53:37).

John Noyes's most famous descendant was our 38th president, Gerald R. Ford (b. 1913), who succeeded to the office as Vice President on the first resignation of a president in history. John^3 Noyes's son John^4 Jr. (454) , and younger brother of our ancestor Mary, had a daughter Elizabeth^5 (227) who married William Adams of Newbury, whose daughter Sarah (113) married Daniel Ayer of Haverhill, their son Samuel (56), had John (28), had George (14), had Adele (7) Ayer who married Levi Gardner (6) , whose daughter Dorothy Ayer Gardner (3) was mother of President Ford (Roberts 88) . Douglas Warren Gould and Warren Gould were thus eighth cousins of the president.

THE POORE FAMILY OF ANDOVER

MARY^2 (Poore) Noyes was daughter of DANIEL^1 POORE and MARY^2 FARNUM, born

Newbury 6 March 1651 (VR 428; Reg. 53:37). She died Newbury after 1716 when she is mentioned in her father's will (Ibid.).

Her father Daniel Poore was born in Wiltshire, England about 1624 (age 14 on arrival 1638, "A Great Oak from a Little Acorn", *Andover Townsman* 28 April 1899, in Charlotte Abbott, ed., *Andover Historical Series* 3:349, [hereinafter Acorn]; Charlotte Abbott, "Early Records of Families in Andover" (orig. in Andover Library, copy in NEHGS mss. cb 137, 13: 1947; Cutter 143). He left Southampton for America in May 1638 on the ship *Bevis,* Capt. Robert Batten, as "Dayell Poore", a 14 year old servant to Richard Dummer, gentleman, who came from Basingstoke, Hampshire, or his farmer brother Stephen Dummer (Sav. 2:79; Banks Planters 200, citing Drake 60) . Also with him as servants to Dummer were his sister Alice, 20, and brothers Samuel, 18, and John. On 20 Oct. 1650 in Boston he married MARY FARNUM (And. VR 2:120, 278).

The Daniel Poores moved to Andover, where he was a husbandman, and pioneer settler of North Andover before 1644 (Hurd 2:1558, 1658) . Poore settled near the Shawsheen River, at the west side of the town (Hurd 2:1660 quoting "Historical Sketches"). He first appears from Andover in the Ipswich grand jury of Sept. 1654 (EQ 1:362). He became freeman there on 27 March 1655 (EQ 1:387; Abbott 1947) . He was given one of the smallest houselots, of four acres, before 1662 (Philip Greven, *Four Generations...in Colonial Andover* [Ithaca: Cornell, 1970], [hereinafter Greven], 46. In all he received over 213 acres from the town (Greven 59). The largest grant was 140 acres in the Fourth Division of 1662, which were laid out 12 March 1677 (Greven 66 citing photostat of Essex Pro. 302:198; "7 score for the last division" in town record, 281).

Their homestead was in North Andover on the east bank of the Shawsheen, near its junction with the Merrimac, between the Andover fields and the pine barrens of Lawrence, called "Moose Country", on the trail from the fords to Concord (Acorn 349-350) , near the railway station at the junction of the Essex Railroad with the Boston & Maine (Cutter 144).

A list of his lands, totalling about 65 acres, follows (Forbes Rockwell, comp., "Andover Massachusetts Early Land Grant Records" [N. Andover Historical Soc., Aug. 1961 in NEHGS F74 A6 A76 1961], 0280-2, corrected by the court record in EQ 8:80-1):

7 acre houselot "with all accommodations" (also on 280).

2 ac. below falls of Shawsheen, south of the Merrimack, east of the swamp, north of John Fry, and west of Richard Barker.

7 ac. on west side of Shawsheen, south of a spring, east of a hill, north of a fence, 4 of which in the Shawsheen Division, and 3 for 2 acres of divisional land.

14 ac. in the plain above Joseph Parker's meadow, east of Solomon Martin's, north of John Stevens, west of Richard Barker, south of John Aslett and a swamp; 2 acres of this granted for house lot, and 12 for Third Division of upland.

8 ac. in Neck of new field, south and east of the Shawsheen, north of the swamp, and west of John Russ and William Ballard and the road to Shawsheen, 5 acres as his division of the new field, and other 3 for fencing.

1 ac. for fencing west of Benjamin Woodbridge, north of the swamp, east of the Shawsheen, and south of his own land.

23 rods for fencing at west end on south side of highway to Shawsheen field.

5 ac. of meadow in Wade's meadow on north side of Mosquito River, south of Richard Barker's meadow, north of Nathan Barker's meadow.

3 ac. of meadow about Shawsheen Field, with a slip of meadow that lies southeast of it.

2 ac. meadow on north side of pond above meadow of John Russ and John Lovejoy, north of the pond.

10 ac. swamp, 6 on west side of way to his house, east of the river; the rest east of the way, west of John Russ, and north of John Farnum.

2 ac. on west side of the Shawsheen by the field fence.

a parcel for an acre of his houselot on the ridge he exchanged with Nathan Parker (sold p. 266), and again for swamp land.

2 ac. for his new field.

1 ac. 20 rods north of the way to his house between the west end of John Farnum's for which he paid the town "30 sh./acre in wheat & Indian corne in equal proportions" (382).

"a parcel of rubbish land on the west side of the Shawsheen River" (281).

In 1681 Poore won a suit against Walter Wright for taking a load of hay from his pond meadow (EQ 8:80-2).

Evidently a member of the local militia, Daniel signed the Andover petition to appoint John Osgood sergeant and militia commander in 1658 (EQ 2:123).

He was on the Grand Jury at Ipswich in 1660, 1669, 1670, 1671, 1681 and 1682 (EQ 2:225; 4:278, 326; 8:373) . He held a number of town offices, including 8 years as Selectman 1665, 1674,5,8, 1683,4,5,7; Constable 1689; Fenceviewer 1669; 7 years Surveyor 1673, 1701-7, and one of the most used Lotlayers 1667 thru 1684 (Rockwell 15, 345) . He was also on the Essex County trial jury for 1680 (EQ 8:1, 23).

Daniel died in North Andover 8 June 1689 (not in VR; Abbott 1947; Greven 60n) . His will of 7 June 1689, probated 24 June 1690, mentions his widow Mary, and his daughter Mary (Noyes; Pope 367). He left a goodly estate of £ 800, including 240 acres, of which 140 acres were "wildernesse land" (Inventory of 23 Sept. 1689 in photo of Essex Pro. 302:198 cited by Greven 60n).

THE FARNUM FAMILY OF BOSTON

Daniel Poore's wife Mary was born in England about 1628 (7 on arrival, died about 85), the oldest child of RALPH[1] and ALICE FARNUM (Russell C. Farnham, "Farnham Genealogical History" [typesc. Lecanto PL, 1991 in NEHGS is the latest, and carefully done, [hereinafter Farnham]; Leora Belknap "'Know Thyself: A Farnum Genealogy" [typescr. Shelburne Falls MA, 1948 in NEHGS F 32] . Mary Poore died Andover 3 Feb. 1713/4, about 85 (VR 2:529). The family name is variously spelled FARNHAM, FARNUM, VARNAM, VARNEHAM, VARNHAM, VARNUM.

Mary had come with her parents on the brig *James,* Capt. John(athan) May, which left England late July 1635, and arrived Boston the last week of Sept., not the ship of the same name which arrived 3 months earlier (contra Belknap 32: Farnham viii; Antoinette Stepanek, "A Farnham Family in America" [typesc., Boulder CO, 1987 in NEHGS. book 4, group 4]; Banks Planters 153).

Ralph was born about 1603, given his age 32 on departure. His occupation is given as barber. Savage says that tradition is that they came from Wales, which he doubts (Sav. 2:143). The family came from Leicestershire according to early records of Andover (Stepanek). However, one family genealogist thought he was the namesake brother of Ralph Farnum who was baptized at St. Peter's, London 25 Aug. 1601, son of a merchant-tailor Ralf Varnham, glover of Liverpool, located in 1600 at the Sign of the Lute Inn in London (Charlotte Abbott, "The Farnum Family of Andover" typesc. in Memorial Library Andover, cited by Stepanek, copy in NEHGS 6:837, 841-2; Farnham vii).

Another unproven theory is that Ralph was the son mentioned in the will of Henri Farnham, merchant of Rochester, dated 1618 and proved the next year (Farnham vi, 25). Ralph may have been related to Henry Farnum of Roxbury and Boston, outside whose workshop the big fire of 1658 began, and who became Deacon in Killingsworth CT. There were other Varnums in the Boston area, but kinship is unknown.

Ralph moved briefly to Ipswich, where he became a Proprietor, and received a grant of land in 1639 (Varneham in Waters 493). The land southwest of Theophilus Wilson's lot beyond Egypt River (ED 16 11th mo. 1639 in EQ 8:154). He became the first Town Crier, paid to ring the bell, clean the meetinghouse, and publish notices (Varnham in town order 11 June 1640 in Hammatt, *Early Inhabitants of Ipswich* text in Waters 66, 107; Farnham x). We have not determined which children were born in Ipswich.

Between 1641 and 1646 the family moved to North Andover, where his son became Proprietor (first record 1681). He died about 1642 in an unrecorded place (Abbott), between the last record of him 1640/1 and the remarriage of his widow in 1648 (Stepanek). A Ralph Farnum, a barber-surgeon used to lecture people on religion while he shaved them (Edward Johnson, *Wonder-working Providence* quoted by Stepanek), and died about 1642 in Roxbury in the snow trying to get to a patient who needed a tooth pulled. Johnson judged this event an act of providence to halt the tongue of Farnum's Presbyterian heresy. It is not known if these were the same persons. Our Ralph is described as a yeoman, and is not recorded as a physician in Ipswich.

Alice Farnum was born England about 1607 (age 28 on arrival). Her maiden name was still unknown in 1991, though Stepanek suggested Harris, and Dr. Richard Clark suggests Abbott, based on IGI marriage London 1 Oct. 1627, which cannot be proven (Farnham 25).

Alice Farnum (Ales Varnam) of Ipswich remarried Gloucester 18 June 1648 (VR 367) to ship's carpenter Solomon Martin of Gloucester and Ipswich (Waters 351) , who had come over at age 16 with the Farnums on the *James.* Solomon's first wife Mary (Pinder) had died 9 Feb. 1648 (VR), a month after delivering a daughter Marie (9 Jan. VR 465). Alice sold her share of Ralph's Ipswich lands (to Thomas Lovell for £ 16, Ips. Rec. 7 March 1652 in Abbott 878), and Martin sold his in Gloucester and Ipswich, and they bought a farm in Andover about 1652 along the old Salem Road along Boston Hill and Den Rock Pastures. Solomon died Andover about 1713. We have not found when and where she died.

Farnum's most famous descendant was President Rutherford B. Hayes (1822-93; Roberts 36, #182). His grandmother Chloe Smith (5) was daughter of Abigail Chandler (11), daughter of Isaac (22), son of Lydia Abbott (45), daughter of Sarah[2] Farnum (91), sister of our Mary (Farnum) Poore. This makes Lydia Ann Gould seventh cousin of President Hayes.

BENJAMIN & SALLY TEEL'S MARRIED LIFE

Having given the background of Sally Teel, we return to their life after marriage in 1803.

Shortly before his marriage in 1803 Lydia's father Benjamin Teel was back home dealing with the estate of his father, who had died 1 May 1797:

18 Jan. 1803 Newburyport "Mr. Rutly this day moved from my small House on Sumer Street I Haveing Sold It to Mr Ebenezer Noyes."

25 June 1803 Newburyport "this day settled with Mr. David Plumer & gave him my Note for $27--Mr. Mills pay'd $44.87 the whole being $ 71.83".

26 Jan. 1804 Teel gave Daniel Fletcher "4 Dozen Crown Soap at 4/6 pr. Dozen wich I prmise to Sell to the best advantig In the West Indies and Return Him the proceeds in West indies produce He alowing me one quarter part for my trouble and Comision."

25 June 1805 Lydia Ann Winship Teel was born Newburyport, named for her two paternal great-grandmothers Lydia (Wood) Teel and Ann (Whitmore) Winship. She was an only child, there being no evidence of any other births to her parents. The family moved to Boston within a year of this.

22 Nov. 1805 John Teel received $1 from Benjamin for all accounts [last entry, Newburyport].

By 15 July 1806 Benjamin had moved to Boston, as his brother Joseph had counselled. There a letter was addressed to him by Levi Mills: "I rec^{d} your favour of the 7th Instant wherein you inform me, that you wish to have your Brother William Teel's estate Setled, so that you may have your part to pay your Debts [.] if the matter should be undertaken it will be one year before it can be Setled--if you want any money, your Sister Sally [Titcomb] will purchase yuor part of what was Sett off to your Mother for her Dower--if she can have it at a fair price--Mr. [Moses] Brown has been to me about his debt, I told him I would write to you if you wish to Sell your part of the dower you will write to me & Send your Lowest Terms...Levi Mills".

On 5 Sept. 1806 Benjamin Teel, baker of Boston sold to Charlestown blacksmith John Tapley for $12 his right in a piece of land in Charlestown, fronting the Training Field on the north 15 feet, 40 feet on the east and 50 feet on the south bordering Aaron Putnam, and 50 feet on the west on Silas Niles's land. This is west of the Gould homestead on the east side of the Training Field. Middlesex Deeds might be checked for source of purchase or inheritance from Teels or Winships. The document is signed by both Benjamin Teel and Sally Teel, his wife.

Benjamin Teal's name first shows in Boston Directories in 1808 when he is shown as soap boiler in the North End at Love Lane, which ran from Middle Street to Salem Street (138, 1809 133). In 1810 the address is Salem Street, which may be the same location (189).

After a gap in 1813 Benjamin has moved to the West End, listed as tallow chandler, that is, a maker of candles from tallow. The address is the south side of Cambridge Street, nine houses east of the West Boston bridge, not a bad neighborhood, for Robert G. Shaw lived on the opposite side of the street, and Daniel Henchman had his shop on the other side (*Directory 1815*, 200, 22).

After the death of his mother on 23 Dec. 1815 Benjamin Teel, baker of Boston, quitclaimed his quarter of the family home in Newburyport. Moses Brown, merchant of Newburyport, to whom he probably owed the money, paid him $130 for his "one undivided fourth part of the dower or thirds, that was set off to my honoured mother Elizabeth Teel, from the estate of my honored father, William Teel, deceased...the whole of said dower consisting of part of a dwelling house with land under it; --and seventeen feet of cellar under the other part of the house, situated in Newburyport, adjoining Merrimac street,--also half of a barn adjoining Summer street, with the land under & adjoining the same, with the privileges of a way from the house to the barn..." 20 Sept. 1816. The other three quarters were probably owned by the other living siblings: Sarah (Teel) Titcomb (1785-1817), John Teel (1786-1848), and Catherine (Teel) Nickerson (b, before 1794-after 1877), the other children having died.

Benjamin Teel, tallow chandler, was still at Cambridge Street in 1816 (200), but is not listed in Boston in 1818.

In 1817 Benjamin founded a soap factory in Louisville, where Proctor & Gamble was to become the world's largest producer of soap. Pressed by debts, Benjamin Teel left Boston at the end of 1817 for Louisville where he was involved in running a candle and soap factory for Israel Munroe, attorney of Boston, (at #2 Tudor's Buildings, *Boston Directory 1818*, 156, 1819, 120,

1820, 175) . John Shaw has four letters to his wife from him in Louisville 1818 which describe his business.

Louisville Jan[y] 18 1818

My Love

I have this moment Rec[d] your Letter of the 7 Dec[r] but what is it you write, my Sister [Sally Titcomb] Dead... [Y]ou are afraid that my morals will be vitiated by boarding at a tavern[.] do not my Love let that Concern you since I do not drink & but very Little [.] wiskey Women Cards & Dice are as much Strangers to me as they were in Boston[.] I have not yet touched none of them and is my determination not to do it depend on that my Love let your advising friends Say what they will. [Y]ou Speak of Distance [;] it is but Small depend on it we Shall meet again in this world when my depts are paid I Shall come to Boston and we will try to do A Little buisiness for ourselfs...

I hope Mr. Sigourney's Conduct has been that of a Gentleman towards you but I mistrusted him when I left Boston but I hope he will be a friend to you but I think he will befriend hiself first[.]...

Give my best respects to Mr. Munroe and tell him he has my hearty thanks for the kindness he Shows toward you which I hope he will Continue in my absence from you. I am glad that I did not take you with me to this place. I shall never again Spend my days here[.] [W]as I in Indiana or Ohio I Should be better Contented but I do not Like Kentucky[.] If it had been my Lot to have gone to St Louis on the Missouri I should have been better Sattisfied or in Alabama Territory I would not Care much[.]

But at any rate I am determined to "Stay here one year if not two, that I may pay of my depts [sic] in Boston...

[Y]ou might write oftener than you do and do not fill up your Letters with Small Scraps of Paper for every one of them Costs 25 Cents[.] *I* paid 75 Cents for your Last Letter of 3 pieces[.] I wish you would put it all in one Sheet of paper as that is only 25 Cents with no Covering like this!.]

M[r] Cotting arrived about Christmas time and Brought your Dear first Letter[.] [H]is Brother Annable Cotting keeps Store not far from you[. Lydia evidently continued to live at the Cambridge Street address in the east end, even though his mail was directed care of Israel Munroe's office. In 1818 Annable & Charles C. Cotting's store was on South Russell Street, which was in the West End, running south from Cambridge Street, *Boston Directory 1818*, 69, 1819, 71; in 1820 the address is Charles Street, which ran from the West Boston Bridge to the west end of Beacon Street, *Directory 1820*, 75] I want you to Send him word that you have heard from Louisville that his Brother is well Satisfied with his Situation but detests the place and says if he ever sees Boston again he will look no further for happiness and I Say so too--I did not expect that Turner would Stay at Livermore' s long he was not able to do the work...

My Love[,] you & Lydia Ann are allways in my mind[.] Tell the Dear Daughter that I will remember the verses She Sent but She must Learn to write the next herself..." (she was 12).

25 cent cover addressed to Mr. Benjamin Teel, Care of Israel Munroe, Esq. Boston:
"Louisville May 10 " 1818

My Love I rec[a] your Letter of March, and am rejoiced to hear that you are well and in good circumstances[.] I was Shocked at the account you gave of Luthers [Titcomb, husband of his deceased sister Sally] Conduct[.] it nearly reconciled me to death of my Sister for I had as Liever She would be in heaven as to Live with a brute on earth--! admire your Conduct with regard to the dificulty you was in and think it the best way you Could persue...

I have my troubles as well as you but I am determined to persue the Line of Conduct you have marked out because I know that a good Conscience is the best friend and Virtue must triumph in defiance of every vicet.]

I gives me great Pleasure to hear that Lydia Ann is a good girl and goes to School[.] I hope you will//try to distill into her mind principles of virtue and paint vice in such Collors as will induce her to Shun it [.]...

[Y] our Say you want Some Cloth [.] I have written to Mr Munroe respecting it and I Conclude you have it before this time--

I have at Last got to work making Windsor & Rose Soap and have gained much Credit by it and I hope Still to Continue to deserve it[.]

Tell Mr Munroe that Mr Peterson has Sent him some white Soap and I think he may as well make you a present of a box of it[;] there is one Box I marked my name on purpose for you[.] [T] ell him that the Factory is doing well. [I]n the month of April I made $800"00 for him Clear of all expence[.] I wrote to him Last Sunday and Shall write again the Latter part of this month!.] Mr Peterson is Sick and will Start into the Country tomrrow..."

Cover addressed to Mr. Benjamin Teel, Boston; no postage, so probably delivered by hand:

"Louisville June 28 "1818

July 12 I hope you will not read nor Show this Letter to"Mr Munroe My Love

I cannot get over your Last Letter It was too Cruel it Stuck daggers in my Soul[.]

I will acknowledge to~you that I have made use of Some ambiguity in writing to you but I was afraid that you would tell Mr Munroe of Some Circumstances if I wrote plain that I did not want him to know[.] But rather than give your dear bosom any more uneasiness I will explain myself trusting to your honor & Secrecy[.]

[T]he fact is there was no Soap nor Candles made in the factory untill *I* Came that was good for any thing and Cap[6] Hawes Seeing the factory runing in dept every day Sold it with all the utensills to Mr Munroe and when I came to the Factory it Looked more Like a tomb than any thing else[;] it was nothing but a Shell and although it was Thursday when I arrived and there was no apparatus for dipping Candles I was able by exerting myself to make on Saturday the third day four hundred & fifty pounds Candles and ever since that I have drove the business in the Same proportion and the business now is Carried on Regular[.]//

The increasing profits of the Factory produced Some enemies friends to the Capt[.] [T]hey try'd to persuade Mr Peterson that the Soap Cost 20m Cents a pound that we wer Selling for 10 Cents at another time!.] [T]hey would Say that the Soap would not wash and again that I must Clear three Hundred Dollars a month to Support the expense of the Factory and try'd everey way to discourage me in every respect[.] [T]hese are but Small things to Some others that were Said and every art was put in motion to Crush the infant establishment[.]

[d] ont this explain my dream and Can you blame me for being sick of this business! [N]o my Love you ought to praise me for my Perseverence and final victory!.]

When Mr Wells first came he went to Board with the Capt [.] [0] ne day at meal time the Capt was damning Mr Munroe and every one that took his part[.] Mr Wells made answer that Mr Munroe was able to take his own part[--]then the Capt began to Swear at Wells who immediately Left the house Saying that he would not board in a house where Mr Munroe was abused[.] Wells is a smart little fellow and a great friend to Mr Munroe and the Factory[.]//

Dont you tell Mr Munroe that I do not Like the Place nor nothing about it[.]

I have made me a hammock which I Sleep in, in the factory[,]m [I]t is very Comfortable but you know were I had rather Sleep[.]

Good night My Love I am Going to turn in[.]

I hope to Sleep with you in 1 year from this[.]

[p.s.] Write me word as soon as possible the particulars of my Sisters Death and how the Children are provided for &c[.]

25 cent cover from Louisville 14 July [1818?] addressed to Benjamin Teel, Care of Mr Israel Munroe Esq, Boston:

[no date or greeting—a page may be missing; it matches 12 July date added to letter above, which has no signature]

"I think this will explain in part the Cause of my discontent when I first came and when you come *I* will Clear up every thing to your Satisf action [.] The business is different now and I am proud to Say that I give general Satisf action [.] The Situation of the Factory is delightfull in a fine Airy place from the Chamber windows we have a view of the falls of the Ohio and the Surounding Scenery which is truly romantic and nothing is wanting but you my Love to make me happy but though I wish for you to Come yet I would have you act your own pleasure but as I have Said before it [s] impossible for me to Live without you and if you will come I will do everything in my Power to make you happy...M[r] Munroe will Settle up with you before you Come away which enable you to pay what Little Depts you may have Contracted and if you want any more money Draw on M[r] Munroe on my account. M[r] Peterson will Pay your expenses on the Passage"

He may have come home to Boston in July 1819 as he hoped. Benjamin appears to have returned to Boston by mid-1820, for he is shown in the 1820 Directory (199, as tallow chandler on Leverett Street, close to his old address) composed the previous year, and the Teel Account book resumed then, recording his wages received from Jno. Dunbar @ $1.25 a day, working 6 days a week, 1 Aug. to 21 Oct. 1820 (at end). Jonathan Dunbar is listed as a soap boiler on Nassau Street in 1818 (45 Orange Street and the Mall, Boston Directory 1818, 83; in 1820 a tallow chandler at the same address (82), and in 1821 again as soap boiler, at #6 Pleasant Street, which runs from Orange Street to the Ropewalks (Directory 90).

The next year there is record of rent of Thomas Haskins' house in Boston from 9 Feb. 1821 to 21 Oct. 1821 @ $7.50 per month. Thomas Haskins had a distillery business on Rainsford Lane (in the South End off Essex Street, Directory 1820, 110, 1821,123, but his residence was on Carver Street in the South End. However, by 1821 a second Thomas Haskins, house and millwright appears at Salutation Alley in the North End (123).

Teel may still have been in the soap manufacturing business, as a notation of 16 March 1821 records John W. Ballard's receipt of 53 pounds of soap on account of Robert Brondson.

The last record of him in Boston Directories is 1821 (223), as tallow chandler on Carver Street in the South End, in today's Park Square. By coincidence, this street was the residence of his grandson T. Warren Gould in the late nineteenth century.

Benjamin Teel's death does not appear in the Boston or state records, but the 1821 directory and the account book are the last evidence. He appears to have died in Boston after March 1821, and probably after 14 July 1821, the last entry in the account book, for $7.50 rent for the month of May.

Sally Teel appears to have been living in her mother Salley Barnard's house at 209 Hanover Street in the North End of Boston in 1824-5, as the last entries in the Teel Account Book show:

" Reed of Mrs. Teel twelve Dolers in full up to November th 25 1824//Boston the 4 1825 Salley Bernard//Received payment" and "Reci[a] of M[rs] Sally Teel twenty Dollars in full for rent to June 8th 1825//Boston June [the] 21. 1825. Salley Bernard//Received pament".

Sally Teel, widow is in Boston Directories for 1825 and 1826 (255, 267) , though Salley Bernard is not in any directory 1789-1831. She appears to have made ladies clothing.

On the last page at the back of the account book is an undated record of ladies clothing and dry goods purchased by Mrs. Yourter probably by Sally Teel (or less likely, Bernard), about 1825:

handkerchief 1 Doller
head Dress 2 Dollers
head Dress 2 Dollers
vandike 75 cents
black Bonet 2 Dollers
pink Luster 3 Dollers

Gren Bonet 3 Shillings

Buf Luster 2 Dollers 25 cents
Yallow Callerco 2 Dollrs 50 cnts
hankerchiefe l Doller
mufer 37 cnts
mufer 37 cnts
gloves 30 into gloves 30 cnts trunkes 12 cnts 2 cnts
gloves 44 cents <u>Coleprteen 15 cnts</u>
Mrs Yourter 1 Doller 3 yards
1 Doller plumes 2 Dollers
1 Doller Mrs. M

50 cents colering head nets 50 cents 5 y
ribon 25 cnts
3
2 ?grilior? *If*
3 Stockings

Another undated entry on an earlier page (on a blank page following 12 July 1793) is in the same handwriting: Received one Ladock Bonet tien and sixpence one Blue Bonet one pink Bonet the same prise

one pair white gloves

Thear

three Black Bonets

Received three mufs 50

cents a peace fore pair of Dark gloves

The final entry in the same hand is this: "Received of Mr.
Dunbar 25 cnt one Botle of drops p 23 cnts
50 cnts"

A Sally Teel died in Boston 26 Aug. 1826, age 58 (Massachusetts VR), but this is probably not our ancestor, for in 1827 and 1828 Sally Teel appears in the Boston Directory as a widow at rear of 64 Salem Street but in 1829 is no longer shown (256, 266) . The last record we have of her is an inscription "Sally Teel' s Book Boston Jan. 1 1828" at the back of Edward Young's *Night Thoughts* [Brunswick ME, 1822] in the possession of Hazel LaPorte 10 Sept. 1968, and left with her daughter Dorothy Pass of Bedford.

It is this Sally Teel whose brief obituary appeared in the Boston paper: "Died on Sat. [16th]...Widow Sarah Teel, 48" (*Columbian Centinel* Weds. 20 Aug. 20 1828, 2) . By pure coincidence the same column reports the death of "John Barnard, 24", with no date, but shortly before the 20th.

She was buried in Boston, probably in the Gould plot in Copps Hill, and moved to the Gould family plot in Mt. Auburn.

There is no record of Salley (Hidden) Barnard's death, though it is probably Boston, sometime after our last notation of her on 21 June 1825, above.

LYDIA TEEL'S LIFE

Lydia Teel grew up in the North End close to the Gould houses. She was three when Benjamin first moved there. The Teel home in the West End was also close to Gould properties. She was 20 when the Teels moved back to the North End, living with her widowed mother and grandmother until they died. The deaths of all of her close relatives within seven years, her father when she was 17, her mother when she was 23, and grandmother shortly before must have been devastating. The death of her nephew Charles (Warren's son) brought back memories 40 years later: "every thing seems so sad my own early troubles come so fresh to my mind it seems as if I lived them all over again" (Diary 15 March 1862).

Lydia Teel was married to Thomas[6] Gould Jr. in Boston 3 Sept. 1829 (VR 1:343), when she was 24, by Rev. James D. Knowles at the Second Baptist Church in the North End of Boston. She was two and a half years older than he.

In 1848 the Gould family moved to Lexington, where her ancestors Edward Winship and Richard Park had settled two centuries earlier, in 1642.

She was 64 years old when her husband died in Lexington 19 Oct. 1869. She continued to live in their homestead, "Grapevine Corners", on the Waltham Rd. for nearly a quarter of a century. She always lived with her daughter Lucy Whiting, and her grandson Thomas "Tomey" Whiting.

Lydia was a habitual diarist, so we get an intimate idea of her life from the seven diaries which survived the 1948 fire at Grapevine Corners (1862, 1877, 1880, 1884 with John Shaw, San Mateo 1995; 1869 and 1874 with Hazel LaPorte, Bedford 1969, inherited by her daughter Dorothy Pass; 1875 with J. W. Gould, Cotuit MA 1995).

Left only a modest $1000 by her husband's father, Thomas Sr., she made ends meet by taking in boarders, some relatives, others not. Among the relatives were her daughter Annie's widower husband, George E. Muzzey (1875; $20 a month in 1880), and her Aunt Katie (Catherine Teel) Nickerson (1877), her son Warren & family ($10 a week 1862), Aunt Betsy ($26 a month 1862). Others were Mr. Hunt ($40 a week, 1875).

She also did some nursing of sick friends, for pay. In 1862 she records: "Anelieno came for me to take care of Pablo//! left every thing and went to the city...found Pablo very sick." (16 May). "June...earned twenty seven dollars for takeing care of Pablo four weeks 27°°". Pablo's last name is not recorded, but we know he was a friend of Annie, Lucy and Sophia in 1860, mentioned in four letters of that year.

Lydia had a regular routine of keeping the house, cooking, washing, sewing and cleaning. One entry described it well: "*I* have been joging on in the same old way cooking, and eating, when it comes night I am tired to death[.] I expect to work as long as I can propell." 22 Jan. 1875. But at age 70 she had some outside help from Eunice Common, who was paid $81.50 in Oct. 1875. When she was older, in 1880, she paid a Mrs. Burck $1.25 to $2.50 a day to work and do the wash (2 April, 14 June, 11 Nov., 15 Dec.) . The same year she had a Miss E. Walls come in to work for a week, her $ 5 pay coming from son-in-law George Muzzey (17, 23 Oct.; address at end of diary).

Washing took three days, every two weeks: "Monday, Jan. 18...Lu & I did a fourtnights Wash"..."Tuesday, Jan. 19 [1875] . . .very cold down to zero we dried our Clothes to day"..."Wednesday, Jan. 20, Lucy lorned to day".

Lydia did most of the cooking for the three in the family, and usually two boarders. She seems to have made a good bit of cash on the side by selling preserves and berries.

Lydia did a lot of sewing, mainly for the family, but she made things for others, as on 22 Oct. 1875: "Lucy cut Eunice an overskirt I have began to make it for her//Oct. 23 "I have worked all day on the overskirt I am always getting into some such scrap" . She made shirts for her husband and sons, dresses for herself and daughters. A special treat was cloth dolls, as the 1862 diary records: "began to make some presents for the children...finished the babys for Warrens children, and a little rabit for the baby." (Dec. 30-31).

Lucy was more involved in the local Unitarian church than her mother, and Lydia shows less religious devotion than her father, attending church irregularly on Sunday. However, when her son lost a child she wrote: "I hope it will lead him to God, and teach him that all his blessings are only lent//God gives and takes as he knows best" (11 March 1862).

She seldom mentions reading, though she scolds herself one day: "I am reading a silly book, just throwing time away." (18 Feb. 1875) .

Lydia wrote occasionally, but only two of her letters survive. Like her diary entries, the punctuation is rare, spelling phonetic, and capitalization saved for nouns of importance. She probably had no more than a grade school education, but a good one in pioneering Boston schools of the 1810s. But she saw that all of her children had more education than she, finishing high school.

Her main pleasure was in family, visiting relatives, or more likely having them come for long visits; there were Gould relatives like her husband's Aunts Lizzie Gould and Sophia Mann, and dozens of cousins like James Gould, who brought news of the exciting Lawrance inheritance (1874), the Dams from California, the Philipses from Somerville, the Adamses, Professor Ezra Palmer Gould of Andover Newton Seminary, the Lawrence cousins the Drews, etc. There were also her own Teel cousins, the Newburyport Merrills, and Boston Knights, Nickersons and Wyeths.

She made an annual pilgrimage to her birthplace, Newburyport, usually staying with her best friend, her first cousin, Annie (Titcomb) Merrill. There were longer trips like the one to New York in 1875 to visit the Gould cousins the Temples: "July 3...this morn we started for Albany, and arrived there ten minutes past three we did not feel very tired. the folks were glad to see us... 4 July... to day we rode to Church with an spann of horses//this eve we rode to see Mr. Corver but he was not at home...Monday 5 July...they are celebrating to day for the Glorious fourth//the procession passed the house of Mr. Temple it looked very <u>much like the processions I have seen in Boston</u>...6 July this morn we started to sail down the Hudson river every thing was delightful until about three O'clock, when we had a terrible thunder shower which lasted about an hour.//it was clear when we reached New York[.] Mr. Charles Temple was there to meet us and took us to his home in Brookline where we have a very nice supper...7 July we started from the grand railroad depot in New York for home at half past eight in the morn.//we got into Boston about five O'clock in the afternoon//took tea with Mrs Hook, then started for home, was two minutes too late [for the last train] went to Mrs. Bradfords staid all night, come home in the half past eight train in the morn for home. . .8 July, we arried home this morn tired enough[.]"

Her husband's first cousin, Frances[6] (Gould) Temple had married Amos[9] Temple of Deerfield, and moved from Vermont to Albany; their eldest son, Charles Amos Temple (1842-1885) lived in Brooklyn.

About once a month there was a big shopping trip to Boston, either by "the cars" (the trolley) or by train, combined with visits to relatives and friends. And there was at least one trip a year to the family plot in Mt. Auburn. The big Boston cultural attraction of 1875 was "the Painting of the Prodigal Son it was very Beatifull" (24 May) , so good that it was worth a second viewing {6 June). Her best educated child Warren took her to the theater in Boston, including a performance by John Wilkes Booth (5 Dec. 1862, also 3 Dec.).

There's not much humor, but an occasional event like this: "Lu and I had a fright this evening, puss had an awful fit. she ran up on the Pictures, on the wall, and made things fly right and left." (23 Jan. 1875).

The expected holidays like Thanksgiving and Christmas are family occasions, and all the patriotic holidays are marked: "the Glorious Nineteenth" (19 April) and the Fourth of July. Birthdays and anniversaries are noted, but not celebrated especially.

What of Lydia Gould's character? My impression is that she was a good Yankee, frugal and hard-working. Her first love and loyalty was to her family, to whom she was devoted. There is a what looks like jealousy of her daughter-in-law Caroline (Goddard) Gould when she criticized her "royal" airs. There may not really have been a difference in attitudes. Lydia herself was clearly proud of her family heritage, her descent from leading families of the colonies. But there was no snobbishness. Perhaps it a touch of envy of her son's economic success, rising into the merchant class. She had a wide circle of friends in the community, including neighbors like the Wellingtons, but her closest friends are her cousins. She does not get involved in any community or church activity.

Politics gets mentioned, but it's not important; rarely does the national news intrude into her commentary, like the collision of the steamers *Stonington* and *Narragansett* in 1880. But she is strongly patriotic, and she loved a good parade. Her interest in history is noted by Edward G. Porter, *Rambles in Old Boston* [Boston: Cupples, Upham, 1887], ix) who acknowledges her contribution. Her politics were Republican, as in 1877 when she heard that Tilden had been elected, she wrote, "I hope not". Her satisfaction with Lincoln's first year in office is marked by the comment: "One year ago to day president Lincoln took his office of state//how well he has filled it the nation knows, but I hope he will go on from prospering to prosper" (4 March 1862).

Her philosophy was a simple one, of accepting the changes of life like the weather. This diary entry tells it:

"March Sunday *2* 1862//
hurah for spring,
I know it is wrong to wish time a way, but summer is so congenial to my feelings I cant help it.
I hope I shant be sick as I was last summer, for I lost all the beuty of the season//Monday 3//stormy again//such is life sunshine and shade, if it were all sunshine we should forget we were mortal//
Thomas went to the City brought home two very large oranges for me to give to a sick friend//thank him"

Lydia died in Lexington 6 Jan. 1893, "of old age", 87 (MDR 437:219).

Her obituary, undated, probably from a Boston newspaper, preserved by her family, reads: "Mrs. Lydia Ann Gould, who died in Lexington Jan. 10, 1893, was born in Newburyport in June, 1805. Removing with her parents to Boston early in life, she married Thomas Gould, Jr., an old-time resident of the North End, who died about twenty-five years ago, and their history was woven with that of the old families of that period. Possessed with a cheerful, loving, and Christian spirit, she bore with patience the infirmities of advancing age, and peacefully passed away, surrounded by her children and loving friends, to whom her life is a most precious memory."

She was buried beside her husband and mother in Mt. Auburn Cemetery, Cambridge.

T. Warren Gould in 1860, age 27

Chapter XI

T.^{7} WARREN GOULD
Textile Merchant
(1834-1895)

25. T(HOMAS)^{7} WARREN GOULD (Thomas^{6,5}, James^{4}, Thomas^{3}, William^{2}, Thomas^{1}) was born in Boston MA 17 Feb. 1834 (Family record; not in Boston VR, nor Massachusetts Arch.), and died in Melrose MA 27 Jan. 1895 in his sixtieth year (MDR 455:313).

.

He was named for his father, Thomas Gould Jr., who never used the middle name. The son reversed the practice, and from youth always signed himself T. Warren, though we will call him Warren, as his parents did.

Warren was born in the North End of Boston, in his father's house near Baldwin Place, behind the Second Baptist Church, now the Knights of Columbus Hall on North Margin Street (Note on clipping of his obituary, probably by Ida, stating he was born on Salutation Alley is wrong, for that is where the Goddards lived before moving to 19 Unity Street (*Boston Directory* (hereinafter Dir.) 1831, 151, and Family record of births), whereas there is no record of Goulds owning or renting there (see prev. chapters).

.

He was the first son, and remained the eldest child, for his sister Ann Maria had died at age seven months almost two years before his birth. His father, then a carpenter, was then building railway cars and depot structures for the new railroads then coming into Boston.

WARREN'S EDUCATION.

Warren was educated thru high school in one of the best public school systems in the world, for Boston was then pioneering in the country under the guidance of Horace Mann, with the support of a citizenry that thought paying for public education the best investment of tax money.

He started in the excellent public schools in the North End. He graduated from Eliot Grammar School on North Bennet Street in 1848. That year the all boys school was headed by Edwin Wright, Grammar Master, assisted by Levi Conant, Writing Master (Dir. 1847/8, 18). The other teachers were all women, assistants Caroline W. Carter, Hannah Damon, Anna S. Carter, Martha West, Eliza L. Felt, and Miss Kent (Dir. 1848/9 list 21).

Eliot School, on the northeast side of N. Bennet Street, midway between Salem and Hanover streets, was one of the oldest in Boston, founded in 1713, for 80 years associated with Boston's most famous school master, John Tileston (1735-1826), as the North Writing School, and renamed for Rev. John Eliot (1779-1813), pastor of the New North Church.

We have three blue notebooks, inscribed "Thomas W. Gould". The earliest is full of practice penmanship, with somewhat shaky "mmm"s, "mine mine mine" and "ssss", "ffff". The second, more fluent, has a pencilled name "T. Warren Gould...10 Yrs Feb", dating it to 1844. In this he practiced the alphabet and numbers as well as difficult words "inconvenience", "Multummultummult..." and "fermentation".

The third bluebook is in a smaller and neater writing, with "T.W.Gould//May 13th 1847...Sep 3^{d}" written on the cover, and "Eliot School. T. Warren Gould" under the first exercise, "May I govern my passions with absolute sway//And grow wiser and better as life wears away." There are similar aphorisms: "Disappointments and distress are often blessings in disguise." "Youth is the season to prepare for a long and happy life.", "Excess is an evil that smiles and seduces enchants and destroys.", "Attainment in learning is gained only by industry. Americans.", "By a commendable deportment we gain reputation. Boston.", "Commendation commonly animates mankind. Commendation.", "Deride not the poor nor triumph over their misfortunes.", "Experience and wisdom are the best fortune tellers. Eastport."

Most interesting, however, is the accounting exercise on page 2. Here the young scribe gives Mr. Henry Leeds's receipt for 145 yds. Mixed Cassimere @ $1.57, 28 yds. Dark Prints @ .42, and 25 yds. Light do. @ .51, totaling $252.16 from John E. Davis & Co. of Boston on May 6, 1847. The second is for an identical amount, an unlikely reality, from Samuel B. Willard on May 14 to Warren Lincoln. Although it does not seem likely to represent actual sales, it is interesting that the 13 year old future merchant of European textiles is already practicing his trade.

From sometime between 1844 and 1847 we have a history paper of three pages signed "Eliot School T. Warren Gould". It is titled "The Battle of Lexington", the schoolboy's version, with his own corrections, and uncorrected misspellings: "baajonets", "thougt", "sentinals", but not badly written.

More original is an essay of about 1845 which is in John Shaw's archive in San Mateo: "Thoughts occasioned by a sight of the Chinese Junk now exhibiting in the city of Boston. On my first obtaining a sight of the junk, then laying between the Charles river and Warren bridges, I compared her with the ship of war Franklin laying below the Charles river bridge, and opposite the navy-yard, And I thought of the many advancements that had been made in the art of ship-building, in the world since the building of the ark by Noah, under the instruction of the Almighty. It also led me to think how frail, and weak, was man, and all his works, compared with God. The great ship with her sails all spread to the wind, her decks covered with men, all in the bloom of health, and manhood, bearing proudly onward to^her home, the locomotive engine with nerves of brass, and muscles of steel and iron, drawing a heavy train swiftly over the land, and two hostile armies approaching battle, are sights truly great. But how much greater than all these ~~sights~~ is God. With but one stroke of his power he can destroy all these works of man, himself. And even man himself is cut down yearly, monthly, weekly, and daily, by God's own agent Death. Therefore let us love and fear him; let us remember that we are all sinners in his sight, let us follow his commandments that we may obtain through his son Jesus Christ, that reward which he has promised us even after Death in the world to come."

The reference to the "two hostile armies approaching battle" after the warship may be allusion to the Opium War of 1839-1842.

In 1848 Warren won the Franklin Medal of the City of Boston. We still have the bronze disc of about an inch diameter which is inscribed "Gift of Franklin//AD. 1788", and on the reverse, "Awarded to T. W. Gould. 1848".

By 1848 Warren's father had begun building a house in the Boston suburb of Lexington, at Grapevine Corners, to which his parents and sisters were to move into by April 1849. Warren, now 14, chose to stay in Boston. He probably stayed with his Grandfather Thomas and Grandmother Lydia at their home on Friend Street, just north of Faneuil Hall.

He was likely guided by the advice of his uncle, Samuel Lawrence Gould, Headmaster of Winthrop School, and one of the educational pioneers in Boston education under Horace Mann. Warren had the choice of the classical Latin School which was oriented toward college, or the almost as prestigious English curriculum. Perhaps because of his interest in business he chose the latter. The official description of English High is, "This school was instituted in 1821, with the design of furnishing young men of the city, who are not intended for a collegiate course of studies...with the means of completing a good English education, and fitting them for all the departments of commercial life." (*Third Annual Report of the Superintendent of Schools* [Boston: The City, 1853], 57).

He entered Boston English High School in 1848, with the class which graduated in 1851 (*Catalogue...of the English High School* [Boston: English High School Assn., 1891], [hereinafter Cat.], 22). Founded in 1821 as the English Classical School, it had moved only four years before to a new building on Bedford Street (Engraving in Cat. 19, torn down 1882, xviii). The Principal was the well-known educator Thomas Sherwin, former Instructor in Mathematics at Harvard after his graduation there in 1825, engineer, and creator of its reputation "as the model school of the United States" (Bishop Frazer of Manchester, England, report to Parliament 1865; Cat. xvi.). One of his successors (in 1881) was Francis A. Waterhouse, who summered in Cotuit (Cat. xxii; photo 79, 90).

Among the outstanding teachers at English High was Charles M. Cumston, who succeeded Sherwin as Principal (Cat. xx). The Sub-Master was Luther Robinson and Francis Williams, the Second Sub-Master, and their two Ushers, or assistants, were Cumston and Samuel M. Weston, who was to become Head of Roxbury Latin School (*One Hundred Years of the English High School* [Boston: Centenary Committee, 1924], 82, 21, 19; *Organization of the Grammar Schools* [Boston: the city, 1850], 5; 1851, 5). Other teachers of the time were John D. Philbrick, who became Superintendent of Boston schools, and Edward Seager.

The demanding curriculum was set forth in the official Regulations (*Organization 1853*, 16; although this is two years after Gould's graduation, the regulations have not changed, and the courses are similar to those at founding in 1821, 3d Report 62).

"*Class* 3. [First year, 1848-49]. 1. Review of preparatory Studies, using the text-books authorized in the Grammar and Writing schools of the city." These included Mitchell's

Geography and Atlas, Worcester's Dictionary, Robinson's Book Keeping, Hall's Manual of Morals, Parker's Compendium of Natural and Experimental Philosophy, and Bullion's Grammar, and Worcester's History.
2. Ancient Geography. 3. Worcester's General History. 4. Sherwin's Algebra. 5. French Language. 6. Drawing.

Class 2. [Second year, 1849-50]. 1. Sherwin's Algebra, continued. 2. French Language, continued. 3. Drawing, continued. 4. Legendre's Geometry. 5. Book Keeping. 6. Blair's Rhetoric. 7. Constitution of the United States. 8. Trigonometry, with its application to Surveying, Navigation, Mensuration, Astronomical Calculations, &c. 9. Paley's Evidences of Christianity, --a Monday morning lesson.

Class 1. [Third year, 1850-1]. Trigonometry, with its applications, &c., continued. 2. Paley's Evidences, continues--a Monday morning lesson. 3. Drawing, continued. 4. Astronomy. 5. Natural Philosophy. 6. Moral Philosophy. 7. Political Economy. 8. Natural Theology. 9. Cleveland's Compendium of English Literature. 10. French, continued,--or the Spanish language may be commenced by such pupils, as the judgment of the master have acquired a competent knowledge of the French....

The several classes shall also have exercises in English Composition and Declamation. The instructors shall pay particular attention to the penmanship of the pupils, and give constantly such instruction in Spelling, Reading and English Grammar as they may deem to be necessary to make the pupils perfect in these fundamental branches of a good education."

French was a required subject at the school since 1832, so Warren started his foreign travels with three years of French. But the primary emphasis, officially stated, was "decidedly scientific, not to say mathematical." (Cat. 1; Superintendent Bishop in 3d Report, 63).

.

Warren had the option of a fourth year, which included more astronomy, plus new topics of Logic, Spanish, Geology, Mechanics, Engineering and Higher Math, and Intellectual Philosophy, as preparation for MIT or another college. But we do not know if Warren took this option, but it seems unlikely, since he is not listed in capitals as graduate in 1851 (Cat. 1).

His mother Lydia recorded at the end of her diary for 1880: "One of Warren's classmates Edward Augustus Lecompte", followed by on obituary clipping that says he was born in Boston 14 Sept. 1835, received the Franklin Medal at Mayhew School and entered Boston English High School; Feb. 1852 Little & Brown bookstore; m. 24 July 1862 Frances Eliza Draper of Winsor CT, and Aug. 1862 pastor of Fourth Baptist Church; 1869 pastor Syracuse; 1874 pastor Baptist church in Lowell; he died 2 March 1880.

HOW WARREN GOT STARTED IN BUSINESS.

We now get a biographical story written by his son John G. Gould from Bass River, Cape Cod, 3 Oct. 1951:

"In about 1840 (I am guessing again) another young man came to Boston to seek his fortune--far better than he could have imagined as he worked on his father's farm in Lexington (Grapevine Corners) Massachusetts. He had dramatically run away from home, determined to face the perils and advantages of the city. By walking and an occasional lift from a friendly dray-driver, he finally reached the then growing mercantile port-center of the New England coast. Making his breakfast of part of a loaf of bread he had stowed away in his jacket pocket, and water from a convenient pump, he began to look about for Dame Fortune herself!" [The family did not move to Lexington until 1849, when Warren had finished Eliot School in Boston, where he had lived all his life. Perhaps he tried farming in Lexington, and then ran away to Boston].

The story continues [5]: "Walking along the streets of the business section, his attention was attracted to a man who was sweeping off the steps of one of the warehouses. Thomas Warren Gould judging from this gentleman's attire and his awkwardness in handling the broom, that he was not used to that sort of labor, asked if he might relieve the sweeper of his task."

"He could, and he did and thus launched himself into a career which was to make him well acquainted with Dame Fortune, take him into many foreign cities and enable him to acquire the education of a college-bred man and the polish of a diplomat. Less than five years after he thus met Mr. Lucius M. Beebe and swept off the warehouse steps of "Beebe Brothers", Warren was made their Foreign Buyer, making several trips annually to England, Ireland, Scotland, Germany, France and Switzerland, in quest of merchandise for that firm."

Lucius Beebe (1810-84) was founder of the oldest cotton brokerage firm in the country, in 1844. As a commission merchant, he first appears in Boston Directory of 1846 at 54 Commercial Street, then as today, the waterfront street between Long Wharf and the Charlestown Bridge (*National Cyclopedia of Amer. Biog.* 25:244; the middle initial "M" was that of his son and grandson, the well-known author and journalist, Nat. Cyc. 55:4). The Wakefield Town Library was dedicated as a memorial to him in 1922. In 1850 Beebe set up a company in his name, and in 1851 moved to 108 State Street, an address that continued thru 1859 (Dir. 1846/7, 12, 1847/8, 52, 247, 1848/9, 70, 1849/50, 71, 1850/1, 88). His biography describes him as "noted for his scrupulous integrity, generosity and hospitality. He was a man of high ideals and tender feelings, fond of children, kind, tolerant, and devoted to his family and home.

T. Warren Gould does not appear in the Boston Directory until 1853, when he his "Warren, clerk, 35 Kilby, boards 24 Hull". He was then 19, probably before he could start on his own, but maintaining his own office from 1853-8 on Kilby Street which is perpendicular to State Street, Beebe's office. The boarding address at 24 Hull Street, opposite Old North Church in the North End, was kept for the next decade, even after his marriage in 1855, he "boarded" there until 1859, and only in 1860-4 listed as his house.

Number 24 Hull Street was the well-known Hartt House, pictured in Reverend Porter's *Rambles in Old Boston* (Dir. 1850 88, 1851 23, 1852 25, 1853 33, 1854 35, 1855 31, 1856 33, 1857 34, 1858 34, 1859 40). This was a gambrel-roofed house of about 1725 with a later shed-roofed addition. The house was owned thru most of the nineteenth century by the Hartt family, the famous shipbuilders who built the frigate *Constitution*. The builder's oldest son Edward bought this house in 1803 from the heirs of the Boston caulker Alexander Baker. He died in Kentucky in 1823 where he was building river boats. His widow, Sally (Webb), daughter of the bookbinder Samuel Webb, continued living in 24 Hull Street with her remarkable sister Mary Webb, both of whom T. Warren and family must have known well, as their landladies.

Rev. Porter tells about Mary: "Mary Webb (born 1779, died 1861), a woman of rare character and great practical benevolence, although of humble means and a helpless cripple. She was an active member of Dr. Baldwin's [Second Baptist] church; and by the energy of her will and the promptings of her heart, she was able to do a charitable work among the poor which is deserving of high praise. Before the development of our city missionary societies, our Sunday-schools, and the organized charities of the present day [1887], Mary Webb was a society in herself, devising plans and executing// [189] them with surprising facility. Many of the former generation can remember her little hand-carriage, covered with green baize, in which she had herself wheeled about town on her errands of kindness to the needy and the suffering. Such an example could not fail to inspire others with her spirit of devotion; and the enterprises which she began in feebleness grew to large proportions by the generous support of the Christian public. The case is somewhat like that of Anna Gurney...too...a cripple, and went about in a perambulator; yet she overcame her natural disability..." to aid shipwrecked sailors, starting a life-boat service that later became the Royal Humane Society. "The life of neither Mary Webb nor Anna Gurney has ever been written, and the two probably never heard of each other; but their trials and their triumphs were singularly alike, and their record is on high."

Overlooking Copp's Hill burial ground, Porter says, "The Hartt estate is defined in an old deed as 'situate in Hull Street near Corpse Hill,' a grim way of spelling the familiar name, and apparently not uncommon even among those who might have known better. Doubtless, in the imagination of some who live in the neighborhood to-day, there is no other way of spelling it."

After the initial entry in Boston Directory of "Warren" in 1853, he is always "T. Warren Gould" thereafter, 186).

We propose that he was Beebe's foreign buyer of textiles 1853-9. Houghton & Dutton is not listed in any of these years.

MARRIAGE TO CAROLINE GODDARD, 1855.

When he was 21 years old T. Warren Gould was married # **29.** CAROLINE GODDARD of Boston. They met at the old Mechanic's Building according to their son's account:

T. Warren Gould, "Hearing of 'The Mechanics' Fair' after return from one of his trips abroad, and alert to keep abreast of technical and mechanical know how, he went to see it. He was now, 'a coming young man' and he neglected no opportunity to familiarize himself with whatever was new or better through skill or research."

"At the 'Fair' he of course saw many wonderful and beautiful sights but it was not until he stood before the exhibit of 'Elias W. Goddard & Sons,' --Coopers, that he became instantly, completely and irrevocably intrigued!"

"In that booth stood a young lady (Miss Caroline Goddard) and for the next 35 years her interests (as his wife) and his interests (as her husband) were mutual!"

The Mechanics Building of 1867 was on the corner of Bedford and Chauncy Streets, near today's Lafayette Hotel (Dir. 1853 123, 1854 134).

This is not far from the homes of his ancestors Thomas^1 and William^2 Gould, and the English High School which he attended.

Warren and Caroline were married in Grace Church, Episcopal. The marriage was performed by Rev. George D. Wildes, on the groom's twenty-first birthday, 17 Feb. 1855 (*Boston Marriages 1855* MMR 89:18, #292; his occupation "clerk"; she is resident of Somerville, daughter of Elias Goddard; also in family record of Ida Gould). The choice of Grace Church over Caroline's father's Old North is perhaps because the Goddards had moved to Cambridge in Aug. 1853.

About 1915, from C.T.& Co. "Souvenir of Boston, Mass.". View taken from Hull St., T.W.Gould's first home in Boston where their first children were born; #24 on the right, was the Hartt House, home of the builder of the U.S.S. *Constitution.* Caroline's father was Senior Warden of Old North Church .

After a honeymoon of two weeks, their first home was Grapevine Corner, Lexington, as we see from a calling card,

"Mr. & Mrs. T. Warren Gould//
Miss Carrie Goddard//
[reverse] At Home Feb. 28th//
Waltham Street--Lexington".

We get a glimpse of the Lexington family's reactions from a letter of his 17 year old sister Sophia to her brother Charles on 3 Feb. 1856: "Have you seen Warren's wife lately? How does she enjoy being in the city? Does Warren ever laugh or joke now? or is he as sober as a deacon--I think the poor boy is to be pitied. Look out that you do not make a like fool of yourself Charles--as for me, I would sooner be an old maid & 'dry up', and 'blow away', than to make such a confounded fool of myself as W----has done--I shall most certainly 'look before I Seven children were born to the couple, first two girls, Ida and Caroline, then five boys, Charles, Frederick, Samuel, John and Warren. Dates of their lives appear at the end of this chapter, and biographies of the adults in subsequent chapters.

Their first born child was Ida Warren Gould, poetess and librarian, born at 24 Hull Street in Boston 10 Oct. 1856 (MBR 98:145, #1007, no name given, female; Family record). The first grandchild was brought out to Lexington in the first year, as we see from the diary of 14 year old Lucy (17-24 Jan.: "The baby has grown lots since I saw her last", "George [Estabrooks] thinks Warren has got a real pretty baby", 11-13 July: "Warren[,] Carrie & the baby came out we went to Sandy Pond".

The Lexington family went into Boston to see the June 17 parade: "Warren was in the procession". Since this is before he joined the Masons, it is unknown in what group he was represented.

A second daughter, Caroline Gertrude, was born in the same North End house in Boston 19 Nov. 1858 (MBR 116:74, #3313, no name given, female; father clerk; name from family record). She died at age 21 in Boston 27 Feb. 1881, of emphysema (MDR 330:58).

WARREN'S BUSINESS SUCCESS IN EUROPEAN TEXTILES.

John Gould's account of his father's business continues, "Subsequently [to working as Beebe's Foreign Buyer], he performed similar services for a well known Boston firm, "Houghton & Dutton". (Their store building has long since been torn down)"

"By a strange coincidence, three decades later, in that same store, the youngest son of Mr. Gould (John) was to meet a gentleman and inaugurate a career of exceptional trust and accomplishment."

"Because of his knowledge of Textiles (Cotton, Linen and Wool) Mr. T. W. Gould became an authority and was frequently consulted to fairly appraise quality of importations made by other concerns."

A marked shift is found in 1859 when D. Beebe appears as principal of L. Beebe & Co. (40), when Lucius's son Decius is taken into the firm (The firm became Lucius Beebe & Sons after 1868 when a son was taken in; Lucius Sr. retired in 1884, *Nat. Ency.* 25:244). (There was an indirect relation between the publishers Edward Dutton (Boston 1852-69) including the Old Corner Book Store under Osgood Co., which was sold to Henry Houghton (Boston 1848 ff.), but I can find no direct connection. Warren Gould showed no publishing interest until his retirement about 1880. John Gould may well have been hired by Houghton, Mifflin, but I find no Houghton & Dutton).

Simultaneously, when Warren is 25, he appears independently as salesman at 60 Franklin Street (173). There is no Houghton & Dutton, but the next year he shows up as salesman at Jordan, Marsh & Co. at Devonshire between Franklin & Sumner (187). In 1861 he is a salesman at 154 Devonshire Street, which is one of Jordan Marsh's addresses, 148-150 (190, 247). We can find no Houghton & Dutton for this era, and propose that his son John has mistaken it for Jordan Marsh, for whom he worked 3 years 1859-1861.

Our first evidence of Warren's foreign travels is an ocean insurance policy that has been kept in the family, dated 18 April 1859, from Connecticut Mutual Life Insurance Co.: "Thomas Warren Gould insured by Policy N° 19419 is hereby permitted to pass by sea in first class vessels from Boston to, & return from any Port in England France or Germany, and to travel in Central Europe, by the usual means of public travel, north of the 42nd. degree of north Latitude, & west of the 30th. degree of east Longitude, during one year from the date hereof, without prejudice to said Policy. Gary R. Phelps Sec'y". This was the time of the famous clipper ships, racing across the Atlantic at record speeds, but also of the rival trans-Atlantic steamers of the British lines.

Warren, being 27 to 30 years old during the Civil War, was surely eligible for military service. According to his granddaughter Caroline Gould, he hired a substitute, the usual price being $100 (Letter to author 28 Feb. 1976). Overseas travel may have been difficult because of the Confederate raids on Northern shipping, but Thomas probably traveled on British ships. The threat of seizure also drove up prices of European goods, so Gould probably did well financially during the war. The progress of his social status is shown in the difference in occupations on his sons' birth records: In Aug. 1860 he is a salesman; but in Feb. 1864 he has become a merchant.

Warren was successful enough in business to be able to afford a summer vacation at the seaside, the first of the family to enjoy such luxury. John Shaw has a letter of Warren's dated 12 Aug. 1861 from Boston urging his parents to visit them at Hull for a night, coming down on the first train from Lexington to catch the 9:15 boat from the foot of Pearl Street over to Hull, or to come down with him on the last boat at 6 pm. This is when he was working as a salesman at Jordan Marsh on Devonshire Street. We have a single photo of a house at Hull, without address or date, which could be almost any year.

Warren was helping his father with finances, by paying a large part of his mortgage payments and buying butter from the Lexington farm. This is seen in Thomas's Cash Book of 1861. Four times in the year Warren gave him cash to pay Glover's interest: $30 on 1 April and 1 Oct, $80 on 5 Nov. and $35 on 2 Dec., totaling $175. He bought a firkin of butter 18 March for $11.14, and $7 on 2 Dec.. Warren returned $15 he had borrowed via Edward Bailey, his daughter Sophia's fiance. On 13 Feb. he paid Warren $2.25 for cloth to pay for rents, and $1.12 in cash for cloth. On 30 Nov. they squared accounts through Frank Harrington, 50¢ for Thomas, and 87¢ for Warren.

DEATHS OF FIRST TWO SONS, 1862-1863.

Caroline and Warren's first son Charles was born at 24 Hull Street in Boston 20 Aug. 1860 (*Boston Births, 1860* #3001 in Boston VR Archives, City Hall (hereinafter VR). The father's occupation is listed as "salesman". Warren's sister Annie who was at Hull Street to help, reported home about the happy birth of a first son:
"Warren says it shall be called Geo. Washington, he is as patriotic as ever. You ask me if it is pretty; it is the very picture of its papa, but we can hardly tell what it looks like yet, at best 'tis a squearming, screaming little piece of mortality." (Annie to Lucy 21 Aug. 1860).. However, it was named Charles Walter Gould, probably for his uncle Charles Winship Gould, lumberman. Annie stayed on to help with the children and reported at the end of the month: "I can't come home 'till the middle of next week perhaps not then...Ida kept me up all night with the earache and I shall feel splendidly by afternoon. I desire never to have any babies." (Annie lost her life giving childbirth to twins in 1872; Annie to Lucy, 31 Aug. 1860).
. On 4 Sept. she reported: "I'm getting terrible lazy, for I have to rock Carrie so much, that it makes me sleepy too....Warren got me a nice hoop skirt, it cost two dollars...."

The sudden death of this child Charles at only 18 months, on 10 March 1862, of pneumonia, was a great blow to the family (MDR 158:34).. Lydia's diary has the following entries: "March 6: note from Carrie all well...March 10 Mrs. Bailey rode up horseback this morning to bring the sad news of Warren's darling boy's death, how will he bear it--he was their pride and hope. God be with them." March 11: "Anna has gone up on the first train. I went in the second train, found Carrie calm but distressed, her darling snatched from her so sudden, sick only three days, dear blessed boy their loss is his gain" March 12: "dear Warren I do pity him, his pride and hope taken from him, but I hope it will lead him to god, and teach him that all his blessings are only lent//God gives and takes as he knows best". March 13 "the dear child was buried yesterday Rev. Mr. Huntington [Frederic Dan Huntington, first rector of Emmanuel Church, Back Bay] attended. the funereal."

This tragedy was lightened ten days later by the joy of the birth of the second son, Frederick, on 20 March 1862 (MBR 159:32, #1386, father merchant; name in family Record).

Frederick may have been named for the Emanuel minister, who spelled his name without a "k". Lydia records the event in her diary: "March 20 Anna arrived in the three oClock train, and brought the happy news, of a darling little boy baby at Warrens may he be a comfort and blessing to them both."

Warren was living at 24 Hull Street in the North End, as shown in Annie's letter reporting baby sitting again, as she closes her letter: "The baby is crying and I must take him--" (Annie to Lucy 16 May 1862. At end under Oct. cash).

.

That summer Warren, Carrie and the three children went out to Lexington to board at Grapevine Corner for three months. "July 12 Warren and his family came here to board for ten dollars per week...Aug 2 Warren paid all up to this date...Aug. 6 Warren went fishing...Oct. 7 Warren went home... Warren's board came to $127".

Lydia also went into Boston and stayed at Warren's: "Dec. 3 Boston...Dec. 4: staid all night with Warren for the first time since he was married [1855]". He took her twice to the Boston theater: Dec. 3 went to see an entertainment with Warren...Dec. 5 went to see Booth with Warren".

Just before Christmas Warren's family went out to Lexington: "Dec. 17 Carrie and the diamonds come to spend the day [;] Warren come to spend the night...Dec. 18 Carrie and the baby went home in the last train//she took three dozen of Eggs of me." Lydia sewed New Years presents for the three: "Dec. 31...finished the babys for Warrens children, and a little rabbit for the baby."

The second boy Frederick was not yet a year old when he died of scarlet fever, in Boston 4 Feb. 1863 (MDR 167:161). Annie reported to her sister: "Our baby, our boy is gone! God pity poor Warren, his cup is full; surely we all have now a hold on Heaven, for where the treasure is, there the heart is also. The funeral takes place Friday afternoon...I shall go to the city early tomorrow. I cannot tell when I shall go to N[ewburyport?]. if ever. Carrie may want me with her for a day or two. Oh Lu! may we be spared such sorrow--" (Annie to Lucy, Lexington 5 Feb. 1863).

From Boston she reported home: "Everything that can be done, has been. Carrie and Warren feel very, very badly, what more can we expect, their only son, their pride and darling, gone. Carrie and Warren both wish you to come in and that you can do in the second tram and go home in the three o'clock. Have Father come by all means--Charlie looks pretty, but like Ida now his eyes are closed. The children have not seen their mother since Friday until today, Ida feels badly, but Carrie asks all sorts of questions to make us cry--Carrie will put on black, and we want you to bring in our Zouave jackets both of them, for her to wear one, you know she cannot put on a dress. Mother wants the black broadcloth cape, hanging in the dining room--Yours in haste--Annie" (Annie to Lucy, Tuesday Afternoon [7 Feb. 1863]).

John Gould recalled: "Memorial stained glass windows for these two boys are now in Em[m]anuel Church (Episcopalian) Newbury Street, Boston. This is in the "Back Bay" district, not far from Arlington Street." (6).

Samuel C. Gould left this note about his brothers: "Charles Walter Gould...Died of Scarlet Fever=Buried in tomb or vault No( )[A] under Old North Church--Salem Street Deed for tomb or vault may be in Melrose together with another of my brothers Frederick ( ) Gould...I do not know Frederick's middle name, but some time in the future when you are in Boston and care to visit Em[m]anuel Church on Newbury Street, you may find some missing information on the two memorial windows in rear balcony window. If memory serves me correctly with the two above mentioned windows you will find a "Lawrence" family represented by one or more similar windows as those for my brothers Charles and Frederick. At the time when my folks lived at 14 Carver Street [later], Boston, both families attended Em[m]anuel Church. Later all moved to Longwood. attended The "Church of our Saviour". The head of the Lawrence family was a Mr. Amos & one of his sons was in the choir with me at the same time. His name was William and has been Bishop of Massachusetts for many years & not only that--but his son also named William is now Bishop of Central Massachusetts." (Undated note from S. C. Gould to D. W.

Gould about 1950?).

.

The memorial windows could not be found in 1963. From the description of their being in the rear balcony, it may be that they were covered up when the Leslie Memorial Chapel was built in 1924 (Harriet Robeson, "Emmanuel Church...The First Hundred Years" (Boston: The Vestry, 1960), 37). The cornerstone of the church was laid in 1861, and it was consecrated 24 April 1862 (Ibid., 9), so it is not unlikely that memorial windows could be dedicated in 1863. No record of the boys' baptism has been found at Emmanuel (Letter to D.W.Gould 8 Feb. 1963).

After the loss of two sons is it any wonder if the next boy was spoiled? Our grandfather, Samuel[8] Clifford Gould, was born in the Hartt House at 24 Hull Street in the North End on 3 Feb. 1864 (*Boston Births, 1864* #4841 in VR). Samuel was probably named for his well-known great-uncle, Samuel Lawrence Gould (1814-81), abolitionist orator and Boston school master. The source of the middle name is probably from his uncle Clifford Wayne Goddard (1837-1903), his mother's younger brother.

Annie wrote home to her sister Lucy: "I suppose you have heard the news-It's a boy-homely as Palmer [her father's first cousin Ezra Palmer Gould, then 13, born 27 Feb. 1841], I will tell him he looks like him, he arrived just as the bells rung nine wednesday eve...Warren is so proud that he allows all his friends to go up and see the boy-something unusual. He says he will call him Earnest,-appropriate dont you think so? Mrs H [the midwife?] did not come till yesterday//[2] morning, so I sat up the night before and took care of the folks. Mrs. Pitman [mother of Caroline's brother Walter's wife] was here too. I have an immense ironing, and an immense sick headache to attend to today. No girl and no prospect of one...Little Carrie is in Waltham [with her aunt Sophie Bailey] to stay a week. Ida spent Wednesday afternoon and night there..." (I date this undated letter as 5 Feb. 1864 which was a Friday, because Samuel was born on a Wednesday as she states, whereas Frederick was born on a Thurs. at 3 pm as previously reported, and Charles on a Monday, before Sophia lived in Waltham).

The next year, 1864, the family moved to 14 Carver Street for a decade, where Sammie began school, between the family trips abroad. When he was 12 they moved to Brookline.

Meanwhile, in 1862, when Warren was only 24, he set himself up in business with a partner under the name Wakefield & Gould, at 8 Arch Street (From 55 Franklin to 28 Summer Street; Dir. 1862, 173, 9). William L. Wakefield, commission merchant, had been working with Gould as a Jordan Marsh salesman (Dir. 1861, 451, 247).. The partnership lasted only six years, for in 1866 the name of the firm became T. Warren Gould & Co. at the same 8 Arch Street address (263), but Wakefield listed separately (513), and disappearing from Boston the next year. The firm continued at different addresses until 1885, for 20 years.

The summer of 1863 was spent in Hull again, as Samuel noted on a letter from Caroline's father Elias Goddard dated 31 Aug., and quoted in a later chapter.

In 1864, when Warren was only 30 years old, we get a clue to what was to kill him at the young age of 60 in this letter in his usual florid handwriting.

"Boston Sept. 14.1864

Dear Sister Lucy

Please accept the accompanying trifle as a slight token of affection from Carrie and myself, and with them our mutual wishes for your happiness today, and for many, many returns of this the anniversary of your birth-day.

The sincere regret that we are unable to present them to you in person, and receive a kiss from you in return, but Sammy's health is such, that we dare not risk the jaunt.

Expecting soon to see you at No 14 [Carver Street]

I remain as ever

You big brother (*weight 217 lbs)*[in mock shakiness]

Warren".

MOVE TO 14 CARVER STREET, 1864-1876.

In 1864 the family made a big move from their childhood homes in the North End, at 24 Hull Street, to the original Gould neighborhood of the South End, at now stylish 14 Carver Street John's biography records, "In Boston, they lived at No. 14 Carver Street (not far from Park Square and then a select section of the city." This was on the east side of the street. Most of Carver Street has disappeared underneath the State Transportation Building in Park Square, but in 1864 ran from the Boston Common south from Boylston Street to Pleasant Street, approximately where Charles Street goes today. This was a fashionable residential district at the time. Edgar Allan Poe was born at 62 Carver Street in 1809 to a pair of actors (Plaque at SW corner of Boylston & Townsend alley; Harris 154). On the other side of the street, at #77 lived the famous educational reformer Horace Mann, and Nathaniel Hawthorne, and their wives the remarkable Peabody Sisters. There is no record in Suffolk Deeds Grantor or Grantee Indexes of any property here for T. Warren or Caroline Gould up to 1900, so the house must have been leased. The owner in 1874 was E. M. Bigelow.

In the twentieth century the old brick house became a restaurant which pictured its entry through a fine iron gate in a pretty brick wall. A review from the twenties reads "Mrs. Shipman has reopened her winter dining room at 14 Carver street, after a summer at Linekiln Lodge, Boothbay Harbor, Maine. This is pleasing news of the first order to the many who know the delight of lunching or dining in the atmosphere of a refined home of the Colonial period.//One can relax to full enjoyment inside the iron gate of 14 Carver street--where candlelight flickers on old glass, and early American furniture. The food is of the sort that calls for exclamations of epicurean delight. Mrs. Shipman is justly famed for her full course dinners at $2, while her special luncheon, from 11:30 to 2 o'clock, has been the talk of town.//14 Carver street is an ideal place at which to entertain one's friends. Phone Hancock 8125 for reservations."

It was here that the second surviving son, John[8] Hogg Goddard was born on Christmas Day of 1870 (*Boston Births, 1870* #3721; father's occupation "dry goods").

.

It was a short three blocks walk northwest to the family church, Emmanuel Episcopal on Newbury Street in the Back Bay. This Gothic revival church had been newly built in 1862 by Alexander Estey (AIA 278). At least one of the children went to Exeter Street School, on the corner of Newbury, for this created the family joke that Warren always signed his letters to the children, "The best Father in the Exeter Street School". The family went out onto the Common for celebrations, like one described by Annie: "I was in the city last Friday [;] carried Warren a boquet, dined with him [,] went on the Common to see the 'Star//[4] Spangled Banner' make pleasure ascencions, got late afternoon train..." (*Boston Atlas, 1874* [Philadelphia: G.M. Hopkins, 1874], 1, pl. R, 77; east side, middle of block).

The Gould family may have spent summers in Hull again, for Sophie met them in Hingham on 28 June looking for a house (Annie to Lucy 11-12 June 1865). Annie adds a frank comment about her brother's wife, saying "the week before I came home [12 June, above] W[arren] told Anna he was not going out of town this summer, and I should think she [Carrie] might be contented with two servants, and her large house, and try to save so much expense for Warren[.] [I]s it not to bad she such an unhappy//[4] thing. Ed [Bailey] said she had her Hull St uniform on the day they met her, he meant her horrid frown, what do you suppose makes her feel so toward Soph and me, I am sure I have not done nor said any thing that I know of [.] they have had Miss Saweyer thxx's there to have a surgical operation performed[.] I should think poor Warren would be discouraged, doing every thing to please her that is in his power with so little thanks from her, but I hope he will enjoy something with his children one of these days, he deserves some comfort for his hard work, poor dear boy may God sustain him..."(Two letters from Annie to Lucy 2 July 1865, 3 of short one, 12 of long).

Carrie accompanied her husband on a trip to New York in July, perhaps to a Masonic convention. Annie reported after her next visit to Boston: "I dined at Warren's on hash and //[2] ice-cream. Helen [Goddard, Carrie's only sister] was there, did not speak to me, Carrie's face looked almost as handsomely as yours last fall, she was quite pleasant, but is provoked with everyone because she has the teeth ache. I asked her what she thought of Jeff Davis' capture, and she replied she hadn't had a chance to think of any one but herself. She went to New York last week with Warren." (Short letter, Annie to Lucy 2 July 1865).

Family relations became quite strained over Warren's administration of the estate of his brother Charles, who died 17 Oct. 1865. Warren's officiousness is clear in an undated letter saved by his mother:

"All of my experience will be lost to Father if he administers.

A trip west will be necessary to obtain satisfactory settlement of the estate, and for this certainly Father is incompetent both by age and experience.

Most of the parties with whom Charles had dealings are personal friends and acquaintances of mine, and men who while they would esteem it a pleasure and a privilege to assist me to the utmost, would not be actuated by similar feeling in dealing with father.

I cannot conduct the entire business to a favorable settlement without the intervention of law or lawyers, with their bills of cost &C. which is more than Father or any other person will be able to do.

Remember Mother, I am not dictating. The dictation is Charlie's, and as such, should be responded to by us all, not only as a duty, but as a pleasure.

Read this well Mother and consider it better, and with the girls.

If you can view the matter in the light of reason, let me know of it by return of bearer to-night or by your personal presense at my house at seven o'clock tomorrow morning, after which time it will be too late for.

Your Affectionate Son

Warren".

The painful settlement of the estate has been related in the account of Charles's life in the previous chapter.

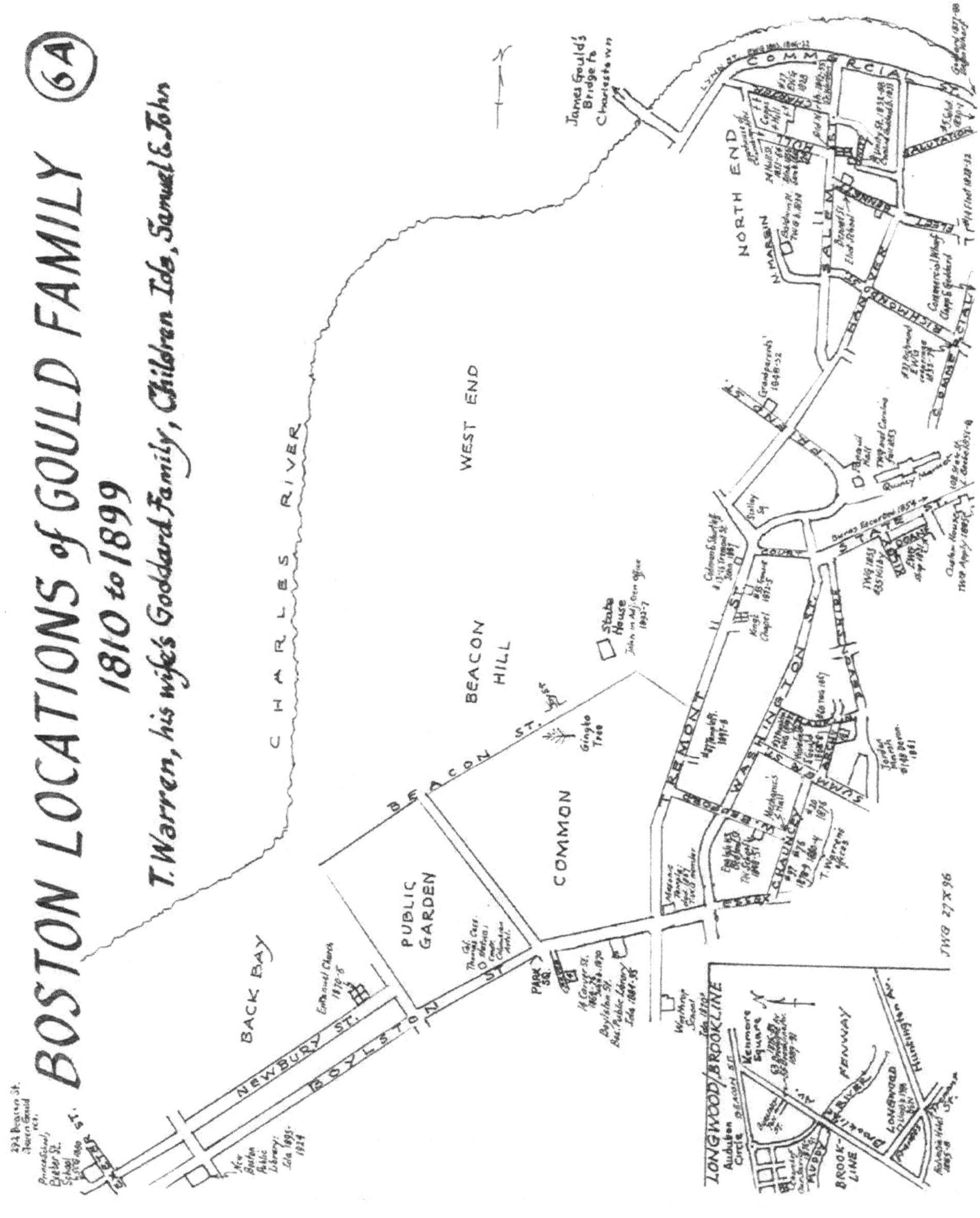

WARREN TAKES HIS WIFE CAROLINE TO EUROPE, 1866.

1866 is the first year we know of any detail of their travels in Europe. A letter from Queen's Hotel, Manchester, England, on 17 June 1866 tells much of Carrie's sadness in leaving her children at home, and her reaction to Paris that will be saved until the next chapter. Here just the details of the trip will be excerpted.

They arrived in Manchester 16 June, having left Paris on Weds. 13th, journeying at several places en route, including Leicester. Even in 1887 Queens Hotel was the best in Manchester, at #2 Piccadilly, "a large and long-established house near the London Road Station" (K. Baedeker *Great Britain*,1887, 341). In Paris she spent three weeks. During that time Warren "went to Germany alone; I was disappointed because I could not go with him; but probably it was quite prudent for me to remain in Paris, as he had to travel very fast indeed." Plans for the next week were unclear: "I dont know where we are going this week. We may go to Ireland, and Scotland, but it is not certain. However, next Saturday, the 23rd of June, we start from Liverpool for America, in the Steamer Cuba."

The steamer Cuba, Capt. James Stone, of the British & North America Royal Mail Steam Packet Co. advertised to leave Liverpool for Boston on 21 July 1866, first class fare £ 22. A woodcut shows a sidewheel steamer (Dir. 1866, 592).

The children, ages 10, 8 and 2, stayed with her sister Helen. This was probably Caroline's first trip abroad with Warren, about a month in length.

On the parents' return the Gould family went down to Hull again for the summer, staying until the last week of September, when school began. They had a day's visit from their grandfather, Elias Goddard, whose impressions are recorded in a later chapter. From this we get the only idea of their location, when Elias refers to "the high land directly in the rear of your House...".

After 1867 T. Warren Gould & Co. made changes of business address every year or two (Dir. pages in parentheses):
1867-8: 8 Arch Street where Wakefield & Gould had been since 1862 (222, 263).
1869: 37 Franklin Street (270).
1870-1: 3 Winthrop Square (between Devonshire & Otis, 294, 307).
1872-5: 55 Tremont Street (east side, between Court Street & King's Chapel, 317, 329, 397,

383).
1876: 20 Chauncy Street (between Summer & Avon, 385).
1877-8: 37 Temple Place (between Washington & Tremont, 383, 383).
1879: 97 Chauncy Street (394).
1880-4: 76 Chauncy Street (412, 430, 444, 455, 462).

The major change in this period was the mention of Jeffrey Hollingdale in the firm in 1873, who lived at 8 Alleghany, and stayed with the firm for several years (Letter of 21 Sept. 1866, 3).

Warren would not have missed the celebration of the fiftieth anniversary of the founding of his English High School, on 2 May 1871, when 1200 graduates gathered at Fanueil Hall, and marched to the Music Hall where a capacity audience was greeted by the Governor, and a bust of Principal Sherwin by the sculptor Thomas R. Gould (no known relation; Cat. xx), a graduate of the school in 1834, was unveiled (Dir. 1874, 397).

We have a receipt for $72.90 premium paid to New York Life Insurance Company for a $3000 insurance on the life of T. W. Gould, at 37 Franklin Street [his office] for policy #33689, 17 Aug. 1869, issued by their Boston branch agent D. W. Russell, 13 Merchants Exchange on 7 Aug. This may have preceded a trip to Europe.

THE WHOLE GOULD FAMILY IN EUROPE, 1871-1872.

In 1871 Warren took the whole family along to Europe, probably for the first time. John was only seven months old, Sammie 7, Carrie 13, and Ida 15. The newspaper clipping of 7 Oct. 1871 reads: "DEPARTURE OF THE CALABRIA. The Cunard steamship Calabria, Captain McMicken, will sail this afternoon for Liverpool direct. She has 47 cabin and 70 steerage passengers, and a valuable cargo of domestic cotton. The following is a list of the cabin passengers:...[listed after 5 names] Mr. and Mrs. T. Warren Gould and infant [John, 7 months old], Master Samuel C. Gould, Miss Ida W. Gould, Miss C. Gertrude Gould and maid, Mrs. Austin, Miss Austin and two Misses Austin..." Among the other passengers were distant cousins J. Amory Codman and James Greene.

In anticipation of the trip Warren had his New York Life Insurance policy 33,689 extended to permit travel in Europe & Elsewhere, Dated Oct. 2^{d} 1871".

We do not have an itinerary, but we do know they spent Christmas of 1871 in Leipzig, Saxony, in the new German Empire, for we have the inscription in Sammie's present, the German book, *Unzerreissbares Bilderbuch* [Stuttgart: K. Thienemann, c. 1871], a nicely illustrated collection of childrens' stories and puzzles. It is rebound, title and first pages missing, inscribed on the cover: "Samuel Clifford Gould, Leipzig, Dec. 25, 1871".

From this period also are three English childrens' books, perhaps brought home on an earlier trip by Warren, or bought on this trip: Anon., *The Good Child's Album* [London: Routledge, c. 1870, four classic childrens' stories with 18 colored plates: "Little Red Riding-Hood", "Old Mother Hubbard", "Cock Robin" and "The Three Kittens". *Aunt Louisa's Gift Book* [London: Frederick Warne, 1867] has four more stories, 24 color plates. The stories are "Nursery Songs", "Edith and Milly's Housekeeping", "Life of a Doll" and "John Gilpin". The third book is *Aunt Louisa's Holiday Guest* [London: Frederick Warne, c. 1870], four stories and 24 color plates. The stories are: "Dame Trot and her Cat", "The Good Children", "Bruin the Bear" and "Home for the Holidays".

One of my childhood favorites was "Home for the Holidays", which had pictures of children travelling by train, just as the Goulds travelled. Under the glass-domed station is the locomotive with a tall stack. The boys wear jackets and slacks, with hats, as Sammie was probably dressed. The full-bearded men have tall stove-pipe hats, or Derbys. The girls have full skirts trimmed with lace, thin bodices, and perched on long hair are tiny hats trimmed with feathers. They are miniatures of their mothers, dressed in gorgeous gowns of costly cloth that Warren imported into the United States.

We have a Swiss souvenir from this period, a 2" x 3½" color picture that was framed for "Ms Gould: Cut Matt and PP No 1//6 Pict Sat SF 1,50", perhaps for Ida. The scene, by "R. Dikenmann, Peintre, Zurich", of Gersau in Canton Schwytz, on the north shore on Lake Luzern. It shows the lake on the right with a steamer at the dock, and on the left a grand four-story hotel, perhaps the Gersauer Hof (K. Baedeker *Switzerland* [Leipzig: Karl Baedeker, 1882], 98). This is beneath the famous Rigi, and only two miles east of Vitznau, where the James Gould family stayed in 1966.

Warren's son John's biography recalls some homes in Europe: "In Paris, their residence was in a fine house not far from, 'The Church of Mary Magdalen'. In Switzerland they resided in a hotel on the shore of Lake Lucern." (6). This might be Gersau or another hotel. The Paris location is probably La Madeleine, in the heart of fashionable Paris, on the first of the Grand Boulevards, and only two blocks from the Place de la Concorde and the Opera (K.Baedeker *Paris* [Leipzig: Karl Baedeker, 1898], 80-1).

Whatever Warren's quarrels were with his family, they loved his sense of humor. His sister Sophie Bailey's letter of 1872 tells of an enjoyable entertainment in Boston:

"Ned [her husband] enjoyed himself too=but most of all Warren's inimitable personation of a 'hot potato' pedlar, who kept warming his hands, nose and ears,//with the 'taters', on the street=corner, when he thought no customers were in sight. If, every good, heartstirring laugh a man causes here on earth, counts one reward of merit in Heaven, what a seat that Warren will have, close by the Throne.

May he be in nor hurry to take it however, till I am off the stage." (Sophia to her mother Lydia 9 Jan. 1872, 3-4).

One of the few letters that survived was written by Warren to his daughter in 1872, probably to 16 year old Ida, who was sketching in the Swiss Alps, at Gersau, while the rest of the family was in Paris, written from his Boston office:

"55 Tremont Street
Boston July 6. 1872

My Dear Daughter

I received your very welcome letter of June 13 a few days since (length of time suggests she was in Europe) but with the mercury at 100 even the pleasure of writing to you failed to tempt me to the necessary exertion.

I have been broiled, stewed. roasted and parboiled so for the past week, that my 'Turkish baths' last night, seemed to me but five degrees warmer than the outside world, although it really was, fifty-five.

The surprise of my appearance at No. 19 was great, although the news of my intended visit was pretty well circulated.

I buckled down to the main pursuit of my life, the acquisition of phosphorus, immediately on my arrival, and since that time, or about seven weeks, I do not think I have eaten meat seven times. But the consumption of Oysters, lobsters, and fish in all variety, baked beans and brown bread, has been as 'the beats' would say, 'perfectly immense.'

At the present time of writing I think my intellect does not require another whale, and as for phosphorus, I have stock enough to start a match factory, either of wood, or of 'the race'.

This last, is entirely new, and you may not 'see the point', unless you lean forward in the pew and look at your mother [who was seven months pregnant with Warren Jr., born Paris 8 Sept. 1872].//

Your account of the sunset on the mountains was interesting and I should have enjoyed it if I had been present but I still maintain and affirm, that

'Not sunny France or fair Italia's skies,
Such beauteous sunsets furnish to our eyes,
As Boston common, when at close of day
Our faces homeward turned from work or play
Towards fourteen, where all our treasures lay
And where I hope we long again may stay
Nor following fickle Goddessess fortune stray
from the corner of Carver and Boyleston streets'

[the reference to fourteen is to the Goulds' home at 14 Carver Street; this may be original with TWG, or an adaptation].

You will see above, what fish will do, for here instead of answering your letter, I find myself soaring into the ninth sphere of machine poetry.

If you think Gersau is good sketching ground for artists, why not 'steal a march on them' all, by filling your own portfolio with 'the gems' before you advertise it to the public.

You and Miss Kuhn and Mr. Gould [Samuel, age 8?] will make it livelier all round in that dismal Gould family when he arrives, which will be in about ten days after this letter reaches you.

'Oh that will be joyful, joyful, joyful,
When we meet to part no more'

Johnnie [age 2] seems to be particularly favored with aches and pains and I think rather more than his share, but I hope by this time he has recovered.

By the bye do you think he will remember me?"

Warren's reference to a diet of phosphorus sounds like a treatment for his diabetes. Prior to the use of insulin in 1923 the only treatment was diet, which we know today to be a third of the triangle of treatment of food-insulin-exercise. The substitution of seafoods for fatty meats and starchy potatoes may have been helpful, but phosphorus itself wouldn't have helped.

The letter suggests that Warren returned to Boston alone from Europe about 1 June, and intended to leave 16 July. Check passenger lists in news.

There was tragedy upon his return to the family in Paris. Caroline gave birth to their seventh child, named for his father, Warren Gould, on 8/9 Sept. 1872. He died four days later. The family buried the baby in the famous Père Lachaise Cemetery, 13 Rue Street André, Paris, in the 19th division, 22d line, 111th grave (card of Auguste Destieux, marble carver). We have a sad reflection on death written by Warren's wife Caroline, probably at this time, which we will quote in the next chapter on her life.

My favorite description of the cemetery is Mark Twain's *Innocents Abroad*, in 1867, only five years before: "One of our pleasantest visits was to Père la Chaise, the national burying ground of France, the honored resting place of some of her greatest and best children, the last home of scores of illustrious men and women who were born to no titles, but achieved fame by their own energy and their own genius. It is a solemn city of winding streets and of miniature marble temples and mansions of the dead gleaming white from out a wilderness of foliage and fresh flowers. Not every city is so well peopled as this or has so ample an area within its walls. Few palaces exist in any city that are so exquisite in design, so rich in art, so costly in material, so graceful, so beautiful…"

"The great names of Père la Chaise impress one, too, [like the royal tombs of St. Denis], but differently. There the suggestion brought constantly to his mind is that this place is sacred to a nobler royalty--the royalty of heart and brain. Every faculty of mind, every noble trait of human nature, every high occupation which men engage in, seems represented by a famous name. The effect is a curious medley. [Napoleon's Generals] Davoust and Massena, who wrought in many a battle tragedy, are here, and so also is Rachel, of equal renown in mimic tragedy on the stage. The Abbé Sicard sleeps here--the first great teacher of the deaf and dumb--a man whose heart went out to every unfortunate...and not far off, in repose and peace at last, lies Marshal Ney, whose stormy spirit knew no music like the bugle call to arms. The man who originated public gas-lighting, and that other benefactor who introduced the cultivation of the potato and thus blessed millions of his starving countrymen, lie with the Prince of Masserano, and with the exiles queens and princes of Further India. Gay-Lussac the chemist, Laplace the astronomer, Larrey the surgeon, DeSeze the advocate, are here, and with them are Talma, Bellini, Rubini; de Balzac, Beaumarchais, Beranger; Molière and La Fontaine, and scores of other men…"

"But among the thousands and thousands of tombs in Père la Chaise, there is one that no man, no woman, no youth of either sex, ever passes by without stopping to examine...This is the grave of Abelard and Héloïse--a grave which has been more revered, more widely known, more written and sung about and wept over, for seven hundred years, than any other in Christendom save only that of the Saviour...Go when you will, you find somebody snuffling over that tomb…"

"Yet who really knows the story...? Precious few..." Clemens then tells the story how the "dastardly seducer" Abelard deliberately debauched a confiding, innocent girl, under the roof a trusting friend.

Warren's refusal of the legacy of his grandfather's estate probably reflects his relative prosperity at this time. When Warren's uncle, Francis Gould, settled his grandfather Thomas[5] Gould's estate in 1872 he mailed checks to all the heirs including Warren. Francis wrote to Lydia from Crosby & Gould, Solicitors of American & Foreign Patents, No. 34 School Street, Boston on 17 Dec. 1872: "At the same time I sent checks to Sophia & Lucy, I sent one to Warren for the same amt. This check he has returned to me, & I endorse it over to you, this in my judgement being the correct way to dispose of it." (Orig. with Ron Shaw).

TRIP TO GREAT BRITAIN WITH DAUGHTER, 1874.

Warren probably made another trip to Europe in 1873. In 1874 he took his 15 year old daughter Caroline Gertrude on a whirlwind business trip thru the British Isles, for five weeks. The rest of the family stayed at their summer place at Hull for a week or so, then moved back to 14 Carver Street, Boston.

Warren and Carrie left Boston on the Cunard steamship *Atlas*, Capt. Hoseason (Clipping dated 15 Sept. 1874). The two are listed among the 17 cabin class passengers, including Mr. & Mrs. Charles Forners, Mr. William Cochran, Mr. & Mrs. H. Simmons Jr. all of Boston, Mr. Thomas Smith & Miss Lina E. Smith of Natick, Mrs. J. Reid and child, Mr. William Gardner & child of W. Roxbury, Mr. J.N. Andrews, son & daughter, Mr. Adamar Winlienmier of Lancaster, and 180 steerage passengers.

Three of Carrie's letters to her sister Ida have survived. The first is on stationery of "Cunard Steam Ship Atlas", "Atlantic Ocean Sept. 16th '74:

"I shall write as much as possible to-day and try and fill the sheet before we get to Queenstown (Cork, Ireland). I have not been sick yet, as it has been remarkably smooth so far, but I expect to be, before long. After the steamer left, yesterday, I went down below and took everything out that I thought Papa or I would want, then went on deck till lunch.

Papa waited till we had passed Hull, and saw Mr. and Mrs. Kellog and Capt. Hale on the beach, waving the American flag. We then sat on deck till dinner, then on deck again till after dark, when we went to the cabin. I felt a little sleepy, and after drinking a bottle of ale, I retired. Papa stayed up for fried sardines. I did not sleep well at all, but rose a half past six, and felt a great deal better after getting on deck. After breakfast, I sat down to write.

Mr. and Mrs. [H.] Simmons are very pleasant people, and I like them very much. they sit next to us//at table, we are next to the Captain [Hoseason].

Mr. [Thomas P.] and Miss [Lina E.] Smith I do not fancy at all, if they <u>are</u> relations to the Vice-President [Republican Henry Wilson of Massachusetts (1812-75), who died in office 1875]. The other passengers are a Missionary [J.N.Andrews] and his two sons and a daughter, a French lady and gentleman [Charles Forners?], and two ladies with two little children [Mrs. J. Reid and Mrs. William Gardner of W. Roxbury]. So you see, we have a very lively crowd of passengers.

Wednesday, Sept. 23rd

After writing the above, I fell asleep in the cabin, and slept till the luncheon bell awoke me. The next night was pretty rough, and in the morning it was as much as I could do to get on deck, with the assistance of the Stewardess. I lay in the chair all day, too sick to open my eyes; the next day I was in by berth all day. Saturday morning, however, I got on deck, and have not been really sick since. Monday I commenced coming to the table, and now am well as any one on board. Papa has not been sick at all,//and I am very glad he was so fortunate, as to escape it.

We are now counting the days till we reach Liverpool, or, rather, I count the nights, as they seem the longest and most tedious. We expect to reach Queenstown (Cork, Ireland) some time on Friday, most likely in the afternoon, and Liverpool on Saturday. If we get there in time for Papa to transact his business, we shall go to Leicester the same day, if not, we will stay in Liverpool over Sunday.

Papa thinks it will be best to put all the things we will want coming home, into the trunk, and leave it in Liverpool; then get all the other things into the valise and bag, and then we won't have the bother of the trunk. I think I can manage it, though it will be close packing.

We think less and less of the Smiths; they make themselves very disagreeable on board, and no one seems to like them except the French man and his wife.

Mr. [H.] Simmons is the gentleman of the firm of Dalney & Co. that Papa heard of as going, in the office. Mrs. Simmons is a cousin to//Miss Heyer who was in Hull, and sister to the Charlie Heyer that Kate Bennett talks so much about. So she seems a little like an old acquaintance. She also knows the Birkmaiers very well.

The Captain [Hoseason] is a very pleasant man, though not so nice as Capt. Mcdowell. He has lent me two books since I got well, one of which I am reading.

I wish, if Mamma thinks of any thing else she wants me to get, that she would write and let me know. I hope my choice will suit you all, and I shall try my best to have it please.

I suppose you will have moved up from Hull when this letter arrives; it must be very lonesome down there now. I wish you all were here, but as it will only be for five weeks, we must make the best of it.

Tell Sammy and Johnny to be good boys, and I will bring them home something nice. The Steamer is getting pretty shaky now; and I think I will go on deck. I <u>may</u> write again to-morrow. Love to all, your affec. sister, Carrie."

Carrie next wrote to her sister Ida from the Washington Hotel, Liverpool 27 Sept. 1874: "We have just returned from Church, and as Papa is writing to Mamma, I shall take this opportunity to write to you, as I may not have another before the mail goes.

Of course you have seen by the despatches that the "Atlas" has arrived safely in Liverpool and of course you feel relieved to hear it.

I wrote that we expected to reach Queenstown [Cork, Ireland] Friday, but, unfortunately for us, a 'dense//fog' settled down in the forenoon, and after sighting land about noon, it faded away, and we saw no more land that day.

We proceeded, and about 8 oclock reached the entrance of Cork Harbor, and, still in a fog, whistling and sounding about ever five minutes, we 'fooled around' for two hours, and, no tender making it's appearance, we headed for Liverpool. So we did not see Mr. Lindsay, but hope to on our return. It was a very anxious night, and, after supper, we stayed on deck till 12 o-clock. The next morning, the fog had cleared away a little, and after lunch, about 1 o-clock, we passed Holyhead. It looked as pretty as ever, especially the bridge, and zigzag path, which the Captain called the lover's walk and I wished you were all here it enjoy it with me [Holyhead is the northwest point of Anglesey, "the chief object of interest near Holyhead is the bold rocky scenery of the *North and *South Stack]("Lighthouse on the latter", K. Baedeker, *Great Britain* [Leipzig: Karl Baedeker, 1906], 306). About 3-4 o-clock we picked up a pilot, and after our usual//supper of fried sardines, we went on deck just in time to see the signals of blue lights and rockets. The tender soon reached us, and, before long, we were safely landed, with our luggage, at Prince's landing stage (Prince's Landing Stage is the major quay on the Mersey; Baedeker 1906, map 340 A3). Hailing a four wheeler, we drove here, and have one of our old rooms (Washington Hotel, shown on the letterhead had five stories, with American and British flags on the rooftop).

We slept pretty soundly till 9, when we were glad to get hot baths. When ready, I went to the Coffee room, and while waiting for Papa, Mr. and Mrs. [H.] Simmons and Mr. [William] Cochrane called (both fellow passengers on the *Atlas*). After breakfast, and a short call at their hotel, Papa and I went to Herr Weissstein's, to deliver Mr. Frankenthal's letter. The aunt can not speak much english, but we were treated to beer and cake. They all send a great many 'greetings' to Mr. Frankenthal, and seemed much pleased to see us.//

We then returned to the North Western station, and saw our friends the Simmons' off, also Mr. [Thomas P.] and Miss [Lina E.] Smith, whom everyone heartily disliked by the time they left the steamer, to London in the same carriage. We expect to join them Wednesday at the Castle and Falcon.

After dinner, we went to church, a little way down the street, and enjoyed the service very much indeed.

We shall, probably, start for Leicester, to-morrow morning at 11.40, and stay there till Wednesday.

I wish very often, to see you all, but as that will do no good, I look at the picture once in a while.

Tell Mamma, that in that little bag of money she gave me, there is only 3½ pence, English mony, and about 2 francs, in French. I am at the end of the paper, and pretty sleepy, so good bye, with love to all.

Carrie."

From this we know that they were in Leicester 28-30 Sept., and London 1 Oct..

Carrie's third letter is from Belfast (Northern) Ireland, Wed. Oct. 16th 1874 on stationery of Alexander Guild & Co., Linen & Cambric Manufacturers:

"Your letter of the 28th has just been read, and as Papa is answering his, I will do the same.

We started from Nottingham on Monday, at noon, arriving at Birmingham at 3 o'clock. Left Birmingham at 10½, in the evening of the same day, for Glasgow, where we arrived at 7 o'clock in the morning. We were very tired, and slept till after 10. It is a very nice city, I think, with very nice stores. We went to the manufactory where the quilted bibs are made. I was shown the process of stamping the patterns on the cloth, and it occured to me that if I had the old cashmere here, that I could have had it stamped very nicely, and perhaps embroidered. Who knows?

We left Glasgow, (Jimmy Scott's native city) last evening at 8 o'clock, and traveled all night, reaching Belfast this morning at 6. It was very smooth crossing the Irish Sea, and no one was sea sick. I am sure I do'nt know what it means, my not being sea sick, unless it's that I am to be sick the whole passage going//home.

After breakfast we drove in a 'low backed car' to Mr. Guild's office, where we found our letters awaiting us. We leave for Dublin probably to night, perhaps stopping at Dundalk (on the east coast of Ireland, about halfway between Belfast and Dublin) for a few hours. Still I can't tell exactly what we shall do, until Papa gets through his business here.

The young lady ^whom you inquired about in one of your letters, was Miss [Lina E.] Smith, 'a relation of the Vice-President's"

I forgot to tell you when I answered your letter. She is going to France to keep house for he[r] brother, who is the United States Consul at Coignac. She is to be introduced into french society by a French lady, who has been Maid of Honor to the queen, or somebody. She couldn't seem to remember which.

We remembered that it was your [18th] birthday Saturday, and wished we were all together to celebrate it. The day after to-morrow we shall sail for America, and in 11 days from then you may expect us. It hardly seems possible that we have been so far//and seen so much in so little time. Papa is very much rejoiced at going home, and counts the nights till we shall be home.

I have had the nicest time I ever had in my life, although I am very tired just at present. It may seem very selfish of me to be here enjoying myself, and you and Mama at home, working so hard, but I can not help it now, and I think the best thing for me to do is to have as good a time as I can.

Give my love to all the folks, and kiss Johnny for me. I will add a few lines before this is posted.

Carrie G. Gould

Dublin.--9 p.m

Good night, too tired to write.
Leave for Cork in the morning,

your affec. sister

Carrie."

In 1878 Warren took his wife on the RMS *Parthia,* of which we have a souvenir of the works of Byron given to her by fellow passenger Horatio McKay (see note below on her biography).

In 1876 the Goulds left 14 Carver Street for a new home on Brookline Ave. near Short Street in Longwood (*Boston Directory 1876*, 385; Short Street, Roxbury, once called Appleton Place, and later Maple Av., (*Record of Streets* [City of Boston, Street Dept., 1891] 424, 14). This is perhaps the same place that is numbered 63 Brookline Ave., where they lived until 1885 (Dir. 1877 383, 1878 383, 1879 394, 1880 412, 1881 430, 1882 444, 1883 455, 1884 462, 1885 466). Brookline Ave. had only been laid out in 1868 across the Back Bay Fens and Muddy River of colonial times, and the low numbers looked out eastward across the street to a canal on the edge of the marshes (*Rec. of Streets*, 75; 1874 Atlas, pl. Z). But this country atmosphere was made socially attractive by Brahmin families that built mansions in Brookline. The Goulds were to live in Longwood for 15 years until they moved out to Melrose in 1891-2.

It is probably at this time that they transferred membership from Emmanuel Church in Back Bay to Church of Our Saviour, Longwood. The church had been built in the country only eight years before, for the Lawrence family, including future Bishop Lawrence, and the Amorys who were descended from Anne^2 Gould Greene (Herbert Fletcher, *A History of the Church of Our Saviour* [Brookline: Parish Council, 1936], 4, 8). The architect of Emmanuel Church designed this church to resemble an English parish church for the Brahmin society of Brookline. It still stands at 23 Monmouth Street, Brookline (AIA Guide 455).

A decade after the death of his brother Charles, Thomas was still criticized by his family for the handling of the estate. A letter of his sister Sophia Bailey from the resort at Temple

Mountain in 1876 responds to her mother's complaints about money: "fretting will not alter the most stubborn facts. It seems hard to be restricted at all when it goes against your nature, but Father did the best that he could for you, I think. That his judgment was far-seeing and wise, we had ample//proof when we rejected his counsels, and prevailed upon him to give up Charlie's affairs, to Warren's exclusive control, and perhaps he saw father, in your case, than we gave him credit for." (Sophia to Lydia 15 Aug. 1876, 3-4).

ILLNESS AND DEATH OF DAUGHTER CAROLINE, 1881.

Carrie, never strong, came down with TB, and in 1878 was placed in a recuperative home in Needham. She was under the care of Dr. James Ayer, who had an office at 135 Boylston Street, around the corner from the Goulds' former Carver Street home (Dir. 1878, 70). Warren wrote to his 19 year-old daughter from their home:

"63 Brookline Ave.
Boston Oct. 20. 1878
10 A.M.

My Dear Gertie

I rec'd your very [c]heerful note last Thursday, but have not, till this moment had an opportunity to acknowledge it.

I am glad to hear from all reports, that the trial trip to Needham has thus far proved a success. Although as you know yourself, yours is a desperate case, yet [in] the providence of God, He may, as in many living witnesses, perform a miracle in your case, and give you yet a long life of health and happiness.

But remember this, that 'God helps those, who help themselves.'

All that can be done for you by Mother and myself, or that Dr. Ayr can suggest, will amount to naught if you do not use the best judgement yourself. I will not repeat my 'crochets' so often given you, but hope you have them all by//heart and will put them in daily practice, and I shall not be surprised in your next report to hear that you weigh 96 pounds instead of 95½. One of my oldest and most "chronic" crochets is, you know, "fresh air, and plenty of it"

By this I do not mean a draft, for you can not stand that as I could, but for you it is the best medicine you can take.

Mrs. Whitney has had ample experience in her own case, and knows just about what you want. When you are out riding some afternoon with Mrs. Whitney, ask her to drive up to Highlandville, to Alexander Bynes hosiery factory.

Ask him to let you have 3 or 4 pairs of stockings to fit you, out of the lot of seconds or imperfect goods such as I had of him last and I will settle with him when next I see him.

Tell him to show you both, through his factory, as it is a sight worth seeing.

Your Grandmother, on your Mothers side [Caroline Garran Goddard, who died 18 months later, of catarrhal fever],//has been very sick for a week or more, but was a little better last evening.

"Pet" [his wife] and "Johann" [her brother John who was probably called that as a baby in Germany] went to the fair yesterday Pa, Sammie and Johann went to the Howard-Friday [.]
Business is goin to the D--- every day
"Jones' cow has had a calf"
"Sauce is higher" and Potatoes have "riz"
"Pet" had a letter from our friend the Captain and has put it in her bosom or stocking. I had a

bundle of papers from him, and sent him a letter to-day.

"Johann" has had his hair cut, and his mother had been learning the hair-cutting trade on him, the man had to give him a close fighting cut to cover up the gaps she made on his scull, and his head now looks like a billiard ball.

I am in hopes to get up to Needham soon, but cannot fix the dates. Write me once in a while and report progress. All send love, joined with that of the best father in the Exeter st school.

Carrie (or Gertie, as her parents called her) was being treated for TB, of which she died 2½ years later, at age 22. John's story recounts, "Caroline, youngest of the daughters, died when about 21 years of age and was buried in Mt. Auburn Cemetery." (6). She died in Boston 27 Feb. 1881, of emphysema, in the official report (MDR 330:38). She was the fourth of the seven children to die, leaving only the three tough ones, Ida and John, who lived to nearly 90, and Sammie, the alcoholic wreck, who lived to 83.

Warren's son Samuel preserved an undated letter which he dated during the summer of 1879 or 1880 and sent from from "The Carrollton", Baltimore, Light & German Sts., Baltimore MD: "Friday 8.30 P.M.

My Dear Children

I have only time to say that we are well, but very tired. It has been a continual "circus" since we started, but ma has souvenirs of every item en route, and will tell all she knows on her return. We are just off to a "grand" reception but they are getting rather common. Leave//here at 8.30 A M for New York and Sunday night leave for Boston arriving about 9.15. Perhaps Sammie would like to see us on our arrival at the depot if he comes up to Boston on Monday

Best love of ma and
Your "best Father
in the Exeter st school"."

SUMMERS AT HULL.

All of the Gould children had fond memories of childhood summers at Hull, Mass. Sammie and Ida recalled staying at the Old Oregon House, opposite the Hull Yacht Club (Photo of "Road to Stony Beach" in Album #11). Ida recalled spending several summers in the Smith Cottage opposite Ed Knight's house on Main St.

SIR THOMAS WARREN GOULD, KNIGHT TEMPLAR?

Samuel penciled this comment on the above letter:
"NOTE June 4th 1938
Douglas.

This letter from my Father was written to my sisters Ida & Carrie & to my brother John while we were at Hull during summer of 1879 or 1880, and my mother & he were on a Masonic ^ trip to Baltimore & Washington D.C. He was a member of the Mt. Lebanon Lodge & also of the De Molay Commandery of Boston & frequently had mother accompany him on pilgrimage.

Father".

The only Masonic souvenir that got handed down was a dress sword with a red cross of Street George on the ebony hilt; it was about four feet long, strait, double-edged steel blade, with no identifying inscriptions, in a brass scabbard. This was found in the attic at 301 W. Foster Street, Melrose, about 1934; I was given it about 1946, and it stayed at my parents' house in Havertown until they moved to Ardmore, where it disappeared, by the time my father left the house after my mother's death in 1973. Perhaps my nephew Jimmy Clark can remember playing with it.

The cross of St. George is the insignia of a Knight Templar of the Commandery, and the local Commandery was de Molay (Robert Homburg, Rm. 704, Masonic Temple, 186 Tremont Street, Boston). However, [Sir] Warren's name is not listed on the cards currently held by the Grand Commandery, nor does his death appear in the *Commandery Returns* under de Molay #7 or Hugh de Payens Commandery, Melrose for 1895 or 1896 (Richard Sleeper, Rm. 405, Masonic Temple; the secretary to the Grand Commandery says that many nineteenth century cards were

destroyed by her predecessor, and current cards cover from only about 1900). Further evidence of his knighting might appear in the Triennial Conclave volumes where there are photos of participants.

The third level Masonic titles and ritual is based upon the Crusades.

Although the evidence of his having reached the third stage of Masonry, by becoming a knight, is only circumstantial, we have proof of the two previous stages.

T. Warren Gould took the first degree 11 Jan. 1858, when he was 23 years old. He took the second degree 17 Feb. [his third wedding anniversary], and third degree 29 March 1858, becoming a "Brother" with rank of Master Mason of the Mt. Lebanon Lodge of Boston ("Hard cards" of the Blue Lodge, Grand Secretary, 2d fl., Masonic Temple). He signed the by-laws of the Lodge 10 May 1858. The Mt. Lebanon Lodge met at Nassau Hall, Common Street, for the first time 8 Nov. 1858. Gould is listed as #48 of living members in the printed by-laws of 1874 (*By-Laws of Mount Lebanon Lodge* [Boston: The Lodge, 1874], 24, 67; in Lawrence Library of the Temple, 2d fl.).

Gould reached the second stage of Masonry by taking the "Fourth Step" of Masonry, becoming "Companion" of St. Paul's Royal Arch Chapter of Boston in the York Rite . (*Chapter Returns*, 1895, "Deaths" in room 704, Grand Chapter records). Unfortunately there are no returns prior to 1865, when the local lodge burned, so we do not know when he joined. Bob Homburg says it could have been as early as 1858. He would have taken at least the fourth step in the Capitular Rite to become Mark Master Mason, and probably the next three steps of Past Master, Most Excellent Master and Royal Arch Mason (Bob Homburg, *The Fourth Step* [Boston: Royal Arch Chapter, 1991].

It is not easy to judge Warren's business success, since there was no income tax, he owned little property, and the family kept no financial records. However, the Boston Directory records a business change in 1885 which seems to show that he retired at age 51. Warren gave up listing an office address that he had given for over 30 years, since 1853, and the office at 76 Chauncy Street he had maintained since 1880. He listed only his home address at 63 Brookline Av., but in the next year gave that up as a home too. There is a photo of a large house with an octagonal cupola labeled “Brookline Ave. Longwood where we once lived” in Sammie’s album #11. The next photo shows a four story brownstone at the end of a row of houses, on the corner of Burlington and Brookline Ave., labeled “Front end view of #63 Brookline Ave”. In 1886 the Goulds moved to 4 Hotel Helvetia, a residential hotel on Huntington Av. at the corner of Tremont Street, in Longwood, near today's Brigham & Womens Hospital (Dir. 518, 1313; 1887 518; 1888 534). 1885 was a year of slight business recovery, it followed two years of depression, and a longer period of "long-wave" poor conditions after 1873.

JOURNALIST AND THE NATIONAL TARIFF DEBATE

Warren became involved in the national debate over the tariff, which was associated with the economic problems of the country. Generally, the Republicans supported higher tariffs, and the Democrats were free traders. In 1882 President Arthur appointed the Tariff Commission, which recommended lowering rates. They were lowered 5% in 1883, but high tariffs remained, and the battle in Congress and press continued.

Gould, as an importer, was obviously in favor of lower tariffs. In 1884 *Boston Post* published a long letter of 9 Feb. from "T. W. G." to the current Democrat who headed the House Ways & Means Committee, titled "Tariff Reform" (Tues. 12 Feb. 1884, on the bottom of which in his handwriting: "With love of the Author"). He makes two arguments against the tariff, the major one its reduction of property values, and a minor one its inflation of prices. On the first, he calls the tariff "an immediate, fixed, arbitrary reduction of valuation of nearly fifty millions of dollars of imported goods...and...about the same amount on home products."

Gould tied this to currently depressed business conditions: "Every industry in our country, with a few rare exceptions, is now suffering a depression which has brought prices and values down to 'bed-rock', and this wiping off one hundred millions of the national wealth at one stroke, will be most serious in its results, not only to the nation as a whole, but to each humble individual owning property. The national government should not be the instrument of such an act of injustice..."

He compared the "immense amount of suffering" this causes to slavery: "The abolition of slavery was attained at a loss of filthy lucre vastly in excess of the value of the bondmen, to say nothing of the millions of sorrow stricken hearts in the land that only Heaven can ever heal."

Gould then picked up the popular theme of currency reform. "The incidental inflation of our currency, and the subsequent reduction to gold values, counts its wrecks of individuals and institutions by thousands and tens of thousands, north and south, east and west, that never will be prosperous again."

He then warned of the growing populist revolt: ""the tariff is paramount over all other subjects and its burdens are oppressive to an extent that when realized by the great mass of the people, will demand redress in such thunder tones as shall receive the immediate and earnest attention of their legislators..."

Warren then pulled out all stops: "The negro is elevated, but the white man is depressed. The rivers and harbors are dredged, but the outlet to the sea is blocked by solid granite custom houses. The Mormon church exacts tributes of tithes, or one-tenth from its deluded members, while our 'paternal government' is not satisfied with four-tenths (about 43 per cent.) [before the income tax 63% of government revenue came from tariffs, 1890, Morris 531]. from a patient, long-suffering people. This question is national and not sectional, it is patriotic and not partisan;

it should be determined by statesmen and not by politicians.

Then he made a partisan appeal to the Democratic chairman of the House Ways & Means Committee by saying that tariff reduction "will demonstrate that the democratic party is not only traditional but practical, and that it can furnish leaders to grapple with the wrong who can practice as well as preach the doctrines of Jackson and Jefferson." Gould asks Congress to show leadership to seize the historic opportunity: "The great mass of the people are aroused on this subject of the tariff, and the dominant party of the future will be enrolled under the banner of reform. This great army of patriots needs leadership only, to organize complete victory. They look naturally to the democratic party for such leaders and if it will not furnish an ideal leader, they will turn in desperation to the republican party."

Gould waxed poetic: "This is a subject that cannot be temporized with by either party and it will not be used as a plank in the platform of either party, as it has timber enough in it to build an entire platform, and it will be spiked together by convictions and facts which will make it large enough and lasting enough to hold 'an army with banners.' Each member of the army is stimulated by the same settled belief in the justice of his cause, which demands

'A man with soul content and brave,
Himself to carve his pathway to the grave,
And caring not for what men think or say,
Makes his own heart his world upon the way.'"

I cannot find this poem in Bartlett. Is it his?

He then came down to earth and offers a compromise on his original proposal for a daily reduction of the tariff, to a monthly one of 2½ %, to meet objections of the disruption of a sudden change.

Gould concluded with an apology for his "seeming prolixity and enthusiasm" caused by "the obnoxious and oppressive operations of our present tariff [which] have, in my own personal experience...served to 'stir a fever in the blood of age and make the infant's sinews strong as steel.'"

Four days later the Boston *Herald* printed a shorter column, also titled "Tariff Reform.", signed "Veritas", whom we know to be Warren from his note at the bottom of a clipping "With love of the Author". (Tues. 8 April 1884, editorial printed on silk). Here he added an argument against the protectionists' claim that the market will be flooded by foreign goods, that the law of supply and demand operates so that importers wouldn't overstock. But he said that if one concedes the flood argument, one should cut off every import, which would drive up prices for the benefit of the few. These are the "wealthy capitalists and corporations" who make the laws. The victims "are the weak mass of the people, the toilers and consumers...[on who falls] the burdens of the tariff, which robs them at every turn, from cradle to the grave, of every part of the pittance granted them in exchange for honest labor. In the mean while they find themselves driven nearer and nearer to the starvation point, while protected monopolists flaunt contemptuously in their faces the evidences of constantly increasing colossal wealth. They see legislation shaped only by the wealthy for the favored wealthy class, while the interests of humanity are blindly ignored. They are without champions of their wrongs, a poor man's chances of a seat in our national Legislature being less than the probability of a rich man obtaining one in the heavenly kingdom."

So here is Gould, the democrat populist, opposing the wealthy manufacturers, championing his own self-interest in cheap imports.

Two months later *Boston Post* reported "T. Warren Gould of this city has just returned from a mission to Washington in behalf of a large number of our leading business houses..." . Gould reported that he had lobbied in Congress against the Treasury's tariff on empty boxes. The climax of his argument is this: "The babe in the cradle should not be taxed for the worthless box which contained the tiny socks which protect its tender feet. Nor should its mother contribute to the dredging of our rivers and harbors by a tax on the box which has contained a cake of soap or a dozen hairpins in her toilet case. Neither should poor Muldoon in his casket, or the proud policeman at the head of the procession, or the rank and file of the mourners, have their sorrows deepened and their grief intensified by a tax on the empty box which contained the white cotton gloves which fit, with such perfection, their immaculate hands."

He mentioned the subcommittee of the Ways & Means Committee giving him a favorable reception, and the cooperation of the Speaker of the House John G. Carlisle and the Committee Chairman William R. Morrison. He also acknowledged the help of T. Leopold Morse, prominent Jewish textile merchant of Boston, who was one of his sponsors for the job in the Customs House (Caroline Gould to author 20 Sept. 1976).

UNSUCCESSFUL TRY FOR POLITICAL APPOINTMENT

Cleveland won the Presidency on 4 Nov. 1884, the first Democrat to win it in 28 years. To the victor belong the spoils, so Democrats looked for appointments.

Gould's lobbying success may have encouraged him to seek a political appointment, but his diabetes may also have been a factor in seeking retirement from active travel in business. We have an undated letter of recommendation in his handwriting:

"We the undersigned, from a long personal acquaintance with, or honorable reputation of, Mr. T. Warren Gould, most cordially recommend him for any position where ability, integrity and business experience are essential qualifications.

Mr. Gould is a graduate of our public schools, and a life long resident merchant of this city.

A physical infirmity obliges him reluctantly to retire from active business life, and we believe the valued services he can offer, will be most thoroughly acceptable in any official or merchant trust that may be tendered him."

There follows 27 signatures.

Gould got Democratic Congressman H. B. Lovering to send the following telegram:

"Lynn Mass 1885
May 28th

To Hon Daniel Manning
Secy of Treas, Wash D.C.

I join with Hon P. A. Collins in asking the appointment of Mr. T. W. Gould of Boston as appraiser in the Custom House in place of Darrah deceased--Papers on file in your department give highest endorsements as to ability integrity and experience HBLovering
M.C."

Then Gould got up a petition of 110 businessmen to the President himself:

"Boston June 5th 1885. To his Excellency
Grover Cleveland"...the signatures follow, and at the end, in Gould's writing:

"The signatures above given, are of gentlemen in active business in Boston, who have known Mr. Gould for many years." Since the purpose is not stated, it may be that this was intended to be attached to the one quoted above.

As he got new supporters, Gould got additional letters, like the one on the stationery of Henry G. Parker, Editor and Publisher of the *Saturday Evening Gazette*, 2 Bromfield St, corner of Washington, Boston, a handwritten letter:
"Aug. 25, 1885.
Hon. H. B. Lovering, M. C.
Dear Sir:

I take pleasure in stating that I have known Mr. T. Warren Gould for twenty five years, & have had occasion to realize that he is a capable business man, that he is a thorough master of the intricacies of Dry Goods & that his reputation in business circles has always been creditable to him. I regard Mr. Gould as being in every way qualified for the position//he seeks as General Appraiser of Dry Goods in the Boston Custom House.

Yrs. Very Truly,
Henry G. Parker."

Nothing came of this during Cleveland's first term, and in 1888 Republican Harrison won back the White House. Gould must have been encouraged by Cleveland's reelection in Nov. 1892 to try again, for we have this letter from former congressman Lovering, now Warden of the Massachusetts State Prison in Charlestown:

"Feby 22nd 1893

Friend Gould

Yours rec^{d}. Sorry to hear you had been sick so long & hope you will soon be around again. I cannot say whether or not your papers filed 8 years ago at Treasy Dept. are in the files or not. A note to the Hon Chas Foster Secy of Treas might bring the desired information. I do not know how else to ascertain. I am rusty on national affairs & hardly know how to advise proceeding in the matter, a new set of men at the front whose wishes would probably have to be consulted. I mean Congressmen & State Central Committeemen--I know very few of the latter, as I have been out of the swim so long. Truly yrs
T. Warren Gould Esq H B Lovering"

Gould followed the advice and got this typed letter from the Division of Appointments of the Office of the Secretary of the Treasury in Washington: "March 9, 1893

Honorable Levi P. Morton

Washington, D. C.

Sir:

In compliance with your request of this date I send you herewith all papers filed in behalf of the appointment of Mr. T. Warren Gould as Appraiser, Boston, Massachusetts.

Respectfully yours
Daniel Macauley
Chief of Appointment Division."

Again, nothing happened.

T.W.Gould, 1895, shortly before his death, age 60

FINAL YEARS AND MOVE TO MELROSE

But in the meantime, after three years at the Hotel Helvetia in Longwood (1885-8), they moved close by to 55 Brookline Av. for the three years 1889-91 (Dir. 538, 547, 557).

Warren reopened an office in town, at 22 Eliot Street, between Washington and Pleasant Sts., near to the old Carver Street home. The children were earning salaries, for the oldest, Ida, had got a job at the Boston Public Library by 1887, while living at home. In 1887 Samuel had a job as a clerk, but lived at home. John got his first job as a clerk in 1891.

The last letter we have from Warren was written in 1889 to his daughter Ida who was then working at Boston Public Library, but boarding at home, but then vacationing with her mother at Easthampton, Long Island:

"55 Brookline Avenue

9.30 P.M. Sunday Oct.27/89

My 'Darling Daughter'

I sent 'Pet' [his wife] a letter four feet long [this sheet is 3 feet long], at 3 o'clock P.M. to-day, which ought to make up, in some degree, for the short supply from me last week. It is raining cats and dogs at this moment, and rats too I should think, by the sound. I have just waded through the 48 pages of Globe and Herald, from the dime museum 'ad' to bargains at 'Jordan's mash'. I see one bargain I shall try and connect with at the Mass B & G store opp. Boylston Street, and that is more of that Old White Castile Soap, at seven (7) cts. a lb. or bar.

It is a positive luxury to use it in #8 or elsewhere//Johnnie has just returned from 'the Durgins', where during the past two hours, he has been administering electricity, to the entire family. Sammie has not returned from the city, which he visited at 7.30 PM.

If 'Marie' (that's our French girl) returns to-night it must be 'by boat', for it is pouring torrents. Everything is running smoothly at home.

We have a good furnace fire and plenty to eat. Mr. Blaisdell said they were getting along as well as possible at the Library, but would be glad to see you home again, as more familiar with the 'routine work', which is now left to numerous substitutes. Neighbors White enquired kindly after you and Ma. He is quite broken up by his loss. Three carriages stopped there to-day with sympathysing friends or relatives, I suppose.

Emily is at home I believe, but do not know when she will return to St. John. I have heard nothing from your 'Ma'. since Thursday last, or rather Friday A. M., acknowledging the receipt of your 'lost or stolen' funds, and stating her intention of leaving Friday A. M. for Easthampton, where I presume you have arrived safely and have resumed your 'giddy round of pleasure'.

I may get news direct in the morning, but if not, my four letters will be returned to me during the week by this P. M. as directed on the envelopes. If you are safely in Easthampton, and have pleasant weather, a climb to the top of some of the hills//in the neighborhood will amply repay you for the time and fatigue.

But, if you do not care to walk, I enclose a fine picture of friend 'Martha', which will enable you to obtain conveyance of some kind for yourself and 'Pet'.

Please note and advise me at what time you receive the letters, and also at what time 'Pet' receives hers, as the post-man, at 3 P. M. advised me this would be collected from our box at midnight.

Good night, with love and kisses from all to yourself and 'Ma.' to whom as well as yourself I subscribe myself as ever

'The best Father in the Exeter Street School'.

I enclose envelope for 'Ma'--a few gems from the papers".

Warren made his only real estate venture about this time, for the sole deed with his name is when in 1891 the city of Boston took 35 feet of a property he owned jointly with several others, to lay out Prospect Street in West Roxbury, between Brandon and Birch.Streets (SD 2093:467, surveyed 14 Nov. 1891).

Ironically, suffering from the complications of diabetes, of which he was to die in less than three years, Warren moved away from the Longwood neighborhood of today's world-famous Joslin Clinic where the care of diabetes was to be pioneered, and his great-grandson James and his daughter Elizabeth were to be treated successfully.

The Gould family moved for the first time to the Boston suburbs. In 1892 Warren is no longer listed in the Boston Directory, though his three children are, but shown as boarding in Melrose (574). So, about 1891-2 they left 55 Brookline Av., Longwood, for 23 Gooch Street, in the northeast part of the suburban town of Melrose. This was formerly North Malden, where Warren's 4th great-grandfather William[1] Teel had land.

Perhaps to avoid inheritance taxes, the title was put in eldest son Samuel's name. Samuel was then living nearby, on Whitman Av. (Msx Deeds 1989:161-6). They bought a 6,104 sq. foot lot with buildings on the west side of "a new street leading Southerly from Grove street", that was to be called Gooch Street, on the northeast corner of Gooch and Third, to be renamed Laurel Street (*Melrose Directory* 1893, 84; *Bluebook & House Guide*, Melrose 1893, 37 says Larrabee off Grove, which is near Whitman; *Town Report* of Melrose, 1892, Polls (bound in Melrose Public Library History Room, places Samuel on Whitman, 103, his father at Gooch, 76). Gooch Street runs parallel to Main Street, a few blocks east of the center of Melrose, and only close to the railroad station, which Ida, Samuel and John must have commuted from to North Station in Boston. This newly developed neighborhood was a couple of blocks south of an area of more impressive and expensive Victorian homes. Only one house on Gooch Street is on the National Register.

Theirs was a three-story Victorian house that is still standing 105 years later. The cost was $250, bought from Nathaniel P. Jones and Alonzo G. Whitman of Melrose on 24 July 1890, but at the same time mortgaged to Jones for $2000 @ 5 % interest, to be insured for the same amount, and a second mortgage for $250 to both Jones and Whitman, @ 6 %, half payable at the end of the second year, and the rest at the end of the third (Msx Deeds 2186:25). Neither Thomas or Caroline's names appear on the deeds, though Samuel's sister Ida, and his wife Laura are witnesses. Jones assigned his mortgage to Anna May Fletcher, who discharged it as paid 29 March 1893 (Msx Deeds 3103:286). The mortgage was paid off at 10:15 16 June 1904. Meanwhile Ida had obtained a new mortgage from the Hingham Institution for Savings 26 July 1899, and from L. J. Ames on 6 April 1904 (Msx Deeds 2754:445, 3089:184).

In the 1893 town directory he is listed as a "journalist"(*Melrose Directory*, 1893, 84). We do not know of any publications other than the tariff letters quoted above. We know from the petition and letters above that Warren's health was declining, though he was not yet 60 years old. He died at 23 Gooch Street, of diabetes 27 Jan. 1895 , three weeks short of his 61st birthday (MDR 455:313).

.

The Boston paper carried this short death notice: "GOULD--At Melrose, Massachusetts, Jan. 27, T. Warren Gould, 60 yrs. 11 mos., 10 days. Funeral services will be held at Trinity Episcopal Church at Melrose, Wednesday, Jan 30, at 3 P.M. Train leaves Boston at 2.15. Friends and relatives invited to attend." (*Boston Evening Transcript*, 29 Jan. 1895, 4, col. 7).

.

His obituary which appeared in the Melrose paper tells of his last illness:
"For the past few years T. Warren Gould, of 23 Gooch street, has been confined to his house most of the time by illness caused by a complication of diseases, prominent among which was rheumatism, and has been unable to perform any work except in a literary way on a small scale, during his illness (*Melrose Reporter,* Sat. 2 Feb. 1895). Within the past few months his physical troubles have taken a more serious turn, and gangrene attacked one of his legs. His physicians did all in their power to relieve his intense suffering, but without avail, and last week it was decided to amputate the limb, which was done on Thursday, not with the hope of saving his life but to relieve his pain to some extent. The shock, however, was more than his system could bear, and on Saturday he died, at the age of 60 years. He leaves a widow, two sons and a daughter.

Mr. Gould was a man of more than ordinary ability, and was thoroughly educated, possessing a knowledge of several languages, and of the affairs of the world. He was literary in his tastes, a great reader, and often wrote articles upon various subjects of interest. In his earlier life he occupied a responsible position in the commercial world as the foreign buyer for sever of the leading business houses of Boston, and his judgment and ability in that line was considered above the average. He has taken a lively interest in Melrose affairs and has made many acquaintances, but owing to his helpless condition, his efforts in any direction have been confined to his home."

Warren was buried in Wyoming Cemetery, Melrose, in the south end next to the woods of Pine Bank Park (Lot NI 54, on the south side of Forest Av., three lots west of the corner of Vesper Av.). The simple granite stone, placed there by his granddaughter Caroline in 1935, says only "GOULD". His was the first burial in the lot, and beside him lie six members of the family: his wife Caroline, his daughter Ida, his son Samuel with his wife Laura, and their daughter Annie, and Laura's sister Minnie Ida Douglas (Wyoming Cemetery cards; Minnie's is the only name inscribed on the stone, on the reverse; cemetery file for lot NI 54 shows that Caroline D. Gould ordered the stone 15 Sept. 1936). Three of his children who died earlier were buried at Mt. Auburn, and one child at Père La Chaise in Paris. His son John was buried in Kensington CT. His grandson Douglas and granddaughter Caroline were cremated in Pomona CA., where they died.

He left three children of their seven, and two grandchildren, Annie and Caroline Gould. His first grandson was born exactly a year after his death, on 27 Jan. 1896, and named Douglas Warren Gould. Only one more grandchild was born, and named Warren for him.

Seven children, born Boston, except for last one:

30. i. IDA[8] WARREN, poetess and librarian, b. 10 Oct. 1856 (MBR 98:145, #1007, no name given, female; family record). d. Melrose MA. 18 July 1946, age 89, unmarried. (See chap. XVII).

ii. CAROLINE GERTRUDE, b. 19 Nov. 1858 (MBR 116:74, #3313, no name given, female; name from family record; d. Boston 27 Feb. 1881 (MDR 330:58) of emphysema (TB); unmarried; buried Mt. Auburn Cemetery, Cambridge.

iii. CHARLES WALTER, b. 20 Aug. 1860 (*Boston Births 1860* # 3001); d. Boston 10 March 1862 (MDR 158:34), age 17 months, of pneumonia. Buried Mt. Auburn.

iv. FREDERICK, b. 20 March 1862; d. Boston 4 Feb. 1863 (MDR 161:163), age 10 months, of scarlet fever.

31. v. SAMUEL CLIFFORD, bookkeeper, b. 3 Feb. 1864 (*Boston Births 1864* #4841 VR). d. Worcester MA 11 Feb. 1947, age 86; m. 1) LAURA KEENE DOUGLAS, 2) CLARA MANGAN. (See chap. XV)

32. vi. JOHN (HOGG) GODDARD, private secretary, b. 25 Dec. 1870 (*Boston Births 1870* #3721 VR); d. Kensington CT. 24 March 1959, age 89; m. 1) JANE BLAISDELL, 2) JESSICA SCHWAB. (See chap. XVI)

vii. WARREN, b. Paris, France 8/9 Sept. 1872; d. 13 Sept. 1872, age four days (Family record and burial card).

CAROLINE GODDARD GOULD
(1833-1915)

29. Caroline Goddard (Elias^{6}) was born at 5 Unity Street in North End of Boston, Tuesday 14 May 1833 ("Family Record" from Goddard Bible, original with author). She died in Melrose MA 13 March 1915 (Family Record).

She was the third of seven children of Elias Waters Goddard, master cooper, and his wife Caroline Garran, for whom she was named. She grew up as the oldest child of five, the first two, Caroline and Andrew Jackson, having died the year before her birth, in 1832.

Her son John told the story of her birthplace, in the shadow of Old North Church (John G. Gould letter from Bass River 3 Oct. 1951). "In those eventful days, at No. 19 Unity Street, Boston, (in the 'North End') there stood a two-story-and-a-half frame dwelling. This was practically opposite the terminus of 'Lamentation Alley' which ran from the North side of Hanover Street (At that time called Robinson Alley, which ran from Unity Street south to Hanover Street, not far from Salutation Alley).

Slightly to the East of the front door of this dwelling, was a high, stout, oak-plank gate, admitting to a narrow passage between No. 19 and its next-door neighbor, which passage opened on to the 'back yard'. This became a very interesting and beautiful spot later by virtue of what transpired in and near it after a certain young gentleman and his bride came to occupy No. 19 as their permanent home (A fine photo of the oak plank gate with #19 to the left, is shown opposite p. 78 of Annie H. Thwing's *The Crooked & Narrow Streets of the Town of Boston 1630-1822* [Boston: Marshall Jones. 1920].

The North side of this yard was then bounded by a very high wall of masonry - the rear wall and foundation of a church which fronted on North Street. As North Street was considerably higher than Unity Street, an extra-solid and deep retaining wall was necessary to amply support the church steeple and to compensate for the difference in elevation between the two roads. High above this back yard then, towered the graceful steeple and belfry which was to become famous for the part i[t] played in the Americans' fight for Freedom and Independence."

The old Goddard house at 19 Unity Street was torn down in 1899, and all that can be seen today is the roof line on the east wall of the neighboring Ebenezer Clough house of 1715, at no. 21 Unity Street The restored Clough house at no. 21 gives us an idea of the appearance of its neighbor (Michael & Susan Southworth, *A. I. A. Guide to Boston* [Chester CT: Globe Pequot Press, 1989], 52-3; original appearance in Jane Holtz Kay, *Lost Boston* [Boston: Houghton Mifflin, 1980], 36).

We have two photos of Elias and Caroline Goddard taken at the house about 1880. The brick front is three stories high, and two bays wide. The appearance is much like the Clough neighbor, except that the doorway is in the right bay, with two windows on the west. Above the 6 over 6 windows is the identical brick detail of lintel and keystone, with raised arch over the windows. The Goddard house appears to be narrower, for instead of three full bays on the second floor, there is a narrow bay over the doorway. Again, on the third floor there are two full bays of 6 over 6 windows, with a narrower 4 over 4 over the entrance. But the Clough house lacks the dark shutters on all the windows. The Goddard house has three lights over the single door, in contrast to the double door and more lights on the Clough's. The Goddard's sidewalk is brick, broken by a cellar trapdoor leading under a low arch under the windows. The Goddard house is flush up against the Clough house, with a passage to the back on the east side, barred from the street by a vertical plank door between two simple pilasters.

The close similarity of the Goddard house to the Clough House suggests that it was built at the same time by Ebenezer Clough, master mason, who also built Old North Church in 1723 (Virginia Bright, "Old North Church Restoring Ancient Church...", *Boston Sunday Globe*, 3 Jan. 1960, 6-A). It is the oldest church in Boston, built six years before Old South, and thirty years before King's Chapel (Edwin M. Bacon, *Boston//A Guide Book* [Boston: Ginn & Co., 1903], 60; John Harris, *The Boston Globe Historic Walks in Old Boston* [2d. Ed. Chester, CT: Globe Pequot Press, 1989], 250). The Clough house the second oldest house in Boston, after Paul Revere's.

The Goddard's librarian granddaughter Ida Gould labeled the photo thus: "House, formerly 19 Unity Street, Boston, torn down in 1899 was once owned by Benjamin Franklin and occupied by his sister Mrs. Richard Dows, who lived and died there. It was owned by Mr. Elias W. Goddard who lived in it over 60 years. It is, or was the only house in Boston, ever owned by Franklin. The garden in which Mr. Goddard took pride in cultivating was directly in back of the house. He is seen sitting there. Tradition relates that the bricks to build the house were brought from England. Further details may be found in Rambles in Old Boston, by Rev. Edward G. Porter, 227-229, Boston. [Copples & Hurd] 1887."

This is Porter's description of the house: "The house next to this [#23] on the right [#21] exhibits some rather eccentric architectural features, one of which is that while the *voussoirs* and keystones of the first-story window arches are generally of brick, those on each side of the key are of solid wood. The reason for this is not apparent. Above the door is a carved brick lintel; and along the whole front is a unique attempt at ornament by an irregular relief in brick. The moulded water-table and the solid plank sills are noticeable. The upper story was not a part of the original building."

"The brick house adjoining this (No. 19), and identical with it in age and style, though not as wide, is the one which Benjamin Franklin owned for many years, and which was the home of his two sisters, Elizabeth and Jane. It came to him as collateral upon a loan which he made, in 1748, to Richard Dowse, the second husband of his sister Elizabeth, who had received the//[228] estate from her first husband, Joseph Berry, who died in 1719. Berry had bought the house, in 1716, of Deacon John Barrett, who probably built it, as he speaks of it as 'newly formed for habitation.'"

"On the death of Dowse, Franklin allowed his sisters, both of them being widows, to occupy the house together. As there was a difference of thirty-five years in their ages, --Elizabeth being the oldest and Jane the youngest of seventeen children,--and a still greater difference in their tastes and habits, they did not get on very well together. The younger sister wrote to their brother in Philadelphia, begging him to provide some other home for Elizabeth, who had become very troublesome in her old age. Franklin sent the following wise letter in reply:--

'As *having their own way* is one of the greatest comforts of life to old people, I think their friends should endeavor to accommodate them in that as well as anything else. When they have long lived in a house, it becomes natural to them; they are almost as closely connected with it as the tortoise with his shell; they die if you tear them out of it; old folks and trees, if you remove them, it is ten to one that you kill them; so let our good old sister be no more importuned on that head. We are growing old fast ourselves, and shall expect the same kind of indulgences; if we give them, we shall have a right to receive them in our turn...*Old age, infirmities, and poverty*, joined, are afflictions enough. The *neglect* and *slights* of friends and near relatives should never be added.'"

"The old lady died soon after; and Jane lived here undisturbed nearly forty years longer. More than any of the family, she is said to have resembled her famous brother in strength and character and practical good sense. She seems to have developed early, for she married Edward Mecom at the age of fifteen. Benjamin, who was only a few years her senior, was interested in the event and sent her a gift, with the following note:-[229]

'...I have been thinking what would be a suitable present for me to make, and for you to receive, as I hear you are grown to a celebrated beauty. I had almost determined upon a tea-table; but when I considered that the character of a good housewife was far preferable to that of being only a pretty gentlewoman, I concluded to send you a *spinning wheel*, which I hope you will accept as a small token of my sincere love and affection.'"

"In 1802 the house was sold by John Lathrop, D. D., and Benjamin Sumner, executors of the will of Jane Mecom. Noah Lincoln bought it and lived here till 1820. For the last fifty-five years it has been the home of Elias W. Goddard, the well-known cooper and one of the few living representatives of the old-time Boston mechanics. His yard, which is directly behind Christ Church, has the best-kept vines and plants of any at the North End, reminding one of the care which was formerly bestowed upon all the gardens in this neighborhood."

"Among former residents in Unity Street may be mentioned...John J. Swift, President of the Fitchburg Railroad...Colonel Peter Dunbar, Commander of the Lancers...and Charles A. Vialle, President of the Bank of the Republic."

"Robinson's Alley--now called Webster Avenue for reasons not given--is one of the narrowest, darkest, and most repulsive lanes in the city, suggesting the Ghetto of Rome or the old Judengasse at Frankfurt-on-the-Main. This used to be the headquarters of the colored people before they migrated to Belknap Street. They kept poultry, ducks, pigs, monkeys, parrots, and //[230] other live-stock in great numbers. When the celebration of peace took place after the War of 1812, the denizens of this alley were not to be outdone in their illuminations. They put lights in all their windows, and then went up town to see what others had done. Meantime their candles burned low and set fire to some of their houses; and soon the whole alley was ablaze, giving them indeed the grandest display of all, but leaving them without a single house for shelter the next morning."

Lamentation Alley has disappeared with the clearing for what is now called The Prado, officially the Paul Revere Mall, through which the tourists follow the red line of the Freedom

Trail (AIA Guide 45-6).

The passageway on the east side of the Goddards' house led into the well-known garden, which we see in the photo shaded with an ailanthus "tree of heaven", the walls covered with ivy on trellises, with numbers of potted plants on the planked terrace. What can be seen of the house appears to be shingled on the north, with 6 over 6 window. Next door, at no. 17, is a frame house with a second floor balcony overlooking the Goddards' garden.

Their son's description continues, "But through that massive wall was subsequently to pass from time to time a very important figure in this story!

[2] In the latter half of the seventeenth century, this house, with its small-paned windows, sharply sloping gables, rather steep front and rear staircases, was well-grayed by the blustery, freezing, rainy, foggy or blistering vagaries of Boston's climate. But it was good enough to be selected as the residence of two unmarried ladies (the Revere sisters)! (I think John has confused the actual owners, who were Benjamin Franklin's sisters. See Harris 250). It is quite out of reason to assume that these estimable spinsters anticipated any of the events that were to take place in that locale; events in which their brother, (one Paul Revere, Silversmith and Engraver by profession and Patriot by choice) was to play such a vital role. Nor, as they looked from the two rear windows of their second-story bedroom and saw the belfry and slender spire of the Old North Church over on North Street, was it likely that they gave more than a casual thought to its graceful lines or its sacred place in the community affairs!

Thus, my tale sets the stage for what happened on that evening of April 18th, 1775 when their brother, waiting on the Charlestown shore of the Charles River saw the twinkling light from a single lantern which suddenly gleamed from the belfry of Old North Church.

"The British are moving---by sea!" it signalled!

With a quick leap, Paul Revere was in the saddle and galloping through hamlet and village on his way to Concord, spreading an alarm that was to bring to arms, every able-bodied man and boy to resist the 'red-coats'.

It was on the next day, that assailed from every tree, stump and stone wall along the line of their retreat from Concord and Lexington, the British, after losing some two thousand men finally escaped to their war-ships in Boston harbor.

Before he took that momentous ride, I am thinking it quite likely Paul Revere first went home to No. 19 Unity Street, to change from civilian clothes to riding-breeches and boots (More likely from his own house at #19 North Square, where he went to get his boots and surtout [overcoat] before rowing across the Charles to Charlestown; Harris 245).

At this moment I cannot place exactly the date when a young couple took residence in that same house (*Boston Directory 1832*, 154 first places him there in 1832). A rough estimate puts it early in the 1800's. (The Revere [Franklin] sisters had long before vacated the premises.)

[3] He was of Boston Town; his bride came from Marblehead, Massachusetts. The family name was 'GARRAN, possibly of French extraction. His was 'GODDARD'. He went into the Cooperage business, a very important trade at that time for supplying oaken butts for holding drinking water on sailing vessels, and hogsheads, casks, barrels and buckets.

In the course of time Elias W. Goddard was able to open his own cooperage shop at the head of 'T.' Wharf, on Atlantic Avenue and when two of his sons (Walter and Clifford) had duly finished their apprenticeships, he took them into the firm which was henceforth to be known as 'Elias W. Goddard & Sons'. When Elias Goddard's household was blessed with a baby girl she was name[d], 'CAROLINE' after her Mother!

She was described, so I have been told, as an extremely beautiful young woman even then and two-score years later I too thought she was the handsomest lady in the whole world. A portrait of her at that time [1870] bears out my opinion. She was my Mother!

Her two brothers worked hard and faithfully and as skilled artisans were eventually admitted to the Cooperage Guild.

Out on Huntington Avenue, Boston, still stands 'The Mechanics Building' (The second Mechanics' Hall, built in 1881 on Huntington Av. on the site of Prudential Center, could well have had contributions from Goddard (who died seven years later) and his sons. That building succeeded an earlier Mechanics Hall on Bedford Street Jane Holtz Kay, *Lost Boston*, [Boston: Houghton, Mifflin, 1980], 203.). It was built through the cooperation of Elias W. Goddard & Sons and of hundreds of other trades-men, representing practically every one then contributing to the progress and renown of New England for skill in woodwork, masonry, building materials, copper, brass, iron, glass and textiles. For many years after its inauguration, 'The Mechanics' Fair' was a mecca for tens of thousands of sight-seeing visitors who flocked to it, not alone from every State in the Union, but from European countries as well!

...As faithful Episcopalians, they attended Old North Church which as I have previously mentioned, was around on North Street, just a few minutes walk from 19 Unity Street

[4] Now it was not very long after, that the Goddard couple came to that neighborhood and became regular members of the Old North Church congregation. Furthermore, the governing Board of the church, recognizing the high integrity and sound character of Mr. Goddard, appointed him Sexton and entrusted him with the care of the solid silver Communion Service! This had been presented to the Church at the time of its dedication, by King George, then ruler of Great Britain."

There is a photo and description of the silver in the church guidebook *Christ Church //Salem Street, Boston//1723* [Boston: the church, 1912], 30-32). "THE COMMUNION SERVICE...of the church is now deposited at the Museum of Fine Arts, where several pieces are always on exhibition. In the time of Captain Thomas Hall it was kept under his bed in East Boston, and it no doubt endured like vicissitudes in the century before his day. It consists of thirteen pieces:

A chalice and paten, made by John Edwards and given by Captain Thomas Tudor in 1724, in place of a 'silver Romish cup' previously given by Tudor, and sold to Edwards.

Two flagons, made by Rufus Greene [1707-77, son of Anne^2 Gould Green, above Chapter II], and given by the congregation in 1729. Engraved by Thomas Sturt White, of Williams's Court, Cornhill, late of London.

A paten, made by John Read of London in 1715, and given by Leonard Vassall, Esq., in 1730. The family arms are beautifully engraved in the center.

A baptismal basin, made by Jacob Hurd [1702-58, ancestor of Anne Garrison Gould; see chart #20/7], and given by Arthur Savage, Esq., in 1732. The family arms were engraved upon it by Thomas Sturt White. This large and handsome piece of silver stood on a large brass stand.

Two flagons, made by Joseph Allen and Mordecai Fox in London, and inscribed: 'The Gift of His Majesty King George II To Christ Church at Boston in New England at the Request of His Excell^{ncy} Govern^{r} Belcher, 1733.' They bear the Royal Arms.

Chalice and paten, makers, donor, inscription, and Royal Arms being the same. Taller than that given by Captain Tudor. The paten refitted by Mr. Hillard.

Alms basin, makers, donor, inscription, and the Royal Arms being the same.//

[33] *A bread dish with cover*, made by Churchill and Treadwell, and presented by Mrs. Hannah Smith in 1815.

A mote spoon (perforated), made by Gooding, and inscribed: 'Presented to Christ Church by H N Baxter Dec^{r}25th 1833.'"

John Gould's account continues, "Mr. Goddard solved the problem of how best to safeguard the Service in the intervals between its use in church rituals. At his suggestion, permission was granted to have a doorway cut in the foundation wall of the church which wall abutted the back yard of Mr. Goddard's residence, No. 19 Unity Street.

From then on, Mr. Goddard might have been seen on every Communion Sunday bringing the King's Service from his house through the little door in the back wall of his yard, into the church, to the altar table! And after each of such trips he would take the Service back into his house! Where did Mr. Goddard keep the Service?

He reconstructed one of the steps of the staircase going from his front door to the second floor of his dwelling, hinged it so that it could be lifted and whenever he was ready to put away the Communion Service, all he had to do was to unlock a small padlock on a certain spot on the stair, raise the stair on its hinges, and deposit his sacred trust in the space beneath, thus disclosed. Tilting down and locking the hinged step, no one could be the wiser. The stairs were carpeted of course and gave no inkling of what they hid!"

Samuel Gould wrote his son about the passage from their house to the church: "When my mother & her sisters & brothers were children there were no chances of offering excuses for not//[2] going to church for there was a passage leading from kitchen to wash room right into basement of the church (Letter of Samuel C. Gould to his son Douglas 16 Nov. 1934). Two of my brothers--Walter & Charles are buried in the vaults under the church."

Family tradition is that the Goddards found various old objects in the walls of the house at 19 Unity Street, including a toy whistle. On what grounds these were assumed to be Benjamin Franklin's I do not know, but they were lent to an exhibition of Frankliniana in Philadelphia, for the 200th anniversary of his birth, on 17 Jan. 1906. We have a nicely inscribed acknowledgment, "Frankliniana. Sundry Relics of Benjamin Franklin and his time//For the Loan Exhibition held at the Masonic Temple from March 6th to April 23^{d} 1906//To Mrs. Warren T. Gould. She apparently donated these to the temple, as the attached receipt reads: "Right Worshipful Grand Lodge of Pennsylvania Free and Accepted Masons Library of Grand Lodge//The Committee on Library has received the donation mentioned on the following page and thanks you for this very desirable addition to the collection of the Library of the Grand Lodge//[signed] Louis Wyman? Chairman. Masonic Temple Philadelphia May first 1906."

Caroline Goddard was educated in the excellent Boston schools of the North End. From her well written letters we can assume she went well beyond primary school. In 1850 she was awarded the City Medal, which we still have, a hexagonal bronze medal about an inch wide, inscribed, "Awarded to C. Goddard 1850".

When Caroline was 19 she made a trip to Troy NY to visit her aunt Sarah (Garran), staying for four months. In the first of six letters, she tells her mother of her plans:

"Troy, April 21st 1853

It is some time since I have heard from home, and although I do not consider that it is my turn to write, I will for I am anxious to hear from you. I sent a letter to Walter [her brother] last week, and one to Julia this week.

I am at Aunt Sarah's today. I spent Tuesday at the St. Charles Hotel with Mrs. Saxe(?). Phebe and John came down in the evening. Last evening, I spent at Elbridges'. He has come back to Troy to stay. They are going to move from North Third Street to Congress Street Mr. Lounsbury, the pastor of St. John's buried his wife yesterday afternoon. She died of//Consumption. Aunt Sarah wants me to ask you if you are getting ready to to come to Troy, and if not she wishes you to set about it immediately, and I wish the same. We shall move in about a week and I suppose it take considerable time to get settled. Aunt Sarah is nearly well now. She has spells of the head-ache, but excepting that, she is perfectly well.

She wants me to stay all summer, or until Phebe goes to Boston, which will be in July, and I want to stay at least till the first of July, because Phebe graduates the last week in June, and I would like to be present, but in that case I shall want my summer clothes, and if you come, I shall wish you to bring them. I shall wait for an answer, and if favorable, shall write again for the things I shall need. It is getting warm here now, so that thin shawls are needed, although in the evening furs are very comfortable. I wish I could sent your tippet and my thick dresses home, but I dont know of any one going to Boston at present. You will have to bring two trunks I//guess, so you had better get up a subscription paper, but I hope you will meet better success than I did. Tell Walter I thought of him on his birthday [24 April, age 18], and wished I had been at home to pinch his ears, but he may expect a double dose, when I get home. I hope you are all as well as I, and have as good an appetite, and you will have a monstrous one to match mine. A week ago last Sunday evening, I went to Christ Church. The minister in the place of Mr. Starky, is very good, but not equal to Mr. L. The service there is discontinued for two Sundays, on account of some repairing. Mr. Starky is expected home soon, and I shall go to hear him. St. John's Church has been torn down, and the rubbish is being removed now. The new church is to be built on Second Street, and in place of the old one, stores are to be erected. Julia wrote me that she read in the paper, that an Indian, would lecture at the N. Street Methodist Church on a certain evening. It was not the one who has been here. He did not go to Boston as he intended. He returned yesterday afternoon from N.York, and left this morning for his home in Canada.

I have reached the bottom of my paper, and wishing ^you to give my love to all the folks, and to tell them to write. I will write good bye. Your affectionate daughter Caroline."

Caroline's second letter tells of Aunt Sarah's new house, and her studying French with her cousin Phebe:

"Troy, May 4, 1853.

My dear Mother,

I know you will excuse me for not answering your kind letter, which I received last week, when you hear in what confusion we have been for the past week. We moved into this house [on Congress Street], last Friday afternoon. It is a very nice house. A basement, cellar &c on the ground floor; two parlors and a dining-room on the next; three large chambers, two bed-rooms and a bathing room on the next; and four rooms above those. There is a very large yard, and there are plum, pear and peach trees in it. When it is all cleaned, it will be very nice. Lucy [her cousin] and I have the back chamber,//and Sarah has a bedroom leading from our room. We are not settled yet, but hope to be in a week or two more. Aunt is very much disappointed at your writing that you cannot come here this month. She says it will do you good, and I think so too. I

wish you would; you would like here, I know. I heard the other day, accidentally of the fire you have had in Boston lately, and the damage done to the roof of Christ Church. I am sorry for that, but I am not sorry that the Catholic Church was burned, and I suppose Billy [?her brother William, age 14?] is glad of it. I was very glad to hear from all at home, and I would like to hear oftener, but I suppose I must content myself with what I get now. I sent a letter to Julia this week, as it was nearly finished before we moved. Aunt Sarah and the folks here want me to stay 'till after the Examination at the Seminary, which takes place the last of June. I would like to stay if you are willing, and I wish you would write me whether you have any objections or not. If I//should stay, I need other clothes, and as Newton Bacon is going to Boston the last of this month, I can send by him for what I wish; I do not think Julia knows anything about his coming yet. Lucy told me the other day, that he was. In the next letter that is written from home, please write whether you think I had better stay or not, and if you are willing I will write what I wish you to send, and perhaps you can borrow a trunk of Mrs. Bogardus to send my clothes in, and Mr. Bacon will take charge of it. It is getting very warm here, and my pink loose-dress would be very comfortable, as my other is not cut yet. Phebe is teaching me French, and I can read it very well. I do not idle my time, for I have done considerable sewing for myself and Aunt Sarah too. She is well now, and I think will keep so. I would like to hear from you as soon as convenient. Give my love to all, Mary [no relative--the maid?] included. If Billy has any horses, tell him to keep one for me. Yours as ever Caroline
Our direction is No. 187. Third Street Troy N.Y. All send their love."

The third letter home thanks the family for the box of summer clothing and gifts, and the rumor that her parents were moving to Cambridge:

"Troy. June 10th 1853.

My dear Father,

You requested me to write as soon as I received the box from home, but I have been unable to write before today, on account of a severe headache which lasted two days. I am as well as usual now. The box and all that therein was, arrived safely Wednesday forenoon. Aunt Sarah said when she saw the pot of beans, 'just like your father'. She is very much obliged, and says she shall have them for next Sunday's dinner. I took a piece of the fish to Mrs. Buswell and she wished me to thank you. I am very much obliged to you and mother and all, for the things sent to me.//The candy I gave directly to Aunt Sarah, because I am not going to eat any more. The oranges I distributed to all in the house and some out of it. They were very nice indeed. I am much obliged to you for the puff combs, for I had broken those I had when I left home. The paper was very acceptable also. They say Yankees are good for guessing and I can venture to guess on the result of your visiting Cambridge. I hope mother will get a house near Aunt Louisa's (Neither Elias nor his wife had a sister named Louisa, but her mother's brother Ebenezer may have married a Louisa).

I am much obliged to Billy for the ring. I like it very much. Why does he not write to me? I am afraid he does not like my lecturing him on bad spelling &c. I wish he would write. I owe Walter [her brother] a letter, and shall ~~answe~~ write very soon. Give my love to the boys, and say I am much obliged for the papers. There is not much news here, just now. We have very fine weather. Uncle Henry is building a house in the rear of this one. All the folks are well and send their love. I want to write a few lines to mother, so I will say good bye. Caroline//

My dear Mother,

I wish to write that the dress suits me very well indeed. It is just what I wanted. The sleeves and handkerchief are beautiful, and I thank you much for them. Julia confirmed the guess I made, when I read father's letter, by writing that you was going to Cambridge to look at a house. I am glad of it, and hope you will get a place near Aunt Louisa's.

I have written a note to Mrs. Dunn, and after you have read it, please seal it, and give it to her. I suppose the boys are preparing for the 4th of July. I am glad I am not there, to be among the crackers and pistols. All send love

Lucy's mitts suited her, she was much pleased with them, and is ^much obliged to you for getting them. Good bye, your aff. daughter Caroline. P.S. I suppose Sis [Helen, age 7] sent the frying pans, I am much obliged to her, but fear she robbed herself. C."

The next letter tells of her confirmation by the local Episcopalian bishop:

"Troy. June 14th /53--

My dear Father,

I write to you at this time, to inform you of a determination I have made, and which I trust will meet your approval. I have long had my thoughts occupied with the serious subject of Confirmation and I have concluded to renew my baptismal vows at the altar on Sunday next, when the Bishop of this Diocese will administer the rite of Confirmation in St. Paul's Church in this city. It would have been more in accordance with my natural feelings to have had <u>our</u> Bishop perform the service in our own church, but shall I neglect//<u>this</u> opportunity of declaring to the world, my determination to serve God, and by waiting for the next (and who knows that I shall have another) grow cold and indifferent to these things?

I have thought a great deal of this subject, and feel assured that you will be rejoiced to know it.

Will you not write as soon as you get this, which will be probably on Thursday noon. If you could [send--crossed out] put a note in the office the same day, I could get it Friday night, or Saturday.

I would like to hear from you very much, before Sunday.

I shall wait anxiously your answer. We are all well.

Give my love to mother and all,

Yours affectionately

Caroline--"

The Goddards had moved about 1 Aug. 1853 to Cambridge, so Caroline's next (fifth) letter is addressed to Mr. Elias W. Goddard

Care of 'Clapp & Goddard'

Richmond Street

Boston, Massachusetts

Troy, Aug. 1. 1853-

My dear Father,

I received your kind letter week before last, and should have answered it sooner, but I wished^to write something definite concerning my return home. I can [olnly--crossed out] only write now, that in the course of three or four weeks, John is going to Boston, and from there to Cape Cod, and he intends to take Phebe with him, and if you think it best, I shall return with them. As I have heard you have moved to Cambridge, I shall not know where to go, without I//should stop in Boston over night, at Julia's. About that of course you will write me.

I wrote you about visiting Gt. Barrington, but I think it will be better for me to stay in Troy. I shall w[r]ite an answer to Mr. Woart's letter, which was a very kind one. Of my debts, I shall only write, they are trifling, and if when you send me my money to return home with, you send me a little over, it will do. I believe all that business is settled. I have been very well considering the very warm weather we have had, but although I do not like to complain, I have had a very bad cold the past week. However, it is almost gone, and I have been quite careful. So you have really moved! What will come of it? Can Christ Church survive without the presence of her Sen. Warden? (Elias was Senior Warden from 1842-1853). I think you must have made a grand move.

Well on the whole, I am glad//of it; this warm weather in the city is not just the thing, but Aunt Sarah says you wont go back again. I dont say anything to that because I dont know.

I have written this in a hurry, as it is getting late, and my lamp is getting dim. It is so unusual to send a letter any where but to No. 5 [Unity Street], that I dont^know where to send, but I will venture to send it to the shop.

We all send love, and give my love to mother, brothers, sister and Aunt Louisa's folks and everybody else.

I remain as ever your affectionate daughter,

Caroline."

She had still not received the new address in Cambridge two weeks later, so sent the last letter to the same business address:

"Troy, Aug. 16, 1853-

Dear Father,

A letter from Julia Friday evening, informed me that you expected me home next month. Perhaps my letter of week before last, was not explicit enough, although it was as much so, as I could possibly make it at that time. I have been expecting a letter from you, but suppose you misunderstood the time of my return. Next Monday, the 22nd, is the time set.//Phebe has decided to go with John, but she will probably stay but a week or ten days. I cannot of course know whether to go with them till I hear from you. Miss Copeland left here this morning for Oswego. She came Saturday. She will return in about two weeks, and urged me very much, to wait till then, and if Phebe was not going to Boston, I would, but it would hardly seem right to do so now. However, I leave that for you to decide. You will probably receive this Thursday; If you will write a line and put it in the office the same day, I shall get it on Saturday, and that will be time enough,. Unless I hear from//you, I shall not go on Monday.

We are all well, that is, as well as can be this hot weather. An east wind would be quite a luxury. I have been preparing to return, consequently I am very busy, and I can write no more at present. Our love to all, and hoping to hear from you on Saturday I remain as ever your affectionate daughter,

Caroline--

P.S. I do not know where I am to go to take the coach for Cambridge, so you will have to write about that. C."

As related in the previous chapter, she had met T. Warren Gould at her father's booth at the Mechanics' Fair in Bedford Street in Boston. They were married on his twenty-first birthday, 17 Feb. 1855 (Massachusetts Marriage Record, 1855, 89:18). She was nine months older than he. They were married by the Rev. George D. Wildes of Grace Church, not on Beacon Hill, but where?

The couple's first home was the groom's former boarding house, at 24 Hull Street, a half a block north of Old North Church and the bride's former family home (he had boarded there since 1853, Dir. 123). They were to live there for a decade, until 1865, when they moved to 14 Carver Street in the South End (Dir. 1855, 129; 1864, 164). The first five Gould children were born there. Samuel related, "I was born, as was your Aunt Ida in the old 'HARTT HOUSE' at No. 24 Hull Street, about where the gas post is shown on page 1 [of the booklet on Christ Church]. The Hartt family I believe built the frigate Constitution." The 1912 photo shows a four story brick residence of three shuttered bays, and granite basement, and a small sign out front, reading "The SEG BOWE SHOP". Edmund Hartt, builder of the famous warship is buried in Copp's Hill, across the street, where the first Goulds were buried (Bacon 62; see prev. chapters).

Aside from the six letters written from Troy in 1853 we have only one other letter of Caroline's, written on what is probably her first trip abroad with her husband in 1866:

"Queen's Hotel, Manchester, Eng.
June 17, 1866.

Dear Ida, & Carrie [her daughters],

You cannot tell, how gratified your papa, and I were last night, on arriving here, at eleven o'clock, to find quite a large bundle of letter and a paper, awaiting us.

You may be sure, they were grabbed up quickly, and read with a great deal of interest. One or two, of them, were due at Paris, before we left, and I was feeling sort of homesick, because they did not arrive, with your pictures. But, I retired to bed, last night, feeling very happy, and thankful that Our Heavenly Father has taken such good care of us all. I have wished a great many times, that I have taken one of you with me. I have seen a great many//children, travelling with their parents, and occasionally, it has made me feel a little homesick. I hope, you have been good children, and have not made your Aunt Helen [her sister] any trouble. I was very glad to receive your letters, last night, also, the letters from the other members of the family. I have written a long letter to Walter [her brother], and should like to answer Clifford's [another brother], but am afraid I shall not have time to answer more than an other. I saw a great deal in beautiful Paris, that would amuse you, and when I return home, I shall tell you all about it, and can read the Rollo books, with you, with a new interest. I have bought you and Gerty [their nickname for daughter Caroline Gertrude Gould], something, but shall not tell you, till I get home. I am a great deal better in health, than when I left Boston, and I am in hopes to continue so. It is a very windy day here, reminding me, very//much of some of the weather, we have at home, and more especially, in the vicinity of Carver Street I spent about three weeks, in Paris, and among other places, went to the 'Jardin des Plants', where you remember, Rollo, went one Sunday. If you will look into the book, called 'Rollo in Paris', you will find out about it; also the Place Vendome, where the column is, and the Place de la Concorde, where the obelisk, that was brought from Egypt, stands. There are a great many things of interest in that delightful City, and I shall take great pleasure in telling you about them. Your papa, went to Germany alone; I was disappointed, because I could not go with him; but probably it was quite prudent for me to remain in Paris, as he had to travel very fast indeed. I was sorry to hear of the death of Mrs. Brown and Miss Hopkins. When you receive this letter,//we shall, Providence permitting, be almost home. I hope it will not be very warm weather, for it is quite cool here, and you know that I like cold weather. I suppose, you have been to Church today, but I have not, for we were so fatigued, after so much journeying since last Wednesday, that I thought it best, to stay in the house today. I dont know where we are going this week. We may go to Ireland, and Scotland, but it is not certain. However, next Saturday, the 23rd of June, we start from Liverpool for America, in the Steamer Cuba.

I have written a letter to Helen, from Leicester, but which will not go until this does. Be good children, and give my love to all the family and friends, not forgetting Mary, from whom I should like to have received a letter. From your loving
Kiss Sammie dear for me." Mother"

Her son Sammie wrote in pencil to his son: :"Note:- To Douglas 6/4/1938. Referring to last lines in my Mother's letter of 6/17/1866 wherein she sent a kiss to me--I suppose I recd it on time, but never realized it until I first saw this letter almost 10 years ago, but believe me I have treasured it ever since Father".

The Gould family's trip to Europe in 1871-2 has been related in the previous chapter. On that trip Caroline gave birth to their seventh and last child, Warren Gould, born in Paris 8/9 Sept. 1872, and buried in Père LaChaise cemetery 13 Sept. 1872. Caroline was then 38 years old.

Caroline traveled again to Europe in 1878, on R.M.S. *Parthia,* we know from a full morocco bound volume of Byron's works given to her by a fellow passenger, who inscribed it "Mrs. C. Gould//From and who has a lively recollection of many kindnesses, in and about her, HM//Boston March 28/78//Horatio McKay//RMS "Parthia". (*Poetical Works of Lord Byron* (London: Gall & Inglis, n.d.) now kept by her great-granddaughter Elinor Gould Krueger, Pinehurst NC, March 2006. Other books that Elinor has preserved from her library include *Poetical Works of Thomas Gray* (Philadelphia: E.H.Butler, 1858) and Jean Ingelow's *Songs of Seven* (n.p., n.d.). Robert Burns's *The Cotter's Saturday Night* (N.Y: Scribner, 1857) with book plate "T.W.Gould" is also in Elinor's possession.

After the death of her husband in 1895, she lived another twenty years until her death in Melrose 13 March 1915 (Family Record). She died of cerebral hemorrhage at age 81, 9 months and 27 days (File record in Wyoming Cemetery). She is buried beside her husband in Wyoming Cemetery, Melrose, in section NI (at south end, on Forest Av.), lot 54 (3 graves west of Vesper Av.), under the granite stone marked only "GOULD". Later two of her children, Ida and Samuel, were buried beside her here.

Caroline was survived by three of her children, Ida, Samuel and John, and four grandchildren, the oldest Caroline, named for her, Annie, Douglas and Warren. Her first and only great-grandson was born ten years after her death, on her 90th birthday, 14 May 1924.

7 children, listed at end of previous chapter XI.

THE GODDARD & GARRAN FAMILIES
Chart 8
GODDARD
WALKER
GARRAN
FLETCHER

Chapter XIII

THE ELIAS GODDARD FAMILY OF BOSTON

Caroline Goddard Gould was the daughter of ELIAS[6] WATERS GODDARD and CAROLINE GARRAN. Her father was the oldest of ten children of ELIAS[5] GODDARD, Senior, sailmaker of Boston, and his wife EUNICE WALKER.

Her father-in-law Jabez Garran had been living (Dir. 1829, 119; 1828, 118). She lived at the rear of 27 Charter Street with her son John, the mast maker until 1835, when she moved to 7 Tileston Street (Dir. 1833). Remaining there until 1837, her name is missing until 1839 when she reappears at 248 Hanover Street (Dir. 1839). Not in the directory 1842-5, she reappears as a nurse in 1846, at 4 Alien Court, then in 1848/9 at 128 Endicott Street (Dir. 1846 246, 1848/9 137; Alien Court opened opposite 323 Alien Street, which ran from Chambers to Brighton Street, Dir. 1846, 35). In 1850/1 Mrs. Eunice Goddard, nurse, has moved to 74 Prince Street, where she remains until 1852 (Dir 1850/1 168, 1851/2 103). She moved from Boston after 1853, and was living on Inman St. in Cambridge in 1854 (Cambridge Directory 1854). She died in Cambridge 24 Feb. 1858, age 75 (MDR 130:39; Family Record merely gives age at death 75).

Elias Goddard Sr. and Eunice (Walker) had ten children, born in Boston's North End:

i. ELIAS WATERS GODDARD, b. 4 Sept. 1803 (All dates from Family Record in Bible of E.W.Goddard). d. Boston 3 Jan. 1888; m. CAROLINE GARRAN.

ii. JOHN, mastmaker, b. 22 Feb. 1805; bp. Boston 20 Jan. 1820; d. Boston 16 Nov. 1878; m. ELIZABETH-----.

iii. JANE, b. 22 July 1806; d. Boston 5 Dec. 1813, age 7 years, 4 mos.

iv. ELIZABETH, b. 28 Sept. 1808; bp. Boston 30 Jan. 1820.

v. WILLIAM WALKER, b. 13 Sept. 1810; bp. Bos. 30 Jan. 1820[4]; m. Old North 29 May 1836 Louisa N. Hatch (CCRec. 144, # 96).

vi. GEORGE WASHINGTON, real estate broker, b. 28 Nov. 1812; d. Boston late 1886, age 71; m., One child, Charles A., b. Nov. 1836, buried Old North tomb #35, 12 Oct. 1838, age 23 mos.(CCTomb 14, #502; CCRec. 176, # 176).

vii. CHARLES, b. 19 June 1815, bp. Bos. 20 Jan. 1820; d. 3 June 1827, age 11 years, 11 months,

viii. SAMUEL, b. 9 Oct. 1817, bp. 20 Jan. 1820; d. 11 Jan. 1886, age 68, 3 months, 2 days.

ix. MARY JANE, b. 11 Nov. 1822; d. Boston 28 Aug. 1882, age 59, 7 months, 15 days; m. 18 Oct. 1842 George A. Dearing, (CCRec. 145, #31). Two children, i. Mary Jane, b. Aug. 1845; bur. Old North tomb 35 23 Dec. 1845, age 4 mos. (CCTomb 24, #714); ii. Mary A. b. May 1849, bur. Old North tomb 35 7 Aug. 1849, age 3 mos. (CCTomb 31, #844).

x. CAROLINE G., b. 2 Oct. 1825; d. 16 Sept. 1826, age 17 mos.; buried Old North 18 Sept. 1826 (CCRec. 207, #236, "child of Mr. & Mrs. Goddard").

ELIAS WATERS GODDARD'S EDUCATION AND WORK.

Elias Waters Goddard grew up in the North End, and probably attended the North Writing

School on North Bennet Street, the only grammar school in the North End, and made famous by the demanding Headmaster John Tileston, who was in charge until 1819. "Master Johnny", as he was known, was called "father of good writing in Boston" (Porter, 140). The students sat on long backless benches, facing long tables, or forms. Among his famous pupils was the orator Edward Everett, who grew up nearby, and recalled having been rapped on the knuckles by the Master. Elias's writing shows the influence of the rigid schooling. He probably went on to another Boston public school.

Elias was baptized when he was 17 at Old North, at the same time as his sister and four brothers. He was probably apprenticed to one of the many coopers in the North End. There were over fifty in Boston in 1827, most in that area.

At the age of 25 Elias married Caroline Garran of Boston at his parents' Old North Church, on Sunday, 5 Oct. 1836 (CCRec. 141, #354).

Elias's occupation as cooper first appears in 1828, at #27 Charter Street, when his father-in-law the ships' rigger Jabez Garran was living at the rear of the house (Dir. 1828 121, 118). Perhaps it is there that he met his wife, for the directory was made in 1827, before their wedding on 5 Oct. 1828 at Elias's parents' church, Old North (Sunday, by Rev. Sebastian Streeter, per Family Bible; Christ Church Register 141 #354).

But the next two years Elias is at 14 Fleet Street, which is on the other side of Hanover Street, with his new bride.

Fleet Street was one of the busiest maritime streets, probably named for the busy London thoroughfare. The North End Street ran down from Hanover to Scarlet's Wharf and later to the East Boston Ferry. Porter's Rambles has a fine picture of the street as it once looked, and a chapter on its interesting residents (Porter 278-88). Among these was one of the first woman doctors, Harriot Hunt, several Boston harbor pilots, the Revolutionary War Commodore Samuel Tucker, Oregon fur-trader Martin Bates, and other Boston merchants and politicians.

For just one year, 1830-1, the Goddards lived at 5 Salutation Alley, where their first child, the first Caroline Goddard, was born on "Sunday Morning June the 6th 1830, a rainy day (Family record)".

The cheerful name of this street, running down from Hanover Street to the North Battery, came from the Salutation Tavern, near the waterfront, where North End mechanics gathered to discuss the politics and to organize the Boston Tea Party and American Revolution under Sam Adams, John Hancock and Dr. Joseph Warren (Porter, 272-6; Drake 176). Outside the inn, which stood near the Goddards' home, was a sign showing "Two Palaverers" formally "bowing and cringing to each other". Porter's chapter tells how individual each of the old houses looked, and gives a glimpse of the Greenwood house. The narrow alley can be seen in an undated photo opposite p. 64 in Annie Thwing's *Crooked & Narrow Streets of Boston*, cited above.

The Goddards were back on Fleet Street when this first surviving letter of Elias's was written to his wife who took baby Caroline, age just a year, to visit her friends the Rices in

Andover:

"Boston Thursday Evening June 23d 1831 Dear Wife

It is with pleasure that i take my pen in hand for the purpose of communicating to you a few thoughts which naturally arise from your absence, and believe me when I say that I feel sad and melancholy. Since your departure, every thing goes on well in the house, but still there is some thing wanting, your presence and that dear Little Caroline I sincerely miss. No one can duly appreciate the worth of another until they are deprived of their society and company, and in the present instance I truly feel the difference,

I have been accustomed heretofore when coming home at the usual times to be greeted by your kind looks and pleasant smiles and the childish pratter of our child, but now how changed is every thing of the kind I do not meet you nor the little babe. Nothing but Empty Rooms, I hope you arrived here safe, and the country air i hope will be of especial benefit to the health of yourself and child. I went to see the diamond, do not Expose yourself too much to the damp airs I wish that your visit may be pleasant and agreeable and your company such as you can converse with freedom.

Mr. & Mrs. Noyse were in the city yesterday and called at the house in the afternoon and asked if you was cuming [sic] to Salem on your return home. I did not see them, but I think that you can go to Salem on your return home; there is not anything now at home that needs your immediate attention, and think you had better go. I want to see you and the little one, but then if it will do you and the baby good and in the meantime be a pleasant visit among your friends.//

I have a lot of business on hand to do this week and this day has been a rainy day which has put us back one day later. I am obliged to say that I cannot come to Andover at this time. But I do advise you to stay until Monday and then start for Salem in the Stage. //

Give my respects to Mr. & Mrs. Rice and Excuse the Matter as well as possible, tell them that I did intent to come but unforeseen circumstances render it imprudent to try it. It is now past 12 o clock at night and I am very sleepy.

And May a kind providence be with you both and protect you from harm and accident is the constant wish and prayer of him who is proud to acknowledge you as his dutiful and affectionate wife.

I remain your affectionate Husband

Elias W. Goddard Fleet St Boston ½

past 12 o'clock at night

[large flourish of quill]

P.S. Morning of 24th

Elizabeth [his sister?] & Ben & all hands from Beezies family are going on a water frolic this day. the house is well fastened and the keys secured.

Mr. Hollis undertook to drownd himself yesterday afternoon but was prevented, & brought home in a chaise, he was quite sick all last night and had watchers [could this have been a relative, perhaps of the Mary E. Hollis who was buried in the Goddard family plot at Mt. Auburn 26 Dec. 1883, age 37 years, 3 months=born Sept. 1856?] .

George [his brother, age 29] will leave Mr. Robbins on Saturday they do not agree he wants to go to Providence or N.York but I shall do all I can to prevent him.

I have added this poscript in haste. I have a plenty of business on hand to day. It is a fine morning but cold.

This done at the Doane Street Shop ½ past Seven. Yours &c E.W.G."

Fleet Street was also the birthplace of their first son, Andrew Jackson, born "August 23^{d} 1831, on Tuesday afternoon, a Rainy day". The political name, instead of the expected repetition of Elias, gives an idea of the enthusiasm of the Goddards Democratic politics.

In 1832 the Goddards moved to #5 (later numbered 19) Unity Street where they were to remain for the next 55 years, with the exception of a brief stay in Somerville in 1854. The historic Franklin house, built about 1725, and its garden have been described in the previous chapter.

SENIOR WARDEN OF OLD NORTH, AND THE SMITHETT SCANDAL

Living directly behind Old North Church, Elias became actively involved in parish affairs. When their first two children died in the summer of 1832, they were both buried in tomb #11 on the east wall of the crypt, one tomb from the rear (Christ Church "Record of Tombs 1829-1853", Book 53 in Diocesan Archives, hereinafter CCTomb, 6 #318, 320). Five years later their father bought tomb #35, on the same east side, but nearest the altar, and had their bodies moved to it (CCTomb 6, #319, 321, June 1837; 12 #463, 464; It may be pure coincidence that the next burial in the Goddard family tomb was five year old James W. Laurence, on 8 July 1836, 12, #468. The Goddards had no connection with the Goulds until 1855, when Ann Lawrance's grandson Thomas married Caroline Goddard. The next burial in the tomb is also a mystery, Sarah Rouse, age 83, 28 Feb. 1838, 13, #468. We have no evidence that she was a relative.

We still have the original deed to this tomb, for which he paid the sum of $200 on 1 July 1836, signed by the Wardens John Bacon and Charles Williams. This was accompanied by a further bond of $400, dated 27 June 1837, by the same wardens, confirming the deed "of a certain tomb under the vestry building of said Church and numbered thirty-five", and Goddard's payment of $200 payable in two years, with interest, on 1 July 1838.

The Goddard family pew was number 15, fourth back from the altar on the left side of the west aisle (Elias Goddard paid $66 for pew #15 on 16 April 1841, Christ Church Pew Records 1806-1853, Book 37, Diocesan Archives, 200. He also is listed for pew 12 at the right side of the altar, but in the Pew Book this is owned by William Munroe 2 Nov. 1841, 202, and sold to John Fox 12 Sept. 1870. Today the Senior Warden's pew is designated at the far rear, on the left side of the center aisle).

Elias became a Vestryman of Old North church in 1837-40 (Christ Church "Hall's Index to the Proprietors Records", Box 6, hereinafter Hall, 159).

In 1841 he was made Junior Warden, and the following year Senior Warden, a post he held for 12 years, until he was deposed on 7 Sept. 1854 (Hall 199, first elected Warden 2 May

1842, p. 199; reelected 8 May 1843, 20 May 1844, 21 April 1845, 27 April 1846, 26 April 1847, 8 May 1848, 14 May 1849, 30 April 1850, 21 April 1851, 10 May 1852, 2 May 1853, Hall pp. 55, 61, 67, 76, 94, 138, 198, 232, 267, 309, 332. W. W. Mair elected Warden 7 Sept. 1854,. 216).

For the last six years he was also Treasurer of the church (Hall 197, with the same dates 1848-53). We told above how he cared for the precious silver communion service, hiding it under the stairway of his house at 5 (23) Unity Street.

Goddard's tenure as Senior Warden the church ended in 1855 when he was deposed after a major scandal about its Rector, Rev. William T. Smithett. Goddard had been Senior Warden when Smithett was hired, but a rumor about the candidate's reputation delayed his invitation. Goddard finally ended the year-long vacancy by sending a letter to him in 1851 (Letter of Elias W. Goddard 14 Oct. 1851, authorized by unanimous vote of Proprietors the previous day, in "Smithett Correspondence", Box 20, Diocesan Archives).

Smithett was then only 29, born in Dover, England 2 April 1822 (Biography from Gleason's Pictorial "Drawing Room Companion" in "Smithett Correspondence", Box 20, and "Biographies of Christ Church Rectors", Box 19, hereinafter Bio, 78 ff).

He had lived in France as a child, and returned to England after the Revolution of 1830. At age 19 he became a missionary in the West Indies, working as a lay reader among the native aborigines of British Guyana, and in the plantations there. He was 23 when he was ordained priest and deacon by the Bishop of Demerara. After several years as minister there he moved to the U.S., where he was rector in Honesdale, a coal mining town of Pennsylvania, then at Redont, a town in the Catskills of New York.

Old North had been without a Rector for over a year since the last sermon of Rev. John Woart in July 1850. The debt at the end of 1850 was over $5000, much of it in notes issued by Goddard and other wardens against the bequest of Catherine Hay, and $2000 in private loans (Ibid., 79). Because of the lack of a preacher, the congregation had dwindled to a small number.

In July 1851 Smithett was invited to preach at Old North, and again in Sept. Although the Proprietors were pleased with him, they delayed action because of "numerous false stories which had been circulated against him by persons who had confounded his identity with another person" (Bios of rectors 78).

Goddard and James Benjamin were appointed a committee on the matter, and reported 2 Oct. 1851: "after hearing Mr. Smithett preach, conversing and consulting with him, and making inquiries in relation to his character and standing, as to which we have a favorable account of him by a distinguished clergyman of New York,-cheerfully and cordially recommend him to your serious consideration as a suitable person to be called to the Rectorship of Christ Church", (Ibid).

The Proprietors accepted this report and unanimously voted to accept Smithett on 13 Oct. Goddard's invitation is apologetic about the delay. But Smithett accepted, and first officiated on the first Sunday in November 1851, and formally installed by the Bishop Eastburn at Epiphany 1852.

Smithett's honeymoon was short. In April 1853 a fire in the Goulds' North Margin Street sent sparks onto the wood shingles of Old North, and almost burned it down (28 April 1853).

The shingles were replaced by slate, and Smithett raised half of the $1200 to reroof and repair the aging church building. Smithett started to solve the financial problems by getting pledges from members of other churches, with permission of the Bishop. He raised $750 in 1852.

A proposal to raise money by selling pews was the cause of the "Smithett Controversy" and Goddard's ousting as Warden. In the long list of Proprietors only ten were eligible to be Vestrymen and Wardens by being regular worshipers and taxpayers. Many nominal Proprietors held deeds exempting them from taxes.

Smithett supported a proposal in 1853 to sell the non-taxpaying pews to members who were then renting them. Goddard and the Junior Warden, William P. Parrott, turned down the applications. Smithett found support of some proprietors who agreed with him "that the refusal to grant pews to applicants was absolutely unwarranted, and the right to grant pews was not vested entirely in the wardens" (Ibid., 81).

This was a direct challenge to the power of the Wardens.

The battle was out in the open at "a stormy meeting" of the Proprietors on 25 Nov. 1853, which the Junior Warden got adjourned by declaring the meeting illegal because all Proprietors had not been notified. The biography of Smithett says Goddard and Parrott then tried to pack the next vote by privately selling or transferring pews.

The next meeting, on 1 Dec. adjourned again after another confusing session. The Smithett faction was led by F. H. Stimpson, an outsider who worshiped at the Church of the Advent, calling for by-laws, which he knew did not exist. Lacking them, he called for a meeting governed by state statutes, and asked if the Clerk, George W. Collamore, had been sworn in. Collamore said no Clerk had been sworn in the 130 years of Old North's history. But Junior Warden Parrott said he was the sworn Clerk, and if the acting Clerk hadn't been sworn everything was illegal, including all the officers, the Proprietors and this meeting. The meeting broke up in confusion.

Nothing was done over the winter, until the Easter meeting of the Proprietors, on 17 April 1854, at which Goddard was elected chairman, with 12 members present (Hall 171, 343). One of the proprietors, Dr. Bacon, read a legal opinion which seems to favor Goddard's view of the validity of non-taxpaying deeds, stating, "that any subsequent purchaser, or any representative of the original grantee takes such pews subject to the conditions expressed in the body of the deeds" (Bio 83, opinion of Ellis Gray Loring, Charles Theo. Russell and George M. Browne).

A "stick-vote" was called to determine the validity of the non-taxpaying pew owners' votes, but efforts to exclude the proxies failed. Parrott then declared the parish disorganized and promised to get a legal opinion by the next meeting.

Junior Warden Parrott produced a legal opinion that the parish was disorganized and could be reorganized only under state rules. Therefore a justice of the peace, J. H. Wakefield, called a Proprietors' meeting on 24 May 1854. The notice of meeting did not mention election of wardens, which was due, and Goddard failed reelection for the first time in 14 years. However, he chaired the Proprietors' Meeting of the same date (Hall 178, 347).

That Proprietors' meeting was adjourned to 8 June, with Goddard again in charge (Hall 179, 349, 479, 481).

Four new Vestrymen were elected from the Minister's faction: John Bacon, Abel H. Coffin, William A. Haslam, William W. Mair and John McKay. Although the hand vote was not challenged at once, Parrott was evidently upset by three voters who had no right to vote, and said he would later move consideration of voting method. Goddard failed reelection as Treasurer.

The newly elected Vestry met with Wardens Goddard and Parrott on 25 June. Two days later they authorized a committee to draw up deeds to be signed by the Wardens, and warned that "in case of their refusal to sign the same, then we do hereby authorize and empower this committee to execute good and lawful deeds in favor of those persons whose names have been presented." Smithett had effectually asserted his authority.

The Proprietors met on the evening of 29 June in a rowdy meeting in which the minister was later convicted of slander (News item, "Court Calendar//In the Justices' Court--Suffolk County. *Parrott vs. Smithett).*

Smithett got up before the Goddard had called order, and read the resolution of the pew committee of the vestry.

When Smithett presented the pew committee deeds Goddard pushed them aside as out of order, and tried to call the meeting to order. Parrott came up, took the deeds off the table, and put them into his pocket, saying he would take care of them. Smithett demanded the deeds unsuccessfully. He then went out of the church, and brought back two policemen, and ordered them to arrest Parrott, saying, "He has committed a theft and has my property." Parrott explained the situation, that these were the Wardens' standard forms. The police then left, but Parrott sued for slander, and won. Smithett's lawyer admitted the accusation in court, and stuck to the charge of theft, so was convicted of slander and fined damages of $75. Smithett appealed.

The Committee later executed new deeds under its authority, by-passing the Wardens. Smithett announced from the pulpit that the old method of collecting pew rent was abolished (Goddard's cross-examination in Boston Police Court 4 Jan. 1855, *Herald* 5 Jan. 1855, "Affairs About Home", para. 4).

The Proprietors' meeting on 29 June formally increased the Vestrymen to 15 (Hall 180, 370).

It was at this turning point in Goddard's influence that he left the Unity Street house and moved to Somerville, in Aug. 1854.

The schism in the church became formal after the last joint meeting of Proprietors on 3 August. The Wardens' faction got a justice of the peace Henry M. Parker to call a meeting on 18

Sept., declaring that they were the legal body of the church pending an opinion of the Superior Court of Massachusetts. This was not handed down for three years, when Justice Dewey declared that the Wardens had been displaced by a legal vestry meeting of 7 Sept. (Copy of opinion 22 June 1857 in Box 10, "Smithett Controversy").

Initially Goddard attempted to avoid public controversy by asking the Supreme Court to give an advisory opinion *quo warranto,* but Justice Shaw ruled in 1854 that they would have to go thru ordinary process of law (E. W. Goddard relator vs. Smithett and others, in Boston *Transcript*, 3 Jan. 1855, "Christ Church--Again", an article signed "Layman", probably a friend of Goddard).

The Minister's faction met on 7 Sept. and formally deposed Goddard and Parrott by electing William Mair and F. H. Sampson as Wardens, and new officers, including a new treasurer and moderator to replace Goddard.

Old North parish deteriorated into brawling at Christmas time, culminating in an open fight before Sunday services in the last Sunday of the year. A Boston paper reported that at Holy Communion Smithett substituted for the offertory a speech which warned the congregation not to give any money to the officer making the collection (*Herald*? 1 Jan. 1855, "Church Troubles").

Goddard brought about a confrontation by insisting upon his right as Treasurer to post pew rents as usual at the end of the year. Before the 10 o'clock Sunday service on the last day of 1854, he began passing out the notices. Goddard's testimony before the police court was summarized in the Boston *Herald:*

"I reside in Somerville; have been connected with Christ Church for the past twenty years; am one of the proprietors of the church; own two pews; have held the offices of Clerk, Senior Warden and Treasurer; was present at Christ Church on Sunday last at 10 o'clock, in company with others; was there to attend divine service and distribute notices of rents due from the several pew holders; [witness then read the form of the notification, which was in the customary style of bills for pew rent, with the --otion that at the bottom of the notification was a request that the rents be paid into the Treasurer's (Mr. Goddard,) hands] Had commenced the distribution of notices into the pews, when on reaching pew No. 17 (Third from the altar on the left side of the west aisle). I was arrested by the Rector, who commanded me to desist; I paid no attention to him, but kept on distributing; he then put his hands around my body and shoulder to prevent my going further; I told him to take his hands off, but he pressed me harder and harder, and said he would make me accountable for what I had done; during all the time the Rector was very vehement in his language; his talk was so loud as to attract the attention of Mr. Collamore, who was distributing notices in another part of the church, and that gentleman came over to where I was; he told Mr. Smithett that he was a Justice of the Peace and wanted no trouble in the church; a scuffle ensued between the Rector and Mr. Collamore, and I went towards them to prevent any disturbance, or rather I was shoved towards them by the crowd; a scuffle ensued, and [James] Lyndes, [Joseph] Parks and [William] Gault took hold of me; they pressed me backwards and forwards, and finally I was pressed over the back of a pew; I became alarmed for the safety of my back, which I feared would be broken; was sick the next day from the effects of the assault".

Another account says that Smithett "seized hold of Mr. G. and whirled him round two or three times, and soon after the other defendants came up and also seized him by his cravat and his coat, handling him quite roughly (*Herald*? 6 Jan, 1855, "The Church Assault Case").

Hubbard supported Goddard's story, and added that "he saw Mr. Parks strip off his coat and say to the others that they must put Goddard and Collamore out of the church; and they all took hold of Goddard, using a great deal of force, and moving him backwards and forwards, frightening him to such an extent that his face assumed a deadly hue." (*Herald* 5 Jan., para. 7).He said Goddard "offered no other resistance than holding on to the pews, which prevented his expulsion until the arrival of the police" (As reported 6 Jan. "Church Assault Case").

Collamore added that "when he went in [to the church he] saw three of defendants near the stove; was distributing his notices when he heard Mr. Goddard say--Don't put your hands on me; that was repeated three or four times; saw Mr. Smithett with his hand on Mr. Goddard's arm; it was by Mr. Smithett's appearing to push him harder and harder; that I went in; as I was passing along saw Mr. Smithett take hold of Mr. Goddard's coat and pull him in the direction of the chancel; I said to Mr. Smithett I am a Justice of the Peace; immediately I was attacked by Mr. S. and the bow of my stock bow broken (Both Webster and OED say this is an obsolete term for a crossbow); Mr. Lynes had Mr. Goddard by the throat in a ferocious manner; Mr. Parks had hold of Mr. G's left collar, and Mr. Smithett of the right side of his coat; Mr. Parks and Mr. Lynes cried out repeatedly, put him out; saw Mr. Gault there, but did not see him touch any one."

Collamore continued that he "Repeatedly asked them to let alone of Mr. Goddard, and as they did not, beckoned to Mr. Hubbard; finding that he did not come went towards Mr. H., and when he went back Mr. Goddard was released. . .Saw no violence or demonstration to violence on the part of Mr. Goddard; [Collamore] used no violence; when Mr. Smithett seized me by the throat, I only raised my hands to protect myself".

Goddard said, "after getting released I kept on distributing the notices in the pews; the Rector followed immediately after, endeavoring to prevent my distribution, taking up my notices as fast as distributed, and calling on some person to take up those already distributed; I finished my distribution, and called to a person in the church Mr. [Josiah W.] Hubbard, to witness that I had done so; I told parties that Gault, Lynde and Parks had assaulted me; I have distributed notices at the end of every quarter previous; they varied slightly from those distributed last Sunday; for the last fourteen years notices have been distributed requiring pew owners to deposit their dues in the collection box."

Collamore concluded the story, saying that "divine service commenced in fifteen minutes afterwards; Mr. Smithett officiates...".

On New Year's Day readers of the paper got the false news of this "disreputable transaction" that Goddard was forcibly ejected, and the police called, with a sarcastic conclusion that "the parties guilty of these strange scenes are *'Christians'*, but by our dictionary they cannot claim to be '*gentlemen.'* The Police Court has jurisdiction over these Sunday fights." (*Herald*, 1 Jan. 1855, "Church Troubles").

Goddard and Collamore preferred charges, and on 4 Jan. Smithett, Parks, Lynde and Gault were arraigned before Police Court in Boston. Goddard had future Governor John Andrew represent him, with his lawyer J. H. Wakefield (*Herald*, 5 Jan. 1855, "Affairs About Home.".)

Smithett and his friends' lawyer George M. Browne maintained the position of the Rector gave him control over church property, and the right to prevent Goddard's illegal activity. Although some of the minister's defenders charged Collamore with "striking the minister in his own church", Smithett denied it ("Church Assault Case" 6 Jan. 1855).

Goddard's faction called a Proprietors Meeting for 8 Jan., but found the locks had been changed. They voted not to break down the door, as some proposed, but to meet at Collamore's house nearby at 73 Salem Street (Hall 184, 481-3).

At issue in court was who had the legal right to control the property of the church. So in early February 1855 Goddard's faction brought suit in Supreme Judicial Court against one of the renters of Christ Church property for back rent. This was *"The Wardens of Christ Church--Ellas W. Goddard and William P. Parrott vs. George W.* Pope" (Begun 19 Feb. 1855 for the quarterly rent of $75 for Chamber Street property from the estate of Jane Keene Richardson, due 15 Dec. 1851., 71 pp. in Box 10, "Smithett Controversy".)

This had the effect of drying up church revenue from other church properties, for fear of suits.

As the biographies of the Rectors states, "With two sets of wardens and vestrymen, two clerks, two treasurers and two sextons" the church was "almost literally torn asunder."

Goddard's group tried to depose the minister on 14 May. Among family souvenirs are two copies of a printed call of Vestrymen and Proprietors by Wardens Goddard and Parrott to discuss the dismissal of the minister. Although they have the same dates, the text has been toned down in one to the Vestry. Here is the text of the first, to the Proprietors, with changes in the second underlined: To GEO. W. COLLAMORE, Esq.

Clerk of Christ's Church:

YOU are hereby authorized and requested to call a Special meeting of the Proprietors [Vestry] of Christs Church, to be held at the Vestry Room of said Church, on THURSDAY, May 24, at 4. [5] o'clock, P. M., for the following purposes, viz:

To take into consideration the late disgraceful transactions at said Church, and to act upon the same.

To consider and to act upon the question of closing the Church for a time as the Meeting may determine.

To consider and act upon the question of taking the required legal steps to terminate the connection between the Church and [the dismissal of] Rev. WM. T. SMITHETT.

E. W. GODDARD, WM. P. PARROTT,

Wardens of Christ's Church, Boston. BOSTON, MAY

14, 1855.

Agreeably to the above Warrant, to me directed, I hereby notify you that a Special Meeting of the Proprietors [Vestrymen] of Christs Church will be held at the Vestry Room of said Church, on THURSDAY, 24TH day of May current, at 4 [5] o'clock in the afternoon, for the purpose of transacting the business named in the said Warrant. Your attendance is respectfully requested.

[signed] Geo. W. Collamore. CLERK. BOSTON,

May 16 1855."

Rev. Smithett continued as Rector for five more years, until 1860. It is clear that he won, and the Senior Warden's resignation shows who lost. North Church Archivist Canon Jonathan Young explains that there is a long history of congregational independence in American Episcopal churches, but the hierarchical tradition usually leads to the victory of the clergy (Interview at the church, 20 Nov. 1995).

But it was a Pyrrhic victory for Smithett, and he lasted only two more years. The income of the church was so reduced by lawsuits and loss of parishioners that his Proprietors could give him no more than $300 a year salary, and let him go on raising extra funds where he could. By 1859 Smithett was looking for a new parish, at the same time the Vestry finally raised his salary to $1000 a year <u>after</u> all other expenses were raised (Vote of 14 July 1859 in Bio 85).

This precipitated his resignation to accept the Rectorate at Galesburg IL, effective 1 Oct. 1859.

This dispute was probably a factor in the Goddards' move to Somerville in Aug. 1854, dated from their daughter Caroline's letters from Troy NY in the previous chapter (Dir. 1854 131, 1855 127; 15 Ashland Street in 1856).

That daughter Caroline was not married in her father's Old North on 17 Feb. 1855 also shows the extent of Elias's disaffection with the church.

They did not sell the 19 Unity Street house, however, and returned to it by 1857 (Dir. 1857 147).

With the decision of the Superior Court in June 1857 that Goddard had lost control in Sept. 1854 the battle was essentially over. The Goddards eventually rejoined services at Old North, but Elias never returned to his former church offices.

THE GODDARD COOPERAGE BUSINESS.

Goddard joined in a business partnership with Benjamin Clapp, for in 1832 the name of the firm Clapp & Goddard first appears (Dir. 1832 159).

As the letter of 1831 says, the cooperage shop was in Deane(?) Street In 1833 they took a seven year lease on a triangular piece of land fronting 83 feet on Richmond Street, with liberty to build (SD 375:220). They paid $150 rent a year, a quarter $37.50, payable quarterly to Boston wharfinger James Bartlett, starting the first of July. The renewal of this lease is not recorded, but appears to have been done for another seven years, for Clapp & Goddard took a ten year lease in 1846, for the same $150 rent annually, payable the first of each quarter, from Benjamin Wheeler, merchant of Boston (SD 587:78, signed 18 July 1846, effective 1 July). They had obviously built their cooperage here, for the lease refers to this as the east end of the building on the premises, with its west end 43 feet long on the northwest

Elias joined the Massachusetts Charitable Mechanics Association in July 1834, becoming its oldest member at his death in 1888 (Obituary in *Boston Transcript* 5 Jan. 1888). Among the souvenirs the family has kept is the silver medal awarded by the Association to him in 1837. An inch and a half in diameter, the front shows a classical woman seated next to the craftsman's tools, the wheel, anvil, hammer and press, with her arm over the shoulder of a young man who holds a scroll. The only words are name of the sculptor, "Goodrecht, F." and "FOUNDED 1795.//INC. 1806." . On the obverse is an oval with the full name of the association, enclosing "AWARD TO" and inscribed, "E. W. GODDARD//FOR A FINE OVAL//HARNESS CASK//EXHIBITION OF 1837.". A harness cask is a nautical term for a wooden tub "with a rimmed cover used on ship for keeping the salt meats for present consumption." (Oxford English Dictionary 2:100, citing Dana's *Before the Mast* xxx, 109 in 1840, and first used in 1818).

Elias and Caroline Goddard in front of their home 19 Unity St.

In 1840 Goddard had made enough to pay $500 down on the Unity Street house from the owners, merchant tailor Caleb C. Hayden and trade Thomas T. Hayden, from whom he had apparently leased it since 1832 (SD 455:180, 14 May 1840, their daughter's seventh birthday).

He paid $2000 for a lot of 1197 sq. ft., measuring 22 feet 9 inches on Unity Street, and the same width backing up to Christ Church and John Hobby's land south of the church, and 59 feet 2 inches deep between John Dodell on the north, and John Brown on the south. The deed records that this was sold by the estate of Benjamin Franklin's sister Jane Mecom (John Lothrop & Benjamin Sumner, executors sold it 14 Dec. 1802 to Noah Lincoln in SD 203:231; Lincoln sold it to the Haydens 13 April 1820 in SD 267:131).

The house was already subject to a mortgage of $3000 made in 1839 (SD 449:120, 9 Oct. 1839, discharged 22 Aug. 1876 by Morton Newcomb to Massachusetts Hospital Life Ins. Co. in SD 1340:265). However, Goddard at purchase in 1840 took a mortgage of $1000 from single woman Elizabeth Hovey, $600 of which was to be paid in two years (SD 455:181, 14 May 1840). Business must have been bad for Goddard, for she foreclosed on this in two years, but he managed to pay it off the next year (SD 487:21, 1 July 1842; discharged 19 May 1843). At the time of purchase Goddard also took a second mortgage for $500 from the Haydens, which he duly paid off in three years (SD 455:182, 14 May 1840). The Hovey and Hayden mortgages were only paid off by taking a single mortgage from Widow Elizabeth S. Danforth for $1200. On Mrs. Danforth's death, the mortgage of $1200 was transferred to the name of Caroline Goddard (SD 1072:281, 4 Oct. 1871, by Elizabeth S. B. Danforth and Mary S. Danforth, executors of estate of Elizabeth S. Danforth).

This was not paid off until after the death of both Elias and his wife, in 1889 (SD 501:135, 18 May 1843, discharged 20 Nov. 1889 by the estate of Caroline Goddard by Henry Buxton, her administrator).

But two years after the first deal, in 1847, he took second mortgage of $500 from Lucy P. Jennings, a widow from Reading (SD 578:284, 21 Aug. 1847, @ 6 % interest, to be insured for $1200, like Danforth mortgage; discharged 9 May 1860).

The long depression of the eighteen forties which had adversely hit the Goulds, also affected Goddard's cooperage business. The foreclosure of 1846 was followed by declaration of insolvency in 1849 (SD 598:283, Insolvency of Elias W. Goddard, cooper, debtor 14 March 1849, George W. Collamore of Boston, assignee, by John M. Williams, Commissioner of Insolvency).

However, the national economy turned around in 1849, aided by the Gold Rush. Goddard evidently prospered, for in 1853 he was able to pay $5500 for a lot on Richmond Street by the Town Slip, where Richmond crosses Commercial Street today. This was called by some “Beer Lane”, near the site of the Red Lyon Inn, whose proprietor Nicholas Upsall took pity on the first Quaker missionaries, by bringing food to them in jail, an act of mercy which earned him expulsion from Boston, to become one of the pioneers of Friends meetings on Cape Cod (Drake 155, 157; SD 643:220, 7 March 1853; Dunbar's title from Curtis S. Dunbar SD 578:134, his from Gilman S. Bow, SD 575:248). The lot fronted 38 feet 4 inches on Richmond, went back 28 feet 5 inches on the east on a passage which separated it from the mansion of Prince Snow Jr., and 30 ft. 7 inches on the west against a brick house, and a passage at the back the same width as on the street side. The property had two liens which Goddard assumed, a mortgage of $1000, and a lease running to 1 Sept. 1855, perhaps Goddard's own. At the same time Goddard gave the seller, gentleman David A. Dunbar, a second mortgage for $3000, at 6 %, with $500 repayable in six months, and the balance in three years (SD 643:221, 1 March 1853). This was paid off in 1871 (To Elizabeth S. B. and Mary S. Danforth, legatees of Elizabeth S. Danforth, 3 Oct. 1871, SD 1072:281). He also took a third mortgage from Melrose gentleman Daniel Copeland for $1500, payable in three years, at 6 % interest (SD 643:222, 1 March 1853). To meet the considerations of the new Homestead Law Elias joined with his wife Caroline-in 1856 to take a consolidated mortgage of $6500 from Charles Horace Hubbard, Gentleman of Boston; this was witnessed by their daughter Caroline and her husband T. Warren Gould (SD 731:66, 7 June 1856; his wife Caroline confirmed this under her rights in the Homestead Act on the same date, SD 731:67-8). This was accompanied with a Declaration of Trust by Goddard, who covenanted with George W. Collamore, who had died, thru his trustees John A. Andrew, counselor at law, who paid Goddard a nominal dollar to convey the property to him (SD 872:75, 7 Feb. 1856; in the previous document, SD 731:67, same date, Goddard paid $6000 as trustee to Hubbard; Collamore transferred this to Andrew on 11 April 1849 for $52.50, as recorded 40 years later in SD 1892:323-5, with Andrew's declaration of trust at the same date in SD 1892:325-6). Andrew was to become Governor of the state during the Civil War. After the death of Governor Andrew and of Goddard, the four Goddard children quitclaimed the old 19 Unity Street house when Andrew's trustee sold it for $4000 to Boston widow Delia Martin (Henry Buxton, trustee of Andrew, sold in SD 1919:580, 9 Nov. 1889; quitclaim of Goddard and Andrew heirs SD 1919:581, 25 Nov. 1889; mortgage of Delia Martin to David Flynn SD 1919:583).

Elias evidently did well in the mid-seventies, when he was able to buy the two old wooden houses to the east of their Unity Street home, at numbers 15 and 17 in 1875 from the Newcomb family for $8100, and took a mortgage from them for $2200 (SD 1274:285-6, 11 May 1875, 5/6 from Thomas C. Newcomb and Charles F. Newcomb of Medford, Norton and George A. Newcomb of St. Louis, and John W. Newcomb of Boston, for $6,833.33, and 1/6 from Thomas C. Newcomb as trustee of the estate of Lydia Ann Goldthwaite of Medford for $1367; then a second mortgage for $2200 from Thomas C. Newcomb SD 1276:205, 1 June 1875).

Since this was for a high interest of 7 %, he paid it off in 13 months, on 22 Aug. 1876. But this was done by taking a new mortgage at 6 % from the Franklin Savings Bank for $2600 (SD 1340:265-7, 22 Aug. 1876; new measurements of the property showed the original 22 feet 9 inches backing up to Christ Church now measured 20 feet and 88/100, 59 feet 2 inches on the east (now Josiah Snelling's) was now 57 feet, and 22 ft. 9 inches on Unity Street now 22 ft. 2/100, and the west side 57 ft. 23/100). These houses were sold after Elias's death by his four children for $3500 each, the west one (#17) to Margaret, wife of Robert Keanelly, and the east one (#15) to Bessie, wife of Michael J. Landrigan (SD 1871:612-615, 18 April 1889, with plan on SD 1871:613).

After Goddard bought the Richmond Street property, it was the workplace of the cooperage business of Clapp & Goddard, from 1857 to 1864 (Dir. 1857 147 #100 Richmond; Dir. 1859 169 #102 Richmond; last entry is Dir. 1864 151, 74 #103 Richmond). Goddard's partner, Benjamin Clapp, resident of Medford, evidently died in 1864. Elias Goddard continued at this location until 1877 (#27 Richmond in 1868 259, 43 appears to be a renumbering). After more than two decades on Richmond Street, Goddard moved his cooperage north on Commercial Street a couple of blocks to Union Wharf, in 1877 (Dir. 1877 376; Richmond was at #117 Commercial; #323 is on the right side of Commercial, at Union Wharf). It remained there until his death in 1888, but the business was not called E. W. Goddard & Son until 1885, when he took in his son Clifford, and 1887 made plural when he took in Walter (Dir. 1885 271; 1887 507; his death recorded Dir. 1888 523).

We have a business card that must date from after his death. It reads: "E. W. GODDARD'S SONS, //COOPERS, //--and manufacturers of--//Water Tanks, Water Casks,//SALT, COAL & OYSTER TUBS.//And all other kind of Work in their line of Business .//Have on hand a General Assortment of New and Second-Hand Casks,//And are Prepared to Cooper Merchandise by the Package or Cargo.//Special attention is also given to Sampling Leaf Tobacco//and preparing if for the African Market,//No. 323 COMMERCIAL STREET,//Corner Union Wharf, BOSTON." There are pictures on the card of three types of containers.

FAMILY RELATIONS

Elias's letters that have been preserved show his love of his grandchildren. The family had gone to the Gould homestead at Grapevine Corners in Lexington for the summer when he wrote his two oldest grandchildren, ages 5 and 3, this letter:

"Tuesday Evening 10 O'clock

My Dear Grandchildren) Boston July 22^D/62.

Ida, & Carrie, }

Your grandpapa Goddard sends his ?liness? love to you, and hopes that you are enjoying yourselves and having a very gay and pleasant time, I suppose that you busy about something all the time. I expect that you run about out of doors a great deal, and I dare say that you take a ride in the chaise once in a while, and I have no doubt that what you have been out, to geather [sic] berries in the woods, and fields,

but *I* really hope that you will not do any mischief, as get into any trouble, and if you are both good little girls, and obey what you are told to do by papa & Mamma, you will not have to be sorry for being careless & disobedient, and then you will <u>not</u> have to be corrected.
I really hope that my little <u>Ida</u> is getting much better than when I saw her last. I hope you are becoming quite strong and Fat. - -1 miss both of you very much, and I long to see you again,--I send you some candy & cocoanut cakes which you must make last as long as you can. it will not do//to eat it all at one time, "Mamma" will give it to you at such times as she may think it best. I will not write any more now but hope that you both will~^be good girls, and you will be kind and affectionate to all those kind folks with whome you are staying. From your Truly

affectionate grandFather

[flourish of pen] Elias W.

Goddard

P.S.I send to Miss Betsey Atkins "My old & Much Respected Friend" My love and kind regard, and that I am in hope of again seeing her, but I cannot now tell when. I sen her a few oranges which I wish her to accept.

E. W. G."

Later the same summer he again wrote the little girls:

"Boston Monday p.m. August 11th/62. My Dear Ida

& Carrie,

Your Grandfather has hurt his foot by getting it jamed under a case of Copper last Week, but it troubles him a little "more this morning""and he thought that it would be best, to stay at home to day, and this afternoon as I feel quite lonesom, I thought that perhaps you would like to get a letter from Me, and therefore I write to say that we are all by "Gods blessing" Very well, and I sincerely pray that both of you are enjoying health and contentment, and that you are having a very fine visit. I begin to miss you now, & more than perhaps you think I do. I dont know as I shall be able to tell you apart, for I expect that you have grown much larger & if you have played out of doors, perhaps you have tanned up some. However I believe I should remember the looks of you both, even in a crowd. It has been very warm the past two weeks, and we have had a good deal of Rain, with Thunder & Lightning, & I dare say that you have had warm weather & Rain at Lexington, as well as in Boston, But one man told me "after we had a great storme one night last week" that they had no Rain at all, up at Lexington, our House is quite still just now [;] Clifford is away, Helen is on a visit to Newburyport & is having a grand time. Abbie Pitman is there too,//6 and both of you are away. Only think of it, how still it must be, when so many are gone at one time.--I thought of you yesterday, but I could not have attended to you much on account of my lame foot, but I was "thinking of you" of Ida & Miss Trott." of how many questions that you would be asking, & that you would ask "gandpapa have got any things good." have you any cocoa nut cake" "any chocolate creams", "any Beans" "give me some water" "I should like some lemon aid" have you got any Candy", and I cannot tell all the questions that you would ask, and then you"would want me to play with you & Run around the yard, and to get upon my Back, and perhaps you would do something that was not exactly right, and I should chide you for it--and then you would say, "I do not like you Grandpapa" and I should say, well I cannot help it, but you must mind~what I tell you to do, and after a while you would come & get up in my arms, & then you would make it all up & be very good children again,--ah! that is the way, "Forgive & Forget, when you do wrong, own up, & make amend, and all will be right. I want you to be good children, and obey your Parents.

give my love & regards to Miss Atkins that I shall send you with this a small package of "Nick Nacks" so therefore be good Children.

your Grandfather"

Elias evidently went out to Lexington to visit the family at Grapevine Corners, and tells of the attractions of shopping in Harvard Square and a walk through Harvard Yard. This letter, written five weeks later, is evidently a not a continuation of the previous letter, but an unfinished one, of four pages, now lost:

"5 Sleepy & Must Stop---Wendsday Evening-10-oclk Sept 17'62

Well, here I am again, My dear Children. Having read the evening paper, I have come up stairs to finish my letter to you, I hope that I shall not tire you all out, with this dry story,--I left off last night "when I got Sleepy" some where near Mr. Frosts House. When I got there, Mr. F. had gone to the Depot for Walter who was coming up to do some work for him, & shortly afterwards he came up in a waggon with Mr. Frost, and you may believe that he "Walter" Stuck his Eyes out when he saw me, as he did not know that I should be there, "Said he to me" "Whear did you come from",--We soon regulated the work & I left him, to [Started?] for Boston, I found that Mr Frost had 5- or 6 men picking Tamatoes & packing for Market,--there was two small Boys who were having fine sport trowing cucmbers [sic] at each other, & the way the peices flew was a Caution to any one who might be in the way.--

I rode to the depot, "with one of the Boys in a waggon, but I concluded to stop at "Camp day" in Brighton or Cambridge. & after looking around the "Camp & Soldiers"[.] I stopped into the Horse Cars and rode into Boston, & at this part of the ride was the most peasantest of the whole trip. the road leading from the Camp to Old Cambridge is Very Broad, & there are very many beautiful residences, and handsomely laided out Gardens on the rout, & then, when you get down to the Colledge [sic] Buildings & Grounds, the Scenery is really beautifull, O how I wished that both of//you, could have been with me then, and have taken a walk around & over the Colledge Common, I think we should have had a fine time, and then all could have just stopped into some of the stores, & perhaps called for an Ice Cream, if we should have wanted one, & we might call for some other things, but you were not there & I did not stop, and kept on through Old Cambridge & passing a great many elegant Houses and delightful Estates on our way down the Maine Street, & passing the head of "Inman Street", where we once lived for a short time, untill we came to the Bridge & in sight of Boston with its great pile of Brick Houses & the Many Steeples--and how soon every thing becomes changed, the scenery; the air, the pleasant quietness of the country, for the narrow streets, and the continual noise of the rumbling cart & carriage wheels, the noise & Bustle of so many people passing too & Fro--

But I soon arrived home & found all well, Helen had gone to School, , & it was working day, so I had to tell your grandmother all about you, & she had a great many questions to ask, if you were well & if your arms & Necks were properly covered, the Season would soon change, that the country air was colder than in the city & it would be better to put on some Flannels &c. I told her all about our ramble in the woods, up the Hill, up the observatory, the Living & the Summer House up to Mr. Johnson' & that Miss Trott went up twice, & that we went up the road & gathered acorns. & I told her that Ida did not appear so hearty, as Carrie, »&~^{she}" Said, "Poor little Dear", I beleive she has worms...".

The letter is unfinished, and unsigned.

The next summer there is a letter evidently written to them in Hull:

"Boston Monday 2% '0 Clock
Agst 31^{Bt} /63

My Dear Grand Children

Ida, & Carrie.

I was very sorry that I did not send you the Sweet Meats on Saturday last, but I forgot them untill it was too late, yet I suppose that they will answer as well to day.

Thinking so, I have sent you a little package, which Mamma, will give you, as she may judge it best. We are quite well at home. Abbys Baby" [his son Walter's wife] is improving Especially in regard to its Eyes.--I thought of you all, yesterday, and that the Sunday before, we took a sail togeather [sic] over to the light House. & had a Very pleasant time, up in the light House & around that barren Rock. Hoping that you will be Very good Children & we shall see you again soon.

I remain Truly your Grand Father"

Elias's grandson Samuel wrote this explanation to his son on the back: "Douglas:-

This note is from my Grandfather Elias W. Goddard to your aunt Ida and Carrie

Ida would probably tell you that they were at Hull at the time & that Light House refd to was "Boston"

Father."

The next letter is written three years later to his eight year old granddaughter Caroline, whom we saw above he nicknamed "Miss Trott":

"Boston Friday Evening

Sept 21st 1866. My

Darling Trott.

It is with great Satisfaction that I now acknowledge the receipt of two loveing letters from you, and I wish to say that it was my intention to drop a line to you at the proper time, but you must see, that when we know that all the little folks are taken care of-We old folks are apt to become somewhat negligent of all our duties to them. And then again, you must remember that I have a "Thousand and One" of other cares upon my mind, all of which have so constantly demanded all my spare time, that I have not found the leisure to write you a single word before this, and perhaps I should put it off a little while longer. If the fact did not stare me right the//face--that you are coming Home to Boston next week, that if I write at all, I must do so now, you, during your Visit to the "City of Hull" I have no doubt [that you, crossed out] have formed very many new acquaintances with the little girls and boys of that place, and in their Company many pleasant Hours has been passed in your Childish Amusements and prattle.

I really hope that all those little folks with whom you have played were good and kind little Children, and that they are always Obedient to what their "Father and Mother" tells them to do. Of course you are dutiful and careful to do all things which you are bidden by "Papa and Mamma" . let me tell you that when you lie down at night, your thoughts and Sleep will be a deal pleasanter *If.* you have done Every thing "as well as you know" as directed by Father & Mother.//you will remember that a few days Since, I in company Mr. John Collamore made you a call at Hull. Well, we had a very pleasant time & enjoyed ourselves during our ramble up the road, along the Beach, around the 'Whale' bones, up the Bank, over the fences and pastures to the high land directly in the rear of your House & here we Sat down, had a chat on Various Matters, such as Sheep wool, Grass, cost of keeping feed, watch dog, pasture land &c, and at the same time had a grand view of the Surrounding Country, the Sea, the Shipping of all Sizes from the Small Sail Boat, to the great Ship under full sail, and I think we were as well Satisfied in the turn our "intended Excursion" took, as though it was carried out in all its previous arrangements.--- But when we returned to the House before going home, I could [not] find you, or Ida//nor "Sammy". but I suppose that you were out amoung the Neighbors children, having a nice frolick. When you get back to Boston, I shall expect a Visit from you at our House; then again, your thought must be turned toward the School House, because you have had a Very long Vacation, and you must not forget your Books [& Studies crossed out] and your lessons, for now, in your Early life, is the best, and most Suitable time to ~~Store~~ "fiii the mind with useful knowledge, as this Early learning will be of very great importance in assisting you to a better condition in Society as you advance along in life--"God" Grant that It may be Smooth and Happy.

your Grandmother is very glad to hear that all of you are coming up again. She thinks that you have had enough of Hull this time, but she wishes & is pleading for your health & comfort.--you see I have filled up this sheet, and it will be of no use to begin another, therefore Adieu. "Grandpapa".

The next letter comes some 14 years later, when Elias is 76 years old, and had lost his wife only three months before. As a distraction, apparently, some friends took him on a trip to Saratoga Springs and to New York City. It has an introduction by his grandson Samuel Gould:

"12/24/1937

Note for Douglas;

This letter of my grandfather's Elias W. Goddard written from Saratoga Springs N.Y 8/25/1880 to his sons, Walter, Clifford (my Godfather), William, and daughters, my Mother Caroline & Helen.

It was when he was on one of his few pleasure trips I ever heard of his having taken. The Mr. Collamore mentioned, was supposed to have been one of Bostons wealthy real estate owners of whom Ida can tell you more about [Collamore is not mentioned by name, but the "John" may refer to him].

As I believe I have already written you, my Grandfathers commissions as Corpl, Sargt, Lt. & Captain of The Old Columbian Artillery Co. may probably be found in Melrose together with other papers which may be of interest to you [The commissions have disappeared].

Father"

"Saratoga Springs, N.Y. Aug 25th 1880. My Dear

Sons, and Others of the Family.

I wrote a few hasty lines on my arrival here & mailed it Saturday last, and I suppose you received it on Monday, a.m. I somewhat expected a line from home this Morning (Wednesday) but did Not. Since I have been here we have been to Several of the Springs & drank of the waters, In fact we go to 3- of them every Morning (The Nearest-"[3]" The "Old Red"_"High Rock"_"Empire" "Star"- and, "Magnetic" Springs. They all have a different taste, and at first they are very disagreeable to many, to drink, but you become accustomed to it. There is a large

Number of Springs all through the Valley, which extends several miles, and quite a large business is done at some of them in Bottling, & in barrels for exportation all though the States & Canada. Hundreds of people of all ages come every morning to get a drink, and many come with bottles, Jugs, Pails, Kettles & Demijons. It is queer to see many old ladies drink 2 & 3 Tumblers full of this water for a Morning draft. No fee is Charged for it at most of the places. Some few, Charge a fee, Where they are inclosed in Hotels Parks. --We have made Several Walks and Visits to the Showey parts of the Town &//(2) vicinity, and have seen many wonderful sights, the customs of the people, and the Structure and Style of the great public Hotel are so differently constructed and arranged, That one is Compelled at once to acknowledge that there is nothing in Boston In the line of Hotel. That has any approach to the Magnificence and extent of Many of the large public buildings of this Town and I think Builders would well to take a pattern from the external architecture of these Grand Hotels.

We[,] that is John, Maria, Mrs. Pierce, Mr. Balfour & son & myself, to[ok] a barge (two horses) coach, and went out to Saratoga Lake which is about 5 to 6 miles out. We took two baskets full of Eatables & some Lager, and started at 9 a.m. and returned home at six p.m. having a first rate time and a grand view of the distant Country and the "Green Mountains" of Vt. This lake is 4^ to 5 miles "in a direct line" in length, and about 25 Miles arount it. We passed the Saratoga Race Course. The Races are now in full blast, but we did~not stop, for want of time, we passed several handsome Estates, and had a very fine view of the lake and all the points of note, and saw the place where the "Regattas" take place. There are two or 3 small Steam Boats on the Lake, which ply from the "Lake House" west to the "White Sulphur Springs", where there is a small public house. They make several trips during the day and carry passengers for 50 C each the round trip, in our Course out//(3) we pass the "White Sulphur" Springs. The half way House, and Stop here for a hour & take a Stroll on foot and then went on untill we come to an old Mill where there was a Stream of clear & pure cold water. The[re] had formerly been a Small woolen Factory in this place, here we came to a halt, fixed up a Table of old boards & had our lunch of Sandwiches, Cake[,] dough Nuts, Plums & Peaches & Lager Beer. here we again Stopped an hour, and"then started on for a long ride back we had to take a more inland route, because there is no road near the Margin of the Lake on this side. We finally reached the "Lake House", having passed the Estate of the late "Frank Leeislee?" he owned a large tract of land in this region. We stopped at the Lake House grounds about one hour, going to the look out at the top of of a 3 Story building which is prepared for a promenade & covered There are Chairs to sit on and a fine view is had of the~LaKe, and all the Surroundings, during our Stay here, one Steam Boat Started for a trip across the lake, and another returned with passengers. We now have made up our Minds//(4) to take the home Stre[t]ch for 534 Broadway going~through the fine and well Kept Carriage road wide enough for 4 teams to pass abreast of each other. This is a beautiful road, which in the Morning, at 9, & again in the edge of the evening from 5-to 6 o/c when hundreds of the wealthy & Fashionable population go out to ride~in their own Carriages and Viacles [sic] of every kind, dressed in the Richest and gayest possible Manner There is indeed very many wealthy Nabobs in the long procession, and they make a gay, Rich and Grand display of the Upper Ten Society.

I will say no more on this point, I have been troubled a great deal with head ache. & the Trouble with the Pain in the Coards of My Neck has been a great anoyance to me. I have however, been abroad on every occasion when required. John & Mr Balfour are doing every to render my Stay pleasant and agreeable. I am unable to say when we will Turn homeward, if we go as the intention is laid out, we are now 234 miles from home, & we have 325 miles farther to go, and as far as I know, I cannot say when we shall start again. *I* assure you all, That I am very anxious to hear from Home. I wish to learn how things are going on, or if any hitch has occurred. Tell Clifford to write,~& Caroline, & Helen, or Ida. Send a paper, Traveler, Journal, or Transcript, dont want the Herald.

Truly & affectionately I remain your

devoted Father

(I shall to get a line from David) Elias W. Goddard".

Elias continued to live as a widower in the old house on Unity Street for the next eight years. A newspaper story which is framed in the Old North Church gift shop describes him and the area well ("Odd Bits of Boston", *Sunday Herald*. 20 May 1888, 17, col. 6).

"Unity street, at the back of Christ Church/ is a bright, quiet, clean, homelike street, with bright, clean, quiet, homelike houses in it. Some of these house date from the first part of the last century, and are built of imported bricks. No. 19 was erstwhile called the Mansion House, and was owned by Benjamin Franklin, whose sister resided there, and to whom he bequeathed it. For the last half-century it has been the home of Mr. Elias Goddard, a well known cooper, and a true representative of the old-time Boston mechanics. Mr. Goddard's garden, which lies between his house and old Christ Church, is renouned as having the best vines and plants known at the North end. [Number] Twenty-three this street is a//good old specimen of colonial architecture of brick, and it had British officers quartered in it during the Revolution, as did many another house at the North end."

Caroline and Elias Goddard in their garden at 19 Unity Street

ELIAS'S DEATH AND ESTATE.

Elias Goddard died at 19 Unity Street, Boston's North End, at 4 pm, on Wednesday, 3 Jan. 1888, at age 84, of pneumonia (Family Bible; Gravestone, Mt. Auburn Cemetery, and obituaries; the page in Massachusetts Death Records is torn off).

The *Boston Transcript*'s obituary stated that he was "The oldest master cooper in Boston, and we believe the oldest native-born resident of the North End, passed away Jan. 3, at the advanced age of 84 years and 4 months. He was born in Charter street, of old Puritan stock...Commander of the Columbian Artillery...one of the oldest members of the Massachusetts Charitable Mechanics Association, since July 1834 (*Transcript,* 5 Jan. 1888).

Memorial services were held at Old North on the sixth. The newspaper account reads:

"EIGHTY-FOUR TIMES

The Passing Bell of Christ Church

Rings.

Simple Services Over the Body of Elias W. Goddard.

A Sketch of the Aged Merchant's Busy Life.

That good old custom, now nearly obsolete, of tolling out the age of the person for whom they mourn, called the sorrowing friends and relatives to historic old Christ Church in Salem street at noon today. It was the funeral of the late Elias W. Goddard, himself a landmark.

For over a quarter of a century he served faithfully in the church and not more fitting could have been the deep tribute paid his memory by the old members of the church than that they voiced in gathering at the church.

The services were conducted by Rev. William H. Munroe, an old friend of the deceased. When the preacher ceased for a moment the ancient clock over the heads of the congregation ticked mournfully on, and seemed to add its voice to that of the mourners when they made response to the readings.

In almost every sense it was an old-fashioned funeral, utterly devoid of all that pomp and display which mark the last rites of a man of this generation who shall do so much good and kindness as did Mr. Goddard in his day.

The hymns sung were not accompanied by the deep tones of the organ, but struck up some [by some] one in the congregation in the olden manner, and sung with more feeling and sincerity than the best trained choir in Boston could have evinced.

Mr. Munroe in his eulogy of the deceased referred not to his life, but stated at the outset that he could say but one thing: "We bury today in a truly literal sense, a father in Israel." He went on to show the great example presented in the life of Mr. Goddard. "So live that when you shall have departed you may go where you will meet your father, your mother, your son, your daughter, your wife or your husband." Keep ever green in your memory that it was through Christ that all this is permitted.

The interment was made at Mount Auburn.

The life of Elias W. Goddard is a page in the history of Boston. Born, reared and educated in Boston, he continued his residence here, until at the age of over 84 years he died.

He was the oldest native-born resident of the North End of the city, the oldest master cooper in Boston and the oldest commander of the old Columbian Artillery, also believed to be the oldest member of the Massachusetts Charitable Mechanic's Association. Mr. Goddard was born in Charter street in September, 1803, of good old Puritan stock, and all through his long life he failed not to exemplify in his deeds and work the spirit which has made the Puritan's marks on the pages of civilization. It is claimed, and indeed, admitted, as a historical fact, that the house in which Mr. Goddard lived for 60 years, and in which he died, was once owned by Benjamin Franklin. It is at 19 Unity street and directly in the rear of Christ Church of historical fame, from which he was buried, and from which, in the words of an admirer, he was separated in interest and piety only by the distance across the yard. In this old church he served all his life faithfully and with an interest unflagging to the end. For many years he held two of the most prominent offices in the church, those of vestryman and warden. These offices he held successively for over a quarter of a century.

Always retiring in his disposition and reticent in his ambitions, content to do good and faithful work, as it came in his way, he never held political office. When in the vigor of life, so great was the friendship of his acquaintances that he was repeatedly urged to accept nomination, and assured of victory, but he steadfastly refused to mingle with political strife. But his methodical and ripe judgment and advice was always given without stint, and greater head than his accepted his counsel. To him a matter which promised public good was a desired end, and always did he labor toward it. In deeds of charity and aid for less fortunate men than himself he was bountiful. His sympathy enlisted, he rested not until good had been done.

Much of the fame of the old Columbian Artillery was due to his efficient services as its honored commander in his early life. His comrades had passed away for the greater part, but the memory of that old North End organization lives on.

But it was as a member of the Massachusetts Charitable Mechanic's Association that he labored hardest. He joined in July, 1834, and all through his connection with its interest he devoted his best energies to the success of the institution. His interest in its welfare was deep, and his record as a committeeman clean and full of good works. He wrote a great many letters, visited a great many men and other associations, and lived to see the association he loved a grand success.

As a business man he was diligent and untiring to the last, and his name was a synonym for probity and integrity. A hard worker always, spotless in his reputation and punctual in his engagements, "his work was his bond." He leaves four children, Walter C. Goddard, Clifford W. Goddard, Mrs. T. Warren Gould and Mrs. R. M. Wilson, all of whom reside in Boston. Besides these he leaves a very large circle of friends, who will cherish with pride the memory of his life."

Elias was buried on 6 Jan. 1888 in the Goddard plot #3882 at Mount Auburn Cemetery, Cambridge, between Elm Avenue and Mount Auburn Street, about 550 feet west of the Main Gate. He had bought the plot in 1878 for his son William, and had already buried his brother John, his wife Caroline, his nephew Sullivan Goddard, his granddaughter Carrie Gould and Mary Hollis there. He lies next to his wife, to the right of the back center of the plot (Mt. Auburn chart #3882, Elm Ave, No. Br). The marble stone reads, "In memory of Elias W. Goddard//died Jan. 3 1888//aged 84 years//sleep in Jesus" (O. M. Wentworth was paid $75 by the estate for the stone; Mr. Tinkham, the undertaker, got $150; Suff. Pro. 79233).

Elias Goddard left a modest estate, consisting of three houses on Unity Street and half interest in the cooperage firm of Elias W. Goddard & Son (Suffolk Probate 79233, 79357, 83387). After all the debts were paid, and the houses sold, there remained only $5,324.84 to divide between the four heirs, Caroline Gould, Clifford W. Goddard, Walter C. Goddard, and Helen R. Wilson. Each got about $1300.

The firm of Elias W. Goddard & Son was valued at $3318.44, mostly in bills receivable $2040.20, with tools and machinery at 323 Commercial Street valued at $365.10, and the rest in cash. Half of this was credited to his estate. Interestingly, there are no debts owed by the firm. There was a loan of $300 to his son Clifford. The furniture in 19 Unity Street was valued at $200, and was distributed among the heirs. Rents for #15 and 17 Unity Street received were $365.43. So his personal estate came to $2509.66.

Real estate totaled at $11500 for the three properties on Unity Street, $3900 for #19, and $3800 each for the wooden houses at #15 and 17. But all of these were mortgaged, #15 for $2,150, #17 for $1950, and #19 subject to the old trust deed of 1849 once held by Governor Andrew (Discharged by Henry Buxton, trustee, Suff. Pro. 83387), #19 netted the most, selling on 4 Feb. 1890 for $4053.

The furniture inherited by the Gould family consists of four pieces in 1995, the first perhaps bought by the Gould sisters, but the last three believed to have been made by Elias Goddard himself:

1. Block front lowboy, eighteenth century, 30 in. high, 32 in. wide, in. deep, with two drawers with 2 ornate brass handles each; the block front center is recessed in a simple 3 centered arch, and the left and right sides bowing out to 1 5/8 in. thickness; 4 clawed feet on bowed legs; mahogany top with scalloped edge, repaired; plain sides; valued at $500-750 in 1977 by a Cambridge antique dealer for Caroline Gould. Although this may have come from the Goddards it is too early, and too fine a piece compared to the following ones known to have been made by Elias:

2. Top of a pine desk, with cubby-holes made from cigar boxes.

3. & 4. Two rectangular prayer stools of pine.

Winterthur Museum was consulted about a possible relation to the famous Goddard furniture makers of Rhode Island, but records show no Elias in that firm or family (Letter of Bert Denker, Librarian, 15 July 1986).. The museum would like to have photos and descriptions of other furniture made by him

The cooperage workbook was passed down from Clifford to his daughter Grace Cook, to her daughter Helen Burke in Belmont MA in 1966. Since this would give us an important insight into the kinds of casks Elias made, his customers, his pay scale, and other important business details, we would appreciate borrowing it. Please contact James W. Gould, Box 161, Cotuit MA 02635, ph. (508) 428-8267 about the workbook, furniture, photos, letters or other records.

Seven children, born Boston:

i. CAROLINE, b. Salutation Street, Sunday Morning, 6 June 1830 (Family Bible); bapt. Old North 25 Sept. 1830 (Christ Church Register, book 30, 85, #89); d. Boston Sunday Morning, 24 June 1832, aged 2 years and 18 days (*Transcript*, 5 Jan. 1888); buried 25 June Old North tomb #11, moved to tomb #35 June 1837 (Christ Church, "Record of Tombs 1829-1853", Book 53, 6 #318, 319, p. 12 #456).

ii. ANDREW JACKSON, b. in Fleet Street, 23 Aug. 1831, Tuesday afternoon, a rainy day (*Transcript*, 5 Jan. 1888); d. Boston, Monday afternoon 2 July 1832, aged ten months and 9 days (*Transcript*, 5 Jan. 1888); buried 4 July 1832 Old North tomb 11, moved to tomb #35 June 1837 (CCTomb Book, 6, #320, 12, #464).

29. iii. CAROLINE, 2^d^, b. Unity St, 14 May 1833, Tuesday (*Transcript, 5* Jan. 1888); d. Melrose MA 13 March 1915 (*Transcript,* 5 Jan. 1888); m. 25. T(HOMAS) WARREN GOULD.

iv. WALTER CHANNING, cooper, b. Unity Street, 24 April 1835, Friday (*Transcript, 5* Jan. 1888); bapt. Old North 19 July 1840 (CCRec. 95 #597-9); buried Mt. Auburn, Cambridge 20 June 1907, age 72 (Mt. Auburn lot #3882); m. twice, (1) C. 1862 ABBIE PITMAN; (2) IRENE PUTNAM HARRIS, b. April 1836, d. 1 Feb. 1907, aged 70 years, 10 months (*Transcript, 5* Jan. 1888); buried Mt. Auburn 4 Feb. (Suffolk Probate 79233, 79357, 83387).One known child, by first wife, born Boston c. 1862-3; a daughter res. with mother Somerville.

v. CLIFFORD WAYNE, cooper & machinist, b. Unity Street, 12 Feb. 1837 (*Transcript, 5* Jan. 1888); bapt. Old North 19 July 1840; d. Arlington MA, Wednesday morn 3 am, 10 Feb. 1904 (*Transcript,* 5 Jan. 1888); m. 24 Dec. 1868 MARY M. KENDALL, b. Nova Scotia 29 Sept. 1848, d. Arlington MA 30 June 1933.

Two children, b. Chelsea:

1. *Helen Grace,* b. 12 July 1872, d. Arlington 25 June 1945; m. 12 Feb. 1896 Calvin Porter Cook; 3 children, i. Ruth Goddard Cook, b. 18 Nov. 1896, d. Cambridge July 1897, age 8 months; ii. Helen Gertrude, b. Boston 7 Dec. 1901, d. Billerica 1 April 1975, m. twice, 1) 21 April 1924 Oscar H. Drake, 2) 31 Dec. 1932 Richard X. Burke, 3 children, see Chart 8

2. *Harriet Gertrude,* opera singer, b. 25 June 1874; d. Arlington 24 Oct. 1949; m. 11 June 1901 diplomat John Quimby .Wood, 1909-32, U. S. Minister to Ethiopia; one child, Manon Godard Wood, b. Paris 24 May 1906, d. Centerville MA 8 Jan. 1993, m. 24 May 1933 Brownell W. Hale, who d. 12 July 1966; for children see Chart 8.

vi. WILLIAM CROSWELL, clerk, b. Unity Street 17 Aug. 1839; baptized Old North 19 July1840, named for the minister; d. Boston Monday 4 March 1878, age 38 years, 6 months, 16 days; buried Mt. Auburn, Cambridge 7 March 1878 lot #3882, Elm Av.. Unmarried.

vii. HELEN RUTHVEN, b. Unity Street, Sunday 7 Feb. 1847; d. Boston 15 Oct. 1924; m. Boston 2 Jan. 1869 RICHARD M. WILSON (MDR 1869, 299:5, #83) b. Boston 28 March 1838, son of William H. & Beulah R. Wilson; d. Newton Center MA 24 April 1902. Four children:

1. *Richard Goddard Wilson,* b. Charlestown, 28 April 1871, d. Chelsea MA 12/22 Oct. 1934, m. ?10 Jan. 1889? Kitty Thurston, 2 children: i. Walter Thurston, insurance agent, b. Boston 13 June 1890, d. Trenton NJ 29 Nov. 1958?, m. Edith May Hibbs (1895- 1968), 3 ch. see Chart 8; ii. Blanche, b. Newton Center MA 15 Feb. 1892, d. Grosse Point MI 29 Nov. 1987, m. 10 Jan. Chester Steeves Redpath, b. 13 Aug. 1896. d. Detroit MI 27 Feb. 1959; 2 ch. see Chart 8.

2. *Howard M.,* b. 17 Dec. 1876, d. Newton Center MA 4 Oct. 1897, age 20, unmarried.

3. *Helen "Nellie" Louise,* ladies' companion, b. Chelsea? 26 Nov. 1878, d. Boston 29 July 1959, unmarried.

4. *Edith* C., b. 28 Sept. 1880, d. Boston 2 March 1920, age 39, unmarried.

ORIGINS OF THE GODDARD FAMILY.

The obituaries of Elias[6] W. Goddard claim that he came from "old Puritan stock". The first ancestor of the name arrived in Boston about 1678. He and his son and grandson married into early Massachussets families of FARRINGTON, PRATT and WILLIAMSON.

Elias[5] Goddard, Senior first appears in the Boston Directory at Charter Street in 1805 (Dir. 55) though his first son was born at Lynn Street in 1803. But the Goddards were probably living earlier in the North End, for the parents were married by the Rev. Samuel Stillman at the First Baptist Church, on North Street on 5/6 Dec. 1802 (VS 101:217; CD 101:217). They moved back to Lynn Street in 1806, and remained there for 16 years, until 1822, listed as a sailmaker (Dir. 1807 76, 1813 129, 1816 115, 1822 112). Lynn Street was on the waterfront of the North End, facing the wharves and big shipyards like Hartt's Naval Shipyard where the frigate *Constitution* was built and launched in 1798.

Elias and Eunice had left the Baptist church and joined Old North, Christ Church Episcopal, by 1820. (Six of their children were baptized there on 30 Jan. 1820, Elias, John, Elizabeth, William, Charles and Samuel; "The Clerk's Register of Christ Church Boston: Christ Church Records, beginning 1703-1851", Book 30, [hereinafter CCReg.] , 72, in Massachusetts Diocesan Archives, St. Paul's Cathedral, 3d fl., 138 Tremont Street, Boston).

In 1826 sailmaker Elias Goddard is located at Power's Court, Ann Street, and listed for the last time in 1827 at Power's Court, 328 Ann Street (Dir. 1825 121, 1826 127). Elias Sr. died there 25 Nov. 1826, at age 48, of pleurisy. Boston Registry, Copy of Death Record, #13412, 25 June 1976). He was buried in Copp's Hill, and perhaps removed to Old North Church (Official copy of death #13412, 25 June 1976, died 25 Nov., buried 27 Nov. in Copp's Hill Cemetery (Christ Church Tomb Book 481; CCRec. 207 #240, "Mr. Goddard".).

Elias Goddard was a Boston seaman in the Revolutionary War, who served twice under Capt. John Foster Williams. The first time was four months, 12 May to 6 Sept. 1779, as ordinary seaman aboard the brigantine *Hazard,* under Captain John Foster Williams (Rev. Records 519; original in Revolutionary Rolls, Massachusetts Archives, v. 39, 140, 192) .This was the third voyage of the ship, which was employed July 1779 on the Penobscot Expedition. (Rev. Rec. 356).

On the payroll we get the only personal detail about Elias, that he was 5 feet 7 inches tall. He was paid £ 7/9/4 for three months and six days (Rev. Rolls 39:192 (B).

The second voyage of seaman Goddard was on board the ship *Protector* captained by the same John F. Williams, from 14 Jan. 1780 to 17 Aug. 1780 (Rev. Rolls 39:49). This was the first of the voyages of the State ship of the American Navy, commissioned 8 Oct. 1779. Goddard was lucky, for he was not aboard the third voyage when the ship was captured by the British.

Another Elias Goddard shows up in Boston serving as a soldier in the War of 1812 (July

1-30 in Capt. R. Hartshorn's Company, and [2?]4 days, 12 Sept.- 10 Oct. 1814 in Capt. E. Norcross's Co., Gardner W. Pearson, ed., *Records of Massachusetts Volunteer Militia...1812-1814* [Boston: Wright & Alter, 1913], 78, 26).

It seems unlikely that the seaman of the Revolution would have missed a chance to go to sea again in the very maritime War of 1812, so this is more likely to be the sail maker father of our Elias W. Goddard. In the U.S. Census of 1820 there are only two Elias Goddards, one in Boston and another in Athol, Worcester County (*U. S. Census, 1820*, 20, 72).

Elias's birth is not recorded in town records, but age at death makes his birth about 1778-1779. This could make him the son of another ELIAS GODDARD, who married MARY GREENE 23 Aug. 1778 in the First Baptist Church, North End of Boston, by the same Rev. Samuel Stillman (CD 101:81; #1646 per official copy 24 March 1983).

Elias and Mary [Eunice?] Goddard who were sponsored by their parents Elias Goddard and Mary Green at Trinity Church (Episcopal) in Boston, with co-sponsors Matthew Baileyand his wife, on 9 Sept. 1781. (Records of Trinity Church, *Colonial Society of Massachusetts.* 61:596; there is record of his father's birth at Trinity, as detailed below).

The connection with two Episcopal churches, Trinity and Old North, makes it worth seeing if Mary Greene was descended from the Greenes who founded Trinity. She is definitely not the Mary Greene, daughter of Benjamin Jr., born Boston 9 March 1762, who died unmarried 5 April 1852 (*The Greene Family* [Boston: Private printing, 1901], 54, chart E).

ELIAS^{6} GODDARD, REVOLUTIONARY WAR SERGEANT

Elias Goddard was a Sergeant in the Revolutionary Army on three different campaigns, at Bunker Hill, Quebec and Saratoga. To have been a sergeant at the start of the war probably had prior military experience, perhaps in the French & Indian War. He first signed up shortly after the opening battles of Lexington and Concord, on 12 May 1775 (Rev. Rec. 519; Rev. Rolls 16:45).

He is the sixth name on the rolls of Capt. Lemuel Trescott's company, under Colonel Jonathan Brewer, with Lt. Nathaniel Gushing and Lt. John Kilby Smith. He was given £ 2 advance wages, and a uniform worth £ 17, and a £ 4 cartridge box. Elias was probably at the Battle of Bunker Hill on 17 June. He was probably at the assembly of the Continental Army when General Washington assumed command on Cambridge Common on 3 July 1775. He was discharged after service of 2 months and 24 days, on 1 Aug. 1775, and paid £ 6/17/10. He was paid for travel of 18 miles, perhaps the round trip from Boston-Cambridge-Charlestown-Cambridge-Boston.

Sgt. Elias Goddard's second hitch of service was on the ill-fated Quebec Expedition of 1775. This came after a month's leave, for on 28 Aug. Gen. Benedict Arnold assembled a thousand volunteers, including some veterans of the capture of Quebec in 1759, at Cambridge, and set forth for Maine 12 Sept., via Gardiner, Augusta, then a trek across the wilderness 24 Sept. But on 6 Oct. 1775, Goddard was still with Capt. Trescott's company at Prospect Hill, Somerville (Rev. Rec. 519; Rev. Rolls 56:33). This historic site was where the first Union flag was displayed with 13 stripes, on New Year's Day 1776, over the strongest fort in the American defenses of Boston, where General Putnam established headquarters after the Battle of Bunker

Hill (Bacon (1903) 143). When Trescott's company joined Arnold is unclear.

Arnold reached Quebec after many hardships 8 Nov., crossed the St. Lawrence 13 Nov. and attacked the fortress on the last day of the year. Goddard was fortunate not to be among those killed, but was taken prisoner by the British in the disastrous siege. We know of Goddard's presence from his claim on return to Boston on 8 June 1776 that he had not received a coat by reason of his being at Quebec 'last year' in Capt. Trescott' s company (Ellas Goddard, Rev. Rec. 560).

Goddard was home in Boston to celebrate the Declaration of Independence on 4 July 1776.

Goddard's third tour in the Revolution was during the climactic Saratoga Campaign of 1777. He enlisted again 15 Aug. 1777, again as sixth man on the muster roll, in Capt. Aaron Smith's company under Col. Benjamin Gill (Rev. Rolls 23:80, 85). The unit was sent west "to Reinforce the Northern Army", which was fighting the battles of Ticonderoga and Bennington, culminating in the great surrender of the British General Burgoyne at Saratoga on 17 Oct. 1777. Goddard was discharged in Boston 29 Nov. 1777, after 12 days travel of 240 miles. He had served 8 months and 25 days, and got paid £ 9/11/8.

His testimony on 7 February 1781 reads:
"This may certify that I was at the siege of Quebeck in the year 1775 with Genl Arnold & that Benja West was also there & taken prisoner, lost his clothes & was left in Captivity. Elias Goddard" [1] General Benedict Arnold was defeated in his siege of Quebec December 1775-March 1776[2]. See the novel *March to Quebec* by Kenneth Roberts 1940.

Elias served in Capt. Lemuel Trescott's company in the Sixth Continental Regiment of Colonel Jonathan Brewer. [3] The American force invading Canada suffered terrible hardships and near starvation as they pushed up the Kennebec River in the winter. It is not surprising that survivors like Elias Goddard died young.

His death is not recorded. He died before his father Giles's death about 1792. The last record before the testimony above was as witness of a deed on 29 July 1777. [4]

---

[1] James Phinney Baxter, testimony of Elias Goddard, The Documentary History of the State of Maine, Portland, Maine: Maine Historical Society, 1914, Vol. 19, p. 122. Internet Archive https://archive.org/details/documentaryhisto19main.

[2] HISTORY.com Battle of Quebec (1775) - American Revolution - www.history.com/topics/american-revolution/battle- of-quebec- 1775

[3] *Massachusetts Soldiers and Sailors of the Revolutionary War*. Boston, Wright and Potter 1899, vol. 6, p. 519; hereinafter Revol. War; Putnam, Charles F., *Ancestry.com public member trees/giles goddard/ stories*.

[4] William and Peter Seaver to Ebenezer Seaver, *Suffolk Deeds* vol. 127, pp. 229-230. It is believed this involved former lands and house of Giles Goddard in Roxbury. There is no record in Roxbury of death or probate.

Elias's baptism is recorded as ISAIS GODDARD on 28 January 1749 as son of Giles[4] and Elizabeth Goddard, sponsors John Brackett and Elizabeth Williamson in Trinity Church, Boston[5].

Elias was son of:
GILES[4] GODDARD, Junior, housewright, was born in Boston 22 December 1721. [6] He was the son of Giles[3] and Hannah PRATT. He died about 1790-2.[i] He was father of "a Bastard Child"[7] born July 1747 to the spinster Elizabeth Trescott of Dorchester. A lower court ordered him to pay her two shillings sixpence a week for the maintenance of the child from birth until the trial, and two shillings a week thereafter. When he failed to pay, Elizabeth Trescott appealed to the Supreme Judicial Court. In 1752 the court calculated he owed £ 7/15 in bills of credit (or £ 4/2/8 in lawful money). The court ordered the sheriff to seize £ 6, and arrest him if was not paid. We have no record of the sex or name of the bastard child.

Giles married 2 December 1747 Elizabeth WILLIAMSON in Trinity Church, Boston. She was born Elizabeth Williamson 16 September 1726.[ii]
Giles owned seven and a half acres of pasture with no buildings in Roxbury which he inherited from his grandfather John Goddard. He also inherited by entailment the south half of the house which was not held by his mother Hannah. In 1758 Giles Jr. sold all his unentailed land to Samuel Phillips, merchant of Boston for £ 40.[8] His half of the house and land was evidently entailed, and remained in his possession. This was located on the Providence Turnpike on the Dorchester line [9]About 1750 Giles claimed title of a quarter of eight acres of pasture in Roxbury which his parents sold to his brother John on 1 March 1750, but his claim was denied by a committee of petition. John sold the property to John Newman of Edgartown on 1 December 1762 for £ 122/10 . [10] John had built his home, a barn and a slaughter house on this land on the east side of the highway, and west of the land of the heirs of John and Joseph Wales of Dorchester.
Giles is listed in the census of 1790 in Roxbury in a household of four, a male over 16 (himself), a male under sixteen, whom Putnam says is probably a servant, and two females, his wife and his unmarried sister Elizabeth. [11] He died within two years, for by 18 August 1792 his son Samuel said he was dead. [12].
Giles and Elizabeth had five children:

---

[5] *The Records of Trinity Church, Boston, Publications of The Colonial Society,* vol. LVI, p. 536, hereinafter Trinity.
[6] Boston, *Report of the Record Commissioners of the City of Boston,* City Document 42, p. 150; hereinafter CD; Massachusetts, *Town and Vital Records, 1620-1988*, ancestry.com Provo, UT: Holbrook Research Institute, Birth, p. 255, 11th line from bottom.
[7] *Massachusetts Supreme Court* 69178 7 April 1752, Putnam, Charles F., *"Some Descendants of Giles Goddard*" typescript c. 1993 p. 15, app. 23; hereinafter Putnam; also Putnam, Charles F., *Ancestry.com public member trees/giles goddard/ stories*) p. 15.
[8] 25 July 1758 *Suffolk Deeds* vol. 92 p. 44; Putnam p. 13, app. 20.
[9] Putnam p. 6.
[10] *Suffolk Deeds* vol. 98, p. 251; Putnam app. 17.
[11] *US Census Roxbury, Massachusetts,* 1790, p. 205; Putnam p. 16.
[12] *Suffolk Deeds* vol. 174, p. 25.

Giles[5] was baptized in Boston 6 November 1748[13]. He married Catharine BROWNE 11 April 1771.[14] , but he died soon after, for in 1777 she married Simon PEARCE/PIERCE. Catharine and Giles's son Giles[6] Brown Goddard [15] who was a Loyalist who fled to St. John, New Brunswick 1783, married to Joanna Wager [16]. His biography and descendants are detailed by Putnam and Kingston Goddard Hadley. [17] Among themis Elias Kingston Goddard who died 12 Nov. 1788 at age 22 in Baltimore after arrival from Jamaica, but born in Massachusetts (Boston *Chronicle* 4 Dec. 1788, 3 reads: "DIED...In Baltimore, Mr. ELIAS KINGSTON GODDARD, late of this state, aged 22."; *Maryland Journal* and *Baltimore Advertiser* on 14 Nov. 1788 read: "GODDARD, Elias Kingston, died Wednesday evening [12 Nov.] last in the 22nd year; a native of Massachusetts, who arrived a few days ago from Jamaica." cited by letter of 15 Jan. 1980 from Enoch Pratt Library of Baltimore).

1.
2. Elias, baptized 28 January 1749 (see above).
3. Samuel Goddard, cordwainer of Roxbury [18] was baptized 8 December 1751. [19] His wife is named Hannah. [20] He and his brother Elias served in the infantry in the American Revolution, with service mainly in Rhode Island. He was the only surviving son at the time of his father's death in Roxbury by 1792, and inherited his grandfather's estate which was partly entailed, that is, not saleable. In 1792 Massachusetts modified its law of enfiefment, so Samuel was able to sell half of seven acres of family land to Ebenezer Wales, Esquire of Dorchester for £ 35 on 18 August 1792.[21] There is no mention of buildings in this deed. The other half was sold to Wales on 1 December 1797 for $ 160 by the 24 heirs.[22] Putnam points out that legally only Samuel and his brothers Elias and Giles (both dead) were entitled to the land although two younger sisters, Elizabeth and Sarah also signed the deed.
4. Elizabeth, baptized Trinity 8 July 1751. [23] Unmarried in 1797.
5. Sarah baptized Trinity 25 January 1760; [24] she married Nathaniel DAVIS.

---

[13] Trinity p. 534.
[14] CD 101, p. 401.
[15] baptized 20 May 1771, Trinity 562.
[16] Putnam p. 17.
. [16] Hadley, Kingston Goddard, *The Giles Goddard Genealogy*, 1931, manuscript on film, Salt Lake City , microfilm Genealogical Society of Utah, Salt Lake City UT 1967, manuscript of original in Historical Society of Pennsylvania; hereinafter Hadley).

[18] *Suffolk Deeds* vol.174 p. 25.
[19] Trinity 539.
[20] *Suffolk Deeds* vol. 174, p. 25.
[21] 18 August 1792 *Suffolk Deeds* vol. 174, p. 26, Putnam app. 22.
[22] *Norfolk Deeds* vol. 10, p.. 258-9; Putnam app. 22.
[23] Trinity 546.

Giles[4] was the eldest son and heir of:

GILES[3] GODDARD, housewright and innkeeper, was born in Lynn 28 December 1698.[25] He died about 1752. [26] He married 23 December 1730 Boston Hannah PRATT of Malden [27]Apprenticcd as a carpenter and housewright in Boston, he probably worked with his grandfather in that trade. [28] He moved to his wife's home town Malden, and later to his father's farm in Roxbury. He was co-executor of his father's estate (more below). Roxbury gave him license to succeed his father as innkeeper 25 July 1745. In 1745 he paid his brother John, the Plymouth mariner, the brother's house and land in Roxbury for £ 132.[29] He built a new house about 1749. [30]In 1750 he and his wife Hannah sold eight acres of unentailed pasture land near his house to his son John. [31]

Giles lived only seven years after his father's death. He left an estate of £ 434/4, of which £ 351/19/4 was real estate, including the house (and inn?) valued at £ 135/6/8 and twenty and a half acres of land. [32] His widow Hannah was given her dower right of one third of his estate, consisting of the chamber over the Great Lower Room on the east part of the house by the road, a quarter of the cellar, use of the well, and 8 ¾ acres next to the road over Gourds Hill.[33] Their eldest son Giles Junior took possession of the remaining two thirds, some his right by entailment, and some held in common.

Since debts exceeded the value of £ 82 personal property by £ 75. [34] Hannah petitioned in 1753 to sell seven acres, representing a quarter of his estate.[35] She was authorized by the court to sell land on 19 February 1754 However, her son refused, claiming that he was entitled by entailment to a quarter of the land that was sold to his brother John in 1750. This was denied by the court after a committee of five found that John owned the eight acres free and clear.[36] The state legislature allowed her on 18 January 1757 to sell the seven acres.

The final division of eleven and three quarters acres gave Giles Jr. seven and a half acres of pasture, and to his mother the house and barn on four and a quarter acres of orchard and plowed land. Hannah's dower of eight and a quarter acres and room in the house, plus the remaining land that had not been contested [37] There being insufficient funds to pay her husband's debts, she sold

---

[24] Trinity 548.

[25] *Lynn Vital Records* vol. 1, p. 160.

[26] Putnam p. 12.

[27] CD 150, p. 89 lists the year 1720, his name Gyles, married by Presbyterian minister John Webb.

[28] Putnam p. 11.

[29] 14 December 1745, *Suffolk Deeds* vol. 71, pp. 118-119; Putnam app. 11.

[30] ***Suffolk Deeds*** vol. 78 p. 88; Putnam app. 16.

[31] This lay east of the highway, south of the apple farmer Josiah Warren, and west of John Wales of Dorchester 30 March 1750, *Suffolk Deeds* vol. 78, p. 88-9; Putnam p. 12; app.16.

[32] *Suffolk Probate* 10004, vol. 46, p. 490.

[33] 15 July 1752, text in Putnam p. 12.

[34] *Suffolk Probate* vol. 49, pp. 36-39.

[35] *Suffolk Probate* 10044 21 August 1753; Putnam app. 18.

[36] *Suffolk Probate* vol. 35, p. 38; Putnam app. 13, 15, committee report 19 May, 1757, approved by court 10 June 1757.

[37] *Suffolk Probate* vol. 55, pp. 18-20, 38-39 .

her half of the house, barn on seven acres on the west side of the county road from Boston to Plymouth at auction to Thomas Stoddard of Boston for £ 173 [38] In 1758 Giles Jr. sold all his right to unentailed land to Samuel Phillips, merchant of Boston for £ 40. [39] His half of the house and land was evidently entailed, and remained in his possession.
Giles and Hannah had four children:

1. Giles[4] Junior born 1721 (see above).
2. John Goddard was born in Boston 10 December 1725 [40], married Malden 3 August 1747 Sarah SARGENT [41]In 1750 he bought eight acres of unentailed land from his brother, near the Dorchester line and the Providence turnpike. He built a house there. Do not confuse him with John Goddard born 30 May 1730 Brookline, wagon-master general credited with victory of battle of Dorchester Heights.
3. Mary born Boston 15 November 1728[42], died 1790; married Malden 17 September 1747 James BUCKNAM of Malden born Charlestown 3 January 1735, died Malden 10 October 1799, and had eleven children. [43]
4. Hannah born about 1731; married Roxbury 23 or 24 November 1751 Major John REED born 1728, died 1813; paymaster of militia before the Revolution[44]. She was living as late as 1797. Three sons: John, William, Thomas.

Giles was the elder son of:

JOHN[2] GODDARD, shoemaker, farmer, innkeeper, and Captain of the Roxbury militia was born 1675 in England, died Roxbury in early 1745 (between 26 March and 16 July when will was executed).[45] He was a cordwainer or shoemaker in Lynn, but became a farmer and innkeeper

---

[38] 20 January 1759, *Suffolk Deeds* vol. 92 pp.195-6 ; Putnam p. 13; app. 19.
[39] 25 July 1758 *Suffolk Deeds* vol. 92 p. 44; Putnam p. 13; app. 20.
[40] CD 43, p. 170.
[41] *Malden Vital Records* p. 236.
[42] CD 43, p. 186.
[42] All born Malden except James II and Sarah who were born in Chelsea: 1. Mary born 16 July 1748, James born 27 March 1751, died 5 February 1753, 3. Phoebe born 17 March 1753, 4. James born 11 August 1755, died Part-au-Prince Haiti 1785, 5, Sarah born 11 April 1757, 6. William born 30 April 1758, died Malden 4 April 1823, 7. Joses born 6 March 1761, died Hillsborough NH 2 July 1849, 8. Ebenezer born 9 November 1762, died 1 Dec. 1797, 9. Elizabeth 3 October 1765, died Cambridge 7 March 1838, 10, 11. Twins born 4 September 1767 Caleb died one month 4 April 1767, Joshua died Charlestown NH 2 July 1849. Source:Reynolds Family Association: James Buckman.

[44] Reed, John, *My Link with the Past,* www.genealogy.mylinktothepast.com/p88396.htm.
[45] *Suffolk Probate* 8288, vol. 38, p. 14; *Suffolk Deeds* vol. 174, p. 25, Putnam p. 6; www.myheritage.com/person-3000243_126754271_126754271/john-goddard says he died: July 4 1745 without source.

in Roxbury.[46] He is named "Capt. John Goddard" in Suffolk Deeds vol. 76, p. 161, and in his inventory of his father's estate [47] but also that he is a cordwainer. This means he was not a marine master, but an officer in the Roxbury militia.

John married three times, first 19 June 1697 [48] in Lynn to Sarah FARRINGTON, born 20 September 1677 Lynn[49], daughter of Matthew[4] Farrington Junior of Lynn (1649-1729) and his wife Sarah.[50] Sarah Goddard died 22 May 1732[51], buried in Eliot Cemetery, Roxbury. [52]

In January 1720 John Goddard was given land in Roxbury by his father who entailed it so that it could not be sold out of the family; this became the source of family disputes.[53] The main part was a house and barn on fourteen acres on the highway to Plymouth, on the Dorchester town line.[54] In addition, Giles sold his son a barn on seven acres of orchard and pasture.[55] Soon John established an inn, and was licensed as an innkeeper

John2 and Sarah had five children[56]:

1. Giles, the oldest, was born Lynn 28 December 1698. See above.
2. Sarah born Lynn 14 November 1700; married Newton 13 April 1720 Rev. James BAILEY, born Roxbury 22 March 1697/8, died 23 August 1766.[57] Graduate of Harvard 1717; teacher in Andover; 43 years as first minister of Second Congregational Church in Weymouth 1723.[58] She died in Boston, probably buried in Boston Common tomb # 14.
3. Mary born about 1710 Hingham, who married 14 October 1725 in Weymouth to Jeremiah CHUBBUCK (1683-1774)[59] . Their daughter Huldah born Hingham 27 February 1730/1 married 1 January 1753 cooper Stephen Gardner. They had ten children, including Silence

---

[46] There were no leather tools in his estate, but a plow, rye, a horse and two cows. *Suffolk Probate* 8288, inventory vol. 38, p.18.

[47] *Suffolk Probate* 7246, vol. 20, p. 298.

[48] Intentions *Lynn Vital Records,* vol. 2, p. 153.

[49] *Lynn Vital Records, Births,* p. 145.

[50] Hanit, Kevin, *Mathew Farrington,* geni.com, www.geni.com/people/Sarah-Goddard/6000000010722660874. Matthew was son of Matthew[3] Farrington (1621-1720) and his wife Sarah. He was son of Edmund[2] Farrington (1588-1671) and his wife Elizabeth. He was son of first immigrant Caldwell[1] Farrington (1565-1682), son of Thomas[A] (1534-1570), John[B] of London (1524-47, Hugh[C] (1484), Robert[D] (c. 1489), Richard[E] Farrington of Hutton Grange, Lancashire. Anderson, Robert, *The Great Migration* Vol. 2, Great Migration 1634-1635, C-F. p. 496. Online database. AmericanAncestors.org. New England Historic Genealogical Society, 2008.)

[51] *Roxbury Vital Records,* vol. 2, p. 534.

[52] Putnam, p. 6.

[53] Putnam, p. 7, *Suffolk Deeds* vol. 174, p. 25.

[54] 7 September 1711, *Suffolk Deeds* vol. 26, p. 51.

[55] 7 September 1711, *Suffolk Deeds* vol. 26, p. 52.

[56] Putnam p. 6.

[57] Sibley, John L., *Biographical Sketches of Graduates of Harvard University*, Boston: Massachusetts Historical Society (1876), vol. 6, pp. 293-8.

[58] Bailey, Morris R., *The Bailey Genealogy,* Somerville, 1899 # 156; CD 150 p. 105 spells his name Baylie.

[59] CD 150 p. 305.

born Hingham 1730 married 6 July 1780 Perez Gardner who survived the Quebec expedition that the Goddards fought in. [60]

4. John , Junior born Roxbury 14 February 1714, died Plymouth 8 February 1747. He was a master mariner. He married Plymouth 10 November 1734 Lydia POLDEN[61], daughter of John Polden and Lydia Tilson. They had four children.[62] In 1745 he sold his Roxbury inheritance to his brother Giles in Malden for £ 132.[63] A John Goddard of Plymouth was witness to the sale of half of the Roxbury homestead from Joseph Wales to Giles on 9 September 1748.[64]
5. Elizabeth born Roxbury 17 February 1716/7.[65] She married in Weymouth 17 February 1734/5 John SHAW, born Bridgewater 13 April 1708, died 29 April 1791.[66] She died before 1736, when Oakes Shaw was born to John Shaw's second wife, Sarah Angier. Rev. Oakes Shaw was the outstanding minister of the West Barnstable church, and father of the famous Lemuel Shaw, chief justice of Massachusetts.

Six months after Sarah's death, on 15 November 1737 John Goddard married Mary (Bunker) SPRAGUE,[67] born about 1689, widow of the Malden innkeeper Jonathan Sprague, who had died in 1730/1. [68] They had no children, though she had a dozen by her first marriage, bringing along a ten year old and a teenager. She died shortly after their wedding, and he married in Hingham 16 November 1738 Susanna (Gill) LINCOLN, another widow. [69] She had five children, adding to his household a ten year old Thomas. Susannah outlived John, dying at age seventy in Roxbury, 21 January 1754.[70]

John left a large estate of £ 1944/8/6 (about $425,000 in 2017) including the house, barn and 20 acres assessed at £ 1,200 and eight acres of orchard and meadow valued at £ 360, plus a personal estate of £ 464/8/6.[71] In his will he left his wife use of his estate for six

---

[60] Bouvé, Thomas T., *History of the Town of Hingham,* Hingham, 1893, vol. 2, p. 249.

[61] Putnam p. 6.
[62] Moore, Stephen P., *Genealogy of Stephen R. Moore*, http://homepages.rootsweb.ancestry.com/~smoore/1874.htm, Lydia Polden.
[63] 14 December 1747, *Suffolk Deeds* vol. 71, p. 118; Putnam app. 11.).
[64] *Suffolk Deeds* vol. 76, p. 161.

[65] Putnam p. 6.
[66] http://www.timjanzen.com/family/groups/gp465.html.
[67] *Malden Vital Records* vol. 1, p. 236.
[68] Putnam p. 6.
[69] *Cohasset Vital Records* p. 143 gives him as Capt. Jno. Goddard of Roxbury, a mariner. Not to be confused with a contemporary John Goddard of Brookline, who was wagon-master-general of the Continental Army.
[70] Putnam p. 6.
[71] *Suffolk Probate* 8288, inventory 30 July 1746, vol. 39, p.465.

months, "a suitable house", a set of mourning clothes, her premarital gift of £ 10, and the chair which Zechariah Trescott made for him, for which she owed the estate £ 20.[72] The chair does not show up in the inventory of his estate, but Zechariah Trescott was known as the keeper of the notorious Suffolk County jail where the nation's first prison revolt occurred in 1737.[73]

To his son Giles and his legal heirs John left "one half and one hundred Pounds of all my Real Estate and Housing & Lands in the Town of Roxbury". He left his son John, the mariner Captain "if ever he should return home again the Remainder of my Real Estate". He did return, though the will gave each of his children £ 100 if he did not. His daughter Sarah Baily, the minister's wife got £ 100, as did daughter Elizabeth Shaw Daughter Mary Chubbock got only a shilling, unless she were widowed, in which she got £ 150; the same sum went to her children if she died before her husband. The daughters' portions were to be paid out of "Indoor Movables", but they brought no more than £ 284.

In the inventory of John's estate the most expensive items were his wearing apparel and shoes (£ 54). [74] There was also a watch, a cane, a gun and a sword. Most interesting is "Cyder Mill and press" (£ 8) which indicates that his orchards were apple trees, like his neighbor Josiah Warren's.
But John's debts of £ 479/19 exceeded the liquid assets. The largest sum owed was £ 100 to his widow "in part of the marriage Contract" [75]"Funeral Charge & for mourning" came to £ 52/16/6; the accountant got £ 40; taxes due were £ 13/17/8; the Roxbury minister Rev. Ebenezer Thayer got £ 19; an item of "Charges of Arbitration in Willm Goddards Affair" £ 7 (presumably the suit of his brother Captain William; see below). Dr. William Holden was owed £ 2/11/6, indicating a short fatal illness; fellow farmer Joseph Warren (£ 19/19/10), who died falling out of an apple tree in 1755, and father of the famous doctor who died in the battle of Bunker Hill, after whom several generations of Goulds were named; and a dozen other creditors made up the rest.

The debts could only be met by selling the entailed property.[76] The executors Thomas Wales Clap and John's son Giles petitioned the Superior Court for sale and were granted permission on 21 February 1747/8.[77] Half of the homestead, including buildings and eight acres southwest of the Dorchester-Boston highway and north of the Dorchester line were sold on 8 September 1748 for £ 535 to the neighbor to the east, blacksmith Joseph Wales of

---

[72] *Suffolk Probate* 8288, vol. 38, p. 15; Putnam app. 10.
[73] Barusch, Amanda, *Empowerment Series:Foundations of Social Policy,* Belmont CA 2017), p. 292.
[74] *Suffolk Probate* vol. 39, pp. 465-6.
[75] *Suffolk Probate* vol. 41, p. 82.
[76] *Suffolk court case* 6117; Putnam, pp. 7, app. 21.

Dorchester. [78] The next day his son Giles bought it back for £ 550. [79] Two years earlier he bought his brother John Jr.'s interest for £ 132 [80]

Putnam sums up the confusing ownership thus: "Whether or not these sales included the parcel of orchard and pasture that John Goddard had purchased from his father as well as the homestead property that he had received as a gift is not clear…At a later date confusion over this matter caused some family problems…As a result of the sale of one-half of the homestead to Joseph Wales and its repurchase directly by Giles Goddard that portion of the real estate came into his possession in fee simple and free of all entailments. His purchase of his brother's half interest (less fifty pounds) gave him one-half (less fifty pounds) of the remaining one-half interest in fee simple and free of any entailments. The remainder of the homestead property, which was Giles' inheritance from his father, was held by him in fee tail [entailed so it couldn't be sold out of the family]. The other parcel, of orchard and pasture land, as it later turned out was owned by Giles Goddard in the same proportion in fee simple and in fee tail." [81]

John was the younger son of:

GILES[1] GODDARD, merchant and housewright, born Clyffe Pypard, Wiltshire 1647-8 [82] He was son of Giles[A] Goddard.[83] He died Boston 29 June 1729. [84] He married in England Mary SPRAGUE who lived about 1653-1721. He immigrated to Boston by 1679 with his wife and servants.[85] In July 1678 he was involved in two court cases in Boston, a suit against Benjamin Ludden for striking him and drawing blood, and conviction for stealing a canoe from Capt. Valentine Decro. [86] His son William was born in Boston in August 1678. Putnam says without source that Giles was apprenticed to a carpenter and became a housewright. In 1683 he appraised the house of his granddaughter's husband John Butler.[87]

---

[77] Putnam p. 7.
[78] *Suffolk Deeds* vol. 76, pp. 160-1; Court files 8171, 8269, 8403, 9925, 9316 per Putnam p. 21 app. 12).
[79] *Suffolk Deeds* vol.76 p. 161, Putnam app. 13.
[80] 14 December 1745, *Suffolk Deeds* vol. 71, pp 118-119, Putnam app. 11.

[81] Putnam p. 7.
[82] Putnam p. 1, citing his deposition giving age 32 on 28 April 1680, *Massachusetts Supreme Judicial Court* (hereinafter Sup. Court, case 1916, Taft v. Bateman, in which he was involved in a building dispute.
[83] Cowdrey, Nathan Luke, *Genealogy of Giles Goddard (1648-1749),* Geni, hereinafter Cowdrey www.geni.com/people/Giles-Goddard/6000000017337440944.
[84] Dowling, Tim, *Tim Dowling's Family Tree*, Giles Goddard, http://gw.geneanet.org/tdowling?lang=en&p=giles&n=goddard&oc=1
[85] NEHGS *Register,* vol. 1, p. 138.
[86] Putnam cites *Colonial Society of Massachusetts.*, vol. 30, p. 938.
[87] *Superior. Court* 2157, 16 May 1683; Sup. Court 42956, 22 June 1736; Putnam app. 3, 9

Putnam also believed that Giles may have come from England on his own ship because he took aboard goods of residents fleeing the Great Fire of 27 November 1678.[88] Samuel and Mary Nowell claimed that there were three trunks with "many rich clothes , Gold Rings, necklaces, many pieces of gold & some of silver, also Silver Spoons with embroidered gloves" amounting to £ 300. The inventory showed only £ 40: "A great Thumb ring worth £ 2/10", two Thumb rings at £ 2/10, one Stone ring of great price £ 9, 2 Stone rings £ 2/10, a very large Golden bodkin £ 2, several pieces of Gold £ 4, One large Carnelian ring, several pieces of O[ld?] England money, 3 pairs of Gloves embroidered in Gold & Silver £ 10, The Nowells' daughter testified there was a great gold thumb ring with the poesy: "Matches were made in heaven and confirmed here on earth". Thomas Price testified that when he was in the island of Nevis Goddard offered to sell a gold ring with the poesy: "The match is made this ring to Show made up in heaven and performed [cemented] below". We don't know how the court ruled.
Giles moved to York County, Maine by 1681 when he was elected Deputy for York County and Surveyor.[89] He was a resident in New Dartmouth (today's Newcastle), which had been destroyed by the Indians in King Phillip's War in 1676. -Perhaps it is another Giles Goddard whom Putnam cites as 1684 Assembly representative of Cornwall, NY, fifty miles up the Hudson from New York, and Justice of the Peace there in 1686.[90] In 1685 he was in Pemaquid, Maine.[91] But in the same year 1685 there is a report of his daughters showing wonderful things in the Goddard house in Boston. [92] In 1689 New Dartmouth was again destroyed. After Indian troubles in Pemaquid he moved back to Boston.
Giles is named a carpenter in a deed of May 1704[93] but a housewright in 1705, and at the time of his death in 1728.[94] He was taxed in Boston in 1691, 1695, 1698.[95] 1694 is the date of the first deed found in Boston, for the purchase of a house at Spring House Yard at the mouth of Sudbury Lane.[96] Sudbury Street lies west of Haymarket, ending north at Distillery House Square, the distillery of Isaac Hall around 1800. The land faced north on the lane, 109 feet on a curve, bounded on the west 154 feet by the land and orchard of Nathaniel Lynd. Giles kept this property for seventeen years, selling it to housewright Samuel Belknap in 1711 for £ 210[97]
In 1705 Giles bought a farm in Roxbury from the Boston painter Thomas Child for £ 55[98]. In 1720 he gave this to his older son John, cordwainer for £ 80[99]. The gift was restricted by enfiefment, that is, it could not be sold out of the family, a restriction that was to cause family problems for nearly a century. The sale included fourteen acres, a messuage (house), buildings,

---

[88] *Superior Court* 2375, 26 March 1685 Nowell v, Goddard, Putnam p. 2, app. 2.
[89] *York County Deeds* vol. 1, p.44, vol. 9 p. 126-7.
[90] Noyes, Sybil, Libby, Charles, and Davis, Walter, *Genealogical Dictionary of Maine,* Baltimore, Genealogical. Publishing.Co. 1979, pp. 266-7, Putnam p. 2.
[91] Hadley, notes.
[92] Noyes p. 345, Putnam p. 2.
[93] *Suffolk Deeds* vol. 22, p. 374,
[94] *Suffolk Deeds* vol. 22, p. 203, *Suffolk Probate* 7246, vol. 34, p. 181.
[95] Hadley.
[96] From Nathaniel and Sarah Newgate or Newdigate, 31 October 1694, *Suffolk Deeds* vol. 26, p. 52.
[97] 6 September 1711, *Suffolk Deeds* vol. 26, p. 52.
[98] 17 March 1704/5, *Suffolk Deeds* vol. 22, pp. 202-4; Putnam p. 2, app. 4 and 5; Child had foreclosed on Henry Gibbs, "plaisterer" of London, now in Boston.
[99] 30 January 1719/20, *Suffolk Deeds* vol. 35, p. 168.

"trees, fences, woods, wells, ways, waters, watercourses, profits", etc..It lay northwest of the Dorchester line southeast of the highway from Roxbury to Fresh Meadow, north of the highway from Dorchester to Fresh Meadow, and southeast of the fence of Samuel Payson.
Two days later Giles added without restriction seven acres of orchard and pasture in Roxbury which he had bought for £ 50 from William and Anna Charter.[100] The sale included a barn, Old [apple] Orchard, a piece of Swamp Meadow and five acres of pasture; it lay west of the [Providence-Boston] Highway, east and north of Deacon Samuel and Stephen Williams, and south of the old orchard and two walnut trees.
In 1713 Giles paid £ 75 for the estate of housewright Edward Taylor estate at Raynsford Lane and Essex St. in the south end of Boston, using his grandson John Slaughter as a front.[101] Giles occupied the northeast part of the house, and his grandson Capt. John Slaughter the other part.[102] In 1722 he sold the whole property for £ 50 to his grandson Elijah Vinall, a housewright of Hingham, reserving the right for Giles and his wife Lydia to live in the northeast part. [103] After his death this became the source of a quarrel between his two daughters' families. In 1736 his daughter Elizabeth Slaughter and her only child Mary, wife of Samuel Butler, petitioned the state legislature for the property, claimed by her deceased sister's son Elijah Vinall. The General Court granted their request the request, signed by the Speaker Josiah Quincy, the patriot leader in the Revolution.[104]
After his wife Mary's death Giles married in Boston 2 August 1721 Lydia CHAPIN.[105] She was born 16 March 1683, daughter of Caleb and Sarah Chapin. In a premarital contract she agreed to pay him £ 50, to be refunded on his death, with right to the northeast part of their house on Raynsford Lane in the south end of Boston [106] Lydia died in Boston 1 March 1725/6.[107] There is no record of children.
Giles died in Boston 29 June 1729 intestate. The inventory of his estate 21 September 1729 showed only twenty pounds and seventeen shillings, since he had already given away most of his property.[108] In the inventory submitted by his son Capt. John Goddard cordwainer the most

---

[100] 25 May 1705, *Suffolk Deeds* vol. 22, pp. 374-6, Putnam p. 2, app.6, *Suffolk Deeds* vol. 36 p. 164, 20 December 1722; the land came from the estate of Joseph Good 1695, father of Charter's wife Anna.
[101] 7 May 1713, *Superior Court* 42956, Putnam app. 9; *Suffolk Deeds* vol. 36 p. 164 describes the land as 59 feet facing the street on the north, 54 feet Elder Raynsford Lane on the east, 49 feet of "a [James] Wort" on the west, and 62 feet on Goddard's land to the south, for which no deed has been found; Putnam also cites court cases relating to it: 12287, 43313, 45155, 45157, 45904, 45907. Putnam points out that his wife did not sign the deed, indicating that she died before 1711.
[102] Putnam, p. 3.

[103] *Suffolk Deeds* vol. 36, page 163; Vinall was to pay Lydia ten pounds within two months of his death.
[104] Clifford, John, *Acts and Resolves of the Province of Massachusetts,* Chapter 93, p. 102; *Superior Court* case 42956, Putnam app. 9; *Suffolk Deeds* vol. 53, p. 170;
[105] CD 150, p. 101, by Rev. Samuel Myles.
[106] *Suffolk Deeds* vol 38, p. 82, 1 July 1721, Putnam app. 8.
[107] Boston, *Inhabitants & Estates of Town of Boston, 1630-1822 (Thwing Collection). Online database www.americanancestors.org/DB530/i/14226/9091/260109139* .
[108] *Suffolk Probate* 7244, vol. 20, p. 298; Putnam p. 3, app. 21.

expensive item on the list was his Feather Bed, Bolster & Pillow at ₤ 7/15. The rest were a "Bedstead with an old Rugg & old Coverlid", Curtain, Andirons, an old Chest & Drawers, some carved Chairs, two plain fore back'd Chairs, an old Chest, two old Iron Potts & potthooks, dishes and a Tramel (to restrain a horse's legs).

His debts came to ₤ 46/13/4.[109] Twenty pounds in silver was due to his son, six pounds "To Nursing and Charges of My father in his last sickness", and the rest in funeral expenses: six pounds two shillings to James Williams for "Digging the grave and other funeral charges", six pounds six shillings to David Colleon for [black mourning] gloves, eighteen shillings to Mr. Weld for the Coffin, ₤ 11/16/4 to Sundries of Mourning, and sixteen pounds one shilling "To Sundries Due to me [his son] per Note".

Giles and Mary had two sons and two daughters. The oldest was

1. Elizabeth, born 1668 in England, married George SLAUGHTER mariner about 1687 [110] They had a son John born about 1688, who married Boston 22 October 1711 Elizabeth BRADSTREET, daughter of John Bradstreet, baptized Rowley 28 January 1693.[111] They had one child, Mary Slaughter who married 20 October 1732 in Boston Samuel BUTLER. [112] Elizabeth remarried in Boston 27 December 1736 Boston tavern keeper John WASS.[113] Elizabeth's suit for her father's Raynsford Lane property is detailed above.

2, The second daughter, Mary Goddard, was born in England about 1670-1.[114] About 1690 she married John VINALL, Junior, born Scituate 7 October 1667.[115] They had eight children, whose names and birthdates 1691-1711 are recorded by Putnam p. 5.

3. John Goddard, Giles's and Mary's third child is detailed above.
4. William, the youngest of four children, was a master mariner who inherited his father's shipping business.[116] He was born in Boston 4 August 1678.[117] On 29 October 1678 he married Elizabeth FAIRFIELD, born 1 March 1674.[118] She was the daughter of Daniel and Sarah (Ludden) Fairfield. She died in late 1707.[119] They had four children:
   1. William, born Boston 24 January 1697/8. [120] William died 1748.[121]

---

[110] Putnam p. 4.
[111] *Rowley Vital Records* vol. 1, p. 30.
[112] CD 150, p. 175.
[113] CD 150, p. 199.
[114] Putnam p. 5.
[115] *Scituate Vital Records*, p. 395.
[116] Putnam p. 2.
[117] Putnam p. 8.
[118] CD 130, p. 132; Dowling, Tim, *Tim Dowling's blog* http://gw.geneanet.org/tdowling?lang=en&pz=timothy+michael&nz=dowling&ocz=0&p=elizabeth&n=fairfield&oc=3.
[119] Putnam p. 9.
[120] Putnam p. 8

2. Giles born Boston 23 August 1703[122], died 1757 married 11 December 1735 Concumscussuc, Rhode Island Sarah UPDYKE (1700-1770). Their son William born 1740 married 25 May 1785 Abigail ANGELL (1758-1845), parents of William Giles Goddard (1794-1846).
3. Daniel born Boston 22 December 1705; died Boston 5 February 1705/6, age one month.
4. John born Boston 5 April 1707, died 1757.

William married again, 21 September 1709 Elizabeth EVERTON by the famous Rev. Cotton Mather.[123] She was killed on a Boston street accident in June 1714 when a cart ran over her in front of Dr. Clarke's shop. [124]

Captain William Goddard's voyages were mostly in the Caribbean, the Azores and Madeira. In 1703 he was master of the sloop *Dart* leaving Boston for Montserrat, a British island in the West Indies, taking along his fifteen year old nephew John Slaughter.[125] Putnam believed that his wife and children may have gone with him [126] He was employed by the Boston merchant John Colman in 1704 as master of the sloop *Speedwell,* until October 1707, when he sold the sloop in Fayal in the Azores. The next year he took a cargo of whale oil and pipe staves to the Azores, and returned with barrels of wine. However, Colman sued Captain Goddard over the sale of the sloop and his conduct of business in the Azores. [127] Litigation lasted four years, starting in Jan. 1710/11 when the court decided against Goddard, who appealed and went to the Azores for depositions which were rejected by the Superior court. When Goddard's home in Boston was seized he fled to New London, Connecticut to avoid being jailed. He went back to the Azores for more evidence, and won on appeal . He lived in New London, probably sailing from there until 1733.[128] Retiring from the sea about 1745 he went west to central Pennsylvania town of Lewistown, where he was living in 1748 (*Superior Court* 64880, 16 Aug. 1714; Putnam p. 9, app. 15).
Giles' father was:
GILES[A] GODDARD born Clyffe Pypard, Wiltshire 1598; died 1660 Wiltshire. [129] The town's name means "piper's cliff". [130]
son of:
JOHN[B] GODDARD born Corsham, Wiltshire. 1580, died there 1644. Married Johanna. Son of:

---

[121] Dowling.
[122] CD 43, p. 25.
[123] CD 150 p. 23; Putnam pp. 1, 8.
[124] (*Suffolk General Court* 9686, 8 June 1714 Inquisition, Putnam p. 9, app. 14).

[125] 11 July 1703, Putnam p. 9 citing court case 6117.
[126] Putnam, pp. 9, 21.
[127] Suffolk court files 8171, 8269, 8403, 9925, 9316, Putnam pp..9, 10, 21.
[128] Putnam p. 21, app.12 citing Frances Caulkins, *History of New London,* New London 1895, pp. 242-4.
[129] Cowdrey.
[130] Ekwall, Eilert, *English Place Names*, Oxford: Clarendon Press, 1947 p. 107.

ANTHONY[C] GODDARD born Corsham, Wiltshire. 1557, died there 5 July 1621, Married Johanna. Son of:

THOMAS[D] GODDARD born Upham, Wiltshire 1521, died Clyffe Pypard, Wiltshire.2 June 1597. Married Jane. He was brother of John Goddard, father of Sir John Goddard, born about.1558. "The arms of the Cliffe Pypard family are : Gules, a chevron vair, between three crescents, argent. Crest, a stag's head, eftronte gules, attired, or ; and the motto, " Cervus non Servus." ("A Hart is no Slave"). [131]

Son of:
JOHN[E] GODDARD born Upham, Wiltshire. 1465. son of:
WALTER[F] GODARD DE CHERHILL son of :
JOHN[G] GODARD born Poulton, Wiltshire, 1393, died 1490 Wiltshire. son of:
JOHN[H] GODARD 1393-1490. son of:
JOHN[I] GODARD DE POULTON, born London 1266, died 1326, son of:
Sir WALTER[J] DE GODARVILLE 1200-1273, castellan of Devizes Castle, son of:
Sir HUGH[K] DE GODARVILLE born Chester about 1175, son of:
Sir HUGH[L] DE GODARVILLE of Chester, born about 1148.[132] Goderville is a town on the coast of Normandy, near Le Havre. The lords of the town were GODARD DE VAULX[133] until 1492. The name Godard probably derives from Good Heart. Vaulx is a town northwest of Godarville, in Pas de Calais.

Elias Waters Goddard's mother was a nurse, EUNICE WALKER, daughter of JOHN WALKER (MDR 130:39). She was born in Boston Sept. 1784, and died in Cambridge 25 Feb. 1858 at age 75. She remained a widow for 32 years after her husband's death in 1826, when she left their home at Power's Court, 328 Ann Street, and moved to 31 Charter Street, next to her son at #27 (Dir. 1828, 121). The next year she was living at the rear of her son's house, where his father

---

[131] Jefferies , Richard, A Memoir of the Goddards of North Wilts., https://archive.org/stream/memoirofgoddards00jeffrich/memoirofgoddards00jeffrich_djvu.txt; nice illustration in Cowdrey.

[132] *www.geni.com/people/**Hugh-de-Godarville**/6000000009645602382.*
[133] *Wikipedia Godarville.*

Caroline Garran Goddard (1807-1880)

Chapter XIV
GARRAN FAMILY

CAROLINE GARRAN was born in Newburyport MA 1 November 1807 to Jabez and Sarah Garran (Newburyport VR 152; Massachusetts Cert. of Birth; Gravestone, Mt. Auburn Cemetery, Cambridge; Goddard family Bible); she died at her home at 19 Unity Street, Boston 24 April 1880, age 72, 6 months and 22 days of catarrhal fever (Goddard Bible); married at Old North Church, in Boston, by the Rev. Sebastian Streeter, Sunday, 5 Oct. 1828 to ELIAS WATERS GODDARD (Goddard Bible; Christ Church record 141, #354).

Our great-great grandmother Caroline Garran is our link to the *Mayflower*, to the first settlers of Barnstable, to three Puritan ministers, and to the founders of Concord, Charlestown, Amesbury, Ipswich, Dracut, Woburn and Chelmsford. Most of her Garran ancestors were seamen or fishermen, and the Fletcher ancestors mostly farmers. But among them were some pioneer craftsmen, including the builders of the first bridge over the Charles, the first iron works on the Merrimac, and the first sawmill in Amesbury. Among her ancestors is Olive Welby Farwell, whose Welby family had a coat of arms as minor gentry in Lincolnshire, and had ancestors who were High Sheriffs and members of Parliament from the county.

We have only three pictures of Caroline, separated by nearly fifty years. In the first, about the time of her wedding, when she was 21, a cutout silhouette shows a profile of a receding jaw and chin, rather frilly bows at the front and back of her thin neck, and a large comb atop her hair, which is pulled back in a bun. The other two are photos, probably taken at the same time, before her death, which show her with her husband in front of their North End house at 19 Unity Street, and in the garden at the back of the house. Here she is a rather severe looking old woman, hair parted in the middle, and pulled back, probably in a bun, a thin neck wrapped in a dark scarf, a checkered dress buttoned tightly up the front, a white apron, and in the garden scene, a dark shawl over her shoulders. Though it is mid-summer, she looks cold.

She was buried in the Goddard plot in Mt. Auburn Cemetery, Cambridge, on the north side of Elm Avenue, which backs up to Mt. Auburn Street The inscription on the white marble stone is badly eroded:

"In memory of CAROLINE GARRAN
Wife of Elias W. Goddard
Born in Newburyport
Nov. 1, 1807 died in Boston April 24, 1880
Aged 72 yrs.

Dear Caroline,
We [rue?] the thought that we shall
See thee no more on earth;
That thou art gone forever,
-ell—ee thee; as the days flow by
At [rest? in?] the bosom of the blest
A token of esteem by friends."

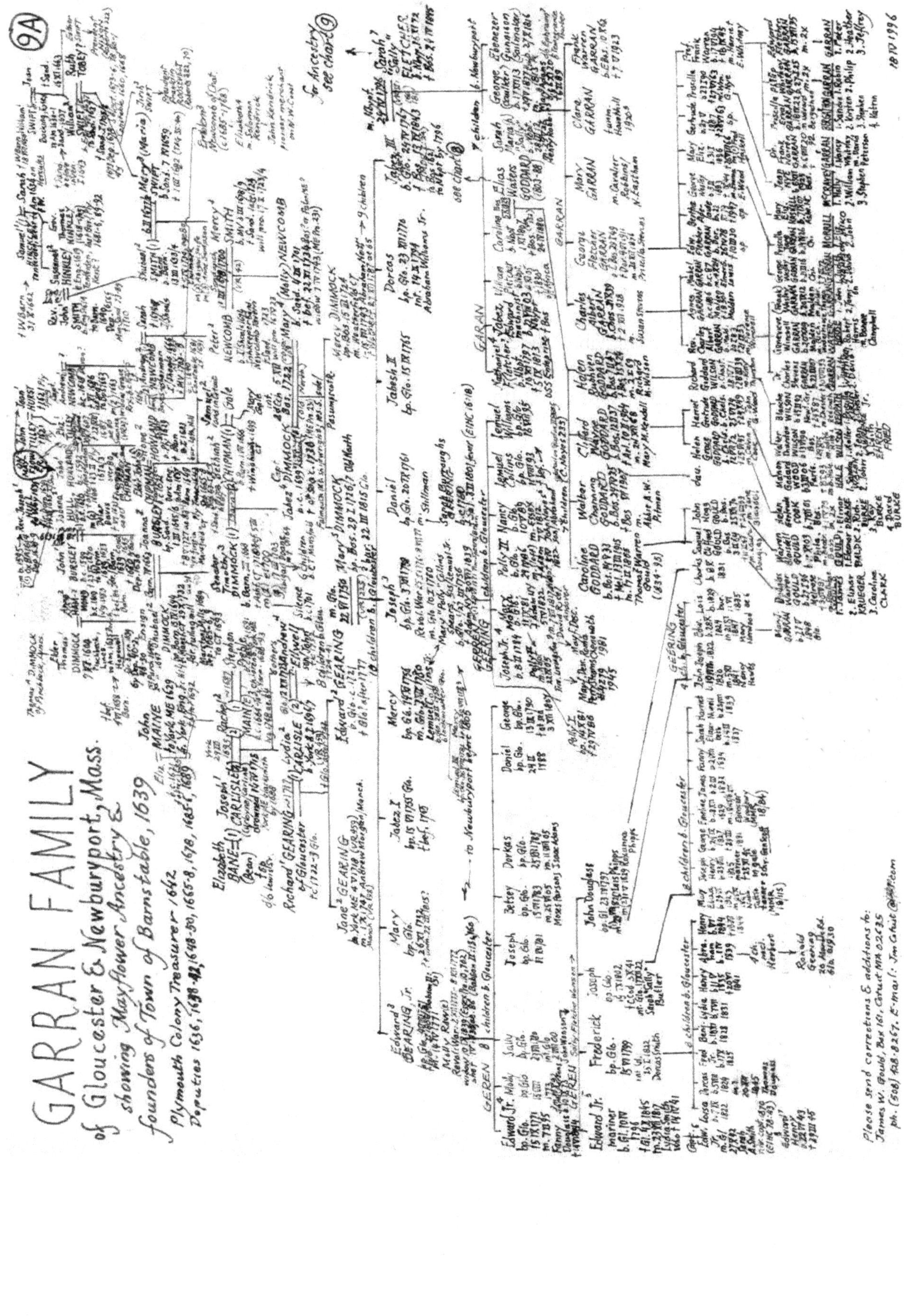
9A
GARRAN FAMILY
of Gloucester & Newburyport, Mass.
showing Mayflower Ancestry &
founders of Town of Barnstable, 1639
Plymouth Colony Treasurer - 1642
18 IV 1996

Caroline's parents were JABEZ^{3} GARRAN and SARAH^{7} FLETCHER of Newburyport. Jabez was born in Gloucester, MA 24 April 1767 (Gloucester recorded in death of son George in Massachusetts Death Records 1877, 293:261, #26; Date recorded in Garran family Bible in possession of Dr. Frank Garran of Barnstable MA, but no place; VR of Gloucester do not record it, but of two earlier births, Jabez 15 April 1755, and "Jabesh" 15 Sept. 1765, who evidently died), the ninth child of EDWARD^{2} GEARING and MARY^{5} DIMMOCK. The evidence of his parents is circumstantial, since no record appears in any town or church record. However, the unusual name appears twice before in the children of Edward and Mary, commemorating her father Jabez Dimmock, and there is no record of the survival of the two younger boys. A further support is the fact that two of Edward's sons (Edward Jr. and Joseph) moved from Gloucester to Newburyport by 1805 (Lester C. Gustin, *The Ancestry of Herbert E. Gustin* [Newton: Modern Press, 1954], 1021), where our Jabez appears in 1796. Another circumstance is that three of seven of Jabez and Sarah's childrens' names at baptism were written Gerring, and the others spelled Garen or Garon. (Mary Adams Rolfe papers, Historical Society of Old Newbury, "Dump Gardner to Hale", 1-2; Newburyport VR 1:152-3; Newbury VR 2:176). The name is also variously shown as Gayran and Garan. Fourth evidence is onosmatic, for their first son is named for Sarah's brother Nathaniel Fletcher, but the second son is named for his father, Jabez, with the middle name of his grandfather, Edward.

Jabez Garran died in Newburyport MA 13 Sept. 1843, age 77 (Massachusetts Death Records 1:24). The family was probably living in Newbury 1813-7, where three of their children were baptized (Three of the children were baptized GARAN in Belleville Congregational Church (organized 1808), 285 High Street, Newburyport per letter of 26 May 1966 of Rev. David Van Strien to Eleanor Baldic). He first appears in Boston in 1821 and remained in that city until 1836. His first occupations are as a ships rigger and stevedore, living at 23 Cross Street in the North End (Boston Directory (hereinafter Dir.) 1821, 104; 1822, 107), where Caroline would meet her future husband, Elias Goddard. Jabez moved to 26 Middle Street in 1823, is not recorded in the directory for a couple of years, until 1827 when he has a boarding house at 5 Hamilton Street (Dir. 1827, 112). In 1828, the year Caroline Garran married Elias Goddard, her father is living at the rear of the Goddard's house at 27 Charter Street, but moved to Battery Street the next year(1828 118; 1829 116), and to Clark Street in 1830 (Dir. 160). In 1831 he is at 205 Hanover, but back in Clark Street the next year (Dir. 1831, 151; 1832, 159). Then comes the longest stable residence, from 1833 to 1836 he is living on Unity Street, near the Goddards. But then he apparently returned to Newburyport in 1837.

However, his youngest son the sail maker Ebenezer G. Garran continued to live nearby at 211 Hanover (1838), Salutation (1839), 205 Hanover (1840), 8 Stillman (1841), rear of 41 Endicott (1842), rear of 42 Salem Street (1843), rear of 8 Prince Street (1844), rear of 41 Charter (1850/1), rear of 63 Charter (1851/2-4, 1856). Another Garran of unknown relationship, perhaps a son, James Garran, appears at 4 Unity Street in 1838. Sarah Garran, Caroline's mother, was living with the Goddards in 1839 at 5 Unity Street.

Jabez married in Newburyport 24 April 1796 (VR 181) SARAH^{7} FLETCHER (1772-1845), of whom more shortly. They had at least seven children, born Newburyport:
i. Nathaniel Fletcher?), b. 10 Nov. 1797 (VR 153). He was supposedly killed in the naval battle between the U.S.S. *Enterprise* and H.M.S. *Boxer* at Monhegan Island off Pemaquid ME 5 Sept. 1813, and was buried at sea off Halfway Rock, although official record is lacking. No record of marriage or children.

ii. Jabez Edward, b. 22 Aug. 1803 (Gamon,VR 152); d. Boston 19 March 1864; m. Carlisle MA 8 Oct. 1829 (VR 53) Mary Proctor of Lowell, who died Carlisle 3 Dec. 1830 (VR 89), and buried in Green Cemetery there. There is no known children or remarriage. He was a machinist in Boston in 1848, living on Wesley Street (Dir. 1848/9, 135).
iii. William Fletcher, b. 4 Nov. 1805 (VR 152); died off Africa in the 1830s; no known marriage or children.
iv. CAROLINE, noted above.
v. Sarah (Sally) Maria(h), b. 28 March 1812 (VR 155); bapt. Belleville Church, Newburyport 26 July 1812; d. Boston? 10 Oct. 1867, age 55; m. Newburyport 29 May 1836 Henry Robbins (*Columbian Centinel* 1 June 1836). They moved to Troy NY by 1853, where Caroline Gould visited them at 137 Third Street, as we have seen in the previous chapter. She may have had children named Julia, Phebe, John and Lucy.
vi. George, b. 17 Dec. 1813 (VR 155) bapt. Belleville Church, Newburyport 12 July 1814; d. of TB, Hyde Park MA 29 May 1877, age 64 (Massachusetts Death Record 293:261, #26); m. Mary^{8} S. Adams, second cousin of President John Quincy Adams, and fourth cousin of waiter Henry Adams, b. Portsmouth NH 2 Nov. 1820, daughter of Ephraim C. Adams (Samuel^{6}, Ebenezer^{5}, Joseph $^{4-3-2}$, Henry^{1}) and Temperance Thurber; d. Medford MA 6 Feb. 1889 (Massachusetts Death Record 1889, 401/182 #22; Andrew Adams, *A Genealogical History of Henry Adams* [Rutland VT: Tuttle, 1898], 444). By profession he was briefly an engraver (1846), then a ships caulker, living in the North End of Boston 1846-51, 1854-6, and later in Medford.
Six children:
i. Charles Alfred, b. Charlestown MA 21 Oct. 1839; d. 2 Dec. 1928, in auto accident; m. Susan Stevens, daughter of Andrew & Elizabeth Stevens, and sister of his brother's wife. He was a painter. Three children born Malden MA., one of whom became a minister. See chart 8 for detail.
ii. Emily A., m. 7 March 1867 Joseph Baker^{8} Higgins (Abner^{7}, Jonathan $^{6-5}$, Samuel^{4}, Jonathan $^{3-2}$, Richard^{1}) b. Orleans MA 24 Dec. 1834 (Katharine Higgins, *Richard Higgins...Eastham* [Worcester: The author, 1918], 446); m. 1) 5 Sept. 1859 Temperance C. Newcomb, daughter of Elnathan S., who died 2 Nov. 1865. Higgins was a mariner, and served two months in the Army in Co. F, Third Massachusetts Heavy Artillery, the Civil War, 24 June to 24 Aug., then transferred to the Navy (*Massachusetts Civil War* 5:797, 8:171). They had three children, Elisa, Eva Smith, and Josephine (Descendants listed in Higgins 446).
iii. Mary Adeline, b. 10 Sept. 1847; d. Eastham MA 24 Nov. 1931, age 84 (Eastham Town Report, 1931, 42); m. Cavalier Houdlette Robbins, b. 25 Feb. 1861, d. Eastham 28 Feb. 1945 (*Eastham Town Report, 1945*, 26). They moved from Chelsea about the turn of the century to Cape Cod, where he was long-time station master at North Eastham for the N.Y.N.H. & H. Railroad's Cape Cod line. They lived in the historic 1750 Doane-Stevens House at 855 Nauset Road, which remained in the Doane family until 1947, so must have been rented by the Robbins family (C. H. Robbins papers in Eastham Historical Society archives EHS 678). His papers have been preserved in the Eastham Historical Society archives in the basement of the public library (This includes the Account Book of Daniel Robbins of Chelsea (his father?) c.1850-67, EHS 684).
iv. George Fletcher, b. E. Boston 29 Jan. 1849; d. Dorchester 4 June 1911; m. 20 Dec. 1876 Priscilla Stevens (Massachusetts Marriage Record 1876 281:217, #35), b. Nova Scotia 23 Nov. 1853, daughter of Andrew & Elizabeth Stevens; d. Dorchester 21 Jan. 1929. George was a paperhanger in Boston, and lived in Chelsea in 1888 (Numerous receipts in Cavalier Robbins accounts in Eastham Historical Soc. EHS 678).7 children, born Dorchester, from whom the Cape

Cod Garrans are descended.
v. Clara, d. unmarried Haverhill in 1920s.
vi. Frank Warren, b. E. Boston 10 Oct. 1862 (Massachusetts Birth Record 152:31, #47); d. 7 May 1923, age 61. He was a dry goods dealer in Gloucester, and owned one of the first autos on Cape Cod, res. Orleans.
vii.Ebenezer Gunnison, b. 27 Oct. 1816 (VR153); bapt. Belleville Church, Newburyport, 11 May 1817. He lived and worked in the North End of Boston as a sailmaker from 1838 to 1853, when he moved to Cambridge.
viii. James? This name appears in the North End of Boston in 1838 Directory, at 4 Unity Street, next to the Goddards; is it a mistake for Jabez?

GLOUCESTER ORIGINS.

Jabez's father EDWARD[2] GEARING, is a person of whom we know little except what appears in the vital records for his marriage and births of children in Gloucester. His birth and death is not recorded, but we assume he was born about 1720, and died after the end of 1770 when his daughter Dorcas was baptized. He married in Gloucester 22 June 1750 MARY[5] DIMMOCK (VR 225; John H. Babson, *History of Gloucester* [Gloucester: M.V. R. Perley, 1876], [hereinafter Babson], pt. 2, 131)((1726/7-1815?), of whom more below. He first appears in Gloucester town records on 27 Jan. 1761 when the town paid him 54 shillings for nine days work of "car [ry] ing up Pools family to Boston", presumably by horse and cart (Order of Selectmen, Town Records, 67). He had apparently some property, for in 1762 he was assessed 15 shillings 8 pence for the year 1760 (15 Feb. 1762, 90). He must have had a hard time paying, for in 1764 his province tax of 8 shillings 4 pence was abated (7 Dec. 1764, 131).His town tax of 10/9 for 1766 was abated in 1768 (16 Feb. 1768, 131?). His tax for 1774 was 4/6 in 1777 (9 Oct. 1777, 449). He may have been living at this date, though this assessment may be on his son Edward.

Edward Gearing's father was RICHARD[1] GEARING of Gloucester, the first known ancestor, though the family may have been here earlier. He married in York ME about 1717 LYDIA[2] CARLISLE, born York ME 8 Jan. 1696/7 (VR 459; spelled Lidiah Carlile or Carliel). They had only two known children, Jane Gearing ,born in York 4 May 1718 (VR 459), who married Gloucester 1 Oct. 1747 Andrew Morgan of Manchester, and our Edward. Richard died about 1722-3, for on 12 Dec. 1723 Lydia remarried in Gloucester to Andrew Ellwell, son of John Ellwell (VR 225; Elizabeth Versailles, *Ellwelliana* [Williamsburg MA: the author, 1974], 14, 23-4, 35, 47; see also 140 for descendants of Sally[4] Garran Wonson). By him Lydia had eight children. She died, probably in Gloucester after the baptism of the last child, Lucy, 16 May 1742.

The origins of the Garran/Gearing family are mysterious. On our Goddard/Garran branch the vague assertion was that Garran was a French Huguenot name like GUERIN, who were refugees from Richelieu's persecution of Protestants after 1640. This was supported by the tradition passed down to Dr. Frank Garran of Cape Cod that they were French river pirates of the river Garonne.

None of this is supported by French given names in the family, or any connection to the Boston Huguenot family of Francis, Nicholas and Leon Guerin, or to Jacobo (James) Garon (Letters of Denization in Suff. Deeds 14:212, about 1688, but not necessarily in Boston, Reg. 35:249, 46:414; Reg. 35:249 cites a letter of a resident of Suffolk County, Boston 20 July 1688, citing

Agnew's *French Protestant Exiles* (London, 1871), 1:46, and Camden Society *Lists of Foreign Protestants and Aliens Resident in England, 1618-1688* ed. by William D. Cooper, London, 1862, 48).

In fact, all of the early given names in this family are clearly English, and the name Gearing shows up in London in 1606, long before the influx of Huguenot refugees, in the merchant Simon Gereing (Reg. 47:398-9; 1637 in 49:37-4; Gustin shows a Simon Gering of London who died about 1651 in Percival Boyd, *Roll of the Draper's Company of London* (Croydon, 1934) , as well as a Henry Gering living 1667, Josh Gerring d. c. 1699, and another Josh living 1727, Thomas Gering d. c. 1730, John F. Gearing 1763, d. c. 1804), and as John Gearing, the merchant in 1626 (*Pub. of Colonial Society of Mass: Transactions* [Boston: Colonial Society, 1910], 11:272). Closer to home is a Richard Gearing in London in 1636, also spelled Gerie and Gery (Reg. 46:451-2), though of no known relation (Also John Geering of London in Reg. 47:497,45:231, and London mercer Thomas Gearing 1719 in Reg. 49:484, from Waters Gleanings).

The first appearance of the name in America is as early as 1645 when "Mr. Gearringe, being very poore" was left a generous bequest of £10 in the will of Richard Bartholomew of Salem (6 Nov. 1645, EIHC 1:5, 51:59; taken from Salem Quarterly Court files, printed in Essex Probate Records I:51, 102). Significantly, this is in Essex County, so we know someone of the name was living in the area long before the Huguenot persecutions. However, in the same year Braintree records show a John Gearing among the first settlers (Pattee, 558). The connection has not been established since there are no wills or deeds, but the family may have come to America well before 1645.

In 1658 a John Garven, a servant, appeared in Salem Court records (20 May, Essex Quarterly Court 2:107; Essex Antiq.. 12:75): "John Garven, Goodman [William Jigles] Gigles servant, fined for abusing Richard Midleton, Servant to John Puttman, by smiting him violently with a stick." His master Jigles died in 1659, and Garven went to sea, perhaps with Jigles' s brother, a sea captain, but died in a wreck in 1662, as the court recorded: "Richard Eliott and John Garven, having been cast away, and no wills appearing, the court granted the administration upon their estates to Mr. George Corwin, and ordered him to bring in an inventory to the next Salem court."(EQ 2:164 (estate inven. 26 March 1659), 369 (25 March 1662). There is no printed record of Garven's estate, though Elliot's was appraised March 1662/3 for a small £ 2/14 EQ 3:181 June 1664). No more is known of this man.

The only evidence of the family in the area between 1645 and 1722 is a Peter Guerin, Gerrin, Gerin or Jerrin, a soldier killed in the Falls Fight on the Connecticut River 18 May 1676. Although he came from Northampton, he does not seem to have resided there, and Savage says came from the eastern part of the state (George M. Bridge, *Soldiers in King Philip's War* [Boston: The author, 1891], 204, 207; same title, [Leominster: the author, 1896], 247, 250; James R. Trumbull, *History of Northampton* [Northampton: Gazette Publ. Co., 1902], 1: 575; George Sheldon, *History of Deerfield* [Deerfield, the author, 1895], 159; Kellogg's *History of Bernardston* does not list the name among claimants for land in 1736. Savage 2: 239).
The death of Peter Gearing also shows up in the Dorchester records of 1675, so he may have come to the South Shore (Dorchester Church records, 261, cited by Gustin 1018).

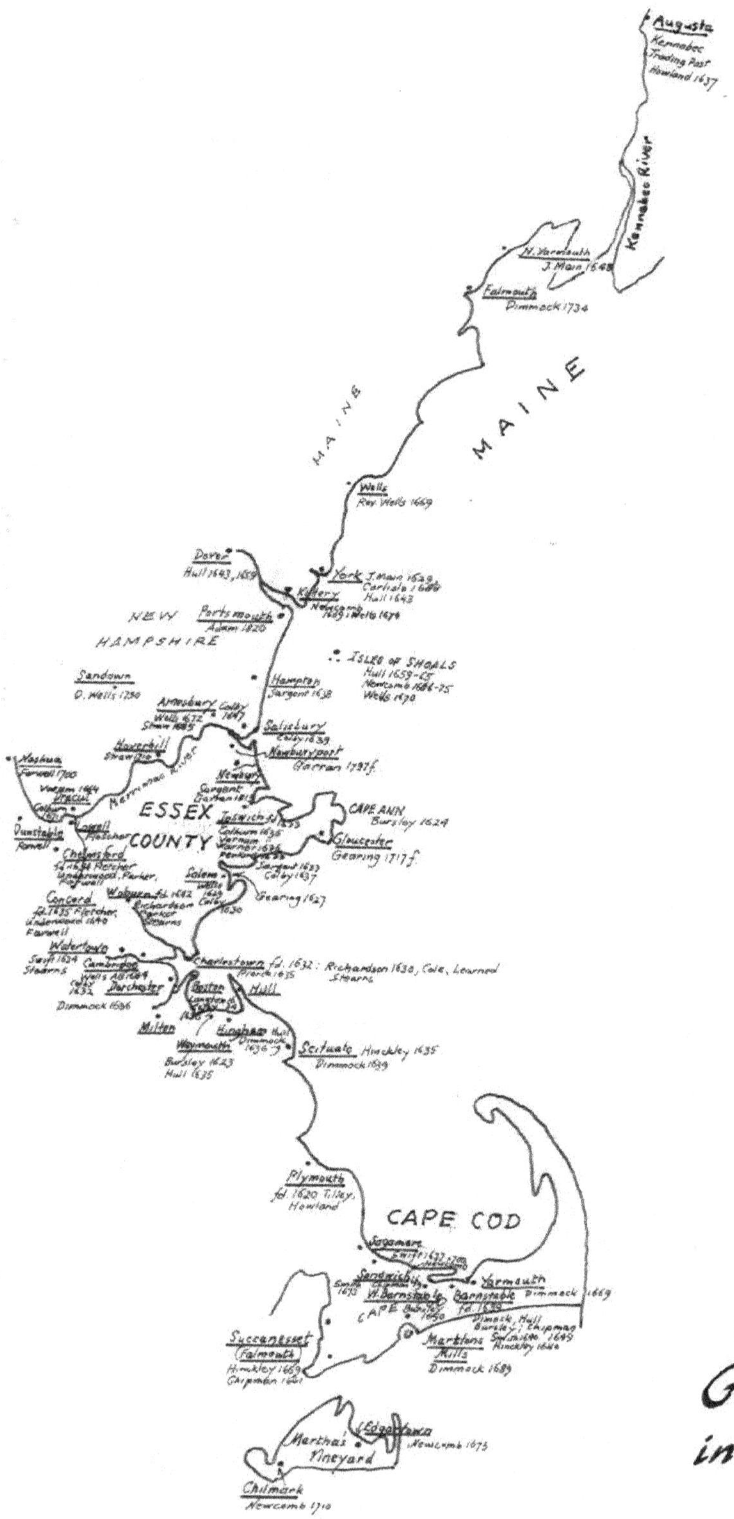

Homes of our Garran Ancestors in New England

TWG 2 IX 96

CARLISLE AND MAINE FAMILIES.

Lydia Gearing's father was JOSEPH[1] CARLISLE (variously spelled CURLOYNE, CARLIEL and CARLILE). He probably lived in Boston before he moved to York, Maine. He first appears in America in 1688, as a blacksmith who brought Charles Brisson to court for assault (Gustin 605---source of quote; Noyes 110, 128-9). In 1691 Brisson was ordered to give Carlisle's stepdaughter's things to his wife Elizabeth, who was thus related to Brisson. Banks found Carlisle in York ME in 1690, as husband of Elizabeth Bean or Bane, daughter of Lewis Bane Sr. (Charles Edward Banks, *History of York, Maine* [Portsmouth, NH: Randall, 1935], v. 2, cited by Gustin 606, Noyes 129).

The next year Carlisle and his wife were indicted in York for not attending church.In 1693 Carlisle was at sea as a smith aboard the ship *St. Jacob*, for on 29 April 1693 Carlisle gave power of attorney to his kinswoman Elizabeth (Dodd) Ryall, wife of John Ryall, victualer of Boston (and York), to sue Capt. Benjamin Ems, Commander of the ship *St. Jacob* for £ 14/0/6 due to Carlisle "for worke and service Done on board the said Ship St. Jacob in her late Salt voyage made under the said Capt. Ems". (SD 7:149, quoted by Gustin 605).

Elizabeth (Bane) Carlisle died before 29 March 1695 (not in York VR; Libby 129a), when Joseph remarried RACHEL (MAIN) Preble, the widow of Stephen Preble. Rachel was the daughter of JOHN MAIN(E) who had come to York in 1629 from York, England. He was born about 1614-1615. (Sybil Noyes, Charles Libby and Walter Davis, *Genealogical Dictionary of Maine and New Hampshire* [Baltimore: Genea. Pub. Co., 1976], [hereinafter Noyes, 453]. He and his wife Elizabeth had settled on 60 acres at Mayne's Point on the west side of the Wescustogo River in North Yarmouth Maine about 1648. They were in York in 1684 and Casco Bay 1687. Elizabeth was living in Jan. 1684/5 when she was about 61, and her husband about 70. He was still alive 14 April 1693, nearly 80. Rachel was born about 1664-70, probably at Mayne's Point, North Yarmouth ME. She had married about 1687 Stephen Preble of York, born about 1656, and died about 1691 when Rachel was given administration of his estate (Noyes 567). They had three children, Rachel Preble, Jemima Rhodes of Dorchester, and Stephen Jr., who may have had descendants that are our cousins.

Rachel and Joseph Carlisle had seven children, including our ancestor Lydia.
In early 1696 Carlisle was granted 30 acres "where he can find it" in York, and made pound keeper the same year (Banks vol. 2, cited by Gustin 606). In 1700 York gave him another 40 acres at Rocky Ground, where he lived. The next year he was Surveyor of Highways.

Joseph Carlisle was drowned 17 March 1717 (York VR 371) while he was crossing a pond near their home, and accidentally fell in. Rachel lived on until at least 1748, when she was 84.

Much of the Carlisle family had moved to Gloucester MA as early as 1723, when the first of four children married a Gloucester spouse. Two of Edward Garran's sons, Edward Jr. and Joseph, served as privates in the Revolutionary War, in the defense of Boston, in Capt. Barnabas Dodge's company of Col. Loami Baldwin's 26th Regiment, in Chelsea and Cambridge (Massachusetts Soldiers 6: 282-3; Massachusetts Muster and Pay Rolls, 58:3 # 16, 5 # 9, 18, 19; 71 # 1; 78, # 1; 79 # 1). This was after the battles of Lexington and Concord, and Bunker Hill, and the expedition to Quebec, but they witnessed the British evacuation of Boston in March 1776. Gustin says both served until 8 Dec. 1777. We do not know the relationship of the British soldier from Nova Scotia named John Garron.

The brothers Edward and Joseph show up in Gloucester with large families in the first U.S. Census of 1790, near each other, and to earlier relatives the Elwells, as well as the Rowe, Witham, Parsons and Soward families.

The Gearing family was evidently relatively poor, for no record of property or wills shows up before 1814. The first probate record for the family is 1814, when a Nathaniel Garran is recorded as a minor (Essex Probate # 10678, 9 June 1814, 385:491), perhaps the child of the eldest son of Jabez Garran, Nathaniel Fletcher, according to family tradition, was killed in the War of 1812 naval battle of 5 Sept. 1813 at Monhegan Island off Pemaquid ME, aboard the U.S.S. *Enterprise* in its fight with H.M.S. *Boxer* and buried at sea off Halfway Rock.. However, he is not listed among crew or casualties of the battle.

We get no specific reference to where the Gearings lived in Gloucester until 1816, when the first deed shows up (ED 209/51). On 28 Feb. 1816 mariner Edward[4] Gearing (1771-1844) sold a one-story house on the Eastern Road in Gloucester for $400 to John Smith. The lot is northwest of the road, measuring only 35 x 100 x 42 x 90 feet, with John Wonson a neighbor on the northeast. It was probably this property that entitled him to vote in 1814 (Gloucester town "List of Persons qualified to Vote 1814", Gloucester Archives), but we do not know how much earlier he had owned the house and lot. This was probably in the area of East Gloucester where Edward Gearing was awarded $30 for taking by the town of a roadway in 1840 (30 Oct. 1840, Gloucester Town Records, book 6:175; the only larger recipients were three Wonsons, which suggests proximity to Wonson Cove). Since 1928 the Gerring name has been commemorated by a road in East Gloucester running east from Smith's Cove from East Main Street to Mt. Pleasant Street (Named 2 May 1928 per city street record, based on previous layout on 6 Feb. 1891 as Geering Street per city record vol. 13, folio 94 on Wonson land). This area, where the Gearings have long lived, is on a hill overlooking the Rocky Neck Art Colony, and some well known views of Gloucester have been painted from the site, such as Frederick Mulhaupt's "An East Gloucester Wharf" (c. 1926) and Max Kuchner's "Gloucester Harbor" (1912), both of which hang in the Cape Ann Historical Association gallery.

DIMMOCK.

MARY[5] DIMMOCK GARRAN was baptized in Old North Church, Boston 29 Jan. 1726/7 (Gustin 1031), daughter of Capt. JABEZ[4] DIMMOCK and MARY[4] "MOLLY" NEWCOMB. Of her mother's family more later under NEWCOMB. Her father was born in Windham CT about 1699 to TIMOTHY[3] DIMMOCK and BETHIAH[2] (CHIPMAN) GALE, granddaughter of two Mayflower passengers. He died "beyond seas", reported at Falmouth ME about 1737-8 (Maine Probate Abstracts, York County, 6: 231, 6:36 "Whereas Capt. Jabez Dimmock of Falmouth, mariner, died about 4 yrs. ago beyond seas. . ."; not Falmouth MA 15 Jan. 1771, as Newton records, 41).

Jabez is first mentioned in 1702 as grandson in the will of Elder John Chipman of Sandwich, who left him £ 5 (Otis 158), which he received in 1708. John's widow Ruth Chipman left Jabez an additional 20 shillings in 1710, received in 1713. By 1722 he was in Boston, where on 5 Dec. 1722 (Int. CD 150, 150) he married, at the Second Church, which became Old North, to "Molly" Newcomb"of Sandich". They evidently lived in Boston, where their two daughters, Mercy and Mary were born, in 1724 and 1727. In 1733 he was in Maine, where he witnessed a deed in York County (York Deeds [hereinafter YD] 16: 274, 282, 570, in Mayflower Soc. Bowman files, microfiche #9 of 18). In June 1734 Jabez Dimmock, shipwright of Falmouth ME

deeded land to Boston merchant Samuel Waldo (YD 16: 530-1, 27 June). This was the same piece of land he received from Samuel Staples of Falmouth, in a deed recorded later in 1734(22 Nov. 1734, YD 17: 195-6). In this deed his wife is Elizabeth, so we assume that Molly had died before 22 Nov. 1734, perhaps in Boston. This may be an error, for in his estate his widow is Mary (Maine Probate Abstracts, York Co. 6: 231, 6/36). In Dec. 1734 Dimmock signed in Boston an indenture to Samuel Waldo on a "Dwelling house with one acre of land situate in Falmouth on the South Side of Pasumpscot river on which the said Dimmock now lives." (YD 17: 193-4, 18: 330-1).
Dimmock apparently took a ship on a deep water voyage on which he was lost, about 1737-8. His widow Mary renounced administration of his estate in favor of his principal creditor, Samuel Waldo of Boston, in Jan. 1742.

Jabez's father, Timothy Dimmock, was born in Barnstable village in the house his father built in 1712, in March 1668, the third son of Ensign SHUBAEL[2] DIMMOCK and JOHANNA[3] BURSLEY of Barnstable (Otis 339). Before 1699, probably in Barnstable, he married Bethiah[2] (Chipman) Gale, of whom more shortly under CHIPMAN. Timothy and Bethiah followed his father's move to Mansfield CT, and to Windham CT, where Bethiah died in l699, about the time of her son Jabez's birth (Robert S. Newton, "The Dimmock Family" (Reston,VT: typescript, 1989 [hereafter Dimmock], 33). Timothy[1] remarried to a local woman, about 1700, but she too died after giving birth to a daughter Silence Dimmock in 1701. Timothy married a third time 17 March 1703 to Abigail Doane, daughter of Daniel Doane of Eastham. By her he had six children, born in Mansfield, CT. He died in Ashford CT before 5 March 1718. His estate was inventoried at £ 56/7 on 26 May and administered by his widow on 8 July 1718 (CT. Probate 72-8 in Mainwaring, 1:377-8, cited by Newton 33). His widow was granted 100 acres in Ashford in his name on 5 March 1718. She remarried ten years later, in the fall of 1728, to Benjamin Follet of Windham, who died there March 1752. Abigail died in Windham July 1764.

Timothy's father, Ensign SHUBAEL[2] DIMMOCK, was baptized by Rev. John Lothrop in Barnstable 15 Sept. 1644 (Spelled "Shubeall", John Lothrop's Diary, copied 1769 by Ezra Stiles from a mss. of Rev. Elijah Lothrop of Gilead CT, hereinafter Lothrop, 332; also in Reg. 9: 279-87, 10:37-43, 345-51), the son of Elder THOMAS[1] DIMMOCK, first settler of Barnstable, and his wife ANNE[2] HAMMOND, born in England about 1610, possibly daughter of WILLIAM[1] HAMMOND. She was still living in 1683, about 73 years old, and probably died before 1686, and was buried in Barnstable.

Shubael was only 18 when in April 1663 he married 17 year old JOANNA[2] BURSLEY in Barnstable, but they were wed for 64 years. In 1669 they were living east of the Barnstable line, in Yarmouth (The original boundary followed the present Indian Trail in Cummaquid, which cut through the original Dimmock grant. The boundary was not moved until later, so Shubael's house was probably on the original grant), but soon returned to live in his father's fort house on Dimmock Hill, by 1686. About 1712 he built a high fronted house, owned by Selleck Hedge in 1888. He was Representative and Selectman of Barnstable 1685-6, and 1689, and Ensign in the local militia. Interested in manufacturing, the town put him on a committee to set up a grist mill powered by wind or water (7 Aug. 1684, Trayser 218). But he turned to wool, and became part owner of the fulling mill in Marstons Mills in 1689.

In 1693 he moved to Mansfield CT, where he became Deacon of the church (one of the six founders), and Lieutenant of the militia (1703-8) (R. Cutter, ed., *Genealogy & Families History of Connecticut* [NY: Lewis Historical Pub. Co., 1911], 4: 1762). The house was still standing 1911) He died in Mansfield 29 Oct. 1732, age 91. His gravestone there reads:

"Here lies ye Remains of thatpious Godly man Dec" Shubael Dimmuck Husband to that Worthy Godly Woman Mrs Joanna Dimmuck who after he had sarved God & his people fell Asleep in Jesus Ocbr 29/ 1732 Ages 90 yrs & one month."

(As transcribed by Newton from Jacobus, *The Cranberry Family* (1945), 210).

His wife Joanna's death there 8 May 1727, age 83, the inscription was:

"Here Lieth ye body of Mrs Joanna
much ye wife of Deacon Shubael
Dimmuck who died May
8 1727 aged 84 years."

The Elder Thomas[1] Dimmock was baptized in Pinchbeck, Lincolnshire 7 Nov. 1604, the son of THOMAS[A] DIMMOCK (DuBourdieu cites Pinchbeck Parish Register 180 in George Cockayne, *Lincolnshire Parish Registers* 1:137; Robert S. Newton, "The Dimick Family" [Reston VA: typescript, rev. 1990], 19, gives Edward as father, citing Lucius Barbour, "Family Record of Dimmock-Manley" (typescript Hartford State Library) . According to family tradition, the immigrant Thomas came from Barnstaple, Devon, Otis 338).. The family name is inconsistently spelled DIMACK, DIMICK, DIMMICK, DIMMOCK, DIMMUCK, DIMOC, DIMOCK, DIMUCK, DYMOCKE, DYMOKE.

Newton shows that Dimmock was probably a member of Rev. John Lothrop's church in London before 1632. He left Weymouth, England 8 May 1635, with "wife and family" on the Hopewell, Capt. John Driver (Peter W. Coldham, "Genealogical Gleanings in England", Nat. Genea. Qtly. 71:173-4, Weymouth port book 876/1 in PRO E190; Newton 19, citing Port Books 876/1), and came to Dorchester. He must have made a good impression, for soon after arrival he is called "Mister", made a Selectman, and appointed to lay out land in Milton, six miles above the mill on the Neponset River (Dorch. TR ijth [11] Nov. 1635, Richard J. DuBourdieu, *Thomas Dimock. His Times* [Masters thesis, Lake Forest College, IL, 1991], [hereinafter DuBourdieu], 19, 20). In Dorchester he was given 20 acres in Jan. 1636, then two acres of marsh in Feb., and two more in June (Newton 21-2, citing NER Quarterly Oct. 1867, 21:333-8, 22:48) He was made freeman in Dorchester 25 May 1636 (Dorch. church rec. xii-xvii in DuBourdieu 26). However, he moved south to the south precincts of Dorchester, to today's Hingham in 1636 (History of Hingham 1:202 per DuBourdieu 47), where Rev. Joseph Hull was preaching.

Somewhere along the line, perhaps in Dorchester about 1636-7, he had married an ANN, whose maiden name is unknown (DuBourdieu 39). It was once supposed that she was daughter of the William Hammond of Watertown, but that is now disproved. It is possible that she was related in some way to another William Hammond who died in London before 1634, and to the Quaker William Penn (Newton 20-21). We get a clue to her character from Lothrop who tells of "(he excommunication of Goody Shelley for slander in saying "Syster Dimmick was proud."(4 June 1649, Lothrop 357). Their first child, John was born perhaps in Hingham about 1636-7 (DuBourdieu 37-8). By 1639 he had gone to Lothrop's town of Scituate briefly before moving on to Barnstable in March 1639 in advance of the Lothrop party.

Their first child, Timothy, was born in Barnstable, baptized by Lothrop 12 Jan. 1639/40 (Lothrop 329, 364), and also the first to die there, buried "in the lower syde of the Calves Pasture" in 17 June 1640 (Lothrop 351).

Otis, the Barnstable historian, credits Dimmock as the founder of the town (Otis 328-345). He was a member of the party of Richard Collicut of Dorchester who received the first grant to the town in 1637-8. On 5 March 1638/9 he was appointed head of the militia of Barnstable. He was the leader in the incorporation of the town on 14 (4 Old Style) June 1639. He was involved in the purchases of the whole north side of Barnstable. He witnessed the First Purchase, of West Barnstable from Serunk, on 26 Aug. 1644 (text in Trayser 30). And he and Isaac Robinson negotiated the Second Purchase of 1648, of the village of Barnstable. His house, the first built in Barnstable, stood on the north side of Route 6A, the Old Kings Highway, following the old Indian Path, on the east side of Dimmock Hill (Trayser 104 places it east of the E.A. Handy house in 1938). This is east of the Ned Handy house at 3674 Main Street (6A) , though sellers of the Isaac Davis house at 3688 Main Street think that the front of that house is on the site, which makes sense as a choice of a south-facing slope. Thomas Dimmock was one of three Deacons ordered to fortify their homes after an alarm in Oct. 1643. We have a description of Dimmock's fort house: "the lower story was built of stone. The second story overhanging the walls of the first story for added protection". (Barnstable Tercentenary Report quoted in NHR form B-58).

A plaque marks the location between 3688 and 3704 Main Street(#33 in Seven Villages 63, map 61) It reads "This Boulder//is erected as a memorial to//ELDER THOMAS DIMMOCK//who with//Rev. Joseph Hull//received the charter for the land//now occupied by the//Town of Barnstable//" //On this knoll//He built a fortification house in 1643//Barnstable Tercentenary 1939. Dimmock's Great Lot of 75 acres, granted in 1654 (Barn. TR 1, DuBourdieu 63), was the easternmost in the village, covering much of Cummaquid from his house east to the Yarmouth line at Mill Creek, the best grazing land in the village, and still productive as the Town Farm.

Dimmock was the leading man in politics, as Representative for six years 1640-2, 1648-50, and first justice in the county, 2 June 1640. He continued to lead the militia, appointed in 1642 to the Council of War, and head of the local band with rank of Lieutenant. On 7 Aug. 1650 he was ordained teaching Elder of the First Church (Lothrop 348, 364; Freeman 2: 247n), of which he had been a founder. This duty involved teaching the gospel, and recording the officers and members of the church. Thomas died in Barnstable before 4 June 1658. He became ill in the summer of 1657, and gave an oral will to Anthony Annable and John Smith (Their testimony of 4 June 1658, after his death in Ply. Wills 75, in *Mayflower Descendant* (1912), 14:230 cited by Newton 26). He is probably buried at Lothrop Hill, the second burial ground started in 1648 to replace the one at Calves Pasture, where his son Timothy was the first burial in Barnstable in 1640 (Lothrop records 17 June 1640, Trayser 13).

Otis's tribute to Dimmock's character is worth quoting: "Few of the first settlers lived a purer life than Elder Thomas Dimmock. He came over, not to amass wealth, or acquire honor; but that he might worship God according to the dictates of his own conscience; and that he and his posterity might here enjoy the blessings of civil and religious liberty. His duties to God, to his country, and to his neighbor, he never forgot, never knowingly violated. In the tolerant views of his beloved pastor, the Rev. John Lothrop, he entirely coincided. If his neighbor was an Ana-Baptist or a Quaker, he did not judge him, because he held, that to be a perogative of Diety, which man had no right to assume." (Otis 337).

_BURSLEY.

Shubael[2] Dimmock married in Barnstable April 1663 Joanna[2] Bursley, baptized in Sandwich MA 1 March 1645/6 (Lothrop 332) daughter of JOHN[1] BURSLEY and JOANNA[2] HULL. John was born in England about 1599. Otis speculates only on the basis of the name he used on arrival, BURSLEM, that he came from Burslem, Staffordshire (Otis 127), but that is hardly persuasive. He appears to have come from a good family, for he is called Mister in many early documents, and gentleman in grants for York, Maine, which attracted West Country gentry like our ancestor Thomas Bradbury.

The Great Migration Project concluded that Bursley came over in the fall of 1623 to what was to become Weymouth, in the company of Robert Gorges (Anderson, 1:280, 282, based on MHSP I:16:197). Banks suggests that he may have come over to Cape Ann in 1624 with the Dorchester Company, on the Katharine, Capt. Joseph Stratton, sent to Weymouth in 1624 by Sir Ferdinando Georges (Banks 56-7). By 1628 in Weymouth the oldest tax bill shows him paying for the arrest of Morton Anderson cites Bradford LB 43; Katharine W. Swift, *The Swift Family* [Whitinsville, MA: the author, 1955], 68). He shows up in 1629 in Weymouth as one of William Jeffrey's party. He became freeman 18 May 1631 (Mr. John Burslin requested 19 Oct. 1630; admitted at Mr. Jo. Burslyn 18 May 1631, Anderson citing MBCR 1:79, 366). He is called gentleman in the grant he got in 1631 for the first and second patents to York ME, but does not seem to have gone to Maine (Anderson 281 cites Council for New England 2 Dec. 1631, 2 March 1631/2, 101, 105 grants for Agamenticus, which became York). He was Deputy for Weymouth in 1636, but was dismissed at his request because the town was so small (Anderson 281: appointed 25 May per MBCR 1:174; dismissed 8 Sept. per MBCR 1:179).

In May 1639 Bursley moved to Cape Cod with Rev. Thomas Hull and Thomas Dimmock, as one of Barnstable's first settlers. Initially he lived in the back of his father-in-law, Rev. Hull's house in Barnstable village, opposite the first meetinghouse, and early meetings were held in his home (Rev. Lothrop recorded 24 March 1644, Freeman 2:258; Trayser 12; a plaque marks the location at 2786 Main Street, today's Capt. Thomas Harris House, NHR E 166).

Although Bursley had property in Exeter (now NH) 1643-5, Hampton and Kittery 1647-52, he remained in Barnstable as its Constable in 1645(4 June 1645 per PCR 2:83 in Anderson 281). In 1650 he moved to West Barnstable, just west of Bridge Creek, where he built a house on the south side of Old King's Highway, where it stood until torn down in 1827. Otis relates the story of a calf becoming stuck in the marsh to the south, and since he had a broken leg, told the women how to get the calf out by attaching it to a rope which pulled toward the house. He died in West Barnstable before the inventory of his estate 21 Aug. 1660 (Anderson 281 citing MD 17:159, PCPR 2:2:63; pro. 2 Oct, in PCR 3:201 gives first name Thomas in error; the death in 1670 per Freeman 2:271 does not refer to his son, who died 1726 per Otis 130,133), at age 61. His widow Joanna was living there in 1686, after her marriage to Dolar Davis, who died June 1673 (Otis 291). Dolar was the father (by a previous marriage) of Nicholas Davis, the Quaker who started the first business in Hyannis.

HULL.

At Sandwich on 29 Nov. 1639 (Lothrop 341) John Bursley was married to JOANNA[2] HULL, born in England, perhaps Colyton, Devon, about 1620 (Age 15 on departure from

Weymouth, England 20 March 1635 on shipping list in PRO, per Charles H. Weygant, "The Descendants of Rev. Joseph Hull" [Hull Family Assn., 1912, reproduced 1979 by Marion McHale] to Rev. JOSEPH[1] HULL, another pioneer of Barnstable, and an unknown mother who died in England.
Hull was baptized at Crewkerne, Somerset on 25 April 1596, son of THOMAS[A] HULL and his wife JOAN PESINGE (Phyllis P. Hughes, "A History of the Ancestors & Descendants of the Rev. Joseph Hull" [typescript, Boulder CO, 1983]. Thomas was buried at Crewkerne 29 Dec. 1636. He had married there on 11 Jan 1572/3 Joan Pesinge, daughter of RICHARD[B] and MARGERY PESINGE, PYSINGE or PEYSSUN. Joan was buried there 30 Oct. 1629. Her father Richard was son of JOHN[C] PYSINGE and ELIZABETH SAMWAYS or SALMON.

Thomas was the son of RICHARD[B] HULL and his second wife ALICE.
Richard[B] Hull's will of 10 Feb. 1558/9 was proved 10 June; he owned half of a cont [punt or barge?] mill. He had married about 1550 Alice ---, buried Crewkerne 20 Oct. 1557, leaving a will of 12 Oct. 1577, proved 25 Nov. 1587.

John, the youngest son in a large family, followed his eldest brother to Oxford, entering St. Mary's College at age 17 in 1612, to earn his MA at Oxford in 1614). It was seven years until he obtained a parish of his own, and may have spent the interim as assistant to his brother Rev. William Hull, who had succeeded the Rev. John Eedes, one of the translators of the King James Bible, as vicar of Colyton, Devon in 1611 (James W. Hull, *Rev. Joseph Hull* [Pittsfield MA: the author, 1898], 3).

He must have married his first wife, whose name is unknown, for he had his daughter Joane about 1620 (Age 15 on departure from England March 1635). One source believed she was named for her mother, JOANNA COFFIN, of a Devon family that came to America, and thus became ancestors of Anne Garrison Gould. Joanna died in England about 1632 (Narragansett Historical Reg. 1:145, in Weygant). It is not known when Hull married his second wife ALICE, born 1610 (Age 25 on departure from England March 1635), nor her family name, but it was probably in the Colyton area.

Then John got his own parish in a nearby town. For a decade 1621-32 he was Rector of the church of St. Giles in Northleigh, Devon (Installed at Northleigh 14 April 1621, Hull 1). Rev. Hull brought 21 families, mostly from Devon and Somerset over the Atlantic, leaving Weymouth, England, to arrive in Boston 5 May 1635. They went at once to Weymouth where he became the first minister of the church. Winthrop recorded the event: "At ...Wessaguscus [Weymouth] was made a plantation [by] Mr. Hull, a minister of England, and 21 families with him allowed to sit down there." (8 July 1635). Hull was made Freeman Sept. 1635. Moving south to Hingham about 1636 or 1637, he settled in the northeast part of town in Nantasket, later called Hull, not for him, but the town in England. He was made Deputy for Hingham 1638-9.

In May of 1639 he followed Thomas Dimmock to the Cape, where he built a house opposite the first church in Barnstable, which was on the west side of today's Lothrop Cemetery. The site of his house is marked by a plaque (2786 Main Street, Capt. Thomas Harris house, NHR E
166). Hull preached his first sermon in the open, on Sacrament Rock, which later rolled down onto the Kings Highway and had to be blasted to make way. Today it is marked by a brass plaque on the north side of 6A near the house of his descendant Dr. Frank Garran, opposite the West Barnstable School. Otis called Hull "the founder of the town of Barnstable." (Otis 2:27). He was chairman of the committee which incorporated Barnstable in 1639, and its Deputy to the General Court 1639-40, as well as first pastor of the church. Hull and his friends appear to have given a

warm welcome to the weary newcomers. The first Thanksgiving was celebrated at his house on a very cold day, 11 Dec. 1639 (Lothrop 351; Trayser 12). He and Dimmock were named Deputies to the Plymouth court starting Dec. 1639 (Named 4 June 1639, Trayser 26).

Yet, soon after the arrival of Rev. John Lothrop in Oct. 1639 Hull was totally eclipsed, and took up ministry in Yarmouth, for which he was excommunicated 1 May 1641 by Lothrop's church (Lothrop 356,364,1 May, Freeman 2:256n), and an order for his arrest issued on 7 May (Ply. Records 1:172 per Freeman 2:256n, 172). His wife rejoined the Barnstable congregation in 1643 after "confessing her evill", in Lothrop's words (Lothrop 350,11 March 1642/3; Freeman 2:256n), and he too later that year (Lothrop 364,10 Aug. 1643; Freeman 2: 256n), after a warrant for his arrest was issued (Plymouth Col. warrant March 1642/3; her submission 11 March 1642; his Aug. 1643 per Swift 70).

Although Hull was out of the ministry, he seems to have engaged in trading and raising of cattle and horses, which were fed on the rich marsh grasses of the area (Otis 24, citing deed of Richard Standuwick of Broadway, Somerset who sent cattle to Hull for a share of the profits, Ply deed 1:160) During the arrest warrant in 1642, Hull's cattle in Yarmouth were confiscated, and his extensive property also lost (Hull 19-21).

But about this time he sought a new ministry in New Hampshire. In 1643 Hull moved north to preach in York Maine, and Dover NH, where Gov. Winthrop protested his presence as a "very contentious man", but stayed until at least 1646. Although he was 50 years old in 1645, a Rev. Joseph Hull showed up as a volunteer in the Narragansett War, and must have given active service, for he was rewarded with lot # 37 in the Cedar Swamp (Volunteer # 116 per Weygant). About 1652 Rev. Hull returned to England and got a living for a decade as minister of the parish of St. Burien at Land's End in Cornwall, where the Quaker leader George Fox found him in 1659 (Hull 27).

Hull returned to America about 1659, and became minister at Dover or Oyster River, where the Quakers invaded his church. When Alice Ambrose and Mary Tompkins stood up "before the old man he began to be troubled; and having spoken something against women's preaching, he was confounded, and knew not well what to say, whereupon Mary standing up declared the truth to the people." (Bishop, *New England Observed* (1667), 386, quoted by Otis 22-23). In the melee of carrying Mary out of the meetinghouse Hull pinched her. The Quakers held a separate meeting that afternoon, which most of Hull's congregation attended.
Now about 65, he fled to the off-shore Isle of Shoals by 1659, and became minister there, where he died, at age 70, 19 Nov. 1665. The name of Hull's first wife, the mother of Joanna Hull, is not known.

OUR MAYFLOWER ANCESTORS, HOWLAND AND TILLEY.

Timothy[3] Dimmock married, probably in Barnstable, BETHIAH[2] (CHIPMAN) GALE, a widow with a daughter Mary Gale. She was born in Barnstable 1 July 1666 to Elder JOHN[1] CHIPMAN and HOPE HOWLAND, daughter of two Mayflower Pilgrims. Nothing is known of her first husband. She died in Windham CT about 1699.

Hope Howland was born in Plymouth in 1629, daughter of JOHN[1] HOWLAND and ELIZABETH[2] TILLEY. John Howland was born in Fenstanton, Huntingtonshire about 1592 (Died "above eighty years" PCR 8:34 in Anderson 1022) to HENRY[A] and MARGARET HOWLAND. He died in Plymouth 23 Feb. 1672/3, over 80. He was evidently well educated, as indicated by his library of about ten books at his death, including works by Tindall and Wilson, and annotations on the Old Testament (Inventory of 3 March 1672/3 in MD 11:73-7, citing PCPR 3:1:51-4)

Howland came on the Mayflower from London as a servant of Gov. John Carver (Bradford 441 in Anderson 1021; Banks 47; Sav. 2:479.), age 28. Crossing the Atlantic Ocean he was nearly drowned in a storm which washed him overboard. Gov. Bradford tells of the rescue of this "lusty young man", as he calls him: "it pleased God that he caught hold of the topsail halyards which hung overboard and ran out at length. Yet he held his hold {though he was sundry fathoms under water) till he was hauled up by the same rope to the brim of the water, and then with a boat hook and other means got into the ship again and his life saved. And though he was something ill with it, yet he lived many years after and became a profitable member both in church & commonwealth." (Bradford 59 in Anderson 1023). He was thirteenth signator of the Mayflower Compact on 11 Nov. 1620 (Sav. 2:479).

His services to the commonwealth were many. John was Assistant to the Governor of the Colony 1633-5 (Elected 1 Jan. 1632/3, 1 Jan. 1633/4, 1 Jan. 1634/5, PCR 1:5, 21, 32 in Anderson 1020), and nineteen times Representative, 1645, 1647-56, 1658, 1661, 1663, and 1666-7 (PCR 2:16, 94, 117, 123, 144, 154, 167; 3: 8, 31, 44, 49, 63, 79, 99, 135, 214; 4: 122, 148, per Anderson 1020). He was at the top of the list of Freemen in 1633, and on the subsequent lists to 1670 (PCR 1:3, 52, 4: 274, 4: 173, 197 per Anderson 1021).Active in the church, he assisted in the ordination of Rev. John Cotton in 1669 (Pope 244).

He was a partner in the colony's trading company, in charge of the Kennebec, Maine fur trading post in 1634, and on the colonial fur trading committee 25 years later (MD 11:10-11, PCR 3:170 in Anderson 1020). While he was leader at the Kennebec post two men were killed in a fight. In April 1634 John Hocking challenged their right to trade and sailed into the harbor. When Howland sent a boat out to warn them off it was taunted and defied by Hocking, so Howland told his men to cut Hocking's anchor line. Hocking responded by threatening to shoot Moyses Talbot, to which Howland bravely replied by asking him instead to shoot him, who had given the orders. But Hocking killed Talbot with a shot through the head, and was almost at once shot in the head (MD 11:10-11 in Anderson 2:1023-4).

Howland's last home was in Rocky Nook, north of Plymouth, but earlier lived in Plymouth village. He was a big landholder, having received grant of four acres in 1623, 40 acres at the west end of Island Creek Pond in 1637, Spectacle Island in Green's Harbor in 1638, six acres in the north meadow on Jones River, and 100 acres on the east side of the Taunton River (PCR 12: 4, 1:70, 102, 110, 168, 11:49, will). He also bought land in Middleborough and at Namassakett Ponds from William White, and a house and land in Middleborough from Capt.Thomas Southworth and from the Sachem Wampatuck (Will and inventory). He also owned land at Satuckett and Paomett, 12 acres at Winnatucsett River, land on the south side of Mill Brook, and a house in Colchester.

He died in his eighties at Plymouth 23 Feb. 1672/3, "a profitable instrument of good; the last man that was left of those that came over in the ship called the May Flower that arrived at Plymouth." (Ply. Col. Rec. 7: 34 cited by Pope 244). His will of 29 May 1672, probated 6 March 1672/3, left his widow Elizabeth their house in Rocky Nook, and 20 shillings to each of our ancestors Hope Chipman and Desire Gorum [Gorham] (PCPR 3: 1:49-50 in MD 2:70-3 in Anderson 1020-1). His estate came to £ 157/8/8 (Inventory 3 March 1672/3 in MD 2:73-4, citing PCPR 3:51-4, in Anderson 1021).

Elizabeth (Tilley) Howland's parents, JOHN[1] TILLEY and JOAN HURST also came over on the Mayflower, but died in the spring of 1621 after the first hard winter, and are buried on the hill above Plymouth Rock, in unmarked graves near the statue of the Indian chief. They came from the parish of St. Andrews Undershaft in London, on the north side of Leadenhall Street in the City (Banks 49). The fifteenth century parish church survived the Blitz. Nearby Elizabeth was probably born, about 1607. Her legacy of several books, including Works of Tyndall, Robinson's "Observations Divine & Moral" and Willson on the Romans, in addition to a Great Bible (Will of 17 Dec. 1686, pro. 10 Jan. 1687/8 in MD 3:54-7 citing BrPR 1:13-14, partially quoted in Anderson 1021-2), marks her unusual education for a woman of her day.

She died in Swansey 21 Dec. 1687, age 80 (VR 27).

Her father may have been with the Pilgrims in Holland before coming to America. Pope found a marriage of a Jan Telly, son of Paulus Tellij in Leiden in 1615, which may have been a first wife who died, followed by his marriage to Elizabeth who may have had a daughter Elizabeth by a previous marriage. Savage points to another John Tilley whom he thinks is probably the same, who had come to Cape Ann with Thomas Gardner in 1624, and oversaw that colony in 1635 before being killed by the Indians on the Connecticut River while he was master of a ship there in Oct. 1636 (Sav. 4:303), citing Winthrop 1:200 for his death).

Hope Howland died in Barnstable 8 Jan. 1683, and lies beneath the fourth oldest gravestone in Lothrop Hill Cemetery (Gustavus Hinckley's copy in Deyo 393; NHR inventory), reading:

HERE LYETH
INTERRED Ye BODY OF
MES HOPE CHIPMAN
Ye WIFE OF ELDER
JOHN CHIPMAN
AGED 54 YEARS
WHO CHANGED THIS
LIFE FOR A BETER
Ye 8TH OF JANUARY
1683."

9C
Origins of our
GARRAN ANCESTORS
in England
JWG 2 IX 96
Lincoln
LINCOLN
Boston
Farwell 1605
Pinchbeck
Harbling
Colby 1605
Moulton
NORFOLK
EAST ANGLIA
SUFFOLK
Colby 1592
Warwick
Hillmarton
Perkins 1538 f.
Gater 1576 f.
Howland 1592
Cambridge
BEDFORD
Henlow
HERTS
Stoke Nayland
Colchester
Wells
1662
Bocking
ESSEX
Oxford
Fletcher 1592
Hull AB 1614
LONDON
Stepney
Southwark
Stearns 1606
KENT
Tenterden
Sandwich
WILTSHIRE
Colburn
SOMERSET
DORSET
Crewkerne
Colyton
Dorchester
Weymouth
Dimmock 1636
DEVON
Barnstaple
Plymouth
CORNWALL
St Buryan
LANDS END
0
25
50
75 mi.
Base map Wld. Geo 193

CHIPMAN.

Elder John Chipman was born near Dorchester, Dorset about 1621, the only son of THOMAS[A] CHIPMAN and ----DERBEY. His father inherited a mill which was taken over by his wife's brother, Christopher Derbey, gentleman (Lovell 121). Thomas died in Brinspittal, Dorset, about five miles northwest of Dorchester (Otis quotes a long legal case 153-5, correcting the version in Reg. 4:22-23). Christopher's son Richard Derbey emigrated to Plymouth, Massachusetts in May 1637, bringing Chipman as a boy, an indentured servant. He learned the trade of carpenter. In Plymouth in 1647 Chipman married Hope Howland.

They moved to Barnstable village, where in 1649 he bought the house built in 1639 by Edward Fitzrandolphe on the southwest corner of King's Highway and Hyannis Road (Old Colony Records 12:180-1, cited by Otis 368, 156). Soon afterward he sold it and bought 45 acres of upland in West Barnstable from his brother-in-law Lt. John Howland, where they moved. As a carpenter, he probably built the high single house with a leanto, now gone, at 1064 Main Street, where the Timothy Chipman house of 1838 now stands (Gustavus Hinckley's description in Trayser, 445; NHR WBWn39).

His wife Hope joined the Barnstable church in 1650, and he followed in Jan. 1653. In 1652 John was one of the collectors of the whale oil owed to Plymouth colony (Freeman 1:206) John may have had surveying skills as well as carpentry, for he was appointed to lay out the boundary between Barnstable and Sandwich in 1661 (Freeman 2:266).In the same year he received some of the first grants in Succanessett, today's Falmouth (Freeman 2:424). Chipman was Deputy for five years 1663-5, 1668-9, and Barnstable Selectman 1665-8. In 1667 he was appointed to the provincial Council on War (Freeman 1:261).

Chipman was one of the pillars of the church. During the Quaker invasion, he was appointed to join the Rev. John Smith "to frequent Quaker meetings to endeavor to seduce them from the error of their ways" (7 June 1659, Freeman 2:265. On 14 April 1670 he and Henry Cobb were made ruling Elders of the church, and he was the last in Barnstable. Trayser says that the duties of the Elder were to teach the doctrine, and the ruling elder was in charge of membership, including excommunication and readmission, and ordination of officers (Trayser, 5).

After the death of his first wife Hope (Howland), Chipman remarried in 1684 Ruth (Sargent) Bourne, born Charlestown 25 Oct. 1642, married first to Jonathan Winslow of Marshfield (son of Josiah), and secondly to Richard Bourne of Sandwich. She was known as a healer of illnesses. They lived in Jarvesville part of Sandwich, the area of the former glass factory (Lovell 121). She died in Sandwich 7 April 1698, age 87, without issue. Before this second marriage, Chipman moved to Sandwich, for he became townsman there in 1679 (Freeman 2:73). The Barnstable congregation so regretted their loss that they offered him both salary and marshlands to continue as Elder. However, he stayed in Sandwich, and was called Elder when he was active in finding a successor to his friend Rev. John Smith in 1688 (Lovell 131). He died in Sandwich 7 April 1708, age 87. His gravestone is in the old town cemetery by the mill pond. His will of 12 Nov. 1702 was proved 17 May 1708.

His son, Deacon Samuel[2] Chipman owned land in Cotuit, but probably never lived there (Barnstable Proprietors Records 144, 188). However, the name is perpetuated in "Chipmans Narrows", as the strait between Grand Island and Cotuit was called in early deeds.
Among the notable descendants of Elder Chipman were the first U.S. Senator from Vermont,

Nathaniel^{5} Chipman (Thomas^{3}, Samuel^{2}), and New Brunswick Chief Justice Ward^{6} Chipman (Ward^{5}, John$^{4-3}$, Samuel^{2})(Reg. 15: 80).

NEWCOMB.

Capt. Jabez^{5} Dimmock married in the Second Church in Boston 5 Dec. 1722 MARY^{4} "Molly" NEWCOMB, born in Sandwich 4 March 1701 (named Mercy, VR 80) . "She died in Maine after 7 April 1743 (Maine Probate 231). She was daughter of PETER^{3} NEWCOMB and MERCY^{3} SMITH. Peter was born on the Isle of Shoals, off New Hampshire 1674 to Lt. ANDREW^{2} NEWCOMB and his wife SARAH. Peter married in Sandwich 11 March 1699/1700 Mercy Smith of that town. In 1702 he built the house that still stands at 8 Grove Street on the north side of the mill pond. Soon thereafter he opened the town's first inn for overnight guests (Lovell 136-7, photo 157). Among the prominent guests was the Rev. Samuel Sewall, who recorded his stays in 1706 and 1714. Newcomb was successful enough to send his son William to Harvard, in the class of 1722. Peter had to pay for William's breakage of glass in college, but the son sobered up to take over the tavern. Peter died there in early 1723. His will was proved 16 April 1723, leaving his estate to his wife Mercy, who died soon after, leaving a will proved on 17 Jan. 1723/4 (John B. Newcomb, *Newcomb Family* [Elgin IL: Knight & Leonard, 1874],[hereinafter Newcomb], 31).

Peter's father Lt. Andrew^{2} Newcomb, a fisherman at the Isle of Shoals in 1666 (shortly after the death of Rev. Hull there), was born about 1640 to Capt. ANDREW NEWCOMB and his first wife, Sarah whose maiden name is unknown; she died at the Isle of Shoals about 1674-7. In 1669 Andrew Jr. was living in Kittery, in a house on Emerys Point, on the southwest side of Spinney Creek, about half a mile north of Portsmouth (Alfred ME, York Co. deed 11:162, 20 April 1669 in Newcomb 14-15). But in 1671 he was Constable on Isle of Shoals, having sold the Kittery house in 1674. In 1673 he and his wife Sarah, whom he had married about 1661, were living on Hogg Island, Isle of Shoals (Exeter NH deeds 3:80, 19 July 1673 in Newcomb 16). His wife Sarah died about 1674, and he moved about 1675 to Edgartown on Martha's Vineyard. There, in 1676 he married Anna Bayes, born about 1658, daughter of Capt. Thomas Bayes and Anna Baker. By her he had eight children, including Emblem Newcomb of Chatham, whose daughter Elizabeth was the mother of the famous John Kendrick, the pioneer merchant on the Northwest Coast of America (Newcomb 20). Anna died in the summer or Sept. of 1731.
He may have retired from the sea to become a merchant. Andrew was a proprietor of Edgartown, which gave him shares in the town land divisions. In addition, in 1677 he bought the dwelling, barns, shops and hovels of the blacksmith John Daggett on the south side of town (13 Feb. 1677, sold 2 Feb. 1702, per Newcomb 17). He also owned land at Sanchacantaket, the site of the present courthouse, and the land that later became the Camp Meeting ground. In 1686 he bought Job's Neck from two Indians, the Sachem and his wife the Queen (13 May 1686, sold to his son Simon 22 Jan 1701/2, per Newcomb 17).

He served as town Constable in 1681, setter of tax rates in 1684, and townsman and overseer in 1693. He was appointed head of the militia in 1691, with rank of Lieutenant, and given charge of the fort (Newcomb 18, citing N.Y. Col. Mss. at Albany 37:230). Andrew died at Chilmark on Martha's Vineyard before 17-- (Sale of lands by Thomas Harlock, Newcomb 18). He died without a will, and there is no record of probate.

The senior Capt. Andrew^{1} Newcomb was born about 1618 in west of England, perhaps

Devon, and came to Boston by 1663, where he married secondly Grace Rix, born about 1620-5, widow of William Rix or Ricks (Newcomb 10; also SD 10:358, 12:46). They lived in the old house of Rix near the water-mill in Boston (Suff. Deeds 14 Feb. 1672, in Newcomb 10).
He was a master mariner for two decades, recorded as master of a ketch in 1667 carrying cattle and horses from Charlestown MA to Virginia (Charlestown records 281, 28 Feb. 1666/7 in Newcomb 9). In 1679 he was master of the sloop Edmund and Martha in New York harbor bound for Boston with a cargo of tobacco, probably from Virginia (N.Y. Col. Mss. at Albany,29: 13, 28 Aug. 1679). In Oct. 1684 he was on his vessel in Saco Harbor, out of Boston (Suff. Court files depos. of Philip Foxwell in Newcomb 9). He made his will in Boston 31 Jan. 1682/3

(Text in Newcomb 10-11; Suff. Probate 11: 48), but does not mention his son Andrew, by then prospering on the Vineyard. He died, perhaps at sea, Nov. 1686 (Newcomb 11; inferred from probate 8 Dec. 1686).

REV. JOHN SMITH.

MERCY[3] SMITH was born on Martha's Vineyard 3 Jan.1678/9 (Banks 3:448) to SHUBAEL[2] SMITH and his first wife MARY[3] SWIFT. She died in Sandwich about a year after her husband Peter Newcomb, for her will was proved 17 Jan. 1723/4.
Mercy's father Shubael styled himself a Gentleman, baptized by Rev. Lothrop in Barnstable 13 March 1653/4 (Written "Shubeall", Lothrop 335), the son of the Rev. JOHN[1] SMITH and his wife SUSANNAH[2] HINCKLEY, sister of the Governor Hinckley. He was evidently friendly with the Wampanoags, for he was appointed in 1695 as a sort of guardian in Shearjashub Bourne's purchase of land in Waquoit and Sandwich, "to assist the Indians in the sale, and to see that they receive a good and valuable consideration." (Freeman 1:332). Shubael moved to the Vineyard, where he died at Chilmark 5 April 1734, age 80 ((Charles E. Banks, *History of Martha's Vineyard* [Edgartown: Dukes County Historical Soc., 1966],[hereinafter Banks], 3:448).

Shubael's father Rev. John Smith appeared in Barnstable very early, in 1640, but little is known of his origins (Otis 2:236-7; Stanley R. Smith, "Direct Line of Descendants of John Smith" (typescript, about 1976) states without source that he came over on the White Angel at age 16 in 1630, but this must be treated with caution because of other errors like repeating Freeman's error of his father). He was born in England about 1614 (He retired in 1688, saying he was 74; Lovell 131) (not in Dorset like the Chipmans), and had some theological training, but it is not known where (Lovell 94, 128; Lovell points to the error in Freeman's (2:80n) giving Smith's father as Thomas Smith of Brinspittae, five miles from Dorchester, in a probate of Thomas Chipman of that place. Smith's parents are still unknown). He appears to have been unusual in his nonconformist views and had difficulty settling down in the ministry, though politically well connected.
He married in Barnstable 13 June 1643 SUSANNAH[2] HINCKLEY, whose brother was a leader of the colony (Intentions recorded by Lothrop, Freeman 2:247n). A hint of the future differences with his brother-in-law came in the engagement ceremony, when Rev. John Lothrop lectured the couple. As the minister recorded it: "John Smith & Susannah Hinckley contracted at ye Syster Hinckleyes house [bef?] me J: to: May 22. 1643. exercised uppon this Scripture Lett yoe: conversation be as becomes ye Gospel Phil:1.27."
The King James text reads: "Only let your conversation be as it becometh the gospel of Christ:

that whether I come and see you, or else be absent, I may hear of your affairs, that ye stand fast in one spirit, with one mind striving together for the faith of the gospel".
The passage is preceded by contrast of two kinds of preachers: "15 Some indeed preach Christ even of envy and strife; and some also of good will: 16 The one preach Christ of contention, not sincerely supposing to add affliction to my bonds: 17 But the other of love, knowing that I am set for the defence of the gospel."
John and Susanna had 13 children. Their first home was in the east side of Barnstable village, east of Lothrop's (Deyo 394).

A mark of Smith's influence in politics is his participation in the first negotiation with the Indians which resulted in the First Purchase of West Barnstable in 1644 (26 Aug., text in Trayser 30).In an unusual delay, Smith was not made Freeman for a decade after his arrival, until 5 June 1651. But Smith served as Deputy for three years beginning in 1656 (Deyo 381), He was appointed with Elder John Chipman to a committee to examine the Quakers in June 1659, and attend their meetings in hope of converting them (Lovell 94). They reported in favor of toleration (Banks's Martha's Vineyard 3:448).

However, the majority of the church disagreed with toleration. Since Lothrop was the principal minister, and Hull forced out, Smith preached only occasionally in Barnstable. By Sept. 1661 Smith had formed in Barnstable a "separate and distinct church", which a regional church council rejected as a schism, and punished with non-communication (Text in Freeman 2:267, subject of church council Sept. 1661, promulgated 4 June 1662).In 1663 Smith withdrew from the Barnstable church "on account of his conscience", but free of charge of "heresy nor morrall scandall" (Record in his own hand 12 Aug. 1663, text in Trayser 37-8). Whether this congregation was physically separated, perhaps in West Barnstable, has not been stated, but by this time Smith had moved to that area, just west of Bridge Creek, where he built a house on the north side of the Old King's Highway, near the Otis memorial and the Irving Paul House of 1910 at 1190 Main Street Smith sold this house to John^2 Otis, grandfather of the patriot in 1667 (21 Oct., NHR WBW 35B).

Smith then went to Long Island, then to New Jersey, where he bought land, and met Quaker emigres from Sandwich (Lovell 128; perhaps at Auchter Kill, now Perth Amboy, per Stanley Smith). The regular church declared him "noe member"in 1672" on account of his being different in opinion from them" (23 (4) 1672, text in Trayser 38), but later took him back on his return from New York, perhaps through the mediation of Barnstable rector Rev. Walley.

Rev. Smith finally got a call in 1673 to the long-vacant ministry at Sandwich, and served as their pastor 1673-89, successfully readmitting those who had been attracted to the Quakers (Lovell 109). Sandwich gave him personally ten acres in Aug. 1673, and then laid out land for the ministry above and below the Town House, and in the swamp by the ford at the site of the present Town Hall, as well as at "Pinguine Hole River" (Freeman 1:278). Smith was harassed by the old Quaker nemesis, Sheriff Barlow, who was fined in 1677 for threatening to drive Smith from town (Cited without source by Stanley Smith, which needs confirmation). Quakers complained that the Congregational meetinghouse was in such ruin that in a great rain Smith's book and clothes were drenched like those of the parishioners (Lovell 110). But Smith's family helped raise funds for repair, to which the town contributed £ 80 in 1680.

He built his saltbox house on Water Street that is now the Hoxie House, which was owned by his descendants until 1857 (Lovell 128). On retiring in 1689 he moved to a colonial house on Dock Lane near Church Street which may have become a boarding house for the Sandwich Glass Factory (Lovell 280). Samuel Sewall was shown around Sandwich by Smith during his visit of Oct. 1676 (Lovell 77). He died in Sandwich (not in VR). Susannah's death in Sandwich is not in VR.

Among Smith's descendants was the author of "Home Sweet Home" (John Howard Payne, grandson of Elizabeth Osborne, daughter of the doctor poet mathematician John, whose mother was Jedidiah Smith, the minister's granddaughter; Lovell 144-5).

HINCKLEY.

Smith's wife, Susannah Hinckley, was born perhaps at Tenterden, Kent, about 1619, the eldest daughter of immigrant SAMUEL[1] HINCKLEY and his wife SARAH (Otis 2:30ff). Samuel Hinckley was baptized in the parish church of St. John the Baptist, Harrietsham, Kent on 25 May 1589, the son of ROBERT[A] HINCKLEY and his second wife, the widow KATHERINE LEESE {or LOOSE?).(Rev. Robert J. Goode, "The Hinckley Entries in the Register of the Parish Church of St. John the Baptist, Harrietsham" (typescript ,1976, in Sturgis Library, Barnstable 929.2 H).

Samuel married at Harrietsham 8 May 1617 SARAH SOOL or SOULE, born about 1600 to THOMAS[A] SOOL and his first wife MARY IDDENDEN (Rev. Charles N. Sinnett, "Hinckley Family History" [typescript, Fertile MN, 1919 in Sturgis Library], 5). They moved to Tenterden, Kent, where their daughter was born.

Robert[A] Hinckley first appeared in Harrietsham in 1570 when his daughter Clemen was baptized. His first wife Elizabeth died 25 Oct. 1574, and he remarried to the widow Leese or Loose 10 Feb. 1575. His will was dated 5 April 1605, and he was buried at Harrietsham 27 March 1606/7 (E. Charles Hinckley, "Hinckley Heritage & History" [typescript, Ft. Worth TX, 3d ed., 1982 in Sturgis Library], 7).

Robert's ancestry can be traced back nine generations to the early XlVth century:
JOHN[B] HYNCKLEYE of Harrietsham, will 1577, son of:
JOHN[C] HENKLE of Lenham, Kent, died after 1522, no will, son of:
JOHN[D] HENKELE of Lenham, will 5 Jan. 1483/4 (In S.F. Hinckley papers in NEHGS; Reg. 75:238), m. MARGARET or MARJORIE; he was born Lenham c. 1435, son of:
JOHN[E] HENCLYE the Elder of Tenham (The switch of spelling from L to T is unexplained; Lenham has existed since Saxon times, and there is no Tenham in Ekwall), will Canterbury 1463/4, son of:
JOHN[F] HENCLINE, Jr. of Tenham, son of:
JOHN[G] HENCLINE of Tenham, son of:
JOHN[H] DE HENCLYNE of Tenham, renter of farms of Gore, Pete & Mellefield, assessed for knighting of Black Prince c. 1346, son of:
ADAM[I] DE HENCLYNE of Tenham, Kent, 1326.

The family of Samuel[1] Hinckley sailed on the Hercules in late March 1635 from Sandwich, Kent to Boston, to join Rev. Lothrop in Scituate. There they built house #19, on Kent Street. Sarah joined Lothrop's church there (#27, 30 Aug. 1635, Lothrop 324). In July 1640 he sold the house in Scituate to join Lothrop in Barnstable, where he built a one-story, thatched-roof house on the east side of Rowley's (today's Coggins or Hinckley) Pond, on land sold to him by Rev. Hull.

Samuel was one of the first to take advantage of the rich pasture of the Great Marshes in West Barnstable, and moved there, west of Bridge Creek, to what is known as the Otis farm, marked by the plaque on a boulder memorial to the birth of patriot Otis .

Samuel's wife Sarah died West Barnstable 18 Aug. 1656 (Otis 2: 32). He remarried 15 Dec. 1657 Bridget, widow of immigrant Robert Bodfish of Sandwich, who died 15 Nov. 1651 (Otis 1:68, VR 22). Samuel died West Barnstable 31 Oct., 1662 (Freeman 2:281) . He was appointed to the committees of 1659 and 1661 to view and purchase land from the Wampanoags at Saconesset, in Falmouth (7 June 1659, 4 June 1661, Freeman 1:239, 2:422).A liberal in religion, he was indicted twice for entertaining strangers (Trayser 182). His will of 8 Oct. 1662 left a large estate, mentioning his daughter Susannah Smith.

Samuel and Sarah Hinckley 's oldest child was Thomas Hinckley (1618-1705) , the last Governor of the Plymouth Colony (1681-6, 1689-92), leading military leader who had been an officer at the Great Swamp Fight in King Philip's War, lawyer, magistrate and politician (Trayser 180-1). He was a strict supporter of the church, and a critic of Rev. John Smith. His third child Meletiah Crocker was ancestor of Anne Garrison Gould through the Weld line (see chart 22) .

SWIFT.

Shubael Smith married Sandwich 6 Feb. 1677/8 (VR 24) MARY[3] or MARA SWIFT, born Sandwich 7 April 1659 (VR19), daughter of WILLIAM[2] SWIFT and his wife RUTH, perhaps TOBEY. Mara died 5 March 1682/3 (Banks 3:448; TAG 35:40 cited by Dodge 21). He remarried the next year Abigail Skiff, born to Stephen & Lydia Skiff in Sandwich 2 May 1666 (VR 47), and, died 7 June 1718 (not in VR, Banks 448) after bearing him four more daughters, and at last, a son Shubael Jr. The father remarried a third time 12 Oct. 1725 (not in Sandwich VR, Banks 448) to Anne Sampson daughter of James and Hannah Sampson of Portsmouth, RI. Shubael Sr. died at Chilmark 5 April 1734 (MV VR, Banks 448), leaving a will dated 10 Feb. previous, proved it the next 7 May.

Shubael's father William[2] Swift Jr. had come to Sandwich in 1637 with his parents, WILLIAM[1] SWIFT or SWYFT and JOAN ?SISSON? (Raymond J. Dodge, "Swift Family Genealogy" (typescript in Sturgis Library, c. 1976), 1 gives no basis for this speculation). He was born in England before 1627, perhaps at Bocking, Essex. He married in Sandwich, a Ruth, perhaps TOBEY (The only evidence for this is Nat. Cyclop, of Am. Bio. 26:356, which has no support in town or church records, or in Tobey genealogies. It does not seem likely that she was a daughter of the founder of the local family, Thomas[1], who appeared in Sandwich in 1644, and married a local woman only a few years before Ruth's marriage to Swift (Rufus Tobey & Charles Pope, *Tobey Genealogy* [Boston: Charles H. Pope, 1905], 15, 17, 22). There were four other Tobeys in the Massachusetts Bay at the time, perhaps related. Was Ruth a sister of the first Thomas Tobey? (Parish records in England might establish the relation). In 1654 he and others agreed to build a mill, which was not done (Swift, 1; R. A. Lovell, Jr., *Sandwich: A Cape Cod Town* [Sandwich: the town, 1984], 37). In 1655 he contributed to the building of a town meeting place. He served as Sandwich Constable in 1660 and 1668, and seven years as Selectman, 1673-6, 1678, 1680-1. He was Deputy for four years 1673-8 (Deyo 288). He died in Sandwich Jan. 1705/6, based on his will of 15 Dec. 1705, presented 29 Jan. 1705/6 (Barn. Prob. 11:217 cited by Dodge).

The senior William[1] Swift or Swyft had come to America from Bocking, Essex, in the Great Migration, about 1630-1634. He received land as a proprietor of Watertown in 1634, when he was given lot #14 of 40 acres, plus five acres in Beaver Brook Plowlands (Bond cited by George H. Swift, *William Swift of Sandwich* [Millbrook NY: Round Table Press, 1900], 1). In

1637 he sold his properties there and moved with his family to Sandwich where he bought the largest farm, on Standish Road in North Sagamore, part of which was still owned by the Swift family in 1900 (Lovell, 129; Swift, 1). He died in Sandwich before the inventory of his estate Jan. 1643, which came to £ 72/11. His widow Joane administered the estate, and lived another 20 years until her death in Sandwich 26 Nov. 1663 (Not in VR). Her will of 12 (8) 1662 was proved 7 April 1664 (Dodge 19 citing MD 16:21, publ. in Ply. Wills 16:21).

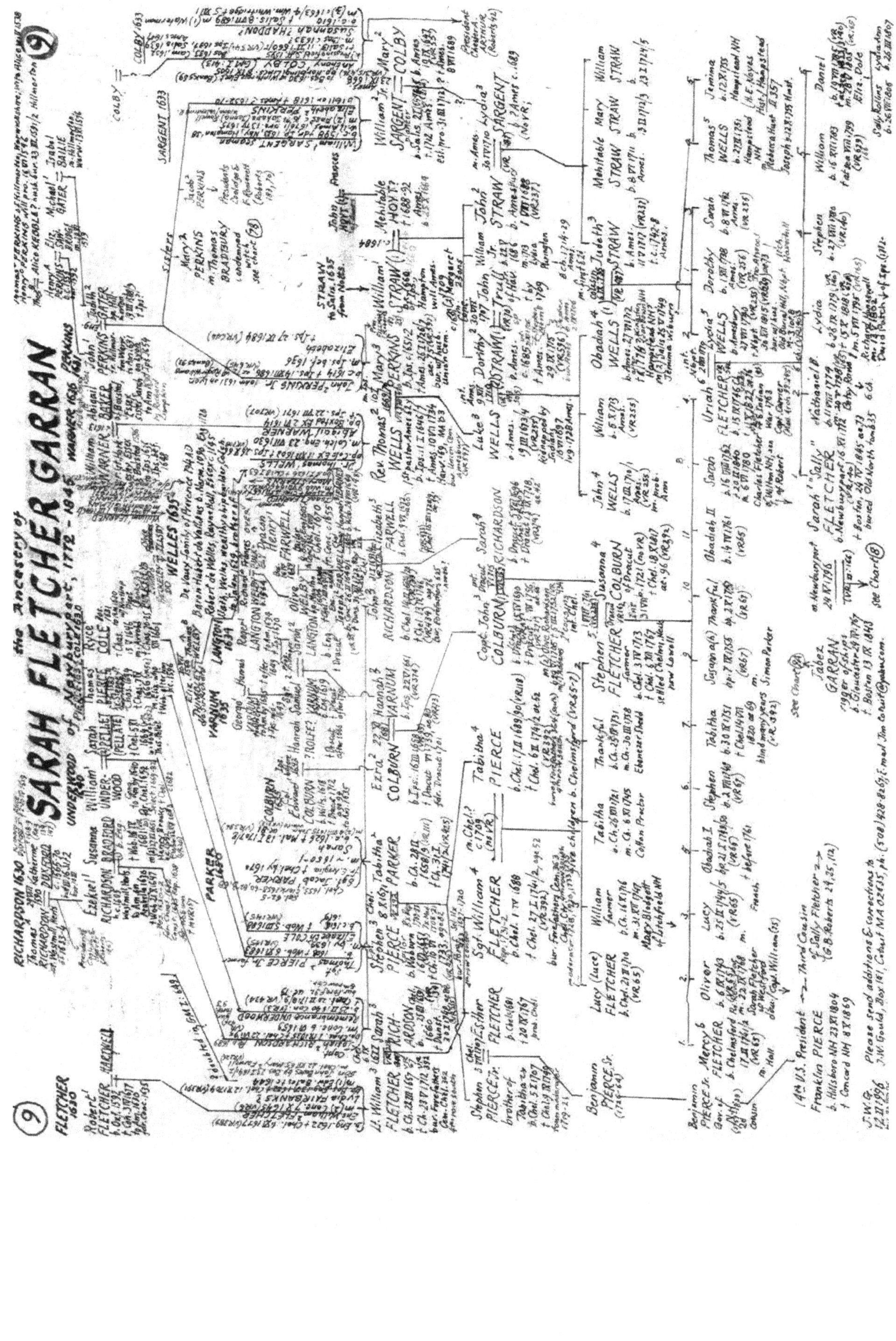

9
the Ancestry of
SARAH FLETCHER GARRAN
of Newburyport, 1772 - 1845

FLETCHER.

Caroline Garran Goddard's mother was SARAH[7] "Sally" FLETCHER, born Newburyport MA 16 Nov. 1772 (VR 140; Massachusetts Cert, of Birth), eldest of six children of URIAH[6] FLETCHER and LYDIA[5] WELLS. She died in Boston 24 April 1845, age 73, and was buried 27 April in tomb 35 of Old North Church.

Sally was third cousin of President Franklin Pierce, through her great-grandmother Tabitha Pierce (Gary Boyd Roberts, Presidents, 24, 25, 112).

Her father Uriah was born in Chelmsford MA 15 Sept., 1746, sixth generation from the founder of Chelmsford and Concord, Robert Fletcher. His parents were STEPHEN[5] FLETCHER and SUSANNA COLBURN of Dracut. His intention to marry LYDIA[5] WELLS of Amesbury was published in Newburyport 2 Aug. 1770 (VR 502) Of Lydia more below.

Uriah was an Indian fighter during the French and Indian War, under Capt. Jonathan Carver, in 1763 (Wilson Waters, *History of Chelmsford* [Lowell: Courier-Citizen, 1917], 178, citing Massachusetts Arch. 99:245). He died in Newburyport 11 Oct. 1822, age 76, and was buried there in Old Burial Hill, row M-3, lot 8.

Uriah's father Stephen Fletcher was a farmer, who settled Chelmsford Neck, now Lowell (Fletcher 126). He was born in Chelmsford 3 April 1713 (VR 67), eldest son of Sergeant WILLIAM[4] FLETCHER and his wife TABITHA[4] PIERCE. He died in Chelmsford 6 Dec. 1767 (VR 392 age 55). Intentions to marry Susanna Colburn were published in Dracut 31 July 1741 and next day in Chelmsford (Dracut VR 163, Chelmsford VR 232). Of her more later.

Sergeant William was born in Chelmsford 1 April 1688 (VR 62) to Lt. WILLIAM[3] FLETCHER and his wife SARAH[3] RICHARDSON. The marriage to Tabitha Pierce is not recorded, but probably occurred in Chelmsford where they both lived, in 1709, the year before the birth of their first child. Of her parentage, more below.

Sergeant William was a political leader in Chelmsford, as Representative to the state legislature 1731-2, and town moderator for four years, 1728, 1730, 1733, and 1735, and town treasurer for seven years, 1717-20, 1725-6, 1728, and frequently Selectman for much of two decades 1713-35 (Waters 757-8). He was on the committee which built the new meetinghouse in 1710-12 (Waters 677). The first schoolhouse in town was built under his supervision in 1718, a brick building east of Forefathers Cemetery, and he was one of the largest contributors (Waters 556; map facing 352).

Sergeant William died in Chelmsford 27 Jan. 1741/2 (VR 392). He is buried with his wife in Forefathers Cemetery, Chelmsford Center.

Lt. William[3] Fletcher was born in Chelmsford 21 Feb. 1656 (VR 67, Ctr.), son of Ensign WILLIAM[2] FLETCHER and his second wife, LYDIA, whose maiden name is unknown (The assertion that she was daughter of Richard Fairbanks of Kiddington, Lincs, and Boston MA, and his wife Elizabeth Dalton of Boston, Lines. has been doubted by Anderson 1:649, who show this couple had no children). He married in Chelmsford 6 Sept. 1677 (VR 307) Sarah[3] Richardson of Chelmsford, of whom more below. He was made Freeman 11 March 1689, and was commissioned Lieutenant in the militia in 1704 (Fletcher 14). Like his father, Lt. William was active in town government, serving as Treasurer of seven consecutive years, 1705-11, and Selectman for three, 1701, 1709-10 (Waters 756). His wealth and prominence are shown by his donation of 50 shillings for the elaborate tombstone of the minister Thomas Clark in 1708 (Waters 71; photo op. 192). Lt. William died Chelmsford 23 May 1712 (VR 392), and was buried in Forefathers Cemetery, Chelmsford.

Ensign William[2] Fletcher was born in England about 1622, and came to America in 1630 with his father ROBERT[1] FLETCHER, born Oxford about 1592 (Theodore C. Bates, *Bates and Fletcher Genealogical Register* (Boston: n.p., 1896), 1, calculating his birth from his death at 85, and his age 38 years on arrival 1630. Source of Oxford birth is not given), and his wife whose maiden name may have been HARTWELL. Robert was a founder of Concord in 1635. Robert died 3 April 1667 (Concord VR 19), age 85.

His son Ensign William became Freeman 10 May 1643 (Edward H. Fletcher, *Fletcher Genealogy* [Boston: Alfred Mudge, 1871], 11). He married in Concord 7 Oct. 1645 (VR 6; recorded as William ffletcher and Lidia Bats the 7th (9) mo. 1645). (2) LYDIA BATES, widow of Edward Bates, who had died about 1644. She died Chelmsford 12 Oct. 1704 (VR 391). Her son by Edward, John Bates was to marry Mary Farwell, daughter of our ancestor Henry[1] Farwell, as related below.

Robert and his son William were among the three who took the initiative on 4 Oct. 1654 to establish a church in Chelmsford, and William and his wife were the first named members on 27 May 1655 (Waters 10, 12). William was one of the founders of the town government of Chelmsford, which first met in his home in 22 Dec. 1654. He was a Trustee of the town for its first six years, then Selectman continuously for the decade of the sixties, and again in 1673 and 1676 (Waters 754-5; 12). He was also the first Constable, chosen in 1655 (Waters 13). His house of 1654, the first frame house in town, was located about 100 feet northeast of the Crosby House, and 900 feet east of the "Bill Fletcher House" just north of the center of Chelmsford (Waters 394, 38; map following 80; photo of Bill Fletcher House facing 608). On the first tax list in 1671 he is the second wealthiest man in town (Waters 59). He died in Chelmsford 6 Nov. 1677. (VR 389).

RICHARDSON.

Lt. William[3] Fletcher married" in Chelmsford 6 Sept. 1677 SARAH[3] RICHARDSON (VR 307), born in Chelmsford 25 March 1659/60 (VR 134) to Capt. JOSIAH[2] RICHARDSON and REMEMBRANCE[2] UNDERWOOD (VR134 spells name RITCHESON, and her mother's name Rememberans). Sarah died in Dunstable MA (VR 215) (Tyngsboro?) 30 Jan. 1748 (under Flatcher, Dunstable VR 215)(buried in Fletcher private burial ground Tyngsboro), age 88. Josiah was baptized in Charlestown 1 Sept. 1635 (not in Charlestown VR), son of EZEKIEL[1] RICHARDSON and his wife SUSANNA BRADFORD. Josiah Richardson came to Chelmsford by 1658, and built the foundation of a house on the Westford-Lowell Road by digging out the bank (Waters 37, 43, 35). He was made Freeman in 1674 (Waters 404), and soon became a leader in town politics. He served as Constable in 1667, for 14 years as town Selectman, in 1668, 1673, 1679-88, and 1694, with the interim of five years as Town Clerk 1689, 1691-4, and as provincial representative in 1689-90 (Waters 755-6). He was made Captain of the Militia 20 June 1689, in charge of the west end of town (Waters 128, 134). Josiah and William Fletcher were given land in 1669 to build the second sawmill in town, probably on Stony Brook, to produce boards at the maximum price of four shillings per hundred (Farwell 55). He died in Chelmsford 22 July 1695, age 61 (VR 436). His gravestone in Forefathers Cemetery reads:

"HERE LYES Ye BODY OF
CAPT IOSIAS
RICHARDSON AGED 61 YEARS
DIED THE 22 OF JULY 1695" (Waters 717).

EZEKIEL[1] RICHARDSON was born at Westmill, Hertfordshire (south of Buntingford) about 1605, son of THOMAS[A] RICHARDSON, who had married 24 Aug. 1590 KATHARINE DUXFORD or DURFORD, born about 1565-70 and died about 1631-2. Thomas Richardson died in Westmill about 1633-4.

The son Ezekiel and his wife probably came to America on the *Arabella* with Winthrop in 1630, or at least with his fleet (Banks 81). They settled in Charlestown 6 July 1630 (Reg. 98:363). He had a houselot on three acres at Highfield (on the way to the Penny Ferry to Malden), on the north side of the highway to the Mystic River, between his brother Thomas on the east, and Thomas Squire on the west (Estate as of 1638, Wyman 810; Richard Frothingham Jr., *History of Charlestown* [Boston: C.P. Emmons, 1852], [hereinafter Frothingham], 90). He also got a dozen other lots, including 90 acres in Waterfield, and 35 acres of woodland in Mystic Field.

Since there was no church in Charlestown, they had to travel to Boston, where they were members of the First Church, from which they were dismissed 11 Oct. 1632 to found the First Church in Charlestown (Sav 3:535; Frothingham 70). He had been made Freeman 18 May 1631. He was Constable in Charlestown 1633, and Representative 1634 and 1635, and Selectman for five years beginning in 1635, when the first government was formed (Frothingham 52), then again in 1637-9 and 1641.

In 1637 he signed the protest against the conviction of the Rev. John Wheelwright for sedition of supporting Anne Hutchinson's doctrine of grace over works, but Ezekiel repented in Nov. 1637 after the protest was also called seditious, and had his name crossed off (Frothingham 73-4).

As Charlestown Selectman in 1640 he led the settlement of Woburn, exploring the site in 15 May 1640 (Samuel Sewall, *History of Woburn*, [Boston: Wiggin & Lunt, 1868],[hereinafter Sewall], 10). and calling the organizing meeting at his house in Charlestown (13 Feb.1640/1 per Woburn Record I:4,on site 16 Feb., Sewall, 15). The family moved to Woburn in 1641, settling in Richardson's Row, later Washington Street, Winchester (Letter from marine biologist Win Richardson 26 Jan. 1996). Ezekiel was on the first board of Selectmen on 9 Nov. 1643 (Sewall 24), (Frothingham 108n). He was one of the founders of the church in Woburn 24 Aug. 1642 (Sewall 20). He died in Woburn 21 Oct. 1647 (VR 157). His widow Susanna remarried to Henry Brooks, and died in Woburn 5 Sept. 1681 (VR 20).

UNDERWOOD.

Josiah Richardson was married by Capt. Simon Willard in Concord 6 June 1659 to Rememberance Underwood, born in Concord 27 Feb. 1639/40 (VR 3), daughter of WILLIAM[1] Underwood and SARAH PELLET (PELLATE). Remembrance died Chelmsford 20 Feb. 1718/9, age 79 (VR 434). Her father William had come to America by 1640, to Concord, and became one of the founders of Chelmsford with the Fletchers in 1654 (Waters 11-12). They settled on the west side, near Francis Hill, on the Stony Brook Path, now the Westford Road (Waters 11-12).Underwood suffered damages from the Indian raids in 1676 (Waters 121). A political leader in town, he served as first Trustee in 1654, and 15 years as Selectman, in 1667, and continuously from 1669 to 1682 (Waters 754-5). He died in Chelmsford 12 Aug. 1697 (VR 452). William Underwood married SARAH, the widow of Thomas Pellet or Pellate. She died in Chelmsford 5

Nov. 1684 (VR 452).

PIERCE.

Sgt. William[4] Fletcher's marriage about 1709 is not recorded, but probably took place in Chelmsford where his wife TABITHA[4] PIERCE and he lived all their lives. She was the daughter of STEPHEN[3] PIERCE and TABITHA[2] PARKER, great-great grandparents of President Franklin Pierce (1804-1869) (Gary Boyd Roberts, Presidents, 24, 25, 112).

Stephen[3] Pierce was born in Woburn 16 June 1651 to Sgt. THOMAS[2] Pierce and ELIZABETH[2] COLE. Stephen married in Chelmsford 8 Nov. 1676 (VR 292) TABITHA[2] PARKER), who was born in Chelmsford 28 Feb. 1658/9 (VR 111) to Sgt. JACOB[1] PARKER and his wife SARAH (VR 118). Tabitha died in Chelmsford 31 Jan. 1741/2, age 81 (VR 425). Following his marriage to Tabitha, in 1671 Stephen was granted "a small parsill to sett a house upon, 20 rods---south west side of beaver brook bridge" in the center of Chelmsford (Waters 541). He was a tailor by trade (Waters 578, 676), and Corporal in the local militia (Waters 676 (1701). He too became prominent in town and state government, holding office as Representative 8 years 1709, 1711-15, 1717, 1721, Town Moderator seven years 1708, 1710-11, 1715-6, 1720-1, and Selectman for 11 years 1697-1700, 1703, 1705-6, 1708, 1718-20 (Waters 757-8). Stephen died in Chelmsford 10 June 1733, age 82, and was buried in Forefathers Cemetery (Waters 740).

Sgt. Thomas[2] Pierce was born in England about 1608, and came to America, perhaps from Stepney, in the East End of London (Biography of Henry Hill Pierce, b. 1875 in *Burke's Landed Gentry* [16th ed., London: 1939], 2866; this gives no source; there is no connection to British landed gentry, just origins of "American Families with British Ancestry"), with his parents THOMAS[1] and ELIZABETH PIERCE to Charlestown 2 l Feb. 1634, when both parents joined the church (Admitted 21 (12) 1634/5, Wyman 756; Pope 361; Cutter 1477). He was on committee to divide land in Woburn 1668, 1677/8 (Sewall l38-9) Committee to build the first Meeting house 1671-2 (Sewall 79); he had Small Pox 1679 (Sewall 123). Thomas[2] died Woburn 6 Nov. 1683 (VR 145). His wife Elizabeth (Cole) died in Woburn 5 March 1688 (VR145).

Thomas the father was one of the founders of Charlestown government in 1635 (Frothingham 51). He became Freeman 6 May 1635 (Sav. 3: 431), presumably a year after their arrival. He was granted four acres of planting ground in early 1636, and probably built there the house in the West End of the village, on the south side of the highway between Richard Sprague and Edward Bruton (Wyman 756). He also had nine other pieces of property, including 62 acres in Waterfield.

The first Thomas, born about 1583-4, died in Charlestown 7 Oct. 1666. Thomas's will of 7 Nov. 1665 was made in Cambridge when he was about 82, leaving a small bequest to Harvard (Probated 22 March 1666/7, Wyman 756). His wife Elizabeth, whose maiden name and marriage date is unknown, was born about 1596, and died in Woburn. They moved to Woburn where he was a proprietor in 1643, and town officer.

COLE.

By 1639 the son, Sgt. Thomas[2] Pierce, had married, probably in Charlestown, to Elizabeth[2] COLE, born in England about 1619 to RYCE[1] COLE and his wife ARROLD (also written Arald, Arrald, Arrall, Harald, Harrald, etc.), whose maiden name is unknown. The couple came with their daughter Elizabeth to Boston with the Winthrop fleet in 1630, although Wyman found him in Charlestown in 1629 (Banks 71; Wyman 228). Ryce became Freeman in Charlestown 1 April 1633 (As "Rise Coles" in MBCR 1:367 per Anderson 426; Frothingham 80). He signed his name Rice Coles in the document establishing Charlestown government in 1635 (Frothingham 51). He and his wife were founding members of the Charlestown church. He was granted four acres of planting ground in 1636, and lived on Middle Row between the Millway and W. Johnson. His will describes his "house dwelling & an acre of ground in the neck" (MPR Misc 106-07 per Anderson 427). He also owned eight other properties.

Ryce died in Charlestown 15 May 1646 (VR 10), and his will of May 1646 was proved 1 April 1663. His executrix was his widow Arrold, who died Charlestown between 20 and 26 Dec. 1661, leaving an estate of £ 92 (Will of 20 (10) Dec. 1661, proved 26th, MPR case #4798 in Anderson 428; Wyman 229). Forty acres of Cole's land located northwest of Mt. Discovery and west of the Aberjohn River [Woburn to Winchester, Mass.] were sold by his son-in-law Thomas Pierce Jr. to Thomas Richardson (Wyman 756).

PARKER.

Stephen Pierce's wife Tabitha[2] Parker was the daughter of Sgt. JACOB[1] and SARAH PARKER of Chelmsford. The Parker family may have come from Ipswich, Suffolk, or Wethersfield, Essex, where they were known (Dawes-Gates 465n), although another source says one brother Abraham Parker was born in Marlborough, Wiltshire (Cutter 1457). His service as town clerk in Chelmsford suggests very good education. Jacob Parker, one of five brothers, the first of whom had come to America before 1640 to Charlestown, but was not there long enough to own property (Wyman 726 does record the death of his brother John Parker in Billerica 14 June 1667, citing relationship in court record, and death in county record), before moving to Woburn by 1650.

Jacob and Sarah Parker probably came to Chelmsford (from Woburn) before the Fletchers, for their child was the second born in town, Jan. 1653/4 (Sarah, b. 14 Jan., Waters 7). They were in Woburn in May 1653 when he and his three brothers James, John and Joseph petitioned to settle in the Chelmsford area (Waters 3). Two brothers moved to Chelmsford early, and Jacob's homestead was in the south part of town, on the Billerica Road, near the town farm of 1917 (Waters 39). They joined the First Church shortly after the Fletchers and Mrs. Underwood, in 1655 (Waters 12). He became the first Clerk of the town in 1658, serving until 1661, again 1662-3 and 1666 (Waters 8, 39, 754). He was also Selectman for four years 1662-5. Jacob died in Chelmsford before 6 April 1669, when his wife SARAH administered his estate.

Sarah Parker was a large taxpayer in Chelmsford in 1671 and 1672 (Waters 60, 616). Her maiden name is unknown. She was born in England about 1626. After his death Sarah Parker remarried in Malden 4 Aug. 1675 to Capt. John Waite of Malden, many years Deputy to the General Court, and its Speaker, as well as one of the compilers of the first Massachusetts laws in 1647-8, and their revision of 1680 (Dawes-Gates 465). She died in Malden on 13 Jan. 1707/8, age 81, and was buried in Bell Rock Cemetery there with the inscription, "Ye Memory of ye Just is blessd."

COLBURN.

The parents of Stephen^5 Fletcher's wife SUSANNA COLBURN are unrecorded (The town clerk permitted us to check the original records against the printed vital records 2 July 1996; church records were searched, with negative report 3 Sept. 1996), and may never be found. We know her year of birth, about 1721, (VR 392). We also know from her marriage record in two places that she was from Dracut (Chelmsford VR 232; Dracut VR 163; microfilm of original in Holbrook microfiche #14, Massachusetts VR: Dracut, 1710-50, 285: "Stephen Fletcher" of Chelmsford Entered With me John Varnum Town Clerk his Intentions of Marriage with Susanah Colburn of Dracutt"), and therefore probably the daughter of one of the many grandsons of Dracut founder Edward Colburn. By process of elimination we believe her to be the daughter of JOHN^3 COBURN and SARAH^3 RICHARDSON. Support for this lies in the four year gap in town and church records for their children, 1720-4, between birth of Sarah on 4 Nov. 1719, and Phineas on 6 May 1725, in which span the couple is likely to have had more than one child. Further support would be found if the name Susanna appeared in any of the immediate ancestors.

Capt. JOHN COBURN was born in Dracut 15 April 1690, to EZRA^2 COBURN and HANNAH^2 VARNUM. He died in Dracut 19 July 1756. His house was on 60 acres of land, the building located about 50 feet northeast of the 1748 meetinghouse, near the corner of Clark and Pleasant Streets (Silas R. Coburn, *History of Dracut* [Lowell: Courier-Citizen, 1922], 190, citing deed of 1 March 1750 of Capt. John Colburn to son Joshua, and 4 Nov. 1757 to Nathaniel Mitchell; later property of Daniel Abbott, Rev. Nathan Davis and George M. Clark).

RICHARDSON.

Capt. John Coburn married twice, first in Dracut (intentions published May 1715, VR163) to SARAH^4 RICHARDSON, born in Dracut 5 Aug. 1696 (Chelmsford VR 132)), to JOHN^3 RICHARDSON and ELIZABETH^2 FARWELL. Sarah died in Dracut 13 Sept. 1738 (VR 274), age 42. John then remarried (intentions 12 Jan. 1744) to his wife's cousin, OLIVE^2 RICHARDSON ADDAMS of Chelmsford widow of Abel Richardson, (VR 171), born 29 June 1706 to Capt. Jonathan Richardson. Olive died in Dracut 5 March 1752 (VR 272).
Sarah's father was JOHN^3 RICHARDSON, son of JOSIAH^2, and thus Sarah and Stephen were second cousins. John Richardson was born in Chelmsford 14 Feb. 1669 (VR133), son of Josiah^2 Richardson and Remembrance Underwood, whom we told of before. He died Chelmsford 13 Sept. 1746 (VR 434), age 76.

John was a pioneer mill owner on the Merrimac River, and anticipated the big iron works there by a century. John lived in North Chelmsford, where in 1700 he bought the first grist mill that had been established there on Stony Brook by Daniel Waldo in 1695, and one sixth right in the nearby sawmill (Waters 52-3). In 1707 the town gave John the right to build an iron works on Stony Brook, and two years later the right to use Newfield Pond for power (Waters 53, 656, citing Msx Deeds 26:277, and town book A, 170, grant of 4 March 1706/7). The attempt to dam the pond failed in "a most remarkable catastrophe". Waters relates, "As the workmen were digging a channel through the bank of the pond the pressure of the water suddenly burst the weakened bank and the water rushing out carried with it a negro [named "Jack"] who was in the ditch at the time and buried him in a mound of sand washed by the water to the meadow below. Thus this pond, covering 100 acres, was all drawn off with exception of about an acre in the lowest part." —Jack's body was never recovered. The pond remained dry until 1824, when someone succeeded in damming the pond, and actually producing iron at a blast furnace from

1825 until 1909 at least. In 1707 the town laid out a road to Richardson's mill, now Mill Street North Chelmsford, to give access to "an inexhaustible bed of bog ore" on Robert Richardson's farm (Waters 54, 658).

John Richardson was one who joined with Lt. William[3] Fletcher on the committee of three that supervised the building of the Chelmsford Meeting house of 1712 (Waters 677). He was the first named on the committee with Sgt. William[4] Fletcher to assign the seats according to rank (Waters 678). He and his brother Jonathan built the belfry and turret of the church in 1719 (Waters 688). John was town Selectman for five years, 1722, 1724-6, and 1731 (Waters 757-8).

FARWELL.

John Richardson married in Chelmsford 31 Jan. 1693/4 (VR 306) ELIZABETH[3] FARWELL, born in Chelmsford 5 June 1672 (VR60) daughter of Ensign JOSEPH[2] FARWELL and HANNAH[3] LEARNED. Elizabeth died in Chelmsford 9 May 1722, age 49 (VR433 age 51). Her father, Joseph Farwell was born in Concord 26 Feb. 1640/1 to HENRY[1] FARWELL and OLIVE WELBY. He died in Old Dunstable (today's Nashua NH) 31 Dec. 1722, age 82. He owned land in Chelmsford, Dunstable and Groton (John Dennis Farwell, *The Farwell Family*, [No loc.: Frederick and Fanny Farwell, 1929],[hereinafter Farwell], 41). From his father he inherited land in Chelmsford in 1670. He was Ensign in the Chelmsford militia 1687-95.

In 1700 Joseph bought the Waldo Farm in Dunstable, and took the southern half, called the Butterfield Farm, in what was later to be Tyngsboro. He moved there with his family from Chelmsford. His was one of the seven garrison houses in 1711. The house was owned by his descendant Joseph Farwell in the 1920's. He was active in Dunstable town government, as Selectman for five years 1701-2, 1705, 1707 and 1710.

His gravestone in the Old Dunstable cemetery (called the Little Cemetery) in South Nashua NH bears a winged skull and a border of rising spirit, and reads: "Here Lyes ye Body// of Ensign// JOSEPH FARWELL// who Decd Decembr 1722 in ye 82nd// Year of his Age."(Photo Farwell op. 44. His will of 13 Nov. 1711 spells his name ffarewell several times (Photo in Farwell facing 42, text 43). Of his wife Hannah see below under Learned.

Ensign Joseph's father, Henry[1] Farwell, the immigrant, was born probably in Boston, Lincolnshire in 1605, son of WILLIAM[A] FAREWELL, tailor of Boston, and his first wife, whose name is unknown. After her death, about 1615, he remarried in Boston 17 July 1617 widow
Joan Cole, who was buried in Boston Jan. 1641/2 (Farwell 19). William was made Freeman of Boston (England) 19 May 1620, a member of the city council, and Sergeant at the Mace 1631. William was buried in Boston 5 Sept. 1637, having made his will four days earlier.
William[A] Farwell was the son of JAMES[B] and KATHARINA FARWELL (Farwell 14). James) made his will 5 July 1593, proved 3 Aug. 1593 (Text from Norwich Archdeaconry Court 1593, p. 185 in Farwell 15). He was buried in Raynham, Norfolk. James's mother was ANNYS[C] FARWELL, whose will was made 10 Jan. 1561/2.

Henry Farwell followed his father's trade of tailor, and was elected a member of the Boston city council, and one of the Sergeants at the Mace in 1635. However, he resigned the last office in Dec. 1635, perhaps with intent of emigration. His name appears in a deed of sale of a house in Boston in Feb. 1636 (Feet of Fines, 15, Lincoln, 9 Feb, 1635/6, with his father and wife, selling a house to his father-in-law, text in Farwell 12).

Henry came to America in 1636 with his wife and two children, to become one of the first settlers of Concord. He was allotted land in the east quarter of town, his son inheriting 28 lots of 280 acres (David-Parsons Holton, *Farwell Ancestral Memorial* [New York: the author, 1879],[hereinafter Holton], 5). He was made Freeman 22 May 1638/9.

After nearly two decades in Concord Farwell became an early settler in Chelmsford, moving north from Concord about 1655 (Waters 578). His home was on the Billerica Road, on the same side of the road as Abraham and Jacob Parker, but closer to the village, near the Timothy Adams house of 1890 (Hurd, cited by Farwell 17). Farwell was named first Deacon of the church in Chelmsford in 1660, "to take charge of the linen & pewter &c." (Waters 21). He was also the town drummer, who signaled the alarm of Indian attack (Waters 22, 48). He was granted six acres in the Newfield in 1667, though this may not have been his original homestead (Waters 836). By trade he was a tailor (Waters 39, 578), and his death in 1670 probably created the vacancy that was filled in that trade by Stephen Pierce's arrival.

Henry and Olive's daughter Mary Farwell married in Chelmsford 22 Dec. 1665 John^{2} Bates, son of Edward Bates and his wife Lydia, who remarried to our ancestor Ensign William^{2} Fletcher. Henry died in Chelmsford 1 Aug. 1670. He made his will 20 days before his death, on 12 July, spelling his name Henery ffarwall (Text in Farwell 26-27, with photo facing 26). He wrote his wife's name Oliff, His estate came to £ 343/11 (Holton 6)

Henry Farwell married in St. Botolph's church, Boston, Lincs. 16 April 1629 OLIVE WELBY or WELBYE, who came from the minor gentry of the area, known as Holland. She was baptized at Moulton, Lincolnshire, 1604, second daughter of RICHARD^{A} WELBY and FRANCES BUCKLEY or BULKELEY (Farwell 30).Olive died in Chelmsford, on 1 March 1661/2, age 88. Although a birth or baptism record cannot be found, it is believed that Frances was one of the 12 unnamed sisters of the Rev. Peter Bulkeley, first minister of Concord church, and son of EDWARD BULKELEY, D. D. and OLIVE ILLSBY of Lincoln (Farwell 31).

An Olive Welby was a legatee of Richard Whittingham, gentleman of Holland, Lincolnshire in 1616, with Mr. Cotton, Dr. Bulckley, and Peter Bulkley, lending credence to the relationship (A. L. Maddison, Lines. Wills, #125, text in Farwell 30-31. Frances (Bulkeley) Welby was buried at Moulton 1610. She had married at nearby Whaplode, Lines. 1595 to Richard^{A} Welby, baptized at Moulton 1564, the second son of THOMAS^{B} WELBY and ELIZABETH THIMBLEY, daughter of Sir RICHARD THIMBLEY of Irnham, Lincs. Richard and Elizabeth were married at Irnham 20 July 1560, she as the widow of John St. Paul of Nettleton.

Thomas^{B} Welby of Moulton died at Bath 1570, and was buried within Stallys church(Farnwell 31).He was the second son of THOMAS^{C} WELBY and CATHERINE BRAY, daughter of Thomas or John BRAY of Middlesex County. She was executrix of her husband's will in 1524, and remarried a ___Hall.

Thomas^{C} Welby was born in 1484, son of THOMAS^{D} WELBY and JOAN LEAKE, daughter of Sir RICHARD LEAKE. Joan (Leake)Welby died 18 Dec. 1400, as recorded in a brass plate in the floor of the Holbeach, Lincs, church: "Orate pro anima Dominae Johannae Welby, quandam Filiae Ricardi Leake, Militis nuper uxoris Thomae Welby, Armigeri. Obiit xviii Die Mensis Decembris, Anno Dom. mcccc.//cujus aminae propitietur Deus."(Text from Farwell). Sir Thomas^{D} Welby was Justice of Peace 1483, High Sheriff of Lincolnshire 1491-3 (Farwell 32). He held lands in Gedney, Lines., Halsted, North Carleton, and Croyle, and gave the lands he bought at Little Herum for the support of a Chaplain at Moulton. He inherited from his brother Richard his lands in Stixwould and Halsted, and Valentines in Moulton. He was buried in the Chapel of St. Mary's in the monastery of St. Guthlace, Croyland 1496.

Sir Thomas^{D} was the son of RICHARD^{E} WELBY and the daughter and heiress of

THOMAS STYNT. She has a memorial in Holbeach, Lincs, church. Richard Welby was Member of Parliament 1450-2 just before the War of the Roses, and J.P. 1451-5, 1461-4 (Farwell 33). His will of 12 Aug. 1464 was proved the same year in Lincoln.

Richard^{E} Welby was the son of Sir RICHARD^{F} WELBY of Multon, Lincs., Richard was Knight of the Shire to Parliament in 1422, at time when the Commons was becoming more powerful. He was son of Sir ROGER^{G} DE WELBY and his wife MARGARET. Roger was High Sheriff of Lincolnshire 1397. His will of 1410 was proved that year, and he was buried at Multon (Text of will in Lincoln Cathedral in Farwell 36). The Welby (Welleby in Doomsday Book) ancestry is traced back to 1066 (Farwell 37, citing Burke's Peerage (1908) and a dozen other sources).

The Welby arms are Sable, a fess 'twixt three fleur de Lys Argent; Crest: "upon the Helm, on a wreath and sables, an armed arm, the hand charnes issuing out of a cloud azure, in a flame of fire, manteled gules, doubled argent"; motto: "Sorte Contentus"(Granted to Ricjhard Welby, "a near Kinsman of Olive Welby" per Farwell) 29; Illus. in Farwell" 30; my translation).

LEARNED.

Ensign Joseph[2] Farwell married in Chelmsford on Christmas Day 1666 (VR226) HANNAH[3] LEARNED, born in Woburn Aug. 1649 to ISAAC[2] LEARNED and MARY[2] STEARNS (Farwell 43). Of Mary more below under Stearns. Isaac was baptized in the south London suburb of Bermondsey, Surrey 25 Feb. 1625/6, the only son of immigrants WILLIAM[1] LEARNED and GOODITH OILMAN. William was born about 1581, and married in St. Olave's church, Southwark, Surrey 22 April 1606 Goodith (a distinct given name, contrary to Bond who would make it Judith or Goodwife) Gilman (Anderson 2:1165) Isaac came over as a boy with his parents in 1630.

They were among the first settlers of Charlestown in 1630 (Chas. TR 6 in Anderson 2:1165) where they had a house just south of the old meetinghouse (the location of the meetinghouse is unclear: Wyman's description is dated 1637, which would be the second site, located vaguely by Frothingham 95 "between the town and the neck", before its removal in 1639 to permanent quarters between the nineteenth century Town House and the entrance to Main Street. Wyman further locates Learned's house NE of Broad Rowe). They were admitted to the church 6 Dec. 1632 (Chas. Church rec. 8 in Anderson 2:1164). The father became Freeman 14 May 1634 (MBCR 1:369 in Anderson 2:1164), and helped establish the Charlestown government (Frothingham 51; Charlestown TR 38 in Anderson 2:1164). In 1636 he was one of the committee of six to draw up a set of laws. In 1637 he joined with Ezekiel Richardson in protesting the conviction of Rev. Wheelwright in his support of Anne Hutchinson, but repented and had his name crossed out when threatened with charge of sedition (Frothingham 73-4; MBCR 1:208 in Anderson 2:1165).

They were among the founders of Woburn, for which he signed the town orders in 1640 (Henry Bond, *Genealogies of. . . Watertown* [Boston: NEHGS, 1860],[hereinafter Bond], 333), was one of the first seven members of the church there in 1642. He was on the first board of Selectmen of Woburn 1643-5, and Constable 1643-7. His wife Goodith, the mother of our Isaac, appears to have died before him, for his widow is recorded as Jane (or Sarah), but we have no record of this marriage, only of Jane's death in Woburn 24 Jan. 1660/1 (MPR #13856 in

Anderson 2:1165). William died in Woburn 1 March 1646/7 (VR 111).

The son Isaac[2] Learned married in Woburn 9 July 1646 Mary[2] Stearns (VR 161, Farwell 44). Isaac sold his Woburn property 2 April 1652 to Bartholomew Pierson, and moved to Chelmsford. There he served as Selectman. He died there 29 Nov. or 4 Dec. 1657, age 31. Administered estate 1658, granted to his widow Mary 1658 (Msx Ct 1:153 per Woburn VR 161n). His widow Mary remarried 19 June 1662 John Burg(e) late of Weymouth. She died Chelmsford 8 or 9 Jan. 1663, age 47 (VR 370).

STEARNS.

Mary Stearns was baptized at Stoke Nayland, Suffolk 6 Jan. 1627 daughter of ISAAC[1] STEARNS and MARY BARKER. Isaac was a near neighbor of the future Governor Winthrop, with whom they were to come to the New World (Sav. 4:173). The mother was daughter of JOHN and MARGARET BARKER of Stoke Nayland. They were married in 1622.

The family came to America with Winthrop on the Arabella in 1630, and were among the first settlers in Watertown, near Mt. Auburn. There, he grew tobacco and wheat, as shown on his inventory. Isaac became a Freeman 18 May 1631, and was Selectman several years. In 1647 he and William Biscoe were appointed to have the first bridge built across the Charles River. Isaac died Watertown 19 June 1671, leaving a will dated five days earlier. The success of his farming is shown by the large amount of cash on hand at his death, £ 335 (Bond 452). He left 14 lots of 467 acres and a large estate of £ 524/4 (Inventory of 28 (4) 1671 in MPR 4: 129-30 quoted by Bond 451n). His widow Mary died Watertown 23 April 1677.

Isaac spelled his name STERNES. Farwell gives a coat of arms for both Stearns and Learned families without evidence of parents or title (Farwell 55, 44).

COBURN.

EZRA[2] COLBURN was born in Ipswich 16 March 1658, seventh child of EDWARD[1] COLBORNE. He died in Dracut June 1739, age 80. He came with his parents from Ipswich to the rugged frontier, on the north side of the Merrimac River, at today's Dracut, about 1671. In 1682 he inherited from his father on eighth of his Webb grant (Silas R. Coburn, ed., *Genealogy of the Descendants of Edward Colburn/Coburn* [Lowell: Courier-Citizen, 1913], [hereinafter Genea.Coburn], 19, and probably built a house there after his marriage to HANNAH[3] VARNUM on 22 Sept. 1681 (Chelmsford VR 338). He grew up in the Colburn garrison house which fought off the Indians in 1676, as an Indian fighter like his elder brother Edward who was killed at the Brookfield Battle of 1675 (Waters 115, 133, 135, 143). The distance from the church in Chelmsford and the danger of travel were probably factors in his failing to attend meeting, for which he was brought to court in 1692 (Waters 410-1). He was one of the citizens who successfully petitioned the General Court to establish the separate town of Dracut in 1701 (Coburn 3). In 1693 he shared with his brothers a fourth of his father's Shatswell grant, and inherited other lands in Bare Meadow and along the Merrimac.

EDWARD[1] COLBURN, the immigrant, was born in Wiltshire, England about 1618, of unknown parents. The family name is always pronounced like the modern spelling, "Coburn", but colonial documents inconsistently spelled it COBAN, COBEN, COBORN, COBUN, COBURN, COLBON, COLBORN, COLBRON, COLBURN, COLBURNE, COLEBRON,

COULBORNE, etc. Later members of the American family pretended to a coat of arms, without any proof (Genea Coburn 4-5).

Edward first appears on the passenger list of the ship *Defence* of London, under Capt. Edward Bostock, which arrived in Boston on 8 Oct. 1635 (Banks 169), 54 days out of Liverpool (6 Sept.)(Dracut 371, Genea Coburn 2). He went north to Ipswich where he was employed as farmer by Nathaniel Saltonstall. He never owned land there, but may have rented the Saltonstall farm of 800 acres (Kenneth L. Bosworth, *Edward Colborne of Ipswich* [Baltimore: Heritage Books, 1994], 5). In Ipswich before 1642 he married HANNAH, perhaps ROLFE (Dracut 371, citing "references in private letters"). Could she have been a daughter of Daniel Rolfe, one of the first grantees in Ipswich, just south of Gov. Dudley on High Street, who was killed at the Narragansett fight in King Philip's War (Thomas F. Waters, *Ipswich in the Massachusetts Bay Colony* [Ipswich Historical Soc., 1905],[hereinafter Waters Ipswich], 203, 377, map facing 338). Edward's name appeared in Essex County court records in 1652 as surety for John Broadstreet, accused of witchcraft, "haveing familiarity with the devill" (Waters Ipswich, 287). On 30 Sept. 1668 he paid £ 1200 to John Webb (alias Evered) for his 1600 acres north of the Merrimac in today's Dracut (Genea. Coburn 6-7). Two thirds was paid in wheat, malt and pease, and the balance in beef, pork and Indian corn. Only £ 50 had to be paid in a year, and £ 70 the next year, then £ 300 yearly each 26 March until paid off. It is clear from this that Colborn was an astute judge of farm potential as well as a skillful farmer.

Edward Colborn was the first person to settle in "ye wildernesse on ye Northerne side of Merrimac River" permanently, though several people bought land around him at earlier dates. A thousand acres of the land lay west of the former Pawtucket Indian reservation, west of the Clay Pit Brook, and extended 3.25 miles up the Merrimac, with the river on the south and west, in today's Pawtucketville (Genea Coburn 9; map Dracut 176). Shortly after the deed was signed the seller John Webb was killed by a whale in Boston Harbor, when he tied the line attached to the harpoon around his waist, and the supposedly dead whale came to life, dragging him from the whaleboat to his death in the water (Oct. 1668, Bradstreet's Journal in Reg. 9:44, quoted by Waters 535). Webb's widow sold Colburn the rest of his lands on the Merrimac (Genea Coburn 11). Colburn was evidently making more than enough to pay off his debt to the Webbs, for in 1671 he bought the so-called Shatswell Purchase of 500 acres which lay west of his lands (3 April 1671, Thomas).

Edward Colburn's garrison house was still standing in 1922, between Varnum Av. and the Boulevard, opposite Totman Road (Dracut 355, photo 288; Genea Coburn 14; photo frontispiece). It had been built as a fortified house in 1664, before Colburn bought it from Webb. Here the Indian Agent Daniel Gookin held an annual court for trials. The site was strengthened during King Philip's War, under Edward, who had the rank of Corporal in the militia (Genea Coburn 13; Waters 826). However, Colburn and his neighbor Samuel Varnum were caught outside on the river crossing over to look after their cattle on the Chelmsford side. During this raid of March 1676, a band of 40 Indians killed two of Varnum's sons before they could recross, and burned the surrounding unfortified Colburn houses to the ground (Waters 133, 135, 538; account of battle from Drake's Hubbard 1:222). The garrison was maintained here under Corporal Colburn to at least 1691, during the first French and Indian War.

It is not known when the first ferry across the river was established, but it was located on Edward Colburn's land, at the Durkee Rd. or Old Ferry Road (Dracut 260).

Edward died in Dracut in 1712, at age 96 (Genea Coburn 15). It is not known where he was buried, perhaps on his farm (Genea Coburn 5), or in the Varnum Cemetery (Dracut 278-9), near the Varnum homestead on the cross street between the Methuen-Dracut roads. Nor is the death of his wife Hannah known, but it occurred after 20 Aug. 1666, the birth of their last child, Lydia.

VARNUM.

Ezra^{2} Colburn married HANNAH^{3} VARNUM of Dracut, born in Ipswich 22 May 1661 (VR 374), daughter of SAMUEL^{2} VARNUM and SARAH^{2} LANGTON. Samuel was born in England about 1619 (He deposed 25 Sept. 1683 his age 64, John Marshal Varnum, *The Varnums of Dracut* [Boston; David Clapp, 1907],[hereinafter Varnum], 16 from Ips. Court Records 5:14),, to GEORGE^{1} and HANNAH VARNUM or VARNHAM. He came to Ipswich about 1635, when he was 16, with his parents. George's name first appeared in Ipswich in 1635 as an abutter southeast of Phillip Fowler's six acres on the hill next to town (Varnum 14; Waters Ips. 493). He also had land in the north part of Ipswich to the southeast of Fowler's six acres in 1636. In 1639 George Varnum was given three acres of Mr. Bradstreet's land. His houselot, however, was in the center of town, on the east side of the High Street, between John Gaines on the north, and Robert Paine on the south, directly east of the meetinghouse (Map in Varnum 16). George Varnham was the first recorded Ipswich Bell Ringer and Town Crier, appointed in 1640 "for ringing the bell, keeping clear the meeting house and publishing such things as the town shall appoint", and to be paid for his "paynes" 6 pence annually by each citizen whose property was under £ 100, 12 pence for £ 100-500, and 18 pence over £ 500 (Waters Ipswich 66, 107).George's will of 21 2nd month 1649 left his house to his wife for her life, and two thirds of the estate to his son and executor Samuel (Essex Probate 1:110 quoted in Varnum 14; photocopy op. 14). He died soon thereafter, for the inventory of 12 8th month 1649 came to a modest £ 87, mostly for the house. His widow Hannah died after 1649 (not in Ipswich VR).

The son Samuel^{2} married in Ipswich before 1658 (not in Ipswich VR) SARAH^{2} LANGTON, daughter of ROGER^{1} LANGTON, LANCKTON or LANKTON. Roger Lankton became a Freeman in Boston 4 March 1634/5, so probably came over in 1634 (Varnum 17n, quoting Hammatt; Sav. 3:56). He went to Ipswich by 1648, when he was a subscriber to Major Dennison, and lived on the east side of Brook Street and John Newman's land in 1655, on land he acquired from George Farlow (Waters Ips. 492, 394, map facing 386). His house was near the home of David F. Dow in 1909. The inventory of his estate was made 14 Jan. 1671 (Varnum 17), so he probably died in Ipswich in late 1670.

In early 1664 Samuel bought from John Webb (alias Evered) half of his 1100 acre farm north of the Merrimac, in what is the first reference to the area as "Drawcutt"(Msx Deed 20: 10 Jan. 1665, text in Dracut 7-9, 19). The origin of the name is from one of the three villages of Draycot in Wiltshire, from which John Webb had come (Ekwall 144; Waters 534-5; Dracut 19; Charles Cowley, *History of Lowell* [Boston: Lee & Shepherd, 1868], 22 gives the alternate of being named for a parish in Wales (none in Ekwall), original home of the Varnums).
At first Samuel did not settle on the land because of its insecurity, but lived on the south side of the Merrimac near Hinchman's garrison house (Dracut 418).With the protection of Colburn's garrison house, they moved across the river by 1671 (Waters 536 shows tax of Varnum north of the river on 30 March 1671), perhaps to one of the houses which they had bought from Webb. The so-called Varnum Garrison house that was torn down before 1922 at Riverside Street was actually built by Thomas Richardson, who sold it to Samuel Varnum's son John (Dracut 55-6, 350, photo 336; Varnum 123; Waters 91). Before this, however, on 18 March 1676, Samuel's two eldest sons, George and Samuel Jr. were killed by the Wamesit Indians as they were crossing the river with their father and sister to milk their cows (Varnum 19, 20, 538, citing Drake's Hubbard,

1:222; Dracut 49, 55; Samuel G. Drake, ed., *History of the Indian Wars. . .* [from the work of Rev. William Hubbard [Roxbury: W. Elliott Woodward, 1865], 1:222, 50, refers also to N. H. Historical Collections 11:271). One of them fell dead into his sister's arms, and Samuel shouted to the accompanying soldiers, "Don't let dead men sit at their oars."(Waters 113). On the following 15 April the Indians burned 14 or 15 houses (Waters 538 citing Drake's Hubbard 1:222), no doubt including the Varnums' so it was probably after this that the new garrison house was built.

In 1691 Samuel had been appointed Sergeant in the militia in charge of four men, probably at his garrison house (Waters 133, 531). The next year Samuel was paid for killing five wolves (Waters 431). However dangerous the north frontier the Chelmsford church did not appreciate his attending meeting just once in the summer of 1692, and brought him to the county court in Charlestown along with his neighbor Ezra Colburn (Waters 410-11).

Samuel and his wife have no gravestones, but are probably buried in the Varnum Cemetery near the Varnum homestead, on the cross street between the upper and lower roads to Methuen (Dracut 278-9). Here also is the gravestone of Gen. Joseph[5] Bradley Varnum (1750-1833; Samuel[4], Joseph[3], Samuel[2]), U.S. Senator, first Speaker of the House of Representatives in Washington D.C. 1807-11, member of the Massachusetts Constitutional Conventions of 1780 and 1820 (Dracut 279). His more famous brother Revolutionary War Gen. James M. Varnum (1748-89), leader at the Battles of Long Island and White Plains, and at Valley Forge, member of the Continental Congress, was buried in Marietta OH where he was Judge of the Northwest Territory Supreme Court (Varnum 141ff.).

.

WELLS.

Uriah[6] Fletcher gave intentions to marry in Newburyport 2 Aug. 1770 LYDIA[5] WELLS, great-granddaughter of Rev. THOMAS[2] WELLS, first pastor of Amesbury, graduate of Harvard 1669, which honored him with an MA in 1703.

Lydia was born in Amesbury 27 July 1740 (VR 255) to OBADIAH[4] WELLS and his first cousin JUDETH STRAW. Lydia died in Newburyport 30 Dec. 1815, age 73 (VR629), and lies next to her husband in the Old Burial Hill, Newburyport, M-3, lot 8.

Lydia's father, Obadiah Wells was born in Amesbury 27 June 1712 (VR 255). He died in Sandown part of Kingston NH 22 Dec. 1777, age 64 (Kingston VR 169 (typescript in NEHGS). He moved to New Hampshire after his second marriage in Salisbury 25 May 1749 to Jemima Wiburn, and by whom he had two children born in Hempstead,NH: Thomas, born 27 Feb. 1751, and Jemima, born 10 Dec. 1755 (Harriette E. Noyes, *History of Hampstead* [Boston: George B. Reed, 1899], 1:431, 2:356-7, (1903); a Jemima Wells married Kingston 23 March 1774 Peter Eastman, Kingston VR 79).

His prominence in the community is indicated by his being given the second pew in the front row of the church in 1749 (31 Aug. 1749, Noyes (1899) 11:24). He formally transferred membership to the church in Hampstead from Amesbury in Nov. 1753, but was living in Kingston NH the following year. In 1776 he signed the Association Test in Hampstead (Hoyt 812; Noyes (1899) 296, 356). He had previously married Lydia's mother Judeth Straw in Amesbury 6 Sept. 1736 (VR 487). Judeth was his mother's niece, so they were second cousins. More on the Straw family when we discuss his mother.

Obadiah's father Luke[3] Wells, was born in Amesbury 19 March 1673/4 (VR 255), son of the Rev. THOMAS[2] WELLS and his wife MARY[3] PERKINS. At the age of 22 he was kidnapped by the Indians. His intentions to marry widow DORITHY[2] (STRAW) TRULL, widow of John Trull of Haverhill , were published in Amesbury 9 Dec. 1710 (VR 505). Of Dorithy more shortly. His death is not recorded, but was after 1728, when he was living in Amesbury. Rev. THOMAS[2] WELLS was born in Ipswich 11 Jan. 1646/7 (Sav. 4:478) to Dr. THOMAS[1] WELLS and ABIGAIL[2] WARNER. He died in Amesbury 10 July 1734, age 87 (g.s.). He was a member of the class of 1669 at Harvard, and was the first person to receive the honorary M.A. in 1703. He was in Wells ME at the end of 1669, and preached in Kittery and the Isle of Shoals the next year. In 1672 or 3 he became minister of the church of Amesbury, and served there 62 years, until his death 10 July 1734 (Ames.VR 597).His will was made 7 Aug 1728 and proved 29 July 1734. His gravestone in Union Cemetery Amesbury reads:

"Interred here the Body of,
the Revd Mr THOMAS WELLS.
first Pastor, of the first Church
of CHRIST in Amesbury. Who
Departed this life, July ye 10th, 1734,
in the 87th. year of his
Age, & 62D, of his Ministry,
having served his Generation by
the will of GOD, he fell on sleep, and
(we trust) enjoys a Prophets reward.
for tho' Israel should not
be Gathered, yet would x
the faithfull ministers of
the Gospell, be glorious
in the Eyes of the Lord."(Hoyt 350).

The Rev. Wells was the son Dr. Thomas[1] Wells, baptized Colchester, Essex 11 Dec. 1602, brother to Nathaniel Welles, wealthy shipbuilder and innholder of that seaport, who left Colchester for Salem 1629 on the *Susan E. Ellen* from London with Richard Saltonstall, became freeman in Boston 17 May 1637, then went to Rhode Island in 1640 (Will of 3 July 1666, died Oct. 1666).

The Welles family claims descent from the DE VAUX family of Provence 794 A.D. (Woodwell 17-19; claims are said to be stated in the Church of Street Clare in Naples), to Harold de Vaux who came from Normandy to England about 1106; his son Baron Hubert de Vallibus, born in Normandy 1090, who came to England 1120; his son William, b. c. 1120, who came to Rayne Hall, Essex which he obtained with the adjoining manor of Wessing from King Henry II; his son Robert de Welles, b. c. 1145 Rayne Hall, Essex, and held the manor of Little Rayne; his son Thomas, b.c. 1175; his son Henry b. c.1200, d. 1293; his son Thomas b.c. 1240, d. 1315; his son Walter, b. Essex c. 1270, d. 1325; his only daughter and heiress Eleanor b.c. 1330, who married John Pyke, whose son Nicholas, b. 1360, died without issue, succeeded by his sister Maud, heiress./J/Dr. Wells came to Salem in 1629, and practiced in the area until his death in Ipswich 26 Oct. 1666.

Dr. Wells had married in Colchester, Essex 23 Aug. 1630 (Warner) ABIGAIL[2] WARNER, baptized at Boxted, Essex 2 June 1614, daughter of immigrant WILLIAM[1] WARNER, of Great Horkesley and Boxted, Essex, who had married about 1613 to ABIGAIL[1] BAKER, whose sister

Sarah Baker also came to America.

William and his wife Abigail came to Ipswich in 1636, where he was given a one acre houselot between Mill Street on the southwest, and the road from Mill Street to High Street on the northeast (Reg. 20:64-5). They probably died in Ipswich, he before 1648 (Hoyt 340). Dr. Wells was given in 1635 a houselot of 1½ acres at the Cove on the south side of the Ipswich river, just below John Proctor's lot on the bend below the footbridge (Waters Ipswich 495, 444-6, 450, 455). Later he got another ten acres of marsh in return for land taken by the town for the Mill Bridge. (7 Feb. 1647/8 in Waters Ips. 441; Reg. 20:67n). He died in Ipswich 26 Oct. 1666, with estate probated 15 Nov. 1666.

Abigail (Warner) Wells died in Ipswich 22 July 1671 (VR 707).

PERKINS.

Rev. Thomas[2] Wells married Ipswich 10 Jan. 1669/70 MARY[3] PERKINS, born Ipswich about 1651-2 to JOHN[2] PERKINS and his wife ELIZABETH, whose maiden name is unknown. Mary (Perkins) Wells died in Amesbury 26 Jan. 1726/7, age 75, and is buried next to her husband in Union Cemetery under a stone reading:

"INTERRED HERE THE BODY OF MRS MARY WELLS
DECd IANUARY the 26th
1727 AGED 75 YEARS
LATE WIFE OF Mr THOMAS
WELLS
DEATH IS NOT DUMB IT BIDS US ALL
PREPARE BEFORE BY IT WE FALL
WE KNOW NOT HOW NOR WHERE NOR WHEN
FIT NOW OR NEUR WE CANNOT THEN"(Hoyt 350).

Mary's father John[2] Perkins, Jr. was born in Hillmorton, Warwickshire about 1614, and died Ipswich 14 Dec. 1686 (VR 645, quartermaster), age 72. He was unmarried when he came to America on the ship *Lyon* in 1631 with his parents and Roger Williams, founder of Rhode Island. He married in Ipswich before 1636 ELIZABETH ----, who died Ipswich 27 Sept. 1684 (Elisabeth,VR644).

John's parents were JOHN[1] PERKINS and JUDITH[2] GATER,
who came from Hillmorton, Warwickshire on the *Lyon* in 1631. The senior John died in Ipswich 1654 (VR 645, age 64). He was the son of HENRY[A] PERKINS (c. 1555-92) who married 29 Nov. 1597 ELIZABETH SAWBRIDGE. Henry was the son of THOMAS[B] PERKINS (buried Hillmorton 23 March 1591/2) and ALICE KEBBLE? Thomas was the son of HENRY[C] PERKINS, whose will was probated 16 June 1546. He was the son of the earliest known Perkins, THOMAS[D] PERKINS of Hillmorton, Warwickshire, whose wife ALICE is named in his will of 1538.

The Perkinses were also ancestors of Lydia Ann Winship Teel Gould, whose biography above gives more detail on the family.

John[1] Perkins's wife JUDITH[2] GATER was baptized at Hillmorton 19 March 1588/9, and may have died in Ipswich. Her parents were immigrant MICHAEL[1] GATER, who had married in Hillmorton 13 Nov. 1576 ISABEL BAILIE.

Their son John[2] Perkins was brother of Mary (Perkins) Bradbury, who narrowly escaped execution in Salem in 1692 after being condemned as a witch. She was an ancestor of Lydia Ann Winship Teel, as described in an earlier chapter, and thus T. Warren Gould and Caroline Goddard were related to each other as distant cousins .

SARGENT.

Another sister of John Perkins was Elizabeth (Perkins) Sargent, great -grandmother of Judeth[3] Straw, and thus second cousin of her husband Obadiah[4] Wells through the Perkins line, as well as first cousin through the Straws. ELIZABETH[2] PERKINS was born in Hillmorton, Warwickshire in either 1611 or 1618, and came to America with her family, settling in Ipswich, where she married about 1640 seaman WILLIAM[1] SARGENT, born in England about 1598. He was a founder of Ipswich in 1633, of Newbury, and Hampton in 1638. His will in Amesbury 1670/1 was probated 13 April 1675. Elizabeth (Perkins) Sargent's death is not recorded, but may have been in Amesbury between 1652 and 1670.

Their son WILLIAM[2] SARGENT, Jr. was born in Salisbury 2 Jan. 1644/5, and died in Amesbury 1712, before probate of his estate on 31 March. In 1670 he was sentenced by the county court for fornication, to be whipped or pay a fine (12 April 1670, EQ 4: 237 per Anderson 415). He took the oath of allegiance in 1677, and was in the local militia in 1680 (Frederick L. Weis, *The Colby Family in America* (Concord MA: the author, 1970],[hereinafter Weis], 10).

COLBY.

William Sargent Jr. married in Amesbury 23 Sept.1666 (VR 476) MARY2 COLBY, born in Amesbury part of Salisbury, 1647 (VR 55) to ANTHONY[1] COLBY and SUSANNAH (HADDON?) WATERMAN. Mary died in Amesbury 8 July 1689. Her father Anthony was baptized in Horbling, Lincolnshire 8 Sept. 1605 (Threlfall in GMC 50:123 per Anderson 415-6; not the son of THOMAS[A] COLBY of Beccles, Suffolk and his wife BEATRIX FELTON, daughter of Sir THOMAS FELTON and his wife MARY GERNON as earlier sources speculated). He was probably a servant of Simon Bradstreet of Horbling, who came to America. Anthony probably came over between May and July 1630 with the Winthrop Fleet to Salem (Banks 69), then to Boston, Cambridge 1632, Ipswich 1637, Salisbury 1639, and Amesbury 1647. He was an early member of the First Church in Boston, by the winter of 1630-1 (Bos. Church Rec. 47 in Anderson 413). While in Boston about 1633 he married the widow SUSANNAH WATERMAN, whose maiden name may have been HADDON (Frederick C. Warner, "The Ancestry of Samuel. Freda and John Warner " (Boston: typescript, 1949), 135 notes that Anthony's membership in the First Church Boston (#93) is next to Jared Haddon), born about 1610 (not in Salisbury VR). She died in Salisbury 8 July 1689, after marrying a third time, about 1663 (not in Ipswich VR) to William Whitridge of Ipswich, who died in 1669. Susannah's sad and lonely condition in old age is described in a county court case in 1682 (EQ 8: 388). Her estate was inventoried 2 Sept. 1691 at £ 151/15, mostly in real estate.

Anthony was granted a houselot and three acres in the west end of Cambridge on the south side of Brattle Street 29 March 1632, but he sold his Cambridge holdings by 1637. He joined the First Church in Boston before 8 Sept. 1633, when their first son John was baptized (Weis, 3). He became a Freeman 14 May 1634 (MBCR 1:369 per Anderson 413). They moved to the North Shore by 1637 when he had become a planter in Ipswich. There he was an appraiser

for Ipswich in 1640. In 1640 he got an allotment of land in the first division in Salisbury, which was supplemented in 1643. He transferred his church membership from Boston to Salisbury in 1646(2 Aug. 1646, Bos. Church Rec. 47 in Anderson 413). But the next year he sold his house and two acres there, and became one of the first commoners of Amesbury, receiving additional grants in 1654 and 1658.
Anthony was probably occupied as a sawmill operator, judging from the number of sawmill tools in his inventory, and his part ownership of Salisbury's first board mill (John Pressy's account about 1651 in EQ 8:250, 373-5 and inventory in EPR 1:407-10 per Anderson 414, 416).
He died Salisbury 11 Feb. 1660/1, and was buried in Golgotha Cemetery there (Bassett-Preston (1930) 66). His estate came to a goodly £ 359, which included the homestead, barn, 14 acres of tilled land, and 70 acres of upland.

STRAW.

It is believed that William and Mary (Colby) Sargent had a daughter LYDIA^3, born in Amesbury about 1689, though she cannot be found in the records. She married in Amesbury 30 April 1710 JOHN^2 STRAW (VR 487), born in Amesbury 1 July 1688 to WILLIAM^1 STRAW of Ipswich, Hampton and Amesbury (will there 3 May 1709, probated 2 Oct. 1712) and his first wife MEHITABLE, who died about 1688-92 before his remarriage to Margaret. John and Lydia Straw's daughter JUDETH^3 STRAW married Obadiah Wells, as we have seen above. William and Mehitable Straw were also the parents of Luke Wells's wife DORITHY^2 STRAW, born in Amesbury about 1685, died there 29 Sept. 1715 (VR 596). She had first married in Concord 30 July 1707 John Trull of Haverhill (VR 70; he was born after 1659, when the first John Jr., son of John Trull Sr. and Sarah French was born, Sav. 4:335), who died by 1710 when she remarried Luke Wells.

Samuel Clifford Gould (1864-1957)

Chapter XV

31. SAMUEL CLIFFORD GOULD (1864-1947)

My grandfather Gould was the black sheep of the family. Because he abandoned his wife Laura and three little children, my Father would never mention his name. The grandchildren never saw him, and the closest we ever came was a brief stopover in Brookfield MA, where my Father parked the car and left us waiting while he walked to a nursing home, where we gather he made the concession of paying a brief visit to the old man. But in his usual taciturn manner, my Father would say nothing about the visit. We knew nothing about him, except that he was unmentionable. This applied to my Mother as well, who knew nothing of him. And it would be unkind to even mention the name to my grandmother Laura, and she never said a word about him or the divorce. My Father's sisters kept the vow of silence as well, so his name was never mentioned in Melrose where they lived, or in Newfields or Claremont later.

So this account is reconstructed entirely from a few tidbits of pathetic letters he wrote to his son, and what we find in the public record.

Samuel[8] Clifford Gould was born in the North End of Boston, in the famous Hartt House that had belonged to the builders of the frigate *Constitution,* now demolished, at 24 Hull Street, opposite Copps Hill Burial Ground, where Samuel's ancestors are buried. This house was just a half a block north of Old North Church, where his grandfather Elias Waters Goddard had been Senior Warden, and the house behind it, where his mother grew up. It was but two blocks from the old Gould development on North Margin Street that his grandfather Gould and his father had built. He was born on 3 February 1864 (Massachusetts Birth Records, 1864, Boston, #4841.), at the end of the Civil War, in which a great uncle was wounded in battle, and a great aunt's husband also served.

Sammy was a specially welcomed baby, though the fifth in the family, the first two children were girls, Ida and Caroline, and the next two were torn from the parents by childhood diseases, Charles by pneumonia at 18 months, and Frederick by scarlet fever at 11 months. The elaborate memorial windows in the family's Emmanuel Church on Newbury Street, and the sad family letters tells how much they were mourned. It is small wonder that the new baby son was spoiled.

We have quoted his aunt Annie's letter to her sister living in Lexington: "It's a boy-homely as Palmer [her father's first cousin Ezra Palmer Gould, then 13, born 27 Feb. 1841, who became a well-known theologian] , I will tell him he looks like him, he arrived just as the bells rung nine Wednesday eve. . .Warren is So proud that he allows all his friends to go up and see the boy-some thing unusual. He says he will call him Earnest, -appropriate dont you think so?" (Annie Gould to Lucy Gould, 5 Feb. 1864).

Whatever his father's preferences, the name chosen was traditional. His first name was from the most eminent living member of this family, Samuel Lawrence Gould (1814-81), the first college graduate, abolitionist orator, and Boston headmaster under Horace Mann's reforms. The name went back to the Samuel Lawrance, the tailor of Boston, who married the sister of the Revolutionary patriot Dawes. His middle name came from his mother's side, her brother Clifford Wayne Goddard (1837-1903), North End cooper,

When the boy was only one, the Goulds moved away from the North End to the newly fashionable South End, to 14 Carver Street, now below the Transportation Building in Park Square, but then close to Edgar Allan Poe's birthplace on Carver Street Here, close to the Goulds' first home eight generations back, Sammy was to spend the next decade, a block from the Swan Boats on the Garden, a block from the Frog Pond on the Common, a few blocks from the theater district, near the Park Street railroad station, and all the exciting events of downtown Boston. On Sunday the family attended the fashionable Emmanuel Church, within easy walk to Newbury Street.

We know that he attended Exeter Street School, on Newbury, now converted to stores like the Nature Store, from a valentine envelope addressed to him there.

From this period of his boyhood he saved an invitation addressed to "Master Sammy

Gould, Carver Street", which reads: "'Little Bopeep' (Belle Botsford) will receive her friends at a 'Mother Goose' party, Wed. Mar, 24th from 4 o'c till 8 oc P.M. You are requested to appear in costume, also to recite the verse belonging to the character assumed by you.

But that social life was not all. When Sammy was seven, his father took the whole family aboard the Cunard liner *Calabria* for a year's residence in the capitols of Europe. We still have the Christmas present to Sammy dated Leipzig 25 bee. 1871, a childrens book in German, which he learned to read. Here too may have begun the family stamp collection, of old German states stamps pasted into an old album.

On their return to Boston in 1872 Sammy may have attended the Winthrop School on Tremont Street, where his namesake uncle had been Headmaster. When he was 12, in 1876, the Gould family moved out to the Longwood section o£ Brookline, then the country suburbs of Boston. There the family joined the Brahmin founded Episcopal Church of Our Savior. In that beautiful Gothic revival structure Sammy and his brother John joined the choir, singing with the future Bishop William Lawrence and his cousins.

In 1880 he graduated from Prince School on Newbury St. (Photo in Album #11). Like his father, Sammy does not seem to have been directed toward college, but to business. We do not know his first job, but he first shows up in Boston Directory of 1887, when he is 23 as "clerk", boarding with his parents in the residential Hotel Helvetia, on Huntington Ave. at the corner of Tremont Street in Longwood (130 W. Brookline Street Apartment 3; *Boston Directory,* hereinafter Dir., 1887, 518).

Samuel never advanced in life much beyond clerk or bookkeeper. His first business address shows up in 1888 as 207 Congress Street, where he is clerk in one of the many businesses in the location.

On 19 Dec. 1889, when he was 25, he married, to Laura Keene Douglas (1864-1945), 9 months younger than he (Massachusetts Marriage records 1897, 471:221). She was born in Stellarton, Nova Scotia, the daughter of a Scottish immigrant, whom New Englanders called "a Blue-Nose", the first person outside the old English Puritan stock that any Gould had married. But the Black Douglas family was one of the most aristocratic in Scotland, second only to the royal Stewarts, and her father was a well paid supervisor of underwater coal mining in Glace Bay, Cape Breton Island, grandson of a banker in Manchester England, and her brother was one of the major provincial politicians who was to become a Canadian senator. Laura was a shy, quiet woman of great outer dignity and inner strength. She was to hold the family together when Samuel gave up.

They were married in her family's church in Stellarton, by Rev. R. Friggens. We have no record that any of Samuel's relatives went to Nova Scotia. Both of her parents had died in 1907, after which Laura may have come to the United States with heir elder sister Elizabeth, whose husband James Bradley had gone to Haverhill MA., probably for work in the textile mills. In 1892 the Bradleys were living at 495 Wilder Street in Haverhill, which became second home to the orphaned Gould children. How Laura and Samuel met is not recorded, better forgotten by all concerned.

Nine and a half months after the wedding, the first of three children was born. Caroline[9] Douglas Gould was born in Melrose 9 Oct. 1890. The first grandchild of the Goulds and Goddards was named for her paternal grandmother Caroline Goddard Gould.

After their marriage Samuel was still working as a clerk at 207 Congress Street, Boston, and boarding with his family at 55 Brookline Av., Longwood. But that year Samuel had changed jobs to 106 High Street in Boston and he and Laura moved out to the Boston suburb of Melrose (Dir. 1890, 547; 1891, 557), where Caroline was probably born.

Fifteen months later a second child, a girl, was born, on 29 March 1892, in Melrose. She was named Annie, probably for her great-aunt, her grandfather's sister Anna Matilda Gould Muzzey (1841-1872), who had died in childbirth with twins. The name Anna Matilda honored her mother's best friend, and first cousin, Anna Matilda Titcomb Merrill of Newburyport. The new baby's middle name was Warren, for her grandfather Gould, now in his final years of fatal diabetes. The two girls, born 15 months apart, were inseparable, and lived together, unmarried, both secretaries, to the and of Annie's life in 1964.

In 1892 Samuel C. Gould, stenographer, age 29, lived on the west side of Whitman Ave., in Melrose (Melrose Town Report, 1892, precinct 3, 103). In the same year his name appears on the deed to his parents home nearby, at 23 Gooch Street (Middlesex Deeds 3103:286, 2754:445). Samuel was apparently responsible enough to take legal title, having bought the house before his first child's birth, paying $250 to Nathaniel Jones and Alonzo G. Whitman for title to the house then "on the westerly side of a new street leading southerly from Grove street", to become Gooch Street (Middlesex Deed 1989:161). But the property was mortgaged back to the sellers for $2,500, which was discharged on 7 March 1893 (Middlesex Deed 1989:161-5; 2186:125). But Samuel did not pay the debt off, for the mortgage was renewed by his sister Ida (MD 2754:445, 3089:184).

In 1892 Samuel suddenly changed occupations for the better, to the best in his life, to, "printer" at 175 Commercial Street (Dir. 1892, 574), near his grandfather's former cooperage on Richmond Street in the North End, now his two uncles' cooperage. He was living in Melrose. The business lasted but one year. Perhaps he had been set up by his prosperous uncles, Walter and Clifford, for whom he was named. The venture was evidently unsuccessful, for his name disappears from the directory for five years until 1897 when he apparently went back to his old job as clerk at 106 High Street in Boston, but no longer at home in Melrose, but Wyoming Av. (Dir. 1895, 609).

He must have been in Melrose some of the time, for on 27 January 1896 his third and last child is born at 88 Whitman Street (Cert. copy of birth record #5045, father "bookkeeper"; Melrose City Clerk, 21 Feb. 1963). Named Douglas for Laura's family, and Warren, the traditional middle name for three generations of Goulds, after the Bunker Hill patriot-martyr Dr. Warren.

That year, 1896 Samuel C. disappears (Dir. 1896, 642), and the next year a Samuel shows up working at 24 Winter Street, living at 143 Hampden, but not surely our man (Dir. 1897, 651). He reappears for sure in 1898, back home in Melrose, working as bookkeeper for the first time at 52 Sudbury Street in Boston (Dir. 657). But a curious entry is another Samuel C. with an address at 6 Hotel Comfort in Boston. The Melrose home and bookkeeper at Sudbury Street continue for five years 1898-1902, perhaps a period of some stability. At one time he was bookkeeper for Isaac Coffin of Newton (Caroline D. Gould to author 30 July 1969).

. But after a disappearance from Boston directory in 1903. Samuel C. shows up as a salesman for the first time at 140 Pearl Street, Boston, living in Melrose (Dir. 1904, 758). In Melrose town directories he is consistently listed as bookkeeper from 1893 to 1902, living at 88 Whitman Av., except for 1893 when the Melrose address is "Larrabee off Gore". Change of occupation to "trav. salesman" comes in 1904. still living at 88 Whitman Av. (Melrose Directory, 1904, 92).

It is about this time of 1903-4 when Samuel became a traveling salesman, like his father, that the Melrose home broke up. By 1905 both houses in Melrose had been given up, the 23 Gooch St, house to Charles W. Barnard, salesman at 151 Federal Street, Boston, and the 88 Whitman Av. house to Erwin Augustus Harvey, bookkeeper at the Boston Globe (Melrose Dir. 1905, 41, 101; 1907, 144, 171). The family disappears from Boston directories as well, until 1910, John having gone to Philadelphia and New York, but Ida continuing at Boston Public Library, and boarding around Boston. The widow Caroline Goddard Gould lived briefly at #225 Mass. Av., a four story brick building above Mathews Brothers store (Photo in Album #11). About 1906-7 she was joined by her daughter-in-law Laura and her three children. She may have lived with Ida until her death in Melrose.

Samuel filed for divorce about 1912, in Middlesex County Court, Lowell. According to

Caroline, her mother Laura did not contest it, given his repeated infidelities, and 17 year old Douglas was a witness.

For a while, about 1906-7, the family sought refuge with her sister Elizabeth Bradley at 496 Wilder St., in Haverhill (Photo in Album #11). At other times they lived in poor rooms in Dorchester, Commonwealth Av. in Boston, Everett and Malden--the sequence in list made by son Douglas d. 1975.

Samuel showed up again in Boston between 1911 and 1914, living in Malden and working at 43 Tremont Street, in various rooms 309, 1113, and 815 (Dir. 1911; 1912; 1914; no listing 1913). Following his divorce he worked for Hind & Deck Paper Company as "commercial traveler", that is, a traveling salesman. Later he worked for Isaac Coffin in Newton, according to his daughter Caroline. This probably refers to the steam and hot water apparatus firm which also made power plant piping, with offices at 52 Sudbury Street in Boston 1913-22 (Bos. Dir. 1913, 430, 2884; 1922, 440, 2536).

Samuel disappears from the Boston directory in 1915. On 3 Feb. 1916 he married in Worcester by justice of peace Charles R. Johnson, to Clara C. (Magnan) SOULE (Massachusetts Marriage Record 1916, 639:605, #468). She was born in Southbridge MA about 1877, daughter of Alexander and Mary (Cantara) Magnum. She was 39, and divorced from George K. Soule, born in Providence RI about 1878 to Edward B. Soule and Sarah E. Gleason; she had married him 7 Nov. 1901 when he was a salesman (Massachusetts Marriage Records 1901, 514:463, # 980). We do not know if the Soules had children. Clara died in 1952, age about 75 (Massachusetts Death Records 1952, 74:445; her birth is not found in Massachusetts Archives 1870-80).

Sam was then 52, and probably had no more children, at least none that we know of. Sam moved into Clara's mother's home at 59 Myrtle Street in downtown Worcester, a block and a half south of the main Post Office *Worcester House Directory. 1916*, 372; *Worcester Business Directory,* 743). Mary Magnan, widow of Alexander had lived at this address since 1909, and Clara moved in the next year, working as an envelope maker in one of Worcester's four companies (Worc. Bus. Dir. 1909, 431; 1910, 632; 1911, 627; 636; 193,3, 660; 1914, 683; 1915, 473, 684). In 1917 Samuel C. had changed occupations from clerk to commercial traveler, and Clara is no longer listed. But by 1918 Samuel has also disappeared, and Mary is no longer listed, perhaps having died. Samuel is no longer listed in Worcester or suburbs, but is believed to have continued to live in the Worcester area, perhaps in Holyoke and North Brookfield, until his death in 1947.

But Samuel was traveling abroad in 1917, just before the outbreak of World War I. He gave his son a glossy printed folder with his own name, on the list of first class passengers sailing on the American twin-screw steamship *Havana* of the New York and Cuba Mail Steamship Company (Ward Line), Capt. R. Campion, sailing from New York, Saturday, July 14th, 1917, probably for Havana.

In 1921 he became a Mason, like his father. He was then a salesman, living in Holyoke, MA. He joined the Whiting Lodge on 4 May 1921, having been initiated on 19 Jan., passed on 23 March. The record shows him suspended 23 March 1933.

A surviving photo of Samuel taken some time in the early twenties, shows him at the wheel of a giant sporting car, in Maine. My Father's reluctant explanation of this photo is that he was doing what he liked best, hunting and fishing. There are two photos of him fishing at Moon Lake Miss. on 19 June 1921 (Album #11). He explained, "One of my friends in Memphis Tenn. is a Mr. Yancey with whom I have done considerable fishing. On June 19, 1921 Mr. Yancey, Mr. Robinson and I made trip from Memphis Tenn to Moon Lake Miss."

We lose track of him for 20 years, during the twenties and thirties, until some letters to his son start showing up about 1938, enclosing family mementoes and souvenirs. Where these relate to family history, we have already quoted them. Then there is this first personal letter, written when he was 65:

" Mar 13- 1939 Dear Douglas:-

I have been "off my feed" for the past two weeks and altho it is one of Our worst days this winter made trip to Dr. and one of the prescriptions he gave me contained word "dig it al is" that I know has to do with something for the heart[.] That's an old story and with me goes back over sixty years.

He said I shouldn't have walked over to his office + if etc I might see him in ten days. following with a few cheerful stories of others in similar condition as I had found trip to be their last.

"However as I said before thats an old story but I'11 play it safe + get some papers together, in some of which you may be interested. I have been in hopes, possibly without reason, of time coming when we might have gone over them together but evidently that was not to be.

When Ida turned a lot of them over to me she said you might appreciate having some of them.

Letters from Aunt Ida to me--Some from Aunt Minnie [Laura's sister] to Ida--Cards from various//friends of Ida; to her—Cards from Ida to me + pictures Of my sisters Ida + Carrie.

I have made notes on some of the papers but Ida will gladly furnish you with any further information--desired.

Today is the 24th anivsy of your Grandmothers death March 13th 1915.

Sincerely Father"

In 1939 Samuel was living in a retirement home in the little shoe manufacturing town of North Brookfield MA., 14 miles west of Worcester. On 1 Dec. 1939 my Father stopped en route froth Philadelphia to Melrose, leaving us in the model A Ford, while he made a brief visit. This was as close as we ever got to "grandpop", as I called him in my diary, but we learned nothing about him, and his name was not mentioned at the big Thanksgiving dinner for 11 family members at Laura's home at 301 West Foster Street in Melrose. Aunt Ida was there--How I would like to ask her now about her childhood with Sammy!

Samuel died in Worcester State Hospital, at 1:15 p.m. 11 Feb. 1947 (Letter of Massachusetts Dept. of Vital Statistics, 16 Oct. 1972, citing 99:257 1947, 24:350 1948; 99:257, #427 gives details), of a heart disease and pernicious anemia, four days after his 83d birthday. He had been living at 34 School Street, North Brookfield before he was hospitalized. Reunited with his family only in death, they brought his body back to Melrose where he had left them, and buried it beside his patient first wife, Laura, in the Wyoming Cemetery (letter of Superintendent Kenneth Malenchini, 15 Aug. 1968).

John Hogg GOULD (1870-1959)

Chapter XVI

32. JOHN^8 HOGG (GODDARD) GOULD

Great uncle John was a remarkable character. He was a hard worker, but humorous; patriotic, but progressive in politics; an idealist and persistent optimist about fellow humans and his own potential, liberal Episcopalian all his life. He was a gifted writer of prose and poetry though he completed only five years of grade school. Nevertheless he was admitted to Tufts Medical School, and helped edit two medical texts.

A man of unusually wide skills who described himself as "a Rolling Stone", he went through at least 47 jobs. The range of his work shows his wide interests: Confidential Secretary to Edward Filene in the first lectures at Harvard Business School, supervisor of building of a dam in North Carolina and a railroad in Maine, Secretary to the feminist President of Bryn Mawr, traveling lecturer on music, private diplomat for a Jewish family at the outbreak of World War I, when he traveled to Germany where he had lived as a boy, and historical researcher for WPA Writers Project, and maker of ball-bearings for World War II aircraft.

But his greatest success was as partner of a Boston advertising firm that promoted direct mail, a venture he gave up just before the Wall Street Crash brought everything down. His last work, when he retired at age 74, was as precision grinder of ball-bearings for the fighter planes of World War II.

He was attracted to men of near-genius, who left him holding the office when they failed. Among his friends were the utopian progressive Ralph Albertson, the inventive promoter Leonard Atwood, and internationalist engineer Carl Davis.

Born with a strong constitution, he lived until he was 88, and worked until he was 74. For recreation he was a hiker, and loved Cape Cod, to which he was the first of our family to return, in 1934.

John^8 Hogg Gould was born at 14 Carver Street in Boston on Christmas Day of 1870 (Boston Births, 1870, #3721). He was the sixth of seven children of T. Warren and Caroline (Goddard) Gould. It is not known from whom he received this name that he disliked so much that he changed it to John Goddard about 1924. He had a living uncle John Goddard (1805-78), his mother's uncle, a North End mast maker. But that John is never mentioned in letters, and does not seem to have been close to the family. So we assume that John Hogg was a friend of the family, perhaps a member of the church who would serve as godfather. We have found such a namesake.

John Hogg (1830-1917) was a highly respected Boston commission merchant in dry goods, like T. Warren, and also Senior Warden of their Emmanuel Church on Newbury Street His obituary in the *Boston Transcript* is headlined OLD TIME BOSTON MERCHANT//John Hogg, Long a Leading Figure in Dry Goods Trade, Retired from Business Activity New Year's Day" (Boston Transcript). Born in Kinrosshire, Scotland, he came to the U.S. in March 1853, and worked for dry goods retailer Turnbull & Kinmouth until that firm was dissolved, when David

Kinmouth made Hogg manager of his firm. On Kinmouth's death in 1857 Hogg formed the firm of Hogg, Brown & Taylor, which became one of Boston's leading dry-goods retailers, at 299-301 Washington Street They built a granite store at the corner of Washington and Temple Place. In 1885, after death of his two partners, Hogg formed a new firm called Smith, Hogg & Gardner, which became retailer for many important New England textile mills. Hogg was not only Senior Warden of Emmanuel, but member of the Union, Algonquin and Merchants clubs. After more than 60 years in business he retired on New Year's Day of 1917, and died of apoplexy two days later.

The place of his birth was then a fashionable street in the South End, where Edgar Allan Poe was born. It was a block east of Park Square, the Providence Railroad station, a block south of the Common's Frog Pond and Boston Garden, with its swan boats, a couple of blocks west of where the Goulds first settled in Boston, at Washington Street, eight generations back, a couple of blocks southeast of the family's Emmanuel Church on Newbury Street in the Back Bay, and five blocks east of the Exeter Street School where John first began about 1876.

We have one fragment of John's memory of his mother and father, Caroline and Warren Gould at Carver Street:

"He remarked, "Oh, Caroline, I've brought you an American cook!" "An American cook, why Warren, what an idea! I have a nice cook now." But well he said, it will only be fair for you to see her. "Well said Mother, remember that if I don't like her, you'll have to send her back. Have her come up.

Readers, you may paint your own picture of what happened when the door was opened and in walked the new "cook" for Mother, her <u>own</u> Mother!"

Her own mother, Caroline Garran Goddard died in 1880, when John was ten.

However, in his first year, when John was only seven months old, their father took the whole family on a year's business trip to Europe. We have described their departure on the Cunard liner *Calabria* in Oct. 1871, their Christmas in Leipzig, Germany, and stays in hotels in Paris and Switzerland. He would have been only 18 months old when they returned, so John probably remembered little of this trip, but heard a lot from his family. We have a fictional account of such a voyage home on the *Saxonia* which John wrote, perhaps filled out from on another trip to Europe in 1914.

"The great ship, with its decks crowded with passengers, slowly edged out by puffing tugs, finally swung its nose into the channel and started on its way into the ocean.

Down in the stokehole, sweating coal-handlers began the task of keeping the ravenous furnaces supplied with fuel.

In the great kitchens and the various dining rooms, preparations went forward for the approaching meal.

In the steerage, crowds of prospective citizens of the new land were getting settled with their baggage and getting acquainted with each other.

In the Intermediate the wealthier of the poor and the poorer of the wealthy began to look over their section of the ship and get acquainted with the limitations of promenade and recreation allowed to them.

The first cabin passengers assumed or were familiar with an exclusiveness they did not hesitate to exhibit toward all others. The wealth of this class was apparent in their dress. Whereas in the steerage many a rough-clad emigrant carried his entire fortune in a belt around his waist, a hold-up man (had there been one on board) would surely have found far less available cash on the upper than on the lower decks, and this despite the fact that there WAS a goodly representation of bankers, brokers, capitalists and other people of means among the Saloon list.

Captain Mack stood beside Pilot Deming as she guided the big craft down the bay. Fourteen years of service--from cabin boy to commander of the Company's newest floating palace, marked him as a man of experience--a self-made man in fact--and although 50 years old still anxious to be strictly up-to-date in knowledge.

This would be his first trip on the Caxonia and he recognized the responsibility that rested upon his shoulders...

Before they had gone far the group was joined by another officer who upon entering greeted the pilot with a smile and a salute. First Officer Tompkins was not over 30 years old, with the face and figure of Adonis, a man who commanded attention from both men and women alike. He fairly worshiped Captain Mackey and it was known throughout the Company that the Captain trusted Tompkins implicitly...

The first three days out were ideal so far as speed and weather were concerned but late in the afternoon of the third day the wind veered into the North and a nasty chop commenced to slap the sides of the ship...

Tompkins stepped over to the telephone and in a moment had set more than a hundred men at work tightening belt fastenings, testing ropes and fastening everything securely in place.

Already the Saxonia had commenced to pitch more than usual. Her enormous length and tonnage made playthings of the ordinary ocean swells but now there was a decided pitch--a noticeable quiver after each plunge and the more violent throbbing that followed the uncovering of her whirling propellers as she would dip over the crest of the mountainous combers that we now rushing down her quarter..."

After laying this scene John gives a summary of the plot to come: "Change to the room of the Plotters. Conversation on injustice of capital, etc. Plotters retire leaving bomb in stateroom of boy who grows inquisitive and accidentally releases clockwork. Bomb will explode in an unknown time, perhaps any instant, perhaps not for days. Frantic with fear he rushes from stateroom to seek help from Levis who has stateroom on same deck but along gallery at end of hall." There it ends. But we have a later draft in which the ship is blown up, and the survivors are wrecked on a tropical island in the middle of the Sargasso Sea. One of these is a man named Gould, who gives us his philosophy of life and how to deal with the varied characters, ranging from banker to burglar, Captain to The Crook, minister to radical. The novel is unfinished, but we can see how the voyage of the *Calabria* was the starting point of John's creation.

SUMMERS AT SEASIDE RESORT OF HULL.

When the Gould family got home in 1873 the family resumed their summer vacations at the seaside resort of Hull, which John often recalled with pleasure.

In his "Thoughts" published in 1924 he recalled these days in a poem,

I AM A BOY AGAIN

The stretch of beach where I was wont to romp and play is mine again today.
The tide is low and at the point I find the self-made rocks--the pools wherein the lazy crabs and crawfish lay,
The lighthouse glistens brightly in the sun,
The bellbouy clangs a welcome lay,
On every hand dear Mother Nature bids me take full joy,--
I am a boy again today.

The gulls and sand-birds skim the blue,
With now and then a friendly dip to me,
They sense the lad who in the days of old
Kept vigil with them through the storm-whipped spray
And with them braved the cold.

Today the sea's at rest. Naught breaks its calm
But straying zephyrs and the slow and rythmic heaving of its breast
Some white-plumed yachts roll heavily
As if asleep and nodding in the swell
The jade-like waves break daintily along the shore,
Each with its whispered "hush" that naught may break the spell,
And I could rest content and say
That God was good
To give me health and joy and such a perfect day." [9]

Or in a different mood, this is the first of six poems printed in "Thoughts" [3]:

THE WIND

O'er spume-swept beach I roar and screech
And the rocks give back my cry;
Till Mother Carey's chicks take wing
And the gulls in terror fly!

My rage I vent on ships strength-spent,
Make shrouds of their straining sails;
In which I bury unnumbered dead
In the deepest kelp-fringed trails.

Out of my way I dash the spray
From snarling, frothing waves--
Rushing on in headlong fright
Like cowardly, craven knaves,

Who shrink from my whip and with curling lip

Scurry away in haste,
Anxious to seek some sheltering cove
Or escape in the Ocean's waste.

Through Seven Seas they know no ease,
They fear me in every port,
They only rest when I decree
To stop my merry sport.

Yet while I'm rude in my rougher mood,
I often compensate
For the wrong I have done in my evil fun
And bless where I showed Hate.

Now those who have sinned are just like the Wind--
Whatever wrong they do--
The strength that was theirs to tear things down
Is theirs to re-build anew! [3]

The seashore town also became the setting of a philosophical piece he wrote later in life, called:

WHAT CAN BE DONE

Down in the little fishing village of Hull (Massachusetts) I have seen old Captain John Smith, two of his sons and half-dozen other stalwart fisher-folk, run the big life-boat down to the water's edge, nose her well through the innermost lines of crashing breakers, wait for the 'back-wash' and then at just the right moment, with a final united shove, leap over the gunwales and man the oars!

Last over the stern would go the Captain, to grasp the long oar and with mighty thrusts of arms and swaying body, keep the craft to the set course.

The mountainous 'rollers' eight to twelve deep and terrifying in height, would be met with equal skill by the oarsmen and steersman and despite lashing and stinging of the spume-flecked and icy brine, the terrific power of the mighty swells [,the] boat slowly but surely would make its objective--a schooner aground on Harding's Ledge, miles off-shore!

Had not the men on either side of the boat pulled steadily and strongly or as the Captain directed from time to time, or had he been less alert to every menacing wave or wind-squall, they would have gotten nowhere,--except to Davey Jones' Locker!

It seems to me that his narrative very clearly depicts the far more thrilling trip that is being taken today by the United States.

On one side of our "Economic life-boat" if it may so be called--is one group of "oarsmen" known as LABOR and on the other side a group known as CAPITAL. The "steersman" we will designate, "Government"...[If] the three "will work and think in harmony, nothing can stop the victorious progress of the craft..." His solution is for Labor to accept a fair wage, Capital to give a guaranteed wage, and Government to help both to make a fair profit and keep taxes down.

CHILDHOOD IN BOSTON AND BROOKLINE.

When John was six, in 1876, the family moved out to suburban Longwood, next to the fashionable garden suburb of Brookline. John probably attended the Boston public school there. He had only five years at Martin School, from which he graduated about 1882 (His draft of application to International Correspondence School, 5 July 1939, hereinafter Corres.)

.

We have a poem written in the late thirties with a memory of childhood called:

The Wonderful Land Of 'Let's Pretend.'

O wonderful Land of, 'Let's Pretend',
Cram-jammed with all good things, without end;
The grandest place you ever did see!
Everything there is perfectly free!
A Princess lives in her castle there
With clear candy windows everywhere.
Doors of rich chocolate open too;
Bit off a knob--or even two!
There are hills of ice cream, lakes of milk,
Spun candy-balls, shiney as silk.
Gum drops will drop on to your table.
Try some, do, if you are able.
Down one side street are hunks of nougat
Stuck on cane-stalks you'd love to chew at.
Now not a cent do you have to spend
'Cause everything's FREE in, 'Let's Pretend'!
And you can ride on the, 'Chew-Chew' train.
(Why there it is now right down that lane)
Loaded high with your favorite gum;
Quite free! Ask the Conductor for some.
Like crunchy nuts without a shell?
(Don't eat too much, they don't digest well.)
All kinds of sundaes, every day.
Free at the fountain; nothing to pay!
Sweet Muscatel Grapes, and Hamburgs plump,
To fill a hollow--make a lump!
If you like this story which I have penned
Perhaps you can visit, 'Let's Pretend'.
Where is this lovely place? Just a rod
The other side of the Land of Nod.
One simple caution before you go
It's quite important you should know:
Don't eat too much there or they may send
You back from the land of 'Let's Pretend.'"

The family joined the Brahmin Episcopal Church of Our Saviour in Brookline, where John and his brother Sammy sang in the choir with blue-bloods like William Lawrence, who was to become Bishop of Massachusetts, and whom the Goulds assumed to be a cousin.

John remained in the Episcopal church all his life. In his resumes he described himself as "Protestant, but broad in thought". Here is the only poem on a religious theme that survived in his writings, written about 1936-40:

An Easter Thought

As the soul of a seed thrust into the earth
Reaches up to the Sun's inspiring light;
Daily growing in stature from its birth
With unswerving faith through each day or night;
So do human souls which follow His lead
With heart and mind in the fullest accord
Become from all doubt eternally freed
Through the great lesson of the risen Lord.
As o'er the world rejoicing bells peal out,
I gladly add to what their tongues do say,-
Their message true of what it's all about;
'To you, my friend, a joyous Easter Day'!

The Goulds moved several times, probably reflecting the tightness of funds as their father's diabetes limited his work, but they were longest in one of the new residential hotels, Helvetia, at the corner of Huntington and Tremont Streets in Longwood. When he first went to work he was living with his family at 55 Brookline Avenue, Longwood.

John did not go to high school in Boston, like his father, which makes his entry into Tufts Medical School remarkable. He did study shorthand at nights at Hickox School to become a stenographer, while he took his first job in 1887, at age 17 [1](To keep track of his jobs we will number each known one in brackets). He started selling surgical instruments for Codman & Shurtleff in Boston (Resume 1915), becoming a clerk there.

STENOGRAPHER FOR MASSACHUSETTS STATE MILITIA.

When he was 20 years old, in 1891, John got his first job as a clerk/stenographer with Mr. Butcher, agent for R. Frybil & Co. which made woodworking machinery [2] Butcher "went away without pay" and John became stenographic secretary to J. W. Stockton, Eastern District Superintendent for the Pullman Car Co. in Boston [3]. It may be this first job that he referred to when he wrote that he was in Houghton & Dutton's dry goods store in downtown Boston when, about 1889, he met "a gentleman and inaugurated a career of exceptional trust and accomplishment."(Letter from Bass River 3 Oct. 1951; the date this occurred is vague, 3 decades after his grandfather's work at Beebe & Co., 1853-9; he places this in Houghton & Dutton which did not exist in his grandfather's day).

In 1892 he worked at 13 Tremont Street. The Goulds left Longwood in 1892, so John was commuting from the family home at 23 Gooch Street in Melrose.

For six years, 1892-7, he was employed by the state of Massachusetts, for Adjutant General Dalton, in the office which managed the state militia [4]. It is possible that he got this job through some friend of his grandfather Goddard's, who had been Captain of the Columbian Artillery which became the famous Fifth Regiment of Fighting Irish in the Civil War. For the first five years he is listed as "clerk", and in the last two as "stenographer". The offices were in the State House itself in 1893-5 and 1897-8 (Room 261), and nearby at 6 Mt. Vernon Street in 1896. He continued to commute from Melrose, probably by train to North Station.

For Christmas of 1895 he gave his five year old niece Caroline a copy of Mrs. Emily Bennett Molesworth's *Cosy Corner Stories* (N.Y.: Dutton, n.d.), which became her niece Elinor Gould's favorite book, and now in her possession in Pinehurst NC.

MEDICAL STUDENT AT TUFTS 1896.

In 1896 John made an ambitious career move, enrolling as a special student in the Freshman class of Tufts Medical School. He took courses in Chemistry, Psychology, Osteology and Dissection for one semester, but dropped out (Application for Federal Employment, Hartford Ct., 12 Nov. 1944, 2, hereinafter Fed. Emp.).

It may be at this time that he became "Editorial Assistant to nationally known authority on Electro Therapeutics [Dr. Fred H. Morse]; Editorial Assistant to well known Boston physician [Dr. J. C. R. Caines] in compilation of Handbook on Emergency Procedure" [5](1938 "The Record and Promise", 2).

John left a vivid account of his medical study in a story typed about 1940, called:

<u>A HORRIBLE MISTAKE</u>

The thickening snowfall, backed by a mounting wind from the North, met me as I left the trolley, two blocks from my destination. Had there been any warning of this storm, which was rapidly smothering the city with its white blanket, I would most certainly have gone directly home from the office of Dow and Company where from 9 A. M. until 5 P.M., as assistant bookkeeper I juggled with the accounts of the firm.

But I was now almost at my objective, an old school building in the attic of which there had been set up temporary dissecting accommodations for the medical college I was attending. A special student, I was permitted to do my dissections in the evening, hence the necessity for being out on such an inclement night.

As I waded through the drifts already barring approach to the building I glanced up at its dark and cheerless bulk. Bleak and desolate indeed! There would be no warmth, I knew where I was to work on the top floor. Cold or not, I must stick it out for the next two hours!

Letting myself into the basement boiler room I locked the door behind me. The janitor always left a single gas jet lighted here but as I mounted the four flights I had to light the burner at each of the landings. Only the first floor was used for school rooms. The rest of the building had been stripped of desks. Except for the rats, it was deserted but as I passed the doors of now vacant class-rooms, I was aware of scurrying feet fleeing my approach!

The front portion of the top floor--the attic--was walled off across its width by a wooden, eight foot partition, this space constituting the "Dissection Room". A door, which I unlocked, led into it from the main part of the attic.

Partitioned from this room was a smaller space in which was located a large open vat wherein were kept the cadavers or 'subjects' upon which we students practised to acquire the surgeon's knowledge and skill. A door from the Dissecting Room led into the, 'Pickle-room' as we called it.

Entering the larger room where I was to work tonight I lighted the two overhead gas brackets supposed to provide illumination for my task. The room was virtually freezing cold for the four windows fronting on Copley Square had been intentionally left slightly open. I closed them, brought out my case of instruments, removed the wet cloths from the head of my subject (already laid out on a table[)], drew up a high chair and prepared to dissect out the maze of nerves in the cheek and jaw! Except for the whining of the wind as it tore across the roof, and the occasional rumble of a trolley taking the switches at the junction of Huntington Avenue and Boylston Street, I was isolated within the silence of Death! With text-book propped up handily, for reference, I was soon busy with scalpels, forceps and clamps, completely oblivious to my surroundings.

And then suddenly, I was brought to rigid alertness by a sound that paralyzed body and mind; the sound of a mighty 'splash' in the 'Pickle-room"! This was instantly followed by other sounds--unmista[ka]bly those of sloshing, dripping, water!

Like a lighting bolt a terrifying thought flashed through my mind! This could mean but one thing! Someone has made a horrible mistake!

Dreading what I might see, I forced my eyes toward the door leading into the room where the 'vat' was!

Closed for the moment but in what instant might it not swing open! What ghastly, groping apparition would confront me!

To describe the sensations that swept my body within the space of seconds, takes longer to relate than the actual elapsed time between that first sound and my physical reaction! Forgetting or ignoring the routine of putting out all lights before leaving the building (to say nothing of locking the dissection-room door) I thought of nothing but to flee from the 'Thing' now doubtless staggering toward its escape through the 'Pickle-room' door.

In a series of leaps I crossed the room and the intervening space to the stairway and as fast as I could go, sprinted down the four flights to the boiler room! It was all my shaking fingers could do to let myself out of the basement door and lock it behind me, before I sank to the snow-covered ground, in a dead faint!

The next morning I telephoned Dow & Company that I would be late getting in and sought my professor of Surgery, Dr. Morse, to whom I related my hair-raising experience of last night. To my surprise and chagrin he laughed long and heartily. Indeed, it was a full half minute before he could control himself. Placing his hand upon my shoulder, he said, 'Son, what your imagination pictured as a terrifying incident, was a perfectly natural happening. The 'splash' which you heard was real enough but it was caused by formation of gases within the cavities of one of the cadavers in the vat. Hence its floating equilibrium was upset and the body flopped over, creating a series of splashes and drippings'.

Yet, while that explanation had to suffice, even today forty years later, I sense chills marathoning up and down my spine whenever I recall that Winter night in the dissection room and what I was sure was a horrible mistake!"

In 1897 John dropped out of medical school and took work for six months in Worcester, as Secretary to the credit manager of Graton & Knight, leather beltings [6].

However, in 1898, he quit to travel for 18 months. "Invited to visit a chum in Colorado...[he] Went and traveled in the West (Was married Nov. 1898), returning to Boston on account of his Mother's wishes (Resume 1915). Colorado had a long attraction to the Goulds: His great uncle Samuel had given up his job as Boston headmaster to go out for the gold rush and become a rancher; his nephew Douglas was to go there in 1921 to start the first oil shale refinery; Douglas's first two children were born there; and James's son Robert went there to school in 1966, and eventually settle there.

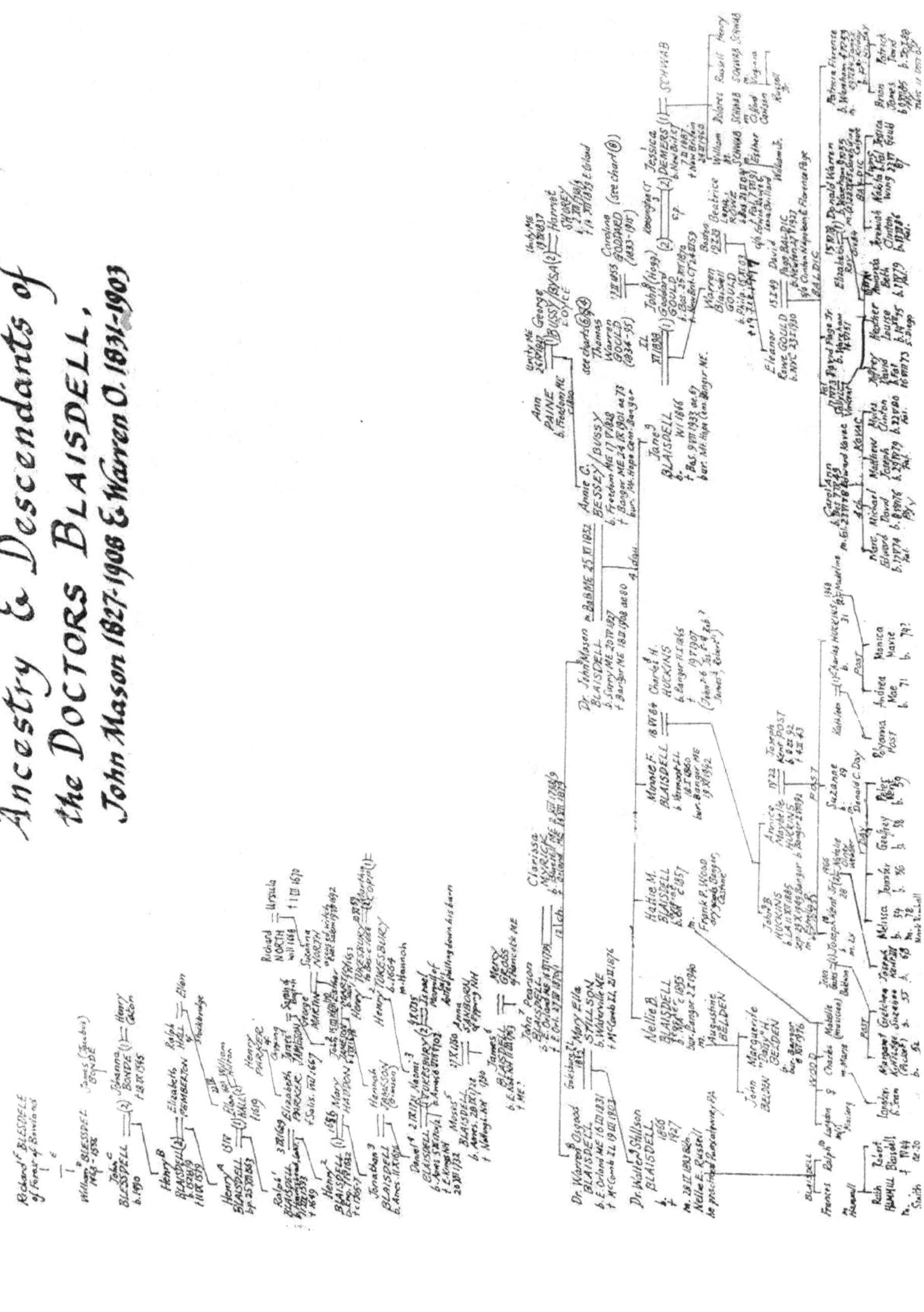
Ancestry & Descendants of
the Doctors Blaisdell,
John Mason 1827-1908 & Warren O. 1831-1903

MARRIAGE TO JANE BLAISDELL: HER ANCESTRY.

It was probably in Illinois that John met and married in Nov. 1898 his first wife, Jane^{9} Blaisdell born in Wisconsin, daughter of homeopathic physician Dr. John^{8} Mason Blaisdell and Annie C. Paine.

Dr. Blaisdell is credited with having first declared that TB was caused by a germ, in 1877, five years before Koch proved it (undated article in Ill. newspaper c. 13 Dec. 1892?, citing Quincy, IL *Whig*, Nov. 1877, reprinted in *Macomb Journal*, April 1878).

He was born in Surry, ME 20 April 1827 to farmer John^{7} Pearson Blaisdell (James^{6}, Moses^{5}, Daniel^{4}, Jonathan^{3}, Henry^{2}, John^{1}) and Clarissa Myrick of Blue Hill ME. Her father was fourth cousin of James Arnold Blaisdell, President of Pomona College, who founded the first college cluster in America, the Claremont Colleges, at three of which James W. Gould was professor 1955-90, and who worked with Dr. Blaisdell in his Blaisell Institute of Religions and Cultures (ancestry and relationship in letter from Pres. Blaisdell 29 May 1916 to Dr. Walter S. Blaisdell, in box of Suzanne Day of E. Dennis).

The Blaisdells had immigrated from Hawkshead, Lancashire (Ralph^{1}, Henry$^{A\text{-}B}$, John^{C}, William^{D}, Richard^{F}) to Pemaquid, York and Salisbury. Among his maternal ancestors were the Parkers of Salisbury, Haddons, Jamesons and Tukesburys of Amesbury, Sanborns of Epping NH, Grosses of Hancock ME. Hannah (Jameson) Gimson, wife of Jonathan^{3} Blaisdell, was a granddaughter of the accused witch Susannah Martin, heroine of Whittier's poem.

Dr. Blaisdell died in Bangor ME 18 Feb. 1908. (Maine death cert. #154). His mother Annie C. Bessey/Bussy was born in Freedom ME 17 May 1828, and died in Bangor 24 Sept 1901 of gastritis.(Maine death cert. #104). Her antecedents have not been clearly determined, but it is probable that her father George Bussy and Ann Boyce were the George Bysa of Waldo Co. Maine who married 26 April 1827 Ann Paine.

It is possible that Dr. Blaisdell remarried after Annie's death in 1901, for his widow is recorded as Emma L. Blaisdell. John was a brother of noted physician Warren Osgood Blaisdell, M.D., who was practicing with him in the town of Vermont IL in 1860, and became the leading citizen of McComb IL, where he was leader of the Republican party and breeder of trotting horses. He was born in East Orland ME 16 March 1831, and died in McComb IL 19 March 1903 (AMA, *Directory of Deceased American Physicians, 1804-1929* (AMA, 19930, I:133, which cites obit. in JAMA 40:930).

Jane died in Boston 9 July 1933, age 67 (Massachusetts Cert. of Death #6143). She had no brothers, but three older sisters who married, and had descendants. Her oldest sister Nellie B. was b. Boston 1855, was buried Mt. Hope, Bangor 2 Jan. 1940, had married Augustine Belden, buried Mt. Hope 11 April 1934, and had a son John Belden and a daughter Marguerite "Daisy" H. Belden who was buried Mt. Hope 8 Dec. 1976.

Jane also had a sister Hattie (Harriet?) M. b. Ohio c. 1857, who married Bangor dry goods merchant Frank P. Wood and lived later in Castine. They had four children, Langdon, a Buffalo stockbroker, Charles, and Mabelle, who studied music in Germany.

Jane's third sister was Minnie F. b. in town of Vermont (Putnam Co.) IL in Feb. 1860 (Both in 1860 Census for Vermont OH). Minnie m. 8 June 1884 Charles^{8} H. Huckins (1845-1907; John$^{7-6}$, Joseph$^{5-4}$, Robert^{3}, James^{2}, Robert^{1}) by whom she had John B. Huckins, coal and lumber dealer in Bangor, born Los Angeles CA 11 Dec. 1885, buried Mt. Hope 29 Oct. 1949, (a wife Estrella R.? buried Mt. Hope 10 May 1953), and Annice Maybelle Huckins, b. Bangor ME 2 Aug. 1892, m. April 1922 Joseph Kent Post (1892-1943), son of George Atwell Post of Providence and Emily Kent.

They had three children, Joseph Kent Jr. b. 1928, m. (1) 1950 Jean Gates Baldwin by whom he had Margaret Kittredge (Picket) b. 1952, and Gretchen Suzanne, b. 1955. They were divorced and he remarried (2) 1966 Natalie Olney Webster b. 1936, by whom he had one child, Joseph Kent Post III, b. 1968.

Annice and Charles's second child was Suzanne, b. 1929, who m. 1931 Donald C. Day, auto sales in Southborough MA, by whom she had four children: Melissa, b. 1954, m. 1978 Mark Kimball Vokey b. 1952, who had daughter Caroline; Jennifer b. 1956; Geoffrey b. 1958; Peter Kent b. 1959; they now reside E. Dennis, on Cape Cod, are active in Wildflower Society, and keep the records of the Hutchins, Post and Blaisdell families.

The third child of Annice and Charles Huckins was Charles, b. 1931, m. (1) Kathleen, by whom he had Pollyanna; div. and m. (2) 1968 Madeleine, by whom he had Andrea Mae b. 1971, and Monica Marie b. c. 1973.

EXECUTIVE SECRETARY FOR TWO RAILROADS.

In 1900 John did return to Boston, to work for the Maine Central, as "Secretary for [a] short while before his death to Payson Tucker, late Vice President of Maine Central R.R.//Assistant Sec'y to G. P. A. of Boston & Maine R.R., Boston [8 mos][7]". At an unknown point in John's life, perhaps about this time, he took courses in Mechanical Drawing at Boston YMCA.

For 14 months he had an "Excellent business proposition [when] invited and was accepted to represent Waterproof Collar Co in Maine, [but the] company failed [8]".

In 1901 he "Was solicited by Met. Life Ins. Co., took agency and won their prize for largest amount of business written in New England in Intermediate Class...3 mos sellg" [9](Resume 1915).

John then worked in his wife's family's home state, Maine, but was living in Philadelphia. John's resume, "A Record & A Promise//The Record" lists his jobs chronologically, and the first is:
"1. Selection of operating crews, surveyors and office force, acting as secretary and assistant to Leonard Atwood, (at that time confidential agent for Morgan interests) building and operating

[small railroad] W.W. & F. R.R. in Main[e].", at a salary of $2000-$2500 a year [10]. Another resume says that in the "Spring of this year [1901 I] met and was employed by Mr. Leonard Atwood, Capitalist of Philadelphia, then projecting a narrow-gauge railroad from Wiscasset, Me. to Waterville, Me. I became his Secretary and upon me later devolved much of the detail for putting this project through. Later I was elected Treasurer of the Company...1 yr 9 mo secy [1901-3].

Leonard Atwood (1845-1930) was an inventor and promoter who had missed making a fortune in the discovery of an oil gusher in the first Pennsylvania oil fields (Ben & Natalie Butler, *The Falls: Where Farmington, Maine, began in 1776* [Farmington Historical Soc., 1976], 16).

He claimed to have invented the first oil pipeline, and the first elevator. He planned to build a narrow gauge railroad from Wiscasset on the Atlantic Ocean across Maine to Quebec. Rails were laid southward from his birthplace, Farmington, toward Waterville, with a station built at Farmington Falls that was converted to the William Gower home. But as the local historians recount, this became the "Railroad that never ran", and "the ambitious project failed miserably" like so many of his imaginative schemes.

John tells of the next step, in "1903...In September of this year I returned from Cape Fear, North Carolina where I had been doing some work for Mr. Atwood, under Pepper & Register, Contractors who were putting a 1200-ft. concrete dam across the Cape Fear River." [11].

"Mr. Atwood's health compelled him to drop all business and I located temporarily with Miss M. Carey Thomas, President of Bryn Mawr College, Bryn Mawr, Pa., until the Spring of 1904 [Secy 1 yr)"[12].

M. Carey Thomas (Info from Caroline Gould 1 April 1962) (1857-1935) was a famous Quaker feminist educator, who had been refused a Ph.D. at Leipzig because she was a woman, about 1880. Perhaps John's first Christmas with his family in Leipzig in 1871 established a common bond. She did get her degree from Geneva in 1882, and became the first woman Dean in the U.S., at Bryn Mawr in 1885 to 1908. She became the college's President 1894-1922. She was a leader in achieving the womens vote in the Nineteenth Amendment, and was also a leader in the peace movement (Helen Horowitz; Robert McHenry, ed., *Liberty's Women* [Springfield MA: G. & C. Merriam, 1980], 411; Peter Brock, *American Peace Movement* [Princeton: 1971], 887; Blanche W. Cook, *Eleanor Roosevelt* [NY: Viking, 1993], 2:343). How we wish we had John's diary of these years, or his recollections of this great woman!

We get a nice portrait of her at this time from James Gould's former colleague in history, Helen Horowitz (Helen Lefkowitz Horowitz, *The Power and Passion of M. Carey Thomas* [New York: Alfred A. Knopf, 1994], 365): "Her dreams of a great college had a chance; but she constantly had to outmaneuver a board of trustees who mistrusted her. She hardened herself to the outside. Inside, however, conflicts roiled. Her passion and her greed entwined her with two women [her lovers Mamie Gwinn and Mary Garrett] who loathed each other, who each had to be satisfied but kept apart. She was in debt personally and collegiately. She was always grabbing, grasping for more; and she had no sense of where the college's needs ended and hers began. As she moved into her forties, the scars of her childhood burn immobilized her and caused her pain;

she fought even harder against the new limits her body imposed. As scandal and personal illness surrounded her, she hid behind a smokescreen of propriety and acquisition..."

The Spring of 1904, when John left Bryn Mawr, Horowitz describes as a "nightmare" in Thomas's life, when her lover Mamie Gwinn walked out on her and married, and Bryn Mawr was in a financial crisis precipitated by the breakdown of the contractor for the new dorm and power plant, Arthur Houghton, who was "careless about money and possibly corrupt."(Horowitz, 365, 329).

This could not have been an easy job for John, and he may have been glad it was only "temporary". He had taken a large reduction in salary, from $2500 with Atwood to $1500 at Bryn Mawr.

While living in Philadelphia, John and Jane had their only child, Warren, born 15 Nov. 1903. He was named for his grandfather, T. Warren, who had died eight years before, in 1895, taking the family name of two generations who recalled the famous martyr doctor-soldier General Warren, killed at the Battle of Bunker Hill. Warren was given the middle name of his mother's family, Blaisdell. The name is reinforced on his mother's side, where her uncle was Dr. Warren Osgood Blaisdell.

In the Spring of 1904 he "Re-entered employ of Mr. Atwood in Philadelphia and Waterville Bangor Me. until September 1904, when he left me and disappeared."[13] The Waterville project may have been Atwood's continuation of the linkage of railroads, which came to disaster for lack of money and the refusal of the Maine Central to permit the lines to cross theirs. (Butler, 18-19).

John was then "selling 1 yr..[when he] Took up agency work for University Course and National Binding Co until Fall of 1905"[14].

We then get a musical interlude in 1906-8 when he was "Traveling in West giving lecture-recitals on music (San Francisco, Little Rock, Ark) and returned to East to give course of lectures for Ivers & Pond Co., Boston...Travel & selling 1 yr" [15]. Elsewhere he explains that he was a "RECITALIST for leading piano houses in exploiting Pianola. This called for LECTURES on Music before prominent musical clubs."

In 1908 he was doing "selling lectures 1 yr...In Milwaukee, Wis. giving lecture-recitals for Edmund Cram."[16].

START OF ADVERTISING CAREER, 1908.

In 1908 he says he "Returned to East on account of death in the family and studied Advertising until Fall of 1908". There was no death in the Gould family that year, so this must refer to the Blaisdells in Maine, probably his father-in-law, Dr. Blaisdell, who died in Bangor on 8 Feb. 1908.

The result of his study of advertising was perhaps a brochure he later sent his son with a cover note: "Warren--This is my first piece of publicity, Dad"[17]. It is titled "The Squirrels on Boston Common", with no date. It says, "Anyone familiar with Boston must be familiar with the squirrels that inhabit that famous piece of ground.

Almost any hour of the day they may be seen, scurrying across the greens or the walks; clamoring up to some man's shoulder or nibbling out of a child's hand; visiting this individual or that group.

To one who will watch and note, a common trait of these 'nut crackers' becomes impressive.

No matter how hungry a squirrel may be, although you seldom see one that looks ill-fed, he is more likely to eat only a portion of what you gave him, and will carry off the balance and hide it.

As soon as he has satisfied his present appetite, Mr. Squirrel 'beats' to one of his many supply depots. Take him by and large, he is the greatest little quartermaster you ever saw and he keeps a very careful record of everything on hand, its location and its capacity.

He knows that the days are coming when from one reason or another, the H.C.L. will be upon him, so he hoards away that which will permit him to sport a warm suit of clothing and the finest kind of overcoat for the Winter, and to set a satisfying if not a bountiful table through the hard times.

And while the proud, stuck-up pigeons must huddle into odd corners and shiver in the wintry blasts and would surely starve to death except for a stray crumb, the spillings from an occasional feed bag or the charity of the good hearted people of Boston, Bunnie Squirrel cuddles down in his hollow tree apartment, while the wind howls and the snow scoots past his windows, and when there is a lull he slips out to one of his cellars and selects what he needs, knowing that he has plenty more salted down.

He is the greatest little SAVER in the animal kingdom.

Why not take a lesson from "Bunnie"?

YOU do not really *need* all the money you earn, do you?

YOU *could* put away just a little of it if you only tried, couldn't you?

Well, let's begin, TO-DAY.

SUFFOLK SAVINGS BANK
FOR
SEAMEN AND OTHERS
1 Tremont Street
BOSTON
Massachusetts"

Chronologically, John's next job after Bryn Mawr was "Assistant to Mr. Ralph Albertson, then Employment Manager, William Filene's Sons Co., Boston, Massachusetts Also Secretary of Filene Cooperative Association."[18]. This began in the fall of 1908. His salary was back to $2000 a year, the figure at which he had started with Atwood. In another place he says he "entered service of Wm. Filene's Sons Co, as Sec'y to Mr. Albertson, Efficiency Manager and Mr. Cory, General Manager. Left them in Fall of 1909 but did some work for Mr. Filene at the 1915 Exposition." In 1912 John is still listed in Boston Directory as "Executive Secretary" at 90 Tremont Street, the same address as Ralph F. Albertson, "Manager" for Filene's (Dir. 1912, 802, 142).

Ralph Albertson was an extraordinary character. Born in 1866, he was an ordained Congregational minister who had founded a commune in Ohio in 1899, and wrote many books on the social gospel (*Nat. Cyclopedia of Amer. Biog.* 15:367-8). He became superintendent at Filene's, then moved to William S. Butler department store in Boston 1910-12 as manager, then moved to New York. He was active in the Single Tax movement that William Lloyd Garrison Jr. was leader in Boston of the day, and active in promoting cooperatives, like the Filenes coop that John worked on.

Albertson left Filenes in 1910, so this may mark John's move to his next job [19], as "Assistant to late Edward A. Filene in conjunction with first lectures on Business Administration at Harvard College." [two years, 1908-10]. Filene (1860-1937) was the progressive department store head who started the bargain basement whose produce was given to charity if not sold in 30 days. In 1901 he and his brother Lincoln founded the Filene Cooperative Association which could veto any management decision. and later had representation of the board of trustees. He and James Jackson Storrow founded the Boston City Club, open to people of all races and classes. In 1909 he began the movement for city planning called the Boston-1915 movement, to which John may be referring above. In the same year he helped organize the Boston Chamber of Commerce. So we can see that John was involved in the great progressive movements of the day. An early internationalist, Filene was founder of the League to Enforce Peace, and promoted the League of Nations and International Labor Organization.

By 1910 the Gould family had returned to Boston, where they lived at 150 St. Botolph Street, in the South End, near the Christian Science Center and Symphony Hall. Perhaps Warren began school nearby. In 1913 the family moved from 17 Cumberland Street (which crosses St. Botolph's) to 42 Ivy Street, Fenway, in Brookline, where his sister Ida had boarded the year before. We do not know if Warren went to school in Symphony Hall area, and changed to Brookline school.

After Filene, John lists a year's work in 1909-10 doing "some investigating and efficiency work" as "Private Secretary to Mr. Clarence Hollander (L. P. Hollander Co., Boston) making Efficiency Survey and re-classifying employes [sic].", making $2000 [20]. T. Clarence Hollander was an executive of L. P. Hollander & Co., whose ad reads: "Importers and Retailers of DRY GOODS, Boston, 202-216 Boylston Street; New York, 550-552 Fifth Av. Newport, Casino Building Paris Office, 5 Cite Rugemont."(Dir. 1914, 2284, 961).

That job ended 1 March 1910, when he did "a few weeks substituting...[at?] Callahan's (Boston) in the Managing"[21].

So, in late March 1910, John got a job at $2500 a year with the Moxie soft drink company, as "Private Secretary to late Frank M. Archer, Vice President of The Moxie Company, Boston; also handled research and assignments for Mr. Archer (an authority on Substitution and Infringement.)...Assisted him in editing his brochure on the subject."[22]. In 1916 Frank M. Archer is listed as Vice President of Moxie Co., at 69 Haverhill Street (Dir. 1916, 190, 1114).

Then, in the fall of 1910, Archer put him in business for himself doing printing and advertising, but this failed when his "partner did not come up to promises"[23].

So, in October 1910 he was taken back by Albertson, who had become General Manager for the department store Wm. S. Butler & Co., at $2000[24]. John lists job for two years as "Assistant Personnel Supervisor for William Butler Stores, Boston; Confidential man for Mr. Butler. General Secretary for "Butler Group" (a six million dollar corporation.)" He says Butler shot himself Nov. 1, 1912" and "At his death, was appointed confidential secretary for the Receivers of his estate"..."I remained with Mr. Albertson...and with the receivers of the bankrupt firm until Feb. 1914."

Butler Co. was famous as the originator of the department store, evolved from the five cent counter in Boston in 1878 (*Nat. Cyclop. of Am. Bio.,* 52). Edward B. Butler, the only surviving partner, was a noted progressive, who supported Jane Addams's Hull House.

MOVE TO NEW YORK 1914: WORLD WAR I.

After 1914 John is not listed in directories again in Boston for nearly a decade, until 1924. Yet they were living in Boston when their son Warren graduated from high school where? in what year?

Soon after Feb. 1914 John moved to New York, for three years, to work as "Confidential Secretary for Mr. Maurice Dimond, President A. D. Matthews Company, Brooklyn, N. Y. (Two million dollar corporation)[25]. Executed commissions abroad for Dimond family calling for exceptional tact and integrity.)". In another resume he says he was "Sent abroad by Mr. D. in 1914 on confidential mission." and in another, "Incidentally transacted extremely important and personal matters abroad for the Dimond family. At this time received high written praise from late President Theodore Roosevelt for certain commissions performed." Another resume gives his job as EFFICIENCY MAN & SECRETARY...Reorganization of personnel//Interviewing and classifying employment of executives".

It may have been in preparation for this European trip that he refreshed his childhood German at the Rosenthal language school. He does not say whether this was in Boston or New York, or give dates.

In Brooklyn John was involved in several community activities, the founding and Presidency of the Matthews Buyers & Managers Club, as Secretary of "Bundle Day", and promoter of truth in advertising. The first was a employee-employer cooperative founded 6 Jan. 1915, as reported by the New York *World* on 10 Jan.: "BUYERS AND MANAGERS ORGANIZE A CLUB.//<u>This Action of Firm's Employees Marks Another Step Along Line of Co-operation.</u>

At the Imperial last Wednesday the Buyer's and Managers' Club of A. D. Matthew's Sons, Inc., was formed. About thirty-six of the executives of this store assembled around horseshoe tables, and in an evening spent in disposing of an appetizing dinner, in fun making and in an interchange of uplifting and interesting speeches, founded the association that marks another step forward in the co-operation existing in the house of Matthews.

The club is composed wholly of buyers and members of the managerial staff of the store, although it has the privilege to include other employees. It is vested with the right at its meeting to make suggestions to the corporation of way and means to better the welfare of the store and its business conditions.

The officers are: John H. Gould, President...Thomas V. Gould, Secretary...". We do not know who Thomas was, but no known relation.

In John's papers is a letter of 2 Jan. 1915, signed John Gould, on the top of which he wrote, "This was the letter, sent to every member, that gave birth to the famous Buyers & Managers Club". It starts with a philosophical reflection, "The future is full of mystery to every one of us. No matter how long we have lived; no matter how much there is behind us, we never know just what is coming. There is no doubt that this is well, for we would be depressed if we could anticipate the sorrows which were to befall us and on the other hand our joys would lose their full value if we knew what they were to be." He then goes on with a pep-talk for the firm, with a goal in red caps: "ONE MILLION MORE in 1915."

The Brooklyn Daily Eagle on Sunday 7 March 1915 carried John's picture as Secretary of the "Committee in Charge of Bundles", under another photo of the "Sorting of Articles for Distribution at Brooklyn "Bundle Day" Headquarters.

The same newspaper carried a long quotation from a speech by Dimond to the Full Copy Club meeting at the Vanderbilt in New York City on 31 March 1915, which John says was "written by J. G. and given by Mr. M. M. Dimond//This was re-printed in every representative Advertising medium and by many newspapers." He saved the *New York Tribune* article headlined, "MERCHANT PLEADS FOR HONEST 'ADS'" on 1 April 1915. A key idea was that "Truthful advertising points to the coming of a new era in advertising.."

But this firm too went into bankruptcy, as he recorded "remained with him [Dimond] and with Mr. John J. Kuhn, Receiver for the firm until September 18, 1915." At that date he was living at 107 Henry Street in Brooklyn. Where had Warren gone? What was their last home in Boston? Did he visit them in NY?

At age 44 John was able to sum up his jobs and conclude with a <u>NOTE:</u> "A Rolling Stone may not gather moss but it gets a mighty fine polish." He philosophizes: "Were this a record of a bum; one who had been kicked out of one position after another; who profited nothing from his experiences-it would be a waste of time to record it, but the man who has passed through this schooling has received a college education in depth and thoroughness."

He follows with a list of his strengths:

"His is now the ability to know and to meet men; to know what and when not to speak; to know that a man cannot do wrong and get away with it-finally; to know the value and the use of the written word; to know how to obey; to know how to obtain service rather than how to command; to know the country in which he is a citizen; to know the advantage of education and be eager to add to his knowledge at every point; to be able to look at all things with optimism; his is now the ability to look for the best in men rather than guard against the worst...[phrase crossed out] and finally his is the unpurchasable blessing of perfect health, a clean conscience, a keen interest in every task he undertakes and real ability to win out. [signed] John H. Gould."

This appears to have landed his next job [26], "1915-19 Started as salesman in N.Y.C. for Elliott Add. Mach. Co. and on the death of their oldest Dist. Mgr. in Cleveland I was appointed D.M., subsequently going to Pittsburgh for them. Left acct. of illness of son requiring residence in Denver." Another version states: "Sales Manager for Elliot Addressing Machine Co., in N.Y.C., Cleveland and Pittsburgh. Had to give up and go West on acct. of son's health." Warren, at age 16 had developed severe bronchitis, and the doctors recommended the mountain cure. Warren told his daughter that he was made to sleep on the front porch in zero degree weather.

RETURN TO BOSTON, 1920; ADVERTISING EXECUTIVE.

No account is given of his work or family events in Denver in 1919, but John is back in Boston in 1919 or 1920. An indication of presence in Boston is the souvenir of an invitation of the New England Music Trade Association's convention at Nantasket Beach on 15-16 Sept. 1920, with a four verse poem which could well have been written by John.

About 1925, at age 45 John reached the peak of his business career and income, as partner of an advertising firm in Boston [27].

His next job description is: "Idea-man and Chief of Copy and Service for Dickie-Raymond Company, Boston. Assisted in building their organization to national prominence in Direct Mail Advertising excellence. Taken into partnership...6 [years], 1919-25". He started at $1500 and ended at $4000. Founded 1 Oct. 1921, with offices at 88 Pearl Street, Boston, it is unclear what John did between 1919 and 1921 (Sixth anniversary celebrated in "Direct Results", Nov. 1927).

In 1925 the firm published 22 page booklet promoting its direct mail services, called "Direct Results". John Goddard Gould's photo is among the five in the frontispiece, probably after he became partner. The opening page repeats his frequent motto, "a Record of Progress and Promise of Performance." The booklet may have been written by him.

"Direct Results" was already the name of the house organ edited by John Goddard Gould on a monthly basis. We have only a few copies which he saved, with articles checked which he probably wrote, including "Just Around the Corner!", a story about Mark Twain in Boston (April 1926), "Travel Planning", "Only a Perfect Fill-in Is a Good Fill-in" (same date), and a poem:

LET HIM IN! QUICK

No matter how busy folks may be,
No matter whom they don't want to see,
There's one man always gets a smile,
Is always greeted in princely style,
At whose approach the whole works goes
To open door and shout,--'Hello's.'
Neatly dressed in suit of gray,
He makes his rounds most every day;
The news he brings may often be

The turning point of your destiny.
Hark! There's his step! Now see them flock
And gather round at the Postman's knock.
--J. G. G."
(Nov. 1926)

In the same issue are "Coordination" and "Persistency Wins Again!". Another issue has his "Revolutionizing Revolutions!" a pun title about selling ball-bearings, and a cartoon "Another Way to Obtain Direct Results" showing a sleepy horse about to be wakened by a diving horse-fly (Sept. 1927). A measure of John's interest in the new medium of radio is an article, "It's Easy to Get the Station When You Know the Wave Length".

One of the services provided by Dickie-Raymond was publication of house magazines distributed to a customer's clients. John Goddard Gould appears as editor of *Leadership News*, a slick four-page "monthly publication devoted to increasing among the Customers and Employees of CHAMBERLAIN & CO. 24 South Market Street BOSTON//WHOLESALE//Beef, Lamb, Poultry, Lard, Pork, Veal, Smoked Meats, Butter, Eggs", all the products on a train of railroad freight cars. In the first issue, of July 1926, John's interest in the history of Boston is shown in his cover page story of the origins of the Chamberlains' store at Quincy Market in 1850, and an inside feature, "Stories of Old-Timers", with an invitation "Let's hear from Old-Timers!", inviting photos of the Market District before the Civil War, and stories about "when Grandfather was a boy." Only a few issues were saved, but continue through Sept. 1927 featuring "Leadership" tips on how to increase retail sales of meat, stories of Faneuil Hall butchers, with fillers of typical John Gould humor.

In 1924 the Goulds were living in Boston next door to their old home at 21 St. Botolph St. near Symphony Hall, and John was working as "advertising manager" at 32 Oliver Street (Dir. 1924, 568).

By 1924 he had changed his middle name from Hogg to his mother's name, Goddard.

In 1926 he published an eleven page booklet of "Thoughts", in poetry and prose he had written for the Dickie-Raymond newsletter "Direct Results". The copy we have is inscribed, "To my brother from "John", Copyright, 1926, JOHN GODDARD GOULD. It starts with this introduction:

"That Life is a wonderful adventure is apparent to anyone who stops to contemplate it. It is a Treasure-hunt in which each indulges according to his desires. But there are two treasures, beside which all others sink into insignificance.
ßRegardless of race, creed, color or ability, he who finds Friendship and Love, have found *everything!*
ßOut of such blessings have been inspired the thoughts in this book.[1]

UNDERSTANDING

By devious paths, highways and trails we have arrived at a common terminus.

In this respect we are helplessly--(but not hopelessly) alike! For however we have toiled or planned, so long as we have held Life's hand, we're rich in having the privilege of standing at this meeting place,--the end of the year.

And then a baby comes across the stage and opens wide the doors that neither age nor strength could move and welcomes us to share in the wonderful possibilities of the coming year.

As we pass through the portals may we be companioned with all the friendships that have come with us thus far and, going forward, may we learn the great lesson of the New Year--to recognize the better nature of the other fellow--in other words, to *understand!*

For through Understanding comes Tolerance; through Tolerance comes Friendship and through Friendship comes Faith!

What more can one ask?

--Reprinted by permission from Dickie-Raymond's "Direct Results." [2] In 1931 John revised this text by replacing the year with the day, and the baby with the Sun.

CRYSTALS AND CHARACTER

If you want to get a bit of inspiration out of your sugar bowl, here's a simple way to do it.

Into about a cup of boiling water pour as much sugar as the water will take up. Make what a chemist calls "a saturated solution."

Pour part of this into a saucer and watch the phenomenon that takes place.

As the solution cools, you will see it solidify into tiny crystals which will spread and increase until, when the water has entirely evaporated, the saucer will be filled with a mass of crystals.

If, instead of sugar, you should take salt, a similar chemical change would take place, but the salt crystals and the crystals of sugar would be entirely different in their character.

Those of sugar would be somewhat flat or tabular, with a generally rectangular outline; those of salt would always be in the form of a cube.

Now the interesting part of this simple experiment is that no matter under what conditions sugar or salt are allowed to crystalize, they will always form true to these figures; the sugar crystals will be flat and those of salt will always be in the form of a cube.

All minerals have their characteristics and each is absolutely true to its own.

The inspirational part of this study in chemistry is that it paints a truth in human character.

If one is careful about the fundamentals of honesty, faith, and morality, he will be unaffected no matter into what surroundings he may be thrown, and always when the test comes, will come through--a man!

--Reprinted by permission from Dickie-Raymond's "Direct Results." [4]

John's sister Ida was a published poet, a skill evidently inherited from the Gould family, where their aunt Annie had written poems, perhaps going back to the Moody family. We have already quoted two poems about the sea, at Hull. Now a nautical theme about his responsibilities as a boss:

THE PILOT

You are the pilot of your own fair ship;
    That ship of Life which God placed in your hands.
How lays the course you've plotted for this trip?
    Do you know the way to the 'Other Lands'?

Be sure you know each member of your crew,
    Their supreme master on this voyage to be.
Command them with an iron hand to do
    Your bidding!--thus you control mutiny!

Some few,--a servile lot of blatherskites
    Schooled by the weak to sneer at discipline
Have deep in their hearts a spark which lights
    And grows to a warming flame, when Love's let in.

If Dishonesty, Hatred, Jealousy
    Or Suspicion, Meanness or other scamps
Among your sailing crew are found to be
    Call them aft to you and discharge these tramps!

They have no place on board if you are bound for port,
    No good can come with them, and woe betide
That mariner who sails with such a sort!--
    His vessel's doomed!--She starts with Death to guide!

Run to the peak your bunting of pure Faith
    Pick crew of Honor, Hope and Charity.
Roam where you will, no storms or fog-made wraith
    Can wreck you on your journey o'er Life's sea! [5]

THE GARDENER

A man toiled in a garden. He was not a young man, and although it was hot, and the sun beat down upon him out of a clear sky, and reflecting from the ground beat up at him fiercely, he still continued to dig and plant.

Considering that this was one of many days spent in the garden one might marvel at the hardiness of the man. The wonder would grow with the knowledge that his labor was not restricted to daylight alone, but often continued far into the night.

Seasons came and went, while, through them all, the soil was turned, new fertilizers tried, several hundred thousand seed crossed and re-crossed, and the effects of moisture and sunshine carefully noted.

Nothing but expense, apparently, until a day fifteen years after he started on his quest, when the gardener picked the first stoneless plum from a tree, and Luther Burbank "had made it good." [6]

Luther Burbank, the famous plant hybridizer, was born in Lancaster MA in 1849, and died the year of these thoughts, 1926. Another poem, which he wrote on 15 Dec. 1919:

SNOWFLAKES

Soft fall the "Petals of Winter"
Winging from dizzy height,
Whitening hill and valley--
Myriad hosts of might.

Might of raging torrents.
Might of waterfall,
Might of ocean surges,
And floods and rains and all

Of Nature's truant forces,
Coming home to rest;
As children turn to their Mother
Who knows and loves them best. [7]

THE THOROUGHBRED

The horse that's bred from a line of fine strain; of clean, full blood on both sides, keenly sensitive, intelligent,--is a thoroughbred.

In which they do not differ from human beings.

In business or society, the man or woman who is not phased by out-of-the-ordinary events, who is not disconcerted at the unexpected; who is able to stand the disappointment of detail or the thrill of victory in a normal way--without breakdown or conceit--is a thoroughbred.

When ideals are shattered and tumbled in the dust; when the last turn in a long, weary trail discloses a yet more heartbreaking path ahead than the one just traversed; he who can rise equal to the need; can plumb depths of yet untouched for newer inspiration, newer courage, and hear and heed naught but the indomitable urge of a conscience which ever whispers, "I can" is

A THOROUGHBRED!

--Reprinted by permission from Dickie-Raymond's "Direct Results" [10]

On the same theme is the poem,

I CAN!

Men cut through the hardest rocks with a drill
And melt pure steel with a flame
And there's nothing impossible in Life's game
To the fellow who says, "I WILL!"

Men tunnel through mountains as they plan
And sail 'neath any Sea
And the fellow who finally comes to BE
Is the fellow who says, "I CAN!" [11]

The last poem is this:

MY CHRISTMAS MESSAGE

Like a blessing rare, divine
May the Christmas Spirit shine
On thee and thine
O friend of mine. [11]

John worked for Dickie-Raymond until at least Nov. 1927, when he edited the last copy of "Direct Results" that we have.

The first Christmas in New York in 1927 he celebrated with fond roast of his former Dickie-Raymond colleagues, in a typed manuscript poem. Logan was senior found Logan B. Dickie; Keysie is senior partner Newell G. Keyes; Caswell joined the firm as head of Service in Sept. 1927; Jack may be John Coolidge Hurd who joined the firm as Merchandising Counsel of Service Dept.; Clarkie is R. G. Clark.

CHRISTMAS 1927

Twas the night before Christmas
But no sound from the Mults
Broke the silence--so we listened
For--"Direct Results"
But with eyes telepathic
I caught visions quite graphic
Of all my associates just as they be
So I write down my copy
While chewing a poppy
Which some accounts for its lunacy.

Logan was sitting, his feet on the table
  Atelling the gang that they'd never be able
To grasp all the ins and outs of his brain
  While he gave new cant to his cigar again
His Bulletin 10 was not in force when
  Bulletin twenty-four nineteen four three
Was made to amend the amount you could spend
  For chewing Gum, Matches or Tea.

Bookkeeper Stewart was trying his new part
  And his voice rang out thrilling and mighty
"I Love my Girl in All her Gowns--
  But Best in a Moonlit Nightie."

A. Remington Caswell "First Nighter" De Luxe
  Recited some chapters from forbidden books
He also declared that he'd make Jack relinquish
  The medal he won for climbing Joe English.

Here Jack in true nautical style cut a caper
  "When Ballbearings Split, why try Middlesex Paper."

Here's Wahoo Keysie--that cute funny chap
  With the incomprehensible, mystery map
Although apathetic, he's also magnetic
  And draws everything to him with a stroke of his flap.

"Now what in the world did I do with that letter
  I am sure 'twas from Jones or else Donnervetter
Although I have searched, I can't find it at all
  "Sh!" don't bother to search--Just call in Miss Hall.

Don't need introduction
  to "Head of Production"
Our Clarkie's the one to speed jobs on their way
  He gets so mad checkin'
That a bridle he wears in
  His muzzle, by biteing his pencil all day.

BACK TO NEW YORK CITY 1928-1930 FOR WALL STREET CRASH.

Leaving Dickie-Raymond and Boston was a major career step downward, but perhaps offered the chance to be more independent.

John next took a job in "1926 to 1931 With J. L. Rouleau, 45 Bromfield Street, Boston, Massachusetts, (then in N.Y.C.) Advertising Associate. Wages, $25. per week."[28]. This is a great loss of income from his previous $100 a week, or $4000 a year at Dickie-Raymond. In another place this is described as "Associate to L. J. Rouleau, eminent Advertising Counsel of New York and Boston.[, and in 1928]...This lead to Assistant Managership of N. Y. Office". He saved a business letter dated 16 April 1929 headed Louis J. Rouleau, Industrial Publications, 347 Fifth Ave, New York, with Gould's name at the top as "Associate".

Rouleau published a four page newsletter which John probably edited, called "*BUY-WORDS*//To attract friends--to prove the POWER of Buy-Words in the Buy-Ways and to present a means of using both profitably, claiming distribution of 20,000 copies in 1928. Along with advertising tips was the Gould humor, like a filler:

Mother Hubbard! 1928

'Twas a sick Mother Hubbard
That went to the cupboard
To get her nice bottle of gin
But when she got there
The cupboard was bare
Her daughter already had been.

The next job he lists is in New York for one year. He describes this as "Confidential Secretary to J. Maxwell Gordon (former head of Gordon Bankers' Publicity Corporation) President Bankers' Exposition, N. Y. City. [29]. Responsible for selection of huge personnel, designing and preparation of Publicity, management of operating plans; carrying through of diplomatic negotiations with Foreign and American bankers and with Governors and Mayors." This came about when Rouleau and Gould's "Buy-Words" announced in 1928 a new customer in the Bankers Exposition, with an "architect's sketch...of the beautiful Reception Foyer" of a center which would provide "the advantage of a central mart where those who have merchandise or service of special interest to this preferred class, may meet those alert in keeping abreast with the times..." It would include exhibits of coin counters, bank furniture, bronze, safety devices, etc. J. Maxwell Gordon's address was 11 West 42d Street, and scheduled for opening in Sept. 1928.

He was still with Rouleau on 16 April 1929 when we have a letter with his name as Associate on top of the Rouleau letterhead at 347 Fifth Avenue soliciting business from a steel firm. On the reverse they offer "*Experienced Editorial Management"...*"It will be edited by Louis J. Rouleau and John Goddard Gould, with an aggregate experience of thirty years in sales-building by this method."

Somehow in connection with Rouleau John then became Associate or "Assistant Manager of the New York office of P. J. O'Keefe Advertising Agency of Boston [30]. Many national and local accounts handled and research work for prominent firms." Major Patrick O'Keefe was the originator of the famous slogan, "Say It With Flowers".

It may be then that he met Charles Davis of Bass River, for he describes work on the Graybar Building west of Grand Central Station: "Here it was my task to create ideas, prepare copy, select art-work, engraving, type and to supervise all advertising campaigns in process. In conjunction with this position it was my responsibility to secure space and lay out offices and equip some in the Graybar Building, N.Y.C. and to pass upon and train executive staffs for another large advertising firm [O'Keefe] and for the Bankers' Exposition in N.Y.C.--about 35 persons."

John saved the blueprint for the O'Keefe offices on the 21st floor of the Graybar Building at 420 Lexington Av. Of the eight offices, O'Keefe got the big corner room, with others for Gould, Rouleau, an Artist and reception. The date is 12 Nov. 1929, approved by J. G. Gould for P. F. O'Keefe. This may actually have gone through, for we have a letter with the P. F. O'Keefe Advertising Agency...Graybar Building, 420 Lexington Avenue, New York dated 24 April 1930, with Rouleau's initials as Manager.

About this time he was living on the Upper West Side, at 419 W. 118th Street, the address he put on the "First Original Copy" of a 3200 word short-story "Red Lead", set in a fishing port near Hingham.

John's only reference to sports is to hiking at this time, with the Appalachian Mountain Club, of which he was still a member in July 1939. He recorded that on 26 Jan. 1929 "a party of the New York Chapter of Appalachian Mountain Club walked out by Hendrik Hudson's monument, near Riverdale and thence along the Hudson. There had been a rain the night before, followed by a sudden drop in temperature, which left each blade, twig, branch and leaf encased in an armor of crystal clearness and jewel-like brilliance. The [poem] was inspired by the scene."

<u>Interpretation.</u>

Along the village byways;
Far from the City's rush,
To the peace of the woodland highways
With their comforting, restful, 'Hush'.

Our steps took us ever higher
'Til we stood where the Great have trod,
And there, like gems afire,
Flashed, 'The Jewelry of God'!

Each branch a prism of color--
Rainbows in every blade;
Emeralds, rubies, saphires;
Diamonds, amethyst, jade!

Like glint of sun on metals
Or the flash of silver sheen,
From a million, million petals
And the spines of the evergreen.

Who labor with brush and palette---
Who strive with chisel and stone--
Not one! Not one shall tell it!
The Art that is God's alone!

Apparently in connection with O'Keefe John was "Selected as Executive Secretary to Mr. M. Martines in planning and promotion of $220,000 publicity campaign for New York Hotels and Restaurants" [31]. In another vita he says Martines was Head of "New York Hosts" (National Hotel Campaign, and his own salary $7500 and bonus..."office has been given up" about 1930-1.

The Great Depression following the Wall Street crash of 1929 must have ended this job, and the following years were obviously hard ones. In 1930 he returned to Boston. Rouleau gave him a strong recommendation which John extracted this:

"Some men do not seem to care where they work so long as eight hours a day are paid for. Others work best among their friends or relatives.

John Gould, who has been assisting me and the O"Keefe Agency for the last five years is one of the latter type and, I might add, it is never a question of hours with him!

With us, he has been constantly at work on booklets, sales letters broadsides, house organs, catalogs, national advertising, etc., creating, directing and supervising <u>every detail</u> from original ideas to type, plates, art work. paper, printing, lists and mailing.

I frankly believe that he will prove a splendid investment for any organization, for he knows direct mail and general advertising intimately and what is equally important, he is experienced in the present day value of complete campaigns, rather than spasmodic attempts.

Gladly, I recommend Mr. Gould, for of scores he alone had the qualities of knowledge and personal integrity to merit a place in our organization.

There are very few men of Mr. Gould's experience, character, energy and ability to be had at any price and we would to a man be sorry to see him go."

Sincerely,

LOUIS J. ROULEAU
N.Y. Manager for P. F. O'Keefe
Advertising Agency, Graybar Building
New York, N. Y."

Rouleau was the kind of loyal friend that John probably had in mind in this undated poem, written in Kensington after 1939:

<u>"Sincerely Yours."</u>

Here's one you know you'll always find
Your friend; to ease your troubled mind;
Always seeing the best in you.
Happy to help in all you do.

Alert to all you may suggest.
        Eager to do what you request.
Staunch help if sorrow comes your way.
        Ready to laugh whene'er your gay.
Proud of the love which you give me.
        With never-failing sympathy;
My signature can't change, because
        It's from my heart, "Sincerely Yours."

HARD TIMES OF THE DEPRESSION, 1930, AND DEATH OF WIFE 1933.

By late 1931 John was back in Boston "associated with Sampson & Murdock, in Direct Mail Dept."[32]. He was employed by J. G. Gordon as Advertising Manager. Sampson & Murdock was located at 111 Summer Street in Boston. A promotional brochure called "*Baldy's Diary*, RANDOM MUSINGS OF AN ADVERTISING MAN", dated 12 April 1931 may have been one of his works for Gordon. The same may be true of The Atwell Company's house publication "Hidden Treasure" for Sept. and Nov. 1931, and the Dixie Electrotype's "Dixietype" of July 1931.

John listed his next job "1931 to 1933 With J. C. Corrigan, Coal Handling Mach., 179 Lincoln Street Boston. Adv. and Sales. Wages $30. per week and trav. exp." [33]. This is actually an increase over the previous $25 a week he made with Rouleau. Elsewhere he gave an annual salary of $1500 and described the job as "In charge of N. E. Sales for J. C. Corrigan Co., Boston, and designed and wrote all advertising, thus establishing more than fifty NEW accounts, including most of Koppers Coke Plants in the east. His nephew Douglas Gould had just left the Koppers Coke Company's research labs in Chicago to work for Atlantic Refining Co. He was living at 57 Pinckney Street in Boston, on Beacon Hill.

At this time, about April 1933, their son Warren was hospitalized for many months after peritonitis developed while he was swimming, but was undiagnosed. Jane came from Boston to Quincy every day to visit him, but was in the last months of her own life, and suddenly died. Warren was not told of her death, and John soon remarried. These events contributed to an estrangement of the family, and a gap between Warren's wife Beatrice, who disliked John intensely, and his new in-laws the Schwabs, who cared for him and their mother to the end of their lives.

John and Jane were living at 87 St. Botolph Street when his wife of 35 years, Jane Blaisdell Gould, died in Boston City Hospital on 9 July 1933, at age 67, having had broncho-pneumonia for four days, and dying of subarachnoid hemorrhage. She was cremated at Forest Hills and her ashes buried in an unmarked grave near her parents in the family plot #39 Eastern Division of Mt. Hope Cemetery, 1038 State Street in Bangor Maine.

Soon after Jane's death in Boston on 9 July 1933 John found a new love, and remarried Jessica Schwab of Kensington CT, where he moved and lived until the end of his life. She was born in New Britain CT 7 Feb. 1887, daughter of Henry DeMers, born in Canada. (Conn. Death Cert. #52, 26 May 1960). We know that by a previous marriage she had a son William B.

Schwab, a dairyman of Kensington CT, to whom they gave the Cape Cod cottage in 1951. William had a son William by his with Esther. Jessica also had a daughter, Delores Carlson, whose son, or husband, Private Clifford Carlson, was in the Army in the Mariana Islands in Nov. 1944. ("Application for Federal Employment", 12 Nov. 1944, 4, #41). There were two other boys, Henry and Russell, married to Virginia, who had a son Russell Jr.

John was "out of work" from Oct. 1933 to 1 Dec. 1933 when "business conditions restricted operations." At this point in life he became a traveling salesman like his father and brother Sammy. He used to show up at our home at 311 Fairfield Ave., in Upper Darby, outside of Philadelphia, in the early thirties, almost always with a different product he was selling. He would fish around in his big overcoat pockets for a treat, and I remember his coming up with a really useful one for a schoolboy, an eraser that would bounce! It was about an inch square, and more rubbery than the drafting gum eraser, and it worked.

To us John was a kind of Santa Claus figure, big in frame, cheerful and hearty, full of laughs and kindness.
Only once do I recall his having brought his wife Jane, who was to die in Boston in 1933, at 67. She was a quiet woman beside John's boisterous jollity, and I can say little about her except that she was kind.

From Jan. to the end of March 1934 he said he had "No steady employment".

But John was back in Boston with Corrigan for the first month of 1934 as Advertising Manager, but at half the salary, $15 per week.

Then, from 1 Feb. to March 1934 he was Advertising Manager for Publix Oil Co., Kenmore Square, at $25 a week [34].

DISCOVERY OF CAPE COD, 1934.

It was in April 1934 that John first became associated with Cape Cod, the first of the family to return to the narrow land that his ancestors the Dimmocks had left 250 years before.

He was hired by E. J. Harris of the Moxie Company of Boston from 1 April to 15 Oct. 1934 as "Special Rep. in charge of sales on Cape Cod. Wages, $30 per week and expenses." [35]. At the end, in 1938 he was making $2080 a year. He detailed this experience as "With Moxie Company for nearly five years, two seasons of which had charge of sales, collections and adjustments in the Cape District. This was very intensive work calling for diplomacy and honesty [and courtesy], as well as strength and endurance. Unaided, a territory was covered and highly developed which now requires three men to take care of."

In another place he gives more detail of the job with Moxie: "including diplomatic settling of old accounts. winning of new trade, the making of sales, delivery of products, collection of empties and the collection of accounts." Headquarters were in Hyannis. The reference to two seasons at this job implies that it was only for the summers of 1934 and 1935. But "Excellence of first season's work won me assignment for another season."

Moxie was one of the five largest soft-drink companies in the world, and the oldest trademarked brand in U.S., having begun as a nerve tonic by Augustin Thompson in Lowell in 1884. (Nat. Cyclop. of Am. Biog. 372-3). But the job on the Cape was seasonal, so he found a job back in Boston.

In the "Fall of 1934 [he] served as Route Builder for C. G. Howes Co., Allston Massachusetts Dry Cleaners and Launderers." [36]. He earned half what he had made with Moxie that summer, $15 a week. He says he "Left them to better my position in Dec. 10th, 1934 to go with..."

"Advertising Associates, 175 Congress Street in Boston as Idea Man and Direct Mail contact man" at $25 a week.[37]. "They were not strong enough financially to keep up the work so I left them to better my condition."

John's name reappeared in Boston directories in 1935, after an six year absence. He is listed as a "salesman", living at 223 Newbury Street, not far from the Exeter School he attended. We have a job application as "Candidate for Local Assignment Supervisor and Interviewer" in which he describes his qualification as "Freedom from influences of any kind tending to interfere with impartial judgment in accurate classification and assignment of those being registered." His address is 223 Newbury Street, phone Circle 6783. Curiously, he lists himself "Married. One boy dependent", for Warren, now 32, was married with his own child.

In April 1935 John was rehired by Moxie Company's E. J. Harrison on the basis of his successful sales on the Cape, working out of Hyannis [38]. "Work so satisfactory, promoted to take charge of sales and advertising in State of Connecticut. During the next period of nearly three years, sales were doubled in this State." He moved to Berlin, Connecticut. He earned $30 a week plus travel expenses. "Have doubled sales and it now takes 5 men to do my work. Have established high record among grocers, etc. in this territory." "I was told", he says, "that I had increased sales in Connecticut by 200%". But the job ended on 30 June 1938 because the "Death of Vice President [Frank M. Archer] brought about change in field work."

In Dec. 1935 John was living at 1158 New Britain Av., Elmwood CT, and applying for a sales job with The Manternach advertising company in Hartford. Some time before 1 April 1936 he had an accident which Manternach refers to with good wishes for "no interruption to complete recovery and good health" in a letter saying they still couldn't hire him.

We still have his layout for a proposed "Universal News for Home Folks", a house organ for the Universal Grocery Co. of New Britain, with himself as editor in Nov. 1937, and a couple of feature articles, "For Diabetics", and "Historic New Britain, No. 1 in a series of short sketches about The Hardware City".

For three months in 1938 he was out of work, and applied for a WPA job. For the last three months of the year he was hired by the Federal Writers Project at the City Hall in New Britain CT. as "Senior Researcher,[39] collecting material for Ethnic History of New Britain [and Hartford]. High commendation from Director of this work." John B. Derby was State Director of the Federal Writers Project. He earned $1056 a year. He was then living at Worthington Ridge, Berlin, CT., but moved to 287 Main Street in Kensington and belonged to Stanley Memorial Church, New Britain. But the historical project was completed.

He was then promoting something he called the Daylight Lamp, as recorded in the first of the surviving family letters: "287 Main Street
Kensington, Conn.
Dear Warren and Beatrice,
and Eleanore [sic], too.

I had to make a hurried trip to Boston last Thursday and returned same night, so did not have time to get in touch with you.

There is no doubt that the DAYLIGHT Lamp is destined to be a big money-maker, just as soon as we can get out with samples. Practically everywhere I have shown it, it is liked and a few orders have resulted and now we are waiting for production and deliveries. I have blown out one set of fuses and one of the lamps had some fault in it so that I have been greatly delayed.

This morning new transformers came and by night I expect to make several demonstrations-with strong likelihood of orders.

Now Warren, I think you have a great chance to show your ability. Try writing articles AT ONCE. Submit them to your paper; to other publications and keep at it. You have the stuff that you cannot get in college,- natural talent for writing and illustration. Try including sketches in your stories. They will tell what you may not be able to tell in words, at first. Later, you will get the hang of it. I'm serious about this and wish you would send me manuscript of ANYTHING you want published and I will see what I can do about it.

Jessica has been quite sick with the prevelant cold and sore throat that has been so general. Better now. Hope you folks got along all right...

There are several good prospects lined up for the lamps and if a few of them will click, everything will be O.K. It is just a matter of being able to hold on..."

So he was unemployed again for the first three months of 1939, until he went back to Boston as salesman of raincoats for Associated Industries of Louisville KY's Fashioncraft, Inc. of 56 Amherst Street, Cambridge, under President Joseph Goodman, from 1 April to 13 May 1939 [40]. He left because "Work [was] distasteful to me." He made only $135 in commissions.

He was out of work again from 13 May 1939 to 30 Sept. 1939, except when he put in a month as salesman for Household Paper Products of Elizabeth NJ, which he soon quit because of "Too much detail, small commission, temporary fill in."[41].

But two weeks in June 1939 unpaid work for International Correspondence Schools of Scranton PA in their Boston office at 38 Chauncey Street under J. B. Whitney of 14 Bay State Av., West Somerville, were to lead to a longer job [42]. He gave it up when "Business matters in Kensington Conn demanded return" and lack of pay. He then applied for a permanent job with ICS, stating his qualifications: "Because I appreciate the value of knowledge and its intelligent application; because I am interested in helping young men and women to better their condition; because I have real appreciation of what the I.C.S. are and of how they assist their students; because my training and experience demonstrate ability to meet all classes of people and to win their goodwill; because of initiative, merchandizing and advertising sense highly developed; because of I have met the advantage of maturity to lend weight to my position and the tact, persistency, honesty and vigor so essential in an I.C.S. Manager. Finally, I have the finest incentive of all to make good, my wife."

This won him the job, and on 19 Oct. 1939 he "became the Hartford Field Representative for International Correspondence Schools "soliciting new students and handling all collections from old" ones, earning only $12 a week. This lasted for a year until his next job.

He must have made enough to buy a lot for a future house on Cape Cod, at 6 Danbury Street, on the west side of Bass River in South Yarmouth. On 18 Sept. 1940 his wife bought a 50 foot by 100 foot empty lot from the widow L. Melva Jones, on which she took a $25 mortgage @ 6 %, which they paid off in three years. (Barnstable Deeds 571:169; discharged 28 July 1943, Deed 672:170, signed by John I. [sic] Gould).

On this and the next lot John was to build a small house, but in the summers before the war camped in the nearby Bass River Camp Ground that had been established about 1938 between Willow and 698 Main Street, at the north end of Breezy Point Rd. by Warren Baker. (The location was identified by his granddaughter Eleanor Baldic; history from Warren Baker's granddaughter Kathy Watson, manager Bass River Trailer Park). John pitched his tent beside a two-wheel box trailer.

The next year when he applied to Canada Dry to be their Cape Cod representative he said he "has lived in Hyannis and would like to live there again,- all the year 'round if desired. (He is interested in a piece of property down there and plans to build)". (Letter from 140 Percival Street, Kensington, 22 March 1941).

On 30 Sept. 1940 John got work [43] as route booster for Bayburn Cleaners, No. 1 Broadway, Arlington, Massachusetts at $20 a week, about what I earned as starting soda-jerk at Rexall's.

WORLD WAR II WORK FOR WPA AND DEFENSE INDUSTRY.

Returning to Connecticut, he was hired again by WPA on the Connecticut Writers Project at 63 Dwight Street in Hartford as Research Assistant at 82.80 a month, from 23 Nov. 1940 to after 23 Feb. 1941, under Mrs. Louise M. Crampton, State Supervisor of Conn. Writers Project [44].

With the fall of France in June 1940 the U.S. had begun a large program of aid to Great Britain, and defense industries in the country were booming. John recorded that "On the outbreak of World War # 2, I entered factory of Fafnir Ball Bearing Co., New Britain and became expert Precision Grinder with three promotions." He started at .55¢ per hour and got raised to .80¢ working on Carrigue grinders under L. Dewey [44]. They were living then at Hartland Terrace in Kensington CT.

Now 70 he went on working from April to 27 Sept. 1941 as cashier and clerk in shipping and service for John P. Nielson & Sons, Ford Agents at 122 Washington Street, Hartford, at $20 a week, but was laid off for "Lack of work" in the business [45]. They were living at 140 Percival Av. in Kensington. His health is still strong, with only a "Slight Inguinal Hernia" to complain of. His weight was 150 at 5 feet 10 inches in height, as it had been in 1938.

During the summer of 1941 he was living at Bass River, for we find a resume typed on stationery of Charles Davis (1865-1951), the extraordinary engineer-internationalist-presidential candidate, descendant of Lucretia Mott and cousin of Anne Garrison Gould. John saved a letter from his old boss Rouleau referring to his construction of a home, "the new bungalow". This is probably the 24 foot by 27 foot one story, 3 room house that stands empty in 1996 at 6 Danbury Street, with a sagging roof and amateur-built brick chimney (Assessor's # 29:110; for sale for $50,000 by Surette Realty in West Dennis for the owners, Nicholas S. and Irene S. Aiello of Worcester, assessed for $60,000, of which the land was $41,100 and the house $18,500, "a tear-down". The Assessor's card says the house was built in 1930, and "Effective year built 1947").

We have a photo of John and Jessica sitting at the front door of the house, with a gaping hole where the fireplace was to be built from piles of used bricks.

Danbury street is about a half a mile west of Davis's well-known "House of the Seven Chimneys". The Gould cottage is the second house west from Breezy Point Rd., a street that leads south to the beach on Nantucket Sound.

Rouleau thanked him for sending a brochure about Carl Davis, then nearly 80, commenting that he "was amazed that a man as old as Mr. Davis should have such a real and active interest in the affairs of life that counts. You and he have one thing in common namely your hold on youth."

After the war, in April 1946, Davis's five page biography was published in *National News Service* #7007. That three copies show up in John's papers strongly suggest that he wrote it for Davis. Davis tried hard to bring the United Nations headquarters to Cape Cod, and the brochure concluded with a strong pitch for World Government: "Mr. Davis believes that the only solution for the famine-breeding Old World wars of death and destruction--or anywhere else on this earth,--and for the creation of opportunity to live in lasting peace and in neighborly fashion with all nations can be found *only* in WORLD GOVERNMENT!"

We have a calling card that he used on the Cape:

Reasonable Terms

A Refined Diplomatic Service

John G. Gould
Claims Adjuster

Box 53
Bass River, Massachusetts

In July 1944 Jessica bought another lot in South Yarmouth from L. Melva Jones, which was registered two years later, in Aug. 1946. (As in the previous purchase it was in his wife's name, signed 20 July 1944, Barn. Deed 653:528). I remember visiting him at Bass River, with my parents, and recall only that he had aged, and seemed less active, and alone. In 1948 my Father took a picture of another, larger house than the one he had built. Perhaps this was a larger rental. The photo shows a double gabled cottage in vernacular style, the gables joined by a center cross gable in which there is a front door and central chimney; at one end is a screened porch; the cottage is shingle-clad with dark trim. In 1951 Jessica transferred her ownership to the two lots and buildings thereon (the small bungalow) to her son William M. Schwab of Mountain View Drive, Kensington CT, reserving rent free occupancy for her life and her husband John G. Gould or survivor. (Barn. Deed 792:29, signed by him 5 Sept. 1951). About 1954 John and Jane consented to Schwab's sale to fellow Kensington residents Per and Elena Pearson. (Barn. Deed 845:186; they sold it in Sept. 1959 to Douglas Forbes of Winchester in deed 1055:271).

Having just turned 73 he was still the optimist, as his New Year's reflection shows: "The doors of 1943's 'TODAYS' are swinging open for you.

Each offers you two stairways: the steps of one descending down--the steps of the other, ascending.

Each of these ways leads to unknown possibilities. It is up to you which of these paths you will follow during 1943,

Every step that takes you 'upstairs' is electric with the mysteries of the Future--a better job, greater comfort for those whom you love, education, better health, etc.

No matter if the yesterdays of 1942 were unsatisfactory--here is the Door of Today!

And be determined, as you stretch out your hand to knock on the portals of Today to ever remember that according to what you ask (and strive for) you shall receive--on the other side of that door!"

John went back to Fafnir Company for whom he worked through the war to the day after V-J Day, 16 Aug. 1945. [46] Fafnir was making parts for Curtiss Warhawk fighters. John contributed this poem to "Fafnir News" of March 1943:

I Am A Fafnir Bearing

World-famous for my daring,
(I've been on fighting front lines everywhere.)
I'm an expert at "eviction"
Of progress-slowing friction,
And for carrying loads to Victory--
well, I'm there!

I've done my bit at stopping
Any evil intent cropping
In the diabolic scheming of the Japs,
Who fear our planes that harry,
So resort to 'hara-kiri.'

Thus silencing their Oriental yaps.

Other partners to the Axis
Have also found the fact is
We're incomparably better than they be.
Plane controls all have a 'slickness'
That makes for quickness.
It's the 'smoothie' Fafnir gadgets--
and that's *me!*

You'll find me in the 'Warhawks,'
In 'Fortresses', whose 'wartalks'
Are *listened to* by those on whom they call!
In flashing, dashing 'Lightnings,'
Who carry death and blightnings
Wherever they may cause their loads to fall.

I'd also like to mention
Other facts for your attention
(Referring now to how our Army's faring.)
Most everything that swings,
Turrets, guns, and other things,
Depends upon the *proper* FAFNIR BEARING!

And then there is our Navy
That thinks that I'm the gravy.
They look to me as one would to a brother.
For when they see me spinning,
They know we're out there winning.
For I know that one good turn deserves another.

So when you hear some grinding,
And the friction starts a-binding,
Remember now to use this magic 'key.'
To satisfy your yearnings,
Increase your weekly earnings:
INSTALL FAFNIR BALL BEARINGS, for that's me!

J.G.G., FR52

February 17, 1943."

RETIREMENT AT 74, AND DECLINING YEARS.

John was 74 at the end of the war, and finally retired. (Application for Old Age Insurance, 18 Sept. 1945, giving Soc. Sec. # 045-03-3536).

He was living at Hartland Drive, Kensington CT in 1945 and 1948. But he was still looking for work, asking for an interview to prove that "You will think I am but 50." For the next decade he was doing free-lance advertising.

In 1947 and 1948 he was producing advertising, as we see from historical notes about old New Britain for a local bank, perhaps not used. His story of the Jesse Hart blacksmith shop, and the 1842 Baptist Church gives us a clue to the historical research he did for WPA.

At 78 he was still writing poetry seriously as we see from the rejection notices from "Good Housekeeping" and greeting card companies. But his tribute to "The Gardener" was published in the Sunday *Standard-Times* of New Bedford 21 Nov. 1949.

An illness of John or Jessica that sent them to the Cape Cod Hospital in Hyannis evoked this extravagant praise of the hospital, and of Cape Cod, published in the *Cape Cod Times* 27 Oct. 1950:

Few of his letters to his family have survived, but this undated one, handwritten late in life, perhaps during the Summer of 1953 when they were living on Mountain View Drive in Kensington, is revealing:

"Dear Son

God bless you! That wish is and always has been close to my heart

Distance makes no differences where we know the speed and the power of prayer and as I say these words to myself I know that you have already felt their impact.

I need no Holy man nor learned men to teach me the value of prayer. Through many years of experience I have <u>witnessed</u> the answers by which God has proved that He exists and hears and <u>replies</u> to one who <u>believes</u> in Him and comes to Him in any trouble or perplexity.

So in this confident spirit I am asking that God shall guide your fine mind and your true heart so that there will come to you the rewards of wealth, health and happiness you merit.

You have been and are a worthy son and I have only the utmost confidence in your future success.

It is not my desire to interfere with your own plans but recognizing as I have the potentials of your talents and training I feel that your greatest and most natural field of endeavor is Advertising.

You should be and can be an A.1. Assistant to some good Agency or as <u>Manager</u> of an Advertising Agency of your own.

Your Grandfather and your Aunt (Ida) and your father have all proved that the Literary streak is strong in the family. There is no barrier to prevent you making <u>your</u> mark in that field.

I still believe that your artist training and ability might be of 'tremendous' value to you in the writing field. Certainly if "Kip" [Colby of Coleman Company equipment] can do it,--you also? And while I think he has shown great persistence I do not yet grant him any marked literary ability.

Within your present environment may be the ultimate jack-pot to your complete success.

But there is not the slightest doubt in my mind that you <u>do</u> possess many of the qualities that you should have to fill a big place in the Publicity field, as Counsellor or Adviser, etc, etc.

However remember that after all Jessica's a very lovely soul and that she and I pray only for your ultimate and complete assurance of prosperity, plenty and comfort of mind body and spirit.

It would be wonderful were you to build and occupy your own house. Wherever this comes true, we are with you 100% and always with deep love from both of us, and this includes 'Be'[atrice, Warren's wife], Jessica Dad

Jessica and I are living in a one room place not far from [her son] Bill's. He is and has been wonderful in his efforts to make us comfortable. He has presented an electric refrigerator, a four burner gas stove and keeps us supplied with water. Quite often too Esther [his wife] brings or sends over something in the way of food. We have to be a trifle careful in what we eat. Jessica has not been any too well but is now much better. I have to avoid salt and take it easy physically,

Our expenses for medical care have been heavy but we have managed by Jessica's guidance to keep outside the red line. Bill is away at the Dairy from 7.30 AM to noon and from 12.30 to 5.45. He is over here frequently as he can be and either he or Billie his son, is constantly ready to run errands for medicines or anything else.

Please pray for Jessica for she has been brave far beyond anything I ever knew and is a lovely soul indeed.

Personally I am doing very well and my ankles are getting pretty near? normal now and my breathing much better. Don't worry about us at all. Probably when the weather gets cool, we will go over to Bill's house for the Winter-2 to 4 months.

We are not sponging on you but if once in a while you could send along a bill, it could be used. Thanks for the subscription to Unity [magazine of the Unity Church to which Warren belonged] and the other publications. We are enjoying them tremendously. That was very thoughtful of you. It will come back to you in deep gratitude from Lovingly

Dad and Jessica".

At 83 he began cleaning up the old files and sent a batch to his son, reminiscing that "Even now, when I lay aside any further thought of continuing this character of work, I cannot think of any other which has given me such real pleasure-and profit.

Even in this parcel of memoranda, copes of letters, manuscripts, ideas, etc., etc. you will I hope find ample evidence to prove that my old slogan had much truth in it,---'He can who thinks he can!'" (Letter from Mountain View Dr., Kensington 10 Sept. 1953).

The next day, 11 Sept. 1953, John wrote another letter to Warren: (Kensington 11 Sept. 1953).

"Just what the future holds for us cannot be foretold but at the present it looks as if we shall go over to Bill's house when the weather gets too inclement. This place we are now in [on Mountain View Drive, Kensington] is not built for Winter's cold or storms and the toilet conveniences are primitive. To correct these conditions would necessitate considerable expense for sheathing around the base of the house and installation of some semblance of a modern toilet, cesspool and drainage connections. Much the better plan will be for us to be located in a couple of rooms somewhere down town in New Britain or possible Kensington, where we could be warm and be able to get some simple meals ourselves and be within easy walking distance of lu[n]ch-rooms, etc. It is roughly planned at present for us to live over at Bill's house during the worst of Winter, but this arrangement could not and should not be contemplated for any lengthy period. It would not be fair to Esther and her family to have us there indefinitely.

Jessica is feeling much better since she went up to Springfield for a week or so, visiting one of her cousins, Bertha Hawthorne. While there she had plenty of steaks, chops, Liver, etc., Was taken out for rides and in general had a grand change of environment. It did her a lot of good and I am very grateful to those who brought this about.

Jessica changed Doctors and this has resulted in her discarding much of her former routine of medicines. She is now getting better sleep and eating better.

Bill has been grand in his efforts to make Jessica comfortable here, got an electric refrigerator, put in a gas stove and is constantly running errands for us and all this while he is trying hard to finish up his garage and attending to the many official duties he is obligated to in connection with Town Affairs, the Lions Club, The Boy Scouts, etc., etc.

Personally, I am much better than I have been altho have to be careful not to exert myself. Take no medicine now but Digitalis and a very little brandy, before meals.

I have been cleaning out much of my old portfolios and brief-cases and have lain aside quite a lot of my records, ideas land samples of advertising pieces. [I] have made a bundle of these and am holding it ready for your call if and when you can get up this way or will mail it to you, if you prefer. I feel sure that you will find much of interest among these papers and if there is anything of mental or spiritual help in the lot, I shall feel thankful indeed. For you of course I hold only the highest and most loving regard and positive confidence that you will be successful in whatever you do. Your faith in God and the fine ideals upon which you were brought up and which you have always maintained, leave no doubt in my mind on that score.

After all is said and done, I pray that <u>always</u> you shall hold in your heart, the utmost tender and respectful and regards for Jessica--to whom I owe so much in success and faith and ambition.

Lovingly and not
forgetting Beatrice--
Dad"

A few months later, on 12 Dec. 1953 John wrote in his ever-optimistic way, his expression of love. Appended is an interesting account of some friends at Bass River.

"Dear Children,
Beatrice and Warren,-

Wherever and however you are at this writing, God bless and grant you both, fullest happiness at this Christmas Season and contentment and prosperity through the new year ahead!

Love is like the phenomenon of Magnetism! You can't SEE it yet you can <u>see and feel its existence</u>! If a bit of soft iron is placed on the upper side of a thick glass plate or on the upper side of a wooden board and then a strong electro magnet is moved back and forth on the UNDER side of either the glass plate or the wooden board, the bit of soft iron will be seen to move in a corresponding direction! Love is like that! Regardless of intervening distance or years! It is ALWAYS THERE, ready and eager to cheer, advise, or help.

Contrasts are what give us values and if we line up our health, mentality, companionship, etc., at the present moment, we find we have acquired quite an impressive array of BLESSINGS!

Age has nothing-to do with! IF one has ambition AND the WILL to back up this ambition, one can be a Gladstone, or a Lincoln or a Churchill or a Helen Keller!

This is only written as a bit of Inspiration and assurance that all is well with us all and only the most optimistic thoughts for you both have a place in our Christmas message.

So go to it, happily and merrily as in the Past and in the many new years to come, please God. With these sentiments I close this note, trying to say what I have not said before,

Jessica and I love you

[signed:] Dad

P.S. You will remember our friends at Bass River, Mr and Mrs. Robert Johnson, who live on Locust Street, there. Well, Mr. Johnson was in an accident some time ago and will (so we understand) have to go to the Cape Cod Hospital, in Hyannis for some further attention in January. Both of these persons have shown their interest in us in many ways and Mrs. Johnson has always been especially sweet to Jessica. I think it would be nice if you could make it a point to call their house and tell them how grateful we are for their fine friendship to us in the days gone bye. [in pencil:] If you could find any way to do a kindness for there good souls, it would be comforting to us. Mr. Johnson built those 8 cottages on the edge of the marsh-at the end of Breezy Point Road. He is also a lawyer.

The next of John's letters that have survived was written in pencil on two sides of an envelope, dated 31 Dec. 1953, the week after his 84th birthday:

"Dear Son Warren,
and Dear Daughter Beatrice

Your letter just came to hand, having been delayed somewhat in the Christmas rush. It was (aside from the 'financial report' which it contains) a most inspiring message and you have brought to this my 84th birthday a very deep gratitude for the love which God has thus blessed me with.

As to your ability to 'make good' I haven't the slightest doubt. In the field of Advertising, Literature, Illustration or Selling, you have a fine background of experience and personal gut and courage not to give up even in the face of obstacles! That is a traditional trait of the Goddards and the Goulds. Keep right on trying-each time profiting from previous attempts.

Whatever 'problems' you may have you will overcome them, Warren. Go ahead, and plan and work for that home of your own [Beatrice and you].

You are absolutely right about your faith in things that are right and based on your belief in your interest in and care for us is a grand proof of your fine character.

Here's hoping that your Christmas was a merry and that your New Year shall bring you all possible happiness and prosperity. Heres to Eleanor and her family and may she have every year increasing happiness.

Believe me, son Jessica and [I] do appreciate your fine wishes for our years to come. It makes our confidence the stronger knowing that we are so loved.

[2] It is most likely that we shall stay here at Bill's at least through the inclement weather months. Esther and he have gone to a lot of inconvenience and expense to provide a place for us.

Jessica is going to the New Britain Hospital Sunday Jan 3d for a very minor operation and will be home here by next Wednesday, so everything will be ok. She has been always wonderful to me and sympathetic and understanding toward my love for you and the memories of the Past. She is a lovely soul and I am very proud to have been her mate for even these few years. In whatever way you can I know that you will not forget her sweet influence on me. I do not hesitate to say I love her.

The best of everything for you and yours. God bless and keep you in His grace.

Lovingly to each of you and with the most optimistic and brightest hopes for the New Year Dad".

John's good health persisted until he was 85, when he suffered his first heart attack. Jessica wrote to his son: "Friday Feb. 25, 1955

Dear Warren & Bea,

Just tho't I'd write you and let you know how Dad is. We have had the Doctor 3 times times week, tho't yesterday he would have to go to the Hospital on account of his heart. We had to stop the Digitalis for a few days as his heart beat was low but it is back to normal to-day. The Doctor gave him a Hi-po to-day and he is now asleep will probably sleep all night. He has had little sleep and all tensed up worrying over his condition but he is going to be alright and should be up & around by Sunday.

Hope you people are well. You surely had winter there while we have been very fortunate in having only 3 in. of snow all winter. We have the month of March to go thro and usually that is our bad [2] month.

Dad was pleased as well as I to get a valentine from the kiddies and Eleanor. It is nice to hear from them [Carol Baldic, born 1949, and David, born 1951].

I should not plan, but ~~we~~ I will try to rent a few rooms or a small place if possible and I can get it cheap enough, up on the Cape for the Summer. I know Dad would like it, but I am only dreaming this and have not mentioned it to him. He would probably say No tho' I know it would be good for him. I think the family here will help us, I mean give us part of our rent, that is [her children] Dolores, Henry, Russ and Bill. If you come across anything reasonable let me know. Perhaps you could send the "Times" down for a month, we could probably find something in the advs.

I shall contact a few of my friends to see what they can suggest. Please remember this is only my idea! I have not [3] mentioned it to Dad. I want to see him happy and to hear him laugh as he used to again. I could get a place near our old Home [on Danbury Street, S. Yarmouth] but it would only bring us unhappiness. That was a dream and is in the Past.

What a beautiful day it is, the sun shines so brightly for which I thank 'God' and for the many blessings we receive.

Our love to you both, Jessica"

John recovered well, but a photo of July 1956 shows him thin and frail. A letter of 13 July from 20 Mountain View Drive says:

"Jessica and I expect to stay at Delores' [Carlson, her daughter] house, in the village of Kensington for a possible two weeks, starting August 6th...

If you can now and then send along any $ it will be greatly welcomed, especially at this time..."

They apparently got down to Cape Cod in the fall of 1956, perhaps at Warren's house at Lyman Rd., South Yarmouth, or his next home in the Octagon House on South Street in Hyannis, as the next letter suggests. John is full of enthusiasm about promoting tourism on Cape Cod.

"October 12, 1956

Your recent newsy letter was evidence of your thoughtfulness-we are always interested in where you are or what you are doing. It was not our intention to leave the Cape so soon but by coming up [to Kensington] with those relatives of Viola, it meant that both Leon and Warren would be spared the trip and the expense.

As Jessica has written you, we thank you for the many pleasant hours we enjoyed at your home. Naturally we would have liked to stay longer, but acted as seemed best under the circumstances. We look forward to the next opportunity to enjoy your fine hospitality.

Note what you say about possibility of being able to look in on us before Christmas but remember that ANY TIME and always, you will be welcome and if we are able to put you up here overnight, so much the better. I do not know just when we will have to move over to Bill's but it will likely be before December.

If you go to Bangore, Me., you will doubtless see [Warren's first cousins] Daisy Belden and Annice Huckins [Jane Blaisdell's sisters Nellie Belden and Minnie Huckins' daughters]. Please convey my respects and deep gratitude for all they have done for me in the past.

Every night I pray for your better health, wealth and happiness and these prayers always include Beatrice.

If you can suggest any way in which my abilities can help you, it will make me happier to be honored by your confidence.

[2] Get that new cosy place on the seashore- or anywhere you please, so long as you and Beatrice, are happy.

IF it is possible - and to me it seem as if it were - why cannot you write up a glowing, enthusiastic description of your present house, in a quiet part of the Town, within easy acces to local grocery stores, meat and fish markets, Post Office, Schools, Churches (?); near Long Pond, an out-door movie and within a very few miles of Hyannis, etc., etc. Run this ad. in the Cape Newspaper with which you are connected or run it in a smaller size in the Hyannis Newspaper as an inducement for folks desiring to get away from the congested Hyannis area?

Suppose that you could get Mr. H. L. Small, who runs that large Filling Station not so very far from your house, to mention your place to people who stop at his place for oil, gas or service. There must be hundreds of such in the course of a month. If he learned that any tourists were interested in settling on the Cape, it would take but a moment to direct them to you. A reasonable commission would satisfy Mr. Small and the many contacts he could make in the course of a month would be sure to produce some worthwhile prospects. This is only ONE idea but you can think up many more, I am sure.

At any rate put out all possible contacts and GOOD LUCK! Lovingly, to both of you. Dad and Jessica."

A couple of months later John wrote another letter to his son, this time started in pencil and finished with a pen, rather than typed as usual:

"Dec. 18, 1956

Dear Warren and Beatrice,

It doesn't seem possible that in seven more days it will be Christmas and I shall be chalking up my 86th birthday!

But while my pace had slowed up so far as <u>running</u> is concerned, my mind is very active

in keeping me reminded of the many blessings God has granted to me through these years.
[2] May your Christmas bring you the fullest measure of its joyousness and good will.

I pray that you may prosper in your work and advance to even greater responsibilities and commensurate income. I am very eager to be of help if I can, in this.

We have not heard from Leon lately. Hope everything is ok with him in Osterville? Hope you see him soon.

It is very possible that Jessica and I will be flying down top Miami in January through kindness of her daughter Dolores. Will advise later.

Please tell me how I can be of help to you to better your income.
[3] Did you have any trouble with that Dec. storm?

Thousands of homes here were without light, heat or power.

Here at Bill's we cooked our ~~scanty~~ meals over a fire in the fireplace! Quite an experience!

God bless you and yours always and all ways and may you have the merriest Christmas ever and a New Year full of real happiness. Lovingly Dad"

AIRPLANE FLIGHT TO MIAMI AND WINTER IN FLORIDA.

After Christmas [29 Dec. 1956] John reported on their circle of family and friends in Kensington, and their anticipated trip to Florida:
"At 'Bill's'
24 Mt View Drive
Kensington, Conn.

Dear Son-

From your last letter I gathered that despite your efforts to provide an atmosphere of good will and cheer on Christmas Day, your anticipated guests failed to gather at your home with Bea and yourself! Never mind! There were two who were there-who will always be with you, wherever and whenever you look for them- Jessica and your Dad to join with you in your spirit of hospitality and friendliness. In fact, there is never a day when we are not there ('in absentia')-by your side! -very ready to help you spiritually morally or mentally to meet and smooth out your problems.

It is 6 P.M. here in Kensington, Conn. and I am reminded that at this same hour only 3 days hence, it is possible that Jessica and I will be having supper in Miami, Florida, with Russell his wife Virginia and his eldest son, Russell, Jr.

Such is the march of travel by air!

We anticipate a warm welcome, climatically as well as emotionally. Jessica has not seen her son for four years!

Of course, while we know they will do everything in their power to make us comfortable [2] while there we are bound to miss our relatives and friends up North, Bill and Esther, Billy and Linn, Leon, Viola and Donnie and Harris Henry Schwab, his wife Gertrude and their two children,-Billie and Diane. Most certainly we will miss Jessica's daughter DOLORES (Mrs. Cliff Carlson) who through her thoughtfulness about my comfort is almost like a daughter to me.

Yet with all we will miss in this separation I pray the change of scene will serve to bring back the smiles to Jessica and her laughter and complete health. Every day of my life, witnessing her unselfish and consistent devotion to me, but serves to increase my admiration, respect and love of and for her!

The snow-storm has drawn a beautiful fleecy white blanket over the previously bare and cold earth.

So son of mine, Ill bid you and your loyal mate Goodnight and God bless you and yours. I'll keep you posted. Sincerely to both Dad
P.S. Warren, we leave at 10 AM. Jan. 1st expect to reach Miami at 3:15 P.M. Love Jessica"

John's report on the trip down was mislaid, and not mailed until 13 Feb. 1957:

"It is almost 1:30 PM, luncheon of asparagus on toast, Tea and peaches has been stowed away and I turn happily to the opportunity to sen you news from this 'place in the sun! The calendar shows that we have been here exactly <u>one month</u> todate and every day has been sunshine!

The transition from cold, rain, high winds and generally inclement weather to day after day of ample sunshine, balmy breezes and cool nights is just a part of the magic-like experiences through which we have passed within so short a time! Most impressive of all were the miles spent far above the earth as our 4-engine air lines sped with dear Mother and me [and about 50 more passengers] from Bradley Field in Conn. to International Airport, Miami, Florida! in something short of 5 hours!

I cannot recall whether or not I wrote to you about this, but if not, let me know and I will promise you at least a second-hand thrill!

Since our arrival, Russell and his wife Virginia and <u>his</u> son 'Russell Jr. have spared nothing in trying to make us comfortable.

As he has the care of some 30 apartments [2] he is a <u>very busy</u> guy and I believe has won the complete confidence of his employer--who owns the two apartment houses <u>here</u> [866 N.W. Third] and another on 33d Street far across the city.

Russells' son, Russell Jr. is returning from the Variety Children's Hospital tomorrow I believe, after undergoing the final operation necessary in his case.

Note: Above letter was written many days <u>prior</u> to the accompanying one of the 13th of Feb ~~but was~~ which was mislaid until today!

Please excuse--
Sincerely Jessica
Dad and
~~Jessica~~"

The next letter, his next to last one, is in a much less legible handwriting, perhaps because he wrote it outdoors:

"Feb. 13, 1957
866 N. W. Third Street
Miami, Florida

Dear Warren and Beatrice

have been sitting outside in the sunshine, until it became a little <u>too</u> warm then changed to the front of the house-which faces North and is shadier. Jessica is ironing Russell has gone out on some errand, Rusty, his eldest son is working on the weekly crossword Puzzle which is run by the Miami News. This week the prize is $700!

Personally, I think this is just a scheme to sell more papers and possibly to get more readers. The puzzles are very tough because there are so many different answers which may be decided upon by the people running the contest.

So far--for several weeks--none have been solved! I suppose that there must be thousands of people trying for their prizes! [a five letter word, second letter J, is tried out in the margin].

But that is like this city anyway. It is the mecca for crooks and gangsters and the newspapers all play up every crime or accident and try to make headlines out of everything they can that it is possible to.

It is 'Playboy' Paradise and they are experts at playing with a 'pair of dice'!

[2] The jails are full--so are a lot of the inhabitants.

Jessica and I wish we could leave but cannot very well just now as it would not be diplomatic to do so.

If we can, we will try to get back North by May. Thanks to the love of Dolores, Jessica's married daughter in Kensington we have our return tickets on The Eastern Air Lines and only need to apply for passage back to Bradley Field, 2 weeks in advance! Everything ok but could use a $ or two, if you can spare any.

Think I wrote you about the trip down. It was nothing less than WONDERFUL! Will write more about that later.

The days are sunny and warm but the evenings are cooler than I thought they would be. Jessica wears a light shawl or sweater in the evenings.

Good night for now. Take good care of yourselves and Eleanors little family too.

Lots of love from

Jessica and Dad."

Their Florida hosts' job having ended, John and Jessica returned to Kensington from Miami before the end of May 1957. John's optimism was still strong, but his strength was failing, as Jessica's next letter tells:

"Dear Warren,

Dad has tried several times to write you but it tires him quite a bit. As you can see, he is not as able to write as of a few months ago. For weeks ago [about May 1] I had the doctor check on his condition & he said he was very good. Russell says, he has grown thinner since he saw us last. I am writing this not to worry you but to let you know how he is. This afternoon Russell took us for a short drive and of course Dad enjoys that. His trouble is shortness of breath and you know there is nothing one can do about that, for that is His heart condition.

Hope you make out in your new work. Free yourself from anxious tho'ts. We know that God answers prayers and we are praying for your success in this new undertaking.

My love to you both Jessica"

On the reverse of this is John's last letter:

"Dear Son Warren

Cont from May 28th Sheet 2

Russell and Virginia (his wife) arrived last Wednesday. The last leg of their journey from West Palm Beach was from S Carolina to here [Connecticut] and the springs of the car were carrying a very heavy load.

Now they must get a roof over them and get partly settled.

Russell's old boss has a job all ready for him in New Britain and his brother Bill found a small apartment for him in Kensington.

They have found a table 2 beds and they are going to sleep there tonight. The apartment comprises a large living Room a bed room and a new bath room.

He will have to work late nights but gets good pay and in a couple of weeks can be quite comfortable. Virginia will also soon get a job.

Now as to your fortunes my prayers and Jessica's also are constantly that you will be shown the right thing to do.

Of course, if you come this way we will do everything we can to help.

In your new job I pray you strike it rich from the start.

Lovingly and very thankfully

Jessica and Dad"

The next letter from Jessica is undated, between June 1957 and Feb. 1959, complaining of John's poor treatment in Ledgecrest nursing home:

"Dear Warren and Bea,

Hope it was as nice at the Cape as it was here. To-day I did not go down to see Dad. I have a very bad cold & a sore throat. It was hard to stay away because, knowing that he depends on me to help him with his supper, I wonder how he will manage. He looks much better, is stronger but the Infection he had before, has developed again and now I know it is from neglect. The Dr. yesterday told me that if I wanted to have him removed from Ledgecrest I could, he would do everything to help me. The minister, Mr. Davis, also would help in locating another place. The trouble in transferring him to another place, is, he might change from something worse. The Hospital in New Britain is the best that we can think of at the present time. There they would treat him as a human being, not let him stay all day, or until I get there, in a condition that would cause all this! I get there and the Nurse lets me, but it should not be that way. The Dr. says his heart is pretty strong lungs good but the Infection is bad. Sunday I asked them (Mrs. Prior) to have the prescription filled, also to get another bottle of powder the Dr. had ordered before. Monday when I went down they had not ordered it. so I asked the Nurse to, stood right by here until she did and it was not delivered until Tues. morning and was not used when I reached there about 4 P.M. They do not answer his calls as they treat others that was too, only a few have special attention. For the present I'll have to wait until I feel better and if they dont want to treat him right, I shall look up some other place. Will let you know if anything else develops, or if he is transferred. Hope you are well.

Love to you all Jessica"

It is hard to date some of the scraps of writings, but we close with this undated credo:

"From an earth-wide range I come born of the souls who, restricted in mind, body and soul in every land, sought a mecca wherein they might express their confidence in a supreme being[.]

[U]nafraid to brave each barrier of God or Man,

they hesitated not to trek vast plains, cleave virgin forests and cultivate break rocky soil or to overcome every hazard of Nature[.]

The very act of winning[,]moving with majestic strides of progress like the foot beats of the Hosts of God ringing through the majestic corridors of Time Eternity the battlecry of indomitable will and changeless purpose, 'I CAN' 'I CAN' 'I CAN' for I am American[.]"

John and Jessie were living with her son William Schwab at 24 Mountain View Drive, Kensington CT until their deaths.

John died in New Britain Memorial Hospital, CT at 6:45 pm on 24 March 1959 at age 88, of circulatory failure due to generalized arteriosclerosis and cerebral fibrosis due to cerebro-vascular accident, with contributory cause of benign prostatic hypertrophy (Conn. Death Cert. #31). His wife sent my Father this telegram:
"JOHN GONE. PRIVATE FUNERAL TUESDAY. LETTER FOLLOWING=
JESSICA=". He was buried in West Lane Cemetery, Kensington CT. As the youngest of seven children of T.Warren and Caroline Gould, John was the last survivor of the eighth generation of the Gould family.

Jessica herself died in the same hospital fourteen months later to the day, on 24 May 1960, age 73, of heart attack, and was buried beside him at West Lane. (Conn. Death Cert. #52). There were no children by this second marriage, and John had only one by the first.

One child, born Philadelphia PA:

i. WARREN[9] BLAISDELL, b. 15 Nov. 1903; m. 19 Jan. 1929 BEATRICE L. ROWE.

Ida Warren Gould (1856-1946)

Chapter XVII

30. IDA WARREN GOULD, LIBRARIAN
(1856-1946)

The first born child of T. Warren[7] Gould and Caroline Goddard was Ida[8] Warren Gould, writer and librarian, born at 24 Hull Street in the North End of Boston 10 Oct. 1856 She died in Melrose MA. 18 July 1946, age 89 (Massachusetts Death Rec. 59:296, #345), unmarried.

Ida was born in the Hartt House at 24 Hull Street in the North End. The famous Hartt House had belonged to the builders of the frigate *Constitution,* now demolished, looking out over Copps Hill Burial Ground, where Ida's ancestors are buried. The house was just a half a block north of Old North Church, where her grandfather Elias Waters Goddard had been Senior Warden, and Goddard home behind it, on Unity Street, where her mother grew up.

I assume Ida had a huge trove of family history that could be tapped, but I never asked the detailed questions. When *I* was eight she wrote my parents this: Ida to Douglas and Elsa, Jan. 4, 1933):

"Now what James wants to know probably is that my grandfather was Elias Goddard. His daughter Caroline Goddard married my father T. Warren Gould, your grandfather.

I do not know what else I can write to make it plainer than that Elias W. Goddard was James' great great grandfather; Thomas Warren Gould was his grandfather; Samuel Clifford was his grand father.

My aunt Lucy [Gould Whiting Harris] once had a genealogy of the Goulds. I do not think it can be in existence now.

So that is all *I* know of family relationship...

If James went to the Phila library he might get more information than I have." [I did, and found nothing]...

P.S. The great great great grandfather was Thomas Gould. Of the Goddards, no record of E. W. Goddards father is known."

Ida, as the first grandchild, was brought out to the Gould homestead in Lexington in her first year, as we see from the diary of 14 year old Lucy (17-24 Jan.: "The baby has grown lots since I saw her last", "George [Estabrooks] thinks Warren has got a real pretty baby", 11-13 July: "Warren Carrie & the baby came out we went to Sandy Pond".

Ida graduated from the Winthrop School on Tremont Street, a four story brick building, long demolished (Fanny G. Patten, *"History of the Winthrop School"* [Boston: the author, 1908], 24). At one time Ida's great uncle Samuel Lawrence Gould had been Headmaster of Winthrop South, and still remembered in Ida's day as "such a pleasant, genial sort of man, that during recess, we girls would cluster around him at his desk, and put our arms around his neck" when he was transferred to Franklin School in 1851 (Patten, 51, 13). Ida was active in the school's alumnae association, serving on its Entertainment Committee in 1905 (Patten, foreward).

In 1864 the family moved from their childhood homes in the North End, at 24 Hull Street, to the original Gould neighborhood of the South End, at now stylish 14 Carver Street Ida's brother John recorded: "In Boston, they lived at No. 14 Carver Street (not far from Park Square and then a select section of the city." In the twentieth century the old brick house became a restaurant, which disappeared when the Transportation Building was built. From here it was a short three blocks walk to the family's church, Emmanuel Episcopal on Newbury Street in the Back Bay, and only a block from the Common and Public Garden.

As we related about the T. Warren Gould family spent its summers at the seashore south of Boston, in Hull. We have an unfinished short story by Ida that gives some flavor of life there, titled Fatality:

"The scene of this story is laid in a little village near the sea. There the first seeds of this romance were planted.

A tall slim young girl knocked at the door of a tiny cottage close to the beach.

"How is he to-day?" she inquired of the woman who cautiously opened the door a few inches.

"Better" whispered the woman. We got a special nurse for him to-day. The doctor says he'll pull through if he lives till sundown. I'm glad you came. He thinks a great deal of you. When he's so he can understand I'll tell him you were here."

"Thanks. I shall come every day until he's well "Good bye for now"

"That's right. Good bye Miss Willa."

More than a week after that call, Willa Dowd strolled to the beach to watch the dancing waves, and came abruptly upon the invalid James Pope[.] He looked a mere shadow of his former robust self. He was//swathed in shawls, half-sunken in the depths of a wheel-chair.

Willa nodded brightly and sat on a log outside the cottage near his chair.

"Getting on splendidly, Willa."

"So I see. I brought you some jelly from our house. Never looked at the label and find it is Chili Sauce."

"Just as good, Willa--thank you for coming every day to inquire too"

Willa laughed infectiously.

"That was the least I could do for my rival at croquet games. You know you always laughed so at my defeat. That made it harder. But it is all wiped off my slate against you Jim. Perhaps in our next game I may laugh at you"

We're moving to town next week Jim, but you may come and see us up there before next season."

Will you come?"

"I hate to promise so far ahead, and I never go to the city after winter sets in Willa. My work is here."

"Very well, I must also work hard up town...["]

The story is unfinished, and we have to imagine how the "romance" was consumated, usually happily in Ida's endings. She doesn't seem to have figured how to get Jim Pope up to Boston to propose.

Some of Ida's memories of Hull are recorded in the 16 photos in her brother Samuel's photo album (#11), in which she identified people and places.

In 1871 Warren took the whole Gould family to Europe on the Cunard steamship *Calabria,* Ida was 15, and may have graduated from Winthrop School.

Ida's brother John's biography recalled some of their homes in Europe: "In Paris, their residence was in a fine house not far from, 'The Church of Mary Magdalen'. In Switzerland they resided in a hotel on the shore of Lake Lucern." (6) . This might be Gersau or another hotel.

We have a Swiss souvenir from this trip, a 2" x 3½" color picture that was framed for "Ms Gould: Cut Matt and PP No 1//6 Pict Sat SF 1,50", perhaps for Ida. The scene, by "R. Dikenmann, Peintre, Zurich", of Gersau in Canton Schwytz, on the north shore on Lake Luzern. It shows the lake on the right with a steamer at the dock, and on the left a grand four story hotel, perhaps the Gersauer Hof. This is beneath the Rigi, and only two miles east of Vitznau, where the James Gould family stayed in 1966.

We already quoted the letter written by Warren to his daughter from Boston in 6 July 1872, probably to 16 year old Ida, who was sketching in the Swiss Alps, at Gersau, while the rest of the family was in Paris:

"If you think Gersau is good sketching ground for artists, why not 'steal a march on them' all, by filling your own portfolio with 'the gems' before you advertise it to the public."

They spent Christmas of 1871 in Leipzig, Saxony, in the German Empire. Ida evidently studied German, which she read, for among the poems in her scrapbook are two in German, written in English script rather than the German script of the day. They are Heine's "Bin Fichenbaum" and what she calls "Gems from the German", six lines from Fr. Ruckert. There is also a cartoon with the initials C. VdP and the quote "Pretty Maud Muller, on von summer day, Raked dot meadow schweet mit hay." The scene is a small figure sitting on a fence holding an umbrella as shade from the bright sun, watching a short hooded figure cutting the hay with a big sickle. Perhaps this was drawn by a German friend of Ida's, mocking her own English accent, recalling a shared event in Germany.

Ida got a job at the Boston Public Library by 1887, while living with her parents at Hotel Helvetia at the corner of Huntington and Tremont Avenues (*Boston Directory 1887*, 518; 1888, 534). We have quoted above a letter from her written in 1889, when vacationing with her mother at Easthampton, Long Island. In 1889 Ida moved with her parents to the new brownstones at the corner of Burlington and Brookline Avenues in Longwood (#55 Brookline Ave., Dir. 1889, 538; 1890, 547; 1891, 557; 1892 moved to Melrose, 574; photos of house in Samuel's album (#11).

Ida's brother Samuel described her hobby of making articles from cigar ribbons: "I am wondering if you ever heard of how Ida used to receive stamped addressed envelopes in his [her father's] handwriting some years after his death.

It came about in this way[:] Along about 1890 Ida together with many others had a "hobby" of making articles--Chamois bags I think--into which were used the yellow silk bands which cigar Mfrs tied their bundles of 25 + 50 cigars. Father used to collect the ribbons + mail them home to her at once, or leave the above mentioned envs to be forwarded later and so some came home to her some years after his passing"(Undated letter in pencil, c. 1938 to his son Douglas, in Ida Gould file.).

Ida moved with her parents to 23 Gooch Street in Melrose In 1893, living there for a decade, until 1904 at least (Melrose Directory 1893, 83; Blue Book 1893, 37; 1899, 37; Directory 1900, 96; 1902, 107; 1904, 92; 1907 nothing)… She probably commuted to the Library in Boston by train. In 1906 she and her mother had moved to the fourth floor of 225 Massachusetts Av. (Photo in Samuel's photo album #11; *Boston Post* 24 Feb. 1908), Boston, and remained there until about 1909, when she was at 148 West Newton St (*Post*, 28 Dec. 1909; Dir. 1910, 789).

Ida was a writer of short stories. We have clippings of four of Ida's short stories that were published. The first, "For Mandy's Sake" was printed in the *Boston Post* 24 Feb. 1908. It is the story of a man whose invention has been stolen. The next, in the *Post* of 28 Dec. 1909 is "Through the Silver Ball", the story of a girl who helps a lame boy. Much later, perhaps about 1928 were two stories printed by the Post. "Vibrations" is about the reunion of a man and woman after 30 years' separation. "Paradise Farm" is about the courtship of a 40 year old spinster and an older man.

In Ida's papers at her death were eight more short stories, typed and revised in pencil, and one in pencil alone. Most of these are romantic stories of how young ladies win a husband. "Red Top" is another story of a spinster who marries an older man. "Miss Tweedie's Wedding" is a tale of the courtship of a woman store buyer and a commercial traveller. "The Hired Man" is the story of a woman who ends up marrying a man she had hired to give her the appearance of having a beau. "The Seer" is the story of a couple who are brought together by the prophecy of an Egyptian fortuneteller who reveals that the man has wrongly inherited the woman's fortune. "Originally Plain" is about a 16 year old who becomes attractive by losing her freckles over a steaming tub of Fels Naptha soap. "Con Amore" is about a courtship that ends after finding an amethyst ring.

"All Alone" tells how a woman brings her husband back home by coming home late from a dancing lesson. "The Blue Parrot" tells of a bird that has been trained to reveal the location of a will.

"The Purity Soap Co., Inc." is a woman writer's reproof of flattering soft-soap from an ad man. "Why don't You do it?" is a draft of an advertisement for life insurance, perhaps suggested by her brother John, who was a successful advertising executive. The unfinished sketch is the one tentatively called "Fatality", quoted above.

In these years before the first World War Ida, probably living with and caring for her aging mother Caroline, changed residences annually, from 148 W. Newton in 1910 to 17 Hemingway for two years 1911-2, 42 Ivy Street in 1913, 21 Cumberland in 1914, finally settling in 1915 thru 1918 at 23 Hancock Street (Dir. 1910, 789; 1911, 826; 1912, 802; 1913, 812; 1914, 833; 1915, 860)

Following the Great War, Ida was active in readings and drama productions at the Library. In 1921 she got her nephew Warren to help her with the second drama put on by the Boston Public Library Staff Club. This was Robert Marshall's "A Wire Entanglement", put on in the staff classroom in the evening of 30 Nov. ("BPL Staff Club", call # T.36.111; *Library Life* 1:2 [24]).

In 1922 there were "clever and enjoyable readings by Miss Ida W. Gould…a responsive audience…with glee at Miss Gould's humorous account of Miss Tweedie's wedding…" (24 Oct. 1922, *Library Life*, 2: #2, 16).

The following fall Ida took the part of a comic Shakespeare character, Mrs. Ford, who succeeds in trapping a lecherous Falstaff in an attempt to woo her, to be driven off dressed as an old women by Mrs. Ford's jealous husband. This was part of a Staff Club celebration of the tercentenary of Shakespeare's First Folio. (*Library Life*, 3:, #3, 32).

At the Christmas pageant a month later Ida took part in "Cavalcade", presented in the Library Lecture Hall (*Library Life*, 3: #4).

In the fall of 1924, when she was 65, she took retirement from the library where she had worked for 41 years. This was the farewell tribute:

"Just one month over forty years ago, Miss Gould of the Catalogue Department, came to work in the Patent Room of the old Library on Boylston Street. This summer, at her own request, she was retired from service."

"The amount of the pension about which there is always an element of doubt, proved in her case to be more than she expected. So, unhampered by financial difficulties, Miss Gould faces the future cheerfully. Many of us remember that she had a literary flair, and used occasionally, to make us all envious by displaying her published work in the pages of the *Boston Post.* With added leisure, she now resumes her short-story writing, when not intrigued by social claims." ("Library Life's Good-Byes" signed "C. H.", *Library Life*, 4: #1-2, 8, 15 Oct.-15 Nov. 1924).

What those social claims were we never knew. We never heard of any friends, male or female, and she lived alone. After retirement, until 1928 she lived at 134 West Newton Street, in the Back Bay (*Boston Directory* 1925-8). About 1928 she moved to Melrose, living finally at 957 Main Street, near her nieces Caroline and Annie Gould, and their mother.

As grand-nieces and nephews, we saw her only on family gatherings like Thanksgiving at 301 West Foster Street We saw none of the humor or playfulness, only a very old quiet and distant woman who had ominous black marks of age on the back of her hands.

The following obituary appeared in the *Boston Globe* (19 July 1946, 6, col. 2): "GOULD--In Malden, July 19, Ida W. Gould, in her 89th year--Funeral service at the A. E. Long Memorial Chapel, 4 Beech Street, corner Mass Av., North Cambridge. Saturday July 20, at 2 p.m. Interment at Wyoming Cemetery, Melrose."

Her niece Caroline worked as a secretary at A. E. Long's undertakers. The death in Malden is unaccounted for; perhaps it was the hospital to which she was taken.

Douglas W. Gould c. 1945, age 49, Havertown PA.

Chapter XVIII

DOUGLAS^9 WARREN GOULD
PETROLEUM SCIENTIST
(1896-1987)

Douglas Gould was a self-made man, an accomplished scientist and writer, who brought himself up from abject poverty to comfortable and respectable upper middle class. Although he came from old Yankee stock, he owed little to his father's side of the family, and showed no pride in it, except for his grandmother Goddard's father, the Senior Warden of Old North Church, Elias Waters Goddard.

He was most proud of his mother Laura Douglas and two older sisters, Caroline and Annie, who sacrificed all to raise him and educate him. He spoke with pride of the Douglases, for whom he was named: His uncle John who became Canadian Senator, his cousin Charlie who became a wealthy Montreal chemical manufacturer, and their distant origins in the clan of Black Douglases, the most prominent family in Scottish history after the royal Stewarts.

He also got his looks and disposition from the Douglases. He looked most like his mother, and her father John Douglas. He had brilliant blue eyes, but the black hair of the Celts. His hair began to recede in his thirties, and by the time he was fifty his photos show him about half bald. By sixty he still had a generous fringe of jet black hair, and a few strays he pulled across the top, and beginning to gray at the temples. His build was thin and wiry like his mother, too, with small bones and small feet. Like his mother, he was relatively short, only 5 feet 6 inches tall at age 23. Of his fifteen grandchildren, Grant Krueger looks most like him.

Like his mother too, Douglas was a very quiet person. It was difficult to have a conversation with him, since he'd never start the discussion, and seldom ask you a question. So he would listen to others talking, and respond thoughtfully when asked his opinion. This reply might be quite independent, or even skeptical, but you couldn't tell ahead from his expression.

So his family really knew very little about his childhood, and nothing about taboo subjects like his father or the war, even if one asked. Even at the twilight of his life when he recorded some childhood memories, and revealed the nightmare of the war, he would not mention his father. So much of what is told here is from inference, or what his wife got out of him. Getting anything personal was, as he would say, "Like pulling teeth".

FAMILY HOME IN MELROSE.

Douglas^9 Warren Gould was born in Melrose Mass, on 27 Jan. 1896, the third and youngest child of Samuel^8 Clifford Gould and Laura Keene Douglas (Certified copies of Record of Birth, Record #5045, copies dated 26 Jan. 1959, 21 Feb. 1963). He was named for his mother's family, and given the name Warren that had been borne by three generations of Goulds in honor of the martyr of the battle of Bunker Hill, Dr. Joseph Warren.

He was born in his parents' home at 88 Whitman Avenue, six blocks east of Melrose center, a two story Victorian house built about ten years before his birth. The area was newly suburban, on the edge of being rural. Many of the nearby lots were still unbuilt, and the woods in which he played as a boy extended nearby out to the rocky Middlesex Fells. A letter of Annie tells of her brother when he was nine: "Douglas and I went blackberrying we have enough to have blackberry short cake and sauce." (Annie to her aunt Minnie from 88 Whitman Ave. Melrose, 9 Aug. 1903, with a pressed clover.)

A letter from Caroline on the same day says: "Next Monday we will probably go to

Lowell! ! ! . . .Douglas is wishing we would go so he can have a good time. He is going to the beach while we are gone, and says he is to have three dollars. (In the neck)" (Caroline to her aunt Minnie 9 Aug. 1903 from Melrose. Could Douglas have been taken to Hull, the former Gould family vacation place, by his father?).

When Douglas was a year and a half his mother took him and the girls to visit her parents and family in Stellarton, Nova Scotia (see photo album #2). They boarded the steamer at Long Wharf in Boston, for the trip to Yarmouth, Nova Scotia. From there it was a long train ride the length of the province to the coal mining village in the north, a mile from the town of New Glasgow. The Douglas home was a two story late Victorian Gothic house. Douglas probably made later visits to Stellarton after the death of his grandparents, surely in 1917.

Melrose was really a middle class neighborhood, far better than downtown Boston. But this life lasted only for a few years, as long as his father stayed home. Samuel Gould never held a job more than bookkeeper, and by 1902 was away from home for long periods, as salesman. The oldest letter of the children that survives is one from Annie that says: "Papa did not go away until Monday morning...Mamma is working very hard." (Annie to her Aunt Minnie 9 March 1902 on stationery of the New Falmouth Hotel, Portland ME.).

The family was reduced to poverty brought on by the desertion of his father by the time Douglas was ten, a source of great bitterness. Grandfather T. Warren Gould had left his widow Caroline with little more than the mortgaged house on Whitman Avenue in Melrose, and that had to be sold before her death in 1915. The only Gould relative who could help out was spinster Aunt Ida, who had a lifetime job as cataloger at Boston Public Library, but was probably poorly paid. Uncle John Gould had his own family responsibilities, as he moved from job to job as private secretary, not doing very well until he got into advertising in the 'twenties.

The other family support was from Laura's sisters, who were far from well to do. Laura's parents in Nova Scotia died in 1907. Her sister Minnie Douglas had modest paying work as ladies' companion. Florence held comparable low paying jobs. Her brothers were ten years younger, and starting their own careers and families. Her brother John C. Douglas was a successful lawyer and newspaper editor just starting on a career as politician, about to run for mayor of Stellarton. He could help out, but Laura may have been ashamed to admit that her marriage had failed, and too proud to ask for help.

About 1904 Laura had to leave the Whitman Street house to move to 324 Swains Pond Av. in Melrose, about half a mile south, near the Malden line. This is one of the most beautiful parts of Melrose today, in the rugged Middlesex Fells woodlands and ponds. Even today it is quite rural, and would have been a great place for a boy to explore (#324 does not exist today, but there is a nineteenth century farmhouse at #314 on the west side of the road, about a quarter of a mile north of Swains Pond.).

At that house he remembered the stirring reports of the Russo-Japanese war of 1904-5, particularly the siege of Port Arthur and the Battle of Mukden in Jan. and Feb. 1905. The children continued in the same George Washington School in Melrose, a long hike from the house.

He left one memory of Melrose in his writings about 1982: "Legend said [there] was an Indian grave and legend is irrefutable when affirmed by the oldest inhabitant. But what likelihood that any member of the poor Pequot tribe (related by some as belonging to the Am...,) could have, would have chosen a brick vault for the final resting place? Skeptics of the legend offered equally implausible explanations of the disputed sepulchre. The immediate area itself once had been a prosperous farm and at its eastern? flank had been a clay pit, now mournfully changed to a dump, the repository of the town's cast off and worthless possessions. The farm's owner had died unmourned and apparently with no relatives but a distant big city cousin who at once establishing legal possession and a look at his acres, figuratively shuddered at the prospect of cultivating and besought local realtors to dispose of the property as a development of small homes." He continues: "But nothing came of this; the opinion seemed to favor the 'Southside' as the likely direction in which the town would grow. Nature asserted herself, and within a short while overgrowth of the soil and decay of the few farm buildings could meet and declare the site no longer a farm. Taxes, often delinquent, reminded the owner of his doubtful legacy...Melrose, Massachusetts"

By the end of June 1906 the family moved to Hartford, CT (postcard from Annie dated 30 June 1906 to her Aunt Ida at 225 Massachusetts Ave.), where they rented at 26 Brook Street, apparently named for a nearby stream which Douglas remembered. The children attended North West School on Asylum Street in Hartford. His father had a job hauling carcasses for Swift & Co. Douglas recorded several memories of Hartford: "As a child I was plucked from the pervasive security of home + relations and set abruptly down in the alien shelter of Hartford. Alien, because we reasoned: Everyone knows the composition of N[ew] E[ngland]: Massachusetts, center of universe, NH, V, M[aine], CT; CT last [therefore] farthest away."

"If the sidewalks are made of flagstones roughly 3 ft. square, and laid end to end with just enough difference in height to assure you tumble at the joint, don't look up, you are in Hartford."

"Panic seized the boy who saw a freight car with ENGLAND stenciled on its side. Heretofore the only RR worthy of being read was the Boston & Maine (curious how he accepted Boston as having precedence over Maine in size, though he knew that the state exceeded his own Mass). Have the British invaded us, taken our RR's and are now 'stamping' the cars as their own? In time the offending car was moved, revealing the full title, CENTRAL NEW ENGLAND. Even this was not wholly assuring--somehow the term 'New England' was etherial--we had New England heritage, customs, authorship. Now it was something material and perhaps the New was a sop to our distant ENGLAND. And CENTRAL! Never heard of [the] place. A map of the New England states was found, and studied: central point seemed to be [elsewhere], belying its name it was the center of nothing, certainly less dens?? noted? than Boston or Hartford."

He went back to visit Hartford with his daughter Elinor, driving by his old home at 26 Brook Street, without stopping. But he did recall that "Samuel Clemens lived in Hartford. He was our author-hero." He added that the town got "civic attention in a bizarre fashion. What other town would have the affrontery to name a principal thoroughfare Asylum Street (actually leading to the institution)." This reminded him of Mark Twain's story of a "diddle", an outrageous lie which the diddler enjoys. Douglas then told his own diddle story of a man who borrows a parking ticket from a neighboring car to avoid getting his own ticket, and puts it back when he leaves.

A WAIF IN BOSTON, 1906.

It was Elizabeth Bradley, three years older than Laura, who by 1906 gave shelter in a warm home to her sister and her three children in Lowell. 496 Wilder Street was a copious and rambling Victorian house where the Goulds played happily with their four Bradley cousins, who were the same ages. The older Ruth had a mothering role. Grace was just Annie's age. Marian was born the same year as Douglas, and James, the baby, was two years younger than he. Douglas and Annie attended Highland School in Lowell.

The first letter of Douglas's that has survived was written from the Bradleys' when he was almost ten, thanking his Aunt Minnie for Christmas presents: [a note from DWG: "Written from 496 Wilder Street in Bad Days. . .Prob. 1906 (This was saved with four letters dated Dec. 26 and 27, 1906 from Caroline, Annie, Grace and Marion, which refer to some of the same presents.)]

Lowell, Massachusetts
Dec. 27, 190-Dear Aunt Minnie

I thank you very much for the game and the book. Besides that I got a game of checkers and

kerchief and a boat we play the Boston game a lot. We built a snow house//a fort and two snow men. We sail the boats in the bathtub.
We were throwing snow balls at Mr. Barren who lives two houses down the street.
Thank Mrs. Mackenzie for the money she sent with which I bought seven presents. Momma came down here less than an hour ago.

Good Bye From
Douglas.

P.S.
Mamma got three handkerchiefs. She got a picture frame from me.
Grace is helping me-new
James now.//
I did not sleep more than half an hour last night, because I had an awful tooth ach and Auntie had only ginger.
In school the class made maps of the United States.
We are started one of New England for a cent.
I won twelve out of thirteen games of tiddle-winks last night with James and three out of three with Grace.
Mamma had a [sugar] cane where she works but brought it to us so Marion, James and I each had a piece.

Good Bye. From Douglas."

Douglas always loved games like checkers and tiddley-winks, at which he was very skillful. At ten one can see his early interest in maps, which he loved too. The letter also shows the expectation that one give presents to every family member, and write thank-you letters, but the poverty is evident. We do not know who the angel Mrs. Mackenzie was, but probably a friend of the family in Stellarton.

The letter gets some elaboration from an undated letter, probably from eight year old cousin James Bradley, which refers to the same events: "Dear Aunt Minnie, I thank you very much for the boat and the picture you sent me. We had a Christmas tree//in the sitting rom full of presents I got ta[?] bookes a boat a handkerchief a picture a Christmas card a game of tiddledy winks a box of candy// Douglas a[nd] I have got a snow fort in the yard. We made a snou man too. We shoveled Mr. Baron's walk and earned fifteen cents. We sail our boats in//the bathtub quite often. Of all my presents I like the picture and the boat the best."

But the Bradleys were not well to do, and Laura did not impose for long. They moved back to the Boston area to one-room flats. When they returned to Boston in 1907 Laura rented single rooms at places such as one in an old brownstone over Mathews Grocery store at 225 Massachusetts Avenue (Mathews Brothers grocery listed at <u>226</u> Massachusetts Av. in *Boston Directory*, 1906, 1257; 1907, 2112.), briefly living with Aunt Ida Gould in the Back Bay, opposite the Mother Church of Christian Science, and just north of Symphony Hall). Then they moved to Lonsdale Street in Ashmont in south Dorchester (Lonsdale runs east-west between Adams Street and Dorchester Av., three blocks north of Ashmont center, *Boston Directory* 1907, 99 and map.), where he attended Mary Hemingway School.

From these days in Boston came a reminiscence he called "Ways & Days of a Boston Waif", which has been reconstructed from a scribbled outline. "Atlantic Avenue to State Street, among Ships Chandlers was the ever beckoning saloon, a workers tavern, marked with a never brightly lighted sign that set its proprietorship in a satisfying light: 'Page's'. Today a sign shouts a name, calling attention to a resort: "You are coming to a place, well known, well established". The <u>place</u> not the person. But this you knew was Page's place, not an establishment flaunting the man Page, but a simple appellation of pride."

"Sometimes a sign said 'No Menu', gathering dust but that was all. Beer at 3C, whiskey 1CK, beer in bottles 10-20C."

"The 'free lunch', was served not all the time, nor on stated days. Plates had sliced ham and beef; sometimes eggs (in shell). Bread (rye, wheat). Stew rarely."

"Unusual 'scene': A man orders a beer, casually or it seems as a minor thought he 'drifts' to F.L. (Free Lunch), builds sandwich and returns to previous group. 2nd helping, possibly 3rd. Barkeep was quiet, observant, never intruded, respected each [customer]. Page entered, bearer of news. All watch. Momentary stir, then each returns to oneself or group."

"A beer dray draws up outside. The driver is big, tired. Two barrels to be put into cellar below the bar. Steps, outside, lead to cellar. How to get barrel down? Rope is laid under, then over the barrel at head of stairs, with two men holding the rope at the street. 'Get out of the way, kid, You want to get hurt?' Remarkable how a man could handle full barrel of beer, weighing 400 pounds. Suddenly effort is made, and barrel is upright. Could this be done unless it was well filled?"

"The appearance of a child with a pail (actually a tin lunch pail up to two quart capacity) would edge up to those at the bar, and fidgeted until noticed [by] 'The bar tender's' eye. 'My father wants twenty four cents worth', and tendered a fist full of mince? rolls? Usually the tender is made without further word, and the barkeeper says quietly to one of the customers, 'Jim, see she ate some? she can make?' He is a keeper of many secrets, and if he makes a living, it is hard earned. It was my business to know the name of the Proprietor and Barkeep. Proprietor was easy. I performed the errand for 1C."

"State Street was vast (certainly for Boston's size). Torrents of commuters pour back and forth, most seem prepared to walk."

"Wyman's eating place (Wyman Lunch Co. advertised ten locations in Boston Directory 1907, 2780, including one at 12 State Street, 2226.) served stew or baked beans. Take both and you have a load. About quality I don't know. But a sure test of a panhandler was to invite him to one of these. If he accepted and wolfed it down, you were on safe charitable ground. Maybe you'd offer a beer."

"Harold Piper, boss of shipping and receiving for Crown Cork & Seal Co. , was ferocious in treatment of draymen who misunderstood size and name of Harold, or ship at Merchants & Miners docks (Merchants & Miners Transportation Co. at Battery Wharf, Boston Directory 1907, 1178.), and great urgency of teamsters to get at job of transshipment. None of today's spread of time. Get it done. All finished exhausted, soon got drunk, others threatened violence against 'them'[1]. Probably this was a suitable line for rising unions."

"C[rown] Cork & Seal seemed to have a monopoly on caps, and machines for closure of soft drinks, etc. I wonder what became of Harold Piper. Sober, and trained, I think he would have been a formidable entry in the boxing world. Of the entry of Gould into his life and home, letter is lost."

"Tom Tyman was a derelict mutually adopted. Poor Tom, those who had compassion for him bought whiskey (no beer) when the man needed bread and meat. Sent to the alley to push a broom, he swept his assignments as assiduously as a hospital housekeeper, performing the task in hours, which would take the dullest maid an hour. Tom's story is not easy to pry out: Good family, 2 years college at Harvard, an accountant, married, he simply let..."

Douglas also wrote two more memories of his boyhood in Boston, which can be read in the legible typescript he submitted them to magazines like the *New Yorker*, but never published. They are "The New England Common" and "India Street as We Knew It".

Childhood was not entirely grim, for he told his children about exciting things for a boy, like the bonfire on the Fourth of July, celebrations on the Common, patriotic parades, traveling circuses, trips to Revere Beach (only three miles east), and explorations of the rocky woods near Melrose.

TEENAGE POVERTY, 1907.

Finally, Laura Gould settled in Malden, a suburb about five miles north of Boston, about 1907, staying there until 1924, but at three different houses, all in the south end of town, almost in Everett. This is the oldest part of town, to which the first settlers came. It has changed little in 90 years, with most of the old Victorian houses in place, some beautifully restored, but with many new immigrant families speaking Cambodian and Spanish.

The first Gould residence was at 150 Belmont Street, on the Everett line, about halfway between Boston and Walnut Streets. Today it is a two story hip-roofed nineteenth century box, white-vinyl sided. Two blocks to the north Douglas went to Belmont School on Cross Street while Cal and Annie were in Malden High. He told James that his father Samuel had invited him to a picnic at a yacht club to which he did not belong, but obviously spent more money than he was giving to support his family.

About 1911 they moved about five blocks west to 27 James Street, Malden. In 1997 this is on the west side of the street between Wigglesworth and Medford Sts., a two story flat roofed shingle warehouse which may have been broken into residential units. This is half a block south of Bell Rock, where the first Malden church was located, and across whose rocky knoll Douglas would have gone to Malden High. The school was five blocks north, in the center of town, where the new building stands today.

Then, about 1915 they moved three blocks southwest to 98 Converse Ave., Malden, where they stayed for a decade until the move back to Melrose, to the Sprague House at 301 West Foster Street The Converse Ave. house is a three story Victorian gable fronted house, with nice gingerbread detail. It is located on the south side of the street, one house from the corner of Green Street, opposite which is Malden's oldest graveyard, Bell Rock or Sandy Road Cemetery. This is under a mile from Malden High, where Douglas graduated, but also a good two mile walk on Medford Street west to Tufts College.

It is not known at what age Douglas first went to work, but it was very early. He probably started by running errands for a penny or dime. When his sister Cal was twelve she said she hoped to have a dollar in her pocket, which she probably earned "when I go on my route with the milk." (Caroline to her Aunt Minnie 9 Aug. 1903, 2.) A note in a photo album by Douglas about a friend named Royal Baker when Douglas was about six says: "add 10 years [=age 15?] or so and Royal was driving a laundry wagon; D[ouglas] helped; not much pay but much fun."

He recorded earning 25 cents on Sundays as organ pumper until electrification, at the Mystic Side Congregational church in Everett, which they attended while they lived in Malden (The church is at 422 Main Street, just across the town line from Malden, at the corner of Belmont Street, only three blocks west of the 150 Belmont Street house, and about the same distance from the James Street and Converse Street homes.)

He commented on John Gould's article "Let the Pealing Organ Blow" in the *Christian Science Monitor:* "My experience about 1912-1916 Mystic Side Congregational Church, Everett Mass, parallel[s] author's. I too, was displaced by electric motor. [The pumper had] Best keep in good graces [of the] organist; otherwise her use of bass notes can exhaust strength of pumper. Heard many a sermon but also got in some good school study."

He did not talk about this painful childhood time when the family lived from hand to mouth, and rented in dingy one-room quarters in poor parts of Boston. Both Annie and Caroline worked, Laura earned money cooking and caring for the children of others, like the Kittridge family in Lowell. Annie wrote to Laura's sister Minnie saying, "Mamma didn't have to prepare [Christmas] dinner at Mrs. Kittridge's as they were going away. Ma got here about 11 o'clock....Ma likes where she is working very much. They have a baby boy 4 mon. old + a little girl 3 1/2 yrs. old. " (Annie to her aunt Minnie, from Lowell 27 Dec. 1906, 1,4.).

Laura did superb cooking and baking, all with a wood stove. Douglas and his sisters raved about her cooking, but never got any recipes, which were all in her head, probably learned at home in Nova Scotia. Among his favorite dishes was a slice of buttered bread soaked in the red juice of roast beef. He did not have a craving for sweets, except penuche, but particularly enjoyed brownies and hot apple pie. Among his best loved dishes were old New England fare like baked beans (with a chunk of fat salt pork) and hot buttered brown bread, oyster stew, codfish cakes, and molasses poured generously over hot corn-bread, fried corn meal mush or waffles. He also loved ox-tail soup and raspberries.

Douglas had learned early not to be greedy, and when offered any portion of food, invariably replied, "Half." If the remaining half were still there when all had finished, he might be persuaded to take it, with urging.

At age 90 he typed out three poems with the explanation: "These were favorites for Cal and me." They are Kirk Munroe's "The Mince Pie Prince", which ends "The moral is this: When mince pies you see, Dear children, beware of gluttony." "The Wolf and the Goslings" is headed: "Forever a favorite with Cal and me." The third one is M. E. Blake's "The Tragical History of Chang Fung Loo", whose rhyme he would repeat to his children:

"For he was a glutton! Just think of that!
In a country with stomachs so small and nice
That they would make a whole meal of one frog--if fat--
Or some infinitesimal grains of rice."

It is probably no coincidence that all three favorite poems are about food, and overeating.

Finally, in Feb. 1915 the long-absent Sam Gould sued for divorce. Douglas was in his last year of high school, and received the legal notice at home on Converse Ave. in Malden while his mother was out working. He could not understand why he was subpoenaed, since he would be a hostile witness, but he went to the hearing at Middlesex County Court in Lowell. As shown in the chapter on Sam above, she did not contest it, except to try to get some financial support, and Sam soon remarried to an envelope maker in Worcester. Sam tried to keep in touch, but Douglas adamantly refused to see him, mention his name, or even let his children know he existed.

The three children went to public schools wherever their mother lived, in Hartford, Dorchester, Lowell, Malden and Melrose. The first one he marked in the photo album was the George Washington school at the corner of Foster and Meridian Streets in Melrose. Boston public schools had been among the first in the nation, and always among the best. All three children finished high school, Caroline attending the last class (1911) for which Greek was a required subject; the others had Latin, and the required curriculum of science, mathematics, history, literature.

Douglas graduated from Belmont Grammar School in Malden on 27 June 1911, in a 2 p.m. ceremony honored by an address from Rev. Richard E. Sykes, and music directed by the one-armed veteran of the Spanish-American War, Melville Chase Program of "Graduation Exercises of the Belmont and Faulkner Grammar Schools Malden, Massachusetts".)

Douglas's interest in science began at Malden High in Tenth Grade. A teacher named Hutchins, who was a former principal but enjoyed teaching better than administration, had a way of making Physics interesting by doing experiments. Douglas recalled one illustrating Archimedes' law of displacement of fluids. (DWG to author 3 Jan. 1974, Diary #41, 118-119.)

But high school brought the bitter memory of the principal Jenkins who refused to certify him as college material, saying that even if he made it he couldn't pay. So Douglas had to enroll in Tufts Chemistry courses on condition and take all the entrance boards in the summer at his own expense.

Douglas graduated from Malden High School on 23 June 1915 at 8:15 p.m. . He was one of the 55 graduates in the "General Course", not the Scientific or College groups.

FIRST IN THE FAMILY TO GO TO COLLEGE, 1915.

There was no money to send Annie and Caroline to college, and beside, no woman in the family had ever gone to college. But they would work and save to put Douglas through college.

Douglas was the first Gould to attend college since his great-great uncle Samuel Lawrence was sent to Brown to prepare for the ministry, and to become a prominent educator in Boston. The other Goulds had commercial careers that required no more than a high school education. His uncle John Douglas, however, had obtained an L.L.B. from Dalhousie University that prepared him for the law and a political career.

Douglas got a scholarship to attend Tufts College in nearby Medford Mass, to study engineering. His picture made the Boston newspaper at the start of college. The photo page of the *Boston Evening Record* of Tuesday 28 Sept. 1915 features the title: "Typical Scenes at a College Opening--Picturesque Stunts Pulled Off at Boston's Franklin Field". Douglas is shown in a beanie cap, jacket and tie in "A Typical Scene on the Tufts Campus on Opening Day...These two Tufts students [unnamed] are seen sprawled on the ground mapping out their courses for the coming year, evidently. Judging from their expressions it seems to have been a solemn task, but they were not alone, for the green was peppered with many another similar group."

Douglas is clearly identifiable, and his companion he said was "R. P. Wood". He added a note in 1986: "R. P. Wood [was a] close friend [from] Everett, Massachusetts, both go to Mystic Side Church. Wood deserted Phi Delta during War. This photo made great stir amongst upper classmen, particularly Sophs. It was forbidden for Frosh to be on grass, and to lie down on it, was beyond measure a crime. Identity not revealed by photographer, if known. . .and how do you like, the cost of paper--!".

He had to work full time through the four years, and wasted little time on campus. The above note implies that he joined Phi Delta fraternity, though he probably wasted little time there or at other clubs, and took few sports. A photo labeled 1917 at 20 Sunset Rd. shows him with 19 other young men, probably frat brothers.

One job he described was being night-watchman in a coffin factory in Boston--a rather spooky job, wandering around in the night among the pine boxes, wondering what would come out from behind the shadows cast by a lantern.

THREE TIME VOLUNTEER IN WORLD WAR I, 1917.

The Great War intervened half way through his college career. He told me he volunteered three times. The first was when he and two Tufts classmates went down to the Navy recruiting station in Boston to enlist. When the first man came out of the physical exam and was told the tour of duty was three years, he said indignantly, "You're crazy! I'll be an old man by then!" So the three walked out and went back to school (DWG to author 12 April 1987, Diary #64, 12-13. DWG to author 11 July 1983, Diary #58, 110-111. Diary 4 March 1966.)

In an unusual moment of talkativeness, at age 87, he told James about the next two episodes. About 1915, while a sophomore at Tufts, some French recruiters arrived to get volunteers as ambulance drivers. Although Douglas spoke no French, he could read a newspaper and volunteered. He was bitterly disappointed to be turned down because he couldn't drive. Two classmates from well-to-do families that had cars were accepted.

He didn't learn to drive until the summer of 1917 when his uncle John Carey Douglas invited him to Glace Bay, Nova Scotia, to drive him around his Senate district. He learned in an Overland, taught by the Senator's secretary (George McDonald?), who anticipated being drafted. A visit to a Hong Kong barber in 1966 caused his "Remembering [an] incident 1917 in Glace Bay, N.S. (lady barber heats water over a kerosine lamp)" (Diary 4 March 1966).

During that summer of 1917 Gould went to the Canadian recruiting office and volunteered for any service available. His uncle was furious, saying he could have at least got him into an officers training camp. But Uncle Sam intervened in the form of a letter from a judge in his home town of Malden, as head of the draft board, ordering him to report for service in the U.S. Douglas couldn't see that it mattered which side of the line you fought on, but the judge was adamant, so his uncle, being diplomatic, wanted to avoid an international incident and to keep good relations with the U.S., and got Gould released from Canadian service.

Douglas cut the summer job short, and showed up in Malden to be kept waiting for months. Lacking money for college and not wanting to eat his mother's food without contributing, he took defense jobs. The first was building barracks in nearby Everett. He then got a job in the Fore River Yard at Quincy, where they were building warships. His job was probably unskilled heavy manual labor.

Finally, he heard that the shipyard was getting deferments for war workers, and asked what would happen if he quit. He would be drafted, they said. So he quit, and went to the Malden draft board and protested his deferment. Three or four days later he was called up for active duty.

He was inducted at L[ocal?]. B[oard?]. Malden 29 April 1918, at age 22 3/12 years, with occupation as a laborer (Discharge, 9 May 1919.)

The draftee was described as having blue eyes, brown hair, fair complexion, and was 5 feet 6 ½ inches tall. Among his souvenirs are the "dog-tags" which he wore around his neck throughout the war, a pair of aluminum discs about the size of a silver dollar, with name "Douglas W Gould. . .USA" on one side and his serial number on the reverse: 2720350.

He was sent for Basic Training at Fort Devens, Massachusetts. There he must have come down with Influenza which had started in an Army camp in the south, and was sweeping the world, for he saved a letter from a former "bedmate":

"Camp Deven
May. 30-18 Hello Kid Gould,

I got your letter and was glad to hear from you. hope you are getting along allright.

Well Gouldie old kid you made a big jump also a big mistake when you thought we were in quarantine as we were transferred the same day as you we are all split up. Patso and Tomlo are together *I* am all alone Swede and Breslin were rejected but will have to do Guard duty till the war is over

I am in F. Co. 301st and it is some company believe me

We had inspection today and I got tipped up but was only//of 54. so I get no pass tomorrow

We expect to get shipped away from here pretty soon. We are having target practise every day and I am some shot. I have not been home since I came here I am always out of luck. They even stopped visitors here Sundays. The camp is like a grave yard every Sunday

Well all the rest of the boys are around here I see them every night. They are all sick of it here and want to move.

Well kid I guess I have no more to say just now so I must close wishing your the best of luck.

From your old bedmate
Timothy J. Galvin
F.Co.301st Inf.
Camp Devens
Ayer Mass

P.S. Write often, Patso is in F.Co. 302nd Inf. so is Tombo xxxxxxxx These are for you from Saltzman. So long Kid."

Douglas was probably released from the hospital soon after this. Among his papers was this surprising account scribbled in ink, called "Then and Now", written in the last decade of his life:

"It is said that today's recruit needs two years of hard training to become a soldier whose skilled use of military gear? embraces perhaps a half dozen weapons. We were scheduled to be battle-ready in a third or quarter of that time, with the proviso that we concentrate our effort on one weapon---the rifle.

At assembly, one morning, the company commander soberly read a communication asking for volunteers to serve in some unstated capacity. It was evident that the prospect was uninviting; that he (the captain) wouldn't like it, but that volunteers or no, a quota would be filled. Those who offered themselves would be honored; why not anticipate this fate and gain a cloak of glory. So we did (another and myself, and away we went entrained with dozens of similar to Camp McClellan,, Augusta, Georgia. (82d Division trained at Camp Gordon, Atlanta GA,5 Aug. 1917 until departure 10 April 1918; *Order of Battle of the United States Land Forces in the World War* [Washington: GPO, 1931-49, reprint U.S. Army Center of Military History, 1988],[; hereinafter OB.]

And so we came into being an integral part of the 82nd 26th division, and therefore called AA (all Keystone) American) presumably because the whole was concocted by random selection (There is some evident confusion here: 26th Div. was the Massachusetts Yankee Division 28th was Pa. Keystone Division, neither of which never trained in the South; OB: 117, 143. The 82d was AA, All-American, Ibid., 349.) That Camp McC. was site of the Pa. N[ational]. G[uard]. named auspiciously. Local folks were ambivalent, indignant that a hated Northerner's memory should be preserved here, but most rejoiced that the butt of derision was a general whose military record was diminished by encounter with "The South's Best".

We now became instructed in M[achine]. G[un] use and tactics. Of the latter, not much was offered. What American troops had ever used a M.G. in battle? Unending oral evidence was given us that we were the fortunate few to whom was given the finest M.Gs in the world--the Browning. "Nothing is too good for the American soldier and Congress has insisted that// 2. the best, and only the best shall be yours." No M[ember of] C[ongress] could face his constituents in the knowledge that the American soldier has a lesser weapon. And so we trained, and were happy that we had the best. Those few who somehow know of the existence of guns with names like Maxim, Vickers, Lewis, wondered how the war could continue in the absence of the Browning. The weeks passed, until one morning as we were about to start for the firing range, Sgt. B. held up a hand and said "Put your guns back in the racks. You are going on a little journey." A triumphant, unified shout, and all discipline forgotten, "Gee, Sarge. tell us where? Are we going over? (alas)". "Can't tell you; but the town is near the ocean and it has a brightly lighted street."

Sure enough, by late afternoon we were crowded on railway cars, each of us with a barracks bag containing all our personal possessions and all else issued to us and charged to our personal account in the minutely perfect records of our Historic Uncle, and two days later we were disembarked at Camp Upton, NY.

A delay of three days while someone found the above mislaid records and we boarded the SS Mauretania. Our immediate squads were assigned a part of the (once) luxurious mahogany of panelled space of the ships library. Even the Bunks, four high, attested to the desire of Washington that the best should be given us.

Scores of books have told of transport: ship life much like ours; the principal difference was in the duration of our on Mauretania was blessedly short. Liverpool (Knotty Ash, Greetings from King George), Southampton to embark on S.S. Harvard (was the S.S. Harvard one of the familiar steamers that operated S.F., LA SD?). Who forgets the discomfort of a rough Channel passage to Le Havre, and a long hike in the rain to a rest camp. Here the first of a million enquiries as to where was "Sunny France?"//

3. A review staged for Gen. Hunter Liggett implied the best awaiting us. It was well known that Gen. Pershing was very busy planning the defeat of Germans without reliance on the armies of France + Britain. Gen. Liggett, it was said would be the man to lead Americans in person. Wonderful was the polish on shoes, remarkable the unison of opinion how puttees should

be rolled; and how pleasing to hear the compliments of the general as he passed along the ranks. "Yes, machine gunners, we need you; need you badly and I have pledged Gen. Pershing that you are ready. By the way, where are your machine guns, I would like to see you demonstrate them?" A deathly silence. "Well, where are your guns?" "Ft. McClellan, sir". "Well I'll xx xxx! Do you mean to say you have no guns?" "Yes, sir. Sgt. B. told us to put them in the rack, and we did." Well, I'll * * * (stars get larger, the general redder in the face, less coherent in his speech). "I don't know what to do with you, whether to send you back to America, or to put you in a labor battalion (all accompanied by interjections and furious gestures). Thereupon a French major valiantly spoke up, "General, my nation gave you the French 75; the British have furnished your army with heavy artillery, I happen to know that there is a supply of M.Gs available; will you permit France to give you these for your troops here?" Gen. Hunter stared; still in the shock of unbelief, he murmured "Take them and do what you like with them" (obviously he meant troops, not the guns. "But", turning to an aide, "You will go with them and report back to me each week. If there is the slightest doubt of competence or the merest interruption to their training, we shall send them to labor battalion, right now they aren't worth their passage home." And the general stalked to other parts of wartime France.

And so, in the custody of the French major, we moved dejectedly to St. Aignon (St. Aignan was replacement depot southeast of Tours, in central France, ABM-445, map 438.) and Selles sur Cher acquiring the Hotchkiss mg and the doubtful reputation to which the revered motto of the Coast Guard could be applied.

Of Hotchkiss MG little need be said. It was of the 'gas piston' type. A small aperture in the barrel allows a portion// [4] of gas from the cartridge explosion to escape at high pressure. The stream of high pressure gas actuates the mechanism (reciprocal) , to effect extracting the empty shell and to insert a new cartridge. It was as reliable as most m.g.s, it had served in France for almost four years, but most unfortunately, we had it [and] could again call ourselves m gunners. With this weapon we went to war, and if we did not love the Hotchkiss, neither could we imagine life without it. I do not know whether Gen. Liggett ever heard of our Phoenix-like rise. We are confident that if he did possess knowledge of our regeneration, he would, general-like, take credit for decision not to sent us into the hands of S.O.S. [Service of Supply.] The apparent happy solution made by giving us the Hotchkiss m. g. was slightly marred in an unexpected manner:---" [no more].

WOUNDED ON THE WESTERN FRONT, 1918.

Gould was sent to France, probably as a replacement, crossing the Atlantic on a troop ship, the converted luxury liner *Mauritania.* He said he was put into the former library of the ship. He saved his meal card, which reads: "Your quarters are on DECK C COMPARTMENT 7 in which you occupy BERTH 32// You draw your food at Station No. 1 Breakfast 6-45 a.m. Dinner 11-45 a.m. Tea 4-45 p.m. <u>NOTE</u> This Ticket must be punched when a Meal is served and no food will be served without it." The punches show the voyage lasted nine days, the eaten meals starting with "tea" on the first day, breakfast the second, but skipping lunch and tea, which probably shows seasickness. But from breakfast on the third day all meals are taken until dinner on the ninth.

The arrival in England was marked by a Red Cross post card he mailed home reading: "The ship on which I sailed has arrived safely overseas. Name Douglas Gould. Organization 2nd Co. July Auto. Replace Draft American Expeditionary Forces Symbol I 725". Laura received this at 98 Converse Ave. Malden on Aug. 8, 1918.

On another letter addressed to his mother in Malden "A Message to you from His Majesty King George Vth. Douglas later noted "I think we were given this to mail home as we prepared to embark Southampton for LeHavre Just to let folks at home know we had safely crossed the Atlantic (on the Mauretania)". The letter inside has the royal coat of arms embossed above

WINDSOR CASTLE all in red, followed by a reprographed message reproducing the royal message:

"Soldiers of the United States, the people of the British Isles welcome you on your way to take your stand beside the Armies of many Nations now fighting in the Old World the great battle for human freedom. The Allies will gain new heart + spirit in your company. I wish that I could shake the hand of each one of you + bid you God speed on your mission.

George R.I. April 1918."

His service with the A. E. F. in France began on 1 Aug. 1918 (Discharge.). He was sent from Le Havre to Selles-sur-Cher, then to the rail marshalling yard and replacement depot at St. Aignan. From there he was sent to the front with the 82[d] "All-American" Division, which had been in France since 17 May 1918. Primarily recruited in the heart of the old South, including Appalachian men like the heroic Sergeant York, it was filled with replacements from New England and the Middle Atlantic, which gave it its "All-American" character, nickname, and AA patch (OB 349.

Gould was assigned to Company D of the 320th Machine Gun Battalion (This was part of the 163d Inf. Brigade, commanded throughout by Brig. Gen. Marcus D. Cronin; OB 346, 347.). He loved his job as a courier-runner, which he shared with a Vermonter named Flanders (could it have been the future Vermont Senator? (This could not have been the Vermont Senator Ralph Flanders (1880-1970), who spent the entire war as an industrial executive, never in the service; *Current Biography* 1948, 212.). He joined the unit at the front in the Flirey Sector (The village of Flirey is 18 miles NW of Nancy, then on the front held by the 89th Division; 82d had just come off the line at the Lucey Sector, and moved to Toul area 10 Aug. , and on 12 Aug. moved to the Marbache Sector on the Moselle, where, on the night of 15-16 Aug. it went back onto the line between the Foret du Bois le Pretre, 2 miles NW of Pont-a-Mousson, eastward across the Moselle to one kilometer east of Port-sur-Seille, under the French XXXII Corps; OB 350-3. It was in immediate reserve on 10 Aug. (American Battle Monuments Commission, *American Armies and Battlefields in Europe* [Washington: GPO, 1938], [hereinafter ABM-1938], 105.), 10-25 August, then was in the Battle of St. Mihiel 12-24 September 12 to 24, and finally 25 September to October 9 in the Argonne-Meuse Offensive. These places are all in Lorraine, the former French province that the Germans had conquered in 1871, and defended desperately to protect the great steel center of Metz.

Gould fought as an ordinary infantryman in the bloody battles of the Argonne and St. Mihiel. He later listed where his company was: "Places Fleville, Apremont, Les Islettes near Street Menehould, Chalons-sur-Marne, Bar-le-Duc, Ligny hike" (All of these are behind the lines, except the first two which formed the jump-off line of the final battle of Argonne-Cornay, in which he was wounded; Les Islettes was the reserve area of the 82d prior to the battle; he mentions being in Bar-le-Duc before this, when he wanted to visit the nearby home of Jeanne d'Arc; Ligny-en-Barois was headquarters of the First Army, 8 miles SE of Bar-le-Duc. The reference to the hike may be to the way the division got from the battlefield of St. Mihiel westward to the Argonne).

Years later he got a list of members of his company, some names which he could not decipher. But the Captain was Archer, and non-coms were Sgt. Murphy, and Sgt. Williams. That the company was racially integrated we only know in his effort to distinguish the two Smiths, one "hard coal", the other "nigger". They are otherwise undistinguished except for Williams, who got T.B.

He would never talk about the war, but made it clear that it was a literal Hell that no sane man would want to repeat. Only at the end of his life he wrote up a public display to remember the final battles as part of his series "Why the Flag Today?" His captions read: "St. MIHIEL 9/12/18 First independent action of American forces against German army. General Pershing had insisted that in principal his armies would accept despite intense pressure by the French and British Allies, to merge the AEF into their armies, all the American troops, G[reat] objections given by the High Command (Foch) but operated solely as an American. Pershing's insistence prevailed, the high success of the operation sustained his position; the experience of staff work found invaluable. American losses were [7,000]."

"9/12/18 Battle of Argonne-Meuse began. The great Allied offensive extended from [September 20] to [the Armistice]. General Pershing's American army held a position fronting the Argonne forest. The attack upon German positions was planned and put into effect wholly by his staff. The objectives were exceeded, and at Armistice (11/11) the American Army was considered equal to and perhaps superior to either of that of France or Britain. American losses were [120,000]." For most of the first month on the line the 82d Division was in trenches in the valley of the Moselle. He joined the unit at Flirey, a devastated ruined village, crisscrossed with trenches and underground dugouts (Photos of Flirey ABM-1938, 132-3.)

They were under the French Eighth Army, XXXII Corps, which later erected a monument in gratitude (Photo, ABM-1938 131.). This area had been a battlefield for four years, since the French had stopped the German invasion here, and there was a highly developed system of trenches and underground dugouts, between barbed wire and a wilderness of shellholes.

The 82d had just made a raid into the No-Man's Land to capture three German machine guns. The division suffered 100 casualties in this month. By Sept. 1 the Americans were taking over sole responsibility for their sectors, and the 82d was transferred from French command to the American First Corps, First Army (ABM-1938, 166.).

None of this structure made much difference to the soldier. Much of their warfare was spent waiting in cold and muddy trenches, which stunk from rats and parts of dead bodies. Periodically the cannon fodder infantrymen were ordered to climb out of the trench, through the protective barbed wire, and run yelling at the invisible Germans in the trench ahead--hoping not to be hit by the machine gun fire, or the mortar and artillery shells crashing into the "No man's land".

As an essentially cautious person Private Gould probably never did any heroics, or anything remotely rash, until ordered out of the trenches by the platoon leader, with whom he must have lived in the same wretched cold mud and filth with the other doughboys, eating the same cold packaged food, cursing the lice, and wishing to be home, but grateful to be still alive.

The American offensive in the Battle of St. Mihiel began in the rain, an hour after midnight 12 Sept. with four hours of saturation by American artillery followed by infantry attack across the trenches (ABM-1938 124.). Fortunately, the Germans had already decided to abandon the St. Mihiel salient that extended south of Verdun, but they defended the main highway of American advance with fierce artillery fire.

The 82d was on the far right of the front, on the both banks of the Moselle, along the main road between Nancy and Metz, just north of the town of Pont-a-Mousson. Their mission was to protect the flank of the 90th, as it advanced on the left, and to raid and patrol, but not permanently advance the first day (ABM-1938 138-141; the corps commander had argued for attack, but was overruled, Major Gen. Hunter Liggett, A.E.F. (New York: Dodd, Mead, 1928), 149-150.).

The next day one unit of the division drove up the left bank of the river to Norroy, where one man won the Congressional Medal for bravery. Gould's brigade, the 163d, raided and patrolled on the right bank, northeast of Port-sur-Seille toward Eply, in the woods of Cheminot, Voivrotte, Tete d'Or and Frehaut (OB 353.). Opposing them was the 31st German Landwehr Brigade (*United States Army in the World War 1917-1919: Military Operations* [Washington: GPO 1948; reprinted by Center of Military History, 1990]; [hereinafter WWI], 8:279.). The 82d remained on the line until 20 Sept., in the old French trenches.

The 82d was thus at the hinge of the whole bloody campaign, placed at a strategic corridor fiercely defended by the Germans, and consequently suffered over 1000 casualties. To have survived must have seemed a miracle.

But only 14 days elapsed before they were thrown into the next battle. Gould's unit then moved some 60 miles westward along the front, from the battlefield of St. Mihiel to the Argonne. This was done by a long circuit around Verdun, as we reconstructed above, a hike near Ligny, to Bar-le-Duc, north to Les Islettes near Ste. Menehould (They may have gone by bus and foot from the front to Nangois-Joinville area; WWI, 10:8; by 22 Sept. they were ordered to Rarecourt area, and were to go to Triaucourt via 1'Iverdun, Ibid., 52, 54; they left the area south of the St. Mihiel front on 24 Sept.; map Ibid., 67; the foot units arrived by motor on the night of 24-25 Sept. near Rarecourt, Ibid. 56; on 25 Sept. the division was moved by bus to the woods south of Clermont, at Grange-le-Compte Farm at Passavant-en-Argonne, 60, 63.)

The Battle of the Meuse-Argonne began 27 Sept. at 5:30 am. The 82d was in reserve of the First Army (Held ready to assist attack and resist counterattacks, and to reconnoiter the roads to Varennes, Ste-Menehould and La Harazee per Field Orders #20, 20 Sept.; WWI 10:83, 85; located in woods south of Clermont (25-29 Sept., WWI 10:162, 168, 177; On 29 Sept. the 82d's 327 Infantry Regiment was moved up to the line at Baulny, WWI 10:181; on 3 Oct. the division was placed in First Corps reserve for "eventual relief of the 28th Division" WWI 10:200; ABM-1938 172.)

The First Army attacked on a wide front between the Argonne Forest on the left and the Meuse River seven miles north of Verdun, driving north to penetrate the Hindenburg Line. It is perhaps then that Gould was at les Islettes, a small village six miles east of Ste. Menehould, on the road to Verdun. As the offensive continued on 4 Oct., the 82d was again in close reserve of the First Corps in the Argonne (ABM-1938 176, 177; the 82d was put on alert 29 Sept. when German infantry started filtering south of Chaudron Farm north of Baulny, and one infantry regiment was moved up, WWI 10:151-2.).

The division under newly appointed Gen. George B. Duncan was finally on 7 Oct. put onto the line at Apremont and Fleville, villages about two miles apart on the Aire River, for a flank attack on the Argonne Forest from the east (Field Order 44, 6 Oct., WWI 10:222.). The German artillery on this ridge were able to harass the American advance to the east.

While Gould's 163d Brigade remained in Corps Reserve, another brigade of the 82d Division moved onto the line in the night of 6 Oct. The next morning they pushed westward into the Argonne Forest, north of the village of Chatel-Chehery, taking Hills 180 and 223 against the strong resistance of some of the best German units of the German Army, the 2d Landwehr, and 5th Guards of the LVIII Corps (Map WWI 10:234; ABM-1938 176, 177; panorama 227, map 228.).

Among the defenders of the Argonne was the Wurttemberg Landwehr (Liggett 168.). Private Gould saved a souvenir of one German soldier, Cadet Leo Flegenheimer of the 7th Battery of the 2d Wurttemburg Field Artillery, which contains a letter in German from a friend in Heilbronn dated 30 Sept. 1918, which places this in the Argonne battle. This soldier had been in the war some time, for there are passes to Heilbronn , Stuttgart and Ulm for 10-22 Dec. 1917, and 25 May to 7 June 1917. Among the triumphs of these last battles was the American capture of nearly a thousand artillery pieces. This soldier was probably one of the gunners.

On 8 Oct. the attack westward was resumed toward the ridge beyond Cornay, where a light railway and a road were the core of German supply into the Forest (ABM-1938 229). It was on this day that Sergeant York of the 82d won the Congressional Medal for his capture of 132 German prisoners in a fight in the valley west of Hill 223 (ABM-1938 229-230). The 82d captured the village of Cornay before dark, but retreated at midnight (ABM-1938 231).

They recaptured the village again 9 Oct. about 11 am, but after noon the Germans shelled it and counterattacked, surrounding the Americans there and killing or capturing 100. The Germans appear to have pushed back into Fleville, and down the road to Apremont (See line of 9 Oct., map ABM-1938 228). The Germans fought hard, despite exhaustion of their front-line troops and lack of replacements, and on 9 Oct. decided to retreat ("Gudrun Movement", WWI 10:542-6).

Finally, the Americans recaptured the town for good on 10 Oct. On the night of 8-9 Gould's 163d Brigade was at last brought up from reserve to relieve the 28th Division two kilometers west of Hill 223 (Called Schlossberg by Germans, WWI 10:541.), in the heart of the Forest, through Drachen (the Dragon) to 2¼ kilometer west of Menil Ferme (OB 355.). This is a line that zig-zags from the heart of the Forest, short of Cornoy to Fleville. The 82d held a front of about three miles west of Fleville, two miles south of Marcq (Map ABM-1938 228.). Near the village were scattered trees, perhaps fruit trees, then open fields before the terrain rose up to the heavily wooded hills of Bois de Cornoy, part of the Argonne Forest (Army photo in WWI 10:142.). The Germans had the approaches protected by machine gun fire as well as mortars and artillery.

On 9 Oct. Gould's unit attacked, reaching half a kilometer south of Pylone to Rau de Louviere. The two ravines in the forest ahead were those of Lancon (running east-west and thus no obstacle), and Chevieres, running north-south, and thus probably the one he was sent to scout with the compass.

It was during this battle west of Cornay on 9 Oct. that Douglas was gassed. He was one of 6,373 American casualties suffered in the battles of Cornoy and Marcq, a figure exceeded only by the First and Third Divisions (ABM-1938 328.).

On Easter before his death Douglas relived the Battle of the Argonne with me (DWG to author 19 April 1987, Diary #64, 16-18.),a story he had never told when he was well. Company D of the 320th M.G. Battalion arrived at Bar-le-Duc, the entrance to the Argonne Forest. He wanted to stop at Domremy to see the birthplace of Joan of Arc, but he was the only one in the group who had heard of her.

He was surprised at the size of the pines in the forest, and how carefully the French had preserved these trees to use Canadian trees for pulp. The terrain was more rugged than expected, cut by a huge defile that was on the topographic maps, but not known to the Americans. He was sent with his Brunton compass (which he brought home as a souvenir) and rifle (the only man with a rifle), to tell the men of the hazard. When he arrived he found the Captain of the company drunk and his second in command in tears because he'd lost all his men. For bringing this news the Captain rewarded the messenger with all the canned beans he could eat. At one point Douglas found a cold spring from which he could drink, but was chided by a soldier who told him there was a dead mule above the spring. He didn't care!

One day Gould was sent as a runner to the front with some hot rations, but when he arrived it had been contaminated by gas, and had to be dumped. They said not to worry, he could take some German prisoners back. He signed for six, and en route was missed by a six inch shell that landed nearby but didn't explode. Farther on one of the prisoners was hit by a shell; all that remained was a boot and a white bone, almost to the knee. At this he vomited and "went crazy". When one of the prisoners tried to run away he shot him. Back of the lines he turned in the remaining four prisoners to the M.P.s who scolded him for looking so unkempt.

Another time they were advancing to a wide German trench, evidently widened more than normal to trap the Allied tanks. He captured a German anti-tank rifleman, thought of killing him, but spared him. So, ironically, he got the German to a safe POW camp, and spared his life so he could serve Hitler!

Douglas was gassed on the front at the Argonne Forest on 9 Oct. 1918, only a month and two days before the end of the war The Americans were authorized to use both phosgene and chloropicrin poison gasses along the whole front of the offensive, and even "If the wind is blowing directly toward our own troops, the gases should be used just the same...", WWI 10:156. Since they were generally winning on 9 Oct., the Americans' need to use gas seems unlikely, unless the heavy German counterattacks on Cornoy justified it.

Why gas-masks were not ordered is unclear, for the Germans had on 2 Oct. fired heavy gas shells with phosgene, chlorine and mustard gas into the rear of another unit, the 32d, only 9 miles east of the 82d, WWI 10:209, also 208, 206.). Jim Clark was told about the event that Douglas would never tell his children (James Clark to author 17 Feb. 1990, Diary #68, 76.). D Company was told that it was about to be pulled to the rear before an expected German offensive, but before they could move out of the trenches men were coughing. Soon they were all coughing, too late to put on gas masks. About 200 victims were evacuated, including Gould, which saved him from battle. They told him that he could never have children, so Elsa's pregnancy with James must have been a surprise!

He was probably taken to Villers-Daucourt, where an annex tent was established for gas victims at the Evacuation Hospital of the First Corps (WWI 10:104.).

He would not talk about his injuries, but it appears that he was hospitalized for some time behind the lines in France. He was one of 190,000 wounded soldiers in hospitals at the end of the war (ABM-1938 502). For many years, until the thirties he suffered problems with breathing, but eventually recovered full health. He smoked an occasional cigarette, but never became addicted.

The only illness that we children ever knew of was a bad case of pyorrhea in the early thirties, when we had to avoid drinking from the same glass to avoid catching his bleeding infection of the gums. He had poor teeth, a result of childhood malnutrition, and had many silver fillings, and a bridge to replace teeth that had to be pulled out. But he never complained about pain anyway, so we would not have known if he were miserable. Even as a young man he endured constipation, which we children knew of only from the blue bottles of Milk of Magnesia in the bathroom. This was an evident failure as a cure, since they were supplanted by large bottles of mineral oil.

In his sixties he suffered from arthritis, and went to the Veterans Administration. There he was treated by Dr. S. Samuel Rovito, chief of geriatrics and arthritics. When Dr. Rovito died in 1973 he left a note: "A kindly man who for years treated my arthritis at V.A. Immediately admitting there was no <u>cure</u> for the disease in all its forms, he did his best to understand the type afflicting the patient. Every time *I* visited him I had a sense of respite." (Note with obit. *The Evening Bulletin*, 19 March 1973, 22.).

None of Pvt. Gould's letters home have survived. But he did save two letters from home, the first from his sister Caroline dated 17 Oct. 1918 must have reached him in the hospital after he was wounded on 9 Oct.:

"Probably you think it is a long time between letters, but do you know it was four weeks before we heard from you. I thought perhaps you were sick again. Gertie Gloom always looking on the dark side.

Of course you know the Liberty Loan drive is on here. It has been going rather slowly up to date, partly because the papers are full of 'peace talk'. There aught to be a law against a decent newspaper//2. suggesting 'peace'. For my part I do not want 'negotiated peace'. I want force of arms to determine this war. And you needn't bother to come back until they are licked. It just makes my blood boil to hear people say with calm certainty that the war will be over by Christmas. I guess the English and French have something to say beside President Wilson.

The influenza has been paying us a visit It did not strike any of us however. Annie had an extra bad cold and had to stay at home for a week. If she had taken a good vacation she might have avoided it. A doctor came in our place the other day, and he said that they had the same kind of epidemic 30 years ago and they called it 'Russian Grip' because it spread from Russia.

Grace Burden has been very sick with pneumonia. She hasn't lost much flesh though. Their uncle is expected to arrive any day now. He will have to drive the car now as Ernest reported for duty today. He will be quarantined for 21 days and when he comes home he is going to bring the Commodore with him, and a young man//3. for Evelyn and an old man for Grace.

Annie had a short note from Ernest [West, Douglas's best friend] . He is one of 5000 orderlies taking care of the sick at his camp. He would make a husky attendant for he could move bed, patient and all at one lick. Annie sent him a box of chocolates, but he didn't say that he liked them. Too busy to eat. Working twelve hours a day.

Things are going along a little slower in business. Only 20% sugar until December. We are working on *a* Government order at present. So perhaps you will see our chocolate in France."

The second letter from home, dated 2 Feb. 1918 is addressed to him at D Co. 320 M[achine] G [un] Bn. A.E.F., which is crossed out with the date "2/26 Sick CPU Bourges (AEF central records office in central France, ABM-1938 443; 82d Division was under First Corps in battle of Argonne.) APU 902", then forwarded to C[orps?] H[ospital] 10", then to B[ase] H[ospital] (This may have been one of the three Advance Sector hospitals, at Baune, Toul or Remaucourt, ABM-1938 442-443) 53, then Perigueux" (Hospital center at Perigueux in central France, ABM-1938 446.), Beau Desert (Beau Desert hospital center in Base Section 2, south and central France, ABM-1938 445.) 705, and B[ase] H[ospital] 1.1 (Base Section 1 hospital for wounded being returned to U.S. was at Savenay, near the coast between Nantes and St. Nazaire, ABM-1939 445.). This probably followed the route of his hospitalization, arriving after the second of March. It was exactly seven months from the time of his gassing to discharge from the Third Convalescent Centre on 9 May.

His sister Annie wrote: "I think we received all the mail in the Malden post-office this last week from you, and are glad to hear that you are out of the hospital." So he must have been discharged from one hospital in time for a letter to get home on Feb. 2--perhaps in January 1919.

He came home across the Atlantic (perhaps from St. Nazaire, the port closest to his last hospital address.) on the U.S.S. *Orizaba,* on D deck, section 7, bunk 1, as his meal card shows. From the 23 punches the crossing took eight days. He received his honorable discharge at Ft. Devens on 9 May 1919, having served one year and ten days. The Army paid him $66.55 back pay and a ticket on the Boston & Maine from Ayer to Boston. Anticipating another war, or not knowing what to do with the surplus, the Army also issued him a brand new helmet, mess-kit and gas mask which he kept until he died. He also brought home a khaki uniform, with the Purple Heart for injury in battle, and the rainbow AEF service medal.

The war did not turn him into a pacifist, for he was a member of the American Legion and joined the Army reserves. He saved a letter from the Kelly-Hanson Post no. 78 of the American Legion in Rifle CO, which tells of his service: "According to our minutes you were 2nd vice Commander during 1927 and occupied the Commanders chair much of the time that year." (Letter of Adjutant E. C. Robertson to D. W. Gould, 3 Nov. 1930.). The letter is in response to his offer to represent the post at the National Convention: "We would be mighty pleased to have you carry our banner at any convention and should you be in a position to do so again let us know in time to get the banner to you."

In 1927 he was commissioned as a Second Lieutenant in Chemical Warfare division and served in the reserves until about 1930. As a boy James enjoyed the photos and cartoons in his father's *Legionnaire* magazine, especially the jokes about the doughboys' transport in France, 40/8 cars, forty men and eight horses.

BACK TO COLLEGE, 1919.

Douglas came home in early 1919 determined to make up the two lost years. He finished his studies at Tufts in a year and a half, earning a BS in Chemical Engineering in June 1921. One of his original classmates, Harold Pinkham, had been killed in the war.

He chose for a thesis the subject of oil shale. As he recalled in 1970: "No one in chemistry department knew anything about it. Any help given was by A.C. Lane of geology."

(D.W.G. Publications, May 1970, hereinafter Pub.) Alfred Church Lane was Professor of Mineralogy and Geology at Tufts 1909-36 (Joseph Morton, ed., *The Book of Tufts People* [Medford: Tufts College, 1942], 378.)

At Tufts Douglas met Elsa Dohne, a Phi Beta Kappa in Mathematics at Jackson College, the women's equivalent, which shared classes with the men at Tufts. She was active in women's sports, and baby-sitter for Physics Professor Nathaniel H. Knight's family who lived on Professors Row (Nathaniel Hobbs Knight was Assistant (Instructor) in Physics Dept. 1911-1920, then Assistant Professor, Morton, 377.). She was four years younger than he, and entered Tufts when he was an upper classman. Elsa probably had to pursue Douglas, who was always shy, and probably had no time for dates in high school.

The Knights offered them both jobs at their family hotel, The Ontio, on the shore at Ogunquit Maine. The two worked at the hotel that summer of 1920, she helping Mrs. Knight who was expecting the birth of Dickey in July, and he the bellboy and "the cook" (See the photo in her album #4; Douglas's note on Mrs. Knight's Christmas card 1946?). They spent their spare hours walking along the picturesque rocky shore, beneath the cliffs and along the sandy beaches. They no doubt talked about the future, both planning graduate work, he in the west, and she teaching mathematics.

It is not known when they became engaged, but it was first recorded in his mother's letter to her first cousin Harriet Rockwell, 9 May 1923: "he has become engaged to a girl to whom he//was paying attention before he went West and they are to be married the last of June. She is a very nice girl and will make a good wife; we have seen her a good deal and we like her very much. I was in hopes that he would come on here to be married; she was a school teacher but lately has been at home preparing for the event, busy at sewing, etc."

He graduated from Tufts on 20 June 1921. His most notable classmate was Leonard Carmichael, a psychology major who was to become the President of the college, and Secretary of the Smithsonian Institution in Washington.

GO WEST, YOUNG MAN, GO WEST! 1921.

"Go West, Young Man, Go West!" was the old call to the boy on the East coast. Douglas loved the West. It had the great open space, the huge vault of a sky, which seemed to dwarf even the huge colored mesas and towering peaks, making Man seem small. In fact, the emptiness of people and the junk of civilization was a great attraction. The air was sparkling clear and pure, the sun warm and bright, the vistas endless, with gaudy sunrises and sunsets.

Douglas went west, as the only other Gould college graduate, Samuel Lawrence Gould had done fifty years earlier. The attraction for Douglas was oil shale, in which he became an expert. He explained it this way: "I was raised in an era that was just beginning to wonder whether our petroleum resources would last forever. Not that we had any shortage for ourselves, but foreign countries were willing and able to buy any surplus. The combined demand was growing. I had the opportunity to take a fellowship at the U. of Utah to do research on oilshale." (Biography before University Club Claremont CA 24 April 1979, [hereinafter Bio.])

On graduation from Tufts Douglas got a graduate fellowship in Chemistry at the School of Mines and Engineering at the University of Utah in Salt Lake City. The fellowship gave him about $60 per month. The offer came on the day after graduation from Prof. Walter D. Bonner, whom Douglas described as "aloof, [with a] Narrow interest in chemistry, [who] urged me to go to Columbia U. for Ph.D." He also recorded comments about four other professors at Utah: "Bradford an intelligent, kindly man I think he had personal troubles...

Peck--a good geologist, very jealous of intrusion in his dept.
Lewis--like him and should have taken more under him Varley--was big man on football team; therefore gave him job of running station."

We have more knowledge of Douglas's activity at this time than almost any time because of all the photos he took and labeled for his fiancee back home.

In a picture of the University campus Douglas noted that there were no dormitories. A photo in Album 4 shows him "At Boardinghouse where I first landed in 1921 on fellowship U. of U....327 East First South Street S.L.C...room $15 per month, board $30" . Fellow boarders in the picture are long-time friend David Sorenson, John Swenson, Fay Hostetter and Iris Kelleher.

About 1982 he wrote a story about this experience, titled *"Irish's Boarding House or Salad Day of I.T."* [his nick-name Itinerant Traveler], SLC 1921-1922".

"Those who spent humdrum existence at home, knew the inexorably routine of mealtime. Differences of opinion can be expressed caustically; it is permissible to flounce from the room in open rage.

Millions attending college were thrown into groups so homogeneous no diversity of opinion prevailed in it.

But the communal boarding house is the closest to heaven we'll ever get. The ?clublet is near as a cross section of a viable community. Courtesy keeps rancor from discussion; all information and opinions are filtered by the group when unlocked for authority may surface to challenge.

The Irish B[boarding] H[ouse] offered an ideal. The shy and unsure were protected; the oracle suffered rebuff of uncooperative fortune and triumphed mightily on occasion. The fives and the spiritual heathen were table fellows. In one respect it was a narrow spectrum:--wealth. If you had little or no money there was no free lunch. Anyone person of considerable means would never insult his systems with the viands which, however filling and possibly nourishing, were unpretentious.//

Insult direct (to addressee): 'This is exceptionally good cake. I presume you had nothing to do with its making.'//

Lou Boehme. Swarthy, needed only a full beard to be a major Hebrew prophet. Understandably proud of physique, would pose as understudy for J[ack] Dempsey, flex all muscles and announce himself a being triturate plus 'nuxated iron'. Who would guess that the physical heart could not match the spiritual generosity and that he would be one of the first to go. Med school student and eager to use each of us as objects of the daily topic he gave lurid treatment to imagine departure from the norm."

A photo dated 31 July 1921 shows his office with a note which reads: "Nowhere to go on Sunday so I went up to school like the motorman who spent his vacation riding around on the cars." On 21 July "Lane and I climbed the hill where the 'U' was.", and took a photo of the valley at sunset. A photo shows "Lane, a Bureau of Mines chemist, from the San Francisco station...is a Bates '04 graduate." at the "U" .

From there he enjoyed geology field trips into the wild parts of Utah.

One of the other fellows was Morris Badt, from Univ. of Arizona, working on flotation. He is shown on 21 Aug. 1921 as the one who "went with me for a short hike up Dry Canyon this Sunday. It was then that we planned to make the Timpanogas hike. All three of us B of M's got to the top." They did this on Saturday August 27 when he took a photo on the way up "from American Fork Trail. They say that from Timp to Mutual Dell is 8 miles but I think they measure miles like the sheep herders do--as far as you can see it one...It took from 11 P.M. till about 4 A.M. to make the trip from Aspen (the start) to the lake".

The next shot is "Temp on right. The glacier we went up is in between the two mountains. Then we turn directly back and follow a ridge to the top. To the left of the base of glacier is the lake, of the coldest and cleanest water you ever saw. We experienced a slight sinking of spirits when we saw the climb in front of us because the lake is only about half way up."

Then two views from the top at sunrise on Sunday Aug. 28, and two shots of the hikers, "Everybody frozen". The next is taken "A short way down the Trail... flowers were growing right beside the snow beds." Farther on, "American Fork Trail down...The snow is mostly on the North side...there is no snow on top, either because the sun melts it or the wind blows it off."

A group of about 50 is shown in a big professional photo at "End of moonlight trip up Mt. Tempanoga, Utah. Location probably American Fork. Waiting for trucks to go back to S.L.C....Mighty weary group, having started on trail late afternoon, climbing glacier by moonlight, to get on top (12000 ft.) at dawn" . Then a shot by Douglas of loading onto trucks at Mutual Dell in American Dell. The last of the series is at the "Mount Service Station", "On the road to Provo. We piled out here and loaded up with pop [soda] . At Provo we stopped and got some watermelons. Can you imagine about 30 people crowded in one truck eating watermelon? We could almost wade around when we got through."

His master's thesis was approved on 2 June 1922, titled: "The Destructive Distillation of Oil-Shale", for the Degree of Masters of Science in Metallurgy at University of Utah (Gould's copy.). The abstract summary gives its purpose "to give information upon the nature of pyrolysis of oil-shale" (Ibid., 9.). Among his conclusions was that "the yield and quantity of oil from shale can be controlled to a certain degree by the operator." The thesis also presented data on the chemistry of a typical American oil-shale, changes caused by application of heat, and nature of the products of the process.

Elsewhere he recorded: "Thesis at U. of Utah received guidance from Karrick, but others were aloof." (Pub. (b)).

"Acknowledgments" at the end tell us of the four people who helped him: "The author wishes to express his appreciation of the constant help and advise [sic] extended to him throughout by Mr. Lewis C. Karrick, Associate Oil-Shale Technologist of the Bureau of Mines. He gave freely of his time in the laboratory and placed much information at the disposal of the writer. Dr. Walter D. Bonner of the University of Utah and consulting chemist for the Department of Metallurgical Research in cooperation with the Bureau of Mines, gave much assistance and constructive criticism. Mr. Frank V. Parry made many determinations of setting points and gravities, and Mr. Richard Watkins assisted in the laboratory work." (Thesis, 11).

A photo shows him beside a car with "Dick Watkins the sole lab assistant...Dick is trying for the fellowship for the coming year." In the thesis Gould stated that the chemical analysis of the standard shale was done by Watkins through combustion (Thesis, 12.).

"An original apparatus [was] designed and constructed by L. C. Karrick and D. W. Gould especially for the purpose." of extracting oil from the shale with carbon tetrachloride (Thesis p. 15 note.). "The apparatus chosen after experimentation was one that employs the principle of upward percolation of the solvent through the substance to be leached, and the filtration of the solvent and the dissolved extract through a medium that will remove the mineral matter held in suspension."

We have his diploma for Master of Science from University of Utah dated 6 June 1922, awarded by President George Thomas. The program lists Gould as one of seven such who were awarded degrees, including a woman, Rebecca E. Cox, a Columbia graduate in 1915. The speaker was Supreme Court Justice Samuel R. Thurman, and the graduates were sent away with a final benediction from Mormon "Apostle Richard R. Lyman".

After graduation he says on a photo that he "continued to stay here to help new fellows. Pay=$125/mo. Zimmerly + Drapeau were new fellows on oil shale. Others had ore-dressing studies...U.S. B[ureau]. of Mines Station U. of U. Campus...Salt Lake City 1922-23 Research fellows Koerner, Baumgartner and Sherman". His graduation program identifies the new fellows in the School of Mines: C.A. Baumgartner (B.S. Univ, of Missouri 1921), Joseph E. Drapeau Jr. (Rensselaer Poly), Carl C. Kessler (M. S. Iowa State 1922), George W. Kuerner (B.S. Penn State 1922), Henry C. Sharman (B. S. Utah 1910).

The broader picture of his work was described in his biography: "The Rocky Mountain states assured the world that their deposits [of oil shale] could supply the world's needs to the end of time. California, too, at Casmalia, had smaller deposits of quite high quality.

At Salt Lake City and later at Boulder and Rifle, Colorado we gathered fundamental information on the recovery and treatment of shale oil. Throughout all this work with the States of Utah and Colorado in cooperation with the U.S. Bureau of Mines, one curious phenomenon was seen: the calculated cost of shale oil in commercial quantities was a bit higher than that of crude petroleum. The years have not changed this much."

Two weeks after graduation, on 18 June he took a hike into Bell's Canyon with his fellow graduates Morris Badt and Charles G. Maier, and a "Me". A photo shows a "Wonderful view of Maier as cook. Note the pail of coffee on the left. Maier is frying the potatoes and soon will broil the steaks."

Perhaps Douglas's oldest acquaintance from these days was L. C. Karrick, his thesis mentor at the Bureau of Mines, whom he later described as "forever a friend...who died VA hospital S.L.C. about 1963." There is a photo of Karrick's log cabin at Brighton, Utah in July 1922, which he labelled "The cheesecloth screens give a queer appearance, but inside it is *a* log cabin de luxe." Douglas sent Elsa a great panoramic series of four shots from Karrick's cabin in Brighton, Utah, above the Big Cottonwood Canyon, looking toward Millicent and Wolverine peaks, with Alta Divide between them. This was taken 12 July 1922, the day they "climbed Mt. Majestic which was reputed to be higher than Wolverine, but proved to be only a fair climb with a good trail most of the way." He was back there again on 25 July when he labels a photo of himself with arms akimbo, "A long drink of water!" An earlier panorama was taken of the Salt Lake water reservoir Lake Mary, above Brighton on the Fourth of July.

On 5 to 7 Aug. 1922 Gould went on a hike to Twin Peaks with several friends, including Charles Maier, who is shown cooling off in an irrigation ditch with "buffy" Blanche Buffington, a scene Douglas labelled, "What a dignified pose for a man ranking as a Professor in the U. of U. "

His first publication came out in Oct. 1922, in the *Journal of the Franklin Institute* in Philadelphia, with Karrick as the primary author. Gould's later description of this was a "Joint contribution by Karrick and self in Jour. Franklin Institute was my idea and Karrick's energy." (Pub.(c).) It was titled "An Extraction Apparatus with Extract-Recovery and Solvent-Regenerative Devices". The four page article describes the laboratory device he had used to separate oil from shale, with a full page diagram. The article concludes that "It has given perfect satisfaction and it is hoped that it will be found equally satisfactory for testing oil sands, leaching salt-laden earths, and for lixiviation purposes in general." Lixiviation, in case you didn't know, is the process of separating a soluble substance from an insoluble one with a solvent.

The Utah fellowship appears to have ended in six months, about Dec. 1922, when he moved to Boulder, Colorado, at the base of the Rockies north of Denver. He had moved to the Bureau of Mines Oil Shale station on the University of Colorado campus in Boulder about Jan. 1923. He lived at 1305 17th Street, in a one room wooden cabin on a field stone foundation, with his bed in a tent behind. Among his colleagues there were Joseph Horne, Willard Finley and Arthur D. Bauer. There is a photo taken on 17 June 1923 in Boulder Canyon showing two cars with Horne and his wife Patsy and his mother, with Finley and his wife. This was just before he took the train home to Massachusetts to be married.

MARRIAGE TO ELSA 1923.

In the meanwhile, Elsa Dohne had finished her degree at Tufts in June 1922, and went on to the state teacher's college, Massachusetts Normal School at Northfield, for a MS degree in teaching of Mathematics. She immediately got a job teaching Math at Cranston R.I. high school, but taught for only one semester, from Feb. to June 1923.

They were married in the Goddard Chapel on "The Hill" of Tufts University by a Unitarian minister on 30 June 1923. There is a certificate of marriage on 30 June 1923 at Boulder CO signed by Lucius F. Reed and witnessed by Charlotte Hammond and Mary T. Reed.). Elsa's matron of honor was her best friend and Jackson classmate Sarah DeWolfe of Medford (Sarah married a Unitarian Minister named Hamer, and lived well into her late nineties at Eaglesmere Retirement Home in Kingston MA.). Her bridesmaid was another Medford classmate, Miriam "Mim" Ford, who was to marry Sarah's brother. Beside family, their professor-mentors and their wives were there: the Knights, and "Uncle" Billy Ransom (Prof. William R. Ransom, was Professor of Mathematics at Tufts 1900 ff.; Titus Mergendahl, Asst. Professor of Math 1919 ff., whom Mother often mentioned, may have been there too.) and his wife. I do not recall having heard of a best man, but it may have been "Westy", his lifelong "chum" from college, Ernest West, who became a correspondent and editorial writer for a major Boston newspaper.

They were married for life, for almost 50 years (just five months under fifty years.). It's hard to believe in this day, but I don't think he ever looked at another woman to lust after her. Elsa was all. She was not only his sole lover, but his intellectual equal, his social secretary, mother of his children, and his best friend for life.

They honeymooned at Niagara Falls, then went by train to Boulder, and had another honeymoon at Yellowstone in August. We have a dozen photos taken in Yellowstone National Park, taken 20-23 Aug. 1923. They probably drove up from Boulder, for the first shots on 20 Aug. are of Shoshone Lake, just outside the park, 30 miles from Cody, Wyoming. On 21 Aug. they took photos of three waterfalls: Twin Sisters, and Lower and Upper Yellowstone Falls. On 23 they did the geysers, Old Faithful, Daisy and Minute Man.

Douglas had found a small bungalow at 655 Pleasant Street, where they began married life. The house faced south, with a view of Flagstaff to the southwest, and sloped back to 7th Street at the rear. It was a one story frame house on *a* stone basement, the first floor clapboarded up two feet, then finished in fancy shingling in alternating narrow and wide bands. The gable front had an open porch in front, up four steps. At the northeast corner was the kitchen, with exit onto an open back porch.

They got their first dog here, an airedale named "Pat", who came to a sad end when he was lying in the driveway asleep and Douglas backed his car over the dog, killing him. He always talked fondly of "Pat", with great remorse for his carelessness. They took exploration trips into the Rockies, up Pikes Peak, and hiked into Estes Park. Pictures taken in July 1923 show Bear Canyon and on 2 August in Big Thompson Canyon before the Yellowstone trip.

Among their friends who visited Pleasant Street were David C. Sorenson, a law student at University of Utah, whom he had met in Salt Lake City, and his wife Lola. Also living on Pleasant Street were his boss Arthur D. Bauer and his wife, but they left when he was transferred east on 15 April 1925. Their neighbor immediately to the rear was *a* Mrs. Byron. Other friends with children the same ages were the McCauleys, Hixsons, Strunks, Goodykoonzes, Thomases and Alvords.

Gould had been employed by the U.S. government Department of Interior in its oil shale laboratory of the Bureau of Mines in Boulder, Colo. This was a big brick warehouse in the Mechanical Engineering Building of the University of Colorado. The Director was Martin J. Gavin, who had published a paper on solvents of shales with Aydelotte, and went on to the Bureau of Mines office in San Francisco. Gould's dislike of his boss is evident from his description on the back of the staff photo: "Gavin an on the make technologist, nominally in charge". There were three professional staff members, Gould, Joseph Horne, and Willard Finley. Amos T. Strunk was the clerk, or office manager.

Karrick supervised the construction of a retort or furnace to refine shale oil in the Boulder lab. The retort was finished and the first products obtained in June 1924 ("Report for Period June 1-30, 1924.", probably by Gould.).

Douglas is shown with Horne and Finley on a trip in Aug. 1923 up Long's Peak, a photo evidently taken by their boss, A. D. Bauer who appears in the next photo.

The next month Gould did a two week "Oil Shale Trip" from 10 to 25 Sept. 1923. He explained to me: "A.D. Bauer, in charge of the Boulder, Colo. office U.S. Bureau of Mines wanted some first hand info on oil shale. I suggested a trip and used this entry to get a marvelous tour of the Basin. Shale, gilsonite, ozokerite oil sands were seen in their natural habitat. We left Boulder by rail to Denver and thence to Mack Colo via D&RGW. Mack is or was a flag stop where the narrow gauge railway from Dragon (I guess) runs MWF south and T,T,S north. Miss connections at Mack and there was literally nothing. See my book 'Story of Gilsonite' Herbert F. Kretchman/ /American Gilsonite Co. SLC 1958. We were met in Dragon by a truck with driver and chemist from S.L.C. office of B of M. No car-hire those days."

In addition to Gould and Bauer, there were also Arthur T. Aydelotte, Bureau of Mines expert whom Gould had cited in his thesis for work on oil-shale solvents, and two younger men, Carl Carlson and Albert Clarke.

Five photos show the Dragon Gilsonite mine, including "a train load of Gilsonite leaving Dragon, Utah for Mack, Colorado." Then a "View of the Western Oil Shale Go's plant near Ute Switch about 4 mi. north of Dragon, which shows that this company had already built a plant before the Rifle one. Another scene on the same trip shows the "Offices of the concentrate plant of the American Hydrocarbon Co. at Soldier Summit, Utah. Then oil shale buttes at Green river Wyoming. And there are two views of the "Uintah Rwy, Narrow gauge over Baxter Pass Looking down valley toward Atchee Colo."

FIRST CHILDREN, BOULDER, 1924-5.

Elsa and Douglas's first child was conceived shortly before he went on this trip. James Warren Gould was born in Boulder on 14 May 1924 . He was probably named for his uncle James Douglas, for then no one remembered the James Gould who built bridges in Boston after the American Revolution. Their second child, Elinor Janet Gould was born there 13 Aug. 1925. There are no ancestors or relatives, or even friends of these names, so her name is a radical departure signifying the freedom of the new life in the west.

They took the children on trips at once: James was taken into Boulder and Chatauga at 3 weeks. At two months they went on a 200 mile auto trip of two days to Colorado Springs, visiting the Cave of the Winds on Aug. 19 and Garden of the Gods the next day. On 22 Aug. Douglas took James on his back up Flagstaff Peak, southwest of their house.

The results of the Boulder experiments in an official report in May 1924, "Assay Retort Studies of Ten Typical Oil Shales", with Gould as third of four authors, W. L. Finley and J. W. Horne as cooperative employees of the state of Colorado, and A. D. Bauer, Associate petroleum chemist, Department of the Interior. This reported the differences in yields of oil shales from Brazil, Scotland and Australia with American ones from Kentucky, Colorado, Nevada and Utah. Gould commented later: "Joint publication...was a queer one. Finley did two thirds of the work; Bauer, as head of station did most of the writing, the other authors got little chance at editing."

At the end of his graduate fellowship at Utah he came up with a proposal for a large laboratory for study of oil shale. This was submitted to A. W. Ambrose, Chief Petroleum Technologist at the Bureau of Mines as a result "of the investigation, instituted at your direction..." His comment on this was: "Already I took it upon myself to push. My superiors hardly dared to address Ambrose. Lab was established (Laramie, Wyo.?) ten years hence, probably not by my effort." The 22 page proposal survives only in outline and Introduction. The latter noted that Congress had already authorized $100,000 for such a lab. It was justified by the need to find a satisfactory equivalent to the gasoline driven engine. Given the likelihood that the gas engine was here to stay, the question was how heavy crudes could be used. Since corporations would be unlikely to invest in this expensive search, he proposed a government lab near shale deposits in Indiana. He estimated the cost within the $100,000 range, $60,000 for initial equipment and building, $28,900 salaries, and $5,000 first year operating costs.

OIL SHALE PIONEER, RIFLE, COLORADO, 1925.

At age 28, in 1925, he was appointed to set up the first government oil shale plant in America. During the war the U.S. government had recognized that dependence upon oil in the ground, which appeared to be limited, was unwise, and proposed to develop the huge potential of oil trapped in rock. This required a process of heating and treatment that was entirely new. Gould's knowledge of hydrocarbons and the geology of the region made him the logical candidate to head the operation. He was probably recommended by Karrick and Bauer.

One gets the impression that much of the mining and construction was done under the supervision of others, and that his job was primarily to supervise construction of the refinery. A photo taken in 1926 shows the staff in front of the corrugated walls of the plant: J. S. Desmond, Head of the Rifle Plant, killed by a bomb; Gould; M. J. Gavin, of the Bureau of Mines San Francisco; Mclntyre, a temporary employee; and Bertrand Landry, of the Bureau of Mines, Boulder, then stationed in Rifle.

The site chosen by the government was Rifle, in the remote northwest corner of Colorado, in the heart of the largest deposit of oil shale in the country, and the huge Naval Oil Shale reserve in the Book Plateau northwest of the town. Private companies were already working the deposits, the March Oil Shale Co. in Parachute Creek, 15 miles west of Rifle, and in Roan Creek 25 miles west were American Shale Refining Co., Monarch, and Index.

This location was evidently chosen after 24 March 1925 when the Rifle Chamber of Commerce made an illustrated pitch for the location there, with Gould's guidance. They specifically suggested "the big open park known as Sherrard Park eight and one-half miles west of Rifle, near Morris Station on the D. & R. G. W. Railroad and the Pikes Peak Ocean to Ocean Highway [now route?] ." The best feature of what the promoters called "the most progressive little city of western Colorado" was "THE BEST YEAR-ROUND CLIMATE ON EARTH - Altitude 5,300 ft." The four room" School House was offered as temporary Headquarters for Offices and Laboratories."

On 27 May 1925 Gould went to Rifle to survey the site for the mule trail to the proposed mine in the cliffs above Rulison, accompanied by Caywood and Dahmer, perhaps local surveyors. By July 1925 he had located a site for the shale plant in a gulch above Rulison.

In Rulison Gould supervised construction of a large retort, or furnace, in which the oil-bearing rock was cooked, and the resultant fumes bled off, into components like kerosine, gasoline and tar.

He later wrote: "We had office in Rifle for about a year [on the ground floor of the High School]. Plant built at Rulison [nine miles west of Rifle, on the Colorado River], and all activity there. Our house in Rifle meant I drove to Rulison. Envied by all, because site at Plant had no amenities...High School...nearby house...we owned...We left Rifle 1927 for Chicago, visited Melrose before taking job Chicago, first time with folks 1921-1927."

When Elinor was only six weeks old the Gould family made the big move west. They took the train from Boulder to Rifle on 29-30 Sept. 1925 (Father's note on graph paper, but James's *Baby' Record* under "Important Events" has his penciled note: "Move to Rifle Oct. 30, 1925", with later comment "Good date".). They stayed first downtown at the Winchester Hotel, 32 rooms, steam heated, hot and cold water, cafe. They then rented a small brick bungalow 200 yards south of the back of the High School where Douglas had his offices. Attached to the front corner of the house was an open porch with shingled railing. There was also a small screened wooden porch at the back. The house faced south, high above the canyon of the Colorado River, and a sharp drop into an escarpment to the east, with a view of the 9,000 foot shale cliffs five miles away. There, at 5,000 feet, they spent their first Christmas. Then, in 1926, Douglas bought his "Estate", the house they owned, and the second home in Rifle. It was located on a hill up a steep street above the Continental filling station, and the First Christian Church. This was also a one story brick bungalow, but hip-roofed, with railed-in front porch, a gable extension in front, and open wooden porch at the back. There was a large flower garden out back, the land rising up steeply behind to a couple of wooden shacks, perhaps a chicken coop and storage shed. His note on a picture of 11 Sept. 1926 says: "This house on steep street. First we ever owned. Lost it via mortgage to a couple who went broke in 1929."

James's first memories, when only four, is the big Mack trucks roaring by, with their shining hubcaps, and the fragrant smell of the sweet alyssum in the garden next to the house. They took the children out in their open car, over the wide open plateaus, and into the canyon of the Gunnison, or shopping at the nearest metropolis, Grand Junction, to the west (Note on graph paper: "Elinor Grand Junction all day Dec. 31, 1925".).

Before leaving Rifle Douglas joined the Chemical Warfare branch of the Army, and was commissioned a Second Lieutenant of 6 April 1927. His commission, with his serial number, 0-241677, has been saved. This required attending summer camp, and in the summers of 1928 and 1929 he went to Camp Custer, MI. He does not seem to have continued this in Philadelphia, so he probably let his commission lapse about 1929.

The Rifle shale refining experiment ran into trouble with unscrupulous lessees and poor management. There are only hints of the problems in a letter from Douglas's friend and colleague in the Boulder office, J. W. Home, dated 24 Sept. 1927:

"Things concerning your affair at Rifle have not quieted down. I thought they would with a little time. One thing is certain, either you or I will have to pay that gang of thieves $52.50 or let the case go to Washington.

I have received from you checks to the amount of $32.50 of which $12.50 plus a bank charge was returned to me, no funds. I was holding everything until it could be paid in full with one check, but the money you gave Alien for stock had already been used to purchase the stock and said stock is valueless today. The mine was found to be a very low grade proposition, and the ore can not be worked. So there is nothing left to do but pay cash.

Desmond wrote a few days ago and asked if she should take the matter up with Washington. If you wish, I will tell him to do so and that will start things going right. In fact you could write first and tell Hill a complete investigation would satisfy you that your indebtedness actually existed, which at present you doubt. This would give you a chance to tell the whole story about the steals they have pulled, including the $100 which Gavin took and how Desmond perjured himself while in Denver for $70.

Because of the short check I have not been able to pay them the $32.50 which I think should be done and then you can light into them with both feet. Please do one thing or the other and get this settled."

MOVE TO KOPPERS, CHICAGO, 1927.

Trouble with his bosses over these accounts probably led Douglas to look for a new job. But 1927 was a boom time in the American industrial economy, and he had no difficulty finding an employer who needed his knowledge of hydrocarbons. His 1924 research paper had revealed an interesting discovery about oil shale: "The most striking difference in behavior of these shales in retorting lies in their relative tendencies to coke...", or fuse (page 4).

His mind was moving toward the question of getting gasoline from coal, as he tells in his biography: "a nagging problem was seen by me---the process for recovering shale oil from shale left a residue of barren rock. For every barrel of oil produced, there remained about three quarters ton of rock. What to do with it? The answer fifty years later is not too clear. It struck me that what one could do with oil shale, could also be done with coal, that is, heat coal as you would oilshale and you get tar (or inferior oil), gas and a residue of useful coke."

Kopper's Coke Company of Chicago was the country's leading maker of coke from coal, but in developing byproducts in which the Germans had pioneered: chemicals and dyes. The possibilities seemed enormous, and the profits great. Douglas was hired by Kopper's in its research laboratory. Here he developed several petroleum products which were patented by Kopper's.

His account of the move is this: "I changed jobs; went with Koppers Company in Chicago, and learned the intricacies of coal processing and manufacture of gas for public utilities, in fact the entire byproduct industry (tars and fertilizers and coke for steel plants) . I was asked to conduct research on the cracking of tars (a subject of which I knew nothing) and became so much interested in acquiring knowledge that I took work with an oil company." (Bio, 1.).

Gould published his second scientific paper as a result of his work at Koppers. He did this jointly with a fellow Koppers researcher A. R. Powell. This was presented at the American Chemical Society meeting in Street Louis , 16-18 April 1928, and published in the Society's journal, *Industrial and Engineering Chemistry* in July 1928. The article reported the results of an experiment testing the ability of coke to stand rough handling. His comment was: "Joint paper...was more satisfactory [than the Boulder report]. I did the work, Powell did most of writing but was quite willing to give me a chance at editing, and he took upon himself the follow through to publication."

His office was in a brick building of the Chicago By-Product Coke Company on Crawford Ave., near the Chicago Drainage Canal.

After taking the children back to Boston to visit their grandmothers, in 1927 the Gould family moved from Rifle to Chicago. They stayed first at "Paradise Arms", near 40th, Mackson and Washington. They then moved to an apartment on the west side, including one on 51st Street in Cicero, the home of Al Capone. Douglas said they read about the gangster's doings, but he caused no problems in the quiet neighborhood, which he described as "Neighborhood strong Slavic ethnic, Quiet despite hdq. of Capone". Cicero was also the site of a big steel mill, but that was not annoying either. They lived on the first floor of a two story brick apartment which had a big living room with four windows looking out onto 51st Street .

In October 1928 they had moved to a five room apartment on the ground floor at the corner of two quiet streets, at 5054 Thomas Street and 51st Street in Austin. This was in a three and a half story brick building, entered through the central dining room, with living room which had three tall windows facing onto the street, two more bedrooms on the outside, but interior kitchen and bathroom. The trolley into Chicago was just a block away. There were good schools nearby, and James began kindergarten in 1929 at the John Hay School on Laramie Street They went to a Unitarian church somewhere on the north side of Chicago, a big neo-Gothic structure.

James remembered only one friend of his Father's, probably a colleague at Kopper's, who came from New Zealand, about which he told stories that have always attracted a boy to go "down under" . His apartment was in a high building with a great night view of downtown Chicago, which featured a huge world which was covered with multi-colored Sherwin-Williams paint, "that covers the globe".

Chicago had lots of cultural attractions: They took the children to the Art Museum to see the Egyptian mummies, and for Spring walks along the lakefront of Lake Michigan. Summers were spent at the Indiana Dunes, which one reached by a long trolley ride through the open countryside, to the southern tip of Lake Michigan, and east into Indiana. Then, one hiked across the sand dunes, through hollows where the sulfur gas accumulated, to the shore--to plunge into the lake, and come out to soak up the sun.

He had to attend Reserve Officers Summer camp in the summers of 1928 and 1929, at

Camp Custer, MI. One of the four pictures taken in July 1928 shows Gould on horseback lined up with other officers in an equitation class. He quotes his group commander, Major Heritage explaining: "Every gentleman should be able to ride."

A rare letter has survived that Douglas wrote from Camp Custer the second summer, to Elsa c/o Johnson at Waverly Beach, Tremont, Indiana was returned to her as no such town. Dated 16 July 1929, he wrote: "Just a few moments before we go out again, and as I know you look forward to a letter as I do, I'll use the time well. The writing paper [blue stock, headed "Reserve Officers Training Corps//Engineers//Camp Custer, Michigan/ /Courtesy The Kellogg Company, Battle Creek, Mich] is furnished by the Kellogg Co. They are good town boosters here, and we have pep or bran or rice crispies every morning. I was "officer of the day" for our group yesterday and could not get away , as the tour of duty is from 7.30 a.m. to 7.30 P.M. The duties are not heavy, but confine one to the vicinity of the tents during the entire period.

An army plane came from Selfridge Field, Detroit and today laid down a smoke screen. An what a flyer he was!//
[2] From a mile high in the air he would swoop down close to us on the ground with the wind whining through the guy wires, and would then zoom up again. The screen was very pretty and effective, but very short. Then he did stunts for our benefit. Flew upside down! Made a barrel roll. Like this [5 sketches of the plane] Loop-the-loops! And when he left he said good-by by wagging his tail!

Already the men are talking of time to go home. Two weeks is almost the limit of endurance where you have no great motive for this style of living. And I, too am looking forward to coming home, and am almost sorry you are not going to be in Chicago. I havn't forgotten your letter of last year where you said//[3] you would be proud to meet me and have supper with me. Believe me if you are by any chance in Chicago Thursday you are to save that date for one of three places--The Steven, Tip Top Inn, or the New Morrison. However, that date holds good for the first opportunity we have if you are not in Chicago Thursday. My first move would be to phone the house.

Evening.

I held this letter hoping to hear from you on one of the two mail deliveries today. It is probable that if I do not hear that you are going to be in Chicago Thursday, I shall wear my civvies instead of the uniform. If, however, you have any plans you can reach me by telegram up to Wednesday night. There is a much larger crowd of men to be cleared out of camp this year than last and we probably won't be lucky enough to get away by 9 or 10 in the morning//[4]

I am surely looking forward to seeing you and the children, and as I said in my last letter, I will probably make my appearance at the beach some time Friday night. If you write me at 5054 Thomas, you can give me any last minute directions necessary.

It seems weeks instead of days since I saw you. Another year you must not let me go away without pictures of my loved ones.

I must mail this now so that you will get it Wednesday if possible.

As ever your lover Douglas."

The reference to Mother's desire to see him in uniform may have been gratified by two photos sent from Camp Custer in July 1929, showing Douglas dressed in khaki, with dark tie tucked into the upper buttons of the shirt, riding pants tucked into polished leather leggings and boots, a campaign hat held on by chin-strap.

At Christmas or Thanksgiving the family would all board the train for the two day's trip to Boston to celebrate the holiday at Gramma Gould's home at 301 West Foster Street in Melrose, to enjoy her wonderful home cooking, concluded with ice cream from Aunt Annie's employer, Hood's, and livened by tales told by Aunt Cal. Aunt Ida was usually included in the family, and sometimes also Elsa's mother Henrietta Dohne, who was then working as housekeeper-cook for the widowed dairy farmer Mr. Hill of West Bridgewater, VT.

MOVE TO PHILADELPHIA, ATLANTIC REFINING CO., 1929.

All good things come to an end, he would say. The stock market crash of 1929 ended the boom economy. Douglas had the foresight to see the boom in the Kopper's company coming to an end, and was looking for a more secure job. He got an offer as a research scientist at the Atlantic Refining Company in Philadelphia. It was chancy to move at this time, but it was a smart move. He stayed with Atlantic until retirement.

His explanation was that he "became so much interested in acquiring knowledge of cracking that I took work with an oil company. This was Atlantic Refining Company now Atlantic Richfield. Do you recall the phrase "Oil for the lamps of China"? It refers largely to the kerosine produced in the Phila. plant. There was also the story told that Atlantic supplied all the aviation fuel use by the U.S. Army in W.W. I. Whether fact or not is beside the point.

With Atlantic I was given exceptional opportunity to explore the operations of refining, of crude oil producing, and of pipe line distribution. Such latitude seldom exists today; the rule is strict compartment at ion, don't encroach on other's affairs." (Bio. 2.).

Atlantic Refining had been one of the biggest processors and shippers of crude oil in Rockefeller's Standard Oil empire, and when the Supreme Court broke up the trust, Atlantic was established as an independent company which then had to go out an find its own markets and sources of oil. But its refining primacy was well established. What new products could be made from oil? And in the Depression, what economies could be made in refining of oil? Were there new processes and catalysts that could produce the by products more cheaply?

There was an element of danger in all this highly inflammable stuff: kerosine, gasoline, benzine, etc. that inspired his second book *Explosion.* Atlantic's laboratory was in a three story building facing Passyunk Avenue, on the north side of the Point Breeze refinery, near the entrance of the dirty Schuylkill River into the Delaware River. The air had the evil smell of the unwanted gasses that were vented into the air, or burned smokily from high stacks. All around were huge storage tanks, with posted warnings: "NO SMOKING". Every now and then there would be a terrible explosion at one of the refineries of the area, at Sun or Gulf or whatever. But Douglas assured his family that Atlantic's safety measures were good. It didn't seem to worry him at all.

In his official reports at work he refers to one fire on the afternoon of 12 Sept. 1931 during the construction of the Jackson gasoline plant. (18 Aug.-30 Sept., Problem No. 91000, 74.)

Among the projects he worked on at the plant were assessing the gasoline recovery plant built by Jackson Engineering Co. (July 1930-July 1931), under R. B. Chillas, Jr. There was his assistance in survey of production of Liquified Fuel Gas done by Dr. J. H. Boyd (March-May 1931). In Jan. 1931 he recommended ways to improve distillation with a Bubble Cup. In Feb. 1932 he reported on a way to produce sodium hydrosulphide to make artificial silk. In Oct. 1931 he began study of hydrogenation of oil to make anti-knock gasoline and hydrogen itself. In 1935 he was studying uses of gas as a by-product. An important innovation was catalytic polymerization of gasses, which he began studying in 1933. The Houdry cracking process was studied that year too.

The Gould family took the Pennsylvania Railroad from Chicago to Philadelphia shortly before Christmas of 1929. They put up at a hotel near 36th Street and Chestnut, where the doorman or concierge favored the two homeless children with toy metal lanterns, with glass windows revealing the contents, red candies. They did their first Christmas shopping at the big department stores downtown: Wanamaker's for the quality, Strawbridge & Clothier for the best buy, and Snellenberg's and Gimbel' s only for the bargains. But the treat was meeting Santa at the end of the road in Santa's Village at Wanamaker's.

Elsa and Douglas soon found a nice apartment at the southeast corner of 42d at 4260 Chestnut Street, to which they moved for Christmas Eve of 1929. The three and a half story brick building had a typical twenties layout of a "U" around a central courtyard. They were on the northeast corner of the first floor, looking out onto Chestnut Street, and the Presbyterian Church across the inbound traffic. The apartment had about four rooms: a living room on the street, dining room, a small kitchen on the back, and two bedrooms. Elinor's only memory of the apartment is the ice box, in which her father's (36th?) birthday cake was securely hidden until she rushed to the door as he came in and gave the secret away--her "Lesson in keeping a secret".

The closets were small, but there was a caged and locked storage area in the basement. There, by the furnace, James struck up friendship with the son of the Black janitor. His liberal parents had some trouble deciding what to do about this friendship, encouraging him not to be racist, but wondering if the influence was really good. When they moved away he perhaps mistakenly attributed the move to a way to end the relation.

They were well enough off to have someone come in once a week to clean the apartment and do the wash--in those days, scrubbing over a washboard in a galvanized tub, and wringing by hand, and carrying the clothes down to the warm basement to dry. At the start of the Depression even a five dollar a day job was a boon to the widow Mrs. (Anna?) West, who lived with a daughter in a brick row house half a block northwest. She stayed with the Gould family for many years, at the Llanerch house on Valley Road, when she must have retired in her seventies.

DOUGLAS'S RELIGION.

Douglas could not be called a religious person, though he was a loyal parishioner of the Unitarian church in Philadelphia, largely through Elsa's interest. His views of the spiritual, as far as one could tell from rare expressions, was a sort of Emersonian rationalism, non-credal, and individual rather than group determined. It is doubtful that he believed in any after-life or psychic connections.

Before Douglas and Elsa discovered the Unitarian church downtown, the family went to the Presbyterian church across the street. There the children started Sunday School and James began Kindergarten again. James absorbed his first image of God the Father from the huge stained glass window that looked across at the apartment: the Presbyterian God was a stern bearded Judge, sternly benevolent but demanding. James was never been able to escape that image of God the Terrible, who has nothing to do with the loving Spirit his parents believed in.

Douglas later told James his dislike of this, and began going to the Friends meeting at 42d and Market Streets, nearby (DWG to author, 27 July 1973, Diary #41, 6.). He never attended a Quaker business meeting, thinking they were only for members, but went to meeting for worship several times.

It was Elsa who probably found the First Unitarian Church, at 26th and Chestnut Streets, just two miles east of the apartment, and only two stops on the subway.

Douglas did not grow up with any strong religious background, except New England Protestantism. The Goulds evidently joined the Mystic Side Congregational Church in Everett when he was in his teens, for there is a photo of the minister Rev. Kilborn date 1 July 1911. His sisters probably stayed with this ancestral Congregational church after they moved to Melrose in 1922, and continued membership in Newfields, NH, probably because it was the center of social life in the village.

Their mother Laura does not seem to have gone to church at all. Her religious background was confused: Her grandmother Carey had grown up in the Anglican church, but took on her husband's Catholic faith when they were married. They were among the first Catholics in the largely Presbyterian Scottish community in Nova Scotia, and when her husband died she went back to her childhood Episcopalianism. But meanwhile her children had married protestants. Laura's father John Douglas came from Anglican stock, but were not particularly religious, and declared themselves Methodists in the census. Then Laura married Sam Gould who had been raised in the Boston Episcopal church, without strong religious leanings. She was religious in a natural way, loving her neighbor and doing the will of God by living a loving life, devoted to family.

Elsa's parents had abandoned their German Lutheran tradition, and her father's Socialism made him anticlerical . But in Boston the Dohnes had been attracted to the Universalist rationalism, and Elsa went with her mother to the high church Unitarian services at King's Chapel, which Thomas Gould had founded as Anglican over two hundred years earlier.

The minister of the First Unitarian Church in Philadelphia was Dr. Frederick R. Griffin, Harvard Divinity School, who gave the Goulds a great connection to the Boston's tradition of rational religion and social reform. He always gave great sermons, logically constructed, with moral inspiration, and delivered in an elevated and intellectual style. The topic was supported by a good Universalist menu of texts, from the Bhagavad Gita and Tao Te Ching, as well as the King James Version of the Bible. Music was always an important part of the service, with a powerful organ that shook the church on the full bass notes, and a fine choir of voices that included the artist Oakley. That the church had been founded by the great chemist, the discoverer of oxygen, Joseph Priestley, no doubt attracted Douglas.

His religion was a very rational one. His son once asked him if he were an atheist or an agnostic, and he could not decide which. He clearly did not believe in the masculine God the Terrible, nor the miraculously conceived Jesus. Nor did the trinity make any sense in scripture or reason. The main point of religion was how one lived one's life, and he managed it quite well.

He was not as active in the social life of the church as Elsa, but in later years he dedicated every Sunday to passing the collection plate, a round wooden dish with green felt on the inside. He was a regular attender, every Sunday of the year, and for special services at Christmas Eve, but was not upset if he had to miss a Sunday while on a trip.

After Elsa's death, interestingly, when he entered Mt. San Antonio Gardens, at age 81, he described himself "Without denominational ties, he, in his own words, feels quite comfortable with Congregationalists, Quakers and Unitarians. " (*The Green Leaf: Mt. San Antonio Gardens.* 16, no. 12, Jan. 1978, 5.)

The Great Depression had a big impact on the Gould family. Although they were lucky that Douglas had the foresight to move to a job that kept him employed through the decade-long crisis, he probably took cuts in salary to hold on. Douglas instilled a Yankee frugality that taught his children not to waste anything they owned, and never to abuse what they had. One sewed up holes in old clothes before one bought new ones, and put cardboard in the holes of old shoes. He would remind the children that he had gone to school in one suit of clothes. Plates had to be completely cleaned before one could have dessert--"Just think of the starving Ethiopians!" There was no such luxury as an allowance that some spoiled kids got--One had to earn it outside. Tasks in the home, like taking out the garbage, dragging up the ashes from the coal furnace, or emptying the trash or feeding the cat, were done as part of sharing the family chores, unpaid, and done cheerfully, or else.

When anyone complained, Douglas would take the child down to the Chinese Wall at 16th and Market Streets and show what many fathers were doing: Holding out cups with new pencils for sale, or apples. On other occasions of disagreeable complaint, he would threaten to take the offender down to South Philadelphia to see what it was like to be poor, living in a slum of row houses. If you had heard that threat before, you quickly assured him you knew what poverty was!

The children were also taught to save, not spend the money we earned. They opened a bank account, where one could watch the interest grow. But to avoid reducing the principal one had to plan ahead to buy birthday and Christmas presents for the family. "Money does not grow on trees", said the old Yankee.

We were made to walk a mile to school, and back, as Douglas and his sisters had walked, rain or shine, snow or sleet. If one had to go farther, one took the "el", the elevated train from 42d Street, as he commuted to work.

Douglas introduced his children to science early, taking us on Saturdays or Sundays after church to the fabulous treasures of the Franklin Institute on the Parkway at 27th Street There he showed us the glorious colors of minerals, the greens of the copper malachites, the vermillions of the mercury ores, the glittering gold of the pyrites. One learned how electricity behaved from the lightning displays, and how chemicals react from the do-it-yourself experiments with catalysts that transformed clear liquid to color. And one rode the great workhorse Pennsy steam locomotives that Douglas loved. And one got astronomy lessons in the Planetarium, supplemented with star searches with Douglas on star clear nights, based on the big blue star atlas he knew so well.

Early on Douglas introduced his son to Penn's annual science open house, where we saw the primitive start of the world's first computer, Eniac.

He also got his children interested in history very early. He took them often to one of his favorite museums, the University Museum at 30th and Locust. There he exposed them to his love of archaeology, in the great tombs of the Egyptian pharaohs, with their mysterious mummies in layer after layer of care for the dead: the stone sarcophagus, the painted wooden case, and the bandaged corpse, and finally, the still-preserved skin of the immortal king himself. One saw the stern Assyrian friezes, the graceful marbles of Athenian gods, the wonderfully woven designs of baskets of the Western Indians, the exotic carvings of the Pacific Islanders.

Art was also a free show in downtown Philadelphia. They often climbed the steps of the city's Acropolis to enter the temple of the art museum, and to wander through the great halls. Douglas's favorites were the ancient classical art of Rome and Greece. He also took us to the nearby Rodin Museum to appreciate the fine bronze sculptures.

Outings were to nearby Fairmount Park, one of the biggest city parks in America, for picnics on the grass, and romping in the open. There too was the Philadelphia Zoo, which had great attraction too, especially the big beasts like elephants and bears.

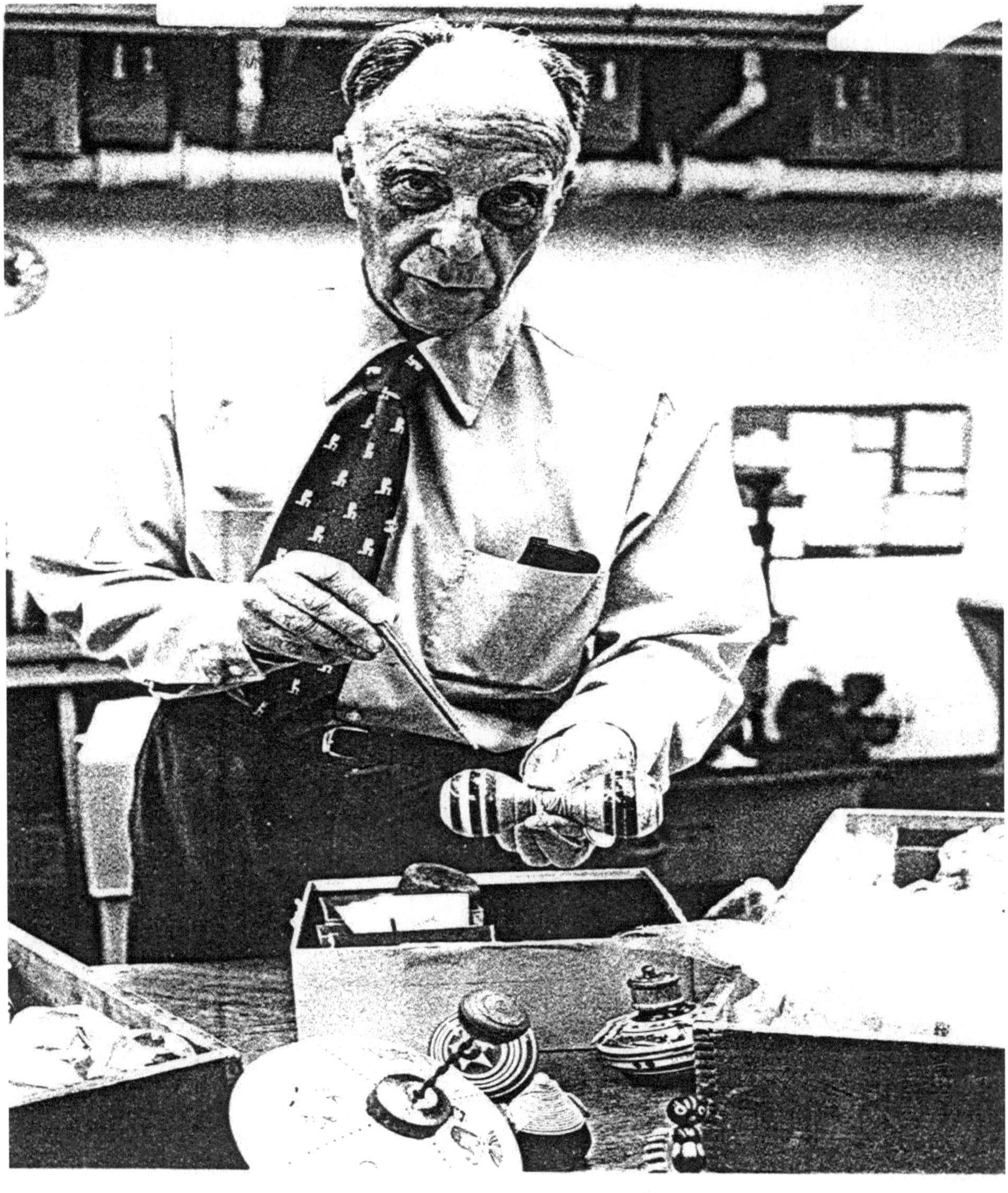

Univ. of Penn. Museum photo
Spring 1980,
age 84

MOVE TO UPPER DARBY, 1931.

In 1931 they moved out of West Philadelphia to their own home in the suburbs. This was at 511 Fairfield Road, in Upper Darby, about four miles west of the old apartment in the city. It was a three block walk down to 69th Street for the el, which Douglas took into town to work. And there were stores, restaurants, banks, movies, etc. much closer than they had been in the city. One night a week the cook (Elsa) got time off, when they went out to Schrafft's restaurant in Upper Darby. This was a treat, but not as much fun as going to Horn & Hardart's automat where three nickels opened a door to a hot beef or chicken pie, and one nickel released a slice of apple pie.

He rented their first house, a two story duplex, on a dressed stone basement, brick on the first floor and stucco on the second. There was an open porch on the front facing the street to the south. One entered a living room, with stairs to the east, dining room in the middle, with a shingled bay looking out onto the vacant lot and the corner. Beyond was the kitchen, with wooden steps out the back door. The stairs from the living room led into an upstairs hall, off which was the one bathroom, with white tiles and appliances. The master bedroom was on the front, over the living room, and two small bedrooms for Elinor and James--in all, one more room than they had in town. Beside, it had a full basement with a storeroom for Elsa's conserves and Douglas's home-made root beer. The insulation between the neighboring house to the east was soundproof, so one was not conscious of being twinned, and we had no knowledge of our neighbors. To the west, on the corner, was a lot that stayed vacant while we were there, and gave us breathing space and a view of the setting sun.

There was a small back yard with some lawn and forsythia bushes, and a garden plot Douglas dug up and planted some vegetables and flowers.

Here he bought their first "frigerator", with the big round cooler on top. This replaced the old ice box that had to be stored with blocks of ice at least once a week, and the pan of melted water dumped from beneath.

Here too, the family got its first "car". It was a brand-new 1932 "Tudor" Model A Ford, a four door "sedan". It was two toned, light tan on top, and darker brown below, separated by a black band with thin yellow line. It arrived one exciting day driven by Arthur Magee, husband of Elsa's first cousin Frieda (Fenn) of Brooklyn. Before the Depression Arthur had done so well selling Ford cars that they could afford a small yacht, and live in a nice house near the championship tennis games in Forest Hills. But all of this was lost in the Depression, and Douglas may have helped out with one of his last sales. They named the car "Steaddie", which had more to do with the driver than the vehicle.

Douglas was a super-safe driver. In the 60 or more years that he drove a car he had only one accident, and James took the blame for that. It was late in the day, and in the twilight he was driving down the four-lane highway at City Line when James suddenly asked him to turn into a side street he was looking for. Douglas responded and got a fender bender with an oncoming car. No one was hurt, and both cars drove away, with the repair costs left to the insurance companies. James apologized, but Douglas made nothing of the event, simply saying he was the driver.

He had not grown up with a car, of course, and learned to drive in 1917 for his Uncle John in Nova Scotia. He did not get his own car until 1923 when he got a government car when he was working for U.S. Geological Survey in Colorado. He drove defensively, teaching us his motto, "Watch out for the other idiot!" It was good teaching, for none of his three children ever had more than a fender-bender.

He also stayed within the law, including the posted speed limits, but may have got trapped by a revenue seeking village where the cop was enforcing an inconspicuous low speed limit.

Douglas always drove, and Elsa never learned. He tried to teach her, but it didn't work. The "car" gave the family a new mobility. On Sundays he drove down Chestnut Street to the

First Unitarian Church in the city. Douglas could drive directly to work via the Darby Creek valley much more quickly than going round about by el. And they took expeditions to the museums and park in town, and out to the suburbs to swimming holes on the creeks like Lake Sharpless, or for the Tufts picnic reunion.

Douglas kept in touch with Tufts through this annual picnic. Every June, shortly after the end of school, he would drive out to the farm of a Tufts alum a few miles west of West Chester for a whole Saturday of fun. Doug usually took part in the baseball game, and pitched horseshoes, at which he was very skilled. After midday there was a picnic in the open near the farmhouse. Their friends the Hoopers were always there, since Allan was a Tufts engineering graduate like Douglas.

Douglas also took the family on day-long trips to places like the Jersey shore, where they found Ocean City to their liking, less commercial than Atlantic City or Wildwood, and "classier", as Elinor put it. For years they stayed at Miss Adams's Virginia Inn. The route of 75 miles went through the city, over the Delaware River Bridge to Camden, and down the Black Horse Pike (or White Horse the same), across the Jersey farmlands, pine barrens, and salt marshes. Going at 30 mph meant an early start at both ends, getting up at dawn and leaving by three or four in the afternoon to beat the rush of traffic. We would occasionally detour north to Lakewood if the big German dirigible "Hindenberg" was there, for that was a wonderful sight.

He loved the salt water, and ducking the waves, even when the water was cold. He was a good swimmer, having grown up near ponds in Melrose, and the beach at Revere. Most of the time at the shore was spent relaxing in the sun, which he always enjoyed. In later years they tried other resorts farther north, like Lavallette in the late forties and Toms River in the fifties. Here their best friends were the Ed Gilliams, who nearly got them to buy a house nearby. Among his enjoyments at Toms River was going out in a rowboat to catch crabs, which were brought home to boil and laboriously pick apart for the last morsel. A good Bostonian, he always loved seafood of all kinds.

A special treat for his son, he thought, was a deep-sea fishing expedition. He would wake him up in the dead of night, and drive down from Philadelphia to a Jersey seashore fishing port, probably Cape May. Arriving at the dock before dawn, they boarded a motor launch. By daybreak they were well out at sea in the Atlantic Ocean, baiting hooks with ready-cut chunks of fish, to cast out into the rolling waves. If there was any roll at all, one threw up breakfast, and that ended the effort. If it was calm it was boring that one seldom got bites, and then only a useless sea-robin that had to be taken off the hook and thrown overboard, injured. But Douglas obviously inherited his own father's love of fishing. He also got seasick if it were really rough, but he was determined to enjoy the sport, and to bring home a good-sized fish for his wife to clean and cook.

The other male privilege Douglas taught his son was boxing. When the local bullies scared James out of going outside, his father bought a pair of boxing gloves, and tried to teach the boy to use them. He was a born coward, he thought, and hated the idea of being beaten up, let alone beating someone else up. Boxing didn't take, and James learned not to provoke bullies.

The car also enabled us to drive to Boston to visit Gramma Gould at Thanksgiving or Christmas, going up old Route One, through Trenton and New Jersey, taking the railroad ferry across the Hudson River to Manhattan, and up the old Boston Post Road--an all-day trip, starting before dawn, with a picnic for lunch, and ending late at night. This was not easy driving on two-lane roads with hazardous passing, frequent stops for traffic lights, and big city congestion. The driver had to concentrate on the unexpected actions of the other "crazy" drivers, as he called them. Elsa's task was to keep us quiet and amused. Douglas joined in the games of scoring for animals (white horses=2000, other horses=1000, cows=100, etc.), or trying to find the license plates of all the states.

Douglas also took us longer trips, like one to eastern Canada to visit cousin Charlie in Montreal, stopping en route at scenic waterfalls or historic sites like Ticonderoga and Lake George. They slept in tourist cabins, or an occasional private "tourist home", as B&Bs were then called. Gas was paid for with Douglas's Atlantic Refining credit card, so he had to plan ahead to get to an Atlantic station, where they could go to the bathroom. There was no such luxury as a soft drink, but a big thermos of lemonade quenched our thirst. Lunch was always a picnic at a grassy spot by the road, preferably beside a moving stream, in the shade. Dinners had to be inexpensive but served in a clean dining room, not an easy combination to find. But they had the Keystone Auto Club to guide them.

It was at this house on Fairfield Road that the third and last child Caroline Nancy Gould was born on 8 Dec. 1931. Her first name came from Douglas's elder sister whom he called "Callie" and the children called Aunt Cal. But she got the name from their paternal grandmother Caroline (Goddard) Gould, who had been named for her mother Caroline (Garran) Goddard. The name fitted well into Elsa's family, for one of her mother's middle names was also Caroline.

The house was getting crowded, and James was getting into trouble. When pregnant with Caroline Elsa once dragged him home by the ear from Upper Darby stores, and turned him over to the family disciplinarian. Douglas was a stern judge who took the prosecutor's evidence as final. The worst punishment was to be ordered to lower one's pants, lie tensely on a chair, as he pulled out his black leather belt, and whopped it over one's bare bottom several times until the tears came, and promised never to do "it" again. After one such beating he said, "Don't just promise--! want you to stop doing it!" "It" was usually failing to come home from school on time. When James got too big for his father to handle physically, the punishment would be exile in the cellar, without a meal.

MOVE TO VALLEY ROAD, HAVERTOWN, 1934.

Douglas must have got a raise even at the bottom of the Depression, for in 1934 he was able to rent a single house farther out in the suburbs, in Llanerch. This suburban village was an ancient Welsh farm settlement in Haverford Township (later called Havertown), about four miles west of their first house in Upper Darby. This was only a block from the stop of the Red Arrow Line than ran into Llanerch and down West Chester Pike to 69th Street.

James was once sent to Lynch, the realtors at the corner, with a check for the month's rent of $75. That was in the late thirties, probably after the rent had been raised. For this sum they got a six room house and garage at 813 Valley Road.

The style of this twenties-built house was Dutch Colonial, with gambrel detail on a side-gabled structure. The exterior was clapboard painted white. One entered the center hall from the south side porch, turned left into a living room, with an open porch beyond, facing the street. One turned right from the front hall into a dining room, with kitchen at the back. The staircase rose from the front hall upstairs to the upper hall, off which was the single bathroom, a master bedroom on the southwest, and two rooms on the back for the children. There was a big full basement for the Maytag washing machine, and a workbench which Douglas built for his tools. He wasn't a great mechanic, but could fix broken things in the house, clean out clogged drains, and repair electrical problems--at least the minor ones.

Outside there were flowering shrubs like quince and forsythia in the front and a good sized back yard for a vegetable garden and grape arbor for the Concord grapes Douglas loved. Though the house was close to its neighbor on the southeast, on the other side was a big shrub filled yard which completely screened the house from the next one, a big place where U.S. Commissioner William S. Wacker lived until his death in 1938. Best of all it backed up to a nursery which gave access to a golf course. They were practically in the country.

In the thirties Douglas's hobbies were stamps, coins and reading. He had inherited a small collection of stamps from his grandfather T. Warren who had begun collecting on trips to Britain and Germany. Douglas cataloged the variations of early British stamps that his grandfather had saved in large quantity. But his main interest was in American issues. He joined the Lansdowne Stamp Club and put on a display of special cancellations and grill-marks of early

American stamps. For his exhibit of U.S. stitch watermarks at the club's eleventh annual show 27-28 Nov. 1936 he got a Third Prize green ribbon. In 1932 he began what became a lifelong collection of every U.S. issue, saving mint plate blocks and marginal inscriptions.

About the same time he began collecting every new American coin, including all from the three mints at Philadelphia, Denver and San Francisco. The collection ran from the copper penny to the silver dollar, but never went into the gold coins. He also collected all the Indian head pennies that he could find by buying rolls at the bank. He also collected small bills of paper currency. He made a point of never buying a coin or stamp from a dealer, so the collection was basically paid for at cost from the post office and bank.

Douglas had a draftsman's neatness and skill, which he applied in designs of refinery complexes, carefully labeled in a natural print style. The most curious inheritance was his frequent use of block caps, so like his father's that he probably would have rejected it if he had been aware of the similarity. His son James got a love of maps and diagrams from him, and probably the taste for calligraphy. But when the boy got an A in his first mechanical drawing class and declared that he wanted to be a draftsman, his father told him it was a low-paying job and career, clearly beneath his talents.

His reading was broad, mostly non-fiction: archaeology, classics, anthropology, astronomy, exploration and discovery. Not that he would discuss his views at home, but the books were around to dip into if curious. He often went back to his childhood favorites, like Sir Walter Scott, Robinson Crusoe or Dickens or ancient myths and epic tales. He often reread 0 Henry and Mark Twain, especially "my old favorite "Roughing It" (Diary 26 Feb. 1966.). Somehow Balzac crept in too.

He did not start writing for fun until after retirement, but he did sing a poem, titled:

"LOVE SONGS (Best sung in the shower) Music from William Tell [,] Back to our Mountains":

Hark to the bob-o-link Sing as he cleans the sink
(Anyone would think He would know better.)

And to the whippoorwill Hum as he gathers swill
"Now I will get my fill, Now or never".

All praise to the sable crow; In France he's le corbeau)
Handsome and in the know; We count him a friend,

Ponder now the low tomtit Alert, saucy and full of wit. He'll win
your heart, (Count on it) By summer's end."

Douglas's job at Atlantic filled a good eight hour day. The family got up at seven every day. He would leave after breakfast about 7:30 for the half hour drive to Point Breeze. He once showed James the time cards and clock where they punched in and out, but his children never saw his work space, presumably a desk in a lab on the second floor. He would have lunch during the hour's break, in the company cafeteria. Then check out at five to be home by 5:30 to 5:45, depending on the weather and traffic. He was commuting by car during rush hours, but in general this was across the west suburbs and the main flow of commuter traffic from the city.

Dinner was promptly at six, and one had better be home, or be punished. The advantage of Douglas's regular hours was that he was usually home in the evening, but he settled down in the living room with the newspaper, and children were supposed to be doing homework.

Sometimes the family would play games like Monopoly, Parcheese or Chinese Checkers, or Douglas would play a game of checkers or chess with the children. Although he was a good player, he could not verbally explain strategy, so one learned tactics by playing him. We all played several card games, starting with "Squeak", a double card game, which he would let Caroline win until she was about five, but after that it was cutthroat. Pinochle was apparently a game he had learned to enjoy as a boy. Pit and Fish were also fun family games.

He seldom brought work home. He would usually read until after Elsa had gone to bed before ten, or go to his "Den" upstairs and pay bills, write letters or work on his stamps or coins. His desk had a pile of "scratch paper", discarded graphs, charts or pages of manuscripts, the back sides of which he reused in Yankee fashion. Pencils were honed to a point by penknife or sharpener.

There were several colleagues at Atlantic whom he saw occasionally outside of work. He always called them by their last names, so his children rarely knew their given names. His boss at Atlantic he called Doc Myers since he had a doctorate in chemistry, and lived in a big house in the northwest suburbs. Cooley had a summer retreat on the river at Collegeville where the Goulds used to visit until their child died of a congenital heart defect. Douglas was surely sympathetic as he could be in his distant manner, but the presence of the Gould children was too painful a reminder for the Cooleys to bear.

Other friends were couples he shared with his wife, the Hoopers, the Merrises, the Kellers, the Gallops, the Houghtons, the Flowers, the Heckmans and the Coburns. Allan and Lorna Hooper were their best friends. They had in common with Allan a Tufts engineering education, a Boston upbringing, and Unitarian faith. Lorna (Austin) graduated from Union, but fit right in. The family had dinner followed by bridge at the Hoopers' at least once a week, alternating weeks at the Goulds'. The kids fell asleep during the bridge game, and got carried home when the game was over at ten or eleven. The Hoopers had children about the Goulds' ages: Alice was slightly older than James, Bobby about Elinor's age, then Margaret, and the youngest Gertie, slightly younger than Caroline. Young Bob inherited his father carrot-red hair and freckled complexion.

Carl Merris was an engineering colleague of Mr. Hooper's at GE in Philadelphia, who lived a few houses east of the Hoopers on Strathmore Road. Carl and Grace's children were older than the Goulds, and knew them less well. Margaret and Hayward Coburn also had older children, their youngest, Carol, was a little older than Caroline. Hayward Coburn was a Philadelphia lawyer with Drinker, Biddle & Reath, who lived across the street from the Hoopers, and also went to the same Unitarian church. Beside bridge and church, the families did a lot of other things together on outings, picnics, birthdays or vacations.

Jack Keller was an engineer at the Baldwin Locomotive Works, until the Depression closed the plant. He had four children the same ages as the Goulds, and went to the Unitarian church.

The Nelsons also went to the Philadelphia Unitarian Church. Oscar was professor of accounting at the Wharton School, and he and his wife Helen and children lived near the Swarthmore College campus.

Other friends were the Ed Heckman, the Finneys, Healds, Morgans, Hydes, Kiehls, Dietrichs. Foulkrods, Moores and Hallowells (This list is compiled from "Fyne Olde Printes", a souvenir of a party 26 Jan. 1946, which Father described thus: "The occasion was a party at our house where those coming were invited to bring inconsequential gifts such as old money, fine prints, objets d'art, etc. the names shown are married and maiden." Each couple is described in a short phrase, a sketch of a ship and thumb prints, not in my Father's handwriting. Ed & Dot Churchill had a "farm" near West Chester, and retired to Lake Winnepesaukee in New Hampshire, where the Goulds visited.

The only club he belonged to was the Delaware County College Mens Club, a monthly luncheon club. Douglas was no joiner or crusader. He belonged to a fraternity in college, the American Legion after the war, the College Men's Club in Havertown, and the University Club in Claremont, but was never a leader. Organization and clubs annoyed him, partly in disgust at the power hunger or ostentation of leaders. He had few close friends, and mostly through his wife. There were superior colleagues like Karrick and Field with whom he worked usually as an admiring and loyal deputy. At the end he felt closest to Dr. Joseph Griggs, with whom he had a close but sometimes contentious friendship and rivalry. Douglas did not seem to need the company of others to sustain him, since his own active mind was the source of stimulus.

Bridge was serious stuff. It was always Contract, never played for money. Douglas and Elsa worked well as a team, each learning the cues the partner was sending about one's hand. They tried to teach their children the game, but the attraction stuck only with Elinor. Douglas occasionally went out to play poker with a group of men, probably from work. He had a set of chips at home, and even taught his children the basics, while warning of the dangers of betting too high. He played for nickels and quarters at most. He scared his son away from the fun, if that is what one gets. He also played billiards with some skill, but too infrequently to say he enjoyed it.

Sports were not important at home. Spectator sports like baseball and football were not things he cared about in the thirties, and James and Elinor were never taken to a game, but by the forties he developed a great interest in the Phillies and the "A's", and took Caroline to many games at Shibe Park, leaving early to get to the balling practice. One had to park on the street in South Philadelphia in front of homes where the enterprising youngsters would try to charge a dollar or two parking fee. Douglas would tell them, "I'm going to park here, but I won't pay you!"

His intense sense of justice is probably the reason he developed one long-term project out of a pet peeve. That was what he called the illogical way that baseball standings were made. He observed that many players like infielders didn't get credit for their skills, and didn't get paid as well as the big-hitters. Defensive ball players might get no credit for saving a game by fielding balls. His identification with the underdog made him indignant about this injustice, so he developed a far more accurate and relevant scoring which he tried to peddle without success. His son-in-law Jim Clark respectfully pointed out that the public paid to see homeruns, but that made it worse. Doug wrote to the management of both Philadelphia teams, without response. He eventually got a Philadelphia patent attorney to patent his scoring system, but could find no intereStreet His grandson Roger Krueger took on the task and still has the details.

Douglas didn't care much for football or hockey, but in the fifties he got interested in cricket, and went with Elsa to games played on City Line. The only sport that he took his son to see was track, at the Penn Relays in Franklin Field. He may have done some running in college, and he encouraged his son to do broad-jumping in a sand pit, and even built a high jump with a bamboo pole between two upright posts. Caroline never persuaded him to put up a basketball hoop, but finally got him to put up a high jump bars over a pit in the back yard. At one time he took the children out onto the abandoned golf course and taught them golf, but he never joined a club, or played much himself.

Elsa and Douglas played singles tennis in Chicago and in Philadelphia (at Fairmount Park), and occasional doubles with some friends like the Hoopers. He belonged to a men's bowling league, to which he went once a week. He was reasonably good at this game, and he later took up bocci for fun. Croquet was a family sport in the backyard, at which my Douglas excelled. He played a competitive game at which he could win if he concentrated. So one always chose him as partner since he would find ways to help you out. But if he greatly outmatched someone he would play casually with one hand and good-naturedly cuss at his bad shots.

Walks were Douglas's style of exercise. He would drive the family out into the country, and hike down some dirt farm road, exploring the woods, and come back for a picnic fire over which were roasted hotdogs and marshmallows. They never camped out as he may have done in the Army and in Geology field trips, but he gladly spent money to send the children to summer camp in the Poconos. At the age of 85 he was still physically skilled, as his winning the Claremont championships in both lawn bowling and in pool shows.

Douglas kept his Boston accent throughout his life, saying "Idear" for idea, "Clea" for clear. He was better at reading foreign languages than speaking them, and often read the professional journals of chemistry in German, and read some Spanish. During the first World war he seemed to have picked up some spoken French, which he could already read. He retained some Latin, probably from high school.

His lack of gregariousness is illustrated by his attitude toward their Upper Darby bank they frequented for many decades. He was insulted that they never knew who he was when he came in, whereas he said his wife was always greeted, "Hello, Mrs. Gould!"

At home Elsa did all the talking, and invited argument from all. Her spouse seldom responded, but appeared to agree with her ideas most of the time. When he had to communicate it was often in brief aphorisms that would usually stop the conversation:

"As Edison said, believe only half what you read, and none of what you hear", or
"You can lead a horse to water, but you can't make him drink!", or
"There are more than two ways to skin a cat!", or
"Try, try again!", or
"Nuff said!"

When he was angry or injured he would let go a profanity, like "Damn!", and quickly change it to "Darn!" a word he often said when he was annoyed if he was careful. "Drat it!" was a common expletive. His usual version of Hell was "What the heck!" Although he must have learned all the other four letter words every Army man uses, he'd cured himself of that, and the children never heard any. But contemptuous persons, were "bastards", of course.

Although Douglas was a man of few words, you knew for sure what he did not like. He had a lot of pet peeves, about which he would comment derisively when the subject came up. Among them were mayonnaise, pigeons and *The Readers Digest.* For unexplained reasons all Dutch things were despised, including tulips, but he seems to have mellowed about the Dutch after visiting their land in the fifties. All hypocrites came in for scathing rejection. Among them were super-patriots, the typical flag waver who hides behind the national symbols like the national anthem (which he could never sing). He also despised wealthy developers who gouged the poor, like Philadelphia's Greenberg.

The press and all advertising was treated with the greatest skepticism. Once when his sister Caroline was bragging about the articles about him in Claremont, when asked if he had provided the facts, he replied: "Half may be true and the other half is the way you heard it." (On his 82d birthday, 27 Jan. 1978, JWG Diary #50, 5.). Most politicians came in for contempt also. He called them "crooks".

Douglas's politics were more conservative than his wife's, but on the liberal side. He was a life-long Republican, based as much on anti-Irish sentiments as anything traditional. The Irish like Mayor Curley controlled the corrupt politics of Boston and Beacon Hill, so all Yankees voted Republican. He hated Roosevelt for no apparent reason than that he was a Democrat. The same sentiment applied to all the Pennsylvania politicians. But as Massachusetts Republican party began with the cause of abolition, and remained liberal in social policy, so Douglas supported the liberal politics of pioneer conservationist Governor Gifford Pinchot of Pennsylvania. His Republicanism was of the Bull Moose sort of Teddy Roosevelt, reforming rather than reactionary.

An example is his reaction to meeting the Garrisons' friend Calvin Wells in Paris in 1963: "At dinner E[lsa] put up good strong defense of [Pennsylvania Governor] Joe Clark as being far from communistic. [I] Suspect G's friend (although frat brother of Clark), is a Bircher. " (1963 Diary, May 10.)

He voted in every election, and usually commented out loud about the corruption of the other side, like Boss Pew, who made his money in Atlantic's rival Sun Oil, and bought his control of local politics. Basically he was very skeptical of all politicians, and wary of power.

The same principles dictated daily newspaper reading: *The Evening Bulletin* was the only paper he would read; the morning *Inquirer* was too corrupt to bother with, and the tabloids not worth contempt. The only exception was made for the mordant political cartoons by Hutton, who was a good friend of Douglas's, perhaps from College Club. The *New York Times* was essential Sunday reading, all Sunday afternoon. Elsa would start the crossword puzzle while he was reading the other parts, and he would try to finish it, sputtering about the mistaken guesses she had written in too boldly. "The News of the Week in Review" was then a real summary of the week's news, not features as today, and that obviated reading opinionated weeklies like Time.

The timely pictures in *National Geographic* and *Life* had attraction, however. They had to take the *Saturday Evening Post* and *Ladies Home Journal* once James began peddling it in the neighborhood, and he enjoyed its Mr. Moto stories. *Collier's* and *Liberty* were around for a while, but he probably did not read much more than an occasional feature article. He subscribed to professional journals like *Chemical Abstracts,* which piled up until he clipped them for relevant articles.

Radio was the main home entertainment, but he didn't listen often, except to some major news event that was breaking, a weather report, or election results, and a Sunday afternoon concert of classical music.

They had a Victrola on which he liked to put the old Victor Red Seal 78 rpm records to play some of his favorites, like operatic overtures, waltzes and folk tunes such as "Drink to me only with thine eyes. . . " . His taste was mainly classical nineteenth century music: Beethoven's symphonies and overtures, Brahms's symphonies and lullaby, Chopin's waltzes and polonaises, Bizet's Carmen and 1'Arlesienne suites, Grieg's Pier Gynt and piano concerto, Liszt's concerto and rhapsodies, Offenbach's Gaite, Rossini's William Tell, Schumann and Schubert, Strauss waltzes and polkas, and Wagner's Ride of the Valkyres. Gilbert & Sullivan fit the same era. He was less fond of singing and modern music, and disliked the sound of the saxophone. Although he never let on that he liked singing, he could carry at tune quite well, as when he'd hum to the dog.

He seldom went to movies, but seemed to enjoy the old silent comedians like Harold Lloyd and Our Gang Comedy. He was a devotee of certain comic strips, like Krazy Kat, Katzenjammer Kids, Popeye, and Gasoline Alley, his favorites. He spent hours reading the Sunday "funnies", as he called them, to the Clark grandchildren.

He loved the circus, especially the big-top and the animal and clown stunts, though we were warned against the shysters in the side-shows. We got the idea that as a boy he had enjoyed going to the circus. Food was rationed to one "treat", usually popcorn, which he enjoyed.

Until the '40s he and Elsa were tee-totallers, out of fear of reviving the devil drink that had ruined Samuel Gould's life. None of their friends were drinkers, but perhaps got them to relax the prohibition a bit, and Doug would have an occasional beer with a friend, and they even bought a bottle of sherry which they served in a decanter to celebrate special occasions. A bottle could last a whole year. In the fifties their son-in-law Don Krueger introduced them to hard liquor iced with fruit juices, like lime and lemon, and these soon became great favorites, but only one an evening.

The job at Atlantic seldom involved any travel, except to the annual meetings of the American Chemical Society. However, in 1937 he had to go to the Atlantic refinery at Port Arthur, Texas for the whole summer (Elinor received a letter from him dated 8 July from Hotel Sabine, Port Arthur).

An indication of his expertise in the field of petroleum chemistry are the five articles which he contributed to the encyclopedia of oil, *The Science of Petroleum*, published by Oxford University Press in three countries, Great Britain, Canada and U.S. in 1938. He is the expert on the heat, density and properties of coke.

He left two commentaries on this work. The first says: "The volumes Technology of Petroleum started out reasonably, but editorial policy on different sides of Atlantic caused some of the intended authors to drop out. Shuffling of subjects to new writers followed, but I never did discover an editor before the manuscript was submitted. H. M. Weir did his best he could as intermediary, but had no authority, and was trying to meet a deadline for a section of his own. Yet this Science of Petroleum might have [been] a splendid thing twenty years earlier. But at the date of issue, it was neither comprehensive nor completely up to date."

The next is: "These several articles in vols. II & IV were written on short notice, and probably assigned to me at suggestion of H. M. Weir. Luckier writers knew a couple of years ahead that they would contribute. Anyway it was an ambitious project. Weir left Atlantic, went to Germany as a consulting engineer, saw the re-arming, and returned to U.S. at outbreak of war[.] Afterward he helped accumulate the contents of technical files (German) from which the reels of film were made (see Article in Atlantic Magazine)."

Gould saved some official Memoranda that he wrote for Atlantic with this comment: "There was a vast amount of 'Progress Reports' or monthly summaries of work done on projects in ARCO. R & D Mostly dry and uninspired, but is really the cold record of what was done.

Segments of the above summaries which seemed to have novelty or interest were issued as "Memoranda["]. Everyone puts his work in a favorable light, hoping that it reaches others in the Department or Company who will take interest and show why further support should be given the project."

The first of these is dated Nov. 1939, "Estimation of Lead Requirements of Napthas". His comment on these is: "Memoranda were means to get your work read other than by monthly summaries. They also served to anticipate shots from those who seemed to be asking "Why?" and "why don't we do this?" Among the recipients were colleagues in the research department whose names are familiar: Hugh W. Field, L. Laskaris, and W. A. Myers.

He saved several official memoranda that reflect Gould's involvement in the defense buildup in 1940, on the capacity of Atlantic to produce aviation gas.

From this era, 1940, he preserved a chart, "Ethyl Fluid Blending Chart" (PE-1243) which he described as : "My brainchild, and thought very good at time. Present motor fuels (1986) so high in octane, they would be considered aviation grade 1940."

He picked up the idea presented by Eastman at the American Chemical Society meeting of 8-12 Sept. 1941 to urge that Atlantic "initiate a cooperative exchange of data with several refining companies leading to a systematic attack and early solution of the problem of lead susceptibility of motor fuels and their components. " (Memo Ml.2361, 5 Sept. 1941.).

MOVE TO PENFIELD, 1938.

As the American economy pulled out of the Depression in the late thirties more gasoline was sold, and Atlantic was doing well. Douglas was able to buy a house for the first time since Rifle, Colorado. They found a nice 1920s Colonial Revival two miles northeast in Haverford Township, in Penfield. The house at 1209 Larchmont Avenue was on a quiet tree-shaded street close to the woodland overlooking Darby Creek, and a five minute walk to the Beechwood station on the Red Arrow Line from 69th Street Station and Allentown. This suburban electric railway he affectionately called the "Pig and Whistle" for its initials P. & W. (Philadelphia and Western).

They moved from the Valley Road house on 1 Sept. 1938. This house was a side-gabled, with a false gambrel detail and apron between the two stories. It was white clapboard, with dark shutters beside the windows. The central entrance was up four brick steps to a Classical Revival portico, supported by two Ionic columns.

The interior was laid out much the same as the Valley Road one, the front door entering into the center hall which had a staircase right ahead, the living room to the left, with fireplace on the far wall, and enclosed sunporch behind that. To the right was the dining room, but the kitchen was in back, and off it a small breakfast nook. A similar plan prevailed upstairs: the one bathroom at the top of the hall, master bedroom over the living room, and two bedrooms on the other side. But this house had a great unfinished attic, which became James's combined bedroom and playroom. Like Valley Road there was a full basement (with a toilet), and detached one-car garage.

The Penfield house had a bigger back yard which opened out to a vacant lot. But their neighbors were closer, to the south a big balloon frame house of about 1910 vintage loomed across the driveway. The other neighbor, the Moore's, was somewhat farther away. In the back yard was a large weeping willow tree, hydrangeas, lilies of the valley, and forsythia. Front and back yards had ample grassy lawns, with a swing set in back.

Douglas lavished love openly on pets that he would be embarrassed to be seen giving to his wife or children. The Goulds' ornery orange tom-cat "Reddy" took almost abusive stroking from Doug to raise electricity on its back.

Although the Welsh Terrier "Ned" was theoretically James's dog, Elsa gave him food and water, and Douglas gave him periodic flea-baths, or tomato juice cleansings after a run-in with a skunk, brushed his wiry fur and stroked his back vigorously. By decree Ned had to sleep at night in the cellar, but might be found cowering under a bed upstairs after a frightening thunderstorm. When James left for college and the war, Douglas took over Ned with great affection. Ned submitted without protest to all kinds of affectionate attention from him, such as being picked up the stump of his cropped tail, or being spun around on the piano stool. Douglas genuinely mourned when Ned had to be put to sleep in 1951. He left a poem "To Ned", to be sung to the tune of Brahms' s Lullaby:

"Mine poor old Neddy Weddy

Why don't you be good to me?

You're nothing but a poodle woodle,

And I think I'll swap you for a poo named Poo."

PRODUCTION OF AVIATION GAS FOR WORLD WAR II.

Before the outbreak of war in 1939 the job at Atlantic became shaky, for one of his friends, Lloyd Smith, was fired, and Gould was threatened by firing on 24 May 1939.

World War II brought great demand for all kinds of oil products, but especially aviation gas. This required redesigning the refining process to get higher octane fragments from the distillation. But most important, the government had to find a substitute for the natural rubber that was lost to the Japanese in Southeast Asia. They turned to the hydrocarbon specialists to find synthetic substitutes. At one point Gould was sent to the Southwest to look at the desert plants that were supposed to be producing rubber latex.

His memoir of the war is brief: "In W.W. II I found time to serve on several committees which sought and got complete cooperation of all refiners in U.S. and as a result of this cooperation this country's armed forces never knew a shortage of aviation fuel nor of toluene for the explosive, TNT." (Bio., 2.).

Elsewhere he elaborated: "In the period 1942-1945 there arose the Technical Advisory Committee (TAG) child of API and Aviation Gasoline Advisory Committee (AGAC) reporting to Petroleum Administration for War (Ickes Of course as nominal head). These organizations did immense good, and I was most astounded at the spirit of rival oil concerns giving up real secrets to the committees who then coordinated the information and converted it into usable operating procedures. Of aviation gasoline and of aromatics as for TNT there was never a critical shortage. Field and myself were on many of the groups, and he was quite willing to leave work and reporting to me; his forte was in enthusing those who had information to give and acceptance of procedures of refinery operation by those who most stood in need of the information." (Pub., 2, (m) .)

Among the technical committees for which there are reports are Aviation Gasoline, Synthesis, Codimer Subcommittees.

He stripped the details of bulky data and charts, but saved several of the basic reports to the Technical Advisory Committee (TAG) , a subcommittee of the Technical Committee of the Petroleum Industry War Council. He comments on his boss at Atlantic: "H. W. Field as chairman, dynamic, good leader, persuasive, glad to assign work to G[ould] who wrote reports signed by Field."

The first is "First Progress Report of the Aromatics Subcommittee of the Aviation Gasoline Advisory Committee: Summary of Information Submitted at the 'Benzine from Petroleum[1] Meeting, Chicago, October 14-15, 1942." Gould's introduction starts with their mission: "The Aromatics Subcommittee of the Aviation Gasoline Advisory Committee is charged with the duties of surveying means for securing adequate supplies of aromatic hydrocarbons for aviation fuel."

The next is three months later, covered with his comment: "Some wartime reports: Largely anonymous, we (committee or subcommittee) did the work...shows diverse involvement of D.W.Gould, Chairman of Aviation Gasoline [sub] Committee. This is "First Progress Report Correlation of Variables in Catalytic Polymerization..." dated 21 Dec. 1942, and issued by the Petroleum Industry War Council, Suite 2017, 50 W. 50th Street, New York. Gould states the importance to the war effort in the first paragraph: "Catalytic polymerization is a very effective means of removing light olefins from gaseous mixtures and of converting the olefins to liquids of lower vapor pressure which may easily be transported from one refinery to another and used directly in the manufacture of components of aviation fuel or synthetic rubber."

Gould was appointed to an API (American Petroleum Institute) wartime committee on synthetic fuels, which met periodically in Washington and New York. The work was supposed to be secret, and surely was from Douglas's standpoint, since he never talked much anyway. All of the reports are classified "Restricted" but distributed to all the refineries in the country plus all the experts. These restricted reports continue even after V-J Day, evidently to prevent their reaching former enemies.

After the end of the war (26 Nov. 1945) the U.S. Navy gave a "Certificate of Achievement" to the Aviation Gasoline Advisory Committee "in recognition of exceptional accomplishment in behalf of the United States Navy and of meritorious contribution to the national war effort.

This was given him by his boss, Hugh W. Field, Chair of the Subcommittee on Aromatics, which the government's Petroleum Administration for War thanked them for with this tribute: "The Aviation Gasoline Advisory Committee was created with one goal in mind; namely, to assure that aviation gasoline would never be lacking on any fighting front...The...Committee is best judged by results --never has there been a claim that the petroleum industry failed the military -- and this most enviable record was achieved during the period when requirements increased tenfold." (Letter of Ralph K. Davies, 7 Sept. 1945 to H. W. Field.) The Committee was disbanded 30 Sept. 1945.

Gasoline was rationed even for those who produced it at Atlantic, but he got top priority. Still, it was the patriotic thing to carpool, so he would share driving to the plant with five other employees who lived nearby. Saving scrap metal and paper came easily to one who had always been frugal from necessity.

Toward the end of the war he began scanning captured German documents for information on their aviation gasoline production. This continued after the war, reading documents in German, dictating his interpretation into a dictaphone, whose results were typed and edited by him. This was described in an illustrated article "Geheim!", the company organ

The *Atlantic Magazine,* vol. 1, no. 4, Feb. 1946, 22-23, with two pictures of him.

The purpose of the search, the article says, is in the hope that "it may save millions of dollars by short-cutting some of the slow, painstaking advances of research and development." But Gould is quoted as saying: "It is too soon to talk about individual discoveries on film as being important. We will learn what Germany knew and thought. There is no reason why America should not profit from the technical advantage it possesses. It will be a long time before Germany can threaten our trade with important technical advances."

He later commented that the article "is not my writing, but is my brainchild. Actually it records some very interesting months when we tried to discover gems of German technology. They just were not there in the form we sought. The miracle of the German technology was carrying on the war with synthetic fuel. Had they possessed petroleum in adequate amount, their chemistry might have taken them to the superior products of the Allies. And the vast effort given to synthetic fuels could have gone into other production. It remains a wonder to me that the Germans held out so long."

The secrecy of the war over, the great progress in development of aviation gasoline could be revealed to the public, and this was done in a professional paper presented at the American Petroleum Institute convention in Chicago on 12 Nov. 1946, and published as Gould[1] s third paper, this one with Hugh Field as first author is was called "Project 6 Spotlights Avgas Progress".

Doug's gloss on this was: "Joint paper with H. W. Field in A.P.I, was my idea and two thirds Field's writing. More important, Field was an excellent talker, and could make the subject sound more profound than it really was. Even so, it was a new concept to most in A.R. Co."

The paper tells of the wartime development of analytical methods for analyzing the chemical properties of the blending agents in making aviation gas.

POSTWAR RESEARCH AND WRITING, 1945.

Following the peace, simultaneous with the review of the captured German documents, he also did research on drilling muds, the lubricant for pushing oil wellheads deep into the earth. A preliminary report of 84 pages presented in July 1946 laid out a plan of research. This took him to the west Texas oilfields for fairly long trips, and to the Atlantic refinery at Beaumont on the Gulf Coast.

In 1948 he was producing Bulletins on a variety of research topics. His explanation was that "Bulletin summarized information and prodded those who could do something to do so..." No. 77 in Aug. 1948 on laid out in plain language the basic facts on "Oil Shale and Shale Oil" and recommended that Atlantic not get rights west of the Mississippi, that deposits in Pennsylvania and Ohio had not been explored, that the company could keep track of developments through contact in the Department of Interior, and shale was no threat to Atlantic's refining business.

Bulletin 76 reviewed the results of research projects by the American Petroleum Institute, to which Atlantic contributed funding. No. 79 reported on Atlantic's production of detergent soap. Another reported on natural gas.

By the late forties he was out of the lab at Point Breeze, and moved up to the corporate headquarters at 260 South Broad Street. There one of his last jobs was editing a newsletter, a skill he seemed to share with his uncle John Gould, who made it a specialty. This involved layout and design at which he was good, as well as writing interesting news about the developments in the oil industry.

The Bulletins soon evolved into a monthly report which Gould edited, called *News Slants.* His covering summary of it was "A monthly publication to inform executives of current developments. Higher-ups lived in perpetual fear that some rival company would suddenly gain advantage from topic appearing in newspaper. I tried to allay their fears...The research was wholly mine. Whole available family was used to assemble and staple the pages. Caroline will remember."

"For several years [1948-51] I issued News Slants on current topics presumably of interest to the petroleum industry. Intended solely for top management, they were framed to explain the significance of the news items which appeared in public media and aroused unreasonable fear that doom was awaiting Atlantic, either because we were not a party or had backed another horse. I think the idea was unique to the industry and could have done immense good. But the controlling parties were horrified that opinions were expressed and might represent the opinion of R. & D. Suppose the conclusion was wrong. The result was a continuous hampering in content, form and of actual reproduction of the copy, even to the extent of putting out a departmental issue extolling the accomplishments of the department. But this worked to my advantage because those responsible for the rival issue were inept to a monumental degree. All the same it syphoned off availability of facilities which I needed; I had to take lower priority. The rival fell of its own inertia; could not maintain a monthly schedule, and gained no friends in its uncompromising praise of R. & D. Quite a scene of interdepartment politics. No wonder that a sweeping reorganization caught up with R. & D. Imagine having three full time photographers for a department of our size." (Pub. 2, para. (1) .)

The index for the first year, 1948, shows a wide range of topics from Solar Energy to Detergents, from Flame Throwers to the Olympic Torch. He covered rival companies in the U.S. and new developments abroad, in U.S.S.R., Persian Gulf and Germany, and even an item on the Berlin Airlift.

The next year seemed to focus more narrowly on current research, with fewer international topics, but the subjects ranged widely from Sewage Disposals to Dry Ice. 1950 had a review of the marine history of Atlantic, rubber roads, and cleanup of the Schuylkill River. In the fourth and last year, 1951, he wrote:"Snow Melting, seems an incongruous topic for July. Yet it is estimated that there are over 500 major installations in the United States. Perhaps by next fall, a number of these can be identified as Atlantic fuel oil customers..." This was followed by a lead article on the new development of the Heat Pump.

GRANDFATHER 1952.

The greatest joy of the fifties was becoming a parent again to the Clark family. The first of fifteen grandchildren, Robert Douglas Gould, named for his two grandfathers, was born in April 1952 half way "round the world, in Medan, Sumatra, where their son was acting Consul. Though they soon came back to U.S., it was to California, Boston and Washington DC. Elinor's children were born on Long Island and New Jersey, near her husband Don's work in Manhattan.

So when Caroline gave them their second grandchild, James Edward Clark, they loved the fact that she could live with them, and they could help bring up the children as their own. As soon as he was born on 11 June 1952 Jimmy became like a fourth child. They shared all the trials and fun of parenting without the sole responsibility it means for a parent. Douglas was much more relaxed about his parenting role, and had more fun with the grandchildren. Linda was born 15 months later, and Barbara only 14 months after that. The Clarks had the upstairs of the Clearfield Road house, and lived with them until they moved to their own house in Broomall.

Even when the growing Clark family moved to their own home Douglas and Elsa were on hand as baby-sitters, counselors, and teachers. This probably gave them a new lease on life, and a new interest as retirement approached.

One of Douglas's favorite entertainments was to tell a small child to stand stiff, while he proceeded to pick the child up by two hands under its chin. Another game was "Button, Button", which involved putting a small object like a button into one closed hand, and asking the child to guess which hand held it; if correct the child could go up a step; if not, down one. He also made bathtub ships out of walnut shell halves fixed with a toothpick mast and square sail.

Early on one grandson called him "Pop-pop", a name that stuck.

To help in the house with cleaning and wash they found a wonderful Black woman to replace the aged Mrs. West. "S. A.", pronounced "Essie", got her name when the mother had used the whole alphabet to "R" on previous children, and had to use the next letter. When Essie grew too old to work a relative or friend named Alice (Yorke?) took her place, helping when Jimmy and the other Clark children were born. She served them until Doug left Philadelphia for California. Because she lived in a dangerous part of West Philadelphia, Doug would often drive her home.

In these years he was active in the First Unitarian church in Philadelphia, taking the collection on Sundays, and in Laymans' League, a mens' group which met monthly. On 14 Dec. 1952 he gave a talk to the Sunday Open Meeting held before the main church service, on the topic "Our Changing Climate". This was announced in the church bulletin thus: "In this talk on weather, Mr. Gould will review the nature of our climate in the past, discuss the kind of climate we have today and venture some opinions as to what the future holds in store for us."

They continued to drive to visit his sisters in New Hampshire and Maine. In the late forties they took a trip to Williamsburg, visiting the Civil War battlefields on the way. Longwood Gardens near Wilmington DE were always a favorite trip.

In June 1954 he took Elsa on their first cruise, to the Bahamas. They sailed the S.S. *Nassau,* Captain Francesco Perilli, 18-21 June to Little Abaco, to visit his English cousins, Brigadeer Gen. Malcolm Douglas and his wife Clare, who had entertained me in England in Dec. 1945.

Elsa's heart attack in Dec. 1954 made it impossible for her to climb the stairs of the Larchmont Av. house to the bathroom, so they sold the house and bought one with a ground floor bathroom. It was at 37 West Clearfield Rd., two miles northwest in the Oakmont neighborhood of Havertown. This was their last home as a couple, and his for over two decades, from 1955 to 1977.

The one and a half story gable fronted house, about two thirds the size, built after the war, was white with dark shutters stucco had four rooms: the front door came directly into the living room; there was one bath, kitchen and two bedrooms on the ground floor, and two more bedrooms and a bath on the second floor under the twin-dormered roof, and a full basement.

Outside there was a good sized lawn, enclosed by a wooden board fence, and the usual garden plot for vegetables and flowers. They missed Ned but soon adopted local dogs and cats who were not really fed, but given special treats like marrow bones, for which they soon made daily visits. The neighbors were friendly. Margaret and Ed Hornketh the plumber lived next door. The people across the street were particularly helpful during Elsa's illnesses.

Douglas had his lawyer friend Hayward Coburn draft a will, which he signed on 30 June 1958. It was a fairly standard text of six pages, leaving his estate to his wife, or on her death to his sisters, and finally equally to his three children. In 1986 he had given each child $25,000 (Note in his estate: "5/24/86 Redemption of funds [he sold T. Rowe Price Prime Reserve Fund (7.4%) for $37,641, U.S. Treasury notes for $21,174, and AARP GNMA U.S. Treasury Account for $13,598] netted $73676.90 This allows 25,000 each to Jim, Elinor, Caroline. Pay E, check #1278, Pay C check #1279, Jim, later or as blue-chip stock to the children, so before his death, he left a net estate of $24,900 after expenses).

The will anticipated leaving a "memorandum with respect to distribution",. and he left a written instruction "James to dispose at discretion//Suggested <u>Disposal:</u> Each grandchild $1000; each gr .Grandchild $500--, Tufts College $2000." (James's letter of 20 July 1994). The children ended agreeing to send Tufts the amount suggested and divide the remainder three ways, and the parent to give the amounts to their children and grandchildren. On his death he left 24 living descendants, three children, 15 grandchildren, and six great-grandchildren (Aidan, Michelle, Jennifer, Michael, Jason and Chris).

When *News Slants* ended in 1951 Gould continued alerting the company to new developments, as in his 1954 Memo 4725 which details about 100 grants for academic research in hydrocarbons in American universities.

In the last years at Atlantic he was applying the new technology of punch cards to retrieve data. This resulted in an article in the professional library journal, *Special Libraries*, in Nov. 1949, describing his idea for retrieval with a template. His explanation is "what was probably a new approach to use of the McBee card for information retrieval. My thought was to aid the smaller user of data, one who couldn't afford a complex system, but possibly in danger of being overwhelmed by having to sort many cards by hand. My system aids him in entering the data; the retrieval is a continuing evil. The article was a much abbreviated version."

This led to a most curious Christmas card, an orange card with no writing whatever, but punched with rectangular holes, and a sketch of the new house. His explanation to me was: "This was Xmas card one year//you may guess the message, but perhaps you can get it read out." How many relatives or friends could get it read? This kind of riddle was typical.

One of his final projects at Atlantic was to work on the second edition of American Petroleum Institute's *Glossary of Terms Used in Petroleum Refining,* which was not published until 1962, after he retired. He left me a comment on his copy: "H. W. Field (later W. A. Myers) was chairman of a Glossary Subcommittee of API. To me fell the work of pushing the project selecting terms, suggesting definitions, leveling differences of opinion within the Subcommittee (Atlantic, Sun, Sinclair executor 6/9/86 Pomona F. E. certificate..." (James's letter of 20 July 1994.) principally. The results appeared dated 1962 . I guess there is about three years actual preparation. We were fiercely against names of authors appearing on the works published." This fierceness about anonymity is characteristic, regardless of the feelings of those who would have liked the praise.

He saved the "second rough" draft of the last project he worked on at Atlantic's Research and Development Department: "Some Common and Uncommon Density Boiling Point Relationships in Crude Oils", commenting on the margin: "This is part of material I worked on toward close 1961. I think it would have been good//There is more, but I don't know where."

NEW LIFE ON RETIREMENT, 1961.

Atlantic had been good to Gould, and he retired on his 65th birthday, 27 Jan. 1961, but being entitled to a month's vacation, his final work was in Dec. 1960. He had served over thirty years. There was a generous pension, but no golden parachute. At his retirement dinner in a Chinese restaurant in Dec. were Doc W. A. Myers, J. C. Martin, Pitts, Brown and Simons.

On retirement Douglas still had a quarter of a century ahead of him, and he made it the most productive, writing two books and several articles, and becoming the world's authority on a neglected topic, the top.

His brief summary of retirement is this: "Since my retirement almost twenty years ago, Atlantic has been getting bigger and bigger, and I have been getting smaller and smaller. I have found satisfaction in Archaeology, caving, flying kites, and the acquisition of a self-entitlement as an authority on the spinning top." (Bio., 2.)

First, retirement freed him to travel to places they'd always wanted to visit: Great Britain, the classical sites of the Mediterranean, Egypt and the Middle East, and back to the American West

First they went back to the West they both loved. An early trip went to the Grand Canyon, where they took the mule trip down Bright Angel Trail on 7 May 1962, and returned to Colorado. It was probably on this trip that they visited a Navaho silversmith, and Douglas bought his string tie with a Thunderbird ornament of lapis lazuli set in a silver clasp, which he once told a Bedouin chief had "rainmaking virtues" . For the next 25 years he always wore this in lieu of a tie, obviously more comfortable.

One trip took them to the Great Bend of the Rio Grande River in Texas. It was wild, deserted country, perhaps like the country around Rifle. He and Elsa bought several acres of sagebrush in a proposed development called Horizon City that had no water, or any other utilities and no access (Three Horizon city lots: 1) Unit 75, block 580, lot 28; 2) Unit 99, block 830, lot 7; 3) In section 2, block 77, twp 4 south half of east half of NE quarter of SE quarter, sec. 2, block 77; Warranty deed 57238, 2 Oct. 1975). For years he paid the dollar or so of taxes because it was so inconsequential. The land was still worthless when he died, and we gave up paying taxes.

Gould joined the National Speleological Society and pursued one of his favorite hobbies, visiting underground caves. He was most enthusiastic about the huge bat population of Carlsbad, and loved the legend of the rival race horse hidden in Mammoth Cave, but visited the smaller caves too.

He took Elsa along to his favorite archaeological sites, like the Lascaux caves of France, the stone circles and barrows of Great Britain, the Neolithic lake villages of Switzerland, and of course, all the museums where ancient relics were displayed. He always went to these sites with more knowledge than the local people, having read everything in the Philadelphia Public Library and the University Museum. He was always armed with the best Ordinance Survey map, or its equivalent. He pursued the construction of Crusader castles in the Near East with the same professional interest, and built a fine collection of the best books on Medieval castles. But he never pretended to any professional expertise in this (or any other field for that matter) , and wrote nothing about it. He had strong opinions about origins of things like Stonehenge and Avebury, however, and could dismiss the myths with strong evidence.

He kept detailed diaries of five trips between 1959 and 1967. Much of it merely records the places visited and photographed (Caroline has his slide collection) . But there are also complaints about the service which their travel agent, Cook's provided, or amusing anecdotes about local customs and signs, and reviews of high points in his typical telegraphic style, omitting pronouns.

His favorite compliment was "wonderful", liberally attributed to museums in Jerusalem and Birmingham, cathedrals at Winchester and Wells, scenic towns like Garmisch-Partenkirchen, an operetta "The Merry Widow", architectural details of the Taj Mahal or Lufullah Mosque in Isphahan, Mont San Michelle, cities like Vienna and Tours, markets in Naples and Perigueux, ancient ruins of Pont du Gard and Luxor, modern wonders of Seattle's Space Needle or Grand Coulee Dam, scenic beauties of the Badlands, Murren, Sorrento, or Kogon Falls, and the Garrisons' Glendora house.

A higher rating was "magnificent" for views like the Himalayas or Beartooth Pass, the museums of Geneva and Damascus, the mosques of Istanbul and Jerusalem, medieval sites like the Doge's Palace or Thetford Priory, or ruins of Persepolis and Isphahan. But "superb" was reserved for only the best museums in Jerusalem, London, Istanbul and Rome, for the scenery of California's Route One and Lauterbrunnen, and for the fort at Agra.

The first diary covers a month traveling in Britain from 27 Feb. to 27 March 1959, flying over by BOAC and returning by the *Queen Elizabeth.* They visited his cousin Muriel Douglas in Saffron Walden. Thetford's Cluniac priory was "Magnificent". They went to York. Edinburgh, the Lake Country, Stratford, Oxford, Salisbury, Winchester, Exeter, Penzance, Hastings, Dover, Windsor, and London. The return home on the *Queen Elizabeth* was notable for a curious event in mid-Atlantic. As he recorded it: "6/20 At Sea. This day, about 6.30 AM, [a] member of crew reported missing. Search, not found. Vessel turn[ed] about heading East to approx. position when report missing man [was] given. Estimate half speed. Many scanning sea. No sign and vessel resumes western course. Concern heard of ship docking late account incident. Sea rougher than yesterday...This holiday at sea is a chancy thing." "6/21 Rumor that there was a burial at sea for person died on board after leaving Cherbourg."

The second diary was for a ten week trip in the Spring of 1961 through Germany, Switzerland and Denmark, centering on a visit to James's family near Munich, where Jim was Fulbright Professor at the University of Munich. They sailed across the Atlantic on a Hamburg-Amerika liner S.S. *America* from New York to Bremerhaven. There they were met by James and Steven and Elsa's second cousins the Müllers. They went to Hamburg and Copenhagen, and to the Danish mainland where he declared "Funen village...is absolute tops of its kind and I do not believe we have anything to compare." (May 4). The "low point" was Hotel Hamburg Stadt, a "Dump" (May 6).

James and Anne's home in Weipertshausen was a "Lovely situation of house in country." (May 13) . He rated the Konigsee "Scenery spectacular" (May 19). "Salzburg...exceeds all expectations. Street Peter's church most decorated church I have visited...catacombs...Castle...Dom...Lunch excellent" (May 26). Munich's Hofbrauhaus was "another highlight" (May 27).

On May 30 they left for Switzerland, visiting Lindau, Konstanz, to Zurich. The expense of the Hotel Sonnenberg elicited the comment: "Pay now worry later, Expression 'I don't want to be a millionaire; I just want to live like one' is relevant" (May 31). Luzern's lake was "splendid", and train ride from there to Interlaken "Spectacular in spite [of] overcast" (June 2) . Lauterbrunnen's falls were the "Only thing I've seen reminding of it is Watkin's Glen, N. Y., but there comparison ends. Tis superb." (June 4). "train to Jungfraujoch. What views stupendous" (June 5).

They spent a week with Anne's parents, Bob and Catherine Garrison, in Interlaken, Bern, and French Switzerland. He loved "Morat, (a fabulously medieval town, arcades, parapet walkways)" (June 10). Then they went to Schaffhausen and Stuttgart ("fabulous" June 12), down the Rhine to Hamburg. They returned on the Hamburg Amerika Line via Le Havre, Southampton to New York (June 30) .

Douglas's descriptions become more detailed with the years. The third trip was for six weeks in the Spring of 1963 when they went back to Britain and Switzerland, but spent most of the time in France, and flew both ways by Pan American. In Paris they met the Garrisons again. He compared the "Louvre and Grand Canyon not amenable to description...Gallery after gallery of magnificence." (May 11) . "Opera (Carmen). . .How [can one] describe opulence of place, lavish yet realistic settings, multitude of figures on stage. Music wonderful...Doubt I will ever see opera again under such good conditions." (May 11) . "Some comments on Paris: Dogs, dogs, dogs; but better curbed than in Munchen. Saw shop nearby, devoted to dogs only. Never saw so many dog dish designs..."(May 12). Near Chartres he noted "Several million dollars with of mistletoe being ignored on trees by French." (May 16)"[I] Don't care if M[ont] S [an] M[ichelle] has name of 'touristy', I think it [a] wonderful piece of structure." (May 16).

The Neolithic stones of Carnac were "very impressive, but not as dramatic or well cared for as Stonehenge or Avebury in England." (May 18).

The Tours Cathedral was "beautiful" (May 19) . There he "called at shop of 'gray cats'...No cats. Shop mistress plays on music box and summons a cat who thinks it is for 'souper'" (May 24) .

Nearby he noticed the only site that he had known as a doughboy in World War I, en route from debarkation at Le Havre to the Replacement Depot. The train passed Selles-sur-Cher, and he commented, "Much change since 1918. Industry has come in. Saw church in distance. I think then that the church was plenty big for town." (May 24) .

Perigueux's markets were "wonderful. Vegetables, fruit, flowers, fowl, rabbits. Carry a heap away in a basket or have it killed and bled right there. This is life as it has been for years." (May 25).

Clermont-Ferrand's cathedral was "impressive" (May 26), but the bells of "Clermont-

Ferrand['s] two churches were not synchronized and the calls to worshipers might begin with the quick eager nun bells followed by the more deliberate most bells or perhaps the deep ones would sound first and a minute later the higher pitched ones would come in out of breath as though knowing they were late but hoped for forgiveness." (recalled May 27).

Millau's old city "exceeds all rabbit warren slums seen to date, not barring Germany, Fantastic." (May 27) . Carcassonne "is the most tremendous extent of walled city I've seen. There is still some permanent population and it is easy to picture Medieval conditions therein." (May 31) .

On the Grand Corniche of the Riviera they had "a fine trip with unbelievably lovely and striking scenes." (June 5) . The Musee Arts Decoratifs in Avignon "may turn out to be tops in museums of its kind", and its companion textile museum with its "marvellous fabrics of last 3 centuries." (June 8).

The "Gorgeous countryside" of Chamounix beats expectations. Mountains seem to hang over town." (June 10) . "Think I am going to like Chamounix. . .Train bringing us from Street Gervais to Chamounix had crates of young, pink and clean porkers, two to a crate (live) . Have seen such pigs in shops with apple fore and lemon aft." (June 10). "June 12 Big day! Trip to Mer de Glace via cog railway... spectacular." "June 13. Elsa looked out window about 4 AM and then woke me. Mt. Blanc a delicate pink in a gray blue, cloudless sky Moon touching Aiguille. You won't catch this again in a year."

Geneva was a "Beautiful city.", its "Musee d'Art et Histoire A magnificent museum; [I] Rate this among tops!" (June 14) . At their Hotel d'Allives their Chateaubriand won the praise "Doubt I ever had better meat." On leaving, his conclusion was: "I vote Geneva the handsomest city I've been in."

Back in London "After touring France's cathedrals & basilicas, [I] can say that Westminster ranks with best" (June 15) . The changing of the guards at Whitehall brought this description of crowd control: "Metro police (women) regulate crowd firmly seize children by heads and thrust them into first rank, while elders are unceremoniously pushed to rear. Fine sense of who was on spot early and later comers are firmly told to go the rear and not encroach on early arrivals." (June 16).

He judged "Kew Gardens Rose gardens particularly lovely." But "Hampton Palace Exceeded expectations." (June 16)...Grounds of Palace breathtaking[ly] compare favorably with Versailles...Grape vines must be hundreds of years old. Said to give black sweet grape fruit forming now. It is said that in Fall, anyone can purchase grapes. This is Democracy!"

They were met on June 21 at Philadelphia Airport by Caroline and the five kids, "and so ends a memorable trip well punctuated by moist kisses as it did begin."

Douglas's fourth trip diary covers a five weeks' tour of California and the Northwest in the Spring of 1965. They flew to Los Angeles on May 27, and stayed with the Garrisons in Claremont. They went back to the former Garrison house in Glendora where they had seen Anne and James married. Douglas declared, "What a wonderful place this is and no one would guess it from the street where the windowless wall and doors confront the visitor. "

They rented a car to drive up the coast of California, finding the "Hearst Ranch House Fabulously furnished." (June 2). They "then set out via Calif 1 along coast. Scenery superb." In San Francisco they took "cable car down to Chinatown and was fascinated even though [he] found no mysterious alleys." (June 4).

Continuing northward their "Unescorted trip thru Pacific Lumber mill at Scotia [was] Tremendous." (June 7) . The "Scenic Highway Latowell Falls, Multnomah Falls, Wahkeena Fall Very good. Switzerland can offer no better." (June 9).

He rated Seattle's "Space needle wonderful; Science center one of the best" (June 11) . At Spokane they took the train to Glacier Park, bussed to Butte to visit the mines, flew to Idaho Falls, then back to a rental car to drive to Twin Falls, Pocatello, to Jackson Lake Lodge, "a lovely place." (June 23).

They drove around Yellowstone, where they had gone when newly married 42 years before, but he made no reference to that first visit or to the changes. But the "Lower Falls [were still] spectacular." "The so-called Cook City-Red Lodge or Beartooth highway is magnificent, Utterly overshadowing the "million dollar highway" trip in Colorado." (June 28).

They took the train and bus to Rapid City SD, then another rental car to the Badlands ("wonderful" July 1) . They flew back to Philadelphia for the Fourth of July.

"Westward to Philadelphia" was what he called their three months' trip around the world, covered in his fifth and longest diary, in two parts. They left Havertown 20 Feb. 1966, and returned xx May. The halfway point was Kuala Lumpur, Malaysia, where James was finishing up a two year tour with the Peace Corps. I excerpt a few comments that give the flavor of his reactions:

"HONOLULU Feb. 23...Fascinating".

"TOKYO...March 1" stayed at Imperial Hotel "Older section of hotel Wright architecture luxurious. Never saw anything like it." "Signs:--Coffee & Curry; Lady Fair Bar" . "Kogon Falls Wonderful. . .from train bus takes us to Shrine. Marvellous."

"HONG KONG March 3...absolutely thrilling". On the way to the New Territories they saw "marvel after marvel of the real manner in which these HK Chinese are living: Sights, smells, sounds beyond belief." (March 4). Shanghai Street in Kowloon "Unbelievable. Returning [I] got rickshaw driver. He asked HK $10 to hotel. I said HK $4 and he took up the burden But I didn't feel so good about it, the human muscle to move me about. Rationalize that if I hadn't employed him, where is his supper coming from for I saw numerous other rickshaws, in fact, no others in use."

"Tiger Balm Garden (fantastic=Disneyland in cement. Garish good humor, wonderful imagination." (March 5) . "royal party (Princess Margaret...passing. Yes, saw the royal escort then the car with princess and husband. M. had fine lavender? dress." (March 5). "Notes of day:--Bamboo scaffolding in construction. Phone in hotel bathrooms beside toilet."

"KUALA LUMPUR...Mar 7... 9 Steven got mumps? [I] Put on Dr. act for kids. Steven has cut in mouth (from popsicle stick?) and slight infection. In afternoon Steve & Kip blacked up with burnt corn. Terrific."

"Mar. 10.. .Market.. .Never saw such an array of animal parts, strange vegetables..." "This day children were duly amused by group participation in ' I see something--' (Red, etc.).

"Mar. 13...You havn't seen KL if you haven't seen Petaling Street Shops and sights beyond belief...Some signs:--Bang Soon; Hung Onn Thye; Kum Sing; Fatt Thin". "I remember some signs in Malaya, often Sultan's residences or gov't quarters [with] visual presentation of a fleeing person being shot in the back by a rifleman." (March 28).

March. 14. . .K[uala] Kemaman. . .Signs :--KL Teksi; Hung On (laundry) .. .Chew Lee." Mar 15 A day of wonders...sunrise over sea...rubber...tapped...Trengganu ...Elsa distributed Chicklets. Kids seem not to understand. Roared with laughter when they see me <u>chew</u> Chicklet."

"Mar. 16 Trengganu-Besut-Kota Bharu More wonders: Batik complex on rafts. Silver Smiths, Textile weaving...Kris maker. Ancient type forge with plunger type piston for blowing...Wayang Kulit (shadow maskers..."

"Mar. 17 Tre[n]gganu-Kuantan Top spinners ... Kite Makers". It was this thrilling scene that he described in his book Tops.

"Mar 19 KUALA LUMPUR. . .I show kids how to dust floor with cat." March 20...to Sedky residence *(Y_2* hr out of P.J. Delightful setting with view mts...Pandemonium on way home. G. kids can not talk or sing except at top of lungs and high pitch. Animal spirits is the name of it."

"I have contributed to Malay proverbs on cloth weaving center toward Kota Bharu: My entry:--'The tongueless stranger <u>feels</u> courtesy in every language."

"March 23 Kuala Lumpur-Bangkok...Never did see so many kites, Literally hundreds and probably thousands ..."(March 24) .

"March 25. ..BANGKOK-SIEM REAP...A group of 5 elephants turns in gate about 100 feet away. Who can eat breakfast and watch elephants?...elephant ride to the Phnom Bakheng...fine view of surrounding jungle and to Angkor Wat; Ride is something to tell your grandchildren. I will pay for it in sores at back of [my] knees." (March 27). "Royal Museum where I signed the guest book with my screed: "The tongueless stranger, etc." (March 28).

"[I] Should mention that on flights Bangkok to Siem Reap and return, none of the air lines Vietname, Royal Cambodge and United Burma furnished maps often found in seat pockets of planes. Only distress bags. So when I asked the U. B. Steward for a map, he disappeared forward and soon returns with the pilot's flight map. I noted the then position and shortly returned this map for delivery to pilot. I want no suspicion that I have caused the plane to lose its way just to satisfy my curiosity." (March 28).

"March 29 BANKGOK-CALCUTTA...Calcutta ad:- 'Last 20 years with repute'...Hundreds sleeping on sidewalks." In Syria he recorded his "Note on solutions to Indian problem: (1) Education, Catastrophe, Ward [of the west?], Birth Control." (April 14).

"March 31...flight to New Delhi with magnificent view of wall of Himalayas."

"April 1 NEW DELHI In car to Agra. . .This was perhaps most interesting day of trip. Here was India. Calcutta was a huge city with deepest slums; Delhi is a showplace...performing bears en route. Camels...Agra fort & palace superb Taj Mahal better than pictures. Whole is a complex [of] workmanship of screens & inlays wonderful. Remarkable echo in dome of Taj."

"April 2 . . .NEW DELHI-TEHERAN-SHIRAZ . . .Near East tour agent...recommends going to Persepolis at once...This is 13th day of New Year and a special holiday. . .He is right. One of most colorful spectacles seen. Crowds of people.. . Picnicing in most forbidden, and unlikely spots...This seems partly an awareness of ancient glories and the rites of spring. Monuments of Persepolis & cliff graves magnificent..."

"Apr. 3 SHIRAZ-ISPHAHAN. . . In retrospect we are very fortunate to witness yesterday's holiday. Unimaginably colorful, simple enjoyment of poor escaping from life's routine May be chance for girls and men to display themselves." "exodus from town is to escape evil, which remains behind. Don't know about those who can't make the trip." "Spent morning touring town: Tombs of Sa'adi and Hafez...The beauty of the tombs beyond belief."

"APR 4 ESFAHAN...Stained glass window rivals European cathedral this may be most beautiful we've seen. Then to King or Shah Mosque Magnificent. Next to Lutfullah Mosque... the mosaics in this mosque are wonderful. . .Royal Covered Bazaar. Never saw anything like it."

"April 5 Esfaha[n]...Never saw such quantities of alabaster. Asked laborer at hotel for loan [of his] hammer to fix catch on [my] money belt. Not a word of English; he watched [with] keen interest my use. Unmistakable refusal of pay for this. I put [a] real in[to] his pocket, and he grinned appreciation."

"April 6. TEHRAN-BAGHDAD...Sign in B:- Killer & Gabriel...on beauty parlor 'Saloons for Ladies'; in gas station:- 'Passengers in excess of 6 must alight before refueling is made.'...Archaeological Museum...was marvellous."

"Apr. 8 BAGHDAD... once you get away from the city...Donkeys the usual transport. Herds of sheep accompanied by many goats. These people are right out of the past with a little intrusion of the metals. . .Scene in Baghdad:- chap on bike with cake of ice behind."

"April 9 BAGHDAD-CAIRO...Went to Museum and am overwhelmed. All else I've seen has been but fragmentary bits of Egyptian relics."

"CAIRO...April 10... Pyramids larger than I had anticipated. Enormous stones."

"Apr. 11 CAIRO-LUXOR. . .Ruins immense wonderful. . .the stupendous scale dwarfs Amesbury & Stonehenge."

"Apr. 13 CAIRO-BEIRUT...Sign dates me--'Klaxon Interdit'"[Horns Forbidden].

"Apr. 14 Beirut-HOMS...Krak des Chevaliers [is] huge, complex and a marvel of human effort."

"Apr. 15 HOMS-PALMYRA. . .Guide asked whether we would like to see Bedouin group. Took us to one. Flock of kids to meet us...curious and friendly. Then by leader and we were invited into tent. Large black, loose weave probably wool. Take off shoes, seated on woolen pads, served hot sweet tea. Delicious. Lambs about ranging from a couple of days to a couple weeks. Offer to have us stay the night, would kill sheep. I believe it. [I] Showed them my Navaho

Thunderbird ornament on tie and explain rain making virtues."

"Apr. 17 BAALBEK-DAMASCUS...National Museum Magnificent and in terms of its objects and their display, it is among tops...bazaars to end all bazaars."

"APRIL 18 DAMASCUS-AMMAN...This place is all steep hills and it's a good thing they do not have ice here in Winter."

"Apr. 20 JERUSALEM (J[ordanian east side])...Museum Wonderful...Apr. 21...Guide says three Christmases celebrated here, Dec. 25, Jan. 7 and 14, makes for a long season. Hope they don't have loud speakers roaring forth canned Xmas carols 12 hours a day as we would have in cities at home.

Dome of the Rock...a magnificent mosque... Stained glass windows can really rival Chartres...the 'working mosque...is magnificent if modern. Sign outside 'Please keep quiescence'."

"April 22...Still think that Jerusalem is tops as place to see native life in the city and to explore the rabbit warrens. Amazingly little stink!" After they walked the Road of the Cross he said: "I think we can lay some claim to title of Pilgrim, and I'll bet few Catholics have a memento that has gone the full route and received full attention at Golgotha [where "a priest blesses crucifixes and passes them before an image"] and the tomb."

"APR. 23 JERUSALEM (I[srael-West] ... Israel Museum...Display of scrolls superb...Museum proper...is a superb and abundant presentation of archaeological finds and a brilliant collection of religious objects."

"Apropos of nothing:--Had haircut yesterday. Barber takes piece of thread and deftly (but not wholly painlessly) removes wild hair on ears."

"April 25 TEL AVIV-ISTANBUL. . .Notes on Arabs-Jews:--Organized Jew has no fear of disorganized Arab. Moslem faith having reduced women to inferior position, [the Jew] fears them i.e., [he] distrusts fidelity. Parallel with treatment [of] Negro in U.S. Inferior, yet feared for possible superiority. Israel has oriented itself to Europe, Arab continues Asian. Jew respects learning and adopts technology avidly."

"April 26 ISTANBUL...Archaeological Museum. Superb material...Constantinople is an exciting city in a beautiful setting...Mosques we visited are magnificent."

"Apr. 27...Topkapi...a wonderful view [of] water...from room to room are treasures...".

"April 28 ISTANBUL-ATHENS...James phoned and with him boys. They are docked at Piraeus on Illyria. . .On map of moon I show[ed] boys cite "GOULD" in sea of clouds. Impressed...Impressions [of Athens]:--Modern city, heavy foot traffic, abundance of flowers...women emancipated."

"April 29 ATHENS...Museum (National) of course excellent..."

"Apr. 30 ATHENS-CRETE-ATHENS...Impressive view [of] snowclad mtns. incl. Mt. Ida Museum excellent but as usual you can hit only high spots. . .Knossos. . . [I] am well satisfied of visit. Favorite pastime seems to be criticism of Evans' reconstruction. But not me, having seen Babylon etc. with little or no reconstruction."

"May 4 ROME...Street Peter's...Picture gallery superb. Throughout it all a sense of annoyance at the prudery (?) of drapery and fig leaves that are more conspicuous than the nudes." In the gift shop a woman asked "'are these medals blessed?' Nun answers 'If you pray they are blessed.'"

"May 5.. .NAPLES.. .Funeral coach looks like royal coach (almost) glass enclosed to show coffin, plumes at 4 corners. Market...a succession of stalls (canvas) and a wonderful display of vegetables, fruit, meats (including horse)..."

"May 6 NAPLES-SORRENTO...Pompeii exceeds expectations. To study Roman life one should concentrate on findings from Pompeii...Drove along a breathtaking corniche to Amalfi...continue wonderful route above sea...to Sorrento. Hotel=Excelsior Victoria, Room 210. This must be tops for Elsa + self. Balcony high over Mediterranean, Mountains, huge (acres) garden with flowers, lemon trees + orange trees both in bloom and bearing fruit...Here is route from room (210) to lobby: Out from room, turn R, 8 steps; turn R, 3 steps; turn L, 10 steps, Left 6, Diagon[al] L 4 steps, Diag R (stairs) 3 steps, Proceed L 18 steps, Left 12 steps, Right 12, Right

6, Eleva[tor] R, Down 2, Out 6, Left 4, R 40" (This was one of his favorite observations, rivalled by the Mitre in Oxford (26 May 1959).

"May 7...Capri wholly unlike anything I had imagined: Seven square miles of ruggedness, Little beach villa on villa climbing hills. Prestige or social status presumably mount too."

"Sunday May 8...FLORENCE...walked to Cathedral... Mass going on for many sick. Beautiful singing. Impressive and touching Picture of crowd at Cathedral front. Everything seems to have touch of years and art that have preceded it."

"May 10...VENICE...Astonished at the square. Arcade on three sides, cathedral on fourth. All shops but you [Continued on separate part 2.] see no advertising on side of arcade facing quare. Astonishing, too, all the way from station to hotel, no advertising. Visited Cathedral (gaudy, grimy, gingerbready), also Archaeological Museum. Technical note--Toilets near lobby marked by figurines (m + f) on large panels of outer wall but not knob or handle. Lo, you push panel and it opens."

"May 11 VENICE...Doges palace magnificent if one can stomach thought of the aristocratic rule."

"May 13 MILAN...Square in front of Duomo infested with pigeons and people who encourage pigeons. To La Scala...Enquired of guide for objects relating to Geraldine Farrar (born Melrose Mass and a name when I was a boy) . Guide had never heard of her. Did she never sing at La Scala? or is the guide not knowledgeable? or is her fame (to me) inflated?"

"May 14...VIENNA...at Opera House and enquired chance to see current performance. It is Lohengrin and all sold out. Chap says 'besuchen' . We do and go to box office area, Buy two tickets from people not able to use. Five galleries. I am in 5th near center (2nd row) Elsa in 4th left (2nd row) . Marvellous performance. Orchestra 75 Chorus estimate 125+. Lasted 6-10 pm."

"May 16 VIENNA...Hofburg, i.e., palace. Very fancy living conditions if one accepts as in Schonbrunn 400 rooms and no baths...Went to Demel for lunch, famous for Konditorei. But little system prevails and a long wait ensued. Fare delicious. Went to stables of Spanish Riding School. Stallions only, I think. Magnificient horses and certainly living in greater luxury than a billion humans."

"May 17 VIENNA. This was day of Superlatives. First to National Library--Papyrus Collections... Beautiful + astounding exhibition of writings. Papyrus, bone, leather, wood. . .National Gallery. . .is probably best I've seen. Certainly Louvre + Vatican get run for money...Painting gallery classic (Egyptian, Greek, Roman, etc.) then the plastic arts outdo anything I've seen...Vienna Woods...Meyerling scene of tragedy of Rudolph and now Carmelite nunnery (no talking)...Sachers...Wonderful."

"May 18 LONDON. . .I went to British Museum. With all the museums seen this trip I think that the Palm goes here--The material, the display, the descriptions are superb... Have come to the conclusion that if you can't visit a designated country for archaeology, etc., next best thing is to visit British Museum."

"May 19...Saffron Walden to see Muriel [Douglas, who] related a story of rooks. They have been building nests for years on one side of common and Muriel has hoped they might build on opposite side (near her). One day she observed that a nest is being built and her hopes fulfilled. But lo, a flock of perhaps 10 rooks appears, circles about the tall tree with new nest and they tear nest to pieces. Astounded, she enquired of a rural friend whether this is unique phenomenon. No; rooks do not permit deviation from flock practice, and the individual who tries to break away is brought into line."

Douglas may have claimed no expertise in archaeology. But it was different with two other favorite topics, tops and kites. He had always loved kites, and Spring often began with Douglas at his workbench in the cellar rigging up the crosspieces, and experimenting with a new way of attaching the paper skin, or a fast-unwinding reel, and a unique tail of cloth and string. He would take these experimental models out to an open field an a breezy day. The abandoned golf course was a perfect take off place. In spite of his skill there was the inevitable tangle in a tree, when too much line was paid out and it dipped with the weight. He read everything that was written on kites, especially Chinese, and tried them all out. The trunk of his car usually had a kite and rig all ready to go if the right spot coincided with a good wind. The reason he wrote nothing on kites was that so many books had already been written on the subject.

WORLD'S EXPERT ON TOPS, 1973.

Not so with tops--an unwritten topic until he retired. It began at the University Museum where he volunteered on Thursdays as a "Mummy Duster" (His photo on a ladder appeared in Philadelphia Inquirer Sunday Magazine, *Today*, 26 Dec. 1971, 8,9 describing the group, "a sort of voluntary lean-up, fix-up group, who used to call themselves the Thursday Night Volunteers…the Mummy Dusters…also string beads, paint signs, pack and unpack vases, move statues, you name it…". He is also mentioned in Mark Jury's account of the Mummy Dusters in *Playtime! Americans at Leisure* [N. Y.: Harcourt Brace, 1977], 86). They put him to work cataloging in the Egyptian collection, which he loved. Among the uncatalogued pieces were some small round stones, tentatively labeled as "fishing weights?"

It was a perfect puzzle for his analytical mind. He knew enough about fishing to be suspicious, and his knowledge of Neolithic objects probably increased his doubts. He began a systematic search for similar objects in the Museum, and wondered if they might be tops. Had the Egyptians played with tops? No one seemed to know.

[108] See his photo on ladder in Philadelphia Inquirer Sunday Magazine, *Today.* 26 Dec. 1971, 8, 9: "a sort of voluntary lean-up, fix-up group, who used to call themselves the Thursday Night Volunteers...the Mummy Dusters. . .also string beads, paint signs, pack and unpack vases, moves statues, you name it..." He is also mentioned in Mark Jury's account of the Mummy Dusters in *Playtime! Americans at Leisure* [N.Y.: Harcourt Brace Jovanovich, 1977], 86. And, unlike kites, virtually no one had ever done any writing or research on the subject. That began a worldwide search for anything written on the topic, which turned out to be minimal. Then, he began a systematic study of the world's tops.

He and Elsa showed up in Malaysia in 1966, on the trip recorded above, and he was in seventh heaven when he was taken to a village on the east coast of Malaya where the village experts showed him a top fight. It was a combat of two wooden tops as big as dinner plates, the object being to knock one's opponent out of a wide ring on the earth without stopping rotation. This took great skill and strength.

He began in 1966 writing a childrens' book on tops, "The Top--Perhaps the First Toy", which was never published. As he said in the introduction, "work was stopped and re-begun to make a more complete story of the top. It was realized that there must be two separate versions: one that would do full justice to the top must use adult wording. The choice for younger people could be all pictures or very simple language; a middle path has been taken."

The outcome of this was the first and only authoritative reference work on tops in every culture, form ancient times to present, but written in very direct language and copiously illustrated. This was published in both Great Britain and U.S. Clarkson Potter of New York City signed a contract 20 Jan. 1971, giving him a $1000 advance, and 10% royalties. *The Top: Universal Toy. Enduring Pastime* was published in New York in Nov. 1973. The English edition was published under the same title by Bailey Brothers & Swinfen of Folkestone two years later, in 1975.

The reviews were enthusiastic and full of praise (*Book Review Digest, 1974* 455.). *Scientific American*'s reviewer Philip Morrison called it an "original and well-informed book"...an "entertaining and substantial volume" (*Scientific American,* April 1974, 124-5). The antiques magazine *Spinning Wheel*'s reviewer, a museum director, praised it as "a serious and scholarly study" which left the reviewer in "awe, so thorough was the task of research done. This is the definitive study of tops, if ever one was written...a labor of love...Gould's enthusiasm for the mundane little toy will sweep you along. Toy collectors will surely want it for their libraries..." (Robert DiBartolomeo in "New Books about Antiques", *Spinning Wheel,* May 1974, 36). The professional librarian's magazine called it "a definitive survey...well indexed and illustrated. " (Sarah Chokla Gross, *Library Journal,* 15 Feb. 1974, 475.)

The book got nation-wide publicity from an article by Desmond Ryan which was distributed by the Knight newspapers, and printed in *The Baltimore Evening Sun* ("His World Spins Around Old Toys", 1 May 1974, 24). The *Miami Herald* ("Engineer's World Revolves in Getting To the Bottom of the History of Tops", 3 May 1974). and *Dayton Daily News* ("Tops Ancient, Fan Says", 27 May, 1974). It also got a plug as "Definitive top book" in Stewart Brand's *The Next Whole Earth Catalog* (N.Y.: Random House, 1980), 546.) It also got articles in two local papers (*Philadelphia Inquirer*, 27 April 1974, sec. B, 2; *Philadelphia Daily News*, 7 May 1974, 2. The Atlantic house organ *the Product Spark,* 2, no. 2, Feb. 1969).

Gould got invitations to give an illustrated lecture on tops to the Atlantic Richfield Pensioners, the annual meeting of the Haverford Township Historical Society, and The Old Guard of Havertown (Atlantic at Engineers' Club, Philadelphia, 17 Dec. 1970; Historical Society at Temple Lutheran Church, Brookline, 17 April, 1975; Old Guard at Nunan Slook's Dugout, Oakmont, 15 Oct. 1969).

Although *The Top* was scholarly, it had been made popularized to sell and publish, and he was dissatisfied. What was needed, he believed, was a reference work to which museum curators could turn to identify tops like his Egyptian mysteries. He began collecting black and white photographs of prototypes of every form of top, with accurate measurements, and descriptions and provenance to match. He carried on this project until his death, contacting every museum in the world, including toy collections which hardly knew what they had.

Then he sought out obscure collectors in places like Paris and Santa Fe, persuading them to have their treasures identified. In the process, he no doubt let owners know for the first time what they had.

By 1981 he had completed *A Reference Guide to the Spinning Top,* hoping to persuade the University Museum to publish it. The problem with the project was that it was too expensive to publish, and he never found any interest. The great collection of photos and descriptions went on his death to the University Museum where it can at least be referred to. It is probably the best archive on tops in the world.

One of the best pieces of publicity for his tops came when the U.S. Postal Service put a top among the toys pictured on a Christmas stamp. He was asked by *Reader's Digest* to write the publicity for the cachet, or special envelope, which it published when the stamp was first issued at Christmas, Michigan, on 31 Oct. 1980.

The success of publishing the top project encouraged his writing, even though he made little money on the sales. He began putting down ideas on other subjects that interested him, like history and explosions. He sent the reminiscences about Boston childhood to magazines like *Yankee.*

Elsa's death on 14 Jan. 1973, at the relatively young age of 72, did not come unexpectedly. She died of a heart attack, having had rheumatic fever as a child. She had long suffered high blood pressure like her mother, and thyroid deficiency, complicated by intolerance for foods like cabbage. Douglas nursed her through the illnesses of the later years, helped by her uncomplaining optimism.

But her death deprived him of a companion of almost half a century--they would have celebrated their golden anniversary the next June. Douglas took the event stoically as he always did with close deaths, showing no outward grief or loneliness. But he was lost.

He never cooked during married life until his wife's last illness. Around the house he had been a typical husband of the generation, who did the heavy chores of maintenance but none of the "women's" work of cooking, sewing, making beds, cleaning, washing and ironing, shopping for groceries, buying clothes and having them dry-cleaned and pressed, or even setting the table, etc. His main indoor contribution was to dry the dishes, though he occasionally washed them.

Even the neighborhood dog deserted him. One of his favorite stories was the "uncanny" fact that his friend stopped coming the day Elsa died. Friends called to commiserate, and he said that one woman proposed to him only a week after her death. He sold the Clearfield Road house with his daughters' help, and moved for less than six months in an apartment about half a mile south, in Oakmont center, at 2323 East Darby Road. Apartment 503 of "Eagle Towers" had three rooms, living room, bedroom and kitchen, on an upper floor. Old friends looked in on him, and he carried on some of the old volunteer work as a Mummy Duster at the University Museum, but his obvious confusion and lethargy was not healthy.

His sister Caroline had made a successful transition from a similar lonely apartment in Cambridge to the sunny climate of southern California. She had thrived in the intellectual atmosphere of Mount San Antonio Gardens retirement home in Claremont, two miles from her nephew James and his family. So again he went west.

LAST DECADE IN CLAREMONT, 1977.

Douglas then joined Caroline at Mt. San Antonio Gardens in Claremont on 15 Dec. 1977, driving his Dodge Dart in an easy pace across the warm part of the country, stopping off in New Orleans to visit the Superdome, Carlsbad Cavern and other caves, and the darks' home in Albuquerque. In Claremont he took a new lease on life for another productive decade. His living unit (A-28) was quite removed from Caroline's (D unit), and he was careful not to intrude on her already established routine. They enjoyed being nearby, but led separate lives. He was on hand all the time when she became ill and when she died 25 Oct. 1981, at age 92.

After coming to Claremont he had another ten years of enjoyment and productivity. The Gardens, as they were called, was full of interesting people like himself: retired professors, artists, writers, musicians, corporate managers, charity administrators, doctors and ordinary people with quirky hobbies. There were so many activities in the Gardens itself that there was little need to go outside for stimulus: painting classes, physical education, a library, movies, etc. But it was easy to get to the academic lectures and concerts and plays in the college town. And there were plenty of ways to get into the museums and cultural events of Los Angeles, 28 miles to the weStreet

Douglas quickly became involved in helping set up the movie projector and sound system for the frequent shows. His writing and editing experience were put to work on the Gardens monthly newsletter, "Greenleaf", to which he contributed his characteristic squibs and anecdotes.

A bit of doggerel he composed when his friend
Dr. Griggs was robbed was called:

"BALLAD OF THE OPEN DOOR by "The
Uninvited"

(naught but chirp of cricket is heard) 'Tis the switching-blade hour of
midnight; Yes, Brother! I don't need no light:

(tut-tut)
Hoped to catch well-heeled reader; instead Found HoJo dead asleep in his bed,

(sotto voce)
(His own, where he just happened to be. I'll be a some; the door-knob turns free!"

(urgent)
As he comes awake, I says "For Pete's sake, "I'm not funning! No phoning! Just money, Joe (or Jake) " .

(calm)
He chew the fat; I'll show my shiv*; He tells his name; I thank the spiv.**

(shaking of hands)
We reach accord (he says ententee) For all I need just now's a twenty

(furious)
Dollar bill. "Okay; my shiv is yours pro tern," And then-"What's this??!! A twenty changed into a ten!!"

(indignant)
"Shame to you! Greek Galen's son, to Cheat a decent burglar of his due.

(satirical)
Call the Fuzz! Security! His Nibs! I say Babes like you should sleep in cribs, alway.

(clairvoyant)
I'11 see you next night and return Your wallet; good money I won't spurn."

1'envoi

To solve this crime (or just a part) Seek Lecoq or Lupin whose art

Will lead them strait as die To variety store, the T G Y.

You've had a good lesson; I'll say no more
But, 'gainst real baddy you should lock your door.

* knife, ** gent, of *a* sort."

In 1981 and 1982 he was champion pocket-billiards (pool) player in Claremont University Club's annual tournament at Claremont Manor (*The Green Leaf,* 20, no. 6, July 1981, 5; University Club news Aug. 1982). In 1981 he was awarded a silver dollar for first prize in Claremont Lawn Bowls Club (Annual meeting 12 Nov. 1981).

He found a vacant plot of ground at the west end of the Gardens, in soil that had been a fertile rose nursery, and began the annual cultivation of his vegetable garden. And, of course, he would grow his favorite Concord grapes, for which he built an arching tunnel arbor. Just short of 90 he enjoyed giving away some 200 pounds of grapes, Concords, Niagras and Delawares, and a bumper crop of tomatoes.

In his room he pursued his encyclopedia of tops project vigorously, continuing a world-wide correspondence with collectors and museum directors and publishers. The University Museum got him to write a scholarly article on tops, which it published in its magazine *Expedition* in the Spring of 1980, and even paid him $100, which he quickly endorsed back to the Museum as a gift. His interest in history is seen in a four page outline of "Warriors of the Revolution: A study of the creation and movements of the American and British military units during 1775-1783." He continued writing his little historical memoirs, and sending them off to magazines, usually turned down with kind regrets.

He was asked to speak on subjects like energy. His son heard him speak publicly for the first time when he was 82 (Mt. San Antonio Gardens, 4 Sept. 1979, JWG Diary #52, 147). His style was deliberate and almost disconnected, but easy to understand. His views of atomic fuel seemed too optimistic, especially on the problem of disposal of the waste. He also seemed a bit disparaging of environmentalists. He put little hope in fossil fuels, including his own baby, oil from shale. He dismissed wind and tidal sources, as well as all solar ones, except for electric generation. But he ended with a prophetic hope for development of the unlimited potential of heavy water in the seas. It was a goodspeech for a silent man, aged 82.

At age 90 he published his second book, *Explosion,* a subject like tops, on which he had some authority. Having worked with explosive gasoline all his life, and seeing oil wells on fire, and other man-caused conflagrations, his interest in explosions was a natural. He always had a great fondness for fireworks, and never missed a Fourth of July show at Fairmount Park, Narberth ballfield and in Claremont. He had also heard heavy artillery on the Western Front in World War I, and knew the fear of the Germans' super-cannon "Big Bertha". Also, his geological interest had always been attracted to volcanoes. He visited ones like Etna and Vesuvius, Mt. Shasta and Crater Lake, and others around the world. The result was *Explosion.* Like Tops, he kept it in popular style, and tried to interest Clarkson Potter in printing this commercially too, but failed. After trying several publishers he ended up subsidizing the book himself, paying $5,475 to have it printed by a vanity press, Vantage Press, which, of course did no advertising, so there were lots of remainders and no reviews (Contract signed 9 Feb. 1985; Receipt for payment of $3,200 to Great Western Publishing Co. of Glendale CA, 11 March 1982; printed at Whitlock Press, Middletown NY; published by Vantage Press of New York City, 26 March 1986, copyright application 29 May 1986, form TX 1 837 621). As his own publisher and publicist he ended up "peddling it" himself, as he put it. There was still a big box full of remainders left over at his death, which his grandson Kip offered free on the Internet, getting requests from as far away as China.

Douglas continued to enjoy traveling to visit new sites, like Machu Pichu in Peru (1980), and Alaska. As ever, he loved traveling by train, taking the Canadian transcontinental to Banff and Lake Louise (Aug. 1984), and across the United States to visit his children and grandchildren in Denver and Albuquerque and summers in Cotuit. Among the highlights of a visit to New Mexico was a flight aloft in a hot air balloon, with a great view of the Rio Grande Valley.

He came back to the Gardens from these trips and wrote up accounts of his mishaps and adventures under the "moniker" of "I.T.", or Intrepid Traveler. A few of these were published in *The Green Leaf,* but most were probably too abstruse for the taste of the editors. One of his last adventures was a "terrible" trip to Yugoslavia in 1985, when he was 89 (Returned before 12 June 1985, JWG Diary #61, 18). He reported fine weather, good health, friendly people, but a poorly organized tour. He complained that was not met at Belgrad airport, but made his way to the hotel with another tour group.

He had been in good health most of his life, despite malnourishment as a child, and gassing during the war, and this strength persisted until he was nearly ninety. A gall-stone attack in Cotuit in 1978 put him into Falmouth Hospital, but he recovered quickly after flying home and having his gall-bladder was removed back in Pomona Valley Hospital. Few of his immediate ancestors had lived so long, though there was one distant forebear who made it to a hundred.

In the end, "the old body just wore out". By the time he was 87 he had angina, anemia, arthritis, high blood pressure, deafness and numbness in his right arm, for which he took medication, but typically, made no complaint. His motto was to keep as active as possible. At Kip and Joan's wedding in the summer of 1983, he got up in the Quaker meeting and said he guessed he was the patriarch of the family, which meant he was the old generation welcoming the new (Chappaqua Friends Meeting, 26 June 1983.)

His mind stayed clear and alert to the end, as he learned computer skills, solved crossword puzzles, and inquired about nature.

He stayed physically active too, playing frisbee with Muffin when he was 90. He even showed up for jury duty at age 87, driving himself to the courthouse to his childrens' dismay. When he failed the written test for his license renewal the compassionate clerk told him to try again, so he dashed off another set off answers, and failed again. This time the clerk could see he was going too fast, and told him to take his time to do it carefully. He passed.

He celebrated his ninetieth birthday at Disneyland with Caroline and Jim Clark, Linda and her son Jason. He took all the rides, and wanted badly to ride the roller coaster on the Matterhorn despite his heart problems. So he popped *a* couple of nitroglycerin pills and lined up, insisting, "I can go!" Caroline replied "No you don't!", and he was finally dissuaded by Jim from going.

At his ninetieth birthday celebration in 1986 he gave this little speech: This was a great occasion; he had been through a couple of difficult times in his life, but the end had turned out well. He appreciated having a good family, and a supportive one. He wished us all as happy a conclusion.

He was in fine humor, making jokes and laughing heartily. His mind was as alert as ever, precise, logical and methodical, absorbing new ideas from reading, testing their validity, and experimenting in his garden. His body was wearing down, but he still walked erect, read without difficulty, and didn't complain about arthritis or angina.

The major cause of his final illness was malfunction of his kidneys. Shortly before his 91st birthday the uncontrolled attacks of angina, dizziness from high blood pressure, and the kidney failure put him into the medical unit of the Gardens where he got great care. The buildup of poisons in his system caused his legs to swell, and to itch all over, and he visibly fought the temptation to scratch the maddening itching. He rejected kidney dialysis, which would have prolonged life a short time, at great cost. Lying in his bed near the end he said typically, "Nobody ever promised me I'd live forever!"

Douglas Gould died quietly in the medical unit of Mt. San Antonio Gardens, Pomona CA, on 30 April 1987. He was 91 years old. His body was cremated, as he wished. Since he cared not where the ashes went, the offer to have the funeral director's uncle scatter them out on the Pacific Ocean from his private plane, off Newport Beach, on 18 May 1987 was accepted. So we can imagine him at last, off in the sunset, in the Channel Islands.

A good life.

His most admirable characteristic was his silence, or better, his control over his speech. Douglas seldom expressed his feelings openly. Perhaps this self-control is what limited his speech, but it also made him seem unsympathetic. He never cried in public. His bottled-up anger would occasionally explode at his children or against public figures. He was openly disdainful of corruption and incompetence, and ill-concealed his disdain. Some this no doubt reflected a high personal standard of probity, honesty and responsibility. The last is something he learned as a boy, to replace his absent father, and in reaction to his father's own irresponsibility.

Douglas had a fine mind for scientific research. He had great skill at systematic organization of materials, and dogged persistence in tracking down the minutest details, such as the name of an obscure author who was known only by his initials. With this he had a mathematical sense, and an ability to translate a visual image onto paper.

Material things were of little importance to him. His daughter Elinor usually had to buy him clothes and keep track of his dress. He was something of a packrat, saving scrap paper and broken pens, as well as "sentimental" cards, letters and photos. His collections of stamps and coins were only partly for value, but probably more for the fun of building a complete run of items at face value, with no more cost than his time. He had quite a few books on a wide variety of subjects, but his favorites were Ekwall's *English Place-Names* and the hundred year old childrens' books with which he grew up. There was not great ambition in Douglas, though there was plenty of pride. He was proud of his family, though not for the Douglas nobility as its "fire" as he put it. He was proud of the work he accomplished at Rifle, at college, at Atlantic during the war, in writing *The Top* and raising a fine family. But one could never get him to speak of these things first; you had to ask. Getting anything personal out of him was "like pulling teeth". You might extract one act with difficulty, but he'd never give you another freely.

Above all, personal considerateness was his greatest strength. At 90 he had bought Christmas presents for all his children, 15 grandchildren, 8 great-great grandchildren, and spouses. Even at the end, consideration was evident.

He died, almost deliberately, after waiting for his daughters to arrive. Although he was miserable in the last weeks, he was always reluctant to ask the attendants for anything, never desiring any special care or consideration, but always expressing gratitude for it. This self-effacing modesty and gratefulness were qualities he inherited from his mother, Laura Douglas. In her there was a quiet self-sacrificing character, as if it were natural that the meek should inherit the earth.

Three children:

i. JAMES[10] WARREN, b. Boulder CO 14 May 1924; m. Anne Wright Garrison.
ii. ELINOR JANET, b. Boulder CO 13 August 1925; m. Donald Martin Krueger.
iii. CAROLINE NANCY, b. Upper Darby PA 8 December 1930; m. James Edward Clark.

Warren Blaisdell Gould (1903-1997)

Chapter XIX

WARREN BLAISDELL GOULD

(1903-1997)

By Eleanor Gould Baldic

Warren[9] Blaisdell Gould was born on 15 November 1903 at the Hahnemann Homeopathic Hospital in Philadelphia, PA. (Dept. of Public Health, Vital Records Department, Philadelphia, PA., Certificate #C 57989). This was the same hospital that his grandfather Dr. John M. Blaisdell graduated from in 1852.

He lived most of his life in or near Boston and the last few years on Cape Cod. He was the only child of John[8] (Hogg) Goddard Gould and Jane Blaisdell, daughter of Dr. John M. Blaisdell and Ann Bessey.

Warren was an impressive figure of a man, 5' 11", medium brown hair, deep blue eyes, a strong face and athletic build, which he kept until his later years. He never looked his age and always looked on the bright side of life so his face was never lined with furrows or frowns.

He was known for his sense of humor, joke telling (some corny but fun), doing magic tricks and most of all for playing his ukulele and singing. One of his favorite magic tricks was the magic mummy. It was a miniature mummy in a tiny coffin, he would tap the coffin and the mummy would mysteriously pop out of the coffin , tap again and it would go back in the coffin. Another one was showing the magic postage stamp book. When he would flip the pages the stamps would appear , do the same and they would magically disappear. This would hold the children's attention as well as the adults.

The collection of stamps, coins, records and music were some of his interests.. He would devote at least one night a week going over his stamps and coins. His records were mostly of Blues and Jazz., and some classical. He played chess and won quite a few matches throughout his life. He loved music and sang in many church choirs and choruses. His greatest pleasure in his later years was playing the ukulele. Each night he would practice for an hour and became an accomplished ukulele player. He would play whenever, wherever and to whom would listen). He loved to visit with people. He was a dreamer, a romantic, a procrastinator, a good father and a devoted husband. He was not one to use profanity except for "damm." When he was in his nineties his favorite expression when he knew he was not in charge of everything he would say "that's a hellofa thing."

During his lifetime he held many jobs. He was always searching for the one that would give him a sense of personal satisfaction. . He wanted to be a writer, an artist, a singer, an actor, photographer, musician, and whatever else he aspired to be. He made many attempts in these fields and others also. He had a great compassion for others and tried his best to bring a little sunshine into their lives.

Warren was a very private person. He was very proper about his dress and manners. He reminded one of a very proper English gentleman. He read constantly and loved discussions about philosophy, religion and world affairs.

There are a few papers, photos and memorabilia that he left and the few stories we remember that he told throughout the years.

We have few pictures of him when he was young. One as a baby in a carriage. From the picture one can see a fancy wicker carriage with a beautiful two tier lace umbrella on the back. His mother is standing next to the carriage. On the back of the picture it says "Warren at two months and mother". The next picture is Warren at one and half years old with an unknown person (an aunt maybe).

There are some pictures taken at the age of about four or five years of age. In one he is sitting down holding a teddy bear and in the other he is standing like a little soldier. He has a Dutch hair cut and is dressed in a high-necked knee length dress of white or ivory cotton with long satin stripes running down the front, pleats on the side and a wide belt buttoned in the front. One can see what are probably knickers under the dress (they are the only part of him besides the haircut that indicates that he is a boy). He has on long white stockings and is wearing high black shoes. His expression depicts a very angelic little boy.

In another picture of about the same age and same haircut he is standing with a very serious expression on his face, He is dressed in a black cloth coat with a mutton collar, white stockings and high laced black shoes. One hand is in his pocket and the other by his side. He has on earmuffs and on his head is a black three cornered hat .

In the next pictures he was about six years old. In one he is wearing a sailor suit sitting next to a little girl of about the same age. The other one is with his Aunt Hattie Blaisdell Woods (his mother's sister).

The last picture of Warren in the early years shows a lad of about ten or twelve years of age. He has a slim build, a fine profile, short haircut, shirt and tie, long jacket with double buttons in front, knickers, long black socks and high shoes.

Information about where Warren lived was gleaned from a biography of his father, John[8] H. G. Gould, in Chapter XVI above.

We find that the family moved many times in Boston. This probably explains why Warren never settled too long in one place all through his life until his later years.

From the biography we find the family living near Bryn Mawr College, PA. where his father John H. G. Gould was working in 1903. Between 1906 and 1908 they traveled to Wisconsin and other places in the West. They returned to the East in 1908 due to the death of his grandfather, Dr. John M. Blaisdell who died the 18 of February 1908 in Bangor, Maine (Maine Vital Records, Cert. #154).

By 1910 they moved to 150 St. Botolph Street near Symphony Hall Boston. By 1911 and 1912 they moved to 17 Cumberland Street and by 1913 they moved to 42 Ivy Street, The Fenway, Brookline.

COLORADO

Warren lived in Boston while growing up except for going to Colorado in 1916 when he became ill with bronchitis. His father was working in New York while he and his mother stayed in Boston. His father left his job in New York and moved the family to Colorado. They had heard that the best cure for this ailment was out West where the air was pure and the climate ideal for the lungs. This idea probably came from his grandfather, Dr. John Blaisdell or his uncle Dr. Warren O. Blaisdell. (Both were homeopathic physicians and believed in natural cures for the body and mind.)

Warren said, "In Colorado we lived in a cabin in the mountains. The temperature was in the teens but at night I slept out on a screened porch all bundled up. In the day time brisk walks in the cool crisp air were in order. Great for the lungs and it would either cure me or finish me." He said. It worked as he lived to the age of 93.

After 1916 we do not know where they lived but in the 1920 Census (U.S.Federal Census, Ward 8, Suffolk, Ma, Roll T625—742; 20B) he is found living with Aunt Ida age 63 (his father's sister) in a boarding house on Hancock St., Warren was 16 years of age. His mother and father were living on Temple St. in a boarding house. One might assume that housing was at a premium in Boston at this time so Warren had to live with his Aunt Ida. For schooling in Boston Warren said he attended the Perkins school, English High, Boston Latin, and the Massachusetts Normal Art College.

Warren had many friends over the years but Kendall (Ken) Crossfield ,Carroll (Kib) Colby, William (Bill) Fenstermaker and Ray Chamberlain are the ones he talked mostly about. He met Kendall while a boy scout and Kib while in art school (more about Kib later), Bill when they were young men courting their "wives" to be, and Ray on Cape Cod. They shared many good times together throughout the years.

Kendall had a problem with bronchitis as did Warren. Kendall's cure was also going out West to work as a lumberjack to strengthen his lungs. This cured him of the problem. Apparently going West was not only to get rich but it provided a great place for health cures according to Warren and Kendall. Warren's parents took he and Kendall to Maine on a steamer out of Boston to Maine several times to visit his Aunt Hattie B. Woods in Castine (pictures of them on the deck of the ship with Eleanor Baldic: hereinafter E. Baldic).

FRYEBURG, MAINE in the early 1920's

Warren and Ken became camp counselors in the summer at "Indian Acres", a Jewish boys camp in Fryeburg, Maine, Warren taught art, archery, swimming, modeling with clay, canoeing, etc.

Warren wrote a story of an experience he had while camping with Kendall (copy in folder 2, with E. Baldic). This gives one an idea of his humorous side.

"Ken suggested we build a platform out of logs and pine slabs for our tents. Finally the tents were erected, and everything stowed away and by then it was time to retire for the night. For lights we used outdoor lanterns which we hung on a hook fastened to the rear tent pole.

On to bed, so I thought. Opening the flap of the tent one had to crawl in on hands and knees (this was a pup tent). Halfway in I looked up and ahead of me, also crawling, was a disheveled looking character. Without a second look I scrambled out of the tent, caught my leg in the guy ropes and toppled into the water (our tents were very close to the water). I let out a yelp and Ken rushed out of his tent and shouted "what's the matter?" I pointed to the tent and said "there's someone in my tent. Ken quickly looked at the partially collapsed tent and it appeared there was a large, long bulge under the canvas. Ken picked up a pine club and shouted "you'd better come out of there, If you don't want to get killed". There was no answer so he lifted the flap open. Nothing could be seen with the light of his flashlight but the sleeping bag and mattress in one corner. "there's no one in here. You must have had a nightmare".

He flashed his light again and drew back with a sudden start. Then he broke into a long chuckle and said, "Well I'll be darned if I ever thought I'd be afraid of my own shadow". "whaat do yoou mean, I stammered". "Come here and see. I'll give you a hand" Ken said. Taking his flashlight again he shone it in the rear of the tent. "Look here, now what do you see". For a moment I almost jumped again. For a face closely resembling my own but a lot more disheveled and wet was looking back at me. "Who is it, I asked?" Ken said, "Why it's your own reflection in the shaving mirror you have hanging up at the end of the tent. "Well I guess I was sort of chicken for a moment", Warren said. Ken said, "If you want to know the truth, I got a start when you yelled so loud telling me that someone was in there and when I looked in the tent and saw myself." "Well," said Ken, "We'd better get some sleep if we are going on tomorrow. If you weren't so darned homely you might not have been so scared".

We found another story he wrote about Indian lore in Maine. Warren and Ken were on a lake called Passamassawamkeag near Bucksport, Maine, better known as Toddy Pond. The lake was named by the Indians like so many were in the regions of Maine. It was said that when white hunters were crossing the lake in the winter with an Indian guide they would pause occasionally for some liquid refreshment, a concoction of rum which they carried in small wooden kegs. The Indian guide was curious about the kegs and asked to sample the warming fluid the hunters seemed to enjoy. He asked the hunters to passa massa wam keg. Warren said "I think that "Toddy Pond" describes the incident more aptly" (We never knew if this was a true story, but there is a copy in Folder 2, with E.Baldic; Toddy Pond is in Orland ME, near Bar Harbor)

Kendall went on to be a Doctor of thoracic medicine, married and had a family. In later years Warren and his family spent many weekends at the Crossfield summer camp on the banks of the Rowley River in Rowley, MA ,clamming, boating, swimming and playing chess.

SCHOOL JOBS

To help defray the cost of school and college Warren worked at several jobs. He used to tell us of his experiences. He was able to laugh at himself so we found the stories quite amusing.

Warren told this story: "While working at an automat restaurant on Boylston Street my job was to clear the dishes off the tables and put them on a cart to take to the kitchen to be washed. To my dismay and great embarrassment the cart rolled down the ramp and the dishes went slowly sliding onto the floor and broke. The manager came out and fired me. Oh well, there was always another job".

The next job he told about was when he was a tour guide on the "old Blue Line" that gave tours of Boston. (Warren had a severe stuttering problem when he was young and when he was nervous this was obvious). He was on the bus pointing out places of interest in the city and he was near the Museum of Fine Arts making his announcement. He said it went like this. "Ladies and Gentlemen we are now passing the Muse.......um of F......ine Ar.......ts". By the time his announcement came they were a block away. Needless to say that job did not last long. He eventually overcame this problem except when when he got too excited about getting his point across.

Another story he told about was while working at the Boston Public Library. His father's sister, Ida[8] Gould, worked at the Boston Public Library in the catalogue department. His job was to take the books off the shelves and dust them. He would don a white coat and mask, take each book over to the window that overlooked the garden courtyard at the library and clap them out the window. How the dust would fly! He said this was the most dirty, dusty job he had ever had.

It was out the window on the second floor that he could observe the people who came to enjoy the quiet of the garden. There were some unsavory characters that frequented the place and always seemed ready to pick a fight. This spoiled the solitude of the garden. Warren was wary of going down there, but he did love to read and was a frequent visitor to the library and always left with an armful of books. One he was most fond of was about Egypt. He took the book out several times and eventually lost it. He looked high and low but the book was never found. As Aunt Ida was well aware of the loss and never let him forget about it!

The Boston Public Library opened to the public in 1895. It still is one of the great treasures of Boston with its great collection of rare books, (such as John Eliot's Indian Bible), the art collection, old newspapers and the great marble staircase flanked by the stone lions by Saint Gaudens and the inner courtyard.

His Aunt Ida had a small apartment near the library and Warren would go over there quite often. His uncle Samuel[8] Gould, a salesman, would visit his sister Ida whenever he was in town. When Samuel came he would always bring the dinner which was usually enough for quite a few meals. Sam was a big man and Warren said that Sam would always eat enough for the three of them. (Warren was not far behind in his later years. He always had a second helping for dinner).

Warren's Aunt Ida became sick a few years later and died. Warren was very fond of her and when she died it really affected him as she had been the most influential woman in his young life besides his mother. He never went to many funerals after her death. (We remember her as a quiet woman with great big brown spots on her face and hands).

EDUCATION

Warren said that he went to the Perkins school, English High, Boston Latin, night classes at the university extension, and the Massachusetts Normal Art School.

We found this paper in Warren's belongings (copy in folder #1 with E. Baldic). This gives a good insight of him as a young man:

"In my early informative period of youth, the longing for answers apparently not given by mortal sense, spurred me to undertake what later proved a profoundly enlightening, if not circuitous quest.

Sunday proved to be the day most free from compulsory endeavor. I used this time to explore both orthodox and unorthodox avenues of approach to my objective. Although the adopted plan varied slightly to coincide with the times that the services of the various meetings were held, it conformed more or less to the following procedure.

It was natural to take the line of least resistance and visit first the church nearest the vicinity where I lived. I'm not certain whether its denomination was Congregational or Baptist as the services were along the usual orthodox line but the last half-hour kept me spell-bound until the conclusion of a selection of some of the finest works of the great composers exquisitely given by an exceptionally accomplished organist----I liked beautiful music.

By walking briskly I was just able to attend the last fifteen minutes of the service held in an edifice whose exterior and interior reflected the finest in old Gothic architecture. The stained glass was among the finest I had ever seen.......... I also appreciate Art.

In the early afternoon I delved into some of the so called esoteric types of beliefs such as the Vedanta presided over by a very distinguished looking Swami and whose origin stemmed from somewhere in the interior of India. Or possibly might wander into the Bahai Temple founded in 1863 by Mirza Husayn Ali (whose teachings emphasized the spiritual unity of mankind). Persia was the land of its original dissemination. And also an occasional visit to a Rosicrucian meeting and maybe to one of the Theosophical Society ....There is a bit of the mystic in many of us.

Later about 5 O'clock, I would attend a meeting of the Men's class in Old St. Paul's Episcopal Cathedral in the heart of down-town Boston. Here in a hear-warming atmosphere of many friends with a cozy fire burning in a grate at the further end of the room we would sit and listen to current and vital topics by prominent speakers. Concluding with an appetizing supper, reasonably priced, it was an affair that I seldom missed; everyone likes friendship, interesting speakers and I have seldom been known to have refused good food.

By careful timing and before I could finish the last morsel of the tasty meal I would dash to the nearest station of the not too rapid transit system and about eight miles and thirty minutes later would find myself at the last scheduled visit of the day.

The Young Peoples Club of this church and another denomination (of both sexes and some, very pleasing to the eye) planned and conducted a very interesting and entertaining program. Occasionally throughout the year there would be outings, dances and amateur plays, in which I was extremely interested. The feminine pulchritude, and social gatherings pleased me almost as much as the possibility of becoming the next "Great Profile". Time had not yet etched my features, raised my forehead and a "36 was still comfortable.

Before the day bade goodnight and there were no other spiritual oasis from which to quaff, I returned homeward reflecting upon as I went, the various impressions I had received. I was still not completely satisfied that I had found the answers to who-what and why.

In retrospect I have found that my early search for Truth gave me a greater sense of tolerance of the beliefs of others and a feeling that an understanding of all of them might give me a picture of the whole. The diamond's scintillation brilliance comes not from the reflection of only one facet, but from the combination of many scores of them. True, some facets are larger than others but they all reflect the light to the limits of their capacity.

Religious faiths to me are like the diamond. Some groups or believers are in a small minority, others are tremendous in scope. Each one can only express the Truth (or light) as they see it. It could be, if seen from a distance with the mind's eye not focused on any particular facet, you might get the awe inspiring view of the greatest treasure in the world today. The Great Diamond of Faith. Who knows?????"

Warren attended night school at the Massachusetts Normal Art School, now called the Massachusetts Art School and was the first state school of art begun in 1873 on the corner of Exeter and Newbury Streets. It is now located on Longwood Avenue in Brookline.

He did not save any school records but we do have a year book called the "Palette and Pen", The Year Book of the Massachusetts Normal Art School, edited in 1924 by the Junior Class. In the year book there is a picture of him in the Glee Club and a short bio of him for the class of 1925. Class of '25: "- Warren B. Gould -25 St. Botolph Street, Boston, Mass., came to us from English High. He is a very obliging soul, ready at all hours to argue upon all subjects, religion, literature, or sport, and this he does with the art of a sophist, the wisdom of a professor, and the experience Rudyard Kipling. He is a prominent Glee Clubber, with a musical comedy voice. Warren is also a member of the Junior Dance Committee".

We have some of his art work (in brown folder, labeled Art Work, with E. Baldic). He was especially proud of one he did using only pencil dots. It is of a man's head depicting a strong swarthy face. He said he received a prize for the detail.

After college he applied for several jobs and we were able to get a general idea of what he did from a resume he wrote (copy in folder 3 with E. Baldic). Printed on parchment paper in green ink the following resume was very impressive.

JOBS 1917-1928

1917-1920 - Three years with the *Boston Daily Record* - selling and sales promotion; Citizen Publishing Co., Brookline -circulation 65,000 -free distribution .(This must have been to earn money for college as a newspaper boy. He would have only been fourteen to seventeen years old.)

1920-1922 - Food Company - 2 ½ years -Best Foods Company, Inc. ,New England Division - Sales promotion for Hellman's Mayonnaise, Nucoa, B&B Pickles, etc. (He worked there part time for college expenses)

1922 - Manufacturer - six months. Gorham Company (Bronze Division), Providence, RI, Sales Promotion Manager in Boston, handling sales and merchandising plans (this also was a part time job to help with college expenses).

1922-1928 - One year with the American Wool and Cotton Reporter, a product magazine, Boston, MASS., advertising and promotion department, handling copy and layout for clients for publication.

James W. Brine Co., Boston, Ma - two years as advertising manager handling copy and layout for magazines and newspapers. (copies of ad work in red scrapbook with E. Baldic)

Warren was still a camp counselor in the summer, working and going to college nights in 1925 when he met Beatrice (Bea) Lena Rowe who became be his wife four years later. They met at the Young Peoples Club in Boston, Mass. Saturday night was dance night for all the young people who cared to attend. They both could hardly wait for Saturday nights to go dancing. The Two Step and the Charlestown were the rage then and the latest songs of the day were "Won't You Be My Honey Bee?, "Paddling Madeline Home", "Everyone's Doing It, Doing What, Falling In Love"," I Met My Love In Avalon". "Smile Awhile" and many others. (Warren sang these songs to his family and we learned to sing them to the strumming of his Ukulele).

Warren had a Model "T" Ford in those days and Bea and he had a great time riding around in it. They also did a lot of canoeing and we have a few pictures of them in a canoe (pictures with E.Baldic).

We have a letter Warren wrote to Bea from Fryeburg, ME in 1925 when he was twenty-two years old. This one shows his sense of humor (with E. Baldic in folder marked personal).

June 14, 1925

Dearest:

Thanks for keeping that date with me Saturday. If your letter had not arrived when it did, I would have felt rather lonesome. Never mind about the news, just write anything, the longer the better, I can stand it if you can stand writing it.

Couldn't get the car this weekend so we didn't take in any dances. Although I did have a haircut for excitement, and some haircut it was. I escaped by a close shave. Everybody's doing it, doing what, doing it, work, work, work, all kinds, shades varieties,)excuse all the ink blotches).

This is quite wild country up here, in fact there's an animal known as the Lizzie, leaping lance or the galloping gee whiz which is quite dangerous as there are so many of Them em. All joking aside though, there are quite a few deer around and every day we see several eagles flying overhead (where else would they fly?

Last year there were anywhere from fifteen to fifty girls staying here in what was known as the adults camp. This year however, it is strictly boys. Tough luck. No Bee, girls don't phase me anymore. At least for the Summer and, (get this) as long as I know you. You can skip this coming paragraph if you want to when you read this letter to the family - if you do, some do.

Now listen honey, this is no oil or applesauce. Do I miss you dear? Say, I think of you every time the stars and moon are out and in between times too. Especially on a nice moonlight night while canoeing on the river. I wish you would send me a snapshot, hon, just to keep me in touch with a little closer. Won't you please.

As I won't write until I hear from you again, please write soon enough for a letter to reach here by Saturday. There is only one delivery here a day and that is at noon. Of course you may be pretty busy moving and can't find time but write early if you can.

Well dear, the candles are waning and this is the last sheet of my present supply of camp stationary, so I'll say Buenos Noches, (Spanish)

With regards to everybody.

Love Warren

(passed by the board of censors)."

Warren was very persistent and courted Bea for four years until she finally accepted his proposal. They married in Boston on the 29 of January 1929. Shortly after that they moved to New York as he had accepted a job with the McGraw-Hill Publishing Co. in New York City in the circulation and promotion department handling direct-by-mail for two engineering publications.

In New York they had an apartment in Hastings on the Hudson, and in Flushing, Long Island. They took many pictures of the area and their trips to Washington, DC (pictures in family album with E. Baldic).

He worked for two years for the McGraw-Hill Publishing .Co. (copies of ad work in red scrapwork with E. Baldic). Soon he left and went to work for the New York, New Haven, and Hartford Railroad Co. (N.Y.N.H.&H.R.R.Co.) as advertising manager handling copy layout, budget control, newspaper ads, direct-by-mail and radio advertising.

During this period on the 23 of January 1930 their only child, Eleanor[10] Rowe Gould was born. (VR City of New York #03218), They were expecting a boy; much to their surprise a girl! They had already had a boy's name decided and it took two weeks to name her. We always felt Warren was disappointed that Eleanor was not the boy that he had longed for.

Warren's last job in New York was for the "Tail Waggers Club" which was located at 545 Fifth Avenue, New York The club was a non-profit organization that originated in London, England. Capt. H. H. Hobbs started the club in 1928. In three months over ten thousand members belonged. The requirements to join the club were to register one's dog, receive a numbered tag for the collar, and pay two shillings & six pence (currency in England) for life membership. One dollar was the fee in the USA or Canada. The purpose of the club was to improve the conditions in which dogs were kept. For all this members would be taught the proper way to groom, feed and train their dogs.

By 1929 the club was so successful it opened an office in New York. By the end of May 1930 the membership was over three hundred and forty thousand and more then ninety one countries were represented. By this time the "Tail Waggers Club" was recognized as the simplest, most economical and most efficient way of promoting dog welfare. Among the elite of the members were Prince of Wales, Princess Mary, Herbert Hoover, Commander Richard Byrd, Calvin Coolidge, The Prince of Monaco and many others.

Warren became the executive secretary of the club. There were a few articles complimenting him on his good work (copies of the club's pamphlets and articles in red scrapbook with E. Baldic).

"Mr. Warren Gould, the new executive secretary of the Tail Waggers' Club of America, is not allowing the grass to grow under his feet. He has been successful in securing the Club much excellent publicity - he is an expert in the publicity game - but, what is of more importance, he has placed the organization on a sound business footing, and club members are now assured of getting the service to which they are rightly entitled".

In another report "Mr. Warren Gould, the new Secretary of the club, is a man full of energy and ideas and has a wide experience of publicity work which will stand him in good stead in his new position; and he is 100 % enthusiastic over the Club and its aims".

He worked at this for some time, and got fired! The reason was that he also collected money when the regular person who did this was either out to lunch or unavailable. At any rate, he forgot to put the money in the drawer when he left one day (he was a always forgetting something). He was putting it back the next day but some one thought he was stealing it. Even though he denied the accusation no one believed him. He always thought that someone was envious of his job or just plain did not like him. Whatever the reason, he was fired!

LIFE IN WOLLASTON, MASSACHUSETTS

By 1933 Warren moved his family back to Massachusetts to 41 Sewall Avenue, Wollaston, MA, a suburb of Quincy. The house was a two-decker, front and back porch, living room, dining room, two bedrooms and kitchen. The move was probably strongly influenced by the fact that Bea's sister Madelaine Basse was living there and taking care of their mother Lena Rowe who lived with Madelaine's family. This enabled Bea to be as close to her family and help out with the care of her mother Lena.

The move to Wollaston was also influenced by the move of their friends William (Bill) and Helen Fenstermaker to Wollaston. Warren and Bea had chummed around with the Fenstermakers all during their courtship days., and Helen and Bea had grown up near each other.

Many grand times were spent with the Fenstermaker family. Their daughter Janet was born in 1930 and her brother Bill came along ten years later. In the winter we all would go to Merry Mount Hill in Wollaston for the best coasting around the area. Warren and Bill would take Janet and Eleanor down the hill on their" Flexible Flyers", racing to see who would come in first.

There was also a pond around the corner and during the Winter would freeze solid. All the local families would be out on the pond Saturdays and Sundays skating with the children- some would be on double runners, the more experienced on single blades. On Saturday nights a bonfire would be lit on the edge of the pond to warm up by. There was a small wooden round house on the edge of the pond and inside there was a small pot-bellied stove in the center with a round steel ring that went all around it. The stove would be blazing hot and one could put their feet up on the ring to warm up . The warmth felt good after being out in the cold.

In the Summer, Warren said his family and the Fenstermakers' would catch tadpoles in the pond. The tadpoles could be taken home in a jar until they grew legs. Then off to the pond with them to grow into frogs.

MERRY MOUNT

We lived around the corner from the famous "Merry Mount" as the area was called. It was made famous by its "Merry" May Pole. Actually Merry Mount was a high hill covered with lush foliage, green grass and magnificent old trees. Merry Mount was a part of Wollaston named for the famous Captain Wollaston.

The idea of erecting a may pole came from a custom in England. On the First of May a May Pole was erected , long streamers attached and people would hold the streamers and go round and round dancing with merriment. As the soldiers were getting bored sitting around with nothing to do, Thomas Morton , one of the soldiers helped the men erect a maypole at Merry Mount.

The pole was a pine-tree eighty feet high with deer horns attached to the top. The Indians would join the soldiers night after night dancing around the May Pole. It certainly was a merry old time. Captain Wollaston returned and heard of the merry time the soldiers and Indians had been having dancing around this pole every night. This was not to be tolerated by Captain Wollaston or the local people so the events were reported to Captain Miles Standish.

Captain Standish was so furious he promptly marched his troops from Plymouth, arrested the soldier, Thomas Morton, and chased the Indians away. From then on "Merry Mount" was no longer merry.

In the thirties "Merry Mount" became merry once more, but instead of a May Pole being erected, a great bonfire was built on the bottom of the hill near the marsh every fourth of July. Set to burn at precisely at 10 p.m. Everyone gathered for this great show. What a splendid affair it was! Every year this was held until the property was sold and houses were built there.

Wollaston Beach in those days was a great place to swim and clam. Today none would dare to clam there let alone swim. The city of Quincy is trying to clean up the bay.

Warren enjoyed many great summers at the beach with his family. Warren and Bea were expert swimmers. The cardinal rule about the water was "swimming lessons or no beach". Warren taught many of the local children how to swim.

HEALTH CRISIS

While swimming one day Warren's appendix burst but he did not realize this until about a week later when he became ill and Bea took him to the hospital.

This part of the story was told to him by Bea as he was so ill he did not remember what happened for three months. He was in the hospital and not expected to live as peritonitis had set in. His bed was slanted, head down and a tube was put in his back to drain the poison. These were hard times for the family with no money coming in.

Warren's mother, Jane Blaisdell came every day to visit him from Boston. When she stopped coming Warren never asked why until he was better. He said "My Mother died didn't she?" Jane Blaisdell Gould died on July 9, 1933 (Boston VR book 50 #359008) in Boston from a stroke. He mentioned her to the family again only once. We found this odd and he made no mention of his father ever visiting him during this time.

Warren recovered quite well from this ordeal and when his grandchildren asked about the deep scar on his back, he would reply, "this was a war wound, I am lucky to be alive." They believed this throughout the years until one day in his eighties while talking about his illness he told them what really happened. They were really disappointed. This was not as exciting as a war wound!

Warren had been working for the "Old Trusty Dog Food Company" before he was ill. He was a good salesman as this letter attests:

"Mr. W. Gould, please accept my sincere thanks and congratulations for the splendid cooperation you have given me during the past year in putting Old Trusty where it rightfully belongs. I am assuring you that a continuation of your past performance is going to mean bigger dividends for us all during this coming year. V.T.Y. W.F. MacQuarrie." (letter in red scrapbook).

Shortly after that, Bea's mother died at her sister Madeline's house. Lena M. Rowe was 53, and died of cancer on 17 September 1935 (VR, Quincy, MASS.) in Wollaston, MA and was buried in Mt. Wollaston Cemetery, Quincy, MA. These again were not happy times with the deaths of both their mothers.

Now it was time to move on to another job. of which he had quite a few. He secured a job at the *Quincy Patriot Ledger* a local newspaper in Quincy, Mass. as a reporter and photographer (copies of his work in gray folder, labeled Publicity with E. Baldic).

The great hurricane of 1938 was quite an event to cover as a reporter. The day of the storm he went out early and when he came home he had some stories to tell. It wreaked havoc in the area. Trees were wrenched from their roots, power lines were down, boats askew on the shores and battered. The water rose at least 15 feet in some places.

After that he worked for the *Boston Herald.* His best work as a reporter and photographer show up here. His photos and stories made the front page many times. One in particular dated January 8, 1940 . There was a photo of a young girl on the ice holding on to #4 channel buoy off Wollaston Beach. "Girl Meets Buoy" was the title of the photo. The story tells of the 9 degree weather, ice freezing the bay and of the many people who were walking out on the ice and ice sailing in boats. As a reporter he covered many events at the Fore River Shipyard, Quincy, Mass., rescues, etc. (all pictures and articles in gray scrapbook with E. Baldic).

These were the best of times for Warren and Bea while living in Wollaston. He had a good job, the family was doing well, the beach was a short distance from the house, the school was nearby and it was a short ride into Boston. Howard Johnson started his first ice cream parlor in Wollaston and Warren would take Bea and Eleanor to the parlor at least once a week for a treat.

Every year the circus would come to town. A great event for all! And of course there was the annual fair at the Nazarene Church in the Summer. All the children would bring their animals to see if they could win a prize for the best groomed, best behavior, the biggest and the smallest. Bicycles would be decorated as well as doll carriages. Eleanor won a blue ribbon for the best decorated carriage.

Warren tells the story of Eleanor proudly marching home with her doll all dressed up in the best carriage of the day, a "real English Coach". On the way home Warren bought a dozen eggs and put them on top of the doll's feet. He said that Eleanor cried: ". My doll carriage is spoiled by the eggs wrinkling the blanket." Warren said Eleanor was very sassy about the eggs and he exploded.!!! "Wait until you get home," he said. when we arrived home he gave Eleanor one of the first spankings she ever got or remembered. The only other time he ever spanked Eleanor was when she was really fresh to Bea.

Neither Bea or Warren could make up their minds as to what religion Eleanor should be brought up in. fact Bea was a Catholic, (not a practicing one as she had enough of being made to go to church growing up) and Warren still had not decided which church he wanted to attend. Eleanor was finally baptized at five years old, at St.Anne's Catholic church in Quincy. They did not send her to church as she was too young to cross the big avenue so she was sent to the Church of the Nazarene which was just around the corner from the house.

Warren took many walks with Eleanor on weekends as Bea worked part-time. He always would look up in the sky on a sunny day to see if there were any fluffy clouds and ask "what shape do you see up there"? This was great fun. When he was in his nineties, we were driving along one day and he looked out at the fluffy clouds and said "Look, there is a great big fluffy teddy bear up in the sky".(this brought back memories of our many walks together looking at clouds)

At Easter, Warren brought home baby chicks one year, the next year a rabbit and the next year a dog. There was an old soapstone sink in the kitchen , around the legs Warren built a wire enclosure for these pets. These pets did not last long as Bea had all the care of them and it was a lot of work.

In the summer Warren would take small pieces of hamburger, put it on the ground near an ant hole and sit there with Eleanor and Bea and watch the ants carry the food to their hole.

There were the trips into Boston nearly every weekend. We would drive in on what is now known as the "Southeast Expressway". In those days it was a pleasure to go in to Boston. Just past Neponset on the right were shacks where the destitute souls and derelicts were living. I remember my Father stopping there and walking through the pathways. These people lived in tin shacks, built out of whatever they could salvage from the nearby dump. They seemed to be happy just to have a roof over their heads.

The next job that he held was for the Quincy Community Fund and again he received more accolades for another splendid job "Well Done!" (articles in red scrapbook)

In 1939 Bea became pregnant again but lost the baby in the second month. They were very disappointed.

BELMONT, MASSACHUSETTS

Shortly after this they moved to Belmont, MA to 22 Knox Street. The house was a typical Cape, two bedrooms, kitchen, breakfast nook, dining room, large living room and a garage underneath. There was a lovely rose arbor at the end of the front walk. The house was one street over from the elite of Belmont Hill, near the exclusive Belmont Hill School for Boys and one street away from what is known as Route Two today. There was a bus line on the corner that went to Harvard Square. From there one could get the subway to Boston. This was convenient for Bea as she worked in Boston, at the Domino Sugar Co., as a bookkeeper.

Warren had the only car and that was used for his work. It was truly a luxury in those days to have more than one car. It surely is different today!

We were lucky to live on a hill . Out in front of the house the road ran down to a dead end and a path from there went through the woods. In Winter, Warren and the men of the neighborhood would take their children down the hill for hair-raising rides, for Warren and Eleanor it was on the old reliable "Flexible Flyer"- down the hill , over the bump and right through the path in the woods. It was always a challenge to see how far we could go. He had more energy than most of the fathers. He was always ready to go sledding or take part in any activity.

At this time Warren had secured a job with the Metropolitan Life Insurance Co. Russell Kerr, the husband of Bea's sister Ruth, worked there and felt that Warren would have job security with the company. Life was good. Bea's two sisters with their husbands, Madeline and Al Basse and Ruth and Russ Kerr lived just over Route Two in Arlington Heights with their families. It was a short fifteen minute walk to get there.

Every Thanksgiving was spent with Aunt Madeline's family and every Christmas with Aunt Ruth's family. These were again the best of times for our family. The men played chess or cribbage; these games were very serious and played with vigor. The family would get together to sing carols, play instruments, and have a grand time.

It was during our stay in Belmont that Warren got caught up in the "Pyramid Craze", which was a form of gambling. He would drive out nights with Bea and Eleanor to several houses, they would wait in the car while he would go in a house and come out quickly and off to the next one. The purpose of the game was that each person would pay a dollar, and slowly work their way to the top, somehow, each dollar being doubled and tripled along the way. If you were really lucky you would win the jackpot.

Along with this so called game Warren also started playing poker. This caused grief for Bea who was quite a penny pincher. She managed money very well and thanks to her things ran quite smoothly. She probably had to learn this rather quickly with all the job changes Warren had made which did not provide much security.

Bea was hoping this job with Metropolitan Life was to be the last and that they would buy the house. But this was not to be. Metropolitan decided to transfer Warren to the Newton office. He could have refused, but he finally had a pretty good job with security and he felt that he'd better stay there. He tried commuting to Newton but it was a long way and in the Winter quite a chore. So it was then they decided to make the move to Newton, MA. in the summer of 1944.

NEWTON, MASSACHUSETTS.

They moved to 611 Washington Street to a two-decker house. There was a living room, dining room, kitchen, pantry, two bedrooms, sunroom, front and back porch. The house was opposite the railroad tracks which was the main route to Boston. (now the Mass Pike) One could smell the smoke from the engines, a smell that permeated the house when the weather was just right and dust was everywhere. The bus stopped one door down from the house. The train station was only five minutes away, as were the schools. And best of all, "Our Lady's Catholic Church" was a convenient two doors away. It was convenient to send Eleanor there.

Bea did not like the house, but the conveniences of transportation outweighed her objections as it was a convenient way to get to her job in Boston.

The house had a coal furnace and Warren would stoke it by night and fill it up with coal early in the morning, shovel by shovel full. In the Spring we would don our old clothes and bandannas for our faces and then sweep out the coal bin in the cellar. It was a yearly ritual.

In the winter Bea would bring the frozen clothes in off the line and put them on the radiators to dry. Warren used to get a good laugh out of the different shapes the clothes would take as they were thawing out.

There was not a weekend in the Summer that we did not go to the beach. either to Swampscott, Nantasket or take the four hour trek to Cape Cod to visit the Fenstermakers who had moved to Falmouth in 1942. Warren and Bea loved the beach and did not mind traveling a long way to get to one.

During the other months on good weekends, if it were not stormy, we were off to Boston , of course only after Eleanor had gone to church at "Our Lady's Catholic Church". Then we were on our way to go to Warren's place of worship. It was called Unity, which is a spiritual study of being one with God. It was in Boston near Park Square. After church we would occasionally go to "Olga's Smorgasbord Restaurant" on Carver Street, off Park Square. This Swedish restaurant was in the very same building where his father John Goddard Gould[8] was born on the 25 of December 1870.

Next it was off to the museums, the Boston Common, a movie or visiting an art gallery. We also would go to the North End of Boston to enjoy the best Italian food to be had anywhere.

During World War II Warren had a Victory garden like most families during the war. He loved to garden and of course enjoy the fruits of his labor. There was rationing for sugar, butter, gas, etc. and Bea was very careful about buying sugar and butter. Warren was very careful about gas consumption so this curtailed unnecessary trips considerably.

Bea was a very good cook and like most thrifty New Englanders nary a morsel of food was wasted. Anything left over either went into the salad or potato pancakes or any other recipe she could dream up. Warren loved to eat and never missed a meal.

COAST GUARD

Warren enrolled as an Apprentice Seaman in the United States Coast Guard Reserve on the 22 June 1944 Newton, MA. (Flotilla #518, Copy in folder 3, Coast Guard, with E. Baldic), and spent one week at the temporary reserve training school in Gloucester, Mass. His service number was 6154-603,S2C - Class E, re-classified as 3A (copy in folder 3 ,Coast Guard, with E. Baldic). He was allotted $136.66 for two uniforms There is a letter from the USCG Custom House, Boston on 1, July 1945 announcing the end of the war due to the surrender of Germany and requirements for the port security in the First Naval District of Boston have been greatly reduced. He was disenrolled on the 30 of September 1945 as a Coxwain (picture and copy of letter in folder 3, Coast Guard, with E. Baldic).

Warren and Bea sent Eleanor to live with her sister Madeline Basse two summers in 1943/44 at Swifts Beach in Wareham, MA. Bea had to go to work again and did not want to leave Eleanor at home. The next two summers Eleanor was sent to live with "Aunt" Helen Fenstermaker and family. (children rarely called family friends by their first name so "Aunt" was quite proper).

While still in Newton Warren joined the Chess Club at the Newton "YMCA". He was very good and won quite a few matches. He played on teams against the Boston College team, the Harvard Club, and others. He called himself Warren Blaisdell or Blaisdell Gould, just for fun or anonymity (copies in folder 1 with E. Baldic).

During the time he worked for Metropolitan Life Insurance Co., many nights while balancing the days collections (his job was to go out to the customers and collect weekly or monthly monies due for their insurance policies), he would sit down and count the nickels, dimes and pennies he received from the customers for their weekly insurance premiums. Many of the people could hardly pay the meager amounts due to keep their policies in effect and he felt sorry for them so he would put in a little extra in their premium so that their families would be insured. Many were poor and had a difficult time just to make ends meet.

It was during this time that Eleanor married 15 Jan. 1949 David Page Baldic, son of Clinton N. Baldic and Florence Page. They bought a house in Newton and Warren and Bea now thought this a good time to move to Cape Cod and find a job.

CAPE COD

They loved Cape Cod and as the Fenstermakers and the Chamberlains lived in Falmouth decided to look there. Bill Fenstermaker and Ray Chamberlain were pharmacists and were in partnership owning Chanberlain & Fenstermaker Drug store in Falmouth. Warren and Bea found a place at Hope Spring Farm on Megansett Rd. in North Falmouth. The farm was named for the natural spring which ran in back of the property. It was a lovely old house with plenty of room to roam. It had a stone fireplace with a cozy nook beside it to snuggle up in, three bedrooms, bath, dining room and kitchen. There was a large barn on the property , more than enough land for a garden and there was an old fashioned croquet court in the yard with a covered viewing stand (which was used many years ago to watch the tournaments).

Warren would till the garden to prepare it for his annual planting .The vegetable crop was unusually good the summer the woodchuck promptly moved in. He was eating everything in the garden. One of Warren's friends, George, owned a shotgun and said he could get rid of the varmit. He waited early each morning and at dusk before nightfall. Nary a sign of the woodchuck.. After his friend left, each night the woodchuck would show up. (He must have known when it was safe to come out). George came back one day and looked for the woodchuck's holes, put sulfur gas in one hole and covered it and did the same for the other hole. The woodchuck was never seen again. This sounds cruel, but that was the only way to save the garden.

Bea kept hearing noises down in the cellar, a walk-out basement. Warren went down to look and there was the biggest rat he had ever seen. He bought a trap and poison and that made short work of the rat.

There were also raccoons, skunks, rabbits, mice ,etc. They had a cat named "Tiger". (they always had cats). He was a good mouser and usually kept that pest under control. He loved to roam at night and usually came home before bed time. One night he did not come home and Warren felt that some large animal killed it.

Well, all was well again for awhile. Warren had a job with the Buzzards Bay Gas Co. as a salesman and collector. This job went well until he injured his back changing a tire on his car. He had to have surgery and was laid up for awhile. The doctor told him to walk as much as possible for a good recovery. This he did and as long as he was careful his back did not bother him until later on at the next house he built stone walls, dug fences, etc., then he would be laid up for awhile.

HYANNIS

Everything seemed to be finally going all right for them until the gas company wanted to transfer him to Hyannis. Bea didn't want to move again but they did! They moved to an apartment on South Street in Hyannis. The house [the famous Capt. Baxter house] was an Octagon shape, cold and drafty. They did stay long enough to make many friends there. In Hyannis Warren joined several churches searching for the choir that suited him. He finally settled on the Hyannis Baptist Church. Its choir was excellent and he was happy to be able to sing again. Bea again went to work.

SOUTH YARMOUTH

Again, another job change. Warren left the gas co. and went to work for the "*Central Cape Press*" in South Yarmouth. He was back reporting and taking pictures again. He really seemed to be happy. He and Virginia Stone shared a column in the paper called "The Sidewalk Forum", which were weekly interviews with people they would meet walking on the sidewalk. (copies in red scrapbook with E. Baldic). He enjoyed this as he loved to meet people. At this time he really felt secure enough to buy their first house.

The house was located on lot 24 off Lymans Lane, Bass River, South Yarmouth. They bought it on the 11 March 1954 for $5000 @ 5% for fifteen years. The mortgage was $40.86 per month (copies in house folder with E. Baldic). Bea was quite happy at owning their first house . They made many friends there and had some good times.

Again all was well, until the newspaper was sold or went out of business. At any rate he decided to go back to work for the Buzzards Bay Gas Co.. They did take him back, the pay was good and benefits were excellent.

FALMOUTH

Another move! The gas company asked Warren to transfer to Falmouth as there was a lot of building going on and they wanted him to sell gas to the new developments. Bea was really disappointed at the news. She had a good job, a lovely house, what more could she want, but she agreed to move. They looked at many houses in the Falmouth area and finally found one that Dad really loved. It overlooked a pond!

The house was located in East Falmouth, 318 Acapesket Road, on a ¾ acre lot, with 100 feet on Green Pond. It was a cement block house, two bedrooms, 1 bath, small den, kitchen, fireplace in living room with a small dinette. They paid $9000 @6% for 16 years at $58.43 (copy in house folder with E. Baldic). Today the property is worth at least $700,000. Not a bad investment!

BARBERSHOP SINGING

Barbershop singing is distinguished by close harmony using a pitch pipe to get started on key, singing without any instrument accompaniment. Warren started singing in a quartet in Hyannis and when they moved to Falmouth he helped organize a chapter there. He had a beautiful baritone voice and it was pleasant to listen to. The first quartet was organized about 1951 and was called the Vineyard Sounders. which included Warren, Walter Swain, Loran Crain and Frank............ The next quartet was called the Cape Chorders with Maurice Appel, James Dufur, Edward Wright, and Howard Cummings.

The first Barbershop parade was held in Falmouth in 1952 and was a great success. They had a newsletter called "Notes "N" Swipes" . Opus 1 No.1, NO. OF PAGES 1, PRICE is attendance at meetings. In the first newsletter (copies of all Barbershop activities and pictures in folder marked "Barbershop Singing" with E. Baldic) an article appeared entitled "CREDIT WHERE CREDIT IS DUE". It goes like this:

"Hats off to Warren Gould, father of barber shopping here in Falmouth. Warren has really worked hard to promote our society here and without his efforts we would not be enjoying the benefits that have come and the more that will come from gathering together and singing the grand old tunes that make barbershop what it is. Warren has had an assist here and there, but I think everyone will admit that the major share of credit is his. May he survive until the society is on its feet and rolling along. As Warren says (Its and awful lot work to go just to sing in a quartet). He's a great worker. So gather around, all of you and help form another quartet".

Warren retired from being secretary of the club and just concentrated on singing with a quartet. He loved Barbershop singing and whenever he could he would start to harmonize with anyone who would join in. In the market, and even at the auto dealership, always with his ukulele in hand. We miss that part of him very much and whenever we hear a quartet singing we think of Warren. Especially when the old songs are playing like: "I Love The Way You Roll Your Eyes", I'd Love To Live In Loveland", "Smile Awhile" and Let Me Call You Sweetheart" and many others.

ROTARY

Rotary is an organization that encourages and promotes good will, peace, and high ethical standards in business and professions among fellow-man. Rotary donates to charity and gives scholarships to deserving students throughout the world. Warren became a Rotarian in 1959 as a representative of the Buzzards Bay Gas Co. He served as Sergeant-at-Arms, Secretary, vice-president, and was elected President in 1970-1971 (copies in Rotary scrapbook with E. Baldic). He was the song leader at all meetings. His greatest honor was being voted a "Paul Harris Fellow" in 1976 for outstanding service (copy of award with E. Baldic). He was awarded many plaques and pins (items with E. Baldic) during the years of service with Rotary in honor of his unselfish contribution to the Rotary organization

He was also a Mason and became quite active when he lived in Hyannis in the Masonic Lodge AF & AM located in Centerville. When he moved to Falmouth he joined the Marine Lodge AF & AM in Falmouth, for awhile but could did not continue as Bea had become ill and he did not like to leave her alone at night.

Warren retired in 1975 from the gas company and went to work for the Falmouth National Bank as a courier. He had to give it up due to an old time knee injury. He finally retired from there in 1978 at the age of 75 years .

After retirement he joined the Senior Center and promptly signed up for the chorus. Each month they would go to a local nursing home to sing, The chorus would go to the hospitals and nursing homes to entertain. He and Bea played cards, shuffle board and traveled a little.

The Fenstermakers, and the Chamberlains would spend many an afternoon with Warren and Bea card playing, shuffle boarding or singing around the piano with Warren and Ray accompanying on his ukulele, which we call "Uke" (Uke with E. Baldic).

Kib and Lila Colby were long-time friends from New York and lived in Briarcliff Manor, in White Plains, New York. Kib was the camping editor for *Outdoor Life* and a writer in his own capacity. When he worked for *Outdoor Life* the company would have him test their equipment that they advertised. such as tents, lights, gear and stoves for the Coleman Co. These jobs enabled him and Lila to travel all over the continent . The books he wrote were published through the Coward-McCann Publishing Co., such as *My First Rifle*, *My First Fishing Trip*, books about World War II planes, equipment, etc. and ghost stories, such as "Stranger Than Fiction". He had over fifty books to his credit along with the illustrations he had done.

Among Warren's papers we found this article that Kib had written for the *Citizen Register*, in Ossining, NY, Friday 25 April 1958 about the bamboo that Warren grew in his yard in East Falmouth. (copy in folder marked Kib Colby). Bamboo is native to Ceylon and other countries where it grows to huge sizes. It was used for fishing poles, animal troughs, crude knives, pipes, even boats were made of bamboo. The inner pulp is used for making paper. The plant grows rapidly especially in the mosit environment of Cape Cod.

In 1979 Warren and Bea celebrated their 50th wedding anniversary with about sixty people attending including most of their long-time friends.

In 1989 they celebrated their 60th wedding anniversary. By this time most of their friends had passed away so it was mostly the family present.

Bea had been disabled since 1985 but managed to get around as best she could. Every year of their life they celebrated Thanksgiving and Christmas with the family but in the year of November 1990 there was a surprise snow storm on Thanksgiving Day and they could not come due to the storm. In the Spring of 1991 Bea fell and broke her hip and did not recover rapidly. She lived to celebrate their 62nd wedding anniversary on 19 of January 1991 and on the 7th of July 1991 she died at the age of 87 years.

After Bea died Warren was very lonely, but carried on like a trooper. If he was sad he did not show it. He would go to the Senior Center on every Friday to sing with the chorus and practice for the birthday party that was held every month at the center for all the seniors having birthdays during that month.

He still drove his car but in 1994 and 1995 he had three car accidents and totaled all three cars. He was quite shaken up by all of them and came close to losing his life. One accident he had while walking was stumbling over a cement abutment at the end of a parking place. He called us at home and said, "now don't get excited, I'm at the hospital and had a little fall, but I'm all right." We went there immediately. He looked as if he had been struck on the head by a bat. His face was swollen and bruised. After that fall and the three car accidents the doctor said he should not drive anymore. This was quite a blow to him, but we think he realized he could get killed or kill someone else.

From then on he lost interest in a lot of things for awhile. He rallied again and each week we took him out to the Senior Center to sing every Friday. They made him a "star" of the show many times. As he was the oldest singer there many of them took him under their wing. And of course he played his "Uke". On Thursdays we would go to have our blood pressure taken and then off to lunch. His favorite place was the "Burger King" where the hamburgers were just right for him.

He was stubborn man which most people who knew him could attest to. He had a hernia years ago which kept growing and refused to have it fixed. It was only small then and he felt that by "praying it away" it would go away (this was also in part to his beliefs, which were very much a combination of Christian Science, and homeopathic healing). It did not go away and that really held his activities to a minimum when he got into his nineties.

He had to use a cane and was all bent over to one side but he still liked to read and played his Uke and sing but one could see that he was failing. When we would visit him he would be asleep with his head down on the table. He finally wasn't able to take care of himself so we had to make a decision to place him in a nursing home, the [J.M.L.Care Center, Falmouth.] This was a very difficult decision to make, but family members were working and could not take care of him.

As usual he rallied even though he realized he was in the nursing home he made the best of the situation. He wheeled around in the wheelchair and visited the other patients, played his uke and still sang with the Senior Chorus when they visited the nursing home. He fell and broke his hip 15 February 1997 and died two days later on February 17, 1997 at the age of 93 years, 3 months and 2 days (VR Falmouth, MA).

When he died, there was an article in the *Falmouth Enterprise* column "As I Was Saying", by Hugh McCartney. Hugh wrote " If they had a barbershop quartet hall of fame and a "music hall of fame" where ever we go, Warren would be in it. Warren's death was a great loss to the community". (copy with with E. Baldic).

THE GRANDCHILDREN REMEMBER

From Carol Ann(Baldic) Kovac - Memories of Grampa Gould

Grampa Gould always thought of me as the fixer of the family. When there was a family crisis he would look to me for information about what was going on. I never thought he especially cared for me one way or another, I was just the informer of family news. As we both got older he would confide in me with little stories about himself at different stages of his life. He enjoyed playing his ukulele and singing songs. He let me know he loved me when he was in his nineties. I enjoyed listening to him tell stories. He used to tell these long jokes that were more thinking then funny. My four sons liked Grampa Gould as he used to pay attention to them and talk with them.

From David Page Baldic, Jr. Memories of Grampa Gould

He always had an unusual handshake for everyone sometimes strong, sometimes comical. He was always the comedian, whether it was a joke or a unique facial gesture. He was always the philosopher, always the showman, ready at will to play a song on the ukulele, break out into a Barbershop song or just use a convenient corner to practice a few low notes using the corner as his amphitheater. All in all Gramps was a very knowledgeable person, searching relentlessly through his National Geographic, or books. He was still strumming his uke at the age of 93. I wonder how I will be at that age?

From Donald Warren Baldic - Remembering my Grandfather- My Fond Memories

I always enjoyed spaghetti dinners at their house and digging clams and quahogs. My very first boat ride was in their small row boat. I liked listening to his nice record collection and keeping time to the music. I loved my grandparents very much. Grampa took the time to teach me the ins and outs of chess and at the age of ninety two he beat me in three moves. I was amazed how quick his mind was. He shared his feelings about God with me. It seems every time we met he still was #1 in my life with his wisdom. May God bless him and keep his soul at peace.

From Patricia Florence (Baldic) Kilday

I think of Grampa Gould as a very funny man who was forgetful as well. I remember Grampa trying to get to work and he would come in and out the door at least three or four times. First he would ask "Where are my keys, glasses, or billfold". He would then return to get a top coat, rain coat, or umbrella . Of course it would not be the item he came in for so back in the house he would come again, still looking for what he came in for. He always had a pen, pencil, pad of paper with him and of course the "Daily Word" (his monthly Unity booklet). I remember him doing lots of tricks and jokes. He had his famous fish hand shake. He used to put his glasses or his hat on backwards to get a laugh. Gramp always had a funny story to tell.

We would go over his house in the Summer and play croquet, darts, or just throw a ball. He loved the outdoors and liked to show us the roses and how he would put the beetles in the jar. He loved flowers and showed us his flower garden with the beautiful tiger lilies. Grampa had some fill put in to make a place to sit out so they could overlook the pond and sit in the shade. He was so proud of this little sitting place that looked out on "his" pond. He loved showing us his lawn mowing job and the paths he made to get down to the water.

I remember Nana and Grampa coming over for Sunday dinner and it seemed like such a long time before he would say grace and we could eat. He loved to eat and would always have two helpings of everything and eat it all. He always used a lot of napkins as well. Gramps loved to sing and would go in the corner to hum. He would have his ukulele with him and we would have sing-alongs. David would play the guitar and Donald would get out the harmonica.

He had style about the way he drove. He would step on the gas and floor it, then he would let up so you felt like you were riding a bronco. We used to all laugh about it as kids. Most of my memories of Grampa Gould are good as he always had a smile or good word to say. He would always see his glass as half full.

This biography was written from what we remember and papers and pictures that we found. He left all of us with the memory of him as being a positive person and yes, he would see life not as a half empty glass but as a GLASS HALF FULL.

ELEANOR GOULD BALDIC

One child: ELEANOR [10] ROWE GOULD, born 23 Jan. 1930 New York City, NY; m. David Page Baldic

---

i